gardening encyclopedia

gardening
encyclopedia

CHANCELLOR
PRESS

Acknowledgements

Revised and updated by Richard Rosenfeld

Black and white line drawings by Ian Garrard, Alan Burton and Charles Stitt

Colour illustrations
Herbaceous plants, trees, climbers and shrubs – Stephen Kirk
Rock Plants – Cynthia Pow
Bulbs – Tim Hayward (Linden Artists)
House Plants – Stuart Lafford (Linden Artists)
Roses – Kristin Rosenberg H.R.M.S.

Colour photographs by *Amateur Gardening*, Pat Brindley, Valerie Finnis,
Photos Horticultural and The Harry Smith Horticultural Photographic Collection.

First published in 1984 by W. H. & L. Collingridge Limited
This edition published in 2001 by Chancellor Press,
an imprint of Bounty Books, a division of
Octopus Publishing Group Ltd.
2-4 Heron Quays, London E14 4JP

ISBN 0-7537-0393-9

Printed & Bound at Ajanta Offset, Delhi, India.

Contents

Preface *7*

Part 1 **Planning a Garden** *page 9*

1 Garden Style *10*
2 Cultivation *13*
3 Working with Soil *19*
4 Draining Problems *23*
5 Creating Paths *26*
6 Manures and Fertilizers *30*

Part 2 **The Ornamental Approach** *page 46*

7 Flowers from Seed *47*
8 Hardy Herbaceous Perennials *107*
9 Rock Gardens and Rock Plants *169*
10 Trees and Shrubs *232*
11 Roses *326*
12 Bulbs, Corms and Tubers *338*
13 Bedding Out *381*
14 Water and Bog Gardens *383*
15 Lawns and their Maintenance *395*

Part 3 **Gardening under Glass** *page 405*

16 Cloches, Frames and Greenhouses *406*
17 Methods of Heating *414*
18 Greenhouse Management *417*
19 Recommended Greenhouse Plants *429*
20 Chrysanthemums Indoors and Out *504*
21 Cacti and Succulents *511*
22 Helpful Tips for House Plants *532*

Part 4 **Vegetables** *page 534*

23 **Planning the Vegetable Garden** *535*
24 **Vegetables and their Cultivation** *543*

Part 5 **Fruits** *page 609*

25 **Making a Fruit Garden** *610*
26 **Fruit Propagation** *617*
27 **Pruning Fruit Trees** *623*
28 **A Spraying Programme** *633*
29 **Cropping Problems** *635*
30 **Fruits and their Cultivation** *638*

Part 6 **Dealing with Foes** *page 716*

31 **Diagnosis and Treatment** *717*
32 **Common Pests and Diseases** *726*
33 **Useful Remedies** *767*
34 **Weeds and Weedkillers** *771*

Index *775*

Colour Plates

Colour in the Garden *49*
Herbaceous Plants *145*
Rock Plants *209*
Trees and Climbers *289*
Bulbs *353*
House Plants *449 and 513*
Roses *521*
Shrubs *577 and 673*
Ornamental Plants *678*
Colour and Produce
in the Garden *737*

Symbols used in the garden plant
information to the colour plates

⊕ Deciduous   ☼ Partial sun

△ Semi-evergreen   ● Suitable for shade

△ Evergreen   ▬ Damp to wet soil

☆ Slightly tender   ▬ Dry soil

⊠ Requires shelter   ▦ Good drainage

❀ Flowering season   ☐ Alkaline soil

♻ Ornamental fruit   ■ Acid soil

☼ Sunny position   ◨ Tolerates any soil

Preface

For many years gardening has been the most popular outdoor hobby in Britain and I do not find this at all surprising. We have a climate that is as good as any in the world for gardening, lacking any great extremes of heat or cold or of wet or dry seasons. Almost the whole vast range of plants from the temperate zones of the world can be grown outdoors in most parts of Britain, so that even supposedly cold Scotland is able to boast some of the finest plant collections to be found anywhere. If a heated greenhouse is added to the garden there is really no limit to the number of plants that can be grown and it is this very vastness of scope which makes gardening so fascinating.

No one ever masters all aspects of gardening and most home gardeners are content to accept a quite modest range of plants or to specialize in one or two types only. This book is not intended for specialists though it may serve as an introduction to specialization. But specialists soon acquire an enthusiasm and an expertise which lead to research in the great volume of specialist books that already exists and is being added to annually. Some may, in time, actually add to that literature themselves for many of the best specialist garden writers started as, and may still be, amateurs.

My main purpose in writing this encyclopedia has been to provide information about a sufficiently wide range of plants, and the methods of growing them, to meet the needs of ordinary, non-specialist gardeners. For this reason I have kept different kinds of plants separate; the flowers which we call annuals and biennials and which we regularly renew from seed, in one chapter, herbaceous perennials, which live for many years, but many of which die down in winter, in another; trees and shrubs, which have permanent woody branches, in a third, and so on. This is the way in which we approach plants in the garden and it determines to a considerable extent the way in which they are grown, though it does not prevent these various classes of plant from being mixed together in many delightful ways. In this scheme of things the lawn and its maintenance get a chapter to themselves. For some a lawn is the greatest pride and joy of the garden and much time is lavished on it. For others it is a time wasting nuisance, or there is just not room for it, and it is reduced to the most perfunctory of elements or is simply replaced by paths and areas of paving. There are no rules about the way in which a garden should be made but, instead, there is endless scope for the expression of individuality and, if desired, the frequent carrying out of change in planting and design.

In any comprehensive book about gardening some technicalities are unavoidable but I have tried to keep them to a minimum and explain them when they occur. For some plants botanical names must be used if only because they are the ones in most general use in nurseries and garden centres and in the plant catalogues from which all of us acquire so much information. One trouble with so called common names is that so many of them are far from common or have been applied to several quite different plants. Still, where it is appropriate, I have used them. It is also fortunate that many botanical names have passed comfortably into the English language so that antirrhinum, aspidistra, begonia, camellia, chrysanthemum, dahlia, delphinium, fuchsia, gladiolus, petunia and rhododendron, all of which are botanical names, seem as natural to most people as forget-me-not, rose and wallflower which are genuinely vernacular.

There has been a great change in the laws relating to the use of potentially dangerous chemicals in gardens, particularly as pesticides for the control of plant pests and disease and as herbicides for the eradication of weeds. Many chemicals which were in use have been banned and the rules are much stricter as they apply to the private gardener than they are for commercial growers and farmers. Because of this, and also probably because there is less reward from advertizing these chemicals, there seems to be a more relaxed attitude towards pests in general and less urgency in rushing out with an appropriate spray or dust directly the first greenfly or the earliest outbreak of mildew is seen. This seems entirely sensible and for a great many ornamental plants treatment with pesticides does seem to be largely unnecessary. Notable exceptions are roses, despite the fact that there is continuous breeding of new varieties one major object of which is to increase natural resistance to disease.

A modern tendency to plant ornamentals closely, in the cottage garden tradition, gives less space for weeds to colonize and the small size of many new gardens also reduces the necessity to use chemical methods of control. Nevertheless, for one reason or another, there are times when pesticides or herbicides should be used and, provided manufacturer's instructions are followed, there is no need to fear that any of the kinds still on sale will have any harmful effects except on the pests, diseases or weeds which they are meant to kill.

Arthur Hellyer 1993

Part 1

Planning a Garden

Chapter 1

Garden Style

Gardens can be of many kinds to meet as many needs. One gardener may be interested mainly in beauty, a second in relaxation, a third in growing flowers or crops for use in the home. Some gardeners are exhibitors, some collectors, some artists, but perhaps the most widespread need of all is for a place in which to pass a leisure hour pleasantly and in which to entertain friends. As gardens have become ever more numerous yet progressively smaller, the concept of the garden as an outdoor room has grown in acceptability and conditions a great deal of contemporary garden planning.

But the really important thing about design is that it must be well suited to the purpose for which the garden is required. The exhibitor and the food grower will require outdoor workshops rather than living rooms. Beds will need to be of sensible size and shape, easy to work and provide access to every plant so that each can be properly cared for. Flower arrangers, of whom there are so many today, will also demand a thoroughly practical disposition of paths and borders so that flowers and foliage can be gathered in comfort, whatever the weather.

Even the would-be artists have many different outlooks. One may see everything in patterns, another in pictures; some are ultra-sensitive to colour, whereas to others form and design are all important.

There can, in consequence, be no hard-and-fast rules about garden planning; no one way that is right or other that is wrong. Books are available filled with plans for plots of all shapes and sizes and many useful ideas can be culled from them, but it is seldom that any one of these ready-made designs will perfectly fit individual requirements. They must be adapted, and usually adapted freely, to meet the particular needs of each gardener and his garden.

The best preparation for garden making (or for garden alteration which can be just as absorbing an occupation) is to visit other gardens, both great and small. Even in the biggest and most lavishly maintained there may be ideas that can be used; particular associations of plants that are pleasing, patterns in paving that are good to look at as well as comfortable to walk on, contrasts of textures that are striking to the eye, even labour-saving devices that can be put to good use at home.

Armed with ideas from these and other sources the amateur garden maker may then prepare some kind of plan, though in my experience it is professionals who try to put everything on paper before they proceed to work on the ground and even they often have to amend mistakes afterwards. Proportion and elevation are vitally important in garden making and both are very difficult to visualize on a two-dimensional plan. Perspective drawings from different angles are far more revealing but much more difficult to execute.

In practice I am sure most amateurs carry out the greater part of their planning and replanning in the garden itself. There, armed with canes and string to mark out terraces, paths, beds and lawns and to indicate the position of prominent objects such as trees, a greenhouse, summerhouse or pergola, the whole thing can be visualized more readily and adjustments made until it all begins to look right. Even so, after a few years it will probably turn out that some of the more permanent plants, such as trees and shrubs, have been planted too closely together and may need to be thinned. Most of us, even the most expert, plant too thickly, though it is no great fault for plants like company and are seldom completely happy in isolation. In any event if a garden is to look well from the outset it needs to be a little overplanted with the slower growing trees and shrubs which take a long time to make their full effect. Nowadays few garden makers are looking much more than ten years ahead and even a relatively fast-growing tree, such as a silver birch or mountain ash, is unlikely to have attained more than half its ultimate size in that time. Even when a longer view is taken at the outset there is advantage to be gained from putting in some trees and shrubs as fillers, just as commercial fruit growers do in their orchards, to give an immediate return in beauty or utility. These can then be removed when they have served their turn. Ten years' service is not to be despised and usually represents a very good return on the money spent. There is certainly no reason to regard every tree, still less every shrub, as a permanent part of the landscape.

Large gardens can often be designed in separate sections each with its own purpose or style. There are splendid examples of this in many of the fine gardens open to the public, notably at Château de Villandry in France, Hidcote in England, and Longwood in North America. Such diversity is impracticable in the very small gardens typical today, though even in these it may be possible to satisfy several interests by growing, for example, rock plants in a stone sink or on a dry wall (that is, a wall bonded with soil in place of mortar), shrubs in tubs or other movable containers and vegetables in neat beds ornamented with edgings of clipped box, lavender or rosemary.

In very small gardens a lawn can be a nuisance unless kept solely to be looked at and never walked on, except for mowing and other care. Paving is more practical, and since many different paving materials are available for use separately or in combination, it also offers more scope for variety. But in this respect even grass has possibilities which are often overlooked. A pleasant variation in texture and colour can be obtained by keeping part of a lawn close mown, say to 12 mm ($\frac{1}{2}$ in), and leaving part rough mown, say to 3.8 cm ($1\frac{1}{2}$ in). This can give an illusion of a natural progression from a well-groomed area near the house to a wilder area at a little distance from it, an illusion made stronger if reinforced by suitable planting with the more formal flowers, including annuals, bedding plants and display roses in the foreground and less formal shrubs, shrub roses and trees further away. Bulbs, particularly daffodils, crocuses and snowdrops, can be naturalized very effectively in the rough-mown grass though it will be necessary to delay the first mowing each year until the bulb foliage begins to die down in late spring or early summer.

Two factors which every garden designer must take into account are soil and aspect. Of the two soil is the more amenable to treatment since even the stickiest clays can be rendered more workable by cultivation and, thanks to modern chemicals, it is now possible to grow lime-hating plants on limy soils. All the same it is much easier, as well as being considerably cheaper, to work with rather than against one's soil. If in doubt some observation of neighbouring gardens and nearby parks will indicate what will (and maybe what will not) thrive in the locality, and serve at least as an initial guide until a greater fund of local knowledge has been acquired.

Aspect is at least as demanding a factor and usually far more varied. Few gardens have more than one type of soil, but most have several different aspects, each with its own potentialities and limitations. Ground immediately to the north (or south in the Southern

Hemisphere) of a building, wall, fence or high hedge is unlikely to receive any direct sunlight, except perhaps for an hour or so in high summer. This is the place for shade-loving plants of which there are many of great beauty and variety. Many evergreens thrive in the shade and so do many early-flowering plants, including bulbs.

To the south (or north in the Southern Hemisphere) of the house there may be places that not only receive a maximum of sunlight but also shelter and reflected warmth. This is the place to plant the sun lovers, such as cistus and helianthemum, and to grow slightly tender plants such as the autumn-flowering nerine and the spring-blooming ceanothus.

There will almost certainly be other places that are part shady, part sunny, some with the sunshine dappled by the leaves of trees. Rhododendrons, azaleas and lilies are among the many plants that revel in these conditions.

There are, in fact, ideal plants for every soil and every situation and a great deal of the fun of gardening consists in finding out which are the ones that best suit your garden, and choosing those that suit your taste.

Chapter 2

Cultivation

It is quite possible to grow plants successfully without any soil at all. This is done on a large scale in some places and for special purposes in others, a kind of gardening sometimes known as hydroponics. There are several different systems but all are alike in providing the plants with some non-nutritive roothold, such as a bed of sand or ashes or a wire framework, and then surrounding their roots with a solution containing all the essential plant foods. A good many advantages can be claimed for this kind of cultivation, but invariably it suffers from one grave drawback, namely that the plant is entirely dependent upon the gardener for everything it requires. One slip or oversight may bring about catastrophe.

In the garden this is not the case. Ordinary fertile soil contains all the ingredients a plant requires for life and health and it is only in comparatively small matters that the gardener's interference is necessary. It is even possible for him to leave the garden alone for considerable periods and still get good results. All the time he is taking advantage of the natural resources of his land instead of relying exclusively on his own skill and knowledge as is essential with so artificial a system as soilless culture.

These comments are not made with any intention of running down soilless culture or belittling its value under certain circumstances. What I am anxious to do is to emphasize, by contrast, the unique value of fertile soil, and the importance of understanding its nature and the means by which it may be maintained.

What is Fertile Soil? That is not an easy question to answer but broadly speaking it will consist of a mixture of sand, clay and humus. The last is the term used by the gardener to describe any well-decayed organic matter, for example leafmould, dung, peat and the dead bodies of small animals. Fertile soil, in addition to containing a number of chemicals, some of them in such minute quantities that it is very difficult to measure them, also teems with microscopic organisms known as bacteria. Like other living things these multiply under favourable conditions and what they require is warmth, moisture and air.

When the soil was first studied scientifically the importance of these living organisms was not recognized and it was only the chemical constituents that were taken into account. As a result many of the age-old practices of the gardener were hard to explain and some of them came to be regarded as mere prejudices. It is only of comparatively recent years that the concept of 'living soil' has become widespread. With it has come the understanding of much that was previously obscure.

This idea that the soil is alive may puzzle the beginner but it is a fact which he must recognize for it explains a great deal of the work which he will have to do. For example, one of the objects of cultivation is to aerate the soil in order that useful bacteria may be encouraged to multiply more rapidly. The dung and other humus-forming materials which he digs into his garden are not only intended to feed plants and improve the texture of the soil but also to stimulate those bacteria which are most beneficial to it.

I can imagine someone saying at this point: 'Are soil bacteria really essential to plant life and if so where do they find a place in the science of hydroponics?' The answer is that they are not essential to plants though they are essential to soil fertility. In hydroponics they are ignored but without them the gardener has to provide his plants with a much greater variety of artificial foods and take elaborate precautions to prevent the accumulation of poisonous substances. Briefly what these bacteria do is to manufacture plant foods from substances which contain the essential elements but in unsuitable forms or combinations, and to neutralize or make positive substances which might do harm. Without bacteria even the richest natural soil would become infertile in time.

By no means all bacteria are beneficial from the gardener's point of view. Some reverse the work of the useful kind, wasting plant foods, producing acids and in other ways damaging the soil. Fortunately these harmful bacteria only get the upper hand in soil that is badly supplied with air or heavily saturated with water. In other words they will only be found in dangerous numbers on those types of land which gardeners refer to as waterlogged, sour, or badly aerated. A great deal of cultural work is directed towards correcting these natural faults.

Frost, Wind and Rain. Weather plays a big part in improving the fertility of soil. Frost penetrates unyielding clods of clay and chalk, expands the moisture within and bursts them asunder just as it bursts our water pipes. Any observant person will have noticed the way in which freshly dug ground tends to crumble on the surface after a spell of frosty weather.

Drying winds have a similar effect. Though some gardeners find them extremely irritating, they are really most helpful in crumbling the surface soil and so preparing it for seed sowing and planting.

Rain is the most vital of all because plant roots can only absorb food in solution and so practically everything they need from the land must first be dissolved by the rain which falls on the soil. I say 'practically everything' advisedly because the root hairs themselves do excrete weak acids which are capable of dissolving some chemicals without the agency of external water. That explains why one will sometimes find the fine network pattern of a root system covering the surface of a soft stone or lump of chalk. The acids of the root hairs have etched themselves into the stone.

The purpose of cultivation is to aid and abet all these natural forces. For example land is dug early rather than late in the winter so that as much of the surface as possible may be exposed for a long period to the beneficial effects of wind and frost.

Drains are made in order to remove surplus water, so warming the soil, allowing air to enter, and encouraging the beneficial types of bacteria. In summer soil is hoed or lightly forked in order to break the surface crust and let in air, so again stimulating bacterial activity and quickening the release of plant foods.

Types of Soil. Briefly one may classify four basic types of soil from which the rest are built up. They are sand, clay, chalk and peat or humus. Loam, of which we hear so much, is a mixture of sand, clay and humus, while marl, famous for its use as a top-dressing for some sport pitches, is a mixture of clay and chalk.

Of course no fertile soil is pure sand, pure clay, or, for that matter, pure anything else. These basic ingredients will not by themselves support plant life. But when the gardener refers to a certain soil as being of this or that type he means that this or that ingredient predominates. In practice all these terms are used extremely loosely.

Loams are of innumerable different types varying from sandy loams in which sand may form 80 per cent of the complete bulk, to heavy loams in which clay is predominant. Lime may be almost entirely absent or it may be present in considerable quantity. Fertile chalk soils are always mixed with a certain amount of sand or clay, sometimes both. Good peaty soils also often contain a high percentage of sand. It is, in fact, not possible to draw a hard and fast line between one type of soil and another and this must always be borne in mind when the terms are used.

The characteristics of the different types are important. Sandy soils are in general rather lacking in plant food and they tend to lose quickly whatever is put into them. In consequence they are in need of frequent feeding with dung, fertilizer, and so on. This is what the gardener means when he describes such soils as 'hungry'. Sandy soils are dry by comparison with other types and, because of this, they are easily worked and become warm early in the year, which means that they are suitable for the cultivation of early crops.

By contrast clays are generally well supplied with plant foods and they hold easily whatever is put into them but they are wet, cold, slow to absorb heat and difficult to work.

Chalk soils have many of the bad points of both sand and clay. Like the former they are often poor and particularly wasteful of one important plant food, nitrogen, for reasons which will be considered later. They have not the compensating earliness of sand though they are not as a rule as cold and late as clay but they are often sticky and difficult to work in winter.

Peat soils, when first cultivated, are usually poor but they improve rapidly and repay the gardener well for intelligent treatment. They are easy to work and, though often wet, can frequently be drained easily. The principal trouble with peat is that it is often very acid and this is a condition inimical to healthy bacterial activity and to much plant life.

The ideal soil is the good loam of which the gardener so often talks but is seldom able to produce. Theoretically it should be a mixture of about equal parts of sand and clay with plenty of humus and sufficient lime to correct any tendency to acidity. In actual fact even the best garden soils are generally a little deficient in one or other of these qualities and one of the gardener's first tasks is to discover just what this deficiency is and then make it good.

Subsoil. When one has walked over a piece of ground and classified the type of soil one has not said all that there is to be said about it. The surface soil is only one part of the problem. What lies beneath is of equal importance. Technically this is known as the subsoil and it may differ strikingly from what appears on top. For example, it is quite possible to have a dark, spongy, humus-laden top soil overlying a bed of solid, cheese-like clay. Not only are the two soils quite different in appearance and texture but they vary in every other respect, chemically as well as physically.

Nor is there any particular level at which the subsoil begins. In some cases it may be within 7·5 cm (3 in) of the surface, in others there may be 1·2 m (4 ft) of top soil before the subsoil begins. Sometimes the change between top soil and subsoil may be sudden and sharply defined like layers in a cake; at others the one may gradually merge into the other, without any clear line of demarcation. The only way to settle these points is to dig a number of deep holes in various parts of the garden, continuing to delve downwards until the subsoil is reached.

Acidity and Alkalinity. Another matter of great importance is the degree of acidity or alkalinity of the soil. For the sake of the non-technical reader let me explain first that acidity is the opposite of alkalinity and that a substance which is neither the one nor the other is described as neutral. Most garden crops, including ornamental plants and fruit trees, thrive best in soils which have a slight degree of acidity or are neutral. This characteristic can be measured in various ways, is expressed numerically and is described as the pH of the substance. pH7 represents neutrality. Figures below 7 denote increasing degrees of acidity, above it increasing degrees of alkalinity. The ideal garden soil will have a pH reading of between 6·5 and 7. Real trouble begins to arise when the reading gets below 5·5 or above 8. Without going into a great deal of unnecessary detail I may say that below the 5·5 limit soils become definitely acid, many crops fail to grow and various undesirable organisms multiply. Plant disorders of one kind or another are also apparent above the 8 limit, some plant foods become locked up or are wasted at an unreasonable rate.

There is, as a matter of fact, a great deal of difference between the tolerance of one plant and another for acid or alkaline soils. To give an example, rhododendrons and many heathers have adapted themselves to grow in regions which are too acid for many other plants and they have to be given these conditions when they are brought into gardens or they fall into ill health. At the other end of the scale there are plants such as chicory and wild clematis which are naturally found on chalk downs and which prefer conditions of comparatively high alkalinity.

An accurate test of the pH of a soil is really a matter for a trained chemist but a rough guide can be obtained by making use of one of the soil-testing kits that can be purchased at most garden shops. A sample of soil is placed in a test tube and a chemical indicator poured in and shaken up, after which it is left for a while for the fluid to clear. It is then matched against a colour card which indicates the pH value.

The value of Lime. When soils are seriously acid they can be corrected by dressing them with lime and that is, in fact, one of the main purposes for which lime is used in the garden. It will be readily understood from what has already been said that an excessive use of lime can be quite as harmful as lack of lime and it is therefore wise before applying it to get some idea of the condition of the soil as well as its relative acidity or alkalinity. This matter is further dealt with in the chapter on manures and fertilizers (see p. 37).

In addition to its effect in counteracting soil acidity lime also has a remarkable physical influence on heavy soils. Clay is sticky when wet because the particles of which it is composed are so fine that they are held together by the surface tension of the water covering them. When lime is added to clay these minute particles group together into small crumbs or flocks less influenced by surface tension and are consequently neither so slippery nor so close in texture. The scientist terms this process flocculation and the gardener uses it to great advantage to improve the working of difficult soils.

Soil Colour. It might not appear that the colour of soil could be of any importance, but practice shows that it has a considerable effect upon the growth of plants. The reason is that dark soil tends to absorb sun heat whereas light-coloured soil reflects the sun's rays. In consequence, other things being equal, dark soils are warmer and earlier than light soils. That is one reason why the addition of humus-forming substances such as compost, dung, leafmould and peat is valuable, because humus is dark in colour. Soot also helps in this respect besides having important manurial properties.

Chemical Analysis. So far I have said nothing about chemical analysis as a means of determining the quality and character of soil. This is not because of any poor opinion of analysis but rather because it may be out of reach of most of my readers. A detailed analysis of even one sample of soil will cost quite a lot. As soil may vary considerably from one part of the garden to another, a single sample is not of much value.

There are other difficulties about soil analysis which are not always recognized. An ordinary, straightforward analysis will give the total quantity of the more important elements which exist in the soil but it will not tell the gardener in what form they exist. It may well be that a great deal of what the analysis shows to be present is in forms which make it unavailable as plant food, at any rate for the time being. This drawback can be overcome to some extent by special methods of analysis designed to show available rather than total plant food, and the ideal is to have both kinds of analysis carried out.

Finally there is the difficulty of interpreting the analysis and using it to devize a plan of action. In many cases this is impossible for anyone but a trained soil chemist, and the best solution would be for the chemist who carries out the analysis to state plainly what it implies in terms of garden practice; for example that there is a marked deficiency in nitrogen and therefore immediate dressings of some nitrogenous fertilizers are required. Unfortunately my own experience is that chemists seldom give such practical advice. However, if the reader happens to belong to a reputable horticultural society he can get his soil analysed by that body for a quite reasonable fee and the experts will interpret the results.

Weed Indicators. I believe that for most gardeners more is to be learned from a general study of the soil and of the weeds and plants that grow in it than from chemical analysis. I will give a few examples of how this works in practice. Clover shows a considerable intolerance of acid conditions so that if clover grows naturally and freely on the ground it is a fairly certain indication that it is not highly acid. In contrast to this most heathers and rhododendrons cannot thrive on an alkaline soil, and do not even like one that approaches neutrality. These plants favour land with a marked degree of acidity. Weeds which may be associated with them are the common sheep sorrel, foxglove, bracken and spurrey. Wild gorse and broom will also be found under similar conditions.

Soils which contain large amounts of lime and are in consequence markedly alkaline will produce the wild clematis freely (this is the plant often known as old man's beard or travellers' joy) while other vegetation that is characteristic is bird's foot trefoil, kidney vetch, centaury, bladder campion and chicory.

Loamy soils that are in reasonably good condition will produce luxuriant examples of the sow thistle. Groundsel will spring up freely and become very strong. Chickweed and fat hen or goosefoot are also likely to be abundant.

On badly drained land rushes and sedges will appear while on peaty soils sphagnum moss may be abundant. Common moss is usually a sign of poverty and/or poor aeration and green scum appears on the surface under similar conditions.

The symptoms of chemical deficiency which crops may show have been dealt with in the chapter on manures and fertilizers.

Weedkillers. One purpose of cultivation is to clear land of weeds but, on occasion, this can be done by other means than digging, forking or hoeing. Weedkillers are available but they must be used with understanding of their individual characteristics. They can be divided into selective and non-selective types.

Selective weedkillers kill particular classes of plants. Some such as 2,4-D and MCPA kill most broad-leaved plants but do not harm grass. They are therefore very useful for clearing weeds from meadow grass and converting it to good lawn turf and they can also be used to keep established lawns weed free. Others, such as amitrole and MCPA, are particularly effective in killing nettles, brambles and thistles and are useful in the preliminary clearing of rough ground. In contrast dalapon kills grass but is much less poisonous to broad-leaved plants so it can be used to get rid of unwanted grass around fruit trees or in shrubberies.

Non-selective weedkillers kill everything, plants and weeds alike. Sodium chlorate was once the most widely used total weedkiller in gardens but it has serious drawbacks. It is readily washed through the soil and may damage plants it was not intended to touch. It is also highly inflammable and the dry crystals can even explode if struck, though these risks are lessened in some proprietary preparations of sodium chlorate by the addition of a fire depressant.

Simazine and dichlobenil by contrast have little tendency to move through the soil and are extremely persistent. They are particularly effective in preventing the growth of weeds on ground already dug or hoed.

Two non-selective weedkillers, paraquat and glyphosate, kill all plants they touch but are rendered innocuous by the soil. They can, in consequence, be used around growing plants so long as they are not permitted to fall on them. Moreover planting or seed sowing can proceed immediately after they have been applied, which would not be possible with sodium chlorate. Paraquat acts rapidly, especially in warm sunny weather, as it is dependent on light to be converted by the chlorophyll in the plant from an innocuous to a toxic substance. Glyphosate does not require this chemical change but is much slower in action. However, it has the additional merit of being absorbed by the plant and carried in the sap even into the roots, which are killed. It is, therefore, more effective in the long run than paraquat against deep-rooted perennial weeds.

Chapter 3

Working with Soil

Soil tillage resolves itself into two main parts: autumn and winter working on the one hand and spring and summer cultivation on the other. As a rule the soil can be far more thoroughly broken up in autumn and winter than at other times of the year.

Autumn and winter cultivation can be subdivided into four distinct operations: forking, digging, double digging and ridging. I will deal with these individually.

Forking and Digging. These operations are very similar. In both cases the object is to break the ground up to a depth of 25 cm (10 in) or so, that is to say to the full length of the prongs of a fork or the blade of a spade. In both cases, also, an attempt is made to turn each spade or forkful of soil right over so that the part which was on top is buried when the operation is completed. In this way weeds are turned in and killed and the lower soil is brought to the surface and exposed to the beneficial influence of weather (see Chapter 2).

In practice it will be found more difficult to turn the soil right over with a fork than with a spade especially if the soil is sandy or crumbles readily. Nevertheless the fork has two advantages. Firstly the work is less laborious and can be done more rapidly; and secondly with a fork it is possible to work ground that is too sticky or hard to be turned over with a spade.

In both cases the same general method should be followed. Start by digging out across one end of the plot a trench approximately 25 cm (10 in) deep and 30 cm (1 ft) wide. This

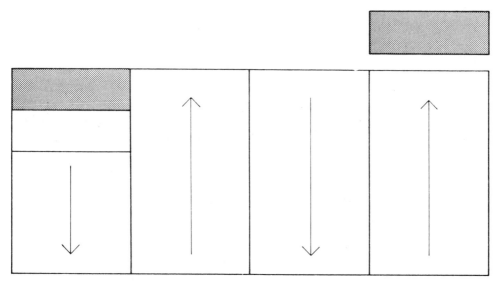

Dividing a large plot for digging. The two shaded rectangles indicate the first trench opened and the position of the soil which has been wheeled from it. The work of digging follows as indicated and the soil from the first trench is used to fill in the last trench

initial trench is most important for upon it depends a good deal of the success of the rest of the work. The soil removed from the first trench is wheeled to the far end of the plot. With a very large piece of ground it is more economical to divide it into several fairly narrow strips and deal with each separately. In this case the soil from the first trench is wheeled to the opposite side of the plot, as shown in the diagram.

Now start at one end of the trench, face it and thrust in the fork or spade to its full depth and about 15 cm (6 in) back from the edge of the trench. Lever the soil up by pulling backwards on the handle. Slip one hand well down the shaft, lift the spadeful of soil and turn it right over, at the same time throwing it forward into the trench. Continue in this way right across the plot until the whole of a 15 cm (6 in) wide strip has been dug forward into the previously made trench. If this work is properly done there will still be a trench 25 cm (10 in) deep and 30 cm (1 ft) wide into which the next 15 cm (6 in) of soil can be turned in the same way. Operations proceed in the same manner, strip by strip, until the whole plot has been dug, when the last trench is filled with the soil removed from the first trench.

One mistake which the beginner frequently makes is that of failing to throw the soil sufficiently far forward so that the trench becomes blocked up and there is no room to work. Another is that he does not turn each spadeful right over, with the result that some grass and weed is left on the top. Yet another point to watch is that the spade or fork is thrust vertically into the soil to its full depth. If it is pushed in at an angle, the ground will be covered more rapidly but cultivation will not be anything like so deep or thorough. The last error to avoid is that of taking too much soil at a time; 15 cm (6 in) is quite enough; more makes heavy going and bad work.

Double Digging. This is a method of breaking up the ground more deeply than by forking or digging, and yet avoiding the danger of bringing relatively infertile subsoil to the top.

Briefly the method is as follows: start as for digging but make the trench 25 cm (10 in) deep and 60 cm (2 ft) wide. As before, the soil displaced should be wheeled to the far end of the plot, or the far side if the plot is big and to be worked in strips. Now get into the bottom of the trench so formed and fork or dig it from one end to the other. To do this it will be necessary to face at right angles to the position adopted for the preliminary digging. In this way the soil is broken up a further 25 cm (10 in) deep but is still left lying in the bottom of the first trench. Mark out another 60 cm (2 ft) strip behind the first trench. Turn the top soil from this, spadeful by spadeful, into the first trench on top of the broken-up subsoil. When this second trench is finished, get into the bottom of it with spade or fork and break it up as before. The work continues in this way, one 60 cm (2 ft) strip after another, until the whole plot has been trenched. Again the soil displaced from the first trench will be used to fill the last one.

Ridging. Another occasionally useful item of autumn or winter cultivation is known as ridging. The object in this case is not so much directly to break up the soil as to expose as large a surface as possible to the pulverizing action of weather.

There are several methods of ridging, but it will suffice to describe one. The ground is first divided into 90 cm (3 ft) wide strips, each of which will be made into a ridge. Start at the end of one of these strips and take out a trench 30 cm (1 ft) wide and about 25 cm

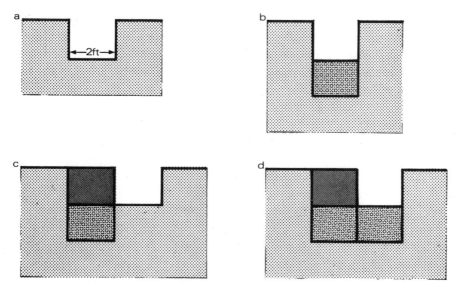

Double digging. (a) The first trench is 60 cm (2 ft) wide and about 25 cm (10 in) deep. The soil is removed and used to fill the last trench. (b) Subsoil is broken up with a fork. (c) Another 60 cm (2 ft) strip of soil is turned over on to the broken-up subsoil of the first trench. (d) The bottom of this fresh trench is broken up and the work is continued in the same way throughout the plot

(10 in) deep across it, i.e. the whole trench will be 90 cm (3 ft) long. Now work back down the length of this strip as for ordinary digging, turning the soil forward and over but bringing the spadefuls from each extremity of the short trench towards the centre. In this way a ridge will be built up as the strip is dug. Each strip is dealt with in the same way until the whole plot is turned up into a series of ridges which should be as steep as possible. The illustration below makes this process clear.

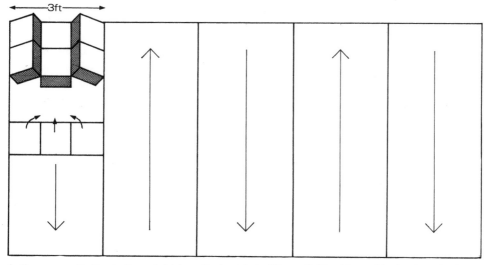

A diagrammatic illustration of ridging. Each strip is 90 cm (3 ft) wide and is dug lengthwise, the central spadeful of soil being turned forwards and the left and right turned inwards. The work is continued up and down the strips as indicated by the arrows

Spring and Summer Cultivations. These mainly consist of forking, raking and hoeing with the object first of breaking down clods left by the winter digging and, secondly, of destroying weeds and maintaining a loose, finely broken layer of soil on the surface.

Clods may be broken down with a fork or special hoe. The latter is rather like a short, three-pronged fork with its tines set at right angles to the handle. It is a very good tool for this particular purpose and it can be used with quick, swinging blows to break down even the stiffest lumps of clay. When using this hoe work forwards across the ground and deal with one small strip at a time.

The fork is used with a swinging motion from side to side when breaking down lumps and it is the backs rather than the points of the tines which do the work.

Do not, at this first breaking down, attempt to get the soil too fine. For a great many plants and even for the sowing of large seeds, very finely broken soil is a drawback rather than a help, as it tends to set badly after heavy rain. It is only when sowing small seeds that an extremely fine seed bed is essential, since otherwise it would be impossible to sow the seeds sufficiently near the surface.

Another important point is that this spring preparation must be done when the soil is in just the right condition, which will be when it is drying out rapidly on the surface as a result of sunshine or wind.

Raking. This is an art which takes a little mastering. The object should be to break up lumps of soil and not just drag them off the surface. To do this the rake should be used with long strokes both towards and away from the operator. Just as much power should be employed in the movement away from the body as towards it and in fact it is in this second part of the action that most of the breaking up takes place. If raking is properly done it will be mainly stones that remain to be gathered up at the finish.

Hoeing. There are three distinct reasons for hoeing: one, to kill weeds by disturbing seedlings and severing larger weeds; two, to thin out plants and particularly to 'single', i.e. reduce seedlings sown in rows to one every few centimetres and three, to break down lumps. A fourth use for the hoe is to draw seed drills.

There are also two main types of hoe, the Dutch hoe with the blade set roughly in the same plane as the handle, and the draw hoe with the blade set at right angles to the handle. The former is used by pushing it away from the body and then drawing it back again, all the time moving slowly backwards across the ground. It is most serviceable for weed eradication between plants. The draw hoe is used by pulling it towards the body with chopping and 'drawing' motions and is most serviceable for singling, breaking down lumps, severing weeds growing in rather stiff soil and drawing soil up towards plants, a process known as 'earthing up'.

Chapter 4

Drainage Problems

Waterlogging is very bad for soil even if it occurs at times of the year when there are no crops actually in the ground. If this seems to require a little explanation the reader should refer to the paragraph about soil bacteria and their activities as described in Chapter 2. I would stress that bacteria, though they are probably most familiar to us as agents of disease, are by no means all harmful. Many are absolutely essential to the health of the soil and without them the best land will soon become infertile. On the other hand there are other kinds of bacteria which are harmful to the soil, wasting plant foods, producing poisons and quickly preventing all satisfactory plant growth. It so happens that the useful bacteria require air, whereas most of those that are harmful only thrive where there is little or no air. If soil is saturated with water air will be driven out of it, the useful bacteria will perish and the harmful ones will obtain the upper hand.

That is just one of the evils of waterlogging. Another is that it chills the soil, while a third and equally vital point is that roots also require air and if deprived of it for long they will die. It is no uncommon thing to see whole groups of trees in low-lying orchards burst into bud in the spring and then suddenly wither and die without apparent cause. So frequent is this in some places and so destructive of trees that it has been dubbed 'The Death' and various causes have been suggested. The true explanation in almost every case is that this particular area has been waterlogged for some period during the winter, that all fine roots have died in consequence, and that the brief burst of activity in the spring was simply made on the stored-up sap in the branches. When this was exhausted, the trees died.

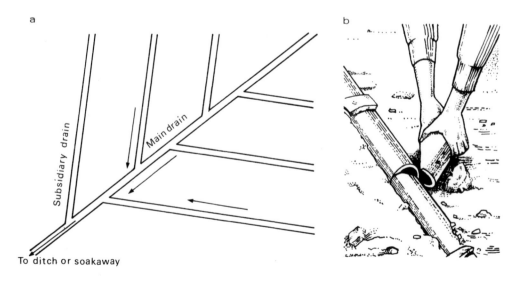

The herring-bone system of drainage. (a) All drains must slope towards the soakaway shown at the bottom left of the diagram. (b) Making a junction between land drain pipes

Cultivation to Improve Drainage. By no means all soils require drainage, nor is this even always necessary on soils which show a certain degree of winter water-logging. Where the trouble is not very serious it can often be overcome by thorough cultivation, particularly if this can be accompanied by generous dressings of dung, well-rotted compost, straw, peat or leafmould, any of which will improve texture and allow water to flow more freely. Heavy liming will often effect a wonderful improvement on clay soils for the reasons I have already explained in the section on lime, p. 37-9. In fact unless there are obvious reasons for believing that such treatment will not effect a remedy, cultivation and the addition of extra lime and humus should always be tried first as a remedy for water-logging because drainage is invariably an expensive undertaking and frequently a difficult one, especially in small gardens with limited outlet for water.

One problem which is often hard to overcome is to find any suitable outlet for the water once it has been collected in drains. In fields and large estates there are either ditches or main drains into which subsidiary drains may be directed but the owner of a small garden seldom has any such facilities. It is against the law to open a sewer for the purpose of running a land drain into it and the only alternative as a rule is to dig in the lowest part of the garden a soakaway which must be of considerable size and depth if it is to be of any practical value in the event of a rainstorm.

Land Drains. The method of draining land is to dig narrow trenches at intervals of about 3·6 m (12 ft) and to a depth which will be dictated by the depth of the subsoil. Soil becomes waterlogged because the subsoil is so hard or close textured that water cannot soak through it and in consequence it forms a pan on which the water lies. A drain, to be effective, must be laid at just about the level of this pan, neither higher nor lower. If the drain is too deep, it will itself be protected by the pan and very little water will get into it. If, on the other hand, it is too high, water will still stand below it and the evil will not be fully overcome. As a rule the top of the really impervious subsoil is anything from 30-60 cm (1-2 ft) below the surface and that is approximately the depth to which land drains should be dug. Each drain must have a continuous slope in one direction, though it need not be greater than 30 cm (1 ft) in 12·2 m (40 ft). Frequently it is most convenient to have a number of subsidiary drains communicating with a central drain, in which case what is termed the herring-bone pattern is generally followed.

When the drainage trenches have been dug, something must be put into them to keep them open at the bottom and provide a free passage for the water. There are several alternatives. The best, but also the most expensive, is the earthenware land pipe which is simply a cylindrical length of earthenware pipe without joints or flanges. To be fully effective it should be laid on a clinker or stone bottom with more hard rubble surrounding and covering it. The pipes are butted end to end but there is no attempt to make the joints between the pipes tight for it is through them that the water seeps into the pipes. The purpose of the surrounding rubble is to prevent earth being washed down into the drain and silting it up. The very best drains have the rubble graded, the coarsest pieces surrounding the pipes and the finer material being used on top to act as a filter. Finally the trenches are refilled with soil.

Where one pipe drain leads into another the joints are made by cracking the pipes with a hammer and covering them with a few crocks.

An alternative to pipe drainage is a plain stone drain. In this case the bottom of the trench is filled for 23 cm (9 in) with fairly large clinkers, brick ends or other coarse rubble. Then the material is gradually graded off to finer samples with breeze or gravel on top to make the filter. The efficiency of stone drains depends a great deal on the type of material used. The harder and more angular it is the better and there is nothing to beat well burned boiler clinkers. If the rubble is too small or smooth the drain tends to silt up after a few years and then has to be re-made.

Very often the cheapest method of all is to fill the bottoms of the trenches with faggots (bundles of brushwood) laid end to end. These can be made from almost any brushwood, but hazel, when available, is preferable to most other kinds. It is a great advantage if turfs can be laid grass side downwards on top of the faggots before the soil is returned to the trenches. Well-made faggot drains will remain effective for years but if insufficient wood is used or it is too soft and unbranched the drain soon collapses and is useless.

The Soakaway. I referred earlier in this chapter to a soakaway. This is a device for collecting surplus water and allowing it to drain away slowly into the more porous layers which often underlie the first subsoil. The effectiveness of a soakaway will depend partly on its size but even more upon whether it can be driven right down through the subsoil to a more open layer beneath. Sometimes it is possible to penetrate the impervious subsoil by digging a hole 1·3 m (4½ ft) deep but in other places – my own garden is an example – one has to go down at least 3·6 m (12 ft) before getting to anything through which water can flow freely. In diameter the soakaway may be of any convenient dimensions but it is seldom wise to have it less than 90 cm (3 ft) across; 1·8 m (6 ft) is a more usual measurement. It is, in effect, a well, but it differs in that once it has been dug it is immediately filled to within say 30 cm (1 ft) of the surface with large stones, clinkers or other hard rubble and is then covered over with soil. The soakaway is, of course, made at the lowest part of the ground to be drained so that all drains may eventually discharge their water into it.

Chapter 5
Creating Paths

Paths are so permanent a feature of the garden and have such a tendency to dominate the rest of the layout that it pays to think carefully before deciding where they should go and of what material they should be made. And yet, having delivered this warning, I find it next to impossible to give any further advice beyond suggesting that common sense is often the best guide. There are, I know, various stock rules about the siting of paths: that they should be centred on a main window or door; that they should lead somewhere and not just meander about aimlessly; that there should not be too many of them and, in particular, that they should not cut the garden up into awkward shapes or leave narrow, useless borders against fences. But there are so many exceptions to all these generalizations that they may be more hindrance than help to the garden planner, and the best advice I can give is to suggest that each problem must be solved in its own way according to the obvious needs of the situation.

When it comes to the matter of path construction it is possible to be far more precise. Even the width of a path is a matter upon which some fairly definite statements can be made. Main paths should seldom be less than 1·2 m (4 ft) wide; 1·7 m (5½ ft) is often better. Side paths can sometimes be as little as 60 cm (2 ft) in width but this is about the minimum except for the little tracks that are often used to give access to out-of-the-way parts of the rock garden.

Again one can dogmatize to some extent regarding materials. Main paths do need to be made of something that will stand up to heavy wear. That rules out thin paving slabs set in sand and also grass paths, attractive though these can be in the right place. Asphalt has the necessary wearing qualities but does not blend well with the garden and in my opinion is suitable only for car drives. Gravel can be costly in upkeep though modern weedkillers have eased this problem a little. Nevertheless I do not favour gravel around the house because it can cling to boots and be carried indoors.

By this process of elimination one is left with three obvious possibilities – thick paving slabs preferably set in cement, paths made entirely of concrete, and brick paths. The last can be charming in the right setting but suffer from one serious drawback, a tendency to become dangerously slippery in wet weather. Concrete by itself is the solution which thousands of small-garden owners have accepted in the past and no doubt will continue to accept in the future. It has the merits of cheapness, durability and safety and the added advantage that any handyman can lay it himself. Its greatest drawback is that it does not look very sightly. This can be overcome to some extent by careful tinting – but beware of overdoing this or the cure can be worse than the trouble. A popular alternative is the precast paving slab available in a variety of sizes and finishes. These can be set in various patterns or may be decorated with panels or edgings of other materials such as bricks or pebbles set in concrete. Good non–slip surfaces are available and though such slabs do not weather as attractively as natural stone paving they are considerably cheaper. Further off, in a vegetable and fruit garden, gravel may prove a perfectly satisfactory material, provided it is of the type that will bind when rolled and not remain permanently loose as is

Making a path. (a) Before surfacing, a good foundation of at least 10 cm (4 in) of hard rubble should be laid. (b) Tamping down concrete. The board is shaped to ride on the shuttering and level off the surface. (c) Bedding paving slabs in cement, using a spirit level to ensure an even surface. (d) Laying circular slabs in a lawn. Each slab should be set 12 mm ($\frac{1}{2}$ in) below the surface of the grass to allow a mower to pass freely over it

the case with sea shingle. I know of nothing more tiring to walk on than this.

Every path needs a good foundation – or, to be more precise, at least 10 cm (4 in) of hard rubble below the surfacing material. Without this there is bound to be trouble in winter when water will collect beneath the surface and heave it up whenever there is a sharp frost. Incidentally, a well-made path with a good depth of clinker or brick ends beneath it can act as a very serviceable garden drain and considerably improve the surface condition of a wet plot, especially if the lowermost part of the path can be made to communicate with a soakaway or ditch.

When gravel is used for surfacing there should be at least 5 cm (2 in) of it on top of the foundation layer, and it should be well watered and rolled as it is spread. A 2·5 cm (1 in) layer of asphalt makes an excellent path provided it is bedded on a solid layer of hard rubble; in fact 12 mm (½ in) of asphalt will do for paths that will not receive a great deal of wear. It must be well tamped down as it is laid and all asphalt paths should be given a distinct camber, that is, slope downwards from centre to sides, so that they throw off water readily. Water collecting and freezing beneath asphalt can cause disaster in no time.

Bricks can be laid in a variety of ways; flat, on edge, in straight rows, herring-bone fashion, in squares and so on. Moreover they can simply be bedded in sand, with more sand brushed down into the crevices between them, or they can be set in cement mortar which makes a far stronger but also considerably more expensive job. Another drawback of cement setting is that it limits the possibility of establishing small creeping plants, such as thymes and sandworts (arenaria) between the bricks. This can be overcome to some extent by leaving unmortared crevices here and there and confining the plants to these chosen spots.

Paving slabs can be bedded in sand or ashes, a method which provides almost endless possibilities in planting and the plants, as they become established, will help to bind the paving slabs in position. Nevertheless there is always some danger of slabs working loose, and even one rocking or sticking up a little above its neighbours can be a source of considerable danger. For this reason it is better to bed the slabs on all main paths in cement, though an occasional pocket can be left in which to introduce a few plants.

The preparation of good concrete, either for path making by itself or as a setting medium for bricks or paving slabs, is not quite so simple as it might appear. The first essential is to purchase really fresh cement. Old cement, though it may still be powdery and apparently in good condition, never gives the hard set possible with a fresh sample. The other two ingredients, ballast and sand, should be mixed in the proportions of two parts by bulk of the former to one of the latter. To this the cement is added at the rate of one part to six of the aggregate.

Be sure that all the ingredients are thoroughly mixed while still dry. Then add water, a little at a time, turning the heap meanwhile and continue in this way until the whole mass is easily worked without being sloppy. This is rather important. If too much water is applied, the cement will tend to float on top of the concrete when it is laid and later it will scale off, leaving a bad surface and the set will not be hard. The correct condition of wetness is sometimes described as 'greasy'. It is a little like that; but perhaps it will help the novice more to say that it should have the consistency of very stiff porridge. It is very important to tamp the surface well with a straight-edged plank to force out the air from between the stones.

When bricks or slabs are laid on concrete it is wise to scrape out the joints as one goes along and fill them up later (this is known as pointing) with a specially fine mixture made with three parts sand to one of cement. This, or the concrete itself, can be tinted by mixing in a very small quantity of any of the painter's recognized pigments, such as Venetian red or yellow ochre. Add this while mixing the dry materials. The right proportions will have to be found by experiment.

When laying crazy paving paths start with the bigger slabs and then fill in the spaces afterwards in the style of a jigsaw puzzle. Sometimes there is a lot of clay adhering to the stones. This should first be removed as if left it will be very difficult to bed the slabs level and firm.

Concrete can be given various finishes by brushing, raking or scoring it when it is beginning to set but is not completely hard. Brushing with a stiff broom will remove surface cement and expose the aggregate, and various effects can be produced in this way according to the particle size and colour of the aggregate. Raking or scoring with the point of a mason's trowel can be used to form patterns in the concrete and, by making it a little rough, will also reduce slipperiness when wet.

Chapter 6
Manures and Fertilizers

No very clear dividing line can be drawn between a manure and a fertilizer. Broadly speaking the term 'manure' is used by gardeners to denote the bulkier soil foods of organic origin such as dung, leafmould, compost, spent hops, etc., while 'fertilizer' is taken to denote more concentrated forms of inorganic food such as superphosphate of lime, sulphate of ammonia and sulphate of potash. But there are plenty of examples which do not fit neatly into either of these groups and in the following notes I shall not attempt to make any distinction between them but simply explain the particular value and the method of use of each substance named in alphabetical order.

At the outset it may be well to consider why it is necessary to apply manures and fertilizers at all. Under natural conditions there is no such addition or, at any rate, it is not very obvious to the casual observer, yet weeds and grasses appear to thrive quite satisfactorily.

The explanation is twofold. First of all even in uncultivated soil manuring of a kind does go on, partly by the agency of earthworms which pull decaying leaves and other vegetation into the soil, and also by the surface decay of vegetation and myriads of small creatures. Second the gardener requires much more intensive cropping than would occur under natural conditions and this exhausts the soil of certain vital plant foods more rapidly than would otherwise be the case.

Every fertile soil, besides containing enough plant food in suitable form for immediate use, also holds considerable reserves of all the essential chemicals which in time will be rendered available by the action of weather and soil organisms, such as the bacteria discussed in Chapter 2. All the gardener has to do is to supplement these natural supplies of essential chemicals and especially to balance them where one tends to be in excess of another or some of the crops he wishes to grow have a particular requirement.

A distinction should be drawn between feeding the soil and feeding plants. Both are necessary in certain circumstances but the former is considerably the more important of the two. By feeding the soil I mean adding to it substances which will enrich it chemically for a considerable time and also, in many instances, stimulate the living organisms which form so vital a part of it. Dung and compost come into this category and so do nitrogenous fertilizers applied with a green manure to assist in its decay.

When the rapid feeding of plants is essential the gardener must make use of chemicals which are either immediately available for absorption by the roots or can be changed into suitable forms by one or two simple stages and in a short time. Nitrate of soda is an example of such a food. In solution it can be absorbed by the roots at once and an effect may be observed in increased growth and deepened colour of foliage in three or four days. Contrast this with the effect of bonemeal which is not soluble in water and only liberates the useful phosphoric acid it contains after a period of disintegration in the soil. Even when bonemeal is very finely ground so that the greatest possible surface is exposed to the action of soil acids and bacteria it may be weeks before any appreciable benefit is observed in the growth of plants.

Essential Foods. It is not known exactly how many chemicals are essential in the soil for the growth of plants but it has been shown that something like fifteen or sixteen substances appear to be required. From the gardener's point of view, however, the four most important foods are nitrogen, phosphorus, potassium (potash) and calcium, with manganese running these a close fifth and sulphur, iron, boron, copper, zinc and molybdenum tagging along somewhere in the rear. It is usual to refer to the first six of these as major and the remainder as trace elements since they are required in smaller quantity, but all are equally essential to healthy plant growth. The first four, nitrogen, phosphorus, potash and calcium, are the most likely to be deficient in soil, and are, in consequence, those which the gardener will most frequently need to supply.

At this point I must explain another matter. Nitrogen, phosphorus, calcium, etc. are elements which, as a rule, cannot usefully be applied to the soil in their pure state. Nitrogen, for example, is a gas which forms a major part of the air that we breathe and it would be quite impractical to put it into the soil as nitrogen. But all these elements combine with others to form salts or organic compounds and it is in these forms that the gardener puts them into the soil. Nevertheless even when it is found that a particular salt of one of these elements is soluble in water, it does not follow that the plant will be able to make immediate use of it. Plants are finicky in this respect. They like their foods in certain well-defined forms and if the wrong form is supplied it must remain in the soil until it is changed into the right form. Sometimes this takes a long time and that is one reason why some fertilizers are quicker acting than others.

Balanced Feeding. Before considering what effect each particular food has upon the plant I must make it clear that lack of any one food may affect the usefulness of all or any of the others, and also that excess of one may produce an apparent shortage of another. Sometimes it is the balance or proportion between foods which is vital. Imagine a soil which contains a normal quantity of nitrogen and potash, both in forms suitable for use as plant food. In consequence plants grow normally and show no signs of starvation. Then for some reason the quantity of nitrogen is greatly increased. As one result there may soon be signs of potash deficiency which will disappear only when the potash content of the soil is also raised above the normal. An understanding of this will explain many otherwise inexplicable soil problems and will also answer the question why it is just as necessary to keep a balance of food in a garden that is in a high state of cultivation as one in which the soil is comparatively poor. It also follows that, although one may speak of this or that effect being the principal one produced by any particular food it is quite wrong to think of it as the only effect produced. A well-balanced soil can be given an all-round boost by applications of Growmore two weeks before sowing or planting out.

Specific Influences. Here are some indications of the way in which some of these foods influence growth.

Nitrogen has its most marked effect upon rate and vigour of growth and colour of foliage. When nitrogen is in short supply plants tend to be stunted, leaves are small and pale or bluish in colour. Add nitrogen in a suitable form and the rate of growth immediately increases, the leaves becoming large, lush and dark green.

Phosphorus also has a considerable effect upon growth though not quite so markedly as in the case of nitrogen. Nevertheless when phosphorus is very deficient there will be many of the symptoms of nitrogen starvation. Perhaps the most spectacular effect of phosphorus is on roots which grow freely when it is abundant but are poor and stunted when it is lacking. That is one reason why fairly large doses of phosphatic fertilizers are always advised for root crops. It is very important that seedlings and other young plants shall have adequate phosphorus so that they can form good root systems. Phosphorus also has a marked effect on the satisfactory ripening of seeds and fruits though curiously enough it does not appear to be very important for orchard cultivation.

Potash is, however, the principal fruit-forming fertilizer. As already suggested there is a close linkage between the effect of potash and nitrogen on plants. When the proportion of nitrogen is increased potash must be added also or it will appear to be deficient though it was present previously in adequate quantity. When there is insufficient potash in the soil in relation to the nitrogen present, fruits tend to be poorly coloured and lacking in flavour, faults which disappear directly potash is added. Potatoes in potash-starved land cook badly, turning black and soapy though others nearby with plenty of this element are white, floury and of first-class quality. Potash also has a striking effect on foliage for when it is deficient leaves, particularly of fruit trees, become scorched at the edges much as they would be scorched by drought or excessive heat.

Calcium is the element which the gardener adds to the soil when he limes it, for quick-lime is calcium oxide, hydrated lime is calcium hydroxide and chalk and limestone are calcium carbonate. It enters into the constitution of all plants and is essential to them, but there is generally sufficient in the soil for their needs. Lime must be regarded as one of the major soil foods because of its importance in the soil itself where, as already explained, it flocculates clay (i.e. turns it into small granules) and corrects acidity, thereby stimulating bacterial activity and aiding the liberation of other plant foods.

Magnesium is used in the formation of chlorophyll, the substance which makes leaves green. When magnesium is in short supply leaves develop purplish or brown patches between the veins and may fall prematurely.

Though iron is said not to occur in chlorophyll it does in some way assist its formation because plants that are short of iron develop yellow or very pale leaves, a condition known as chlorosis. Similar symptoms are produced by shortage of manganese.

Boron is one of the so-called trace elements, that is to say it is only required in very minute quantities above which it acts as a plant poison. Some conditions which were once regarded as diseases, such as brown heart in turnips and swedes, cracking in celery and death of the shoot tip in sunflowers and some other plants, have been shown to be due to lack of this element. Nevertheless the amateur must go carefully in using boron because the maximum dose required does not usually exceed 56 g per 25 sq m (2 oz per 30 sq yd) and even this may prove too much. It is difficult to distribute 56 g (2 oz) of any material evenly over 25 sq m (30 sq yd) of ground, so first mix it thoroughly and evenly with a suitable carrier such as fine sand.

Zinc, copper and molybdenum also come into this class of trace elements but are best left alone by the gardener unless he is certain they are required.

Complete or Compound Fertilizers. These general terms are used to describe any mixtures of chemicals which provide nitrogen, phosphorus and potash in reasonable quantity. It will be observed that such mixtures are not complete in the sense of supplying every single food which may possibly be deficient in the soil. In fact the description arose many years ago when it was supposed that these three elements were the only ones about which the gardener need trouble. It still remains true that they are the three most likely to be in short supply so that the all-purpose fertilizer like Growmore is the best general standby for the gardener. Manufacturers are generally required to declare the amount of available nitrogen, phosphorus and potash in the fertilizer which they produce. Sometimes a fertilizer will be described solely in the terms of this analysis, in which case the quotation will be for nitrogen, phosphoric acid and potash in that order. A fertilizer described as 6:8:4 will contain 6 per cent nitrogen, 8 per cent phosphorous and 4 per cent potash.

Mixing Fertilizers. Not all chemicals which are themselves suitable as fertilizers can be mixed satisfactorily. In some cases there is an immediate and very noticeable chemical reaction, as, for example, when sulphate of ammonia is mixed with lime, the result of which is to liberate quantities of ammonia gas which is most unpleasant, causing choking and watering at the eyes. Ammonia lost is nitrogen lost. In other instances the reaction is less obvious though not necessarily less serious. For example, if lime is added to super-phosphate of lime much of the soluble phosphoric acid will be converted into insoluble calcium phosphate which will not become available as plant food for a very long time. For these reasons it is wise to stick to well-tried or properly recommended formulae.

Another important point about mixing one fertilizer with another is that each ingredient must be ground as finely as possible and that the whole lot must be mixed thoroughly. If this is not done one part of the soil will get an excess of one chemical, another of some other chemical. That is one advantage of purchasing proprietary compound or complete fertilizers. These are ground and mixed by machinery with better results than can be obtained by hand. Many fertilizers, even those of an organic nature, are now available in granular form which is much pleasanter to handle since there is no dust and they are much easier to distribute evenly.

LIST OF MANURES AND FERTILIZERS

Though you won't be able to obtain all of the following, it is still useful to know the different ways in which soil can be improved.

Bark. Pulverized or shredded bark can be used as a soil conditioner to improve the soil texture and increase its humus content and also makes a good surface mulch to retain moisture, protect roots and suppress weeds. It can be used in potting composts too in the same way as peat and is specially useful for epiphytic plants like some orchids, many bromeliads and a few cacti. Bark is improved by being composted and partly rotted after shredding. Most commercial supplies come from coniferous forests and are much cheaper if they can be bought direct in bulk rather than in bags. Bark contains little available plant food and may even cause a temporary reduction of available nitrogen in the soil so it is usually advisable to give some nitrogen-rich fertilizer at the time of use or soon after. As a surface mulch pulverized bark can be spread 2·5 cm (1 in) thick or as a soil conditioner dug in at the rate of 3·2-6·4 kg per 0·8 sq m (7-14 lb per sq yd).

Blood. Dried blood is not as a rule fully soluble in water but can be used to make liquid manure if it is well stirred and applied at once. A good sample will have an analysis of about 12 per cent nitrogen. This is readily available and in consequence dried blood can be used as a spring and summer fertilizer either before sowing or planting or to plants in growth. Increased growth may be observed within a week of application which makes it one of the quickest acting organic fertilizers. Rates will vary from 28-85 g per 0·8 sq m (1–3 oz per sq yd), or 14–28 g per 4·5 l (½–1 oz per gal) of water.

Bonemeal. This is a favourite phosphatic fertilizer with gardeners and has the merit of being extremely steady in action. The phosphorus which it contains is liberated slowly over a long period, the rate of its release being increased by fine grinding and an acid soil. The analysis varies from about 20–25 per cent phosphoric acid. Bonemeal is most useful for autumn and winter applications and has little immediate effect on growth. It can be used at rates of from 113–170 g per 0·8 sq m (4–6 oz per sq yd), or 85–113 g per 36 l (3–4 oz per 8 gal) of potting soil.

Chelates. See **Sequestrols** (p. 43).

Coal Ashes. These have no value as a fertilizer though gritty ashes from a furnace with a quick draught are useful for lightening heavy soil. Ordinary domestic coal ashes are too soft and fine in texture to have any useful effect.

Compost. This is a general name given to any decayed organic matter, for example leaves (leafmould), grass mowings, hedge clippings, refuse from the vegetable garden, etc. All these materials may be dug into the soil in their natural state but it is usually better to convert them into compost by one of the controlled processes of decay. In practice there does not appear to be much difference between the results obtained from any of these methods. Provided the final result is a dark brown or blackish mass in which there is little trace of the original ingredient such as undecayed leaves or stems, the compost may be applied in the same way and amounts as animal manure with similar results.

As air is necessary for healthy decay it is inadvisable to make compost heaps too wide or too high, though they may be of any convenient length. Usually 90 cm (3 ft) should be regarded as the maximum width and height of a heap when first built.

The rate of decay can be increased and the quality of the compost improved by treating it with nitrogen and lime in one form or another. The purpose of the first is to feed and thereby stimulate bacteria and of the second to counteract acidity. A number of excellent proprietary accelerators are marketed or use can be made of one of the fertilizers which provide these substances, for example calcium cyanamide, nitro–chalk or nitrate of lime. A third alternative is to dust alternate layers of the heap as it is built with a nitrogenous fertilizer such as sulphate of ammonia and some form of lime such as quicklime or hydrated lime, but the two should not be mixed or brought into direct contact with each other or ammonia gas will be released and its valuable nitrogen content lost.

Other essentials to satisfactory and rapid decay are warmth and moisture. In consequence the compost heap should be built in a sheltered position, though not a sunny one, and any parts of it which appear dry should be thoroughly soaked with water. More even decay results if the heap is completely turned after about one month, the interior portion being brought to the outside and the latter turned inwards. At the same time any parts which appear dry should be thoroughly moistened with water or liquid manure.

Cow Manure. The value of cow manure as plant food will depend partly upon the way in which the cattle from which it was obtained have been fed and also upon the manner in which it has been stored. Fresh cow manure from cake-fed beasts will have the highest analysis and may contain something like 0·8 per cent of nitrogen, 0·4 per cent of phosphoric acid and 0·7 per cent of potash. It is, therefore, a well-balanced plant food.

There tends to be a rapid wastage of plant food elements, and particularly of nitrogen, if the manure is exposed to air and rain. The best method of storing farmyard manure so that it does not deteriorate is to build it into a compact stack under a roof of some kind and then to cover it all over with at least 15 cm (6 in) of soil beaten down hard.

As animal manure decays it loses bulk and it is possible, because of this, that an old sample may show a higher chemical analysis than a fresh sample, but this should not be allowed to obscure the fact that some of the valuable plant food originally contained in the manure has been lost. Undoubtedly the most economical method of using this or any other form of animal manure is to dig it in fresh. Unfortunately there are two drawbacks: first that the plant foods contained are not immediately available but must first be liberated by bacterial action, and second that in the process of decomposition acids may be formed in the soil and prove harmful to plant life. In time they may be washed out or neutralized but the use of fresh manure is not desirable on soils that are known to be already acid.

Where it is essential that the manure used shall have an immediate effect on plant growth it is necessary to use samples that have already decayed to a condition where they are of an even texture throughout, without any straw or other bedding remaining readily

Making a compost heap in a special steel wire container. The compost is built up in 15 cm (6 in) layers each of which is sprinkled with a proprietary compost accelerator or nitrogenous fertilizer. To ensure even decay the heap should be turned after about a month and any parts which appear dry should be thoroughly moistened. Other kinds of compost bin can be bought from garden centres. Or you can make your own with wood slats.

identifiable. Such manure can be used as a topdressing to plants in growth either alone or mixed with an equal bulk of soil, or can be dug into the ground at rates up to 50 kg per 5 sq m (1 cwt per 6 sq yd).

Fresh cow manure is best applied to vacant ground in autumn or early winter.

Feathers. All types are rich in nitrogen and in consequence valuable as a soil dressing. A 50 kg (1 cwt) pile of feathers is sufficient for 200-250 sq m (240-300 sq yd) of ground, or a plot about the size of an ordinary allotment. The average analysis is about 8 per cent of nitrogen, which is slowly released.

Fish Waste. This, like other organic matter, contains a lot of potentially valuable plant food. The flesh and offal are particularly rich in nitrogen while the bones contain a high percentage of phosphorus. Fresh fish refuse of all kinds may be dug into the soil as a substitute for animal manure and is estimated to have approximately the same chemical value, though its mechanical effect upon the texture of the soil is not so good as that of stable or farmyard manure prepared with plenty of straw. It is very unpleasant stuff to have lying about for any length of time and the best method of using it is to keep a trench open on a vacant plot of ground and throw the refuse into this as it becomes available, turning soil on top of it at once. The rate of application will be the same as animal manure, that is to say 50 kg (1 cwt) may be spread over from 5-20 sq m (6-24 sq yd) of ground according to the poverty of the soil and the type of crop to be grown. As a rule such refuse will contain more nitrogen than either phosphorus or potash and so for crops which require a balanced food supplementary dressings of phosphoric and potassic fertilizers should be given at the appropriate season.

Fish Guano is a name given to fish waste prepared in specific factories. It is dried and granulated and can be kept for long periods without decaying or becoming unpleasant. It is much richer in plant food than fresh fish waste and analysis will vary from sample to sample within the range of nitrogen 5-10 per cent, phosphoric acid 6-14 per cent, potash 0·5-0·8 per cent. It should be used like a fertilizer as a dressing at the rate of 85-113 g per 0·8 sq m (3-4 oz per sq yd) in late winter or early spring on ground that is about to be planted or sown.

Fish Manure is a name given to a mixed or complete fertilizer prepared with a fairly high percentage of dried fish guano but with added phosphorus and potash to make it a better balanced plant food. As the formula will vary according to the ideas of the manufacturer his instructions regarding use must always be followed.

Guano. This is rarely sold but is well worth a mention. Originally this name was applied solely to the dried deposit left by sea birds on certain points along the coast of Peru. This is an almost rainless district and as a result the bird droppings remain for many years and retain their manurial value. Similar deposits occur in other areas such as the Persian Gulf, Red Sea and coastal regions of south west Africa.

This natural guano is a rich, complete manure varying in analysis according to the region from which it comes, that from very dry areas containing the highest percentage of nitrogen. Analysis may show differences as wide as 2-12 per cent nitrogen, 10-20 per cent phosphoric acid and 2-3 per cent potash and should be valued accordingly. Guano can be used in the preparation of ground at the rate of 56-113 g per 0·8 sq m (2-4 oz per sq yd), but is particularly valuable as a summer feed or topdressing to plants in growth at rates of about 28 g per 0·8 sq m (1 oz per sq yd), or 28 g per 4·5 l (1 oz per gal) of water.

Hoof and Horn Meal. Ground hooves and horns make a valuable fertilizer containing an average of 12-14 per cent nitrogen, the rate of availability depending on the fineness of the grinding. Coarse-ground hoof and horn may decompose slowly over a period of several years, gradually liberating its nitrogen, whereas finely ground hoof and horn may be completely used up in a few months. It is a rather expensive fertilizer but is especially valuable for potting composts with which it may be used at rates varying from 42-113 g per 36 l (1½-4 oz per 8 gal). Outdoors the usual rate of application is 56-113 g per 0·8 sq m (2-4 oz per sq yd). It may be used at any time of the year.

Hops. Spent hops as obtained from the brewery have not much value as plant food but they have a most useful effect upon the texture of most soils. They tend to lighten heavy clay and yet make light, sandy soils more retentive of moisture. Hops should always be allowed to weather for three or four months before use, after which they can be dug in at any time of the year at rates up to 50 kg per 12·5 sq m (1 cwt per 15 sq yd).

HOP MANURE is quite a different proposition since the hops it contains have been treated chemically to improve their value as plant food. As treatment varies considerably, analyses will also differ widely. All should be applied strictly in accordance with manufacturer's instructions, which may vary from 113-340 g per 0·8 sq m (4-12 oz per sq yd). As the chemicals used are generally of a very soluble character, hop manures are not particularly suitable for autumn or winter application but are excellent in early spring and may also be used as topdressings to plants in growth.

Horse Manure. Weight for weight, horse manure is usually richer than cow manure but once again samples are likely to vary a great deal according to methods of feeding and the way in which the manure has been stored. All the remarks made in this connection about cow manure apply equally to dung from the stable. Horse manure is drier and more open in texture and therefore better in its mechanical effect upon heavy soils. It is also the only kind of natural manure which is reliable for the cultivation of mushrooms. However, it should be noted that it is now possible to grow mushrooms on straw or chaff compost prepared by rotting with special chemicals (see p. 570). Horse manure that is to be used for mushroom culture must be fresh, prepared with straw bedding, and from animals that are in good health. (Note, this is only necessary if you are not using a special mushroom kit.) For other purposes horse manure is used like cow manure.

Lime. As already stated in Chapter 2 lime is not just a plant food, it is very much more, and this point must not be ignored. It is also used to correct acidity by neutralizing acids formed in the soil and to improve soil texture by flocculating the very fine particles which characterize clay soils.

Strictly speaking lime is the popular name for calcium oxide (quicklime) and calcium hydroxide (slaked lime). The latter is obtained by slaking quicklime, also known as burnt lime or lump lime. In the garden 'lime' is used more broadly to cover practically any substance which has the same general effect upon the soil. Thus when the gardener applies chalk or ground limestone he still says that he is 'liming' the soil.

There is a good deal of misconception as to the relative value of the different forms of lime, using the term in this broad sense. It is often stated that quicklime is swifter in action than any other form of lime and that chalk and limestone are comparatively slow. In practice this is not found to be the case to any marked degree, provided the chalk or limestone is sufficiently finely ground. The main advantage of quicklime is that, directly it comes in contact with moisture, even the moisture of the atmosphere, it very rapidly crumbles to an extremely fine powder which can be mixed most intimately with the soil. It takes good machinery to grind chalk or limestone to anything like the same degree of fineness, and coarser samples cannot be mixed so evenly and thoroughly with the soil; therefore they do not affect it so rapidly. Quicklime and slaked lime (calcium hydroxide), the form in which lime is usually applied in gardens, are more beneficial in their action on the soil than chalk or limestone.

When applied to soil all types of lime tend to turn rapidly into one of two distinct forms. If the soil to which the lime is applied is acid, a certain percentage, sufficient to correct this acidity, is absorbed into the soil and becomes combined with the humus and finest particles of soil (colloids). All this absorbed lime is termed 'active' lime (sometimes it is referred to as exchangeable lime) and this is the only part which is of immediate value to the soil and the plants growing in it. It is this active lime which reacts with other chemicals in the soil, liberating plant food, stimulating bacterial activity and itself becoming available as plant food. The remaining, or surplus, lime after acidity has been corrected is rapidly converted into chalk or, more technically, calcium carbonate. This surplus lime has no immediate effect on plants or soil but forms a store from which more active lime can be absorbed as required.

Though a little free lime does no harm to many crops, an excessive amount of it may cause a lot of trouble. It will tend to destroy humus, waste nitrogen, lock up iron and bring about various conditions of plant starvation, some of which may be revealed by the foliage turning yellow or white (chlorosis). It is just as easy to do harm by giving too much lime as by not giving lime at all.

Applications of lime can be directly related to the known pH reaction of the soil provided the character of the soil is also taken into account. One cannot say straight away, for example, that because the pH is 5·5, 340 g per 0·8 sq m (12 oz sq yd) of burnt lime must be given to make the soil neutral. As already explained, active lime combines with the humus and very fine particles of soil. There are far more fine particles in a clay soil than in a sandy one and the largest amount of humus is likely to be found in peaty soil. It follows from this that soils which contain a lot of clay or peat can absorb more lime than soils of a more sandy and consequently coarser nature. Thus clay or peat soils require more lime to bring about a required rise in pH but also take longer to revert to a condition of acidity. It is very similar to the difference between filling and emptying a large reservoir and a small one. That is why the gardener's rule must be little and often when liming sandy soils though he can afford to give heavier applications at less frequent intervals on clay or peat. I have attempted to show how this works out in the following table. A level of pH 6·5 has been chosen as this is considered ideal for a great variety of plants.

The principal types of lime in use in the garden are burnt or lump lime, also known as quicklime (calcium oxide); slaked or hydrated lime (calcium hydroxide); limestone and chalk, both of which are regarded by the chemist as having the same chemical constitution, namely calcium carbonate; and magnesium limestone, a valuable mixture of

TABLE FOR LIME DRESSINGS

Dressings of ground quicklime necessary to raise acid soils to pH 6·5.
All figures are for grammes per 0·8 sq m (oz per sq yd)

pH	Sand	Light Loam	Loam	Peat or Clay
6·0	6	10	12	16
5·5	14	18	20	26
5·0	22	28	30	36
4·5	31	36	38	44
4·0	40	46	48	54

magnesium carbonate and calcium carbonate which may be obtained in natural, burnt and hydrated forms.

The table of lime requirements shown here is based on finely ground quicklime but this is not often used in gardens as it is unpleasant to handle, is apt to burn its bags and may scorch any foliage with which it comes in contact. Hydrated lime is most frequently used, and to produce an equivalent effect the recommended rates for finely ground quicklime would have to be multiplied by 1½. If either finely ground chalk or limestone is used the figures would be multiplied by 2. As a rule magnesium limestone is only applied when there is a known magnesium deficiency since magnesium in excess can damage plants. When used, each type of magnesium limestone (natural, burnt or hydrated) is applied at the same rate as the equivalent type of lime or limestone.

Lime in any form should be worked as thoroughly and evenly as possible into the upper soil, to a depth of 10 cm (4 in). It will in general be easier to do this properly in the autumn or early spring than in the winter or summer, but lime should not be applied at the same time as dung, particularly if the dung is fresh, nor at the same time as certain fertilizers, notably sulphate of ammonia. Lime liberates nitrogen from dung and sulphate of ammonia in the form of ammonia gas, which passes into the atmosphere and is lost. It is possible without much loss to give a moderate dressing of lime two or three months before or after applying manure or sulphate of ammonia, but it is better policy to make the applications in separate years. Where rotation is carried out (see Chapter 23) it is good policy to apply lime annually but only to the plot that is not being manured, so that all the ground will receive lime once every three years.

Liquid Manure. This may be prepared in a variety of ways. Originally the term was confined to the liquid drained from stables and cow sheds which was allowed to run into underground cess pits from which it was pumped on to the land from time to time. This kind of manure was valuable and contained approximately 0·18-0·23 per cent nitrogen, 0·017-0·03 per cent phosphoric acid and 0·40-0·46 per cent potash.

A very good substitute for this kind of natural liquid manure can be made by steeping a small sack of well-rotted dung in a tub of water and using the fluid in place of ordinary water for plants in full growth. It must be well diluted, approximately to the colour of straw. For a liquid feed high in potash and ideal for tomatoes, use comfrey and even stinging nettles.

Liquid manures can also be prepared with most soluble chemical fertilizers but great care must then be taken not to increase the strength too much. In the case of proprietary fertilizers the manufacturers generally give instructions for the preparation of liquid

manures and these must be followed to the letter. Failing any such instructions it is generally safe to use a complete fertilizer containing up to 10 per cent each of nitrogen, phosphoric acid and potash at the rate of 28 gr per 4·5 l (1 oz per gal) of water, though more
dilute solutions employed in greater quantity may actually give better results. Single
chemicals such as nitrate of soda, sulphate of ammonia, etc. should seldom be employed
at a strength above 14 g per 4·5 l (½ oz per gal).

Since most of the plant foods in dung are only liberated after fairly prolonged decomposition it is useless to prepare liquid manure from animal droppings which are not fully
decayed.

Muriate of Potash. Chemically speaking muriate of potash is potassium chloride and
because it contains chlorine it is liable to cause leaf scorching in some plants, notably
tomatoes, lettuces, red currants, strawberries and roses. For this reason muriate of potash
is not quite as safe or satisfactory a fertilizer as sulphate of potash which it resembles in
other respects. The potash analysis is 50 per cent. Muriate of potash is well held in the
soil and can therefore be applied at any time of the year. Rate of application is from
14-56 g per 0·8 sq m (½-2 oz per sq yd).

Mushroom Compost. The compost from spent mushroom beds is a useful organic soil
dressing which will improve the texture of most soils by raising their humus content. It
also contains plant foods including nitrogen, phosphates, potash and some trace elements,
but how much of each will depend on how the compost was originally made, how much, if
any, animal manure it contained and how it has been stored. An average for straw compost
without horse manure would be 2 per cent nitrogen, 0·3 per cent phosphoric acid and
1·5 per cent potash. Mushroom compost can be used as a surface mulch at any time or
dug in at a rate of up to 9 kg per 0·8 sq m (20 lb per sq yd).

Nitrate of Potash. This chemical is better known as saltpetre, once an ingredient of old-
fashioned gunpowder. It is rather too expensive for widespread use as a fertilizer but as it
contains both nitrogen and potash in readily available forms, it is a useful food for special
purposes. In particular it makes a first-rate liquid manure used at the rate of 14 g per
4·5 l (½ oz per gal). Dry, it can be applied at rates up to 56 g per 0·8 sq m (2 oz per sq yd).
The analysis is nitrogen 12-14 per cent, potash 44-46 per cent.

Nitrate of Soda. This is one of the two most used nitrogenous fertilizers in the garden.
It is readily soluble and one of the quickest acting of all fertilizers. Under favourable conditions some effect may be observed three or four days after use. Because of its ready
availability care must be taken not to use too much at a time, nor should it be applied in
autumn or winter when it would be washed out of the soil before the plants have had time
to benefit from it. If applied direct to foliage it is inclined to scorch and it makes clay soils
even stickier than before. Nevertheless it is one of the best fertilizers for giving a quick
boost to backward crops in spring and summer. Rates of application are up to 28 g per
0·8 sq m (1 oz per sq yd), or 14 g per 4·5 l (½ oz per gal) of water. The analysis is 16 per
cent nitrogen. It is extremely deliquescent, that is to say it attracts moisture, even from
the atmosphere, and the crystals will soon dissolve unless stored in a very dry place.

Nitrate of Lime. This is a granular fertilizer which contains both nitrogen and lime and is consequently particularly suitable for application to the more acid types of soil. In many respects it resembles nitro-chalk with which it should be compared and it contains 15·5-16 per cent nitrogen. It is used as a topdressing to crops in growth at rates up to 28 g per 0·8 sq m (1 oz per sq yd) and, like every fertilizer containing both nitrogen and lime, is a useful accelerator of decay in the compost heap through which it may be sprinkled thinly. Like nitrate of soda it must be stored in a very dry place.

Nitro-chalk. This is a proprietary fertilizer which has the merits of being extremely clean and pleasant to handle, easy to spread evenly and containing both nitrogen and carbonate of lime in readily available form. It is most suitable for use on the more acid types of soil in spring or early summer. It attracts moisture readily and must be kept in a very dry place or it is soon reduced to an unpleasant wet paste. It should be used at rates up to 56 g per 0·8 sq m (2 oz per sq yd). The analysis is 15·5 per cent nitrogen, 48 per cent carbonate of lime.

Peat. Milled peat is excellent for improving the texture and humus content of soil. For horticultural use it should not be too acid unless the soil is markedly alkaline and the pH needs reducing. Two types of peat are commonly marketed, moss and sedge, but there is no clear division between them. Moss peats contain a higher percentage of decayed sphagnum moss and are fluffier in texture than sedge peats in which the remains of decayed sedge predominate. Neither contains much available plant food and so should be regarded as soil conditioners rather than as feeds. They can be spread over the surface as mulches up to 2.5 cm (1 in) thick at any time or can be dug in at the rate of 2·7-5·4 kg per 0·8 sq m (6–12 lb per sq yd). Peat is a good insulator and so a winter covering could be used to protect the crowns and roots of rather tender plants. Moss peat is also used for pot plants with added fertilizers and usually with sand, vermiculite or perlite and possibly also soil. See Potting compost (p. 423). Concerns that peat is a fast disappearing resource have led to experiments with peat-free composts, see p. 426.

Phosphate of Potash. This is a highly concentrated and very soluble fertilizer which is too expensive for general use though it is useful for application to special plants or crops, particularly as a liquid manure during the season of growth. It contains both phosphoric acid and potash in readily available form, the analysis being phosphoric acid 51 per cent, potash 35 per cent. Use at the rate of up to 14 g per 4·5 l (½ oz per gal) of water, or 28 g per 0·8 sq m (1 oz per sq yd) of ground.

Pig Manure. Chemically pig manure has very much the same value as that obtained from cattle; all the remarks made under the heading 'Cow Manure' regarding influence of feeding and storing on the value of the manure apply equally to this substance. The important difference is that pig manure is much wetter and closer in texture than manure from the stable and is therefore less suitable for the heavier types of soil. For the same reason it is a particularly good dressing for light, sandy soils which dry out rapidly in summer. Pig manure may be used either fresh, to vacant ground only, or rotted, either on vacant or cropped land. Rates are the same as for cow manure.

Potash Nitrate. This fertilizer generally has an analysis of 15 per cent nitrogen and 10 per cent potash but there are variations. Both potash and nitrogen are readily available and as the potash nitrate is very soluble in water it is best applied in spring or early summer. The rate of application is up to 56 g per 0·8 sq m (2 oz per sq yd), or 14 g per 4·5 l (¹/₂ oz per gal) of water.

Poultry Manure. Fresh poultry dressings contain a lot of valuable plant food though, as with other animal manures, the exact analysis will vary according to the method of feeding, the amount of bedding and water content. The highest grades are likely to be from birds that have been fattened under intensive conditions and these may reach 2·5 per cent nitrogen, 1 per cent phosphoric acid, and 0·5 per cent potash. This analysis is for the moist droppings. When droppings are dried slowly they lose bulk but not quality and therefore the analysis goes up. Taking the above sample as an example, when air dried the analysis would rise to 5-6 per cent nitrogen, 2·5-3 per cent phosphoric acid and up to 1·7 per cent potash. Careful kiln drying would result in an even further extraction of moisture and a slight upward trend in the analysis. An air-dried sample of poultry manure is therefore worth nearly three times as much as the same manure before drying.

There is a popular prejudice against poultry manure which is mainly unjustified. The only drawbacks to the use of poultry droppings are that they have not the useful mechanical effect of bulkier manures, they tend to make soil acid rather more rapidly and are, by comparison, somewhat poorly supplied with potash. The first drawback can be overcome by adding straw, leafmould, peat or compost, the second by giving more frequent applications of lime and the third by supplying extra potash in the form of wood ashes, sulphate of potash, etc.

Fresh droppings can be dug in at any time of the year at rates up to 50 kg per 64 sq m (7 cwt per 80 sq yd); dry droppings are most suitable for application in spring or summer at rates of 170–226 g per 0·8 sq m (6-8 oz per sq yd), or they may be used as topdressings to plants in growth at from 56–113 g per 0·8 sq m (2-4 oz per sq yd).

Seaweed. In seaside areas seaweed is often abundant and can either be collected by the gardener or purchased very cheaply. Analysis varies greatly according to the kind of seaweed which predominates and whether it is wet or dry. The seaweed richest in plant foods is that known as laminaria, with long, broad fronds, usually with crinkled edges. Next in merit come the bladder seaweeds. The least useful are the very fine, fern-like seaweeds. Dried seaweed will contain three or four times as much plant food per tonne as a wet sample. An average analysis for fresh bladder seaweed is 0·3 per cent nitrogen, 0·1 per cent phosphoric acid and 1·0 per cent potash. Note the comparatively high potash content which makes it an especially valuable manure for fruit trees and tomatoes. Fresh seaweed can be used at rates up to 50 kg per 5 sq m (1 cwt per 6 sq yd) and dry seaweed up to 100 kg per 25 sq m (2 cwt per 30 sq yd).

There are also a number of proprietary fertilizers prepared from seaweed including liquefied forms very useful for liquid and foliar feeding, that is, spraying on to plants so that the food is absorbed by their leaves. Since such products vary greatly in strength and may have other fertilizers mixed with them, they must be used according to manufacturers' instructions.

Sequestrols. Some chemicals required by plants become insoluble in certain soils so that they are not available as food. A familiar example is iron in chalk or limestone soils. As a result of the lack of available iron the leaves become yellow, growth is weakened and some plants, notably the so-called lime haters such as many rhododendrons, heathers, camellias and lupins, may even die. It is no use giving soil dressings of ordinary iron salts as these are almost immediately rendered ineffective as well. Feeding through the leaves by spraying with dilute solutions of iron salts may help but must be repeated frequently. A more lasting remedy is to apply the iron in particular chemical combinations known as chelates or sequestrols, in which the iron is held immune from the normal reaction with the calcium carbonate in the soil, and so is available to plants. Various chelating agents are used, some more effective than others.

Chelated iron (iron sequestrols) are applied like any other fertilizer to the soil and are entirely safe provided the rate of application advised by the manufacturers is not exceeded. They can be applied at any time of year and can be used for pot plants as well as for plants grown in the open. Marketed products usually contain manganese as well as iron as this is another chemical which can be locked up in chalky soils, resulting in chlorosis. They may also contain magnesium.

Sewage Sludge. This varies greatly in its value as a plant food. Several types are available differing according to the treatment they have undergone. Raw sludge is seldom offered to garden owners but may be used by farmers and commercial growers. It is a bulky material rather difficult to handle and should be used in much the same way as farmyard manure. Do not apply to vegetables which will be eaten raw. Digested sludge and activated sludge are sometimes commercially available, and are easy to handle. The former may have about 6 per cent nitrogen, the latter rather more. Neither contains much phosphorus or potash. Rates of application are from 0·6–1·1 kg per 0·8 sq m (1½–2½ lb per sq yd).

Soot. As a fertilizer, soot is valued solely for the amount of sulphate of ammonia it contains. This may be as much as 30 per cent in a good sample, yielding 6 per cent nitrogen, whereas a poor sample of soot, for example one which has been exposed to rain for some months, may contain as little as 1 per cent nitrogen. Secondary advantages are that soot darkens the soil so enabling it to absorb more heat from the sun and that, when fresh, it deters pests, especially slugs and snails. It can be used at any time of the year as it becomes available at rates up to 170 g per 0·8 sq m (6 oz per sq yd).

Sulphate of Ammonia. This chemical and nitrate of soda are the two most popular quick-acting nitrogenous fertilizers. Sulphate of ammonia contains 20·6 per cent nitrogen. It is not quite so rapid in action as nitrate of soda but under favourable conditions will show an effect on the colour and vigour of growth in about a week. Unlike nitrate of soda it does not damage the texture of clay soils but it does tend to make acid soils even more acid. It must not be mixed with lime or ammonia gas will be given off which means the loss of nitrogen from the fertilizer. On the other hand it is most effective on soils which contain an adequate quantity of available lime (see Lime, p. 37). It is the best nitrogenous fertilizer for mixing with superphosphate of lime, sulphate of potash and muriate of potash and in consequence is employed in a great many compound fertilizers. It is most suitable for spring or early summer application and can be used by itself at rates up to 56 gr per 0·8 sq m (2 oz per sq yd), 14–28 g (½–1 oz) being the usual dose. It is readily soluble in water and can be used in this way as a liquid manure at rates up to 14 g per 4·5 l (½ oz per gal). Sulphate of ammonia is not quite so deliquescent as nitrate of soda but nevertheless it must be stored in a dry place.

Sulphate of Iron. Iron is an important plant food and if it is deficient in the soil the plant fails to develop chlorophyll and in consequence has yellow or white leaves. When this condition is known to be due to lack of iron in the soil, dressings of sulphate of iron at rates up to 28 g per 0·8 sq m (1 oz per sq yd) will serve as a corrective. However, iron deficiency is generally due to alkalinity of the soil rather than actual lack of iron and under these conditions soil applications of sulphate of iron are of little use since the iron will rapidly become locked up in insoluble forms. Better results may be obtained by spraying leaves with a solution of sulphate of iron at 14 g per 4·5 l (½ oz per gal), but the usual practice is to apply iron sequestrols (see Sequestrols, p. 43).

Sulphate of Magnesium. Besides its medicinal value it is a useful fertilizer where magnesium is lacking. It is soluble and fairly quick acting and consequently most suitable for spring and summer application. The commercial salt contains 10 per cent magnesium and should be used at the rate of 56 g per 0·8 sq m (2 oz per sq yd) or in liquid manures at 28–56 g per 4·5 l (1–2 oz per gal) of water. This liquid feed can also be sprayed over plants to be absorbed through the leaves. In some countries it is known as Epsom salts.

Sulphate of Potash. This is the most generally useful form of potash and is safer to use than muriate of potash. It can be mixed with such chemical fertilizers as superphosphate of lime and sulphate of ammonia. The analysis of pure sulphate of potash shows 48 per cent potash. It can be used at rates up to 113 g per 0·8 sq m (4 oz per sq yd) or in water at 14 g per 4·5 l (½ oz per gal). As it is held well in the soil it can be applied at any time of the year.

Superphosphate of Lime. This is the most popular and useful fertilizer where phosphates are deficient. In spite of its name it contains no free lime and consequently it cannot be used to correct soil acidity though it does add calcium to the soil. Its value as a manure lies solely in the phosphate which it contains and this varies according to sample from 12–18 per cent measured in the form of phosphoric acid. Some manufacturers quote the phosphate content of this fertilizer on the basis of the amount of phosphate of lime it contains which gives to the uninitiated an exaggerated idea of the quality of the sample. The phosphate of lime content of any sample will always be just over twice that of the phosphoric acid analysis. For example, a sample of superphosphate of lime described as containing 40 per cent phosphate of lime is the equivalent of another sample quoted as containing 18 per cent phosphoric acid. Bear this in mind when comparing prices.

Superphosphate of lime is a quick-acting fertilizer and is reasonably soluble in water. It can be mixed with safety with sulphate of ammonia, sulphate of potash, muriate of potash and bone flour. There is a tendency for mixed fertilizers containing superphosphate of lime to set after three or four days but the lump can easily be broken up by a blow with the back of a spade and the fertilizer will not set a second time unless it gets very damp.

Superphosphate, either by itself or in combination with other fertilizers, is most suitable for spring or early summer application. Alone it can be used at rates up to 113 g per 0·8 sq m (4 oz per sq yd), or in water at 28 g per 4·5 l (1 oz per gal).

Urea. This contains 46 per cent nitrogen which becomes rapidly available when applied to the soil. Urea is a crystalline substance easy and pleasant to handle and readily soluble in water. It is an excellent quick-acting nitrogenous fertilizer for use at 14 g per 0·8 sq m ($\frac{1}{2}$ oz per sq yd), or 28 g per 31·5 l (28 oz per 7 gal) of water, but because it is so readily available care must be taken not to use it to excess.

Urea formaldehyde, also known as urea-form, has been produced to overcome this danger. It is a combination of urea and formaldehyde and is an insoluble powder. It is consequently much slower-acting than urea, the nitrogen it contains being released in the soil over a period of several months. It contains 36 per cent nitrogen.

Wood Ashes. A very useful source of potash which is present in the form of carbonate of potash. Unfortunately samples vary so much in the amount of potash they contain that it is impossible to give any general instructions regarding rate of application. A lot will depend upon the age of the wood burned, the rate of burning and the method of storage. In general old wood contains more potash than young growth, slow burning preserves more of the potash than rapid combustion and storage must be in a dry place or much of the potash will be lost. Best samples may contain as much as 15 per cent potash, the poorest as little as 4 per cent. Wood ash can be used at the rate of 113-226 g per 0·8 sq m (4-8 oz per sq yd) at any time of the year. It is an alkaline material which can be used to correct soil acidity but in soils that are already alkaline it should be used with caution.

Part 2

The Ornamental Approach

Chapter 7

Flowers from Seed

I hope that the heading of this chapter will not prove misleading. It is, of course, true that most flowering plants can be raised from seed if one has the facilities and the patience to deal with them correctly. But it is not my purpose here to enter into a general discussion of seed germination in all its more difficult aspects. On the contrary, this chapter concentrates on plants that are so readily reared from seed and so quickly and satisfactorily attain flowering size that it has become the usual practice to renew them annually by this means.

The chapter includes all those plants known as annuals because they complete the cycle of their growth in one year and then die, leaving their seed-produced offspring to perpetuate the race. But it goes beyond the rather narrow limits set by this definition and embraces in addition many plants not strictly speaking annuals though usually treated as such. Antirrhinums and heliotropes are plants of this type which can be raised from cuttings but are now more usually raised from seed. It also includes biennials, that is, those plants which complete their life in two years and then die like annuals, having distributed their seed to germinate in due time. This group is also swelled by plants not strictly belonging to it though usually treated as biennial in gardens. The wallflower and the forget-me-not are two familiar examples. Despite the fact that biennials live for two years, it is necessary to sow seed every year if an annual display of flowers is to be produced.

All these plants which are so readily raised from seed have one point in common; they are comparatively cheap to produce. Hardy annuals and biennials in particular can be raised in hundreds from packets of seed with little tax upon the gardener's skill beyond the preparation of a fine, crumbly seed bed. The half-hardy kinds need a little more care and must in most cases be raised under glass, though often an unheated frame will provide sufficient protection. Millions of these plants are raised annually by nurserymen and offered for sale in the spring and early summer. They often provide the best means of making a bright display during the summer and can be used with equal effect in formal bedding schemes or in the more natural forms of gardening.

Bedding Out. This is the name given to the practice of planting for a short term or seasonal display. It is a method of obtaining more continuous colour in the garden than would be possible with permanent plants. In public parks and large gardens bedding-out plants may be renewed several times a year but in the main two seasons are observed, 'spring bedding', usually planted in autumn for spring display, and 'summer bedding', planted mainly in late spring for summer display. It is in summer bedding that annuals, particularly half-hardy kinds, play a very important part together with some greenhouse plants such as pelargoniums and fuchsias (see Chapter 19). Spring bedding is carried out very largely with biennials or plants treated as such, for instance forget-me-nots, double daisies and wallflowers, all described in this chapter, together with tulips, hyacinths, daffodils and other bulbs (see Chapter 12).

Special Hybrids. It will be observed in seed catalogues that many varieties of annuals carry the prefix F_1 hybrid or F_2 hybrid. These are special hybrids which bear the twin merits of greater vigour and greater uniformity than non-hybrid varieties. F stands for filial, meaning 'generation', and 1 or 2 for first year or second year. Thus an F_1 hybrid is a first-generation hybrid, that is, the seed is produced by crossing two dissimilar parents and the seedlings are the first generation resulting from that cross. An F_2 hybrid is a second-generation hybrid produced by growing on an F_1 hybrid and allowing the plants to pollinate themselves or one another, then saving the seed from them and sowing it the following year. It is more costly to produce hybrids of either type than ordinary open-pollinated varieties, and also more costly to produce F_1 than F_2 hybrids. This extra cost is reflected in the price of the seeds. Normally seedsmen do not sell the parent strains from which these hybrids are produced and since these hybrids cannot be grown true to type from their own seed the seedsman retains an exclusive ability to produce his own varieties.

For the purpose of cultivation all these seed-raised plants may be most readily considered under three headings:

1. Hardy annuals and plants treated as such.
2. Half-hardy annuals and plants treated as such.
3. Biennials and plants treated as such.

HARDY ANNUALS

These are all plants which are hardy enough to be sown out of doors in spring without any protection in most parts of the country. Some, though not all, are hardy enough to pass the winter out of doors without protection. All complete their growth in a year or less. If they are sown in the spring they flower the following summer and ripen their seed before the winter. If they are sown about early autumn they make small plants before the winter, almost stop growing from late autumn to early spring when they start to grow rapidly again, and flower in late spring or early summer. Only the hardiest kinds should be chosen for this latter method of cultivation if it is intended to leave the plants outdoors all the winter, but any hardy annuals can be early autumn sown for overwintering in a frame or cool greenhouse. Many of them make delightful pot plants grown in this way and can be potted from mid-autumn to early spring, and flower at the start of the high season.

Soil. Most hardy annuals will succeed in any ordinary soil. Germination is likely to be most rapid and successful in the lighter types of sandy loam, particularly those soils which readily break down to a fine seed bed in spring yet do not easily set on the surface after a few heavy showers. Heavy, wet soils and those very liable to cake or 'pan' are the most unsatisfactory for this type of plant though they can be improved a lot by the free use of peat, pulverized bark, leafmould and sand.

A rich soil is not as a rule desirable as it tends to encourage leaves at the expense of flowers. For this reason dung should be used rather sparingly and so should the quicker-acting fertilizers, but slower kinds such as bonemeal and hoof and horn meal may prove useful, especially on poor, sandy soils.

Beds for hardy annuals should be well dug or forked and then given a week or so to settle. If this is impossible, tread them well, first in one direction and then in another, choosing a day when the surface is fairly dry and not sticky, to get a firm seed bed which will

An established colony of winter aconites, *Eranthis hyemalis*, like golden buttercups each with a green ruff, is an uplifting sight in early spring. They love a cool, moist leafy soil

Any early colour is welcome in the garden, but crocuses naturalized in the grass under white-stemmed birches are particularly lovely. They come up automatically year after year

This double-flowered Kanzan cherry, heavy with blossom, accompanied by generous plantings of bright tulips and white narcissi, is an excellent start to spring

Spring flowers seem to rejoice at the passing of winter, whether azaleas in mixed colours (above)
or the traditional aubrietia, yellow alyssum and tulips (below)

The bright red young leaves of *Pieris formosa forrestii* Wakehurst which develop in spring are its most decorative feature. It should also produce clusters of white bell flowers

Besides onions, leeks and garlic, the alliums offer a rich choice of decorative flowers of all sizes and many colours. *Allium giganteum* is one of the most striking

Faced with a plot of bare soil in spring and wondering how to fill it? How about a mixture of hardy annuals like this for quick colour?

If you prefer paving to beds and borders, you can still cram a lot of colour in baskets and tubs –
pelargoniums and petunias particularly

A variety of summer-flowering annuals can give you a remarkably colourful display. Here are petunias, alyssum, tagetes and yellow *Mimulus moschatus*

A rock garden can be surprisingly colourful at peak flowering time in late spring. Here are
Penstemon pinifolius, an orange helianthemum, pinks, thyme and silver *Artemisia schmidtiana* Nana

What are the secrets of an interesting garden? Certainly water – a pool, stream or fountain – is one. Another is a vertical effect, perhaps a pergola. The little rose is The Fairy

The beauty of a waterlily bloom is almost too perfect to be real, whether it is the ordinary white one or a choice variety like Marliacea Chromatella

Contrast is the secret here: Above, silver stachys, pink viscaria and white flag iris. Below, white-flowered *Hydrangea paniculata* Grandiflora is set off by blue agapanthus lilies

No reason why you should not grow your own grapes given enough room. This is Foster's Seedling. Chrysanthemums like Buckland will yield masses of bloom in autumn

The warm autumn tints of *Smilacina racemosa* are set off by smart *Hebe x franciscana* Variegata,
above. Below: Even bare shoots – here *Salix alba vitellina* – add colour in winter

Midwinter colour can be surprisingly showy. Here the pale-flowered witch hazel, *Hamamelis mollis* Pallida, is underplanted with winter heathers, *Erica herbacea*

not sink unevenly at a later date. Rake the surface level and leave it loose and crumbly on top.

Sowing. It is of vital importance to choose a good period for sowing. As a rule from early to mid-spring is the best time but condition of soil matters far more than date. I would delay sowing until late spring rather than put seed in when the ground is wet and lumpy.

Seed can either be sown in shallow drills, 15-46 cm (6-18 in) apart according to the variety of annual to be grown, or scattered thinly all over the surface, a method known as 'broadcasting'. The former is usually best for formal beds and borders and the latter method for irregular groups and patches, either in borders of annuals by themselves or where annuals are grown with permanent plants such as herbaceous perennials and shrubs. If the seed is sown broadcast it can either be raked in or covered by sprinkling fine soil over it. Old potting soil is excellent for the purpose but ordinary garden soil can be used if put through a 12 mm ($\frac{1}{2}$ in) mesh sieve.

Germination is usually rapid. The seedlings must be thinned out directly they can be handled conveniently which is usually when they are 2.5 cm (1 in) high. It is most important to give them sufficient room. One of the commonest mistakes is overcrowding which results in drawn, half-starved plants which have a brief and comparatively poor flowering season. Thinnings of many kinds can be replanted to fill gaps or make further beds, but annuals with tap roots seldom transplant well. This is true of poppies, eschscholzias and godetias.

Summer Care. Very little further care is required beyond occasional hand weeding or hoeing and the removal of faded flowers. The latter is important because it greatly prolongs the flowering season. An annual's life is over once it has ripened its seed. If by the constant removal of faded flowers it is prevented from setting any seed it will often persist in the attempt to do so and go on producing more and more flowers.

Most hardy annuals will stand a good deal of sunshine and drought but in very dry weather it sometimes pays to water the beds thoroughly. The only drawback to this is

Marking out a bed in preparation for broadcasting seed

Sowing seed. Notice the box of fine soil ready for covering

that, once one starts to water, it is usually necessary to continue as the plants are encouraged to make more roots near the surface than they would otherwise do and so are less able to find their own supplies deep down in the soil.

Seed Saving. If desired, seed can be saved from some of the plants to be sown the following year. All that is necessary is to cut off the seed pods, heads or whatever they may be when they turn brown or yellow, place them in paper-lined trays in a sunny window, frame or greenhouse for a week or so, and then shake or rub out the seed and store it in a cool dry place until sowing time. The drawback of home-saved seed is that the different colours and forms of any one kind of annual usually intercross very readily and so, as a result, the next year's seedlings are hybrids of very mixed appearance. As carefully selected seed from specially isolated plants can be purchased quite cheaply it is seldom worth the trouble of saving seed at home.

However, this applies mainly to garden varieties and hybrids. Unimproved wild plants (species) usually come true to type from seed even when the parent plants are grown in mixed company. This is true not only of annuals and biennials but also of perennials and seed does provide an easy and cheap means of increasing many plants, even large ones such as shrubs and trees.

If it is decided to save seed it should be cleaned, at any rate roughly, before it is sown. With seeds in fairly large dry pods or capsules it may be possible to shake them out without much debris. This may be much more difficult with seeds carried in smaller receptacles or in soft fruit and berries. The former, when quite dry, can be passed through an ordinary household sieve to get rid of dust and much of the larger chaff can be gently blown away. Another simple cleaning device is a sheet of blotting paper or fairly smooth-textured cloth on a sloping board down which the seeds can be made to roll. Dust will be held on the surface, but the seeds will roll down to the bottom.

Berries of hardy plants, including trees and shrubs, are often best mixed with sand in pots or boxes and placed out of doors for one winter, suitably protected from mice. By the spring the flesh will have largely decayed and can be gently rubbed or washed from the seed. This exposure to cold is sometimes necessary if the seed is to germinate.

Fruits of tender plants such as tomatoes must not be exposed to frost but can be soaked in water for a few days when the flesh will disintegrate and the seeds float to the top, from which they can be skimmed off and subsequently dried.

If seeds have to be kept for any length of time before they are sown they should be stored in a cool, dry place, preferably in well-sealed envelopes or packets.

HALF-HARDY ANNUALS

The chief difference in cultivation between these and hardy annuals is that most of the seedlings are raised under glass. Greenhouse sowing begins in mid-winter but the main sowings are seldom made before the end of late winter or the first week in early spring. In either case a temperature of around 16°C/61°F is desirable to ensure quick germination. A few weeks later seed can usually be germinated satisfactorily in a frame. Outdoor conditions are seldom sufficiently settled to justify sowing without protection before the first week in late spring and that means the plants will be late in flower. Nevertheless some kinds do well treated in this way and it is a useful way of extending the flowering season.

Sowing and Early Care. Details of seed sowing and germination are exactly the same as for greenhouse plants. Fill well-drained seed trays or 7·5 cm (3 in) plastic pots with John Innes seed compost. Sow very thinly, cover lightly with fine soil and protect with panes of glass and brown paper to cut down evaporation. When germination occurs remove this covering and keep the seedlings in as light a place as possible.

When they can be handled conveniently, prick them off into deeper trays and a slightly richer compost such as J. I. No. 1 or peat potting compost. After a further week or so in the greenhouse to get them growing strongly, remove them to a frame and gradually harden them off by increasing ventilation a little at a time as the weather improves. The object should be to get the plants thoroughly accustomed to the open air not later than the end of late spring. Many kinds can be put out of doors several weeks earlier, especially in warm-climate gardens.

Soil and Planting. The soil for final planting should be prepared in the same way as for hardy annuals but need not be quite so finely crumbled as the plants are by this time sturdy and better able to fend for themselves. Plant with a trowel giving the roots plenty of space. Make firm and water in freely. Thereafter treat exactly like hardy annuals.

Hardening Off. The main difficulty with these half-hardy kinds is to get them thoroughly hardened off before they are put outdoors. If they are rushed along too quickly and are not gradually inured to the outside air they may receive a severe check after planting out. They will eventually flower so late that they give only a fraction of the display of which they are capable.

BIENNIALS

These are almost invariably raised in a reserve bed or in a frame from which they are first transplanted to another reserve bed, and only to their flowering quarters when they have made quite big plants.

Two methods of cleaning seed. (a) By rolling them down a sheet of blotting paper or a rough-surfaced cloth. (b) By sifting through an ordinary household flour sieve

Sowing seed in boxes. The top of the packet is cut cleanly across. A thin layer of soil is sprinkled over the seeds, and the box is then covered with a sheet of glass and paper to cut down evaporation and light and so encourage germination

Sowing and Care of Seedlings. Early summer is the busiest sowing month for biennials though some gardeners like to get their seeds in about a month earlier. This, I think, is wise on those soils which tend to delay germination. Seed can be sown in drills or broadcast as for hardy annuals but drills are better as it is easier to recognize seedlings from weeds and to keep the bed clean.

The seedlings must be transplanted as soon as possible to the nursery bed in which they will grow on. This should be sheltered and the soil should be reasonably rich and crumbly. Lift the little plants with a small fork after first giving them a good soaking if the ground is dry. Replant them firmly with a trowel, spacing them several centimetres apart so that they will have plenty of room to make strong plants. As a rule this transplanting can be carried out during mid- and late summer.

Planting. By October most of the plants should be ready for their final quarters. Here they should be planted just like hardy perennials, either in straight rows if the object is a formal display or a supply of cut flowers, or distributed in irregular drifts if the aim is a natural effect.

A SELECTION OF THE BEST KINDS

Adonis (Pheasant's Eye). Plants belonging to the buttercup family and with distinctly buttercup-like flowers. These are deep crimson in colour in both the annual species to be found occasionally in catalogues. *Adonis aestivalis* flowers in early summer and *A. autumnalis* (also known as *A. annua*) flowers principally in late summer. There is also a yellow-flowered species, *A. vernalis*, but this is a perennial for the rock garden or part of the border in well-drained soil, flowering in spring. The annuals average 45 cm (18 in) in height, have finely cut foliage which sets off the brilliant flowers charmingly, and succeed best in fairly warm places and well-drained soils. Sow where wanted to flower and thin to 20 cm (8 in).

Agathea. See **Felicia** (p. 82).

Ageratum. One of those plants treated as half-hardy annuals though they are in fact perennials (in this case half-hardy perennials). Ageratums are for the most part compact, low-growing plants with soft, feathery heads of tiny bluish flowers. They are grand plants for edgings and carpeting for which purposes they rival the blue lobelia. The best forms do not exceed 15 cm (6 in) in height but there are taller varieties up to 45 cm (1½ ft). Colours include lavender and purplish mauve. All can be raised very readily from seed sown in a warm greenhouse in late winter/early spring, or in an unheated frame in mid-spring. Prick the seedlings off 4 cm (1½ in) apart each way into shallow boxes, and harden them off to be planted out along with the other summer bedders in late spring.

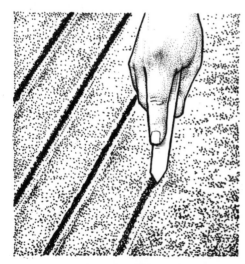

Marking out a seed drill. By sowing in drills it is easier to keep the bed tidy and to sort out the weed seedlings from young plants

Planting out seedlings in a nursery bed using a small dibber

Ageratums will succeed in any ordinary soil and sunny or partly shaded place and should be planted 15 cm (6 in) apart. If desired, specially good forms can be increased by cuttings of young growth overwintered in a frost-proof greenhouse.

Agrostemma (Corn Cockle). The common corn cockle, *A. githago*, is a hardy annual weed of cornfields but a purplish form with fine lilac, purple or white flowers, known as Milas, is popular as a hardy annual. It has slender stems about 76 cm (2½ ft) high and quite large single pink flowers. Sow in spring or early autumn where the plants are to flower and thin seedlings to 20 cm (8 in).

Alonsoa. These very cheerful plants are regarded almost exclusively as subjects for the greenhouse, yet they will succeed well outdoors in sunny, sheltered places. For this purpose they should be treated as half-hardy annuals and raised under glass from a late winter/early spring sowing. Prick off in the usual way and plant out late in late spring, 8 cm (7 in) apart. Heights vary from 30-76 cm (1-2½ ft) for the species such as *Alonsoa acutifolia* and *A. warscewiczii*, but there are improved garden forms of more compact habit, some of which do not exceed 23 cm (9 in). Colours range from pink to bright scarlet and flowers are produced all summer. When grown as greenhouse pot plants alonsoas are usually sown in late summer/early autumn and then flower in spring. Only sufficient warmth is required to give protection from frost.

Althaea. See **Hollyhock** (p. 86).

Alyssum. The yellow-flowered alyssum is a perennial described under rock plants (see p. 177) but the sweet-scented alyssum (*A. maritimum*, though now known as *Lobularia maritima*) is a true hardy annual. It is probably the best carpeting annual with white flowers especially as there are now specially compact forms which do not exceed 10 cm (4 in) in height. There are also lilac and reddish-purple varieties. All may be grown from seed sown in mid-spring where the plants are to flower or, if preferred, seed may be sown in boxes in a frame or greenhouse in early spring. The seedlings are transplanted several centimetres apart into other boxes when they can be handled and hardened off for planting in flowering quarters in late spring. This is one of the hardy annuals which transplants well. Plant or thin to 15 cm (6 in). This alyssum will grow anywhere – sun or shade, heavy soil or light.

Amaranthus (Love-lies-bleeding, Prince's Feather, Joseph's Coat). There are several species but the one most commonly seen is *Amaranthus caudatus*, popularly known as love-lies-bleeding. This makes a bushy, leafy plant 60-90 cm (2-3 ft) in height producing flowers in numerous, very long, thick, catkin-like trails. In colour they are a deep plush purple, very striking if somewhat sombre. There is also a variety with pale greenish-yellow flowers. This is a plant that can be used effectively as an isolated specimen dotted about here and there in bedding schemes. Raise the plants from seed sown in greenhouse or frame in early spring and give the usual half-hardy treatment of pricking off (or better still potting singly) and hardening for late spring planting. Alternatively *A. caudatus* can be treated as a hardy annual, seed being sown out of doors in mid-spring where the plants are to grow. Either way, plants should be spaced 25-30 cm (10-12 in) apart.

A. hypochondriacus, the prince's feather, with branched upright red or crimson flower spikes to a height of 90 cm (3 ft), can be grown in the same way, but a third species, *A. tricolor*, is rather more tender and is always best raised in a greenhouse and not planted out until danger of frost is past. It is known as Joseph's coat because of its green, yellow and crimson leaves. There are several improved garden varieties.

A warm, sunny position and open but rather rich soil suits all these plants best.

Anagallis (Pimpernel). Everyone knows of the Scarlet Pimpernel and the pretty little native plant which provided his name, but many remain unacquainted with the far more showy garden pimpernels of which *Anagallis linifolia*, also known as *A. monellii*, is the best. There are blue, pink and scarlet-flowered forms of this plant. The colours are very good and clear, the flowers are produced in profusion for a long time and the plants are easy to grow in any sunny place. They are perennials best treated as hardy annuals and raised each year from seed sown thinly in mid-spring where the plants are required to grow. Pimpernels are sprawling in habit and well fitted for the rock garden, for use as edgings or for making a groundwork beneath taller plants. They seem to do particularly well in seaside gardens.

Anchusa (Alkanet). These are mostly hardy perennials but one is treated as a hardy annual. This is *Anchusa capensis*, a perfect miniature of the big perennial kinds with masses of bright blue, forget-me-not-like flowers on bushy plants 38-45 cm (1¼-1½ ft) high. It will bloom in summer if sown in mid-spring out of doors, preferably where it is to grow. It is not faddy about soil but likes a sunny place, as might be expected from a South African. Thin to 20 cm (8 in).

Antirrhinum (Snapdragon). Antirrhinums are nearly hardy perennials, that is to say they will live and flower for a number of years and will pass the winter out of doors without protection in some places. But antirrhinums are not reliably hardy and often disappear in winter especially if the weather is wet as well as cold and the ground is inclined to be heavy. In any case old plants tend to get straggly and are not so attractive as first-year specimens. For these reasons, and also because antirrhinums are very readily raised from seed sown in moderate warmth and flower profusely in a few months, they are almost invariably treated in gardens as half-hardy annuals.

Seed is sown very thinly from mid-winter to early spring. Early sowing is advisable provided the necessary temperature of about 15-18°C/59-65°F can be maintained as the early seedlings make the best plants and have the longest flowering season. Sow very thinly in well-drained boxes and germinate on the greenhouse staging, covering with glass and paper. Prick off the seedlings when they have their first true leaves, spacing them 5 cm (2 in) apart in ordinary seed trays or similar boxes using a slightly richer compost (see p. 423). Early-sown plants may need to be potted singly into small pots when they are about 7½ cm (3 in) high but as a rule early spring sown antirrhinums can be grown on in the boxes until planting out time. Water moderately throughout, give plenty of light and air, and get the plants into an unheated frame as soon as the spring weather permits. Harden them off steadily so that they can be planted out when the weather is favourable in late spring. In their beds the plants should be spaced 30 cm (1 ft) apart, or 20 cm (8 in) for the dwarf varieties.

Some gardeners pinch out the tip of each plant when about 15 cm (6 in) high. This gives a very branching plant but the central spike, which is the biggest, is sacrificed. It is probably better to allow the plants to grow naturally and then remove the central spike directly the flowers fade, so encouraging side spikes to develop and extend the flowering season. Dwarf varieties branch early and do not produce a central spike.

The only summer care needed is the constant removal of faded flower spikes. Rust, a disease which attacks the foliage, first producing many rusty spots on the undersides of the leaves and then causing them to wither, is troublesome in some seasons particularly those that are hot and dry, and is difficult to keep at bay. Frequent spraying from mid-spring to late summer with copper fungicide will help to keep plants healthy; rust-resistant varieties are also available.

Varieties are very numerous and may conveniently be classified under three main headings: tall, intermediate and dwarf. The first are 90 cm (3 ft) high, the second 38-45 cm (1¼-1½ ft), and the last 15-23 cm (6-9 in). There are also double-flowered varieties and others with an open, trumpet-like flower in place of the normal lipped version. This type is sometimes known as penstemon flowered. In all these classes there is a great range of colour from white through pink, yellow and apricot to intense crimson. There are no better plants for summer bedding.

Arctotis. A pretty half-hardy annual well worth growing. The flowers are like delicately formed moon daisies on slender stems and they vary in colour from silvery with blue reverse in the species *Arctotis grandis* to white, yellow, orange and red in the numerous hybrids. *A. grandis* is 60-76 cm (2-2½ ft) tall and the hybrids are mostly about half this height. All flower from mid-summer to early autumn. They should be raised from seed sown in a warm greenhouse in late spring, the seed being covered very lightly and watered rather sparingly at first. Prick the seedlings off 5 cm (2 in) apart and harden them off for planting out towards the end of spring. Space them 30 cm (1 ft) apart and give them a warm, sunny spot in particularly well-drained soil. These are good plants for hot, dry banks as they are used to the heat of a South African summer.

Argemone (Prickly Poppy). These are sun-loving American poppies. The best is *Argemone mexicana*, 60 cm (2 ft) in height with prickly leaves and big, lemon-yellow or orange flowers of the usual poppy type. Another is *A. grandiflora* with white flowers and no spines on the leaves. Seed should be sown in early spring in a warm spot out of doors and in light or ordinary soil. Do not transplant the seedlings but thin to 23 cm (9 in) apart. The plants begin to flower in mid-summer.

Arnebia (Prophet Flower). Those interested in novelty may like to have these plants with their unusual yellow, black-spotted flowers. *Arnebia cornuta* is the species usually offered. It is 45-60 cm (1½-2 ft) high and is a half-hardy annual. Sow in a warm greenhouse in early spring and plant out of doors in a warm, sunny place in late spring. Space them 23 cm (9 in) apart. There is also a hardy perennial species named *A. echioides* (now listed as *A. pulchra*).

Asperula (Woodruff). A big family containing a few remarkably pretty garden plants of which one, *Asperula azurea* (or *A. orientalis*) is a hardy annual with myriads of little sky-blue, sweet-scented flowers. It is about 30 cm (1 ft) high, and can be raised from seed sown outdoors from early to late spring where the plants are to bloom. Thin to 15 cm (6 in).

Aster. The asters considered here are all true half-hardy annuals and not to be confused with the hardy perennial asters (Michaelmas daisies) described on p. 118. Botanists call the annuals callistephus, though the name has not really caught on.

Annual asters are of many types but all can be raised from seed sown in a slightly heated greenhouse in late winter/early spring, in an unheated frame in mid-spring, or in a sheltered place outdoors in late spring. Cover the seed very lightly and be sparing with water at first. Damp and heat are the enemies of seedling asters and will soon bring on an attack of damping off if permitted. For the same reason sowing should be specially thin and the seedlings pricked off as soon as possible. Personally I never sow asters until mid-spring even in a warm greenhouse because with the longer days there is less trouble from damping off.

Space seedlings a good 5 cm (2 in) apart when pricking off. Avoid checks to growth especially from chills or drought. Harden off steadily and plant out in late spring, 25-30 cm (10 in-1 ft) apart. Asters like a sunny place but will often do quite well in light shade. The singles in particular will put up with a good deal of rough treatment.

If seed is sown outdoors in late spring scatter it where the plants are to grow and so cut out the checks to growth caused by transplanting. Cover the seed with a thin sprinkling of fine soil. Thin out the seedlings to 25-30 cm (10-12 in).

Summer care consists solely in removal of faded flowers. If any plants wilt off in the beds, going black at or a little above soil level and quickly collapsing, they should be removed and burned at once and the soil soaked with a solution of Cheshunt compound. Where this wilt disease proves troublesome it is best to grow wilt-resistant varieties.

There are a great many different types, some with double and others with single flowers. The latter are suitable for cutting as well as for garden display though some, such as Californian Giants, are grown principally for the former purpose. Ostrich Plume asters have big, fully double, rather shaggy flowers. Comet asters are also double but the flowers have a firmer, more regular appearance. Both are about 45 cm (1½ ft) in height. The Californian Giants and Mammoth asters resemble Ostrich Plume varieties in flower but the plants are nearly twice as tall. There are Dwarf asters, usually about 30 cm (1 ft) in height, with double flowers of medium size. Another race of below medium height has small, button-like flowers and is known as Pompon. Then there are several strains of single-flowered asters with flat, daisy-like flowers in a variety of colours.

Balsam. See **Impatiens** (p. 478).

Bartonia. See **Mentzelia** (p. 90).

Begonia. Most of the begonias are dealt with as greenhouse plants but one important species, *Begonia semperflorens*, has become a very popular summer bedding plant and, though a half-hardy perennial, is almost invariably raised anew each year from seed. It is treated as a half-hardy annual, the seed being germinated from late winter to early spring in boxes at a temperature of about 15-18°C/59-64°F and pricked off 5 cm (2 in) apart into deeper trays to be hardened off in a frame ready for planting out in early summer. The best plants can then be potted singly as advised for forward antirrhinums, so that bigger plants are available for putting out in the beds. The secret of success with these begonias is to use a rather open, leafy or peaty compost throughout and to give them plenty of sunlight and moisture. Plant out 20-23 cm (8-9 in) apart. There are many varieties with flowers ranging from white to scarlet, some with green and others with bronze leaves. All flower continuously until stopped by frost and if some plants are lifted in early autumn, potted and brought into a greenhouse they will continue to flower as long as the temperature remains above 10°C/50°F.

Bellis (Daisy). The common daisy is a perennial and a tough one at that, but the garden varieties to which it has given rise are often treated as biennials. There are some very good plants amongst these with fully double flowers, often of such size and deep colour that it is difficult to associate them with the humble lawn daisy. They make grand edgings or carpetings especially for spring bedding schemes with daffodils, tulips and hyacinths. The method of culture commonly used is to sow seed out of doors in late spring, prick off seedlings several centimetres apart in mid-summer in a nursery bed, also in the open, and remove the well-grown plants to flowering quarters in the autumn after the beds have been cleared of their summer occupants. The giant kinds may be planted as much as 23 cm (9 in) apart but the smaller varieties should be set 15 cm (6 in) apart. All will grow in practically any soil and place. There are white, pink and red-flowered varieties.

Brachycome (Swan River Daisy). *Brachycome iberidifolia* is a pretty little half-hardy annual which makes a bushy plant 15-20 cm (6-9 in) high with thin, wiry stems, feathery leaves and produces masses of small white, lavender or blue daisy-type flowers. It is a sun lover and should be raised from seed sown in a greenhouse or frame in early spring, or out of doors later in the season. The plants should be spaced 15 cm (6 in) apart.

Browallia. Though really a greenhouse perennial this may be treated successfully as a half-hardy annual particularly in a good summer or a sheltered garden. Raise under glass in early spring and plant out as soon as all danger of frost is past. The best kind is *Browallia speciosa* which has showy white, lilac or deep blue flowers during late summer. It grows just over 45 cm (1½ ft) in height. Alternatively, seed may be sown in mid-summer, the seedlings potted individually and grown in a frost-free greenhouse to flower in winter and early spring. *Browallia viscosa* has smaller soft blue flowers and a more compact habit.

Calandrinia (Rock Purslane). These are plants for the warmest places in the garden. They do well on sunny ledges in the rock garden or sown on dry walls. Few of the species are true annuals but they may be treated as such and either be sown in greenhouse or frame for planting out in late spring or directly in the open several weeks later where they are to flower. The two best kinds are *Calandrinia grandiflora*, with showy reddish-purple flowers on 30 cm (1 ft) high stems and *C. umbellata* with smaller but very numerous flowers of a penetrating shade of magenta. The last is a sprawling plant not exceeding 15 cm (6 in) in height. Both flower in high summer.

Calendula (Pot Marigold, Scotch Marigold). The most easily grown of hardy annuals but not to be despised on that account. The modern calendula is a really magnificent hardy plant, 15-60 cm (6 in-2 ft) high, with fully double flowers of great size and in a variety of fine shades of yellow and orange. Some have quilled and others flat petals. All can be raised with the greatest of ease from seed sown in spring or early autumn where the plants are to flower. Cover the seeds with 12 mm (½ in) of soil and thin out the seedlings to at least 23 cm (9 in). Most people leave calendulas far too thick with the result that they get starved and finish blooming sooner than they should do. The flowering period can also be lengthened if all faded blooms are removed. There is really no place in which calendulas will not grow but they are happiest in well-drained soils and full sun.

Californian Poppy. See **Eschscholzia** (p. 81).

Callistephus. See **Aster** (p. 73).

Calvary Clover. This mat-forming hardy annual is named *Medicago echinus*. It is grown for the tripartite clover-like leaves, each with a conspicuous blood-red blotch, and for the curious, spirally coiled spiny seed heads. It can be grown out of doors, from seed sown in early spring where plants are to flower and seedlings thinned to about 20 cm (8 in), but it is more commonly grown as a pot plant for a sunny window ledge or unheated greenhouse.

Canary Creeper. See **Tropaeolum** (p. 104).

Candytuft. See **Iberis** (p. 86).

Canterbury Bell. To be correct I should call the Canterbury bell by its botanical name *Campanula medium*, but this might be very confusing to readers in view of the popular association of campanula with the perennial members of the race. The Canterbury bell is a true hardy biennial.

Seed of the ordinary biennial Canterbury bell is sown in late spring/early summer in a frame or sheltered border outdoors. The soil should be rather light and as fine as possible. Sow in drills 6 mm (¼ in) deep and about 15 cm (6 in) apart. Prick off the seedlings into a bed of fairly rich, light soil when they have made three or four leaves each. Give them a watering first and another afterwards and space them 15 cm (6 in) apart. They will soon grow into good, strong plants and can be put into their flowering beds either in mid-autumn or the following spring. Here they should be spaced a good 30 cm (1 ft) apart for they will grow from 45-90 cm (1½-3 ft) tall according to variety and make big, branching plants. They like well-dug, fairly rich soil and will succeed in a sunny or partially shaded position. Flowers are produced in summer.

Canterbury bells are available in a variety of colours including white, pink, rose, light blue and dark blue, and in single-flowered, double-flowered and cup-and-saucer varieties which are really semi-doubles with a second ring of petals behind the main bell forming a 'saucer' to its 'cup'.

Carnation. In addition to the border and perpetual flowering carnations described on p. 121 there is an interesting and useful group of so-called annual carnations which will flower the first year in late summer from seed sown in a warm greenhouse in mid- to late winter. They should be pricked off into deep seed trays as soon as they can be handled, hardened off for planting outdoors early in spring and given an open, sunny position in reasonably good soil. Some of the best plants can be potted and used for cool greenhouse decoration in the autumn and winter. All flower very freely, have double flowers with fringed petals and they include a good range of colours such as white, pink, scarlet and yellow.

Castor Oil Plant. See **Ricinus** (p. 97).

Celosia. One of the more difficult half-hardy annuals requiring a good deal of heat and moisture. It is more often seen as a greenhouse plant than out of doors but it can be used most effectively for summer beds if good strong seedlings are obtained by sowing in early spring in the greenhouse at a temperature of 18 to 21°C/65 to 70°F. Keep the atmosphere of the house rather moist by frequent syringing and damping of the walls and floors. Pot the seedlings singly in small pots filled with John Innes No. 1 or similar compost as soon as they can be handled conveniently. Harden off very slowly and carefully, and plant out of doors when all danger of frost is over and the weather is mild. It is usually wise to wait till at least the second week in summer.

Give as sunny and sheltered a position as possible and keep the plants really well watered in dry weather.

The flowers of celosias are extraordinarily graceful and brilliant, feathery plumes in bright yellow, scarlet or glowing crimson. They are 30-45 cm (1-1½ ft) in height and borne throughout the late summer and early autumn. There is another form, popularly known as Cockscomb, with stiff, curiously congested clusters of crimson, pink or yellow flowers.

Celsia. See **Verbascum** (p. 105).

Centaurea. See **Cornflower** (p. 78) and **Sweet Sultan** (p. 103).

Cheiranthus (Wallflower). In addition to the wallflower, the botanical name of which is *Cheiranthus cheiri*, a few other species of cheiranthus can be raised from seed. The best is *C.* × *allionii* (sometimes listed as *Erysimum hieraciciifolium*) a brilliant, orange-flowered plant usually known as the Siberian wallflower. It has the bushy habit of an ordinary wallflower, small, single, vivid orange flowers and an exceptionally long flowering season lasting from mid-spring and often continuing till mid-summer. In fact practically the only difficulty likely to be encountered with this fine plant is to make it fit into the rotation of bedding. If it is put out along with the other spring-flowering plants it will be practically impossible to get it cleared away in time for the normal summer occupants of the beds, unless one can bring oneself to sacrifice it while it is still in full bloom. *C.* × *allionii* is not fragrant; all varieties of *C. cheiri* are.

All wallflowers are really perennials but they tend to get straggly when old and are only reliable, year after year, on poor, exceptionally well-drained soils. In good garden soil such as is necessary to make them give their best display the first season, they are apt to grow lush and disappear the winter following flowering. In consequence they are almost always treated as hardy biennials. Seed is sown in late spring in an open position in drills 12 mm (½ in) deep and 15 cm (6 in) apart. The seedlings are transplanted when 7½ cm (3 in) high to another similar bed and spaced at least 10 cm (4 in) apart in rows 23 cm (9 in) apart. The tip of each plant is pinched out a few weeks later to make it grow bushy. In mid-autumn the plants are finally removed to the beds in which they are to flower where they are spaced 25 cm (10 in) apart.

The common wallflower can be obtained in double-flowered as well as single forms but the latter are the more popular. In addition to the more familiar yellow and crimson varieties there are many other more unusual shades such as rosy lilac, purple, ruby, orange, ivory and fiery red. Average height is 45 cm (1½ ft) but there are also dwarf varieties only 30 cm (1 ft) high.

Chrysanthemum. The familiar perennial chrysanthemums have their counterpart in the world of annuals. These species are quite hardy and can be sown outdoors in early spring where they are to bloom. Broadcast the seed very thinly or sow in drills 30 cm (1 ft) apart, and cover with 6 mm (¼ in) of fine soil. Choose a really sunny position for these plants. They can be grown in most soils but prefer those that are fairly light and open. With really good drainage it is possible to sow in early autumn as well as in spring and let the seedlings stand outdoors all winter. They will then flower early the following summer before the spring-sown seedlings begin. All plants, autumn or spring sown, should be thinned to about 30 cm (1 ft) apart. Varieties derived from *Chrysanthemum carinatum*, the tricolor chrysanthemum, have single or double flowers with contrasting rings of colour, white, yellow, red or purple, all about 60 cm (2 ft) high. Varieties of *C. coronarium*, the garland chrysanthemum, are 30-90 cm (1-3 ft) high, single or double flowered, in shades of yellow and white. Varieties of *C. segetum*, the corn marigold, are 45 cm (1½ ft) high, yellow or white, often with a dark central disc. *C. spectabilis* is a hybrid between *C. carinatum* and *C. coronarium*, 90 cm (3 ft) high, with single or double flowers in shades of yellow and white. *C. parthenium*, the feverfew, is really a perennial but is usually grown like those above as a hardy annual. Seedsmen generally offer it as *Matricaria eximea*, which is rather confusing. It grows 30 cm (1 ft) high and has masses of yellow or white flowers like tiny balls. One variety, named *aureum* and often known as golden feather, is grown for its golden ferny leaves and is clipped to prevent it flowering.

Cladanthus. A hardy annual with golden-yellow daisy flowers and attractive, finely divided leaves. The kind grown is *Cladanthus arabicus*. Each flower terminates a stem which then produces several branches radiating from beneath the flower, each of which shortly develops a flower of its own, then more branches and so on to the end of the summer. Sow in the first half of spring in well-drained soil and a warm, sunny place where the plants are to flower. Thin seedlings to 20 cm (8 in).

Clarkia. Very easily grown hardy annuals which will thrive in practically any soil and sunny, or even partially shady positions. All the garden varieties have double flowers carried in what, in the non-technical sense, would be called slender spikes. From successional sowings made throughout spring plants may be flowered from mid-summer to mid-autumn. An early autumn sowing made in a fairly sheltered place will provide flowers in early summer the following year. All sowings should be made where the plants are to flower as clarkias do not transplant well. Sow thinly 12 mm ($\frac{1}{2}$ in) deep and thin the seedlings to 15-20 cm (6-8 in). Some seeds can also be sown in small pots and potted on for flowering in the cool greenhouse.

There are many varieties in shades of pink and red and there is also a good pure white. Heights range from about 45-76 cm ($1\frac{1}{2}$-$2\frac{1}{2}$ ft).

Cleome (Spider Flower). *Cleome spinosa* is a handsome and highly distinctive half-hardy annual with large clusters of purple, pink or white spidery looking flowers on sturdy 90 cm (3 ft) stems. Sow in early spring in a greenhouse or heated frame, prick off seedlings or pot singly in small pots and harden off for planting out of doors in early summer in good soil and a sunny, sheltered place. Keep well watered in dry weather.

Cobaea. One of the few good annual climbing plants, *Cobaea scandens*, is not, strictly speaking, an annual at all but a half-hardy perennial. It is much more convenient to raise it anew each year from seed rather than try to protect it during the winter. Seed is sown in late winter/early spring in a greenhouse or frame and the seedlings are potted singly in 7·5 cm (3 in) pots and hardened off for late spring planting. Given good soil and a sunny place they will grow very rapidly and a plant may easily produce numerous stems 3-4·5 m (10-15 ft) long. The flowers are not unlike those of the Canterbury bell and are either a rather pale violet-purple or white. A drawback is that, unless plants are raised early and kept growing steadily, flowering may start rather late in the summer.

Collinsia. *Collinsia bicolor* is a pretty little hardy annual with 20 cm (9 in) spikes of lilac and white flowers all summer. It should be sown thinly where it is to flower and be thinned out to 10-15 cm (4-6 in). Successional sowings can be made all through spring with a further sowing in well-drained soil in early autumn to stand the winter out of doors and flower the following summer.

Convolvulus. *Convolvulus tricolor*, sometimes listed as *C. annua*, is a showy hardy annual sprawling in habit, with wide funnel-shaped blue or pink flowers often with a white or yellow centre. It is easily grown in any ordinary soil and sunny place, sown outdoors in early spring or even early autumn where it is to bloom. Thin seedlings to at least 23 cm (9 in) and leave to cover the ground with their spreading growth and flower all summer (See also **Ipomoea**, p. 87).

Coreopsis. In addition to the perennial varieties of coreopsis described in Chapter 8 there are some excellent hardy annual varieties of *Coreopsis tinctoria*. All have very showy flowers like big, broad-petalled daisies on slender but surprisingly strong stems 30-90 cm (1-3 ft) in height according to variety. In some the flowers are wholly yellow; others are crimson, while yet others combine yellow and crimson. All flower from mid-summer to early autumn. Sow successively through spring outdoors where the plants are to flower. Cover lightly and thin the seedlings to at least 23 cm (9 in) apart. These annual varieties of coreopsis do best in a sunny place and are not in the least fussy regarding soil. They are excellent for cutting as well as being first-rate bedding plants.

Cornflower. This favourite hardy annual has numerous varieties in colours from white, lilac, rose, carmine to blue, some the normal 90 cm (3 ft) high of the wild cornflower, others dwarfs no more than 30 cm (1 ft) high, some single, some double flowered. The dwarf varieties are excellent for bedding. The tall varieties can also be used for garden display but need careful staking. Their prime value is as cut flowers for which purpose they are unexcelled by any hardy annual. Sow seed thinly in early spring or early autumn in drills 12 mm (½ in) deep and 45 cm (1½ ft) apart; 23 cm (9 in) for the dwarf varieties. Thin the seedlings to at least 23 cm (9 in) – for the dwarfs 15 cm (6 in) – and place bushy twigs in the ground around the tall kinds to give them support. They will grow up through the twigs and soon hide them from view. An alternative is to strain a length of twine or wire between stakes down each side of the row, but this is not so neat. If the flowers are required for cutting gather them regularly and do not let any form seed as this will shorten the flowering season. Seedlings from the autumn sowing will stand the winter out of doors without protection provided the soil is fairly light and well drained. These seedlings will start to flower the following summer about a month ahead of the spring-sown plants. In spring sowing can be carried out in almost any kind of soil though light, not too rich soils give the best results. The position chosen for these plants should be open and sunny.

Cosmos (Cosmea). There are two distinct kinds of cosmea, but both are half-hardy annuals requiring similar treatment in the garden. Varieties of *Cosmos bipinnatus* have ferny foliage and flowers in a variety of shades of pink, rose, wine red, white and yellow. Double-flowered varieties are also available. All grow about 90 cm (3 ft) tall. Varieties of *C. sulphureus* are shorter, about 60 cm (2 ft) high, and rather stiffer in habit with yellow or orange single or double flowers. Seed should be sown at a temperature of 15-18°C/ 59-64°F in late winter and the seedlings pricked off and hardened for planting out during early summer. Space them at least 23 cm (9 in) apart in a sunny place and reasonably good soil. Some strains of *C. bipinnatus* start to flower very late in the summer and should be avoided. This fault is often erroneously put down to faulty culture. A good strain will start to flower in early summer and continue till early autumn if faded flowers are removed regularly. Varieties of *C. bipinnatus* are first rate for cutting because of their long, slender stems.

Cuphea (Cigar Plant). The popular name for *Cuphea ignea* refers to the little tubular scarlet flowers each with a ring of black and white at the mouth. This is a neat half-hardy annual 30 cm (1 ft) high to be sown in a warm greenhouse in late winter or early spring and either grown on as a pot plant or planted out of doors in a warm, sheltered place in early summer.

Cynoglossum (Hound's Tongue). *Cynoglossum amabile* has brilliant blue forget-me-not flowers. It can be treated as an annual sown in early spring in a greenhouse, temperature 15-18°C/59-64°F, for planting out in late spring to give mid-summer bloom. Alternatively, it can be sown in late spring to flower the following year, but seedlings need well-drained soil to overwinter safely. The plants are bushy and about 60 cm (2 ft) in height and will be all the better for a little support from, for example, the tops of twiggy sticks pushed into the ground around them while they are still fairly small.

Dahlia. The double-flowered dahlias are dealt with elsewhere (see p. 346). Here I want only to mention the dwarf, single, collerette, semi-double or double-flowered bedding types which are readily raised from seed and are usually treated as half-hardy annuals. They are very easy to manage and make an unsurpassed display from about mid-summer to mid-autumn or even, in a very favourable season, until late autumn. The best results are obtained by sowing seed in a greenhouse with a temperature of 15-18°C/59-64°F in early spring but seed can be sown as late as mid-spring in an unheated frame and will produce plants which will flower freely the same year. Early-raised seedlings must be pricked off 7·5 cm (3 in) apart or potted singly in small pots but, if mid-spring sowings are made very thinly, the plants can often be allowed to stand undisturbed in the seed trays until planting-out time. This must not be before the first week in early summer as dahlias are very easily injured by frost. Give the plants a sunny place in good, rich soil and space them at least 30 cm (1 ft) apart. They will attain a height of from 45-76 cm (1½-2½ ft). If desired the tubers can be lifted in autumn as soon as the top growth has been blackened by frost and be stored like other dahlias, to be replanted or increased by cuttings the following spring. As a rule this is only worth while with exceptionally good colours or with plants that are outstanding in some other way. Sometimes these seed-raised dahlias do not make very good tubers and it is a waste of time to store them. Colours are very varied, including scarlet, pink, yellow and white. Seed can be purchased in mixture or separate colours.

Daisy. See **Bellis** (p. 74).

Delphinium. See **Larkspur** (p. 87).

Dianthus. Most dianthuses are perennials and they will be found in other sections, but the genus includes one important group of half-hardy annuals. These are forms of *Dianthus chinensis* and its variety *heddewigii*. They grow 15-30 cm (6 in-1 ft) high and look very much like perennial pinks but are extraordinarily bright and varied in colour. There are vivid scarlets, rich crimsons, good clean pinks, salmons and various effective combinations of these. Flowers are also very varied in form, some being double, some single; some smooth petalled and others deeply slashed or fringed.

All can be sown in a warm greenhouse (15-18°C/59-64°F) in late winter to be pricked off 4 cm (1½ in) apart in deep seed trays as soon as possible, and subsequently removed to a frame in spring for hardening off and planting outdoors later in the season. They will then flower in high summer. Those who have no heat can sow in a frame or unheated greenhouse in early summer, overwinter the plants without heat and plant out the following late spring. For a massed display plant about 23 cm (9 in) apart.

Digitalis. See **Foxglove** (p. 82).

Dorotheanthus. What was once known as *Mesembryanthemum criniflorum* is now known as *Dorotheanthus bellidiformis*. It is an outstanding half-hardy annual, a trailing plant a few centimetres in height with many large, brilliantly coloured flowers which might suggest showy daisies to the unbotanical observer. Penetrating shades of rose are common, also crimsons, apricots, softer shades of pink and even buff. This is a grand plant for edging sunny beds and borders or for planting on south slopes and ledges in the rock garden. In shade the flowers refuse to open and they will remain closed everywhere on a dull day.

Sow the seed in boxes in a greenhouse or frame in early spring, prick off into deeper boxes as soon as the seedlings can be handled and complete the hardening-off process in time to plant outdoors, about 20 cm (8 in) apart, in early summer. This is one of those rare plants which seems to prefer poor soil to good, but it does need good drainage.

Eccremocarpus. *Eccremocarpus scaber* is a vigorous, half-hardy, perennial climber which, like *Cobaea scandens*, can be so readily raised and flowered from seed in one season that this is the usual method of growing it. It is a slender, twining plant with tendrils, the flowers are small, tubular and scarlet or orange and they are at their best in late summer. The plant thrives in a warm, sunny place such as the side of a porch or an arch. Sow seeds in a greenhouse, temperature 15-18°C/59-64°F, early in spring, pot the seedlings singly in 7·5 cm (3 in) pots and harden them off for early summer planting. If the soil is reasonably good the plants will easily reach the top of a 3 m (10 ft) trellis in one season.

Echium (Viper's Bugloss). These plants have the merit of thriving in very hot, dry places and poor soils, which improve rather than spoil them by keeping growth compact and encouraging the freest production of flowers. Those grown as annuals in gardens are mostly dwarf hybrids of *Echium plantagineum* with purple, rose, mauve, lavender, blue or white flowers about 30 cm (1 ft) high. These can be raised from seed sown in mid-spring where the plants are to bloom. Thin them out to about 23 cm (9 in) apart.

Emilia (Tassel Flower). The plant frequently called *Cacalia coccinea* is really *Emilia flammea*. It is an annual with tassel-like clusters of orange-scarlet flowers on 30 cm (1 ft) stems and can either be raised in a frame or greenhouse, temperature 15-18°C/59-64°F, in early spring for planting out in late spring. Or, sow in mid-spring where it is to flower. It likes a warm, sunny place and well-drained soil. Thin them to 15-20 cm (6-8 in) apart.

Erysimum. Wallflower-like plants, mostly hardy perennials which are almost always treated as hardy biennials. Culture is exactly the same as for cheiranthus (see p. 76). *Erysimum linifolium* is about 45 cm (1½ ft) high and has mauve or purple flowers. There are also good forms of *E. suffruticosum* which are a little taller and have clear yellow or bright orange flowers. *E. perofskianum* is a hardy annual also 45 cm (1½ ft) high with yellow or orange flowers. It can be sown outdoors in spring where it is to flower, seedlings being thinned to about 25 cm (10 in). All bloom in late spring and early summer.

Eschscholzia (Californian Poppy). For a warm, rather dry place there is no more easily grown or brilliantly coloured hardy annual than this. The wide open, poppy-like flowers are vivid shades of yellow, orange and red. They have the high gloss that one associates with buttercups and are admirably set off by the finely divided, grey-green foliage. Eschscholzias grow from 23-30 cm (9 in-1 ft) tall, spread rather widely and should always be sown where they are to bloom as they resent root disturbance. Sow any time through spring in the sunniest and warmest spot available. Thin the seedlings to 20 cm (8 in) and then leave them to look after themselves. It faded flowers can be removed from time to time it will help but it becomes an almost impossible task after a while because of the freedom with which they are produced. Poor soil is an advantage as it increases the rate of flowering and prevents undue growth of leaves. There are double-flowered as well as single-flowered forms.

Evening Primrose. See **Oenothera** (p. 93).

Felicia (Blue Marguerite, Kingfisher Daisy). Daisy-like flowers which have obvious affinities with the Michaelmas daisies. As with the true asters blue is the prevailing colour and some of the shades represented are exceptionally beautiful. One of the best in this respect is *F. amelloides*, a popular greenhouse pot plant, sometimes known as *Agathaea coelestis*. It is a half-hardy perennial but will flower the first year from seed if sown in warmth in early spring and it can then be hardened off for planting out of doors. *F. bergeriana*, the kingfisher daisy, is an annual and can be treated in the same way. The average height of these dainty, free flowering plants is 30 cm (1 ft) and when planted out in the border they should be spaced about 23 cm (9 in) apart.

Forget-me-not. See **Myosotis** (p. 91).

Foxglove (Digitalis). A plant so well known under its popular name that one almost forgets it has a botanical one. In gardens the common magenta-red foxglove of our wood- and wasteland has been transformed almost out of recognition. The flowers are not only bigger but their colours are much more varied, embracing fine shades of pink and cream, besides white and many handsome spotted forms. The Excelsior race has flowers which are held out almost horizontally all round the stem instead of hanging downwards on just one side only. All can be raised without the least difficulty from seed sown outdoors in early summer in a cool place. Plant out the seedlings in mid- to late summer in good rich soil and a half-shady place, spacing them at least 15 cm (6 in) apart, and they will grow into sturdy plants for removal to flowering quarters in mid-autumn or early spring. They will grow anywhere but are seen at their best in fairly rich, leafy or peaty soil and partial shade. Space them at least 38 cm (1¼ ft) apart as they will make big plants averaging 1·2 m (4½ ft) in height. They are at their best in early summer.

Gaillardia. There are perennial gaillardias described in Chapter 8 but here we are concerned with the half-hardy annual varieties. They are all showy plants with the large, daisy flowers typical of the family. Some are wholly crimson and some wholly yellow but most are bicolored with red flowers tipped with yellow or white. Most of the best are varieties of *Gaillardia pulchella* while Picta with coppery red and yellow flowers is especially good. All flower over summer from an early spring sowing under glass, temperature 15-18°C/59-64°F, and should be planted in a sunny place and ordinary soil. Height averages 45 cm (1½ ft). The plants should be spaced 30 cm (1 ft) apart.

Gazania. These are rather tender half-hardy perennials which can be increased by summer cuttings but are commonly raised from seed sown in a greenhouse or frame, temperature 15-18°C/59-64°F, in early spring. Seedlings are pricked off or potted singly and hardened off for planting out in early summer. They are low-growing, spreading plants with large daisy-type flowers, orange, yellow, cream, rose and ruby, often with a zone of maroon or almost black at the base of the petals. They are sun lovers and will thrive in a hot, dry place.

Gilia. The finest species, *Gilia coronopifolia*, is a half-hardy biennial which needs to be sown in a greenhouse in summer to be grown on in pots protected from frost until it is safe to plant outdoors the following spring. The plants have finely divided leaves and the scarlet, pink, salmon or yellow flowers are borne in long slender spikes 1 m (3½ ft) high. Easier, hardy annual species, such as *G. tricolor* with white lavender-edged flowers on 30 cm (1 ft) high stems and *G. capitata* which is blue and about 60 cm (2 ft) high may be sown out of doors in mid-spring where they are to flower. All like sunny places and are not particular regarding soil. The plants once commonly known as leptosiphon, and described under that name in this chapter, are actually species or hybrids of gilia. See also Leptosiphon (p. 88).

Glaucium (Horned Poppy). *Glaucium flavum* (or *luteum*) is a handsome British biennial which is worth a place in the garden especially in hot, dry sites. It has yellow poppy flowers and grey-green foliage and is known as the horned poppy because of the extraordinarily long, curved seed pods which suggest attenuated horns. It grows about 60 cm (2 ft) in height and flowers in summer. Sow seed at this time of year directly in the open ground where the plants are to flower the following year and thin the seedlings to 30 cm (1 ft) or thereabouts.

Godetia. This is one of the most useful of hardy annuals. It will succeed practically anywhere, in sun or shade, light soil or heavy, and there are heights for all purposes. Varieties of the tall type may be anything from 60-90 cm (2-3 ft) high and they carry their flowers in long spike-like sprays. In contrast there is a dwarfer type in which the plants seldom exceed 38 cm (1¼ ft) and are very bushy, the flowers being carried in short clusters all over the plant. There are also ultra-dwarf varieties of the same general habit but not exceeding 18 cm (7 in) in height. In each type there are both single and double-flowered forms, and the colour range, though mainly in shades of pink and magenta, also includes crimsons and white. Seed of all kind may be sown any time through spring or in early autumn in any ordinary soil. Cover lightly with fine soil and thin the seedlings as soon as possible to 20 cm (9 in) apart (15 cm (6 in) for the very dwarf kinds). The seedlings do not transplant well as they have tap roots. Flowers are produced all summer if several sowings are made.

Golden Feather. See **Chrysanthemum** (p. 77).

Grasses, Ornamental. A number of grasses are worth growing for their ornamental leaves or flower heads and some of these are annuals, either half-hardy or hardy. Seed of the half-hardy kinds should be sown in early spring in a greenhouse or frame, and the seedlings hardened off for planting out of doors by early summer. Seed of the hardy kind can be sown from early spring out of doors where the plants are to grow and the seedlings thinned to about 15 cm (6 in). Most ornamental grasses succeed best in light, open places though they will grow in partial shade. Those with attractive inflorescences are often used for cutting.

Among the best hardy annual kinds are *Agrostis nebulosa*, the cloud grass, so called because of its large inflorescence of tiny flowers like a cloud, height 45 cm (1½ ft), *A. pulchella*, the bouquet grass, 30 cm (1 ft); *Avena sterilis*, known as animated oats, because the flowers change position according to the moisture in the air, 76 cm (2½ ft); *Briza minor*, the little quaking grass, with hanging, pearl-like flowers; *B. media*, is similar but larger, 30 cm (1 ft); and *B. maxima*, the largest flowered of the quaking grasses, 45 cm (1½ ft); *Bromus briziformis*, with drooping sprays, 45 cm (1½ ft); *Eragrostis elegans*, the love grass, also known as *E. interrupta*, with graceful sprays, 60 cm (2 ft); *Hordeum jubatum*, the squirrel-tail grass with little nodding spikes and long beards like a tail, 76 cm (2½ ft); *Lagurus ovatus*, the hare's tail, with soft, ovoid spikes, 30 cm (1 ft); *Panicum violaceum* with curling plumes of green and violet flowers, 90 cm (3 ft); *Setaria italica*, with dense heads of yellow or purple flowers, 90 cm (3 ft); and *Tricholaena rosea*, the wine grass, with fluffy purplish heads, 60 cm (2 ft).

Good half-hardy kinds are *Coix lachryma-jobi*, known as Job's tears because of the curious bead-like seeds, 90 cm (3 ft); *Pennisetum villosum* (also known as *P. longistylum*) with feathery spikes of whitish or purplish flowers, and ornamental varieties of *Zea mays*, the maize or Indian corn, with variegated leaves or coloured seeds in cobs – 1m (3½ ft).

Gypsophila. In addition to the perennial varieties described in Chapter 8 there is a fine hardy annual species named *Gypsophila elegans*. This has single flowers each about 12 mm (½ in) across borne in loose, lavish and very slenderly built sprays. It is an ideal plant for cutting and is grown in immense quantities for market, especially for sale with sweet peas with which it associates well. It is also a pretty plant for massing in the garden though it does not last very long. Average height is 45 cm (1½ ft). There are white and pink-flowered varieties. In order to ensure a succession of bloom from early summer until the autumn frosts, four or five sowings should be made at intervals of about a fortnight through spring with a final sowing in early autumn to withstand the winter and flower early the following summer. Choose a sunny spot and any ordinary, not too heavy soil. Sow thinly either broadcast or in drills 23 cm (9 in) apart and cover with 12 mm (½ in) of soil. Thin the seedlings to at least 15 cm (6 in) apart.

Helianthus. See **Sunflower** (p. 101).

Helichrysum (Strawflower, Double Everlasting). There are perennial kinds of helichrysum described elsewhere, but *Helichrysum bracteatum* is a half-hardy annual with chaffy petals which will last most of the winter if the flowers are cut in the right condition and dried slowly by being hung in small bunches head downwards in an airy shed. The flowers of the best garden forms, usually sold as *Helichrysum monstrosum*, are like big double daisies in a great variety of bright colours including yellow, pink and scarlet. They are borne in profusion on bushy plants 76 cm (2½ ft) in height. Helichrysums may be sown in late spring out of doors where they are to bloom but better results are obtained by sowing under glass in early spring for an end of season planting. Give the plants a sunny, open position in well-drained soil, cover the seed lightly and thin the seedlings (or plant out those raised under glass) 25 cm (10 in) apart. Cut the flowers for drying just before they are fully developed. For winter decoration their stems should be replaced by florist's wires. Average height is 60 cm (2 ft).

Heliophila. *Heliophila longifolia* is a 45 cm (1½ ft) half-hardy annual which can be grown out of doors as an edging or ground-cover plant. It has slender, branching stems terminating in loose sprays of small, bright blue, white-eyed flowers. It can be sown in early spring in a greenhouse or frame and after being potted, with two or three seedlings in each 7·5 cm (3 in) pot, should be hardened off for late spring planting in small groups just as it comes out of the pots. Space these groups 20 cm (8 in) apart and give them a sunny position in light, open soil. Alternatively sow in late spring out of doors where the plants are to flower and thin seedlings to 20 cm (8 in).

Heliotrope (Cherry Pie). Though this plant is a half-hardy perennial and is included amongst greenhouse flowers, it is so frequently treated as a half-hardy annual that I must mention it here also. When grown in this way seed should be sown from mid-winter to early spring in a warm greenhouse (15-18°C/59-64°F) and the seedlings pricked off into boxes and later potted singly just like antirrhinums. Be very careful when hardening them off as they are sensitive to cold. For the same reason do not plant out until early summer and then give as sunny a position as possible in reasonably rich and well-drained soil. If desired some of the plants can be lifted and potted in early autumn and transferred to the greenhouse to be propagated by cuttings the following spring. The greenhouse must, at the very least, be frost proof.

Heliotropium arborescens (once known as *H. peruvianum*) is the wild Peruvian plant from which the garden varieties have been developed. It will grow 1·2-1·8 m (4-6 ft) high and the flat heads of small violet or lavender flowers are intensely fragrant. Garden varieties are mostly shorter, more compact and deeper in colour but not all are so richly scented. All flower throughout the summer.

Helipterum. What was once called *Acroclinium roseum* is now known as *Helipterum roseum*. It is a hardy annual with a pretty, everlasting flower. The blooms can be dried and will then retain their shape and colour for many months. The plant grows to about 30 cm (1 ft) high and flowers from early to mid-summer after an early spring sowing. Or it flowers from mid- to late summer after a late spring sowing. The flowers are daisy-like and the colours mainly shades of pink together with cream and white. Seed should be sown in late spring where the plants are to flower and covered very lightly. Give the plants a warm sunny place and lightish soil. Plant out greenhouse-raised seedlings in early summer or thin outdoor seedlings to 15 cm (6 in). Cut the flowers for drying just before they are fully developed, tie them in small bunches and hang them upside down in a cool, airy shed.

H. manglessi, once called rhodanthe, is an 'everlasting' grown for drying and subsequent use in winter decorations. The flowers are pink and smaller than those of the better known helichrysums. It is a half-hardy annual and should be grown in exactly the same manner as acroclinium.

Hibiscus. The hibiscus of romantic novelists is a tropical shrub or small tree and could not under any circumstances be treated as an annual but the family, which is a big one, contains several true annuals of which the best from the garden standpoint is *Hibiscus trionum*. This is a rather straggly plant, about 45 cm (1½ ft) high, which produces masses of fleeting, silken-textured flowers, sulphur yellow with a showy central blotch of maroon. The flowers are followed by attractive bladder-like fruits. It should be treated as half-hardy, that is, seed should be germinated in a greenhouse or frame in early spring and the seedlings passed through the usual stages of pricking off and hardening in time to be planted out of doors in a sunny place and rather poor, sandy soil at the end of spring. Space them about 30 cm (1 ft) apart.

Hollyhock (Althaea). This hardy perennial is often treated as a biennial, seed being sown out of doors in late spring to provide seedlings which are transferred to a nursery bed in summer and to flower beds the following autumn or spring. Sow very thinly in drills 12 mm (½ in) deep and 18 cm (7 in) apart. Plant in the nursery bed at least 15 cm (6 in) apart in rows 30 cm (1 ft) apart and in final quarters at least 60 cm (2 ft) apart. Both double and single-flowered varieties can be raised from seed and great variety of colour can be obtained in both types all of which will breed reasonably true to type if the seed has been carefully saved. The best plants can be retained for flowering again in later years and may be propagated a hundred per cent true to type by means of root cuttings (see p. 111). It is also possible to flower some varieties of hollyhock the same year if seed is sown in late winter in a warm greenhouse. Seedlings are pricked off into deep seed trays or potted singly and then carefully hardened off for planting out at the end of spring.

All hollyhocks are most likely to prove really permanent in sunny, sheltered places and rather poor, well-drained soils. The flowers may be bigger and finer in richer soils but the plants grow too lush and are apt to rot off in winter. For this reason and particularly in cold districts, some gardeners prefer to overwinter their summer-raised seedlings in frames and plant them out in mid-spring. Hollyhocks suffer severely from rust disease in some places but occasional spraying with thiram over summer will check this.

The common hollyhock is *Althaea rosea*. The fig-leaf hollyhock, *A. ficifolia*, has similar flowers and deeply lobed leaves.

Honesty. See **Lunaria** (p. 89).

Humulus (Hop). Hops are perennial climbers but the Japanese hop, *Humulus japonicus*, can be grown as an annual if seed is sown in greenhouse or frame in early spring so that the seedlings can be potted singly in 7·5 cm (3 in) pots and hardened off in time to be planted out towards the end of spring. It is also possible to sow in late spring directly in the open ground where the plants are to grow but they will not get so big from such a late sowing. Given good soil and an early start the plants may easily climb to a height of 4.5 m (15 ft) before the end of the summer forming a decorative screen for an arch or pergola. The leaves are light green.

Iberis (Candytuft). This family includes several outstanding rock plants (see p. 194). There are, in addition, two exceptionally fine annuals, the common candytuft (*Iberis umbellata*) with flattish heads of white, lilac or purple flowers, and the rocket candytuft (*I. amara coronaria*) with big columnar spikes of pure white flowers. The first ranges from 23-38 cm (9 in-1¼ ft) according to variety, the second averages 45 cm (1½ ft). All are quite hardy and can be sown outdoors in early autumn to stand the winter without protection and give a mid-summer display the following year. For summer flowering it is quite sufficient to sow in mid-spring where the plants are to bloom. Thinnings can be transplanted elsewhere. Space at least 20 cm (8 in) apart (more for really big blooms) and give a sunny position in ordinary or moderately rich soil. The common candytuft can also be used for filling blank places in the rock garden.

Impatiens. See p. 478.

Ionopsidium (Violet Cress). *Ionopsidium acaule* is a tiny hardy annual which may be used to make a carpet of little leaves and pale violet or white flowers or to grow in the crevices of paving or in rock gardens. Sow seed thinly from spring to summer where plants are to grow. Little thinning is required. This is a plant that will do well in shady places.

Ipomoea (Morning Glory). These twining plants are much confused with convolvulus and are sometimes included under that name. *Ipomoea purpurea* is a half-hardy annual and *I. tricolor* (sometimes called *I. rubro-caerulea*) a half-hardy perennial usually grown as an annual. Both have slender, twining stems and funnel-shaped flowers in various shades of pink, purple and, in the case of *I. tricolor*, a very pure blue called heavenly blue. All are raised from seed sown in spring under glass at a temperature of 18°C/66°F. Seedlings are best potted singly and hardened off for planting outdoors in early summer in a warm, sunny place or they may be grown throughout under glass in a greenhouse or conservatory in large pots or a bed of soil. Plants must be given canes, trelliswork or taut wire as support.

Jacobaea. The hardy annuals commonly known as jacobaea are varieties of *Senecio elegans*. They are easy to manage and make a great display with their highly coloured flowers borne in clusters on 45 cm (1½ ft) stems throughout the summer. The best strains produce nothing but fully double flowers – small but showy pompons in bright shades of rose, purple and crimson. There is also a pure white variety for contrast. Seed of all may be sown very thinly in mid-spring where the plants are to flower, while, for an earlier display, seed can be sown in the greenhouse in early spring and given the usual half-hardy treatment. Out of doors cover 12 mm (½ in) deep and thin seedlings to at least 20 cm (8 in) each way. Jacobaeas succeed best in warm, sunny places and rather well-drained soils. They are first class for cutting.

Kochia (Summer Cypress). One of the few annuals grown exclusively for its foliage. *Kochia scoparia trichophylla*, the best variety, makes a little pyramidal bush like a miniature conifer up to 90 cm (3 ft) high, bright green at first but slowly changing to purplish crimson as the summer draws to a close. The colour is most highly developed in rather poor, dry soils. Sow seed in shallow boxes in a frame or airy greenhouse early in spring, prick off the seedlings 5 cm (2 in) apart directly they can be handled and transfer them to summer beds in early summer. They are most useful dotted here and there among low-growing plants. They also make pretty pot plants for the unheated greenhouse.

Larkspur. Really a hardy annual species of delphinium named *Delphinium ajacis* but I have kept to the popular name to avoid confusion. Larkspurs carry their flowers in long spikes not unlike those of a perennial delphinium though considerably smaller, but they have very finely divided, ferny leaves. There are both single and double-flowered forms but the latter are the more popular and certainly the more effective. Normally they are about 90 cm (3 ft) in height but there are shorter varieties. They flower in the second half of summer from a spring sowing or in the first half from an early autumn sowing. Mid-spring and early autumn are the best times for sowing. Seed is usually sown directly in the beds in which the plants are to flower, the seedlings being thinned to 27 cm (11 in) apart, but an alternative method is to sow in boxes in a frame or greenhouse, prick off like stocks or asters and plant out in early summer. Larkspurs do best in full sun and will succeed in most ordinary garden soils though they prefer those of an open-textured but fairly rich nature.

Lavatera. There are shrubby kinds of lavatera but *Lavatera trimestris* (sometimes known as *L. rosea*) is a vigorous hardy annual which looks very much like a mallow. The flowers are shaped like wide funnels and in the common type are a rather crude rose pink, but there are improved forms including Loveliness and Silver Cup, in which the colour is both brighter and purer. There are also white varieties. All are plants for the back of the border or the centre of large beds. They grow about 90 cm (3 ft) high and if given space, a single plant will cover 0·8 sq m (1 sq yd) of ground. Sow very thinly in mid-spring where the plants are to grow and thin to at least 45 cm (1½ ft). Give as sunny a position as possible. This plant will grow in practically any soil but flowers most freely in those that are well drained and not too rich.

Layia (Tidy Tips). Only one species, *Layia elegans*, is much grown; a hardy annual with daisy-like flowers mainly yellow but each with an outer rim of white. The plant is bushy and about 30 cm (1 ft) in height. Layia lacks the brilliance to make it a really popular plant but it is a useful addition to the garden in summer and is easily grown in a warm, sunny place and rather light soil. Sow seed in mid-spring where the plants are to bloom and thin the seedlings to 20 cm (8 in).

Leptosiphon. An unhackneyed annual and a dwarf plant for warm, sunny spots, suitable as edgings, carpeting or in rock gardens. The name leptosiphon is a garden one and these plants are in fact hybrids of *Gilia lutea*. Their fragile stems are smothered by the small but showy flowers in a great variety of colours. Seed should be sown in mid-spring where the plants are to bloom and the seedlings thinned to 10 cm (4 in). No further attention is required.

Limnanthes (Poached Egg Flower). One species is grown, *Limnanthes douglasii*, a delightful hardy annual which will flower in early summer from a spring sowing or in spring from an early autumn sowing. It is a great favourite with bees, and bee-keepers often grow it from an early autumn sowing so as to have something in bloom to stimulate activity at the beginning of the season. *L. douglasii* is a low-growing plant with masses of pale yellow and white flowers. It makes a charming edging to a bed or border and is a welcome change from more popular subjects. Soe thinly 12 mm (½ in) deep where the plants are to grow and thin the seedlings to 15 cm (6 in). It likes a sunny place but is not particular about soil.

Limonium. The annual plants are grown principally for cutting. The flowers have the papery texture which distinguishes the 'everlasting' and, if carefully dried, will retain their colour for many months. The kinds commonly grown are *Limonium sinuatum* in shades of white, blue and pink, and *L. psylliostachys*, yellow. All are readily raised from seed in the same manner as annual stocks or asters from late winter/early spring sowings. After hardening off, plant them out in late spring or early summer in beds in the reserve or kitchen garden from which their flowers may be cut without loss. Plant 23 cm (9 in) apart in rows 45 cm (18 in) apart in as sunny a place as possible and well-dug, open, but not over-rich soil. For drying cut just before the flowers are fully open and hang head downwards in a cool, airy shed for several weeks.

All these plants were once known as statice and may still be found under that name in some catalogues. There are also hardy perennial kinds.

Linaria (Toadflax). In addition to the perennial linarias (see p. 136), there are some excellent annual varieties derived from *Linaria maroccana*. These have slender spikes of small, snapdragon-like flowers in a great variety of very striking colours including rich purples, wine reds and bright pinks and average 30 cm (1 ft) in height. All are excellent for cutting besides making a grand display in the garden. So through spring in a sunny place where the plants are to flower and thin to 20 cm (8 in). No special soil or preparation is necessary.

Linum (Flax). Another genus which, besides perennials, includes one fine hardy annual. This is *Linum grandiflorum*, the scarlet flax. It is a fragile-looking plant with thin, wiry stems 30-45 cm (1-1½ ft) in height clothed with narrow leaves and terminating in loose sprays of vivid scarlet flowers which individually do not last long but are produced in never-ending succession through the second half of summer. Seed should be sown sparingly in spring in a warm sunny place and ordinary soil. Thin the seedlings to 15 cm (6 in).

Lobelia. The blue bedding lobelia, of which there are also white and magenta forms, needs no introduction since for generations it has been the most popular of all edging plants for summer bedding schemes. Strictly it is a half-hardy perennial but it is almost invariably grown as a half-hardy annual. Seed is sown in boxes late winter/early spring in a greenhouse at a temperature of about 15-18°C/59-64°F. The seedlings are pricked off 5 cm (2 in) apart into other seed trays while quite small and are removed to a frame towards late spring. If steadily hardened off the plants will be ready for putting out of doors around early summer. Plant 15 cm (6 in) apart in any ordinary soil and in a sunny or even partially shaded position. Lobelias are excellent town plants withstanding the grimy atmosphere better than most. They can also be grown in pots and hanging baskets, though for the latter purpose the trailing varieties derived from *Lobelia tenuior* or those sold under the name *L. hybrida pendula* are to be preferred to the compact type derived from *L. erinus* and favoured for bedding.

Love-in-a-mist. See **Nigella** (p. 93).

Lunaria (Honesty). This old-fashioned plant is grown for the seed vessels which are like 2.5 cm (1 in) wide parchment discs. They will last most of the winter and make an attractive indoor decoration especially when associated with scarlet berries. But honesty is also attractive in the garden. The magenta flowers are freely produced in late spring and early summer after which they are quickly followed by the distinctive seed vessels. There is also a variety with white variegated leaves. The plant has been known by botanists both as *Lunaria annua* and *L. biennis*, reflecting their uncertainty whether it is an annual or a biennial. It is usually grown as a hardy biennial and raised from seed sown in early summer in a partially shaded place out of doors. Sow thinly and plant out the seedlings about 30 cm (1 ft) apart when they have two or three rough leaves each. No further attention beyond occasional weeding will be necessary. It can also be grown as an annual from an early sowing under glass. Height is about 90 cm (3 ft). For winter decoration cut in late summer when the seed vessels look like parchment.

Lupinus. The perennial lupins are described on p. 137. The hardy annual varieties with which we are concerned here are by no means so beautiful, their flower spikes tending to be small and ineffective by comparison with those magnificent giants, but improvements have been and still are being made and good strains are worth a trial especially in poor, sandy soils for which selection of suitable plants is necessarily restricted. Sow the seeds 2.5 cm (1 in) deep in spring where they are to flower. The seeds are big and easily handled so it is usually most convenient to drop them in singly about 15 cm (6 in) apart and subsequently remove surplus plants to leave the rest standing 30-45 cm (1-1½ ft) apart. Transplanting is seldom very satisfactory as the plants take too long to recover. These lupins are 45-90 cm (1½-3 ft) tall and flower in the second half of summer. There are white, blue and pink varieties.

Lychnis coeli-rosa. See **Viscaria** (p. 106).

Maize. See **Grasses, Ornamental** (p. 83).

Malcolmia. See **Virginian Stock** (p. 105).

Malope. *Malope trifida* is a hardy annual much resembling *Lavatera rosea* and, like it, a member of the mallow family. It makes a bushy plant 76 cm (2½ ft) high. The flowers are rather crude in colour, a bright but harsh shade of rosy red with darker stripes. There are improved forms and a white one, *M. t. Alba*. Seed should be sown very sparingly in early spring where the plants are to bloom and the seedlings thinned out to at least 38 cm (1¼ ft) apart. Malope likes plenty of sun and warmth but is not the least particular regarding soil.

Marigold. See **Tagetes** (p. 103) and **Calendula** (p. 74).

Matthiola. See **Stocks** (p. 100).

Matricaria. See **Chrysanthemum** (p. 77).

Medicago. See **Calvary Clover** (p. 75).

Mentzelia. The only species grown is *Mentzelia lindleyi* (formerly known as *Bartonia* *aurea*), a showy hardy annual with yellow, poppy-like flowers produced throughout most of the summer. This is an easily grown annual which deserves to be a good deal better known than it is. It revels in light soils and sunny places and should be sown thinly in mid-spring where it is to flower. Thin the seedlings to at least 23 cm (9 in) as the plants make a good deal of growth and will eventually be 45 cm (1½ ft) in height.

Mesembryanthemum (Livingstone Daisy). See **Dorotheanthus** p. 80.

Mignonette. This is one of the most fragrant of hardy annuals. It does especially well in chalky or heavily limed soils but will grow in most soils, preferring an open, sunny position. Although not a showy plant the best varieties are quite attractive with broadly conical spikes of small green and dull red or orange flowers 30 cm (1 ft) in height.

Sow seed successively through spring where the plants are to flower and thin the seedlings to at least 20 cm (8 in). Most people leave the plants much too thick and spoil the effect.

Mignonette also makes an excellent pot plant for the cool greenhouse. For this purpose the seeds are sown in boxes and transferred singly to 7·5 cm (3 in) pots while still quite small. Later they can be moved on into 10 cm (4 in) pots for flowering. Seed sown in late summer will give flowering plants in early spring.

Mimulus (Musk, Monkey Flower). The true musk, famous for the scent which it lost, it is said, through hybridization with another species, is *Mimulus moschatus*. This is purely a greenhouse pot plant but there are some other species of mimulus which are excellent plants for the open garden, some of them hardy perennials, some true annuals but all readily raised from seed sown in greenhouse or frame in early spring. All like moist, fairly rich soils and will thrive in sun or some shade. Many are first class by water. The best of all for annual treatment are the large-flowered hybrids with brightly coloured and usually spotted or blotched flowers which may be sold as *M. tigrinus*, *M. cupreus*, *M. guttatus* or simply as plain mimulus. They are, in fact, hybrids 23-30 cm (9 in-1 ft) high flowering in mid-summer. Seedlings should be raised under glass from an early spring sowing and planted out, 23-30 cm (9-12 in) apart, in late spring where they are to bloom.

Myosotis (Forget-me-not). The spring bedding kinds are usually described as biennials. Actually they are hardy perennials though they often flower themselves to death or succumb to wet and cold in their second winter. In consequence, and also because young plants give the best display, they are almost always treated as hardy biennials. Seed is sown outdoors in an open or half-shady place and ordinary soil in the first half of summer. The seedlings are pricked off 10 cm (4 in) apart in rows 20 cm (8 in) apart as soon as they have made two or three leaves and are removed to their flowering beds in mid-autumn. Plant 20 cm (8 in) apart for a massed display or use as an under-planting or edging for tulips, wallflowers, etc.

Forget-me-nots can often be naturalized in the wild garden, thin woodland or shrubbery and will seed themselves and soon cover all the ground. If plants removed after flowering are scattered over the ground where forget-me-nots are required they will shed their seeds and give a good crop of seedlings.

Nasturtium. The plant we all know as nasturtium is not really a nasturtium at all but a tropaeolum and the true owner of the name nasturtium is quite a different thing – none other than the refreshing watercress. But here I am following the popular usage of the name 'nasturtium'. Listed as a hardy annual it is really only half-hardy but it can be sown out of doors from mid-spring without protection and will then flower from mid-summer until the frosts of autumn finish its gorgeous display. It is a useful ground-cover plant with its large, rounded leaves.

Yellow and scarlet are the typical nasturtium colours, both separately and together in a variety of brilliant combinations but other and more unusual shades are available including salmon pink, orange pink and cherry. There are both tall and dwarf varieties with single flowers as well as semi-tall and dwarf varieties with double or semi-double flowers and at least one variety, Alaska, with white variegated leaves, and some varieties that have lost the characteristic spurs from their flowers.

All will grow in any soil – in fact the poorer it is the more they seem to flower – and in practically any position, though they do better in sun than in shade. The tall kinds make good coverings for fences, trellises, screens, etc, while the semi-tall and dwarf kinds are excellent bedding plants. Tall and semi-tall kinds should be thinned to at least 30 cm (1 ft) or planted that distance apart. Dwarfs may be as close as 15 cm (6 in).

An alternative method of cultivation to sowing where they are to bloom is to sow the seeds singly in small pots, or space them 5 cm (2 in) apart in seed trays, germinate them in a frame or sheltered place out of doors and plant them out in their flowering quarters in late spring/early summer. They transplant well.

Nemesia. One of the loveliest half-hardy annuals. Varieties of *Nemesia strumosa*, the kind commonly grown, vary in height from 15-30 cm (6 in-1 ft) and will bloom out of doors at any time from early summer to mid-autumn. They also make excellent pot plants.

For summer bedding seed should be sown thinly in boxes in early spring in a greenhouse or frame at a temperature of 15-18°C/59-64°F. Prick off the seedlings 5 cm (2 in) apart as soon as possible and harden them off steadily for planting out late in late spring. The secret of success is to keep the plants growing steadily all the time without any checks which may easily occur in the boxes through lack of water, poor soil or rapid fluctuations of temperature. Use a good compost (see p. 423) with enough peat to prevent rapid drying out, and do not leave the seedlings so long in the boxes that they begin to flower before they are put out. In the garden give them rather richer soil than is advised for most bedding plants, a sunny or half-shady position and plenty of water in hot weather.

The short, trumpet-shaped, broad-lipped flowers are carried in showy clusters and include a great range of good colours such as blue, scarlet, crimson, yellow, orange and white.

For winter flowering seed is sown in late summer in a frame and the seedlings potted and later taken into a cool greenhouse. Spring flowers can be obtained in the same way by delaying sowing until about early autumn.

Nemophila (Baby Blue Eyes). Lovely hardy annuals for edgings and carpetings. *Nemophila menziesii*, also known as *N. insignis*, is the best species. It grows 15 cm (6 in) high, has small, sky-blue flowers in great profusion and may be sown successively through spring where it is to bloom in any ordinary soil and sunny position. Broadcast the seed thinly and thin seedlings to at least 10 cm (4 in) apart. The plants will start to flower from ten or twelve weeks after sowing and continue for several weeks.

Nicotiana. The commercial tobacco is a species of nicotiana but the kinds usually grown in our gardens for ornament are varieties of *Nicotiana alata* (also known as *N. affinis*), the sweet-scented tobacco and also of *N. sanderae*, a hybrid from *N. alata*. These vary from 30-90 cm (1-3 ft) in height, have long, narrowly tubular flowers widely expanded at the mouth; and include white, lime-green, pink, carmine and crimson forms. The white varieties tend to be the most sweetly scented. Typically the flowers of *N. alata* only begin to open towards evening but by hybridization with other species it has been possible to raise varieties with flowers that remain open by day.

Nicotianas will grow in any ordinary soils and sunny or partially shaded positions and are all treated as half-hardy annuals. Seed may be sown in boxes at a temperature of 15-18°C/59-64°F any time from mid-winter to early summer but for outdoor planting early spring sowing is most satisfactory. Prick off 7·5 cm (3 in) apart in deep seed boxes when the seedlings have their first true leaves and harden off for planting outdoors around late spring. Nicotianas also make excellent pot plants for flowering in the greenhouse during spring, summer or early autumn.

Nigella (Love-in-a-mist). *N. damascena* is a hardy annual with ferny foliage and blue, pink, rose or white flowers produced during most of the summer. *N. hispanica*, sometimes called the fennel flower, is similar but lacks the fine green filaments around the flower. Seed of both should be sown sparingly where the plants are to grow and the seedlings thinned to at least 23 cm (9 in). Sow in the first half of spring with a final sowing in late summer to stand the winter and flower the following summer. Spring sowings give flowers in high summer. The flowers are excellent for cutting as well as for garden decoration.

Oenothera (Evening Primrose). A big family including excellent perennials for the herbaceous border and rock garden, but the true evening primrose, *Oenothera biennis*, is a hardy biennial which will grow in the poorest and lightest of soils and either sunny or shady places. It is easily raised from seed sown in late spring/early summer, either directly where the plants are to bloom, or in a nursery bed for the seedlings to be pricked off when large enough and finally transplanted to flowering quarters in mid-autumn or early spring. It is about 90 cm (3 ft) tall when full grown, with masses of large, lemon-yellow flowers with red sepals which help to set them off. The flowers open towards evening and are individually short-lived though they follow one another for many weeks, the flowering season being right through summer. *O. lamarckiana* is similar to *O. biennis* but with bigger flowers and more robust growth.

Osteospermum. South African daisies, some of which are genuine annuals and others perennials treated as annuals. They love warm places and light well-drained soils. Rightly treated they grow very fast and will begin to flower in early summer from a mid-spring sowing outdoors. Sow very thinly where the plants are to bloom, cover with a thin scattering of fine sandy soil and thin out the seedlings to 20 cm (8 in). Alternatively seed can be sown in early spring in greenhouse or frame, pricked off, hardened and planted out in late spring and this is a more reliable method in cold districts or where the soil is heavy.

O. ecklonis is white with a blue disc, and is probably the hardiest for leaving outdoors over winter. *O. Cannington Joyce* is a particularly attractive white flowered variety.

Pansy. To the botanist this is simply another species of viola and even to the novice gardener the similarity between the pansy and the bedding viola must be obvious. But to avoid confusion and because pansies are so commonly raised from seed I am using the popular name here and have dealt with violas elsewhere. Because the two plants have been so much interbred, even experts have difficulty in separating them. Some of the major differences are described under Viola (p. 167).

Pansies can be treated as perennials and propagated by cuttings just like the best violas, and this in fact is just what is done with some of the outstanding show varieties. But pansies for summer bedding are generally treated as hardy biennials and discarded after flowering.

The method is to sow the seed in early summer in a frame or in seed trays stood in a sheltered place outdoors. The seedlings are pricked off a month or six weeks later into a bed of finely broken but rather rich soil in a cool, shady position. If a little very old dung or mushroom compost can be worked into the bed some time before, this will hold the moisture which the plants need besides giving them plenty of nourishment. In exposed places the seedlings are usually pricked out in frames so that frame lights may be used to protect them from the most severe winter weather and, still more, from sudden alternations of rain and frost which could easily kill them.

In mid-spring the plants are put out in their flowering quarters, still in fairly rich soil in either sun or shade. They are planted 15-23 cm (6-9 in) apart and subsequently all faded flowers must be removed regularly before seed sets. In this way the flowering season will be extended well on into the summer instead of being confined to late spring/early summer.

For a late summer display a further sowing can be made in a cool greenhouse or frame in early spring, the seedlings being treated like half-hardy annuals and planted out in early summer. Yet a third method is to treat pansies like hardy annuals, sowing them outdoors in early spring where they are to flower and thinning to 15 cm (6 in) with no transplanting. The winter flowering pansies are best sown in early summer for early autumn planting. They flower intermittently in winter, but freely in spring.

Papaver (Poppy). The big oriental poppies are perennials, and have been dealt with elsewhere (see p. 140). Here I am concerned with the Iceland poppies, which although also strictly perennial are almost always treated as annuals or biennials in gardens, and the true annual poppies which come mainly from two sources, our own native scarlet field poppy and the big carnation or peony-flowered poppy of the East.

The Iceland poppy, *Papaver nudicaule*, is an outstanding cut flower and a useful garden plant. It can be raised from seed sown very thinly in boxes of fine soil in early spring, barely covered, and germinated in a cool greenhouse or frame. The seedlings are then pricked off 4 cm (1½ in) apart like half-hardy annuals (see p. 66) and are hardened off for planting out of doors in late spring. They like a sunny position and well-drained, though not too dry soil. An open, sandy loam with some leafmould or peat suits them admirably. Plant at least 30 cm (1 ft) apart. Water well for the first few weeks should the weather be dry. Once established the plants grow very fast and will start to flower in mid-summer. If the position is not too cold or badly drained many of the plants will survive till the following year when they will have made big clumps and will begin to flower in early summer. Alternatively seed can be sown in early/mid-summer out of doors or in a frame, the seedlings pricked out a few centimetres apart in a nursery bed and transplanted to their flowering quarters in autumn or spring.

Colours are both brilliant and delicate ranging from vivid orange to soft shades of pink, cream, apricot, and maize.

The true annual poppies are among the easiest of plants to grow. They will thrive in almost any soil and sunny position, in fact they seem to have a preference for the poorer and drier places. Seed, which is extremely small, should be broadcast as thinly as possible during spring where the plants are to bloom, and covered with the merest sprinkling of fine soil. Thin the seedlings to 23 cm (9 in) apart for the Shirleys or 30 cm (1 ft) for the carnation or peony-flowered varieties. The seedlings do not transplant well. If flowers are required for cutting it is a good plan to char the ends of the stems directly they are gathered, otherwise the blooms may fade very quickly.

There are double as well as single forms of the Shirley poppies, while as a rule it is only the fully double varieties of the carnation or peony-flowered poppy that are grown. The latter is about 90 cm (3 ft) high and the leaves are greyish green. The Shirleys are 45-60 cm (1½-2 ft) high with green foliage. Colours are extremely varied in both groups. Both types grow freely from self-sown seedlings but without the careful selection carried out on seed farms they gradually revert to the basic types and many of the most attractive colours are lost.

Annual poppies can also be sown in the same way in early autumn to flower the following early summer.

Perilla. One of the few annuals grown for its foliage and not for its flowers. *Perilla frutescens nankinensis* is a bushy plant, about 60 cm (2 ft) high, with oval purplish-bronze leaves which look very effective in summer bedding schemes. A variety named *P. atropurpurea laciniata* has deeply divided leaves. All varieties are grown from seed sown in a warm greenhouse (15-18°C/59-64°F) in late winter, the seedlings being pricked off and hardened like any other half-hardy annual for final planting out in late spring when danger of serious frost is past. Plant 30 cm (1 ft) apart for massed effect or use as dot plants between dwarfer subjects.

Petunia. These gorgeously coloured half-hardy perennials are almost always grown as half-hardy annuals in the garden. There are single and double-flowered forms but the former are the more popular and generally useful. The singles may be further subdivided into large-flowered (grandiflora) and bedding (multiflora) types, the latter being particularly floriferous though the large-flowered varieties can also be used most effectively for summer bedding. Garden varieties range in height from 23-38 cm (9 in-1¼ ft). Colours are mainly in shades of purple, violet, wine red, rose pink and soft yellow, together with white and various combinations of these colours with white.

Sow seed in a greenhouse, temperature 15-18°C/59-64°F, in late winter or in a frame in early spring. Prick off the seedlings into deep seed boxes when they can be handled and harden off for planting out in late spring/early summer. Some of the most forward plants can be potted singly if desired to keep them growing freely until planting-out time.

Petunias like sun, warmth and good drainage. They need a moderately rich soil and should be planted 23 cm (9 in) apart for a mass display.

All varieties may be used as pot plants for the greenhouse but the large-flowered and double types are particularly suitable for this purpose.

Phacelia. Only one species is commonly grown purely for ornament. This is *Phacelia campanularia*, one of the outstanding blues among hardy annuals. It is, in fact, a real gentian blue without trace of amethyst or mauve. The plant grows 15-23 cm (6-9 in) high and from a mid-spring sowing will be in full glory by summer but the display is rather short-lived. A late spring sowing can be made for succession. Sow thinly where the plants are to flower and thin out to 15 cm (6 in) apart. This phacelia likes a sunny place and an ordinary but reasonably well-drained soil. *P. tanacetifolia* is a taller and less showy hardy annual largely cultivated by bee-keepers because of the quantity of nectar the flowers contain.

Phlox. Most of the phloxes are perennials for border or rock garden (see pp. 141 and 202) but one important species, *Phlox drummondii*, is a very showy half-hardy annual. Seed is sown very thinly from late winter to mid-spring in shallow seed trays, and germinated in a greenhouse or frame at a temperature of about 15-18°C/59-64°F. The seedlings are pricked off 5 cm (2 in) apart each way into deeper trays as soon as they can be handled conveniently and are steadily hardened off for planting in the open garden towards the end of early summer, spaced about 23 cm (9 in) apart.

Flowers are very similar in shape to those of the herbaceous phloxes but are borne in smaller clusters on much thinner sprawling stems. Colours are varied and often extremely brilliant including shades of scarlet, crimson, carmine, rose, pink, violet, mauve, pale yellow and white. The plants bloom in the open from mid-summer to early autumn or may flower a couple of months earlier in pots from an autumn sowing.

Platystemon (Cream Cups). *Platystemon californicus* is a 30 cm (1 ft) high hardy annual with pale yellow poppy-like flowers. Sow in spring or early autumn where the plants are to flower and thin to about 20 cm (8 in). It likes sunny places and well-drained soil.

Polyanthus. The right of this plant to be included in the present section is questionable. However it is so often raised from seed and not retained after flowering that I have included it. None the less it is a true perennial and one which may be grown as such with complete satisfaction.

Botanically it is a primula as is also our native primrose of which it is a hybrid, possibly with the cowslip, *Primula veris*, as its other parent. It is quite possible to keep polyanthuses for many years and to propagate them by division and this is the only practical method when some particular form must be kept exactly true to type. But for ordinary spring bedding it is simpler to raise stock from seed, and seedlings are far less likely to fall into ill health.

Polyanthuses grow rather slowly and so the finest plants are produced from sowings made in a cool greenhouse or frame in early spring, but seed can be sown later to produce smaller plants. Germination is often slow and irregular, so do not give up hope. Prick the seedlings off as they appear into good, rich, finely broken soil in a cool, shady position out of doors, spacing them 7·5 cm (3 in) apart in rows 18 cm (7 in) apart. Water them freely in dry weather. By mid-autumn they should have made strong plants which can be lifted, with as much soil as possible, and transferred to the beds in which they are to flower. These may be in sun or shade and the soil should be good and well supplied with leaf-mould or peat. For a mass display plant 23 cm (9 in) apart. In some gardens it may be necessary to thread black cotton between short sticks over the beds in spring as a protection to prevent birds from pecking off the flowers.

Another way of growing polyanthus is to sow in a frame in early autumn, prick out in a frame and plant out of doors in spring. Such forward plants will often start to flower in the autumn.

A good mixed strain will give a great range of colours in shades of crimson red, orange, bronze and yellow. Separate colours can also be purchased and good varieties of pink and blue exist but sometimes prove less robust than those of other colours. Some of the very large-flowered varieties are less hardy and more suitable for cultivation as pot plants in cool greenhouses or frames.

Polygonum (Knotweed). Most polygonums are perennials but *Polygonum capitatum* is a half-hardy annual, a small, neat carpeting plant with bronzy leaves and small heads of pale pink flowers. Sow seed in early spring in a greenhouse or frame and harden off seedlings for planting out 15 cm (6 in) apart in late spring.

Poppy. See **Papaver** (p. 94, 140).

Portulaca. *Portulaca grandiflora* is a showy half-hardy annual which needs a warm spot and rather light, well-drained soil to do itself justice. The flowers are single or double in a wide range of colours including magenta, crimson, scarlet, orange, pink and yellow. The bushy plants are about 15 cm (6 in) in height. Sow seed in a warm greenhouse in early spring and, after pricking off 4 cm (1½ in) apart in light soil, harden off for planting out in early summer. This is a good annual for a sunny rock garden.

Primrose. When used for spring bedding, primroses may be treated in exactly the same manner as the polyanthus. The colour range is only slightly less extensive and some very fine strains of blue primrose exist. Some varieties cluster all their flowers in the centre of the plant and are specially useful as pot plants in cool greenhouses or frames.

Primula. See p. 203.

Reseda. See **Mignonette** (p. 91).

Rhodanthe. See **Helipterum** (p. 85).

Ricinus. The castor oil plant of commerce, *Ricinus communis*, is occasionally grown in this country for ornament on account of its big leaves, which are finely cut in some varieties and handsomely coloured bronze, crimson or green with white veins in others. The plants grow very rapidly and may reach a height of 2·4 m (8ft) and a diameter of 1·3 m (4½ ft) in one summer. Seeds are best sown in early spring but should first be soaked in

.warm water for at least 12 hours and then germinated in a temperature of 18-21°C/64-70°F. The seedlings are potted singly in 7·5 cm (3 in) pots and hardened off for late spring planting. This plant is chiefly valuable for the sub-tropical effect which it can give to big summer bedding schemes.

Rudbeckia (Coneflower, Gloriosa Daisy). Most of these are perennials and are described elsewhere (see p. 161), but there are also hardy annual species, and though some of these are rather coarse and unattractive there are a few excellent garden hybrids. These have showy yellow, bronze or crimson daisy-like flowers, often blotched or ringed with maroon, carried on branching stems from 45 cm-1·2 m (1½-4 ft) in height. Seed may be sown in mid-spring where the plants are to bloom and the seedlings thinned to 40 cm (1⅓ ft) apart, but earlier flowers can be obtained by sowing in a frame or greenhouse, temperature 15-18°C/59-64°F, in early spring, with seedlings treated like half-hardy annuals for late spring planting outdoors. These annual rudbeckias are not particular about soil but like plenty of sun and good drainage.

Salpiglossis. Half-hardy annuals 76 cm (2½ ft) high, with wide trumpet-shaped blooms delightfully veined in contrasting colours. Growth is slender and branching and the whole plant is slightly sticky. The salpiglossis belongs to the same family as the nicotiana and bears a general resemblance to it, though the flower colours and markings are totally different. It is more popular as a cool greenhouse pot plant than for the open garden but is, none the less, a good bedding plant in sunny sheltered places. Too much wind will damage the rather slender growth. Amongst the many combinations of colour – dark blue and gold, crimson and gold, and rose – crimson and gold are particularly effective.

All should be grown in exactly the same manner as nicotiana except that the plants do not have the same tolerance of shady places, preferring sun and warmth. Sow in the first half of spring at a temperature of 15-18°C/59-64°F. Prick off seedlings 5 cm (2 in) apart and harden off for planting out in late spring.

Salvia. This big genus includes the herb sage, many sub-shrubby and usually rather tender plants, some good herbaceous perennials and the brilliant *Salvia splendens*, a normally scarlet-flowered, half-hardy bedding plant. The last is a true perennial and for long was propagated by cuttings like a geranium or marguerite. Gradually this practice has given place to seed rearing and the plant is now treated as a half-hardy annual. There are pink, salmon and purple-flowered varieties.

Sow in early/late winter at a temperature of 18°C/64°F, pot the seedlings singly in small pots when they are a couple of centimetres high and move them on into 10 cm (4 in) pots by late spring. All this time they need greenhouse protection and an average temperature of at least 15°C/59°F. By early spring they may go to a frame for hardening off but it is seldom wise to plant outdoors before the first week in summer. They should then be spaced at least 30 cm (1 ft) apart in any ordinary, not too rich soil and a sunny, warm position. They will then begin to produce their spikes of tubular flowers in mid-summer and continue until the autumn frosts. At their best no plants, not even scarlet geraniums, are capable of making a more striking display.

Very different is *S. horminum*, a hardy annual with flower spikes bearing large purple, deep blue, rose or white bracts. The plant grows 45 cm (1½ ft) high and is easily grown in any ordinary soil and sunny position. Sow seed in early spring where the plants are to flower and thin the seedlings to about 30 cm (1 ft) apart.

A third kind is *S. farinacea*, with slender spikes of lavender or violet-blue flowers. It is a perennial but commonly grown as a half-hardy annual from seed sown in a greenhouse or frame in early spring, pricked out into boxes and hardened off for planting out of doors a few weeks later.

Saponaria (Soapwort). This, now botanically named *Vaccaria pyramidata*, is a slender-stemmed hardy annual 45 cm (1½ ft) high or rather more with masses of dainty pink or white flowers which are almost as useful for cutting as those of the annual gypsophila and have much the same decorative effect. Sow seed sparingly in spring and early autumn for succession and thin the seedlings to 23 cm (9 in). A sunny place and ordinary, not too heavy soil suits this annual soapwort best. *S. calabrica* is less familiar, only 15-30 cm (6 in-1 ft) high with pale rose flowers.

Scabious. The Caucasian scabious is described on p. 162, but the equally popular sweet scabious, *Scabiosa atropurpurea*, is usually treated as an annual or biennial and renewed each year from seed. It is an attractive plant and not at all difficult to grow. Sow it in boxes in a greenhouse or frame early in spring and make a further sowing a few weeks later directly in the bed or border in which it is to flower. A last sowing can be made in the first half of autumn in a frame or cool greenhouse, the seedlings pricked off into boxes, overwintered under glass with protection from frost and hardened off for planting out of doors the following spring. In this way a succession of bloom will be obtained. The box-raised seedlings will be pricked off 5 cm (2 in) apart each way and hardened off for planting out 30 cm (1 ft) apart each way. The open-ground seedlings will be thinned to 30 cm (1 ft) and the thinnings can, if desired, be replanted elsewhere. In this way there will be flowers for the garden and house from summer to autumn.

The plants average 90 cm (3 ft) in height, like sun but are not fussy about soil. The flowers are in a great variety of colours including some particularly rich shades of purple and crimson, good pinks, mauves, lavenders and a useful white.

Silene (Catchfly). *Silene pendula* is a rather fragile hardy annual which, nevertheless, will grow in most places without any fuss. The flowers are pink, salmon, crimson, lilac or white, single or double, and the plants vary in height from 15-20 cm (6-8 in). Seed should be sown successively through spring for an all-summer display directly in the open ground where the plants are to flower and the seedlings thinned to about 15 cm (6 in).

Silene armeria is taller, about 30 cm (1 ft), with clusters of single rose-pink or white flowers. It is grown like *S. pendula* or can be sown in early autumn to overwinter out of doors and flower the following year.

Silybum (Blessed, Holy or Our Lady's Milk Thistle). This remarkable hardy annual is grown for its large leaves, waved and glossy like those of a sow thistle to which it is related, but heavily veined with white. It is a handsome foliage plant much used in flower arrangements. The thistle-like flowers are rose-purple. It is easily raised from seed sown in spring where the plants are to grow. Thin the seedlings to 30 cm (1 ft).

Specularia. See **Venus's Looking Glass** (p. 104).

Statice (Sea Lavender). See **Limonium** (p. 88).

Stocks. The showy garden stocks of today, all produced from a common parent, *Matthiola incana*, may conveniently be split into three main races or types. First there are the Ten-week stocks and Beauty of Nice stocks all of which are half-hardy annuals. The Brompton stocks are hardy biennials and the Intermediate or East Lothian stocks may be grown either as annuals or biennials. Very different from these is the inconspicuous but intensely fragrant night-scented stock which is a species known as *M. bicornis* and a hardy annual.

The Ten-week stocks are the familiar fragrant and very handsome stocks of the summer garden. There are many varieties from 30-45 cm (1-1½ ft) high in white, primrose, pink, rose, crimson, purple, blue or lavender, single or double flowered. Since it is the double-flowered varieties that are most admired, strains have been raised in which seedlings that will produce double flowers can be recognized by the lighter green colour of their leaves if grown in very cool conditions. To produce the maximum contrast between light and dark seedlings seed germinated at 12-15°C/54-59°F should be cooled to below 10°C/50°F once the first pair of leaves has formed. The lighter seedlings can be retained and the darker green seedlings that will produce single flowers discarded.

These Ten-week stocks are raised from seed sown during early spring in boxes in a greenhouse or frame with an average temperature of 15°C/59°F. Do not sow too early and avoid high temperatures and stuffy atmospheres. Ten-week stocks need to be grown steadily, without checks, but also without undue forcing. They damp off readily in a hot or stuffy place.

Prick them off 5 cm (2 in) apart into deep seed trays directly they show their first true leaves. Give them as light a place as possible, not too far from the glass, and harden them off steadily for planting out towards the end of spring. In the garden give them an open, sunny place in moderately rich but fairly porous soil. Space them 30 cm (1 ft) apart. Do not pinch out the tips of the plants as this will prevent them from forming their central and best flower spikes.

The Beauty of Nice stocks can be grown in exactly the same manner as the Ten-week stocks but they are also excellent for winter flowering under glass for which purpose seed is sown from early summer in an unheated greenhouse or frame. The seedlings are pricked off as already described and later are potted singly, first into 7·5 cm (3 in) pots and, when these are nicely filled with roots, into 13 cm (5 in) pots in which they will flower. Throughout they should be kept in a frame or greenhouse with as much ventilation as is compatible with the maintenance of a minimum temperature of 4°C/40°F. Heights average 60 cm (2 ft) and the colours are as for Ten-week stocks.

The Intermediate stocks can be grown in two ways. One is to treat them as a half-hardy annuals but to sow about a month earlier than the Ten-week stocks. Otherwise the treatment is the same and the plants, put out towards the end of spring, will flower in late summer after the Ten-week stocks have finished. Alternatively seed can be sown in late summer, the seedlings transferred to an unheated frame or greenhouse in mid-autumn, and potted singly to flower under glass during the winter and early spring. The plants are 30-45 cm (1-1½ ft) high. White, mauve, purple, pink and red are the principal colours.

The Brompton stocks have spikes of flowers similar to those of the annual stocks but the plants have a more shrub-like habit. They are grown from seed sown out of doors around mid-summer, the seedlings being treated in exactly the same way as wallflowers (see p. 76) except that when planted in their flowering quarters, they should be spaced at least 38 cm (1¼ ft) apart. Though fairly hardy they will not stand very cold winters in damp places so here or on heavy soils overwinter the plants in a frame and do not finally plant them out until mid-spring. They flower in spring. Heights average 60 cm (2 ft). Colours are white, rose, scarlet and purple.

There is nothing showy about the small, dull lilac flowers of the night-scented stock and by day one might easily ignore this plant. It is towards evening that it begins to exhale its powerful perfume. Sow it freely through spring in any soil or situation, but particularly near the house and below living-room windows where its fragrance can be appreciated to the full. Thin the seedlings to about 15 cm (6 in).

Sunflower. The immense sunflower, *Helianthus annuus*, in which cottagers delight, and from the heads of which vast quantities of seed can be removed to feed poultry and parrots, is a true hardy annual. It is really astonishing that so large a plant can complete its life cycle in one short season of five or six months yet such is the case. Seed can be sown outdoors in mid-spring where the plants are to bloom and within four months the stems will be anything up to 3 m (10 ft) in height, each terminated by one huge yellow flower which may easily measure 30 cm (1 ft) across. By early autumn the petals will have faded and the seeds will be starting to ripen, and it is likely that by the end of that month the seed heads can be cut off and brought indoors to dry. They should certainly be cut directly any of the seeds show signs of loosening.

There are a number of varieties of this sunflower differing in height (some are as dwarf as 60 cm (2 ft), colour range (now including various shades of yellow, lemon, bronze, gold, and crimson), and flower form (most are single but some are double or semi-double and with twisted or slashed petals), but all need exactly the same treatment. They like rather rich soil and plenty of sun and, though they can be transplanted when still tiny, do better when allowed to grow on where sown. For this reason it is best to sow the seeds in twos or threes about 60 cm (2 ft) apart and then single out the seedlings to the strongest of each group.

Swan River Daisy. See **Brachycome** (p. 74).

Sweet Pea. No annual is more widely grown by both professionals and amateurs and certainly none has given rise to such keen rivalry in the production of super-excellent blooms. Every summer show has a class for sweet peas and they are grown in great numbers for cut flowers as well as for garden decoration.

There is a considerable difference in the methods necessary to produce exhibition blooms and those of ordinary quality. Where the object is simply to have a good show in the garden and some attractive cut flowers for the house it will be quite sufficient to treat the sweet pea much like any other hardy annual but to give it rather richer soil. Reduced to its bare outline this means that seed is sown out of doors in early spring where the plants are to bloom, in a sunny place and soil that has been well dug and moderately enriched with dung or a compound fertilizer. No further attention is given, beyond staking with brushy sticks in late spring and occasional weeding and hoeing. It is best to sow the seeds nearly 2·5 cm (1 in) deep in double drills about 25 cm (10 in) apart, with at least 1·2 m (4 ft) separating each pair of drills. The seeds are spaced 7·5 cm (3 in) apart and no thinning is necessary.

Much more elaborate methods are used by the exhibitor. As a rule he sows his seeds in mid-autumn, two or three each in 7·5 cm (3 in) pots filled with an ordinary seed mixture (see p. 427). The pots are placed in a frame but the lights are used more to protect the plants from wind and keep off excessive rain than to raise the temperature.

At the end of the year the tip is pinched out of each plant. As a result it will make several side growths but only one of these is retained, the rest being removed at an early stage.

Meanwhile the ground in which the peas are to be planted is very thoroughly prepared. It is dug deeply and plenty of well-rotted dung is worked in together with bonemeal and wood ashes. The grower will probably finish off with a dusting of a good compound fertilizer. Often only a narrow strip of ground is prepared, sufficient for a double line of plants 28 cm (11 in) wide. The one drawback to this method is that a strip prepared in this way is apt to be surrounded by comparatively hard ground, to which it can act as a drainage trench with disastrous results to the plants grown within it.

The seedlings are thoroughly hardened off for planting out during mid-spring. The seedlings are planted singly, not in twos or threes as they come out of the pots. They are spaced at least 23 cm (9 in) apart and each plant is provided with a bamboo cane or similar support at least 2·1 m (7 ft) high.

Each sweet pea is kept to a single stem and trained up its own cane. All side growths are removed, also tendrils. Even the flower buds are picked off until the plants have climbed about 90 cm (3 ft) up the supports, or until a few weeks before the date of the principal show. In this way the whole strength of the plant is concentrated upon the production of comparatively few flowers each of which may be expected to develop to the fullest possible extent. Flower stems 30 cm (1 ft) or more in length carrying four to six flowers each are obtained.

Feeding of these exhibition plants is usually generous. It starts about late spring and continues all the time the plants are in bloom. As a rule the food is given in liquid form. Dried blood may be alternated with a compound fertilizer, with natural liquid manure made by steeping a bag of rotted manure in water for variety. A close watch is kept upon growth and, if this appears to be getting too coarse, sulphate of potash is applied at 28 g per 18 l of water (1 oz per 4 gal) for a 3·6 m (4 yd) row.

An alternative to autumn sowing is to raise the seedlings in a slightly heated greenhouse in mid-winter and harden them off for planting out in mid-spring. The seedlings are stopped, in the same way as already described, when they are about 7·5 cm (3 in) high. In other respects treatment is exactly the same as for the seedlings raised in the autumn.

If plants reach the top of their canes and still appear vigorous and capable of producing good flowers, they are carefully untied, the bottom 1 m (3½ ft) of stem is laid along the ground and the top is secured to another stake further along the row. In this way more head room is obtained and the season further extended.

There are a great many varieties of sweet pea and also several quite distinct classes. Old-fashioned sweet peas have relatively small, sweetly scented flowers with unwaved petals. Spencer sweet peas have larger flowers and waved petals. Galaxy and Multiflora sweet peas have up to seven flowers per stem. Knee-hi and Jet-set sweet peas only grow about 90 cm (3 ft) high and Bijou or Bush sweet peas are only about 38 cm (15 in) high. The type known as Snoopea has no tendrils so that more of its energy goes into flower production but, unless tied to supports, will sprawl on the ground.

Sweet Sultan. This is a species of centaurea, known as *Centaurea moschata*, and is related to the cornflower. It is a hardy annual, excellent for cutting and for beds and borders. Sow it out of doors in the first half of spring where it is to bloom and thin the seedlings to 23 cm (9 in) apart. Give it as sunny a position as possible and be careful to sow when the surface is reasonably dry and crumbly, otherwise germination may be poor. Apart from this there is nothing special to be said about the cultivation of this lovely, old-fashioned plant with its deeply-fringed flowers in shades of mauve, purple, wine red, blue, yellow and white. Average height is 45 cm (1½ ft) and the plants bloom from mid-summer to early autumn from spring sowings. For early summer flowering sow in early autumn in a sheltered place and particularly well-drained soil so they survive the winter and thin out the following spring.

Sweet William. An old-fashioned plant with fine flat heads of showy flowers on 15-45 cm (9 in-1½ ft) stems, according to variety. Its botanical name is *Dianthus barbatus* and it is closely related to the garden pinks and carnations. It is a perennial but is usually treated as a hardy biennial and is grown from seed sown out of doors in late spring. Sow in drills in the same manner as wallflowers and subsequently prick off the seedlings into a nursery bed also like wallflowers, so that they grow on into sturdy plants for putting into their flowering quarters in mid-autumn or early spring. Final planting distance should be at least 30 cm (1 ft) apart, and the plants should be given as sunny a position as possible in ordinary well-cultivated soil. Pink, scarlet, crimson and white are the basic Sweet William colours and in the auricula-eyed types each flower has a clearly defined eye of a contrasting shade to that of the rest of the bloom. All flower in high summer and are useful for cutting as well as bedding or filling gaps in the herbaceous border. Some varieties of Sweet William can be grown as annuals, sown outdoors in mid-spring where they are to grow, or a month earlier under glass to be pricked out and hardened off for a late spring planting.

Tagetes (Marigold). Those showy half-hardy annuals, the French marigold, *Tagetes patula*, and the African marigold, *T. erecta*, and that bright edging plant, *T. signata pumila*, belong here, but not the pot marigold which is a calendula (see p. 74). All are lovers of sun and warmth. They will grow in practically any soil except, perhaps, one that is excessively damp, but they are happiest in a light, well-drained soil particularly if it is also fairly rich.

Seed should be sown in a greenhouse in early spring at a temperature of about 15-18°C/59-64°F, the seedlings being pricked off 5 cm (2 in) apart in deep seed boxes (or potted singly for show purposes) as soon as they can be handled, and are then carefully hardened off for planting out in late spring 30 cm (1 ft) apart for the larger kinds and 23 cm (9 in) for the smaller ones.

The African marigolds have very big, double or semi-double flowers in shades of yellow and orange. There are both single and double-flowered forms of the French marigold and most combine yellow and chestnut-red, the markings often being very beautiful. The regularity of these markings is of importance in blooms required for show and, as this is a hereditary characteristic great care must be taken to obtain seed only from perfectly marked plants. African and French marigolds have been much interbred and there are now so many intermediate varieties that it is difficult to draw any hard-and-fast line between them.

T. signata pumila makes a low mound of finely divided leaves covered with small single flowers, lemon, yellow or orange-red according to variety.

All marigolds have a long flowering season extending from mid-summer to early autumn.

Tithonia (Mexican Sunflower). *Tithonia rotundifolia*, once known as *T. speciosa*, is a vigorous half-hardy annual 90 cm (3 ft) or more high with orange-scarlet daisy-type flowers. Sow in early spring in a greenhouse or frame, prick off seedlings into boxes or pot singly and harden off for planting out of doors in late spring, 45 cm (1½ ft) apart in good soil and a sunny place.

Tropaeolum. Most species are described under the garden name nasturtium but one popular annual climber must be included here. This is *Tropaeolum peregrinum*, the yellow-flowered Canary creeper. It can be raised from seed sown in a warm frame or greenhouse in early spring, with the seedlings potted singly and hardened off for planting out at the end of spring where they are to flower. Alternatively seed can be sown in late spring out of doors where the plants are to flower, and the seedlings thinned to about 30 cm (1 ft). This plant needs a trellis, wires or other support to cling to with its coiling leaf stalks.

Ursinia. A family of South Africans with bright, daisy-like flowers. They are half-hardy annuals to be raised in the same way as cosmeas and others of this class or, alternatively, they may be sown out of doors in late spring in especially warm, sunny places and, after thinning, left to grow and flower where they stand. If given 23–30 cm (9 in-1 ft) space from plant to plant they will bush out and make a better display than if overcrowded. One of the best is *Ursinia anethoides*, 30 cm (1 ft) tall, with particularly vivid orange flowers each a couple of centimetres across with a central band of crimson. Other good kinds are *U. anthemoides*, yellow to orange but purplish on the backs of the petals – 30 cm (1 ft); and *U. versicolor*, also known as *U. pulchra*, yellow to orange with a crimson central zone – 23 cm (9 in).

Vaccaria. See **Saponaria** (p. 99).

Venidium. Another family of brilliant South African daisies. All species have big, showy flowers in which a ground colour of orange, yellow or buff is contrasted with a central zone of black, maroon or crimson. Heights range from 60 cm (2 ft) for *Venidium decurrens* and its variety *calendulaceum* to 90 cm (3 ft) for *V. fastuosum*. All may be raised from seed sown in a warm greenhouse in mid-spring but *V. calendulaceum*, which is hardier than the rest, can be sown directly in the open ground at this time like a hardy annual. Some venidium are now listed as arctotis.

Venus's Looking Glass. The botanical name of this attractive hardy annual is *Specularia* *speculum*. It has slender 23-30 cm (9 in-1 ft) stems and violet-blue bell-shaped flowers freely produced. Sow in spring where the plants are to grow and thin the seedlings to 15 cm (6 in). It will grow in sun or partial shade and often renews itself from year to year by means of self-sown seed.

Verbascum (Mullein). While many verbascums are hardy perennials (see p. 166) a few are hardy biennials which must be renewed each year from seed. This is true of *Verbascum thapsus*, a giant of 2·1 m (7 ft) with densely grey woolly leaves and narrow spikes of yellow flowers; also of the hybrid Miss Willmott (white) and Harkness Hybrid (yellow) both 1·8 m (6 ft) or more in height, and of *V. bombyciferum*, also known as *V. broussa*, with pale yellow flowers (same height), the whole plant densely covered in grey hairs. All can be raised very easily from seed sown in ordinary soil and an open position out of doors in late spring. Seedlings should be transferred to a nursery bed in mid-summer and from there to flowering quarters in mid-autumn or early spring. These flower in mid-summer. Plants once listed as Celsia now appear as verbascum. They have long, tapering spikes of flowers standing well up above the basal clusters of leaves. Though not true annuals they can be treated as such and this is the best method of culture when they are to be grown out of doors. Sow in a greenhouse or frame in early spring, pot up the seedlings singly and harden off in time for planting out in late spring. They will then flower in the summer. The two best kinds are *Celsia arcturus* with 45-60 cm (1½-2 ft) spikes of yellow flowers, and *C. cretica*, which is 1·2 m (4 ft) or more high with larger flowers, yellow spotted with brown.

Verbena. This family includes hardy perennials (see p. 167) but here I am only concerned with the half-hardy hybrids which are used for summer bedding as well as for greenhouse culture in pots. These are all perennials and can be kept from year to year and increased by cuttings, but in practice this is seldom done except with a few very choice varieties. The usual method is to treat the plants as half-hardy annuals and raise a fresh stock annually from seed sown in a warm greenhouse any time from late winter to early spring. Germination may be slow and irregular unless a temperature of 15°C/59°F or more can be maintained, otherwise cultivation is much the same as for antirrhinums. The seedlings, either pricked off or potted singly, are hardened off for planting out from late spring.

Verbenas are somewhat sprawling in habit and look their best when planted fairly closely, about 23 cm (9 in) apart, so that they make a complete carpet over the soil. Every so often one plant can be tied up to a short cane to break the level. The flowers are borne in compact clusters all the summer and colours are both varied and brilliant, including many shades of pink, blue, purple and scarlet.

Virginian Stock. This pretty little annual, botanically known as *Malcolmia maritima*, has confetti-like flowers and is one of the most easily grown of plants. It is only necessary to sprinkle the seed thinly any time from early spring to early summer where the plants are to flower, and either rake it in or cover with a thin scattering of soil. No thinning or after-care is required. Plants average 15 cm (6 in) in height and colours range from white through pink and mauve to crimson. There are few better annuals for sowing in crevices, between paving slabs or in odd corners where few other plants would find living room.

Viscaria (Rose of Heaven). This is a hardy annual botanically known as *Lychnis coeli-rosa* and is both dainty and effective for garden or cutting. Seed can be sown in spring or early autumn where it is to flower. The autumn sowings will stand the winter out of doors without protection and flower in the following summer, while the spring sowings will keep up the display until late summer. Stems are thin and wiry, not unlike those of the annual gypsophila which the plant also resembles in flower, though colours are more varied, including pink, carmine, scarlet and blue as well as white. Heights vary from 15-30 cm (6 in-1 ft). All should be thinned to 15 cm (6 in) and will do best in a sunny place and open, well-drained soil.

Wallflower. See **Cheiranthus** (p. 76).

Xeranthemum (Common Immortelle). *Xeranthemum annuum* is an everlasting flower with chaffy, daisy-like flowers which can easily be dried and kept for winter decoration. Colours are varied. The plant is a hardy annual and seed can be sown in mid-spring in any sunny, sheltered place and porous soil. Thin to 18 cm (7 in) and support with short, bushy hazel twigs. Alternatively sow in early spring in a greenhouse or frame at a temperature of 15-18°C/59-64°F, prick off seedlings and harden off for planting out in late spring.

Zea (Maize). See **Grasses, Ornamental** (p. 83).

Zinnia. This gorgeously coloured annual is a plant which well repays careful cultivation. The best modern varieties of *Zinnia elegans* will produce fully double blooms, large, medium or small according to variety, which are equally effective in the border and as cut flowers. Colours include white, yellow, pink, orange and scarlet and there are also a great number of intermediate shades, some of them exceptionally beautiful. Some varieties have quilled petals like those of a chrysanthemum. *Z. haageana*, botanically known as *Z. angustifolia*, has smaller single or double flowers, often combining two colours.

To be seen at their best zinnias need rich but porous soil and must be grown steadily without check from start to finish. It is a mistake to sow seeds very early. Mid-spring is soon enough and a frame will often give better results than a heated greenhouse; indeed, some of the best blooms can be raised from seed sown out of doors in late spring, the seedlings having been left to grow on undisturbed like hardy instead of half-hardy annuals. In any case avoid rapid changes of temperature, do not let the plants receive a setback through lack of water and, if they are to be planted out, do this before they become starved in the boxes or pots in which they were pricked out. Give them good soil and a sunny place and water them freely in dry weather. The plants will grow from 15 cm-1 m (6 in-3 ft) high according to variety. Some of the short kinds have miniature ball-like flowers. If two sowings are made, one in mid-spring and the other a few weeks later, a continuous display of blooms may be obtained right through the summer.

Chapter 8
Hardy Herbaceous Perennials

A herbaceous plant is one that is soft in growth as distinct from a plant that is woody and therefore classified as a tree or shrub. A perennial is any plant which continues to live for a number of years irrespective of whether it flowers or not. In this it contrasts with the annual, which completes its life cycle in one year and then dies after flowering and producing seed, the biennial which has a similar life cycle but takes two years to complete it, and the monocarpic plant which also dies as soon as it has flowered and ripened seed but may take an indefinite number of years before it finishes the cycle.

From this it will be seen that a herbaceous perennial is a plant which is soft in growth and continues to live and flower for a considerable time. There are a great many plants which come into this category and they are subdivided again into hardy, half-hardy and tender kinds. These are relative terms with no very hard-and-fast dividing line between them. Broadly speaking, a plant is regarded as hardy when it will normally live out of doors in most parts of the country without protection. It is said to be half-hardy when it can be grown out of doors in summer but must be put into a greenhouse or frame for the winter, and tender when it needs protection throughout the greater part of the year. It should be made quite plain, however, that hardiness varies considerably even in one plant according to the condition of its growth. Young shoots are almost invariably much less hardy than those which are older and riper. It is not uncommon to see the young growth of even native trees such as oak and ash cut by frost in the spring and in exceptional circumstances young trees may even be killed in this way, yet no one on that account would call oaks and ashes half-hardy.

In this chapter I am solely concerned with the hardy herbaceous perennial, a most important type of plant from the gardener's point of view. Most of its members can be grown with very little difficulty and do not require to be frequently renewed. It can also be moved about, discarded or replaced fairly easily and without much expense.

Herbaceous Borders. It is only during the present century that the hardy herbaceous perennial has played a really big part in English gardening. It was largely due to the prolific writings of William Robinson (1838–1935) that the worth of the herbaceous perennial became widely recognized and the herbaceous border, devoted to the cultivation of this type of plant, began to be a feature of every garden. At one stage this process probably went too far, for a border devoted entirely to herbaceous plants became so popular a feature that it was often included in even the smallest gardens.

Yet it is very questionable whether the herbaceous border can be a really satisfactory feature unless plenty of room is available. Personally I would not attempt to plant one in a space less than 9 m long × 1·8 m wide (30 × 6 ft), and I would add that the width is even more important than the length. The reason for this is that a great many herbaceous plants have a short season of flower. They are magnificent while they last but the show is over in a few weeks with nothing to come till the following year.

There are two ways of overcoming this drawback. One is to plant a border entirely with varieties which flower at approximately the same time and arrange matters so that this border is a feature at its own season and can be ignored for the rest of the year. That works well enough in big places, but it is obviously impracticable for the small garden. Alternatively the plants may be assorted so that between them they cover a reasonably extended season and arranged so that the later flowering kinds grow up around the earlier varieties and thus screen their bareness from view. This is the scheme most commonly employed and it works well provided there is room to plant on a generous scale, not single plants of each kind but in groups of five, six or more. This is why width is even more important than length for it is impossible to have several sizeable groups of plants one behind the other in a border that is not more than 90 cm or 1·2 m (3 or 4 ft) wide.

Mixed Borders. There is an alternative to the pure herbaceous border which for want of a better name may be called the mixed border. Here any type of plant is welcome, the only qualifications being that it will add to the general display and not interfere with its neighbours. Annuals, biennials and monocarpic plants can be mixed together with shrubs, roses and even, on occasion, small trees. Bulbs may figure quite prominently and are particularly useful because their foliage takes up little room so that they can sometimes be established under a carpet of other plants. The danger with a mixed border is that, with such a mass of material, the gardener becomes bewildered, has no idea what to put in or what to leave out and probably ends up with too many plants in too small a space to the detriment of all. However, with a little extra forethought and particularly if expert advice is called in this need not occur.

The best method of setting about the planting of any border is first to draw its outline to as large a scale as possible on a sheet of paper and then to write down the names of the favoured plants together with their height, colour and season of flowering on small slips of paper which can be moved about on the plan like the pieces of a jigsaw puzzle. In this way one can carry out experimental planning on the dining-room table, by shifting the pieces around until they make what appears to be a pleasing and satisfactory arrangement.

Specialized Borders. There are other ways in which hardy herbaceous perennials may be used in the garden. Some of the most free-flowering kinds, and particularly the comparatively limited number which have an extended flowering season, are excellent for massing by themselves. In fact they can be used instead of the more usual bedding plants such as geraniums, marguerites, heliotropes and antirrhinums with the advantage that they do not have to be renewed every year or lifted in the autumn and replanted in the spring. Care must be taken, however, to see that the plants chosen really have a reasonably extended flowering season so that the border will continue to maintain its interest.

Herbaceous Perennials as Cut Flowers. Quite a number of herbaceous plants are also excellent for cutting. Some of them are so good for this purpose that they have become popular with market growers and will be found in every florist's shop at their correct season. Examples of this type are pyrethrums, Shasta and moon daisies, Caucasian scabious and the double-flowered gypsophila. In addition to these there are many other charming hardy perennials suitable for cutting which for one reason or another would not be a success commercially but can be grown in private gardens. It is an advantage if plants required specifically for cutting can be grown by themselves in a reserved part of the garden in straight rows where they can be easily reached and their flowers will not be missed when they have been taken indoors.

Arranging Perennials. The actual arrangement of individual plants in the herbaceous border requires some thought. I have on rare occasions seen them planted in straight lines with reasonably satisfactory effect but usually it is much more effective to plant in irregular groups. In a general way the taller plants should be kept at the back and the dwarfer varieties in front, but allowance must be made for the screening of earlier blooming kinds and also it is a good plan to bring some groups of taller plants forward to break up the border into a series of irregular bays.

Soil Preparation. The general cultivation of the majority of hardy herbaceous perennials is simple and follows the same basic plan. The ground need not be very rich but for most plants it should be well-drained and contain sufficient humus to preserve it from severe drying out during hot weather. It must be borne in mind that once planted the border is not likely to be seriously disturbed for several years and that during that period it will only be possible to carry out superficial cultivation and feeding. The initial preparation should therefore be as thorough as possible and in particular great care must be taken to eliminate all persistent weeds such as couch grass, coltsfoot, ground elder and bindweed.

In new gardens it may be best to delay the planting of the herbaceous border for at least one year and use the ground for vegetables or annuals during the first season. In this way at least two diggings can be given before the border is permanently planted. An alternative is to dig, allow sufficient time for weeds to grow, and then kill them with a non-persistent herbicide such as paraquat or glyphosate.

Planting. There are two principal seasons for planting herbaceous perennials, one the period when they are just starting into growth in the first part of spring, and the other when they are just coming to the end of their growth in early autumn. It is not so satisfactory to plant late in the year when the ground is cold and wet and roots are no longer active. A few kinds can be planted successfully in the height of summer as soon as they have finished flowering but this always necessitates a considerable amount of attention for the first week or so after planting. The plants must then be watered freely and frequently if the soil is at all dry.

The actual details of planting are much the same as for other types of plant. It is important to choose the right kind of weather or at any rate to avoid really bad conditions when the soil is wet and sticky. If plants arrive from a nursery when the soil is unfit for planting, line them out in a shallow trench and cover their roots with soil. Heeled in like this they will keep in good condition for several weeks but should be planted permanently directly the soil is fit.

It is very important to make holes sufficiently wide and deep to accommodate all roots spread out in a natural manner. A trowel will be the usual tool, but for big plants a spade may be even better. A dibber should never be used. It makes far too narrow and deep a hole.

Depth can best be gauged by the old soil mark showing on the plants. This should be covered with about 12 mm (½ in) of soil. If the soil mark cannot be seen, make certain that the uppermost roots are covered with at least 2·5 cm (1 in) of soil or that the crown of the plant, that is the point from which most of the basal shoots grow, is at or very slightly below soil level.

Spacing will, of course, vary according to the habit of the plant but it will probably be somewhere between 15-23 cm (6-9 in) for edging plants, 30-45 cm (1-1½ ft) for mid-border plants, and 60-90 cm (2-3 ft) for the occupants of the back of the border.

Though one should never plant when the soil is wet it may sometimes be necessary to plant when the soil is rather too dry. Whenever there is doubt as to there being sufficient moisture to keep the plants going, a thorough watering should be given immediately after planting. Use a can without a rose for this job but break the rush of water with a piece of sacking tied loosely round the spout. One does not want to wash the soil off newly planted roots but at the same time they must be given sufficient water and the trouble with water-ing-can roses is that they invariably give the surface a deceptively wet appearance, leaving the lower soil comparatively dry.

Thinning. Some herbaceous perennials are all the better for a little thinning in the early stages of their growth. This applies particularly to free-growing plants such as Michael-mas daisies, delphiniums and golden rod (solidago). Left to their own devices these make so many shoots in the spring that they become so overcrowded before their flowers open that quality and display suffer. A little experience is necessary to learn how many shoots should be taken away but frequently a reduction of as much as 75 per cent can be made without harm, especially in the second year after planting.

Staking. Tall plants will almost all need some staking, particularly those which have been highly developed by breeding and have, in consequence, very big, heavy heads or spikes of flowers. This applies to all the modern delphiniums and also to quite a number of the taller, double-flowered Michaelmas daisies.

As far as possible try to arrange stakes so that they are concealed by the growth as the stems lengthen. In general three or four stakes should be used per plant if it has more than one stem and these stakes should each be driven into the ground so that they lean out at the top, so tending to open the growth like the feathers of a shuttlecock rather than bunch it together as inevitably happens if only one stake is used. Another good method of support, particularly to plants of medium height, is to push some bushy branches (hazel is excellent) into the soil around the plants when the shoots are still only several centi-metres high. Then the young growth will find support as it grows up through the twigs and conceal them too.

Propagation. The majority of hardy perennials can be increased readily by division of the roots at the planting season. Division simply means that the original large root is split into several pieces, each of which must be provided with at least one growing shoot or crown and some good roots. Small plants can usually be divided by hand but big, old clumps often get so tough that they must be split by some other means. One excellent scheme is to thrust two small border forks back to back through the centre of the clump and then lever their handles apart. Hand forks can be used in an identical manner for smaller plants. Very occasionally a knife may be required but should be used only to sever the hard, central crown of such a plant as a delphinium or peony. The trouble with knives is that they nearly always do more harm than good, severing roots from shoots in an unexpected manner.

When dividing very old clumps, particularly of free-spreading plants such as Michaelmas and Shasta daisies and heleniums, it is usually wise to discard the central portion of each clump altogether and retain only the outer pieces which are younger, more vigorous and less likely to be diseased or pest ridden.

Most herbaceous perennials can also be raised from seed. This is sometimes a slow method of increase for seedlings may take a couple of years to reach full flowering size; in fact in a few instances they may take at least one year to germinate. Seedlings can also be disappointing, especially in the case of highly developed plants such as many of those already mentioned. These are very hybridized and because of this mixed origin seedlings are apt to differ considerably from their parents. Sometimes this does not matter and some perennials do come relatively true from seed but it is wise to enquire into this before purchasing if uniformity is important.

Seed can be a useful method of perpetuating those herbaceous perennials that are naturally short lived, such as hollyhocks, lupins, delphiniums, verbascums and aquilegias and those with which a certain degree of variation in colour, stature, etc., does not matter very much. Seedlings have the merit of being almost always vigorous and healthy and as a rule they can be raised cheaply.

In general, seed of herbaceous plants can be sown either in a cool greenhouse or frame during early spring, or out of doors in late spring/early summer. The former seedlings will sometimes flower a little in their first year but this is the exception rather than the rule. In most cases it will not be until the second year that there is anything like a full display.

In every instance the seedlings should be transplanted from the seed boxes or bed as soon as they can be handled conveniently and immediately replanted in a bed of reasonably rich, finely broken soil situated in an open position. Give them plenty of space to grow on into sturdy plants by the following autumn or spring, by which time most will be ready for transplanting to permanent positions.

A third method of propagation is by cuttings. Far more herbaceous plants can be raised in this way than many amateurs believe. Most people know that lupins and delphiniums can be increased by stem cuttings secured in early spring but not so many are aware that scabious, coreopsis and phlox, besides a great many other plants, can also be easily increased in the same manner. The method is to make cuttings from young shoots when 7·5-10 cm (3-4 in) long. The shoots are cut off low down, even below soil level if possible, the essential point being that each must be firm and solid at the base. Each cutting is trimmed cleanly just below a joint and inserted in a bed of rather sandy soil. It should be put in just deep enough to keep it upright, which generally implies a hole 4 cm (1½ in). Press the soil firmly around the base of the cutting and, when the whole bed is full, water thoroughly. Shade from direct sunlight until the cuttings no longer flag. Thereafter simply water regularly until sufficiently well rooted to be transplanted. Most of these cuttings do best in a frame but they can be rooted in the open if the weather is kind.

Root cuttings offer another very valuable means of increasing many herbaceous perennials and not, surprisingly enough, only those with thick, fleshy roots. Phloxes, which have comparatively thin roots, grow freely from root cuttings and so do gaillardias. More obvious kinds for this method of propagation are anchusas, hollyhocks, verbascums,

Dividing herbaceous perennials. Small plants can usually be divided by hand

To divide larger clumps two forks may be used. These are thrust in back to back and levered apart. Occasionally a knife may be needed to sever the crown

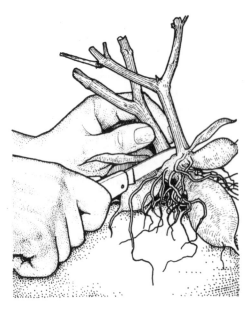

Removing a young shoot from a lupin to prepare as a cutting. The stem should be severed close to the crown

Preparing a root cutting from an anchusa plant. The lower end has been cut at an angle to distinguish it from the top

oriental poppies and perennial statices of all kinds. It is odd that gypsophilas and lupins, which have likely looking roots for the purpose, fail completely.

Propagation by root cuttings is extremely easy. All that is necessary is to lift a good plant at any time between early winter and early spring, cut up the roots into pieces 4 cm (1½ in) long and place them in the soil. The thicker roots are, I think, most satisfactory when pushed into the soil vertically the right way up but as all the cuttings look exactly alike when prepared it is necessary to make some mark on them to know which is the top end. My method is to make a sloping cut at the bottom of each cutting and a square cut at the top. This gives the base of the cutting a pointed end which can be pushed into the soil easily. These vertical cuttings should be just covered with soil. The alternative, most suitable for thin cuttings, is to lay them horizontally on a flat bed of soil and cover with a further 12 mm (½ in) of soil. Water moderately until shoots appear above ground. Then give more water and finally transplant to a nursery bed in late spring/early summer.

One advantage of raising perennials from cuttings, either stem or root, rather than from division is that less of the old plant is carried over to the new individual and in consequence there is less likelihood of its being troubled with the pests or diseases which have afflicted its parent. This is very marked in the case of phloxes which have been crippled by eelworms. Completely clean stock can be raised even from heavily infested plants if root cuttings only are employed.

Botanical Names. In the following list as in most others in this volume some botanical names are necessary because many of the best flowers have no true popular names and even where common names are well established they are sometimes applied loosely to several quite different plants. It is therefore impossible to be precise either in describing or ordering such plants unless their botanical names are specified.

Botanists identify plants by at least two names, the first a generic name and the second a specific name. The generic name identifies the bearer as belonging to a certain 'genus' or group of allied, but by no means identical, plants. The specific name pinpoints it more accurately as a particular 'species' or member of that group. Thus *Lupinus* is the generic name of all of the different kinds of lupin, the annual lupin being distinguished as *Lupinus hartwegii*, the herbaceous lupin as *Lupinus polyphyllus* and the tree lupin as *Lupinus arboreus*. In this instance the popular names annual lupin, herbaceous lupin and tree lupin are just as satisfactory for garden identification as the botanical names, but it is by no means always so. Nursery catalogues use botanical names for a great many plants and that is another reason why the gardener needs some familiarity with them.

Frequently a third name makes its appearance. Sometimes this follows the botanic style and sometimes it is of purely popular origin. In either case it serves to distinguish some special form or variety of a species. As an example there are a great many varieties of *Paeonia lactiflora* differing mainly in the colour of their flowers and distinguished by such names as Felix Crousse and Sarah Bernhardt. Botanically such garden varieties are known as cultivars, and their names can only be used once in any genus; this, together with the generic name, is adequate for identification. So when ordering it is sufficient to ask for Paeonia Sarah Bernhardt, not *P. lactiflora* Sarah Bernhardt, though that is often how it will be listed.

In this alphabetical list of herbaceous perennials I have not attempted to include everything that might be grown but only plants of real merit which can be cultivated without undue difficulty. They are available from most garden centres and specialist nurseries.

A SELECTION OF HERBACEOUS PERENNIALS

Acanthus (Bear's Breeches). A small family of plants grown mainly for their foliage. The leaves rather suggest a milk thistle on an enlarged scale and it is said that one species served as a model for the scroll-like capital of the famous Corinthian column. The flowers of acanthus are curious rather than beautiful – stiff spikes of hooded blooms in a dull shade of purplish lilac and white, about 90 cm (3 ft) in height. There are two species in common cultivation, *Acanthus spinosus* and *A. mollis*, both equally worth growing. *A. mollis* also has a fine group named *Latifolius* with extra large leaves and taller flower stems. All will thrive in any ordinary soil in sun or partial shade. Plant in autumn or spring. Propagate by seed or division in the spring, or by root cuttings in winter.

Achillea (Yarrow, Milfoil). One species of achillea is a well-known weed which can be a great nuisance on lawns. This is the common milfoil with soft, finely divided leaves and creeping stems which hug the soil and root as they go. In addition there are numbers of ornamental species mostly for the rock garden, though a few are suitable for the herbaceous border. All have iron constitutions, will grow anywhere and prefer sunny positions. Curiously enough some of the best have arisen as varieties from *Achillea millefolium*, the weed just referred to. Like many other wild plants it is susceptible to improvement and such forms as Cerise Queen and Fire King, with flattish heads of carmine flowers on 45 cm (1½ ft) stems, make a fine display in mid-summer. Other good kinds are *A. filipendulina* Gold Plate, 1·2 m (4 ft) in height with mustard yellow flowers in heads as big as saucers, *A. filipendulina* Coronation Gold, not quite so large but flowering for a long time, *A. taygetea*, 45 cm (1½ ft) high with silvery leaves and primrose-yellow flowers and *A. ptarmica*, best planted in one of its double-flowered forms such as The Pearl or Perry's

White. These individual blooms are perfect white pompons, 12 mm ($\frac{1}{2}$ in) across in loose heads on 60 cm (2 ft) stems. All flower throughout the summer and may be planted at any time in autumn or spring. They are best propagated by division at either season.

Aconitum (Monkshood). The popular name refers to the curiously hooded flowers which suggest the cowl of a monk. They are carried in spikes not unlike those of the delphinium though on a smaller scale. All thrive best in rather moist soil though they will grow tolerably well under drier conditions. They will succeed in sun or partial shade and some species, including *Aconitum napellus*, may even be naturalized in thin woodland. This, incidentally, is the source of the drug aconite, a poison which permeates the whole plant. It is a handsome plant producing deep purple flowers on 90 cm (3 ft) spikes in midsummer. There are also varieties such as bicolor, with white flowers edged with blue and Spark's Variety, in which the normal purple colour deepens to indigo. The plants known in gardens as *A. fischeri* and *A. wilsonii* both flower in early autumn, the first with rather stout, 90 cm (3 ft) spikes of pale blue flowers and the latter nearly twice as high and varying from pale blue to violet. There are some yellow aconitums, the best of which is *A. lycoctonum*, popularly known as wolfsbane – height 1·5 m (5 ft). There is also one kind, *A. volubile*, which has blue flowers and slender, twining stems climbing to the same height if sticks or other supports are provided. All make underground tubers and dislike root disturbance. They are best transplanted in spring and may be increased by seed or division at the same season.

Agapanthus (African Lily). Plants with fleshy roots, strap-shaped leaves and more or less ball-shaped heads of blue or white flowers. One of the finest is *Agapanthus africanus* (once called *A. umbellatus*) but it is only fully hardy in milder gardens. It is often grown in large pots or tubs which can be stood out of doors in summer but carried into a frost-proof greenhouse or conservatory in the autumn and left there until the following spring. The flower stems are 90 cm (3 ft) high and it flowers in mid-summer. A species with smaller flowers named *A. campanulatus* is considerably hardier and from this the Headbourne hybrids have been produced, most of which can be planted permanently out of doors in warm, sunny places. All can be increased by division in the spring or from seed, but selected garden varieties only by division.

Alchemilla (Lady's Mantle). *Alchemilla mollis* is a low-growing plant with soft, downy grey-green leaves and large sprays of small, greenish-yellow flowers in early summer. It is about 30 cm (1 ft) high and will grow in sun or partial shade in any reasonably well-drained soil and can be increased by division in spring or from seed. It makes excellent ground cover but is rather difficult to remove. One plant will provide countless self-sown seedlings.

Allium. See p. 340.

Alstroemeria (Peruvian Lily). All alstroemerias are extremely showy plants and would undoubtedly be much more widely grown were they easier to establish. It is the first couple of years that are difficult, for all dislike root disturbance, are slow to re-establish themselves and often do little or nothing at first. Being South American plants they delight in all the sun and warmth they can get and require deep, well-drained soil. The rather fleshy roots should be spread thinly at the bottom of a 15 cm (6 in) deep trench and covered with soil. Mid-spring is the best month for this work and thereafter the plants should be left severely alone for as many years as possible, with occasional hand weeding the only attention necessary.

The easiest kind is *Alstroemeria aurantiaca* with vivid orange flowers like small lilies in close spikes. It is in bloom in mid-summer and is about 90 cm (3 ft) high. Other fine kinds of similar height are *A. chilensis*, in various shades of pink and salmon, and *A. haemantha* in which the blooms are blood red with an orange throat. Both plants are now rarely sold, unlike *A. psittacina* and *A. ligtu*, a pink-flowered species which has also produced a number of grand hybrids in shades varying from pink to flame. Other hybrids between *A. aurantiaca*, *A. violacea* and other species have a long flowering season and are grown under glass for cutting. Some of these have been sold as Princess lilies and are very beautiful. These are all rather more tender and difficult to grow than *A. aurantiaca*.

All can be increased by division in the spring but it is easier to start with seed for the Ligtu hybrids, grow the seedlings individually in small pots for the first year and plant out from there in spring with a minimum of root disturbance.

Althaea. See **Hollyhock** (p. 86).

Anaphalis (Pearly Everlasting). The leaves of these plants are covered with short white hairs which give them a silvery appearance and the small white flowers, carried in heads in summer, have chaff-like petals which last a long time. The best kinds are *Anaphalis margaritacea*, 45 cm (1½ ft); *A. nubigena*, 23 cm (9 in); *A. triplinervis*, 30 cm (1 ft); and *A. yedoensis*, 60 cm (2 ft). They enjoy sunny places and well-drained soil and can be increased by division or cuttings.

Anchusa (Alkanet). These handsome plants precede the delphiniums by a week or so, being at their best in early summer, at which season they provide the best blue to be found in the border. The tall anchusas, varieties of *Anchusa azurea*, might be likened to enormous forget-me-nots with flowers nearly 2·5 cm (1 in) across and stems 1·2-1·5 m (4-5 ft) in height. They make stout tap roots which thrive best in a rather light soil and dislike disturbance. Propagation by division is impossible. Seeds germinate readily but seedlings vary quite a lot in the colour of their flowers. The best method of increase of named kinds is by root cuttings. There are numerous varieties such as Morning Glory and Loddon Royalist differing mainly in the precise shade of their flowers. The plant commonly sold as *A. caespitosa* is much smaller, about 30 cm (1 ft) high, with gentian-blue, white-eyed flowers from late spring to early summer. It needs especially well-drained soil. The plant sometimes called *A. myosotidiflora* should more correctly be *Brunnera macrophylla*, under which name it will be found.

Anemone (Wind Flower). Many of the anemones are woodland or alpine plants but one hybrid, commonly known as *Anemone japonica* but correctly *A. × hybrida*, is a fine border plant. At its best during early autumn it is a first-class partner for the Michaelmas daisies. Height varies from 45 cm-1·2 m (1½-4 ft) according to variety, and colour from pure white and palest pink to a rather deep wine red. None of these Japanese anemones likes root disturbance. All are best transplanted in spring and can be propagated by division at that season. They will thrive in any ordinary soil in a sunny or half-shady position. Outstanding varieties are Whirlwind and Louise Uhink, semi-double, pure white; Lady Gilmour, bright pink; and Alice, a deeper pink with semi-double flowers. *A. hupehensis*, dwarf and pink, is closely allied.

Anthemis (Chamomile). Here again there are many species for the rock garden but also some useful material for the herbaceous border. Unlike most hardy perennials nearly all the chamomiles have a long flowering season. The flowers are daisy-like, either white or various shades of yellow and carried on long, stiff stems which make them very suitable for cutting. All do best in rather light,well-drained soils and full sun. They can be propagated by cuttings of firm, young growth rooted in spring or early summer in much the same manner as marguerites which they resemble in many respects without sharing their tenderness.

One of the best species is *Anthemis tinctoria* which makes a compact, bushy plant 60 cm (2 ft) in height. There are several varieties, notably E.C. Buxton in which the colour is near lemon yellow. *A. sancti-johannis* is similar in habit but has larger, deeper yellow flowers.

Anthericum (St Bruno's Lily and St Bernard's Lily). These are graceful plants with white, lily-like flowers in early summer. All will grow readily in any ordinary soil and reasonably open position. They have grassy foliage which dies down in winter and are best planted in spring, at which season they can also be increased by division. The two most usually seen are *Anthericum liliago*, the St Bernard's Lily, which is about 30 cm (1 ft) in height, and what is now known as *Paradisea liliastrum*, the St Bruno's Lily. This is rather bigger and taller. A third kind, *A. ramosum*, spreads more rapidly than either of the others by means of underground stems which throw up fresh tufts of foliage all round the parent plant.

Aquilegia (Columbine). The common columbine will need no introduction to most readers. It is one of the most delightfully dainty of all border plants and its one drawback is that it is somewhat short lived. However it is readily raised from seed sown outdoors in late spring/early summer and an excellent range of colours can be obtained if seed is saved from a good strain. The old-fashioned columbine, *Aquilegia vulgaris*, has short spurs to the flowers and has been largely replaced in gardens by the more modern, long-spurred hybrids in which the spurs are delicately formed and often as much as 4 cm (1½ in) long. Colours are mostly in pastel shades of salmon pink and yellow but there are also blue, red and crimson forms. *A. v.* Nora Barlow is red and white. *A. longissima* has extra long spurs and pale yellow flowers. All bloom in late spring/early summer. Selected varieties may be increased by careful division in spring. Mixed strains raised from seed sown outdoors or in a frame in spring can be planted the following autumn or spring. All do well in sun or partial shade and like a light, but not excessively dry soil.

Armeria (Thrift). Most of the thrifts are rock plants but one species, *Armeria plantaginea*, is a handsome border perennial though it is now rarely sold. It makes compact tufts of grassy foliage from which, in mid-summer, appear bare stems 30 cm (1 ft) or more long terminated by globular heads of bright rose flowers. This is the plant which has produced the even better and more widely grown Bee's Ruby with flowers of increased size and richer, almost crimson colour. All armerias can be increased by division in spring, the best planting season, and thrive in full sun and rather light soils.

Artemisia. For the herbaceous border one of the best kinds is *Artemisia lactiflora*, a really handsome plant of shuttlecock habit, 1·5 m (5 ft) high, each stem terminating in a loose plume of creamy flowers in late summer. It will grow anywhere but does best in fairly rich soil and does not mind some shade. *A. ludoviciana* is a useful, grey-leaved plant for a position towards the front of the border and is equally easy to grow, but prefers a sunny place and well-drained soil. It has a larger-leaved variety named *latiloba*. Both these artemisias can be increased by division in spring.

A. absinthium is a bushy plant, 76 cm (2½ ft) high, with finely divided, aromatic, silvery grey leaves. A specially good variety is Lambrook Silver. *A. stelleriana* is of similar size with white, woolly leaves, and *A. schmidtiana* has the most finely divided silvery leaves of all. It is 60 cm (2 ft) high but a variety named Nana is only 15 cm (6 in) high. If no rooted offsets can be found for propagation, root some cuttings in a frame during the summer.

Aruncus (Goat's Beard). *Aruncus sylvester* is now known as *A. dioicus*. It is a vigorous perennial with handsome, divided leaves and large plumes of small creamy-white flowers carried on 1·5 m (5 ft) stems in mid-summer. It likes most soils, will grow in sun or shade and is easily raised by division in spring or autumn. Alternatively, it can be grown from seed sown in spring or early summer.

Asphodeline (False Asphodel). *Asphodeline lutea* is a plant with bold tufts of narrow leaves, a little like those of a red-hot poker. From these spear up in early summer a few stiffly erect 90 cm (3 ft) spikes, rather sparsely set with starry yellow flowers. It would be wise to see the false asphodel in bloom before deciding to plant it. Culture presents no difficulty in any ordinary soil and sunny aspect, and increase can be either by seed or division in spring.

Aster (Michaelmas Daisy). We are not here concerned with the annual or China asters which are dealt with in Chapter 7 but with the perennial species of which the well-known Michaelmas daisy is the most familiar kind. There is great variety in this family both in habit and flower. Best known are the true Michaelmas daisies raised from *Aster novi-belgii* or *A. novae-angliae*, and the early flowering forms which trace their parentage to *A. amellus*.

This Amellus group flowers in late summer/early autumn. The plants are seldom above 60 cm (2 ft) in height, freely branched with big single flowers. Good examples are King George, bluish violet; Sonia, pink, and Violet Queen, violet purple. *Aster frikartii* is a hybrid of *A. amellus* and similar to King George in colour. Spring is the correct season for moving or dividing all these plants which tend to die if transplanted in the autumn. All other asters can be planted or divided either in autumn or spring.

Varieties of the Novae-angliae and Novi-belgii groups have smaller, often semi-double or fully double flowers in massive branched heads. The main difference from the gardener's point of view is that the Novae-angliae varieties have slightly hairy, rough foliage and flowers which tend to close at night whereas the leaves of Novi-belgii varieties are smooth and glossy and the flowers are open day and night. It is this latter group which has been most highly developed. Examples are Carnival, semi-double, red, 60 cm (2 ft); Jenny, double, violet-purple, 30 cm (1 ft); Gayborder Royal, semi-double, purple, 76 cm (2½ ft); Lady in Blue, semi-double, blue, 25 cm (10 in); Marie Ballard, double, light blue, 90 cm (3 ft); Patricia Ballard, semi-double, pink, 90 cm (3 ft); Raspberry Ripple, double, purplish-red, 76 cm (2½ ft); Snowsprite, semi-double, white, 23 cm (9 in); and Winston Churchill, semi-double, carmine, 76 cm (2½ ft). There are not nearly so many varieties of the Novae-angliae group and they are 1·2–1·8 m (4–6 ft) high. Two of the best are Harrington's Pink, pink, 1·2 m (4 ft), and September Ruby, ruby red, 1 m (3½ ft).

Then there are small-flowered Michaelmas daisies, such as *A. ericoides* which branches stiffly and in mid-autumn smothers itself in tiny white or mauve diasies. *A. cordifolius* and its varieties have similarly small and numerous flowers but in loose, arching sprays often 1·5 m (5 ft) long. Others of interest are *A. acris*, with narrow leaves and starry, blue flowers, and *A. linosyris*, often known as Goldilocks on account of its masses of small, golden-yellow flowers. *A. tongolensis* Napsbury has large, blue daisies on 45 cm (1½ ft) stems in early summer.

All these perennial asters grow readily in any ordinary soil and sunny or partially shady position. They can be increased by division and the vigorous growing kinds are best divided fairly frequently before the old clumps become overcrowded.

Astilbe (False Goat's Beard). This plant used to be popularly but incorrectly called spiraea, since the latter form a distinct genus of shrubs. Astilbes are all true herbaceous plants. They have very elegant, fluffy plumes of small flowers and bloom during the second half of summer. Though not fussy regarding soil they succeed best in fairly rich, moist loams and are excellent for planting at the waterside. They will grow either in sun or partial shade. Most of the numerous varieties grown are hybrids, often collectively known as *Astilbe × arendsii*, raised by crossing four species – *A. davidii*, with narrowly erect, magenta-crimson panicles 1·2 m (4 ft) in height; *A. astilboides* with wider and shorter plumes of creamy white; *A. japonica* which is similar in habit but soft pink in colour and *A. thunbergii*, white. The hybrids have, in consequence, a wide range in colour and type, from white to crimson and from spreading plumes to quite narrow columns. There are all manner of intermediates in colour and shape, some of the loveliest being those with graceful pink or salmon flowers obviously closely associated with *A. japonica*. All these make useful pot plants for the cool or unheated greenhouse and can be brought into bloom a couple of months ahead of their season by gentle forcing. There are also much shorter astilbes described in Chapter 9.

Astrantia (Masterwort). These are unusual looking plants with each cluster of small white, pale pink or purplish rose flowers surrounded by a little ruff of bracts like a Victorian posy in miniature. They enjoy rather moist soil and semi-shade, grow from 30–45 cm (1–1½ ft) in height and flower in early summer. The three species most usually grown are *Astrantia maxima*, *A. major* and *A. carniolica* which has a purplish rose variety named *rubra*. All can be planted in spring or autumn and increased by division at these times. There is a variety of *A. major* named Sunningdale Variegated with cream-splashed leaves. *A.* Hadspen Blood is dark red.

Baptisia (False Indigo). The true indigo, from which the famous dye was once obtained, is *Indigofera tinctoria*. The false indigos are related and one, *Baptisia australis*, is occasionally planted for ornament. It will grow in rough places, does not object to some shade and makes a very leafy plant 76 cm (2½ ft) high carrying a lot of small spikes of blue pea-type flowers in early summer. Plant it in spring or autumn and increase when necessary by division in spring, or sow seeds in a frame or greenhouse in spring.

Bergenia (Large-leaved Saxifrage). The bergenias are plants with very large, undivided leaves and clusters of pink or white flowers in mid-spring. They are worth growing for their foliage alone quite apart from their early blooms. Moreover they have the merit of thriving in shady as well as sunny places and are first-class town plants. There are a number of species and varieties, many of them much alike although they differ in the precise shade of their flowers or size of their leaves. *Bergenia cordifolia*, *B. purpurascens* and *B.* Bressingham White are specially recommended. All may be planted and divided in spring, immediately after flowering, or alternatively in early autumn.

Betonica. See **Stachys** (p. 164).

Bocconia (Plume Poppy). See **Macleaya** (p. 138).

Brunnera. *Brunnera macrophylla* used to be called *Anchusa myosotidiflora*. It is sprawling in habit, has heart-shaped leaves and large, loose sprays of small blue flowers like forget-me-nots in late spring/early summer. It will grow almost anywhere in sun or shade and is increased by division.

Buphthalmum. Only two species are much grown, *Buphthalmum salicifolium*, a 60 cm (2 ft) high, fast-spreading plant with yellow flowers in shape not unlike those of the familiar moon daisy, and *B. speciosum*, 1·2 m (4 ft), with large leaves and orange-yellow flowers. The plants are in bloom from mid-summer until early autumn. They are very hardy and will grow anywhere, being particularly suitable for chalky soils. They can be planted and divided in spring or autumn.

Campanula (Bellflower). A great many of the campanulas are rock plants but there are also numerous showy kinds for the herbaceous border. All are easily grown and several, notably *Campanula lactiflora* and *C. latifolia*, will thrive in shade. All can be planted in spring or autumn and are increased by division at either season. They should be divided every third or fourth year.

    C. carpatica is 23-30 cm (9 in-1 ft) in height, with blue, lavender or white cup-shaped flowers of considerable size throughout the summer. *C. latiloba* is very sturdy with numerous saucer-shaped, purplish flowers close set on 90 cm (3 ft) spikes in mid-summer. *C. lactiflora* is pale blue, mauve or white and the flowers are carried in loose sprays on 1·5 m (5 ft) stems, but there is a variety named Pouffe which is only about 30 cm (1 ft) high. All flower in high summer. *C. latifolia* has the habit of *C. latiloba* but with bell-shaped, drooping flowers. *C. persicifolia* varies from 60 cm-1·2 m (2-4 ft) in height with erect spikes of widely open, bell-shaped flowers in mid-summer varying in colour from clear blue to deep blue and white. There are also double-flowered forms. *C. caespitosa* is primarily a rock plant, but useful in the border as an edging. It suggests a neat harebell with the thinnest of wiry stems terminated by nodding blue or white flowers in mid-summer. *C. glomerata dahurica* has closely clustered heads of violet flowers on 45 cm (18 in) stems in early summer.

Carnation Border. The tree or perpetual carnation needs the protection of a greenhouse in winter so it is described in the chapter on greenhouse plants (p. 442). Here I am concerned only with the hardy, or border, carnation which can be left out of doors all the year, though when grown for exhibition it is sometimes given greenhouse protection to keep the flowers as clean and perfect as possible.

The border carnation has been very highly developed with the result that there are a large number of named varieties to which newcomers are constantly added. The would-be winner of prizes must keep right up to date in this matter for success greatly depends upon growing the right kinds, carnations having a nasty habit of deteriorating after a few years. That is one reason why no selection of varieties will be found in this book. It would be out of date too soon. If you cannot get good advice any other way place order plants with one of the well-known specialists and leave it to him to send you the best.

Culture is fairly simple; indeed it is quite possible to grow good carnations simply by planting in ordinary, loamy soil in a sunny herbaceous border. The exhibitor usually gives them a bed to themselves, in a sunny place for preference, and prepares the soil by deep digging, moderate manuring and the generous use of bonemeal and wood ashes. The plants are renewed annually from layers; that is, non-flowering shoots pegged down into the soil around the parent plant in early summer. The method is to slit the young shoot for about 12 mm (½ in) right through a joint with a sharp penknife. This hastens rooting by checking but not stopping the flow of sap and forcing the formation of a callus from which the new roots will grow. The layered joints are then pegged to the soil but not severed from the parent plants until they are well rooted, a process which usually takes no more than six or eight weeks if the soil is kept nicely moist.

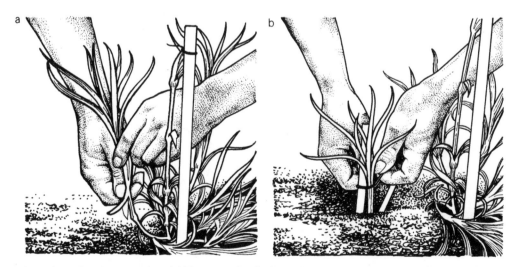

Layering a border carnation. (a) The stem is slit through a joint with a sharp knife. (b) The prepared carnation layer is half buried in sandy soil and secured to a stake. After about six or eight weeks the layer should be well rooted and can then be severed from the parent.

When they are rooted the layers are severed from the parent plant and a week or so later are lifted with plenty of soil and either planted straight away in the beds in which they are to flower, or else potted singly in 10 cm (4 in) pots in ordinary soil (see p. 422). Overwinter in a frame with plenty of ventilation whenever the weather is neither very wet nor very cold. This method is recommended in cold districts or where the soil is not too well drained. The potted layers are planted out early the following spring.

In either case space them at least 30 cm (1 ft) apart and make them really firm. As the flower stems lengthen stake them singly but let the last tie be a good 15 cm (6 in) below the topmost bud so that the stem arches over at the top and the expanding flower hangs a little on its side, shooting off rain and escaping the full glare of the sun.

If the largest possible flowers are required remove all side buds so that the whole strength of the plant is concentrated in the terminal bud which will give the finest flower. It may be necessary to shade or otherwise protect the bloom for the last few days if it is being prepared for a show for no blemish can be tolerated.

For garden display disbudding is unnecessary and plants may be allowed to remain undisturbed for several years. Exhibitors usually discard all their plants as soon as layers have been secured, relying exclusively on year-old stock for their show flowers.

Catananche (Cupid's Dart). The effect of *Catananche caerulea* in bloom is very much that of a short cornflower and it is, in fact, a member of the same family. It is a true perennial, 60 cm (2 ft) in height, and flowers from mid-summer to early autumn. The variety Major has flowers of increased size and substance. All are first class for cutting. Plant in spring or autumn and increase by division in spring. The catananches succeed best in full sun and well-drained soil.

Centaurea (Knapweed). Another family of plants for a sunny position and light soil. All the garden knapweeds are very easy to grow and several are extremely handsome. The best known, *Centaurea montana*, 60 cm (2 ft) in height, is much like a cornflower. There is a white form in addition to the typical blue and both are good for cutting. *C. dealbata* is a taller plant producing bigger, rosy-pink flowers. Even more striking is *C. macrocephala*, with yellow flowers almost as big as tennis balls on 1·4 m (4½ ft) stems. All flower in the first half of summer with the exception of *C. montana* which starts in late spring. All may be planted in spring or autumn and increased by division at either season.

Centranthus (Red Valerian). The common red valerian is a native plant which grows in great profusion in some parts of the country, particularly on limestone cliffs. It is extremely handsome and delights in warm, dry places. For the garden there are deeper coloured forms such as *coccineus* and also a white variety named *albus*. All flower in the first half of summer. They should be planted in spring or autumn and increased by division then. Seed germinates readily but seedlings may vary in colour.

Cephalaria (Giant Scabious). *Cephalaria tatarica* is often known as the yellow scabious. The flowers are like those of the familiar blue scabious, but bigger and coarser and on a larger scale, often 1·8 m (6 ft) in height and branching freely. Unlike the blue scabious it has only a short flowering season in mid-summer. It grows easily in any ordinary soil and sunny position, and can be planted in spring or autumn but should only be divided in spring.

Cerastium (Snow-in-summer). See p. 183.

Ceratostigma. These plants are closely related to the Cape leadwort, *Plumbago capensis*, a popular cool greenhouse climber, and are sometimes called plumbago. Only one is a true herbaceous plant, *Ceratostigma plumbaginoides*. It has clusters of rich blue flowers on 15-23 cm (6-9 in) stems from late summer to early autumn and is an excellent plant for a warm sunny place in well-drained soil. Plant it in spring and increase by cuttings or careful division. *C. willmottianum* has similar flowers but is a shrub 76 cm (2½ ft) high.

Cheiranthus. The common wallflower is a species of cheiranthus and so is the Siberian wallflower. *Cheiranthus × allionii*, but both are bedding plants described elsewhere in this book (see p. 76). There are, however, one or two useful herbaceous kinds which should be considered here. Notable among these are the cheerful yellow Harpur Crewe, with double flowers, and *C. mutabilis*, with single flowers that are yellow at first, becoming bronze and purple. Both like sunny places and lightish, well-drained soils. They should be planted in spring and increased by cuttings in spring or early summer.

Chelone (Turtle Head). These plants are closely related to penstemons and *Penstemon barbatus* is sometimes known as *Chelone barbata*. Two of the best kinds are *C. obliqua*, 60 cm (2 ft) high with short spikes of rosy-magenta flowers and *C. lyonii*, 30 cm (1 ft) high, with even shorter spikes of purplish flowers. Both flower in the first half of summer and should be given a warm, sunny position in well-drained soil. Plant in spring and increase by summer cuttings made from non-flowering side growths or by careful division in the spring.

Chrysanthemum. The familiar greenhouse and border chrysanthemums are outside the scope of this chapter though border varieties can be used in the herbaceous border to increase the late summer and early autumn display. For the moment I am concerned solely with the entirely hardy and herbaceous kinds of which the Shasta daisy (*Chrysanthemum maximum*, also known as *Leucanthemum maximum*) is the best-known example. It grows 76 cm (2½ ft) high and typically has large white single daisy flowers with golden centres. There are also double and semi-double varieties. All bloom in high summer and will grow in practically any soil and reasonably open position but the double flowered kind need winter drainage. All are easily increased by division in spring or autumn and some varieties also come reasonably true from seed.

Another useful species is *C. uliginosum* (*L. serotina*). This has 1·5 m (5 ft) stems bearing single white flowers which do not begin to open until early autumn. Culture is as for *C. maximum*.

C. rubellum (or *Dendranthema rubellum*) is closely allied to the familiar border chrysanthemums and flowers from mid-summer to mid-autumn. It has multitudes of soft pink single flowers on branching, 76 cm (2½ ft) stems. Numerous forms have been raised, some with double flowers, which are almost indistinguishable from the dwarfer forms of Korean chrysanthemum. They are reasonably hardy and in many parts of the country may be grown in the herbaceous border without special protection. They can be increased by cuttings or division in spring.

Cimicifuga (Bugbane). In spite of their unattractive name bugbanes are very graceful and decorative plants, particularly valuable for the late summer border. They produce slender spikes of feathery white flowers and thrive in sunny or partially shady positions. Though they are not particular about soil they prefer moist places. The best kinds are *Cimicifuga japonica*, 90 cm-1·5 m (3-5 ft) in height with erect spikes of flowers which may be branched at the base; *C. racemosa*, similar in stature and colour but with drooping flower spikes, and *C. simplex*, growing to 90 cm (3 ft) with slender, usually unbranched flower spikes. All flower in late summer/early autumn and *C. racemosa* may continue even later. Cimicifugas may be planted in spring or autumn and divided at either season.

Clematis. In addition to the familiar climbing clematis there are two or three not so well-known herbaceous species. Of these the best are *Clematis heracleifolia davidiana*, with spikes of tubular, blue flowers on 1 m (3½ ft) stems; *C. integrifolia*, a rather shorter plant with urn-shaped blue flowers and requiring a few twiggy branches to hold it up, and *C.* × *durandii*, a showy blue-flowered hybrid still more in need of support. All bloom in mid-summer. Plant in spring in ordinary soil and a sunny position and increase by division at that season or by layering in early summer. Prune back dead or thin growth each spring.

Convallaria. See Lily of the Valley (p. 136).

Coreopsis. These are among the most free-flowering plants for the herbaceous border; in fact they tend to flower themselves to death and may need to be renewed from cuttings or seeds fairly frequently to maintain vigour. All have showy flowers on slender stems which are admirable for arranging in vases. They require a fully sunny position and rather light, well-drained soil if they are to be permanent. In heavier soils they are more than ever inclined to die out after the first summer. The most reliable and truly perennial is *Coreopsis lanceolata*, 90 cm (3 ft) in height and yellow. *C. grandiflora* has larger flowers and also several forms, some with double flowers. A grand kind, known as *C. auriculata superba* has a crimson blotch at the base of each yellow petal. *C. verticillata* is very different in appearance, with fine ferny leaves and small but very numerous yellow flowers on freely branched 60 cm (2 ft) stems. It flowers right through summer, the other kinds continuing even later. All should be planted in spring. Propagation is by division, cuttings or seed; cuttings taken in mid-spring are most satisfactory for double-flowered varieties.

Cortaderia. See Pampas Grass (p. 140).

Crambe. (Seakale). *Crambe cordifolia* is a very handsome plant for the back row of the herbaceous border. It grows 1·8 m (6 ft) or more in height, has big, rounded leaves which are themselves an ornament to the garden and, in early summer, bursts into immense cloudy masses of small, white flowers giving rather the impression of a giant gypsophila. It is very easy to grow for it is not fussy regarding soil or situation. Plant it in spring and, if more plants are wanted, lift an old clump and divide at that season or sow seed in spring.

Delphinium. This is one of the most important families of border plants and one which has been completely transformed by plant breeders. There are two main races for the herbaceous border, the giant delphiniums with massive spikes of bloom, often 1·6 m (5½ ft) in height, known as the Elatum group, and the branching delphiniums known as the Belladonna group. These latter have much smaller and looser spikes and are fine for cutting or for the middle and front of the border. No useful purpose would be served by giving lists of varieties as these change fairly frequently as old ones lose vigour and new ones take their place.

All delphiniums thrive in light, loamy soils and sunny, open positions. They dislike bad drainage, particularly in winter, and are best planted in spring or, in the case of rooted cuttings, early summer. Propagation of named varieties must be done either by division or cuttings in spring the latter being preferable as the plants are healthier and more vigorous. The important point is to secure young shoots as cuttings before they have become hollow at the base, that is when they are about 10 cm (4 in) long. They will root very readily in sandy soil in a shaded frame. Seed sown either as soon as ripe in the second half of summer, or in spring, preferably in a frame but otherwise in a sheltered border out of doors, germinates well and will produce small flowering plants the following season, but seedlings may show wide variation from their parents. However, good seed strains giving a reasonable degree of uniformity are available. When grown for exhibition the large-flowered delphiniums are usually restricted to one spike for year-old plants and two or three spikes for two-year-old plants. Staking needs to be carefully done, one stake being used for each spike in the case of the large-flowered kinds. The Belladonna delphiniums can often be most effectively supported by means of short pea sticks pushed in around them at an early stage of growth.

Dianthus (Pinks). Under this name the botanist includes plants more familiarly known to gardeners as border carnations and Sweet Williams. As these are the names which readers will most likely use instinctively when requiring information, it is under these names that the plants are to be found in this book, and I shall refer here only to the species which are commonly called dianthus or pinks in gardens. A great many are rock plants and these are dealt with in Chapter 9.

The herbaceous border kinds of dianthus are not numerous. *Dianthus plumarius*, parent of the garden pinks, is the most important. It is a variable plant, always with the narrow grey leaves of the familiar pink but sometimes compact, at other times straggling, with fragrant white, pink or carmine flowers, often deeply fringed though there are plain-petalled forms as well. The garden pinks themselves, developed from this plant, have usually larger and often double-flowered varieties in a range of colours. They vary in height from about 23-45 cm (9 in-1½ ft). Popular varieties are Bridesmaid, double pink and salmon; Dad's Favourite, double white and maroon; Doris, double salmon; Emperor, double red; Inchmery, semi-double soft pink; Mrs Sinkins, double white; Paddington, double pink and crimson; Pink Mrs Sinkins, also known as Excelsior, double pink; Ursula Bloom, mulberry red, and White Ladies, double white. All flower in early summer.

D. allwoodii is a hybrid between *D. plumarius* and *D. caryophyllus*, parent of the carnations. There are many varieties, closely resembling the garden pinks but with a longer flowering season. They require similar treatment but vary in their resistance to winter wet and cold and are not always so permanent as pinks.

Then there is *D. superbus*, a plant which might be grown in the rock garden but is also quite big enough to take its place in the front row of the herbaceous border. It looks like a rather slender pink, with big single pink or lilac, deliciously fragrant flowers the petals of which are deeply, repeatedly slashed.

All these herbaceous dianthuses will grow in any reasonably good soil that is neither stagnant with moisture in winter nor parched by the first burst of summer heat. Most like lime but it is not essential to any though pinks are unlikely to thrive in very acid soils. All the species can be raised very readily from seed, which may be sown in a greenhouse or frame in spring but seedlings can vary in character. Cuttings of especially fine forms, including the garden pinks and varieties of *Dianthus allwoodii*, can be rooted in sandy soil in a frame or under a handlight in early summer.

Dicentra (Bleeding Heart). Three species of dicentra are commonly grown, namely *Dicentra eximia, D. formosa* and *D. spectabilis*. All are graceful plants with delicate, fern-like foliage and arching spikes of pendant flowers, rose-pink in *D. eximia* and *D. formosa*, which are both about 30 cm (1 ft) tall, but pink and white or all white in *D. spectabilis* which is twice this height. All three succeed best in rather cool, shady places and ordinary soil. They are in bloom in late spring/early summer, may be planted in spring or autumn, and divide equally well at either season.

Dictamnus (Burning Bush). The popular name refers to the peculiar habit this plant has of giving off a vapour in hot weather which can be ignited and will burn briefly. *Dictamnus albus* is a distinctive plant which should be more widely grown for its handsome, ash-like leaves and tall spikes of quite showy flowers in mid-summer. These vary from white to plum purple, one deep-coloured variety being listed as *D. a. purpureus*. All will grow in any sunny position and are not at all particular regarding soil. Seed sown in early spring in a frame usually germinates freely, or old plants can be lifted and carefully divided at the same period.

Digitalis (Foxglove). Though other species are occasionally found in gardens it is selected garden forms of *Digitalis purpurea* that are most valuable. This is a biennial and is described in Chapter 7 under Foxglove.

Other perennial kinds of foxglove occasionally grown are *D. grandiflora*, also known as *D. ambigua*, 76 cm (2½ ft), yellow; *D. ferruginea*, 1·2-1·8 m (4-6 ft), russet red and *D. mertoniensis*, a hybrid between *D. grandiflora* and the common foxglove, 90 cm (3 ft) high with crushed-strawberry flowers.

Doronicum (Leopard's Bane). *Doronicum plantagineum* is one of the best early-flowering border perennials. It has big, yellow, daisy-like flowers on 90 cm (3 ft) stems which open through the second half of spring. They are excellent for cutting besides being very decorative in the border. There is an improved form known as Excelsum, which has bigger flowers. Other good kinds are *D. austriacum*, 60 cm (2 ft) high; *D. orientale*, 30 cm (1 ft); and *D. columnae*, 15 cm (6 in).

All doronicums grow freely in any ordinary soil and sunny or half-shady position and can be increased by division in early spring. Plant in spring or autumn.

Dracocephalum. See **Physostegia** (p. 142).

Echinacea (Purple Cone Flower). In many gardens echinaceas are called rudbeckias and the relationship between the two genera is certainly close and obvious. *Echinacea purpurea* is the species grown but there are several forms of it, all showy plants flowering in late summer/early autumn. They average 1·2 m (4 ft) in height, have stiff, stoutish flower stems each terminated by a big daisy-type flower that has purple petals and a black central disk and are easily grown in any ordinary soil and open place. In some of the named varieties to be found in gardens and nurseries the colour of the blooms is deeper and richer. All can be planted and divided in either spring or autumn.

Echinops (Globe Thistle). Possibly it is the rather coarse foliage which prevents the globe thistle from becoming really popular for it is handsome, easily grown and well worth a place in the border. The flower heads are completely spherical, rather larger than a golf ball in good varieties and either some shade of blue or white. There are several species of which the best are *Echinops bannaticus*, 76 cm (2½ ft), blue; the now rarely available *E. humilis*, 1 m (3½ ft), deep blue; *E. ritro*, 90 cm (3 ft), blue, and *E. sphaerocephalus*, greyish white or white. All flower in high summer. They make long tap roots and will therefore grow in soils too dry for many perennials. They like sunny, open positions and can be planted in spring or autumn and increased by careful division in the spring, by root cuttings in winter or from seed.

Epimedium (Barrenwort). The barrenworts are not showy perennials but they have a quiet beauty of foliage and flower which can be very attractive. An added merit is that they will thrive in quite dense shade, even under shrubs and trees, particularly if the soil contains plenty of peat or leafmould. They are dwarf, bushy plants with yellow, pink, red or white flowers in spring and glossy, dark green leaves which turn to fine shades of bronze in autumn. Plant in spring and increase by careful division at the same time. All kinds are worth growing. Those most likely to be available are *Epimedium alpinum*, red, *E. pinnatum*, yellow, *E. grandiflorum*, in various shades of pink and *E.* × *versicolor* Sulphureum, sulphur yellow.

Eremurus. See Chapter 12.

Erigeron (Fleabane). The fleabanes have the appearance of dwarf Michaelmas daisies. Few exceed 45 cm (1½ ft) in height. One species, *Erigeron aurantiacus*, has orange-coloured blooms and from this some useful hybrids in shades of pink and salmon have been raised. Another species *E. philadelphicus*, has masses of small pink flowers. However, the most popular are the numerous hybrids with fancy names such as Dignity, violet mauve, Foerster's Liebling, rose pink, Merstham Glory, lavender blue, and Quakeress, pale blue. All are at their best during mid-summer and succeed in sunny, open positions and ordinary soils. They are suitable for the middle or front position in the border and can be planted and divided when required in either spring or autumn.

Eryngium (Sea Holly). These are most familiar as everlasting flowers for autumn and winter decoration for which some species are grown on a commercial scale but they are also excellent border plants with handsome, spined foliage and teasel-like heads of flowers surrounded by spiky bracts often of an extraordinary steely shade of blue. All succeed best in rather deep, light, well-drained soils and sunny positions. They do not like being disturbed and are best transplanted in spring at which season they can also be increased by careful division. They bloom from early summer to early autumn. When required for winter decoration the flowers should be cut just before they are fully developed and suspended head downwards in a cool, dry, airy place to dry. Amongst the best of the numerous species are *Eryngium alpinum*, metallic blue *E. a.* Amethyst, amethyst; *E.* × *oliverianum*, violet blue; *E.* × *zabelii* Violetta, one of the darkest in colour, *E. planum* and *E.* × *tripartitum*, both of which have comparatively small but very numerous steely-blue flower heads. An exceptional species with immense heads of creamy white flowers is *E. giganteum*. This is usually treated as a biennial raised from seed sown in spring, planted out in summer and discarded after flowering the following year. The truly perennial kinds can also be increased by sowing seed.

Euphorbia (Spurge). This is an immense family of plants most of which are weeds from the gardener's point of view but a few are effective on account of the handsome bracts which surround the inconspicuous flowers. *Euphorbia cyparissias* is a graceful plant, 30 cm (1 ft) high, with narrow, heather-like foliage, slender stems and bright yellow bracts in crowded heads. By contrast *E. characias* and *E. c. wulfenii* are bold plants, 1 m (3½ ft) high and often double the width with stout, glaucous-green foliage and immense heads of greenish-yellow bracts. Other kinds are *E. griffithii*, 60 cm (2 ft) high with orange-red flower heads, *E. sikkimensis* with red young shoots and leaves, *E. pilosa major* and *E. epithymoides*, both about 45 cm (18 in) high with soft yellow bracts, and *E. biglandulosa*, low growing, grey-blue with pale, greenish-yellow flower heads in spring. All enjoy sunny places, are not fussy about soil and can be increased by division in spring or autumn.

Filipendula. With one exception, *Filipendula hexapetala*, the dropwort, all are moisture-loving plants. *F. rubra*, popularly known as queen of the prairie, has plumes of pink flowers on 1·6 m (5½ ft) stems in the second half of summer. *F. palmata* is a similar colour on 1·2 m (4 ft) stems. *F. purpurea* is similar in height but a deeper cerise colour. *F. hexapetala* Flore Pleno is the best form of the dropwort with loose heads of little double creamy-white flowers on 45 cm (1½ ft) stems in the first part of summer. Unlike the others it enjoys sunny places and rather dry, well-drained soils. All can be planted in spring or autumn and divided at either season.

Gaillardia. These are amongst the most strikingly coloured flowers in the perennial border. The blooms are big and daisy-like, some plain yellow, some scarlet ringed with yellow and some a bronzy tangerine. Unlike most perennials they flower continuously throughout the summer. One drawback is that they tend to exhaust themselves in one season and die out the following winter. They are most permanent on light, well-drained soils and in very sunny positions, but even so it is advisable to maintain a succession of young plants either raised from seed or, in the case of named varieties, by careful division in spring or by root cuttings in winter. Heights average 60 cm (2 ft) and as the stems tend to be too weak to support the heavy flowers it is advisable to supply some support such as the brushy tops of pea sticks pushed into the soil around the plants during spring. Typical varieties are Ipswich Beauty, scarlet and gold, Mandarin, reddish orange, Wirral Flame, reddish bronze and Croftway Yellow, yellow.

Galega (Goat's Rue). These are rather coarse perennials, considered by some too weedy to be admitted to the garden, but useful for rough places and particularly for soils too dry for choicer things. *Galega officinalis* makes a bushy plant 1 m (3½ ft) high, 76 cm (2½ft) wide, smothered throughout the summer with small pea-like flowers of rather too pale a shade of lavender. Better kinds are Her Majesty, which is a really good, soft blue and Lady Wilson, pale lilac. All can be planted in any soil and sunny position in spring or autumn and can be divided at either season.

Geranium (Cranesbill). Do not confuse these hardy geraniums with the pelargoniums used for summer bedding. Geraniums are nearly all quite hardy plants and can be left in the border summer and winter. For the most part they are rather spreading and leafy with showy, saucer-shaped flowers produced freely throughout the summer. Some, such as *Geranium psilostemon*, 90 cm (3 ft), are a rather crude magenta or port-wine red, but others, notably *G. endressii*, 60 cm (2 ft), which is bright rose, *G. grandiflorum*, 45 cm (1½ ft), blue, Johnson's Blue, 60 cm (2 ft), blue, and *G. pratense* and its double-flowered form Flore Pleno, 60 cm (2 ft), a deep lavender blue, are entirely charming and easily accommodated. *G. macrorrhizum* is sprawling, has small purplish pink flowers in late spring and strongly scented leaves. It makes excellent ground cover. All grow readily in any ordinary soil and sunny or partially shady position. Early summer is the main flowering season. Plant in spring or autumn and increase by division at the same season.

Geum. Like the gaillardias, geums suffer from the very freedom with which they flower and in rich soils tend to bloom themselves to death in one summer. They are happiest in rather light, well-drained soil and sunny positions. Unlike gaillardias they do not make good cut flowers as the blooms soon wither in water. Geums average 60 cm (2 ft) in height, bloom from late spring to mid-autumn and are among the best plants for the front of the border. There are a number of garden-raised varieties which must be increased by careful division in spring, the best planting season. Seed germinates readily in spring or early summer, either out of doors or in a frame, but seedlings tend to vary from their parents unless great care is taken in selection. Amongst the best kinds are *G. chiloense* Mrs Bradshaw, vivid scarlet; Lady Stratheden, golden yellow, and Fire Opal, an effective coppery red. A notable species is *G. Borisii* with small, single but very vivid orange-red flowers on 30 cm (1 ft) high stems.

Gunnera. The gunneras are grown for their leaves. These are immense and very handsome, the general effect being that of an unusually beautiful rhubarb magnified five or six times. Obviously these are plants that must be given plenty of space. They are seen to best advantage as isolated specimens and, as they like plenty of moisture, they are frequently planted at the waterside. A few well-placed gunneras, royal ferns and bamboos will give an almost tropical luxuriance to the margin of any fairly large pool or stream. The species usually grown is *Gunnera manicata*.

Gunneras are just a little tender and in all except the mildest parts it is a wise precaution to build a shelter over them of twigs or wire netting covered with straw or bracken after their leaves have been removed in late autumn. Do not let this covering press heavily on the crowns and be sure to remove it in mid-spring by which time the plants will be starting into growth again. Apart from this precaution gunneras are not difficult to grow, thriving in any good, loamy soil that does not dry out too much in summer. Spring is the best planting time and also the season for division when further plants are required.

Gypsophila. From the ordinary gardener's point of view there are two gypsophilas which really matter, one the annual with which we are not concerned in this chapter and the other *Gypsophila paniculata*, a perennial which makes a solitary tap root going 1 m (3½ ft) down into the soil, and a bushy, freely branching plant with narrow, grey-green leaves and an immense number of tiny white flowers produced in cloud-like sprays. It is the ideal foil for sweet peas and similar delicate summer blooms. The most popular forms of gypsophila are those with double flowers like tiny white pompons of which Bristol Fairy is the most popular. Yet other varieties such as Flamingo and Rosy Veil, the latter only 30 cm (1 ft) high, have pale pink flowers. All need a deep, well-drained soil and sunny position. They like lime but can grow without it though they are unlikely to succeed in very acid soils. They should be planted in the spring.

It is impossible to divide the solitary tap root so propagation must be from seed, which is unreliable with the double kinds; by grafting small shoots of the double forms on to pieces of root of the single in early summer (not really a task for the amateur), or by cuttings taken in the following rather special way. A good plant is lifted and potted in spring and stood in a greenhouse or frame. All shoots are pinched when 10 cm (4 in) long. Secondary shoots are pinched again when the same length. The next lot of shoots to appear are taken as cuttings when about 4 cm (1½ in) long and are inserted in pure sand in a frame or under a handlight. They must be watered freely.

Helenium. These are among the most useful of summer-flowering perennials, for they make a magnificent display from about mid-summer until the early days of autumn. The garden varieties which are numerous, are nearly all derived from one species, *Helenium autumnale*. They vary in height from 60 cm-1·5 m (2-5 ft), and in colour from yellow to bronzy crimson. Typical of these are Butterpat and Pumilum Magnificum, both yellow, 90 cm (3 ft), Moerheim Beauty, bronzy red, 90 cm (3 ft), and Wyndley, orange flecked bronzy red, 60 cm (2 ft). Their peak is late summer but some will start to flower in mid-summer and some will continue well into the autumn. All grow readily in any ordinary soil and sunny position and can be planted and divided in spring or autumn.

Helianthus (Sunflower). There are both annual and perennial sunflowers but the former are dealt with separately in the chapter on annuals. Almost all those for the herbaceous border are big plants with massive golden-yellow flowers. One of the most handsome is *Helianthus atrorubens* Monarch with single golden flowers as big as tea plates, each with a small black centre, produced in early/late autumn. It is more difficult than most sunflowers to grow, needing good drainage and, possibly, some winter protection. *H. decapetalus (multiflorus)* is a dwarfer, bushier and less invasive plant 1·3 m (4½ ft) high, flowering in late summer. It has both single and double-flowered varieties and all are excellent garden plants, of which Loddon Gold, double, 1·5 m (5 ft), is one of the best. All kinds of helianthus like sun and, with the one exception mentioned, are not particular regarding soil. They can be planted and divided in spring, or in autumn after flowering.

Heliopsis. To the gardener these plants are extremely like the sunflowers just described.

They average 1·2 m (4 ft) in height, have stiffly erect stems and large, deep yellow flowers in high summer. *Heliopsis scabra* is the most useful kind and it has several varieties, some with large or double flowers. Some of these have been given Latinised names such as *gigantea* and *zinniaeflora* and may appear in catalogues under these names as if they were distinct species, which they are not. All are useful for the middle and back of the border and should be treated in exactly the same manner as perennial sunflowers.

Helleborus (Christmas Rose, Lenten Rose). There are a number of species of helleborus but two particular favourites are *Helleborus niger*, the Christmas rose, and *H. orientalis*, the Lenten rose. The first has pure white, saucer-shaped flowers on stout 38 cm (1¼ ft) stems. Some varieties really bloom at Christmas time in the open air and continue well on into the new year, others flower a little later. There is a form of it named *altifolius* (or *maximus*) which is bigger, has flowers slightly spotted with rose and starts to bloom nearly a month earlier.

H. orientalis has many varieties and these are more familiar in gardens than is the true species. All are a little taller than the Christmas rose, similar in general appearance but with flowers which are more often some rather subdued shade of purple or maroon or white spotted with purple. All the same there are pure white Lenten roses and yellowish ones into the bargain, while some of the purple shades are very rich and certainly welcome in the months preceeding spring.

Other kinds are *H. atrorubens* with deep purple flowers on 45 cm (1½ ft) stems from mid-winter to early spring; *H. foetidus* with apple-green flowers edged with purple in early spring and *H. corsicus*, the tallest of the genus, 60 cm (2 ft) high with handsome leathery leaves and large clusters of yellowish-green flowers from late winter to mid-spring.

All these hellebores like good, rich loamy soils and most prefer cool, rather shady places but *H. corsicus* does well in full sun. Most object to root disturbance so should be left alone as long as possible. When they finally get overcrowded they can be lifted and divided very carefully after flowering, which is also the best planting time. They can also be raised from seed but they are sometimes slow in germinating. Self-sown seedlings of *H. orientalis*, *H. corsicus* and *H. foetidus* are commonly found round the plants.

Hemerocallis (Day Lily). These plants are known as day lilies because the individual flowers last for only one day. This matters little as fresh buds are produced in seemingly endless succession and the plants make a good display throughout the first part of summer. The flowers are trumpet-shaped and in various shades from yellow to a deep bronzy crimson. All have the merit of thriving equally well in sun or partial shade. They are not particular regarding soil but do best in a good loam. There are a great number of named varieties differing mainly in the size and shade of colour of the flowers and at least one very old variety, Kwanso Flore Pleno, has double flowers. Heights vary from 45-90 cm (1½-3 ft). Typical varieties are Golden Chimes, small but numerous yellow flowers; Marion Vaughan, yellow; Pink Damask, soft pink and Stafford, deep red. Planting can be done in spring or autumn and division can be done at either season. Plants can also be raised from seed but seedlings of garden varieties are likely to differ quite a lot in colour, shape and size.

Hepatica. Low-growing early flowering plants often classed with anemone. The two most popular kinds are *Hepatica angulosa*, 15 cm (6 in) high, with single blue flowers and *H. triloba*, about 10 cm (4 in) tall with blue, pink or white single or double flowers. All like soils containing plenty of leafmould or peat and partially shady positions, and all flower in late winter/early spring. Single-flowered kinds can be increased by seed and all by division after flowering.

Hesperis (Sweet Rocket, Dame's Violet). It is very easy to grow both the purplish lilac and the pink and white single-flowered varieties of *Hesperis matronalis* since the seed germinates readily if sown outdoors in spring. Where plants are already established, self-sown seedlings often appear in considerable numbers. This is just as well because although this plant is a perennial, it is usually rather short-lived, flowering itself to death in a few years. Unfortunately the more effective double-flowered varieties, Alba Plena, white, and Flora Plena, lilac pink, produce no seeds, must be increased by cuttings in summer and have become very scarce. Both singles and doubles look rather like tall stocks, reaching a height of 1·2 m (4 ft) and flowering in late spring and early summer. They thrive in porous soils and like chalk or lime. Double-flowered kinds must be increased by cuttings in a frame in summer. Very highly scented.

Heuchera. Very graceful plants with sprays of small but numerous flowers on slender stems up to 76 cm (2½ ft) in height. The colour range is from palest pink to crimson. The most freely grown are forms of *Heuchera sanguinea*, such as Scintillation, pink and red; Firebird deep red, and Pluie de Feu, scarlet. *H. × brizoides* is a particularly dainty hybrid, pale pink in colour. All bloom in the first part of summer, like sunny positions, are not fussy about soil and can be planted and divided in spring or autumn.

Heucherella. *Heucherella tiarelloides* is a hybrid between heuchera and tiarella which looks very much like a heuchera with 38 cm (1¼ ft) sprays of small pink flowers in late spring/early summer. It requires identical treatment to heuchera.

Hollyhock. See Chapter 7.

Hosta (Plantain Lily). The plantain lilies have handsome, broad, plantain-like leaves of a grey or glaucous colour in some kinds, shining green or variegated with white or cream in others and varying greatly in size. They also have spikes of tubular and as a rule not very showy flowers, though there are a few exceptions, notably *Hosta plantaginea (subcordata)*, in which the flowers are white, fragrant and quite striking. Other good kinds are *H. lancifolia*, with pale mauve flowers and ribbed shining green leaves; *H. sieboldiana*, with broad, grey-green leaves and white flowers, and the now rarely available *H. undulata medio-variegata* in which the wavy-edged, glossy green leaves are striped with creamy white. All will thrive in any reasonable soil and place but the best foliage is produced in fairly rich, slightly moist soil and a partially shaded position. All can be planted in spring or autumn and divided at either season. They flower in high summer.

Incarvillea. When these do well they never fail to attract a great deal of attention for their big gloxinia-like flowers have a tropical appearance, unusual in a hardy plant. Yet they are perfectly hardy, if given a situation with good winter drainage and plenty of sunshine but not too dry in summer. All have tuberous roots which need sun warmth to ripen properly. The best kinds are *Incarvillea mairei grandiflora*, rosy-red, 30 cm (1 ft); and *I. delavayi*, rosy magenta and 60 cm (2 ft) in height. There is also a hybrid of medium height named Bees' Pink with soft pink flowers. All flower in the first part of summer and should be planted in spring and increased by careful division at the same time, or by seed sown in a frame or greenhouse in spring.

Inula. Rather coarse perennials with big, showy, daisy-like flowers. Some kinds may be naturalized in the wild garden or thin woodland while others may be used in the middle of the herbaceous border. One of the best is probably *Inula royleana* with large, orange-yellow flowers on 60 cm (2 ft) stems in the second half of summer, but there are several others worthy of consideration including *I. magnifica*, with large yellow flowers on 1·8 m (6 ft) stems, late summer to mid-autumn, and *I. oculus-christi* with yellow flowers on 60 cm (2 ft) stems in summer; *I. ensifolia*, yellow, 30 cm (1 ft), late summer, and *I. hookeri*, yellow, 76 cm (2½ ft), summer. No inula is particular as to soil or situation and all can be planted and divided in spring or autumn.

Iris. This is an immense family including plants with bulbous roots which are dealt with separately in the chapter on bulbs. Here we are concerned only with those having ordinary fibrous roots or with fleshy rhizomes as in the common German or flag iris. It is from this last-named species *Iris germanica*, hybridized with other kinds such as *I. pallida* and *I. variegata*, that a great number of the best garden varieties have been and still are being produced. Colours have been greatly extended beyond the prevailing purple of the common flag and now include excellent yellows, pinks, pale blues, coppery shades, wine colours and combinations of these. All these flag irises suffer the drawback of a rather short flowering season in late spring/early summer. Heights vary from 60 cm-1·5 m (2-5 ft). All grow readily in any ordinary or rather light soils and sunny positions. They like lime but it is not essential to them – though they are unlikely to thrive in very acid soils. Contrary to popular belief they do not like shady places. They are best planted immediately the flowers fade but can also be planted in spring or early autumn. They are increased by division of the rhizomes and special care should be taken to break off all the old half-dead pieces when dividing, keeping only about 6·2 cm (2½ in) of rhizome from the base of the leaves. Plant firmly but only just cover the rhizomes with soil. This is their natural position where the sun can ripen them.

The dwarf Crimean irises obtained from *I. chamaeiris* and *I. pumila* look and behave very much like dwarf flag irises and require identical treatment in the garden except that, as they are no more than 23 cm (9 in) in height they must be planted at the very front of the border or, if preferred, in the rock garden. They flower in the second half of spring.

Then there is the race of very beautiful but difficult irises known as *regeliocyclus* and *oncocyclus*. *I. susiana*, the mourning iris, so-called because of its sombre colour scheme of heavy, almost black netting on a white ground, *I. hoogiana* with large grey-blue flowers and *I. gatesii*, greenish white with purple veins, are typical of the Oncocyclus irises. These and their kind are not for beginners. They need a gritty, well-drained soil and plenty of sun and warmth. In particular their rhizomes must be thoroughly ripened in late summer and for this reason it is an advantage to plant them on a sun-baked ledge or on top of a terrace wall or bank where the soil is likely to dry out thoroughly as the summer advances. Sometimes it may prove necessary to cover them with cloches after flowering to help this ripening process. All have very large flowers and are of medium height.

Apart from these types with thick rhizomes which store food and so help the plants over dry spells there are a great many irises with ordinary fibrous roots and these also vary greatly in their requirements. Some of them like plenty of moisture in the soil and may be planted near a pool or stream but with their crowns a few centimetres above the water. This is true of the so-called Japanese iris, *I. kaempferi*, with its very large, flamboyant, widely opened flowers in various shades of purple, violet, blue and pink. It grows 90 cm (3 ft) high and flowers about mid-summer.

I. laevigata, also sometimes known as the Japanese iris and rather similar in appearance but slighter in build, is even more of a moisture lover and may be planted actually in a pool or slow stream with its crown 6·2 cm (2½ in) below water level. It revels in a good, rich, loamy soil. Such conditions will also suit our own native yellow flag iris which grows 1·3 m (4½ ft) high and flowers in early summer.

Either moist soil or quite ordinary border conditions will please the very graceful *I. sibirica* with its big clumps of grassy foliage and numerous small blue, violet or white flowers in mid-summer that are so delightful for cutting. *I. ochroleuca* with narrow, corkscrewed leaves and 1·2 m (4 ft) stems is terminated by pale yellow and white flowers. This is another of these accommodating irises for moist or ordinary soil.

Finally there are many species which will thrive best in porous soils and sunny positions. Good drainage is a first essential for most of these and the smaller kinds are as happy on the rock garden as in the border. A representative selection would include *I. gracilipes*, with grassy leaves and, in late spring, small lavender flowers on slender 23 cm (9 in) stems; *I. douglasiana*, 15-30 cm (6 in-1 ft) high with cream to lilac-purple flowers in early summer; *I. innominata*, rather similar to the last but in shades of yellow or buff veined with brown, and *I. unguicularis (stylosa)*, the winter-flowering Algerian iris, with fine lavender or white flowers sometimes partly hidden amongst the abundant grassy foliage, a fault which can be overcome by planting it in poor, sandy or gravelly soil. Given a sunny place and well-drained soil, it may be left for many years without being disturbed.

Unlike the rhizomatous irises all these fibrous-rooted kinds should be planted in spring and can be divided at the same season.

Kirengeshoma. *Kirengeshoma palmata* is a striking plant freely branched, about 90 cm (3 ft) high, with long, hanging, bell-shaped yellow flowers in late summer/early autumn. It enjoys good rich, rather moist soil and some shade, is best planted in spring and can be increased by division at that season.

Kniphofia (Red-hot Poker). These are all handsome plants with sword-like leaves and usually sturdy stems topped by poker-shaped heads of scarlet or yellow flowers, but there are some much smaller kinds, mostly species, such as *Kniphofia rufa* and *K. galpinii*, both 60 cm (2 ft) in height with narrow, grassy leaves and comparatively slender flower stems. Unfortunately these are in the main more tender and difficult to grow than the bigger kinds. Of the latter the best are *K. uvaria*, 1·5 m (5 ft) high, with scarlet and yellow flowers in late summer and the many varieties or hybrids obtained from it, including *erecta*, which is similar in height but has flowers that gradually erect themselves from the bottom of the spike upwards, a peculiarity which gives it a curiously rocket-like appearance. *K. caulescens* makes a large, branched plant 90 cm (3 ft) high with blue-grey leaves and rather dull salmon-red and cream flowers in late summer and *K. triangularis* Tuckii, 1·2 m (4 ft) high, has yellow and red flowers in early summer and is one of the first to flower. There are even creamy white kniphofias of which Maid of Orleans, 90 cm (3 ft), and Little Maid, 60 cm (2 ft), are good examples. All should be grown in full sun and reasonably rich but well-drained soil. They need plenty of moisture while the flower spikes are forming but dislike a waterlogged soil in winter. They may be planted in spring or autumn, but are best divided in spring and can also be raised from seed.

Lamium (Yellow Archangel, Dead Nettle). Two kinds of lamium are useful as ground cover but not in this common wild form. One, *Lamium galeobdolen*, the yellow archangel, has a variety named Variegatum with silver and yellow variegated leaves and yellow flowers. It is a rampant plant which must be kept firmly in hand but can be useful in rough places and will grow in woodland. The other kind, *L. maculatum*, is the dead nettle, a common weed which has two decorative varieties with variegated leaves, one named Aureum with yellow leaves, the other Beacon Silver with silvery leaves and pink flowers. They are not invasive and make excellent ground cover in almost any place. The golden colour of Aureum is best developed in semi-shade. All can be increased by division.

Lathyrus (Everlasting Pea). A familiar sight in cottage gardens in summer is the so-called perennial pea, *Lathyrus grandiflorus*, a herbaceous climber, in habit not unlike the sweet pea though somewhat more robust and with numerous pea-flowers which are commonly a rather harsh shade of rose, though there are also paler pink and white varieties. It is a pretty and useful plant which will grow in almost any soil and place. The perennial pea will climb to a height of about 2·4 m (8 ft) and can be used to clothe walls, arches, screens, or sheds. It can be raised readily from seed sown in a frame in early spring or out of doors in late spring.

Lavatera. See p. 88 and p. 280.

Liatris (Blazing Star, Gay Feather, Button Snakeroot). These striking plants never fail to attract comment because of their handsome but unusual appearance. They make a number of stiffly erect stems 76 cm (2½ ft) high, clothed for half their length in fluffy, bright-mauve flowers which have the curious habit of opening from the top downwards. The two best species are *Liatris pycnostachya*, which is 1 m (3½ ft) high and *L. spicata*, which is considerably shorter, and there are also garden varieties, some of which may be hybrids. All enjoy sunny places and good well-drained soil which is nevertheless not liable to dry out badly in summer. They should be planted in spring and increased by careful division of their tuberous roots at that season.

Ligularia. These plants were once known as senecio and may still be found under that name in old catalogues. One of the best is *Ligularia dentata*, also known as *L. clivorum*, a bold plant 1·3 m (4½ ft) high and with big, roundish leaves and heads of large, orange-yellow daisy-like flowers in late summer/early autumn. There are garden varieties and hybrids such as Gregynog Gold, with extra fine leaves and flowers and *L. dentata*

Desdemona with purple leaves. All are easily grown in any soil and situation and do particularly well in damp places. *L. stenocephala* carries yellow flowers in slender 1·5 m (5 ft) spikes on nearly black stems and has large jagged leaves, which flag badly if short of water. Plant all kinds in spring or autumn and increase by division at either season.

Lily of the Valley. The lily of the valley, *Convallaria majalis*, is seldom grown in the herbaceous border though it is a true herbaceous plant. This, no doubt, is largely because, since it is so valuable for cutting, it is more convenient to give it a bed to itself, often in an out-of-the-way place from which blooms can be picked freely without spoiling the general garden display. Certainly the lily of the valley responds well to such treatment which permits it to be mulched liberally with well-rotted manure and leafmould early each spring. Plant the crowns singly in mid- to late autumn about 5 cm (6 in) apart in rows 23 cm (9 in) apart and cover them with 2·5 cm (1 in) of soil. Thereafter leave them to spread and multiply for years until the bed becomes so overcrowded that there is a definite falling off in the quality and quantity of bloom. Then lift in autumn, divide to single crowns and replant as in the first instance. The soil should be rich and deeply cultivated, the position shaded or at any rate not very hot and dry. Alternatively lily of the valley can be naturalized in thin woodland. There is a rare form of this plant with pale pink flowers but it is not, in my opinion, as lovely as the common white variety.

Limonium (Sea Lavender). The statice, now known as limonium, is called sea lavender because one species with lavender-coloured flowers does really grow so close to the water's edge that the tide often washes over it. The best perennial kind for the border is *Limonium latifolium*, a grand plant for cutting because its masses of tiny lavender flowers will last for months if cut and dried. The rarely available *L. incana* is a rather dwarfer plant with bigger, whitish-pink flowers. Both are in bloom in late summer/early autumn and will grow in most soils though they must have an open, sunny situation. Plant and increase by seed in spring or by root cuttings taken in winter.

Linaria (Toadflax). The only two species of this very large family of interest for the herbaceous border are *Linaria dalmatica*, with narrow, grey-green leaves and slender spikes of bright yellow flowers rather like tiny antirrhinums, and *L. purpurea*, which is similar but with purple flowers. Both bloom continuously from mid-summer to early autumn. The plants thrive in any ordinary soil and sunny position and may be planted and divided in spring or autumn. Several other linaria are now listed as cymbalaria.

Liriope. Evergreen plants with tufted grassy leaves and stiff 23 cm (9 in) spikes of small, crowded, lilac-purple flowers, the whole effect being rather that of an elongated grape hyacinth. The plants flower in late summer/early autumn when they are especially welcome. There are several species, of which *Liriope muscari* appears the best and hardiest. It enjoys a warm, sunny position in reasonably well-drained soil, should be planted in spring and may be increased by division at this season.

Lobelia (Cardinal Flower). Many gardeners think of lobelias solely as cheerful edging plants for summer bedding, but there are also some excellent hardy or nearly hardy kinds for the herbaceous border. In well-drained soil these often stand the winter without protection in mild districts. Elsewhere they should be lifted and placed in a frame over winter. Among the best of these are *Lobelia cardinalis*, with slender 90 cm (3 ft) spikes of vivid scarlet flowers; *L. fulgens*, similar but with beetroot-red foliage; *L. syphilitica*, which is a little shorter, less graceful and with rather washy blue flowers and *L. vedrariensis*, a hybrid with 90 cm (3 ft) spikes of purple flowers. All may be planted and divided in spring. They flower from late summer to early autumn and like plenty of moisture during the growing season; so much so that in summer they can be given semi-bog conditions, though good drainage is essential in winter.

Lupinus (Lupins). There are two very distinct species of perennial lupin in addition to the annuals dealt with in Chapter 7. One is the tree lupin, *Lupinus arboreus*, which is almost a shrub, with a semi-permanent, woody framework. It has comparatively small spikes of yellow or white flowers in late spring/early summer and makes a big bush 1·5 m (5 ft) high and wide. The other perennial species, *L. polyphyllus*, is a true herbaceous plant, producing its flower spikes at the same time on 1 m (3½ ft) stems, but dying down each autumn and sprouting up again the following spring. It has been much improved by breeders, a notable improvement being that made by Mr Russell of England when he raised seedlings in which the upright or standard petals spread out fanwise, so giving the whole spike a much more solid appearance than formerly. The present colour range includes white, yellow, mauve, lavender, purple, pink and crimson, in addition to a multitude of intermediate shades and combinations.

All dislike lime, enjoy good drainage and do best in rather sandy or porous soils. They usually tend to flower themselves to death in a few years, and so they should be renewed constantly from seed sown out of doors in spring or early summer, or by cuttings rooted in a frame in early spring. The cuttings are made from firm young shoots severed close to the crown of the plant. Selected or named varieties will not breed true from seed but must be increased by cuttings. All lupins like a sunny position and are best planted in spring.

Lychnis (Campion). Several kinds are showy herbaceous perennials, among the best being *Lychnis coronaria*, once called *Agrostemma coronaria*, 60 cm (2 ft) high with grey leaves and branching heads of crimson-magenta flowers in summer; *L. chalcedonica*, 1 m (3½ ft) in height with flattish heads of geranium-red flowers in late summer; and *L. viscaria* Splends Plena, 30 cm (1 ft) in height with double, carmine flowers, also in summer. All enjoy soil which is well-drained even to the point of poorness. They should be planted in spring and may be divided carefully at that season. All except those with double flowers can be raised from seed sown under glass in early spring or out of doors in late spring.

Lysimachia. The well-known Creeping Jenny is a species of lysimachia, but it is with the taller kinds that we are concerned at present. Three of the best of these are the common *Lysimachia vulgaris*, a rather rare European plant found by stream sides with 90 cm (3 ft) spikes of bright yellow flowers in the first half of summer; *L. punctata*, flowering at the same time and rather similar in effect but more elegantly formed and with flowers and leaves in whorls; *L. clethroides* with white blooms in arching spikes in late summer/early autumn; and *L. ephemerum*, with slender spikes of white flowers in high summer and blue-grey leaves. All these like damp, fairly rich soils and cool, half-shady positions. They can be planted and divided in spring or autumn.

Lythrum (Purple Loosestrife). Spike-flowered perennials for sunny or half-shady places and ordinary soils. The flowers of *Lythrum virgatum* are small, rose magenta and carried in close, slender spikes 90 cm (3 ft) in height. *L. salicaria* is a rather looser, less compact plant with similarly showy but crudely coloured flowers. There are improved garden forms of each with clearer or more richly coloured flowers. All flower in high summer, may be planted in spring or autumn and divided at either season.

Macleaya (Plume Poppy). The two species commonly cultivated in gardens are *Macleaya cordata* and *M. microcarpa*, both once known as *Bocconia*. Both are very handsome plants worth growing for their heart-shaped, grey-green leaves alone. The flowers are small and amber coloured in *M. microcarpa*, white in *M. cordata*, not very remarkable individually but handsome in the mass. They are carried in loose plumes on stems at least 1·8 m (6 ft) high from mid-summer onwards for several weeks. These plants will thrive in either sun or half shade. Plant in spring and when new plants are required increase by division at the same season. *M. microcarpa* spreads rapidly by radiating roots, whereas *M. cordata* remains a more compact clump.

Meconopsis (Himalayan Poppy). See p. 197.

Mertensia. This is a family frequently recommended but seldom seen. Not all its numerous species are good border plants but a few are, notably *Mertensia pulmonarioides*, once known as M. *virginica*, with ample tufts of blue-green leaves and loose sprays of sky-blue flowers in mid-spring, after which it dies down and remains dormant until the following year. The plant is about 60 cm (2 ft) high and grows readily in ordinary, well-drained soil and a sheltered, partially shady position. It dies down during mid-summer and can then be easily destroyed while cultivating. It can be increased by careful division in spring but does not like root disturbance so leave alone as long as possible. It comes from Virginia and is there known as the Virginian bluebell. *M. sibirica* and *M. ciliata* are similar plants but not quite so distinguished. They do not die down early.

Mimulus (Musk). When one has ruled out the musks which are annuals or treated as such (see p. 91) and those dwarf kinds which are grown mainly in the rock garden one is left with a few kinds for the herbaceous border or the edge of stream and pool. Of these one of the best is our own native *Mimulus luteus* which delights in very moist soil and in such places soon makes big, leafy clumps producing freely almost all summer bright yellow, pouched flowers on 45 cm (1½ ft) stems. There are several colour forms in which the yellow is more or less heavily splashed with crimson or maroon. *Mimulus cupreus* is similar but shorter and more tufted and also has numerous varieties, some of which are crimson or scarlet e.g. Whitecroft Scarlet. *M. cardinalis* has taller stems of scarlet, scarlet and yellow or pink flowers in summer. All can be increased by division in spring, the best planting time.

Miscanthus (Eulalia). Hardy perennial grasses grown for their foliage. *Miscanthus sinensis* is 1·6 m (5½ ft) high and has several good varieties such as Variegatus, with a narrow yellow band to each leaf, Zebrinus with cross bands of yellow and Gracillinus with very narrow leaves. *M. sacchariflorus* has broad leaves and is 1·9 m (6½ ft) tall. All can be grown in any reasonably good soil, can be planted in spring or autumn and divided at either season.

Monarda (Bergamot). The leaves of these plants are very fragrant and the tubular flowers are produced in showy whorls, one above the other. The species commonly grown in gardens is *Monarda didyma*, 76 cm (2½ ft) high, flowering from mid-summer to early autumn. Typically it is scarlet but there are numerous garden varieties or hybrids with another similar species, *M. fistulosa*, some pink, some lilac or purple and at least one good white. All should be grown in ordinary soil and sun or partial shade. Plant in spring or autumn and divide at the same season.

Morina. One rather striking species, *Morina longifolia*, is grown in borders. It has spiky, thistle-like leaves and stiff 60 cm (2 ft) spikes of pink and white tubular flowers produced on and off throughout the summer. It enjoys a sunny place and well-drained soil and is best increased by seed. Out of flower it can fairly easily be mistaken for a rather handsome thistle so label it well in case it is thought to be a weed and pulled out.

Nepeta (Catmint). The very popular edging plant commonly known as *Nepeta mussinii* is not, apparently, the true bearer of this name but an improved hybrid from it which should be known as *N. × faassenii*. It makes a dense mass of slender stems set with small, grey leaves and terminated by spikes of lavender flowers. The whole plant has a distinct mint-like fragrance when crushed. It is in bloom throughout the summer and early autumn and its one fault is that, like many other free-flowering perennials, it is inclined to die out in winter, particularly if the soil is very rich and poorly drained. It is seen at its best in rather light, poor soils in sunny positions. One form, known as Six Hills Giant, is larger and looser in all its parts. These features are also characteristic of *N. sibirica*, or the garden variety known as Blue Beauty or Souvenir de André Chaudron, all of which require identical treatment. Plant in spring and increase by careful division at that time or by cuttings of firm, young growth taken at practically any time in spring or summer.

Oenothera (Evening Primrose). The true evening primrose, *Oenothera biennis*, is, as its name implies, a biennial and is described in Chapter 7, but there are some excellent perennial kinds, notably *O. tetragona* and its varieties such as Fireworks and Yellow River. These are bushy, branching plants, 45-60 cm (1½-2 ft) high, with innumerable golden-yellow flowers each as big as a large coin throughout the first half of summer. These are all plants for full sun and well-drained soil, in fact in a dry season they are likely to give the best display in the border. Plant in spring for preference and increase by careful division at that time.

Omphalodes. The plants belong to the same family as the forget-me-not and resemble it in many ways. *Omphalodes verna*, a fast-spreading plant with sprays of bright blue or white flowers on 20 cm (8 in) stems in mid- to late spring, is sometimes called the creeping forget-me-not, and also blue-eyed Mary. *O. cappadocica* is a more compact plant with fine blue, white-eyed flowers on 20 m (8 in) stems mainly in late spring/early summer. Both will grow in any reasonably good soil, prefer cool, shady places, can be planted in spring or autumn and are increased by division in spring.

Paeonia (Peony). There are two quite distinct classes of peony, the herbaceous ones which interest us in this chapter and the tree peony which is dealt with in the chapter on trees and shrubs. The herbaceous peonies are in the main derived from two sources, the European species *Paeonia officinalis*, and the Chinese one, *P. lactiflora*, once known as *P. albiflora*. Both are hardy plants not in the least difficult to grow in ordinary soil and sunny positions, though they all dislike root disturbance and sometimes take a year or so to get fully established after a move. For this reason they should be given permanent places where they need not be disturbed even when other plants have to be lifted and divided. Plant in early autumn, just covering the crowns with soil. Propagation can be effected at either season by carefully dividing the roots, but a sharp knife will be required to cut through the hard, fleshy crowns. There are a great many varieties of *P. lactiflora*, some with single flowers, others fully double and yet others with an outer ring of broad petals as in a normal single flower, containing a central ball of narrow petal segments often in a contrasting colour. Most are fragrant, all flower in early summer, are about 90 cm (3 ft) in height and often rather more through. Typical varieties are Bowl of Beauty, pink and cream; Duchesse de Nemours, white and cream; Felix Crousse, deep carmine; Festiva Maxima, white and red; Globe of Light, rose and yellow; Karl Rosenfeld, crimson; Kelway's Brilliant, carmine; Kelway's Lovely, rose; Kelway's Majestic, cherry and cream; Marie Crousse, pink; Mons. Jules Elie, rose; and Sarah Bernhardt, pink. There are fewer varieties of *P. officinalis* but there are double white, pink and red forms. All flower in late spring and early summer. *P. peregrina* has single salmon-flame flowers and *P. mlokosewitschii* has single yellow flowers, both in late spring. Other good species are less frequently seen.

Pampas Grass. One of the few ornamental grasses which everyone knows as the pampas grass, *Cortaderia selloana*, with its fine silvery plumes in early and mid-autumn. There are several varieties ranging in height from 1·2-2·4 m (4-8 ft). All delight in light but fairly rich soils and warm, sunny places. Pampas grass can be planted at the back of the herbaceous border but looks better grown in a group or by itself in a prominent spot such as a circular bed on the lawn. It can be increased by division in spring but clumps should not be pulled apart too severely or they may be very slow in recovering. Allow the leaves to remain all winter on established plants as they serve as a protection to the crowns, but remove withered leaves in the spring.

Papaver (Poppy). A great many poppies are annuals and are dealt with in Chapter 7 but there are in addition perennial kinds of which the oriental poppy, *Papaver orientale*, is the most important. This is a bold plant with large scarlet and black blooms on 76 cm (2½ ft) stems in early summer. Its one fault is that it is apt to sprawl about, particularly after flowering when it gets rather untidy. There are numerous named varieties, some scarlet and black like the type but more vivid in colour or larger in bloom, others crimson, pink or white. All grow freely in any ordinary soil and full sun. They will also grow in places too dry and hot for many other perennials. Plant in spring and propagate either by seed sown out of doors in late spring or by root cuttings taken in winter. Named varieties do not come true from seed so root cuttings must be used.

Paradisea. See **Anthericum** (p. 117).

Penstemon. The majority of penstemons are partially tender plants mainly used for summer bedding but several are hardy enough to be grown out of doors throughout the year, some in the rock garden and others in the herbaceous border. Of the last group the best are *Penstemon barbatus*, once called *Chelone barbata*, *P. heterophyllus* and *P. isophyllus*. The first is 90 cm (3 ft) high, with slender spikes of tubular scarlet flowers from mid-summer to early autumn. *P. heterophyllus* is more branching, usually about 38 cm (15 in) high with amethyst or sky-blue flowers all the summer. *P. isophyllus* is erect, 90 cm (3 ft) high and has scarlet tubular flowers with white throats all summer. The range of shades and colours is now quite large, from white (Snowstorm) to purple (*P. glaber*).

All kinds delight in loamy soils, good drainage and plenty of sunshine. Plant in spring and propagate by cuttings of non-flowering shoots taken at practically any time they can be obtained. These cuttings should be rooted in sandy soil under protection.

Phlox. In addition to the true herbaceous phlox discussed here there are many rock garden species to be found in Chapter 9. The most important of the herbaceous kinds is *Phlox paniculata* which flowers from mid-summer to early autumn and has given rise to many varieties. Typically this is a plant 90 cm (3 ft) high, but there are shorter and taller forms. All have big trusses of very fragrant blooms. Colours range from white, through pale pink and soft lavender to scarlet, crimson and purple.

Phloxes grow best in rather rich, loamy soils with plenty of moisture during the growing season. They will succeed in either full sun or partial shade. They can be planted in spring or autumn and increased by division at either season or by root cuttings in winter. The latter are particularly recommended when plants become infested with eelworms, minute pests which cause the foliage to become distorted or even, in severe cases, thread-like, eventually shrivelling as if parched.

Phormium (New Zealand Flax). *Phormium tenax* is a large plant with stiff, sword-like leaves as high or higher than a man and forming a clump which can easily be 2·1 m (7 ft) wide. From this several stout stems spear up in summer to a height of 3·3 m (11 ft), branching towards the top to carry maroon and yellow flowers which are unusual rather than beautiful. It is the tropical luxuriance of the plant which makes it so valuable in the right place. This should be sheltered and warm, in soil well drained but rich, so that the plant develops its full proportions. Plant in spring. Division is possible but it is better to rely on seedlings which can be raised in a frame or greenhouse; all activities occur in spring. There are also varieties, known respectively as *atropurpurea* and Variegatum, with reddish-bronze and cream striped leaves. Others, possibly less hardy, are Bronze Baby, reddish bronze, 60 cm (2 ft) high; Dazzler, reddish bronze striped with brighter red; and Sundowner, purple, cream and pink. *P. cookianum*, has broader, less stiff leaves which are bright green in the wild type but cream banded in Cream Delight and deep purple in Dark Delight.

Phygelius (Cape Figwort). These are handsome plants for very sunny, warm positions in well-drained soil. *Phygelius capensis* makes numerous stems 76 cm (2½ ft) high, branching out to carry many tubular, scarlet flowers, curved and downward hanging in a rather curious fashion. Trained against a sunny wall it will grow considerably taller and can be treated as a climber. It is continuously in flower from mid-summer to mid-autumn and is a plant that never fails to attract attention. It is surprising that it is not more widely grown as it is not difficult in the right situation. *P. aequalis*, with salmon-pink flowers on 60 cm (2 ft) stems from early summer to mid-autumn is less striking but also worth planting for its long season and unusual appearance. It has an excellent yellow flowered variety named Yellow Trumpet. Plant both in spring and increase by division at the same season.

Physalis (Cape Gooseberry). Cape gooseberries are more useful as plants for cutting than for the herbaceous border as they are untidy in growth and not very attractive until the autumn when their seed vessels develop into the blown-out, brightly coloured lanterns which are so familiar as Christmas decorations. The cultivated species is *Physalis alkekengi*. There is also a variety with particularly large lanterns which is usually sold as *P. franchetii grandiflora*. The true Cape Gooseberry, *P. peruviana*, is a tender plant grown for its edible fruits. *P. alkekengi* should be grown in ordinary soil and a sunny, sheltered position. It can be planted in spring and divided at that season. It is a good plan to stick some bushy twigs around the plants in late spring as support for their rather weak stems. When planting spread out the thick roots and cover them with 5 cm (2 in) of good soil.

Physostegia (Dragon's Head or Obedient Plant). The physostegias got their name of obedient plant because the tubular, pink flowers which are carried in a narrow spike appear to be jointed at the stalk and will stay in whatever position they are set. *Physostegia virginiana* is a rather tall, straggling plant with flower spikes diminished in effectiveness by its leafiness but there are shorter, more compact varieties such as *alba*, white, *nana*, pink, and Vivid, rosy red, which are 45 cm (1½ ft) high and excellent border plants, flowering in the first half of autumn. Summer Snow is a pure white variety 1 m (3½ ft) high.

Phytolacca (Pokeweed, Pokeberry). These are rather coarse plants grown for their close spikes of white or purplish flowers followed by deep purple berries. *Phytolacca americana* is the kind usually grown, a plant 1·2-1·8 m (4-6 ft) high thriving in any ordinary soil and sunny position and readily raised from seed or by division in spring, which is also the best planting season. It often spreads by self-sown seedlings.

Platycodon (Balloon Flower). These are very attractive plants which deserve to be better known. They suggest campanulas and are in fact sometimes included with them. *Platycodon grandiflorum* is about 60 cm (2 ft) high, with wide bell-shaped flowers, deep blue in the type and white in the form *album*. There is also a variety named *P. mariesii* which is dwarfer, more compact and has deeper blue flowers, a white-flowered variety named *P. m. albus* and a lilac-pink named *P. m. rosens*. The flower buds of all these are particularly striking as they are inflated like small balloons or Chinese lanterns. The plant thrives in well-drained soils and sunny positions, should be planted in spring and blooms in high summer. It can be increased by careful division in spring or, better, by seed sown in a frame or greenhouse in early spring.

Podophyllum. It is only occasionally that one meets a podophyllum outside the gardens of collectors yet these are attractive, unusual and useful plants which, far from being difficult to grow, will thrive in shady places where many other plants would fail. They like soils with plenty of peat or leafmould and moisture without actually approaching the conditions of the bog garden. The best is *Podophyllum emodi*, about 38 cm (1¼ ft) high with broad, lobed leaves, white but not very showy flowers followed by extremely striking scarlet fruits almost as big as tomatoes. Plant in spring and divide when necessary at planting time.

Polemonium (Jacob's Ladder). These plants are pretty in a quiet way and have the merit of thriving in any soil in sun or partial shade. They make compact tufts of fern-like foliage from which arise erect 60 cm (2 ft) stems carrying spikes of blue or white flowers from late spring to early summer. The best known is *Polemonium caeruleum* but a better plant is *P. foliosissimum* with lavender-blue flowers and an even longer flowering season. All can be planted in spring or autumn and divided at either season, or raised from seed. They may be short-lived but often renew themselves by self-sown seedlings.

Polygonatum (Solomon's Seal). These well-known plants are ideal for positions too shady for most perennials. They will even thrive in quite close woodland and few are particular as regards soil. The plant grown in gardens as *Polygonatum multiflorum* is really a hybrid between that species and another named *P. odoratum* and should be called *P. × hybridum*. It makes 90 cm (3 ft) arching stems with leaves suggesting those of the lily of the valley and pendant, creamy-white, tubular flowers in late spring/early summer. Plant this and other kinds in spring or autumn and leave alone for as long as possible as they improve with time. Propagation is readily effected by division at planting time.

Polygonum (Knotweed). This is one of those unfortunate families which contain more weeds than useful garden plants, so the amateur is apt to be discouraged by trying the wrong species before finding the really useful ones. However, the rarely sold *Polygonum campanulatum* is an attractive plant 90 cm (3 ft) high with deeply veined leaves, reddish stems and masses of tiny, pale pink or white flowers which continue from late summer to mid-autumn. It spreads rapidly in moist soil but chiefly on the surface so that it can be dug up quite easily if it goes too far. *P. amplexicaule* has little spikes of ruby-red flowers held aloft on 1 m (3½ ft) stems from mid-summer to mid-autumn. *P. bistorta* is a little shorter and variable in colour but the variety known as *P. superbum* is a good deep pink. *P. affine* and *P. vaccinifolium* are trailing or creeping plants more suitable for the rock garden or dry wall than for herbaceous borders. Plant all these in spring or autumn and propagate by division at planting time. For the plant sometimes called *P. virginianum* see Tovara (p. 165).

Potentilla (Cinquefoil). This is another family which contains an unfortunately high percentage of weeds but also includes some good garden material. There are many hybrids of *Potentilla atrosanguinea* and *P. argyrophylla*, mostly with double or semi-double flowers in various shades of scarlet, crimson and yellow. One form which almost all nurseries offer is Gibson's Scarlet, a good plant almost prostrate in habit and with the most vivid single scarlet flowers imaginable. Most of the hybrid potentillas are taller than this, often 60 cm (2 ft) high and rather straggling. All should be grown in full sun and will succeed in any soil, even those too dry for most perennials. Plant in spring or autumn and divide then if necessary.

143

Primula. See p. 203.

Pulmonaria (Lungwort). These have two outstanding merits – they flower very early in the year and will succeed in shady places. They are low-growing plants, seldom exceeding 30 cm (1 ft) in height and therefore suitable for the front row of the border or as ground cover. Some are, perhaps, a little too leafy for the rather small flowers, carried in clusters on short stems in the first half of spring. One of the best kinds is *Pulmonaria angustifolia*, sometimes known as the blue cowslip though it really has very little resemblance to a cowslip. There are several varieties differing mainly in the colour of their flowers, *P. azurea* and Munstead Blue being a really rich bright blue. *P. saccharata* is a coarser growing plant notable for the large white spots on its leaves covering almost the whole leaf in *P. argentea*. The flowers are purplish pink becoming blue. None of these is in the least particular as to soil. Plant in spring immediately after flowering or in early autumn, and increase by division in spring or autumn.

Pyrethrum. A certain degree of confusion reigns over the name. The plant has been listed as a chrysanthemum, though it is now botanically called tanacetum. However, since it is popularly called pyrethrum, it is dealt with here. The flowers are showy and particularly serviceable for cutting on account of their long, stiff stems and the way in which they last in water. All make pleasant-looking clumps of fine, ferny foliage and have showy, daisy flowers in late spring/early summer. There are fully double forms which rather resemble small, double chrysanthemums, and also single and semi-double or anemone-centred varieties in shades varying from white and palest pink to deep crimson. All transplant rather badly in autumn except on the lightest and best-drained soils. They are best moved either in spring or in summer as soon as possible after flowering, but if the latter season is chosen they must be well watered for the first few weeks. They can be divided either in spring or summer and succeed best in rather light, loamy soils and sunny positions. Where drainage is bad they can often be grown well by raising the beds a little above round level or planting along the summit of ridges and on shallow mounds.

Ranunculus (Buttercup). The buttercup family has not only given us beautiful, if infuriating, weeds but has also provided our gardens with delightful and innocuous plants, notably the Turban and French ranunculus which are described in Chapter 12. Here I want to call attention to some beautiful perennials for the herbaceous border. *Ranunculus aconitifolius* and its double-flowered variety Flore Pleno, often known by the pleasant name fair maids of France, and also white bachelor's buttons. Both are freely branched plants 60 cm (2 ft) in height with white flowers freely produced in late spring/early summer, the first with single flowers, the second with each bloom converted into a perfect globe of petals. There are also two handsome double-flowered varieties of common wild buttercup which produce no seed and so do not become a nuisance. *R. acris* Flore Pleno grows 45 cm (1½ ft) high and is a variety of the meadow buttercup and *R. bulbosus pleniflorus*, sometimes called *R. speciosus plenus*, is shorter and has larger flowers, particularly as they start to open in spring. All these buttercups thrive in damp, loamy soils but can be grown in almost any soil that does not dry out too quickly in summer. They flower in early summer and the plants are readily increased by division in the spring.

Achillea filipendula Gold Plate

Acanthus mollis Latifolius

Achillea millefolium
Cerise Queen

***Acanthus mollis* Latifolius** (Bear's Breeches), is architectural in flower and foliage. Its roots can be divided in autumn or early spring ✤ ❀ Summer ☼ ◑ ▨ ■

***Achillea filipendulina* Gold Plate**, a bold 1.2 m (4 ft) Yarrow, looks striking in a border or can be cut and dried for winter decoration ✤ ❀ Summer ☼ ▨ ■

***Achillea millefolium* Cerise Queen** is a choice 45 cm (1½ ft) tall form of our native Yarrow or Milfoil ✤ ❀ Summer ☼ ◑ ▨ ■

Aconitum napellus

Anaphalis cinnamomea

Alchemilla mollis

Agapanthus Headbourne hybrid

Aconitum napellus (Monkshood), is a valuable but poisonous 90 cm (3 ft) perennial growing from fleshy tuberous roots
⊕ ❀ Summer ☼ ◔ ● 🗹 ▮▯

Agapanthus **Headbourne hybrids,**
76 cm-1 m (2½-3 ft), are hardy forms of the blue lily of South Africa. A fine tub or border plant ⊕ ❀ Summer ☼ 🗹 ▮▯

Alchemilla mollis (Lady's Mantle), 30 cm (1 ft), is valued for its mustard-yellow flowers and shapely grey-green leaves
⊕ ❀ Summer ☼ ◔ 🗹 ▮▯

Anaphalis cinnamomea (Pearly Everlasting), has silver foliage surmounted by flowers which can be dried for winter decoration
⊕ ❀ Summer ☼ 🗹 ▮▯

Aquilegia McKana hybrids

Anemone x hybrida
Honorine Jobert

Anemone x hybrida
Bressingham Glow

Artemisia arborescens

Anemone x hybrida Honorine Jobert 1.2 m (4 ft) and **Bressingham Glow**, 90 cm (3 ft), are choice varieties of the Japanese anemone, which spreads by its fibrous roots. These can be divided to make new plants
⊕ ❀ Late summer ☼ ◐ 🌣 ❚ (Glow ⬆)

***Aquilegia* McKana hybrids**, 76 cm (2½ ft), are superior long-spurred columbines in an attractive range of colours, best raised from a good strain of seeds ⊕ ❀ Summer ☼ ◐ 🌣 ❚

Artemisia arborescens makes a handsome 60 cm (2 ft) shrubby silver foliage plant which can be raised from stem cuttings taken with a heel in late summer
⊕ ⬇ ❀ Summer ☼ ◐ ◼ 🌣 ❚

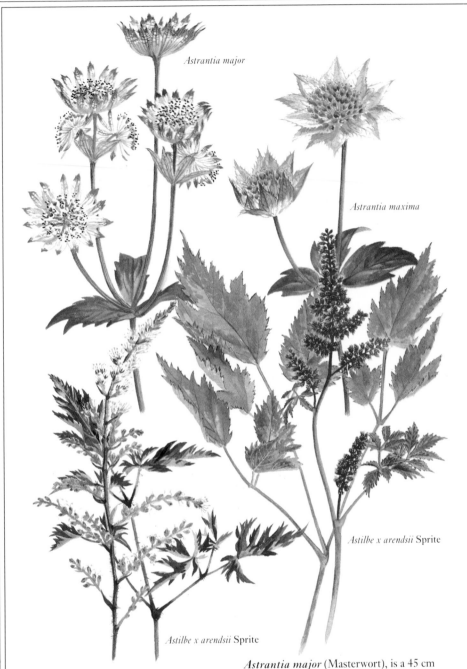

Astrantia major

Astrantia maxima

Astilbe x arendsii Sprite

Astilbe x arendsii Sprite

Astilbe x arendsii Fanal, 60 cm (2 ft) tall, is the darkest red of the many hybrids of this moist-soil loving plant, which include soft pinks, white, peach and pale lilac ⊕ ❈ Summer ☼ ◐ ▭ ♥ ▮

Astilbe x arendsii Sprite belongs to the same range of hybrids, but is a 25 cm (10 in) dwarf ⊕ ❈ Summer ☼ ◐ ▭ ♥ ▮

Astrantia major (Masterwort), is a 45 cm (1½ ft) tall European wild flower, known in gardens as Hatty's Pincushion. Its handsome lobed leaves are surmounted by quaintly constructed flowers ⊕ ❈ Summer ◑ ● ▭ ♥ ▮

Astrantia maxima, a cousin of the last plant, is of similar fascinating shape but its flowers are a little more colourful ⊕ ❈ Summer ◑ ● ⬢ ♥ ▮

Campanula glomerata Alba

Campanula persicifolia

Centaurea dealbata steenbergii

Catananche caerulea

Campanula glomerata Alba, 45 cm (18 in), opens bold upward-facing bells, purple in another form ⊕ ❀ Summer ◐ ▦ ◨

Campanula persicifolia (Peach-leaved Bellflower), 90 cm (3 ft), in blue and white forms is easy to increase by division ⊕ ❀ Summer ● ◐ ▦ ◨

Catananche caerulea (Cupid's Dart), 60 cm (2 ft), is useful in the border and as a cut flower. Easy from seed or by division ⊕ ❀ Summer ◯ ◐

Centaurea dealbata steenbergii, 76 cm (2½ ft), is an aristocratic cornflower for mid-border and a fine cut flower ⊕ ❀ Summer ◯ ▦ ◨

Dicentra spectabilis

Dianthus Mrs Sinkins

Echinops ritro

Doronicum Miss Mason

Dianthus Mrs Sinkins, 25 cm (10 in), best known of the old-fashioned pinks, bears richly scented double blooms ▲ ✤ Summer ☀ ▨ ▮

Dicentra spectabilis (Bleeding Heart or Dutchman's Breeches), 60 cm (2 ft), forms dainty leaves and arching stems with heart-shaped flowers ⊕ ⬇ ✤ Spring ☀ ▨ ▮

Doronicum Miss Mason (Leopard's Bane), 45 cm (18 in), opens its cheerful daisy blooms early in spring ⊕ ✤ Spring ☀ ● ▨ ▮

Echinops ritro (Globe Thistle), 90 cm (3 ft), with its tall-stemmed flowers is valuable for mid-border ⊕ ✤ Summer ☀ ▨ ▮

Euphorbia characias, 1.2 m (4 ft), is one of many herbaceous spurges, whose clustered 'flowers' each consist of a central female bloom with a ring of males, all encircled by coloured bracts △ ❀ Spring ☼ ⬒ ⛉ ◧

***Euphorbia griffithii* Fireglow**, 60 cm (2 ft), makes spreading clumps with heads of deep orange-red bracts ⌽ ❀ Summer ☼ ⬒ ⛉ ◧

Euphorbia myrsinites forms long trailing stems with glaucous leaves and yellowish bracts. Fine for a bank
⌽ ❀ Summer ☼ ⬒ ⛉ ◧

Euphorbia robbiae, 60 cm (2 ft), another spurge, spreads by underground stems to form useful ground cover △ ❀ Summer ☼ ● ⛉ ◧

Filipendula ulmaria Aurea

Gaillardia x grandiflora

Gentiana asclepiadea

Geranium wallichianum Buxton's Variety

Filipendula ulmaria Aurea, the golden-leaved form of Meadowsweet, 90 cm (3 ft), makes a pleasant foliage plant. The insignificant flowers are best cut off
✿ ❀ Summer ☼ ◐ ▭ ◧

Gaillardia x grandiflora (Blanket Flower), opens brilliantly coloured daises on 76 cm (2½ ft) stems. These are popular as cut flowers as well as garden blooms
✿ ❀ Summer ☼ ▭ ▧ ◧

Gentiana asclepiadea (Willow Gentian), 15-76 cm (6 in-2 ft), forms erect arching stems bearing bell-shaped flowers. Raise from seeds, spring cuttings or divisions
✿ ☘ ❀ Summer ☼ ▧ ◧

Geranium wallichianum Buxton's Variety forms effective ground cover with shapely lobed leaves and distinctive flowers. It can only be propagated by division
✿ ❀ Summer/Autumn ☼ ◐ ▧ ◧

Helleborus niger

Helleborus corsicus

Helleborus foetidus

Heliopsis scabra

Helianthus Loddon Gold

Helianthus Loddon Gold, a 1.5 m (5 ft) perennial sunflower, can form a cheerful clump in the border and is a fine cut flower ✤ ❀ Summer ☼ ▥ ▤

Heliopsis scabra opens many large yellow daisy flowers on 1.2 m (4 ft) stems, useful in a border and as cut flowers ✤ ❀ Summer ☼ ◑ ▥ ▤

Helleborus corsicus, 45 cm (1½ ft), is decorative alike for its shapely spiny-edged leaves and clusters of greenish flowers △ ❀ Spring ◑ ● ▥ ▤

Helleborus foetidus (Stinking Hellebore), is 60 cm (2 ft) high with purple and green flowers △ ❀ Early spring ◑ ● ▥ ▤

Helleborus niger, the much-loved Christmas Rose, 38 cm (1¼ ft) high, usually opens its blooms a week or two after Christmas ✤ ❀ Winter ◑ ▥ ▤

Hosta fortunei
Albopicta

Hosta sieboldiana
elegans

Hosta lancifolia

Hosta fortunei Albopicta, 60 cm (2 ft), a variegated Plantain Lily, is bright yellow and green in spring, duller later. Fine by the waterside ✤ ❊ Summer ☼ ◐ ▣ ▨ ◧

Hosta lancifolia, 60 cm (2 ft), a daintier Plantain Lily with narrower leaves, opens deep lilac bells in late summer
✤ ❊ Summer ☼ ◐ ▣ ▨ ◧

Hosta sieboldiana elegans (Plantain Lily), 60 cm (2 ft), forms deeply veined glaucous leaves, lovely from spring to autumn. Mauve and white bells open in mid-summer. Hostas like moist soil, but stand drought. Slugs are their chief enemy
✤ ❊ Summer ◐ ● ▣ ▨ ◧

Kniphofia
Maid of Orleans

Liatris spicata Kobold

Kniphofia
Torchlight

Kniphofia **Torchlight**, 1 m (3½ ft), and **Maid of Orleans**, 90 cm (3 ft), (Red Hot Pokers). Though South African they are surprisingly hardy provided the soil is well drained. They can make the most striking clumps in a border. Their roots can be divided in spring to make more plants ⊕ ⚇ ✿ Summer ☼ ▨ ▮

Liatris spicata **Kobold** (Kansas Gay Feather or Blazing Star), 60 cm (2 ft), grows from tuberous roots and forms unusual spikes of flowers in high summer that open from the top downwards ⊕ ✿ Summer ☼ ▨ ▮

Paeonia officinalis Rosea Plena

Monarda didyma Prairie Dawn

Oenothera missouriensis

Monarda didyma **Prairie Dawn** (Oswego
Tea or Bergamot), 76 cm (2½ ft), is striking in
large groups. Scarlet, pink and white forms
too ✥ ❀ Summer ☼ ◑ ▬ ▨ ◧

Oenothera missouriensis, 15 cm (6 in) high
but spreading to 60 cm (2 ft), is a sprawling
plant for the front of the border. Opens its
flowers in the evening
✥ ❀ Summer ☼ ◑ ▨ ◧

Paeonia officinalis **Rosea Plena**, 60 cm
(2 ft), the familiar cottage garden paeony, is
magnificent in bloom though its season is
short. There is a rich scarlet form too. Its
tuberous roots can be divided
✥ ❀ Spring ☼ ◑ ▨ ◧

Phlox paniculata Border Gem

Paeonia lactiflora
Sarah Bernhardt

Papaver orientale Mrs Perry

Paeonia lactiflora **Sarah Bernhardt**, 60 cm
(2 ft), opens fine double blooms above shapely
foliage, though its season of beauty is brief
⊕ ✿ Spring ☼ ◐ ▨ ▮

Papaver orientale **Mrs Perry** (Oriental
Poppy), 90 cm (3 ft), opens magnificent double
poppies in early summer. Mask its untidy dying
foliage in summer by planting later developing
plants in front of it.
⊕ ✿ Spring/Summer ☼ ◐ ▨ ▮

Phlox paniculata **Border Gem**, 90 cm (3 ft),
is one of many choice varieties of this high
summer favourite which favours a cool, moist
spot ⊕ ✿ Summer ☼ ◐ ▨ ▮

Polemonium caeruleum

Polygonatum x hybridum

Polygonum bistorta Superbum

Potentilla William Rollison

Polemonium caeruleum (Jacob's Ladder), 60 cm (2 ft), is clothed in fine leaves topped by soft blue flowers ⊕ ✿ Summer ✿ ▦ ▢

Polygonatum x hybridum (Solomon's Seal), 1 m (3½ ft), is a delightful shade–lover that forms long arching stems from which its bell–like flowers hang ⊕ ✿ Summer ✿ ● ▦ ▢

***Polygonum bistorta* Superbum** (Bistort), 90 cm (3 ft), likes damp soil and a position by water, forming attractive spikes of pink flowers ⊕ ✿ Summer ✿ ✿ ▦ ▢

***Potentilla* William Rollison**, 38 cm (15 in), is a choice Cinquefoil of unusual colouring ⊕ ✿ Summer ✿ ✿ ▦ ▢

Sedum telephium

Sedum spectabile

Solidago Goldenmosa

Sedum Autumn Joy

Sedum Autumn Joy, 45 cm (1½ ft), is similar to *S. spectabile* but with deeper-coloured flowers decorative even when brown ✦ ❀ Autumn ☼ ◐ ▨ ■□

Sedum spectabile (Ice Plant), 45 cm (1½ ft), has fleshy grey-green leaves and bright pink flowers much loved by bees and butterflies ✦ ❀ Autumn ☼ ◐ ▨ ■□

Sedum telephium (Orpine or Live For Ever), 45 cm (1½ ft), is a more slender plant but resembles the other sedums ✦ ❀ Autumn ☼ ◐ ▨ ■□

Solidago Goldenmosa, 76 cm (2½ ft), is a choice variety of Golden Rod that blooms in late summer ✦ ❀ Summer ☼ ◐ ▨ ■□

Trillium grandiflorum

Thalictrum delavayi
Hewitt's Double

Verbascum phoeniceum

Tradescantia x andersoniana Osprey

Thalictrum delavayi Hewitt's Double
(Meadow Rue), 90 cm (3 ft), has pleasant
aquilegia-like foliage and feathery flowers
✤ ❋ Summer ☼ ❂ ▽ ◼ ◻

Tradescantia x andersoniana Osprey
(Spiderwort), 45 cm (1½ ft), opens short-lived
three-petalled flowers for several weeks. Also
blue and magenta varieties
✤ ❋ Summer ❂ ▬ ◼ ◻

Trillium grandiflorum (Wake Robin), 45 cm
(1½ ft), is a woodland plant with leaves and
petals in threes
✤ ⤒ ⬇ ❋ Spring ☼ ❂ ▽ ◼ ◼ ◻

Verbascum phoeniceum (Purple Mullein),
1.5 m (5 ft), forms a slender spike of flowers. A
group could form a strong focal point in a
border ✤ ❋ Summer ☼ ❂ ▽ ◼ ◻

Red-hot Poker. See **Kniphofia** (p. 134).

Rheum (Rhubarb). The common rhubarb is, of course, a plant for the vegetable plot alone but it has close relatives with foliage and flowers of such beauty that they are welcome inhabitants of the ornamental garden where they may be planted in big beds and borders, by the waterside and in thin woodland. Typical of these is *Rheum palmatum* with immense, deeply divided leaves which are red at first but become greener on top with age and red flowers on 1·6 m (5½ ft) stems. Specially good varieties are named *R. p. rubrum* and *R. p.* Bowles Crimson. All will grow readily in any fairly rich soil and can be increased by careful division in spring.

Rodgersia. This is another family of plants grown quite as much for beauty of foliage as of flower. All are happy in damp soils though most kinds can also be grown successfully in ordinary soil. *Rodgersia pinnata* is the species most often planted. It has compound leaves a little like those of a horse chestnut in shape and deep green in colour. The flower stems are close on 90 cm (3 ft) high, terminating in dense plumes of small creamy pink flowers strongly resembling those of an astilbe. There is a variety with even deeper coloured flowers and bronze leaves named *R. p.* Superba. *R. aesculifolia, R. podophylla* and *Astilboldes tabularis* (once called *R. tabularis*) have white flowers and the leaves of the last named are rounded and in one piece. All bloom about mid-summer and like best a cool, partly shaded position. Plant in spring and increase by division at the same time of year.

Romneya (Californian Tree Poppy). These plants are as likely to be found in shrub catalogues as those devoted to herbaceous plants since they make woody stems. However, in cold climates most of these are usually killed to ground level each winter and the plant grows again from the roots in spring like a herbaceous perennial. Two plants are cultivated but they are so much alike in all but botanical details that the gardener will probably regard them as identical. One is *Romneya coulteri* and the other *R. c. trichocalyx*. Both are extremely beautiful and not difficult to grow once established but they hate root disturbance. They have enormous, pure white, poppy-like flowers, each with a big boss of golden anthers in the centre, and they are carried from mid-summer to early autumn on 1·8-2·4 m (6-8 ft) stems clothed with grey-green foliage. Romneyas thrive in sunny, warm positions and poorish soils; in fact I have seen them doing well in a gravel path. Propagation is best effected by root cuttings taken in winter and inserted singly in small pots, or plants can be raised from seed. The young plants are then potted on carefully until they reach 10 cm (4 in) pots, from which they are transferred to their permanent flowering positions in spring with the minimum of root disturbance. Dead or damaged growth should be cut out each spring.

Rudbeckia (Coneflower). These are easily grown plants of the daisy family, mostly tall, back-row subjects, though one excellent species, *Rudbeckia fulgida*, varies from 30-90 cm (1-3 ft) high and can be used as a front-line plant. Different varieties of this plant have at various times been given botanical names which can be confusing. However, all have showy yellow or orange-yellow flowers with a neat, nearly black central disc and all flower from early summer to mid-autumn. *R. laciniata* and *R. nitida* are much taller and they, too, have produced numerous varieties some of which have double flowers. Good examples are Golden Glow, 2·1 m (7 ft) high with fully double, golden-yellow flowers in great profusion, and Herbstsonne, 1·8 m (6 ft) high with clear yellow single flowers each with an upstanding pale green cone, both flowering in late summer/early autumn. All will grow in any ordinary soil and sunny position. They can be planted and divided in spring or autumn. For a specially warm and sunny place *R. maxima* is a handsome species with grey-green leaves and large yellow flowers, each with a tall black cone in the centre. It is 1·2 m (4 ft) high. For the plant which is sometimes known as *R. purpurea* see Echinacea p. 127.

Salvia (Sage). A good many of the sages are half-hardy plants useful for bedding out or growing in the greenhouse and one is, of course, the familiar herb. But there are also a few good kinds for the herbaceous border, notably *Salvia nemorosa superba*, a grand plant, 45-90 cm (1½-3 ft) high with masses of erect stems clothed for fully half their length with small Oxford-blue flowers set off by purple bracts. *S. uliginosa* is twice as high and considerably more open in habit with rather small spikes of sky-blue flowers. *S. patens*, which is about as true a blue as anything in the garden, unfortunately requires winter protection in most districts. It makes tubers not unlike those of a dahlia which can be lifted and stored dry in a cupboard over winter or be left undisturbed in mild districts and well-drained soils. It is in flower throughout the summer whereas the other two are for late summer/early autumn only. *S. haematodes* has slender 90 cm (3 ft) spikes of lavender-blue flowers in mid-summer and *S. sclarea turkestanica*, the clary, is a handsome plant with hairy leaves and stout 1·2 m (4 ft) spikes of pink and blue flowers in late summer, but the latter is a biennial which dies after flowering and *S. haematodes* often does the same. *S. argentea* which is white woolly all over and has white flowers in summer on 90 cm (3 ft) stems needs a sunny place and well-drained soil.

All the other salvias will grow in any ordinary soil and sunny position. They are best planted in spring and the truly perennial kinds can be increased by division then, the rest from seed.

Sanguisorba. Once commonly known as poterium (burnet), these dainty plants make low mounds of compound leaves from which ascend, in late summer/early autumn, slender stems terminated by bottle-brush spikes of feathery flowers. These are white in *Sanguisorba canadensis* and soft pink in *S. obtusa*. Both kinds are readily grown in a sunny place and in ordinary soil. Plant in spring or autumn and increase by division in spring.

Saponaria (Soapwort). Species of saponaria will be found in both Chapters 7 and 9. Here I want to call attention to *Saponaria officinalis*, the common perennial soapwort or bouncing bet, in its two double-flowered forms, one pink and the other white. Both have heads of quite big and showy, fully double flowers on 45 cm (1½ ft) stems in late summer/early autumn and though a little coarse are worth planting in the rougher parts of the garden. They have no special requirements regarding soil or position and can be readily raised from seed as from division.

Scabiosa (Scabious). The so-called yellow perennial scabious is described under Cephalaria, but the most important of the hardy perennial species for the garden is *Scabiosa caucasica*. The wild type has pale blue flowers but white and deeper blue or purple varieties are also available. All bloom from mid-summer until mid-autumn and average 90 cm (3 ft) in height. They do not make a very great display at any one time and are, in consequence, more useful for cutting than for border display. They like a well-drained limy or chalky soil and a sunny position. They should be planted or divided in spring or, better still, can be propagated by cuttings of young growths severed close to the crown in mid-spring and rooted in sandy soil in a frame. Seed germinates fairly easily in a pan of well-drained soil in the first half of spring but seedlings may differ from their parents. One of the best blue varieties is Clive Greaves. There is also a good variety of *S. columbaria* named Butterfly Blue, 45 cm (1½ ft) high with lavender blue flowers produced all summer.

Schizostylis (Kaffir Lily). Only one species is grown, *Schizostylis coccinea*, and this is invaluable because it flowers in the second half of summer when practically everything else in the border is over. Typically it has spikes of scarlet flowers not unlike miniature gladioli but there are also pink varieties such as Viscountess Byng and Sunrise. Yet another variety, Major, has scarlet flowers of greater size. *S. c. alba* is the rare, pure white form. All are a little tender, needing a warm, sunny position and well-drained, but not dry soil. Plant in spring and increase by division at that season. Plants spread by underground runners.

Scrophularia (Figwort). One kind, *Scrophularia aquatica* Variegata, is cultivated for its foliage, the leaves being broadly edged with cream. It grows 90 cm (3 ft) high, likes a fairly rich, rather moist soil. Increase by cuttings or division in the spring.

Sedum (Stonecrop). Many of the stonecrops are creeping or tufted plants most suitable for rock gardens and walls but some are good border perennials. *Sedum spectabile* has fleshy greyish-green leaves, variegated with cream in one variety, and flat heads of pink flowers on 45 cm (1½ ft) stems in late summer/early autumn. *S. telephium maximum* Atropurpureum is 76 cm (2½ ft) high with fleshy beetroot-purple leaves. *S. telephium* is rather like *S. spectabile* but the flower heads are a dull purplish red and there is also a fine hybrid named Autumn Joy with extra large, reddish-pink flower heads which change to russet red and last until late autumn. All like sunny places and well-drained soils, may be planted in spring or autumn and divided at either season.

Senecio. See **Ligularia** (p. 135).

Sidalcea. These are plants which have been greatly improved by breeders. The species tend to be rather weedy in habit and lacking in variety of colour, but garden forms now have a wide range from white and palest pink to rosy crimson and make compact plants, throwing up slender spikes of bloom 90 cm-1·5 cm (3-5 ft) in height. All flower through the second half of summer and do well in all soils, particularly those that are well drained. They like sun, should be planted in spring and may be divided at the same season, or can be readily raised from seed, though seedlings may differ from their parents.

Sisyrinchium. Most kinds are small plants more suitable for the rock garden than for the herbaceous border (see p. 228) but *Sisyrinchium striatum* is a bold plant with narrow upstanding leaves rather like those of an iris and stiff 60 cm (2 ft) spikes of straw-yellow flowers in early summer. It has a handsome variety with white-striped leaves named *S. s. variegatum* also known as *S. s.* Aunt May. It will grow in any soil in sun or half shade and can be increased by division in spring or autumn.

Smilacina. *Smilacina racemosa* is a good hardy plant for a shady place. It has bright green, shiny leaves, plumed, creamy-white flowers and a general appearance of elegance. It grows 76 cm (2½ ft) high, likes cool soils as well as cool spots and is happiest in a moist, rather rich soil – in fact it can be planted in the bog garden as long as it is safe from inundation during wet seasons. As it creeps about underground in a moderate manner it is especially easy to increase by division, which should be done in spring, which is also the best planting season.

Solidago (Golden Rod). In addition to the common golden rod, *Solidago canadensis,* with its large sprays of golden-yellow flowers on 90 cm-1·5 cm (3-5 ft) stems in late summer/early autumn, there are now quite a number of named forms, some comparatively dwarf and compact in habit, others even bigger and more impressive than the type. All have the merit of thriving everywhere, even in soils too poor for many plants, and flower equally well in sun or partial shade. Planting and division can be carried out in either spring or autumn; these plants repay frequent lifting and division.

Solidaster. × *Solidaster luteus,* once known as *Aster hybridus luteus,* is really a hybrid between a perennial aster and a solidago. It makes a bushy plant 76 cm (2½ ft) high covered in late summer/early autumn with small canary-yellow flowers. It likes a reasonably open space, is not fussy about soil and can be planted and divided in spring or autumn.

Stachys. One kind, *Stachys lanata,* is frequently grown in gardens for its grey, densely woolly foliage. It is often known as lamb's ears and the leaves certainly are as soft and hairy as any animal's coat. The flowers are nothing to look at and it is solely for its foliage that the plant is grown. It will thrive anywhere, in rich or poor soil, sun or shade and can be planted and divided at practically any time of the year. The plant commonly known in gardens as *Betonica grandiflora* is also a stachys, its correct name being *Stachys macrantha.* It grows to 60 cm (2 ft) and has good solid spikes of hooded purple, pink or white flowers in the first half of summer. It is also easily grown in any reasonably open place and can be planted and divided in spring or autumn.

Statice. See **Limonium** (p. 136).

Stokesia. The only species grown, *Stokesia laevis,* looks very much like a small annual aster when in bloom and is useful because of its late season, the large, single lavender-blue daisy-like flowers being carried on 45 cm (18 in) stems from mid-summer to mid-autumn. There are also deeper blue and white varieties. All are easily grown in any ordinary soil and sunny place. Increase by division in spring, which is also the best season for planting.

Sweet William. See p. 103.

Thalictrum (Meadow Rue). Very graceful plants mostly with finely divided foliage not unlike maidenhair fern in some species. The majority are easy to grow in any ordinary soil and sunny half-shady position but the most beautiful of all, *Thalictrum dipterocarpum*, is a trifle more exacting. It needs a deep, fairly rich, well-drained but not dry soil and should be renewed quite frequently from seed. It grows 1·2-1·8 m (4-6 ft) high, is sparse and open in habit and has the daintiest imaginable violet-coloured flowers, each with a tassel of yellow stamens, hanging on thin, wiry stems in large, loose sprays. It is a plant deserving every care and attention and is unrivalled for cutting. There is also a form with fully double flowers named *T. delavayi* Hewitt's Double, which is equally desirable but cannot be raised from seed. Roots may be carefully divided in spring. Other good kinds are *T. aquilegifolium*, 90 cm (3 ft), with lilac flower heads in early summer; *T. flavum glaucum*, 1·2 m (4 ft), with milky green leaves and pale yellow flower heads in the second half of summer; and *T. minus adiantifolium*, 30 cm (1 ft) high with greenish-yellow flowers from early summer to early autumn. All these can be planted and divided in spring or autumn.

Thermopsis (Mock Lupin). With its abundant divided leaves and short spikes of yellow pea flowers it is difficult to persuade people that *Thermopsis montana* is not an inferior lupin, yet it is a pretty enough plant with the unspoiled grace of the wilding and a useful habit of thriving in dry, poor places once it gets established. It likes best light, sandy soils and sunny places. Old plants can be divided in spring but as they are rather slow to recover from a move it is better to rely on seed for propagation. This germinates readily out of doors in late spring/early summer.

Tiarella (Foam Flower). Foam flower is an appropriate name for *Tiarella cordifolia* for when it is in bloom little can be seen of it except low, foaming masses of tiny white flowers, the effect being very much that of a white London pride. The rounded leaves make neat, low clumps and are attractive for months after the spring flower display is over. The foam flower will thrive in most soils and prefers cool shady places. It can be planted and divided in early spring.

Tovara. The plant known as *Tovara virginiana variegata* is now listed as *Persicaria v. v.*, though at times it has been linked with polygonum. It is grown for its leaves which are broadly lance shaped and heavily variegated with cream and reddish brown on a green base. There appear to be several different forms of this plant, one of the most highly coloured being *P. v.* Painter's Palette. Tovara likes fairly rich rather moist soil and will thrive in sun or partial shade. It is best planted in spring and can be increased by division at that season.

Tradescantia (Spiderwort, Moses in the Bulrushes). The best hardy kinds suitable for the herbaceous border are hybrids of *Tradescantia virginiana* and other species, the hybrids collectively known as *T. × andersoniana* though in catalogues they are usually listed as *T. virginiana*. All are remarkable for the fact that each bloom consists of three petals only. The flowers, surrounded by spidery-looking green bracts, are produced a few at a time in constant succession from early summer to early autumn. The foliage is grassy and the whole plant 60 cm (2 ft) in height. There are several varieties differing mainly in the colour of their flowers which may be blue, rose, purple or white. All grow readily in ordinary soil, in sun or shade. Planting and division can be carried out equally well in spring or autumn.

Trollius (Globe Flower). Plants for damp places thriving in either sun or partial shade. The flowers resemble enormous, globular buttercups and appear in late spring with sometimes a second crop in mid-summer. There are numerous named varieties mainly derived from *Trollius europaeus*, a plant about 60 cm (2 ft) in height, but also from other species not commonly cultivated now. Other garden varieties have come from *T. ledebourii* which may reach 90 cm (3 ft) and has more widely open orange flowers produced a little later. A third species, *T. pumilus*, is only about 23 cm (9 in) high. The garden varieties differ mainly in the colour of their flowers which may be anything from palest yellow to orange. Plant in spring or autumn and increase by division, preferably in spring.

Tropaeolum (Nasturtium). The common nasturtiums are annuals which are dealt with in Chapter 7. The genus also includes some excellent perennials, several of them being half-hardy but a few are quite hardy. The loveliest of them is *Tropaeolum speciosum*, well named the flame flower. It is a vigorous climber with light green leaves and small nasturtium flowers in the brightest imaginable shade of scarlet. It likes a cool, moist atmosphere better than a hot, dry one. A good method of growing it is to plant its straggly roots in rich, leafy soil at the foot of an evergreen shrub, such as a holly, and allow it to ramble up into the branches above. It can be trained on walls with a northerly aspect or indeed anywhere except in a hot, dry place.

Very different is *T. polyphyllum*, a sprawling plant with blue-grey leaves and wreaths of yellow flowers in summer. This loves sun and warmth and its tuberous roots should be planted 14 cm (5½ in) deep in light, sandy loam, but it is extremely difficult to transplant. *T. tuberosum* also has tuberous roots but the flowers are red and yellow and come in late summer. *T. t.* Ken Aslet appear earlier.

The flame flower can be increased by spring division of its mat-forming roots, but seed sown in a frame or greenhouse in spring or cuttings in summer provide the only satisfactory method of propagating *T. polyphyllum* and *T. tuberosum*.

Uvularia (Bellwort). *Uvularia grandiflora* is a charming little plant for cool partly shaded places in humus-rich soil. It looks a little like a very small, 30 cm (1 ft) high Solomon's seal (polygonatum) with quite large dangling yellow flowers in spring. It can be increased by division in spring but really prefers to be left alone to spread slowly.

Veratrum (False Hellebore). These are plants with big, oval, glossy pleated leaves and tall, stiffly branched spikes of flowers which are greenish white in *Veratrum album*, an almost black maroon in *V. nigrum* and yellowish green in *V. viride*. The first two are 1·3 m (4½ ft) high, the last rather more, and all flower in the second half of summer. They like good rich soil and sunny places with plenty of moisture while they are growing in spring and summer, are best planted in spring and can be increased by division then or by seeds. Slugs and snails can damage their leaves severely and may need to be killed with slug bait.

Verbascum (Mullein). A good many of the mulleins are biennial plants which need to be renewed from seed every year and are described in Chapter 7. There are, however, true perennial forms as well, such as *Verbascum densiflorum*, 1·5 m (5 ft), yellow. *V. phoeniceum* is dwarfer, 76 cm (2½ ft), with flowers in shades of purple or violet. The Cotswold hybrids include Cotswold Beauty, biscuit coloured, Cotswold Queen, terra-cotta and Gainsborough, primrose, all are 1·2 m (4 ft); Pink Domino, rose and violet, 90 cm (3 ft). All prefer sunny positions and rather poor, dryish soils but will grow practically anywhere. They flower in the first half of summer, can be planted in spring or autumn, and are best raised from seed or named varieties or propagated from root cuttings taken in winter. Root cuttings will reproduce all characteristics of their parents and do not vary as seedlings do.

Verbena. Almost all verbenas are half-hardy plants suitable for bedding out in summer or for greenhouse culture but *Verbena rigida*, once known as *V. venosa*, is a good hardy perennial making a bushy plant about 30 cm (1 ft) high with stiff spikes of small lavender-purple flowers from mid-summer until autumn. It needs a sunny position and well-drained soil, should be planted in spring and divided then if necessary. *V. bonariensis* is a loosely branched, much taller plant, up to 1·5 cm (5 ft), each stem terminating in a little head of lavender-purple flowers in late summer/early autumn. It needs similar treatment and is easily raised from seed.

Veronica (Speedwell). This large family contains much useful material for the rock garden as well as for the herbaceous border. There is a great deal of variety even in the herbaceous species, all of which will grow in any ordinary soil and sunny positions and may be planted and divided in spring or autumn. Among the best kinds are *Veronica gentianoides*, 45 cm (1½ ft), with glossy light green leaves and slender spikes of Wedgwood blue flowers, early spring; *V. longifolia subsessilis*, 45 cm (1½ ft), violet purple, late summer/early autumn; *V. spicata*, 45 cm (1½ ft), blue, pink or white, the second half of summer, and *V. virginica*, 1·5 m (5 ft), with leaves in whorls and slender spikes of white or pale blue flowers in the second half of summer.

Viola. The bedding viola is very closely allied to the pansy, in fact botanically the pansy is a species of viola. But the viola differs in important garden features, notably its compact, tufted habit which makes it a more permanent and satisfactory bedding plant, its longer flowering season and the prevalence of self colours, or one colour blending into another rather than the strong and sharply defined contrasts characteristic of pansies.

Violas can be raised from seed and some varieties come reasonably true to colour and type in this way, but the most certain method of increasing selected varieties is by cuttings taken in late summer/early autumn. A few sturdy plants are cut back with sharp scissors to within a few centimetres of the roots and are topdressed lightly with fine soil, sand and peat in about equal parts. In a few weeks new shoots will come sprouting from the roots through this topdressing and can be pulled out, often with a few white rootlets attached. Dibbled into similar rather sandy and peaty soil in a shaded frame and kept well watered they will make further roots in a few weeks and be ready for planting out the following spring. The prevalence of root rot disease in many gardens has made it increasingly difficult to propagate violas from cuttings or by division and has resulted in greater reliance on seed.

Violas succeed best in moderately rich, rather moist soils and partially shaded positions. If faded flowers are picked off and plants are well supplied with water during dry weather they will flower from late spring to late summer, or even later. There are numerous garden varieties and a few beautiful species most of which are more at home in the rock garden than the border (see Chapter 9).

The sweet violet is derived from the wild *Viola odorata*. There are numerous varieties differing in the size, form and colours of their flowers. Double-flowered forms (Parma violets) are weaker in growth and more difficult to manage than the singles. All can be grown in the open, winter and summer, but for winter flowers the plants require frame protection over winter. Small rooted pieces are planted in early spring in rich soil and slightly shady positions. They should be kept clear of runners and free of red spider during the summer, lifted with plenty of soil in early autumn and placed in a frame. Protection will probably not be required until mid-autumn and advantage should be taken of mild winter days to open the frame and ventilate. Summer planting distances for singles are 30 cm (1 ft) by 45 cm (1½ ft); for doubles 23 cm (9 in) by 30 cm (1 ft). In the frames the plants can just touch one another. Propagation is by division in the second half of spring or by cuttings prepared in late summer/early autumn from runners and inserted in sandy soil in a frame. New varieties of viola are constantly being grown and it is well worth attending specialist horticultural shows to spot the latest forms.

Chapter 9

Rock Gardens and Rock Plants

Here is yet another example of the gardener's genius for inventing vague and indefinable terms. It is quite impossible to give any exact meaning to either 'rock garden' or 'rock plant'. To one person any heap of soil bestrewn with stones is a rock garden; to another it is rank heresy to apply the term to anything less than a carefully conceived and painstakingly made structure in which the soil has been specially prepared to meet the requirements of various mountain plants and each rock has been placed as it might have been found in its natural state on a mountain side. And if at this point it might be argued that at least a rock plant can be defined as a plant that in nature grows on rocks, it should be remembered that there are good rock plants from woodland homes (cyclamen and some anemones, for example) others from the stream side (*Nierembergia repens* and some primulas), and a great number from meadows, alpine or otherwise, which are not necessarily rocky. I have even seen rock gardens planted with geraniums and marguerites, geums, gaillardias and bedding violas but I would not say that any of these were good rock plants. So one appears to be left with the rather unsatisfactory definitions that a rock garden is any part of the garden in which rocks play a prominent part and that a rock plant is any plant which looks at home in such a setting – and that, of course, is a matter of opinion.

Dry Wall Gardening. This variation on ordinary rock gardening has far greater possibilities than are generally realized. The dry wall is one made without mortar or cement. In many upland districts such walls are used by farmers in place of hedges but these are usually made by building the stones one on top of another with no matrix of any kind. In the garden the dry wall must be built with soil packed firmly between the stones, certainly if plants are to be grown on it. To be really satisfactory for a wide range of rock plants the wall should have a good core of soil. Unless it is used to retain a terrace of soil into which the plants can root, a good scheme is to make the wall double-sided with a space of 30 cm (1 ft) or more between and to pack this space with good soil of the type recommended for

A section through a double-sided dry wall showing the core of good soil. Alpine and trailing plants can be grown in the crevices between the stones as well as along the top of the wall

169

the rock garden itself. It will then be possible to plant alpines of many kinds in the crevices between the stones on both faces of the wall and to establish still more, including some good trailing kinds such as aubrieta, yellow alyssum, arabis and helianthemum, along the top.

When building dry walls always start by excavating several centimetres to accommodate a foundation layer of carefully chosen and rather big stones well bedded down into the soil. Build on these in layers similar to those in an ordinary wall and bond the stones so that the vertical crevices are not in line. In this way the stones will bind together and the wall will have considerable strength even though it is not mortared.

Almost any stones, or even bricks, can be used for dry wall building, but quarried sandstone and limestone in pieces about twice to three times the size of ordinary bricks are ideal. It is not, of course, essential that all the stones are of one size or shape nor even that they shall be squared or dressed, though this does make the task of building much easier.

Raised Beds. These are a development of the double dry wall with a core of soil. The raised bed can be of any size but, for convenience, it should not be more than 1·8 m (6 ft) wide, or 90 cm (3 ft) high so that the plants on top are easily accessible. The bed is retained by dry walls built as described and is filled with a good mixture of soil, peat, grit and sand to suit the plants to be grown. These can be planted in the face of the walls and all over the top of the bed and, if desired, a few flattish slabs of stone may be half sunk in the surface so that some plants may creep over them. Many plants thrive in such beds. It is not difficult to change the soil every six or eight years and if the bed is made of a suitable height and width planting and weeding can be done with a minimum of stooping.

Creating a Rock Garden. Though any heap of soil into which stones have been stuck at random is, to some people, a rock garden, it must be stressed that it is scarcely likely to prove a very satisfactory one. The selection of plants which can be grown is likely to be limited to the sturdiest and most indestructible.

If the object of building a rock garden is to enjoy a wide range of the astonishingly varied plants that may be called rock plants (and one of the merits of this form of gardening is that it does enable one to enjoy so much variety in a little space) then it is important that great care be taken in the preliminary work. In the first place it will be wise to choose an open spot clear of the overhang of trees and to make certain that drainage is good. If there is any doubt, excavate all the soil from the proposed site to a depth of at least 45 cm (1½ ft), put in a good layer of clinkers or brick ends and then, before returning the soil, make a drain leading to a soakaway or ditch. If there has to be considerable excavation and building up to get the right contours remove the top soil before starting on this work and replace it afterwards so that there is an even depth of fertile soil all over.

The soil itself is almost certain to need some improvement – in texture rather than in plant foods. Peat of the granulated type, coarse sand and stone chippings are the ingredients which will help to make ordinary garden soil suitable for choice rock plants. The proportions may be varied indefinitely to suit particular groups of plants but a good foundation mixture on which to base these variations is one very like the John Innes potting compost (see p. 423), namely about three parts of good soil to one of sand and one of peat. For plants that need especially good drainage a further part may be added of limestone or sandstone chippings passed through a 2·5 cm (1 in) mesh sieve. If the natural soil

170

of the garden is known to be poor it may be advisable to replace half the peat with well-rotted dung or old mushroom compost, but the latter contains a lot of chalk and is therefore unsuitable for plants that dislike lime.

Moraine and Scree. A special feature of some well-made rock gardens is a moraine or scree. The names are practically synonymous except that provision should be made to water the moraine from below ground whereas the scree lacks this refinement. In both cases the soil mixture is even more stony than usual, the proportions often being as much as ten parts of stone chippings to one of soil, one of peat and one of sand. There must be at least 60 cm (2 ft) depth of this compost for the diet is spartan and plant roots will need to roam far to obtain the nourishment they need. It is also an advantage if the moraine can be on a slight slope but this is not so necessary for the unwatered scree. The moraine water is supplied from a pipe laid 30 cm (1 ft) beneath the surface at the top of the slope. This pipe must be drilled with a few very small holes and connected to a water supply with a tap so that the flow of water can be carefully regulated or cut off entirely. In practice, it will be used only in early summer during the comparatively brief period at which the plants are making their growth. Moraine and scree are invaluable for cultivating many of the more difficult rock plants, particularly those which really are high mountaineers, accustomed to excessively stony soils and the abundant moisture provided by melting snow.

Choice of Rocks. Many show gardens are made with naturally weather-worn stone dug out of hillsides but this is inevitably expensive and carriage often adds greatly to the initial cost. There is no reason why good rock gardens should not be made from stone quarried in the ordinary way provided it is not so hard that it will not weather easily. If a good

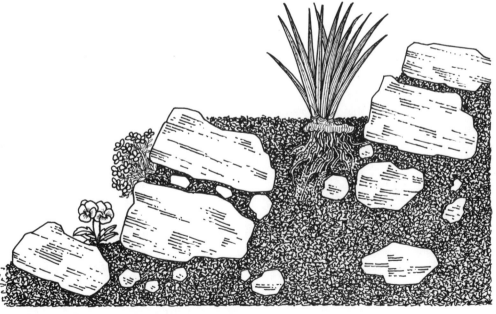

Cross section of a rock garden, showing the rocks well bedded into the soil to give the effect of natural strata and the provision of flat pockets of soil for planting

171

limestone or sandstone of this type can be purchased cheaply near the site it should certainly be considered. In any case try to include at least a few really big pieces because some bold spurs add greatly to the effect of the rock garden. Though these can be built with several stones one upon another a better effect is obtained if the component parts are not too small and numerous.

Always build from the bottom up and be careful to bury the majority of the stones well into the soil. The aim should be to give the garden, directly it is well clothed with plants, a natural appearance as if it really belonged to the site and this it can never have if many of the rocks are perched on the surface of the soil instead of emerging from it.

Many rock gardens are built on the model of the natural outcrop, examples of which may be seen on almost any hillside. It will be noted that such outcrops generally have a definite angle of emergence which is common to the whole formation, due to the strata tilt which the rock follows far back into the earth. One advantage of following this pattern is that it gives unity to the whole design, but care must be taken that this unity does not degenerate into monotony. All kinds of variations can be introduced by varying the spacing of the outcrops, making some bigger than others, changing their outline while retaining the same main angles, and constantly varying the slope and contour of the ground. While building always bear in mind the plants for which the rock garden is being made and leave a variety of suitable homes for them, some flat and wide for the carpeters, others steep and craggy for those plants that like to grow out of crevices and in deep fissures.

For the same reason see that every nook and cranny is filled with soil so that plants may be able to find a root hold even between the largest boulders. Ram soil behind every rock so that there are no pockets to cause trouble and provide homes for mice and other vermin.

Avoid unnecessary use of concrete. When it must be employed to cement together rocks which would otherwise be insecure, it should be tinted to simulate the rock itself and, if possible, the plants should be arranged so that they will soon completely hide the joint.

Peat Wall and Beds. An alternative to a rock garden is to build low walls of peat blocks such as those used for fuel and to fill the space behind them with good-quality granulated peat and sand. The blocks can be built to form shallow irregular terraces much as in a rock garden proper, or they can be simple terrace walls or walls retaining raised beds as described on p. 170. Many plants that like acid soil will thrive in such beds and they require on average rather less weeding and care than ordinary soil-filled rock gardens or dry walls.

Trough and Sink Gardens. Very attractive miniature gardens can be made in old stone sinks or troughs or in reproductions of them made specially for the purpose. These can be of any size and should be at least 10 cm (4 in) deep and provided with one or more holes in the bottom for drainage. Some gravel or broken crocks are placed in the bottom to allow surplus water to escape easily; the trough is filled with a mixture of good loam, peat and sand (John Innes potting compost will do well). Some pieces of rock are partly sunk in the surface to simulate an outcrop or perhaps a little crag, and then the whole is planted with rock plants and small bulbs such as crocuses, scillas and chionodoxas. A final scattering of stone chippings all over the surface can improve the appearance and also help the

Shallow, irregular terraces can be made from peat blocks and the beds filled with good quality granulated peat and sand

plants by keeping the soil beneath cool and moist. The smaller growing alpines should be used such as thymes, sempervivums, androsaces, cushion saxifrages, aethionemas and so on. For preference the troughs should be raised a little on stones or pillars to allow water to escape freely. They make excellent ornaments for a terrace or patio.

Gravel Gardens. It was probably from the scree that the idea was borrowed to make beds of quite ordinary soil and then cover them with a 5 cm (2 in) thick layer of gravel. This discourages weeds, keeps the soil beneath cool and moist and provides excellent drainage around the collars of plants where decay often starts if they remain wet and cold for long periods especially in autumn and winter. Though gravel beds can be used for rock plants they have a much wider application and there are few things that cannot be grown in them. They are particularly suitable for succulents and grey leaved plants. Any gravel can be used that will remain loose and not bind like a path.

Planting Rock Plants. Nurserymen grow almost all their saleable stocks of rock plants in small pots and this enables them to be moved with little or no root disturbance. In consequence it is possible to plant at almost any time of the year, except when the soil is frozen or very wet. In the case of seedlings it is usually wise to plant these permanently as soon as they are of reasonable size while it is usually best to plant other plants in the first half of spring or, if this is their flowering season, directly it is over.

If roots are bound into a tight pot ball it will be wise to loosen them slightly with the fingers before planting. In all cases a little of the new soil should be worked in among the roots. Plant firmly and water in if the weather is dry.

When planting in dry walls and in crevices between boulders it is wise to begin with very small plants or else to build them into position as the wall or rock garden is made. It is impossible to push the roots of a big plant into a narrow space without damage.

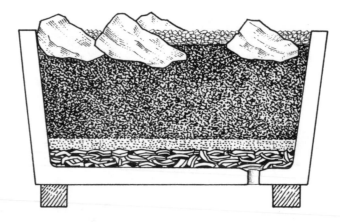

Preparing a sink garden. Put crocks and coarse gravel in the bottom and cover with a mixture of good loam, peat and sand. Sink pieces of rock in the surface like an outcrop

A well-planted sink garden. It has been raised on bricks to allow free outlet for surplus water

Propagation. Many rock plants can be raised from seed and the best time for sowing is almost always as soon as it is ripe. Unfortunately seed can seldom be purchased quickly enough for this and then it is, as a rule, best to wait until the first half of spring when seed will germinate fairly readily in a frame or unheated greenhouse. Ordinary seed composts (see p. 427) can be used but very small seeds should have practically no covering.

Seedlings are potted singly before they get overcrowded in the seed trays. Subsequently they are grown on in a frame till planting time. Always treat rock plants as thoroughly hardy – which is what the majority of them are.

A good many alpines can be divided just like herbaceous perennials and this, too, can be done in spring, or immediately after flowering in the case of spring-flowering plants.

Planting in the crevices of a dry stone wall. To avoid damaging roots, it is wise to place the plants in position as the wall is being made

Avoid pulling the plants apart too drastically and, after replanting, keep them well watered for a few weeks if the weather is dry.

Cuttings provide a method of increasing many shrubby plants that cannot be divided and some herbaceous rock plants are also more satisfactory from cuttings than from divisions. Firm young growths secured in early summer generally provide the best material and the cuttings should be rooted quickly in gritty sand or a mixture of sand and peat in a small cold frame, or under mist. Cuttings prepared from pieces of root and treated in the same way as those of herbaceous plants (see p. 110) are effective in a few instances, such as morisia, while leaf cuttings may be used to increase ramondas and haberleas.

Protection. While very few rock plants are in any way tender in the sense that cold will kill them, many suffer from damp winters. This is particularly true of those with very downy foliage, such as androsaces and *Asperula suberosa*. These may be protected over winter by panes of glass or plastic supported on bent wires, or notched sticks so that they are held well above the foliage with the sides open for free circulation of air. Some choice and early flowering alpines are seen at their best when grown in pots or trays plunged to their rims in a sand or peat bed for the greater part of the year and given gentle warmth in winter or while they are in flower. Alternatively they can be placed in a cool greenhouse, which will give them sufficient protection during the winter months and perhaps make them easier to appreciate.

A SELECTION OF ROCK PLANTS

Acaena. Lowly plants, useful chiefly for growing in the crevices of crazy paving though they also make a good carpet in the rock garden and can be used as a ground cover round early bulbs such as crocuses. The thin stems creep along the ground and root as they go. The leaves are small, sometimes finely divided, and the tiny flowers are clustered in burrs, often most attractive.

Acaenas will grow in any ordinary soil and sunny or partially shady position. They can be increased by division at any time. Among the best kinds are *Acaena buchananii*, with grey-green leaves; *A. microphylla*, which has bronzy foliage, very deeply divided and *A. novae-zelandiae*, with bronzy green foliage.

Acantholimon (Prickly Thrift). These compact, tufted plants have neat rosettes of narrow, spiky leaves and flowers in small heads on 7·5-15 cm (3-6 in) stems in the first half of summer. They are useful to give a succession of colour after the earlier flowering rock plants.

Prickly thrift likes a sunny place and well-drained, gritty soil. It can be increased by careful division in spring, though seed sown in trays in a frame or greenhouse in early spring is preferable. The best kind is *Acantholimon glumaceum* which has bright, rose coloured flowers.

Achillea (Yarrow, Milfoil). This is one of the big genera of the garden world and includes weeds, excellent herbaceous plants (see Chapter 8) as well as a number of useful rock plants. Achilleas are noted for their hardiness and the ease with which they can be grown in practically any soil and situation. They are mostly trailing plants and some are apt to spread quickly and overrun smaller subjects. Propagation is easily effected by careful division in the spring.

Excellent kinds are *Achillea ageratifolia*, with finely divided silvery leaves and small white flowers in summer; *A. clavennae*, similar but larger, to 23 cm (9 in) high; *A.* × *lewisii* King Edward, a neat and showy hybrid with clusters of pale yellow flowers throughout the summer, and *A. tomentosa*, which looks much like our native yarrow, except that it is smaller, neater and has golden-yellow instead of white flowers.

Aethionema. These are all very lovely plants, bushy in habit, with neat spikes of pink flowers in spring and early summer. They are related to the candytufts (iberis) but are choicer and more refined. Grow them in good, well-drained soil and full sun. They make ideal plants for a dry wall or a crevice in the rock garden and, once established, should be left alone for they do not like disturbance. Propagate by seed sown in a frame or green-house in spring, or by cuttings of firm young growths inserted in very sandy soil in a frame in mid-summer.

All kinds are lovely, but three of the best are *Aethionema grandiflorum* which is 30 cm (1 ft) high and has clear pink flowers; *A. armenum* which is a little dwarfer but similar in colour, and Warley Rose, which is particularly neat and bushy in habit and has deep rose flowers.

Ajuga (Bugle). One species, *Ajuga reptans*, is an attractive European wild plant known as bugle. This has produced several varieties that are worth a place in the rougher parts of the rock garden. Among the best of these are *A. r.* Atropurpurea with deep purple foliage, *A. r.* Tricolor with green, white and rose-tinted foliage, *A. r.* Multicolour with green, bronze, yellow and pink foliage, *A. r.* Variegata with green and cream leaves, and *A. r.* Burgundy Glow, leaves in shades of wine red. All will grow in any soil and situation. These plants may be propagated by division of the roots in either spring or autumn.

176

Alyssum (Gold Dust). These are not on the whole very choice plants judged by the standards of the rock-garden enthusiast but there is none that makes a better display than *Alyssum saxatile*, the familiar golden-yellow species which comes into bloom in spring at the same time as aubrieta and arabis and contrasts so admirably with them. It grows easily and spreads rapidly but does need good drainage if it is to prove permanent. It is seen to best advantage in a dry wall or planted in a sunny crevice or ledge in the rock garden. There are numerous forms, including *A. s.* Flore Pleno, with double flowers and *A. s. citrinum*, with lemon-yellow flowers. There are many other species but none quite rivalling *A. saxatile* in display. One of the best is *A. spinosum*, which forms a small, compact, definitely spiny bush covered with a mass of white flowers (pink in var. *Roseum*) in early summer.

Increase by seed sown in a greenhouse or frame in spring or by cuttings of firm young growths rooted in sandy soil in a frame in spring or early summer.

Androsace. These are real rock plants and amongst them are numbered some of the most beautiful and difficult of the high alpine flora. For example there is *Androsace imbricata*, a plant about which the experts talk with bated breath. If you can grow it there is no alpine with which you cannot succeed for it needs the sunniest and driest of places in deep, sandy soil and usually disappears the first winter. *A. carnea* is not so difficult and an excellent plant to grow in a scree or a pan of gritty soil in the alpine house. It is small, tufted and with pink or white flowers on 7·5 cm (3 in) stems in spring.

Fortunately there are also other species which are, by comparison, easy and very beautiful. Of these *A. sarmentosa* is a tufted Himalayan alpine with rosettes of downy, grey-green leaves which slowly spread into a wide clump from which, in late spring/early summer stand up thin, 10 cm (4 in) stems, ending in clusters of clear pink, confetti-like flowers. It will grow in any open, well-drained soil and sunny position but may with advantage be protected in winter by a sheet of glass. There are several varieties varying slightly in flower colour and all equally easy to grow.

Then there is *A. lanuginosa*, looser and trailing in habit and flowering in the second half of summer. It thrives under similar conditions and also has pink flowers. There is a pretty variety named *leichtlinii*, in which the flowers are white with a deep rose centre.

All these androsaces can be increased by careful division in spring. Seed can be sown in a frame or greenhouse in spring and will reproduce the species true to type, but not always the varieties.

Those who want to try their hand at the more difficult androsaces should plant them in the scree or moraine (see p. 171) in the stoniest of mixtures and be particularly careful about winter protection from rain. Alternatively they can be grown in very well-drained pans filled with a scree mixture and housed in the alpine frame or greenhouse.

Anemone (Windflower). One of the great families of the plant world in which are included many excellent herbaceous plants (see p. 116) and bulbs (see p. 341). There are, in addition, some good rock garden kinds, notably *Anemone apennina* which forms wide, mounded clumps of foliage above which stand in early spring the fragile, sky-blue flowers. *A. blanda* is much like it in appearance but flowers several weeks earlier and it has several colour forms from pale to deep blue, white, pink and rosy red. Both species will grow in any ordinary soil and like partial shade. *A. nemorosa*, the European wood anemone, with

177

fragile white or pale blue flowers in spring, can also be planted in shady parts of the rock garden but is not a true rock plant. Propagate all these by careful division immediately after flowering.

Genuine mountaineers are *A. sulphurea* and *A. alpina*. According to some authorities the former is merely a variety of the latter, the one having pale yellow flowers and the other pure white flowers. Both are difficult to grow, the best method being to sow seed where the plants are required or to obtain small seedlings and establish these in spring in a very well-drained bed of light soil containing plenty of peat or leafmould. They bloom in early summer.

For the plants sometimes known as *A. angulosa* and *A. hepatica* see Hepatica, p. 193, and for *A. pulsatilla* see Pulsatilla, p. 205.

Antennaria. Not an important genus but it contains one pretty rock plant, *Antennaria dioica*. This makes a close carpet of grey-green leaves and produces in early summer an abundance of small white flowers on 7·5 cm (3 in) stems. There is also a variety known as *A. d. tomentosa* in which the hairiness of the leaves is more pronounced, and another more valuable, named *rosea* which has pink flowers. All are easily grown in ordinary lightish soil and a sunny place. They can be increased by division in the spring.

Anthemis (Chamomile). There are lots of weeds in this family and the novice should be rather wary about buying any anthemis which he has not seen and about which he has no reliable information. About the best for the rock garden is *Anthemis cupaniana*, a sprawling plant with silvery, deeply divided leaves and pure white, daisy flowers carried with the utmost profusion from spring to autumn. It will grow in any well-drained soil and open place. *A. marschalliana* is smaller, neater, has yellow flowers all the summer and is happiest in a scree or moraine. All can be increased by division in the spring.

Anthyllis (Kidney Vetch). A small race of pea-flowered plants of which one, *Anthyllis vulneraria*, is a pretty English wild flower commonly known as ladies' fingers. This is showy but not choice enough to be admitted to the garden. However, *A. montana*, an alpine species, is well worth planting on a sunny ledge. It will quickly make quite a carpet of small leaves densely covered with silvery hairs. On these sit closely the rather large, deep red flowers which appear from mid-spring to early summer. It does well in a rather limy, well-drained soil and open position. Seed provides the easiest means of propagation.

Antirrhinum (Snapdragon). Though by far the showiest are the so-called annuals, described elsewhere (see p. 71), there are a couple of useful rock plants in the family, *Antirrhinum asarina*, now known as *Asarina procumbens*, and *A. glutinosum*. Both are a little tender and should have a very sunny position and perfect drainage, otherwise they are not difficult to grow in ordinary soil. Both trail about and have typical snapdragon-like flowers, but much smaller than those of the bedding kinds. In *A. asarina* they are white marked with yellow or pink and in *A. glutinosum* yellowish white. They flower most of the summer. It is wise to root a few cuttings in a pot of sandy soil each mid-summer in case the parent plants fail to survive the winter.

Aquilegia (Columbine). Many aquilegias are herbaceous plants and these have been described on p. 117. For the rock garden there are several outstanding species. *Aquilegia glandulosa*, with very large blue and white flowers on 30 cm (1 ft) stems in the first half of summer, is rather difficult to establish though once growing it usually does well in deep, rather light but not dry soil containing peat. The secret appears to be to start with really small plants which should be put out in mid-spring. *A. caerulea*, a really delightful plant with very big, pale blue and white flowers is just as easy to grow as an ordinary border columbine and requires similar treatment. It grows just over 30 cm (1 ft) in height so is quite at home in the rock garden, but some garden varieties listed under *A. caerulea* are really hybrids, considerably taller and more vigorous and better suited to borders. Seed of aquilegias sown out of doors in late spring will give flowering plants the following year.

Arabis (Rock Cress). Though there are quite a number of species of arabis there is only one which immediately leaps to mind when the name is mentioned. This is *Arabis albida*, now known as *A. caucasica*, the remarkable white-flowered, trailing plant which, together with aubrieta and alyssum, fills every rock garden and dry wall with bloom in spring. Though it grows very vigorously and spreads quickly it seldom becomes a nuisance as it has no underground stems to sprout up in unexpected places. It will grow anywhere but is seen to best advantage in not too rich a soil and a fully sunny situation. The double-flowered form, *A. c.* Flore Pleno, is if anything even better than the single kind and quite as easy to grow and there is also a pink-flowered variety named Rosabella and two varieties with cream-variegated leaves, one with single the other with double white flowers. Old plants can be carefully divided after flowering but a better method of propagation is by cuttings made from the young growths and rooted in sandy soil in a frame. Single arabis, including the pink variety, can also be raised quickly from seed sown in a frame in early spring or out of doors later in the season.

Arenaria (Sandwort). These are mainly dwarf plants, grown for their close carpets of tiny green leaves, but *Arenaria montana* is a trailer of looser habit with big white flowers, like those of a refined stitchwort, in late spring/early summer. It will grow in any ordinary soil and sunny position. *A. balearica*, the best of the carpeters, is also most attractive when smothered with its tiny, white blooms on thread-like stems no more than 12 mm (½ in) high. This is a grand plant to use as a ground cover over choice garden bulbs such as crocuses and miniature daffodils. It likes cool, moist but not stagnant places and spreads very rapidly.

Other useful kinds are *A. caespitosa* now listed as *Minuartia verna* and its golden-leaved form *aurea*, both mounded, moss-like plants useful for carpeting in sun or shade. *A. purpurascens* is coarser in growth than *A. balearica* with pinkish-lilac flowers. It needs the same treatment. All may be increased by careful division.

Armeria (Thrift). There are thrifts sufficiently robust to be planted in the herbaceous border (see p. 117) but the common type is a true rock plant which can be found wild on cliffs in many parts of this country. It is an attractive, tufted plant with narrow, grassy leaves and globular heads of small pink flowers on 15 cm (6 in) stems. Its botanical name is *Armeria maritima* and from the garden standpoint it is surpassed by its more highly coloured varieties such as *A. m.* Vindictive (crimson) and *A. m.* Laucheana (deep rose).

All will grow easily in well-drained soil and a sunny place. *A. caespitosa* (now called *A. juniperifolia*) needs more care for it is a true alpine from fairly high levels and must have perfect drainage. It does well in full sun in the scree or in a vertical crevice where it will form a slowly spreading and very close tussock of foliage on which sit the pale pink flowers.

All these thrifts flower in late spring/early summer. Increase by cuttings in very sandy soil in spring or, in the case of the species, by seed sown in a frame in the first half of spring.

Artemisia. In addition to border species there are some useful artemisias for the rock garden, all easily grown plants in any sunny place and poorish, well-drained soil, and all with silver or grey leaves, often beautifully dissected like those of a fern. Names are numerous and not always very reliable. *Artemisia glacialis*, 7·5 cm (3 in); *A. caucasica*, 5 cm (2 in); and *A. schmidtii* Nana, 15 cm (6 in), are a few worth collecting. All can be increased by careful division in spring. Flowers are insignificant. (See also Chapter 8).

Asarina. See **Antirrhinum** (p. 71).

Asperula (Woodruff). A very variable family, containing a good many weeds besides some really lovely gems for the rock garden. Outstanding amongst the latter is *Asperula suberosa*, which makes dense tufts of very slender stems and tiny leaves all densely clothed with grey-green silken down, and suddenly, in early summer, becoming completely covered with tiny, tubular, soft pink flowers. The whole plant grows no more than 10 cm (4 in) high. It must have full sun and perfect drainage and in winter it is advisable to protect its downy growth with a pane of glass supported well above it so that there is free circulation of air beneath.

Less exciting but easier to manage are *A. gussoni* and *A. hirta*, both with pale pink flowers throughout the early summer, and *A. odorata*, with white flowers from late spring to mid-summer but chiefly remarkable for the hay-like perfume of its leaves. All will grow in any porous soil and open place.

Propagate by seed in a frame or by careful division in spring, except for *A. suberosa*, which cannot be divided because of its solitary main root.

Aster. Most of the perennial asters are herbaceous plants (see Chapter 8) but there are some rock plants in the family, notably *A. alpinus*, *A. farreri*, *A. forrestii*, *A. purdomii* and *A. subcaeruleus*. *A. alpinus* is low growing and compact with lavender-blue, daisy flowers solitary on 15 cm (6 in) stems in late spring/early summer. There are several forms, including one, Roseus, that is nearly pink, another, Albus, that is pure white and a third, Beechwood, that is deep blue. *A. farreri* is a bigger plant, at least 30 cm (1 ft) and sometimes more in height with big, rather ragged flowers each with a striking orange centre to set off the violet-blue ray petals. *A. forrestii* is similar to the last in colour but is half as high and *A. purdomii* is similar again but 15-20 cm (6-8 in) high. *A. subcaeruleus* might be described as a big *A. alpinus* with bluish-mauve flowers. *A. sedifolius nanus*, which makes 30 cm (1 ft) high little bushes of thin stems and narrow leaves simply smothered in late summer with small blue daisies, is another which may be admitted to the rock garden.

All grow readily in ordinary soil and an open situation and require no special care.

180

They can be increased quite easily by division in spring. Seed sown in a frame in the second half of spring usually germinates readily but may not reproduce the various forms of the species entirely true to type.

Astilbe (Spiraea). There are four small astilbes which are suitable for rock gardens but they are not really rock plants. All are miniature spiraeas with the same fluffy flower plumes as the big, herbaceous border species but diminished to the scale of rock plants. *Astilbe chinensis pumila* is 15 cm (6 in) high and has rosy-mauve flowers. *A. × crispa* is a hybrid 15-30 cm (6 in-1 ft) high with white, pink or carmine flowers. *A. glaberrima saxatilis* (or *saxosa*) is even shorter, 9 cm (3½ in), with pale pink flowers. All are mid-summer flowering and like rather damp, cool spots. They are ideal for massing in valleys between the spurs and outcrops of the rock garden. Increase by careful division in spring or by seed sown in trays of rather peaty soil in early spring and germinate in a cool greenhouse or frame, but seedlings of *A. × crispa* may show considerable colour variation.

Aubrieta (Purple Rock Cress). This plant should need no introduction for it is the best known of all rock plants. It is the aubrieta which makes those great drifts of purple and lavender in the spring rock garden at the time the white arabis and yellow alyssum are in bloom. Thanks to hybridization and selection the colour range has been greatly widened and there are now pink and even purplish-crimson aubrietas to brighten the garden. All the same, there are none, in my opinion, to beat some of the old purple varieties, such as the well-known Dr Mules which is easy to grow, exceptionally free flowering and always reliable. The same cannot be said for some of the later seedlings which though big and showy in bloom are sometimes stingy with their flowers.

Aubrietas love sun and do best in rather limy soils. They are seen at their best planted at the top of a cliff or ledge, or on a dry wall or bank down which they can cascade.

Seed sown in fine soil in a frame or greenhouse in spring germinates readily but the seedlings seldom come true to colour. In consequence named varieties must be increased by cuttings which are not always too easy to root. They should be prepared from young, non-flowering shoots taken in mid-summer. Root them in very sandy soil in a frame which should be kept closed for the first week or so but must be ventilated freely as soon as the cuttings are rooted or many may damp off.

Auricula. See **Primula** (p. 203 and p. 491).

Bellium (False Daisy). The species grown in rock gardens, *Bellium bellidioides*, is very like a lawn daisy but without that plant's incurable habit of spreading and coming up where not wanted. It is free flowering, pretty and capable of blooming from spring to autumn. It requires no special care and will grow in sun or partial shade. Propagate by division in spring or early autumn.

B. minutum is similar but smaller and needs a little more care if it is not to be smothered by more robust plants. Give it good soil on a ledge by itself in full sun.

Calamintha (Calamint). Most calamintha now go by other names, either clinopodium or acinos. None are particularly choice plants but they are useful everyday alpines which have the merit of growing almost anywhere and never fail to give a good display. The kind most usually seen is *Acinos alpinus*, with dull violet purple flowers. Plant in a sunny place and open, gritty soil. Propagation is by seed in a frame or greenhouse or by careful division, both in spring.

Calandrinia (Rock Purslane). These, to be satisfactory, need very dry, extremely well-drained soil and good warmth. They should be planted in the scree or in a really sunny crevice between vertical rocks. They are worth a little trouble for at their best they are brilliant plants, the best being *Calandrinia umbellata*, with loose clusters of vivid magenta flowers all the summer. It grows about 15 cm (6 in) high. Raise from seed which should be sown in very sandy soil in a cool greenhouse in early spring, the seedlings being planted out while they are still quite small.

Calceolaria. While most of the calceolarias are greenhouse or bedding plants one delightful species, *C. polyrrhiza* is well suited to planting in the rock garden where it will enliven the damper, half-shady spots with its mats of broad leaves from which ascend 15 cm (6 in) stems ending in one, or sometimes two, big, baggy, yellow flowers in early summer. Given moisture and a rather humus-rich soil it is perfectly easy to grow. It can be taken up and divided in spring when extra plants are required. *C. darwinii* has quite large yellow and chestnut-brown flowers carried singly on 7·5 cm (3 in) stems but is more difficult to grow, requiring plenty of moisture in summer and drier conditions in winter.

Callirhoë (Poppy Mallow). Plants for sunny places, they have brightly coloured, poppy-like flowers and make a good show in the garden. For early/mid-summer flowering sow in a frame or greenhouse in early spring and plant out later that season. For late summer flowering sow out of doors in mid-spring and thin out the seedlings to about 30 cm (1 ft). The plants are a little over 60 cm (2 ft) in height. The best perennial kind is *Callirhoë involucrata*, with vivid magenta flowers on 15 cm (6 in) stems.

Campanula (Bellflower). This is one of the big families of the rock garden world. Species and varieties run into hundreds and there are certainly several dozens which are worth a place in any rock garden. They do not lend themselves to easy generalization regarding culture and numbered amongst them are difficult as well as easily managed plants. The expert will take delight in trying his skill on *Campanula alpestris*, which will thrive in the moraine in the grittiest of soils but with plenty of moisture beneath. The blue flowers look something like Canterbury bells sitting singly on a carpet of foliage. Then there is *C. excisa*, a plant from the high alps and a good choice for the alpine house or frame in the grittiest of lime-free soils. A third species much admired by connoisseurs is *C. zoysii*, with flowers curiously puckered at the mouth. It would not be so difficult to grow if only slugs would leave it alone. Zinc collars 5 cm (2 in) high round each plant are said to be the best protection but are unsightly.

There are many more of the difficult types but the ordinary gardener will probably be content to plant such easy kinds as *C. carpatica turbinata*, *C. cochlearifolia* (often sold as *C. caespitosa* or *C. pusilla*), *C. garganica*, *C. poscharskyana* (but this can run far and wide), *C. portenschlagiana* (formerly known as *C. muralis*), *C. pulla*, *C.* × *pulloides*, *C. raddeana*, *C. tommasiniana*, *C. waldsteiniana* and several more which will grow in any reasonable soil and open position. In fact quite a lot of these will even tolerate a fair degree of shade though, contrary to popular belief, very few campanulas are real shade lovers. Many of these are trailing plants which should be placed where they can spread for 30 cm (1 ft) or so in all directions, but *C. raddeana*, *C. tommasiniana* and *C. waldsteiniana* make compact little bushes, branching freely but not spreading far.

Blue is the typical colour of the campanula family but there are many variations from palest lavender to deep violet, with a few excursions into mauvy pink and a great number of albinos. They flower for the most part in early summer, though some continue until autumn or give a second display in the autumn. *C. portenschlagiana*, one of the finest for dry walls or rock gardens, is notable among these.

All campanulas can be increased rapidly from seed but as this is very small it should be sown in the finest possible seed compost and either covered very lightly or else simply have a pane of glass and a sheet of brown paper over each tray. Sow home-saved seed as soon as harvested; purchased seed must usually be sown in early spring. Germinate in an unheated greenhouse or frame. Seed will not as a rule reproduce selected colour forms true to type and these, together with double-flowered campanulas (which may produce no seed), can be increased by division in spring, a method which can be applied to many other kinds though it is not so rapid and cheap as seed.

Cerastium (Snow-in-summer). The two kinds commonly offered, *Cerastium biebersteinii* and *C. tomentosum*, are plants which really should not be allowed in the rock garden proper for, though beautiful, they are rampant weeds which are quite capable of annexing the whole garden if given a chance. Nevertheless in the right place they are undeniably useful. There are no better plants for covering a difficult wall or bank. They will grow anywhere, even in the poorest and driest of soils, and will soon cover the ground with soft masses of grey-green leaves which disappear in early summer beneath a cloud of big white 'stitch-wort' flowers. Both are very alike and can be increased by division at practically any time.

Cheiranthus (Wallflower). See **Erysimum** (p. 189).

Chiastophyllum. See **Cotyledon** (p. 184).

Chrysogonum. The only species grown is *Chrysogonum virginianum*, a very showy little plant, 18 cm (7 in) high, freely branched and producing from late spring onwards starry, golden-yellow flowers. It will thrive in any reasonably good soil in sun or half shade and can be increased by division in spring.

Codonopsis. Trailing or twining plants of which a good number have been listed from time to time, though only two, *Codonopsis clematidea* and *C. ovata*, appear to have been widely planted. Both suffer from the rather unexciting pale blue of their bell-shaped flowers. Otherwise they are attractive plants 30 cm (1 ft) or more in height flowering freely in late summer/early spring when flowers are particularly welcome in the rock garden. They grow readily enough in any ordinary, well-drained soil and sunny place but they transplant badly so are best raised from seed, the seedlings being potted singly quite early and grown on in pots until large enough to be planted out.

Colchicum. See p. 343.

Convolvulus. No doubt this family suffers from having produced one of our most troublesome weeds, the all too familiar bindweed. All the same there are excellent species for the garden which if they have a fault at all, are surprisingly rather too difficult to keep.

Convolvulus mauritanicus is a glorious trailer, soon covering a large patch of ground and producing generous numbers of lavender-blue flowers of the typical convolvulus funnel shape. It is in bloom most of the summer and is at home in a warm, sunny place where it can cascade over rocks or down a wall. Perfect drainage is part of the secret of success but it is not really quite hardy and it is advisable to strike a few cuttings annually in a frame in late summer just in case the parent plant should disappear in winter.

C. cneorum also lacks full hardiness though in other respects it is very different, being a compact bush 30 cm (1 ft) or more high with narrow, silvery leaves and white flowers tinged with pink. It also needs a sunny place and good drainage so it faces no risk of waterlogging.

Propagation of either plant is by summer cuttings in sandy soil in a frame or under a handlight.

Corydalis. You can see *Corydalis lutea*, now known as *Pseudofumaria lutea*, growing in practically any cottage garden and a very pretty plant it is, though a bit of a nuisance in the rock garden because of its habit of spreading everywhere by means of self-sown seedlings. Individually it is delightful, 30 cm (1 ft) high with fern-like, grey-green leaves and little clusters of bright yellow, spurred flowers at their best in late spring/early summer, but continuing spasmodically most of the summer.

A choicer plant for the garden is the Chinese species, *C. cheilanthifolia*, with showier clusters of flowers and a far less invasive habit. It has the same long flowering season.

Both can be increased very readily by seed sown in a frame in early spring or out of doors later in the season. They are not particular as regards soil and will grow in either sun or partial shade. *C. thalictrifolia*, which is much like *C. cheilanthifolia* in appearance and culture, may require a little protection in winter as it is not quite hardy, and *C. cashmeriana*, with peacock-blue flowers in 15 cm (6 in) sprays in spring, needs a partly shaded place in peaty soil.

Cotoneaster. See p. 260.

Cotula. Most cotula are now listed under *Leptinella*. See p. 195.

Cotyledon (Pennywort). The true pennywort *Cotyledon umbilicus* has thick, circular leaves and narrow spikes of greenish-yellow flowers. It is not worth planting in the garden though it is attractive in a subdued manner when naturalized on an old wall.

Very different is *C. simplicifolia*, a really cheerful plant with a long flowering season. It suffers from a superfluity of names, botanists now listing it as *Chiastophyllum oppositifolium* while some gardeners call it *Cotyledon oppositifolia*. The small flowers are carried on arching stems 15 cm (6 in) high, and they are bright yellow, well set off by the shining pale green foliage. It is a plant that grows easily, without special requirements, though it likes a sunny place. It will withstand a good deal of heat and drought and looks its best on a dry wall or in a sunny crevice. It can be increased by careful division in spring.

184

Crepis. Most species of crepis are weeds and all have flowers like small dandelions. In one species, *Crepis aurea*, these are orange and very showy. In good soil the plant is too leafy and rampant but established in poor, sandy soil it is curbed satisfactorily and encouraged to bloom with the greatest freedom. *C. incana* has grey leaves and pink flowers and requires similar treatment. As both plants bloom in later summer they are useful for extending the season. Propagation, by division, can be carried out at almost any time or plants can be raised from seed.

Crocus. See p. 344.

Cyananthus. Creeping plants related to campanula. *Cyananthus lobatus* has wide open blue or white flowers in late summer/early autumn. It likes scree conditions but with plenty of peat or leafmould mixed with the grit and not too hot and dry a place. *C. microphyllus* is said to be a little more tolerant of drought. Plants can be raised from seed but seedlings may vary in flower shade, so especially good forms are propagated by cuttings in early summer.

Cyclamen. See p. 345.

Cymbalaria. Fragile trailing plant for walls and the crevices between paving slabs. *Cymbalaria aequitriloba* is the best kind, like a refined Kenilworth Ivy (*C. muralis*) with small lobed leaves and lilac flowers from late spring to late summer. *C. pallida* is similar but the flowers are paler and the leaves rounder. Both kinds will grow in sun or shade and can be increased by division at almost any time.

Cypripedium (Lady's Slipper). The best-known cypripediums are greenhouse plants now named paphiopedilum, amongst the most popular of orchids. There are, however, several quite hardy kinds, still correctly called cypripedium, which will grow well in the rock garden, particularly in the damper spots. They like peaty soil, but lime may have to be added for *C. calceolus*, and should be planted carefully from pots in spring, thereafter being left undisturbed for as long as possible.

Two of the best species are *C. spectabile*, also known as *C. reginae*, a really grand North American orchid, with fine rose and white flowers of the typical lady's slipper shape and *C. calceolus* with distinctly handsome chocolate and yellow blooms. Both are 30 cm (1 ft) or a little more in height.

Propagate by careful division at planting time.

Cytisus. See p. 262.

Daphne (Garland Flower). Apart from the truly shrubby daphnes which are described elsewhere (see p. 263) there are several dwarf kinds to be planted in the rock garden. Of these, the showiest is *Daphne cneorum*, which makes a low, dense bush of wiry stems and narrow leaves, each stem terminated in early summer by a cluster of deliciously scented brilliant pink flowers. It is one of the outstanding glories of the rock garden but not, unfortunately, one of the easiest to grow. In some places it thrives like a weed, in others it soon fades away. The secret seems to be a good, deep, loamy soil which drains well in winter but does not dry out excessively in summer. The position can be in full sun or slight shade but the plants flower most freely in sun.

Very different is *D. blagayana*, which trails about rather ineffectively and then surprisingly produces terminal clusters of lovely, waxy white flowers which are even more fragrant than those of *D. cneorum*. It delights in warm, sunny places but is not difficult in rather stony soil.

A third species, harder to manage, is *D. petraea* which forms a close, dense hummock of growth only several centimetres high. This disappears completely in spring beneath the big, deep rose, deliciously fragrant blooms. It is a plant for the scree or it can be grown successfully in gritty, quick-draining soil in the alpine house.

Plant all these daphnes from pots with as little root disturbance as possible. The first two can be increased by cuttings in summer rooted in sand in a frame. *D. rupestris* is sometimes grafted on to one of the other kinds, a very undesirable policy. It is better to detach pieces from the parent clump in the spring and start them into growth in almost pure sand with just a little leafmould and loam.

Delphinium (Larkspur). Of course the familiar, hybrid delphiniums with their giant spikes of bloom are quite out of place in the rock garden but there are two or three species which, though not actually alpine plants, can be included here.

The best is *Delphinium nudicaule*, a showy plant with 30 cm (1 ft) high stems terminating in short spikes of terracotta-red flowers. It has a habit of disappearing in the winter unless planted in very well-drained soil and sheltered position, but it can be raised easily enough from seed sown in sandy soil in a frame in early spring.

Dianthus (Pink). Here is another big family, both in numbers and also in importance. Species are very numerous and many have given rise to almost equally numerous varieties and forms. The family has its representatives in the herbaceous border and in the greenhouse. The carnation represents the peak of its man-made development. But the rock gardener is only interested in unimproved species and the simpler garden variations of them.

Dianthus deltoides is a miniature pink which sprawls about in lush green mats and produces without fail each summer myriads of bright rose flowers. There are garden forms in which the colour deepens to near-crimson.

Then there is the Cheddar pink, *D. gratianopolitanus* (once known as *D. caesius*) which is found on limestone rocks in the famous Somerset gorge and is a grand plant for the dry wall or a sunny crevice. Imagine a garden pink reduced to quarter scale but with fine, single flowers of a soft, gleaming rose from late spring to mid-summer and you have a fair idea of it. Both the above pinks are easy to grow in any sunny place.

A little more exacting but still quite practicable for the beginner are *D. alpinus* and *D. pavonius*, both tufted plants but the second making particularly close hummocks of narrow leaves. It has big, short-stemmed flowers, glowing rose on top and shiny buff beneath. *D. alpinus* is a little taller with flowers that are clear rose throughout save for a darker central eye. Both will grow in any gritty soil but are seen at their best in the scree, and enjoy full sun which is really essential for the whole race.

Others that may go with these in the scree and are sure to please are *D. glacialis*, white flowered and no more than 5 cm (2 in) high normally with rose-pink flowers but with a white-flowered variety; and *D. freynii*, which is either white or pink and even more dwarf and mat-forming.

D. superbus returns us to the realms of garden pinks which it much resembles in habit though it is rather soft and weak. Still, the deeply fringed lilac flowers are very beautiful and have the true pink fragrance into the bargain.

In addition to these and many more excellent species there are scores of hybrids combining the charms of the species in as many new ways. Most of these are easy to grow though a few prove a little impermanent particularly if the soil lies damp and cold in winter.

All dianthus can be raised from seed sown in frames in early spring or as soon as ripe in summer but hybrids are unlikely to come true by this means. Early summer cuttings may be taken to propagate them and for the species if more convenient, while some of the more mat-forming kinds can be divided with care in the spring.

Diascia. Charming South African plants which need a sunny place and well drained but not dry soil. *D. cordata* is a perennial, creeping and sprawling in habit with little rounded leaves and loose spikes of salmon-pink flowers for most of the summer. *D. barbaria* is similar but appears to be an annual and is raised from seed sown under glass in spring, whereas *D. cordata* can be increased from seed or by division in spring. Ruby Field is said to be a hybrid between these two species but more nearly resembles *D. cordata* and is reliably perennial. *D. rigescens* is much more upright and less spreading and carries its salmon-pink flowers in closely packed spikes on 30-45 cm (1-1½ ft) stems in summer. It requires the same conditions as the others, is perennial and can be increased from seed or by division in spring.

Dodecatheon (American Cowslip, Shooting Star). One more often sees these charming plants at shows than in private gardens and they are undoubtedly difficult to get going. All should be planted in damp, peaty soil near the water's edge and left to increase until overcrowded.

All have cyclamen-like flowers hanging on slender stems 20-30 cm (8 in-1 ft) in height in late spring/early summer, and all die down after flowering, remaining dormant until the following spring. In *D. meadia* they are in various shades of rosy purple and lilac and there is also a good white.

Division is not very desirable and seed sown in sandy peat in the spring is the best method of increase. Spring is also the best planting time.

Draba. In my opinion these get more praise than they are really worth. They are, on the whole, somewhat insignificant plants, neat and cushion-like in habit and useful for planting in crevices but not of outstanding beauty.

Draba bruniifolia, which makes compact tufts not unlike those of a cushion saxifrage with small yellow flowers in late spring is typical. *D. dedeana* has innumerable heads of tiny, white flowers and is pretty and neat. *D. rigida bryoides imbricata* looks like a hummock of moss studded with tiny yellow flowers in early spring. It really requires scree treatment or it can be planted in very gritty soil in the alpine house.

The other species named can be grown in ordinary, porous soil and a sunny place. All should be increased by careful division in spring, which is the best planting season.

Dryas. There are several very lovely trailing species of which the best known is *Dryas octopetala*. This makes wide carpets of dark green, leathery leaves on which lie the wide open, white flowers, rather like dog roses. It is at the height of its splendour towards the end of early summer just at the time when the rock garden tends to become dull. Plant it in full sun and open-textured soil and leave alone, for it takes a good time to recover from root disturbance. It can be raised from seed sown in a tray of sandy soil in spring, and it is a good plan to establish the seedlings in their flowering quarters while still quite young, before their woody roots penetrate too far. Cuttings can also be rooted in sand during late summer.

Other kinds are *D. drummondii* with nodding yellow flowers and a hybrid between this and *D. octopetala* named *D. × suendermannii*, with yellow buds opening to white flowers.

Edraianthus. These are closely allied to campanulas and have often been confused in catalogues with wahlenbergias. *Edraianthus graminifolius* is a flopping plant with very fragile stems, narrow leaves and big, bell-shaped blue flowers most of the summer. *E. pumilio* makes a cushion of growth with violet flowers in late spring/early summer; *E. serpyllifolius* is one of the best with large purplish-blue flowers in mid-summer. All need more care than most campanulas and are fully at home in the scree though they can also be grown in deep, cool, gritty soil in any sunny place. Plant in spring and raise from seed sown in spring (or as soon as ripe) in a frame.

Epilobium (Willow Herb). The true willow herbs are native weeds, very beautiful but not to be permitted in the garden. There is, however, an alpine kind, *Epilobium dodonaei*, which is quite a pretty, inoffensive plant with slender, bronzy stems and leaves and small, rosy purple flowers in late summer. The whole plant is perhaps 18 cm (7 in) high, less if the soil is very gritty, and it can be grown in any decently drained soil and open place. *E. glabellum* has glossy leaves and creamy white flowers produced freely all summer. Seed is the simplest method of increase and can be sown in a frame in spring.

Eranthis. See p. 348.

Erica. See p. 265.

Erinus. This is a small family of small plants but it must not be overlooked on either count. *Erinus alpinus* is the species that matters. It is a dainty little plant with 5 cm (2 in) spikes of purple flowers in spring and early summer. It is surpassed by several of its varieties of which quite the best is Dr Hanele (sometimes spelt Hähnle). This is similar in all respects except that the flowers are a really telling shade of carmine and there is also a white-flowered variety. The plant likes dry walls or may be used to clothe crevices between large boulders. Seed of the type can be sown where the plants are to grow but Dr Hanele will not reproduce true to colour from seed and must be propagated by careful division in the first half of spring.

Eritrichium. Every writer agrees in describing *Eritrichium nanum* as the king of alpines but I am prepared to wager that many have never seen it. Certainly that is my own position. This is because it is a plant of exceptional difficulty in cultivation and even when a specimen can be induced to survive for a few months it has no chance to reproduce its alpine habit of making close hummocks of silk-coated leaves from which sprout, when the snows melt, tiny stems terminated by clusters of intensely blue forget-me-not flowers.

If anyone is fortunate enough to obtain a plant it should be tried in granite scree or, better still, in an exceptionally stony mixture, entirely lime free, kept throughout the year in the alpine frame or house. But really there is little use in writing cultural notes about a plant of which even the experts despair.

Erodium (Heron's Bill). This brings us back to the realm of possible alpines, in fact a good many of them are so easy to grow that unless one takes care they become weeds. All the same there are some good things in the family, notably the charming carpeter *Erodium chamaedryoides (reichardii) roseum*. It will soon cover a large patch of ground with a mat of neat, rounded leaves freely speckled from spring to autumn with small almost stemless soft rose flowers. It will grow practically anywhere and loves a sunny ledge and is very easily increased by division in the spring.

Others needing similar treatment are *E. guttatum*, with white, purple-stained flowers; *E. glandulosum* in which each pink flower has a maroon blotch to enliven it; *E. corsicum*, pink, veined red and *E. chrysanthum*, with deeply divided, silvery leaves and sulphur-yellow flowers. All are summer flowering.

Erysimum. These are wallflower-like plants, mostly too big for the rock garden, though one or two can be included with safety. *Erysimum alpinum* makes a low, spreading plant covered in sulphur-yellow flowers from spring to early summer. It has produced several hybrids such as Moonlight with purple buds and Pamela Pursehouse, deep yellow. *E. linifolium* is about 45 cm (1½ ft) high with purplish-lilac flowers from late spring to mid-summer. Both are sometimes sold as cheiranthus and grow readily, like perennial wallflowers, in any well-drained soil and sunny position. They can be increased by cuttings in spring or summer and also by seed, but seedlings may vary in flower colour. *E. pumilum* is only 6 cm (2½ ft) high, has yellow flowers in mid-summer and should be planted in a scree or moraine, or grown in the alpine house or frame.

Erythronium. See p. 349.

Euphorbia (Spurge). A family that has produced a surprising number of weeds but has also given us a few excellent garden plants. Most of these are too big for the rock garden though *Euphorbia cyparissias*, *E. myrsinites* and a few others are useful in the right kind of place. They will withstand drought and *E. cyparissias* in particular gives its best colour when well baked. It has very fine, almost ferny-looking foliage, pale green at first but becoming coppery red in autumn. The greenish-yellow flowers are in loose sprays in summer. Unfortunately it is very invasive. All species can be increased by division in spring.

Euryops. *Euryops acraeus* is a neat little bush about 38 cm (1¼ ft) high with grey leaves and yellow daisy-type flowers in early summer. It needs a warm, sunny place and well-drained soil and can be increased by cuttings in summer. It is often wrongly called *E. evansii*.

189

Frankenia. *Frankenia laevis* is a fragile plant with trailing stems and small, pale pink flowers in the early summer. It can be used as a carpet for choice bulbs, is not fussy regarding soil but likes best a fairly sunny place. *F. thymifolia* is also mat-forming and has grey, hairy leaves and pink flowers in summer. When more plants of either species are required, detach a few rooted pieces in spring.

Fritillaria. See p. 349.

Fuchsia. One species only is suitable for the rock garden, the rest being comparatively large shrubs, described on p. 270. This is a completely prostrate plant, known as *Fuchsia procumbens*. The flowers are small, yellow and not particularly showy but they are followed by crimson berries which remain for a long time. It is not very hardy so should be planted in a warm, sunny, sheltered spot in rather light, sandy soil or in a frame or unheated greenhouse. New plants can be raised from seed saved from the ripe berries or rooted pieces can be detached in spring from the parent plant. Fuchsias can be planted either in spring or autumn.

Galanthus. See p. 350.

Galax. The solitary species grown, *Galax urceolata*, is a tufted plant with glossy green leaves which become bronze red in autumn. The white flowers are produced in fluffy spikes about 30 cm (1 ft) high in mid-summer. The plant likes a little shade and a cool, deep soil with plenty of leafmould or peat and no lime; in fact it is a woodland rather than a true rock plant. When necessary, divide in spring.

Gentiana (Gentian). This is one of the big and important rock garden families, which ranks with primula and saxifraga for the wealth of wonderful material with which it has provided our gardens. It is almost impossible to generalize about a family with such an extended range and with so many varied requirements and certainly impossible to do it justice in the space available.

Everyone knows the gentianella, *Gentiana acaulis*. The diminutive 'ella' does not, as might be supposed, indicate that this is small as rock garden gentians go for it is used in contrast to the large, yellow-flowered herbaceous gentian (*G. lutea*). The 5 cm (2 in) long, rich blue trumpet flowers of the gentianella are one of the outstanding sights of the rock garden in spring. In some places it thrives so readily that it is grown in borders and beds without special treatment. In others it grows freely but refuses to flower, though often this difficulty can be overcome by importing a little soil from another garden in which it does bloom. Contrary to the general rule with rock garden plants this gentian likes a rich soil and may even have some well-rotted farmyard manure dug in prior to planting. It also likes lime and I have seen it doing well in a garden where there was no more than 9 cm (3½ in) of soil over pure chalk. All the same this is not the ideal site for it but rather a deep, cool, well-fed soil of the sort one might expect would suit roses.

G. verna is a very different plant, much smaller in all its parts, with narrow star-tipped trumpets no more than 2·5 cm (1 in) long but of an exceptionally pure blue. It flowers in mid-spring and likes an open, rather spongy soil with plenty of sand and peat ensuring good drainage in winter but plenty of moisture in summer. It grows wild on limestone.

There are a number of varieties and species closely allied to it of which *G. bavarica* is one of the most beautiful.

Then there are two autumn beauties, *G. farreri* and *G. sino-ornata* and a hybrid between them, *G. × macauleyi*. These have flowers almost as large as those of the gentianella, clear sky-blue in colour streaked outside with white, most noticeable in *G. farreri*. This particular species is difficult in many places though it does well in cool, damp atmospheres. *G. sino-ornata* and *G. macauleyi* are much easier and seldom fail to give a good display if planted in a deep mixture of about equal parts of lime-free loam, peat and coarse sand. They will soon carpet the ground and rooted pieces can be plucked from this mass in spring or early summer to be dibbled in elsewhere and grow into fresh plants.

Very different in style is *G. asclepiadea*, the willow gentian, with arching stems 45 cm (1½ ft) high and rather dark purple flowers almost all the way up. It is a woodlander, thriving in thin shade and cool, leafy soils.

Useful summer-flowering kinds are *G. freyniana*, *G. lagodechiana* and *G. septemfida*, with trailing stems and terminal clusters of the typical blue trumpet flowers of the family but neither so big as those of the gentianella nor so blue as those of *G. verna*. They are comparatively easy plants, thriving in most reasonably well prepared rock garden soils.

Where possible, with the exception of the autumn-flowering species, seed should be used for propagation, but *G. acaulis* usually divides readily enough after flowering and division can be used for other kinds as well.

Geranium (Cranesbill). Most people immediately think of scarlet bedding geraniums when you mention this name, though in fact these plants have no true right to the name at all. Bedding geraniums are in fact pelargoniums and are described in Chapter 19. All the true geraniums are hardy plants, some big enough for the herbaceous border (see Chapter 8) while others are pleasant, easily grown rock garden plants.

Typical of these is *Geranium sanguineum*, which really deserves the name for the flowers are a rich, blood red, and the very distinct form of it known as *G. lancastriense*, with pink flowers all through the summer. *G. argenteum* is 7·5 cm (3 in) high and has grey leaves and pink flowers in the second half of summer. *G. dalmaticum* is 15 cm (6 in) high, spreads rapidly and has soft pink flowers in late spring. *G. cinereum subcaulescens*, often sold as *G. subcaulescens*, is more tufted, 20 cm (8 in) high and has brilliant carmine flowers all summer. It is one of the best to grow. The unfortunately named *G. pylzowianum* has thin, floppy stems and showers of astonishingly big rose-pink flowers in summer.

All grow readily in any reasonably drained soil and sunny place; in fact *G. sanguineum* and its forms can be planted as edgings to the herbaceous border or used to fill the crevices between paving slabs. All can be divided in spring or raised from seed sown in spring in a frame.

Geum (Avens). The best-known geums are border plants but there are some smaller growing and very showy species which make excellent rock garden specimens. *Geum montanum*, with big, single, bright yellow flowers on 20 cm (8 in) stems from late spring to mid-summer is perhaps the best, but *G. reptans*, a trailer with yellow flowers in the first half of summer, is good if it can be obtained true to type. Inferior species are often supplied under its name. The true species needs a very porous gritty soil.

Then there is the water avens, *G. rivale*, with nodding heads of old-rose flowers. This is a plant for the stream side in dampish soil, whereas the others like gritty, open soil in a sunny, even dry position. All except *G. reptans* are easy alpines; they spread rapidly and can be raised from seed or division in spring.

Globularia. These are not very striking plants but they are attractive in a quiet way and have the merit of being very easy to grow. The fluffy flower heads have somewhat the appearance of ageratum and are a similar soft, blue-mauve in colour. There are several species not differing greatly in appearance and all are about 15 cm (6 in) in height. Perhaps the best are *Globularia bellidifolia* and *G. cordifolia*. Plant in any ordinary well drained soil and sunny place and increase, as necessary, by division in spring or by summer cuttings.

Gypsophila. The big, white gypsophila is a herbaceous plant described in Chapter 8 and there is another popular species which is an annual, to be found in Chapter 7. Here I am only concerned with a few dwarf, trailing perennials which grow well in rather dry sunny places and are seen to good advantage in the face of a wall or in vertical crevices. Of these *Gypsophila repens* is the best. It has masses of small white flowers in summer and there are even prettier varieties named *G. r. rosea* and *G. r. fratensis* with pink flowers. There is no difficulty about its cultivation and it can be increased readily from seed or by cuttings in summer struck in sand in a frame. *G. r.* Monstrosa is a slightly bigger plant and needs identical treatment.

Haberlea. This is one of those rare families of rock plants which do best in the shade. Haberleas make flat rosettes of leathery, dark green leaves. They are happiest when planted almost vertically so that moisture does not settle in these rosettes. A cliff face with a northerly aspect is ideal if there are plenty of fissures in it connected with a good bulk of humus-rich soil behind, for the haberlea, though it resents too much moisture on its leaves, likes a reasonable amount at its roots. The flowers, which appear in early summer, are like tiny gloxinias carried in loose sprays on 18 cm (7 in) stems. They are a bluish lilac in the most familiar species, *Haberlea rhodopensis*, but there is also a beautiful, rather rare white-flowered variety of this named Virginalis. *H. ferdinandi-coburgii* is similar to *H. rhodopensis*. All can be increased by leaf cuttings in a frame or in early summer, or by seed on the surface of peaty soil in the greenhouse in spring.

Helianthemum (Sun, Rock Rose). These are among the most vividly coloured of rock plants. Most are low-growing, rather sprawling shrubby plants with single or, in a few cases, double flowers borne in great profusion during late spring/early summer. Most of the varieties grown are garden selections with fancy names such as Jubilee, double yellow; Fireball, double red; Ben Heckla, coppery yellow; Cerise Queen, cerise; Wisley Pink, soft pink; Wisley Primrose, light yellow; and Wisley White. All enjoy sunny places and light, well-drained soils and benefit from a light trimming with shears or scissors immediately after flowering. They can be increased by cuttings rooted in sand in a close frame in mid-summer.

Helichrysum. This name will be most familiar to readers as belonging to the everlasting annuals but the perennials should not be overlooked. I think the best is *Helichrysum* *bellidioides*, with rather rapidly spreading tussocks of stiffly erect, 10 cm (4 in) stems terminated in early summer by the daintiest imaginable white everlasting flowers. It grows readily in any light, sandy soil and warm, sunny place and when new plants are needed the old ones can be lifted and pulled to pieces in mid-spring.

Helxine. See **Soleirolia** (p. 228).

Hepatica. These plants were once known as anemone and their flowers are much like those of some of the small species of anemone. They make low mounds of growth with rounded, rather leathery leaves, each composed of three lobes, and dainty flowers on 15 cm (6 in) stems from late winter to mid-spring. Two species are commonly grown, *Hepatica americana* with normally blue flowers though there are also white and pink and double-flowered varieties, and *H. transsilvanica* (once known as *H. angulosa*) with blue flowers. *H.* × *media* Ballardii is a hybrid with extra fine lavender-blue flowers. All thrive in shady places and like plenty of leafmould or peat in the soil. They can be increased by division after flowering and the species by seed.

Herniaria. *Herniaria glabra* is another of the dwarf carpeting plants useful in the rock garden to give a cover of tiny green leaves to the soil under choice bulbs. It will grow in any ordinary soil and open but not dry place, and can be increased by division in spring.

Hieracium (Hawkweed). Most hawkweeds are weeds that soon take up more room than can be spared. Even the best of them, such as *Hieracium aurantiacum*, with vivid orange-red, dandelion blooms, or *H. villosum*, with yellow flowers and leaves whitened by silky hairs, must be placed with some care or they will soon over-run less vigorous plants. They are ideal for sun-baked places and poor, dry soils which tend to keep them within bounds.

Frequent division is an advantage with such rampant plants and they will recover from this with the greatest alacrity in either spring or autumn.

Hutchinsia. *Hutchinsia alpina* makes cushions of small, shining dark green leaves covered with masses of tiny white flowers in spring. It is pretty enough in its way, though a little lost among the showy alpines of its season. Being very small it makes a useful carpeting plant over bulbs and it will grow in any soil in either sun or partial shade. Pull the old growth to pieces in spring to make way for new plantings.

Hypericum (St John's Wort). There is a sharp division in this family between the big, shrubby plants which I have described in Chapter 10 and the small, often trailing species whose proper place is the rock garden. There are a lot of these, of very unequal merit. In some, the flowers are too small to be really effective but this does not apply to such grand plants as *Hypericum repens*, *H. reptans*, *H. fragile*, *H. nummularium*, *H. coris* and *H. polyphyllum*, all of which are showy, dwarf and more or less spreading (*H. reptans* is a true trailer) nor to the more erect and bush-like *H. olympicum* which is 30 cm (1 ft) height and has both deep yellow and pale yellow varieties. All have flowers in some shade of yellow, very bright and luminous, and all grow in any reasonable soil and open place. Seed germinates readily in a frame in spring or old plants can be carefully divided at that season.

193

Iberis (Candytuft). When choosing candytufts for the rock garden be careful not to get confused with the annual kinds described in Chapter 7 which, though attractive enough, will last only one season and must be renewed each spring from seed. The real rock garden species are true perennials which will continue for many years without renewal. They are very fine plants; common, perhaps, but making a big display worthy of comparison with aubrietas and arabis.

The two best species are *Iberis saxatilis* and *I. sempervirens*. The first is a compact, low-growing plant with very dark, glossy leaves and innumerable thimble-shaped heads of shining white flowers in late spring/early summer. It will grow anywhere but to see it at its brightest and most compact it should be given rather poor, stony soil and a fully sunny position.

I. sempervirens is a much bigger plant, spreading in time over 0·8 sq m (1 sq yd) of rock garden or wall. These are 23–30 cm (9 in-1 ft) high stems set with evergreen foliage and terminated in spring and early summer by bold spikes of showy white flowers. Personally I think there is no better white-flowered alpine at this season. There are plenty of varieties on the market with names such as Snow Queen, Snowflake, Little Gem, etc., differing in minor details and all desirable. Moreover all will grow anywhere and will put up with the poorest of soils but they do like sun and warmth.

I. correaefolia is intermediate between the other two in size and is said to be a variety of *I. semperflorens*.

In a rather different style is *I. gibraltarica*, a loose, bushy plant with drawn-out spikes of flowers which fall between pink and lilac and are not, in my opinion, very effective. Moreover the growth is soft and liable to be killed in winter but it usually does well in a sheltered place and fairly sandy soil.

All perennial candytufts can be raised from seed but selected forms which might vary from the seed can be increased by cuttings of firm, non-flowering shoots rooted in sandy soil in a frame in early summer.

Inula. Most of these plants are vigorous perennials for the herbaceous border or woodland but *Inula acaulis*, a mat-forming species with big, daisy blooms of a bright golden colour in the second half of summer, is worth planting in sunny places in the alpine garden. It likes good drainage and a light soil, and can be increased by careful division in spring.

Iris. It is inevitable that a very big and varied family such as this should be spread about in different sections of this book. Those who are interested in the big flag irises will find them in Chapter 8, while the bulbous-rooted irises, many of which are small enough to be grown in the rock-garden, are dealt with separately in Chapter 12.

This leaves a few non-bulbous but dwarf species to be accounted for, notably *Iris pumila* and *I. chamaeiris*. The two are much confused and are sometimes regarded as synonymous but whereas the flowers of *I. chamaeiris* are always carried on stems, often 15–25 cm (6–10 in) high, those of *I. pumila* are almost stemless. Both resemble miniature flag irises in all other respects. Most catalogues offer numerous named varieties, differing slightly in height but far more in colour. The range includes purple, mauve, lilac, yellow and white. All do best in freely drained or even rather dryish soils and full sun, and all like lime. There is no reason why they should not be used at the front of the herbaceous border as well as in the rock garden.

Other small and attractive kinds are *I. cristata* with lilac-blue flowers on 15 cm (6 in) stems in late spring; *I. lacustris* which is very similar and was once considered to be a variety of *I. cristata; I. gracilipes*, with lilac-mauve flowers on 20 cm (8 in) stems in late spring; *I. innominata* and its hybrids, with flowers in all kinds of unusual combinations of buff, coppery bronze and purple on 20-30 cm (8 in-1 ft) stems in early summer; and *I. tenax*, also in unusual shades of grey-blue and wine-purple, to 30 cm (1 ft), flowering in late spring. *I. cristata* and *I. lacustris* appear to prefer some shade and a rather moist soil. Transplant all these immediately after flowering and increase by division then.

Jeffersonia. The best species is *Jeffersonia dubia*, which looks like a fragile anemone with milky green lobed leaves and cup-shaped blue flowers on 20 cm (8 in) stems in spring. It likes plenty of sharp sand and peat or leaf mould in the soil and a semi-shady place, for it is a woodland plant. It can be increased from seed or by careful division in spring.

Lamium (Dead Nettle). These are mostly weeds and not to be tolerated in select parts of the rock garden but the variegated dead nettle, *Lamium maculatum*, is sometimes useful to clothe rough places or heaps of stones in odd corners; in fact it is a typical 'rockery' as opposed to 'rock garden' plant which will put up with any rough treatment. Its beauty, such as it is, lies in the small, nettle-shaped leaves, darkish green except for a central stripe of pale cream. There are several varieties with coloured leaves: Aureum, yellow; Beacon Silver, silvery; and Chequers, marbled. All these have pink flowers. Old plants can be pulled to pieces and replanted at practically any season.

Lathyrus. *Lathyrus vernus* is a useful and attractive plant for reasonably good soils and sunny places where it will make a leafy plant 30 cm (1 ft) high, covered in the second half of spring with purplish, pink or white flowers like dainty vetches. Seed germinates readily in a frame or even out of doors in spring and old plants can be carefully divided at the same season. It was once also known as *Orobus vernus*.

Leontopodium (Edelweiss). *Leontopodium alpinum* is the plant which every tourist brings back as a memento from the Alps. It has acquired a reputation out of all proportion to its genuine merit. All the same it is a reasonably attractive plant, not difficult to grow in a porous, gritty compost and producing in early summer 15 cm (6 in) spikes terminated by curious white woolly flowers shaped rather like a starfish. The leaves are also densely silvered with white hairs which tend to collect moisture in winter, so that it is a kindly act to protect the plants with a sheet of glass over winter.

Edelweiss can be propagated by seed or division in spring.

Leptinella. Two species are grown, mainly as crevice plants in crazy paving, *Leptinella reptans*, in which the leaves are entirely green and *L. squalida*, in which they are more or less flushed with bronze. They have the merit of keeping very close to the ground and withstanding a considerable amount of wear. Neither has any beauty of flower but both have attractive ferny leaves. Both will grow in any soil and can be increased with the utmost ease by division at any time.

Lewisia. With these we return to plants of really outstanding beauty. The lewisias all have big, wide-open flowers mostly in shades of orange, salmon and pink. They are not too easy to grow as most of them come from warm, sunny regions and find our climate too damp and dull for their liking. They should be planted in stony mixtures such as those of the scree or in vertical crevices between rocks and on dry walls, but not where they are too baked by the sun. Once established they should definitely be left alone as they do not quickly recover from root disturbance, but they must be regarded as short-lived plants which may need fairly frequent renewal, preferably with seedlings which have a new lease of life.

Lewisia tweedyi and *L. cotyledon howellii* are two of the best, the first seldom above 10 cm (4 in) in height and with very big, soft apricot flowers, the second nearly 30 cm (1 ft) in height and with smaller but still ample blooms in various shades of pink, rose and lemon.

Other kinds are *L. cotyledon*, *L. columbiana* and *L. rediviva*, but perhaps most useful of all are the numerous hybrids of garden origin. Seed, when available, can be sown in spring in a tray of very sandy soil in a greenhouse but seedlings may vary in colour and habit so specially selected varieties must be increased by the most careful division, also in spring.

Linaria (Toadflax). This is a family which contains a great many weeds and only a few worthwhile garden plants but fortunately the few really are worth having. The best for the rock garden are the several forms of *Linaria alpina*, a tiny, slender plant with narrow, grey-green leaves and spikes of hooded flowers which look like antirrhinums seen through the wrong end of a pair of opera glasses. There are pink, white, purple and prawn-coloured varieties and all grow readily from seed sown in gritty soil in spring. Give them a sunny place in light soil full of small stone chips; in fact they are excellent beginner's plants for the scree. They flower from late spring to late summer. For the plants sometimes listed as *L. aequitriloba* and *L. pallida*, see Cymbalaria (p. 185).

Linum (Flax). This is a family which has given us one of the most important of economic plants, the flax from which linen fibre and linseed are obtained. The gardener has to thank it for one brilliant annual described in Chapter 7 and several charming rock plants of which one of the best is *Linum arboreum*. This is a miniature shrub 30 cm (1 ft) or more high, freely branched with saucer-shaped yellow flowers which continue to appear most of the summer. The rarely available *L. campanulatum* and *L. elegans* (or *iberidifolium*) are tiny shrubs in the same style resulting in Gemmell's Hybrid.

L. flavum is rather similar in bloom but has softer, less shrubby growth. Like the others, it flowers all the summer.

For colour contrast there is *L. perenne*, with slender, wiry stems 45 cm (1½ ft) high, terminating in loose clusters of fragile, sky-blue flowers at their best in the first half of summer. Similar, but slightly stouter in growth, is *L. narbonnense*, while a more spreading plant with palest pink flowers is *L. suffruticosum salsoloides*.

All like gritty, well-drained soils and sunny places but *L. perenne* is so easy that it will usually grow anywhere. All the species can be raised from seed sown in a frame in spring but Gemmell's Hybrid must be increased from cuttings in a propagator in summer.

Lithospermum. The star of this genus is *Lithospermum diffusum*, known as *Lithodora diffusa*, a grand plant to establish in crevices between large boulders or in the face of a sunny wall. It is really a spreading, evergreen shrub, usually no more than 20 cm (8 in) high, but covering maybe 0·8 sq m (1 sq yd). It has narrow, stiff, dark green leaves and clusters of forget-me-not-like flowers which are a real gentian blue in the best forms, such as Heavenly Blue and Grace Ward. It is at its best in late spring/early summer. *L. graminifolium*, with tufted bright green leaves and deep blue flowers and *L. intermedium* which is much like it are now regarded as species of moltkia, an allied genus, but the old name lithospermum lingers on in gardens. *L. rosmarinifolium* has rosemary-like leaves, the flowers being blue and the plant none too hardy. All can be increased by seed but seedlings may vary in quality of flower; the best forms should be kept true by cuttings in summer.

Lychnis (Campion). The red and white campions found in North European hedgerows in summer give a very fair idea of the style of the whole family. The rock garden campions are smaller and have bigger flowers so that the whole effect is more showy.

Outstanding among them is *Lychnis* × *haageana*, a startlingly vivid plant with coppery-scarlet flowers as big as large coins carried on 30 cm (1 ft) stems. The plant would be grown much more widely were it more permanent but it has an unfortunate tendency to disappear in winter. The secret of success is to grow it in rather dry, well-drained soil, in fact something approaching the conditions of a scree, and to renew frequently from seed. Full sun is essential. The plant flowers all summer. *L. flos-jovis* is 23-30 cm (9 in-1 ft) high, has silvery-grey leaves and rose-pink flowers, paler in Hort's Variety, in the first half of summer. It also likes sunny places and well-drained soils but is easier to keep. Seed of both may be sown in sandy soil in frame or greenhouse either in spring or as soon as ripe.

Lysimachia (Loosestrife). The only loosestrife of interest for the rock gardener is Creeping Jenny, *Lysimachia nummularia*. No doubt this would get far more praise if it came from the Himalayas or Andes. In fact it is often regarded as a weed and it will certainly thrive almost anywhere, even in damp, shady places, where little else would grow. It makes carpets of trailing, pale green growths set with bright buttercup-yellow flowers all summer. There is a form with yellow leaves which spreads more slowly. Both are readily increased by division at practically any time.

Mazus. Three species are commonly grown, *Mazus pumilio*, *M. reptans* and *M. radicans*. All are dwarf, carpet-forming plants, with small, hooded blue and white flowers. They grow readily and can be used as edgings to beds and borders, but their real home is the rock garden in rather leafy or peaty soil and a sunny position. All flower in summer.

Meconopsis (Himalayan Poppy). A chapter is required in which to deal with the many species of meconopsis and only the fringe of the subject can be touched on in a few paragraphs. This is one of the big families both in the number of its species and their importance in the garden. Many are rather difficult plants to grow and most succeed best in deep, cool soils rich in humus yet porous and open, conditions which can be secured by working in plenty of granulated peat and flaky leafmould. Partial shade suits many of them and for this reason they are often seen to better advantage in the open shrubbery or thin woodland than in the rock garden despite the fact that they are generally regarded as rock plants.

One of the most beautiful and widely grown is *Meconopsis betonicifolia*, once known as *M. baileyi*, the blue Himalayan poppy. It will grow 1 m (3½ ft) high in favourable conditions, each stem carrying several wide-open poppy flowers which are sky blue in the best forms with a golden cluster of anthers in the centre. Unfortunately it is a variable plant from seed, yet seed is the only satisfactory method of propagation, as is the case with most meconopses. Often seedlings turn out to have blooms of a poor shade of amethyst and these should be discarded.

M. quintuplinervia has flowers like large harebells on slender, 30 cm (1 ft) stems. *M. paniculata* and *M. napaulensis* are both 1·6 m (5½ ft) high, the first with pale yellow blooms, the second blue, pink or red. *M. integrifolia*, also yellow, is anything from 30-90 cm (1-3 ft) in height, with very large and showy flowers. *M. grandis*, with blue or purple flowers, is of similar height and there is a fine blue-flowered hybrid between this and *M. betonicifolia* named *M. × sheldonii. M. regia* is notable for its rosettes of large leaves covered in silver or golden hairs. The flowers are yellow on 1·5 m (5 ft) stems and hybrids between this fine plant and *M. napaulensis* extend the colour range to pink. All these flower in the first half of summer.

Any good catalogue of alpine plants may list a dozen further species all worth growing, but I have no space to mention any more except the Welsh poppy *M. cambrica* which is rather like a dwarf Iceland poppy with single or double flowers in various shades of yellow and orange produced from late spring to late summer. It will often naturalize itself in cool, shady places.

All species can be raised from seed sown directly it is ripe on the surface of fine, peaty soil in a well-drained tray. Seedlings must be transferred to flowering quarters while still small as later they transplant very bady. Many of the species die after flowering, so regular renewal from seed is a wise precaution.

Mentha (Mint). Most mints have no business in the rock garden, but one, *Mentha requienii*, is always welcome because of its neat, carpeting habit, tiny purple flowers and refreshing mint perfume when bruised or even lightly brushed. It likes a cool, rather moist but sheltered position and can be increased by careful division of the roots in mid-spring.

Moltkia. See **Lithospermum** (p. 197).

Morisia. *Morisia monantha* is the only species and it is often known as *M. hypogaea*. It is a very neat plant which makes a rosette of dark green, deeply slashed leaves in the centre of which nestles in spring a cluster of small but very bright yellow flowers. The whole plant grows close to the ground or presses itself flat against the rocks if it is planted in a crevice, the ideal spot for it. It will stand any amount of sun and heat and likes a deep, open soil. It can be propagated by seed in spring or by cutting up some of the thicker roots into 2·5 cm (1 in) long pieces in mid-winter, strewing these thinly in a seed tray filled with sandy soil. Cover with 12 mm (½ in) of similar soil and place in a cool greenhouse or frame.

Myosotis (Forget-me-not). The common forget-me-not is a plant for bedding schemes rather than for the rock garden but there are some good alpine species, particularly *Myosotis alpestris*, which is exactly like the common forget-me-not but on a smaller scale and with a neater, more tufted habit. The flowers are bright blue with a small yellow eye. It should be grown in gritty soil and a sunny position and may be increased from seed, though specially selected forms, such as the very fine Ruth Fischer, should be kept true by careful division in spring. *M. rupicola* (now known as *M. alpestris*) is a forget-me-not reduced to 5 cm (2 in) stature, and should be grown in the scree.

Nertera (Bead Plant). *N. granadensis*, also known as *N. depressa*, the only species grown, is a quite prostrate plant with very slender, trailing stems and the neatest of circular leaves. On this almost moss-like carpet of pea green lie in late summer a profusion of small, globular, coral-red berries. The plant is so different that it is worth a place in the rock garden despite the fact that it is a little tender and may need the protection of a frost-proof winter greenhouse. It should be grown in a moist soil containing plenty of leaf-mould or peat and it is an advantage if the position is partially shaded. Division in mid-spring provides a ready means of increase.

Nierembergia. The two species usually grown in rock gardens are very different in character. One, *Nierembergia repens* is a trailing plant with widely opened, white flowers which continue to appear most of the summer. It likes plenty of moisture and yet must have good drainage, a paradox which can be resolved by planting it in sandy soil near a stream or in the moraine with an underflow of water all the summer. The other kind, *N. caerulea*, often wrongly known as *N. hippomanica*, is bushy and branching with innumerable slender stems and masses of cup-shaped lavender flowers, also produced throughout the summer. It is not fully hardy, likes a warm, sheltered place and gritty soil and is often treated as a half-hardy annual being raised from seed sown in early spring in a greenhouse or frame. *N. repens* is increased by careful division in spring.

Oenothera (Evening Primrose). There are evening primroses for the herbaceous and mixed borders, and woodland and, in addition, there are a few dwarf forms which make delightful plants for the sunny rock garden. One of the best is *Oenothera missouriensis*, a sturdy, trailing plant with grey-green leaves covered with silken hairs and very large, canary-yellow flowers from mid-summer to mid-autumn. The plant can stand any amount of warmth and is happiest in the lighter, grittier types of soil. Another lovely dwarf kind is *O. speciosa childsii*, often listed as *O. berlandieri*. The flowers are soft pink and the plant neat and dwarf. It requires similar treatment to *O. missouriensis* but may need winter protection with free ventilation. *O. acaulis*, once known as *O. taraxacifolia*, with white flowers and dandelion-like leaves, and *O. caespitosa*, blush white and spreading, are other desirable kinds requiring warm sunny places and gritty, well-drained soil and flower from late spring to early autumn.

All the rock garden oenotheras are best increased by seed sown in sandy soil in a frame or greenhouse in spring.

Omphalodes. The gem of this genus is *Omphalodes luciliae*, a plant which looks rather like a neat forget-me-not, with blue-grey foliage and the usual forget-me-not-blue flowers. It does in fact belong to the forget-me-not family but is far more difficult to grow, requiring perfect drainage and yet an abundant supply of moisture in summer and lime in the soil – in brief, this is a plant for the moraine or alpine house and is not for the beginner. Moreover slugs love it.

In quite a different category is *O. verna*, often known as the creeping forget-me-not, or blue-eyed Mary and a lovely, sprawling thing with loose sprays of small blue flowers in the second half of spring. It will grow anywhere, even in the herbaceous border, and in the rock garden the only point to observe is that, if not carefully placed, it may over-run some less vigorous plants. It is as happy in shade as in sun and can be increased by division in spring. *O. cappadocica* needs similar treatment, is neater in habit and flowers in the second half of spring.

Ononis. One of the best examples for the rock garden is *Ononis rotundifolia*, a bushy plant 30 cm (1 ft) or rather more in height with abundant bright pink flowers all summer. It loves sun and warmth, is not particular about soil and can be increased by seeds sown singly in small pots in spring. Transplant the seedlings when big enough with as little root disturbance as possible.

Onosma. Onosma belongs to the same family as the comfrey and looks rather like it but on a very much reduced scale. It has the same arching stems terminated by several drooping, tubular flowers which give one species its popular name golden drop. But the onosmas are mostly below 30 cm (1 ft) in height, are neat in habit, and ideal plants for the dry wall or a crevice between boulders in the rock garden. The best known and in some ways the most useful is *Onosma echioides* with golden-yellow flowers in early summer. *O. stellulatum* and *O. tauricum* are similar. *O. alboroseum* is a little more difficult to grow, needing especially good drainage, and it has even more markedly silvered foliage to set off its white flowers which change to pink as they age. All kinds may be increased by seed sown in trays of sandy soil in a greenhouse or frame in early spring, or as soon as ripe, while cuttings of firm young shoots will usually root in sandy soil.

Origanum (Marjoram). The common marjoram *Origanum vulgare* is suited only to the herb garden but its yellow-leaved variety *O. v. aureum* is attractive but rather invasive, useful in sunny places where there is room for it to ramble. *Origanum pulchellum* is an attractive, bushy plant with sprays of tiny pink flowers in summer. It grows about 23 cm (9 in) in height, likes sun and is not at all fussy about soil. Other useful kinds, rather similar in appearance, are *O.* × *hybridum* and *O. dictamnus*. But the gem of the genus is *O. rotundifolium* with grey-green rounded leaves clasping the stems and drooping clusters of pink flowers surrounded by parchment coloured bracts. Unlike the rest it is said to dislike lime. Cuttings can be struck in sandy soil in a frame in summer or seed sown in a frame in spring.

Orobus. See **Lathyrus** (p. 195).

Oxalis (Wood Sorrel). The native wood sorrel, pretty though it is, is far too invasive for the rock garden, but there are two very fine foreign species which are real gems. They are *Oxalis enneaphylla* and *O. adenophylla*. The first enjoys a cool, partially shaded place and plenty of peat or leafmould in the soil; the second a gritty soil and sunny position. Both flower in early summer. *O. enneaphylla* has pure white flowers, though there is a pale pink form, while *O. adenophylla* is lilac pink.

Another point of difference is that whereas *O. enneaphylla* slowly spreads by means of underground rhizomes and little bulbs, *O. adenophylla* stays put, having a solitary corm which does not split up. In consequence whereas *O. enneaphylla* can be increased by division of corms in spring, *O. adenophylla* must be propagated by seed sown in very sandy soil in a greenhouse in early spring. Both are prostrate plants. *O. floribunda* is much looser and more lush in habit, with abundant pale green shamrock leaves and fine sprays of gleaming rose-pink flowers all the summer. Grow it in poor, stony soil and a hot, sheltered place and, when you want more plants, divide the old ones in spring.

Papaver (Poppy). *Papaver alpinum* suggests an Iceland poppy reduced to 13 cm (6 in) in height, with genuine miniature poppy flowers in various shades of yellow, orange and pale pink, together with a clear white. Like most poppies it delights in sun and good drainage and will thrive in the grittiest soils; in fact I recommend it to the beginner with a scree. It is readily raised from seed which, being very small, should be sown on the surface of fine, sandy soil and germinated in a frame in mid-spring. Transplant the seedlings to their flowering quarters while still small for later they resent root disturbance; or, if preferred, sow directly where the plants are to flower.

Parochetus. *Parochetus communis* is a rather rampant trailer which makes lush masses of clover-like leaves among which sky-blue flowers appear all summer. It really is a very pretty plant, but rather a nuisance because it grows too fast in summer, smothering other plants and then in winter, being not quite hardy, is apt to die out completely. Give it a sheltered place and pot up a few pieces each autumn so that they can be overwintered in a frame. Then there will be no danger of losing it. The plant can be increased by division at practically any time, is not fussy about soil and likes sun.

Penstemon. This large genus hovers on the borderline of hardiness, which limits its usefulness in the rock garden. All the same there are some excellent rock plants, four of the best being *Penstemon rupicola*, dwarf, spreading and small leaved with glowing magenta flowers; *P. davidsonii*, similar to the last but with rose-pink flowers; *P. menziesii*, 15-25 cm (6-10 in) in height with lavender-blue flowers and *P. fruiticosus scouleri* which is similar to the last but nearer 30 cm (1 ft) high. Six Hills Hybrid is about 20 cm (8 in) tall and has rose-lilac flowers. All these bloom in the first half of summer and are plants for sunny places and porous soils. *P. pinifolius*, a little bush with very narrow leaves, has scarlet tubular flowers from mid-summer to mid-autumn. *P. rupicola* looks its best on a ledge and will stand any amount of heat. All can be increased by cuttings of firm, young growth struck in very sandy soil in late summer. They can also be raised from seed sown in the greenhouse in early spring, but colour is apt to be variable.

Petrorhagia. *Petrorhagia saxifraga* is the only species of importance. It is a very dainty plant which might easily be mistaken for an alpine gypsophila for it has similar thin, wiry stems, narrow leaves and loose sprays of pale pink, starry flowers. There is also a variety with double flowers. This is an admirable plant for a wall or a sunny crevice in the rock garden. It is not fussy regarding soil and can very readily be raised from seed sown in the greenhouse or frame in spring.

Phlox. The family which has given us the gorgeous summer phloxes of the herbaceous border has also provided a great deal of useful material for the rock garden, especially *Phlox subulata* and the numerous forms and hybrids usually grouped under this name. These all form loose mats of growth, spread fairly rapidly and can be planted either on the flat or in crevices between boulders or on the face of a dry wall. They delight in sun and prefer light soils but are not really particular. Some of the best forms, such as the white-flowered *P. s.* Nelsonii, are exceptionally compact, whereas others, such as the pale mauve *P. s.* G.F. Wilson, are distinctly sprawling. Heights vary from 7·5-15 cm (3-6 in) and all bloom in late spring and early summer. Colours include lilac, mauve, pink, carmine and white.

Very similar to the last and often confused with it is *P. douglasii* which has violet, lilac, pink and white varieties and requires identical treatment. A taller plant but still suitable for the rock garden is *P. divaricata*, of which the best variety is named *P. d. laphamii*. In habit this is more like a border phlox, erect and tufted, with 30 cm (1 ft) stems ending in loose heads of lavender flowers in early summer.

Phlox stolonifera is a mat-forming plant with light blue or purple flowers in late spring/early summer. *P. adsurgens* and *P. amoena* are others of similar habit, the first salmon-pink, the other lilac-pink or purple.

The mat-forming phloxes can be increased by cuttings in sandy soil outdoors or under a handlight in early summer. *P. divaricata* and varieties can be divided in spring.

Phyteuma. These very curious-looking plants belong to the campanula family though one would hardly guess it by looking at them. They make tufts or rosettes of leaves from the centres of which appear in early summer circular heads of small, beaked flowers. The best for the rock garden is *Phyteuma comosum* (now known as *Physoplexis comosa*), which is not more than 7·5 cm (3 in) high and has deep blue flowers. It would not be difficult to grow were slugs not so fond of it. Give it a sunny place and open gritty soil with plenty of lime and either surround it with a zinc collar or be generous with slug killer. It can be increased by seed sown in a frame or greenhouse once ripe.

Polygala (Milkwort). The common milkwort is a minute but decidedly attractive weed of meadows, particularly hillside meadows. It is scarcely a plant for the garden but it has an alpine cousin that is much more showy and well worth inclusion. This is *Polygala chamaebuxus*, a dwarf, spreading, shrubby plant with small, evergreen leaves and abundant cream and yellow flowers, or yellow and purple in *P. c. grandiflora* in late spring and continuing intermittently for most of the summer. It is happiest in a mixture of about equal parts sand, peat and lime-free loam in sun or partial shade and it can be increased by careful division in the spring.

Polygonum (Knotweed). This vast family has been generous in producing weeds or plants which, however beautiful, behave like weeds in the garden. Every new polygonum should be examined with care before it is admitted but no qualms need be felt about either *Polygonum affine* or *P. vaccinifolium*, both low-growing plants making wide carpets of evergreen leaves, which in the case of *P. affine* become delightfully tinted with bronze and crimson in the autumn, and from which spring a multitude of short, neat spikes of flowers in late summer/early autumn. These are pale pink and slender in *P. vaccinifolium*, deeper rose and stouter in *P. affine* or nearly red in Lowndes Variety and Darjeeling Red. Both will grow in any ordinary soil and sunny place and can be increased by division in spring or by cuttings in summer. Many polygonum are now listed as fallopia or persicaria.

Potentilla (Cinquefoil). Another family which has produced far more weeds than good garden plants but has nevertheless given us gold amongst the dross. One of the loveliest species is *Potentilla nitida*, a very dwarf, carpet-forming species with small silvery leaves and almost stemless pink flowers all summer but unfortunately it is often shy flowering. It is likely to do best in rather dry soil. Other useful kinds are *P. nepalensis*, which has a fine variety named Miss Willmott, producing masses of cherry-red flowers on 30 cm (1 ft) high stems from mid-summer to autumn; *P. alba*, low growing, spreading and white flowered but rather too invasive; *P. aurea*, another mat-forming species with green leaves and yellow flowers, and *P. tongei*, prostrate with almost stemless apricot flowers all summer. All these potentillas will grow in any reasonably good, well-drained soil and sunny place and can be divided at practically any time.

Primula (Primrose). This is another of those genera about which the experts write volumes and still leave something unsaid. It contains hundreds of species and a great many garden varieties, and these vary greatly in their appearance and requirements. Some are natives of meadows, others grow in woodlands, yet others by the sides of streams or in bogs, while many are found high up on the mountain sides often growing out of apparently barren rocks with no visible root hold till one realizes that they are established in a deep crevice filled with rich soil which is mainly composed of decayed vegetation.

It is extremely difficult to give useful information about so great a genus in a limited space. There is danger that in condensing and generalizing the final impression left may be misleading and I would certainly advise anyone who intends to embark seriously on the culture of the choicer primulas to study the subject in specialized volumes before spending a lot of money.

Broadly, from the standpoint of culture, primulas can be split up into three groups: (1) those that thrive in ordinary, loamy soils and cool positions as, for example, those partly shaded by trees or buildings; (2) bog or stream-side types which like deep, rich, porous soils abundantly supplied with moisture and (3) alpine types which should be planted in positions containing plenty of leafmould or peat with abundant stone chippings and coarse sand to keep the soil open. Those of the last group like to be in full sun so long as this does not imply excessive dryness in summer, but rather than risk that evil it is better to place them where they are shaded from the hottest mid-day sun by boulders or neighbouring plants.

The first group contains the primrose and polyanthus and, provided the soil is well drained, the conditions will also suit some choicer subjects such as *Primula denticulata*, with globular heads of mauve, purple or white flowers on 23 cm (9 in) stems in mid-spring; *P. capitata*, a delightful plant with mealy leaves and stems and little cartwheels of cowslip flowers the colour of violets; and *P. mooreana*, very like it but with bigger heads and a heavier powdering of meal. In *P. vialii* the heads are elongated into little pokers, purplish red in bud and lavender when fully open, which is not until mid-summer. The plant is notoriously difficult to raise year after year and needs a damp, shady spot. *P. flaccida* has heads of nodding, sweetly scented lavender-blue flowers powdered in white in early summer but is more difficult to grow, since it requires a peaty soil, moist in summer but nearly dry in winter. It is a plant for the peat wall or peat garden. *P. juliae* brings us back to the easy-going kind. It is a mat-forming species with glossy, rounded leaves and claret-coloured, almost stemless primrose-type flowers and *P. × pruhoniciana*, also known as *P. juliana* is a race of hybrids with flowers in all shades of rose, claret and ruby. *P. sieboldii*, with softly downy leaves and clusters of rose-pink, purple, blue or white flowers looks more like a greenhouse primula but is hardy.

Group 2 includes *P. japonica* and *P. pulverulenta*, both very similar in appearance, making bold clumps of primrose leaves from which stand up stiffly in early summer 60 cm (2 ft) stems with tier upon tier of flowers normally crimson magenta though there are also pink and white varieties. *P. prolifera* has similar whorls of flower in yellow and *P. bulleyana* repeats the same candelabra pattern in orange-yellow; *P. cockburniana* is coppery orange. *P. florindae* is the giant cowslip of Tibet, a splendid plant with broad leaves 15 cm (6 in) across and 30 cm (1 ft) long, and stout, 1 m (3½ ft) stems terminated by wide clusters of big, pendant, clear yellow blooms which have the fragrance of cowslips. Rather smaller but otherwise similar is *P. sikkimensis* from the uplands of western China while *P. secundiflora* has nodding heads of wine-red blooms and *P. alpicola* has white, primrose or purple flowers. *P. rosea*, in marked contrast to all these, is a dwarf plant seldom more than 15 cm (6 in) high with flower stems which appear in mid-spring just before the leaves and carry small heads of the most brilliant carmine flowers imaginable. A good drift of this near the pool or stream side is one of the outstanding sights of the rock garden in spring. *P. farinosa* has 5 cm (2 in) stems bearing clusters of pink or rose flowers in mid-spring and *P. frondosa* is similar but twice the size.

The truly alpine species in Group 3 include *P. auricula* in all its innumerable forms; *P. marginata*, with similarly leathery leaves and clusters of bluish-lilac flowers on 15 cm (6 in) stems; *P. × pubescens*, a race of hybrids of *P. auricula* with flowers in various shades of lavender, blue, pink, purple, crimson, terracotta and yellow, and *P. hirsuta*, like a neat, tawny-leaved auricula in various shades of pink or mauve. *P. edgeworthii*, which resembles *P. marginata*, blooms in late winter/early spring and needs a specially sheltered place. *P. latifolia* has slightly viscid leaves and clusters of lilac or purple scented flowers on 5-13 cm (2-5 in) stems in spring and *P. glaucescens*, with rosettes of milky green leaves and neat clusters of purplish flowers on 10 cm (4 in) stems is one of the few truly alpine primulas that appreciate a little shade from a boulder or spur.

I have only given the briefest of selections in the above lists and many more equally attractive species and varieties will be found in any good catalogue. All should be propagated when possible from seed, which germinates readily if sown as soon as it is ripe in gritty soil with some granulated peat to hold moisture. Seed is very small so should be given the lightest of coverings. Old clumps which have made numerous crowns can be lifted and divided in spring or immediately after flowering, but this is not such a good method of propagation as seed except in the case of selected forms which will not breed true from seed.

For Polyanthus see p. 96 and Primrose p. 97.

Prunella (Self-heal). The common self-heal, *Prunella vulgaris*, is a pretty little wild plant making carpets of growth covered all summer in short spikes of purple flowers. It is too widespread to be worth cultivating but it has an attractive variety named *P. v. laciniata*, with deeply slashed leaves and white flowers. A plant once sold as *P. incisa* (but now *P. vulgaris*) is similar but has reddish-purple flowers. *P. grandiflora* is also similar to *P. vulgaris* but has several colour forms including white, pink, rose and there is an especially attractive lavender form named Loveliness. All these will grow anywhere in sun or shade and are useful for carpeting and for planting in the crevices of paving and similar purposes. All can be increased by division at almost any time.

Pulsatilla (Pasque Flower). *Pulsatilla vulgaris*, the beautiful North European wild plant found on chalk downs, was formerly known as *Anemone pulsatilla*. It makes a clump of stems and leaves covered in silken hairs and the quite large, anemone-like flowers appear in the first half of spring on 20 cm (8 in) stems. Typically they are pale violet but there are also purple, reddish, lilac and white varieties. All enjoy sunny places and well-drained soil containing chalk or lime. They can be raised from seed sown in spring, but seedlings may vary in colour so specially selected varieties are increased by careful division after flowering.

Ramonda. The rock gardener owes the ramondas a double debt of gratitude for they are both very beautiful and shade lovers – and it is none too easy to find good rock plants for the shady spots that almost inevitably occur even in the best-made rock gardens.

Ramonda myconi, also known as *R. pyrenaica*, is the species most widely planted and is typical of the genus. It makes a big, flat rosette of dark, leathery, wrinkled leaves from the centre of which, in late spring, appear several ascending stems 18 cm (7 in) high, each ending in a small spray of blue-lilac, yellow-centred flowers. There are several forms, one with white and one with soft pink flowers while there are also two or three quite distinct species of which the best is *R. nathaliae*. It is neater, freer flowering and bluer than even the best forms of *R. myconi* but unfortunately it is also a good deal more difficult to purchase.

Plant all these ramondas on their sides in vertical crevices but always where they have a deep root run into cool, leafy or peaty soil containing enough sand to keep them open at all times yet not enough to make them dry and harsh.

Ramondas can be raised from seed sown on the surface of sandy peat or a fine compost containing plenty of sand and peat, but as seedlings may prove variable, especially fine forms, raise them from leaves detached carefully in early summer and pushed a little way into a similar compost to that used for seed raising. Keep in a cool, shaded frame or greenhouse and each leaf will in time make a new plant.

Ranunculus (Buttercup). The common buttercup of our meadows is a ranunculus, but there are also several excellent ornamental plants in the family including border plants (see Chapter 8) and very showy tuberous-rooted, double-flowered ranunculus which are described in Chapter 12. For the rock garden there is a choice species named *Ranunculus alpestris*, which is best planted in the moraine, as it needs a very gritty soil with abundant moisture in summer. It keeps close to the ground and has small, white flowers about midsummer. Much easier is the grass-leaved buttercup, *R. gramineus*, with narrow leaves and branching sprays of typical buttercup flowers, though the plant has none of the butter-cup's inclination to ramble further than it should. This species will grow in any ordinary soil and looks well in a dry wall. *R. amplexicaulis* has large white flowers on 20 cm (8 in) stems in late spring/early summer and likes a sunny place. There are also several attractive varieties of the common celandine, *R. ficaria*, which will grow in sun or shade. There are at least two double-flowered forms, one all yellow, the other yellow and green, also a coppery-yellow variety named *R. f. aurantiacus* and a giant-flowered variety named *R. lingua grandiflorus*.

All rock garden buttercups can be increased by division in spring.

Raoulia. These are carpeting plants of the greatest merit, the best species being *Raoulia australis*, which has very tiny, silvery leaves and keeps absolutely flat to the ground. It is ideal cover for the choicer and smallest rock garden bulbs such as snowdrops, miniature narcissi and crocuses. It likes gritty, well-drained soils and sheltered sunny positions and can be increased by a portion of the mat being lifted in spring and pulled to pieces.

Rhodohypoxis. *Rhodohypoxis baueri* is a very beautiful but rather difficult bulbous-rooted plant which should be grown in a compost of equal parts lime-free loam, course lime-free grit and granulated peat. It should have plenty of water in summer but be kept rather dry in winter. It makes compact little tufts of grassy leaves, spangled all the summer with carmine, pink or white flowers looking like tiny butterflies. Increase this and other kinds by seed sown in sandy peat in the greenhouse or frame in spring, or by offsets in spring.

Rosa (Rose). The only rose which really belongs to the rock garden is that exquisite miniature, *Rosa roulettii*. Botanists say that it is a miniature variety of the China rose and that its correct name is *R. chinensis minima*. Imagine a pink polyantha rose reduced to 15 cm (6 in) in height with all its parts in perfect proportion, and you have an excellent idea of its charm. It will grow in any ordinary soil and sunny place and can be increased by cuttings of firm, young growth inserted in a frame in the late summer or autumn.

Roscoea. A deep, cool, moist yet porous soil is required to grow roscoeas well. They are worth a little trouble for they are very unusual in appearance and distinctly beautiful plants, with hooded flowers packed closely together on erect stems, varying from 15 cm (6 in) in the dwarf species *Roscoea alpina*, to 30 cm (1 ft) in the case of *R. cautleoides* and *R. purpurea*. The first is pink, the second pale yellow, the third purple and white. All flower in the first half of summer. They can be increased by careful division in spring, though seed sown in a frame at the same season is really a better method.

Rosmarinus (Rosemary). The common rosemary is a shrub, too big for the ordinary rockery, but there is a smaller form named *Rosmarinus × lavandulaceus*, also known as *R. officinalis prostratus*, which spreads slowly along the ground and has the typical fragrant foliage and pale blue flowers of rosemary. It will grow in any ordinary soil and sunny place but is rather more tender than the common rosemary and unsuitable for cold localities. It can be increased by summer cuttings in sandy soil.

Sanguinaria (Bloodroot). *Sanguinaria canadensis* is the only species, a trailing plant with grey-green leaves and wide-open, white flowers. There is also a fine double-flowered variety. It is a member of the poppy family but unlike most of its kind it inhabits moist, shady places and delights in cool, leafy soils. It is a good plant to place near a stream side or in the better drained portions of the bog garden. It flowers in spring and can be propagated by division immediately after flowering.

Saponaria (Soapwort). The common soapwort is a herbaceous plant (see Chapter 8), and there is one annual species (see Chapter 7). For the rock garden there is a trailing kind named *Saponaria ocymoides*, which will soon cover 0·8 sq m (1 sq yd) of ground with rather lush masses of soft, green leaves and clouds of rose-pink flowers during the first half of summer. It will grow anywhere and give no trouble beyond, possibly, over-running some smaller and choicer plants in its way. It can be raised easily from seed sown in a frame in early spring or out of doors later in the season, but seedlings may vary slightly in colour so specially selected varieties are increased by summer cuttings.

Saxifraga (Saxifrage). This vast family of plants should really be regarded as a collection of quite separate groups of plants, each with its own particular characteristics and requirements. Even botanists agree that the name has been stretched to cover plants very distinct in type and it is customary to subdivide the genus into as many as sixteen sections. Some of these are of no great significance from the garden standpoint, but there are at least seven groups with which the gardener should be familiar. These are as follows:

(1) Mossy saxifrages, with soft cushions of growth and flowers carried on slender stems in the second half of spring. These all like cool positions and may be grown in shady places and ordinary soils provided they do not dry out quickly in hot weather. It is an advantage to add leafmould or peat and perhaps a little well-rotted manure before planting, particularly if the soil is by nature inclined to be poor or dry.

(2) Silver or Encrusted saxifrages, many of which make compact, flat rosettes of stiff leaves, often heavily silvered. From these arise, in late spring/early summer, plumes of flowers often 60 cm (2 ft) in height. These are all true alpines, delighting in light, gritty soils and full sun. Many are seen to best advantage when planted on their sides in vertical crevices or on well-made, dry walls with an ample core of good rock garden compost.

(3) Cushion or Kabschia saxifrages, which are also true alpines but on the average very much smaller and more compact than the Silver saxifrages. As their name implies they make compact cushions of growth which is firm and sometimes almost spiky, not soft like those of the Mossy saxifrages. These, too, need true alpine conditions with quick drainage coupled with an ample water supply in spring and summer. The choicest are plants for the moraine. Almost all flower very early, some starting late winter in a favourable season.

(4) A small group which has no popular name so it must be known by its botanical title, Engleria. These are rather like small, neat Silver saxifrages with very compact rosettes. Their flowers are often insignificant but in some species the flower stems are adorned with brightly coloured bracts, quite as showy as any blooms. They need exactly the same conditions as Cushion saxifrages.

(5) Another group without a popular name which I will call Oppositifolia after its best-known species. These are prostrate, mat-forming plants which appreciate very gritty soils but a little shade from the mid-day sun. They are good subjects for the moraine and

flower in the first half of spring.

(6) The London Pride group, well typified by the popular species whose name I have used to describe the section. There are neater forms, however, than the London Pride itself. All are easily grown in any ordinary soil and sunny or partially shaded position. They flower in late spring/early summer.

(7) A group known botanically as Diptera or Ligularia, with rather stout leaves and sprays of flowers in the autumn, an unusual flowering period for saxifrages. They like cool, moist but open soils and partially shaded places.

One could multiply examples in each group almost indefinitely and I must confine myself here to a few only of the best or most widely planted.

Mossy saxifrages are now chiefly represented in gardens by hybrids which pass under fancy names, such as Pompadour (crimson), James Bremner (white), Marshal Joffre (red), Gaiety (rose pink), and so on. Catalogues should be consulted for these for many nurserymen have their own specialities.

There are also a few species or sub-species of the Mossy group which are worth planting, notably *Saxifraga hypnoides* which is exceptionally close growing and moss-like with small, white flowers in great profusion; *S.* Sanguinea Superba, a hybrid of *S. decipiens* with bright crimson flowers on 10 cm (4 in) stems; *S. moschata* and *S. muscoides*, similar in name and in appearance which make dense cushions of growth and have numerous varieties, some white, some pale yellow and some pink; *S. camposii*, rather loose in growth with white flowers; and *S. trifurcata*, known as the stag's horn saxifrage because the leaves look like tiny stag's horns. The flowers are large and white.

All these Mossy saxifrages can be increased by division after flowering. It is often advisable to divide and replant every second or third year to prevent the plants becoming starved and brown at the centre. The species can also be increased from seed sown in a frame or greenhouse in spring but garden varieties, though also growing readily from seed, are likely to vary considerably when propagated in this way.

Not a true Mossy saxifrage but rather like one in appearance and thriving under similar conditions is the meadow saxifrage, *S. granulata*. The flowers, on 15 cm (6 in) stems borne from mid-spring to early summer, are white and there is a very fine double-flowered form which needs to be increased by division.

The four outstanding Silver saxifrages are *S. paniculata*, *S. cotyledon*, *S. callosa* and *S. longifolia*. Each has given rise to numerous garden varieties, often more beautiful than the species itself *S. paniculata*, for example, which has small rosettes multiplying rapidly and soon covering quite a considerable area of ground, is white flowered, but has pink and yellow-flowered varieties. Personally I like the pink form best of all. There is also a variety named *S. paniculata baldensis*, in which everything is reduced in size so giving almost the effect of a Cushion saxifrage.

S. cotyledon is a much bigger plant with rosettes often as large as a tea plate and plume-like sprays of white flowers on 45 cm (1½ ft) stems. One of the best forms is Caterhamensis in which the flower sprays are almost twice as big as normal and the flowers are heavily spotted with red.

S. callosa has narrower leaves than the last and arching plumes of flowers which are especially graceful. The flowers are white. There is an exceptionally fine form named Albertii which is bigger and broader in leaf and has especially fine flower trusses.

S. longifolia itself is a difficult plant as it dies after flowering and in any case needs very

Acantholimon glumaceum

Achillea clavennae

Aethionema Warley Rose

Ajuga reptans Burgundy Glow

Acantholimon glumaceum, 15 cm (6 in), a dwarf tufted evergreen with sharp-pointed leaves, opens many bright red starry flowers in late summer △ ⚇ ❀ Summer ☼ ▬ ▦ ▮

Achillea clavennae, 15 cm (6 in), a charming silver-leaved perennial, bears clusters of white flowers in summer ⊕ ❀ Summer ☼ ▦ ▮

Aethionema Warley Rose, 15 cm (6 in), a sub-shrubby perennial, has glaucous foliage and pink flowers ⊕ ❀ Summer ☼ ▦ ▮

Ajuga reptans Burgundy Glow, 15 cm (6 in), is grown primarily for its vari-coloured foliage but also bears rich blue flowers ▲ ❀ Summer ◐ ▦ ▮

Aquilegia bertolonii

Anthyllis montana

Androsace primuloides Chumbyi

Antennaria dioica Rosea

Androsace primuloides Chumbyi, 10 cm (4 in), a tufted plant, forms rosettes of lanceolate leaves and flowers in long-stemmed umbels ✦ ✳ Spring ☼ ▬ ♨ ■ ▯

Antennaria dioica Rosea, 7.5 cm (3 in), is grown for its mat of grey woolly leaves, easily divided to make more plants ✦ ✳ Summer ☼ ♨ ■ ▯

Anthyllis montana, 10 cm (4 in), forms a miniature prostrate shrub with silver-haired leaflets and dense clusters of pink flowers ✦ ✳ Spring ☼ ♨ ■ ▯

Aquilegia bertolonii, 15 cm (6 in), a dwarf columbine, has ferny glaucous leaves and short-spurred flowers ✦ ✳ Summer ☼ ♨ ■ ▯

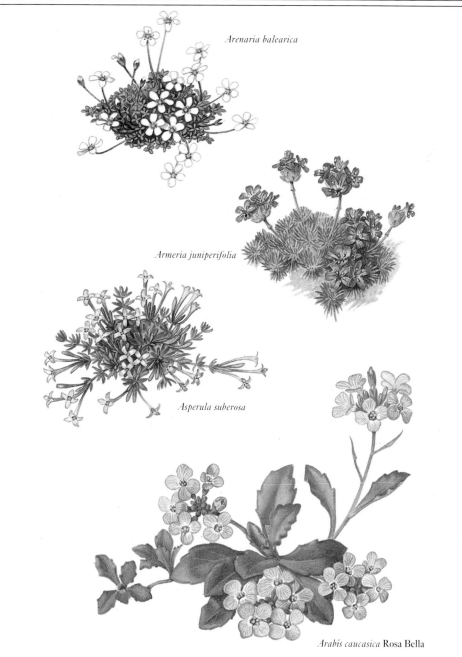

Arenaria balearica

Armeria juniperifolia

Asperula suberosa

Arabis caucasica Rosa Bella

Arabis caucasica Rosa Bella, 15 cm (6 in), a prostrate hairy-leaved perennial, opens heads of reddish purple flowers in spring. Easy from seed or by division ⊕ ❀ Summer ☼ 🖳 ■ ▮

Arenaria balearica, 12 mm (½ in), a tiny creeping perennial, sports its long-stemmed flowers for several months. Easily divided but can become invasive
⊕ ❀ Spring/Summer ☼ ● 🖳 ▮

Armeria juniperifolia, 5 cm (2 in), a densely tufted pink-flowered thrift, is fine for a scree, wall or container △ ❀ Summer ☼ 🖳 ■ ▮

Asperula suberosa, 10 cm (4 in), a tufted silver-haired perennial, opens spikes of tubular pink flowers. Protect its foliage from damp in winter
⊕ ⬇ ❀ Summer ☼ 🖳 ■ ▮

Campanula carpatica

Campanula cochlearifolia

Cassiope Muirhead

Cotoneaster dammeri radicans

Campanula carpatica, 30 cm (1 ft), a vigorous-growing bellflower, forms spreading clumps with masses of wide-open blooms in high summer ✤ ❀ Summer ☼ ◉ 🛡 ◧

Campanula cochlearifolia, 5 cm (2 in), a tiny bellflower spreading by underground runners, bears dainty bells on slender stems ✤ ❀ Summer ☼ 🛡 ◧

Cassiope **Muirhead**, 15 cm (6 in), an evergreen shrublet with stems clothed in overlapping, scale-like leaves, bears delectable white bell flowers △ ⚘ ❀ Spring ◉ 🛡 ◧

Cotoneaster dammeri radicans, 15 cm (6 in), a handsome little prostrate shrub, fine on a scree or over a rock
△ ❀ Summer ♻ Autumn ☼ 🛡 ◧

Cyclamen hederifolium

Crepis incana

Daphne cneorum

Dianthus alpinus

Crepis incana, 15 cm (6 in), a dainty hawkweed, forms compact tufts of leaves crowned with pink daisies in summer ✿ ❋ Summer/Autumn ☼ ☀ ▦ ▮

Cyclamen hederifolium, 10 cm (4 in), opens its charming pink or white flowers in autumn, followed by silver-patterned green leaves that persist into spring ✿ ❋ Autumn ☼ ☀ ▦ ▮

Daphne cneorum (Garland Flower), 15 cm (6 in), a tiny trailing evergreen shrub, opens rose-red flowers in summer. Raise from seed or summer cuttings △ ❋ Summer ☼ ▦ ▮

Dianthus alpinus, 5 cm (2 in), a tiny mat-forming pink, bears large rick pink or white flowers, darker purple at the centre ✿ ❋ Summer ☼ ▦ ▮

Dryas octopetala

Edraianthus serpyllifolius

Erinus alpinus

Dianthus La Bourbrille

Dianthus La Bourbrille, 7.5 cm (3 in), a delectable little pink, forms close tufts of narrow silvery leaves ⊕ ❀ Summer ☼ ▣ ▮

Dryas octopetala, 15 cm (6 in), an evergreen sub-shrub, forms mats of growth from which arise white rose-like flowers and fluffy seedheads. Easy from seed, divisions or cuttings △ ▼ ❀ Summer ☼ ▣ ▮

Edraianthus serpyllifolius, 10 cm (4 in), a compact mat-forming plant, bears lovely blue bells. Fine for a limestone scree ⊕ ❀ Summer ☼ ▣ ▮

Erinus alpinus, 5 cm (2 in), forms leafy cushions and opens spikes of small pink, mauve or white flowers in spring. Fine for crevices. Increase by division, seeds or self-sown seedlings ⊕ ❀ Spring ☼ ▣ ▮

Erodium chamaedryoides roseum

Gentiana verna

Geranium cinereum Ballerina

Gentiana sino-ornata

Erodium chamaedryoides roseum, 7.5 cm
(3 in), is a densely tufted cranesbill. Raise from
seeds or cuttings ✦ ❀ Summer ☼ ▨ ☐ ▮

Gentiana sino-ornata, 15 cm (6 in), a
prostrate gentian fine for ground cover, opens
gorgeous funnel-shaped flowers. Easy from
seed or division ✦ ❀ Autumn ☼ ▨ ▮

Gentiana verna, 10 cm (4 in), is a neat tufted
gentian with solitary flowers. Easy from seed
or divisions ✦ ❀ Summer ☼ ▨ ▮

Geranium cinereum Ballerina, 15 cm (6 in),
an almost stemless cranesbill, forms tufts of
glaucous leaves and distinctive crimson-veined
pale pink flowers ✦ ❀ Summer ☼ ◉ ▨ ▮

Haberlea rhodopensis

Helianthemum Wisley Primrose

Helianthemum oelandicum alpestre

Hepatica americana

Haberlea rhodopensis, 13 cm (5 in), produces clusters of pale lilac flowers from its leaf rosettes. Ideal for a shady part of the rock garden ⊕ ❀ Spring ☼ ▼ ▯

Helianthemum oelandicum alpestre, 7.5 cm (3 in), a tiny ground-hugging rock rose, is fine for a raised bed △ ❀ Summer ☼ ▼ ▯

Helianthemum Wisley Primrose (Rock Rose, Sun Rose), 30 cm (1 ft), a lax semi-shrubby plant, flowers profusely. Trim it back after flowering △ ❀ Summer ☼ ▼ ▯

Hepatica americana, 23 cm (9 in), a cousin of the anemones, opens pink or whitish flowers before its shiny leaves △ ❀ Spring ☼ ● ▼ ▯

Lewisia cotyledon hybrid

Linaria alpina

Iris pumila Cyanea

Lamium maculatum Salmonae

Iris pumila Cyanea, 5 cm (2 in), a miniature bearded iris, propagated by dividing its rhizomes after flowering
⊕ ❋ Spring/Summer ☼ 🛡 ∎

Lamium maculatum Salmonae (Dead Nettle), 38 cm (1¼ ft), is a trailer grown primarily for its silver-variegated leaves
△ ❋ Summer ☼ ◑ ● 🛡 ∎

Lewisia cotyledon hybrid, 15 cm (6 in), forms generous heads of flowers from its dense leaf rosette. Best grown in a pan protected from excessive wet ⊕ ⚑ ❋ Summer ☼ 🛡 ∎

Linaria alpina, 15 cm (6 in), is a miniature prostrate toadflax. Increase from seed, divisions or softwood cuttings.
⊕ ❋ Summer/Autumn ◑ 🛡 ∎

Lithodora (Lithospermum) diffusa
Heavenly Blue, 20 cm (8 in), a prostrate sub-shrub, bears many deep blue flowers. Trim back after flowering △ ❀ Summer ☼ ⛉ ■

***Lysimachia nummularia* Aurea** (Creeping Jenny), 10 cm (4 in), a golden creeper, opens yellow buttercup-like flowers. Good for ground cover △ ❀ Summer ☼ ◐ ⬓ ⛉ ◧

Mazus reptans, 5 cm (2 in), a tiny prostrate plant whose stems root as they go, forms carpeting growth ⦶ ❀ Summer ☼ ⛉ ◧

***Mimulus cupreus* Whitecroft Scarlet**, 15 cm (6 in), a brilliant musk, likes to be very moist in summer, dryish in winter
⦶ ⚘ ❀ Summer/Autumn ☼ ◐ ⛉ ◧

Myosotis alpestris

Oxalis adenophylla

Oenothera pumila

Origanum rotundifolium

Papaver alpinum

Origanum rotundifolium (Marjoram), 45 cm (1½ ft), a leafy aromatic plant, is good in a pan. Increase by division or softwood cuttings ◈ ◙ ❋ Summer ☼ ◐ ▣ ◪ ◼

Oxalis adenophylla, 15 cm (6 in), forms a rosette of silver-green leaves from a bulb-like base, crowned by pink flowers ◈ ❋ Summer ☼ ▣ ◼

Papaver alpinum (Alpine Poppy), 13 cm (6 in), a charming tufted plant with glaucous leaves, opens white or yellow flowers. Good in a pan ◈ ❋ Summer ☼ ◐ ▣ ◪ ◼

Myosotis alpestris, 15 cm (6 in), a miniature forget-me-not, opens slightly scented flowers in spring. Increase by seed or division ◈ ❋ Spring ☼ ◐ ▣ ◪ ◼

Oenothera pumila, 30 cm (1 ft), an easily pleased herbaceous perennial, raised from divisions in early spring or early summer cuttings, opens lovely evening primrose flowers in summer ◈ ⚘ ❋ Summer/Autumn ☼ ◐ ▣ ◼

Physoplexis comosa

Phlox hoodii

Penstemon rupicola

Phlox stolonifera

Penstemon rupicola, 10 cm (4 in), a prostrate evergreen shrub from Western USA, makes a good rock garden plant. Propagate from late summer cuttings △ ❀ Summer ☼ ▼ ▮

Phlox hoodii, 5 cm (2 in), a tiny narrow-leaved tufted plant from N. America, can be increased from seed or cuttings △ ❀ Summer ☼ ◐ ▼ ▮

Phlox stolonifera, 18 cm (7 in), a creeping plant which roots as it spreads, opens clusters of charming flowers. Increase from seed or summer cuttings △ ❀ Summer ☼ ◐ ▼ ▮

Physoplexis comosa, 10 cm (4 in), forms a tufted plant with clusters of flask-shaped flowers. Protect it from slug attack ◈ ❀ Summer ☼ ▼ ▮

Primula marginata

Primula denticulata Ruby

Primula juliae Wanda

***Primula denticulata* Ruby** (Drumstick
Primula), 20 cm (8 in), forms a largish rosette
of mealy leaves and tight heads of flowers. Also
mauve and white forms ⊕ ✤ Spring ☼ ▉ █

***Primula juliae* Wanda**, 10 cm (4 in), a
favourite early-flowering primula, is easy from
seed or divisions. Protect its blooms from
pecking birds ⊕ ✤ Spring ☼ ▉ █

Primula marginata, 10 cm (4 in), so named
after the silvery margins of its farina-covered
leaves, opens fragrant lilac flowers
⊕ ✤ Spring ☼ ☼ ▉ █

Ramonda myconi

Pulsatilla vulgaris

Pulsatilla vulgaris

Pulsatilla vulgaris (Pasque Flower), 15 cm (6 in), is valued alike for its mauve flowers succeeded by fluffy seedheads and its deeply segmented downy foliage. Easy to raise from seed ✤ ⚘ ❀ Spring ☼ ◐ ▦ ◧

Ramonda myconi, 18 cm (7 in), a stemless hairy-leaved Pyrenean plant, thrives in a cool, moist shady position. Easy from seed, division or leaf cuttings ✤ ❀ Summer ☼ ◐ ▦ ◧

Ranunculus alpestris, 10 cm (4 in), a neat little buttercup with solitary white flowers, comes readily from seed
✤ ❀ Late Spring/Summer ☼ ◐ ▦ ◧

Saxifraga oppositifolia latina

Saxifraga burseriana

Saxifraga longifolia Tumbling Waters

Saxifraga grisebachii Wisley Variety

Saxifraga burseriana, 5 cm (2 in), a tiny silver spiny leaved cushion plant, is best in a pan or raised bed ⊕ ❀ Spring ✿ ▨ ☐ ▮

Saxifraga grisebachii Wisley Variety, 23 cm (9 in), forms a cushion of 6 cm (2½ in) rosettes crowned by flower stems clothed in red-haired leaves ⊕ ❀ Spring ✿ ▨ ☐ ▮

Saxifraga longifolia Tumbling Waters, 45 cm (1½ ft), most vigorous of the saxifrages, produces spectacular flower clusters △ ❀ Summer ✿ ▨ ☐ ▮

Saxifraga oppositifolia latina, 5 cm (2 in), a tiny mat-forming creeper with silver-green leaves, opens large pink flowers in spring △ ❀ Spring ✿ ▨ ☐ ▮

Sempervivum arachnoideum

Sedum spathulifolium Capablanca

Silene acaulis

Sedum palmeri

Sedum palmeri, 20 cm (8 in), a Mexican trailer which roots as it spreads, forms rosettes of glaucous leaves. Easily increased from rooted pieces △ ❀ Summer ☼ ◐ ▨ ◧ ▮

Sedum spathulifolium Capablanca, 13 cm (5 in), a stonecrop, forms a cushion of silvery rosettes crowned with yellow flowers △ ❀ Summer ☼ ◐ ▨ ◧ ▮

Sempervivum arachnoideum (Cobweb Houseleek), 5 cm (2 in), a rosette-forming plant covered with cobweb-like hairs, opens flowers on erect stems △ ❀ Summer ☼ ◐ ▨ ◧ ▮

Silene acaulis (Moss Campion), 5 cm (2 in), a tiny tufted plant, opens red, pink or white flowers. It favours sharp drainage. ◍ ⚘ ❀ Summer ☼ ▨ ◧ ▮

good drainage and a deep root run, but it hybridizes easily with other Silver saxifrages and there are some especially fine hybrids between *S. longifolia* and *S. callosa*, in which only the flowering rosette dies and the plant is renewed by offsets. One of the best of these is Tumbling Waters which produces enormous plumes of white flowers from stiff, densely silvered rosettes of leaves.

Another Silver saxifrage worth noting is *S. cochlearis*, which makes a firm, dome-like mound of tiny silver leaves and has white flowers. It is so small that it might be mistaken for a Cushion saxifrage and it has an even more compact, huddled form named *minor*.

All these can be propagated by seed sown in a greenhouse or frame in spring but seedlings of hybrids and selected garden varieties may vary in character. All except *S. longifolia* may be divided by careful division in the spring or immediately after they have flowered.

The Cushion saxifrages have been very highly developed, with the result that catalogues teem with fancy or pseudo-botanical names designating all manner of hybrids and garden seedlings. These include × *apiculata*, primrose yellow; *boydii*, golden yellow; Cranbourne, pink; Myra, lilac pink; × *irvingii*, pale pink; × *elizabethae*, yellow; Haagii, bright yellow and Jenkinsae, rose-blossom pink. The best species for garden cultivation, from which some of these garden hybrids have been developed are *S. burseriana*, with slender red stems and flowers like white cherry blossom, *S. lilacina*, which is absolutely prostrate with almost stemless lilac flowers and *S. marginata*, a very variable plant usually white flowered, sometimes making very tight hummocks of growth and sometimes more open in habit. All may be divided after flowering and species can also be raised from seed at the same temperatures as for other saxifrages.

Far and away the best Engleria is *S. grisebachii*. This makes numerous very compact silver rosettes, each of which erupts in spring into a short, arching stem clothed throughout in crimson plush bracts. It needs exactly the same treatment as any of the choice Cushion saxifrages.

The best of the Oppositifolia group is *S. oppositifolia* itself. It sprawls about making mats of slender stems closely clad with tiny leaves and bearing heather-red flowers in the first half of spring. There are a good many varieties, some with bigger blooms, one white, another purplish crimson. All can be increased by careful division after flowering.

The member of the London Pride group which I like best is the dainty variety known as *S. umbrosa primuloides*. It has loose sprays of small flowers like those of *S. umbrosa* itself but the whole plant is reduced to 15 cm (6 in) in stature, very neat in growth and with flowers in an extra warm shade of pink. It blooms in May and can be pulled to pieces and replanted at almost any time. There are varieties of both *S. umbrosa* and *S. umbrosa primuloides* with yellow variegated leaves. Botanists consider that the plants grown as *S. umbrosa* are not the true species but hybrids which should be known as *S. urbium* but the old name is still commonly used in gardens and nurseries. Another useful plant in this group is *S.* × *geum*, with stout, heart-shaped leaves and loose clusters of pink flowers on 23 cm (9 in) stems in late spring.

Lastly, by far the best of the Diptera group is *S. cortusifolia fortunei*, a handsome plant with quite large, rounded, shining leaves bronzy red beneath and 30 cm (1 ft) high sprays of white flowers in the first half of autumn. It is a woodland rather than a rock plant and can be easily increased by division in the spring. The leaf colour is even richer in varieties Rubrifolia and Wada.

Scabiosa (Scabious). The best-known varieties of scabious are either plants to be treated as annuals (see Chapter 7) or herbaceous perennials (see Chapter 8). There are, however, in addition one or two dwarf species which make pretty rock garden plants, notably *Scabiosa perennis* and *S. graminifolia*. The first forms a cushion of soft, grey-green leaves, the second makes tufts of very narrow, silvery-grey leaves and both produce a profusion of small, mauve, scabious blooms throughout the greater part of the summer. A plant which passes in gardens as *S. alpina (Cephalaria alpina)* is much like *S. perennis* but with lavender flowers. All will grow in any ordinary soil and sunny place and look especially well in the dry wall or planted between big boulders. They can be increased by division or by seed in the spring.

Schizocodon (Japanese Moonwort). See **Shortia** (p. 227).

Scutellaria (Skullcap). These are for the most part small and not very attractive plants but *Scutellaria alpina* is reasonably neat in growth and free with its small, blue-purple flowers which have the merit of coming in the latter half of the summer when colour is scarce in the rock garden. *S. indica parviflora*, requiring similar treatment, is also worth planting for its abundant short spikes of violet-purple flowers. A third species, *S. scordifolia*, makes small tubers and has deep blue flowers on 23 cm (9 in) stems in summer. All will grow practically anywhere provided the position is open and the soil porous, and can be increased by seed or division in the spring.

Sedum (Stonecrop). This is a family of the highest merit for the rock garden, though it also includes some weeds. Most of the sedums are cheerful plants which will grow in the hottest situations and with the minimum amount of soil. There is great diversity in the family, from the tiny, chubby-leaved forms typified by our own natives, *Sedum album*, *S. acre* and *S. anglicum*, the first with white, the second with yellow, and the third with pink flowers, to the big, flat-leaved types such as *S. spectabile* and *S. telephium maximum*, plants more suited to the herbaceous border than the rock garden on account of their size.

There are a great many species and varieties of which I can give no more than a brief selection here. Those which I specially recommend are *S. cauticolum*, sprawling with blue-grey leaves and rosy-purple flowers in the first half of autumn; *S. dasyphyllum*, with tiny crowded leaves making a little hummock of growth studded with pinkish-white flowers in early summer; *S. ewersii*, 15 cm (6 in) high, with grey-green leaves and purplish flowers in late summer/early autumn; *S. hispanicum*, with very tiny, pale grey-green leaves and pink-tinged flowers, the whole plant being no more than 5 cm (2 in) high; *S. kamtschaticum*, quick growing and carpet forming, with shining dark green leaves and orange-yellow flowers and a form of this known as *S. k. Variegatum*, in which the leaves are edged with cream; *S. lydium*, which is like *S. hispanicum* except that the leaves turn bronze when the plant is grown in a dry, warm place; *S. middendorfianum*, narrow leaved, yellow flowered, and non-invasive; *S. pulchellum*, trailing, with rose-purple flowers and one of the few sedums which like a cool, shady, slightly moist place; *S. reflexum*, with sprawling stems densely set with narrow, grey-green leaves and terminating in crosier-heads of yellow flowers; *S. spurium*, with great spreading mats of more or less evergreen leaves and pink or rosy-magenta flowers from mid-summer to early autumn; and *S. spathulifolium*, which I have kept to the last because it is in my opinion the best of all, particularly in its colour forms. It is quite prostrate, spreads quickly, has fleshy, spoon-shaped leaves which are grey-green in the type, purplish crimson in the variety *S. p. pur-pureum* and grey-white in Cappa Blanca (Cape Blanco). All have yellow flowers but are grown for the effect of the slowly spreading mats of foliage.

These sedums can be increased by careful division in spring. There is in addition a charming pale blue-flowered species named *S. caeruleum*, with sprays of pale blue flowers in the second half of summer, which is an annual and should be sown in spring where it is to grow, and another, named *S. pilosum*, which looks like a sempervivum, has rose-red flowers, is a biennial and so, like the last, should be re-sown each year as soon as the seed is ripe rather than in spring.

Sempervivum (House Leek). Many house leeks are among the hardest wearing of all rock plants. It is not uncommon to see *Sempervivum tectorum* happily growing on an old roof with apparently no soil whatever, though closer examination will always reveal a thin covering of drifted grit and dead leaves caught in an angle of the tiles. All kinds are admirable plants for walls, ledges in the rock garden or other hot and dry positions where there is little soil, but in order to start them it is wise to prepare a mixture of rather rich soil, possibly with some dry cow manure crumbled into it, and spread this 2·5 cm (1 in) or so thick over the stones which are to be covered. Later, when firmly rooted, the semper-vivum will look after itself.

House leeks can be most readily increased by division at practically any time of the year, though spring is the best season. All make stiff rosettes of succulent leaves which gradually spread into wide masses. From these appear curious, stiff flower stems in late summer terminated by big, flattish clusters of starry and usually pink or purplish flowers which, though not so effective as the leaves, are arresting because of their unusual appearance.

There are a great many species, of which a few of the best are *S. arachnoideum*, with small, purplish rosettes covered all over with white, cobweb-like filaments, and *S. a. tomentosum*, or *S. a.* Laggeri with an even denser covering of filaments; *S.* × *calcaratum* with large glaucous-green leaves tipped with purple; *S. heuffelii* with medium-sized green rosettes and pale yellow flowers; *S. montanum*, with small, close-packed rosettes which may be green, purple tipped or all purple according to variety; *S. reginae-amaliae*, another variable species with large rosettes which in the finest forms are purplish red though there are also green varieties; *S. soboliferum* (now listed as *Jovibarba sobolifera*) and often known as the hen and chickens because of its habit of throwing out a number of quite long stems from the main green rosette, each terminated by another smaller rosette; and *S. tectorum*, the common house leek, normally green but with grey-green, red-tipped and reddish-brown varieties, *S. t.* Triste being an especially fine example of the last.

Shortia. These are not really rock plants but woodlanders, though they are so small and neat and need such special care that they are almost invariably planted in the rock garden. They should be given a partially shaded place in a deep bed of leafmould containing a little sand and scarcely any soil, or in peat beds. The two best are *Shortia galacifolia* and *S. uniflora*, both with shining green leaves and pale pink flowers on 10 cm (4 in) stems in spring, but the colour is a shade warmer in *uniflora*. Both can be increased by careful division in spring. *S. soldanelloides* closely resembles soldanella and requires identical treatment. It is a small plant, tufted in habit with shining, evergreen leaves and pink, fringed flowers on 15 cm (6 in) stems in spring. Increase is by division in spring or by seed sown in sandy soil and germinated in a frame.

Silene (Catchfly, Cushion Pink, Moss Campion). There is a silene for the annual border (see Chapter 7) as well as those described here for the rock garden. Some of these latter are disappointing plants, notably *Silene acaulis*, which makes cushions of narrow green leaves and should produce numerous pink flowers in early summer but often fails to do so, perhaps because the soil is too rich. An easier plant is *S. alpestris* which makes loose tufts of shining leaves and has abundant starry, white flowers on 15 cm (6 in) stems in the first half of summer and often longer. There is a double-flowered variety. *S. schafta* is a little loose and untidy in habit but has the merit of flowering from mid-summer to mid-autumn. The blooms are a rather harsh rose pink. All will grow in ordinary rock garden soil and sunny position and all can be increased by division in spring. *S. schafta* is also very easily raised from seed sown in a frame, or even out of doors, in spring or as soon as ripe.

Sisyrinchium. Some of the sisyrinchiums are disappointing plants but the family includes a few real gems, notably *Sisyrinchium douglasii*, also known as *S. grandiflorum*, with narrow, rush-like leaves and very slender flower stems 23 cm (9 in) high, terminated by drooping, amethyst flowers which have the texture and sheen of satin. There is a pure white form which is equally beautiful. Both flower in early spring and are so fragile that they merit the protection of a pane of glass. They should be planted in deep, peaty soil with plenty of coarse sand and stone chips. More robust are *S. angustifolium*, often known as the blue-eyed grass and really very like grass with starry, blue flowers in early summer and *S. bermudianum*, which is rather larger and paler. These easy kinds grow in ordinary well-drained soil and open position. Propagation in all cases can be by division after flowering or by seed sown in a frame or greenhouse in spring. For *S. striatum*, a larger plant, see Chapter 8.

Soldanella. In the Alps one may see the violet-blue, fringed flowers of the soldanellas forcing their way through the snow before it is fully melted, yet in our gardens they sometimes need the protection of a pane of glass in late winter and early spring. This is not because they lack hardiness but because they will flower so early that their fragile blooms become prematurely spoiled by rain, mud splashes and alternating frost and thaw. These are good plants for the scree or for any very porous soil and open position. The two species commonly grown, *Soldanella alpina* and *S. montana*, are much alike in appearance except that the last named is considerably larger – 15 cm (6 in) high against 7·5 cm (3 in) – and blue-lilac rather than violet. Both can be increased by very careful division in spring or by seed sown in sandy soil and germinated in a frame in spring.

Soleirolia. In cool shady places in the garden (and sometimes under the greenhouse staging too) one may perhaps see wide-spreading carpets of little, roundish, bright green leaves that are sometimes vaguely, and quite erroneously, referred to as moss. This is *Soleirolia soleirolii* (once called *Helxine soleirolii*), a plant which is easy to grow provided it is never baked or dried or exposed for long to very severe frost. It can creep into everything though, which is why it is called 'mind your own business'. It can be increased at any time by division.

Stachys (Woundwort). These plants, closely related to the dead nettles, are for the most part weeds, but there is one delightful species for the rock garden which in a warm, sunny place will form close carpets of tiny leaves on which sit small, pale pink, practically stemless, flowers all summer long. This is *Stachys corsica*, and because it comes from Corsica it is just a little tender, particularly if the weather happens to be alternately wet and cold. Give it good drainage and place a pane of glass over it all winter. It can be propagated by division in spring.

Synthyris. *Synthyris reniformis* is not very well known but it would almost be worth planting for its leaves alone, they are so exceptionally bright and shining. It is quite a tiny plant, seldom more than 10 cm (4 in) high, running about readily in any ordinary soil and sunny or shaded place, and producing numerous fluffy spikes of blue flowers in early summer. This is one of those easily managed rock plants that require no particular precautions except that it does not like being dry in summer. It can be increased by division in spring.

Thymus (Thyme). The common thyme is not a plant for the rock garden but rather for the herb garden. There are, however, a number of smaller species which make very good rock plants. Of these one of the best is *Thymus serpyllum* (which may really be *T. drucei*), which is now listed as *T. praecox articus*, a carpet-forming species with tiny, fragrant leaves and sheets of small, reddish-purple flowers in early summer. It has a number of garden varieties such as *T. s. coccineus*, with brighter red flowers; *T. s. albus*, white flowered and *T. s. lanuginosus*, with leaves so hairy that the whole plant has a silvered appearance. The last is doubtfully a true variety of *T. serpyllum* and may appear in some lists as *T. pseudolanuginosus* but it has all the garden qualities of *T. serpyllum*. All will grow in any ordinary soil and sunny position. They are excellent for forming a carpet over choice bulbs. A bigger plant, rather like a neat, very erect and compact form of the common thyme, is *T. carnosus*. This makes a little bush 18 cm (7 in) high, smothered in white flowers in early summer. It is usually sold as *T. nitidus*, a name that belongs to a variety of *T. richardii*. *T. herba-barona* is yet another small bushy thyme about 15 cm (6 in) high, its leaves smelling of caraway, while the leaves of the hybrid *T. × citriodorus* are lemon scented and there is also a yellow-leaved variety.

The mat-forming kinds can be increased by division at almost any time, the bushy kinds by cuttings of firm young growths in a frame in summer. All can be raised from seed but hybrids and garden varieties may show variation if increased in this way.

Trillium. These very beautiful plants are woodlanders rather than rock plants but they are frequently planted in shady parts of the rock garden. They need deep, cool, peaty or leafy soil but otherwise are not difficult to grow. All reach a height of about 30-45 cm (1-1½ ft), have broad, three-parted leaves and showy, three-petalled flowers. Good kinds are *Trillium grandiflorum*, which is pure white; *T. sessile*, purple and *T. erectum*, reddish purple. All bloom in the second half of spring. Increase by very careful division in the second half of summer just before the plants become dormant.

Tunica. See **Petrorhagia** (p. 201).

Verbena. There are only one or two verbenas which have any place in the rock garden. Of these the best is not a true rock plant, nor is it quite hardy, but it keeps so close to the ground and makes such a brilliant display with its clusters of scarlet flowers that it is well worth planting in any sunny place and well-drained soil. Its name is *Verbena peruviana*, though it is now listed as *V. chamaedrifolia*. Cuttings of non-flowering shoots will root very readily in sandy soil in a frame in late summer/early autumn and it is always wise to strike a few in this manner every year in case the parent plant is killed by a hard winter.

Veronica. As well as many fine plants for the herbaceous border this very large family contains a number of excellent dwarf kinds for the rock garden. These are all trailing or mat-forming plants or neat little shrubs. All will grow in any ordinary soil and open place. Typical is *Veronica prostrata*, which also appears in some lists under the name *V. rupestris*. It will soon form a mat almost 0·8 sq m (1 sq yd) with small, dark green leaves and little spikes of bright blue flowers throughout late spring/early summer. There are pink and white varieties, neither so good as the type. Rather similar is *V. prostrata* Trehane with golden leaves and blue flowers.

    V. filiformis carries the free-growing habit of the family to any extreme, making such enormous carpets of growth that it smothers everything in its way. It has thread-like stems, abundant, pale blue flowers in late spring/early summer and will grow in sun or shade but it usually becomes a troublesome weed after a year or so. *V. fruticans*, also known as *V. saxatilis*, is another little sprawling shrub up to 15 cm (6 in) high, with blue, red-eyed flowers from mid-summer to early autumn. *V. cinerea* and *V. spicata incana* both have grey leaves and blue flowers but the first is a small plant for a good place where it will not be over-run and it flowers the first half of summer. *V. spicata incana* is a sturdy plant that can be used to edge borders, flowering in late summer/early autumn.

    The trailing kinds can be increased by careful division in spring; the shrubby ones by cuttings of firm, young growth in sand in a frame in summer.

Vinca (Periwinkle). *Vinca major*, the large English periwinkle and its cream variegated variety are a little too rampant for the ordinary rock garden though they are useful for a rough corner, particularly as they will grow in shade *V. minor* is a neater plant with the same trailing stems set with glossy, privet-like leaves and ending in clusters of showy flowers, normally blue though there are also purple, white and double-flowered varieties, and also varieties with variegated leaves. All will grow in any soil and practically any position. They flower from mid-winter to late spring and can be increased by division after flowering.

Viola. The highly developed garden violas have no place in the rockery, their proper position being beds and borders of more formal character, but some of the species are first-class rock plants. One of the best is *Viola gracilis* which in habit is rather like a good, mat-forming, bedding viola with very narrow leaves. It has small, exceptionally graceful and very rich purple flowers from mid-spring to early summer. The true species has become very scarce but there are a number of garden hybrids in various shades of yellow and blue. More vigorous is *V. cornuta* which makes big, loose mounds of thin stems and has spurred flowers rather like those of a very large violet. The normal colour is mauve but there are many varieties including a good white and a deep purple. *V. bosniaca*, also known as *V. elegantula*, with very tiny, rosy-lilac flowers like miniature pansies is also charming but needs more care and a well-drained soil. It is very readily raised from seed and can be treated as a biennial. *V. labradorica* is a small violet with purple leaves and flowers which rambles far and wide and is a useful ground-covering plant for partly shady places, but rather too invasive for the rock garden itself. *V. cucullata* is another attractive species with violet flowers.

All can be raised from seed sown in spring in a frame but selected forms must be kept true to type by division in spring or by cuttings of basal, non-flowering shoots taken in late summer/early autumn, like those of bedding violas. Most may also be divided carefully in spring.

Wahlenbergia. See **Edraianthus** (p. 188).

Zauschneria. *Zauschneria californica* is a brilliant, half-shrubby plant about 30 cm (1 ft) high with tubular, scarlet flowers in the first half of autumn. It would be more valuable if it were a little hardier. Though it is often lost in winter it is likely to be most permanent if grown in rather poor, sandy soil and a hot, sunny position and is first class in a wall or in a narrow, south-facing crevice between boulders. It can be increased by cuttings of non-flowering shoots struck in sand in a frame in late summer or by seed sown in the greenhouse in early spring. *Z. microphylla* (also known as *Epilobium canum*) is similar but has much narrower leaves.

Chapter 10

Trees and Shrubs

In this section I only include trees and shrubs generally sufficiently hardy to be grown out of doors. In themselves they are an imposing collection and one which might easily fill several volumes. Obviously, therefore, in this chapter careful selection is essential and in this preliminary consideration it is necessary to group the bewildering wealth of material in the broadest and simplest possible manner.

An obvious first division can be made by separating evergreen from deciduous (leaf-losing) varieties. This is quite an arbitrary division and one which cuts right through some genera, berberis for example, which have both evergreen and deciduous species, but it is a useful distinction for both culture and ornamental use.

Trees and shrubs may also be divided into conifers (cone bearers) and broad-leaved types, or may be regarded as lime haters as opposed to lime tolerators. These are not sub-divisions of the first grouping, for there are both evergreen and deciduous conifers as well as evergreen and deciduous broad-leaved trees and shrubs, while lime-hating and lime-tolerating kinds are to be found in all the other divisions. The gardener must learn to recognize these distinctions if he is to begin to understand the needs of trees and shrubs in any kind of ordered manner, for each has a distinct bearing on culture.

Taking the evergreen v. deciduous division first, the cultural distinction resolves itself largely into a question of the time at which they are planted and, to a lesser degree, the time at which they are pruned. With a small number of exceptions, of which magnolias are the most important, deciduous shrubs are most safely planted directly they have lost most of their leaves in the autumn, but before the soil has become very wet and cold – roughly in the second half of autumn. Work can continue during any mild and fairly dry weather throughout the winter until early spring, but the later it is left the more risk there is likely to be, especially if the spring happens to be hot and dry.

Evergreens, by contrast, with the notable exception of evergreen conifers, do not transplant very satisfactorily during this period because their roots recover too slowly and are unable to keep pace with the demands of the leaves which are constantly evaporating water even in mid-winter. This peculiarity makes evergreens as a class a little more difficult to transplant than deciduous trees and shrubs. As a consequence it pays to purchase some kinds in (or recently removed from) containers so that they suffer the minimum amount of root disturbance. Nevertheless most kinds can be transplanted from the open ground either in late spring or early autumn in an average season. At these periods roots are still sufficiently active to take hold of the soil reasonably quickly whereas the weather is not, as a rule, so warm that leaves are losing an excessive amount of water. The danger of death can be lessened by lifting the trees or shrubs with a good ball of roots and soil, replanting firmly and with as little delay as possible, and watering freely for the first few weeks. If the weather turns hot after spring planting it may pay to syringe leaves daily with water and perhaps even to shade them with a screen of sacking, hurdles, evergreen boughs or fine plastic netting. After autumn planting a similar screen may prove of value to keep off cold, drying wind.

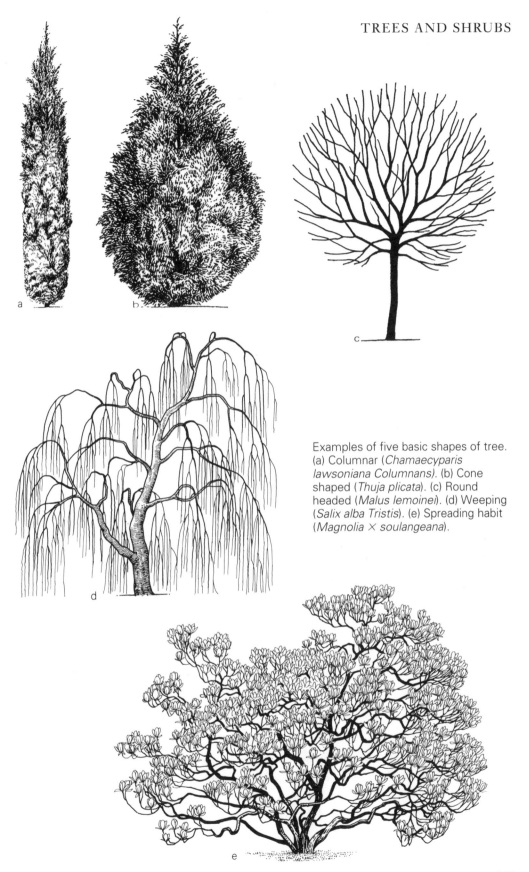

Examples of five basic shapes of tree.
(a) Columnar (*Chamaecyparis lawsoniana Columnans*). (b) Cone shaped (*Thuja plicata*). (c) Round headed (*Malus lemoinei*). (d) Weeping (*Salix alba Tristis*). (e) Spreading habit (*Magnolia × soulangeana*).

All conifers have comparatively narrow and often very small leaves which do not give off moisture anything like so rapidly as those of broad-leaved trees and shrubs. For this reason the objections to the transplanting of other evergreens in the winter period do not apply to evergreen conifers, most of which can be moved during mild weather and when the soil is in good working condition throughout this period. All the same a few conifers prove difficult to transplant at any time, apparently because they resent root breakage, and these must either be established while still quite young and small or else be purchased in pots. *Cupressus macrocarpa* is a familiar example.

Nowadays it is customary to grow shrubs and even a few trees in containers of various kinds, including plastic bags, so that they can be planted without any root disturbance. Such plants can be put in at practically any time of the year when the soil is in workable condition but may need frequent watering for some weeks if planted in summer.

The distinction between lime-hating and lime-tolerating shrubs is one about which the amateur is likely to hear a lot, yet in many ways it is the most unsatisfactory of these loose divisions and the least understood. Some varieties which were once supposed to dislike lime have proved, on closer investigation, to be distinctly tolerant and much more work of this character remains to be done. It is broadly true that the majority of shrubs belonging to the heather family (erica) are happiest in soils that contain no free lime, that is, have a pH below 7 (see Chapter 6). The heather family includes not only the heathers themselves but also the rhododendrons and numerous less important genera such as pieris, leucothoe and kalmia. Obviously when preparing ground it is wise to avoid all use of lime and, so far as possible, to choose land that is itself inclined to be acid. Leafmould, peat, old cucumber-bed compost and similar humus-rich dressings can be used to decrease the pH of soils that have too much lime to be satisfactory for these shrubs.

Soil Preparation. This brings us to the general methods to be employed when preparing ground for either trees or shrubs. The guilding principle in all cases must be thoroughness, for the first cultivation is also likely to be the last, so far as any deep stirring of the soil is concerned. Once planted many trees and shrubs will form roots quite close to the surface making it impossible to do more than hoe or prick the top soil very lightly with a fork.

Dung can be used to enrich poor soils and improve the texture of both light and heavy ones. Dressings in excess of 50 kg per 8 sq m (1 cwt per 10 sq yd) will seldom be desirable as too much manure may cause excessive growth, probably at the expense of flowers or fruits. Of concentrated fertilizers those that are slow in action are most valuable, notably coarse bonemeal and hoof and horn meal which may be worked in at normal rates while breaking down the surface in preparation for planting. Preliminary digging should be completed at least a month before planting time to give the ground an adequate chance to settle.

Planting. This does not differ in any material respect from the planting of fruit which is described in Chapter 25. When shrubs or trees are obtained in pots, plastic bags or other containers they must be removed carefully without disturbing either the soil or roots. This can only be done if the plants are well established in the containers so that the roots hold the soil together. Plants recently put into containers are not suitable for planting out of season.

Pruning after planting is by no means always essential but it is usually desirable with trees and shrubs which are required to make strong growth from the outset, such as those required for hedges and windbreaks. Without such pruning the strength of the plant is liable to be dissipated the first year and weak shoots will result. The only course then is to prune more severely the following year. An exception must be made in the case of conifers which should not be pruned after planting as this may spoil their natural habit.

Spacing is very important as in my experience most beginners err on the side of planting much too closely. If the full spread of the specimen is known the minimum spacing should be three-quarters the ultimate spread, but if it is not known, perhaps as good a guide as any is to allow between plants at least two-thirds of their normal height when full grown, a figure which is given in most nursery catalogues. Note that these are minimum spacings which can usually be increased with advantage, particularly if it is desired that the various trees and shrubs should display their individual shape and not eventually merge into one continuous mass.

This consideration of spacing naturally links up with the method of grouping used. Frequently trees are treated as isolated specimens and then the more room they can be allowed, within reason, the better. Shrubs are sometimes planted in the same way, particularly big shrubs such as lilacs and viburnums. More often, where a special display of one kind of shrub is wanted, a small group is planted in a bed by itself on a lawn or in some similar position which will give it due prominence.

Shrub borders should be planned and planted in much the same way as herbaceous borders except that far more single specimens will be used and fewer and smaller groups. There should be the same care in associating types of varied habit, colour and flowering time, in avoiding set lines and achieving a pleasing varied contour by setting some of the taller varieties towards the front and a few of the dwarfer kinds towards the back. Avoid the use of too many evergreens or the result may be heavy and displeasing, but ignore this rule when planting solely for some particular display, as, for example, when making a border of rhododendrons. It will usually pay handsomely to include a fair proportion of berry-bearing shrubs in the border to carry colour well on into the winter. A similar object can be achieved by planting some shrubs which assume brilliant foliage colour in the autumn and also varieties with coloured barks such as some of the willows, dogwoods and brambles.

Shrubs are also often used in mixed borders in association with bulbs, herbaceous perennials, roses, annuals, dahlias and other bedding plants. The shrubs provide the permanent framework, the other plants increase and extend the flowering season.

Climbers. Many of our best climbing plants are shrubs in the sense that they have perennial and more or less woody growth. Some are, in fact, shrubs in the narrower sense and will make bushy plants if placed in the open; they only display a climbing habit when planted against a wall or fence and even then may need considerable pruning to keep them in shape. Honeysuckle, clematis and jasmine are examples of the true climber, *Cotoneaster horizontalis* of the shrub which will climb if given half a chance, while *Chaenomeles speciosa* and *Pyracantha coccinea* are shrubs which can be trained and pruned to fill a wall space.

The true climbers all need something to support them, be it wires, trellis work or for those provided with adhesive roots or pads, (eg ivy and Virginia creeper) a wall to which to cling. Climbers with tendrils or twisting leaf stalks (eg vines and clematis) prefer fairly thin supports, but real twiners like honeysuckle can lash themselves around stout supports. The more woody shrubs which can be used as climbers will frequently support themselves with no more help than that afforded by the protection of a wall and, perhaps, an occasional tie to guide them.

The general observations to be made about climbers are the same as those for other shrubs. Some are evergreen, some deciduous and the same remarks about planting apply. Spacing cannot be decided by the ultimate height of the climber nor even by its maximum spread which may be a very variable factor depending much upon situation. All the same it is desirable not to overcrowd climbers and it is seldom wise to plant them closer than 1·8 m (6 ft) while 2·7 m (9 ft) might be regarded as a fair average.

Pruning. This is by no means so essential a feature of the cultivation of trees and shrubs as many gardeners appear to imagine. Provided they have sufficient space and do not fall into ill health a great many kinds can be left well alone for the greater part of their lifetime and will continue to grow happily and produce their flowers, fruits or ornamental foliage in season as by nature ordained. It may be good policy occasionally to remove a badly placed branch which is rubbing against another or creating an unbalanced look, but nothing in the way of systematic pruning is necessary.

Pruning is most likely to be of value in the early years, when a little discreet shoot regulation may help to build up a shapely plant and, later on, in the case of shrubs grown for some specific purpose – producing a few very large flowers or filling a special position. Then one must learn to achieve this object with the minimum interference with the natural growth of the shrub.

Evergreen shrubs can be pruned with greatest safety in the second half of spring but if they are in flower then, pruning should be delayed until the flowers fade. As a rule it is wise to prune only when the shrubs have to be shaped for some particular purpose as, for example, to form a hedge or to cover a wall, and to restrict the pruning to the minimum necessary for this purpose.

Deciduous shrubs which flower before mid-summer should be pruned immediately after flowering while those that flower after mid-summer should be pruned in late winter if quite hardy, or in mid-spring if the young growth is inclined to be tender, eg *Buddleia davidii* and *Hydrangea paniculata.*.

As regards the early-flowering group a fairly safe general rule is to shorten each stem that has just been carrying flowers to a point from which a young shoot is starting or has already grown. These will then have the rest of the summer in which to grow and ripen in readiness to flower the following spring.

The later flowering shrubs can generally be thinned by the removal of some of the oldest stems, particularly those that are not carrying much new growth, while the younger and stronger branches can often be shortened a little without seriously interfering with the floral display. In a few cases, notably *Buddleia davidii* and *Hydrangea paniculata*, all branches can be shortened to within several centimetres of ground level as the result will be a few very strong new growths each of which will produce a flower truss of extra size. Note, however, that even in these cases hard pruning, or even any pruning at all, is not essential as more numerous if smaller flower trusses will be carried if the bushes are allowed to grow unrestricted.

236

Top: (a) Roses trained up a pergola will need the support of some ties. (b) Wisteria, a vigorous twining plant, can be trained up a pillar or wall or over a pergola

Bottom: Examples of the different methods of support of three types of climber. (a) Suckers (ivy). (b) Twining stems (honeysuckle). (c) Tendrils (cobaea)

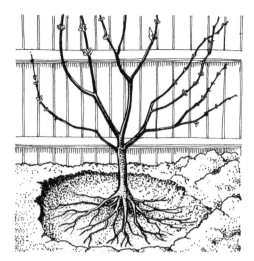

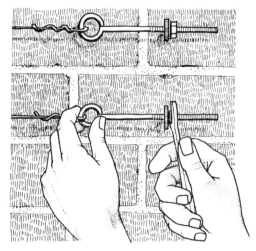

Planting a shrub against a fence. Care should be taken not to plant too close to the fence, or moisture will not reach the roots

Adjustable wire strainers suitable for use with wall-trained trees and shrubs. Tension is increased by the tightening of a nut

Deciduous hedges can have a thorough shaping in the first half of spring and may have one or two light trimmings during the summer. Evergreen hedges may get their main clipping in late spring with subsequent occasional trimming every few weeks until early autumn.

Climbers fall into much the same groups as shrubs, the early-flowering kinds being thinned and shortened a little after flowering, whereas the summer-blooming kinds are dealt with in late winter. True climbers tend to be spoiled by much pruning though the large-flowered clematises, particularly those of the Jackmanii type, can be cut back quite hard each early spring as this will help them to produce still bigger, though fewer, blooms.

Shrubby climbers which are made to cover a wall by training and pruning need the most careful attention. Very often the problem of restricting growth without unduly reducing the flower display can be solved by shortening to 18 cm (7 in) all side growths directly they begin to get really hard and woody at the base (usually some time in mid-summer). If they are berry-bearing kinds take care not to remove the young berries while doing this work.

Propagation. Trees and shrubs are increased by division, cuttings, layering and grafting (including budding) and seeds. I will deal with these in order.

Division is the least general method and yet the simplest. Unfortunately it is only possible with those shrubs or trees which produce numerous shoots or suckers direct from the roots, eg *Mahonia aquifolium*, cotinus and lilac (but if lilac is grafted the suckers will have the character of the stock, not of the variety grafted on it). All that is necessary is to lift the shrub or tree at the normal planting season and pull off some of the stems complete with roots; or, if it is too big and old for this, to dig out some of the suckers with roots attached but without unduly disturbing the parent plant.

Cuttings are of two main kinds: summer cuttings made from shoots beginning to get hard and woody at the base, and autumn cuttings made from fully grown shoots of the same year.

Summer cuttings must always be rooted fairly quickly and for this purpose a propagating box is useful. Very sandy soil or a mixture of sand or perlite and peat is used as the rooting medium and the cuttings are watered fairly freely, shaded from strong sunshine and only ventilated for a few minutes daily until they are rooted, a state which they will indicate by looking much perkier and immediately beginning to grow.

A development of this system is mist propagation, by which the cuttings are kept constantly moist by frequent automatically controlled water spraying. The most sophisticated apparatus is electrically controlled by a moisture sensor placed among the cuttings. This is charged with a low-voltage current which flows between electrodes so long as the surface separating them is moist. When it becomes dry the flow of current stops and a solenoid valve is operated to turn on the water which is ejected through misting nozzles. The spray wets both cuttings and sensor so that the low-voltage current starts to flow again, the solenoid valve closes and the water supply is cut off. Less elaborate apparatus is also available.

Cuttings growing under mist need not be kept close but can be on the open greenhouse bench, nor need they be shaded, but rooting is more rapid and certain if the sand or soil is warmed from below to a temperature of about 20°C/68°F, for example by an electric soil-warming cable.

A simple method of keeping summer cuttings firm while they are rooting is to insert them in pots, then put a polythene bag over each pot, holding it tight to the side of the pot with a rubber band to retain all moisture. The bag should be removed as soon as the cuttings commence to grow again.

Flowering stems of early-summer flowering shrubs, such as weigela or forsythia, should be removed after they have bloomed, leaving the young growth to grow on

For later flowering shrubs that flower on current year's growth, such as purple buddleia and *Hydrangea paniculata*, shorten year-old stems to within several centimetres of the old wood

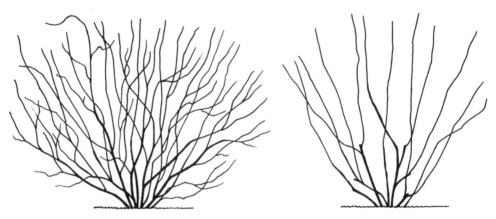

Thinning a typical medium-sized bushy shrub to let in light and air and increase the quality of the flowers or fruit. The sturdy young growth of the shrub is retained

Autumn cuttings can be allowed to root slowly over a period of months and can often be handled out of doors without protection, though the covering of a cloche or frame is a help with the more difficult kinds. In this case no watering is likely to be necessary after the initial watering in and the cloches can be left in position from the time the cuttings are inserted in autumn until the following spring when they will probably be rooted and starting to grow.

Summer cuttings should be potted in ordinary potting soil as soon as rooted and then accommodated in a frame for the next few weeks while being hardened off. Subsequently they can be potted on or planted out. Autumn cuttings are usually left undisturbed till the following autumn when they may be transplanted to a nursery bed or their permanent quarters.

Layering means that the shoots are rooted first and removed afterwards. It has the merit of being particularly safe and easy and is therefore especially recommended to the

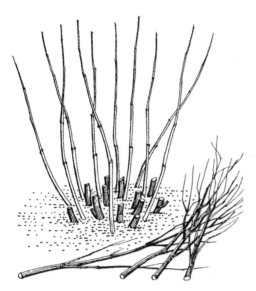

Older branches can be cut to ground level
in autumn or winter, a useful method for
many shrubs that become overgrown such
as deciduous berberis, ordinary
hydrangeas, spiraeas and viburnums

The flower heads of shrubs such as
rhododendrons and lilacs should be
removed as soon as they fade to prevent
seeds forming

beginner. Well-grown young stems are best, though older branches can sometimes be
rooted successfully. Autumn is the best season, spring the second best, though layering
can be practised at any time because shoots will root eventually.

The method is to bend the shoot down so that it touches the soil at a point a little
behind its tip (occasionally the tip itself may be used) and either peg it there or weight it
in position with a heavy stone. A little soil can first be drawn over the shoot to encourage
it to root and it may be given a sharp twist to rupture the bark where it will be buried and
then bent sharply upwards to restrict, but not stop, the flow of sap. Layers pegged down
in the autumn should be well rooted by the following autumn when they can be severed
from the parent and lifted for planting on their own.

Air layering is another form of layering and is done without bringing the shoots to
ground level. A knife is drawn around the branch or stem to be layered, cutting through
the bark and cambium only whereupon the cut is dusted with hormone rooting powder.
Moist sphagnum moss is then placed around the cut and enclosed in a sleeve of polythene
film, tightly tied at each end. Roots grow into the moss and when there are plenty the
polythene is removed and the layer is severed and potted or planted. Air layering can be
done at any time but is usually most effective in spring and early autumn.

Grafting and budding are used to propagate some choice garden varieties of highly
developed shrubs such as lilacs and rhododendrons and are common methods of increasing ornamental apples, cherries and plums. The systems employed are closely similar to
those used for fruit trees (see Chapter 26) and as a rule seedlings or suckers of the common form of the shrub or tree to be increased are used as stocks, for instance common
lilac suckers are used for choice lilacs, seedlings *Rhododendron ponticum* for the big-flowered, hybrid rhododendrons, seedling crab apples or layered apple stocks for ornamental
crabs, and so on. Occasionally it is necessary to graft or bud in the greenhouse, the stocks
being potted and brought inside for this purpose and subsequently placed in a propagating frame until a union has been made.

241

Seeds are not much used by amateurs as a method of propagation probably because of the long time that must elapse before a specimen is obtained of reasonable size for the shrub border. Nevertheless there are a good many trees and shrubs which can be raised quite readily from seeds sown in a frame in spring or even out of doors in a sheltered place at this time. All the deciduous barberries (berberis) come into this class and so do most of the cotoneasters and rose species as distinct from the highly developed garden roses. Here it should be noted that though most species of any kind can be raised reasonably true to type from seed, hybrids always show a degree of variation when increased by this means.

Seed should be sown in the same type of soil as that favoured by the shrub or tree, that is peaty soil for peat lovers, ordinary loamy soil for the great majority that will grow anywhere, and so on. If pots or trays are to be used they must be very well drained. Outdoor seed beds should be thoroughly cleaned of weeds as germination may in some cases be slow and irregular. Early spring is usually the most favourable month for sowing but it often pays to place berries or heps, as soon as ripe in the autumn, in shallow sand-filled boxes and place these out of doors, protected by fine-mesh wire netting to keep off mice, voles and rats, to be chilled during the winter. This hastens the decay of the flesh and is

Layering a climber. The stem is slit and a small wedge inserted to hold it open, then the layer is pegged down into the soil. Layers treated in the autumn should be well rooted and ready for severing from the parent plant by the following autumn

essential to break the dormancy of some species of seeds and make them ready for germination. Then in early spring sand and berries together can be rubbed between the palms of the hands to separate the seeds after which the whole mass can be sown in drills about 2·5 cm (1 in) deep. Alternatively, mix the seeds with moist peat and put them in a polythene bag, seal it and keep in a domestic refrigerator for three months. Seeds should as a general rule be covered with soil to twice their own depth, for example, 6 mm (¼ in) diameter seeds in 18 mm (¾ in) deep drills and so on.

Leave the seedlings undisturbed till they are several centimetres high and then transplant them at the normal planting season for the species, placing them 7·5 cm (3 in) apart each way in a bed of well-broken soil. Here they can grow on for at least a further year by which time they may be large enough to go to their permanent quarters, or shift them to a similar bed but with a little more room.

CHOICE AND CARE OF HEDGES

Appropriately selected and well-cared-for hedges can add greatly to the attractiveness of almost all gardens. The choice of suitable hedge plants is great and there is certainly no reason for the monotonous repetition of any one subject, however good – and I will not deny that privet is a good hedge plant for it has the merits of neatness, hardiness and adaptability to a marked degree and withstands clipping well. Moreover the broad-leaved green privet (*Ligustrum ovalifolium*) has a good appearance and its golden-leaved form must certainly be reckoned amongst the brightest of variegated shrubs. But because of these qualities both have been over-planted to an extent which makes many discriminating gardeners determined to plant almost any hedge shrub rather than either of the popular privets.

Lonicera nitida is one of the possible substitutes. It is exceptionally neat in leaf but apt to be a little straggly in habit unless it is pruned fairly severely. For a small hedge, say up to 1·3 m (4½ ft) in height, it is difficult to beat amongst moderately-priced shrubs.

Those who are prepared to pay more for something of greater quality should consider yew or holly, both unsurpassed for appearance and permanence. They are often referred to as slow growing but this is not so in reasonably rich soil.

For large hedges and windbreaks some of the cypresses are excellent, notably *Chamaecyparis lawsoniana* and its numerous forms, and the hybrid × *C. leylandii*. The last is exceptionally quick growing and quite hardy, unlike *C. macrocarpa* which is one of its parents and which it should replace except in the mildest areas. *Thuja plicata* and *T. occidentalis* are rather similar to × *C. lawsoniana* in appearance and are both hardy and reasonably quick growing.

Cherry laurel, Portugal laurel and aucuba, both spotted and plain green, all make fine boundaries or screens but are not desirable where small, closely trimmed hedges are required.

Beech and hornbeam are remarkable in that, though both are large trees when left to grow naturally, they will submit to drastic pruning and make fine hedges no more than 45-60 cm (1½-2 ft) deep and anything from 1·2-6 m (4-20 ft) in height. Moreover, though deciduous, they will retain their dead leaves all winter when hard pruned and then make fine windbreaks besides providing a pleasant variation in colour from the evergreens.

Cherry plum (*Prunus cerasifera*) and quickthorn (*Crataegus monogyna* and *C. oxyacantha*) are useful for outer boundaries to large estates but are scarcely choice enough for small gardens. Many better flowering or berry-bearing shrubs are available, notably *Berberis darwinii, B.* × *stenophylla, Cotoneaster simonsii, Escallonia rubra* and some of the hybrids of this shrub, lavender or rosemary for a small hedge, the sweet briar (*Rosa rubiginosa*, now listed as *R. eglanteria*), shrub roses and vigorous cluster flowered (floribunda) roses. Some climbing roses can also be used for making wide, rather informal hedges. In seaside districts tamarix makes a delightful hedge while *Atriplex halimus*, though rather untidy, has good silver-grey foliage and will grow in the sandiest soils and most exposed places.

Ground Preparation. This is often neglected with the result that the hedge is hampered from the outset. A strip of ground at least 90 cm (3 ft) wide should be dug a good 30 cm (1 ft) deep and be well manured with dung or, failing this, with generous quantities of such fertilizers as bonemeal and hoof and horn meal. A month or more should be allowed to elapse to give the soil time to settle before planting.

Planting. The two commonest faults are to crowd roots into narrow, carelessly dug holes and to space the shrubs too far apart. It is usually best to dig out a trench 38-45 cm (15 in-1½ ft) wide and 23-30 cm (9 in-1 ft) deep along the whole length of the proposed hedge site. Then the plants can be properly spaced 23-30 cm (9 in-1 ft) apart for privet and quickthorn; 30-45 cm (1-1¼ ft) for *Lonicera nitida*, beech, hornbeam and cherry plum; 38-45 cm (15 in-1½ ft) for yew and holly, and 76 cm (2½ ft) for cupressus and thuja. Moreover there will be plenty of room to spread the roots properly and cover the uppermost with 6 cm (2½ in) of soil. Make this really firm around and over the roots and, if possible, stake the newly planted shrubs or tie them to horizontally trained wires so that they will not be disturbed by wind.

Subsequent Care. Hedges are usually grossly neglected after planting, except for pruning or clipping. They are seldom fed yet they need this almost more than most other shrubs because of the keen competition between their rather closely placed roots. It is wise to give the hedge an annual spring mulch of rotted dung, vegetable compost or hop manure, and this may be supplemented occasionally by a compound chemical fertilizer containing nitrogen, phosphorus and potash. Pruning should be done as described on p. 236.

A SELECTION OF TREES AND SHRUBS

Abelia. These are not very brilliant or showy shrubs and on that account will probably never be widely popular but the best kinds such as *Abelia* × *grandiflora* and *A. schumanii* are graceful and refined and will always appeal to connoisseurs. The first is evergreen with small pinkish-white flowers, the second deciduous with warmer pink flowers, both from about mid-summer to mid-autumn. Both are about 1·5 m (5 ft) high and in spread. *A. schumanii* is a little tender so give it a rather sheltered position, at any rate in cold districts. *A. floribunda*, an evergreen with short trails of carmine flowers in the first half of summer, is by far the most showy of the genus but also one of the least hardy. It should be trained against a sunny, sheltered wall except in the mildest localities. All require ordinary, reasonably well-drained soil and no regular pruning, though old stems can be removed in spring if bushes get too large. Propagate by cuttings in the second half of summer.

Abutilon. Most of these are dealt with under Greenhouse Plants (see Chapter 19) but one kind, *Abutilon vitifolium*, is a beautiful, hardy, deciduous shrub for a sunny sheltered position out of doors. It has an open habit, will grow 3·6 m (12 ft) high and 3 m (10 ft) wide, but is often less, and has soft, grey-green leaves and pale lavender or white mallow-like flowers in the first half of summer. It likes well-drained soil and needs no pruning as a rule, though overgrown branches can be shortened in early spring. *A. × suntense* is similar but more bushy and has deeper violet flowers. *A. megapotamicum* has thin, lax stems bearing hanging yellow and crimson flowers like little Chinese lanterns from mid-summer to mid-autumn. It is rather tender but will usually succeed if trained against a sunny, sheltered wall. Propagate by seed sown in a greenhouse in spring or by cuttings in summer.

Acer (Maple). The maples are deciduous trees, many of great size though the numerous forms of the Japanese maple, *Acer palmatum*, are seldom above 3·6 m (12 ft) in height and are often almost shrub-like. One, named Senkaki, has coral-red bark. The common sycamore is an acer, *A. pseudoplatanus*, and it has several garden varieties with coloured leaves such as *A. p.* Brilliantissimum, young leaves pink and yellow; *A. p.* Leopoldii, leaves blotched with salmon and pink, and *A. p.* Purpureum, leaves reddish purple. *A. platanoides*, the Norway maple, is a similar tree of large size with several coloured-leaved forms, of which one of the best is Crimson King with shining beetroot-crimson leaves. Goldsworth Purple is similar.

The true sugar maple, *A. saccharum*, does not as a rule grow well in northern countries. *A. negundo* is a tree of medium size with bright green stems and leaves. It is chiefly represented in gardens by *A. n. variegatum*, whose leaves are blotched with white.

Yet another group of acers has the additional attraction of bark which is handsomely coloured or marked. Notable amongst these is *A. griseum* with reddish-brown bark which peels like that of a plane tree to reveal lighter cinnamon-coloured bark beneath. The snake-bark maples are so called because their bark is striped longitudinally in light green on darker green. There are several species with this attractive feature, including *A. capillipes*, *A. davidii*, *A. grosseri*, *A. hersii* and *A. pennsylvanicum*. All these are trees of medium size.

The Japanese maples all have leaves that colour well in autumn, some to crimson and some to yellow. There are varieties with leaves that are purple in summer and some varieties of *A. palmatum* have finely divided leaves.

All the acer species should be raised from seed while the garden forms must be increased by grafting or budding on to seedlings of the same, or an allied, species. They thrive in ordinary soils and, for the most part, open positions but the Japanese varieties, being less hardy, should be given a sunny and sheltered spot. They do not like cold, wet soil and, if drainage is poor, are best planted on low mounds so that water does not collect around them.

Aesculus (Horse Chestnut). Trees for the most part of large size – too large, in fact, for many modern gardens, though they are very beautiful for planting in open, spacious places. The showy spikes of white flowers of the common horse chestnut, produced in late spring, are too well known to need description. Besides this species known as *Aesculus hippocastanum*, there is the pink horse chestnut, *A.* × *carnea*, a rather smaller hybrid tree with deep rose flowers, and its variety *A.* × *c.* Briotti, with deeper coloured flowers, popularly known as the red horse chestnut. Other less well-known kinds are *A. parviflora*, which is not much more than a large shrub 3 m (10 ft) high and 3·6 m (12 ft) wide with white flower spikes in the second half of summer and *A. pavia*, the red buckeye, a small tree to 6 m (20 ft) with crimson flowers in early summer. *A. indica*, the Indian horse chestnut, is much larger, to 18 m (60 ft), with fine spires of pink, white and yellow flowers in the first half of summer.

All can be raised from the seeds or conkers, but the hybrids such as *A.* × *carnea* and its varieties show variation from seed so especially desirable forms of these must be increased by budding or grafting on to the common species. They are not fussy about soil or position and need no regular pruning.

Ailanthus (Tree of Heaven). *Ailanthus altissima*, sometimes called *A. glandulosa*, is the only species commonly planted. It is a tree of considerable size with large leaves composed of many leaflets like those of an ash but at least twice as long. It makes a handsome specimen with an ultimate height and spread of something like 18 × 12 m (60 × 40 ft). It will grow in ordinary soil. Pruning is not necessary but, if desired, branches can be cut back in late winter fairly severely, the result being a considerable loss in beauty of habit but a gain in the size of individual leaves. Increase by digging up rooted suckers in autumn or by inserting cuttings made from short pieces of root in late winter in a frame filled with sandy soil.

Alnus (Alder). The alders are deciduous trees of medium size most of which thrive in damp places but are not of the first merit for garden planting. *Alnus glutinosa*, the common British alder, is worth planting in wild boggy places and near streams for its long, dull purple catkins in late winter. There are cut-leaved varieties and one with golden leaves. *A. incana*, the grey alder, has similar catkins and leaves which are grey beneath. It, too, has a cut-leaved variety and another, named *A. i.* Aurea, in which the catkins are more markedly red and both young shoots and leaves are yellow. The species can be increased by seed sown out of doors in early spring but the varieties do not come true from seeds so must be increased by cuttings in summer or autumn or by grafting on to the common kinds.

Amelanchier (Snowy Mespilus, June Berry). The amelanchiers are all very beautiful deciduous trees of small to medium size or large bushes with very abundant white flowers in the second half of spring and brilliant autumn foliage colour. They might well be planted more freely in gardens as they will grow in any ordinary soil and are a pleasant change from more hackneyed kinds. The best are *Amelanchier laevis*, about 4·5 cm (15 ft) high and dense, with leaves which are bronze when young; *A. canadensis*, similar; *A. lamarckii*, once known as *A. grandiflora*, and probably a hybrid, with leaves which are distinctly white when young; and *A. stolonifera*, the shortest, only about 1·6 m (5½ ft) high. None of these requires pruning. All can be increased by layers or rooted suckers removed in autumn, and the species (but not the hybrid) also by seeds sown in a frame in spring. Seeds, however, sometimes take a year or more to germinate.

Andromeda (Bog Rosemary). Many of the shrubs which were once known by this name have been transferred to other genera such as pieris and zenobia under which names they should be sought. *Andromeda polifolia* is a pretty, dwarf evergreen with pale pink, heather-like flowers in late spring/early summer. It likes a moist, peaty soil devoid of lime. No pruning is desirable. Seeds can be germinated in sandy peat in greenhouse or frame in spring or by cuttings prepared in late summer from the tips of branches and rooted in similar compost in a close frame or under mist.

Arbutus (Strawberry Tree). The true strawberry tree is *Arbutus unedo* and it gets its popular name from the red, rather strawberry-like fruits which hang on the tree all summer and only colour up in the autumn, at which season the small white or pale pink, bell-shaped flowers also open. It has evergreen, laurel-like leaves and makes a big, freely-branched shrub or small tree anything from 3·6-9 m (12-30 ft) and certainly as dense. It will thrive in most soils including those on limestone. By contrast, *A. menziesii*, the madrona, dislikes lime in any form and prefers peaty soils. It will reach 15 m (50 ft) or more, has large, erect clusters of white flowers in the second half of spring and very handsome cinnamon-red bark peeling to show a lighter colour beneath. It is not sufficiently hardy for the coldest localities. *A. andrachne* is even more tender but the hybrid between this and *A. unedo*, named *A. × andrachnoides*, is quite hardy and a very beautiful tree with smooth, cinnamon-red bark and white flowers in spring.

All the species can be increased by seeds in spring, by cuttings in summer or by layering in spring or autumn, but the hybrid will only come true from cuttings or layers.

Artemisia (Lad's Love, Southernwood). Many of the artemisias are plants for the herbaceous border or rock garden (see Chapters 8 and 9) but one, *Artemisia abrotanum*, is a shrub with a height and spread of about 90 cm (3 ft) and finely divided, grey leaves which are strongly aromatic when bruised. It likes a warm, sunny place and well-drained soil and can be increased by cuttings struck in sandy soil in a frame in late summer/early autumn.

Arundinaria. See **Bamboo** (p. 249).

Ash. See **Fraxinus** (p. 269).

Atriplex. The most useful species is *Atriplex halimus*, a rather loose, untidy shrub 2·2 m (7½ ft) high and certainly of equal spread with silver-grey, evergreen leaves. It is especially useful for planting near the sea as it will withstand salt spray and thrive in the sandiest and poorest of soils and is frequently used as a windbreak for seaside gardens. Inland it is occasionally injured by frost. Increase is by cuttings of firm young growth in summer. It can be pruned in late spring as much as is necessary to maintain shape.

Aucuba. *Aucuba japonica* was once a favourite evergreen shrub for hedge making. It is far less popular now, no doubt because of the room it takes up, for it is a big, freely branched bush up to 3 m (10 ft) high and the same wide, though capable of being restricted to half those dimensions. It has big, glossy, evergreen leaves, plain green in the type but more commonly heavily spotted and blotched with pale yellow (hence the name 'spotted laurel' sometimes applied). A variety named Sulphurea has leaves irregularly edged with yellow. There are two sexes and if both are planted the female bushes will produce showy scarlet berries in autumn. Aucubas will grow in any soil, and sunny or even very shady position. They are a little liable to be damaged by hard spring frosts and cold winds but otherwise are hardy. Propagation is by cuttings in summer or autumn.

Azalea. Strictly speaking, the shrubs known in gardens as azaleas are rhododendrons but to simplify matters for the general reader I have retained the common name. The family is a big and varied one, including evergreen as well as deciduous species. Almost all are very showy, with bold trusses of brightly coloured flowers in late spring. All like peaty, lime-free soils and do best in partially shaded positions though they can also be grown successfully in full sun.

Most popular are the innumerable hybrids usually grouped under the names Mollis and Ghent, the latter with fragrant flowers. These vary from 1·2-2·4 m (4–8 ft) in height and spread. They are deciduous and have especially fine clusters of large flowers in many shades of pink, salmon, orange and red. The Rustica hybrids are allied to the Ghent azaleas, are also sweetly scented and have double flowers. The Exbury and Knap Hill hybrids are especially fine selections of the Mollis and Ghent types.

All these are at their best in late spring/early summer and are closely followed or even overlapped by hybrids of *Rhododendron occidentalis* which are similar in appearance but are mainly in delicate shades of pink, cream, apricot and soft orange. The yellow *R. luteum* (or *Azalea pontica*) also belongs to this group and is part parent of the Ghent hybrids. Though its flowers are smaller than those of the best hybrids they are an especially good yellow and are richly perfumed. The foliage of this fine and easily grown shrub turns to brilliant hues of scarlet, crimson and copper in the autumn.

Then there are the dwarf hybrids, often known as Kurume azaleas, with little rounded, evergreen leaves and clusters of small pink, rose, scarlet, lavender or white flowers, the whole bush being little over 60 cm (2 ft) high and perhaps 1 m (3½ ft) dense. Hinomayo, salmon pink, and Hinodegiri, bright scarlet, are well-known varieties of this type which, with others of the same class are often planted in the rock garden. They are partly derived from *Rhododendron kiusianum*, a Japanese species which has numerous variations such as *A. amoenum*, with vivid magenta flowers and *R. obtusum*, once regarded as a species in its own right. Another parent, *A. kaempferi*, taller and notably hardy and some of its hybrids inherit these qualities. The Malvaticum hybrids are notable for the size of their flowers.

All azaleas can be increased by layering in peaty soil in spring or autumn and the evergreen kinds by summer cuttings in a propagator. The deciduous varieties are also readily raised from seed but seedlings vary in the colour of their flowers. None requires any regular pruning. The deciduous kinds should be planted in autumn, the evergreens in spring. The dwarf kinds can often be obtained in pots, which makes transplanting a particularly easy task as root disturbance can be kept to a minimum.

Bamboo. The plants familiarly known as bamboos in gardens belong to several different families of which the two most important are arundinaria and phyllostachys, but nomenclature is confused and the same plants may appear under different names in different catalogues. The commonest is *Arundinaria japonica*, once wrongly named *Bambusa metake* and now correctly called *Pseudosasa japonica*. It is an excellent plant, vigorous, hardy and thriving in any fairly rich and not too dry soil. It will soon attain a height of 3·3 m (11 ft) and, like others of its kind, will spread into a very large clump by means of underground stems. Even bigger is *Semiarundinaria fastuosa*, which, under favourable conditions, may attain a height of 7·5 m (25 ft). For the smaller garden *Sinarundinaria nitida* is preferable. This averages 2·4 m (8 ft) in height and has slender, arching canes and comparatively small leaves. *A. viridi-striata* (now called *Pleioblastus auricomus*) has purplish stems and leaves striped with yellow. It is usually under 1·2 m (4 ft) high. *A. murielae* (now *Thanocalamus spathaceus*) is very hardy yet graceful with slender canes and narrow leaves. *Phyllostachys flexuosa* is moderate in growth and graceful in habit, and *P. nigra* has canes that become almost black and very luxuriant foliage. It has several varieties including *P. n. henonis* with greenish-yellow canes and *P. n.* Boryana with yellow canes spotted purple.

All these bamboos, including those varieties described as quite hardy, appreciate some shelter from cold winds which are apt to disfigure their foliage. They will thrive in sun or shade and prefer fairly moist soils. All can be increased by careful division in the second half of spring which is also the best planting time.

Bay. See **Laurus** (p. 279).

Berberis (Barberry). This is a very big and also a very important family of shrubs. It includes both evergreen and deciduous kinds some of which are grown mainly for their flowers, others for their berries and yet others for foliage. All will grow in a wide range of soils.

All barberries can be raised from seeds sown in a frame or sheltered place out of doors in spring, but it takes some years to obtain flowering bushes in this way and selected varieties, including those with coloured leaves, do not breed true from seed. These are increased by cuttings of firm young shoots taken in late summer for the deciduous kinds, early autumn for the evergreens.

Species and varieties are very numerous. Here are a few of the best.

Deciduous kinds with scarlet or coral berries in autumn are *Berberis aggregata*, 1·3 m (4½ ft); *B. prattii*, 2·2 m (7½ ft); *B. thunbergii*, 1·6 m (5½ ft), with beautiful scarlet and orange autumn foliage tints as an additional attraction; *B. thunbergii atropurpurea*, similar in every respect except that the leaves are purple from the outset; and several other varieties including Rose Glow with purple leaves splashed with pink; Rubrostilla, a hybrid producing fine crops of coral-red berries; *B. jamesiana*, very tall with arching branches and large, pendulous clusters of berries; *B. wilsoniae*, 1 m (3½ ft) with good autumn leaf colour. There are also many hybrids such as *B.* × *carminea* Barbarossa and *B.* × *c.* Buccaneer and *B.* × *ottawensis* Purpurea which is similar to *B. thunbergii atropurpurea* but with arching stems.

Evergreen kinds with small to medium leaves and yellow or orange flowers in late spring/early summer are *B. buxifolia*, 2·7 m (7 ft), deciduous in a hard winter; *B. darwinii*, 2·7 m (9 ft), a grand shrub and excellent for hedge making as well as for border planting; *B. empetrifolia*, 30 cm (1 ft) with yellow flowers in spring; *B. gagnepainii*, 1·6 m (5½ ft);

B. pruinosa, 1·6 m (5½ ft), berries heavily covered with a whitish bloom; *B. sargentiana*, 1·9 m (6½ ft), very long, sharp thorns; *B.* × *stenophylla*, a hybrid between *B. darwinii* and *B. empetrifolia*, 2·7 m (9 ft), useful for the same purposes as *B. darwinii*; and *B. verruculosa*, like a small edition of *B. darwinii* not above 1·5 cm (5 ft) in height. There are also dwarf varieties of *B.* × *stenophylla* such as Coccinea, Gracilis and Irwinii.

Betula (Birch). The graceful silver birch, *Betula pendula*, needs no introduction. It is one of the few forest trees which may be admitted to the ordinary garden. It is very variable and the best forms for garden planting are those with white bark and drooping branchlets. *B. p.* Dalecarlica has deeply lobed leaves and *B. p.* Youngii, or Young's weeping birch, is a slow-growing, relatively dwarf variety with a very elegant weeping habit. Other kinds are the paper birch, *B. papyrifera*, which has stouter branches and an even whiter trunk than the silver birch, *B. ermanii*, with white, pink-flushed bark; *B. utilis* var. *jacquemontii* with very white bark; *B. lutea* with yellow bark; *B. albo-sinensis* with orange bark; and *B. nigra* with dark, peeling bark.

All are deciduous, will grow in ordinary soils and situations and need no pruning. The species can be increased by seed sown out of doors in early spring or as soon as ripe, but garden varieties do not come true from seed and are increased by grafting on to seedlings of the species from which they are derived.

Birch. See **Betula** above.

Box. See **Buxus** (p. 251).

Brachyglottis. These are evergreen shrubs from New Zealand, none of which is completely hardy in severe winters. They were listed as senecio. One of the toughest, which will survive quite a lot of frost, is a hybrid named *Brachyglottis* Sunshine, one of its parents being *B. greyi*. Both are much alike, low, rather wide bushes with grey leaves and clusters of bright yellow daisy flowers in summer but Sunshine appears to be the hardier of the two. *Brachyglottis compacta* is also similar but shorter, 60-90 cm (2-3 ft) against 90 cm-1·5 m (3-5 ft) and with wavy-edged leaves. It is not as hardy as *B. greyi*, nor is another species, *B. laxifolia* which differs mainly in having narrower leaves. So Sunshine is the one to plant where there is room for it and *B. compacta* is the best for small gardens. All should have sunny places and well drained soils. They can be thinned or cut back a little in the first half of spring. Increase is usually by summer cuttings which root easily in a propagator but plants can also be increased from seed.

Broom. See **Cytisus** (p. 262), **Genista** (p. 271) and **Spartium** (p. 318).

Buddleia. *Buddleia davidii* is a popular deciduous shrub 3·3 m (11 ft) high and equally wide, producing from mid-summer to early autumn long, tapering spikes of pale purple, fragrant flowers which are a great attraction to butterflies. It has several fine varieties, including some with white and some with deep violet-purple or reddish-purple flowers, and some with yellow variegated leaves.

All are very easily grown in any ordinary soil and sunny place, but cold spots and frost pockets should be avoided as the young shoots are a little tender. Very severe pruning can be carried out in early spring if desired, even to within 30 cm (1 ft) of soil level, and the result will be the production of fewer but larger flower spikes.

B. alternifolia is similar in height and spread but lighter and arching in habit, with the small purple flowers produced in early summer in little clusters all along the stems instead of being gathered into big spikes. No pruning is required.

B. fallowiana is much like *B. davidii* except that its leaves are grey with down. It is also less hardy. Lochinch is said to be a hybrid between the two, has grey leaves and is reasonably hardy.

B. globosa is semi-evergreen, 3·6-4·5 m (12-15 ft) high and equally dense with, in early summer, small orange flowers gathered into compact balls each about 18 mm ($^3/_4$ ft) in diameter. Like *B. davidii* its young growth is rather tender. There is a hybrid between the two named *B.* × *meyeriana* with orange flowers flushed with purple.

All can be increased by cuttings of firm shoots taken in mid-autumn and rooted in a frame or sheltered place out of doors. *B. davidii* also grows very readily from seed and self-sown seedlings are apt to spring up all over the place but are usually variable in colour and quality.

Buxus (Box). The familiar *Buxus sempervirens*, with its densely branched habit and multitude of little, rounded leaves is one of the best hardy evergreens for clipping. It has been a favourite with gardeners for centuries for making complicated topiary specimens representing peacocks, bears and many other fantastic shapes. It is less popular for hedge making but a dwarf form of it, named Suffruticosa, is used for edgings in many gardens and can be clipped to a height and breadth of several centimetres. There are also several golden variegated varieties and others with larger or smaller leaves than normal. All kinds will grow in ordinary soils in sun or shade.

The common box is increased by cuttings of firm shoots 13 cm (5 in) long inserted in sandy soil out of doors or in a frame in autumn. The edging box can be divided in the first half of spring and the divisions should be replanted several centimetres apart to form a continuous line. Other varieties are increased by cuttings in summer or autumn. Clipping of all kinds can be continued from late spring to early autumn but any hard cutting should be done at the beginning of this period.

Calluna (Heather or Ling). It must be a little disconcerting to the beginner to discover that, though the common heather which covers so much of the English and Scottish countryside is botanically calluna, all other heathers despite their obvious similarities belong to a different genus with the name erica. *Calluna vulgaris* is the solitary representative of its family and is a dwarf, evergreen shrub with small flowers packed into slender spikes. There are numerous varieties of it, some with white flowers, others crimson, others double flowered. There are also varieties with golden, coppery or grey leaves; the differences in height and habit range from almost prostrate plants to taller growing varieties up to 60 cm (2 ft) in height.

All grow in peaty soils, show a marked dislike for lime, flower in late summer/early autumn and can be increased by cuttings of short, non-flowering shoots taken in midsummer and rooted in sandy peat in a close frame or under mist. An easier method is to cut back the old plant fairly severely in spring, mound it up with a mixture of sand and peat and leave it to form its new shoots in this soil. It can then be lifted and divided the following mid-autumn or early spring which are also the best planting seasons.

Camellia. The common camellia, *Camellia japonica*, is frequently regarded as a greenhouse plant and does in fact succeed well in a cool greenhouse (see Chapter 19). Nevertheless it is also sufficiently hardy to be grown out of doors in milder rural regions and even some cities. It should have a sheltered or even partly shaded position in loamy, non-alkaline soil and requires no pruning, though if plants become too large they can be cut back as severely as necessary in late spring with no damage other than the probable loss of a season's bloom. It will make a shapely evergreen shrub or small tree occasionally up to 9 m (30 ft) high, though plants 2·4-3·6 m (8-12 ft) high and as dense are normal. Flowers, which may be single or double, pink, red or white, are produced in spring.

Camellia × williamsii is a hybrid between *C. japonica* and a species named *C. saluenensis*. There are numerous varieties, some with single flowers, others double, mainly in various shades of pink plus white. The faded flowers fall off, which is an advantage over those of *C. japonica* which tend to remain on the bushes and look untidy. *C. reticulata* has larger flowers than either *C. japonica* or *C.* × *williamsii* and those of the variety Captain Rawes are semi-double and deep rose pink, but all forms of this camellia are rather tender, so they are usually trained against a sheltered wall. Varieties of *C. sasanqua* flower from mid-autumn to mid-spring but need a very sheltered place as the flowers are destroyed by frost though the plant is hardy.

Increase of all these kinds is by cuttings of firm, young shoots rooted in peat and sand in a propagating frame or under mist within the greenhouse in summer.

Campsis (Trumpet Creeper). Very showy climbers, often known as tecoma or bignonia, but not fully hardy and only suitable for the mildest parts of the country, where they should be planted against sunny, sheltered walls. Both *Campsis grandiflora* and *C. radicans* have large, trumpet-shaped, orange-scarlet flowers in late summer. *C. grandiflora*, which is the handsomer and also the more tender of the two, has some aerial roots but usually needs a trellis or wires for additional support, whereas *C. radicans* has more aerial roots by which it can attach itself to a wall. There is also a hybrid between these two species known as *C.* × *tagliabuana* and the best form is Mme Galen, with salmon-red flowers. All can be increased by layering in spring or autumn. When wall space is filled, further growth can be cut back annually in early spring at which time any frost damaged growth should also be removed.

Carpenteria. *Carpenteria californica* is a beautiful evergreen shrub growing 1·8-2·4 m (6-8 ft) high with showy white, fragrant flowers in the second half of summer. It needs a sunny, sheltered place as it is not very hardy. It also likes light, well-drained soil and is easily killed in winter in wet conditions with poor drainage. No pruning is required but frost-damaged growth should be removed in spring. It can be increased by seed, summer cuttings and also sometimes by digging out rooted suckers. Since plants vary considerably in the quality of their flowers buy when in bloom so you can see what you are getting.

Carpinus (Hornbeam). The chief garden value of the hornbeam, *Carpinus betulus*, is as a hedge shrub for which purpose it rivals, and closely resembles, beech. Though deciduous it will, like the beech, retain its brown autumn foliage throughout the winter when clipped to form a hedge. It has the merit of thriving in practically all soils, even those that are comparatively poor, and of standing any amount of wind. In fact it is an ideal plant with which to form an outer windbreak for the exposed garden. For this purpose plant young hornbeams 30 cm (1 ft) apart in autumn or late winter and prune them in late winter to make a narrow hedge. In addition to winter pruning the hedge can be clipped occasionally, but not too severely, in summer. Planted as an individual specimen, the hornbeam makes a big, rounded tree 15 m (50 ft) or more in height and with corresponding branch spread, but *C. Fastigiata* is neatly erect and pyramidal in form becoming broader with age and makes an excellent street tree. Common hornbeam is raised from seeds sown out of doors in spring, the pyramidal variety by grafting on to seedlings of common hornbeam.

Caryopteris. Several species are widely grown in the milder regions and are attractive, deciduous shrubs 90 cm–1·5 m (3-5 ft) in height. They make numerous, rather soft stems, with small greyish leaves but their great value is that they carry their spikes of bright blue flowers in late and even mid-autumn when colour is scarce in the shrub border. The best kinds are *C. incana*, once known as *C. mastacanthus*, and *C. × clandonensis*, a hybrid of exceptional beauty between *C. mastacanthus* and a rather unreliable species named *C. mongolica*. Some are inclined to be killed back by frost each winter with the result that they never make more than small shrubs, but *C. clandonensis* usually behaves in a thoroughly reliable manner. It is best hard pruned in mid-spring, the previous year's growth being cut back almost to the base. There are several selected forms such as Arthur Simmonds, Ferndown and Kew Blue. Cuttings of firm, young growth root readily in a propagating frame in summer.

Castanea (Chestnut). These are the true chestnuts in contrast to aesculus, the horse chestnuts. The best as an ornamental tree is undoubtedly the sweet chestnut, *Castanea sativa*. This is very big, sometimes 30 m (100 ft) high and with branches spreading 16·5 m (55 ft). It has big, shining, deciduous leaves, small yellowish-white flowers in long rats' tails in early summer, followed by the familiar nuts, each in a large, spiky, green case. The bark of this tree, with spiral furrows on old specimens, is notably handsome.

The sweet chestnut thrives in ordinary soils and will survive in many that are too dry and sandy for most other trees. It grows quickly from seed, which can be sown outdoors in spring. No pruning is required.

Catalpa (Indian Bean). *Catalpa bignonioides* deserves to be better known for it is a quick-growing tree with very handsome foliage and, under favourable conditions, showy spikes of white, yellow and purple-spotted flowers which are a little like those of the horse chestnut. These appear in late summer. The Indian bean will usually thrive well in town gardens and it makes a tree 9-12 m (30-40 ft) high and equally wide. The leaves are rounded, pale green and up to 30 cm (1 ft) in diameter. Pruning is not essential but, if desired, branches can be cut hard back in early spring with the result that a much smaller tree is maintained but the individual leaves are considerably bigger. The two drawbacks are that it comes into leaf rather late, often not until the end of spring, and young shoots are occasionally injured by late frost, so it should not be planted in frost pockets. The variety *C. Aurea* has yellow leaves. The ordinary form can be increased by seeds sown in a warm greenhouse in spring or by cuttings of firm young shoots in mid-summer in a propagating frame or under mist. The golden variety cannot be grown from seed but from cuttings in summer in a propagator.

Ceanothus. There are both evergreen and deciduous species of ceanothus and while most of the former flower in late spring/early summer, the latter bloom towards the end of the summer. Many of the evergreen kinds are a little tender, needing the protection of a sunny wall in most parts of the country. One of the hardiest is *Ceanothus thyrsiflorus*, with thimble-like clusters of pale blue flowers. In the open it will make a shrub up to 4·5 m (15 ft) high and almost as dense, but it is more commonly seen as a wall-trained tree, in which position it is very beautiful. Even better is *C. rigidus*, with brighter blue flower clusters, but this is considerably less hardy and really does need a sheltered position. *C.* × *veitchianus*, a hybrid between the last two, is intermediate between them both in brightness of colour and in hardiness. *C. dentatus* is a good wall shrub with bright blue flowers. *C. impressus* is only 1·5-2·7 m (5-7 ft) high but twice as much through, relatively hardy, with deep blue flowers. It is one of the best kinds to grow as a bush in the open, though it is rivalled by the hybrid *C.* Burkwoodii which is also unusual for an evergreen ceanothus in flowering from early summer to mid-autumn. *C. arboreus* is one of the largest, to 6 m (20 ft), and also one of the most tender. Its variety Trewithen Blue has brighter lavender-blue flowers.

Of the deciduous kinds the most important are the hybrids between *C. americanus*, white, and *coeruleus*, blue. Collectively these are known as *C.* × *delineanus* but individual varieties have distinguishing names such as Gloire de Versailles (bright blue), Indigo (deep blue) and Perle Rose (pink). The flowers are individually small but produced in rather big, loose clusters.

All will grow in ordinary well-drained soils and sunny positions. The evergreens need no regular pruning unless grown against walls, when side growths should be shortened to several centimetres immediately after flowering. The deciduous kinds can, if desired, be pruned hard back in early spring, when they will make fewer stems but with bigger flower trusses. Alternatively they can be left unpruned in which case they will form loose specimens about 1·8 m (6 ft) high and dense. Propagation of all kinds is by cuttings of firm, young growth rooted during the second half of summer in sand in a propagating box or under mist.

Cedar. See **Cedrus** below.

Cedrus (Cedar). All the cedars are evergreen, cone-bearing trees of the largest size and consequently quite unsuitable for small gardens, though they are admirable where there is space for specimens 18-27 m (60-90 ft) high with branches spreading 6-9 m (20-30 ft) in all directions. There are three valuable species, *Cedrus libani*, the famous cedar of Lebanon, distinguished by a flat-topped habit when mature with horizontally held branches; *C. libani atlantica*, the Mount Atlas cedar, which is more conical, and *C. deodara*, the deodar of the Himalayas, the ends of whose branches hang down. This last is the least hardy of the three but is very beautiful. The Mount Atlas cedar has a particularly attractive form named *C. l. a. glauca*, in which the young leaves are blue-grey, and there is also a golden-leaved form which is slow growing and a weeping variety. There is a silver variegated variety of the deodar, also slow growing.

All should be grown in good, loamy soils with first-class drainage. Some protection, such as that afforded by neighbouring trees, is advisable when the cedars are young but later these should be removed so that they can stand alone. No pruning should be attempted at any time. Increase of species is by seeds sown in a frame in spring; increase varieties by grafting on to seedlings of the appropriate species.

Celastrus. *Celastrus orbiculatus* is a very vigorous deciduous climber with insignificant, greenish flowers followed by small fruits which split open to reveal scarlet seeds on a yellow interior in the autumn. This deserves to be better known for it is easily grown in ordinary soil and a sunny position and is one of the brightest climbers in the autumn and early winter. It can be used to cover a shed or outhouse or allowed to ramble up into the branches of a dead tree. The plant is unusual in having some flowers unisexual, some bisexual. Sometimes a plant seems to have almost exclusively unisexual flowers and then no fruits will be produced unless another plant with flowers of the opposite sex is planted nearby. It is, therefore, wise to buy plants only from a reliable nurseryman and to seek an assurance that they are bisexual.

No pruning is necessary but if it strays too far it can be cut back in winter. Increase is readily effected by layering in autumn.

Ceratostigma (Plumbago). Small semi-shrubby plants valuable for their bright blue, phlox-like flowers in late summer and autumn. The best is *Ceratostigma willmottianum* which in very favourable warm and sheltered places can grow to 1·2 m (4 ft), but it is usually killed to ground level each winter and shoots up again in spring to make a spreading 45 cm (18 in) plant. Cut off all dead or damaged shoots in mid-spring and increase by summer cuttings.

Cercis (Judas Tree). *Cercis siliquastrum* is known as the Judas tree because there is a legend that it was on this tree that Judas hanged himself. It is a beautiful deciduous tree of freely branching habit, about 6 m (20 ft) high and dense, with elegant, rounded leaves and clusters of magenta, pea-type flowers in late spring. It likes a warm, sheltered, sunny position and ordinary, well-drained soil. No pruning is required. Propagation is by seeds sown in a slightly heated greenhouse or frame in spring. The Judas tree transplants badly when old so it is advisable to start with quite small specimens, preferably grown in containers. These should be planted in late spring.

Chaenomeles (Japanese Quince). These deciduous shrubs were formerly known as cydonia. By far the best known ornamental species is *Chaenomeles speciosa* (formerly *Cydonia japonica*), the scarlet flowers of which are a familiar sight very early in spring. This is a fine shrub to train against a wall and it will also make a bushy specimen in the open 2·2 m (7½ ft) high and eventually as wide as it spreads by suckers. There are numerous forms with white, salmon and crimson flowers. Another useful species is *Chaenomeles japonica* (formerly *Cydonia maulei*), a branching, spiny shrub only 76 cm (2½ ft) high but often 2·4-3 m (8-10 ft) wide, with scarlet or blood-red flowers from mid-spring to early summer. Both have large apple-like fruits which have the true quince perfume and can be used to make quince jelly. They will thrive in any ordinary soil, prefer sunny positions but will grow in the shade, and can be increased by layers or rooted suckers.

Chamaecyparis (Cypress). These cypresses were formerly known as cupressus, but now that name is reserved for a particular section of the family. Chamaecyparis is a genus of evergreen, cone-bearing trees containing a large number of species and even more varieties, some of which are amongst the most useful of their kind in gardens. One species alone, *Chamaecyparis lawsoniana*, known as Lawson cypress, has provided a whole range of excellent varieties, some, such as Lutea, Lane, Stewartii, and Winston Churchill with golden leaves; others, such as Erecta, Columnaris and Kilmacurragh, columnar; others, such as Intertexta, weeping; yet others with blue-green foliage (Alumii and Triomphe de Boskoop). Many are fast-growing trees eventually reaching 18 m (60 ft) or more but there are also very dwarf forms which can be grown in the rock garden, such as Nana and Minima Aurea, while Elwoodii, Pottenii, and Fletcheri grow slowly to 4·5 m (15 ft) or thereabouts and make medium-sized columns of feathery foliage. The vigorous types make excellent hedges or windbreaks as they are quick growing, hardy and not particular about soil or situation.

Another group of cypresses was formerly known as 'retinospora'. Of these the two most important are *C. obtusa*, a rather broad, spreading tree of medium size and *C. pisifera*, which is similar in habit. Both are most frequently represented in gardens by their numerous varieties, many of which are excellent shrubs of quite modest proportions. Two of the most beautiful are *C. pisifera* Plumosa and *C. pisifera* Squarrosa, both with fine, ferny foliage, grey-green in colour. By contrast *C. pisifera* Filifera has slender, cord-like shoots, yellow in *C. p.* Aurea.

Chamaecyparis nootkatensis is rather like Lawson cypress but more pendulous, is very hardy and has a beautiful variety, *C. n.* Pendula with even more weeping branches.

All these cypresses will grow in ordinary soils and open or partially shady positions. Pruning is not essential but most will submit to very severe pruning if carried out early in mid-spring. They can, in addition, be clipped during the summer though this should only be done when they are used as hedge plants as it spoils their natural habit.

The best method of increase for the species is by seeds kept in moist peat outdoors in winter (or in a polythene bag in a refrigerator) and then sown in a slightly heated greenhouse in early spring, but selected forms do not reproduce true to type from seed and must either be grafted on to seedlings of the parent species or be raised from cuttings struck in sandy peat in a propagating frame in late summer or autumn.

Cherries. See **Prunus** (p. 307).

Chestnut. See **Aesculus** (p. 246) and **Castanea** (p. 253).

Chimonanthus (Winter Sweet). *Chimonanthus praecox* flowers in mid-winter but nevertheless one might easily pass it by were it not for its exquisite fragrance, for the flowers are a very pale yellowish green, maroon at the centre, with petals so thin that one can quite see through them. However, this deciduous shrub is well worth growing for its perfume alone. It is fairly hardy but should have a sunny, sheltered position to protect its blossoms. Grow it in any reasonably good, well-drained soil and if it is trained against a

256

wall, which is a popular method, shorten the side growths and remove any weak shoots in spring as soon as flowering is over. Full-grown specimens are 2·5 m (8½ ft) high and the same in spread. Propagate by layers.

Choisya (Mexican Orange Blossom). The best species is *Choisya ternata*, a very beautiful evergreen shrub with white, fragrant flowers not unlike orange blossom. It makes a dense, rounded specimen 1·6 m (5½ ft) high, slightly bigger in spread, and is at its best in mid-spring but will sometimes flower spasmodically all the summer. There is a good yellow leaved variety named Sundance. Both should be given a fairly sheltered, sunny position in good, well-drained soil. No pruning is required. Cuttings can be rooted in summer or early autumn.

Cistus (Rock Rose). All rock roses are evergreen shrubs, most of them of medium or small size, and flowering very freely mainly in the first half of summer. They have, in fact, all the qualities required for the small garden except hardiness. Few will survive really hard winters, though many are satisfactory in gentle climates. Among the hardiest are *Cistus × corbariensis*, 90 cm (3 ft) high, wide spreading and white flowered; *C. laurifolius*, 1·6 m (5½ ft) high, and slightly wider, has white flowers; *C. × cyprius*, similar in habit with white flowers each with a central blotch of blood red; Silver Pink, a delightful hybrid no more than 90 cm (3 ft) high, with rose pink flowers; and *C. ladaniferus*, to 1·5 m (5 ft), with very dark green, sticky leaves and white, red-blotched flowers. In some ways the most beautiful of all is *C. × purpureus*, with bright rose, maroon-blotched flowers 7·5 cm (3 in) in diameter. Unfortunately it needs a distinctly sheltered position. So do *C. crispus* and *C. incanus* both with grey leaves and rose flowers deeper and brighter in the last named. There is a hybrid between them named *C. × pulverulenta* and a good garden variety of this named Sunset with deep magenta flowers.

    All succeed in ordinary soils, preferring those that are well drained even to the point of dryness. They are unsurpassed for dry, sunny banks and usually succeed particularly well near the sea. No pruning is needed. All can be raised from cuttings of firm young shoots and can also be raised from seed but do not always come true, as some are hybrids and some readily cross with one another.

Clematis. This is an immense genus of plants, mostly climbers though a few are herbaceous (see p. 124). A great number of hybrids and garden forms have been raised, often with very large flowers in bright and varied colours produced over a long period. Typical examples are *Clematis* Jackmanii Superba, with rich purple flowers in mid-summer; Nelly Moser, with mauve flowers each with a band of red down the centre of the petal, blooming in late spring/early summer and sometimes again in late summer; Comtesse de Bouchaud, with pink flowers in mid-summer, and Henryi with huge white flowers in early and late summer. There are double-flowered varieties as well, such as Belle of Woking, mauve, Duchess of Edinburgh, white, and Beauty of Worcester, violet blue, which has the odd characteristic of producing double blooms on the older growth and single flowers on the young stems. Equally attractive are the small-flowering kinds such as *C. montana*, with innumerable white flowers in late spring/early summer; its pale pink form *C. m. rubens*, and the late-flowering *C. flammula*, with masses of tiny, white fragrant flowers. These are more rampant than the large-flowered varieties and *C. montana*, in particular, requires a lot of space. One of the first to flower is *C. armandii*, which, unlike most of the others, is evergreen. The small white flowers are produced in clusters in mid-spring, but the plant is a little tender and prefers a wall facing south or west. *C. macropetala* is very distinctive with nodding, narrow-petalled, semi-double flowers in late spring, lavender blue in the common form, soft pink in Markham's Pink. *C. tangutica* also has rather bell-shaped yellow flowers. They are produced from early summer to mid-autumn, accompanied and followed by silken seed heads which are highly decorative. There are a great many other beautiful species and varieties to be found fully described in nursery catalogues.

All clematises thrive in chalky soils but will grow in neutral and moderately acid soils provided they are moderately well drained without being really dry. They like to have their roots in the shade and their leaves and flowers in the sun, opposites which can be reconciled by planting in a sunny place but near an evergreen shrub which will throw shade over the base of the plant. The growths are very slender and brittle and should be given good support over which to ramble, for example the trunk of a dead tree or a well-made trellis.

Regular pruning is not essential but flowers of extra size can be obtained in some varieties, notably those of the *C.* Jackmanii type that flower after mid-summer, by cutting fairly hard back in late winter. In other cases thinning and shortening, sufficient to keep the plants within bounds, can be carried out without harm, in late winter in the case of summer-flowering kinds, or immediately after flowering in the case of those varieties which finish blooming by early summer.

Nurserymen frequently propagate clematis by grafting in the greenhouse in the spring, using seedlings of the wild British clematis as stocks. This is an unsatisfactory method and if plants of this type are purchased they should be planted rather deeply so that the point of union is buried 2·5 cm (1 in) or so below the surface enabling the scion to make roots of its own. The amateur should increase his plants by layering vigorous young shoots any time from spring until autumn.

Clerodendrum. The value of the hardy clerodendrums (there are also tender kinds described in Chapter 19) is that they flower very late in the summer. Their drawback is that most have foliage that is distinctly unpleasant in odour when bruised. The best is *Clerodendrum trichotomum*, almost a tree in habit, 3 m (10 ft) or more high and of equal spread, loosely branched, deciduous and with fragrant white flowers in late summer/early autumn, followed in a favourable season by small, turquoise-blue berries. It will grow in any ordinary soil and is moderately hardy but prefers a sheltered position. *C. bungei* has rounded heads of purplish-red flowers in late summer/early autumn. In very mild places it will make a shrub 1·8 m (6 ft) high but is often killed to ground level each winter and then sends up sturdy stems in spring, 1 m (3½ ft) high by flowering time. Cut out dead or damaged growth each spring. The simplest method of increase is to remove rooted suckers in the autumn, but it can be raised from seed and from root cuttings in winter under glass.

Colutea (Bladder Senna). These are showy, deciduous shrubs with clusters of small, pea-type flowers followed by inflated seed vessels which look like small bladders. They have the merit of thriving in poor, stony soils and hot, dry places and are among the easiest of shrubs to grow. One of the showiest is *Colutea arborescens*. This can grow to 3 m (10 ft) high, spreading to 2·2 m (7½ ft), but can be kept much smaller by thinning out in late winter. The flowers are yellow and continue all summer. Increase by seeds sown in a frame in mid-spring or by cuttings of firm, young growth taken in mid-summer and rooted in a propagating frame with gentle bottom heat.

Convolvulus. The only truly shrubby species is *Convolvulus cneorum*, a delightful plant 60 cm (2 ft) high, sometimes with a greater spread, very branching, with silvery leaves and blush-white flowers for most of the summer. It should have a light, well-drained soil and sunny, sheltered position. It is a good dwarf shrub for the rock garden. Increase by summer cuttings in a propagator.

Cornus. From the gardener's standpoint this family splits up into two distinct groups, one composed of those species grown mainly for the beauty of their bark in winter or of their foliage effects in summer, and a second consisting of those cultivated for their flowers, though in the last it is often the bracts surrounding the flowers that make the real show.

The best of the bark species are *Cornus alba* and *C. stolonifera*. Both are deciduous, grow to 3 m (10 ft) high, make numerous strong shoots from the base, and are seen to best advantage if hard pruned each spring. The bark is typically red and most highly coloured on year-old wood, but there is a yellow-barked variety of *C. stolonifera* named Flaviramea. These easily grown shrubs delight in moist places and are ideal plants for the stream or lake side.

Of the foliage varieties, *C. sanguinea*, the common dogwood, is sometimes worth a place for its autumn colour but the two best are varieties of *C. alba* named Spaethii, which has leaves heavily variegated with yellow, and Variegata, with white variegation. These are very bright shrubs, well worth including in every shrub border, and ones which will grow in ordinary or moist soils. They need not be pruned if large specimens are required.

Of the species grown for their flowers, *C. mas* is, perhaps, the best. It is a small, deciduous tree 4·5-6 m (15-20 ft) high and of equal spread, branching and also suckering freely; there are numerous small yellow flowers in late winter/early spring on the bare branches. They are followed by bright orange fruits, hence the popular name, Cornelian cherry. A typical example of the type grown for the bracts surrounding the flowers is *C. kousa*. This is a small tree or large shrub with spreading horizontal branches lined in late spring/early summer with tiny clusters of flowers each surrounded by four large, creamy-white bracts which look like petals. Rather similar are *C. florida*, also with white bracts, its lovely variety *C. f. rubra* with pink bracts and *C. nuttalii*, whose bracts are cream but later flushed with pink. All are a little tender and need a place fairly free of spring frosts. All give fine autumn foliage colour and need good loamy soils.

C. alba, *C. stolonifera* and *C. sanguinea* can be increased very easily by cuttings of well-ripened wood or by rooted suckers or layers. Other kinds should be layered or raised from seed sown in a frame or unheated greenhouse in early spring.

Corylopsis (Winter Hazel). These are attractive shrubs or small trees which flower early. *Corylopsis pauciflora* has little clusters of pale yellow flowers and is 1 m (3½ ft) high. *C. spicata* is similar in colour, has tassels or catkins of flowers and is up to 1·8 m (6 ft) high. *C. sinensis* and *C. sinensis sinensis* have still longer tassels of pale yellow flowers and are about 3-3·6 m (10-12 ft) high. All thrive in ordinary soils and sheltered positions and need no pruning. Increase by seeds, summer cuttings or layers.

Corylus (Hazel, Filbert). Though the common hazel and filbert are not shrubs for the ornamental garden they have several forms which are worth planting both for their foliage and catkins. The handsomest of these is *Corylus maxima* Atropurpurea, a variety of the filbert with deep purple foliage. Left to itself it will make a dense shrub 3·6-4·5 m (12-15 ft) high and in spread, but it can be kept a good deal smaller by pruning each spring immediately the catkins fade. *C. avellana* Aurea, a variety of the hazel, has soft yellow leaves while another variety, named *C. a.* Contorta, the corkscrew hazel, has twisted branches. All will grow in any ordinary soil and sunny or shady position and can be increased by layering or from rooted suckers.

Cotinus (Venetian Sumach, Smoke Tree, Wig Tree). These large deciduous shrubs were once called rhus and may be found under that name in nurseries and gardens. *Cotinus coggygria*, the most popular kind, will grow to a height of 3·6 m (12 ft) and may exceed this in diameter. It has clusters of small purplish flowers which develop beige-coloured filaments giving the whole inflorescence a smoky appearance. The leaves colour well in the autumn though not so brilliantly as those of *C. obovatus*, also known as *C. americanus* which, however, is far inferior in flower. There are varieties of *C. coggygria* with purple leaves. All like warm, sunny places and well-drained soil. The purple-leaved varieties can be hard pruned in early spring to get larger leaves. All can be increased by layering, the species also by seed.

Cotoneaster. There are a great many cotoneasters and almost all are useful shrubs or small trees for the garden. There are both deciduous and evergreen kinds and they range in stature from the absolutely prostrate *Cotoneaster dammeri* to the 7·5 m (25 ft) high *C. frigidus*. Most are grown principally for their scarlet or crimson berries which make a fine display in the autumn, but some are also very attractive in flower and almost all have good foliage. They will grow in ordinary soils and sunny or, in many cases, slightly shaded positions. A few make fairly good hedge shrubs and some are first class for the rock garden. All can be increased by seed sown in a frame or even out of doors in a sheltered position in March but selected garden varieties do not breed entirely true from seed so must be increased by cuttings.

Here are a few of the best roughly in order of size, the largest first: *C. frigidus*, deciduous, 4·5-7·5 m (15-25 ft) high and a little less spread, with flattish clusters of white flowers followed by scarlet berries; *C. salicifolius*, to 4·5 m (15 ft) high and of equal spread with narrow, evergreen leaves, white flowers and bright red berries; *C. henryanus*, to 3·6 m (12 ft), semi-evergreen, narrow leaved and with dark red berries; *C. franchetii*, 2·4 m (8 ft) high and more in spread, with oval evergreen leaves and good clusters of whitish flowers followed by orange-red berries; its variety *C. sternianus*, often wrongly named *C. wardii*, with leaves that often turn scarlet and crimson in the autumn; *C. simonsii*, 2·7 m (9 ft) high, spreading to 1·9 m (6½ ft), partially evergreen with neat, box-like leaves, small white flowers and scarlet berries, a good kind for hedge making, either alone or mixed with privet, hawthorn, etc.; *C. dielsianus*, 1·8 m (6 ft) high and in spread has small clusters of whitish flowers and scarlet berries; *C. conspicuus* Decorus, making a dome-shaped bush 90 cm (3 ft) tall, with evergreen leaves and long-lasting scarlet berries; *C. microphyllus*, with narrow, dark green, evergreen leaves and making a stiff, densely branched bush 90 cm (3 ft) high and 1·3 m (4½ ft) in spread, or against a wall, climbing to a height of 2·7 m (9 ft), with solitary white flowers followed by deep red fruits; *C. horizontalis*, which is so called because its branches are spread out flat in herring-bone fashion enabling it to spread widely over the ground or climb against a wall, in either of which positions it will display its deciduous, box-like leaves turning red in autumn, solitary, pinkish flowers and red berries; its variety *C. h.* Variegatus with cream-edged leaves; *C. adpressus*, like a miniature version of *C. horizontalis*, no more than 30 cm (1 ft) high, though often 1·3 m (4½ ft) in diameter; *C. thymifolius*, which is really a dwarf form of *C. microphyllus*, similar in habit but practically prostrate; and *C. dammeri*, which will mould itself to every contour of rock and soil and produce abundant coral-red berries in autumn.

Crataegus (Thorn, Hawthorn, Quick). The common hawthorn or quick is a species of crataegus or, to be exact, two species, for botanists distinguish between *Crataegus monogyna* and *C. oxyacantha* (now known as *C. laevigata*), though to the layman both are equally hawthorns. The best hawthorns for garden display are the double-flowered varieties of *C. laevigata*, known as Paul's Scarlet and Rosea Flore Pleno, according to the colour of their flowers. There is also a double white form, less frequently seen. These all make densely branched trees up to 6 m (20 ft) in height with corresponding branch spread, but the common species can be planted close together and pruned hard to form hedges and are still favourites with farmers for this purpose. For hedge making, seedlings should be planted not more than 30 cm (1 ft) and preferably 23 cm (9 in) apart.

Other ornamental kinds are the Glastonbury thorn, a variety of *C. monogyna*, which opens its white flowers in winter or at the latest by mid-spring; *C. crus-galli*, the cockspur thorn, a small tree with white flowers, large red berries and enormous thorns; *C.* × *lavallei*, with leaves and berries much larger than those of the hawthorn and the berries remaining until the spring; and *C. persimilis* Prunifolia, not unlike the last but the berries usually drop in autumn and the leaves colour brilliantly before they fall.

All these will grow in ordinary soils and open positions and are among the hardiest of ornamental trees. No pruning is required, though badly placed or overcrowded branches can be removed in winter.

Propagation of the species is usually by seed sown 2·5 cm (1 in) deep out of doors in early spring, but double-flowered thorns must be grafted in spring or budded in summer on to seedlings of the common hawthorn and so must hybrid thorns such as *C.* × *lavallei*.

Crinodendron. *Crinodendron hookerianum* is a beautiful evergreen shrub or small tree with hanging crimson lantern-shaped flowers in late spring/early summer. It is usually 2·4-3 m (8-10 ft) high but can be twice as tall. It enjoys good, rather peaty, lime-free soil well supplied with moisture in summer and needs a sheltered place in sun or partial shade. It is too tender for cold, northerly gardens though it can often be grown successfully against a wall. Propagation is by seed or summer cuttings.

Cryptomeria. *Cryptomeria japonica* is one of the most beautiful of evergreen, cone-bearing trees but unfortunately it is just a little tender in its young state. The tree makes a particularly dense, cone-shaped specimen up to 21 m (70 ft) in height though as a rule it is rather smaller. Even more graceful is the form known as *C. j. elegans*, a slower growing and more bushy variety in which the foliage is feathery and turns reddish bronze in the autumn. These trees succeed best in deep, rather rich soils with plenty of moisture during the spring and summer. No pruning is required. Propagation of the species is by seeds sown in a frame in early spring, and of garden varieties by grafting on to seedlings of *C. japonica*.

× **Cupressocyparis** (Leyland Cypress). *Cupressocyparis leylandii* is a remarkable natural hybrid between *Chamaecyparis nootkatensis* and *Cupressus macrocarpa*, which combines the best features of both species. It is a very fast-growing and hardy evergreen coniferous tree which will make a broad column or pyramid 30 m (100 ft) or more in height or can be clipped to form a large hedge, screen or windbreak. Cultivation is as for chamaecyparis but being a hybrid it must be increased by cuttings taken in summer or autumn. Castlewellan and Robinson's Gold are varieties with pale yellow foliage, the latter more compact in habit.

Cupressus (Cypress). These are evergreen conifers, most of which are fast growing and will, if allowed, make large trees. However, *Cupressus macrocarpa*, the Monterey cypress, stands clipping quite well and was at one time a popular hedge plant but its habit of dying or becoming patchy has told against it. It does well in seaside districts, is very fast growing and often used as a windbreak. There are good golden-leaved varieties such as Donard Gold, Goldcrest and Golden Pillar.

C. arizonica, the Arizona cypress, is hardier, neater in habit and in *C. a.* Pyramidalis it makes a tall, narrow column of blue-grey foliage. There is considerable confusion about the naming of this cypress, which often appears in nurseries and gardens as *C. glabra pyramidalis* or *C. arizonica bonita*.

C. sempervirens, the Italian cypress, varies greatly in habit from forms with spreading horizontal branches to narrow spires, the type associated with Italian gardens. Unfortunately it is not very hardy, particularly when young.

All like well-drained soils and reasonably open places. They can be pruned or clipped if desired in spring or summer. The species can be raised from seed but garden varieties must be raised from summer or autumn cuttings, or be grafted on to seedlings of the parent species.

See also Chamaecyparis (p. 256) and Cupressocyparis (p. 262).

Cydonia (Quince). See **Chaenomeles** (p. 255).

Cytisus (Broom). Because of their bright green branches many people regard brooms as evergreen, though in fact they are deciduous; many, in fact, are leafless practically all the year, the green stems performing the functions of leaves. These are amongst the most free-flowering and brilliant of hardy shrubs. A number of valuable hybrids have been produced, mostly derived from *Cytisus scoparius*, an open, loose-habited shrub 1·6 m (5½ ft) high and about the same in diameter. It blooms in late spring/early summer, the type having yellow, pea-like flowers but the forms and hybrids derived from it are in all shades of yellow, crimson, maroon and reddish pink, with many combinations of these shades.

Other good species are *C.* × *praecox*, with sulphur-yellow flowers in late spring;

C. multiflorus, which is taller and more pendulous than *C. scoparius* and has small pure white flowers; *C. ardoinii*, a prostrate shrub for the rock garden with yellow flowers in the second half of spring, the equally golden *C. × beanii*, which is, however, just a little less prostrate than the last though still a rock garden kind; and *C. × kewensis*, almost prostrate with cream flowers. The mauve-pink *C. dallimorei* is really a hybrid between *C. scoparius* and *C. multiflorus*. *C. purpureus* is prostrate, spreads by underground stems and has light purple flowers in late spring/early summer.

C. battandieri is a tall, loosely branched shrub with grey leaves and short, erect spikes of yellow, pineapple-scented flowers in the first half of summer. Its flexible branches can be easily trained against a wall if desired. *C. × spachianus*, a hybrid of *C. canariensis*, is the lemon-scented 'genista' sold by florists as a pot plant. In the open it makes a big bush flowering mainly in spring, but it is not very hardy and does best in mild seaside localities. A hybrid from it named Porlock is a good deal hardier and more suitable for general planting. The other parent of this hybrid is *C. monspessulanus*, much like it in appearance but hardier and less fragrant.

All these brooms delight in sunny places and light, well-drained soils. Contrary to popular belief they do not like lime and thrive best in slightly acid soils. They transplant badly and so should be purchased while young in pots from which they can be planted with a minimum of disturbance. Plant in late autumn or early spring; making very firm and staking the larger kinds as they are very liable to be disturbed by winds.

The species can be increased by seeds sown outdoors in the first half of spring, but selected varieties and hybrids must be raised from cuttings which are rather difficult to handle. Prepare them in late summer from firm young side growths removed with a heel of older wood, and root in very sandy soil in a frame.

The larger kinds benefit from an annual pruning immediately after flowering when the flowering stems can be shortened to 1 in (2·5 cm) or so, but do not cut back into hard old wood.

Daboëcia (St Dabeoc's Heath, Irish Heath, Connemara Heath). *Daboëcia cantabrica* is a compact, evergreen shrub which looks very much like a bell heather. The ordinary form has heather-purple flowers but there is also a beautiful pure white form and a curious variety, named Bicolor, in which some flowers are white, some purple and some combine both colours. All bloom from mid-summer to autumn. They require precisely the same conditions as calluna (see p. 251).

Danaë (Alexandrian Laurel). *Danaë racemosa* is a graceful, evergreen shrub about 90 cm (3 ft) high with narrow, pointed 'leaves' which are really flattened stems. It makes an excellent foliage subject both for the garden and for cutting and it has the merit of thriving in very shady places and moist soils. The flowers are insignificant. No pruning is necessary but branches can be cut for foliage at practically any time of the year without damaging the shrub. It can be increased by careful division in mid-spring, which is also the best planting time.

Daphne. There are both evergreen and deciduous species in this family and they vary greatly in size. Almost all are beautiful shrubs, many with intensely fragrant flowers, but some are a little too tender to be reliable out of doors in all parts of the country. One of the best is *Daphne mezereum*, a deciduous shrub about 1·2 m (4 ft) high and in spread, with a stiff, erect habit and small, very fragrant, wine-red or white flowers produced along the bare branches in late winter in a favourable season, followed by bright red or yellow berries. *D. mezereum* thrives in rather rich, loamy soils with plenty of moisture during spring and summer and is a little apt to die off suddenly for no apparent reason.

Another fine kind is *D. × burkwoodii*, sometimes known as *D*. Somerset, a semi-evergreen shrub about 90 cm (3 ft) high with clusters of very fragrant soft pink flowers in late spring/early summer.

D. odora is evergreen, 60 cm-1·2 m (2-4 ft) high and has clusters of very fragrant purple flowers in the first half of spring. A variety named Marginata has a yellow edge to each leaf and is a little hardier than the type but both these shrubs need a sunny, sheltered position.

D. collina is also evergreen with purple, scented flowers in the second half of spring. It is about 45 cm (18 in) high and quite hardy. The dwarfer daphnes are described in the chapter on rock plants (see Chapter 9).

D. × burkwoodii, *D. odora* and *D. collina* can be increased by layering or by summer cuttings, *D. mezereum* by seeds sown in a frame or out of doors as soon as ripe. No pruning is necessary for any of these.

Davidia (Dove Tree, Pocket Handkerchief Tree). *Davidia involucrata* is a large deciduous tree notable for the big white bracts which accompany the rather inconspicuous flower clusters at the end of spring. It is easily grown in reasonably good soil but is slow in coming into flower. No pruning is required. It can be increased by seed or by summer cuttings.

Deutzia. These are deciduous shrubs, mostly of vigorous growth, which produce small but abundant white or rose-coloured flowers mainly in early summer. The best known and in many ways the most beautiful is *Deutzia scabra*, which grows 2·1-3 m (7-10 ft) high, spreading the same distance; it is erect in habit and has graceful clusters of white, pink-tinged flowers just after mid-summer. There are several fine double-flowered forms or hybrids which are even more attractive than the type, two of the best being Pride of Rochester, in which the flowers are almost purple, and Candissima, pure white. *D. × elegantissima* is looser and more graceful in habit and has lilac-pink flowers in late spring/early summer. There are also numerous hybrids with flowers of various colours, such as Magician, pink single and white; Mont Rose, rose pink; Perle Rose, pink; Contraste, lilac and purple; and Magnifica, double white.

All these shrubs thrive planted in warm, sunny places and ordinary soils and require little pruning though old branches can be cut out in mid-spring. It is generally sufficient to do this every second or third year. Propagation is by summer or autumn cuttings, layering, or species by seeds, but garden varieties and hybrids do not come true from seed.

Elaeagnus. There are both deciduous and evergreen shrubs in this family but the latter are the more important from the gardener's standpoint. Easily the best are the variegated varieties of *Elaeagnus pungens* of which there are several. All make dense bushes 3 m (10 ft) or more high and of equal spread with shining, bright green leaves each with a central band or margin of yellow. Two of the finest are *E. p.* Maculata with an irregular blotch of yellow on the centre of each leaf and *E. p.* Dicksonii with a broad band of yellow in each leaf. *E. × ebbingei* has leaves silvery beneath and makes an excellent windbreak. A fine variety named Gilt Edge has a yellow margin to each leaf. All grow well in ordinary soils and sunny places and are perfectly hardy. *E. commutata*, also known as *E. argentea*, is an attractive deciduous species. The flowers are small, silvery, and not very showy but have an extremely pleasant fragrance while the silvery leaves are very handsome. It spreads by underground stems.

No pruning is required for any of these. Propagation of *E. pungens* is by cuttings of firm, young growths in summer or early autumn, and of *E. argentea* by rooted suckers detached in autumn.

Embothrium (Chilean Fire Bush). These are very handsome evergreen or semi-ever-green shrubs or small trees which would be planted far more widely if they were a little hardier. As it is, they are seldom seen outside mild climate gardens where they do well in sunny, sheltered positions. *Embothrium coccineum* will reach 7·5 m (25 ft) in height and has handsome, glossy evergreen leaves and clusters of narrowly tubular, scarlet flowers pro-duced with great freedom in late spring. A variety named *E. c. lanceolatum* has narrower, semi-evergreen leaves, is more erect and tree-like in habit and carries its scarlet flowers all along the branches. It is also considerably hardier. Plant them in good, well-drained lime-free soil and leave them alone, as neither needs pruning except to remove dead or dam-aged growths in spring. Both can be increased by cuttings in summer in a propagating frame or under mist with bottom heat.

Enkianthus. These are shrubs belonging to the heather family and, like their relatives, need lime-free, preferably peaty soils. They also prefer moist soils, particularly in sum-mer. The best kind is *Enkianthus campanulatus*, a deciduous shrub as a rule about 1·8 m (6 ft) high and in spread, though it can become tree-like. The flowers are small, bell shaped, cream with a flush of orange or bronzy red and appear in mid-spring. The foliage takes on rich autumn tints. This refined shrub should be planted in a sheltered position, such as thin woodland, as it is liable to be damaged by late spring frosts. No pruning is needed. Increase is by seed sown in sandy peat in a frame in early spring.

Erica (Heather, Heath). The value of heathers in gardens is greatly enhanced by the fact that hardy species are available to flower almost throughout the year. All heathers are evergreen and all have small, bell-shaped flowers. In other respects they vary greatly, some being dwarf, spreading shrubs less than 30 cm (1 ft) high, while others are erect and up to 3 m (10 ft) in height under favourable conditions. Almost all dislike lime and suc-ceed best in light peaty soils, but *Erica carnea*, a dwarf species with pink or white flowers from mid-winter to mid-spring, will succeed in almost any well-drained soil, even those containing some lime. There are numerous varieties of this heather, some with much deeper coloured flowers than this type.

Other good species are *E. cinerea*, about 30 cm (1 ft) high, and producing its purple flowers from mid-summer to early autumn (there is a white and an almost scarlet form); *E. × darleyensis*, a hybrid from *E. carnea*, which is similar in character and will also toler-ate lime but is nearly 60 cm (2 ft) high; *E. mediterranea* (now known as E. *erigena*), the other parent of *darleyensis*, yet another lime tolerator, a handsome shrub 1·9 m (6½ ft) high with rosy red or white flowers all spring; *E. tetralix*, about 30 cm (1 ft) high, flowering from early summer to mid-autumn and either heather pink or white; *E. ciliaris*, the Dorset heath, pink flowered and sprawling in habit; *E. vagans*, the Cornish heath, which blooms from mid-summer to mid-autumn and has pale purple or white flowers; and *E. arborea*, the tree heath, 3 m (10 ft) or more high with fragrant white flowers in spring. There are numerous garden varieties of almost all these heathers, differing chiefly in the colour of their flowers which are often much brighter or richer than those of the wild species but some have yellow, coppery or grey leaves.

Heathers can be grown mixed with other shrubs or plants in the shrubbery or rock garden, but are probably seen to best advantage if kept in beds by themselves or planted to form a heather garden with just a few other shrubs, dwarf conifers and perhaps one or two birches for contrast. Rich soil is a distinct drawback. To keep plants neat and compact they should be trimmed in mid-spring, or immediately the flowers fade if they are still in bloom, but only the previous year's growth should be cut. Heathers may die if pruned back into hard old wood.

Propagation is usually by short cuttings of young growth rooted in pure sand or sandy peat in the second half of summer in a propagating frame, but with the dwarfer kinds it is often possible to work sandy soil around and over the branches in spring which encourages roots so that later on the whole plant can be lifted and divided.

See also Calluna (p. 251) and Daboëcia (p. 263).

Escallonia. Some of these handsome mainly evergreen shrubs are a little too tender to be planted in colder regions, though most succeed elsewhere. Two of the most popular are *Escallonia rubra macrantha*, with deep green glossy leaves and clusters of bright rose flowers in the first half of summer, and *E.* Langleyensis, a hybrid from it which has rather smaller leaves, and lighter rosy carmine flowers at the same period. Both grow about 2·4 m (8 ft) high and wide, but *E.* Langleyensis has a more graceful, arching habit, *E. rubra macrantha* being more stiffly erect and, in consequence, popular for hedge making in mild districts for which purpose *E. rubra* with pink or red flowers, and the other parent of *E. langleyensis*, is also used. *E. rubra macrantha* is fully evergreen whereas *E.* Langleyensis often loses many of its leaves in a cold winter. Nevertheless the latter is really the hardier of the two and can be planted in the open in places where *E. rubra macrantha* would need the shelter of a warm, sunny wall. *E. virgata*, a deciduous species with white flowers is probably the hardiest of all. There are also a number of garden varieties and hybrids ranging in colour from white and pale pink to crimson.

All escallonias grow in ordinary soils and sunny positions. Regular pruning is unnecessary though hedges or trained plants can be pruned after flowering. Cuttings of firm young growth root readily in a propagating frame in summer.

Eucalyptus (Gum Tree). Very fast-growing evergreen trees, some of which also have attractive bark. Most are rather too tender to be planted out of doors except in the mildest parts of the country but *Eucalyptus gunnii* is reasonably hardy and in favourable places will make a tree 15-24 m (50-80 ft) high. The leaves on young trees are rounded and blue-grey in contrast to those on older trees which are lance shaped and grey-green. *E. niphophila*, the snow gum, with peeling grey and cream bark, is also fairly hardy. Others that may be tried are *E. coccifera*, a small tree eventually reaching about 9 m (30 ft) high with smooth, white bark and blue-grey leaves; *E. dalrympleana*, with blue-grey leaves and peeling white and pinkish-buff bark; *E. urnigera*, one of the smaller species and *E. viminalis*, one of the few kinds that enjoy damp soil. All can be raised from seed and thrive in open, sunny places. All transplant badly and resent root breakage at any stage. A good way to start is to purchase seedlings in late spring/early summer in containers and plant straight away from these where the trees are to grow, even though the seedlings may be only a few centimetres in height. Kept well watered at first they can make nearly 1 m (3½ ft) of growth by the autumn. It is important to stake securely for the first four or five years and to ensure that neither stakes nor ties cause damage to the bark.

Eucryphia. The best eucryphia for the garden is *Eucryphia × nymansensis*, a very beautiful evergreen tall shrub or small tree. The foliage is deep green and shining and the flowers, which are pure white and rather like dog roses, are produced with great freedom in the second half of summer. It thrives in cool, leafy or peaty soils though good specimens are to be seen in quite ordinary, lime-free soils. Unfortunately it transplants badly so a start should be made with very small specimens, or, better still, it should be purchased in pots and planted from these with a minimum amount of root disturbance. The first half of spring is the best time for planting. It is a hybrid between two fine species, *E. glutinosa*, which is deciduous and hardy and *E. cordifolia*, which is evergreen and rather tender and it combines the best qualities of both, including reasonable hardiness, though it should be given a fairly sheltered position. All can be increased by summer cuttings or layers, and the species also by seed.

Euonymus (Spindle Tree). This genus has provided one of the best evergreen shrubs for hedge making near the sea, *Euonymus japonica*, a densely branched shrub or small tree which will sometimes grow 6 m (20 ft) or more high. It is more often seen at half that height and can be kept still smaller by regular clipping. The foliage is dark green, leathery and handsome and there are several forms variegated to a greater or lesser degree with white or yellow. All thrive in ordinary or poor soil and will put up with a considerable amount of salt spray. For hedge making young plants should be spaced 45 cm (18 in) apart.

Very distinct from this is *E. fortunei*, a creeping, evergreen shrub which can be used as ground cover or may be planted against a wall to grow vertically up it like a climber. There are several varieties of this shrub and the creeping or climbing variety just described is known as *E. f. radicans*. More bushy, erect forms are sold as Carrierei. There are also silver and yellow variegated forms such as Silver Queen, Emerald Gaiety and Emerald 'n' Gold. All will grow in any ordinary soil and sunny or shady position.

For further contrast there are several deciduous species of which the two best are *E. europaeus* and *E. latifolius*, both grown mainly for their rosy-red fruits and orange seeds, freely produced in the autumn. The first named is the spindle tree found in hedgerows. Both are large bushes or small trees 3-4·5 m (10-15 ft) high and wide with a loosely branching habit and leaves which usually take on fine autumn tints before falling. *E. alatus*, a deciduous bush 1·8-2·4 m (6-8 ft) high and with curious winged stems is grown primarily for its scarlet and crimson autumn leaf colour.

The deciduous species require no regular pruning; the evergreens can be pruned hard in mid-spring if necessary and trimmed at any time from then until mid-autumn.

Propagation of the deciduous kinds is generally by seeds sown out of doors or in a frame in early spring; of the evergreen kinds take cuttings of firm shoots rooted in summer or early autumn, while creeping forms of *E. fortunei* can be divided in spring.

Exochorda. These are deciduous shrubs of which the most popular is *Exochorda racemosa*, a bushy plant 2·4 m (8 ft) or so high and rather wider, with numerous pure white flowers in short spikes along the arching branches in late spring. A bush in full flower is a very fine sight and the shrub deserves to be more widely planted. It is quite hardy, thrives in most soils except those that are very chalky and likes a sunny place. No pruning is needed though flowering branches can be shortened to side growths after the flowers fade. It can often be increased by suckers removed with roots in autumn, or cuttings of young growth will strike in summer in a propagating frame or under mist.

Fabiana (False Heath). The species usually grown, *Fabiana imbricata*, is often mistaken for a giant heather, though in fact it has no connection with the family, and is related to the potato. It is an evergreen shrub 2·2 m (7½ ft) high, 1·3 m (4½ ft) wide, erect in habit with tiny, pointed leaves and masses of small, tubular, white flowers in early summer. Its one fault is that it is a little tender and must be given a sheltered position. A variety named *F. i. violacea* has pale mauve flowers and another, *F. i.* Prostrata, is short but wide spreading with mauve flowers. Both like well-drained soils and sunny, sheltered places, need no pruning and can be increased by cuttings of firm young growth in summer.

Fagus (Beech). Common beech makes an excellent hedge or screen (see p. 243). Grown naturally it makes a handsome tree of the largest size but deprives the soil of so much food and moisture that little can be grown beneath it. There are numerous varieties including copper and purple-leaved forms, weeping forms both green and purple leaved, the fern-leaved beech with deeply cut leaves and the Dawyck beech, which is narrowly erect like a Lombardy poplar and yellow and purple-leaved varieties of this named Dawyck Gold and Dawyck Purple. These are the only kinds suitable for planting as specimen trees in small or medium-sized gardens as the others are too big to be accommodated.

Common beech can be raised from seed, and seed of copper and purple-leaved varieties will give a proportion of seedlings with coloured leaves; selected varieties will not come true to type from seed and are increased by grafting on to seedlings of the common kind.

Fallopia. One of the most vigorous and quick-growing climbers is *Fallopia baldschuanica* (previously listed as a polygonum), a grand subject for covering unsightly outhouses, tree stumps and fences. It will soon make vines 6 m (20 ft) or more in length, spreading in all directions or climbing upwards, according to their position. The plant makes a mass of twining shoots and smothers itself in late summer beneath a cloud of small white or pink-tinged blossoms. If necessary it can be cut back hard in late winter or it may be allowed to grow without pruning if space permits. It is propagated by fairly long cuttings of firm growth taken with a heel of older wood in late summer or early autumn and rooted in a propagating frame, or under mist, or by heel cuttings of mature growth in late winter.

× **Fatshedera**. *Fatshedera lizei* is a hybrid between the erect-growing Irish form of the common ivy and *Fatsia japonica*. It has sprawling stems a good deal thicker than those of ivy and no aerial roots with which to cling to anything, but it can be tied to any available support. Its leaves are more like those of fatsia than of ivy and it is a handsome, fully hardy evergreen foliage plant which will grow in any reasonably fertile soil in sun or shade. If it gets too big it can be pruned any time from late spring to late summer. It can be increased by summer cuttings in a propagator or by layering from spring until early autumn.

Fatsia. *Fatsia japonica* is sometimes mistaken for a fig with its big, leathery, deeply divided leaves, often over 30 cm (1 ft) across, but unlike those of the fig, they are evergreen. The spherical clusters of creamy white flowers are produced in stiffly branched sprays in late summer and are followed by small black fruits. This plant is frequently cultivated in pots in cool greenhouses but it is hardy enough to be grown in the open in most parts in ordinary soil in a sheltered, sunny or semi-shady position. Increase by cuttings of young growth in the propagating frame with bottom heat in spring or summer. Pruning is unnecessary.

Forsythia. There is no better yellow-flowered shrub than *Forsythia* × *intermedia*. It is deciduous and makes a big, broad bush with many long whippy shoots and the bright golden-yellow flowers are borne along the length of the year-old branches in the first half of spring. There are numerous varieties, of which Lynwood and Spectabilis are particularly good. Another fine kind is *F. suspensa*. This has paler yellow flowers and a looser, more arching habit. Again there are several distinctive forms, such as *F. s. atrocaulis* with young stems deep purple, *F. s. fortunei*, the most erect, and *F. s. sieboldii*, the most slender stemmed which makes it suitable for training as a climber against walls or fences. All forsythias will grow in ordinary soil in sun or partial shade. They can be pruned in mid- to late spring by cutting out stems that have just flowered and can be increased readily by cuttings in summer or autumn.

Fraxinus (Ash). All ashes are deciduous and most are trees of large size, though a few are big bushes. The two most important from the garden standpoint are the common ash, *Fraxinus excelsior*, which has a number of good varieties including a beautiful weeping form, and the flowering ash or manna ash, *F. ornus*. Both will grow in any ordinary soil and open position. The common ash may eventually attain a height of 30 m (100 ft) with a branch spread of 16·5 m (55 ft), while the flowering ash is considerably smaller, seldom over 15 m (50 ft) in height, rounded in habit and with a spread of 7·5-9 m (25-30 ft). It is a most useful ornamental tree with plumes of greenish-white, scented flowers produced freely in late spring. The common ash is too big and too quick growing for ordinary gardens, but the weeping form of it is often worth planting and will make an excellent natural arbour as its branches come right down to ground level. No pruning is needed for any of these. Propagation is by seeds or by grafting selected forms on to seedlings of the common form.

Fremontodendron. Semi-evergreen shrubs with leathery, aromatic leaves and fine yellow flowers produced from spring to early autumn. Two kinds are grown, *Fremontodendron californicum* and *F. mexicanum*, both very similar, rather tender and in cold countries usually trained against sunny walls where they will reach a height of 3 m (10 ft) or more. There is also a fine hybrid between the two named Californian Glory. All prefer well-drained soil. Damaged stems can be cut out in mid-spring and the species can be increased from seed or by summer cuttings, which is the only means of propagating the hybrid.

Fuchsia. Most fuchsias are too tender to be grown outside except in the mildest regions, but a few, notably *Fuchsia magellanica* Riccartoni with medium-sized scarlet and purple flowers and *F. magellanica gracilis*, which is more arching and spreading in habit, can be grown in the open in many districts and, even when severely cut by winter or spring frost, will usually throw up new shoots from the base to make a good display in late summer. There are good variegated varieties of *F. m. gracilis*, one named Variegata with cream-edged leaves, the other Versicolor, greyish, cream and pink. This is also true of some of the hybrid garden varieties with flowers of superior size and varied colouring such as Margaret, scarlet and purple; Brilliant and Brutus, both cerise and violet-purple; Chillerton Beauty, pale pink and purple; Mrs Popple, light crimson and blue-violet; Rufus, bright red; Tom Thumb, a small plant with little rose and violet-purple flowers; Lady Thumb, similar but rose and white; and Madame Cornelissen, carmine and white.

Give these hardy fuchsias as sunny and sheltered a position as possible in fairly rich but well-drained soil. Cover the plants in winter with bracken or dried straw and prune away all frost-damaged growth in mid-spring. Increase by cuttings of young growth rooted in a propagating frame in a greenhouse in spring or summer.

For the greenhouse kinds, see p. 472.

Garrya. The most important species is *Garrya elliptica*, a rounded, evergreen shrub, 2·4-3 m (8-10 ft) high and in spread, and remarkable for its long, grey-green catkins produced in mid-winter. There are two sexes, one bearing male and the other female catkins; the former is the more ornamental on account of the yellow stamens and longer, more slender catkins. It is reasonably hardy but should be given a fairly sheltered and sunny position or can be trained against a sunny wall. It will grow in any ordinary soil but transplants badly so pot or container-grown plants should be purchased. No pruning is needed but if plants get too large stems can be shortened in late spring. Propagation is by cuttings of firm young shoots taken in summer and rooted in a propagating frame or under mist.

Gaultheria. These are evergreen shrubs for peaty, lime-free soils. The two most useful are very distinct in appearance. One, *Gaultheria procumbens*, is completely prostrate with small, rounded leaves and little pinkish-white flowers in summer soon followed by showy red berries. It is a good shrub for the rock garden or for clothing banks, especially in moist, partially shaded places. The other, *G. shallon*, is a dense, branching shrub 1·3 m (4½ ft) in height and rather wider with leathery leaves and short clusters of pinkish-white flowers in late spring/early summer. It will grow in dense shade and enjoys a moist soil, particularly in summer. It is often planted as game cover. Neither requires any pruning, and both can be increased by seeds sown in sandy peat in a frame in spring, or by digging out rooted pieces in spring or early autumn. The plant once listed as *Pernettya mucronata* is now *Gaultheria* mucronata. It is a most attractive evergreen belonging to the heather family. Small white flowers in late spring are followed by very showy marble-like berries in a variety of colours including pink, puce, crimson, purple and white. Height varies from 90 cm-1·5 cm (3-5 ft) and the shrub spreads over quite a large area by underground shoots. This habit makes it easy to propagate by division in late spring, which is the best planting time. It enjoys peat but will grow in a wide range of lime-free soils and will succeed in sun or partial shade. It is best to plant several bushes together as this ensures proper pollination and fruiting. Pruning is not necessary but bushes can be clipped in summer and this makes it possible to use as hedge plants, as befits their neat foliage.

Genista (Broom). The popular garden brooms are divided by botanists into three distinct families, genista, cytisus and spartium. Some of the showiest of the genistas are greenhouse plants (see Chapter 19) but there are several useful hardy species, such as *Genista hispanica*, popularly known as the Spanish gorse, a compact, spiny bush 45 cm (1½ ft) high and 76 cm (2½ ft) broad with very numerous, golden-yellow flowers in late spring/early summer, and *G. tinctoria*, a wild British shrub of semi-prostrate habit and with the typical yellow broom flowers in mid-summer. This latter has several varieties of which the double-flowered one is the most useful for garden planting. *G. aethnensis*, the Etna broom, grows 3·6 m (12 ft) or more high, has thin hanging stems wreathed in yellow flowers in mid-summer. *G. cinerea* is 2·7 m (9 ft) high and has fragrant yellow flowers mainly in the first half of summer, and *G. virgata* is similar. All revel in warmth and sunshine and will usually grow in the poorest of soils. They require no special treatment and most can be raised from seed sown in spring either out of doors or in a frame, but the double-flowered form of *G. tinctoria* must be increased by cuttings in summer.

Ginkgo (Maidenhair Tree). *Ginkgo biloba* is one of the most distinctive of trees. It grows to a great height – over 30 m (100 ft) in time – is not very spreading and has leaves which are very much the shape of the leaflets of a maidenhair fern but 5 cm (2 in) across. They turn pale yellow before they fall in autumn. Though the tree is not that common in cool climates it is not difficult to grow if planted in good soil and given a sheltered, sunny position. When young it may be cut back by spring frosts but as it matures it becomes perfectly hardy. No pruning should be attempted at any time. Seed, which can be sown in a cool greenhouse in spring, provides the method of propagation but good forms, including the male (there are two sexes) which is preferable, are increased by summer or early autumn cuttings.

Gleditsia (Honey Locust). *Gleditsia triacanthos* is a deciduous tree with finely divided leaves which are very elegant. There are several varieties, one named Elegantissima which is particularly ferny and also slow growing, and Sunburst, with yellow leaves. All enjoy well-drained soils and sunny places. The species can be increased by seed but garden varieties by grafting.

Griselinia. An evergreen shrub with stout, oval, light green leaves, *Griselinia littoralis* grows well by the sea and is often used as a windbreak or hedge in maritime localities. In very cold inland gardens it may be damaged by frost but it is a good deal hardier than is often supposed. It will reach a height of 6 m (20 ft) but is more commonly seen as a bush 2·1 m (7 ft) tall. There are golden and cream variegated varieties. All will grow in any reasonably good soil and can be increased by cuttings in summer or early autumn.

Halesia (Snowdrop Tree, Silver Bell Tree). Very attractive deciduous trees with hanging clusters of bell-shaped white flowers in late spring. They like reasonably good lime-free soil and need no regular pruning. They can be increased by seed which needs to be exposed in moist sand or peat for a winter before sowing, or for three months in a refrigerator. Good kinds are *Halesia tetraptera* growing to 9 m (30 ft) and *H. monticola* which is taller and is said to reach 30 m (100 ft) in its native habitat, the south-eastern part of the United States. In dissimilar climates it is unlikely to reach even half that height.

Halimium. Evergreen shrubs very closely allied to cistus and requiring identical treatment. (See p. 257). Three of the best kinds are *Halimium commutatum*, a neat bush 30–45 cm (1–1½ ft) high with yellow flowers; *H. lasianthum*, 76 cm (2½ ft), yellow with a purple blotch and *H. ocymoides*, similar to the last but with an even darker blotch. All flower in early summer.

Hamamelis (Witch Hazel). These are large shrubs or small trees, all deciduous and flowering in mid-winter. The flowers themselves are curious rather than showy, rather ragged little clusters of narrow, strap-shaped, yellow petals all along the length of the bare twigs. They make up in numbers what they lack in individual brilliance and make a very pleasant picture on a dull winter's day. The best species is *Hamamelis mollis*, in which the flowers are bright yellow and sweetly scented. It has a fine variety named Pallida with larger lemon-yellow flowers. In some other species the flowers are rather dull or pale red or yellow. All like good, loamy soil and will grow in any sunny or semi-shady position. No regular pruning is necessary. Nurserymen usually increase by grafting in spring on seedlings of *H. virginiana*, but rooted suckers can sometimes be detached in autumn from old specimens that are growing on their own roots (not grafted) and young branches can also be layered in spring or summer.

Hawthorn. See **Crataegus** (p. 261).

Hazel. See **Corylus** (p. 260).

Heather. See **Calluna** (p. 251) and **Erica** (p. 265).

Hebe. These evergreen shrubs were formerly known as veronica and may still be found under that name in some nurseries and gardens. It is a pity that many of them are on the borderline of hardiness and are therefore only reliable for outdoor planting in the milder regions. This is certainly true of most of the handsome forms or hybrids of *Hebe speciosa* which make rounded evergreen bushes 1·3 m (4½ ft) high and of equal spread with showy spikes of blue, purple or crimson flowers in late summer. Autumn Glory, which is smaller and has deep purplish-blue flowers, is hardier and will thrive in many inland gardens. *H. × franciscana* is a hybrid often listed as *H. elliptica*, which is one of its parents, the other being *H. speciosa*. It is also distinctly tender but grows well by the sea. Flowers vary from pale blue to deep purple and there is a variety named *H. × f.* Variegata with cream-edged leaves.

One of the loveliest of all, *H. hulkeana*, needs the protection of a sunny wall in most places. It grows 1 m (3½ ft) high, has a loose, almost herbaceous habit, and produces graceful sprays of bluish-lilac flowers in early summer. A hybrid from this named Fair-fieldensis has slightly larger flowers.

H. salicifolia, a bushy species up to 3 m (10 ft) high with narrow, light green leaves and narrow spikes of white flowers in mid-summer, is hardier but may be damaged in cold places. The hardiest species is *H. brachysiphon* which has neat, rounded leaves, makes a dense bush to 1·5 m (5 ft) high and has rather small but very numerous spikes of whitish flowers in mid-summer.

H. × andersonii Variegata, 76 cm (2½ ft) tall, is a handsome hybrid with lavender flowers and cream-margined leaves like a large *H. × franciscana* Variegata. *H. ochracea* has tiny leaves like those of a cypress, golden bronze in colour. It is often listed as *H. armstrongii*, similar in habit but yellower in leaf colour. Other dwarf, small-leaved varieties are *H. cupressoides* and *H. pimeloides* which are fairly hardy, as are *H. pinguifolia* Pagei and *H. albicans* with grey leaves and white flowers.

There are also a number of garden varieties in a range of colours, such as Midsummer Beauty, Carl Teschner and Great Orme, from white, lavender and pale pink to intense purple and crimson. Many of these have a very extended flowering season in summer and autumn.

Though hebes do not require any pruning they can be cut back moderately in spring, if they grow too large. They are not fussy about soil, prefer sunny places and can be increased by cuttings in summer or early autumn. Many are also readily increased from seed but seedlings of garden varieties are likely to vary considerably.

Hedera (Ivy). The botanical name of the common ivy is *Hedera helix* and it has produced so many varieties that whole books have been written about it. These varieties differ in size and shape of leaf and also in leaf colour, some being plain green and others variously variegated with silver or gold.

Among the most useful are Buttercup, leaves wholly pale yellow; Goldheart, dark green with central yellow blotch; Marginata Elegantissima, also known as Tricolor, grey-green edged with cream and flushed pink; Glacier, similar to the last, but no pink; Conglomerata erecta, dwarf, slow growing and erect with small crowded leaves; Cristata, green leaves crimped around the edges; Green Ripple, green leaves with deep jagged lobes; Sagittifolia, leaf lobes very narrow; and Hibernica, the Irish ivy, leaves large and dark green. When ivies start to flower they become bushy and cease to climb. Cuttings taken from this growth retain this shrubby habit and that obtained from the common ivy is known as *H.* Arborescens. Such ivies make handsome evergreen shrubs of rounded shape with a height and diameter of 1·9 m (6½ ft).

H. colchica, the Persian ivy, has very large leaves which are heart-shaped rather than lobed and there is a handsome heavily cream variegated variety of this named Dentata Variegata.

H. canariensis is less hardy than the others but can be grown outdoors in mild places. *H. azorica* Variegata has bright green leaves and *H.* Variegata has greyish green and cream leaves.

With the exception of the arborescent and flowering forms all are self-clinging by means of aerial roots. They will grow in sun or shade and, contrary to popular belief, do not harm brickwork or stonework though they can block gutters, get under and dislodge tiles and do similar damage. Poor brick or plaster work may flake or fall off when ivy is pulled off it but in general ivy keeps masonry dry and protects it from the weather. Ivy can be used as a climber or as ground cover, also to conceal old tree stumps.

It often pays to clip ivy closely with shears in mid-spring and then brush out dirt and dead leaves. Apart from this no attention is required once planted. Propagation is by cuttings of firm growth rooted in summer or early autumn.

Hibiscus. *Hibiscus syriacus* is a deciduous, freely branched shrub, 2·4–3 m (8–10 ft) high, though rather slow growing, and one of the best of the late-flowering shrubs. In the type the flowers are single like those of the mallow in shape, but there are also double and semi-double varieties, all in a range of colours including white, blue, purple and red. Typical varieties are Blue Bird, single violet-blue; Duc de Brabant, double purple; Hamabo, single white and crimson; Lady Stanley, semi-double, white, pink and crimson; Violet Claire Double, semi-double, purple; and Woodbridge, single purplish red and maroon. All are at their best in early autumn and continue into mid-season. They should be planted in a sunny, sheltered position in rather rich, well-drained soil. No regular pruning is required, but overgrown plants can be reduced in mid-spring. Propagation in nurseries is often by grafting, but amateurs should try layering in autumn.

Hippophaë (Sea Buckthorn). The true sea buckthorn *Hippophaë rhamnoides*, is a very beautiful British bush with narrow, silvery, deciduous leaves and masses of small, vivid orange berries in late summer and early autumn. It seldom exceeds a height of 4·5 m (15 ft) and is usually densely branched. As its popular name suggests, it likes coastal districts and will put up with the worst sea gales, but it will also thrive in inland gardens providing it is given reasonably good soil and first-class drainage. There are two separate sexes, some bushes bearing male and the others female flowers. Only the females will produce berries and then only provided they have been pollinated by a male, so for every five or six female bushes one male should be planted not too far away, since pollination is by wind. Pruning is unnecessary. Seeds can be used for propagation but there can then be no certainty about sex, whereas if plants are increased by layers they will be of the same sex as their parents.

Hoheria. Fast-growing but not, as a rule, very long-lived deciduous trees and shrubs all with white flowers freely produced for a few weeks in summer. The species most commonly planted is *Hoheria lyallii*, usually from 3·6–4·5 m (12–15 ft) high but it can exceed this, with attractive leaves covered in grey down. It is not completely hardy but will withstand a fair amount of frost particularly if growing in a warm, sunny place where the rather soft stems get well ripened in late summer. It is easily raised from seed which may sow itself around the trees or can be germinated in a frame or greenhouse in spring. Damaged growth should be cut out each spring.

Honeysuckle. See **Lonicera** (p. 281).

Holly. See **Ilex** (p. 276).

Hornbeam. See **Carpinus** (p. 252).

Horse Chestnut. See **Aesculus** (p. 246).

Hydrangea. For really cold gardens there are only two hydrangeas that are fully reliable for outdoor planting, *Hydrangea paniculata* in its various varieties and *H. arborescens* Grandiflora. The first makes many strong growths, terminated in late summer by cone-shaped clusters of creamy-white flowers. It is a really magnificent shrub, seen at its best when planted in rich soil and hard pruned in early spring. Grandiflora is notable for the size of its flower clusters and *H. paniculata* for its earliness. Grandiflora also has more globular heads of flowers, thinner stems and lighter green foliage; it can be hard pruned in early spring.

The hydrangeas so familiar in greenhouses are varieties of *H. macrophylla* and closely related species and many are unreliable out of doors except in mild climate gardens. It is not that they are extensively damaged by frost but the terminal buds are so injured that few or no flowers are produced unless the position is very sheltered. However, in the less cold places they do make magnificent shrubs up to 3·6 m (12 ft) high and in spread, although they are usually less than half this size, covered with large, dome-shaped heads of flowers in mid-summer which persist throughout the autumn and winter, changing colour as they fade and eventually becoming brown but refusing to fall. Some varieties flower even when all terminal buds have been destroyed and these are to be preferred for outdoor planting. Blue flowers are produced only in acid soils and then only from certain varieties of which Générale Vicomtesse de Vibraye is one of the best. In alkaline soils the coloured varieties such as Hamburg, Parsifal, Sir Joseph Banks and Westfalen produce pink, rose or reddish-purple flowers but white-flowered varieties such as Madame E. Moullière are unchanged. Mariesii, Bluewave, Whitewave and Veitchii are very distinct forms in which only the outer flowers in each cluster are big and showy, the rest being small and closely clustered. This type is sometimes called 'Lacecap' in contrast to the globular headed, or Hortensia, type. No pruning is required by any forms of *H. macrophylla* except for the removal of dead growth and faded flower trusses each spring, but overgrown bushes can be cut back in early spring with the loss of one year's flowers.

There are also a number of attractive species such as *H. sargentiana*, a sparse-looking bush 1·8 m (6 ft) high with hairy stems and enormous heads of dull pink flowers in mid-summer, and *H. aspera villosa*, a large, spreading shrub with softly downy leaves and flat heads of lilac-blue flowers. *H. anomala petiolaris* is a self-clinging climber for a sheltered wall with flat clusters of white flowers in early summer. All these have the Lacecap type of flower and prefer partially shady situations.

All hydrangeas can be increased by cuttings of firm young growth in spring or summer.

Hypericum. Some of the best shrubs for the beginner are in this genus, such as the easily grown *Hypericum forrestii*, often called *H. patulum*, a twiggy bush 1·2 m (4 ft) high and as much in diameter, with big, yellow, saucer-shaped flowers in the second half of summer. Hidcote is probably a hybrid with larger flowers produced until mid-autumn and in milder regions it is semi-evergreen. *H.* × *moserianum*, also a hybrid, is only about 45 cm (18 in) high, with a variety named Tricolor which has leaves variegated with white and pink, and *H. calycinum*, the Rose of Sharon, is sprawling and spreads indefinitely by underground stems. It is fully evergreen and its flowers are 9 cm (3½ in) across, golden yellow, with a central tuft of golden stamens. It is one of the best carpeting shrubs for banks and beneath trees and will also grow in hot, dry places and in very chalky soils. Another distinctive kind is *H. inodorum* Elstead, a 90 cm (3 ft) shrub with small yellow flowers followed by shining reddish bronze seed capsules.

All hypericums are easily grown in any reasonably good soil and sunny or partially shady place. None requires pruning except for the removal of dead growth in spring and all can be increased by summer cuttings; *H. calycinum* can also be divided in mid-spring.

Ilex (Holly). There is no better ornamental evergreen shrub or tree than the holly, *Ilex aquifolium*. Its principal drawbacks are that it grows rather slowly and is a little difficult to propagate. Seed germinates readily enough either in a frame or out of doors in spring, but seedlings cannot be guaranteed to reproduce the particular features of their parents such as size and colour of leaf or freedom of fruiting. Moreover hollies usually produce male and female flowers on separate plants. It is the females which produce the berries but only after fertilization with pollen from males, so at least one male bush should be planted for every five or six females and preferably within 13·5 m (45 ft) of them. Seedlings may be of either sex and can only be identified when they start to flower.

The common holly and also a hybrid between it and the Madeira or Azorean holly, *I. perado*, which is named *I. × altaclarensis* and typically has extra large leaves, have between them produced a considerable number of garden varieties. Some such as Golden King, Golden Queen and Madame Briot have yellow variegated leaves; others, such as Argentea Marginata, Argentea Medio-picta (often called Silver Milkmaid) and Silver Queen have white variegated leaves. Oddly, with the exception of Madame Briot, those with male names are female plants and vice-versa, but both male and female forms of Argentea Marginata are available. Camelliifolia, a female, has very large leaves with hardly any spines and Hodginsii, a male, also has large leaves and grows well in industrial areas. Bacciflava has yellow berries. There are also varieties with a weeping habit and one of these, Argentea Pendula, also known as Perry's weeping, is variegated with grey-green and cream. It is female.

An odd variety is Ferox, which has clusters of spines on the blade of the leaf as well as around the edge and so is known as the hedgehog holly. There are white and yellow variegated varieties of this.

All these hollies are completely hardy. They grow best in deep, rather rich, loamy soils and will thrive in sun or shade. Most make excellent hedge shrubs if planted about 60 cm (2 ft) apart and may then be pruned to shape in late spring or lightly cut at any time during the summer. When grown as specimens no pruning is necessary.

Propagation of selected forms is by grafting in spring on to seedlings of the common holly, or by cuttings of short side growths taken in summer and rooted in a propagating frame or under mist with bottom heat.

Indigofera. An attractive deciduous shrub flowering in late summer, *Indigofera heterantha gerardiana* is 1 m (3 ft) high with abundant small, rosy-purple flowers of the pea type. It likes warm, sunny positions and good but rather light soils. Propagation is by cuttings rooted in summer in a propagating frame with bottom heat, or by seeds sown in a warm greenhouse or frame in spring. Dead or frost-damaged growth should be cut out each spring.

Ivy. See **Hedera** (p. 273).

Jasminum (Jasmine). The two most popular jasmines are the summer-flowering climbing species, *Jasminum officinale* which has white, fragrant blooms all summer, and the winter-flowering *J. nudiflorum*, which opens its bright yellow flowers all winter. Both are deciduous and hardy. *J. officinale* likes a warm, sunny position, while *J. nudiflorum* will grow in either sun or shade. It is a loose, sprawling shrub, but is usually grown trained to a wire or trellis and is one of the best climbers for a fairly exposed wall or fence. Though regular pruning is not desirable, overgrown shoots can be cut back in spring. These jasmines are not fussy about soil and will thrive in town as well as in country gardens. Increase by layering in spring or autumn or by cuttings of firm shoots in summer.

Juglans (Walnut). The common walnut, *Juglans regia*, is sometimes planted for ornament and makes a very handsome specimen tree, slow in growth but eventually attaining a height of 15 m (50 ft) or more with a spread of 9-12 m (30-40 ft). Cultivation is as described in the fruit section, see Chapter 30. The black walnut, *J. nigra*, grows more rapidly and has more attractive leaves composed of up to twenty-three leaflets. It does not produce edible nuts. Cultivation is the same as for the common walnut.

Juniperus (Juniper). The junipers are evergreen, cone-bearing trees, some of which are of great ornamental merit. The most important as garden plants are *Juniperus communis*, normally a spreading shrub or small tree 3-4·5 m (10-15 ft) in height but with numerous forms, some of which are quite erect; *J. chinensis*, the Chinese juniper, a tree with many different forms: *J. horizontalis*, the creeping juniper, a completely prostrate shrub; *J. sabina*, popularly known as savin, which is seldom more than 2·4 m (8 ft) high with spreading branches; and *J. virginiana*, sometimes called the red or pencil cedar, which is a tree 12 m (40 ft) or more high with branches spreading 6-9 m (20-30 ft) and a conical outline. This is a very handsome specimen tree which thrives particularly well on chalky soils. It has numerous varieties, some of which, such as Skyrocket, are slow-growing and spire-shaped, while others such as Grey Owl are wide spreading. These and others are sometimes listed as varieties of *J. scopulorum*, a species much like *J. virginiana*. Of the numerous varieties of *J. communis* the most important are Compressa, which is so slow growing that after 10 or 12 years it may be no more than 30 m (1 ft) in height and a perfect, compact column of tiny, spiny leaves; Hibernia, known as the Irish juniper, has the same erect habit as the last but soon reaches a height of 3 m (10 ft) with a spread of perhaps 60 cm (2 ft). It makes a striking specimen and may be used most effectively to form an avenue. Varieties of *J. sabina* and of a natural hybrid from it named *J.* × *media* include Pfitzeriana which makes a low, spreading shuttlecock of growth and a flatter golden-variegated form named Old Gold. Tamariscifolia, with horizontal layers of branches making a wide bush only about 60 cm (2 ft) high is a variety of *J. sabina*.

All the junipers are easy to grow, thriving in most soils but preferring those with some lime or chalk. Pruning is not required but the erect forms should be circled with several bands of string in winter to prevent their branches being pulled out of shape by snow. Increase of the species is by seed which may be very slow in germination, unless kept in moist sand or peat for about four months at a temperature of 18-21°C/64-70°F and then for a further three months at 3-4°C/38-39°F. The garden varieties do not breed true from seed and must be increased by cuttings of firm shoots in late summer or autumn, under a cloche.

Kalmia. These evergreen shrubs belong to the heather family and like most of their tribe succeed best in rather acid soils and strongly object to lime. A deep, peaty soil with plenty of moisture in summer is ideal. The most striking species is *Kalmis latifolia*, sometimes known as the calico bush. It makes a rounded shrub 2·4-3 m (8-10 ft) high and rather more in spread, with leathery, dark green leaves and large clusters of pink, lantern-shaped flowers in early/mid-summer when it is very beautiful. No pruning should be attempted. Propagation is by seed in spring, cuttings in summer or layering at any time.

Kerria (Batchelor's Buttons). Usually seen in its double-flowered form, *Kerria japonica* is a loose, rather straggling, deciduous shrub which is generally grown as a climber and trained against a wall or fence. It is very handsome in such a position when covered in the second half of spring by its large, golden-yellow blooms. The single-flowered variety only grows 1·3 m (4½ ft) high and spreads freely by suckers. It has a good white-variegated variety named Variegata. All varieties will grow anywhere, even in quite dense shade, but young growth may be cut by frost if in a very exposed position. Kerria can be pruned when the blooms fade, the flowering growths being cut back to young, non-flowering side shoots. Propagation is by layering in autumn, by taking cuttings in summer or by digging up rooted suckers in autumn.

Kolkwitzia (Beauty Bush). *Kolkwitzia amabilis* is a very attractive deciduous shrub with pink, yellow-throated bell-shaped flowers freely produced in late spring/early summer. It reaches 1·8-2·4 m (6-8 ft) high and in spread and can be grown in exactly the same way as weigela, which it somewhat resembles. As with weigela, increase is by cuttings in summer or autumn.

Laburnum. These are among the most useful and beautiful ornamental trees for the garden. They succeed everywhere, grow rapidly and flower while quite young. A drawback is that they are not usually very long-lived trees and are sometimes liable to die suddenly without apparent cause. Also the seeds are poisonous and as they are usually produced in great numbers the laburnum is not a very good tree to have in a garden in which young children play. The common laburnum, *Laburnum anagyroides*, which flowers in mid-spring, is surpassed in beauty by the Scotch laburnum, *L. alpinum*, which has longer trails of golden-yellow flowers in early summer. *L.* × Watereri is a hybrid between these two species and *L.* × *m.* Vossii is a selected form of it with superior flower trails up to 60 cm (2 ft) long. All will eventually reach a height of 7·5-9 m (25-30 ft).

A curious relation is *Laburnocytisus adamii*, which produces flowers of three different colours and growth of two different types. It is what is known as a graft hybrid, and it contains the tissues of two different plants, the common laburnum and the purple-flowered broom. In general appearance it is a tree resembling an ordinary laburnum but with tufts of thin, broom-like growth here and there along the branches. Some of the flowers are in trails and yellow like those of the laburnum, others are in similar trails but yellow and purple while yet others are carried along the thin branches like those of broom and are purple.

No laburnum requires pruning, though misplaced branches can be removed in winter. Seed sown out of doors in spring provides the readiest method of increasing the species but garden varieties and *Laburnocytisus adamii* must be increased by grafting in spring on laburnum seedlings.

Larch. See **Larix** below.

Larix (Larch). The common species is *Larix decidua*, a familiar cone-bearing tree of the largest size, specimens being known which are well over 30 m (100 ft) in height and with an almost equal branch spread. Because of its size and quick growth it is unsuitable for small gardens. Unlike most cone-bearing trees it is deciduous and in spring the new foliage, which is very light green, is particularly beautiful. Equally attractive and also deciduous is the Japanese larch, *L. kaempferi*, which is similar in general appearance but has stouter branches. *L. × eurolepis* is a hybrid between the two and very fast growing. All these larches thrive in a great variety of soils and require no special treatment. Pruning is undesirable. Propagation is almost invariably by seeds, which will germinate readily out of doors in spring if sown in peaty soil.

Laurus (Sweet Bay, Laurel). *Laurus nobilis* is the true laurel of classical times but not what is commonly meant by present-day gardeners, who use the term loosely for the cherry laurel, *Prunus laurocerasus* and the Portugal laurel, *P. lusitanica*. *L. nobilis* is usually called sweet bay, or simply bay, and is most familiar as a shrub for clipping into topiary specimens to be grown in tubs or large pots. It has fragrant foliage, sometimes used for flavouring soups, milk puddings and sauces, is an evergreen, stands clipping well and will put up with the grime of city pollution. It would be even more useful were it a little hardier. In exposed places it may be quite severely damaged during cold winters and if grown in pots or tubs it is wise to move it to a sheltered spot in late autumn. In other respects it is easy to grow in any good loamy soil and sunny or partially shady position. Grown naturally, it will make a broadly conical tree up to 12 m (40 ft) high. It can be pruned severely in late spring and clipped at any time from then until early autumn. Propagation is by cuttings of firm growth in summer or early autumn.

Lavandula (Lavender). The garden lavenders are almost all forms of *Lavandula angustifolia*, also called *L. spica* and *L. officinalis*. This is an evergreen shrub of rounded habit about 60 cm (2 ft) high and usually slightly more in diameter. The fragrant flowers in the second half of summer are too well known to need description. The garden varieties differ chiefly in size and depth of colour, Munstead Dwarf and Hidcote being comparatively dwarf, with deep purple flowers; Twickel Purple, medium height and rich purple; and Grappenhall, 90 cm (3 ft) and normal in colour. *L. stoechas*, the French lavender, is 60 cm (2 ft) high and has purple flowers in dense heads in the second half of spring; and *L. dentata* has saw-edged leaves and spikes of lavender flowers in summer and early autumn but is rather tender.

   All like well-drained, rather light soils and warm, sunny positions. If desired the common lavender and its varieties can be grown as small hedges, clipped in mid-spring to keep them trim. If flowers are required for drying they should be cut just before they are fully open, tied in small bundles and suspended head downwards in a cool, airy place not in direct sunshine. Propagation is by cuttings of non-flowering shoots taken in summer and rooted in a frame, or by firmer cuttings taken in the first half of autumn and inserted out of doors in a sheltered place.

Lavatera. Some of the best lavateras are annuals (see p. 88) but *Lavatera olbia* is a big, loosely branched bush about 1·6 m (5½ ft) high and nearly as much in diameter, with large, soft leaves and numerous big rose-pink flowers of the typical mallow type. It is in bloom from mid-summer to mid-autumn, likes light, well-drained soils and warm, sunny places and is seldom very long lived. It may be cut back considerably by frost in winter but usually breaks out again in spring in time to make a big bush once more before the flowers open. Dead or damaged shoots should be removed each spring. Propagation is by seed sown in early spring or by summer cuttings. *Lavatera* Barnsley flowers pink all summer long.

Leptospermum (South Sea Myrtle, Manuka, New Zealand Tea Tree). *Leptospermum scoparium* is an attractive evergreen shrub, a native of New Zealand and not reliably hardy in cold districts. It will reach 3·6 m (12 ft) but is usually considerably less erect in habit with narrow, heath-like leaves and branchlets clothed in small flowers in late spring. These are white in the ordinary form, glowing carmine in *L. s.* Nicholsii and double as well as carmine in *L. s.* Red Damask. Dwarf varieties are about 30 cm (1 ft) high. These shrubs dislike lime and require a sheltered, sunny position. Propagation is by cuttings of firm young side shoots taken in mid- to late summer and rooted in a propagating frame or under mist, or by seed sown in a warm greenhouse or propagator in spring, but seedlings are likely to vary in character.

Leycesteria (Himalayan Honeysuckle). *Leycesteria formosa* is half way between a herbaceous plant and a shrub. It makes long, semi-woody stems from the upper part of which, in late summer, hang short trails of white flowers surrounded by maroon bracts which persist even when the deep purple berries are ripe. This is not a showy shrub but it is distinctive and decorative. It does best in rich, moist soil and the older or weaker stems can be cut out in early spring, treatment which will encourage it to produce strong new growth. The average height is 2·7 m (7 ft). This shrub is readily increased by division in autumn or by seed sown out of doors in spring. It often spreads by self-sown seedlings.

Ligustrum (Privet). The common hedge privet is a species of ligustrum named *Ligustrum ovalifolium*. This must not be confused with the wild British privet, *L. vulgare*, which has smaller, narrower leaves and is not nearly so effective in its green-leaved form, though it has a very attractive variety with white or cream-edged leaves. Both species are liable to lose their leaves in a really hard winter but as a rule *L. ovalifolium* retains its foliage for a longer period. It is, despite over-planting, still one of the best hedge shrubs, particularly for the town garden for it will stand any amount of ill treatment and grow anywhere, in sun or shade, light soil or heavy. Moreover its golden-leaved form is really bright and attractive. For hedge-making, young plants should be used and placed no more than 30 cm (1 ft) apart. They can be clipped at any time from late spring to early autumn.

Other species worth noting are *L. delavayanum*, a shrub which is also called *L. prattii* and *L. ionandrum*, with small, rounded leaves, a good deal firmer than those of the common privet; *L. japonicum*, the Japanese privet, a tall, evergreen shrub or small tree worth growing for its large, handsome foliage and sprays of small white flowers in late summer/early autumn; and *L. lucidum*, much like the last but even taller and occasionally tree-like. When in bloom these two privets have rather the appearance of lilac, but they are a little tender and not suitable for cold districts.

All can be increased by cuttings of well-ripened shoots taken in early autumn.

Lilac. See **Syringa** (p. 319).

Lime. See **Tilia** (p. 322).

Lippia (Lemon-scented Verbena). Most lippia now go by another name, phyla or alaysia. *Lippia citriodora*, has become *Aloysia triphylla*, a deciduous shrub or, in some cases, a small tree. Being on the borderline of hardiness it is grown as a wall-trained shrub in cool-climate gardens. Since it delights in warm positions it is ideal for a sunny wall, though it can be planted fully in the open in mild districts. The flowers are small, purplish, not very striking and appear in late summer. The plant is grown mainly for its lemon-scented leaves which can be used in the preparation of perfume and pot pourri. Plant in a sunny position and well-drained soil. Early each spring cut out all growth which has been damaged by frost during the winter. Propagate by cuttings of firm young side shoots in a propagating frame in summer.

Liquidambar (Sweet Gum). *Liquidambar styraciflua* is a handsome North American tree which may eventually grow to a height of 18-21 m (60-70 ft) but is usually considerably less and it is only about half as broad as it is high. It has maple-like leaves which turn crimson and purple in the autumn. It does not thrive in markedly alkaline soils but succeeds in moist, neutral or moderately acid soils and is such a fine shapely foliage tree that it deserves to be much more widely planted. No pruning is required. Propagation is by seed sown in a slightly heated greenhouse or frame in early spring. Young plants should be protected from late spring frosts.

Liriodendron (Tulip Tree). The true tulip tree is *Liriodendron tulipifera*, though the name is often wrongly applied to various species of magnolia. The family is related to magnolia and has somewhat similar requirements, certainly a similar dislike of root disturbance at any stage. If possible young plants should be obtained in containers in late spring and planted in good, loamy soil with as little injury to the roots as possible. The tulip tree will eventually reach a great size, possibly over 30 m (100 ft) in height with corresponding branch spread. The yellowish-green and orange flowers are shaped like tulips and open in the first half of summer. The leaves, which are a rather curious shape, as though the ends had been cut off, turn yellow in the autumn before they fall. Some pruning may be necessary in late winter to keep branches well spaced; remove any broken by wind or snow as the wood is rather brittle. Seed provides practically the only method of propagation but germination may be poor even when seeds are sown as soon as ripe in a slightly heated greenhouse as many appear to be infertile.

Lonicera (Honeysuckle). This is the genus to which the honeysuckles belong but it contains many species which have little outward resemblance to the familiar honeysuckle of British hedgerows, *Lonicera periclymenum*. This is a beautiful and vigorous twiner but is surpassed for garden purposes by two of its forms, known respectively as Early Dutch and Late Dutch. These have larger and showier clusters of flowers, the early form flowering in late spring with some more flowers in late summer, the late from mid-summer to mid-autumn and both sharing the fragrance of the common honeysuckle. Another climbing species is the evergreen Japanese honeysuckle, *L. japonica*. It is as vigorous as the British variety, similar in habit with flowers in the first half of summer which are white at first but become creamy-yellow as they age. In gardens it is most familiar in its variegated form, *L. j.* Aureoreticulata, in which each leaf is netted with gold and in a green-leaved variety, *L. j.* Halliana which is particularly sweetly scented. Other fine climbing honeysuckles are *L. sempervirens* and its hybrid *L. × brownii*, known as trumpet honeysuckles because of the shape of their orange-scarlet flowers produced from early summer to early autumn, and *L. tragophylla* together with its hybrid *L. × tellmanniana*, with orange-yellow flowers in the first half of summer, but all these are scentless.

Then there are several good shrubby honeysuckles, some of which flower in mid-winter or early spring. One of the best of these is *L. fragrantissima*, a deciduous bush of loose habit, 1·8 m (6 ft) high and rather more in spread, with small, creamy white, highly fragrant flowers produced over winter. It needs a sheltered position to protect its blooms. *L. standishii* is very similar.

In contrast to these kinds grown for their flowers are the honeysuckles used for hedge making and to form topiary specimens. The best known of these is *L. nitida*, an evergreen shrub of densely branched habit with small, rounded leaves not unlike those of a box. It makes an ideal hedge where the height is not to exceed 1·5 m (5 ft). It will grow taller but then becomes rather weak and is apt to sag. The variety *L. nitida* Fertilis is stiffer in habit and Baggesen's Gold has yellow leaves. Honeysuckles used for hedge-making should be planted 38 cm (1¼ ft) apart. Like most evergreen hedge plants, they can be clipped at any time from late spring to early autumn.

All honeysuckles will grow in any reasonably good soil and in sun or shade but the climbing honeysuckles are sometimes badly attacked by aphids if in too hot a place, and *L. tragophylla* and *L. × tellmanniana* prefer shady places. Climbing honeysuckles require no regular pruning but when overgrown some of the oldest vines can be cut out in early spring. Propagation is by layers in spring or autumn. The shrubby kinds can be increased by cuttings of firm young growth in summer in a propagating frame or under mist and, if only a few plants are needed, it is often possible to divide old plants of *L. nitida* and its varieties in spring.

Lupinus (Lupin). *Lupinus arboreus*, the tree lupin, is an evergreen shrub, though rather soft wooded and usually rather short lived. In a well-drained soil and fairly sheltered, sunny position it will make a big bush 1·5-1·8 m (5-6 ft) high and of equal spread. The flower spikes are produced freely in early summer and are shorter than those of the familiar herbaceous lupin, usually pale yellow or white but occasionally bluish. Tree lupins can be raised from cuttings struck in sandy soil in a frame in spring or from seed sown in a frame or out of doors in the first half of spring. Winter-damaged stems should be removed in early spring when overgrown bushes can be shaped.

Magnolia. Magnolias are sometimes known as tulip trees though this name really belongs to liriodendron (see p. 281). Magnolias are mostly deciduous though there are a few evergreen species. Some make quite big trees but the majority of the popular garden varieties are big bushes or small trees.

Among the best kinds are *Magnolia denudata*, the common yulan, a deciduous tree of spreading habit up to 9 m (30 ft) high, with big white flowers in the second half of spring; *M. × soulangiana*, a hybrid from the last, similar in habit but with a number of varieties differing in colour from white to wine purple; *M. stellata*, with small, pure white blooms very freely produced in the second half of spring on a compact bush 3·3 m (11 ft) high and of equal spread; and *M. grandiflora*, the best evergreen kind, which has large, laurel-like leaves and, in late summer, fragrant white flowers rather like water lilies. In mild districts, *M. grandiflora* can be planted as a specimen and allowed to develop into a tree up to 9 m (30 ft) in height, but is more commonly seen in cool climates against a sunny wall. *M. kobus* makes a tree to 9 m (30 ft) or more but far less spreading than *M. denudata* or *M. × soulangiana*, and *M. salicifolia* is similar in habit. Both produce rather small white flowers very freely in mid-spring.

Of the big tree species the best is possibly *M. campbelli mollicomata*, to 15 m (50 ft) high with pink or purple flowers in early spring, but it is rather slow in coming into flower, though not as slow as the nearly allied *M. campbellii* which may take 20 years to bloom.

Another group, typified by *M. sieboldii*, *M. sinensis* and *M. wilsonii*, make small trees with spreading branches and pendent saucer-shaped, fragrant white flowers, each with a central boss of crimson stamens in early summer. *M. sinensis* is one of the kinds most tolerant of lime or chalk.

All like warm, sheltered positions and deep, well-drained loamy soils. Most prefer moderately acid soils but a few will tolerate lime. All are difficult to transplant. May is the most favourable month and small plants should be obtained, preferably in containers, from which they should be transplanted with a minimum of root disturbance. Keep really well watered for the first few months. Pruning is as a rule quite unnecessary except in the case of wall-trained specimens which can be thinned and shortened a little to keep them shapely, in early spring in the case of the deciduous kinds, in late spring for the evergreens. Propagation is by seed, by layering and by grafting on to the seedlings of the parent or nearly related species.

Mahonia (Oregon Grape). Evergreen shrubs with handsome, divided, rather holly-like leaves. *Mahonia aquifolium* grows 1 m (3½ ft) high and has clusters of yellow flowers from late winter to mid-spring; *M. japonica* makes a bigger bush 2 m (6½ ft) high and in spread with cartwheel sprays of pale yellow, lily-of-the-valley scented flowers in the first half of spring. *M. lomariifolia* makes stout, upright stems topped by large rosettes of long, compound leaves with erect clusters of yellow flowers in the centre of each rosette in winter, but unfortunately it is not very hardy. *M. × media* is a hybrid between *M. japonica* and *M. lomariifolia* which combines some of the best qualities of each. Specially good forms are Charity, Buckland and Lionel Fortescue.

All will grow in any reasonably good soil and in sun or partial shade, but with a preference for shade, and can be increased by layers or by summer or early autumn cuttings. Some may be divided or rooted offsets can be detached in autumn and the species can be raised from seed.

Malus (Crab Apple). These are deciduous trees, hardy and of moderate size; in fact the familiar apple of the fruit garden may be taken as typical of the family.

One of the most popular species grown in gardens is *M. floribunda*, the Japanese crab.

The flowers are small but make up in numbers what they lack in size. They are deep red in bud, pink when fully open and the tree is at its loveliest in the half-and-half stage. It is comparatively slow growing, very freely branched and makes a slightly weeping tree about 6 m (20 ft) high and 45 m (15 ft) in spread.

M. coronaria, the American crab, has big, blush-pink flowers which are fragrant and open quite late in spring, usually missing the frosts. There is a variety of this with semi-double flowers and also of the rather similar *M. ioensis* which is sometimes confused with it. *M. spectabilis*, the Chinese crab apple, has large flowers in the second half of spring, red in bud and pink when open and semi-double in the form cultivated.

The hybrids can be divided into those grown primarily for their flowers and others valued mainly for their ornamental fruits. In the first group are *M. × atrosanguinea*, with wine-purple flowers and green leaves; Eleyi, Lemoinei and *M. × purpurea*, all with similar flowers and purple leaves, and Profusion also similar in blossom and early leaf but the leaves becoming greener with age. All are highly decorative, medium-sized trees flowering in mid-spring. Small purple fruits may be produced but do not make a great display.

Among fruiting kinds, all white or pink tinted flowers, are Dartmouth, with globular crimson fruits; Golden Hornet with yellow fruits; John Downie, with egg-shaped orange and scarlet fruits, and Veitch's Scarlet, with scarlet and crimson fruits. There are also hybrids of the Siberian crab, *M. baccata*, usually listed as *M. × robusta*, with small, cherry-like fruits produced very freely. *M. × r.* Red Siberian has red fruits, *M. × r.* Yellow Siberian, yellow fruits. Both have pink buds opening to white flowers and are shapely, medium-sized trees.

Many more fine varieties will be found in nursery catalogues but the foregoing are representative of the genus. Few kinds are fussy about soil, though a good, well-drained, loamy soil is ideal. Regular pruning is, as a rule, unnecessary after the early years but at the outset pruning can follow the lines recommended for young fruit trees (see Chapter 27).

Seed offers an easy method of propagation for the species and can be sown in a frame or out of doors in early spring, but garden varieties do not breed true from seed and must be propagated by grafting or budding in the same manner as apples and using the same rootstocks (see Chapter 26).

Metasequoia (Dawn Redwood). The beautiful, fast-growing deciduous conifer, *Metasequoia glyptostroboides*, was believed to be extinct until it was discovered in 1941 growing wild in China. Since then it has proved itself a highly satisfactory tree, much like the swamp cypress (taxodium) in appearance but growing at least twice as fast. The feathery leaves turn pinkish-brown or yellow before they fall. It is likely to exceed 30 m (100 ft) when fully grown and is of conical shape, not very broad in relation to its height. It prefers rather moist, loamy soils but will grow practically anywhere. It can be raised from seed or by cuttings in summer or early autumn.

Mock Orange. See **Philadelphus** (p. 287).

Mountain Ash. See **Sorbus** (p. 317).

Myrtus (Myrtle). These beautiful evergreen shrubs are just a little too tender to be entirely reliable out of doors in cooler climates. The common species, *Myrtus communis*, thrives in mild districts or can be grown in the shelter of a sunny wall. It makes a neat, rounded shrub 2·4-3 m (8-10 ft) high when full grown and 2·1 m (7 ft) in spread, with dark, shining, fragrant leaves and small, white, scented flowers in the second half of summer. *M. luma* is taller, more tree-like, up to 7·5 m (25 ft) tall and has peeling tan and cream bark but is more tender than the common myrtle. All grow best in good, well-drained loamy soils. No pruning is essential but they can be trimmed in mid-spring if necessary to restrict growth. Propagation is by seed or by cuttings of firm young growth in mid-summer preferably with gentle bottom heat.

Oak. See **Quercus** (p. 309).

Olearia (Daisy Bush). This family of evergreen shrubs contains numerous good plants which are a little too tender to be grown out of doors with safety except near the sea or in mild places. There are exceptions, however, notably in *Olearia × haastii*, a grand shrub 2·1 m (7 ft) high and in spread, with small, oval leaves and very abundant white, daisy-like flowers in the second half of summer. It grows well in town gardens, likes sunny places and is not particular regarding soil. Rather smaller but similar in general habit is *O. phlogopappa*, also known as *O. gunniana*, which has grey leaves and white, daisy flowers in the type but has produced numerous forms with variously coloured flowers including pink and blue. This and its white-flowered hybrid, *O. × stellulata* flower in late spring. They are rather tender and frequently killed to the ground in winter. A third good species is *O. macrodonta*, with much bigger greyish, holly-like leaves and heads of white flowers in the first half of summer. It will reach a height of 6 m (20 ft) in favourable places and is sometimes used for hedge making in mild districts. All can be increased by summer cuttings. Pruning is unnecessary except for hedges, which can be trimmed in late spring.

Osmanthus. Another family of evergreen shrubs or small trees. The best is *Osmanthus delavayi*, a stiffly branched, rather spreading shrub, seldom much above 1·8 m (6 ft) in height though often 2·7 m (9 ft) in spread, with small, very dark green leaves and clusters of little tubular, white flowers in mid-spring. These blooms, though not very showy, are intensely fragrant. A hybrid from it named *O. × burkwoodii* grows faster, is hardier but not quite so free flowering or strongly scented. Also occasionally planted is *O. heterophylla*, also known as *O. ilicifolius*, a bigger bush grown mainly for its holly-like leaves which in some varieties are variegated with yellow or cream. All thrive in sunny, sheltered positions and like ordinary, well-drained soils. No pruning is required but overgrown bushes can be cut back in late spring. Increase by summer cuttings in a propagating frame or under mist.

Pachysandra. Two species, *Pachysandra procumbens* and *P. terminalis*, are grown as ground cover. Both are evergreens with shining green leaves on stems usually about 23 cm (9 in) high. *P. terminalis* has a variety named Variegata with white variegated leaves. All kinds like rather moist, humus-rich soil and will grow most freely in shade. They have no beauty of flower and do not always spread so freely as one would wish but where they succeed they do cover the ground densely. Increase by summer cuttings in a propagator.

Paeonia (Peony). In addition to the herbaceous peony (see Chapter 8) there are also shrubby species. *Paeonia suffruticosa* is known as the tree peony, though it is in fact seldom above 1·5 m (5 ft) in height in cool-climate gardens. It is deciduous, freely branched, and produces abundant large, very showy flowers in late spring/early summer. There are single and double-flowered forms and the best varieties are quite as effective in bloom as the finest herbaceous peonies. *P. lutea* (now *P. delavayi lutea*) grows more rapidly and makes a big bush up to 2·4 m (8 ft) high and in spread with single yellow cup-shaped flowers in late spring. A variety named *P. d. ludlowii* exposes its flowers above the deeply divided leaves better than the common kind. *P. delavayi* is about 1·5 m (5 ft) high with deep crimson flowers in late spring. *P. suffruticosa* and its varieties need a very sheltered position and good, loamy, well-drained soil. They should not be planted in low-lying places where frost is likely to be severe in spring as the young growth is distinctly tender. The best method of propagating is by layers in autumn or spring. Commercially, grafting is practised on a large scale, the herbaceous peony being used as a stock but grafted plants are seldom as satisfactory as those produced by layers. *P. delavayi ludlowii* and *P. delavayi* will grow in any reasonably good soil, are quite hardy and can be readily increased by seed sown in spring.

Parrotia. *Parrotia persica* is a tree 6 m (20 ft) or a little more high and rather wide spreading with leaves that colour richly before they fall in the autumn. The grey bark peels in flakes and the flowers, which come in early spring, are curious, rather than beautiful, little clusters of crimson stamens on the bare stems. This is a good foliage tree for acid soils but is not satisfactory on chalk or limestone. It needs no pruning and can be increased by layering in spring or autumn.

Parthenocissus (Virginia Creeper, Ampelopsis, Boston Ivy). These are deciduous climbers closely allied to the grape vine and sometimes listed as vitis. Two kinds are commonly called Virginia creeper, both with slender stems and five-lobed vine-like leaves which turn scarlet before they fall in the autumn but differing in the way in which they climb. One, named *Parthenocissus quinquefolia*, has little suckers by which it can cling to a smooth wall surface as well as tendrils by which it can climb trellis, wires or branches. The other has tendrils only and is variously called *P. quinquefolia vitacea*, *P. inserta* and *P. vitacea*. Another species, *P. tricuspidata* is the ampelopsis or Boston ivy, with three-lobed leaves which also colour magnificently in autumn. It is abundantly supplied with suckers and is a splendid wall climber especially valued in its small-leaved varieties such as *P. t.* Veitchii. *P. henryana* has velvety green leaves which are pink and white along the veins and become purple in autumn. It climbs by suckers but is less hardy than the others.

All will grow in almost any soil in sun or shade but with the exception of *P. henryana* which colours best in shade, all colour best in a sunny place. Pruning is not essential but overgrown plants can be reduced in late winter/early spring and should be kept out of rainwater gutters and from growing beneath roof tiles. Propagation is by summer or autumn cuttings or layers.

Passiflora (Passion Flower). *Passiflora caerulea* is the only passion flower hardy enough to be grown out of doors in cool-climate gardens. It requires a very sunny, sheltered position. It is a vigorous climber with curiously formed white and blue flowers produced spasmodically throughout the summer. There is also a pure white variety named Constance Elliott. Grow in ordinary, well-drained soil and train against a sunny wall. Remove frost-damaged growth in the spring. Propagate by summer cuttings, preferably with bottom heat, or by seed sown in a warm greenhouse in spring.

Paulownia. Deciduous trees 7·5-15 m (25-50 ft) high with large rounded leaves and erect spikes of heliotrope-blue flowers in late spring. The young growth is rather tender so these are not suitable trees for cold localities. *Paulownia tomentosa* is the kind usually seen but *P. lilacina*, usually wrongly called *P. fargesii*, is hardier and more reliable. They enjoy good loamy soils and sunny, sheltered positions. If branches are cut hard back in mid-spring leaves of extra size will be produced but the flowers will be sacrificed. Propagation is by seed, cuttings of firm young shoots and root cuttings.

Pear, Ornamental. See **Pyrus** (p. 309).

Pernettya. See **Gaultheria** (p. 270).

Perovskia (Russian Sage). The beautiful sub-shrub *Perovskia atriplicifolia* would, no doubt, be planted more widely were it a little hardier. It has grey-green stems and leaves and small, violet-blue flowers carried in loose, branching spikes in late summer and each year it throws up many 1·5 m (5 ft) stems from the base. When in bloom it has a slight resemblance to a very large and loose lavender. It should be planted in light, well-drained soils and sunny, sheltered positions. In early spring it is advisable to cut back to a few centimetres all growth made the previous year. Propagation is by root cuttings in winter.

Philadelphus (Mock Orange). Many gardeners call these shrubs syringa but this is really the correct botanical name of lilac. Mock orange is, in fact, a far more suitable name for philadelphus for the large, white, wide-open flowers are frequently heavily scented and do resemble the blossom of the orange.

Some of the best deciduous shrubs for the garden are to be found in this genus, which contains many species and varieties, most of them useful. Among the best are the following: *Philadelphus coronarius*, 3-3·6 m (10-12 ft) and more in spread, with creamy-white, very fragrant flowers in early summer, a good yellow-leaved variety named *P. c.* Aureus and a white variegated variety named Variegatus; *P. pubescens*, which is sometimes sold as *P. grandiflorus*, a still more vigorous shrub with pure white fragrant flowers in the second half of summer; *P. intectus* which closely resembles *P. pubescens* and is regarded by some authorities as a variety of it; *P. delavayi*, 3 m (10 ft) high, remarkable for the purple calyces of its very sweetly scented white flowers in early summer; *P. microphyllus*, 1 m (3½ ft) high, with small white fragrant flowers very freely produced in early summer and *P. × purpureo-maculatus*, 1·8 m (6 ft) high with fragrant white flowers, each with a central purple blotch, in early summer. *P. × lemoinei* is a hybrid between *P. coronarius* and *P. microphyllus* with numerous varieties and there are other garden hybrids of which the parentage is not clear. Some have single flowers, some double, some are all white and some purple blotched. There is also considerable variation in fragrance and descriptions will be found in nursery catalogues. Beauclerk, Belle Etoile, Sybille and Virginal are typical and excellent.

Most philadelphuses are quite hardy and not at all fussy about soil or situation. All can be pruned after flowering, if it is desired to restrict size, the method being to cut back the flowering stems as far as good, non-flowering side growths. The simplest method of propagation is by cuttings of young growth taken in summer and rooted in sand in a propagating frame or under mist, but riper and longer cuttings will root in a frame in the autumn.

Phlomis (Jerusalem Sage). *Phlomis fruticosa* is a bushy 1·2 m (4 ft) evergreen shrub, with rather soft stems which may be cut back by frost in winter. It is a good plant for a fairly dry, sunny position in poorish, well-drained soil. The leaves are downy and a little like those of the common sage, while the yellow, hooded flowers are carried in showy whorls in late summer/early autumn, when colour is particularly welcome. Straggly stems can be shortened in mid-spring. *P. chrysophylla* is similar but there is a yellowish tinge to its leaves.

Photinia. Evergreen shrubs or small trees grown in cool, northern gardens primarily for the reddish-bronze colour of their glossy young leaves. In warmer climates they produce in mid-spring clusters of small creamy flowers, rather unpleasantly scented. The best species is *Photinia serrulata* which can reach 6 m (20 ft) or more, but more popular because of its smaller size is *P.* × *fraseri*, a hybrid from *P. serrulata* which is particularly good in a form named Red Robin. Moderate pruning in early summer as soon as the leaves change to green promotes young growth which will produce fine leaves to colour the following spring. Photinias will grow in all reasonably fertile soils but the young stems are a little tender so plants should be kept out of places subject to severe or repeated spring frost. The species can be grown from seed but the hybrid must be increased by summer cuttings in a propagator.

Phyllostachys. See **Bamboo** (p. 249).

Picea (Spruce). Evergreen cone-bearing trees mostly of considerable size and of neat, conical shape. Typical of the genus is *Picea abies* (Excelsa), the Norway spruce, which provides Christmas trees. This will eventually grow to a height of 30 m (100 ft) or even more, but it has several forms of which one, known as Clanbrassiliana, grows so slowly that after many years it is only 76 cm (2½ ft) in height. *P. a.* Inversa is also low growing with stems that curl over and touch the ground. A choicer tree for the garden is *P. pungens*, the Colorado spruce. This has stiffer, more horizontal branches and though the type is green, it has produced several beautiful forms with blue-grey foliage, the colour being most marked when the leaves are young. One of the best of these is *P. pungens* Glauca. This is a highly ornamental tree for planting as an individual specimen on a large lawn or in a similar prominent position. There are numerous forms selected for their good colour or dwarf habit as in *P. p.* Globosa. *P. omorika*, the Serbian spruce, resembles the Norway spruce but makes a more slender cone or a slender column in *P. o. pendula*. *P. sitchensis*, the Sitka spruce, is fast growing and has blue-green needles.

All spruces will grow in any ordinary soil and open position, but they like best a soil that is well supplied with moisture in summer and do not like very chalky soils. Propagation of the species is by seeds sown in peaty soil in spring and of selected forms by grafting on to seedlings of the species.

Acer platanoides Drummondii

Aesculus x carnea Briotii

Acer griseum

Acer pseudoplatanus Brilliantissimum

Acer griseum (Paper Bark Maple), 9 m (30 ft), has flaking bark which reveals young orange-brown bark beneath. Leaves turn flaming scarlet in autumn ✤ ☼ ✿ ▣ ■

Acer platanoides Drummondii, 15 m (50 ft), a handsome variegated Norway Maple, makes a round-headed tree ✤ ☼ ✿ ▣ ◨

Acer pseudoplatanus Brilliantissimum, 10.5 m (35 ft), is a choice sycamore whose peach-pink young leaves turn pale bronze then greenish ✤ ☼ ✿ ▣ ◨

Aesculus x carnea Briottii (Red Horse Chestnut), 13.5 m (45 ft), shows yellow autumn tints
✤ ❀ Summer ↻ Autumn ☼ ▣ ◨

Betula pendula Youngii

Catalpa bignonioides

Amelanchier lamarckii

Arbutus unedo

Amelanchier lamarckii (Snowy Mespilus), 7.5 m (15 ft), boasts coppery young foliage, white blossom and fiery autumn tints
⊕ ❀ Spring ↻ Summer ☼ 🏵 ◫ ◨

Arbutus unedo (Strawberry Tree), 6 m (20 ft), is clothed in dark green leaves with white bell flowers and red 'strawberries'
△ ❀ Autumn/Winter ↻ Summer/Autumn
☼ ◐ 🏵 ◫ ◨

Betula pendula Youngii (the graceful Weeping Birch), 4.5 m (15 ft), has a white trunk and golden autumn colour. Train its trunk to the required height ⊕ ☼ ▬ 🏵 ◼ ◨

Catalpa bignonioides (Indian Bean Tree), 9 m (30 ft), forms a spreading tree with large leaves and delightful flowers
⊕ ❀ Summer ↻ Autumn ☼ 🏵 ◨

Liriodendron tulipifera

Malus Golden Hornet

Laburnum x watereri Vossii

Laburnum x watereri Vossii, 7.5 m (25 ft), is the best form of this popular spring-flowering tree. Its seed pods are poisonous ⊕ ❀ Spring ♺ Autumn ☼ ◉ ● ▨ ◧

Liriodendron tulipifera (Tulip Tree), to 22.5 m (75 ft), makes a fine plane-like tree but with truncated leaves which turn gold in autumn. Mature trees open magnolia-like flowers ⊕ ❀ Summer ☼ ◉ ▨ ◧

Malus Golden Hornet (Ornamental Crab), to 9 m (30 ft), is planted mainly for its clusters of tiny golden apples but it is a useful pollinator for culinary apples ⊕ ❀ Spring ♺ Autumn ☼ ◉ ▨ ◧

Malus floribunda

Nyssa sylvatica

Parrotia persica

Prunus cerasifera Pissardii

Malus floribunda (Japanese Crab Apple), to 9 m (30 ft), flowers prolifically, its white flowers opening from crimson buds on somewhat pendulous shoots ⊕ ❀ Spring ↻ Autumn ☼ ◐ ▥ ▮ ▯

Nyssa sylvatica (Tupelo Tree), to 18 m (60 ft), is planted solely for its magnifcient scarlet autumn leaf tints ⊕ ☼ ◐ ▥ ▮ ▯

Parrotia persica (Iron Tree), to 10.5 m (35 ft), is primarily an autumn colour tree, but opens tiny blooms on bare branches in spring ⊕ ❀ Spring ☼ ▥ ▮ ▯

***Prunus cerasifera* Pissardii** (Purple-leaved Plum), 7.5 m (25 ft), opens ruby foliage, dark purple in summer, and white blossom ⊕ ❀ Spring ☼ ◐ ▥ ▮ ▯

Prunus serrula (bark)

Prunus serrulata Amanogawa

Prunus serrulata Kanzan

Prunus serrula, to 9 m (30 ft), is planted
mainly for its peeling bark and gleaming trunk,
a feature in winter ✦ ❀ Spring ☼ ◐ ▦ ◼

Prunus serrulata Amanogawa (Japanese
Cherry), to 7.5 m (25 ft), is quite distinct, having
an upright Lombardy poplar shape. It takes up
little space in a small garden, but its blossom is
a very pale pink ✦ ❀ Spring ☼ ◐ ▦ ◼

Prunus serrulata Kanzan (Japanese Cherry),
to 9 m (30 ft), is the most widely planted of
this group for its heavy crops of double pink
blossom. Gives colourful autumn tints too
✦ ❀ Spring ☼ ◐ ▦ ◼

Prunus serrulata Ukon

Pyrus salicifolia Pendula

Prunus subhirtella
Autumnalis

Prunus serrulata Tai Haku

Prunus serrulata Tai Haku, 9 m (30 ft), one
of the best white-flowered cherries, has yellow
and orange autumn tints
⊕ ❀ Spring ☼ ◑ ▣ ◼

Prunus serrulata Ukon, 9 m (30 ft), has
unusual greenish-white blossom and fine
purplish-red to rust-red leaf tints
⊕ ❀ Spring ☼ ◑ ▣ ◼

Prunus subhirtella Autumnalis, to 13.5 m
(45 ft), opens sweet-scented white and blush-
pink flowers in mild spells in winter
⊕ ❀ Winter ☼ ◑ ▣ ◼

Pyrus salicifolia Pendula (Willow-leaved
Pear), 6 m (20 ft), is grown for its silver foliage
and weeping habit. Best staked as a standard
⊕ ❀ Spring ↻ Autumn ☼ ▣ ◼

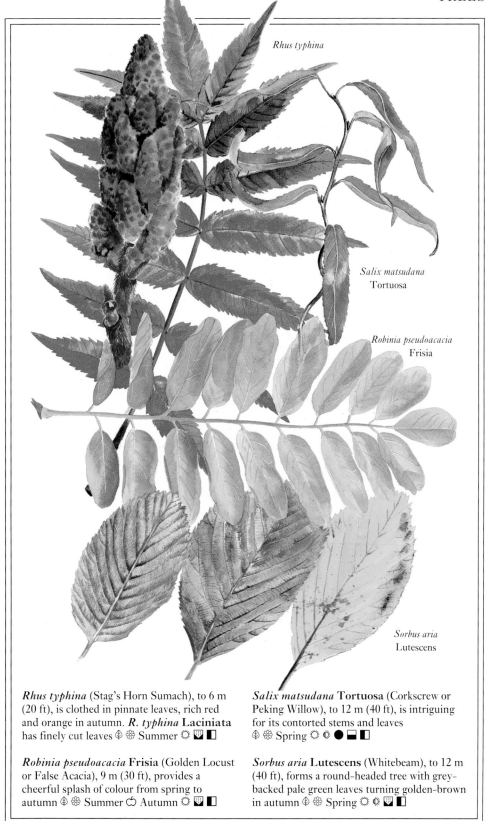

Rhus typhina

Salix matsudana
Tortuosa

Robinia pseudoacacia
Frisia

Sorbus aria
Lutescens

Rhus typhina (Stag's Horn Sumach), to 6 m (20 ft), is clothed in pinnate leaves, rich red and orange in autumn. **R. typhina Laciniata** has finely cut leaves ✦ ✿ Summer ☼ ▣ ▮

Robinia pseudoacacia Frisia (Golden Locust or False Acacia), 9 m (30 ft), provides a cheerful splash of colour from spring to autumn ✦ ✿ Summer ↻ Autumn ☼ ▣ ▮

Salix matsudana Tortuosa (Corkscrew or Peking Willow), to 12 m (40 ft), is intriguing for its contorted stems and leaves ✦ ✿ Spring ☼ ◐ ● ▭ ▮

Sorbus aria Lutescens (Whitebeam), to 12 m (40 ft), forms a round-headed tree with grey-backed pale green leaves turning golden-brown in autumn ✦ ✿ Spring ☼ ◐ ▣ ▮

Abutilon megapotamicum

Actinidia kolomikta

Ceanothus thyrsiflorus

Ceanothus Topaz

Actinidia kolomikta, 5.5 m (18 ft), an ornamental vine, is grown for the sake of its pink-and-white variegated leaves, which develop on mature plants grown on a warm wall ⊕ ☼ ◑ ▣ ■

Abutilon megapotamicum, 1.8 m (6 ft), semi-evergreen, is rather tender but opens many 'lanterns' given a warm spot ▲ ⚘ ❀ Spring ☼ ◑ ▣ ■

Ceanothus thyrsiflorus (Californian Lilac), over 4.5 m (15 ft), a strong-growing wall shrub, opens pale lilac flowers in spring △ ❀ Spring ☼ ▣ ■

Ceanothus Topaz, 1.5 m (5 ft), a deciduous species, bears larger clusters of deep blue flowers in summer ⊕ ❀ Summer ☼ ▣ ■

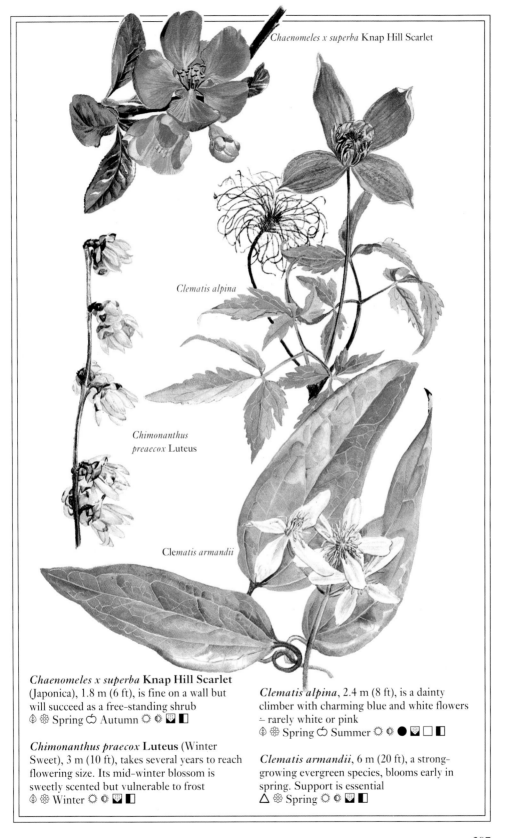

Chaenomeles x superba Knap Hill Scarlet

Clematis alpina

*Chimonanthus
preaecox* Luteus

Clematis armandii

Chaenomeles x superba Knap Hill Scarlet
(Japonica), 1.8 m (6 ft), is fine on a wall but
will succeed as a free-standing shrub
⊕ ❀ Spring ↺ Autumn ☼ ☼ 🛡 ▫ ▮

Chimonanthus praecox Luteus (Winter
Sweet), 3 m (10 ft), takes several years to reach
flowering size. Its mid-winter blossom is
sweetly scented but vulnerable to frost
⊕ ❀ Winter ☼ ☼ 🛡 ▫ ▮

Clematis alpina, 2.4 m (8 ft), is a dainty
climber with charming blue and white flowers
– rarely white or pink
⊕ ❀ Spring ↺ Summer ☼ ☼ ● 🛡 ▫ ▮

Clematis armandii, 6 m (20 ft), a strong-
growing evergreen species, blooms early in
spring. Support is essential
△ ❀ Spring ☼ ☼ 🛡 ▮

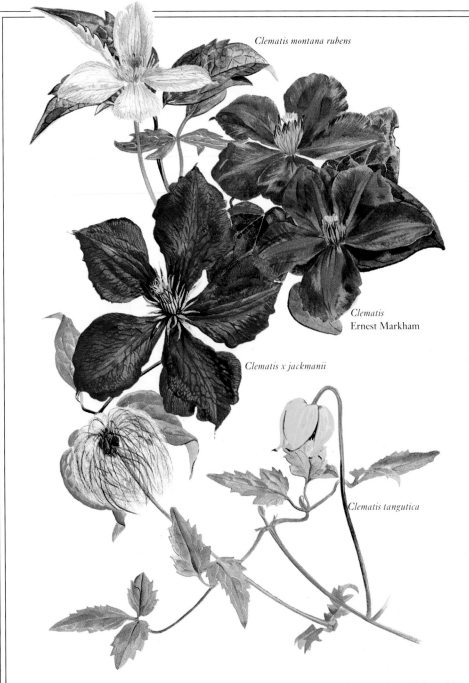

Clematis montana rubens

Clematis
Ernest Markham

Clematis x jackmanii

Clematis tangutica

Clematis Ernest Markham, 4.5 m (15 ft), is one of the finest red varieties. Prune as *C. x jackmanii* ⊕ ❋ Summer ☼ ◑ ▥ ◼

Clematis x jackmanii, 4.5 m (15 ft), a favourite variety, is a vigorous grower that needs cutting back in early spring ⊕ ⚇ ❋ Summer ☼ ◑ ▥ ◼

Clematis montana rubens, to 9 m (30 ft), with masses of small flowers. Fine for walls and trees ⊕ ❋ Spring ☼ ◑ ▥ ◼

Clematis tangutica, 4.5 m (15 ft), a charming yellow-flowered Chinese kind, also forms intriguing fluffy seedheads that persist for months ⊕ ❋ Summer ♋ Summer ☼ ◑ ▥ ◼

Eccremocarpus scaber

Garrya elliptica

Escallonia Iveyi

Hedera canariensis
Gloire de Marengo

Eccremocarpus scaber (Chilean Glory Vine), to 4.5 m (15 ft), can be grown as an annual from seed but will overwinter. Orange and red forms
△ ⚘ ❀ Summer ♻ Autumn ☼ ◑ ▦ ◧

Escallonia **Iveyi**, 3 m (10 ft), is a white form of a usually pink-flowered seaside shrub
△ ⬇ ❀ Summer ☼ ▦ ◧

Garrya elliptica, 4.5 m (15 ft), bears greenish catkins – males 30 cm (1 ft) long – in winter. Good free-standing, better against a wall
△ ❀ Winter ☼ ◑ ▦ ◧

Hedera canariensis **Gloire de Marengo**, 6 m (20 ft), a vigorous variegated ivy, is invaluable for clothing walls and as ground cover
△ ⬇ ☼ ▦ ◧

Hedera colchica Dentata Variegata

Hedera helix
Little Diamond

Humulus lupulus aureus

Hedera helix Goldheart

Hydrangea petiolaris

Hedera colchica **Dentata Variegata** (Persian Ivy), 7.5 m (25 ft), has bold handsomely variegated leaves △ ⚘ ☼ ● 🗔 🗌

Hedera helix **Little Diamond**, 4.5 m (15 ft), is a choice variegated variety of the Common Ivy. *H. helix* **Goldheart**, 4.5 m (15 ft), is similar but with a bold yellow blotch on each leaf △ ☼ ☼ 🗔 🗌

Humulus lupulus aureus, 4.5 m (15 ft), a gold-leaved form of Hop. Cut to ground level after leaf fall ⊕ ❀ Summer ☼ ☼ 🗔 🗌

Hydrangea petiolaris (Climbing Hydrangea), to 18 m (60 ft), opens its white Lacecap flowers in summer ⊕ 🔽 ❀ Summer ☼ ☼ 🗔 🗌

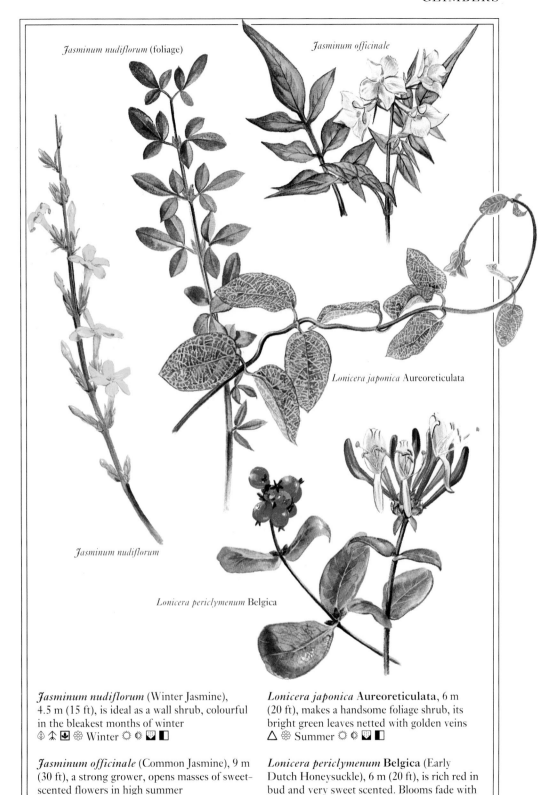

Jasminum nudiflorum (foliage)

Jasminum officinale

Lonicera japonica Aureoreticulata

Jasminum nudiflorum

Lonicera periclymenum Belgica

Jasminum nudiflorum (Winter Jasmine), 4.5 m (15 ft), is ideal as a wall shrub, colourful in the bleakest months of winter ⊕ ⚘ ⬇ ❀ Winter ☼ ◐ ▥ ▮▯

Jasminum officinale (Common Jasmine), 9 m (30 ft), a strong grower, opens masses of sweet-scented flowers in high summer △ ⚘ ⬇ ❀ Summer ☼ ▥ ▮▯

Lonicera japonica Aureoreticulata, 6 m (20 ft), makes a handsome foliage shrub, its bright green leaves netted with golden veins △ ❀ Summer ☼ ◐ ▥ ▮▯

Lonicera periclymenum Belgica (Early Dutch Honeysuckle), 6 m (20 ft), is rich red in bud and very sweet scented. Blooms fade with age ⊕ ❀ Summer ♺ Autumn ☼ ◐ ● ▥ ▮▯

Lonicera x tellmanniana

Lonicera periclymenum Serotina

Parthenocissus henryana

Lonicera japonica halliana

Lonicera japonica halliana (Japanese Honeysuckle), 9 m (30 ft), a semi-evergreen, is a useful coverer with scented pale summer flowers ▲ ❀ Summer ♻ Autumn ☼ ◐ ▥ ▯

Lonicera periclymenum Serotina (Late Dutch Honeysuckle), 4.5 m (15 ft), is a twiner spreading 6 m (20 ft) and useful for camouflage. Scented flowers and red berries ⊕ ❀ Summer ♻ Autumn ☼ ◐ ● ▥ ▯

Lonicera x tellmanniana, 4.5 m (15 ft), an abundant flowerer, is not scented ⊕ ❀ Summer ☼ ◐ ▥ ▯

Parthenocissus henryana, spreading to 12 m (40 ft), clings by means of tendrils. Its variegated leaves turn bright red in autumn ⊕ ♻ Autumn ◐ ● ▥ ▯

Passiflora caerulea

Polygonum baldschuanicum

Parthenocissus quinquefolia

Parthenocissus tricuspidata

Parthenocissus quinquefolia (Virginia Creeper), 12 m (40 ft), another vigorous grower with brilliant autumn leaf colour. Fine through a tree ⊕ ♻ Autumn ☼ ◐ ● ▦▮▯

Parthenocissus tricuspidata (Boston Ivy), 18 m (60 ft), a very vigorous self-supporting climber, fine on a large wall. Brilliant autumn tints ⊕ ♻ Autumn ☼ ◐ ▦▮▯

Passiflora caerulea (Passion Flower), 4.5 m (15 ft), a strong-growing semi-evergreen with most intriguing flowers. Somewhat tender ▲ ❀ Summer ♻ Summer ☼ ▨▮▯

Polygonum baldschuanicum (Russian Vine), 12 m (40 ft), a vigorous, even invasive climber, useful for quick cover. Showy white blossom ⊕ ❀ Summer ☼ ◐ ● ▦▮▯

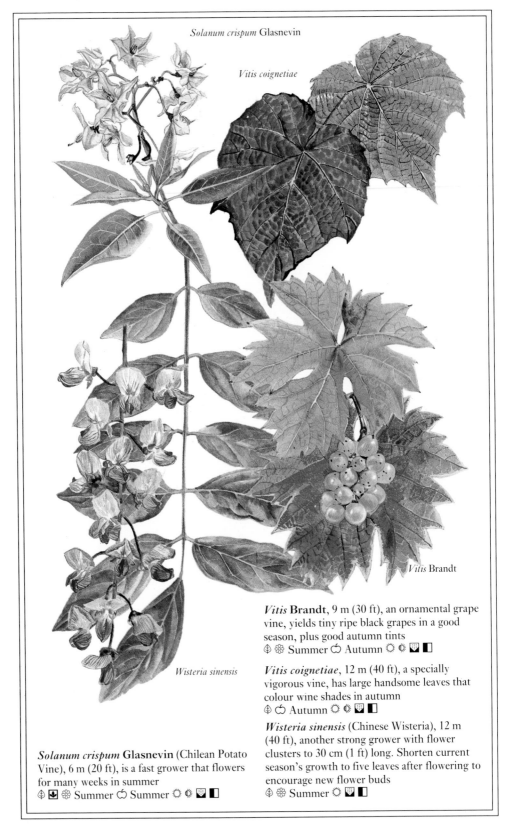

Solanum crispum Glasnevin

Vitis coignetiae

Vitis Brandt

Wisteria sinensis

Vitis **Brandt**, 9 m (30 ft), an ornamental grape vine, yields tiny ripe black grapes in a good season, plus good autumn tints
⊕ ❋ Summer ⟳ Autumn ☼ ❀ ▧ ▊

Vitis coignetiae, 12 m (40 ft), a specially vigorous vine, has large handsome leaves that colour wine shades in autumn
⊕ ⟳ Autumn ☼ ❀ ▧ ▊

Wisteria sinensis (Chinese Wisteria), 12 m (40 ft), another strong grower with flower clusters to 30 cm (1 ft) long. Shorten current season's growth to five leaves after flowering to encourage new flower buds
⊕ ❋ Summer ☼ ▧ ▊

Solanum crispum **Glasnevin** (Chilean Potato Vine), 6 m (20 ft), is a fast grower that flowers for many weeks in summer
⊕ ▼ ❋ Summer ⟳ Summer ☼ ❀ ▧ ▊

Pieris. These are handsome, evergreen shrubs with small, urn-shaped white flowers in spring carried in sprays or drooping clusters, a characteristic which has caused some gardeners to call them lily of the valley bushes. Three of the most outstanding are *Pieris floribunda*, 1·2–1·8 m (4–6 ft) high and in spread; *P. japonica*, which is about twice as big and *P. formosa*, which is a little less hardy but in very mild and favourable places will reach a height of 6 m (20 ft). The first two flower in the first half of spring, *P. formosa* later in the season. It also has bright red young leaves and shoots, a characteristic most highly developed in *P. f. forrestii*, of which Wakehurst is a selected form. Forest Flame is a hybrid between *P. japonica* and *P. formosa* whose young leaves change from red to pink, cream and finally green. *P. taiwanensis* is 1·2–1·8 m (4–6 ft) high and carries its flowers in horizontal spikes.

All thrive in lime-free soil of the type which suits rhododendrons and heathers, to which they are related. They like plenty of moisture during the summer, should only be pruned when overgrown and then immediately after flowering, and may be increased by layering in autumn or spring.

Pine (Pinus). There are a great many species of pine almost all of which have some value in the garden though most grow too rapidly to be serviceable where space is at all restricted. Very typical of the family is the native Scots pine, *Pinus sylvestris*, which will reach a height of 30 m (100 ft) and, though neatly cone shaped at first, usually becomes curiously contorted with age when the trunk is often bare for 15 m (50 ft) with a one-sided head of branches at the top. Two that are frequently planted are the Austrian pine, *P. nigra* and the Corsican pine, *P. nigra maritima*. Both will reach 30 m (100 ft) but the Austrian variety has longer individual leaves and a more spreading habit. The Weymouth pine, *P. strobus*, is seldom over 18 m (60 ft) in height and an attractive species with slender leaves. So is *P. wallichiana* with long, greyish-green needles, but the most beautiful of all is *P. montezumae*, with needles up to 30 cm (1 ft) long. Unfortunately it is too tender to be grown in any but the mildest garden. *P. radiata* also needs a mild climate but is distinctly hardier, very fast growing and an excellent shelter tree in maritime districts. One of the smallest kinds is the European scrub pine, *P. mugo pumilio*, which is often no more than 60 cm (2 ft) or so high, though it may spread over an area of 3–3·6 m (10–12 ft). It must not be confused with *P. pumila*, the dwarf Serbian pine, a distinct species of semi-prostrate habit. The Mexican white pine, *P. ayacahuite*, has slender, drooping needles, makes a large tree and is quite hardy, but *P. patula*, which also has this graceful, needle-weeping habit of growth, is less hardy and needs to be planted in a mild, sheltered place.

All these pines will grow in a great variety of soils though they prefer those that are light and well drained. No pruning should be attempted at any time, except for the removal of dead branches. Where possible trees should be planted while still very young. Propagation of species is by seeds sown in sandy soil either out of doors or in a frame in spring but garden varieties are increased by grafting in spring.

Piptanthus (Evergreen Laburnum). *Piptanthus laburnifolius* (now known as *P. nepalensis*) is an attractive evergreen shrub of open, branched habit up to 3 m (10 ft) high with three-parted leaves and short spikes of yellow laburnum-like flowers in late spring. It is a little tender, needs a sunny, sheltered place or may be trained against a wall. Damaged growth can be cut out in mid-spring. Propagation is by seed.

Pittosporum. There are some extremely beautiful evergreen foliage shrubs and small trees in this genus but unfortunately most of them are a little too tender to be grown out of doors in this country except in the mildest districts. One of the most reliable is *Pittosporum tenuifolium*, which has black stems and shining, bright green leaves. It is very popular with florists for cutting and mixing with flowers, and in the garden will make a shapely shrub or small tree to 9 m (30 ft) high. It has a good variety named Silver Queen in which the leaves are grey-green edged with white. *P. tobira* is usually no more than 3 m (10 ft) high but broad, with bigger, dark green leaves and fragrant creamy-white flowers in spring and summer. Neither is fussy about soil but should have a warm, sheltered position. Overgrown bushes can be cut back in late spring. Propagation is by summer cuttings.

Platanus (Plane). The London plane, *Platanus × acerifolia* (now listed as *P. × hispanica*), is a great favourite for town planting. It has the merit of thriving anywhere, even in the most heavily grime-laden atmosphere, but it grows too quickly for small gardens, soon making a big tree, 18 m (60 ft) or more in height with corresponding branch spread. Though it can be pruned severely this usually spoils its shape. A peculiarity is the peeling bark, which gives the trunk a rather attractive piebald appearance. Although the mature tree is absolutely hardy, young plants are a little tender and occasionally severely cut by late spring frosts. The oriental plane, *P. orientalis*, has more deeply lobed leaves, makes an even larger, more spreading tree, and is very long lived. Propagation is by seed or by summer or autumn cuttings, or by stooling, i.e. cutting the plant almost to the ground and then drawing soil around the young stems to get them to root.

Plums, Ornamental. See **Prunus** (p. 307).

Polygonum (Russian Vine). See **Fallopia** (p. 268).

Poncirus (Hardy Orange). *Poncirus trifoliata* is an evergreen flowering shrub (in some cases almost a small tree) with angular, heavily spined branches and a dense, bushy habit which would make it a good subject for an impenetrable hedge were it a little easier to buy. As it is, one seldom sees more than an isolated bush or two in the garden of some connoisseur by whom it is valued for its unusual appearance, abundant white flowers in late spring and occasional crops of small, orange-like fruits. It likes a warm, sunny position and well-drained soil. Propagate by cuttings of firm young shoots in a warm propagating frame in the second half of summer. This plant was once known as *Aegle sepiaria*.

Populus (Poplar). There are many kinds planted for ornament but all are too big and quick growing for any but the larger gardens. The well-known Lombardy poplar, *Populus nigra italica*, so popular as a roadside tree in France, is occasionally planted as a screen, but is apt to become a nuisance, particularly as it spreads its roots widely. It will reach a height of 30 m (100 ft) with a spread of no more than 3-3·6 m (10-12 ft).

The common aspen, *Populus tremula*, is so called because its thin leaves are constantly on the move even in the lightest breeze. It is an elegant tree 12-15 m (40-50 ft) high and as much in diameter. Another ornamental species is *P. alba*, the white poplar, with leaves that are greyish-green above and almost pure white beneath. This looks particularly attractive on a windy day. It will reach a height of about 24 m (80 ft) with a spread of 9-12 m (30-40 ft) but there is a fastigiate variety named *P. a.* Pyramidalis which makes a narrow column like the Lombardy poplar. The balsam poplars are also worthy of attention because of their fragrant winter buds and young leaves. Three species with these characteristics are *P. candicans*, 15-24 m (50-80 ft) high, *P. balsamifera*, 30 m (100 ft) and *P. trichocarpa*, which can be over 30 m (100 ft) high. *P. × euroamericana* Aurea Serotina (once *P. serotina aurea*), the golden poplar, is one of the best large, fast-growing trees with yellow leaves. The colour is best when the leaves are young, as they become greenish yellow with age.

All poplars are deciduous, none requires regular pruning and all can be increased by cuttings of ripened growth in autumn. They will grow in most soils but prefer those that are fairly rich and not liable to dry out severely.

Potentilla (Shrubby Cinquefoil). In addition to the herbaceous and alpine plants and numerous weeds which make up the greater part of this genus there are a few good shrubs of which the best are *Potentilla fruiticosa* Elizabeth and *P. fruticosa*. These are very similar rounded and well-branched deciduous shrubs seldom over 90 cm (3 ft) in height and of equal spread, with little divided leaves and a constant succession of yellow, white, pink, orange or red flowers throughout the summer. There are numerous varieties mostly with flowers of increased size or improved colours. Abbotswood is a good white, Goldfinger and Katherine Dykes are yellow; Tangerine, orange; Red Ace, orange-red; Royal Flush, rose-red; and Daydawn, cream and pink.

All will grow readily in any reasonable good soil. They prefer sunny places but will grow in partial shade. They can be pruned almost to the ground in early spring or alternatively old stems may be thinned out then. Seed germinates readily if sown in a frame in spring, but seedlings may vary in quality so selected varieties are increased by summer cuttings.

Privet. See **Ligustrum** (p. 280).

Prunus. A genus which includes many highly ornamental trees and shrubs. Popularly the family is split up into numerous groups under such headings as cherries, plums, apricots and almonds. Most are deciduous but the family does include evergreen species, of which the two most important are the cherry laurel, *Prunus laurocerasus*, and the Portugal laurel, *P. lusitanica*.

One of the first of the genus to bloom is *P. cerasifera* Pissardii, the purple plum. Its small, pale pink flowers begin to open in early spring slightly ahead of the leaves. The foliage is purple and ornamental. Even better is *P. × blireana*, a hybrid in which the flowers are fully double, considerably larger and bright pink. *P. × cistena*, the purple-leaved sand cherry, is a dwarf hybrid from *P. cerasifera* with similar flowers and purple leaves but slow growing and not even waist high.

These early-flowering plums are followed very closely by the almond, *P. dulcis*, once known as *P. amygdalus*. This has large, bright pink flowers all along the bare stems and is one of the most beautiful of spring-flowering trees.

The peach, *P. persica*, resembles the almond in many respects but flowers about a fortnight later in mid-spring. For ornament the double-flowered forms are usually planted, such as Klara Meyer, which has big, rose-pink flowers, Russell's Red, double crimson, and Iceberg, double white. There is also a fine hybrid between the almond and peach known as *P.* × *amygdalo-persica*, which has large single pink flowers in the first half of spring. *P. glandulosa*, the dwarf-flowering almond, is a bush only 1·2 m (4 ft) high with single or double, white or pink flowers in mid-spring. *P. tenella*, the dwarf Russian almond, is also 1·2 m (4 ft) high and has single white, pink or crimson flowers in mid-spring. A good rose-red variety is named Fire Hill.

Not unlike *P.* × *blireana*, but less hardy and in consequence more satisfactory against a sunny wall than planted in the open, is *P. triloba flore pleno*. This is a fine shrub for forcing in pots in the greenhouse and its long sprays of double pink bloom can be had soon after the New Year with very little heat. Out of doors it generally starts to bloom in early spring at approximately the same time as the almond. *P. mume*, the Japanese apricot, also flowers in the first half of spring and has pink or white single or double flowers but needs a warm, sunny place.

The Japanese cherries are mainly derived from two species, *P. serrulata* and *P. lannesiana*. The colour range is from white, lemon and palest pink to rose; the flowers, single, semi-double or fully double, are for the most part very large and borne in marvellous profusion in mid-spring. There is also great variation in habit, from the narrowly erect Ama-no-gawa to the spreading Fugenzo (James H. Veitch) and weeping Cheal's Weeping Cherry also known as Shidare-Sakura. In many the foliage colours well before it falls.

These Japanese cherries are fairly big trees, up to 9 m (30 ft) in height. The so-called dwarf cherry, *P. cerasus*, from which the Morello cherry of the fruit garden is obtained, seldom exceeds a height of 6 m (20 ft) and is a good tree for the small garden. Its best ornamental variety is Rhexii with pure white, fully double flowers.

Not to be confused with the last named is the double white form of the wild British cherry or gean, *P. avium*. This makes a very much larger tree, sometimes reaching a height of 18 m (60 ft) with corresponding branch spread.

P. subhirtella is a small-flowered cherry which blooms in mid-spring but it is chiefly remarkable for its variety Autumnalis, which gives one crop of small pale pink flowers in late autumn/early winter and sometimes a few more in the spring. There is also a beautiful weeping variety named Pendula Rosea. Accolade is a fine hybrid between *P. subhirtella* and *P. sargentii* with semi-double pink flowers in mid-spring.

P. sargentii is a Japanese species, a shapely tree to 18 m (60 ft) high with single pink flowers in early spring and brilliant foliage colours in autumn. *P.* × *yedoensis*, another of the Japanese cherry group, and sometimes called Yoshino, is a smaller tree with abundant white flowers in the first half of spring. It has a lovely weeping variety named Perpendens. *P. incisa*, the Fuji cherry, is bushy, to 4·5 m (15 ft) high with small flowers, pink in bud, white when open, and very freely produced in the first half of spring.

The bird cherry, *P. padus*, may attain 21 m (70 ft) and has long, narrow trails of small white flowers in late spring. Wateri is a variety with flower trails of extra length.

P. serrula is grown principally for its bark, which is smooth and shining, like polished mahogany.

The cherry laurel, *P. laurocerasus*, has numerous forms such as *P. l.* Caucasica, with long, dark green leaves; *P. l.* Schipkaensis, low growing and narrow leaved; *P. l.* Otto Luyken, compact in habit and with narrow leaves; *P. l.* Zabeliana, almost horizontally branched and with very narrow leaves; and *P. l.* Magnoliifolia, in which the leaves may be as much as 30 cm (1 ft) in length. All have slender spikes of white flowers in spring.

The Portugal laurel makes a big, rounded shrub, often 6 m (20 ft) high and as much through, with reddish shoots and oval leaves a little like those of the bay tree. It is a fine shrub to form a screen or shelter belt but is rather hungry and exhausts the soil for a considerable distance. Its white flowers in slender, erect spikes come in early summer.

Almost all kinds of prunus are hardy and easily grown in a great variety of soils but it is wise to give the earliest flowering kinds a sheltered position so that their blooms have a chance of survival. Pruning is on the whole undesirable, at any rate with the deciduous kinds, but the cherry laurel and Portugal laurel will stand any amount of cutting about, provided it is done in mid-spring. Any pruning that is essential to maintain the shape or reduce the size of deciduous kinds should be done immediately the flowers fall.

Propagation of the deciduous kinds is as a rule by budding or grafting and plum or cherry stocks are commonly employed. The evergreens can be increased by summer or early autumn cuttings.

Pseudotsuga (Douglas Fir). In its home, North America, specimens of *Pseudotsuga menziesii* occur well over 60 m (200 ft) in height. It is a very handsome cone-bearing tree, conical in habit with wide, spreading, horizontal branches. There are several forms including one named *P. glauca* with blue-grey foliage. It is not always a satisfactory tree as it needs plenty of moisture during the growing season; it is therefore most likely to succeed where rainfall is high. It should not be pruned for fear of spoiling its highly distinctive shape. Propagation is by seeds in spring.

Pyracantha (Fire Thorn). These are evergreen shrubs with dark green, shining leaves, and flattish clusters of white flowers in early summer, both of which are attractive, but the plants become really spectacular in late summer when covered with crops of red, orange or yellow berries. Planted in the open they make bushy specimens 3·6-4·5 m (12-15 ft) high and rather more in spread, but when planted against a wall they shape themselves to it quite readily and require only a little pruning of side growths each summer to keep them in shape. There are several good species, including *Pyracantha coccinea*, with orange-red berries; its variety Lalandei with berries of greater size; *P. atalantoides*, with smaller but very numerous scarlet berries; *P. rogersiana flava* with yellow berries and Orange Charmer with orange berries. All will succeed practically anywhere, on chilly walls as well as warm and in most soils, including those containing a lot of lime.

Propagation is by seeds sown in a frame or unheated greenhouse in spring, or for selected garden varieties by summer cuttings in a propagating frame or under mist.

Pyrus (Pear). The best species of pear to plant as an ornamental tree is *Pyrus salicifolia* Pendula, the weeping willow-leaved pear. It makes a very attractive small tree up to 7·5 m (25 ft) high, but usually less, with narrow, silvery-grey leaves and branches weeping to ground level. It will grow in any reasonably good soil, prefers a sunny position and can be moderately pruned in autumn to keep it in shape. It is increased by grafting on to pear stocks.

Quercus (Oak). The common British oak, *Quercus robur*, a grand tree for parklands is much too big for the ordinary garden but it has a good variety named *fastigiata* with erect branches forming a broad column 15-18 m (50-60 ft) high when full grown but only 4·5-5·4 m (15-18 ft) in diameter. There are many exotic species which will thrive in cooler climates of which perhaps the two best for the ordinary garden are *Q. ilex* and *Q. coccinea*. The first is familiar as the holm oak, an evergreen tree of considerable size which can, however, be restricted by frequent clipping to form a hedge or windbreak. It does well in seaside localities and the milder parts of the country and delights in light, well-drained soils. *Q. coccinea* is known as the scarlet oak because of the vivid autumn colours assumed by its large leaves. It is deciduous and will eventually reach a height of about 15 m (50 ft) with a branch spread slightly bigger. With the exception of the holm oak all kinds thrive best in good loamy soils and open positions. They make fine individual specimens, are best left unpruned except for removal of misplaced or diseased branches, and may be increased by collecting the acorns in autumn and sowing them 5 cm (2 in) deep out of doors in spring.

Rhododendron. This is one of the biggest genera of evergreen shrubs. From the botanist's standpoint the family also includes deciduous species but these are dealt with separately under azalea (see p. 248).

Whole books have been devoted to the rhododendron and several world-famous plant collectors have spent years of their lives collecting new species in various parts of the world, particularly in the mountain ranges between India, China and Tibet. In addition a vast amount of hybridization has been carried out in nurseries in this country, in Europe and in America. There are as a result rhododendrons of every conceivable type, size and colour from small, spreading shrubs with tiny leaves and neat clusters of flowers, to trees with leaves in some cases 30 cm (1 ft) long and magnificent, funnel-shaped flowers borne in heavy trusses.

On the whole hybrids provide the best material for ordinary garden display since they are generally hardier, and are also more tolerant of industrial air, than the species. The so-called Hardy Hybrids combine some of the flower quality and colour variety of the Himalayan rhododendron with the extreme hardiness of *Rhododendron catawbiense* and other American species. They make fine rounded bushes up to 4·5 m (15 ft) in height and diameter with large, dark green leaves and magnificent trusses of showy flowers in a great variety of colours including white, pink, scarlet, crimson, mauve, pale yellow and apricot. The best of these hybrids have been given garden names such as Pink Pearl, Britannia, Cynthia, Dairymaid, Elizabeth, Purple Splendour, Susan and White Pearl. There are hundreds of merit, and descriptions can be found in any good nursery catalogue.

Of the species the following are among the most useful, taking them roughly in order of size, but again there are many more which can be found in the catalogues of nurserymen specializing in rhododendrons:

R. hanceanum Nanum is less than 30 cm (1 ft) high and has small, yellow flowers in the first half of spring.

R. hippophaeoides is 60-90 cm (2-3 ft) high with small, lavender flowers in late spring.

R. yakushimanum makes a compact bush 60-90 cm (2-3 ft) high with fine clusters of pink or white flowers in late spring.

R. praecox is a hybrid between two species, grows 90 cm-1·2 m (3-4 ft) in height and breadth and opens its pink flowers in mid-spring. It is more tolerant of lime than many species.

R. williamsianum makes a neat dome-shaped bush 90 cm-1·2 m (3-4 ft) high and has pink bell-shaped flowers in the second half of spring.

R. moupinense grows 60 cm-1·2 m (2-4 ft) high and has white or pale pink flowers in early spring. Cilpinense is a hybrid between it and *R. ciliatum* which is nearly prostrate and has white or pink-flushed flowers in the first half of spring.

R. russatum is 90 cm-1·2 m (3-4 ft) high with small leaves and clusters of small blue-purple flowers in mid-spring. Song Bird is a good hybrid from it.

R. racemosum has small but attractive pink flowers in the first half of spring and makes an erect bush 1·6 m (5½ ft) high.

R. campylocarpum and *R. wardii* are 1·8-2·4 m (6-8 ft) high and have yellow flowers in the second half of spring.

R. orbiculare makes a dome-shaped bush 1·2-1·8 m (4-6 ft) high and has bell-shaped rose-pink flowers in late spring.

R. cinnabarinum is 1·8-2·4 m (6-8 ft) high and has hanging clusters of tubular flowers in late spring/early summer. These may be vermillion red, plum-red or red and yellow. There are also hybrids very similar in character with orange-red, yellow, amber, apricot or rose-pink flowers according to variety.

R. griersonianum grows 1·8-3 m (6-10 ft) high and has scarlet flowers in early summer. It is the parent of some fine flowering hybrids, such as Tally Ho, May Day, Fabia, Fusilier and Vanessa.

R. augustinii will reach 3 m (10 ft) and has blue flowers in the second half of spring. It is variable in colour so it is desirable to see plants in flower when buying it. Electra and Blue Diamond are good hybrids from it.

R. yunnanense is similar in habit to the last and has white or pink flowers in late spring.

R. ponticum will reach a height of 4·5 m (15 ft) with a spread of 6-9 m (20-30 ft) when well grown. The flowers vary in colour from mauve to rosy purple and make a brave show in late spring/early summer.

R. thomsonii is valuable for its earliness and the brilliant blood red of its flowers which begin to open in early spring. It needs a sheltered position and will make a fine bush up to 3·6 m (12 ft) high and 4·5-6 m (15-20 ft) in spread. This species together with *R. fortunei*, which is similar in height and spread and has fragrant, blush-pink flowers in late spring, have been used to produce a number of beautiful hybrids which flower earlier than the Hardy Hybrids.

Hybrids which bloom after the Hardy Hybrids have been obtained from *R. discolor*, a species which may eventually reach 4·5 m (15 ft) in height. Its flowers are white or pink-tinged, and appear in the first half of summer.

R. loderi is a splendid hybrid between *R. fortunei* and *R. griffithianum*, a slightly tender species with large white flowers in late spring. *R. loderi* itself will make a large bush to 4·5 m (15 ft) high with clusters of very big, funnel-shaped white or pink flowers in late spring. They are fragrant.

R. falconeri is tree-like, sometimes 9 m (30 ft) high, with a similar branch spread and large, creamy-white purple-blotched flowers in late spring. It is distinctly tender and therefore only suitable for the milder garden. The leaves are very handsome, large, dark green above, rust coloured beneath. Not unlike this is *R. sinogrande*, which also has creamy flowers and grows well in mild areas.

R. arboreum is a fine tree up to 12 m (40 ft) high. The flowers are blood red, pink or white according to variety. Like the other tree rhododendrons, it needs a sheltered place.

Rhododendrons thrive in a great variety of soils provided they contain no free lime but they like best reasonably well-drained, peaty soils, or mixtures of peat and lime-free loam. Very dry soils are not good. Many kinds will grow in full sun though almost all are happiest in partial shade. They do not stand up very well to cold winds and this is particularly true of some of the Himalayan species and also some of the continental hybrids. Many of these can be grown in thin woodland in districts which would be too cold were they planted fully in the open.

No regular pruning is desirable but faded flower trusses should be removed when possible. Bushes which have become overgrown can be cut back severely in late spring but this means the sacrifice of one year's flowering.

New plants can be raised from seed, cuttings, layers and grafts. Hybrids will not breed true to type from seed, and seed in any case is small and a little difficult to handle. It should be sown on fine, sandy peat in a cool greenhouse or frame in spring and given the lightest covering with silver sand only. Grafting is done in spring, usually under glass, seedlings or *R. ponticum* generally being used as stocks. Layering in the spring or autumn is one of the most satisfactory methods of increase for private gardeners. Cuttings of firm young side growth can be rooted in sandy peat in a propagating frame or under mist with gentle bottom heat in the second half of summer.

Rhus (Stag's Horn Sumach). The small deciduous tree or large shrub, *Rhus hirta* (previously *R. typhina*), is known as the stag's horn sumach because of the stiff, angular branching of the stout stems which are covered in brown down. They are terminated in summer by dense columns of greenish flowers which develop into velvet-textured reddish-purple fruits. The long leaves are made up of numerous segments which are further cut up into smaller segments in *R. h. laciniata*. The leaves turn yellow, orange-red and crimson before they fall in the autumn. It will reach a height of 3-4·5 m (10-15 ft) and can spread indefinitely by suckers which can be dug out with roots attached in the autumn and provide an easy means of increase. Overgrown specimens can be shaped and reduced in early spring.

Ribes (Flowering Currant, American Currant). The red, black and white currants of the fruit garden belong to this genus, which has also produced a few species of value in the ornamental garden, notably *Ribes sanguineum*. In habit this looks a little like a large black currant up to 3 m (10 ft) in height with similar, short, hanging trails of flowers in mid-spring, but bright rose instead of pale, greenish yellow. There are even better varieties, notably Pulborough Scarlet and King Edward VII, both of which have crimson flowers, Brocklebankii, with pink flowers and yellow leaves, and Carneum, pink. Other kinds are *R. speciosum*, an ornamental gooseberry with small tubular, deep red flowers in spring, and *R. laurifolium*, a smaller bush to 90 cm (3 ft) high, with evergreen leaves and short trails of greenish white flowers in late winter/early spring.

These are all very easily grown shrubs which will thrive in any soils and in sunny or partially shaded positions. *R. sanguineum* succeeds well in town gardens and, if it gets too big, can be cut back without harm immediately after flowering. Propagation is by summer or autumn cuttings.

Robinia (False Acacia, Rose Acacia). Some years ago the false acacia, *Robinia pseudoacacia*, was one of the most freely planted of road trees in this country and was a favourite ornament for small front gardens. Usually the variety Inermis was planted. This lacks the spines of the common type, has much shorter branches and makes a mop-headed specimen instead of a fine, spreading tree up to 24 m (80 ft) in height with a branch spread of 9-12 m (30-40 ft). The foliage of both type and variety is graceful. The mop-headed form seldom flowers but the type, when established, produces in early summer laburnum-like trails of fragrant white flowers.

There is a highly decorative variety named Frisia, with golden-yellow foliage, which floods the garden with sunshine throughout spring, summer and early autumn, and another named Pyramidalis with erect, spineless branches which make a columnar tree.

Other species are *R. hispida*, the rose acacia, and *R. kelseyi*, both of which are deciduous shrubs with fine rose flowers in early summer. They grow 2·4-3 m (8-10 ft) high and can be trained as small standard trees. They often produce suckers freely but these can be removed.

All will thrive in quite poor soils and like sunny places. They can be increased by suckers and the false acacia grows readily from seed. *R. hispoida* is sometimes grafted on to stems of the false acacia to make a small standard tree on a better stem than it would produce itself. *R. pseudoacacia* Frisia is also increased by grafting, so suckers from grafted trees will be like the rootstock, not the variety grafted on it.

Romneya (Californian Tree Poppy). *Romneya coulteri* is midway between a true herbaceous plant and a shrub, since it makes many strong growths each year which become woody and permanent at the base though the upper parts usually die back in winter. It has grey-green leaves and stems and enormous white, poppy-like flowers each with a showy central cluster of golden-yellow stamens, at their best in late summer. It enjoys well-drained soils and warm sunny positions, transplants badly and so should be established from pots while still quite young. It spreads widely by suckers. All damaged growth should be removed each spring. Propagation is by root cuttings taken in winter and inserted singly in small pots, or by seed sown in a frame or greenhouse in spring.

Rosa. See Chapter 11.

Rosmarinus (Rosemary). The common rosemary, *Rosmarinus officinalis*, is a beautiful evergreen shrub, occasionally 1·8 m (6 ft) high and of equal spread, though usually rather less, with lavender-blue flowers all spring. It does well in all soils except those that are very heavy and badly drained and it likes warm, sunny, even rather dry positions. Flowering stems can be cut well back when the flowers fade but not into the hard old wood. There are several varieties including *R. o. pyramidalis*, also known as Miss Jessup's Upright, which is narrower and more erect and *R. o. × lavandulaceus*, which is prostrate and rather tender.

Propagation is by seed or summer cuttings but garden varieties such as *R. o. pyramidalis* will not come true from seed.

Rubus (Bramble). This is the family to which the fruit garden brambles and raspberries belong. From time to time various species have been recommended as ornamental plants for the shrubbery but a great many of them are too vigorous and straggly to be really sat-isfactory except in big gardens. Almost all are hardy and easily grown in practically any soil, and a good many can be increased readily by rooted suckers removed in the autumn or by digging up old plants and dividing them. In some cases layering is easily effected in spring or autumn. Most can be pruned hard after flowering without suffering any injury and this is one method of preventing them from occupying too much space.

Two of the most beautiful are *Rubus deliciosus*, which may attain a height of 2·4 m (8 ft) with an even greater spread, and has large, white flowers in late spring, and *R. trilobus*, which is similar but has large leaves. There is also a good hybrid between these species named Tridel. *R. cockburnianus* is much like a blackberry in habit, and has stems which look as if they had been whitewashed. *R. ulmifolius* Bellidiflorus is like a bramble in habit and has warm pink, fully double flowers. It and *R. spectabilis*, a suckering shrub with single magenta flowers, are useful for shady places.

Ruscus (Butcher's Broom). *Ruscus aculeatus* is an evergreen shrub 60-90 cm (2-3 ft) high and spreading to a considerable extent by means of suckers. In autumn it produces round, scarlet berries which persist all the winter. Flowers of different sexes are produced on dif-ferent plants so if berries are required it is necessary to select females, but include at least one male to every six or seven planted. This is one of the best shrubs for growing in densely shaded places. It is not fussy about soil and can be increased by division in spring or autumn. The stems are often cut in autumn and dyed or gilded for use as winter deco-rations.

For the shrub sometimes known as *Ruscus racemosus* see *Danaë raceriosa* (p. 263).

Salix (Willow). There are a great many kinds of willow ranging from completely pros-trate plants suitable for the rock garden to large trees which should be planted as isolated specimens if they are to be seen at their best, but there are relatively few varieties of real importance for garden decoration. By far the most popular is the familiar golden weeping willow, which has been listed under many names including *S. alba* Tristis but is now *S.* × *sepulchralis* Chrysocoma. This magnificent tree will eventually reach a height of 24 m (80 ft) with a similar branch spread. It is one of the most graceful of weeping trees with long, whip-like branchlets which touch the ground. It is at its best in the spring when the young leaves are a particularly tender shade of yellowish green and the young wood is also yellow. This is a tree for moist soils and one which is undoubtedly seen to best advantage by the pool or stream side though it will often thrive far removed from water. It is attrac-tive planted as a specimen provided it has sufficient room.

Salix alba, the white willow, with grey-green leaves and green young branches, does not weep but thrives in similar places. *S. a. vitellina* and *S. a.* Britzensis, are varieties of the white willow with respectively orange-yellow and bright red bark on the young stems. Though also trees of considerable size if left to their own devices, they are often cut back so severely each year that they never exceed the dimensions of a large shrub. The object of this severe pruning is to get the maximum annual development of young shoots or osiers to provide decorative bark in winter. *S. babylonica pekinensis* Tortuosa is a tree of medium size, 9-12 m (30-40 ft) high, with narrow, soft green leaves and curiously twisted branches.

Smaller kinds are *Salix fargesii*, a shrub to 2·4 m (8 ft) high with reddish brown stems and winter buds and grey catkins; *S. herbacea*, quite prostrate; *S. hastata* Wehrhahnii to 1·8 m (6 ft) high with silvery grey catkins becoming yellow if male; *S. lanata* to 90 cm (3 ft) with grey silky young leaves and yellow catkins; and *S. purpurea* to 3 m (10 ft) with purple young stems becoming yellow or olive-green with age. Pendula has hanging stems and makes a small weeping tree if grafted on an erect willow stem.

All willows can be interested by summer or autumn cuttings. The hard pruning of those willows grown for bark effects should be carried out in early spring and may be practically to ground level. Other willows need no regular pruning.

Sambucus (Elder). The common elder, *Sambucus nigra*, though a handsome hedgerow shrub with its flat clusters of white flowers in early summer followed by black berries, is not sufficiently choice for inclusion in the garden, but it has a golden-leaved form, Aurea, which is among the best of the variegated shrubs. It is similar in habit to the common form, deciduous, 3 m (10 ft) high and rather more in spread, and it thrives in most soils and places including those that are moist and shady. It is actually improved by rather hard pruning each spring which increases the size of the leaves and keeps the shrub a moderate height. There is also a variety named *S. n. laciniata* in which the leaves are the normal green but deeply and handsomely cut. It will thrive under similar conditions. The American elder, *S. canadensis*, has very large flat heads of small white flowers in the first half of summer, which are up to 45 cm (18 in) across in *S. c.* Maxima. There is also a golden-leaved variety. *S. racemosa* grows to 3 m (10 ft) and has two striking varieties, Tenuifolia with very fine divided leaves, and Plumosa Aurea deeply divided yellow leaves. All these elders can be increased by cuttings of fully ripened shoots taken in the autumn and rooted out of doors; the species, but not the garden varieties, can also be increased by seed.

Santolina (Lavender Cotton). The lavender cottons are only half shrubby and are as frequently seen in the herbaceous border as in the shrubbery. The best is *Santolina chamaecyparissus*, also known as *S. incana*, a grey-leaved bush usually under 60 cm (2 ft) in height but spreading to as much as 90 cm (3 ft). It is worth growing for its foliage alone but also has considerable beauty when covered in mid-summer with its globular, golden-yellow flowers rather like daisies without the ray petals. It likes well-drained, even poorish soils and sunny places and can be trimmed in early spring if it becomes straggly. *S. rosmarinifolia* has bright green leaves and lighter yellow flowers, particularly in variety Primrose Gem. *S. pinnata* closely resembles *S. chamaecyparissus* but has much lighter yellow flowers, particularly in varieties Sulphurea and Edward Bowles. Propagation is by summer or autumn cuttings.

Schizophragma. *Schizophragma hydrangeoides* is an interesting climbing plant with flattish heads of small greenish flowers on each branch of the cluster with one conspicuous creamy-white bract. The bracts are at their best in mid-summer. The white bracts of *S. integrifolium* are even larger, up to 8·7 cm (3½ in) long. These are plants which cling by means of aerial roots like those of any ivy and in a congenial position will reach a considerable height. Plant it in good, rich, rather moist soil and a sheltered position where it can climb up a wall or tree trunk and then leave alone. It can be increased by seed, summer cuttings or by layering, which is the quickest method of obtaining a good sized specimen.

Sciadopitys (Umbrella Pine). The only species grown, *Sciadopitys verticillata* is a particularly interesting and beautiful evergreen cone-bearing tree. It is perfectly hardy, slow growing and unlikely to exceed 6 m (20 ft) in height in this country though in its native Japan it reaches 30 m (100 ft). The habit is pyramidal and compact. Plant in lime-free soil similar to that in which rhododendrons would thrive. Increase by seed or by summer or early autumn cuttings either in a propagating frame or under mist with bottom heat.

Senecio. See **Brachyglottis** (p. 250).

Sequoia (Redwood). The evergreen coniferous tree *Sequoia sempervirens* is closely related to the wellingtonia (sequoiadendron) and requires similar treatment. It rivals or even exceeds the wellingtonia in height and has a very handsome trunk with reddish-brown bark.

Sequoiadendron (Wellingtonia, Giant Sequoia). *Sequoiadendron giganteum* is one of the largest trees in the world, an evergreen conifer of which specimens over 90 m (300 ft) in height have been reported in California. Even in less congenial climates this tree will grow over 42 m (140 ft), making a very shapely Pyramid 9-12 m (30-40 ft) in width. It is rather tender when young but quite hardy later. It likes rich, loamy and rather moist but not badly drained soils and is best planted as an individual specimen with plenty of room so that its full beauty can be displayed. No pruning should be attempted at any time. Propagation is by seed.

Service Tree. See **Sorbus** (p. 317).

Siphonosmanthus. See **Osmanthus** (p. 285).

Skimmia. Small evergreen shrubs grown for their foliage, flowers and scarlet berries. The best known is *Skimmia japonica*, 90 cm-1·2 m (3-4 ft) high and a little more in diameter densely branched, with dark green leaves and heads of small, fragrant white flowers in mid-spring. The flowers are of two sexes and these are borne on separate bushes. Only the females produce scarlet berries and then only when pollinated from a male-flowered plant, one of which should be planted for this purpose to every five or six females. Fragrans and Rubella, the latter with distinctive red-purple buds in winter, are males, Nymans female. *S. reevesiana* is similar though seldom above half the size and with darker red berries. It has the advantage of carrying flowers of both sexes on every bush so that there is no need to plant special pollinators. Both thrive in good, rather moist soils and like partial shade. No pruning is required. Propagation is by seed, summer cuttings with bottom heat, or layers.

Solanum. The family which has given us the potato has also provided gardens with two of their loveliest, though unfortunately not their hardiest, climbers. These are *Solanum crispum*, with violet-blue flowers borne all through the summer, and *S. jasminoides* Album, which has a similarly extended season but is pure white. Of the two *S. crispum* is the hardier but also the more shrubby; an evergreen with long, flexible stems which can be allowed to make a big, loose bush in the open or can be trained against a sunny, sheltered

316

wall or fence. *S. jasminoides* will easily reach a height of 6 m (20 ft) but may be kept smaller by judicious pruning each spring. They like well-drained soils but these need not be rich. Increase by layering in spring or autumn.

Sophora. Deciduous shrubs or small trees with attractive compound leaves formed of numerous small leaflets and clusters of dangling, yellow tubular flowers in mid-spring. The flowers are unusual in shape, some of the petals larger than others and the whole capped by a bell-shaped calyx. These plants come from New Zealand and are a little tender in cooler climates. They may be trained against sheltered but sunny walls. They like fertile, well drained soil and the only pruning normally required is the removal of frost-damaged growth in mid-spring but if plants grow too large stems can be shortened or removed after flowering. Increase by seed sown in spring in a temperature of 18°C/65°F or by cuttings of firm young growths in summer in a propagator. The two best kinds are *Sophora tetratera* and *S. microphylla*, the latter with smaller leaflets and a bushier habit when young.

Sorbaria. These deciduous shrubs were formerly known as spiraea and may be found under that name in some gardens. They make big bushes spreading by suckers, the stems terminating in the second half of summer in large plumes of creamy-white flowers. Good kinds are *Sorbaria sorbifolia*, to 1·8 m (6 ft), *S. tomentosa*, to 3 m (10 ft) high, and *S. kirilowii*, to 4·5 m (15 ft).

All can be pruned practically to ground level in early spring which will restrict their height and increase the size of their handsome divided leaves and flower plumes. They are easily grown in any reasonably good soil and sunny or partially shaded place and can be increased by seed, summer or autumn cuttings, root cuttings or by digging up rooted suckers in the autumn.

Sorbus (Mountain Ash, Rowan, Service Tree, Whitebeam). These are all deciduous trees and the popular names distinguish quite distinctive groups. The common mountain ash or rowan, *Sorbus aucuparia*, has compound leaves, clusters of small white flowers in late spring/early summer, followed by scarlet berries in autumn. It makes a neat tree to 18 m (60 ft) and 9 m (30 ft) in spread. There are numerous varieties, one, named Fastigiata, narrowly erect, another named Xanthocarpa with orange-yellow berries. *S. hupehensis* and *S. vilmorinii* are Chinese mountain ashes, with smaller leaves and fruits which are white or pink flushed in the former and pink becoming white in the latter. They are not eaten by birds quite so soon as the berries of *S. aucuparia*, nor are the amber-yellow berries of *S.* Joseph Rock.

S. scopulina resembles the mountain ash but has stouter, more erect stems and large orange-red berries. *S.* Embley, sometimes called *S. discolor*, also closely resembling *S. aucuparia*, is notable for its brilliant coppery-red autumn foliage colour. *S. essertauana* makes a more open branched tree with either red or orange-yellow berries. *S. sargentiana* has larger leaves than other rowans and colours richly in autumn. Its red berries are small but carried in large clusters.

The service tree, *S. domestica*, resembles *S. aucuparia* but is larger and has less decorative reddish-brown pear or apple-shaped fruits. The whitebeam, *S. aria*, is grown primarily for its foliage, the oval leaves being bright green above and white below. It makes a shapely rounded tree to 15 m (50 ft) high, and it has numerous varieties, some, such as Lutescens, with the upper surface of the leaf yellow or creamy-white and one, named Pendula that is weeping. *S. intermedia*, the Swedish whitebeam, often planted as a street tree, has deeply lobed leaves, grey beneath, and clusters of bright red fruits.

All are hardy and easily grown in a wide variety of soils, including those that are chalky. If they become too large they can be thinned in autumn or winter. Propagation of the species is by seed and of selected varieties by grafting on to seedlings, usually of *S. aucuparia.*

Southernwood. See **Artemisia** (p. 247).

Spartium (Spanish Broom). The only species, *Spartium junceum*, is a quick-growing shrub soon reaching a height of 3 m (10 ft) or thereabouts with a somewhat smaller spread and a rather loose, leggy habit. It makes ample amends for this fault by producing from mid-summer to early autumn innumerable spikes of bright yellow, pea-type flowers which have a very pleasant fragrance. It is one of the few shrubs well worth planting especially for cutting and it also makes a good display in the shrub border. The shoots are bright green which gives the shrub an evergreen appearance though in fact it is deciduous and has very few leaves at any time of the year. It thrives in light soils and sunny places and can be readily raised from seed sown in spring. It is wise to grow the seedlings on singly in pots until they are planted out as they resent root disturbance. It can be pruned moderately in mid-spring but not into hard wood.

Spiraea. These are deciduous shrubs, hardy and easily grown in a variety of soils and situations. From both the cultural and decorative points of view they may conveniently be considered in two groups, one composed of early-flowering kinds and the others of those that flower in summer. Of the first group excellent examples are *Spiraea* Arguta, sometimes called foam of May, 1·3 m (4½ ft), with small white flowers all along the thin, arching twigs in the second half of spring; *S. thunbergii*, which is very similar but a little earlier; *S. prunifolia* Plena, the bridal wreath, 1·8 m (6 ft) with clusters of double white flowers in the second half of spring; and *S.* × *vanhouttei*, 2·4-3 ft (8-10 ft) with small clusters of white flowers all along the arching stems in early summer. All these may with advantage be thinned out annually immediately after flowering, some of the older branches being cut out to make room for younger wood.

The later flowering group includes *S. douglasii*, *S.* × *billiardii* Triumphans and *S. salicifolia*, all of which make thickets of long, erect shoots, terminated about mid-summer by short, fluffy-looking spikes of pink flowers. They average 1·8 m (6 ft) in height and spread indefinitely. They can be increased by division in autumn as they produce a lot of suckers. Little pruning is needed though stems can be cut down in early spring.

S. japonica is one of the smallest of the late-flowering group, seldom above 1·5 m (5 ft) and often less. The flowers are produced all summer in flattish heads, rosy red in the type but a really brilliant carmine in the fine variety Anthony Waterer which has some leaves creamy white. Other varieties are Bullata, dwarf with small puckered leaves, Little Princess, also dwarf, and Goldflame with young leaves coppery yellow. Fairly severe spring thinning of old wood is desirable to keep these shrubs in full vigour.

Where suckers are not available propagation is by summer or autumn cuttings.

Spruce. See **Picea** (p. 288).

Stachyurus. These are deciduous shrubs with slender trails of pale greenish-yellow flowers in the first half of spring. There are two very similar kinds. *Stachyurus chinensis* and *S. praecox*, both 2·4-2·9 m (8-10 ft) high. Both are easily grown in reasonably well-drained soils in sun or half-shade and can be increased by seed or cuttings. No regular pruning is required but stems can be thinned or shortened after flowering.

Stewertia. This is sometimes spelled Stuartia. They are deciduous shrubs or small trees grown for their white flowers in the second half of summer and their brilliant yellow and red foliage colour in autumn. All like reasonably good, lime-free soil and require no regular pruning. Good kinds are *Stuartia malacodendron*, 3·3 m (11 ft), and *S. pseudocamellia*, which under favourable conditions may reach 15 m (50 ft) but is usually only half this height. All can be increased by seed, summer cuttings or layers.

Stranvaesia. Evergreen shrubs or small trees grown for their handsome shining leaves, clusters of white flowers in the first half of summer followed by scarlet berries. *Stranvaesia davidiana* is the kind usually grown. It will eventually reach a height of 6 m (20 ft) and some of the large laurel-like leaves turn scarlet in the autumn. It will grow in any reasonably good soil in sun or partial shade and needs no regular pruning. Propagation is by seed or summer cuttings.

Styrax (Snowbell). Deciduous shrubs or small trees grown for their trails of white flowers in the first half of summer. They require similar conditions to Stewertia. Good kinds are *Styrax hemsleyana*, to 6 m (20 ft); *S. japonica* to 7·5 m (25 ft); and *S. obassia* 9 m (30 ft). The flowers of the last two are fragrant. Propagation is by layers, by summer cuttings in a propagator or by seeds, but these need to be placed as soon as ripe in moist peat or sand and a temperature of 20-30°C/68-86°F for five months followed by three months at 4°C/40°F before being sown.

Symphoricarpos (Snowberry). The common snowberry, *Symphoricarpos albus*, is a branching, very twiggy, deciduous shrub well worth growing for its abundant crops of pure white berries in autumn. It has the added merit that it will grow practically anywhere, in sun or shade, good soil or poor, and needs no attention. It makes quite a good hedge, especially if mixed with something of stiffer habit such as hawthorn or myrobalan plum. It reaches a height of 2·5 m (8½ ft) and spreads indefinitely by suckers, which also provide a ready means of increase.

S. orbiculatus, the coral berry or Indian currant, is so called because the berries are rosy red. It will grow from 90 cm-2·7 m (3-7 ft) high but only producing good crops of berries in a warm, sunny place. There are also some good hybrids known as the Doorenbos Hybrids, up to 1·8 m (6 ft) high with variously coloured berries, white in *S. × doorenbossi* White Hedge, pink and white in *S. d.* Mother of Pearl and lilac-pink in Erect.

Syringa (Lilac). *Syringa* is the correct botanical name of the lilacs. In gardens it is often applied to the philadelphus, but this is entirely incorrect, the popular name of this genus being mock orange.

The garden lilacs are all deciduous shrubs or small trees. The most important are *Syringa vulgaris*, the common lilac, and its numerous varieties, many of which have been given garden names. There are single and double-flowered forms and the colour range is from white and palest mauve to a rich wine red. A few outstanding varieties are Mme Lemoine, double white; Congo, single, reddish purple; Souvenir de Louis Späth, single, deep purple; Katherine Havemeyer, double, deep mauve; Maud Notcutt, single, white; Charles X, single, purplish red; President Grévy, double, bluish lilac; Michel Buchner, double, pinkish lilac and Primrose, single, pale yellow. All make fine shrubs 4·5 m (15 ft) or so in height and about 3·6 m (12 ft) in diameter. All succeed best in rather good, loamy soils and open positions.

These choice garden lilacs are often propagated by nurserymen by grafting or budding, sometimes on to common lilac and occasionally on to privet. In either case suckers, which are generally produced freely, must be removed as they will not have the same character as the rest of the bush. For this reason it is better to increase by layering in spring or autumn, or, in the case of bushes already on their own roots, by detaching suckers with roots in autumn.

Syringa × persica, the Persian lilac, makes a graceful shrub 1·9 m (6½ ft) high and of equal spread with fragrant, lilac or white flowers in small sprays in mid-spring.

Hybrids between this and *S. vulgaris* are called *S. × chinensis* or the Rouen lilac. They grow about 3 m (10 ft) high and have drooping trusses of white, lilac-pink, lilac-red or lavender scented flowers in mid-spring. *S. microphylla* is 1·2-1·8 m (4-6 ft) high with small leaves and little trusses of lilac-purple scented flowers in early summer.

Two other species, *S. josikaea*, with slightly scented lilac flowers, and *S. reflexa*, with drooping scentless purplish pink flowers, have been crossed to produce a race of Canadian hybrids known as *S. × josiflexa*. These differ from the common lilacs in having looser and more lightly formed flower clusters. Colours are mainly in shades of mauve, one of the best being Bellicent with reddish-purple scented flowers.

None of these lilacs requires regular pruning except for the removal of faded flower heads in the case of single-flowered varieties, but occasional removal of some of the oldest wood will stimulate vigour.

Tamarix (Tamarisk). These deciduous shrubs or small trees all have a loose, branching habit and feathery leaves which give them a most graceful appearance. One of the best is *T. ramosissima* which will eventually reach a height of 3·6 m (12 ft) if allowed to but can be kept very much smaller by hard annual pruning. The flowers are small, pink and carried along all the upper shoots so that a large specimen has somewhat the appearance of a very fine astilbe. It is at its best in late summer/early autumn. *T. parviflora* , sometimes confused with *T. tetrandra*, is rather similar in appearance but flowers in mid-spring. It can also be kept much below its full size by hard annual pruning but the work must be done immediately after flowering. *T. gallica*, sometimes called *T. anglica*, is up to 3 m (10 ft) high with pink flowers in late summer and early autumn. It does very well by the sea and is often planted in seaside gardens to form a windbreak. It can be hard pruned in early spring if desired.

All will grow in most reasonably well-drained soils but dislike chalk. They can be increased by cuttings in autumn, struck out of doors in sandy soil.

Taxodium (Swamp Cypress, Deciduous Cypress). *Taxodium distichum* is one of the few deciduous cone-bearing trees and is also one of the few that will thrive in very wet places even with its roots completely covered by several centimetres of water. It has feathery foliage and makes a shapely, pyramidal tree occasionally over 30 m (100 ft) in height. The young leaves are light green, becoming darker with age, and turn cinnamon red before they fall in the autumn. Seed sown in pans of moist peat in spring provides the best method of propagation but cuttings can be rooted in a frame in mid-autumn.

Taxus (Yew). The common yew, one of the most famous of British evergreen trees, is *Taxus baccata*. Left to grow unchecked it will make a broadly pyramidal tree up to 12 m (40 ft) in height and more in spread. It bears pruning well, however, and for this reason and also because of its dense, dark green growth it is used as a hedge plant and for topiary. There are numerous varieties, some dwarf; the Irish yew (Fastigiata) erect and column-like; Semperaurea with yellow leaves. There is also a golden Irish yew, columnar and yellow, and a smaller, narrower yellow variety named Standishii.

All thrive in most soils and do particularly well on rich loams overlying chalk. They are rather slow growing, though not so slow as some people imagine. Hard pruning is best confined to mid-spring but yews can be lightly pruned at any time during the summer.

The common yew can be raised from seed sown out of doors in spring but selected forms will not breed true in this way and must be increased by summer or autumn cuttings.

Tecoma. See **Campsis** (p. 252).

Teucrium (Shrubby Germander). *Teucrium fruticans* is an evergreen shrub 1 m (3½ ft) high and rather spreading in habit, with grey leaves and lavender-blue flowers in summer. It is not very hardy and should have a warm, sunny position in well-drained soil. *T. chamaedrys* is a much smaller plant, only 15-20 cm (6-9 in) high but spreading, with small aromatic leaves and spikes of purplish pink flowers in early autumn. It is only partly woody. Both kinds can be increased by seed or by summer cuttings.

Thuja (Arbor-vitae, White Cedar, Western Red Cedar). A genus of cone-bearing trees with many similarities to chamaecyparis. Two of the most popular species, *Thuja occidentalis*, the white cedar, and *T. plicata*, the western red cedar, are frequently used as hedge or screen plants in the same way as *Chamaecyparis lawsoniana*. The first named is a little apt to get thin and the foliage sometimes turns a bad colour in winter, but *T. plicata* makes a first-rate windbreak or large hedge and has fine, dark green foliage. Left to grow unpruned these thujas will make pyramidal trees to 18 m (60 ft) high in the case of *T. occidentalis*, more than twice as much in the case of *T. plicata*. *T. orientalis*, the Chinese arbor-vitae, will also reach 18 m (60 ft). There are numerous varieties of all three species, some dwarf and slow growing, some variegated. Rheingold is a slow-growing, bronzy-yellow, dwarf variety of *T. occidentalis* which will reach 1·8 m (6 ft) in height.

The species can be raised from seed but varieties are increased by grafting in spring on to seedlings of the type species, or by summer or early autumn cuttings in a propagator.

Thujopsis. An evergreen coniferous tree, *Thujopsis dolabrata* reaches 15 m (50 ft) high but is more often seen in gardens as a handsome shrub 4·5-6 m (15-20 ft) tall. The foliage is dark, shining green above, silvery beneath. It will thrive in most soils and likes a fair amount of moisture though it should not be planted in damp hollows likely to be frost pockets. In other respects culture is identical with that of thuja.

Tilia (Lime). The limes are all large, deciduous trees, more suitable for parks and wood-lands than for garden planting. The common lime, *Tilia × europaea* will reach a height of 30 m (100 ft) or even more and a spread of 15 m (50 ft). The greenish flowers, produced with great freedom in mid-summer have a sweet fragrance and are much sought after by bees. They are also often severely attacked by greenflies. A better ornamental tree is *T. × euchlora* which seldom exceeds 18 m (60 ft) in height and is not subject to greenfly attack. The pendent white lime, Petiolaris, is also very attractive because of the whitish under-surface of the leaves and drooping branches but it will reach 24 m (80 ft). The large-leaved lime, *T. platyphyllos*, another big tree, has several varieties including Rubra, the red-twigged lime, a great favourite for pleaching.

All these limes will thrive in any ordinary soil. The species are increased by seed, the varieties by grafting on seedlings of the species from which they are derived.

Trachycarpus (Chusan Palm). *Trachycarpus fortunei* is the hardiest palm tree and quite suitable for planting out of doors in mild regions. It makes a stout trunk to 7·5 m (25 ft) or more in height surmounted by a head of large, fan-like leaves. It is not fussy about soil, prefers sunny places and is easily raised from seed, though seedlings grow slowly at first.

Tsuga (Hemlock Spruce). Large evergreen coniferous trees with shining dark green leaves like those of a yew. *Tsuga canadensis*, the eastern hemlock, will reach 30 m (100 ft) and likes most soils including those that are chalky. It has a weeping variety, Pendula, which is unlikely to exceed 1·8 m (6 ft) in height, though it may grow twice as wide. *T. heterophylla*, the western hemlock, is even larger than *T. canadensis*, similar in leaf but more regularly conical in habit. It is not suitable for chalk soils. All will grow in sun or shade and can be increased by seed.

Tulip Tree. See **Liriodendron** (p. 281).

Ulex (Gorse). The common gorse, though beautiful, is too common to be worth planting in gardens but its double-flowered form, *Ulex europaeus* Flore Pleno, is a very different proposition. When in full bloom in late spring no shrub is capable of making a more solid splash of golden colour. It will thrive in poor, sandy soils and dry places and makes a rounded, densely spiny bush 1·3 m (4½ ft) high and rather more in diameter. It is apt to die out without warning particularly in rich or damp soils and, as it sets no seeds, it must be increased by summer cuttings. No pruning is required but it can be clipped in mid-spring to keep it tidy or create a hedge.

Ulmus (Elm). In general the elms are too big and they send out hungry roots too far to make good garden trees. However, some exception may be made in the case of the weep-ing varieties of the wych elm, *Ulmus glabra* Camperdownii and Pendula, which make handsome specimens on a lawn, and seldom exceed a height and spread of 6 m (20 ft). *U. stricta*, the Cornish elm, is erect in habit and will reach a height of 18-21 m (60-70 ft) with a spread of little more than 6 m (20 ft) and its variety *U. s. wheatleyi*, the Guernsey or Jersey elm, is even narrower. All elms like rather rich, loamy soils. No pruning is required. Propagation of species is by seed and of varieties by grafting on to seedlings of related species. Dutch elm disease attacks all these species, so it is unwise to plant where this disease is epidemic.

Viburnum. Evergreen and deciduous shrubs are included in this genus and several species are notable for the perfume of their flowers. Of these one of the best is *Viburnum carlesii* which makes a well-branched bush about 1·5 m (5 ft) high and in spread, bearing dome-shaped heads of white, pink-tinted flowers in early spring. It is deciduous and rea-sonably hardy. *V. utile* is a little like this but evergreen, flowering in mid-spring and devoid of perfume. *V. × burkwoodii*, a hybrid between the two, combines many of their good points, having the fragrance and earliness of the one and the evergreen character of the other. Another fine hybrid with *V. carlesii* as one parent is *V. × carlcephalum*. It is deciduous, grows to 2·4 m (8 ft) high and has large heads of fragrant white flowers in mid-spring.

V. opulus is the guelder rose of British hedgerows, a pretty shrub with flattish heads of white flowers followed by currant-red berries. For the garden a better shrub is the variety of this known as Sterile or popularly as the snowball tree because of its large, globular heads of white flowers. These are at their best in early summer. The guelder rose and snowball tree both make big shrubs 3-3·6 m (10-12 ft) high and of equal spread, but there is also a dwarf variety of guelder rose named Compactum which is only 1·8 m (6 ft).

V. plicatum is deciduous and has small 'snowball' heads of white flowers. It is some-times known as the Japanese snowball and is a very beautiful shrub. A variety named *V. p. tomentosum* has flat clusters of white flowers carried on nearly horizontal branches. Both are at their peak in early summer and have a rather open habit, make bushes up to 3 m (10 ft) in height and diameter and flower in late spring/early summer.

V. farreri, sometimes known as *V. fragrans*, and *V. grandiflorum* both flower from mid-autumn to mid-spring, the first having clusters of pale pink flowers, the second deeper pink and larger blossom. *V. × bodnantense* is a hybrid between them intermediate in character. All will reach 3 m (10 ft).

An old favourite is *V. tinus*, more familiar as laurustinus. It is evergreen, dense in habit, 2·8 m (9½ ft) high and of equal spread with dark green leaves and flattish flower heads which are pink in bud, white when open. The laurustinus is often in bloom by mid-autumn and continues until mid-spring. It is quite hardy.

V. rhytidophyllum is also 3 m (10 ft) high with large, handsome evergreen leaves dark green and wrinkled. The big, flat, flower heads in early summer are rather a dingy white and are followed by red berries which later turn black. *V. davidii* is only 76 cm (2½ ft) high but may be 1·5 m (5 ft) across. It has leathery dark green leaves with strongly marked veins, abundant clusters of white flowers in early summer followed by turquoise-blue berries, provided both male and female bushes are planted.

All these viburnums grow well in ordinary soils. No pruning is essential but the laurustinus can be trimmed or cut back after flowering and may be used as a hedge or screen. Propagation is by seed for species or by summer or autumn cuttings or layers.

Some kinds, notably *V. farreri*, layer themselves and rapidly increase in spread by this means.

Vinca (Periwinkle). Evergreen trailing shrubs which make excellent ground cover and will grow in almost all soils, in sun or shade. *Vinca major* is the strongest growing kind with quite large blue flowers all spring. There is a variety with cream variegated leaves. *V. minor* has smaller leaves and flowers and does not spread so far or so rapidly. Typically blue flowered, it has several varieties including white and plum-purple kinds and some with double flowers as well as both white and yellow leaf variegation. All can be increased by division, layering or cuttings and usually spread widely by layering themselves wherever their long stems touch the ground.

Virginia Creeper. See **Parthenocissus** (p. 286).

Vitis (Vine). These are all deciduous climbers, mostly clinging by means of tendrils. The grape vine itself is *Vitis vinifera* of which several varieties are suitable for planting for ornament. Among the best are Brant with small, purplish-black grapes and leaves that turn crimson and orange in autumn, and Purpurea which has reddish-purple leaves. *V. coignetiae* is a very strong-growing Japanese vine with large, rounded leaves which colour brilliantly in the autumn. All will grow in any reasonably good soil including that of a chalky character. They require the support of trellis, wires or poles or may be allowed to scramble over sheds and outhouses or into trees but they cannot cling unaided to walls like some of the closely allied Virginia creepers (see parthenocissus). All can be pruned in winter as necessary to keep them within bounds or the tips of shoots that are extending too far can be pinched out in spring or summer. They can be increased by autumn cuttings or 'eyes' (see p. 670) or by layering.

Walnut. See **Juglans** (p. 277).

Weigela. These are beautiful, deciduous shrubs with bell-shaped flowers very freely produced. The two best are *Weigela florida*, 1·9 m (6½ ft) high and a little more in diameter, with arching branches and deep rose flowers in late spring/early summer, and *W. floribunda*, which is similar in height but more erect in habit and with deeper, reddish blooms in early summer. There are numerous good garden varieties ranging in colour from white to ruby red and also a form of *W. florida* named *W. f.* Variegata with attractive cream-edged leaves.

   All thrive in ordinary soils and open positions. If desired, flowering branches can be cut back as far as non-flowering side shoots immediately the blooms fade. Increase by cuttings in summer or autumn.

Whitebeam. See **Sorbus** (p. 317).

Winter Sweet. See **Chimonanthus** (p. 256).

Wisteria. These are vigorous twining plants which require plenty of room if they are to do themselves full justice. The most popular species is *Wisteria sinensis* with 27 cm (11 in) trails of lilac-blue flowers and there is also a good white-flowered form and a double-flowered blue purple variety named Black Dragon. *W. floribunda* is rather similar in its common form but it has produced a number of good varieties of which one, Multijuga, or sometimes Macrobotrys, has the longest flower trails of any wisteria; they are occasionally 90 cm (3 ft) in length. Other varieties are Alba, with white flowers, Rosea, with pink flowers, and Violacea Plena, with double violet-blue flowers. Less well known is *W. venusta* with white flowers. All flower in late spring/early summer.

All these wisterias thrive in any ordinary soil and like a sunny position. The finest flowers are obtained by allowing the plants to produce a number of strong growths and then shortening all subsequent side growth in two operations, first to a length of five leaves each in mid-summer and later to two dormant growth buds in mid-autumn. Alternatively this pruning can be started quite early in the life of the plant so that it is shaped into a wide-spreading bush or even a standard instead of being allowed to climb. *W. floribunda* or one of its varieties is best for this purpose. Propagation is usually by layers. Seeds will germinate in a frame or greenhouse in spring but only the species come true from seed; seedlings also vary greatly in their freedom of flowering.

Witch Hazel. See **Hamamelis** (p. 272).

Yew. See **Taxus** (p. 321).

Yucca (Adam's Needle). These plants give a very tropical look to the garden with their large rosettes of stiff sword-shaped leaves and tall spikes of showy, cream-coloured flowers. *Yucca gloriosa* will make an almost tree-like specimen 2·4-3·3 m (8-10 ft) high with a trunk and branches. Most kinds, however, have quite a short main stem and do not exceed 1·2 m (4 ft) in height except when in flower. One of the smallest and most attractive is *Y. filamentosa*, so called because of the thread-like filaments which are attached to the leaves. *Y. flaccida* is similar. All flower in the second half of summer. They will grow in ordinary or even in poor, sandy soils, are first-rate seaside shrubs and require no pruning. They can be increased by seed which should be germinated in a warm greenhouse in spring, also by offsets detached in autumn or spring, or by root cuttings in a warm propagator in mid-spring.

Zenobia. *Zenobia pulverulenta* is a beautiful, peat-loving shrub belonging to the heather family. It grows 1·2 m (4 ft) or so high and rather more in spread, has greyish, evergreen leaves and clusters of pendent, white, scented bell-shaped flowers in the first half of summer. No pruning is necessary. A semi-shaded position is most favourable. Propagate by seed, layers or summer cuttings.

Chapter 11

Roses

The rose has been very highly developed, probably more so than any other flower. At the same time many of the original species have been retained in cultivation with the result that a great number of totally different types are available for the adornment of our gardens.

Types and Races. The species are themselves very numerous. By no means all are of value in the garden but a number of them have some decorative merit. Many are grown principally for their flowers, such as *Rosa spinosissima, R. hugonis* and *R. × alba*. Others are grown mainly for their foliage, for example *R. willmottiae* and *R. rubrifolia*; yet others for their fruits or hips, such as *R. moyesii, R. setipoda* and *R. pomifera*. There is even one astonishing rose, *R. sericea pteracantha* which is grown for its translucent thorns.

Most of these species make informal bushes but some, such as *R. filipes, R. longicuspis* and *R. multiflora*, are vigorous climbers which can be grown up into trees or trained over large screens and pergolas. Their flowers are almost always single though they vary in every other conceivable manner and have a most extensive range of colour, size and form. The place of the bushy kinds is the shrub border rather than the formal rose garden but they may sometimes be used there effectively as a surround or hedge.

It is to the hybrid roses which have been built up by crossing certain of the species that the gardener must turn for his finest material. Six groups may be distinguished as being of particular value for garden display. They are known as Large-Flowered or Hybrid Tea, Cluster-Flowered or Floribunda, Shrub, Old Garden, Climber, and Miniature, and though they are not always sharply defined, one tending to merge into another, each has its own characteristics.

Large-Flowered roses have the finest flowers, shapely, usually double, often with a high-pointed centre to the bloom. Flowers are carried singly or in small clusters on the stems and are produced successively from mid-summer to mid-autumn. Plants are moderately bushy but with a marked tendency to renew themselves by strong young stems.

Cluster-Flowered roses have smaller flowers produced in larger clusters. Some are single, some semi-double and some fully double. There is also great variation in the form of the flowers, which may be comparatively flat or loosely formed or like rosettes or shapely and high centred like the Large-Flowered varieties. Plants are generally bushy and freely branched and flowers are produced successively from mid-summer to mid-autumn.

Shrub roses have many of the characteristics of Cluster-Flowered roses but make larger, even more freely branched plants. Some varieties flower successively but others flower only once, usually in early or mid-summer.

Old Garden roses may be broadly described as those raised before the Hybrid Tea roses were developed in the last quarter of the 19th century. Most of them flower only once each year in early or mid-summer and they are very varied in habit and flower shape. Some have large, globular, fully double flowers. Others are fully double but cup shaped, flat topped or quartered. Moss roses have a moss-like outgrowth on the flower stems and the green calyx segments which surround the flower bud. Many of these Old Garden roses are very sweetly scented. Many make good bushes like shrub roses and can be used in the garden in the same way but some have poor, lanky or weak growth and need good cultivation if they are to prove satisfactory.

Climbers are of many different types, the one common factor being that they make long, more or less flexible stems which can be trained against walls, fences, over pergolas and screens, or up pillars. They have no means of clinging other than thrusting their thorny stems through the branches of other shrubs or trees so they must usually be tied to suitable supports. Some climbers have flowers of the Large-Flowered type, some more nearly resemble Cluster-Flowered or Shrub varieties in bloom. Many modern varieties flower successionally from mid-summer to mid-autumn but some flower once only and this is particularly true of the ramblers which have small to medium-sized flowers in large clusters. Ramblers are climbers with very flexible stems which can be allowed to sprawl or even hang downwards if wished.

Miniature roses are under 45 cm (1½ ft) in height and have small flowers, often of a rosette type and borne in clusters successionally from mid-summer to mid-autumn.

Besides being grown as bushes, Large-Flowered and Cluster-Flowered roses may also be grown as standards or half standards by budding them on to a stock grown as a straight stem anything from about 60 cm-1·2 m (2-4 ft) in height. By this means miniature trees are produced with a bare trunk or main stem and a head of branches on top. Standards and half standards may be planted among bush roses to give a double tier of blooms or they may be used on their own to line paths, form little avenues or serve as prominent features in a design. Climbers are also sometimes budded on to strong briar stems in a similar manner to make weeping standards with branches arching over, sometimes right down to soil level.

Soil and its Preparation. Contrary to what is often stated roses can be grown successfully on many different types of soil and not only upon the heavier loams and rich clays. I have seen highly successful rose gardens close to the sea coast in places where the soil was extremely sandy. Naturally more feeding is necessary under such conditions than on soils of better quality and greater precautions must be taken in hot weather to prevent excessive drying out.

Because of their permanent nature it is necessary to prepare the ground for roses with particular thoroughness. This does not simply mean that the soil must be deeply dug and well supplied with manures or fertilizers. Preparation also involves the elimination of all deep-rooting perennial weeds such as bindweed, coltsfoot, ground elder and horsetail.

Digging should be as deep as possible but there is no point in going down into stone, chalk or other such medium which would obviously do roses no good at all. Dung, if available, should be used in the preparation of the ground but it must either be well rotted or applied a good three months before the roses are to be planted. Fresh manure used late may check root growth.

If no manure can be obtained, chopped turves make a very good substitute; in fact they can be used in addition to manure with excellent results. Turn them in, as far as possible grass side downwards, under about 25 cm (10 in) of soil. This will ensure that they rot properly and yet are near enough to the roots to feed them when they need it most.

Whether manure, turves or both are used give, in addition, coarsely ground bonemeal at 113 g per 0·8 sq m (4 oz per sq yd), forked in when the beds are finally prepared for planting.

Planting. This is best done in late autumn though it is possible to plant roses from about the middle of autumn to early spring in an average season in a mild climate. In colder regions it may be practicable to plant a little earlier and later but there is more likelihood that a prolonged break will be imposed by weather in the middle of the planting season. Roses purchased well established in containers can be planted at any time of the year provided they can be removed from the containers without damage to the roots or disturbance of the ball of soil around them.

All instructions regarding the planting of shrubs apply with equal force to roses. Several different stocks (see p. 333) are used for roses and these vary in the character of their root system. This in turn will affect the shape and size of the hole required, but if the planter takes care always to allow the roots to assume a natural position without bending and cover the uppermost with about 5 cm (2 in) of soil, he will not go far wrong. Usually when roses arrive from the nursery the soil mark can be seen quite clearly on the stem. It is wise to plant so that this soil mark is about 2·5 cm (1 in) below the surface when planting is completed. Contrary to practice with fruit trees it is an advantage if the point of union between stock and scion of bush roses can be covered with soil as this encourages

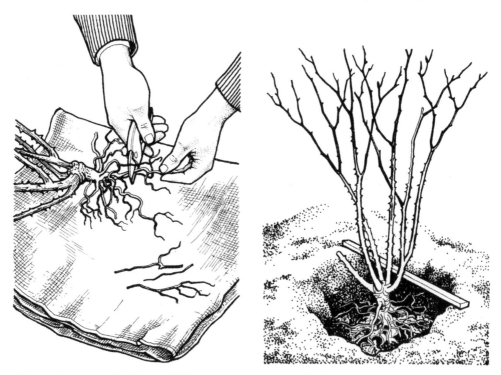

Planting a rose bush. Before planting, damaged or straggling roots should be removed. The planting hole should be wide enough for the roots to be spread out and deep enough for the union to be just covered with soil

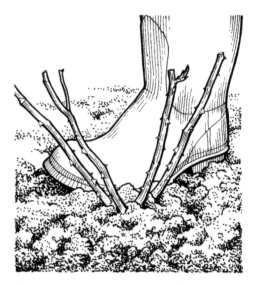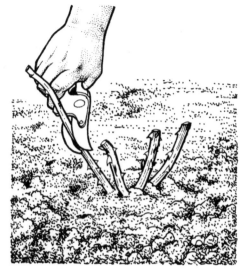

Plants should be well firmed in and given a severe initial pruning for best results. Make each cut immediately above an outward-facing bud

the good growth from the lower part of the plant upon which roses depend for their renewal.

Put three or four handfuls of moist peat with which a little bonemeal has been mixed around the roots before returning the displaced soil. Plant firmly and make certain that standards are staked at once. Climbers and ramblers should be tied to some kind of support even though most of the growth treated in this way is to be cut away within a few months. Wind rocking can do as much harm to newly planted roses as to fruits.

Pruning Newly Planted Roses. Most roses need rather severe initial pruning if they are to give the best results. The reason is that after transplanting roots take some time to recover and meanwhile the supply of sap is curtailed. If it is distributed over too many shoots, all will be starved; if it is confined to a few of the most promising, growth will be strong and will, in turn, stimulate increased root activity.

The general rule is to shorten all strong shoots of bush and standard roses to about 7·5 cm (3 in) and to eliminate weak shoots entirely. Make each cut immediately above a growth bud. These buds will be seen as small lumps on the bare stems or where leaf stalks join the stems and they are arranged spirally a few centimetres apart. Climbers, including ramblers, are treated in much the same way except that it will be sufficient to shorten strong shoots to about 30 cm (1 ft) and weaker ones to 15-20 cm (6-8 ins). The one exception to this general rule of hard pruning is made for those climbers known as climbing sports. These are only lightly tipped to get rid of shoot ends which have suffered damage from one cause or another. The reason is that climbing sports are simply very vigorous forms of bush varieties, forms which have the climbing habit fairly well ingrained but may revert to bush type once more if given any encouragement to do so. These sports always have the word 'Climbing' prefixed to their names, for example, Climbing Cécile Brunner and Climbing Golden Dawn.

All this first-year pruning is best done in early spring if roses are planted in autumn or

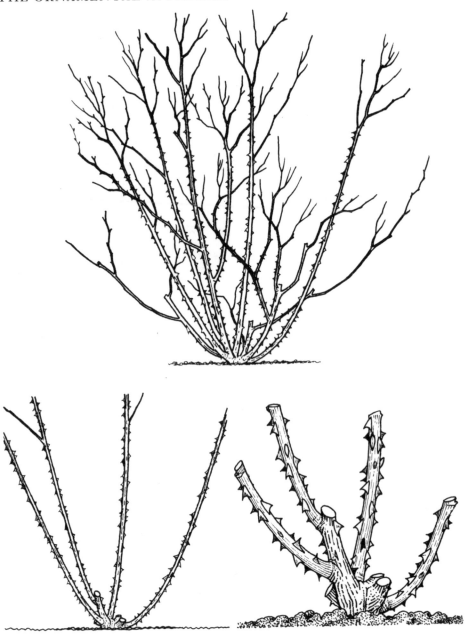

Pruning an established rose. Dead, diseased or damaged stems are first cut out, then as much as possible of the old wood that is not carrying good new stems. Species and miniature roses will require no further attention, but the stems of other types should be further shortened, moderately if the roses are for garden display, more severely if large flowers are desired

winter or even in early spring. Container-grown roses planted in the summer need not be pruned before the following winter or early spring.

Pruning Established Roses. Roses bear their flowers on young stems produced the same season and the best of these stems will grow from branches that are themselves no more than a year or two old. So pruning, especially of the highly developed Large-Flowered and Cluster-Flowered types, is mainly intended to dispose of useless old growth and encourage the production of strong new growth. Once roses are established pruning can be done any time between late autumn and early spring though in cold districts it may be better to leave it until the latter when it can be seen what growth has been killed or damaged by wet, frost and disease during the winter.

Always start by cutting out any stems that are dead, diseased or damaged. Follow this by cutting out as much as possible of the old wood that is not carrying good new stems. Old wood can be distinguished by its darker, tougher and rougher bark.

When this work has been completed the roses will probably look a good deal thinner and less complicated, and in the case of species and miniatures this is usually all that need be done. Other types will require some shortening of the remaining stems much as they were shortened after planting, but not necessarily so severely. How much they are cut back will depend partly on the variety of rose, partly on the purpose for which it is required and partly on the way it has behaved the previous year.

A good general rule to remember is that the harder a stem is cut back the stronger is the new growth. So naturally vigorous roses need not be pruned quite so hard as naturally weak roses. A second result of hard pruning is that it tends to restrict the number of flowers produced but to increase their size. So when individual size is important, as it may be if roses are being grown for show, pruning can be rather more severe than when the roses are being grown solely for maximum display in the garden.

Finally, if a rose is growing badly and failing to make satisfactory new growth it will be necessary to prune it harder than another of the same variety which is growing well.

To reduce all this to some kind of rule of thumb, three grades of pruning may be distinguished: hard, medium and light. Hard pruning is most likely to be necessary for Large-Flowered roses, especially when grown primarily for fine blooms. Medium pruning may be applied to Large-Flowered roses required primarily for garden display and also for most Large-Flowered and some Climbers and Old Garden roses. Light pruning will be used mainly for vigorous Cluster-Flowered roses and Climbing roses and for Shrub roses.

For hard pruning shorten every strong growth to about one third its length and cut back weaker stems to 6·2 cm (2½ in).

For medium pruning shorten every strong growth to half its length and shorten weaker stems to 8·7 cm (3½ in).

For light pruning shorten every strong growth to two thirds its length and weaker stems to a half or third their length.

In all cases a clean, slanting cut should be made immediately above a growth bud without leaving a snag above it, as this will die back. The growth bud chosen should be outward pointing as the new growth will tend to follow the direction in which the bud is pointing; also, outward growth will avoid congestion in the centre of the bush and allow the free circulation of air and maximum amount of light to reach the plant.

Some rambler roses make a great deal of strong new growth right from the base. Cut out all the old flowering stems right to the bottom as soon as the flowers fade and train in the young stems either at full length or shortened to suit the available space.

Summer Pruning. Repeat-flowering roses of the Large-Flowered and Cluster-Flowered types repay a fairly drastic thinning out in summer immediately after the first flush of bloom is over. The stems carrying faded flowers are cut back as far as good growth buds or young shoots, the object being to encourage strong new growth as quickly as possible and so give the plants a chance to build up suitable wood for autumn flowering. In the case of roses grown mainly to supply cut flowers, sufficient summer pruning is usually given by the mere act of cutting the flowers with good long stems.

Suckers. These are stems growing directly from the stock on which the rose is budded. As they will produce only the small, single flowers of the particular species of stock (such as *Rosa canina*, *R. rugosa*) and not those of the budded rose they must be removed as soon as they are seen. Any shoots coming directly from the roots or from the main stem of a standard rose are suckers but if in doubt, suckers can be distinguished by comparison with the normal growth of the rose. They are always different, the leaves usually smaller and possibly of a different colour, the stems thinner and longer. Trace suckers back to the roots from which they grow and sever them cleanly at the base. Shoots coming directly from the roots of roses that have been grown from cuttings will produce just as good flowers as other shoots and need not be removed.

Disbudding. This is really a branch of pruning. It is only necessary in the case of Large-Flowered roses and then only if fine individual blooms rather than a good general display are required. Disbudding means that only one flower bud is left per stem, all other buds being cut out at as early a stage as possible. Usually it is best to retain the terminal bud and remove the smaller buds just below it, but there are occasions when one of the side buds may be retained in preference to the terminal one. This will occur if the terminal bud has been damaged in any way or if it appears to be deformed. It may also be wise with very large, full roses, especially early in the summer or if the weather is very wet. Under such conditions the terminal bud often fails to open fully, beginning to decay when partly open, a condition known as 'balling'. Side buds are not so prone to this fault.

Mulching. A mulch of lawn mowings spread all over the rose beds in spring and renewed from time to time throughout the summer is often of the greatest value in maintaining growth especially on thin, dry soils. It may also help to decrease infection by black spot disease, the spores of which may overwinter in the surface soil and be splashed or blown on to the foliage in spring or summer. The mulch, if it is not disturbed, appears to prevent this infection passing from soil to leaves.

Feeding. Once they are established, the best method of feeding roses is to spread a good dressing of well-rotted dung around them in the first half of spring. This may be supplemented, or replaced when not available, by any commercial rose fertilizer or a general garden fertilizer containing approximately equal percentages of nitrogen, phosphoric acid and potash. A second application of fertilizer may be given in early summer just as the roses are beginning to bloom.

Spraying. Garden roses are subject to attack by various pests and diseases including greenflies, black spot and mildew. These are more fully described in Chapter 33, but as they recur with some regularity almost every year it is wise to carry out routine spraying to prevent them. Special preparations for roses containing both an insecticide and fungicide can be obtained and will save time. Application should be started in mid-spring and should then be continued at fortnightly intervals until the end of summer.

Exhibiting. There are classes for roses at most flower shows and at many of these the standard necessary to win prizes is high. The essentials for a prize-winning Large-Flowered bloom are that it shall be as large and full as possible, in colour typical of its variety, well developed, and free from blemishes such as split, double centre and deformity, spotted or faded petals. To produce such blooms with any degree of certainty a few special precautions are necessary. Much the same applies to exhibition flowers of Cluster-Flowered roses except that with these it is the whole truss of blooms on each stem that is required, not just one fine flower.

First the fertility of the soil must be high and manuring must be generous. Next pruning should be more severe than for garden decoration and subsequently the number of shoots per plant may need to be reduced considerably. The precise number retained will depend upon variety, strength and age, but should seldom exceed half a dozen. Disbudding of Large-Flowered roses must be rigorous and with Cluster-Flowered varieties it may pay to remove the central flower bud from each cluster and leave the surrounding ones to develop, since the central one may open before the others. In the last stages of development the opening bud may be protected with a conical rose shade held a few centimetres above it by a wire clip attached to a stake. This will keep off rain and protect the bloom from strong sunlight which might fade or burn it, but too much shading is harmful and may spoil the colour of the flower.

The last precaution is to place a tie of undyed wool around each Hybrid Tea bloom just before it is cut. This tie will prevent the flower opening too quickly while being taken to the show. It should be left round the bloom until the exhibitor has to leave the hall prior to judging.

Propagation by Budding. Most roses are increased by budding on to one or other of several different types of rootstock. The wild English dog rose, *Rosa canina*, is the stock most frequently used but *R. rugosa* stock is much used for standards. Others used are *R. laxa* (*R. canina froebellii*) and *R. multiflora*.

Stocks can be raised from seed sown out of doors in early spring or from cuttings in autumn 23-30 cm (9-12 in) long, prepared from well-ripened young stems severed just below a joint or leaf. Remove the lower leaves, if any, and line the cuttings in a straight-backed trench about 10 cm (4 in) deep in any well-drained soil. Return the soil and make very firm. By the following autumn the cuttings should be well rooted and ready for removal to a reserve bed in which they may be planted 23-30 cm (9-12 in) apart in rows at least 76 cm (2½ ft) apart. In this they will be budded the following summer and will grow on for a further fifteen months by which time the roses will be ready for removal to their flowering quarters.

Standard roses are best worked on strong briar stems cut from wild plants with as much root as possible. Do this in autumn and transplant the stems immediately to the nursery bed in which they will be budded the following summer. The stems should be from 60 cm-1·2 m (2-4 ft) long – 1·5-1·8 m (5-6 ft) for weeping standards. In the spring they will probably each produce a number of shoots. Retain three only per stem as nearly

Pruning a rambler. After the flowers have faded the old flowering stems are cut right out at the base, and the strong new shoots trained in their place. If there is insufficient new growth, some of the old stems may be retained, in which case the side growth should be shortened to within 6·2 cm (2½ in) of the main stem

as possible where the head of branches is required. Rub out all others at an early stage. If rugosa stock is to be used strong stems are best purchased and planted in autumn for budding the following year. One advantage of this stock is that the bark is so thin and pliable that buds can be inserted directly on the main stem instead of on young side growths.

Budding is done in mid- to late summer. The 'buds' are growth buds, not flower buds. One will be found in the angle made by each leaf stalk with its stem. By mid–summer many of these buds, especially towards the middle of stems that have already flowered, should be fat and prominent. These are the kind of buds required.

Stems bearing such buds are cut from the parent plant and the leaves are removed but the leaf stalks left. They are then stood upright in a jam jar containing a little water.

The stock is prepared by making a T-shaped incision in the bark and lifting the flaps

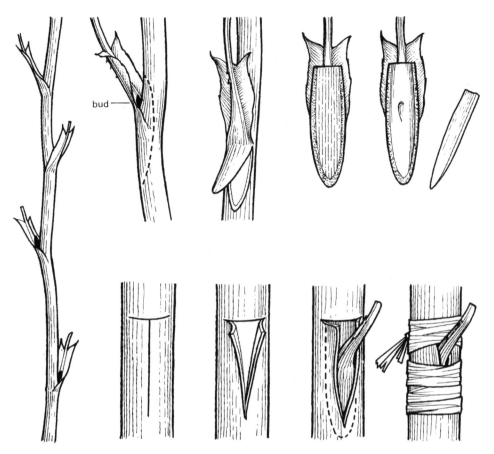

Budding a rose. The bud is cut from the shoot together with a shield-shaped piece of bark about 2·5 cm (1 in) long with a thin slip of wood inside, which is then removed. The bud is inserted in the stock, which has been prepared by making a T-shaped incision in the bark and lifting the flaps. It is then bound firmly in position with soft raffia or twist

of bark on each side of the downstroke of the T. The bud is cut from the stem with a shield-shaped portion of bark about 2·5 cm (1 in) in length which will include a thin slip of wood inside it. This wood should be stripped out, leaving the bark and bud only. This is slipped down under the flaps of the T incision so that the inner surface of the shield lies snugly against the wood of the stock. It is bound firmly in this position with soft raffia or twist, or special budding ties.

No further treatment is necessary until the following early spring when the whole top growth of the stock should be cut off just above the point of budding. This will divert all the rising sap to the bud which will start into growth and so lay the foundation of a new rose plant. Sometimes buds start to grow the first summer within a few weeks of being inserted. This does not matter much, though 'shot eyes' as they are called do not always come through the first winter so well as buds which remain dormant in the normal manner.

For bush roses one bud only is inserted low down on each stock – below soil level is possible. A little soil is scraped away for this purpose and should not be returned after-

---

A CLASSIFICATION OF ROSES FOR GARDEN PURPOSES

Modern Garden Roses

Climbing		*Non-climbing*	
Recurrent	*Non-recurrent*	*Recurrent*	*Non-recurrent*
Rambler	Rambler	Repeat-flowering Shrub	Shrub
Climber	Climber	Miniature	
Climbing miniature	Climbing miniature	Bush	
		Large-Flowered (Hybrid Tea)	
		Cluster-Flowered (Floribunda)	
		Polyantha	

Old Garden Roses

Climbing	*Non-climbing*	
Ayrshire	Alba	Gallica
Boursalt	Bourbon	Moss
Climbing Tea	Boursalt	Portland
Noisette	Hybrid Perpetual	Provence (Centifolia)
Sempervirens	China	Sweet Briar
	Damask	Tea

Wild Roses

Climbing	*Non-climbing*

---

wards. Standard and half-standard roses are budded high up, one bud being inserted near the base of each young side shoot retained for the purpose or direct into the main stem of rugosa stocks. This means that as a rule three buds are inserted on each standard stock.

Cuttings. Garden roses may be increased by cuttings in exactly the same manner as rose stocks (see p. 336), and also by summer cuttings of half-ripened young stems inserted in a propagating frame or under mist. Ramblers and species succeed especially well in this way but many modern Cluster-Flowered and Shrub varieties can also be successfully propagated in the same manner. Miniature roses, which cannot be budded because of the thinness of their stems, may also be raised from cuttings though nurserymen usually increase them by grafting in greenhouses in spring.

Seeds. Garden roses do not breed true to type from seed however carefully it is produced. All new roses are raised in this manner, the seed being obtained from hand-made crosses between selected parents, but out of thousands raised only a very few are likely to prove of sufficient merit to be perpetuated. The hips are gathered in mid-autumn, placed in shallow, sand-filled trays and stood out of doors exposed to natural cold during the winter. In early spring the seed is separated from the now rotten pulp and is sown thinly in 12 mm ($\frac{1}{2}$ in) deep drills in well-broken soil out of doors.

The New Classification. As explained earlier, roses have been so interbred that one class tends to merge with another. In particular, there was a lack of any clear and generally accepted criteria by which new roses could be allocated to their most appropriate classes. To rectify these defects The World Federation of Rose Societies has adopted a new and more logical system of classification which embodies brief but adequate definitions of the characteristics of each class. From the viewpoint of the gardener intent on buying and planting roses this new classification does not involve much change except that the roses formerly known as Hybrid Teas may now be called Large-Flowered and those that used to be Floribundas may appear as Cluster-Flowered, both names which aptly describe their principal decorative differences. The new classification (see p. 336) may also be extended to accommodate any new types that may arise as a result of further breeding.

Chapter 12

Bulbs, Corms and Tubers

The subdivision of plants which I have adopted as a heading for this chapter has neither botanical nor cultural significance. Plants with bulbous or tuberous roots are to be found in many families and are of very diverse types. Some are hardy, some tender. Some are bedding plants, others appear most at home in the herbaceous border; yet others are purely for greenhouse cultivation.

Why, then, adopt the classification at all? Because it is such a familiar one to the ordinary gardener and one which will always be used by nurseryman and seedsman. Bulb catalogues will continue to drop through our letter boxes and it might be confusing for the reader of a popular book such as this to find them classified in more scientific but completely unfamiliar ways. And so in this chapter I have included all those plants which might be found in a comprehensive bulb list plus a few more, such as dahlias, which do not readily fit into any other category. Those kinds mainly grown under glass will be found in the section on greenhouse plants.

Definitions. First a very brief description of the distinction between bulbs, corms and tubers. Bulbs are always composed of a number of scales more or less tightly packed one on top of the other. The onion and the daffodil are typical examples. These scales are frequently the thickened bases of the leaves.

A corm is solid flesh right through and is, in fact, a thickened stem. It is covered by membranous sheaths and the presence of these is perhaps the surest means of distinguishing the corm from the tuber for this is also solid flesh throughout but without any sheath.

Characteristics. Because of their diverse origins and relationships it is not possible to generalize about the treatment of bulbs, corms and tubers in the way one can with most other groups, but a few observations can be made which apply in some measure to all.

The most obvious and also the most important of these is that bulbs, corms and tubers are storage organs which permit the plant to sustain quite long periods of dormancy or semi-dormancy during which it may often be entirely deprived of food and water without suffering any injury. Many of these plants actually benefit from being kept quite dry for a period each year and some are best lifted and shaken free of soil during this resting period, but this is not true of all. Some are better kept in the soil though allowed to get dry for a time while there are some which need a little moisture even during their time of greatest dormancy.

The second generalization which might be made is less universal in application but still applies to a substantial proportion of bulbs, corms and tubers. It is that they often have enough stored nourishment to carry first season flowers with very little extra assistance beyond a supply of moisture. Not infrequently the flowers are already formed in embryo in the bulbs (but not in corms or tubers) before they are planted and the first season's results depend very little on the skill of the gardener. It is in subsequent years that he will find out whether his methods are good or bad. A good deal of disappointment and

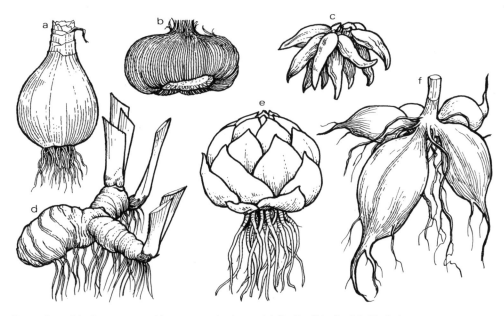

Examples of bulbs, corms, rhizomes and tubers. (a) Daffodil bulb; (b) Gladiolus corm; (c) Ranunculus tubers; (d) Iris rhizome; (e) Lily bulb; (f) Dahlia Tubers

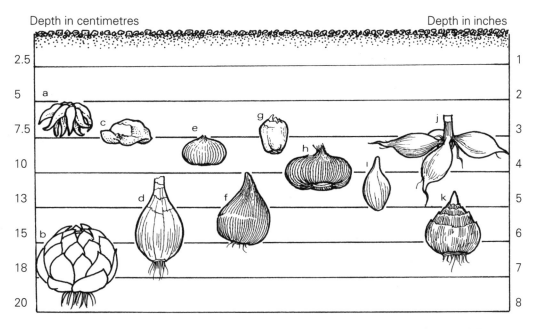

Planting depth table. (a) Ranunculus; (b) Lily; (c) Anemone; (d) Narcissus; (e) Crocus; (f) Tulip; (g) Scilla; (h) Gladiolus; (i) Bulbous iris; (j) Dahlia; (k) Hyacinth

misunderstanding is due to failure to appreciate this point. Novices buy fine bulbs, plant them in an unsuitable environment and yet get very good blooms the following spring or summer. Subsequently results become worse and worse year by year until eventually there are no flowers at all and probably, soon after, no bulbs either.

And so leaving generalities let us get down to a subject-by-subject description of the plants to be grown and their individual peculiarities.

THE ORNAMENTAL APPROACH

THE BEST KINDS TO GROW

Achimenes. See Chapter 19.

Acidanthera. This is rather like a gladiolus (and plants are listed as such) with 90 cm (3 ft) stems carrying short spikes of sweetly scented white and maroon flowers in late summer/early autumn. Plant corms in the second half of spring 7·5 cm (3 in) deep and 15 cm (6 in) apart in a sunny position. Lift in late autumn, cut off the tops 12 mm (½ in) above the corms and store in a dry, frost-proof place.

Allium. The familiar onion of the vegetable garden is an allium but here we are concerned only with its purely ornamental relatives. There are a number of these and very beautiful some of them are though almost all suffer from the characteristic onion smell. However this is only noticeable when they are crushed or cut so it is no handicap to their use in the garden.

All will grow readily in any ordinary soil and most prefer sun and good drainage. Bulbs should be purchased in early autumn and planted 8·7 cm (3½ in) deep and 15-45 cm (6 in-1½ ft) apart according to the size of the full-grown plants. Leave undisturbed until obviously overcrowded, then lift in late summer, divide into single bulbs and replant.

Among the best kinds are *Allium christophii* with large globular heads of lilac flowers on 60 cm (2 ft) stems in early summer; *A. caeruleum* with compact heads of blue flowers on 60 cm (2 ft) stems in the first half of summer; *A. giganteum*, large greyish blue heads, mid-summer flowering and 1 m (3½ ft) in height; *A. cernuum*, with nodding clusters of purplish-pink flowers on 30 cm (1 ft) stems in the first half of summer; *A. karataviense*, with broad green and purple leaves and purplish-white flowers on 20 cm (8 in) stems in mid-spring; *A. moly*, buttercup yellow, flowering in the first half of summer, and 30 cm (1 ft) high; *A. neapolitanum*, with loose clusters of white flowers on 30 cm (1 ft) stems all spring; *A. areophilum*, with big heads of pinkish flowers on 20 cm (8 in) stems in the first half of summer; *A. carinatum pulchellum*, with small heads of lilac-pink flowers in late spring/early summer; *A. rosenbachianum*, with large heads of purplish-violet flowers on 60 cm (2 ft) stems in the first half of summer; *A. siculum* (now listed as *Nectaroscordum siculum*), with 76 cm (2½ ft) stems bearing clusters of hanging, bell-shaped green and reddish-amber flowers in late spring/early summer; and *A. sphaerocephalum*, with egg-shaped heads of maroon flowers on slender 60 cm (2 ft) stems in the second of summer.

Alstroemeria. See p. 115.

Amaryllis (Belladonna Lily). This name has been applied to quite distinct groups of plants at different times and is used by some for the plants correctly named hippeastrums. Here I am concerned only with the belladonna lily, *Amaryllis belladonna*, a plant that will thrive out of doors in a warm, sunny position and deep, well-drained soil (See p. 476 for the greenhouse kind, p. 352 for the hardy.) It usually does well at the foot of a warm wall or against the outside of a greenhouse in a sunny position. The bulbs should be only just covered with soil but in cold places may need the protection of a cloche or a covering of peat in winter. If the natural soil is heavy it should be replaced with a lighter mixture containing plenty of sand and leafmould or peat. Plant in the second half of summer and subsequently leave the bulbs alone. Mulch in late spring with well-rotted stable manure and peat, or leafmould mixed in equal parts with some bonemeal added. It will probably be many years before they become so overcrowded that they need to be transplanted. Meanwhile, if the position suits them, and in particular if they receive enough sun to ripen the bulbs fully, they will give a delightful display each early autumn of showy and very fragrant, trumpet-shaped, pink flowers borne several together on stiff, 60 cm (2 ft). The flowers appear before the leaves.

Anemone (Windflower). There are many anemones and they vary greatly in character, some being herbaceous plants and some rock plants. There are also tuberous-rooted kinds and it is with these that we are concerned here. Among the most useful to the gardener are the Poppy anemones, derived from *Anemone coronaria*. They like good, fairly rich, well-drained soils with ample moisture while they are in growth but good drainage at all times. They should be planted either in mid-autumn or from late winter to mid-spring and may then be left undisturbed if the position is really well drained. Should there be any doubt about this it is better to lift the tubers in late summer when leaves turn yellow and store them away in a cool dry place until the following spring. Plant 6·2 cm (2½ in) deep and 10-15 cm (4-6 in) apart for a massed display. These plants are first rate for cutting and flowers can be had out of doors from mid-spring to early summer.

The season can be lengthened by planting some tubers in an unheated frame but no attempt should be made to force them with artificial heat. Plant in mid-autumn and use the lights to protect the plants from severe weather but ventilate fairly freely at other times.

A. coronaria varieties can also be raised easily from seed sown out of doors in early summer. Choose a sunny place and rather light, open soil. Sow thinly in drills 6 mm (¼ in) deep and leave the seedlings to flower in the seed bed the following year, after which the tubers should be lifted and replanted with the usual amount of room.

All varieties of *A. coronaria* have brightly coloured, poppy-like flowers on 23-30 cm (9 in-1 ft) stems. The St Brigid strain has double flowers and the petals are often deeply slashed, whereas the De Caen varieties are single and have broad petals. Colours are very varied including scarlet, violet, blues, pinks, white and various combinations.

Other attractive tuberous-rooted anemones are *A.* × *fulgens*, with vivid scarlet flowers on 30 cm (1 ft) stems in late spring; *A. apennina*, a low-growing plant with dainty blue flowers on slender 15 cm (6 in) stems in the first half of spring; *A. blanda*, which is very similar but has pink and rose varieties; and any good forms of the British wood anemone, *A. nemorosa*, such as the silvery-blue Robinsoniana and large-flowered Allenii, all of which flower in mid-spring.

A. × *fulgens* is a lover of sun and well-drained but rather rich soils. The others will grow best in light shade and open soils containing plenty of humus. All should be planted 5 cm (2 in) deep and 15-20 cm (6-8 in) apart in the first half of autumn.

Anthericum. See **Chlorophytum** (p. 444).

Babiana (Baboon Root). These are often treated as cool greenhouse pot plants but in mild districts they may be planted in the open in sunny, sheltered positions and rather sandy soils. Plant the bulbs 7·5 cm (3 in) deep and 18 cm (7 in) apart in the first half of spring, and protect in winter with peat, straw or bracken. The flowers are trumpet shaped and borne in close spikes on 15-30 cm (6 in-1 ft) stems. Blue, purple, scarlet, crimson and creamy yellow are the commonest colours. The plants flower out of doors in late spring/early summer.

Bulbocodium. *Bulbocodium vernum* has purple, crocus-like blooms on short stems in the first half of spring and should be planted in warm, sheltered places and well-drained soils. It is a suitable bulb for the rock garden. Plant in early autumn, 7·5 cm (3 in) deep and 13 cm (5 in) apart and leave undisturbed for a number of years.

Calochortus (Butterfly Tulip; Mariposa Lily). These very beautiful hardy bulbs are not well known probably because they are not easy to grow in cool climates. They require good drainage and regular sun and warmth. In ordinary conditions they are apt to disappear for good in the first winter, but they will usually do well in a sunny frame and make good pot or tray plants for the unheated greenhouse.

Plant or pot in the second half of autumn in a warm, sunny position and rather light, sandy soil with plenty of leafmould or peat to retain moisture in summer. Cover the bulbs with 7·5 cm (3 in) of soil (less in pots). Leave undisturbed for three or four years, then lift when the foliage dies down, separate the bulbs and store in a dry place until planting time. Protect bulbs from severe weather in winter and also raise the temperature and dry the soil after flowering to ripen the bulbs.

The flowers are like very delicately formed tulips on slender stems 15-60 cm (6 in-2 ft) high according to species. Colours are varied and bright, including yellow, lilac, purple and rose and some are handsomely blotched. *Calochortus venustus*, 60 cm (2 ft), white, yellow, purple or red with a blotch of dark red on each petal, is one of the most readily available and flowers in the first half of summer. *C. splendens* has lilac flowers on 30 cm (1 ft) high stems in late spring/early summer.

Canna. See p. 442.

Cardiocrinum. See **Lilium** (p. 371).

Chionodoxa (Glory of the Snow). These delightful hardy bulbs produce sprays of small starry blue flowers in early spring. They may be grown in the border as an edging, in beds as a groundwork for taller spring flowers such as daffodils, or in the rock garden. There are several kinds, the best for general cultivation being *Chionodoxa luciliae*, with blue, white-centred flowers and *C. sardensis* which is blue almost throughout. Both are 10-15 cm (4-6 in) in height.

All are easily grown in ordinary soil and sunny position. Plant 7·5 cm (3 in) deep and 14 cm (5½ in) apart in the first half of autumn. Leave undisturbed for several years, then lift in mid-summer when foliage dies down and, after cleaning off, replant in a new place.

Chionodoxas also make pretty pot plants if grown five or six in a 10 cm (4 in) pot in ordinary potting soil. Pot in late summer/early autumn, keep in an unheated frame until late autumn/early winter, and then bring into the cool greenhouse. Repot annually.

Clivia. See p. 446.

Colchicum (Meadow Saffron, Autumn Crocus). Superficially the colchicums bear so much resemblance to crocuses that it is sometimes difficult to convince people they have no connection whatsoever. The popular name 'autumn crocus' applied to colchicums is also very misleading for there are true crocuses which flower in the autumn.

Colchicums require a reasonably good soil and sunny or partially shady position. They can be established in thin woodland or under trees that are not too dense and can be naturalized in grass, but should not be planted in pasture land as the foliage and flowers are poisonous to cattle. The tubers should be planted in the second half of summer 15 cm (6 in) apart. They are large and need holes deep enough to allow the top of the tuber to be covered with 5 cm (2 in) of soil. Leave them undisturbed until over-crowded, then lift in mid-summer, separate to single tubers and replant at once. The two best known species are *Colchicum autumnale* and *C. speciosum*, both of which are lilac pink and have pure white forms. There are double-flowered varieties of *C. autumnale* in both lilac pink and white and a very large double rosy-lilac variety named Water Lily which is said to be a hybrid between *C. autumnale* and *C. speciosum*. In addition there are numerous other species besides varieties and hybrids in a range of colour from soft to deep pink.

Convallaria (Lily of the Valley). *Convallaria majalis* is one of those plants far better known by its popular than by its botanical name. The rhizomes (fleshy underground stems) are unable to stand long periods without water and so they should never be dried right off but should be treated more like ordinary herbaceous perennials, lifted when overcrowded, divided and replanted without delay. Mid-autumn is the best time, but it can also be done in early spring. Just cover the points of the crowns with soil and space them 8·7 cm (3½ in) apart. The best soil is one that is cool and leafy. A little well-rotted dung can be worked in when preparing it. The position should be shady or, if in full sun, plenty of moisture must be supplied while the plants are in growth.

Out of doors flowers are produced in the second half of spring. Earlier blooms can be obtained by covering the bed with portable frames in mid-winter, while winter blooms can be had by forcing strong crowns in a heated greenhouse. These are planted close together in shallow boxes filled with granulated peat instead of soil and are immediately introduced to a temperature of about 25°C/77°F but without light. Plenty of moisture must be supplied. When flower stems can be seen, light is gradually admitted to colour the leaves. The crowns are useless after forcing. An alternative method is to pot, in early autumn, strong outdoor roots, place these in a frame until early winter, and then bring them into a cool greenhouse. The temperature may be raised to 20°C/68°F when the flower spikes start to grow, but before this should be kept to about 13-15°C/56-59°F. The flowers will be later than those produced by forcing but the crowns will be less damaged and may be planted back in the garden.

Crinum. Very showy plants with large, trumpet-shaped, lily-like flowers on stout stems usually about 90 cm (3 ft) in height. Many suffer from the drawback of being on the borderline of hardness – just too tender to be grown safely outdoors and yet sufficiently hardy to tempt many gardeners to take a chance, and then probably suffer disappointment. *Crinum × powellii*, a hybrid with flowers in various shades from white to rose pink from mid-summer to early autumn is one of the best for outdoor culture and will usually succeed in mild gardens if given a sunny, sheltered position. *C. bulbispermum*, also known as *C. capense*, with white or pale pink flowers, will also succeed under identical conditions. All other species should be treated as greenhouse plants unless there is good evidence that they will thrive out of doors in a particular garden or district where conditions may be exceptionally mild.

All should be grown in rather light loamy soil. Plant the big bulbs in early or mid-spring in holes deep enough to allow the whole bulb to be covered except the last 2.5 cm (1 in) of the neck or tip. A good position is at the foot of a warm, sunny wall. It is wise to cover the spot with straw or bracken over winter as a protection against frost. Bulbs can usually be left undisturbed for a number of years and require little attention beyond weeding. Feeding is apt to cause leaf growth at the expense of flowers but may occasionally be useful, especially with old plants.

Crocosmia (Montbretia). The familiar montbretia with its arching sprays of orange, yellow or coppery-red flowers on 76 cm (2½ ft) stems in late summer/early autumn is a hybrid botanically known as *Crocosmia × crocosmiiflora*. It spreads rapidly in almost any soil and place, is particularly happy in light, well-drained soils and warm, sunny places and can be increased by division in autumn or spring. Dry corms are offered for sale in the spring but do not always start well as this is a plant that should never be out of the ground for long. They can be laid in damp peat in boxes in a frame or greenhouse and planted out when they are growing well. Some of the large-flowered varieties are not so hardy and in cold districts are best lifted in late autumn and protected in a frame until the following mid-spring when they can be split up and planted out. *C. masonorum* is a different species with good reddish-orange flowers on 90 cm (3 ft) stems in the second half of summer. There are also hybrids such as *C. paniculatus*. Other valuable plants include Spitfire, orange red, and Lucifer, deep red flowers. All require similar treatment to montbretia and should be planted in well-drained soil in a sunny, sheltered place.

Crocus. For the purpose of cultivation it is necessary to draw a distinction between the large-flowered hybrids which are used for massed displays in beds and borders and are sold either under fancy names such as Striped Beauty, King of the Purples, etc. or merely under colour and the usually smaller though often more beautiful species, usually sold under their botanical names.

The hybrids are all very easy to grow. They are not particular as to soil though a lightish but rich loam suits them best. Most of them can be naturalized in grass quite easily if the grass is not too coarse and is not cut until the crocus foliage dies down in early summer.

A good deal more case is necessary with some of the species. In general these are plants for the rock garden and they are also delightful in pots for the unheated greenhouse or alpine house. They like well-drained soils and sunny positions and are too fragile to rough it with coarse-growing plants, though they may be grown with advantage under a carpet of low-growing alpines such as *Arenaria balearica* or *Thymus serpyllum*.

The hybrids all flower in the first half of spring but the species vary quite a lot, some starting in mid-autumn, others blooming in mid-winter and yet others in spring. All are hardy but the winter-flowering kinds are apt to be battered by rain and wind unless given some protection. This need be no more than a sheet of glass supported on wires or sticks a few centimetres above the blooms.

Autumn-flowering crocuses should be planted in the second half of summer. The winter and spring-flowering kinds may be planted in early or mid-autumn but early planting is always an advantage.

Cover the corms with 4 cm (1½ in) of soil and space them 13 cm (5 in) apart. They usually multiply fairly rapidly and soon form good clumps. These need not be disturbed until they become overcrowded, when they should be lifted as soon as the foliage dies down in summer, separated into single corms and replanted without delay. This division of old plants provides the most satisfactory means of increase.

Hybrid crocuses are continually being bred by specialists so that lists of names quickly date. The latest favourites are to be found in any bulb merchant's catalogue. The species are not susceptible to change in this way and the following are a few of the best:

Autumn flowering: *Crocus pulchellus*, lavender blue, with orange-yellow throat; *C. speciosus*, violet blue with orange stigmas; *C. speciosus albus*, pure white with scarlet stigmas; *C. kotschyanus zonatus*, lilac with a yellow throat.

Winter flowering: *C. chrysanthus*, typically in various shades of yellow, but there are a great many varieties including some that are white, blue and orange, sometimes feathered or striped with bronze; *C. imperati*, violet within, fawn outside, with orange stigmas; *C. tomasinianus*, typically silvery lilac, but there are numerous varieties in a range of colours from pale lavender to reddish purple.

Spring flowering: *C. biflorus*, white to lavender, often striped or feathered with purple; *C. sieberi*, typically bluish lilac but again there are many variations including feathered and banded colours and quite deep purples; *C. susianus*, rich yellow (this species is often aptly named Cloth of Gold); *C. vernus*, white, lilac or purple (parent of the big-flowered garden hybrids); *C. versicolor*, white or pale blue, fathered purple.

Cyclamen. From the garden standpoint a sharp distinction must be made between *Cyclamen persicum* and the numerous other species. The first, though a pretty plant occasionally seen in warm, sheltered, well-drained places out of doors, is rather overshadowed by the wonderful race of garden forms raised from it. These are exclusively treated as greenhouse plants and are dealt with in Chapter 19.

Here I am only concerned with the hardy or near-hardy types that can be grown with reasonable success out of doors. These are all much smaller than the greenhouse varieties, in fact most of them are dwarf plants which make a delightful carpet beneath the boles of large trees, beside paths or in cool rock gardens. All resent root disturbance, which makes them rather difficult to establish. Though they make big tubers which look as if they could stand a long time without moisture this is not borne out by experience. I think the custom of treating hardy cyclamen as bulbs and offering them for sale as dry tubers in autumn is wrong and accounts for many disappointments. it would be far better to regard them as alpines, grow them in small pots and offer them for sale in spring. They could then be transferred to the ground with a minimum amount of root disturbance.

The tubers should be covered with no more than 12 mm (½ in) of soil. The best position is one that is reasonably sheltered and a little shady. The soil should be cool and leafy with enough sand to ensure good drainage without risking severe drying out in summer. They will usually do well in cool parts of the rock garden or may be naturalized in open woodland or at the edge of shrub borders. They do not like dense shade and must not be overgrown by coarser plants. Once established they should be left severely alone as they are unlikely to become overcrowded for many years.

Seed provides the only means of increase. It should be sown in open, leafy soil in a frame or greenhouse during late winter/early spring. Self-sown seedlings often appear freely and clusters of these can be lifted, separated and replanted in spring.

Among the best species are *Cyclamen coum* with rounded, dark green leaves frequently marbled with paler green or silver and with white, pink, rose or magenta-crimson flowers on 7.5 (3 in) stems from late winter to early spring; the plant sold as Atkinsii, a good form of *C. coum*; *C. europaeum*, with pink to carmine flowers on 10 cm (4 in) stems from mid summer to early autumn and leaves sometimes marked with bright green; *C. libanoticum*, with fine salmon-pink flowers on 10 cm (4 in) stems in late winter/early spring and ivy-like leaves combining dark and yellowish green; *C. hederaefolium* and its form *album*, the former bright pink, the latter white, both 15 cm (6 in) high, autumn flowering and with very heavily marbled leaves; *C. pseudibericum*, with crimson flowers on 13 cm (5 in) stems from mid-winter to early spring; and *C. repandum*, which has marbled leaves and bright crimson, pink or white flowers in the second half of spring.

Daffodil. See **Narcissus** (p. 374).

Dahlia. This is now almost certainly the most freely planted of all perennial summer bedding plants. It flowers freely in a great variety of places and soils. Some skill is required to produce exhibition flowers, but results quite good enough for garden display can be obtained with a minimum of effort. Though a decidedly tender plant it has the convenient habit of becoming quite dormant in winter with sufficient food and moisture stored in its large tubers to carry it through without soil in any frost-proof place until spring.

Experts distinguish many different classes of dahlia but with the exception of some 'seed' strains of dwarf dahlias which are annually raised from seed (see p. 80) all are grown in the same way. Tubers are placed in pots, boxes or even direct on the greenhouse staging in the first half of spring and are surrounded and almost covered with any old potting soil. This is watered, rather sparingly at first, and the temperature of the house is kept around 15°C/59°F. In a short time shoots appear and directly these are 6·2 cm (2½ in) long they are severed nearly, but not quite, at the base. The lower leaves, if any, are removed and the bottom of each cutting trimmed just below a joint.

The prepared cuttings are inserted singly in small pots, or several around the edges of bigger pots, but the first method is better. Rather fine, sandy soil is used for this purpose, mixed with plenty of peat or leafmould. The pots are then plunged to their rims in peat in a propagating frame within the greenhouse.

The cuttings are kept moist and in two or three weeks will form roots and start to grow again. The plants can then be removed to the greenhouse staging and after a few days potted on singly into 10 cm (4 in) pots in any good potting compost. They grow rapidly in a temperature of 13-15°C/56-59°F with plenty of water and in a further week or so may be removed to a frame for hardening off. By the beginning of early summer they should be safe to plant out of doors.

Meanwhile the soil should have been prepared for them by thorough digging and the addition of some well-rotted dung or decayed vegetable refuse. This can be used freely for exhibition plants provided it is thoroughly dug in, as it will then serve the dual purpose of feeding the plants and holding moisture against a dry spell. A sunny position is most favourable but dahlias will succeed in partially shaded places. Tall kinds should be planted

90 cm (3 ft) apart; those of medium height 60-76 cm (2-2½ ft), and dwarf bedders 45 cm (18 in).

Little further attention is required except secure staking for the taller varieties. As a rule one strong stake is sufficient for each plant, driven firmly into the ground, and all shoots should be looped to it separately. The dwarf bedding dahlias do not need staking.

When big blooms are required for exhibition it is necessary to restrict the number produced. As a rule the shoots are reduced to about three per plant, the rest being rubbed out at an early stage. Each of these three shoots is restricted to a single flower – the terminal one. Any other flower buds are rubbed off. The plants are watered very freely whenever the soil seems dry and frequently weak liquid manure is substituted for plain water.

Thinning and disbudding are not necessary when the object is simply a plentiful supply of blooms for garden display or cutting.

Dahlias generally start to flower in late summer and continue until frost puts a stop to them in the autumn. They can be left out of doors until their foliage is blackened by frost and then must be lifted and brought into a frost-proof shed or room for a few days to give the top growth a chance to dry off. When it is well withered it is cut off 2·5 cm (1 in) or so above the tubers which are then stored away in any dry, frost-proof place. If it is cool and airy so much the better as this will reduce the risk of moulds growing on the roots during the winter. No soil or other covering is required and it does not matter if the store is dark or light. The tubers are left in store until it is time to start them into growth in the spring.

Those who have no facilities for starting dahlias in warmth may still grow them by planting the roots in an unheated frame in mid-spring and then transferring them to the open ground in early summer. The roots may be either planted whole or cut up into several pieces provided each has at least one shoot.

Yet another method is to plant the tubers just as they are out of doors in late spring. If they are covered with 7·5 cm (3 in) of soil there will be little danger of their being damaged by frost. When the shoots first appear they can be covered at night with inverted flower pots if frost threatens.

Commercial growers prepare dry small tubers (pot tubers) for sale in the spring. These can be potted singly, started into growth in a frame or greenhouse and planted outdoors in early summer, or planted straight outdoors. They will make good flowering plants.

Dahlias can also be raised readily from seed but this method is most suitable for the dwarf bedding types. The seed is sown thinly in an ordinary seed compost (see p. 427) in a warm greenhouse during late winter/early spring, in a frame during mid-spring or in a sheltered position out of doors later in the season. The seedlings are pricked off 10 cm (4 in) apart in similar soil as soon as they can be handled or, potted singly in 7·5 cm (3 in) flower pots. They are hardened off for planting out in early summer.

Of the many types of dahlia the most important are as follows: Decorative, with broad petals; Cactus, with rolled or quilled petals; Ball, with globular blooms made up of short petals giving a honeycomb appearance to the flower; Pompon, similar to the last but under 5 cm (2 in) in diameter; Single, with broad, flat petals surrounding a disc of yellow florets; Anemone-flowered, similar to the last but with a pad of short, coloured tubular florets in the centre; Collerette, similar to Singles but with a ring of short, coloured florets around the central yellow disc; Paeony-flowered, similar to Singles but with several rows of petals; Dwarf Bedding, with flowers of various types but plants under 76 cm (2½ ft) high. For exhibition purposes the Decorative, Cactus and Ball types are further subdivided according to the normal size of their flowers. All have the wide range of brilliant colours characteristic of the dahlia and all flower freely.

Varieties are extremely numerous and new ones are constantly taking the place of old. Lists of names should be sought in up-to-date trade lists.

Dierama (Wand flower). *Dierama pulcherrimum* is a graceful, cormous plant which makes long, reed-lilke arching stems bearing in late autumn/early winter short, pendant trails of funnel-shaped flowers. These are magenta in the common form but there are white, pink and crimson varieties. The wand flower should be grown in reasonably good, well-drained but not dry soils and sunny positions. Plant the corms 7·5 cm (3 in) deep in mid-autumn and cover the soil in winter with a little dry litter as protection against frost. They dislike disturbance and one established should be left alone. They often spread by self-sown seedlings, but seedlings may vary in colour so selected forms are increased by division of the corm-clusters in autumn.

Eranthis (Winter Aconite). A small family of pretty carpeting plants very suitable for naturalizing in thin woodland or under deciduous shrubs. The tubers should be planted 5 cm (2 in) deep and 7·5 cm (3 in) apart in the first half of autumn and thereafter left alone. They do not like disturbance and usually take a few years to settle down and make a carpet of golden, buttercup-like, green-ruffed flowers in late winter/early spring. The small bright green leaves are also most attractive and soon cover the ground. This plant does best in rather moist, loamy soils but is not really fussy. The most popular species is *Erthantis hyemalis. E. cilicica* is very similar but not quite so easy to grow, and *E. tubergenii* is a hybrid between the two with larger flowers.

Eremurus (Fox-tail Lily). It is a pity that these exceptionally handsome plants are being increasingly regarded, and treated, as bulbs for their spoke-like clusters of fleshy roots suffer if left out of the ground for long. It is better to treat the fox-tail lilies as herbaceous perennials and to plant them in the first half of autumn with as little delay and consequent drying as possible. Allow the roots to spread out in a wide, rather shallow hole and cover them with 8.7 cm (3½ in) of soil. Cover the whole site with a good thick layer of bracken or straw for winter as a protection against frost or, alternatively, place a low mound of silver sand over the crown of each plant.

The best place for eremuri is a sheltered, warm sunny spot where the soil is light and open but rather rich. They do well in chalky soils. An annual spring dressing of well-rotted stable manure or a sprinkling of compound fertilizer will keep them growing strongly and reduce the need for transplanting, for it is generally some years before the roots become fully established and the less disturbance they have the better.

Propagation can be effected by very careful division of the roots at planting time but this checks growth still more. A better plan is to raise seedlings from freshly harvested seed sown in light, open soil in a frame in early autumn or in a warm greenhouse in spring. Grow the seedlings on with frame or cloche protection in winter for a couple of years and then plant them in their flowering quarters. In some very favourable places seedlings appear naturally around the parent plants.

Eremuri make bold clumps of strap-shaped leaves from which stand up in summer the stiffly erect stems terminating in long, tapering spikes of saucer-shaped flowers. In habit and dignity they are fit companions for the giant hybrid delphiniums. Among the best are

Eremurus stenophyllus stenophyllus, 30-90 cm (1-3 ft) tall with orange-yellow flowers in early summer; *E. himalaicus*, 90 cm-1·5 m (3-5 ft), white, late spring flowering; *E. olgae*, white, 76 cm (2½ ft), mid-summer; and *E. robustus*, the giant of the race with pale pink flowers in early summer often on stems from 2·1-3 m (7-10 ft) tall. There are also numerous hybrids intermediate in height and colour to the species and some of these are easier to grow.

Erythronium (Dog's-tooth Violet, Trout Lily). These very attractive plants are nothing like violets and have no connection with them but belong to the lily family. The nodding flowers are borne singly or, at most, two or three together on slender stems and they mostly have attractive silver-mottled leaves. All should be planted in cool, rather moist places but not where water will stand around their roots in winter. A soil containing a good deal of peat or leafmould is ideal and the position should be at least a little shaded. Plant the bulbs 7 cm (3 in) deep and 15-23 cm (6-9 in) apart in early autumn and let them grow on for years undisturbed if the situation appears to suit them.

The best-known species is *E. dens-canis* which has several colour forms including pink, violet, purple and white. The stems are 10-15 cm (4-6 in) in height and the flowers appear in the first half of spring. *E. californicum* is a bigger plant, 23-30 cm (9 in-1 ft) high with creamy-white blooms in the second half of spring. *E. revolutum*, the trout lily, is 20 cm (8 in) high, mid-spring flowering and variable in colour from white and pale lavender to quite a deep pink, two of the best forms being Pink Beauty, a clear, pale pink, and White Beauty, cream and white. *E. tuolumnense* carries its fine yellow flowers in mid-spring on stems up to 30 cm (1 ft) high, Pagoda being a superior form.

Freesia. See p. 472.

Fritillaria (Crown Imperial, Fritillary). From the garden standpoint the crown imperial and the smaller fritillaries need to be considered separately as, although they belong to the same genus, they have a very different appearance and different cultural requirements. The crown imperial, *Fritillaria imperialis*, is a big upstanding plant which makes a bold clump of strap-shaped leaves from the centre of which appear in late spring stout leafy stems 90 cm (3 ft) high each terminated by a tuft of small leaves and a close cluster of showy, nodding, bell-shaped flowers. These may be yellow or orange-red according to variety. It enjoys fairly rich soil and a sunny place and should be planted 11·5 cm (4½ in) deep and at least 45 cm (1½ ft), apart in the first half of autumn.

Most of the fritillaries are much smaller plants. The best known is the snake's-head fritillary, *F. meleagris*, which makes a great display in the second half of spring. It will grow in any ordinary garden soil which is not liable to dry out to quickly in hot weather or become waterlogged in winter and may also sometimes be naturalized satisfactorily in grass. Some of the foreign species require drier and warmer positions if they are to prove permanent. Almost all have slender flower stems 23-30 cm (9 in-1 ft) high, each terminated by one or several drooping, lantern-shaped flowers with colours mainly in subdued shades of purple, maroon and greenish yellow. In *F. meleagris* the quite large flowers are either yellowish white or intricately chequered with purple on a whitish ground. All should be planted about 7·5 cm (3 in) deep and 10-15 cm (4-6 in) apart in the first half of autumn.

Galanthus (Snowdrop). Another of those plants so well known under its popular name that its botanical name is unfamiliar to many people. The lovely snowdrop is *Galanthus nivalis* and it has several varieties of which two of the most useful are the double-flowered snowdrop which makes a particularly good display in the mass and *atkinsii*, an exceptionally vigorous snowdrop with large flowers. All thrive in shade. Some snowdrops such as *G. byzantinus, G. ikariae ikariae, G. elwesii* and *G. plicatus* have notably fine flowers and since *G. byzantinus* starts to flower in mid-winter and *G. elwesii* continues into early spring they help to extend the flowering season. They need a little more care, except *G. elwesii* which is very easy, prefer fairly sunny positions and are more suitable for good places in border and rock gardens than for naturalizing in grass and woodland. All grow in most soils with a preference for those that are moderately rich and heavy. Bulbs should be planted 6·2 cm (2½ in) deep and 7·5-15 cm (3-6 in) apart in late summer/early autumn but it is far better to treat snowdrops like herbaceous plant and transplant them in early spring as soon as the flowers fade. They will be in full growth so they must not be allowed to get dry between lifting and replanting. Clusters of bulbs can be split up at the same time. Leave undisturbed for a number of years, but give an occasional light summer mulch with leafmould or peat and a dash of hoof and horn meal and bonemeal to maintain vigour.

Galtonia (Summer Hyacinth). *Galtonia candicans* is sometimes known as *Hycacinthus candicans* and certainly looks rather like a hyacinth though very much larger in all its parts. The flower spike is 1 m (3½ ft) in height and the creamy-white, pendent flowers are in proportion. They are at their best in the second half of summer. This is a perfectly hardy plant and one which may be left undisturbed for a number of years. It will grow in any ordinary soil and sunny position and is quite suitable for the herbaceous border. Plant the bulbs 15 cm (6 in) deep and 30 cm (1 ft) apart in autumn. Lift and divide in early autumn when the bulbs get overcrowded and the quality of the flowers suffers in consequence.

Gladiolus. This has become one of the most important corms grown in the garden. There are many species but most are of interest to the collector rather than to the ordinary gardener, for whom the hybrids are the most important. So numerous are these garden varieties that for convenience of classification they are divided into fairly clearly defined groups. Most important of these are Large Flowered, with spikes of closely placed, wide-open flowers usually about 1·2 m (4 ft) high; Miniature and Small Flowered, with smaller flowers and often rather shorter spikes; and Early Flowering or Nanus, with loose, more slender spikes of flowers with pointed petals produced from mid-spring to early summer, whereas all the others flower from mid-summer to early autumn. Primulinus varieties have hooded flowers usually rather widely spaced on a slender spike and Butterfly varieties have medium-sized flowers, often in two or more sharply contrasted colours.

The early-flowering or Nanus varieties must be planted or potted in autumn, and since gladioli are all readily damaged by frost this means that in cold climates the Nanus varieties must be grown in frost-proof greenhouses. They can be planted with four or five corms in each 15 cm (6 in) pot or spaced 7·5 cm (3 in) apart in boxes at least 10 cm (4 in) deep. Either John Innes potting compost or a good peat potting compost can be used. The plants are watered moderately, given as much light as possible and a minimum temperature of 5°C/41°F. After flowering watering is reduced, growth is allowed to die down and the new corms are then separated from the old, withered corms and kept in a cool, dry place until it is time to start them into growth again.

The outdoor gladioli all do best in open, well-drained, but not dry soil. Those that are too heavy or too light can be improved by working in liberal quantities of peat. Manure should be used sparingly and must always be well rotted and thoroughly worked in some time in advance of planting. Bonemeal at 113 g per 0·8 sq m (4 oz per sq yd) and hoof and horn meal at 56 g to the same area (or a compound fertilizer) may be raked into the surface before planting and are specially valuable on poorer types of soil.

Planting should be started in early spring and may be continued until later in the season. It is a good plan to plant successively as this lengthens the flowering season. Cover the corms with 7·5 cm (3 in) of soil and space them at least 15 cm (6 in) apart – more if grown for exhibition, for which purpose it is customary to plant in straight double rows about 30 cm (1 ft) apart with a 60 cm (2 ft) alleyway between each pair of rows. The corms are spaced about 23 cm (9 in) apart in the rows. The same general plan is used when gladioli are grown for cutting, a purpose for which they are well suited. In borders and beds it is better to avoid straight lines and space the corms more or less evenly in all directions.

Very little further attention beyond weeding is necessary when gladioli are grown for garden display but for cutting and exhibition plants must be staked. One stake is used for each flower stem and should be in position by mid-summer. Make all ties with soft raffia or fillis below the lowest flower bud and be careful not to allow the stake to rub against the flowers and damage them. For exhibition spikes plants may be fed with weak liquid manure every week from early summer onwards.

When cutting gladioli be careful to leave some leaves on the corm, otherwise it will be starved and unable to form a satisfactory new corm to flower the following season.

Lift the plants six or seven weeks after the flowers fade or are cut. Sever all top growth just above the corm, shake off any remaining soil and pull the old, withered corm from the base of the new ones. This old corm is of no further use and should be thrown away but the new corms, provided they are reasonably plump, will flower the following year.

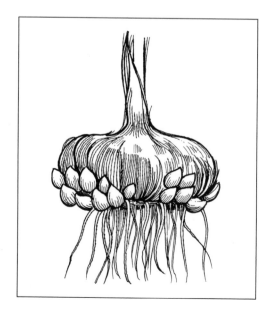

Small cormels or tiny corms may be found clustered round the new gladiolus corms. They can be grown on to flowering size if planted in good soil

There may also be some spawn or cormels, that is, tiny corms, clustering around the new corms. These will not usually flower the following year but they can be grown on to flowering size in a year or two if they are planted in good soil. The best policy is to get them planted at once in fairly deep seed boxes filled with good potting soil (see p. 423) and placed in a frost-proof frame or greenhouse for the winter If kept just a little moist they will soon start into growth and may then be watered with gradually increasing freedom. By late spring they can be stood out of doors.

When their leaves die down they should be shaken free of soil and stored until the normal planting time the following spring, when they can be put out of doors just like the ordinary corms.

The sizeable corms, after autumn cleaning, should be stored in a cool, airy, frost-proof place such as a spare room or well-ventilated cupboard. Avoid damp, heat and frost, all of which will do much damage. Examine the corms occasionally and remove any which show signs of decay. If in any doubt it is safe to peel the dry outer sheath from a corm to examine the flesh beneath, which should be firm and yellow. If it is soft or much pitted or scabbed it is probably diseased and should be dusted with sulphur or quintozene, or be destroyed.

When selecting gladiolus spikes for exhibition choose those that are well formed, with a good number of flowers open, none faded, and the spacing and placing of the flowers as even as possible.

Sometimes plants will be found with flowers that are wrongly splashed and streaked with colour. This is usually due to virus disease and such plants are best destroyed.

Varieties are extremely numerous and fashions change rapidly so study up-to-date trade catalogues. Varieties may simply be offered in different colours without distinguishing name.

Gladiolus byzantinus is a hardy species which can be grown out of doors without lifting and winter storing. The flowers are of medium size, funnel shaped and a bright magenta, borne on 76 cm (2½ ft) stems in the second half of summer. This species likes a sunny place and well-drained soil and when well suited can spread rapidly. When overgrown, plants may be lifted, divided and replanted in the first half of spring.

Gloriosa. See p. 473.

Gloxinia. See p. 473.

Hermodactylus (Snake's Head Iris). *Hermodactylus tuberosus* is very like some of the small bulbous-rooted irises and is sometimes called *Iris tuberosa*. The flowers are purplish-black and green and produced on 20-25 cm (8-10 in) stems in the second half of spring. It likes a warm, sunny place in well-drained soil, should be planted in early autumn and left undisturbed until overcrowded, when it can be lifted as soon as the foliage dies down in summer, divided and replanted.

Hippeastrum. Most of the hippeastrum are tender bulbs which need to be grown in warm greenhouses, but one species, *Hippeastrum pratense*, is sufficiently hardy to be grown out of doors in very sheltered places and well-drained soils. The foot of a sunny wall or a sheltered border outside a greenhouse will suit it well. Plant the bulbs 15 cm (6 in) deep

Allium oreophilum

Allium christophii

Allium moly

Allium christophii, 60 cm (2 ft), one of the choicest ornamental onions, has a head of starry flowers like some floral firework
⊕ ❋ Summer ☼ ▽ ▣

Allium moly (Lily Leek), 30 cm (1 ft), is a strong grower with glaucous leaves and bright yellow flowers ⊕ ❋ Spring/Summer ☼ ▽ ▣

Allium oreophilum, 25 cm (10 in), a compact ornamental onion best planted in generous groups ⊕ ❋ Summer ☼ ☀ ▽ ▣

Alstroemeria ligtu

Amaryllis belladonna

Anemone apennina

Anemone coronaria
De Caen

Anemone coronaria
St Brigid

Alstroemeria ligtu, 60 cm (2 ft), is a charming border or tub plant and cut flower. Plant tubers 15 cm (6 in) deep to protect them from frost ⊕ ⚘ ✲ Summer ☼ ▦ ◼

Amaryllis belladonna, 60 cm (2 ft), flowers on leafless stems in autumn. Plant 15 cm (6 in) deep ⊕ ⚘ ✲ Autumn ☼ ▦ ◼

Anemone apennina, 15 cm (6 in), is a charming miniature for the rock garden ⊕ ✲ Spring ☼ ◑ ▦ ◼

Anemone coronaria, 23 cm (9 in), a familiar cut flower and border plant, grows from tubers or seeds. De Caens are single, St Brigid double ⊕ ⚘ ✲ Spring ☼ ▦ ◼

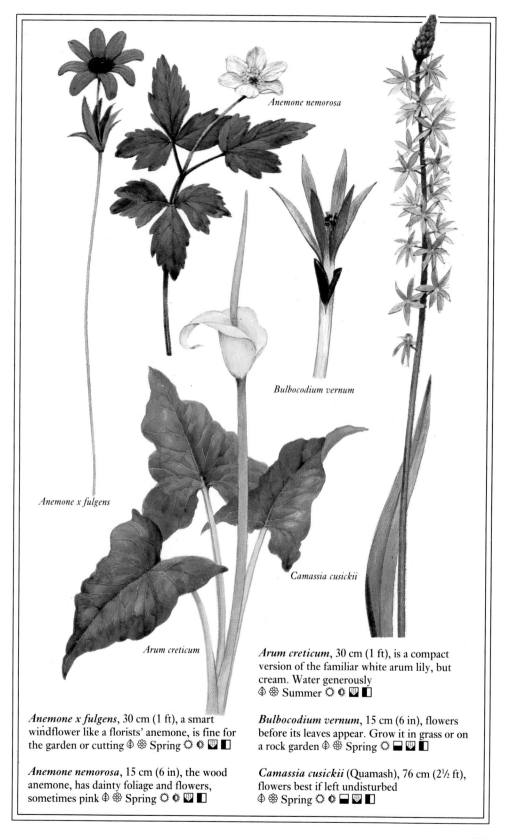

Anemone nemorosa

Bulbocodium vernum

Anemone x fulgens

Camassia cusickii

Arum creticum

Arum creticum, 30 cm (1 ft), is a compact version of the familiar white arum lily, but cream. Water generously ⊕ ❀ Summer ☼ ◑ ▨ ▮

Anemone x fulgens, 30 cm (1 ft), a smart windflower like a florists' anemone, is fine for the garden or cutting ⊕ ❀ Spring ☼ ◑ ▨ ▮

Bulbocodium vernum, 15 cm (6 in), flowers before its leaves appear. Grow it in grass or on a rock garden ⊕ ❀ Spring ☼ ▭ ▨ ▮

Anemone nemorosa, 15 cm (6 in), the wood anemone, has dainty foliage and flowers, sometimes pink ⊕ ❀ Spring ☼ ◑ ▨ ▮

Camassia cusickii (Quamash), 76 cm (2½ ft), flowers best if left undisturbed ⊕ ❀ Spring ☼ ◑ ▭ ▨ ▮

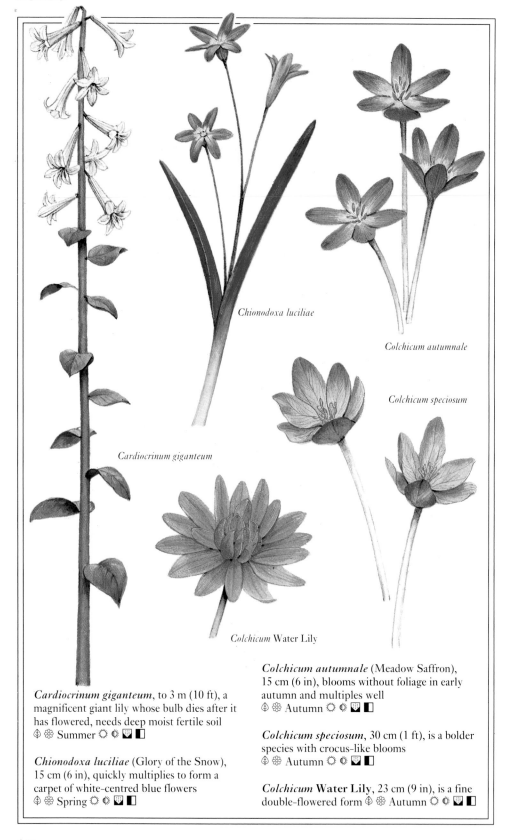

Chionodoxa luciliae

Colchicum autumnale

Colchicum speciosum

Cardiocrinum giganteum

Colchicum Water Lily

Cardiocrinum giganteum, to 3 m (10 ft), a magnificent giant lily whose bulb dies after it has flowered, needs deep moist fertile soil ⊕ ✿ Summer ☼ ◐ ▨ ◼

Chionodoxa luciliae (Glory of the Snow), 15 cm (6 in), quickly multiplies to form a carpet of white-centred blue flowers ⊕ ✿ Spring ☼ ◐ ▨ ◼

Colchicum autumnale (Meadow Saffron), 15 cm (6 in), blooms without foliage in early autumn and multiples well ⊕ ✿ Autumn ☼ ◐ ▨ ◼

Colchicum speciosum, 30 cm (1 ft), is a bolder species with crocus-like blooms ⊕ ✿ Autumn ☼ ◐ ▨ ◼

Colchicum Water Lily, 23 cm (9 in), is a fine double-flowered form ⊕ ✿ Autumn ☼ ◐ ▨ ◼

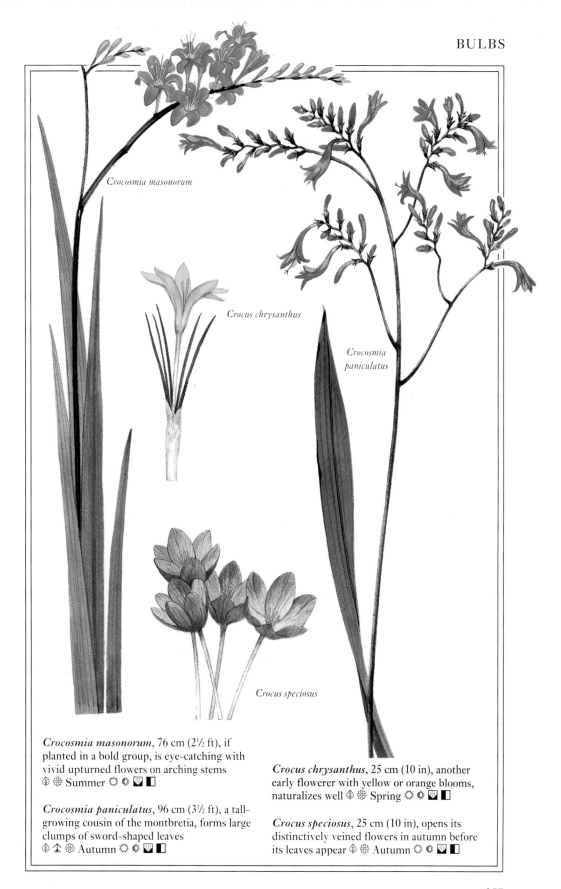

Crocosmia masonorum

Crocus chrysanthus

Crocosmia paniculatus

Crocus speciosus

Crocosmia masonorum, 76 cm (2½ ft), if planted in a bold group, is eye-catching with vivid upturned flowers on arching stems ✤ ❄ Summer ☼ ◐ 🎴 ▮

Crocosmia paniculatus, 96 cm (3½ ft), a tall-growing cousin of the montbretia, forms large clumps of sword-shaped leaves ✤ ⚘ ❄ Autumn ☼ ◐ 🎴 ▮

Crocus chrysanthus, 25 cm (10 in), another early flowerer with yellow or orange blooms, naturalizes well ✤ ❄ Spring ☼ ◐ 🎴 ▮

Crocus speciosus, 25 cm (10 in), opens its distinctively veined flowers in autumn before its leaves appear ✤ ❄ Autumn ☼ ◐ 🎴 ▮

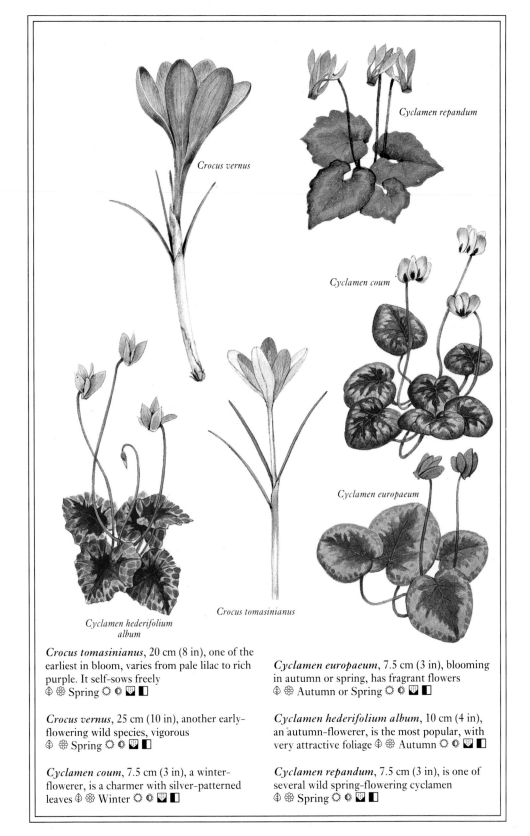

Crocus vernus

Cyclamen repandum

Cyclamen coum

Cyclamen europaeum

Cyclamen hederifolium
album

Crocus tomasinianus

Crocus tomasinianus, 20 cm (8 in), one of the
earliest in bloom, varies from pale lilac to rich
purple. It self-sows freely
✥ ❀ Spring ☼ ◔ ▦ ◼

Crocus vernus, 25 cm (10 in), another early-
flowering wild species, vigorous
✥ ❀ Spring ☼ ◔ ▦ ◼

Cyclamen coum, 7.5 cm (3 in), a winter-
flowerer, is a charmer with silver-patterned
leaves ✥ ❀ Winter ☼ ◔ ▦ ◼

Cyclamen europaeum, 7.5 cm (3 in), blooming
in autumn or spring, has fragrant flowers
✥ ❀ Autumn or Spring ☼ ◔ ▦ ◼

Cyclamen hederifolium album, 10 cm (4 in),
an autumn-flowerer, is the most popular, with
very attractive foliage ✥ ❀ Autumn ☼ ◔ ▦ ◼

Cyclamen repandum, 7.5 cm (3 in), is one of
several wild spring-flowering cyclamen
✥ ❀ Spring ☼ ◔ ▦ ◼

Dahlia (pompon)

Dierama pulcherrimum

Dahlia (formal decorative)

Dahlia (cactus)

Erythronium dens-canis

Eranthis hyemalis

Dahlia hybrids, 90 cm (3 ft), grow from tubers and flower profusely from mid-summer to the first frosts if well tended. There are various flower shapes
⊕ ⚑ ❀ Summer ☼ ◐ ▬ ▨ ▮

Dierama pulcherrimum (Wand Flower or Angel's Fishing Rods), 1.3 m (4½ ft), have arching stems with pendulous blooms
△ ❀ Autumn ☼ ▨ ▮

Eranthis hyemalis (Winter Aconite), 10 cm (4 in), opens buttercup-like flowers in mid-winter ⊕ ❀ Winter ☼ ◐ ▨ ▮

Erythronium dens-canis (Dog's Tooth Violet), 15 cm (6 in), opens dainty drooping flowers above brown-mottled leaves
⊕ ❀ Spring ◐ ▨ ▮

Fritillaria meleagris   *Galanthus elwesii*

Fritillaria imperialis

Galanthus nivalis

Fritillaria imperialis (Crown Imperial), 90 cm (3 ft), grows from a very large bulb, producing magnificent heads of yellow or coppery bells ⊕ ❁ Spring ☼ ▨ ▮

Fritillaria meleagris (Snake's head), 30 cm (1 ft), is so named after its intriguing chequered flowers. Specially charming on a rock garden or in grass ⊕ ♠ ❁ Spring ☼ ◉ ▨ ▮

Galanthus elwesii, 25 cm (10 in), is treated just like the Common Snowdrop but is larger in all its parts ⊕ ❁ Winter and Spring ◉ ▨ ▮

Galanthus nivalis (Common Snowdrop), 20 cm (8 in), is best allowed to naturalize under trees, but also makes a fine pot plant ⊕ ❁ Winter and Spring ◉ ▨ ▮

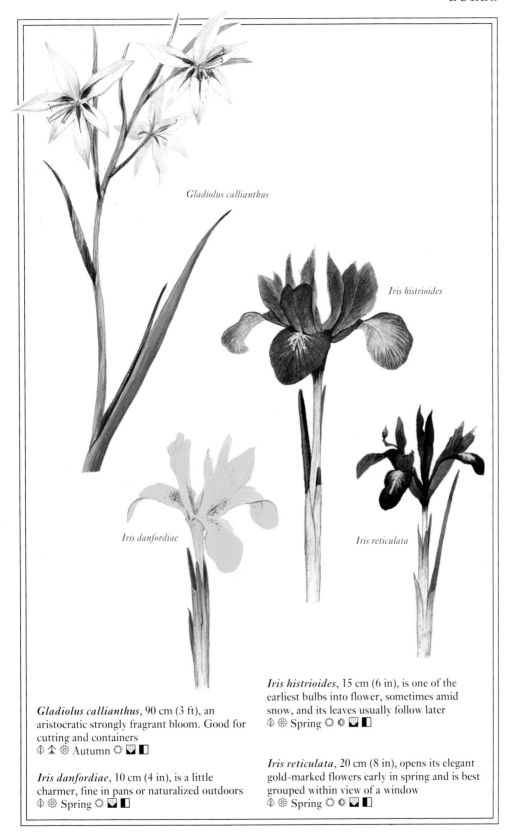

Gladiolus callianthus

Iris histrioides

Iris danfordiae

Iris reticulata

Gladiolus callianthus, 90 cm (3 ft), an aristocratic strongly fragrant bloom. Good for cutting and containers
⊕ ⚶ ✿ Autumn ☼ ▧ ▮

Iris danfordiae, 10 cm (4 in), is a little charmer, fine in pans or naturalized outdoors
⊕ ✿ Spring ☼ ▧ ▮

Iris histrioides, 15 cm (6 in), is one of the earliest bulbs into flower, sometimes amid snow, and its leaves usually follow later
⊕ ✿ Spring ☼ ◐ ▧ ▮

Iris reticulata, 20 cm (8 in), opens its elegant gold-marked flowers early in spring and is best grouped within view of a window
⊕ ✿ Spring ☼ ◐ ▧ ▮

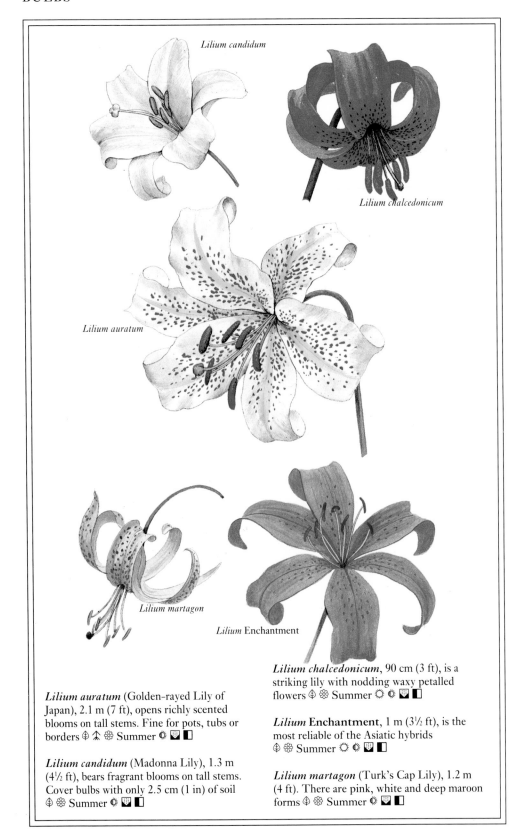

Lilium candidum

Lilium chalcedonicum

Lilium auratum

Lilium martagon

Lilium Enchantment

Lilium auratum (Golden-rayed Lily of Japan), 2.1 m (7 ft), opens richly scented blooms on tall stems. Fine for pots, tubs or borders ⊕ ⚘ ❋ Summer ☼ 🛡 ◻

Lilium candidum (Madonna Lily), 1.3 m (4½ ft), bears fragrant blooms on tall stems. Cover bulbs with only 2.5 cm (1 in) of soil ⊕ ❋ Summer ☼ 🛡 ◻

Lilium chalcedonicum, 90 cm (3 ft), is a striking lily with nodding waxy petalled flowers ⊕ ❋ Summer ☼ ◐ 🛡 ◻

Lilium Enchantment, 1 m (3½ ft), is the most reliable of the Asiatic hybrids ⊕ ❋ Summer ☼ ◐ 🛡 ◻

Lilium martagon (Turk's Cap Lily), 1.2 m (4 ft). There are pink, white and deep maroon forms ⊕ ❋ Summer ☼ 🛡 ◻

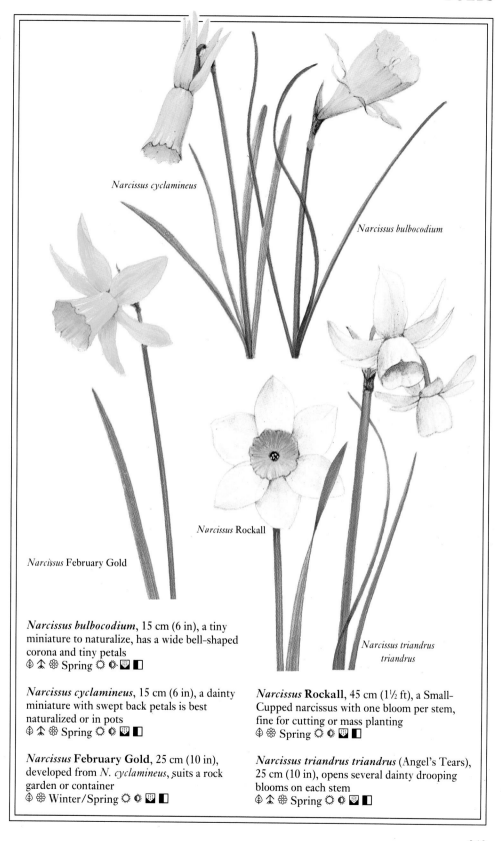

Narcissus cyclamineus

Narcissus bulbocodium

Narcissus Rockall

Narcissus February Gold

Narcissus triandrus triandrus

Narcissus bulbocodium, 15 cm (6 in), a tiny
miniature to naturalize, has a wide bell-shaped
corona and tiny petals
⊕ ⛁ ❀ Spring ☼ ◐ ▦ ◧

Narcissus cyclamineus, 15 cm (6 in), a dainty
miniature with swept back petals is best
naturalized or in pots
⊕ ⛁ ❀ Spring ☼ ◐ ▦ ◧

Narcissus February Gold, 25 cm (10 in),
developed from *N. cyclamineus*, suits a rock
garden or container
⊕ ❀ Winter/Spring ☼ ◐ ▦ ◧

Narcissus Rockall, 45 cm (1½ ft), a Small-
Cupped narcissus with one bloom per stem,
fine for cutting or mass planting
⊕ ❀ Spring ☼ ◐ ▦ ◧

Narcissus triandrus triandrus (Angel's Tears),
25 cm (10 in), opens several dainty drooping
blooms on each stem
⊕ ⛁ ❀ Spring ☼ ◐ ▦ ◧

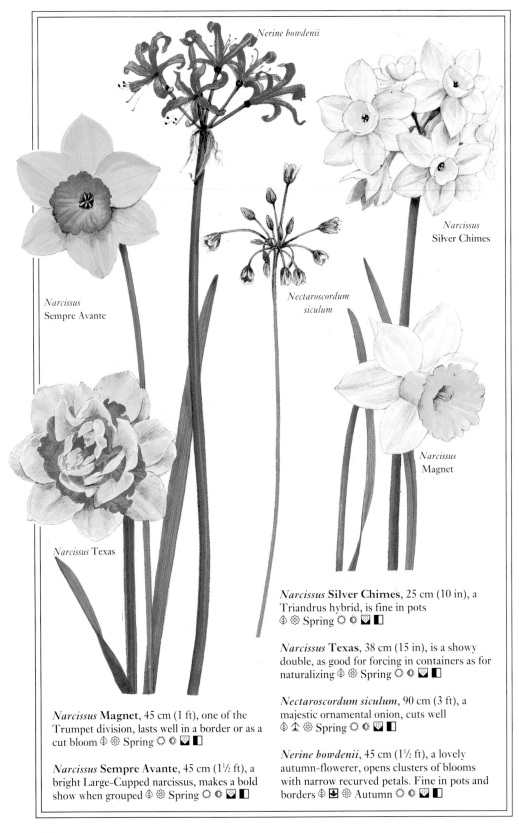

Nerine bowdenii

Narcissus Silver Chimes

Narcissus Sempre Avante

Nectaroscordum siculum

Narcissus Magnet

Narcissus Texas

Narcissus Silver Chimes, 25 cm (10 in), a Triandrus hybrid, is fine in pots ✤ ❀ Spring ☼ ✿ 🔲 ▮

Narcissus Texas, 38 cm (15 in), is a showy double, as good for forcing in containers as for naturalizing ✤ ❀ Spring ☼ ✿ 🔲 ▮

Nectaroscordum siculum, 90 cm (3 ft), a majestic ornamental onion, cuts well ✤ ⚘ ❀ Spring ☼ ✿ 🔲 ▮

Nerine bowdenii, 45 cm (1½ ft), a lovely autumn-flowerer, opens clusters of blooms with narrow recurved petals. Fine in pots and borders ✤ 🔽 ❀ Autumn ☼ ✿ 🔲 ▮

Narcissus Magnet, 45 cm (1 ft), one of the Trumpet division, lasts well in a border or as a cut bloom ✤ ❀ Spring ☼ ✿ 🔲 ▮

Narcissus Sempre Avante, 45 cm (1½ ft), a bright Large-Cupped narcissus, makes a bold show when grouped ✤ ❀ Spring ☼ ✿ 🔲 ▮

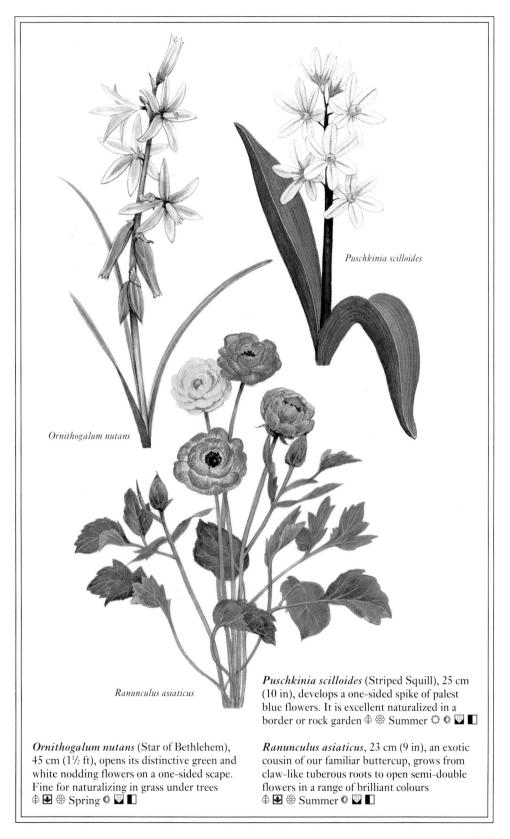

Puschkinia scilloides

Ornithogalum nutans

Ranunculus asiaticus

Puschkinia scilloides (Striped Squill), 25 cm (10 in), develops a one-sided spike of palest blue flowers. It is excellent naturalized in a border or rock garden ⊕ ❀ Summer ☼ ◐ ▦ ▮

Ornithogalum nutans (Star of Bethlehem), 45 cm (1½ ft), opens its distinctive green and white nodding flowers on a one-sided scape. Fine for naturalizing in grass under trees ⊕ ⬇ ❀ Spring ◐ ▦ ▮

Ranunculus asiaticus, 23 cm (9 in), an exotic cousin of our familiar buttercup, grows from claw-like tuberous roots to open semi-double flowers in a range of brilliant colours ⊕ ⬇ ❀ Summer ◐ ▦ ▮

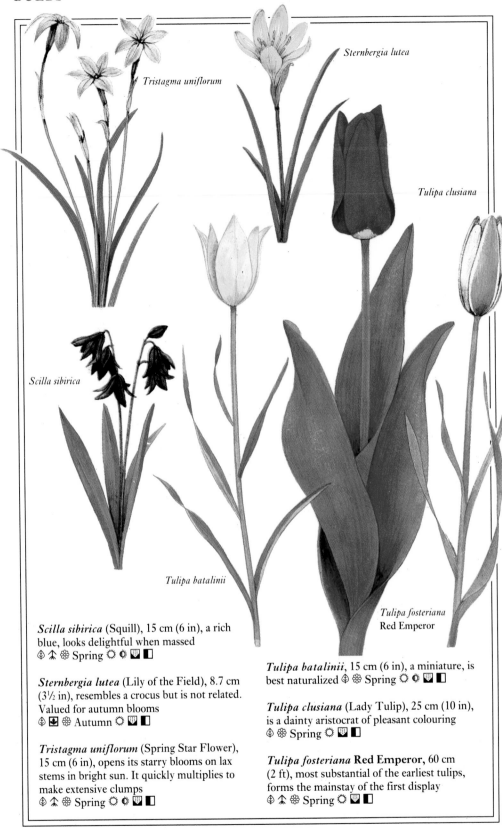

Tristagma uniflorum

Sternbergia lutea

Tulipa clusiana

Scilla sibirica

Tulipa batalinii

Tulipa fosteriana
Red Emperor

Scilla sibirica (Squill), 15 cm (6 in), a rich
blue, looks delightful when massed
✦ ✿ ❀ Spring ☼ ◑ ▣ ▮

Sternbergia lutea (Lily of the Field), 8.7 cm
(3½ in), resembles a crocus but is not related.
Valued for autumn blooms
✦ ▣ ❀ Autumn ☼ ▣ ▮

Tristagma uniflorum (Spring Star Flower),
15 cm (6 in), opens its starry blooms on lax
stems in bright sun. It quickly multiplies to
make extensive clumps
✦ ✿ ❀ Spring ☼ ◑ ▣ ▮

Tulipa batalinii, 15 cm (6 in), a miniature, is
best naturalized ✦ ❀ Spring ☼ ◑ ▣ ▮

Tulipa clusiana (Lady Tulip), 25 cm (10 in),
is a dainty aristocrat of pleasant colouring
✦ ❀ Spring ☼ ▣ ▮

Tulipa fosteriana **Red Emperor,** 60 cm
(2 ft), most substantial of the earliest tulips,
forms the mainstay of the first display
✦ ✿ ❀ Spring ☼ ◑ ▣ ▮

Tulipa Keizerskroon

Tulipa Holland's Glory

Tulipa kaufmanniana
Stresa

Tulipa greigii Red Riding Hood

Tulipa greigii Red Riding Hood, 20 cm
(8 in), is a smart dwarf for formal planting with
dazzling blooms and purple-striped leaves
✧ ❀ Spring ☼ ▣ ▮

Tulipa Holland's Glory, 76 cm (2½ ft), is a
fine Darwin hybrid, a mid-spring-flowerer for
formal bedding displays ✧ ❀ Spring ☼ ▣ ▮

Tulipa kaufmanniana Stresa, a Water-lily
tulip, opens its smart star-shaped blooms very
early in spring ✧ ❀ Spring ☼ ▣ ▮

Tulipa Keizerskroon, 30 cm (1 ft), is an old
favourite Single Early bedding tulip
✧ ❀ Spring ☼ ▣ ▮

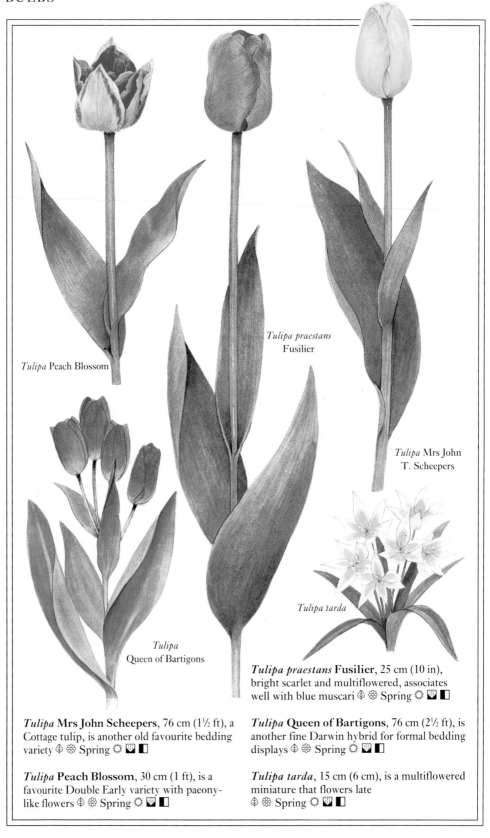

Tulipa Peach Blossom

Tulipa praestans
Fusilier

Tulipa Mrs John
T. Scheepers

Tulipa tarda

Tulipa
Queen of Bartigons

Tulipa praestans **Fusilier**, 25 cm (10 in),
bright scarlet and multiflowered, associates
well with blue muscari ⊕ ❀ Spring ☼ ▨ ▮

Tulipa **Mrs John Scheepers**, 76 cm (1½ ft), a
Cottage tulip, is another old favourite bedding
variety ⊕ ❀ Spring ☼ ▨ ▮

Tulipa **Queen of Bartigons**, 76 cm (2½ ft), is
another fine Darwin hybrid for formal bedding
displays ⊕ ❀ Spring ☼ ▨ ▮

Tulipa **Peach Blossom**, 30 cm (1 ft), is a
favourite Double Early variety with paeony-
like flowers ⊕ ❀ Spring ☼ ▨ ▮

Tulipa **tarda**, 15 cm (6 cm), is a multiflowered
miniature that flowers late
⊕ ❀ Spring ☼ ▨ ▮

in early autumn and cover the ground with dry litter during the winter.

The flowers of this showy plant appear in early summer. They are trumpet-shaped, brilliant scarlet and carried several together at the top of stiff, 30 cm (1 ft) high stems.

For other hippeastrums see Chapter 19.

Hyacinthoides. Bluebells were once listed as endymion but now go by this new name. Two kinds are commonly grown in gardens, the English bluebell, *Hyacinthoides non-scripta*, and the Spanish bluebell, *H. hispanicus*, with larger flowers, stouter stems and broader leaves. There are white, blue and pink varieties. Both kinds can be naturalized in grass or woodland but the English bluebell is better for this purpose, whereas the Spanish bluebell excels for display in the garden. Plant in autumn, 8·7 cm (3½ in) deep and leave undisturbed for years. Bluebells will thrive in most soils, prefer those that are fairly rich and moist and will grow in sun or shade. They can be divided in autumn and increase from self-sown seed.

Hyacinthus (Hyacinth). These need little introduction as they must be familiar plants to everyone, not only in the garden but also in bowls and glass jars for home decoration. There are a few species such as *Hyacinthus amethystinus* (now listed as *Brimeura amethystina*), with slender spikes of light blue or white flowers in the first half of spring, and *H. azureus*, (now *Muscari azureum*) with short, crowded spikes of small, deep blue flowers appearing at the same time, but by far the most important to gardeners are the large-flowered hybrids of which there are scores of varieties of cultivation. Many of these have been raised in Holland in parts of which the light, alluvial soil with water not far beneath the surface is ideal for the cultivation of hyacinths. In many English gardens hyacinths do well for a season or so and then gradually dwindle away, usually because the soil is too close in texture or dry in summer. Matters can be improved by working in plenty of peat with sand particularly in the case of heavy soils.

A little well-rotted manure may be used on poor soils but it is better to rely upon fertilizers such as bonemeal, at 113 g per 0·8 sq m (4 oz per sq yd), and hoof and horn meal at 85 g to the same area applied immediately before planting and well raked or forked in. Plant in mid-autumn and cover the bulbs with 8·7 cm (3½ in) of soil. In badly drained places or on very heavy soils it often pays to raise the hyacinth beds a few centimetres above the level of the surrounding ground. Space the bulbs at least 20 cm (8 in) apart.

Little further attention beyond weeding will be necessary until the following mid-summer when the bulbs should be carefully lifted as soon as the foliage dies down. Place them in a cool dry place for a few weeks, then shake the soil from them, cut off the withered tops and store the bulbs in a cool, dry place, such as a shed, until planting time. It is only worth keeping good, plump, weighty bulbs.

Hyacinths for indoor culture should be placed in their pots or bowls in late summer/early autumn. If the bowls have no drainage holes, special fibre containing charcoal and crushed oyster shell must be used in place of soil. It is very important to moisten this thoroughly before use. Bulbs can be set almost shoulder to shoulder and need barely be covered. For eight to ten weeks after potting the bulbs should be kept in a cool, dark place. Thereafter they can be brought into the light and if required they can be forced gently but too much heat will result in long, weak flowers stems. The Roman hyacinths, which are naturally early flowering and have looser, more slender flower spikes, are particularly good for growing in pots. Prepared hyacinths are stored at controlled temperatures to make them grow and flower very rapidly and can be had in flower by Christmas but the effect only lasts for the one flowering. Subsequently they grow and flower just like other hyacinths.

Incarvillea. See p. 132.

Iris. This is another big genus and one which includes many fibrous and rhizomatous-rooted members as well as true bulbs. Only the last are included here and for other sections of the family the reader should see the chapters on herbaceous flowers, rock plants and aquatics.

Bulbous irises are numerous and varied both in appearance and requirements. The easiest and also the most popular are the so-called Spanish, English and Dutch irises derived from *Iris xiphium*, *I. latifolia*, and *I. tingitana fontanesi*. These flower during the first half of summer, average 60 cm (2 ft) in height, are ideal for cutting and also very attractive for garden display. They will grow in any ordinary garden soil but prefer those that are not liable to dry out quickly in hot weather. They should be planted 8·7 cm (3½ in) deep in early autumn in a sunny position. Space them at least 15 cm (6 in) apart and leave them undisturbed for a year or so. Then, directly they show signs of being overcrowded, lift the bulbs in the second half of summer, when the foliage dies down, allow them to dry off for a few weeks in an airy shed, clean, divide into single bulbs and replant.

Almost as popular is the early-flowering *I. reticulata* which has violet-coloured, sweetly scented flowers on 20 cm (8 in) stems in late winter. There are several varieties, some a light blue and others dark blue or reddish purple. *I. histrioides* has shorter stems and stouter, paler blue flowers which start to open in mid-winter and continue until the end of that season. *I. danfordiae* has smaller, bright yellow flowers on 10 cm (4 in) stems in late winter but it is not as easy to grow as the others and needs good soil with plenty of bonemeal. All need a warm, sunny position and rather light, well-drained soil. They are excellent for the rock garden and should be planted 5 cm (2 in) deep in early autumn. Leave them undisturbed for a number of years, but when overcrowded lift, dry off, divide and replant as for Spanish irises. They also make excellent plants for an unheated greenhouse or frame grown in pans in a good soil or peat-based potting compost.

Ixia (African Corn Lily). It is a pity that these very graceful bulbous plants are on the borderline of tenderness and cannot therefore be relied upon to succeed out of doors except in very sheltered places and well-drained soils. Ixias flower in late spring/early summer, the starry flowers being borne in slender spikes on wand-like stems about 45 cm (1½ ft) in height. They make excellent cut flowers with colours mainly in yellow, orange, red and carmine plus white, often with a contrasting centre.

The corms should be planted 7·5 cm (3 in) deep in light, sandy soil, the ideal position being at the foot of a warm, sunny wall. Plant in the second half of autumn. After flowering cover the plants with panes of glass or open-ended cloches to keep off rain for a couple of months and so give the bulbs a chance to become fully ripened.

Ixias also do very well in pots in the cool greenhouse for which purpose they should be potted in autumn, five or six corms in a 10 cm (4 in) pot, watered sparingly at first, more freely as growth progresses and kept throughout in a light greenhouse with minimum temperature of 5°C/41°F. Gradually reduce the water supply after flowering and keep quite dry in late summer to ripen the bulbs.

Propagation is by seed and division of bulb clusters at planting or potting time.

Ixiolirion (Ixia Lily). *Ixiolirion montanum* is a pretty plant with starry heads of blue or rosy-purple flowers on 30-45 cm (1-1½ ft) stems in late spring/early summer. Names such as *I. ledebourii* and *I. pallasii* which appear in catalogues are simply varieties of *I. montanum*. Plant in autumn 7·5 (3 in) deep and about 15 cm (6 in) apart in good, reasonably well-drained soil and a sunny position and leave undisturbed until overcrowded. Increase by seed or division of the bulb clusters.

Lachenalia. See p. 480.

Leucojum (Snowflake). These pretty plants are nothing like so well known as the snowdrop, which they resemble in many respects, yet they are not difficult to grow. They enjoy reasonably rich, slightly moist soil in sun or partial shade but, with the exception of *Leucojum autumnale*, they do not like hot, dry places. Sometimes the bulbs do not flower for a year or so after planting. There are three principal kinds, the spring snowflake, *L. vernum*, which has nodding white and green flowers on 15 cm (6 in) stems in the second half of spring, the summer snowflake, *L. aestivum*, with similar flowers on 45 cm (1½ ft) stems in late spring, and the autumn snowflake, *L. autumnale*, a much frailer plant with white and pink flowers on 15 cm (6 in) stems in early autumn. Plant the first two in early autumn; the third in mid- or late summer. Cover with 7·5 cm (3 in) of soil and leave undisturbed for a number of years as frequent disturbance checks growth and discourages flowering. Propagation is most easily effected by dividing the clusters of bulbs when transplanting old plants.

Lilium (Lily). This is one of the biggest genera of hardy bulbs. There are hundreds of species and varieties and whole books have been written about them. It is not possible for me to do more than skim over the surface of so big a subject.

A few lilies are too tender to be reliable out of doors in cool climates and there are other species which, though apparently hardy enough have proved very difficult to acclimatize. But in addition to these there are a great many beautiful kinds which will grow well in colder climates without a great deal of trouble.

The first thing to understand about lilies is that some make roots from the base of the flower stem as well as from the bulb. These roots spread out near the surface and must not be damaged by forking or deep hoeing. It is a good plan to spread a mulch of peat or leaf-mould over lilies each spring to feed and protect these surface roots.

Another point is that while a good many lilies will grow in any reasonable kind of soil there are others which dislike lime and these can be grown only on soils that are at least a little acid. In general these lilies like best a soil containing a fair amount of peat or leaf-mould and a little sand.

No lilies like being out of the ground for a long time. Some of the most successful growers treat them like herbaceous perennials rather than bulbs, transplanting them with plenty of soil around the roots in spring just as they are starting into growth. But whatever may be said about this as a method of culture, it is impractical advice for the beginner who must buy his bulbs from a merchant in the autumn when they are offered for sale. The best thing to do then is to get them as early as possible and plant them at once. If they are delivered after late autumn it is probably best to start them in pots in a frame or greenhouse, then plant them out in spring.

Some lilies make no stem roots, only roots from below the bulb, and some of these need to be planted very near the surface. The most important are the Madonna lily, *Lilium candidum*, which needs to be covered with only 2·5 cm (1 in) of soil and will work its way out on to the surface after a time; the Nankeen lily, *L. × testaceum*, which should be covered with 8·7 cm (3½ in) of soil, and *L. giganteum* which should be planted with the top of its bulb level with the surface, though usually some protection such as bracken or heather is required in winter. Incidentally the Madonna lily and the Nankeen lily should both be planted very early in the second half of summer, if bulbs can be obtained then, as they start into growth quickly.

Other lilies, including the stem-rooting kinds, should be covered with 10-15 cm (4-6 in) of soil. It is a good plan to mix a little bonemeal with moist peat and sharp sand and place two or three handfuls of this around each bulb when planting.

A good many lilies will succeed best if they have their 'heads in the sun and feet in the shade'. This is certainly true of the very beautiful Japanese lily, *L. auratum*. The apparent contradiction can be achieved by planting the bulbs among low-growing evergreen shrubs or leafy plants which will shade the ground over the lily roots and keep them cool and yet allow the flower stems to grow up through the coverage into the sunlight. Dwarf rhododendrons and peonies are two suggestions for this kind of interplanting.

Lilies should not be disturbed. If they are growing reasonably well leave them alone and give the beds a good mulch of peat or leafmould each spring when growth appears.

Animal manure should not be used on the lily beds, but bonemeal and hoof and horn meal can be applied to stimulate plants on poor soils.

Lilies are increased by dividing the clusters of bulbs, by growing single bulb scales into new bulbs, and by seed. The first is the slowest but also the easiest. The gardener has only to wait until one of his lilies has formed a good clump producing several flowers, and then lift it in early autumn (or mid-summer for *L. candidum* and *L. testaceum*), carefully divide the clump into single bulbs and replant with the least possible delay.

Scales for propagation are also obtained in the autumn. Any number may be taken from one bulb, in fact the whole bulb may be pulled apart into separate scales, but take care to damage them as little as possible. Press them, right way up, into seed boxes filled with coarse sand and peat mixed in equal parts and cover them with 12 mm (½ in) of the same material. Make them moist and stand the boxes in an unheated frame or greenhouse. Bulblets will form at the base of the scales and by the following autumn it will be possible to shake these out of the sand and plant them in a nursery bed of sandy soil out of doors. Meanwhile the boxes should be watered moderately. Some lilies also make tiny bulbs, or bulbils, all up the flowering stems in the axils of the leaves. These may be detached, planted in soil, peat and sand in pots or boxes and grown on into flowering-size bulbs. Alternatively the whole stem can be laid on the soil and the little bulbs allowed to grow naturally.

Seed is the quickest method of increasing numbers and is very satisfactory with some lilies. The great popularity of the regal lily, *L. regale*, is partly due to the fact that it can be raised so freely in this way, that the bulbs have been put on the market at a very cheap rate. As a rule seed is sown in a mixture containing a lot of sand and peat in well-drained pots or pans in early spring. It is germinated in a frame or unheated greenhouse and the seedlings are not disturbed during the first season. The following autumn they are transferred to a nursery bed in which they are grown on until they reach flowering size.

For the purpose of garden decoration lilies may be grouped according to the character of their flowers. Four principal types may be distinguished: Trumpet lilies, in which the large flowers are shaped like a trumpet or funnel; Turk's Cap lilies, with smaller pendent flowers, the petals of which are normally curved backwards at the tips; Bowl-shaped lilies with very large, usually outward-facing flowers shaped like a bowl or plate and Upward-facing or Cluster lilies in which the flowers face upwards and are clustered together in fine heads. The following are typical examples of each group, but there are many more to be found in the catalogues of specialists, including hybrids and garden varieties which are in an almost constant state of change as new and better ones are raised and older ones are discarded.

TRUMPET LILIES. *L. brownii*, white-flushed purplish-brown outside, 90 cm (3 ft), midsummer; *L. candidum*, the Madonna lily, white, 1·3 m (4½ ft), mid- to late summer, does not mind lime; *L. formosanum*, white, 1 m (3½ ft), late summer/early autumn, rather tender and often grown in pots in greenhouses; *L. giganteum*, white, 1·8-3 m (6-10 ft) midsummer, but this fine plant is often placed in another genus and called *Cardiocrinum giganteum*; *L. japonicum*, pale pink, 76 cm (2½ ft), mid-summer; *L. longiflorum*, white, 76 cm (2½ ft), early to mid-summer, tender and often grown in pots for spring flowering in greenhouses; *L. monadelphum*, yellow, 1·3 m (4½ ft), early to mid-summer, does not mind lime; and *L. regale*, the Regal lily, white, flushed outside with maroon and with yellow inside, 1·3 m (4½ ft), mid-summer, does not mind lime.

TURK'S CAP LILIES. Bellingham Hybrids, yellow, orange or red spotted with maroon, 1·6 (5½ ft), mid-summer; *L. canadense*, orange-yellow, 90 cm (3 ft), mid-summer; *L. chalcedonicum*, scarlet, 90 cm (3 ft), mid-summer; does not mind lime; *L. davidii*, cinnabar red spotted black, 1·2-1·8 m (4-6 ft), mid-summer; *L. hansonii*, yellow, 1·2 m (4 ft), early

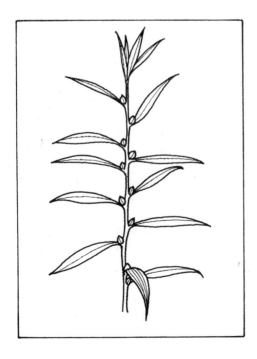

Small bulbils are produced by some lilies in the leaf axils along the flowering stems. These can be grown on into bulbs of flowering size.

summer, does not mind lime; *L. henryi*, orange-yellow, 1·8-24 m (6-8 ft), late summer; *L. martagon*, white or various shades of purple, 1·2 m (4 ft), the first half of summer, does not mind lime; *L. pardalinum*, orange-red, spotted with brown, 1·5-2·1 m (5-7 ft), enjoys a moist soil and does not mind some lime; *L. pyrenaicum*, yellow, 1 m (3½ ft), late spring/early summer, does not mind some lime; *L. speciosum*, white more or less flushed and spotted with pink according to variety, 1·6 m (5½ ft), late summer/early autumn, rather tender and often grown in pots in greenhouses; *L.* × *testaceum*, apricot, 1·6 m (5½ ft), the first half of summer, does not mind lime; and *L. tigrinum*, the tiger lily, orange-red spotted maroon, 1·6 m (5½ ft), mid–summer to early autumn.

BOWL-SHAPED LILIES. *L. aurantum*, the Golden-rayed lily of Japan, white, more or less spotted with crimson and flushed with gold and red according to variety, 1·5-2·1 m (5-7 ft), late summer/early autumn, also numerous hybrids.

UPRIGHT-FACING LILIES. *L. bulbiferum*, orange spotted with purple, 76 cm (2½ ft), the second half of summer, and *L. b. croceum*, the orange lily; *L. maculatum* (also known as *L. hollandicum* and *L. umbellatum*) with yellow, orange or crimson flowers on 30-76 cm (1-2½ ft) stems in the first half of summer; Mid-century Hybrids, lemon to crimson flowers on 60 cm-1 m (2-3½ ft) stems in the first half of summer. All these grow well in full sun and they do not appear to mind some lime in the soil.

Lily of the Valley. See **Convallaria** (p. 343).

Montbretia. See **Crocosmia** (p. 344).

Muscari (Grape Hyacinth). Delightful early-flowering bulbs for carpeting under trees and shrubs or for the very front of the border. The best known and most generally useful finds are *Muscari botryoides* and *M. armeniacum*. Both have compact spikes of sky-blue flowers on 15 cm (6 in) stems but *M. armeniacum*, and particularly its fine variety Heavenly Blue, spread more rapidly. *M. aucheri* has taller flower spikes than these, up to 20 cm (8 in) high and they are light blue at the top of the spike, darker blue at the bottom. A similar gradation in colour, but even more strongly contrasted, is found in *M. latifolium*, which also differs from most muscari in the breadth of its leaf. *M. comosum* Plumosum, popularly known as the plume hyacinth, is a very different plant with much bigger, looser, arching spikes of small blue flowers, the whole spike having quite a feathery appearance. It is a good subject for sunny ledges in the rock garden.

All grape hyacinths should be planted in sunny places and ordinary soil. Plant in the first half of autumn, 6·2 cm (2½ in) deep and 11·2 cm (4½ in) apart, except for *M. c.* Plumosum which should be given twice as much room. Leave undisturbed for a number of years till the bulbs get overcrowded when they should be lifted in mid-summer as soon as foliage turns yellow, separated to single bulbs and replanted with as little delay as possible.

Narcissus (Daffodil). A good many people still seem to regard the daffodil as different in some ways from the narcissus, keeping the first name for the trumpet varieties and the second for those with smaller cups or crowns. But the gardener and botanist recognize no distinction between the two and use daffodil merely as the popular name and narcissus as the botanical one when they are referring to the same group of plants.

These are eleven possible headings which provide a useful survey of the variety found in the family.

Division 1 includes all those varieties with true trumpets longer than, or as long as, the background perianth segments (petals).

Division 2 is known as Large Cupped and includes those varieties in which the cup is more than one third the length of the perianth segments but less than their full length. Next comes the Small Cupped varieties in Division 3. These have cups less than one third the length of the perianth segments.

Division 4 is made up of the Double-Flowered varieties. Division 5, known as Triandrus, is named from the species *Narcissus triandrus* which has small, nodding flowers with very reflexed perianth segments. All garden varieties and hybrids of this species come into this section. Not unlike it is *N. cyclamineus*, so called from the superficial resemblance of its small blooms to those of a cyclamen. Garden varieties and hybrids of this species form Division 6, known as Cyclamineus.

Division 7 is made up of garden varieties and hybrids with the characteristics of the jonquil, *N. jonquilla*, and allied species. They have small to medium-sized flowers, often borne in clusters and very sweetly scented. Division 8 takes in the extremely decorative Poetaz hybrids which have several good-size flowers on each stem and are especially useful for cutting. These were obtained by crossing the poet's narcissus, *N. poeticus*, with a species named *N. tazetta* which has clusters of small, sweetly scented flowers and the division is known as Tazette. Division 9 is made up of garden varieties and hybrids of *N. poeticus* and known as Poeticus.

Division 10 takes in all the species as well as varieties and hybrids that occur in the wild. Division 11 is reserved for garden varieties and hybrids which do not fall into any of the other divisions. Varieties with split cups or trumpets, sometimes called Orchid Flowered, belong here.

Several of the divisions are further subdivided according to the colouring of cups or trumpets and perianths.

So much, then, for the classification of this great family. Fortunately cultural instructions need not be so varied. With the exception of a few of the species which are most at home in the rock garden in rather light, well-drained soil, almost all narcissi will thrive in any ordinary soil. They are perhaps happiest in good loams and fairly rich soils but there are few places in which they cannot be made to thrive with a little encouragement. Ground should be dug thoroughly. Well-rotted dung may be used sparingly on poor soils but as a rule it is better to rely entirely on fertilizers such as bonemeal at 113 g and hoof and horn meal at 56 g per 0·8 sq m (2 oz per sq yd), or a compound fertilizer used according to the maker's instructions if the quality of the soil is doubtful.

Plant as early in the autumn as possible. If bulbs can be obtained in late summer so much the better. Planting can be continued till mid-winter but the later it is delayed the less satisfactory results are likely to be. Cover the bulbs with 7·5-10 cm (3-4 in) of soil. Keep the beds free of weeds and pick off flower heads as they fade. Leave the flower stems, however, as sap will pass back from them into the bulbs later in the summer.

It is unnecessary to lift narcissi every year. Leave them to grow and multiply until they become overcrowded, when they should be dug up carefully in mid-summer directly foliage dies down and cleaned in the same manner as hyacinths. Do not leave them lying about for long however, but plant them again as soon as possible.

If narcissi must be lifted immediately after flowering to make way for other things, replant them at once in a reserve bed – they can be placed quite close together – and leave them to finish their growth until mid-summer when they can be lifted and cleaned.

Many narcissi can also be naturalized very successfully in grass. It is wise to start with good-sized bulbs as smaller ones are apt to be starved by the grass before they become well established and able to look after themselves. A special tool for planting in grass can be obtained or, alternatively, the bulbs can be placed beneath lifted turves which should be replaced at once. It is most important that the grass immediately over the bulbs should not be cut until the narcissus foliage has died down; this must not be removed until it has fulfilled its function of feeding the bulbs in preparation for the next year's flowering.

Strong-growing Trumpet and Large Cupped varieties are especially suitable for naturalizing while many of the species such as *N. cyclamineus* and *N. bulbocodium*, the hoop petticoat daffodil, will succeed in fine, short turf.

Nerine. See p. 485.

Ornithogalum (Star of Bethlehem, Chincherinchee). These are attractive bulbs which are not very well known. The two best are *Ornithogalum nutans*, with 30-45 cm (1-1½ ft) spikes of nodding, silver flowers marked outside with pale green, and *O. umbellatum* with loose heads of starry white flowers on 15-20 cm (6-8 in) stems. Both flower in mid- to late spring. They will grow in any ordinary soil and partially shaded place.

O. arabicum, up to 45 cm (18 in) high with heads of quite large white flowers in late spring/early summer, needs a warmer, more sheltered place than the others. So does the chincherinchee, *O. thyrsoides*, with 60-90 cm (2-3 ft) spikes of papery, everlasting-type white flowers in the first half of summer. It is too tender for cold districts and is usually grown as a pot plant in the cool greenhouse, with four or five bulbs in each 10 cm (4 in) pot. Plant all ornithogalums in autumn 10 cm (4 in) deep and at least 20 cm (8 in) apart and leave undisturbed for a number of years.

Oxalis. See p. 200 and 487.

Pancratium. See p. 487.

Polianthes. See p. 491.

Polygonatum. See p. 143.

Puschkinia (Lebanon Squill). As its names implies, *Puschkinia scilloides* is like a scilla. The small, loose spikes of white or pale blue flowers striped with deeper blue, 10-15 cm (4-6 in) high, appear in mid-spring and this plant is a good one to choose for edgings or for planting in the rock garden. There is also a white-flowered variety. Select a sunny position and good, well-drained soil. Plant the bulbs 7·5 cm (3 in) deep in the first half of autumn and leave them undisturbed until they become overcrowded when they should be treated in exactly the same way as scillas.

Ranunculus. The tuberous-rooted ranunculus grown in gardens are varieties of *Ranunculus asiaticus*. They are commonly known as Turban, French or Persian ranunuculus and have fully double flowers on 23 cm (9 in) stems in late spring/early summer. They are not unlike the double-flowered Poppy anemones to which they are related and like them make useful cut flowers. They may also be used for a bright display in beds or at the front of borders in the garden but are not so easy to grow.

They need a rather open, loamy soil containing a fair amount of peat or leaf-mould. Damp and cold are their enemies. The warmer and more freely drained the position the better so long as it is not the sort of place that becomes arid early in summer. Moisture is needed to complete growth and fatten the small, clawed tubers. As a rule it is best to lift these annually in mid-summer when the leaves have died down. They are allowed to dry for a while in any airy shed after which they are cleaned off and stored in a cool, dry place until planting time from late winter to mid-spring.

Plant under 5 cm (2 in) of soil with the claws of the tubers downwards, spacing them 13 cm (5 in) apart. It is a good plan to surround the tubers with a little sharp sand especially if there is any doubt about the drainage of the land. Ranunculus also make attractive pot plants if potted in autumn about three or four together in a 10 cm (4 in) pot in John Innes or peat potting compost, and placed in a frost-proof greenhouse or frame.

Richardia. See **Zantedeschia** (p. 503).

Salvia. The only important tuberous-rooted species is *Salvia patens*, notable for the pure blue of its large, sage-like flower carried on 60 cm (2 ft) stems from mid-summer to early autumn. It is a handsome plant for a sunny spot in the herbaceous border in any ordinary soil. Plant the tubers under 11 cm (4½ in) of soil in mid-spring, or, better still, start them into growth in large flower pots in the greenhouse or frame a few weeks earlier and harden them off for planting out at the end of that season. Space them at least 38 cm (15 in) apart. Lift the tubers about the middle of autumn, allow them to dry off for a week or so in an airy but frost-proof shed and then store them quite dry in a cool airy place in the same manner as dahlia tubers. The roots are reasonably hardy but frost is liable to damage the young growth when it first appears.

For other species see p. 98.

Schizostylis (Kaffir Lily). The attractive plant *Schizostylis coccinea* suffers from the drawback of being not quite hardy enough to be reliable in all places out of doors in winter. It is most likely to thrive in a warm, sheltered spot. Plant in the first half of spring, 7·5 cm (3 in) deep and, if possible, start with growing tufts rather than dry rhizomes. Leave the plants undisturbed until overcrowded and cover with a little bracken or straw in winter. The type has spikes, 45 cm (1½ ft) high, of bright scarlet flowers but there are several pink varieties of which the two best are Viscountess Byng and the larger, earlier-flowering Sunrise. Major has scarlet flowers of extra size. Flowering time extends from early autumn to early winter according to variety.

Scilla (Squill). These are small plants useful in the rock garden, as edgings to beds and borders or for underplanting beneath taller growth. *Scilla sibirica*, the Siberian squill, is very typical with small, loose spikes of starry, bright blue flowers, the whole plant being no more than 8·7 (3½ in) in height. Planted freely it makes a wonderful carpet of colour in the first half of spring. *S. bifolia* is similar but starts to flower in late winter. These are white varieties of both. *S. tubergeniana* is also early flowering and pale turquoise blue.

S. peruviana is quite different, with a broad, rather short conical cluster of blue flowers in late spring/early summer. It needs a warm, sunny place. All will grow in any reasonably good soil and prefer sunny places. Plant in autumn 6·2 cm (2½ in) deep and leave undisturbed until overcrowded, when they may be lifted in late summer, divided and quickly replanted.

For bluebells, formerly known as scilla, see Hyacinthoides (p. 369).

Snowdrop. See **Galanthus** (p. 350).

Sparaxis (African Harlequin Flower). All that I have said regarding the cultivation of ixias applies equally to sparaxis, a related family of South African plants with brightly-coloured flowers in loose spikes on slender stems 15-30 cm (6 in-1 ft) in height. They make excellent pot plants for cool greenhouses but are too tender to be really reliable out of doors except in the mildest regions, and even then only in really well-drained, open soils and warm, sunny places. Most varieties grown are hybrids sold in mixed colours including cream, pink, purple and red, often with rings of sharply contrasting colours in the same flower. All bloom in the second half of spring.

Sternbergia (Lily of the Field). Despite its name and the legend that it is the authentic 'lily of the field' of the New Testament, *Sternbergia lutea* bears no resemblance to lilies as we know them but might easily be mistaken for a fine yellow crocus. It flowers in mid-autumn and has dark green, strap-shaped leaves. It likes a sunny warm place in reasonably rich but well-drained soil. The bulbs should be covered with 10 cm (4 in) of soil – rather more if the soil is light – and a pane of glass supported on sticks several centimetres over the site will give protection over winter. Plant in the second half of summer and thereafter leave the plants alone for a number of years. When they do get overcrowded, lift and divide in mid-summer and replant at once.

Tecophilea (Chilean Crocus). The small, funnel-shaped flowers of the little bulb *Tecophilea cyanocrocus* appear in the first half of spring and are brilliant gentian blue. Unfortunately the plant, though hardy, is difficult to manage in many places outdoors because it starts to grow too early. In consequence it is usually grown in pots or trays of gritty soil in a light, airy, unheated greenhouse. It can be tried out of doors in specially well-drained soil and a sunny place, planted 6·2 cm (2½ in) deep in early autumn and protected with an open-ended cloche during late winter/early spring.

Tigridia (Tiger Flower). These rather tender corms produce brightly-coloured and curiously-shaped flowers which appear to have only three petals until one looks more closely and realizes that there are six, the other three being very small. Colours are bright and varied and the flowers, on 45-60 cm (1½-2 ft) stems from mid-summer to early autumn, are usually blotched and spotted towards the centre, a feature which accounts for their popular name, tiger flower. Each flower lasts only a day but buds open successively to keep up a display for many weeks. All should be planted in mid-spring in a warm, sheltered place and light, sandy soil containing just a little well-rotted manure. Cover with 7·5 cm (3 in) of soil. Lift all the corms in mid-autumn, dry them off like gladioli and store them in a similar manner until planting time the following spring. Tigridias can be raised from seed and in mild districts sometimes increased by self-sown seedlings. In such places there is no need to disturb the plants which can be left until they become overcrowded.

Trillium. See p. 229.

Tristagma. *Tristagma uniflorum* is a pretty plant with starry blue flowers on 15 cm (6 in) stems in the second half of spring which will grow readily enough in any ordinary, nicely drained soil and sunny position. It makes a good edging to beds and borders or may be used effectively in the rock garden. It should be treated as a herbaceous plant rather than as a typical bulb, and planted, while starting into growth, in early spring.

Tulipa (Tulip). For centuries tulips have been esteemed by gardeners and hybridized to obtain new forms and colours. As a result garden races bear little discernible relationship to particular species, though others, especially those of recent introduction, are of known parentage which may be revealed in their group names. There are also some exceptionally beautiful plants among the species, but they are more the province of the specialist than of the ordinary gardener to whom 'tulip' nearly always means the gorgeous garden varieties which make such a splendid display during the second half of spring; they can be grown so easily in a great variety of solids and situations.

For like so many other cross-bred plants, the garden tulips are hardier and more long suffering than their wild ancestors. There are few gardens in which they cannot be induced to flower for at least a few years, though, if they are to prove really permanent, the soil should be fairly rich and well-drained.

Prepare tulip beds by digging them thoroughly and working in a little dung or decayed garden refuse, plus bonemeal at the rate of 113 g per 0·8 sq m (4 oz per sq yd). Choose a sunny position where possible or at least one not actually overhung by trees. Tulips will not put up with shade to the same extent as daffodils. Plant in mid-autumn about 10 cm (4 in).

Unlike daffodils, tulips benefit from an annual lifting, drying off and replanting. It is best not to disturb the bulbs until the foliage has died down naturally, but if the beds are required for other plants they should be lifted immediately after flowering and replanted temporarily elsewhere. They can be laid close together in shallow trenches, the bulbs and roots covered with a little soil.

When the leaves have withered, lift the bulbs carefully and lay them in trays in a dry shed for a week or so. Then twist off the tops, shake off any remaining soil, remove the small bulbs, which are seldom worth growing on, and store the rest in a dry place such as a shed or spare room until the normal planting season in autumn.

Garden varieties of tulips are subdivided into numerous sections for convenience of classification. There are the Early Single tulips which flower in mid-spring and are seldom much over 30 cm (1 ft) in height; the Early Doubles which are similar in every respect except that the flowers are double; Darwin tulips which flower in late spring, have stems 60 cm (2 ft) and more in height and bold, rather squarely built flowers; Cottage tulips, similar in height and flowering time but with variously shaped flowers; Lily flow-ered tulips, which have elegantly waisted flowers; Rembrandts, resembling the Darwins in all respects except colour which is striped and blotched instead of being mainly plain; Old English or Breeder tulips which are remarkably regular and refined in form; Parrot tulips with curiously twisted and slashed petals, blotched with green; Mendel and Triumph tulips which are in many respects intermediate between the early-flowering singles and the Darwins in season, height and character of bloom; Late Double tulips with large, peony-like flowers on 60 cm (2 ft) stems in mid-spring; Darwin Hybrids and Fosteriana Hybrids, rather like the Darwins but with larger petals; Kaufmanniana Hybrids, sometimes called Water-lily tulips because of the shape of their flowers which are produced in the first half of spring on quite short stems; Greigii Hybrids or Peacock tulips, hybrids between the Kaufmanniana and Greigii races, with chocolate-striped leaves often spread out almost flat and flowers in the second half of spring on 20-30 cm (8 in-1 ft) stems; Multi-flowered tulips, with several flowers on a stem; Viridiflora tulips, all of which have green as some part of their flower colour; and Fringed tulips, in which the edges of the petals are serrated or fringed. Varieties within these groups are extremely numerous and detailed descriptions should be sought in trade catalogues.

There are in addition the numerous species already referred to, which vary from the 7·5 cm (3 in) high, soft pink *Tulipa* to the giant *T. fosteriana*, part parent of the Fosteriana Hybrids and Darwin Hybrids and, with its immense glowing scarlet blooms, as showy as any garden hybrid. Another that should not be overlooked is *T. kaufmanniana*, part parent of the Kaufmanniana Hybrids, for this blooms in early spring and has very gracefully formed short-stemmed but large flowers, creamy white within and flushed with carmine outside. It is a gem for the rock garden. Other outstanding species are *T. acuminata*, with long, very narrow twisted petals; *T. linifolia batalinii*, with elegant primrose-yellow flowers on 15-25 cm (6-10 in) stems; *T. clusiana*, the lady tulip, with white, rose-flushed flowers on 20 cm (8 in) stems; the scarlet, 30 cm (1 ft) high *T. undulatifolia*; the similarly coloured but variable *T. greigii*; *T. linifolia*, deep scarlet and only 15 cm (6 in) high; *T. orphanidea* with small flowers of an unusual orange-buff colour; *T. praestans*, with several small scarlet flowers on each 30 cm (1 ft) stem; *T. saxatilis*, with lilac-pink flowers which has the extraordinary habit of spreading by underground stolons or runners; and *T. tarda*, with clusters of little yellow and white flowers on very short stems.

Vallota. See p. 502.

Veltheimia. See p. 502.

Zephyranthes (Flower of the West Wind). The funnel-shaped flowers of these graceful, bulbous plants are a little like those of a crocus. Unfortunately the plants themselves are far more tender and difficult to manage than crocuses and it is only in warm, sheltered places and sandy soils that they should be risked out of doors in cold climates. Elsewhere they should be grown in pots in a cool greenhouse or frame. Plant in autumn 7·5 cm (3 in) deep and protect with dry litter in winter. *Zephyranthes candida*, with snow-white flowers on 15 cm (6 in) stems in early autumn, is the one most likely to succeed.

Chapter 13

Bedding Out

Bedding out means planting for temporary display. It is the method by which the beds and borders in public parks are kept continuously bright for months on end and to achieve this effect some plants may be changed or renewed several times each year. This involves a good deal of expense and means also that greenhouses, frames and reserve beds must be available in which young plants can be grown until they are removed to the display beds when they are about to come into flower.

In private gardens such elaborate bedding out is seldom possible and if practised at all it is divided into two seasons: spring bedding, and summer bedding.

Spring display beds are planted in the autumn, usually more towards the beginning than the end of the season, as soon as the summer bedding plants have been removed. Summer bedding plants are planted out from late spring to early summer, as soon as the spring bedding plants have finished flowering.

For the spring display wallflowers, forget-me-nots (myosotis), double daisies (bellis), primroses and polyanthuses may be used together with tulips, hyacinths, narcissi and crocuses. For the summer display there is a wide choice of half-hardy annuals and other plants readily raised from seed sown in a greenhouse from late winter to mid-spring, together with half-hardy perennial or shrubby plants such as pelargoniums, dahlias, tuberous-rooted begonias and fuchsias.

The cultivation of these plants is described in other chapters. All the plants required for summer bedding can also be purchased as young plants in late spring and early summer. It is a mistake to buy the more tender kinds too early since severe frosts may occur until quite late in late spring which can easily kill the plants, especially if they have not been well hardened off before being offered for sale.

Bulbs used for spring bedding can be lifted carefully and heeled in elsewhere to complete their growth. Wallflowers, forget-me-nots and double daisies are not worth keeping but good primroses and polyanthuses can be lifted, divided and replanted in a reserve bed to grow on for another year.

Similarly, when the summer bedding flowers have finished many of the plants should be discharged – certainly all the half-hardy annuals which will die anyway. But good pelargoniums and fuchsias are expensive to buy and may well be worth keeping if a frost-proof greenhouse is available. They can be lifted, their stems and roots pruned quite a lot to save space and then potted in J.I. No. 1. or peat potting composts, using the smallest pots that will contain them. The brighter the place in which they are kept the better; the temperature must never fall below freezing point and preferably not below 7°C/45°F and until early spring they must be watered sparingly.

Good dahlias and tuberous-rooted begonias can be stored more readily since, after the plants have been been lifted, the tops can be cut off and the tubers kept dry in any place that is dry and frost-proof but not too warm, such as a cupboard in an unheated room.

Traditionally, bedding plants are often used in patterned displays in formal beds but they can be planted wherever they will contribute pleasingly to the overall effect. They can, for example, be used in mixed borders of shrubs and herbaceous perennials, or low-growing kinds may be used around or beneath rose bushes. They are excellent for window boxes, hanging baskets, tubs, troughs, ornamental vases or urns, and roof or balcony gardens – anywhere, in fact, where a little extra colour is welcome.

Grey- and silver-leaved plants can also be specially valuable in summer bedding schemes as a foil for concentrated flower colour. There are many varieties of artemisia, some helichrysums and centaureas and *Senecio cineraria*.

Helichrysum petiolare is a half-hardy shrub with grey, heart-shaped leaves, *Plecostachys serpyllifolia* has much smaller, more silvery leaves and spreads less rapidly. Both need winter protection and like well-drained soil. They can be increased by summer cuttings in a propagator or in a pot of soil, peat and sand covered with a polythene bag.

Senecio cineraria is much more bushy, as much as 90 cm (3 ft) high, with deeply divided, white wooly leaves. It is hardier than the two plants mentioned above but is unreliable outdoors in cold winters or in poorly drained soils, so it is wise to overwinter some young plants raised from cuttings in a frost-proof greenhouse or framed from which they will be replanted outdoors in late spring or early summer after proper hardening off.

The centaurea commonly used is *Centaurea cineraria cineraria*. It is also bushy with very finely divided white wooly leaves and requires the same treatment as *Senecio cineraria*.

Use soil- or peat-based composts in plant containers. Hanging baskets should be lined with sphagnum moss to prevent the compost trickling out. All container plants need regular watering – perhaps daily in warm weather – as the compost must never dry out. Plants in peat compost will need weekly feeding four to six weeks after planting, but soil composts usually contain more plant food and may not need feeding for about eight weeks. It is best to use a liquid or rapidly soluble compound fertilizer containing about equal percentages of nitrogen, phosphates and potash in water at the concentration recommended by the maker.

Chapter 14

Water and Bog Gardens

Water can add greatly to the beauty and interest of most gardens. It can be used as a new texture, contrasting with that of plants, soil and turf; as a mirror to reflect the sky as well as nearby plants and ornaments; to introduce movement and the pleasant sounds of flowing, spouting or splashing water; and as a medium in which to grow a whole new range of plants which thrive in or near water. It should be noted, however, that few plants, least of all water lilies, will thrive in running water. A very slow-flowing stream may be all right but a still pool is far better for them. Depth of water is also important since the larger water lilies and some floating plants, such as the water hawthorn, will thrive in a depth of 45-60 cm (1½-2ft) of water, but the majority of aquatics prefer the shallow margins of pools and streams where their crowns are covered by, at most, 10 cm (4 in) of water.

Some people are reluctant to introduce water to their gardens in case it will encourage mosquitoes and gnats in summer. It is perfectly true that a badly stocked water garden can become a breeding ground for these pests but the danger can be minimized by introducing sufficient fish.

Occasionally it may be possible to make use of natural pools and streams, but in most instances the gardener will have to construct his water garden. Clay is seldom satisfactory as a building material. Well-prepared concrete is far better and it is wise to include one of the advertised waterproofing preparations because, without this, there will be a slow seepage of water even through quite thick concrete. Alternatives are specially prepared plastic or rubber sheets with which the pool can be lined or pre-formed glass-fibre pools which only have to be placed in a hole of appropriate shape and size.

The design of the water garden may range from the completely formal pool, which forms a centre-piece to the lawn or paved garden, to the natural pool so often used as a charming adjunct to the rock garden. In the former case the lines are likely to be severely geometric and the sides of the pool vertical, or nearly so, whereas the informal pool will have an irregular shape and the sides will slope like those of a saucer. This saucer shape is very easy to construct and also relieves the gardener of many winter problems, as expanding ice will exert less pressure on the sides. With the formal pool it is advisable to build what is virtually a shelf right round the edge, and 23-30 cm (9 in 1 ft) below the surface on which soil can be placed or pots stood to accommodate the marginal plants which like to grow in shallow water. Pre-formed glass-fibre pools usually have such a shelf.

Constructing the Pool. The construction of a small pool in concrete is well within the scope of any handyman. The secret of success is to work with really fresh cement and to prepare the concrete with just enough but not too much water. If it is too dry it will not mix and set properly, while it if is too wet much of the cement will tend to rise to the top and then flake off when dry.

The bottom layer of concrete, even in a small pool, should be not less than 10 cm (4 in) thick. In large pools it is better to have 15-20 cm (6-8 in) of concrete. The sides should be of the same thickness as the base but may taper a little towards the top, though

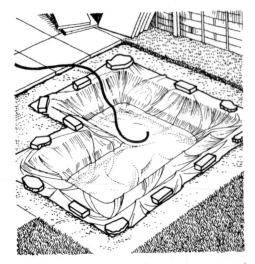

Constructing a pool with a plastic or rubber lining. After the soil has been excavated the base is smoothed with the back of a spade and all stones or sharp objects removed. The sheet is then placed in position, held down by stones and filled with water, the weight of which will mould the sheet into place. Finally the edges are trimmed and covered with rocks or paving slabs for a natural effect. Alternatively you can buy ready-made plastic basins in various ornamental shapes from most garden centres

even at the rim there should be not less than 7·5 cm (3 in) of concrete.

Concrete for pool making should be prepared with no less than 1 part of cement to 4 of ballast. A good general mixture is 3 parts by bulk washed gravel, 1 part builder's sand and 1 part cement, but I recommend lining a pool made with this mixture with a further 5 cm (2 in) thickness of concrete prepared with 1 part of cement to 3 parts builder's sand, to which has been added waterproofing powder or liquid used according to manufacturer's instructions.

Mix all the ingredients dry to begin with, turning them four or five times to make certain that they are thoroughly compounded. Then throw the mixture into a broadly cone-shaped heap, make a crater-like hole in the top, pour in water and turn the mixture inwards. This process can be repeated several times, more water being added at each turning until the whole mass assumes the consistency of rather thick porridge. The concrete is then ready for use and should be thrown into the pool with a shovel and worked to a rough level with a short plank held on edge.

An alternative to mixing the concrete at home is to purchase ready-mixed concrete, specifying what it is to be used for. However, it must be borne in mind that the concrete will start to set from the moment that it is dropped on the site and will probably be too stiff to be worked after three hours, so it is useless to have too much delivered at a time.

If a second application of finer cement is to be made as described above, the first layer should not be smoothed off but should be left with the rough board marks showing on the surface. These will give a key to which the final grout will cling. If, however, only the one application of cement is to be made, it should be smoothed off with the flat of a spade or a builder's trowel. Complete the bottom of the pool first and then build the sides. If these are sloping the concrete can be laid on just as described for the bottom, but in the case of vertical sides it will be necessary to make use of shuttering, that is, planks built on edge one above another to form a temporary wall to hold the concrete in place while it is setting.

The ideal time for doing this kind of constructional work is during mild but rather damp weather. Work should be discounted if frost threatens, because if concrete freezes before it is set it will be quite useless. In very hot, dry weather it is advisable to cover the concrete with damp sacks and keep these moistened for a day or so to prevent over-rapid drying, which may cause cracking.

If two layers of concrete, one coarse and the other fine, are to be laid the second should go on just before the first is fully dry, though firm enough to be walked on. If for some reason there is a delay and the preliminary layer does dry right out, it should be wetted thoroughly before the grout is laid.

In formal pools the raw edge of the concrete can be concealed by setting paving slabs in concrete as a surround and allowing these slabs to overhang the pool by several centimetres. With the informal pool it may be possible to arrange some rocks to overhang the edge, but it is seldom that the whole of the pool can be screened in this manner. Usually it is pleasant to have grass going down to the water's edge, at least around part of the pool, and then the turves may be laid to overlap the edge of the concrete.

Ordinary concrete made without one of the waterproofing compounds is not fully waterproof so unless treated in some way, such pools will gradually empty. The finished pool can be given two or three coats of one of the elastic bitumen compounds to prevent this happening.

The alternative method of making a pool is with a plastic or rubber lining. First a sheet must be obtained sufficiently large to cover the bottom and sides with a good overlap. Manufacturers will weld sheets together to any required size. The site of the pool is excavated and the soil smoothed down with the back of a spade and all large stones or other hard, sharp objects that might puncture the sheet are removed. The whole surface can be covered with a 2·5 cm (1 in) thick layer of sand to make a really smooth bed for the sheet, but this is not essential. The sheet is then placed in position, roughly pressed down to follow the contours of the pool and the edges held in place with a few stones or bricks, but not too firmly. Water is then run in and its weight will settle the sheet on to the soil or sand base, probably drawing in the edges a little in the process. Finally the edge of the sheet is trimmed off 15-30 cm (6 in-1 ft) beyond the lip of the pool and is buried under rocks, paving slabs or turf for several centimetres to conceal and secure it.

It is advisable to fill and empty a concrete pool once or twice before stocking it with plants or fish, though this precaution is not so necessary if bitumen is used for the final coat and is not necessary at all if pools are made of glass-fibre or are lined with plastic or rubber sheeting. The reason is that there may be certain chemicals in the concrete which will be dissolved by the water and prove harmful to plants or fish. Bitumen, by sealing the concrete, stops these chemicals being dissolved.

If chemical purification of the pool is preferred this can be done before stocking by filling it with water and stirring in sufficient syrupy phosphoric acid to turn blue litmus paper pink. It will be found that after a time the water becomes alkaline again, turning pink litmus paper blue. Add more acid daily until the water remains acid, and pink litmus dipped into it remains pink, for at least 24 hours.

Stocking the Pool. The best time for planting water plants is late spring when many aquatics are just starting into growth. Fish, snails and other small water creatures should not, as a rule, be introduced at the same time as the plants. It is better to wait a few weeks to give the plants a chance to become established and allow the water to settle after the disturbance and muddying which is almost certain to occur at first.

Soil must, of course, be provided for the plants, though the way in which it is used may be varied. Many people adopt the simple method of spreading good loamy soil all over the bottom of the pool to a depth of at least 15 cm (6 in), covering this with about 2·5 cm (1 in) of clean gravel or sand and planting directly into this bed of soil as if it were a border on dry land. In this case the water is not added until planting is completed. The drawback to this method is that, if the pool is a big one, it takes rather a lot of soil to cover it completely. An alternative is to build up small mounds of soil here and there where plants are required, holding the soil in position with fine-mesh wire netting. A variation on this scheme is to plant everything in plastic baskets filled with soil and then sink the baskets in position where required.

The ideal soil for any of these methods is a rather heavy, fairly rich loam. Avoid mud from pond bottoms and stream sides and do not use dung or artificial manures.

Water plants vary greatly in the depth of water in which they like to grow. There are some vigorous water lilies which thrive with their roots 60 cm (2 ft) beneath the surface and many pond weeds, such as the Canadian pond weed and the charming English water violet, *Hottonia palustris*, also grow well in quite deep water. In contrast there are a great many plants, particularly those found naturally towards the edges of pools and streams, which would soon be killed if submerged more than 15 cm (6 in) deep. These are often at their best when no more than just awash with water. The flowering rush (butomus), water plantain (alisma), marsh marigold (caltha), and water forget-me-not (*Myosotis scorpioides*), are familiar examples of this type.

Sometimes it will be inevitable that plants must go into their full depth of water straight away, but often it is possible to fill the pool gradually, and this is certainly the ideal method. After planting run in water to a depth of 6·2 cm (2½ in) over the plants and then, as they grow, gradually add more until, after three or four weeks, the pond is filled.

Do not be surprised if there is considerable muddying at first. This is quite natural and due to the unbalanced condition of life in the water at the outset. It may be some months before the water becomes reasonably clear and, even then, one can never expect a pool containing growing plants to be crystal-clear – it is rather like expecting a plot of fertile soil never to produce weeds. However, by stocking a pool wisely with a good mixture of plants, including submerged plants which give off oxygen to the water and, in addition, by having enough fish in the pool to keep down minute animal life, it is possible to have water which will remain fresh and reasonably clear without being changed at any time.

Under these conditions all that is necessary is to bring the water up to its normal level from time to time as it becomes lowered by evaporation. Roughly speaking allow one submerged aquatic (oxygenating plant) per 0·8 sq m (1 sq yd) of water surface, one water lily to every 2·4 sq m (3 sq yd), one marginal plant every 45 cm (1½ ft) around the edge of the pool, and one fish to every 27 l (6 gal) of water. The number of gallons in a pool can be calculated approximately by multiplying the length by the breadth by the depth, measured in feet, and the result by 6¼. Then convert to litres.

Fish are important not only for the interest they add to the pool but also because they devour the larvae of mosquitoes and gnats so preventing the water from becoming a nuisance to the whole neighbourhood. There are many highly ornamental varieties of fish hardy enough to be established in a pool but none better than the common goldfish and the golden orfe. In winter, if the weather is very cold and the pool is a small one, there may be some danger of it freezing solid. No fish will survive this so either they must be removed in good time to the safety of an inside aquarium or the pool must be well covered with planks and sacks as protection. Alternatively an electric immersion heater can be used to prevent the surface of the water from freezing over completely.

Moving Water. Fountains can be used effectively even in the smallest gardens or water can be made to bubble up through a bed of pebbles, to splash out or trickle from wall fountains or to race over waterfalls and down cascades. All these effects are best engineered by circulating the water in the pool by means of a pump which may either be submerged in the pool itself or be installed near it. Completely waterproofed submersible pumps are available and are entirely satisfactory for small fountains, cascades or waterfalls, but where a larger flow of water is required it is necessary to install a pump nearby and for this expert help should be sought. The reason for re-circulating the water in the pool rather than drawing fresh water from an outside supply is that by this means the balance of chemicals and living organisms in the pool is not disturbed and the temperature is also kept reasonably steady.

Unstocked Pools. When water is used primarily as a mirror or as a silvery texture in the garden it may be better to dispense with plants and fish altogether. The water can then be

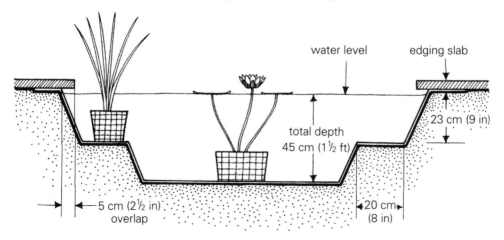

Cross-sectional diagram of a finished pool showing two planting depths

387

kept crystal clear by chemical means, as in a swimming pool, or by frequent changes. A simple chemical method of keeping water clear of blanket weed and other algae is to add 50 g (1·7 oz) of copper sulphate per 4,500 l (1,000 gal), repeating the dose every five or six weeks from early summer to early autumn.

WATER PLANTS

Acorus (Sweet Flag). *Acorus calamus* has strong, sword-like leaves, similar to those of the common yellow flag iris and the whole plant is scented when bruised. It is grown solely for its foliage and, in addition to the type which is green, there is a variety with white, pink and golden variegations. Either will grow in very wet bog or in 6·2 cm (2½ in) of water and can be propagated by division in early spring.

Alisma (Water Plantain). The wild plant, *Alisma plantago-aquatica*, is worth a place in large water gardens but is not quite choice enough for small ones. It has big, dock-like leaves, and loose 60-90 cm (2-3 ft) sprays of pink flowers which are just a little too small and too pale to be really effective. It thrives best in shallow water and is suitable for the margin of a pool or the wettest parts of a bog garden. Propagation is by division or by seed in spring.

Aponogeton (Water Hawthorn). *Aponogeton distachyus* is one of the most beautiful of floating aquatics, in fact it almost rivals the water lilies. It has narrow, dark green leaves which lie flat on the surface of the water and form a carpet to display the small clusters of snow-white flowers which have a marked perfume of hawthorn. The water hawthorn is hardy, easily grown and will do equally well in water of a depth from 15-45 cm (6 in-1½ ft). There is a form known as *A. aldenhamensis* which has purplish foliage and even larger flowers tinged with pink. Both species and variety can be increased by careful division of the tuberous roots in late spring.

Arundo (Giant Reed). A very strong reed-like plant with broad, grey-green foliage, *Arundo donax* will reach a height of 2·4 m (8 ft) or more and is really too sturdy for any but the larger pools. Where it can be accommodated, however, there is no more handsome foliage plant for shallow water or very boggy soil. Propagation is by division in spring.

Butomus (Flowering Rush). *Butomus umbellatus* is a very beautiful wild plant, colonies of which can be found in many canals, slow-moving streams and bogs. It makes a sturdy clump of narrow, grass-like leaves from which rise, in the second half of summer, stout, 90 cm (3 ft) leafless stems terminated by flat clusters of shining pink flowers. This is a really good plant and, despite its height, one which can be accommodated in quite small gardens as it does not spread unduly. It will grow in 2·5-15 cm (2-6 in) of water. Propagation is by division in late spring.

Calla (Bog Arum). *Calla palustris* is very like the greenhouse arum lily on a reduced scale. It has the same bright green, heart-shaped leaves and similar but much smaller white 'flowers', but it does not exceed a height of 30 cm (1 ft). It is quite hardy and easy to grow in 2·5 cm (1 in) or so of water. Increase by dividing the rhizomes in spring.

Callitriche (Water Starwort). Submerged plants useful because they give out oxygen to the water and provide protection for young fish. Two species are grown, *Callitriche verna* which makes a dense curtain of light green shoots in summer and *C. autumnalis*, which continues to grow all the winter and so is more useful for indoor aquaria than for outdoor pools.

Caltha (Marsh Marigold, Kingcup). The common marsh marigold, *Caltha palustris*, is a very beautiful aquatic. Everyone must be familiar with the enormous, buttercup-like flowers on 30 cm (1 ft) high stems which fill water meadows and stream sides with colour before most plants have come fully out of their winter rest. It has a number of forms, including a double-flowered variety which loses in grace what it gains in solidity. There is also an interesting species known as *C. polypetala* in which the flowers are of even greater size and the stems are up to 60 cm (2 ft) long. All thrive in very shallow water or boggy ground. Propagation is by division immediately after the plants have flowered.

Carex (Sedge Grass). This is a large genus of plants all with narrow, grass-like leaves and clusters of small green or brownish flowers similar to those seen on many types of rush. None is of the first merit for the garden, but such kinds as *Carex pendula* and *C. pseudocyperus* are worth planting for foliage effect at the margin of the pool in shallow water. Propagation is by division in spring.

Cyperus (Umbrella Grass). The leaves of these plants are grass-like and the straight flower stems carry clusters of small flowers which in some kinds are themselves surrounded by more leaves. The best of these is *Cyperus involucratus* whose flower leaves are arranged like the ribs of an umbrella and the stems are 60-90 cm (2-3 ft) high. It is rather tender and must be brought into a frost-proof greenhouse for protection in all but the mildest winters. It will grow in shallow water, boggy soil or even quite ordinary soil and can be increased by division or seed. Increase it by dividing the roots carefully in late spring.

Elodea (Pond Weed). One species, *Elodea canadensis*, grows so freely that it soon becomes a troublesome weed in pools and streams. Others are less vigorous and, as they are good oxygenators, are worth planting for this purpose and to provide shelter for fish. All grow completely submerged. Two of the best are *E. crispa* (now listed as *Lagarosiphon major*) and *E. densa*. Almost any piece detached in spring will grow into a new plant. Some species may be listed as anacharis and not elodea.

Eriophorum (Cotton Grass). Before they start to seed there is nothing very striking about any of the cotton grasses which look like rather ordinary rushes 30-60 cm (1-2 ft) in height. The whole picture changes at seed time when it appears that every blade of grass has become tipped with a snowy tuft of cotton-wool. When in seed they provide a sight not easily forgotten.

The best species to choose for the garden are *Eriophorum angustifolium*, *E. latifolium* and *E. vaginatum*, but really there is not a great deal of difference in the decorative value of any of the hardy kinds. All thrive in bog and can be increased by dividing the roots in spring.

Hottonia (Water Violet). One of the prettiest of submerged water plants is *Hottonia palustris*, the British water violet. It makes masses of finely divided, light green foliage and in summer thrusts above the surface of the water slender stems bearing pale lilac flowers. It is perfectly hardy, will grow in anything up to about 45 cm (1½ ft) of water and can be divided in late spring.

Hydrocleys (Water Poppy). The attractive plant *Hydrocleys nymphoides* is a floating aquatic for water 30–45 cm (1–1½ ft) in depth. The flowers are yellow and undoubtedly poppy-like, though there is no botanical connection between this plant and the poppy. It is none too hardy for which reason it should be given a sunny, sheltered position and, in cold districts, some extra protection in winter, or it may be removed to the greenhouse over winter. Propagation is by division.

Iris. This great genus, in addition to giving us fine plants for the herbaceous border and rock garden, also includes several moisture-loving species of which at least two may be truly regarded as water plants. These are the yellow water flag, *Iris pseudacorus*, a rather too vigorous plant with sword-shaped leaves and bright yellow flowers on 90 cm (3 ft) stems in early summer, and *I. laevigata*, which is only about 60 cm (2 ft) high and has notably showy flowers in a range of colours including blue, purple, pink and white. Both these will thrive in 5–7·5 cm (2–3 in) of water. There is a good variety of *I. pseudacorus* with white variegated leaves. *I. kaempferi*, the Japanese iris or clematis-flowered iris, often regarded as a water plant, really likes moist soil only and may be killed by water standing over its crowns. It has been very highly developed in gardens and there are many named varieties in shades of blue and purple with white. *I. sibirica* (see p. 134) also does well by the water side. All these irises can be divided in spring.

Juncus (Rush). On the whole rushes are not very beautiful plants but a few of the best species such as the variegated form of *Juncus follicularis* in which the green leaves are banded with white, and *J. glaucus* which, as its name implies, has greyish-blue leaves, are worth planting at the margins of pools and streams. *J. effusus* Spiralis has stems twisted like a corkscrew and is sometimes planted for its oddity. They thrive in 5–7·5 cm (2–3 in) of water and are easily increased by division.

Limnocharis. See **Hydrocleys** (above).

Mentha (Mint). One species of mint thrives either in a shallow water or a very wet ground at the edge of the pool. This is *Mentha aquatica* which has the typical mint aromatic foliage and little, dense clusters of purplish-mauve flowers in early summer. It is a very easy plant to grow but not notably beautiful. Propagation is readily effected by division in spring.

Menyanthes (Bog Bean, Buck Bean). There is no question about the hardiness of the bog bean, *Menyanthes trifoliata*. This is a plant to grow in not more than 30 cm (1 ft) of water, preferably planted in wet soil at the edge and allowed to grow out as it chooses. The leaves are three-parted and the white or blush-tinted flowers are individually small and produced in short spikes in mid-summer. Plants can be divided in late spring.

Mimulus (Musk, Monkey Flower). The monkey flower, *Mimulus guttatus*, will thrive in shallow water or very wet ground and so will the very similar *M. luteus* and the Allegheny musk, *M. ringens*. These are very showy plants with brilliant yellow flowers, in some varieties of *M. guttatus* splashed with crimson or maroon. There is also a variety with semi-double blooms. *M. ringens* has soft blue, pink or white flowers on branched stems up to 60 cm (2 ft) high. All flower in summer and can be raised from seed in spring but as a rule division will provide all the plants necessary.

Myosotis (Water Forget-me-not). The water forget-me-not, *Myosotis scorpioides*, is very like the bedding variety but looser in habit and, as a rule, with smaller paler flowers, though there can be considerable variation and finely coloured forms may be selected. It is a plant for very shallow water or wet ground. It can be increased rapidly by seed sown in spring or by division at the same time and flowers from mid-spring onwards.

Myriophyllum (Water Milfoil). This genus, which has provided some of the best oxygenating plants for indoor aquariums, has not been lavish with hardy kinds but at least two species are suitable for planting out of doors. These are *Myriophyllum verticillatum* and *M. spicatum*, both with very finely divided leaves. They grow completely submerged except for the flower spikes which are not conspicuous. Propagate by division in spring.

Nuphar (Brandy Bottle). In some north-west European pools and slow-moving rivers a plant with cup-shaped yellow flowers in summer is to be seen and is frequently erroneously termed water lily. This is *Nuphar lutea*, which has large, heart-shaped leaves floating on the surface of the water, very much like those of a water lily. It has the merit of thriving even in running water, to which the true water lilies object, but it is very vigorous and unsuitable for small pools. It will thrive in water up to 60 cm (2 ft) deep and does not mind a certain degree of shade. Culture and propagation are the same as for nymphaea. A much smaller kind, *N. pumila*, also known as *N. minima*, can be grown in several centimetres of water.

Nymphaea (Water Lily). This is the biggest and the most important genus of aquatic plants. The are a number of species and these have been crossed and inter-crossed to produce hundreds of hybrids, many of the greatest beauty. Water lilies vary widely in size, vigour, colour and the depth of water in which they thrive. There are miniature types, such as *Nymphaea tetragona*, *N.* Pygmaea Alba (now listed as *N. tetragona*) and *N. candida*, all white flowered, which will grow happily in 11·2 cm (4½ in) of water and can be established in small tubs or old stone sinks. At the other extreme are very vigorous water lilies, such as *N. alba* and Gladtoniana also with white flowers, which like to grow in 60-90 cm (2-3 ft) of water and will soon cover a large area; in fact they can become a nuisance in any but the largest pools.

It is the intermediate varieties that are of greatest interest to the gardener and these are mostly hybrids of garden origin. Some are derived from *N. odorata*, known as the fragrant water lily because of the sweet scent of its white flowers. The following are also mostly fragrant and some bear the specific name of the parent, such as *Odorata gigantea*, with very large white flowers; Odorata Helen Fowler, rose pink; *Odorata minor*, with small white flowers and small leaves; *N. odorata rosea*, rose pink and *N. odorata sulphurea*, sulphur yellow. Others are called Marliacea after a French breeder, Mons. Marliac, who raised them. These include Marliacea Albida, white; Marliacea Carnea, white flushed pink; Marliacea Chromatella, yellow; Marliacea Rosea; Marliacea Flammea, magenta; and Marliacea Zgnea, carmine. Others simply have fancy names. Amongst the best are Albatross, white; Escarboucle, bright crimson; James Brydon, rosy crimson; Froebeli, blood red; Rose Arey, pink; and Sunrise, yellow. All these will grow in water 30-60 cm (1-2 ft) in depth and should be planted at least 1·2 m (4 ft) apart. Where space is more limited the several forms of the hybrid *N. laydekeri* are useful. These include Laydekeri Rosea, pink; Laydekeri Purpurata, wine red; and Laydekeri Lilacea, deep rose. They like about 30 cm (1 ft) depth of water.

All these water lilies are best planted in late spring. It is advisable to overhaul them every two or three years and to remove dead leaves annually in the autumn. Old plants can be divided like herbaceous perennials, though it will be found that some varieties are much easier to handle than others. Those with tuberous roots need special care and the occasional use of a sharp knife.

Nymphoides (Floating Heart). The only species of importance to the owner of an outdoor pool is *Nymphoides peltata*, once known as *Villarsia peltata*. It is a very attractive plant thriving in 15-30 cm (6 in-1 ft) of water and having dark, floating leaves surmounted by yellow-fringed flowers. Propagation is by division of old roots in late spring.

Orontium (Golden Club). *Orontium aquaticum* is an interesting plant for the centre of the pool in a depth of 7·5-45 cm (3 in-1½ ft) of water. The blue-grey leaves project out of the water and the tiny yellow flowers are clustered along a spadix similar to that in the centre of an arum lily, though there is no conspicuous white spathe to surround them as in the arum. Propagation is by division in spring.

Peltandra (Arrow Arum). The popular name refers to the arrow-shaped leaves and arum-like flowers which are white in *Peltandra alba* and green in *P. undulata*. They are suitable for shallow water at the edge of the pool and can be increased by division in the second half of spring.

Pontederia (Pickerel Weed). Good blue pond flowers are not too numerous and *Pontederia cordata* has the twin merits of having light blue flowers borne in dense spikes on 45 cm (1½ ft) stems and really handsome broad and shining green leaves. It flowers in mid-summer. This is a plant to grow in a few centimetres of water. It can be increased by careful division in late spring.

Sagittaria (Arrow Head). The popular name of these plants also refers to the arrow-like shape of the leaves. They would be worth growing for their foliage alone but all have the additional attraction of showy white flowers in branched spikes. Among the best are *Sagittaria sagittifolia* which flowers in the second half of summer and its double-flowered form Flore Pleno which is often sold as *S. japonica*. Other species are *S. lancifolia*, with narrow leaves, and *S. latifolia*, with broad leaves. All are plants for fairly shallow water. Propagation is by division in the second half of spring.

Sarracenia. These are interesting and beautiful plants, the interest lying in the fact that they are carnivorous. Each plant in addition to producing ordinary leaves has several pitcher-shaped leaves which serve as traps to insects, which are then digested. The sarracenias are bog plants, requiring damp, peaty, acid soils. Good kinds are *Sarracenia flava*, with yellowish-green pitchers, and *S. purpurea*, with pitchers which are green at first but later become red. Careful division in late spring provides the best method of propagation. As these plants are on the borderline of hardiness it is usually wise to grow them in pots, stand them in the shallow water at the edge of a pool, or plunge them to their rims in boggy soil from late spring to mid-autumn but bring them in to a cool but frost-proof greenhouse for the winter.

Scirpus (Bulrush). What most people call bulrush is really reed-mace or typha. These are the plants with long, cigar-like inflorescences. The true bulrushes (scirpus) are far less conspicuous with their small, brownish spikes of 'flowers'. One species, however, is well worth planting for its foliage, in fact it is one of the most popular of foliage plants for the pool. This is *Scirpus tabernaemontani* Zebrinus, the pointed, rush-like stems of which are pale green widely banded with cream. It is popularly called the zebra rush. The whole plant is compact and reaches a height of about 90 cm (3 ft). It thrives in shallow water and can be divided in spring.

Thalia. If *Thalia dealbata* were a little more reliably hardy it would be much more widely planted, for it is a handsome plant with broadly lance-shaped leaves standing high out of the water and clusters of purple flowers on 1·9 m (6½ ft) stems. It thrives in shallow water and is likely to need winter protection in cold climates. For this reason it is best grown in pots so that it can be taken into a frost-proof greenhouse in mid-autumn without serious root disturbance and kept there until mid-spring when it may be repotted and divided if desired.

Typha (Reed Mace, Cat-tail). These are the plants which are so frequently, but incorrectly, named bulrushes. They all have cigar-like inflorescences and are handsome but as a rule somewhat invasive. One of the best for the small garden is *Typha minima* which does not exceed 45 cm (1½ ft) in height. *T. angustifolia* grows to about 1·5 m (5 ft) and has a very slender inflorescence. All are plants for quite shallow water. Division in spring provides the best means of increase though some kinds seed themselves freely.

Vallisneria. Submerged oxygenating plants of which the best for outdoor pools is *Vallsneria spiralis*. The leaves are long and narrow like lengths of almost transparent pale green ribbon. Bubbles of oxygen can be seen forming on them freely on any warm day. However, vallisneria does not provide such good cover for young fish as some of the more densely growing plants such as hottonia and callitriche. Increase by division in spring.

Villarsia. See **Nymphoides** (p. 392).

BOG PLANTS

In the very damp ground surrounding the pool or stream many of the moisture-loving plants described in other parts of this book can be used with good effect. Thus from the herbaceous perennials we can borrow astilbe, aconitum, cimicifuga, hemerocallis, lythrum, lysimachia, podophyllum, rodgersia, *Saxifraga peltata*, and trollius. From the rock garden we can take dodecatheon and the moisture-loving primulas such as *Primula denticulata, cashmireana, microdonta, japonica, pulverulenta, beesiana, bulleyana, prolifera, sikkimensis, florindae, alpicola, rosea* and *veitchii*. The shrub garden can supply bamboos in variety, also *Cornus sanguinea*, many willows, alders and taxodium. Nor must the gunneras and rheums (ornamental rhubarbs) be overlooked. No plants give a more tropical appearance to the water garden. The leaves of *Gunnera manicata* are often 1·8 m (6 ft) in diameter. The crowns are rather tender and should be protected with bracken or dry leaves in winter. Amongst the ferns *Osmunda regalis* is the best for the water garden.

Chapter 15

Lawns and their Maintenance

It is customary to say that there are two methods of making a lawn: either from seed or from turf, but this overlooks a third possibility which, I believe, is the most usual course chosen by the owner of a small garden, and that is to make a lawn out of the turf which already exists on the site.

I have seen some good lawns made in this manner. I remember, for example, an excellent tennis lawn which had been made by the simple process of mowing the meadow in which the owner's house had been built, filling up small hollows and levelling out bigger depressions and bumps by cutting the turf in the form of an H with a sharp edging tool, folding back the flaps and then adding to or scraping away some of the soil underneath.

One advantage in making use of the grasses native to the site is that they are certain to be of a kind which thrives reasonably well under the existing conditions of soil and climate, and this cannot always be said for imported grass. Home-made lawns of this type are therefore often trouble free.

On the debit side, the natural lawn seldom has the fine finish and soft, even texture of lawns specially made with fine-leaved, slow-growing grasses. There are likely to be many small weeds mixed up with the grass and the grasses themselves will probably include kinds of a comparatively coarse type, such as meadow grass and perennial rye grass, but many unsuitable grasses may disappear after a time and many weeds can be eliminated with selective lawn weedkiller.

LAWNS FROM TURF

When we come to consider 'made' as distinct from 'natural' lawns, the classification into turf and seed construction holds true. At one time there were more lawns made from turf than from seed, though this is probably no longer true for several reasons. There have been such great improvements during the present century in the selection and supply of suitable grasses for lawn making, and so much has been learned about their cultivation that this has become the most popular and cheapest method of producing lawns.

There are many people who, for one reason or another, prefer to use turf. It has the merit of being extremely quick, a hard-wearing sward being obtainable in a matter of weeks instead of months. Added to this it is not so essential to rid the ground so thoroughly of weeds as in the case of sites required for seeding. Good turf will smother quite a number of the weeds, particularly those of an annual character such as chickweed and groundsel, which are often such a nuisance on new sites. And though it may be argued that there really is no need to worry about these annual weeds since they will be eliminated by mowing, it must be admitted that they can interfere seriously with the seedling grass.

The great drawback of turf is that it usually contains an unknown combination of grasses together with many weeds; in fact, in this respect it is no improvement on the natural lawn. This is not surprising because supplies of turf are often obtained from meadows which have been earmarked for building sites. It is possible to purchase cultivated turf, that is to say turf specially raised for lawn making by sowing suitable mixtures of grass seed on properly prepared ground, but the price is likely to be higher than that of meadow turf.

Sea-Washed Turf. There is another special class turf of which my criticisms regarding weeds and coarse grasses do not apply. Sea-washed turf grows on salt marshes near the sea and salt water does occasionally flow over it at extra high tides. Because of these peculiar conditions and the fine, silty nature of the soil, only certain grasses can survive, and these are of a very fine, close-growing character. Sea-washed turves are unrivalled for all purposes where an exceptionally fine sward is required, but they are not so suitable for ordinary lawn making where there is to be hard wear and perhaps a minimum of attention. Because of the character of the soil, which may become excessively close with rolling and heavy wear, the turf often dies out and becomes patchy after a few years. Sea-washed turf is difficult to maintain and only suitable for special purposes.

Preparation. The soil should be turned right over to a depth of at least 30 cm (1 ft) and all perennial weed roots picked out. If the site has to be levelled it is essential to keep the fertile top soil on top; that it so say any alteration in levels must be done by moving the lower soil, and the top soil to a depth of at least 23 cm (9 in) must first be stripped off and then replaced when the levelling has been completed. This is because the lower soil is seldom suitable for the cultivation of good grass, lacking the fertility and texture of top soil. If this preliminary work can be completed in the spring and the soil left fallow all summer it will be an advantage and give an excellent opportunity to eliminate weeds by frequent hoeing or the use of non-persistent weedkillers.

If the soil is naturally poor it will pay to dig in dung or compost generously with dressings up to 50 kg per 4·8 sq m (1 cwt per 6 sq yd). Bonemeal, or some other slow-acting phosphatic fertilizer can also be added to encourage early root growth, but not too generously as phosphates in excess will stimulate clovers at the expense of fine grasses, and although clovers make a very dark green drought-resistant lawn, they also make an extremely slippery one and are a real menace on lawns that are to be used for sports or similar activities.

In any case the soil, after digging, should be allowed to settle for at least a month, and preferably longer. Even then, before the turf is laid, the surface should be trodden, when dry, first in one direction and then at right angles. Finally it must be broken down reasonably finely with fork and rake. This will give a final opportunity to pick out any weed roots which may have been overlooked and will also destroy any small weeds which have survived previous cultivations, besides giving a smooth, fine surface on which the turf will be laid.

Laying Turf. The best time to purchase turf is in the autumn, but it can also be laid in early winter or spring. It is not usually wise to attempt turfing in mid-winter unless the weather is particularly mild, nor between late spring and late summer, when conditions are usually too dry.

As a rule turf is cut in rectangles 90 cm (3 ft) long, 30 cm (1 ft) wide and about 3·8 cm (1½ in) thick, and these long strips are rolled up for easy transport. The drawback to this method of cutting is that the rolling almost always breaks the soil to some extent so that the result is less even than that obtained by cutting turves in 30 cm (1 ft) squares and transporting them flat. The small square turf is therefore frequently favoured by experts, particularly when engaged in the construction of lawns requiring a very true surface. A drawback is that there are more turves to be handled for any given area, and therefore more labour is involved in laying them.

Before turf is laid it is wise to examine it closely and remove any weeds likely to prove troublesome, such as dandelions and plantains. Next the turves should be trimmed to an even thickness. The simplest method is to make a shallow trough 3.8 cm (1½ in) deep, just enough to take one turf, and open at one end. The turves are slid into the box upside down one at a time and trimmed with a large knife (an old carving knife is ideal) to exactly the depth of the box.

The turves are laid in straight rows starting from one end of the lawn, but the turves in each row are staggered in relation to those in the preceding row, in fact the whole effect is precisely the same as may be observed in any properly made brick wall. The idea is to get a good bond before the turves actually grow into the soil beneath them.

As they are laid the turves may be lightly beaten down on to the surface with a smooth wooden block. A special turf beater can be purchased for this purpose, though it is seldom an investment which the amateur gardener is prepared to make. The back of a spade can be used for beating the turves but it is not as good as a wooden block because it is more likely to bruise the grass and, in any case, a spade back is seldom quite flat. Beating is more likely to be useful in light soil than on heavy and should always be omitted if the turf is very wet. Never use the beater to level inequalities in the surface. These should be made good by scraping away or adding soil as necessary.

It is impossible for every row to be finished with a whole turf. Half turves, or even smaller pieces, may have to be used to fill up but these should always be laid inside the row, not at the ends where small pieces may work loose and be kicked out.

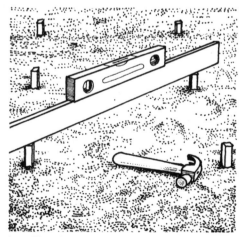

Levelling the site for a lawn using a levelling board, pegs and spirit level. Soil is moved from the higher places to the lower until the surface is even, as determined by the height of the pegs

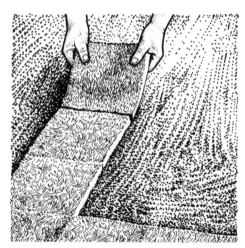

Turves are laid in rows starting from one end of the lawn. The joints are staggered like the bonding of bricks in a wall, but full-sized turves should be laid at the edges as smaller pieces may break away

When all the turves have been laid, sprinkle a little fine soil mixed with sand and peat along the joins, and brush it in with a broom to fill up any cracks remaining between the turves. A week or so later the turf should be knitting nicely to the soil and can be lightly rolled and then mown with the cutters set rather high.

LAWNS FROM SEED

After using the site's natural grass, seeding provides the cheapest method of making a lawn and is usually the most satisfactory. This is because the number of grass species capable of making the finest type of lawn is extremely limited and the best results are obtained with mixtures of two or three kinds, specially chosen to suit the soil, situation and purpose for which the lawn is required.

For high-quality lawns the fescues and bent grasses (agrostis) are unsurpassed. For a wide range of purposes an excellent mixture is seven parts by weight Chewing's fescue and three parts by weight *Agrostis tenuis* (a bent grass popularly known as browntop). Those who prefer a slightly more elaborate mixture, on the principle of not putting all one's eggs in one basket, may use three parts Chewing's fescue, four parts creeping red fescue (*Festuca rubra genuina*) and three parts browntop.

In dry, hot places crested dogstail (*Cynosurus cristatus*) may be employed, either by itself or in association with the smooth-stalked meadow grass (*Poa pratensis*), another grass which withstands drought. It is even possible to find a grass for those awkward damp and shady spots which usually remain bare or grow nothing but moss. The wood meadow grass (*Poa nemoralis*) is just the thing for them.

Perennial rye grass is usually included in the cheaper lawn seed mixtures. It germinates rapidly and grows strongly but does not survive very close mowing nor does it knit together as well as some of the finer grasses. Yet another drawback is that the flower stems or bents are long and tough and apt to be missed by cylinder mowing machines, though rotary machines will slash them off easily enough. Many of the drawbacks have now been removed by breeding and selection; pedigree rye grasses are available that will make lawns of excellent quality. Rye grass is specially useful for lawns that are required for ornament only and will be cut much of the time with a rotary machine set no closer than 18 mm ($^3/_4$ in) above soil level.

Numerous special varieties have been selected which have superior qualities for lawn making to ordinary rye grass. They can be very satisfactory for ornamental lawns but grow faster than the fescues and bent grasses and so require more frequent mowing.

Preparation. The very finest lawns are almost always found on distinctly acid soils. If the soil is already of an acid character (see Chapter 2) there is no need to do anything further, but if it is naturally alkaline it may be desirable to work in plenty of dung, compost, leafmould or peat, and it will certainly be wise to avoid all alkaline dressings such as lime, basic slag and wood ashes.

The initial preparation of the ground is the same for seed as for turf, and even more care should be taken to break the soil up thoroughly and eliminate all weeds before seed is sown.

The best time for sowing grass seed is, as a rule, from late summer to early autumn, though of course it will depend upon the weather since moisture is essential for the

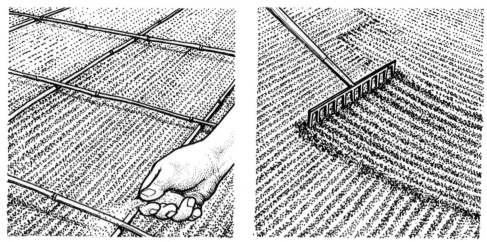

Sowing lawn seed by hand. It is helpful to mark off the area in yard-wide strips or, as shown, in squares, to ensure even distribution of seed. After sowing, cover seed by cross raking

germination of the seed. Next to early autumn, spring is the best season for sowing lawn seed.

Before sowing, the surface must be broken down to a really fine and crumbly texture or tilth, and this means waiting for suitable weather. It is impossible to get the right kind of tilth when it is very dry or very wet, and certainly not if the surface is frozen. The final preparation should be made with a rake. All lumps and big stones must be removed from the surface, and at the same time a good compound fertilizer containing approximately equal percentages of nitrogen, phosphoric acid and potash should be worked into the surface at the rate recommended by the manufacturers.

Seeding. Grass seed should be sown at the rate of from 28–56 g per 0·8 sq m (1–2 oz per sq yd). A heavy rate of seeding will usually give a lawn in shorter time and has the added advantage of smothering weeds more thoroughly. However, if the expense of the 56 g seeding is too great, a 28 g sowing will usually give excellent results provided the gardener is prepared to wait a little longer and take a little more care in the elimination of weeds.

As it is important to distribute the seed as evenly as possible, it is sometimes advised that the whole area to be seeded should be divided into 0·9 m (1 yd) squares with garden lines pegged down at right angles. Personally I think that, unless the area is very big, in which case it may pay to divide it into 0·9 m (1 yd) wide strips, a more practical scheme is to weigh out the right quantity of seed for the whole lawn, divide this into two equal portions and sow half moving up and down the length of the lawn site and the other half moving from side to side across its width.

Another method is to sow with a wheeled fertilizer distributor, which will also be very useful for spreading the pre-seeding fertilizer as well as for feeding the lawn once it is growing. A little experimenting will be necessary to find the correct setting to distribute the seed at the desired rate, and the best way to do this is to run the distributor over a sheet of paper measuring 0·8 sq m (1 sq yd) and weigh the seed that falls on to the paper.

When sown, the seed is covered by careful raking and then cross-raking, or by sprinkling finely sifted soil over it at the rate of 90 kg per 0·8 sq m (2 lb per sq yd). Nowadays most grass seed is pre-treated with a bird deterrent and no further protection should be necessary.

Early Care. If the weather should become very dry after seeding and germination is delayed much beyond a fortnight, it may be necessary to water the lawn, but this should be avoided if possible. If watering does become essential use a lawn sprinkler or a hose fitted with a really fine spray nozzle. As a rule, however, germination proceeds quite normally in seven to fourteen days and a few weeks later the grass will be 5 cm (2 in) high and ready for its first cutting. This can be done with an ordinary lawn mower provided it is really sharp and set high. A blunt mower will drag the seedling grasses out of the ground. Rolling is not likely to be necessary for the first month, but after that, when the grass is beginning to run together and form a real carpet, a light roller can be used when the soil is fairly dry. Before rolling or mowing be careful to remove all worm casts.

Little by little, the blades can be set to cut nearer to the ground, though very close cutting is not desirable (unless the lawn is needed for games demanding a very true surface) as it tends to weaken the grass and does not really improve its appearance. For ordinary use mowing to within 1 cm ($\frac{3}{8}$ in) of the soil level gives a tidy appearance and rye grass lawns thrive best when cut to 18 mm ($\frac{3}{4}$ in).

ROUTINE MANAGEMENT

Once the lawn has been made, whether from seed, turf or from the native grass of the plot, it can, of course, be left alone apart from mowing, but this kind of treatment will not produce the best results. Good lawns are looked after better than that. They must be fed at regular intervals, watered when the weather is dry, rolled occasionally when conditions are right, opened up with a spiked roller or fork at other times and raked and swept practically all the year round.

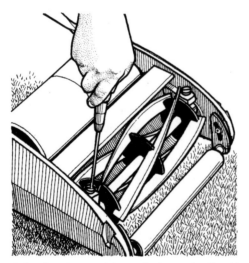 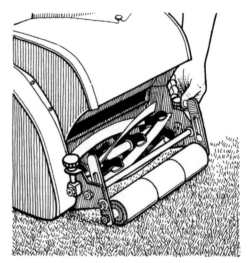

Adjusting the revolving cylinder to the fixed bottom blade (left) and the height of the cutting blades in two types of cylinder

Most amateurs tend to put their lawn mowers away over winter. That is a mistake. Grass does grow, even in late autumn and winter, and occasional cutting is desirable though it may perhaps only be needed two or three times during the whole of that period. Moreover it is essential to choose a day when the surface is nearly dry. If you cut when the grass is very wet you will probably do more harm than good. For this winter cutting the cylinder or revolving blades can be set fairly high to leave the grass about 18 mm (¾ in) long or 2·5 cm (1 in) for rye grass. As it starts to grow rapidly in the spring the blades can be lowered and cutting will become much more frequent. Remember that regular mowing not only keeps the lawn looking nice, but it is also one of the best methods of getting rid of weeds and keeping a good sward, though over-close mowing, by killing the grass, may encourage weeds and moss. Tidy edges of lawns also greatly improve their appearance.

If using a cylinder mower note that a machine with four blades gives about 25 cuts per 0·9 m (1 yd) whereas the finest power-driven machines for smooth lawns may have ten blades and give over 130 cuts. For ordinary home use five- or six-bladed power machines are satisfactory with a cutting rate of 60-70.

Rolling is more necessary for lawns used for games than for ornamental lawns. For home use it is seldom necessary to use a roller weighing more than 100 kg (2 cwt) and it is likely to be most needed in the spring when the grass is growing fastest. Always use it when the surface is moist but not thoroughly wet. Early morning is often the best time for this work.

Towards the end of summer, and sometimes much earlier in the season, lawns which are subject to heavy wear may become too hard in places, particularly if they are used for games. This can be overcome by using a spiked roller or turf aerator equipped with hollow tines which punch out little holes in the turf. Alternatively an ordinary garden fork can be used pushed into the turf for about 5 cm (2 in) and then levered backwards a little, but not enough to break the surface. It is rather a laborious job because a fresh set of perforations has to be made every 7·5 cm (3 in) over the whole area of the lawn.

The spring-toothed grass rake is an invaluable tool which will weaken creeping weeds and expose them to the mower, and will also prevent the turf from getting clogged up with dead grass. Use it immediately before rolling or mowing so that the rather rough surface left by the rake is immediately corrected. Rake the lawn in different directions, working lengthwise, and then across. Sometimes so much dead material collects between grass and soil that even a rake will not drag it out and then a special slitting tool must be used to cut through the mat or thatch and so make it easier to rake.

Brushing is a supplement to raking and, like it, will dispose of a lot of the dead material which otherwise covers the surface of the soil and prevents the grass roots from breathing. It will also remove worm casts which otherwise are flattened out by roller and mowing machine and will kill the grass beneath. The best kind of broom is made from birch branches, but an ordinary yard broom can be used if necessary. Regular brushing is particularly essential in the autumn when worm casts are most abundant.

Feeding. The grasses in a lawn are so crowded and, for the most part, their roots are so near the surface that they soon exhaust the soil, and unless a regular and considered system of feeding is carried out the quality of the lawn is bound to suffer. Careful feeding will not only maintain the strength of the grass but will also have a selective effect, encouraging the finer grasses and eliminating weeds, clover and coarse grasses. The thing to aim for is a fairly high concentration of nitrogen, preferably in the form of ammonium salts and a definite acidity. Regular small dressings of sulphate of ammonia will help to achieve this but it is not wise to rely on this chemical alone or the feeding will become too unbalanced. Moreover the lawn needs humus, so bulky organic dressings must be used as well as chemical fertilizers.

A satisfactory system of feeding is to use either a special lawn fertilizer or a well-balanced general fertilizer (one containing approximately equal percentages of nitrogen, phosphoric acid and potash) according to manufacturers' instructions. Do this each mid-spring and give a second application at half that rate in early summer and possibly a third at this half rate in late summer if the grass shows signs of losing colour. Then in early autumn a special seasonal lawn dressing containing a very low percentage of nitrogen but plenty of potash is used, again according to makers' instructions, plus a good topdressing of finely milled peat. If there is a drainage problem sharp grit can be added, but then the lawn should first be hollow tined so that peat and grit can be brushed down into the holes.

Weeding. For broad-leaved weeds such as plantains, daisies and self-heal (prunella) use one of the proprietary selective weedkillers containing 2,4-D, MCPA, dicamba or meco-prop. Dicamba or mecoprop is necessary if there is much clover to be killed. Some difficult weeds that do not yield to the selective weedkillers can be spot treated with lawn sand which can be purchased ready for use or can be made at home. The ingredients are 3 parts sulphate of ammonia, 1 part sulphate of iron, 20 parts fine silver sand, all by weight. Lawn sand is applied dry directly to the weeds or at 112 g per 0·8 sq m (4 oz per sq yd) if any considerable area has to be covered. Selective weedkillers are usually used diluted with water according to label instructions. A watering-can fitted with a wide dribble bar is best for application. Care should be taken not to exceed the recommended dose and to keep the chemical off other plants. Some manufacturers also sell combined lawn fertilizer and selective weedkiller for dry application.

The growth of moss, and the little weed known as pearlwort which is often mistaken for moss, is sometimes an indication that the soil is poor but may easily be encouraged by mowing too closely so that the grass is unduly weakened. Moss is particularly likely to occur in damp, shady corners, and very often there is no satisfactory method of getting rid of it permanently unless the conditions can be improved by cutting down overhanging trees or removing branches.

Special preparations are also available for killing moss. Prepare 1 part by weight sulphate of iron and 7 parts fine sand and dust this over the moss-infested areas at the rate of 112 g per 0·8 sq m (4 oz per sq yd). However, while such treatment will kill the moss, it will not eliminate the conditions which caused the growth of moss, nor will it encourage grass, so unless appropriate steps are taken the result may simply be a bare patch for a time and then a renewed growth of moss.

Repairing Worn Patches. Lawns which receive a lot of wear are almost certain to become bare in places, particularly towards the end of a dry summer. The quickest way of dealing with this damage is to mark out a rectangle a little larger than the worn place, lift the turf either with a special turf cutter or with a sharp spade, and re-lay with new turves. The drawback is that unless spare turves can be cut from another part of the lawn it will mean that alien grass, and possibly weeds, will be imported, and the patch could become a centre of trouble for the rest of the lawn. It is therefore better to re-seed with the same grass mixture as that used in the first place. The worn place should be loosened with a fork, the points of which need not be driven in more than 7·5 cm (3 in) and, when a fine crumbly surface has been obtained, the seed is sown and covered in the ordinary way.

Watering. The finer grasses from which the best lawns are made are not very deep rooting and tend to suffer quickly during hot, dry spells in summer. The only preventive is timely and adequate watering, and the only satisfactory method of watering a lawn is with a sprinkler. Few amateurs realize how long it takes to get the soil under the turf really moist to a depth of 7·5 cm (3 in), and nothing less will serve. To go out for twenty minutes or so with a hose and spray the lawn is worse than useless, while heavy drenchings from an open hose tend to wash the soil away from the grass roots and expose them to scorching. A sprinkler can be left in position for an hour or so without attention and will deliver a fine rain-like spray over a large area. Lawns which have become very hard should be perforated with a fork or spiked roller before being watered.

Worms and Leatherjackets. These are the two worst lawn pests. The leatherjacket is the grub of the familiar daddy-long-legs and is a sluggish, dirty grey, caterpillar-like creature (though it has no legs like a true caterpillar) which lives in the soil just beneath the surface and devours roots particularly of grass, causing it to die in patches.

There are several ways of destroying leatherjackets. One of the simplest is to soak the lawn very thoroughly with plain water and then cover the surface for a few hours with tarpaulins, polythene, boards or anything else that will exclude air. As a result the leatherjackets are half suffocated and come up to the surface. If the treatment is carried out towards evening and the covering material is removed the following morning, many leatherjackets may be discovered on the surface from which they can be swept up and destroyed.

Another way is to broadcast HCH insecticide over the surface at the rate recommended by the manufacturers and water it in well.

Worms do not injure the grass directly; in fact, in some ways, they are beneficial as they drag decaying leaves into the soil, so enriching it and also tunnel into the turf and aerate it. Unfortunately, worm casts can become a positive menace for in wet weather they become flattened in pasty masses on top of the grass and kill it. The worm population must therefore be strictly limited. This can be done by watering the lawn with worm killer following label instructions. The worms will die in the soil without coming to the surface so there is little risk to birds.

An alternative is to broadcast mowrah meal over the surface at 112 g per 0·8 sq m (4 oz per sq yd) and then water in heavily. The worms come to the surface to die and must be swept up after each treatment. All worm-killing measures are likely to be most successful in fairly warm, moist weather. Mid-spring and early autumn are the best times.

Moles. In some districts moles become very troublesome, not only on the lawn but also in other parts of the garden, particularly in seed beds and frames. Moles are useful in the garden up to a point as they live on worms, leatherjackets and other small creatures in the soil, but they tunnel in all directions just beneath the surface in search of their food, loosening the roots of plants and grass and causing the surface to collapse. Moreover, every few yards they throw up the displaced earth in a big heap, the familiar molehill, and this is not only unsightly but, if left, will kill the grass beneath.

Moles can be gassed with special smoke bombs. A special smoke bomb is ignited and placed in a run, the opening being immediately sealed with a turf or wet sack. Alternatively sprinkle an aluminium ammonium sulphate based chemical in the run. Brambles spread across the entrance to the run may force the moles to move on, with luck.

Fairy Rings. Sometimes one will see a ring of bright green, strong-growing grass on the lawn and immediately inside this a ring of dead or dying grass. Country people call these fairy rings because of the old superstition that this is where the fairies dance at night. The symptoms are in fact due to one or other of several different fungi which do not actually live on the grass but deprive it of moisture and so slowly kill it. The bright green appearance immediately beyond this ring is apparently due to the fact that the fungus liberates nitrogen in the soil and so temporarily enriches it. The best method of dealing with these rings is to dig them out to a depth of at least 30 cm (1 ft), replace with fresh soil and re-seed or turf.

Grass Diseases. Various diseases attack grass, particularly in autumn and winter if the lawn has been too heavily fed late in the season with fertilizer containing a good deal of nitrogen. Special lawn fungicides are available which may be used according to label instructions but the best preventive is to care for the turf properly throughout the year and not to use fertilizer containing much nitrogen after late summer. See also Chapter 32.

Part 3

Gardening under Glass

Chapter 16

Cloches, Frames and Greenhouses

There are several advantages to be gained by adding glass in some form to the garden equipment. Many tender plants can be enjoyed, including vegetables and fruits, which will not survive outside all-year round. There is also the possibility of having crops out of season, either earlier or later than would otherwise be possible. Nor must one overlook the advantage of being able to propagate many plants which would otherwise have to be purchased. Seeds can be germinated earlier or more successfully in a greenhouse or frame, or even under simple cloches, than in the open, and some seedlings from outdoor sowings can be transferred to the glasshouse during the winter and replanted out of doors in the spring, so gaining a better chance of survival.

The precise form in which the glass is added will depend to a great extent on the money that is to be spent on it. Frames and cloches provide the cheapest means of making a start and are also very useful adjuncts to a greenhouse. There is certainly a good deal to be said for making a modest start, because the principles of glass cultivation are the same whatever the structure, and it is good policy to make mistakes and gain experience on a small scale before launching out more adventurously.

CLOCHES

The original cloche or handlight was, I believe, devised by French market gardeners, who used it to bring on early lettuces, etc. Often it took the form of a plain bell or a rectangle of glass in a metal frame with a pyramid-shaped cap. The continuous cloche was a later development and an immense improvement on the old handlight. There are a number of types, each with some point of excellence to recommend it. The qualities to look for in a good cloche of this type are rigidity, portability and roominess.

These continuous cloches are always open at each end, the idea being that they can be set one against another to cover any length of row. Generally it is not necessary to block the ends of the rows, but where they are short and there is danger of a cold draught blowing right through, a pane of glass can be stood vertically against each end and held in position with a stick.

A development of the continuous cloche is the tunnel cloche, made by stretching a length of polythene film over strong half-hoop wire supports with thinner wire half-hoops on top to hold the polythene down. At each end the polythene is folded together and tied to a stake driven firmly into the soil. Tunnel cloches give little or no frost protection but protect well against wind and help keep the air moist, conditions that favour some vegetables such as lettuces and also cuttings of many plants.

Cloches are principally used to bring on early seedlings in the vegetable garden, but they can also be used for the same purpose in the flower garden and can be turned to good account to complete the growth of plants when the weather has become too cold for them to mature without protection; for example, outdoor tomatoes are often ripened in this way during the first half of autumn.

If the ground is properly prepared before cloches are to be used, it is often possible to dispense with watering under the cloches throughout the growth of the crop. This is because the width of soil covered by the cloche is not very great and rain or water from overhead irrigation is deflected by the glass on each side of the row and soaks inwards to the roots of the plants. In order that this may work well the soil itself must be of a rather spongy texture. This is assured by working in plenty of peat, decayed vegetable refuse or dung prior to planting, and also by cultivating the soil as deeply as possible. Moreover the soil must be thoroughly moistened to a good depth before seeds or plants are put in. However, if the ground under the cloches does become dry and the plants show signs of suffering in consequence, there should be no hesitation in removing the cloches and watering in the ordinary way.

As there is bound to be a slight crack between each glass cloche some air is admitted all the time. This is often enough to give adequate ventilation but it is not possible to lay down hard and fast rules, and if cloches are to be left in position after the weather gets really warm in spring, it may be necessary to remove one here and there and space the remainder out. I have seen severe leaf scorching occur through leaving unventilated cloches over tomatoes throughout the summer, and far better results obtained by removing one of the side glasses from each cloche to leave the row completely unprotected on one side. Tunnel cloches can be ventilated by slipping the polythene up on one side, preferably the leeward side.

There is really no end to the ingenuity which can be shown in the use of cloches. Cuttings can be rooted under them, strawberries can be ripened several weeks earlier than in the open air, lettuce seedlings brought through the winter and induced to heart in mid- and late spring, and practically every type of vegetable or flower seed germinated at least a month earlier than in the open. A use sometimes overlooked is that of drying off ground sufficiently to enable sowing to proceed.

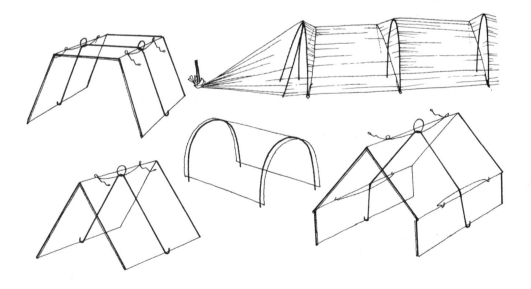

Some popular types of glass, plastic, and polythene covered cloches

407

Those who are interested in food cultivation often practise an extremely intensive rotation of cropping under cloches. Here is a typical programme. Winter lettuces are sown early in mid-autumn, either alone or with onions. The cloches remain over these until about mid-spring when they are transferred to tomatoes previously reared in the greenhouse. By early summer the cloches are taken from the tomatoes and placed over the autumn-sown onions to ripen them off. From these they go to shallots with the same object, and from them to the spring-sown onions, finishing up over the tomatoes again during early autumn to hasten the ripening of the top trusses. For this purpose the tomatoes are untied from their stakes and laid lengthwise along the rows on clean straw.

FRAMES

A well-made frame will keep out more cold than a cloche and so enable the gardener to grow an even wider range of plants throughout the year. The drawback of the frame by comparison with the cloche is its lack of portability, though this can be overcome to a great extent by using fairly small glazed frames and detachable wooden sides. Frames of this latter character are often known as Dutch frames because they have been highly developed by the Dutch market gardeners. The standard pattern Dutch light (that is, the glazed portion of the frame) measures 1·5 m × 87 cm (62 × 35 in), and is glazed with one pane of glass. The sides of the frame are made of 2·5 cm (1 in) thick planks, the back being about 25 cm (10 in) in height and the front 20 cm (8 in). Various methods are employed for bolting or clipping these sides together so that they can be taken down quickly and moved to other parts of the garden.

The more usual type of frame in gardens is a much more permanent affair often with brick or concrete sides, though cheaper patterns are made with grooved and tongued boarding. The standard size of light is 1·8 × 1·2 m (6 × 4 ft), but a small-sized light, 1·2 m × 90 cm (4 × 3 ft), is popular, particularly with amateurs, because it can be handled by one person. The amount of tilt given from back to front varies greatly with different makes and may be anything from about 4 to 15 degrees. Personally I favour a rather flat type of frame because then it is possible to have a perfectly level bed within the frame and yet keep all the plants within reasonable distance of the glass. Moreover, if the sides of small frames are too high they cut off a considerable amount of light and plants become drawn in consequence.

It is of vital importance that the walls of any frame should be solid and reasonably thick so that they withstand cold and do not admit draughts. Wooden frames, if made of more than one plank vertically, should always be tongued and grooved or rebated, for plain boards, even if they fit closely at first, are almost certain to gape after a while. Undoubtedly brick or concrete walls give much better protection but they cannot be taken with you when you move house.

Plastics of various kinds may be used in place of glass for frames. Some manufacturers make frames in such materials, or corrugated plastic sheets, suitably stiffened with a light wooden framework, can take the place of glazed lights.

A good frame can be of use in a variety of ways. It will do everything that the cloche will do and is to be preferred for seed germination and striking cuttings because of the greater control it affords over temperature and atmospheric moisture. In addition it can

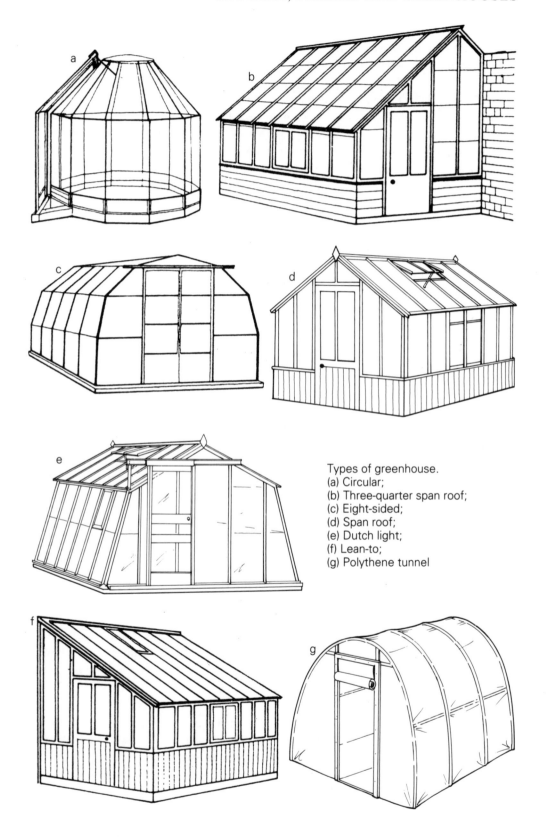

Types of greenhouse.
(a) Circular;
(b) Three-quarter span roof;
(c) Eight-sided;
(d) Span roof;
(e) Dutch light;
(f) Lean-to;
(g) Polythene tunnel

be used to harden off plants raised in the greenhouse and to overwinter many half-hardy plants that would not be safe under cloches.

It is also possible to heat frames in a variety of ways, one of the most satisfactory being with special air or soil-warming electric cables. This may be low-voltage cable operating through a transformer or a normal domestic voltage cable operating directly from a mains power socket. All installations must be completely waterproof and it is desirable that they should be installed by an electrician with experience of this work. Manufacturers' instructions regarding installation should always be followed. Electrical heating of any kind can be controlled by a thermostat and this not only saves much time and worry but also money, since the current is switched on only when it is really required. Moreover this close control of temperature is good for plants which dislike violent fluctuations.

Hardening Off. Most plants have a wide range of adaptability regarding temperature and other factors. The process works both ways. For example, if a plant is grown over a long period in comparatively low temperatures it will become tougher than normal and, in consequence, will quite likely be able to stand even more cold without injury. Conversely, if a plant is grown in a warm greenhouse for some time it will become more tender and easily injured by temperatures which it would normally endure.

In order to bring seedlings and cuttings along rapidly in the early part of the year it is often necessary to start them in warmth, perhaps a good deal more warmth than that to which they are normally accustomed. If, later on, these same plants are to be transferred to the open air it is essential that they should be acclimatized to lower temperatures by gradual stages. It may be possible to go a long way towards achieving this object in the greenhouse, first by cutting out artificial heat and then by giving increased ventilation, but it is never possible to get conditions identical with those outside. In the frame this limitation can be overcome because, when the hardening process has gone sufficiently far, the gardener can remove the frame lights altogether, first of all by day only and then by night as well. Skill in hardening off is one of the secrets of success with a great many half-hardy or greenhouse-raised plants required for growing out of doors.

GREENHOUSES

There are many different types of greenhouse and many uses to which they may be put. It would be impossible to deal with them all in the space available, but here are a few of the most important.

First of all greenhouses can be broadly classified as span-roofed, three-quarter span-roofed, lean-to and circular. These main types can be further subdivided as ordinary greenhouses and forcing houses, while a further classification can be made into hot houses, intermediate houses, cool houses and cold houses.

The Span-roof. These have an ordinary apex or barn type of roof in which both sloping sides are of equal length. The span-roofed house is the commonest type in private gardens and the one with the widest range of uses. It can be used for almost any purpose and is as serviceable for growing utility crops, such as tomatoes, winter lettuces or even choice fruit trees, as it is for ornamental plants grown in pots or planted out in greenhouse borders. The vertical, or nearly vertical, sides may be glazed to ground level on each side, or

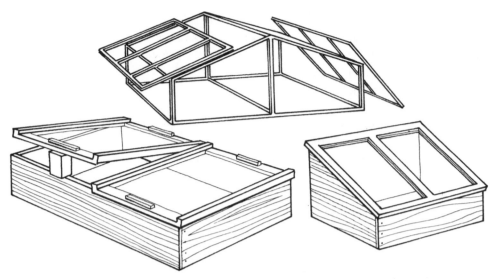

Three types of garden frame. Aluminium, wood and plastic frames have the advantage of portability over those made of brick or concrete

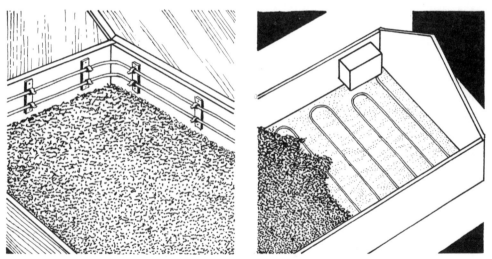

Garden frames may be heated by air-warming cables clipped to the side of the frame or by cables laid under the soil

may have walls of brick, concrete or wood to a height of 90 cm (3 ft) with glass above, or may be glazed to ground level on one side and be half glazed on the other. The advantage of glazing to ground level is that plants can be grown right from the floor of the house with good light. The advantage of the half-walled house is that it loses less heat in cold weather and gains heat more rapidly in sunny weather. The lack of light low down does not matter if plants are grown on staging. This is convenient for small pot plants, seedlings and cuttings which can be inspected, handled and watered easily. The house glazed to ground level on one side only is a compromise which allows plants to be grown from the floor on that side and on staging on the other side.

There is some advantage in siting span-roofed houses to run as nearly as possible north and south so that each side receives an approximately equal amount of light, but when houses are glazed to ground level on one side only it may be better to site them with this side more or less facing the sun.

Three-quarter Span. This differs from the full span-roofed house in having one sloping side considerably longer than the other. The shorter side terminates on a wall and the three-quarter span-roofed house is most serviceable where a fairly high wall, say 2·1-3·6 m (7-12 ft), already exists in the garden. It is a type which is going out of fashion, though it can be found in many old private gardens. Where possible the three-quarter span house should always face the sun, unless it is to be used for ferns or shade-loving plants, when it may face away from the sun. It was at one time extremely popular for vines and fruit trees permanently planted in borders within the greenhouse.

Lean-to. This type resembles the three-quarter span house but with the short side eliminated, the roof sloping down from the wall. Where a wall 2·4 m (8 ft) or more in height exists a lean-to glasshouse is often the cheapest structure of all. A drawback is that unless the wall faces the sun the plants within the house inevitably go short of light and may suffer in consequence. If it can be placed against a dwelling house this type of greenhouse is likely to gain warmth and it may be possible to heat the greenhouse from the domestic system.

Circular Greenhouses. These are usually hexagonal or octagonal with a peaked roof. They take up little room and can be more ornamental than the other types but their size is strictly limited.

Tunnel Types. These are rather like tunnel cloches but much more robustly made, covered with flexible plastic sheet and large enough to work in. They give little frost protection but do protect from wind. In time they will need running repairs, perhaps even complete replacement.

The Forcing House. This type may be of any of the three preceding types but differs from an ordinary greenhouse in having no vertical glass sides, that is to say the sloping roof comes practically to ground level. In small forcing houses this results in so little head room that it is necessary to excavate a path down the centre and enter the house by descending three or four steps. Examples are now rare, and were once known as a forcing pit. The true pit has a rather limited range of usefulness and is mainly employed by market growers for cucumbers, melons, ferns and other moisture-loving plants as well as for very early forcing of all kinds.

Framework. This can be of wood or aluminium. The wood will occasionally need to be treated with a preservative. Examples look good but are more expensive than the aluminium types.

Hot House. The term was once synonymous with the word 'stove' and is used for any class of house in which the temperature range in spring and summer is between 21-27°C/70-81°F and does not fall below 18°C/65°F even in winter. In cold winter climates such temperatures are expensive to maintain and are only necessary for some tropical plants.

Intermediate House. This is a greenhouse in which the spring and summer temperature ranges between 16-21°C/61-70°F, and in winter does not fall below 13°C/56°F. It is still a fairly expensive house to heat but one in which a very wide range of plants can be cultivated.

Cool House. This may be defined as one in which the spring and summer temperature will range between 12-18°C/54-65°F and the winter temperature will not fall below 7°C/45°F. From the amateur's standpoint it is the most useful class of glasshouse, enabling him to grow a considerable range of plants without too much expense. It is possible in most parts of the country to maintain a cool house at the correct temperature for seven or eight months of the year without artificial heat, and only during the coldest periods is continuous heating likely to be required.

Cold House. The name may be somewhat misleading for no one wants to keep a greenhouse intentionally cold. By 'cold house' the gardener simply means one that is not provided with any permanent heating apparatus. A special portable paraffin heater may be used occasionally to keep out really severe frost, but most of the time the gardener must maintain the necessary temperature by skilful manipulation of the ventilators and possibly by the use of canvas blinds pulled down at night to retain some of the heat trapped by day. Inevitably the cold house is of somewhat limited use as it will usually be impossible to exclude frost entirely throughout the winter, and this means that really tender plants will succumb.

Summer Temperatures. The summer upper temperatures suggested in the preceding paragraphs are ideals to be aimed at but they may sometimes have to be exceeded. When the outdoor temperature is over 27°C/81°F it is very difficult to make a greenhouse cooler than the air outside. Occasional rises above the upper limits do not matter but what should be avoided is constant high day temperatures due to sun heat with insufficient ventilation and shading.

Chapter 17

Methods of Heating

Directly the gardener considers seriously the question of heating the greenhouse he is confronted with a large number of possibilities both as regards fuel and apparatus. Coal, electricity, gas, oil and paraffin can all be used as sources of heat and there are many ways in which each may be employed. But whichever method you use, insulate the greenhouse with some kind of bubble sheeting to reduce running costs and increase efficiency over winter.

Hot-water Boilers. For the larger type of greenhouse there is much to be said in favour of a solid fuel or oil-fired boiler heating the greenhouse by means of hot-water pipes. Such boilers are economical to run and, if properly managed, they give the right kind of heat, neither too drying nor too concentrated in source. Very small boilers are not so satisfactory as they tend to behave erratically and often go out if left unattended for many hours at a stretch. Some improvement can be made by surrounding the boiler with a simple shelter to protect it from direct wind. Another scheme is to build a potting shed on the end of the greenhouse and install the boiler in this.

Whenever possible 10 cm (4 in) diameter pipes should be used rather than 5 cm (2 in) pipes as, within reason, the bigger the surface from which the heat is radiated the better will be the result. For the same reason it is advisable to have the pipes extending at least the full length of the greenhouse and, in bigger houses, running round three sides. There should be at least one flow and one return pipe, while in big installations it is often an advantage to have two returns, so ensuring a steadier flow of water. In small or medium-sized installations this flow is almost invariably obtained by the thermo–syphon system, that is, on the principle that hot water rises and cold water falls, involving a steady rise in the outflow pipes from the boiler to the farthest point, and an equally steady fall from this point back to the boiler. Ups and downs must be avoided as they will interfere with the flow of water. The rise and fall respectively need not be more than 2·5 cm (1 in) in 3 m (10 ft), but it can be greater than this with advantage, the result being a quicker circulation of water.

The boiler itself should be well cased in with bricks or cement and, if the boiler is alongside or built into the wall of the house, any length of pipe connecting it with the house should be heavily lagged or covered with soil to conserve heat. It is usually most convenient to have the pipes almost against the wall of the house and low down under the staging, but occasionally pipes are slung overhead immediately under the roof rafters, this system being most desirable where the purpose is to dry rather than to warm the atmosphere, such as in carnation houses.

Some coal boilers can be obtained with automatic stokers of various designs, some thermostatically controlled so that the temperature of the house is maintained within narrow limits. Oil-fired boilers are usually thermostatically controlled.

Boiler makers usually indicate the maximum number of metres of 10 cm (4 in) diameter pipe each size of boiler will heat efficiently. The following table indicates the number of metres of 10 cm (4 in) diameter pipe required to give a reasonable margin of safety if certain minimum temperatures are to be maintained in houses of various sizes. These are guides only, since much will depend on the construction and siting of the greenhouse and the degree of cold experienced.

Electrical Heating. Electricity – which must be installed by a professional – has many advantages, including cleanliness and the ease with which it can be installed and controlled. Its principal drawback is cost of running which can be considerably higher than that of solid fuel or oil-fired boilers. However, if electric radiators are controlled by a thermostat there is little or no waste heat for the radiator is automatically cut off directly the heat exceeds the required temperature. This results in a considerable saving in current but, even so, it would have to be a badly managed coal boiler which cost as much to run as an electric heating system, except on the lowest current rates. A second drawback of electricity frequently overlooked is that any mains failure will cause an immediate (and perhaps unnoticed) cessation of heating.

Broadly speaking there are three ways in which electrical heating may be applied: by low-temperature radiators using current on normal mains voltage, usually 220/250; high-temperature, fan-assisted heaters operating on mains voltage; low-temperature cable or wire which may be high or low voltage. The first two types are the most popular for ordinary greenhouse heating and there is little to choose between them on the score of efficiency. The fan-assisted heater scores on portability and the low-temperature radiator perhaps on heat distribution in fairly large houses. Cable or wire heating is most favoured for heating frames and again there are two alternatives, insulated cable operating on mains voltage or bare wire operating on low voltage, usually either 6 or 12 volts. Cable or wire is simply wound around the sides of the frame or it may be used to warm the soil from beneath by coiling it, serpentine fashion, in the bottom of the frame and covering with sand to a depth of 6·2 cm (2½ in). Where low-voltage heating or soil warming is employed, a transformer will be necessary. All electrical installations in greenhouses should be of a type able to withstand wet and should be installed by an electrician used to this specialized work.

For soil warming about 6 watts should be allowed for every 0·09 sq m (1 sq ft) of soil. For air warming in frames allow about twice this for every 0·09 sq m (1 sq ft) of frame.

HOT-WATER HEATING OF GREENHOUSES

Floor area of house in sq m (sq ft)		Approximate length of 10 cm (4 in) piping required in m (ft)							
		7°C (45°F)		10°C (50°F)		12°C (54°F)		15°C (59°F)	
5·5	(60)	3·6	(12)	4·8	(16)	6	(20)	7·2	(24)
7·4	(80)	4·5	(15)	6	(20)	8	(27)	9	(30)
9	(100)	6	(20)	8·5	(28)	10·2	(34)	12	(40)
10·8	(120)	7·5	(25)	10	(33)	12·6	(42)	15	(50)
12·6	(140)	9	(30)	12	(40)	15	(50)	18	(60)
14·9	(160)	10·5	(35)	14	(47)	17·5	(58)	21	(70)
16·7	(180)	12	(40)	16·2	(54)	20	(66)	24	(80)
18·6	(200)	13·5	(45)	18	(60)	22·5	(75)	27	(90)

Hot Water Pipes and Gas Heating. Gas boilers are ideally sited outside the greenhouse because if there's a malfunction inside the leakage of fumes can ruin a plant's health. But the advantage of this form of heating is that it can be controlled by thermostatic devices. Regular maintenance is essential.

Natural Gas. Since the by-product is carbon dioxide and water vapour the plants benefit enormously. Also, natural gas heaters are economical to run, easy to install, and can be thermostatically controlled (the accuracy should be checked with a maximum-minimum thermometer). However just enough ventilation should be given to prevent a build-up of harmful gases, while regular maintenance is essential because a malfunction increases the likelihood of dangerous fumes. Certain kinds of natural gas heater will run off bottled propane gas.

Paraffin Heating. Makes specifically designed for the greenhouse are the simplest form of heating and enable plants to survive a frosty winter's night when there's no other source of heat. These heaters are enormously popular with amateur gardeners. The principal danger is of fumes (even at this dormant time of year), lack of oxygen and excess humidity which means you must leave the greenhouse roof ventilator slightly ajar. Even when the outside temperature plummets to below freezing the plants should survive because it's reckoned the heater will keep inside temperatures 7°C (10°F) above the former. The figure varies according to make and model.

There are two basic kinds of heater, the blue- and the yellow-flame. If the wick is too high on the latter you will fill the greenhouse with fumes. The blue-flame is said to be less prone to this problem, though individual experiences do vary, while it is more efficient at heat production. But whichever kind you choose opt for the highest grade of paraffin which will have the cleaner fumes. And always keep the heater spotlessly clean, a precaution which equally applies to oil heaters.

Chapter 18
Greenhouse Management

The manner in which a greenhouse is managed will naturally depend to a great extent on the kind of plants that are grown within it. For this reason it is advisable to select plants which will thrive under similar conditions. It is, for example, a mistake to grow ordinary greenhouse cucumbers and tomatoes in the same house because the first like a very damp atmosphere and the second a comparatively dry one. Admittedly there are one or two varieties of cucumber which will put up with drier conditions and can be used in a tomato house, but that doesn't change the argument. Also, tomatoes and grape vines are not a very satisfactory combination as both like plenty of sun, so that the grape vines must be trained quite close under the rafters of the greenhouse, and this cuts off much of the light from the tomatoes below.

Nevertheless some general principles of greenhouse management can be enumerated and are most conveniently considered under the headings of temperature control, ventilation (including humidity control), watering, and shading.

Temperature Control. There is, no doubt, an optimum temperature for every plant at every season of the year but it is almost impossible for the ordinary gardener to fulfil such requirements. As a rule his greenhouse contains several different types of plant, sometimes many different kinds, and although it is possible to choose kinds that associate well there is sure to be some discrepancy between their temperature requirements. Fortunately plants, like human beings, are very adaptable and, provided certain extremes are not exceeded, satisfactory results can be expected.

Temperature control can be obtained in a variety of ways, the most obvious being by the use of a heating apparatus. This should not be employed unnecessarily, for if the required temperature can be obtained by natural means without making the atmosphere too stuffy, this is to be preferred. Too much artificial heat will tend to draw plants, that is to make them grow tall and spindly with pale leaves and little stamina. This is particularly true over winter when days are short and light is diffused. It is a popular illusion that heat is a substitute for light. In fact, the two are complementary and heat without light is liable to cause disaster. That is one reason why it is so difficult to get good winter crops of tomatoes or lettuces. The difficulty can be overcome with artificial lighting but this introduces added expense and complications. It has not as yet been greatly used except for special crops and in special areas in which sunlight is completely replaced by artificial light.

Because of this balance between heat and light, the average temperature of the greenhouse should be lower in winter than in summer. Big fluctuations, and particularly rapid fluctuations, are to be avoided at all times but are more harmful in winter than in summer.

The amateur who has no heating apparatus can control temperature, often to a remarkable degree, by skilful use of sun heat. In cold weather ventilators, if opened at all by day, should be closed an hour or so before the sun sets, and then at sundown heavy canvas blinds may be pulled over the glass, or screens clamped in position, to prevent the escape of heat trapped within the house. Care must be taken not to put such devices in position too early and to remove them early in the morning, for their purpose is solely to hold heat and they must not be allowed to rob the plant of the scanty winter daylight. Sheets of quilted polythene can be used as a permanent lining in winter but they do cut down light a little and are apt to produce heavy condensation which can be harmful.

If a heating apparatus is available and is thermostatically controlled the gardener has little to worry about, for he has merely to set the dial at the desired figure, which should be chosen to suit the most tender plants he is growing. Even so it is wise to have a maximum and minimum registering thermometer in the greenhouse and to set and read it daily as a check on the accuracy of the apparatus.

If the heating apparatus is not under thermostatic control the gardener's task becomes more arduous and a maximum and minimum thermometer is even more essential. It should be read at least morning and evening, preferably midday as well, and the heating apparatus and ventilators regulated accordingly. Bear in mind that too much heat is quite as damaging as too much cold. Incidentally plants which have been scorched in a high temperature look almost exactly like those which have been damaged by frost, a point which the gardener emphasises by referring to frost-damaged plants as 'scorched'. In both the tissues of the younger leaves and more tender shoots are destroyed, quickly turning brown and withering as a result.

In small houses temperature control in summer is usually a battle against high temperatures and rapid fluctuations. The difficulty with the small house is that it contains such a small volume of air that it very quickly acquires heat and as readily loses it. The result may be a rise of 11-17°C/20-30°F in the morning when the sun first shines directly on the glass and perhaps before the gardener is about, with a correspondingly rapid fall after dusk. This kind of thing is extremely damaging and must be countered by early and adequate ventilation coupled, if necessary, by shading for a period to slacken the rate at which the temperature rises. At night it may occasionally be necessary to use artificial heat in small houses even in early summer to check the sudden chilling which otherwise occurs.

Ventilation. Ventilation has two main objects, to control temperature and atmospheric moisture.

The first of these points has been mentioned in the preceding section and I would only add that as regards temperature control most small greenhouses are inadequately provided with ventilators. For example, in a 3·6 × 3 m (12 × 10 ft) house with only one ventilator in the roof it is almost impossible to prevent excessively high temperatures on bright summer days even if the door is kept wide open, a policy which, though often essential, is seldom entirely satisfactory as it is apt to cause serious draughts. The minimum top ventilation which should be regarded as adequate is that the ventilators should total the length of the house, half being on one side and half on the other side of the ridge in span-roofed or three-quarter span-roofed houses. Side ventilators in houses with vertical glass should at least total half the area of the top vents while, in addition, in houses with walls it is useful to have a few small ventilators in these areas below the level of the staging.

Automatic greenhouse ventilators are a 'must' and are sold by the weight of window which they can open. Test yours by balancing the open ventilator on a kitchen scale. The automatic mechanism is worked by a compound which expands in hot weather, so operating a plunger which forces the ventilator open.

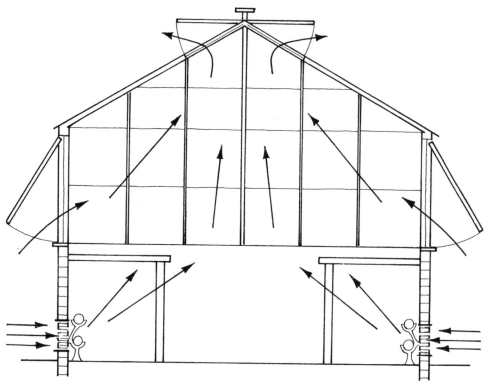

Diagram showing how the flow of fresh and warmed air in a greenhouse can be controlled by the judicious operation of side and roof ventilators

Humidity control is often overlooked completely by the beginner and yet, in some ways, it is the most vital of all. Plants vary greatly in their response to moisture in the atmosphere. Those, such as cacti and succulents, which in nature inhabit desert regions thrive best in dry air and very quickly fall into ill health if kept in a damp atmosphere, whereas many foliage plants from tropical forests revel in very damp air. This again demonstrates the necessity for choosing plant companions with care but, having chosen them, something at least approaching the ideal atmospheric conditions must still be maintained. This is done partly by manipulating the ventilators but also by the processes known as damping down and syringing, the first of which refers to the wetting of floor, path and walls and the second to the direct syringing of the plants themselves. In both cases the net result is to increase the amount of moisture in the atmosphere. Where a very damp atmosphere is required shallow trays which can be filled with water are fitted over the hot-water pipes or radiators. Additional help can be given by covering stages with coarse sifted boiler ashes or small gravel which will hold plenty of moisture when syringed or watered, giving it off steadily by evaporation; a capillary bench (see p. 421) also achieves the same end.

By opening ventilators and encouraging the entry of air it is often possible to decrease the dampness of the atmosphere, though this does not hold true during foggy weather, nor during periods of heavy rainfall. In practice it means that if the house is filled with plants which appreciate a more or less normal degree of atmospheric moisture, ventilation is decreased when the weather is very damp or foggy; alternatively, ventilation is maintained at normal with artificial heat to dry the air. In this case it will be the top ventilators that will be kept open and the side ventilators shut. When the weather becomes hot, top and side ventilators will be opened to create a through current of air, while if the air within shows signs of becoming too dry, with the result that plants need water with undue frequency and show signs of flagging on every hot day, damping down is carried out at least each morning and possibly more frequently.

To adapt these normal conditions to plants which require above or below the normal amount of humidity is purely a matter of common sense. The dry-air plants will receive even more ventilation during mild weather and will seldom get any damping down, while the wet-air plants will have less ventilation and particularly less side ventilation, which causes a drying current of air, together with more damping down and direct syringing.

A problem which frequently arises in unheated or slightly heated greenhouses growing a normal collection of plants is that there is heavy condensation on the glass inside at night. This collects and drips on to the plants, staining flowers, and sometimes leaves as well. The remedies are to avoid watering after midday and unnecessary splashing of water at any time, and to give a little top ventilation even at night, though this may necessitate the use of artificial heat to maintain the minimum temperature.

Shading. This is required for two quite distinct purposes. Some plants do not like strong sunshine, especially in summer, and must be shaded to reduce the light intensity. The amount of shading will depend on the character of the plant and here is yet another reason for growing plants with similar requirements in a small greenhouse since it is difficult to give some parts more shade than others.

The second reason for shading is to control temperature and particularly to check the sudden upsurges that can occur on bright days. It may well be that the plants would appreciate the sunlight if it could be given without the danger of excessive heat so shading used for this purpose should be readily movable. Blinds mounted either inside or outside the roof are ideal whereas when the shading is needed – because the plants grown prefer it that way – it can be of a semi-permanent character such as lime-wash or special shading compound sprayed or painted on the glass. As a rule shading for either purpose is only required on the sunny side – or sides – of the house, and for heat control only at periods between late spring and early autumn, inclusive. In the short days of winter most plants can do with all the light that is available.

Watering. This is a matter which, I think, gives the beginner more headaches than any other, though in point of fact incorrect heating and ventilation are quite as likely to damage plants. There is a general desire to have watering reduced to rule of thumb but unfortunately this is quite impossible. One cannot say 'Give so much water every so often' about any plant at any time of the year because so much depends on the weather conditions prevailing at the moment, the position and character of the greenhouse and the type of soil in which the plant is growing. All the same there are a few general rules which can be laid down.

Firstly, when a pot plant requires water it should always be given in sufficient quantity to moisten all the soil in the pot. If in doubt lift the pot up and keep on applying water until it begins to trickle out of the drainage hole in the bottom.

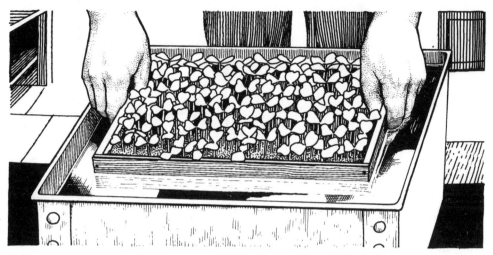

The best way to water small seedlings is to hold the seed tray in water so that the moisture soaks up from below

There are four ways by which one can gauge the moisture of the soil in a pot. One is to scratch the surface with finger nail or pointed stick. This is seldom practicable because of the root disturbance involved. The second is to lift the pot and judge by its weight, for wet soil weighs more than dry. This requires just a little experience, but if you experiment with a couple of pots of the same size both filled with soil, one thoroughly dry, the other wet, you will soon get the idea. The third method is to tap the pot with something hard, such as a small wooden hammer or the leg bone of a chicken. Provided the pot is made of clay and is not cracked, it will give a ringing sound when the soil within it is dry and a dull, heavy note when the soil is wet. This method does not work with plastic pots. The fourth method is to use one of the probes sold for the purpose, which registers the moisture of the soil on a dial.

My last piece of advice about watering is never to use a rose on the watering-can except when dealing with small seedlings or newly potted plants. A rose tends to give a deceptively wet appearance to the surface while leaving the lower soil inadequately moistened. There is also the danger of wetting the foliage too much or of water collecting at the heart of the plant. This is fatal to many plants, such as winter-flowering primulas and greenhouse calceolarias. Even in the case of small seedlings, or seed trays before the seed germinates, it is often better to water them by holding the pan almost to its rim in a bucket of water so that the moisture soaks up from below through the drainage holes than it is to give it from above through a fine rose. Established plants should always be watered direct from the spout which should be held close to the soil to avoid splashing.

Capillary Watering. This technique relies on the fact that water will rise from below by capillary attraction through particles of fine sand or closely packed soil. The capillary bench is a greenhouse staging covered with some impervious substance such as strong polythene film. This in turn is covered with a layer of fine sand 4 cm (1½ in) thick. Alternatively a mat of plastic fibre, manufactured for the purpose, can be used. This has the merit of not encouraging weed growth so much as moist sand. Some device must be

A capillary bench equipped with an automatic watering device controlled by a ball valve

arranged for keeping this constantly moist and various equipment is marketed for this purpose. Pot plants are then placed on the damp sand and absorb water from it. If the plants are in clay pots a wick of cotton or glass fibre must be passed through the drainage holes to carry water from the sand to the soil within, but plants in flat-bottomed plastic pots do not require wicks. It will be seen that plants on a capillary bench are kept uniformly moist at all times. This is contrary to traditional beliefs about what pot plants require but seems to suit most plants admirably with the exception of succulents and plants which have been newly potted. These should be watered by hand until they are fully established, when they can be removed to the capillary bench.

The capillary action is started by giving each plant a thorough soaking with water as the water will not rise if the pots are dry. It is also possible to arrange for capillary watering from the floor of the house. One method is to cover the floor with polythene film, place a good layer of sand on the sheet and a trickle irrigation line on top which can be used to flood the sand once or twice daily. Alternatively if the water is fed from a tank itself filled by a controllable drip feed, water can be applied continuously but slowly and the watering becomes completely automatic, freeing you for other activities.

POTTING

Pots used for greenhouse plants must be clean and also well drained. Cleanliness is important because roots will stick to the sides of a dirty pot and it will then be impossible to remove any plant without injuring its roots. Drainage is vital because unless there is a free outlet for surplus moisture the soil in the pot will become waterlogged, air will be driven out and roots will die.

Old pots, whether of clay or plastic, should be scrubbed or at the very least rubbed clean with a rag. It often pays to spray them with a sterilizing fluid such as formalin to kill any disease germs they may contain. If this treatment is adopted leave the pots out of doors for a few days before use.

Drainage takes place through a hole or slots formed in the base of the pot. These must be open and unclogged by soil, worm casts, etc. It used to be considered essential to put some broken crocks in the bottom of each pot, one large piece over the drainage hole if the pot was bigger than 7·5 cm (3 in) in diameter, and a few smaller pieces of broken pot on top of it. The first crock had to be a little curved and placed with its convex side uppermost so that it kept the drainage hole open. This crocking of pots has been largely discontinued since the development of porous composts such as those made to the John Innes formulae or the various peat composts. Yet crocking is still desirable for many plants, and is harmful to none. It is a slightly old-fashioned technique which has been discarded commercially mainly to save time and labour and may well be continued by amateurs in search of perfection. But crocks and other drainage material must not be used if plants are to stand on a capillary bench as it is then essential that there is good contact between the soil in the pot and the damp sand or mat on the bench.

Many beginners are puzzled by the constant insistence on 'potting on', that is moving plants from one size pot to another stage by stage, instead of placing them straight away in the biggest pots they are likely to require which might save much unnecessary labour. The objection is that, even with good drainage, the soil confined in a pot is apt to become stagnant unless it is reasonably filled with roots to draw moisture through it. In practice it is found that overpotting is one of the commonest causes of failure unless very open composts of the John Innes type are used. In general it is unwise to exceed the following steps in potting on, the approximate figures being for pot diameters measured at the rim 6·2 cm (2½ in), 10 cm (4 in), 17·5 cm (7 in), 30 cm (1 ft).

Composts. At one time it was considered necessary to have a different mixture of soil, sand and other ingredients for almost every family of plants and every gardener had his own pet recipes, some of them closely guarded secrets. A series of experiments carried out at the John Innes Horticultural Institution with the object of finding out whether any simplification of this practice was possible showed that one basic mixture, with very slight modification, could be used for practically every type of greenhouse plant. This basic mixture is prepared as follows:

Seven parts by loose bulk medium loam; 3 parts by loose bulk granulated peat; 2 parts by loose bulk coarse lime-free sand.

The loam should be top soil cut from a meadow and containing plenty of fibrous roots. It should be stacked for at least a year before use so that it may be well rotted, and it is an advantage if it can be sterilized though this is not essential.

Any good-grade horticultural peat will do provided it is reasonably free from dust and lumps. Sphagnum moss peat usually has the right fluffy texture.

The sand should be angular and coarse, many particles only just passing through a 0·3 cm (⅛ in) mesh sieve. Sea sand is not good as it contains too much salt and sometimes lime.

The compost is fortified with fertilizers and again a standard mixture is recommended. This is:

Two parts by weight hoof and horn meal, 0·3 cm (⅛ in) grist. (13 per cent nitrogen); 2 parts by weight superphosphate of lime (16 per cent phosphoric acid); 1 part by weight sulphate of potash (48 per cent pure potash).

For most potting up to 10 cm (4 in) pots, and for all potting of delicate plants, 113 g (4 oz) of this fertilizer mixture is added to each 0·03 cu m (1 bushel) of the mixed potting compost. This is known as John Innes Potting Compost No. 1 or for short, J.I. No. 1. For

GARDENING UNDER GLASS

Repotting a greenhouse plant.
(a) To remove a plant from its pot, tap the pot on the edge of the potting bench so that the ball of soil slides out intact.
(b) Crocks are placed in the bottom of a clean clay pot to allow free drainage. Plastic pots do not need crocks.
(c) Before the ball of soil is set in place, some compost is placed over the crocks in the bottom of the pot.
(d) Fill the compost in round the root ball while holding the plant in place.
(e) Finally, press the compost firmly in place with the fingers. If a large pot is being used, a 'ramming' stick may be needed for soil composts, but not for peat composts

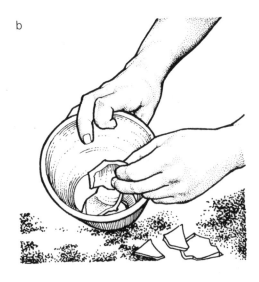

potting on from 10 cm (4 in) to 17·5 cm (7 in) pots for all except delicate plants 226 g (8 oz) of the fertilizer mixture is added to each 0·03 cu m (1 bushel) of potting compost. This is known as J.I. No. 2. For sturdy plants needing 20 cm (8 in) pots or larger, but still with the exceptions already made, 340 g (12 oz) of the fertilizer mixture is used per 0·03 cu m (1 bushel) of potting compost. This is known as J.I. No. 3. In my cultural notes I have referred to the strength of compost best for established plants. Young plants in small pots should always be in the weakest compost.

In addition 2·1 g (¾ oz) of ground chalk or limestone (not hydrated lime) should be added for each 113 g (4 oz) of fertilizer except where the loam used already contains a fair quantity of lime. This addition should not be made in the case of lime-hating plants.

It has become increasingly difficult to get loam of the quality demanded by the John Innes experts and when less fibrous soil is used more peat may be required. There is also a growing tendency to use slow-release fertilizers containing essential trace elements instead of the John Innes mixture. Always use in the quantities recommended by the manufacturers. Peat composts can also be made at home, a satisfactory formula being equal parts by bulk of medium grade peat and fine but not binding sand, to each litre of which is added 1.5 g (0·04 oz) of hoof and horn meal, 0·15 g (0·005 oz) of nitrate of potash, 1·5 g (0·005 oz) of superphosphate of lime, 4·5 g (0·15 oz) of finely powdered magnesium limestone and 1·5 g (0·005 oz) of finely powdered chalk or limestone. A richer mixture for hungry or fast-growing plants can be made by doubling the amount of hoof and horn meal. These mixtures should be used freshly made. Proprietary fertilizers are also available for mixing with peat to prepare seed or potting composts.. They should be used according to manufacturer's instructions.

Recent slow-release granular fertilizers save a lot of time. They release the appropriate quantity of nutrients, often according to the temperature, and need only be applied at the start of each season.

Soilless Composts. The success of the John Innes composts depends to a great extent upon the quality of the loam and this is the most difficult material to standardize. Partly to overcome this difficulty and also because of the shortage of good-quality loam many experiments have been made with soilless composts. Some of these contain simply carefully selected peat plus fertilizers, some have in addition sand or even small quantities of clay. Soilless composts are sold ready for use and should be used strictly according to manufacturer's instructions.. As a rule they should not be firmed much, only well settled around the roots of the plants by finger pressure and a few smart raps of the pot on a firm surface such as a wooden potting bench. They tend to hold more water than soil composts and dry out more slowly. As a rule they contain less food reserves and so feeding must start earlier and possibly be carried out more frequently than with soil composts. Good soilless composts suit a wide range of plants and are particularly suitable for encouraging the growth of plants.

Sieving. When dealing with seedlings and small plants it is necessary to sieve loam but it is unwise to overdo this. Very fine soil tends to clog and become waterlogged or hard more readily than coarse soil. In consequence, when dealing with fairly big plants and pots over 13 cm (5 in) in diameter, it is often best to dispense with the sieve altogether and simply chop the loam up or pull it apart with the fingers into fairly small pieces. Even when dealing with smaller plants it is seldom that a sieve with a mesh below 12 mm ($\frac{1}{2}$ in) will be required.

Peat-Free Composts. Worries that huge areas of peatland, many of special scientific interest, are being depleted has led to an interest in peat-free and low-peat composts for pot plants.

But the search for an all-purpose alternative is difficult. Peat is highly valued because of its uniformity, high degree of sterility, slow decomposition rate, and ability to hold moisture and air. Furthermore it is relatively easy to handle and lightweight, and is cheaply available. It is unlikely that a direct substitute will be found which is equally fool-proof and versatile, with exactly the same physical, chemical and nutritional characteristics. Instead alternatives will be more suited to specific applications, and must be used in different ways with their own watering and feeding rates.

The current peat alternatives divide into the organic (e.g. manure, woodfibre), and inorganic (perlite and vermiculite). Furthermore these alternatives subdivide into those with an artificially derived nutrient source, and those from which nutrients are derived from the microbiological breakdown of organic material.

The artificial nutrients of the former include coir (the leftover material after fibres are stripped off coconuts to make matting), and processed bark. Depending on the level of nutrients added, feeding may be necessary after several weeks' growth. When nutrients derive from microbiological breakdown there may be such a high level of food that some dilution is required.

The most highly favoured peat alternative to-date is coir. Its advantages (lightweight, high porosity, pH of 5·8-6·4, slow decomposition rate, furthering good root growth, can be sterilized, and can be mixed with straw for seedlings, etc), are offset by the fact that coir is at an early development stage, and that it is unclear what impact its use would have on the Sri Lankan economy (where it is produced). Other peat alternatives include pumice, farm waste, and sewage sludge.

Loosening and Firming Roots. When potting plants avoid disturbing their roots over-much but, if the roots are wound into a tight ball, loosen them gently with the fingers or tease out some of the outer ones with a pointed stick so that the new soil can be worked around them. Always remove the old drainage crocks from the bottom of the ball.

Firmness of potting will vary according to the nature of the plant and the character of the potting compost. When using John Innes composts a good general rule, though it has exceptions, is to firm in proportion to the hardness of growth, plants with hard, woody stems being made firmer than those with soft stems. Also there should be a general tendency to pot more firmly as the bigger pot sizes are reached. Up to 15 cm (6 in) diameter, size adequate firming can almost always be obtained with the fingers pressed into the soil around the edge of the pot, and also by rapping the pot sharply on a wooden bench or table. Above 15 cm (6 in) pots it is sometimes necessary to use a potting stick, a short length of stick about as thick as a broom handle, rounded at the end and used to force the soil down around the edge of the pot. Peat composts only need light firming with the finger tips and a few sharp taps on a firm bench to settle in the compost.

Never fill pots with soil right to the brim. Space is necessary so that water can be easily applied. After potting it is usually desirable to water a little more sparingly than usual for a few days and to keep the plants in a slightly warmer and moister atmosphere. This aids quick root growth and prevents unnecessary flagging of foliage.

PROPAGATION UNDER GLASS

Though the methods of increasing plants under glass are the same as for outdoors there are certain differences in the technique employed for seeds and cuttings.

Seed. This will be sown in boxes, trays or pots instead of in the open ground, and the same comments about providing them with good drainage which have been made about potting apply with at least equal force. Boxes should have at least one good slit in the bottom running their whole length and be well covered with pieces of crock and the roughage left in the sieve when preparing composts. In pots and trays it pays to have a good wad of sphagnum moss over the crocks.

According to the John Innes Horticultural Institution the most suitable compost in which to germinate seeds is as follows: two parts (loose bulk) medium loam; 1 part (loose bulk) peat; and 1 part (loose bulk) sand.

The quality and nature of the ingredients are the same as for the potting composts. To each 0·03 cu m (1 bushel) of the mixture are added 50 g (1½ oz) superphosphate of lime and 21 g (¾ oz) ground chalk or limestone. The loam should first be sterilized. This John Innes Seed Compost is commonly referred to as J.I. seed. There are also soilless composts for seed sowing and these resemble the soilless potting composts but contain less fertilizer. All that has been said regarding the differences in handling of soil-based and soilless potting composts applies equally to soil-based and soilless seed composts.

Watering of small seeds needs to be done with great care to avoid disturbance and often the most satisfactory method is to hold the whole receptacle almost but not quite to its rim in a tub of water until the water, soaking up from below, darkens the surface.

It frequently pays to cover seed trays with a pane of glass and a sheet of paper to lower the rate of evaporation and so lessen the need for watering, but the paper must be removed immediately seedlings appear, the glass itself being tilted a day or so later to admit air and removed altogether a few days after that.

Cuttings. Under glass cuttings can often be placed with advantage in a propagator or close frame which may be no more than a deep box with a sheet of glass on top. If this is stood in the greenhouse over the hot-water pipes or heating apparatus, or is provided with an electric soil-warming cable, the soil in which the cuttings are inserted will be warmed from below (bottom heat) and this is found greatly to hasten the rooting of many cuttings. A propagator will also be found most useful and economical for germinating seeds that require a higher temperature than that normally maintained in the greenhouse. Care must be taken not to overdo the heating nor to keep the frame unventilated for unnecessarily long periods or the cuttings or seedlings may be dangerously weakened.

The propagator or close frame, with or without bottom heat, is also a suitable place in which to keep some small grafted or budded plants until they have made a union. Often the frame is partly filled with peat in which pots or pans containing grafts or cuttings are plunged. This filling serves the dual purpose of conducting heat evenly to the compost and holding moisture.

A standard John Innes compost has been devised for cuttings and consists of: 1 part (loose bulk) medium loam; 2 parts (loose bulk) peat; 1 part (loose bulk) sand. No fertilizers are added. However many skilled gardeners prefer their own mixtures. Some use nothing but sand, others various proportions of peat and sand, perlite or vermiculite.

Mist Propagation. Various appliances are now available for keeping cuttings constantly moist by automatically spraying them with water at fairly frequent intervals. Broadly these devices may be divided into two types, those that are controlled by the actual rate of water evaporation and those that work on a simple time basis. Some of these require an electrical mains supply for control but there are a few very simple devices which operate without electricity.

The cuttings are not kept in a normal propagating frame but are usually rooted on the floor or staging of a greenhouse. Coarse sand is the most satisfactory rooting medium and the best results are obtained when this is warmed to about 18-20°C/65-68°F from below as, for example, with an electrical soil-warming cable. Cuttings should be removed to ordinary compost of soil, sand and peat as soon as they are rooted.

Polythene Bag Propagation. A very simple method which suits many spring and summer cuttings is to insert them in pots filled with any of the recommended cutting composts, then slip a polythene bag over the pot and secure it round the sides with a rubber band. If the drainage holes are not covered by the bag the pot can be stood on a capillary bench. The thin polythene retains moisture but permits a very slow exchange of air.

Chapter 19

Recommended Greenhouse Plants

In this chapter the more popular or generally useful greenhouse plants are arranged alphabetically and a short account of the cultivation of each is given. Information about the John Innes and peat-based composts to which frequent reference is made can be found in the preceding chapter.

Abutilon (Chinese Bellflower). These are shrubs with long, flexible stems that can be trained easily as climbers to clothe a greenhouse or conservatory wall. One or two are hardy enough to be grown in the open air all the year round, particularly in milder climates (see Chapter 10). All can be put out of doors in summer; the shrubby kinds with leaves variously mottled with silver or gold like *Abutilon striatum thompsonii* are quite popular for summer bedding. *A. megapotamicum* has red and yellow flowers like little Chinese lanterns, but many of the greenhouse varieties are hybrids with large bell-shaped flowers in white, yellow, pink, red or maroon. All will thrive under cool house conditions and with a little extra warmth may well flower almost throughout the year.

Grow them all in J.I. No. 2 and use 20-25 cm (8-10 in) pots for the majority, though small plants can be accommodated in 15 cm (6 in) pots. Alternatively plant directly into a bed of good soil on the greenhouse floor. Repot when necessary in late winter, and during the same month trim the plants to shape. Stems can be shortened by a half or more to prevent plants becoming straggly. Water freely in summer, sparingly in winter. Propagate by seed, though there will be variation in the seedlings and the variegated-leaf characteristics are not transmitted by seed, or by cuttings or firm young shoots in summer.

Acacia (Mimosa, Wattle). *Acacia dealbata*, is a small tree which can be grown out of doors in specially favoured places, or may be planted in the greenhouse in a big tub or direct in the greenhouse border. It is, however, rather big for the average greenhouse for which shrubby species such as *A. armata*, *A. baileyana*, *A. drummondii* and *A. longifolia* are preferable. All these can be grown in large pots or tubs and will produce masses of tiny yellow flowers in pompons on short spikes mainly in late winter and early spring.

Grow them in J.I. No. 2 and water fairly freely in summer but very sparingly in winter. Artificial heat is only necessary to exclude frost and the atmosphere at all times should be rather dry. In summer plants may be stood in a dry frame or a sunny place out of doors. Acacias do not need frequent repotting, but when pots become overcrowded with roots they should be moved to a size larger immediately after flowering. No regular pruning is required but large plants can be cut back moderately after flowering. Propagate by cuttings in summer or by seed.

Acalypha (Chenille Plant, Red-hot Cat's-tail, Copper Leaf). From the gardener's point of view acalyphas may be split into two groups. One, typified by *Acalypha godseffiana* and *A. wilkesiana*, the copper leaf, is grown principally for its foliage, while the other, of which *A. hispida*, the chenille plant or red-hot cat's-tail, is a good example, has long, catkin-like trails of crimson flowers. All make excellent pot plants requiring warm house treatment and should be grown in J.I. No. 2 or soilless compost. They need plenty of water from mid-spring to early autumn and a moderate supply the rest of the year. Repot, when necessary, in early spring. Most can be propagated quite easily from early spring cuttings, provided these can be given a fairly high temperature, about 20-23°C/68-74°F, with bottom heat.

Achimenes (Hot Water Plant). These are tuberous-rooted plants which can be grown as pot plants but are more frequently treated as trailers to be planted in baskets suspended from the rafters. They look very pretty in this way with cascades of thin stems carrying numerous tubular flowers in showy colours such as red, blue and purple. By potting the little cylindrical tubers every few weeks from late winter to late spring it is possible to have the plants in bloom all summer, even into early autumn.

Pot the tubers five or six in each 11·2 cm (4½ in) pot or 5 cm (2 in) apart in baskets in J.I. No. 1 or soilless potting compost, just covering them. Water sparingly at first and place in a temperature of 15-18°C/59-65°F. Maintain a fairly moist atmosphere and water freely until a few weeks after flowering when the water supply should be gradually discontinued and the tubers allowed to dry off. Feed with weak liquid manure all summer and shade from direct sunshine. The tubers are stored perfectly dry in the pots or baskets in which they have been growing and in a temperature of about 10°C/50°F until it is time to start them again, when they are shaken clear of soil and planted. Achimenes can also be raised from seed sown in a temperature of 18-20°C/65-68°F from mid-winter to early spring.

Aechmea. These handsome plants make rosettes of stiff, leathery leaves and carry spikes of flowers surrounded by showy bracts which remain decorative for weeks or even months. *Aechmea fasciata*, with leaves banded in several shades of grey and grey-green and pink bracts, and *A. fulgens*, with green or green and purple leaves and scarlet, berry-like sepals, are the two kinds commonly seen. Both enjoy intermediate or warm house conditions and should be well shaded in summer. They make excellent house plants. They should be watered fairly freely in summer, moderately in winter, but at all seasons the vase or cup formed by the leaves in the centre of each rosette should be kept full of water. Maintain a moist atmosphere in summer. Grow in a soilless compost or a mixture of equal parts peat, sand and osmunda fibre in the smallest pots that will contain the roots. Only repot when really necessary and then in early spring. Increase by division when repotting.

Agapanthus (African Lily). *Agapanthus africanus* is most familiar as a pot or tub plant for standing out of doors in sunny places during the summer months but is too tender to be left outside in cold winters. It makes a fine subject for the unheated or slightly heated greenhouse. It has strap-shaped leaves and large, almost globular heads of blue or white flowers in summer. Grow it in big pots or wooden tubs in J.I. No. 2 and only repot when it is obviously overcrowded. Then shake it out in early spring, divide the roots into two or three pieces and repot them in the same mixture as before. It likes plenty of water in summer, little or no shade, and should have plenty of air. Heat need only be used in winter to exclude frost and over winter little water should be given. Plants can be raised from seed.

Agave. Agaves are natives of desert regions and look like it. They make large, stiff rosettes of long, pointed succulent leaves, obviously well fitted to withstand periods of extreme drought. It is for their foliage that they are grown in the garden and many of them are hardy enough to be planted out of doors during the summer. Used in this way they are a popular feature of sub-tropical bedding schemes. Most agaves are rather large plants, the biggest of all being *Agave americana*, with leaves up to 1·8 m (6 ft) long and 20 cm (8 in) wide. There are several handsome variegated varieties and smaller kinds such as *A. filifera* and *A. victoriae-reginae* which can be grown in 21·2 cm (8½ in) pots. All need frost protection only and can be grown without heat for the greater part of the year. Plant them in rather light sandy soil, water moderately in summer and scarcely at all in winter. Do not shade at any time and maintain a rather dry atmosphere. Repot when necessary in early spring and increase by removing offshoots at the same time.

Aglaonema. Quite small perennials belonging to the same family as the arum lily. *Aglaonema commutatum* and Silver Queen, the kinds most commonly grown, have spear-shaped leaves in two shades of green, or silvery grey. All are grown solely for their foliage. Grow them in an intermediate or warm greenhouse or in a room in J.I. No. 1 or peat potting compost. Water fairly freely in spring and summer but keep the soil only just moist in autumn and winter. Shade from direct sunshine and maintain a moist atmosphere in summer. Increase by division at potting time in early spring.

Aichryson. *Aichryson × domesticum* Variegatum is a bushy little plant only several centimetres high with fleshy, rounded, green and ivory leaves, often more ivory than green. It can be grown in a cool greenhouse or in a fairly light place indoors and will thrive in J.I. No. 1. Water fairly freely in spring and summer, very sparingly in autumn and winter and repot when necessary in early spring. Increase by cuttings in spring or summer.

Allamanda. *Allamanda cathartica* is a showy climbing plant, but it requires intermediate or warm house temperatures. It is a fairly vigorous plant which may be grown in large pots or tubs in J.I. No. 2 or be planted directly in the greenhouse border in fairly rich soil. Water freely from mid-spring to late summer, moderately from early autumn to early spring and feed it with weak liquid manure from early summer to early autumn. If grown in pots, repot every third or fourth year in late winter. Shoots can either be trained on wires or trellis work or over a crinoline frame. The yellow flowers are trumpet shaped, and with good management the flowering season is from mid-spring to early autumn. Increase is by cuttings of the previous year's growth taken in early spring and rooted in a propagating frame, in a temperature of 25°C/77°F.

Alocasia. These are very handsome tropical plants grown solely for their foliage. The leaves are like big shields, dark green, variously veined with lighter green and milky white. All require warm house treatment with plenty of moisture; in fact just the conditions one would expect in a tropical jungle. Otherwise they are not difficult to grow. Repot when necessary in early spring. Grow them in J.I. No. 2 or soilless compost and water freely in summer, moderately in winter. Frequent damping down and syringing will be needed in summer and the glass can be shaded permanently on the sunny side from late spring to early autumn. Well-grown plants will produce suckers around the main stem and if further stock is required these can be detached at potting time.

Aloe (Partridge-breasted Aloe). The popular name of the succulent, *Aloe variegata*, refers to the curious buff and white mottling of the leaves. It is an ideal pot plant for the beginner for it is practically impossible to kill and it will succeed in quite a small pot, say 10–13 cm (3–5 in) according to the age of the plant. Keep it almost dry in winter, water moderately in summer and give it as much sun as possible and frost protection. If necessary it can be stood out of doors all the summer or used as a house plant. Old plants produce offsets which can be detached in early spring, the proper potting season. Use J.I. No. 1 compost with a little extra sand. Other aloes need similar conditions but most of them take up far more room.

Aloysia. What was once known as *Lippia citriodora* (Lemon Verbena) is now called *Aloysia triphylla*. It is a deciduous shrub grown for the fragrance of its leaves, and is hardy enough to be planted out of doors in a sheltered place, as described on p. 281. It can also be grown in J.I. No. 3 in unheated greenhouses and conservatories, but should then be watered and ventilated freely in summer to prevent attacks by red spider and thrips and syringed daily with water during warm weather. Prune to shape in the autumn. Increase by cuttings of young shoots in early summer.

Amaryllis. See **Hippeastrum** (p. 476).

Ananas. These are the pineapples of which two varieties are worth growing as ornamental foliage plants. These are *Ananas bracteatus striatus*, a coppery green and cream variegated variety of the red pineapple, and *A. comosus* Variegatus, a variegated form of the common pineapple with leaves edged with cream, flushed with red at the centre of the rosette and with red spines. Both kinds make rosettes of narrow leaves. They grow well in a mixture of 3 parts peat, 2 parts loam and 1 part sand with a dusting of slow release fertilizer and can either be grown in a warm room or in a greenhouse with minimum temperature of 15°C/59°F. Water fairly freely in spring and summer, moderately in autumn and winter. Increase by detaching rooted suckers in spring or cutting off the tops of plants in summer and rooting them like cuttings in peat and sand in a warm propagator.

Anthurium. These are precisely the queer, vivid plants which one might imagine would grow in tropical places. They produce very big, handsome, shield-shaped leaves and the flowers (or spathes, to be precise) look like coloured leaves themselves, being oval and flattish, each with a long rat's tail (the spadix) at the top. The colours of the spathes are very bright and include flamingo red, scarlet, rose and orange-red, with white for contrast. The two kinds usually grown are *Anthurium andreanum* and *A. scherzerianum*, the former with larger leaves and spathes but the latter freer flowering and easier to grow.

All anthuriums are plants for the warm house with a very moist atmosphere in summer. Water freely, syringe and damp down frequently from mid-spring to early autumn, more moderately for the rest of the year. Grow in soilless potting compost or J.I. No. 1 plus one quarter its bulk of peat. Repot, in early spring, only when absolutely necessary, which may be every second or third year. Offshoots can be removed at the same time and potted separately, or root cuttings can be prepared and started in a propagating box with plenty of bottom heat.

A. scherzerianum and its varieties may be grown in rooms, at any rate for a few months at a time as they are not so seriously affected by dry air.

Aphelandra. The kind commonly grown, *Aphelandra squarrosa louisae*, is a bushy perennial with shining dark green leaves with ivory stripes and stiff spikes of yellow flowers produced when the plant has really filled its pot with roots. It likes intermediate house conditions and also makes a good room plant, at any rate for periods, though after a while the dry air of rooms may affect it adversely. Grow it in J.I. No. 3 or soilless compost, water freely in summer, moderately at other times and shade from late spring to early autumn. Repot when necessary in early spring and increase by cuttings from late spring to early autumn rooted in a propagator with bottom heat.

Araucaria (Norfolk Island Pine). A close relative of the monkey puzzle tree, *Araucaria heterophylla* makes a useful pot plant for the greenhouse or home. It has a similar stiffly branched habit, but the leaves are much smaller and softer, the whole plant looking like a rather formal Christmas tree. It likes cool treatment throughout with no more than frost protection in winter and plenty of light and air at all times. Grow in J.I. No. 1 and repot in early spring, moving on to larger sizes as the smaller pots become filled with roots, but avoid overpotting at any time. Water freely in spring and summer, moderately in autumn and winter. This is a good home plant for a light, sunny room. The best method of increase is by seeds sown in light soil in pots or trays in a warm greenhouse in spring.

Ardisia. A good pot plant for a cool or intermediate greenhouse is *Ardisia crispa*, a small evergreen shrub worth growing for its fine crops of scarlet berries which last from early autumn to late winter. Grow in J.I. No. 2, repotting in late winter. Water rather freely in summer, moderately in spring and autumn and rather sparingly in winter. Syringe frequently in summer and shade lightly. When plants become too large they can be cut right down at potting time. The best method of increase is by seed but seedlings take two or three years to flower. Quicker results can be obtained from summer cuttings in a warm propagator but these are not easy to root.

Argyranthemum. What was once listed as a chrysanthemum, and marguerite, is now *Argyranthemum frutescens*. Though it makes quite a good pot plant to flower in the unheated greenhouse in summer, it is far more commonly grown for summer bedding and window boxes. For all purposes it is best to propagate by means of cuttings of young, non-flowering shoots, which root readily in a propagator in spring and summer, early spring or late summer usually being the most suitable months. When rooted, pot the cuttings singly in 7·5 cm (3 in) pots in J.I. No. 1, moving on to larger pots and No. 2 as necessary until, by late spring, they are planted out or reach the 13·7 cm (5½ in) pots in which they will bloom. In autumn and winter water very sparingly and keep in a sunny greenhouse with frost protection only. No artificial heat is required from late spring to mid-autumn. Old plants can be kept from year to year and will eventually make quite big bushes though, alternatively, they can be pruned severely each autumn to keep them smaller. If desired, some plants can also be lifted before mid-autumn from the summer beds and potted for return to the greenhouse. The common argyranthemum is white but there is also a good yellow form, Jamaica Primrose.

Aristolochia. This is a big family but not many of its members are of much importance to the amateur. The best known is *Aristolochia aurior*, also known as *A. macrophylla*, hardy but too rampant for most greenhouses. It is popularly known as the Dutchman's pipe because of its curious, yellowish-green and brown flowers shaped like a meerschaum. A far better greenhouse plant is *A. elegans* with large, widely funnel-shaped, dull white flowers heavily mottled with maroon. It is a slender climber enjoying a sunny greenhouse, where it can be trained under the rafters, or up the back of a lean-to. It likes a rather rich soil, is best planted directly in the greenhouse border and needs intermediate house conditions. Cuttings prepared from firm shoots in late summer will root in sandy soil in a propagator provided with bottom heat.

Arum. See **Zantedeschia** (p. 503).

Asclepias. *Asclepias curassavica* is a perennial grown for its clusters of orange and purple flowers on 60–90 cm (2–3 ft) stems in mid- to late summer. It will thrive in a cool or intermediate house and can be raised from seed sown in early spring to flower the same year. Alternatively plants can be divided in spring or cuttings can be taken in late spring/early summer. Grow in J.I. No. 2. Water freely in spring and summer, moderately in autumn and very sparingly in winter and give it full light.

Asparagus. The vegetable garden asparagus has two decorative relatives both needing the protection of a frost-proof greenhouse. They are *Asparagus plumosus*, familiar to most gardeners as asparagus fern, and *A. sprengeri*, which in gardens is frequently known simply as sprengeri. The first is a climber, though there is a dwarf variety. Both forms have flat, very finely divided leaves and wiry stems and are most useful for cutting and mixing with flowers. *A. sprengeri* is a trailing plant with small, shining green leaves. It is popular for hanging baskets and also for cutting and various decorative uses such as winding round the handles of ornamental baskets. Both like J.I. No. 2 compost, a fair amount of light and not too much heat, though *A. plumosus* can be gently forced in a temperature of 18°C/65°F in spring to get early growth. Repot in early spring when the pots are overcrowded with roots. Old plants can be divided if they become too big, and this is a useful method of propagation, though these plants can also be increased by seed sown in a greenhouse in spring or early summer. Shoots can be cut in moderation at any time for decorative purposes, but a plant should never be stripped of its foliage.

For *Asparagus medioloides (asparagoides)* see Smilax (p. 496).

Aspidistra. A useful foliage plant in its plain green or variegated varieties, *Aspidistra elatior* is practically indestructible, thriving in shade too dense for most subjects, and one of the best plants for a living room. Give it J.I. No. 2 compost, water it moderately at all times of the year, and in summer sponge or syringe the leaves frequently to keep them free of dirt. Plants can be repotted in spring when they become overcrowded and big plants can, if desired, be divided at the same time. The aspidistra does not require any artificial heat except to protect it from frost.

Astilbe. The ordinary astilbes of the herbaceous border (see Chapter 8) make useful pot plants and, if potted in the autumn in J.I. No. 1 or soilless compost, placed in a frame for the winter and brought into a slightly heated greenhouse in late winter, can be had in bloom in the second half of spring. They should be given plenty of water while making their growth. After flowering the pots should be plunged to their rims outdoors in a cool sheltered position and the roots can then be planted out in the autumn. They should not be forced two years running. These are perfectly hardy plants and heat is only used to force them into early flower.

Azalea. As explained in Chapter 10 azaleas are really particular kinds of rhododendron. Most are hardy shrubs but numerous varieties derived from *Rhododendron simsii* and known by gardeners either as *Azalea indica* or as Indian azaleas are tender and make excellent greenhouse pot plants. They are evergreen shrubs with big, showy, mostly double flowers in various shades of pink, red and crimson and combinations of these colours, together with white. There are a great many named varieties which are divided into three groups according to time of flowering. The early group is suitable for gentle forcing from mid-autumn onwards for flowers in early and mid-winter. The mid-season group can be forced from early winter onwards to bloom in late winter/early spring and the late group is for mid-winter forcing to bloom from early to mid-spring.

Obtain strong plants in the autumn, pot them up in the smallest pots that will contain their roots, running peat around the balls of soil. Then place them in a frost-proof greenhouse where they should have plenty of light and as much ventilation as is consistent with a minimum temperature of about 5°C/41°F. When forcing time arrives the temperature can be increased gradually to 13-18°C/56-65°F. During this period water freely, feed every 14 days with weak liquid manure and syringe daily with tepid water. After flowering harden the plants off and stand them out of doors in a shady place over summer. Keep on syringing with water during hot weather as this prevents attacks by red spider, to which the plants are very subject; also keep them well watered and continue to feed until midsummer. Repot, if necessary, in mid-spring. Return to the greenhouse before frost occurs. Plants can be increased by layering or by cuttings of firm young shoots inserted in sand in a frame in the first half of summer but propagation is not easy.

Begonia. This is one of the really important genera for the amateur's greenhouse. There are a great many kinds of begonia and a number of them make excellent pot plants, though a few need a little more heat than most amateurs can command. This is particularly true of the winter-flowering begonias which can make such a splendid display from late autumn to late winter.

From the cultural standpoint the family can conveniently be divided into two groups, one tuberous rooted and the other fibrous rooted. The first is represented principally by the many magnificent hybrids with enormous double flowers in various shades of pink, rose, scarlet, crimson, orange, yellow and white. The catalogues of specialists are filled with named varieties of these.

All these tuberous-rooted begonias are summer flowering. The tubers become completely dormant in the winter and should be kept dry in a cool, frost-proof place. They are started into growth in moist peat or leafmould in early spring at a temperature of 16-18°C/60-65°F. The tubers can be arranged quite close together in ordinary seed trays and should be only just covered. Leaves will appear in two or three weeks and when about 5 cm (2 in) high the tubers should be potted singly in J.I. No. 1 in 10-15 cm (4-6 in) pots. Water moderately at first, more freely as they become established. Damp the staging daily and from late spring onwards give shading by day. From early summer it may even be

435

advisable to shade the glass permanently but not too heavily. Throughout maintain a temperature of around 16-18°C/60-65°F. The secret of success with these plants is a mild, slightly damp atmosphere: they do not like excessive heat or drought. Very careful staking is required because of the weight of the flowers. Flower buds may drop off if the plants are kept too dry or the temperature is too cold at night. After flowering gradually withhold water until, by late autumn, the soil is quite dry and the tubers can be shaken out and stored as before in a cool, frost-proof place.

These begonias can also be raised very readily from seed sown in mid- to late winter at a temperature of 18°C/65°F, though seedlings vary in colour and flower quality. The seed is extremely small and so should be sown on the surface of a particularly fine seed or peat compost. Do not cover at all with soil but place a sheet of glass and one of newspaper over each pan. Remove the paper directly germination occurs, tilt the glass a little the next day, remove it two or three days later. The seedlings should be pricked off into ordinary seed boxes filled with seed compost directly they can be handled, spaced 2·5 cm (1 in) apart each way. Pot them singly in small pots in J.I. No. 1 or peat potting compost as soon as the leaves touch in the boxes. Subsequently grow on like plants raised from tubers.

There is another class of tuberous-rooted begonia in which the growths are pendant and the plants are, therefore, ideal for culture in baskets suspended from the greenhouse rafters. All details of culture are the same as for the upright class except that, instead of the tubers being potted after they have been started into growth in boxes, they are placed in baskets lined with moss and filled with J.I. No. 1 compost. No staking is needed.

The fibrous-rooted begonias are even more varied, including both species and hybrids. Of the latter the most important is the winter-flowering group derived from *Begonia socotrana* and typified by Gloire de Lorraine. This has small pink flowers produced in fine sprays. There are other named varieties with deeper pink or white flowers. These are usually raised from cuttings prepared from basal shoots in late winter and early spring. Such cuttings root readily in very sandy soil in a propagating box with gentle bottom heat. They should be potted singly as soon as rooted, first in 5 cm (2 in) pots, then in 7·5 cm (3 in), and finally in 13·7 cm (5½ in) pots in J.I. No. 1. During the summer temperature and treatment are the same as for the tuberous-rooted begonias. It is equally important to avoid cold draughts and to maintain a rather moist atmosphere and mild temperature averaging 18°C/65°F. Any flower buds which appear in late summer or early autumn should be removed. Shoots may be pinched once or twice to encourage branching. These begonias are not allowed to dry off in winter, the soil is kept fairly moist throughout and the temperature maintained at the summer level until immediately after flowering, when it may drop to 6°C/10°F for a couple of months to give the plants a partial rest. No shading will be required after early autumn. Plants should be staked neatly and allowed to start flowering in late autumn. After the resting period the plants are repotted, though not necessarily in a larger pot as overpotting is bad. As soon as new basal shoots appear propagation can be resumed.

Yet another group of begonias is grown principally for their leaves which are handsomely marbled and often very beautifully formed. The best of these are the Rex varieties which, if permitted, will make quite big plants. They have large, heart-shaped leaves in many combinations of green, purple and silver. These foliage begonias are all fibrous rooted. They can be raised from seed sown in early to mid-spring and treated in the same way as seed from tuberous varieties. Alternatively they can be increased by leaf cuttings, that is, ordinary mature leaves pegged flat on the surface of sandy soil in a propagating box with bottom heat. A few incisions are made with a sharp knife through the veins of the leaves where they touch the soil. Roots are formed from these cuts and, in time, tiny new plants appear. Rex begonias will thrive in cool or intermediate house conditions, should be grown in J.I. No. 2 or peat potting compost and be kept moist even in winter. They will put up with a lot of shade and can even be grown under the greenhouse staging but the best foliage colours are produced with more light.

Begonia manicata with big, handsome leaves and quite tall spikes of small pink flowers in spring is grown like a Rex variety and so is *B. masoniana*, often known as the Iron Cross begonia because of the almost black mark in the shape of a cross on each green leaf.

Others requiring similar treatment are *B. haageana* and *B. lucerna*, both pink-flowered, the former blooming mainly in summer and autumn, the latter most of the year provided the temperature stays above 12°C/56°F.

The popular summer bedding varieties of *B. semperflorens* (see p. 73) can also be grown as pot plants in the greenhouse with no difference in treatment except that they are potted singly instead of being planted out. Cool moist treatment with shade from hot sun is needed. If desired plants can be retained for several years.

Billbergia. At one time it was supposed that these plants required a lot of heat, but experience proves that they can be grown successfully in a cool or intermediate house and also make good indoor plants for a light room. Billbergias have stiff, spiky leaves in rosettes and flowers carried in heads, not in themselves very showy, but surrounded by coloured bracts. The most popular is *Billbergia nutans*, 30-45 cm (1-1½ ft) high with slender, arching spikes of red, green and blue bracts all summer. Water freely in summer, very sparingly in winter and repot in early spring in J.I. No. 1. No shading is required. Plants can be increased by removing offsets at potting time.

Boronia. These are evergreen shrubs of small size with narrow leaves and an abundance of small, scented flowers from late winter to early summer. The best known is *Boronia megastigma*, in which the flowers are brownish-red and yellow. They make neat plants in 13-18 cm (5-7 in) pots and should be grown in J.I. No. 1, but with lime-free loam and a little extra peat. Pot very firmly. Boronias need a rather dry atmosphere with plenty of ventilation and a minimum temperature of 7°C/45°F in winter and an average of 15°C/59°F in summer. Let them have as much sun as possible and water with care, keeping the soil moist throughout but never sodden. Repot annually immediately after flowering but never move them into a pot more than one size larger than that already occupied, as overpotting is bad. Propagation is by cuttings of young shoots removed in summer and rooted in sand in a propagating box. The rooted cuttings will need occasional pinching to encourage a bushy habit.

Bougainvillea. Anyone who has visited the Mediterranean region in early summer will have been struck by the magnificent, magenta-flowered climbers which drape so many of the buildings. These are bougainvilleas and they have been developed in gardens so that there are now forms with pink, rose and orange-coloured flowers as well as the natural magenta. All are excellent climbers for the greenhouse. They thrive in a cool or intermediate house in J.I. No. 2 compost. Water fairly freely in spring and summer but gradually reduce in autumn and keep almost dry in winter. In late winter prune the previous year's growths back to within a few centimetres of the main vines. Repot at the same time if necessary, but it is really better to plant bougainvilleas direct in the greenhouse border. During warm weather syringe daily with tepid water. Cuttings a few centimetres long prepared from firm young shoots pulled off with a heel of older wood in summer will usually root readily in a propagating box with a fair amount of bottom heat, temperature 20°C/68°F.

Bouvardia. There are few evergreen shrubby plants to surpass the bouvardia for greenhouse display, more particularly as they bloom continuously throughout autumn and winter. They are not difficult to grow provided a winter temperature of not less than 10°C/50°F can be maintained. The intermediate house is ideal for them from early autumn to late spring and in summer they can be stood out of doors in a deep frame with the glass removed for most of the time when the weather is mild. Water freely in summer, moderately in autumn and winter. Cut back fairly severely at the end of winter and place the plants in a temperature of about 15°C/59°F to restart them into growth. Syringe daily with tepid water at this period and throughout the spring and summer. Pinch out the tips of the shoots occasionally until the end of summer to encourage a bushy habit. Feed occasionally with liquid manure in summer. Repotting, when necessary, should be done in mid-spring using J.I. No. 2 compost but do not overpot. Bouvardias can be increased by cuttings made from young shoots in spring or early summer, rooted in sandy soil in a propagating box with bottom heat. Alternatively root cuttings can be made, each about 2·5 cm (1 in) long and inserted in late winter/early spring in very sandy soil in a propagating box, but not all varieties come true to colour from root cuttings.

Browallia. The two kinds commonly grown are *Browallia speciosa* Major, 30-38 cm (1-1¼ ft) high, and *B. viscosa*, 23-30 cm (9 in-1 ft) high, both with blue and white flowers in summer. Both are perennials but are best grown as annuals. Plants can be had in flower at almost any time from mid-summer to late winter by varying the time of seed sowing, but as autumn flowers are valuable and easily obtained the usual practice is to sow in early spring in a slightly heated greenhouse. The seedlings are potted on stage by stage, usually two or three in a pot until, by mid-summer, they occupy the 13 cm (5 in) pots in which they will flower. During summer they can be accommodated in a frame in a sunny position out of doors. Syringe daily during warm weather. Just before mid-autumn take them in to a cool or intermediate greenhouse. It is an advantage to pinch growths occasionally during the early stages to encourage a branching habit.

Brugmansia (Angel's Trumpet). Several species (most previously known as datura) are grown, all big, showy plants with large leaves and equally large trumpet-shaped flowers, white and very fragrant in *Brugmansia arborea*, *B. cornigera* Knightii and *B. suaveolens*, orange-red in *B. sanguinea*. They are often seen in sub-tropical summer bedding schemes but are also useful greenhouse plants where there is room for them. Grow them in big pots or plant them out in the greenhouse border. Give plenty of water from mid-spring to early autumn and syringe and damp down frequently when the weather is warm. In winter water moderately and keep a fairly dry atmosphere. Winter temperature should not fall below 7°C/45°F. In summer no artificial heat is needed, in fact plants can stand out of doors in a sunny, sheltered place. Repot annually in early spring in J.I. No. 3. Increase by cuttings prepared in spring or summer from the ends of shoots and rooted in sandy soil in a propagating box with bottom heat, in a temperature of 21°C/70°F, or by seed in late winter/early spring. There are also pink-flowered varieties of uncertain origin.

Brunfelsia. *Brunfelsia pauciflora* is an attractive evergreen shrub with big, flattish, deep blue flowers for most of the year. It will thrive in a large flower pot or small tub in J.I. No. 2 and, though usually described as a hothouse plant, will succeed quite well in an intermediate greenhouse with minimum temperature of 13°C/55°F. A variety named Floribunda is specially good for year-round flowering. Water freely in spring and summer, rather sparingly in autumn and winter, and syringe in warm weather only. Repot, when necessary, as soon as the flowers fade. At the same time shoots can be shortened a little to prevent the plants becoming straggly. Propagate by cuttings of young shoots in summer rooted in a propagating frame with gentle bottom heat.

Caladium. These are amongst the most beautiful of greenhouse foliage plants. They have very large shield-shaped leaves in an almost bewildering variety of colours, some mainly green, some almost white, others mottled with white, pink, purple, etc. All are plants delighting in a warm, moist atmosphere. They can be grown in J.I. No. 2 in pots 18-30 cm (7 in-1 ft) in diameter, according to the age and variety of the plant. Temperatures of the warm greenhouse are really necessary for them to do well though they will survive in an intermediate house. Water freely during the season of growth in spring and summer and, at this period, syringe frequently and damp floors, walls and stages daily. A little shading from strong sun is desirable but should not be overdone. In the autumn gradually reduce the water supply and, when the leaves have died down, keep the tubers quite dry and in a temperature of about 12°C/54°F until early spring when they can be restarted in a temperature of 21°C/70°F and, if necessary, repotted. Propagation is by careful division of the roots when repotting.

Calathea. Fairly small perennial plants grown for their highly ornamental leaves. These are in various shades of green on top and of purple beneath. *Calathea makoyana* is one of the best kinds and was once known as *Maranta makoyana*, the two genera being closely allied. All varieties do well in intermediate or warm greenhouses in peat potting compost. Shade from direct sunshine at all times of the year, water moderately and maintain a moist atmosphere, particularly in summer. Increase by division when repotting in early spring. These are good house plants and may also be grown in bottles.

Calceolaria. Calceolarias are of two main kinds: semi-shrubby varieties, some of which are used for bedding, others for greenhouse display, and true herbaceous plants without woody stems. The latter have been very highly developed by breeders and the best strains produce enormous trusses of big, pouched flowers in a variety of brilliant colours. There are no showier plants in the greenhouse at their season, which is mid-spring to early summer. These herbaceous calceolarias are invariably raised from seed each year, sown from late spring to mid-summer on the surface of very fine soil in a well-drained tray. Scarcely cover the seed and place a sheet of glass and paper over each tray. Germinate in an unheated, shady frame. Prick off the seedlings into seed boxes filled with seed compost as soon as they can be handled, and pot them singly in 6·2 cm (2½ in) pots in J.I. No. 1 directly they have made four or five leaves each. Throughout this period grow them in an unheated, shady frame with plenty of ventilation on mild days and a fair quantity of water. By mid-autumn the plants can be moved on into 13 cm (5 in) pots, still in the same compost, and should be taken at the same time to the greenhouse. Give them a good light place not too far from the glass. Ventilate fairly freely and maintain a temperature of 7-12°C/45-54°F. Water carefully at this period, keeping soil moist but not sodden, and avoid wetting the leaves and crowns unnecessarily. Repot the larger varieties into 19 cm (7½ in) pots in late winter/early spring using J.I. No. 2 and maintain the same temperature avoiding wide fluctuations. The secret of success with calceolarias is a cool, equable atmosphere throughout. Shade lightly in spring if the sun shines strongly.

The most important greenhouse shrubby kinds are John Innes Hybrids, *Calceolaria burbidgei* and *C. profusa* (also known as *C. clibranii*), all with yellow flowers in winter. These are usually raised from cuttings of firm young shoots struck in autumn for the summer-flowering kinds and in spring for the winter-flowering kinds. Seed can also be used and should be sown in the first half of spring in a cool house. Grow in a frost-proof greenhouse with plenty of light and ventilation and an average quantity of water. If desired plants can be stood in a frame all summer or even outdoors in a sheltered place but they must be kept well watered.

The bedding calceolarias, varieties of *C. integrifolia*, can be grown from seed or cuttings. They need the protection of a greenhouse, or at least a well-made frame in winter, but are sufficiently hardy to withstand a few degrees of frost without injury. Colours range from yellow to chestnut red. These are bushy plants 30-45 cm (1-1½ ft) in height with innumerable little pouched flowers in showy clusters throughout the summer and have the merit of thriving in shady as well as sunny places. They are increased by cuttings of firm, non-flowering shoots struck in sandy soil in a frame in late summer/early autumn, or can be raised from seed sown in a temperature of 16-18°C/60-65°F in late winter/early spring. Once rooted, cuttings should be ventilated fairly freely, except during cold weather, and with seed-raised plants hardened off in time for planting out of doors mid-late spring. Bedding calceolarias can also be grown as pot plants for summer flowering in a cool, lightly shaded greenhouse.

Callistemon (Bottle Brush). The popular name is a good one because the fluffy spikes of red or yellow flowers are exactly the shape of the brushes used to clean bottles. Callistemons are Australian shrubs with narrow leaves and they need to be grown in a sunny greenhouse with plenty of ventilation and a rather dry atmosphere. Winter temperature need be no more than an average of 10°C/50°F and plants may be stood out of doors in a sheltered, sunny spot all summer. Grow established plants in J.I. No. 2 and water fairly freely from mid-spring to early autumn, but sparingly for the rest of the year, particularly in cold weather. Repot in early spring, but only when the pots become crowded with roots, which may be every second or third year. *Callistemon citrinus* Splendens with scarlet flowers and *C. speciosus*, crimson, are two of the best-loved kinds. *C. salignus* is one of the hardiest and has pale yellow flowers. After flowering prune lightly to keep plants from becoming straggly. Increase by cuttings of firm young shoots in mid-summer or early autumn rooted in sandy soil in a propagator within the greenhouse. Callistemons can be grown out of doors in mild areas.

Calomeria. What was once known as *Humea elegans* is now listed as *Calomeria amaranthoides*. It is not often seen in amateur collections but frequently figures in groups of greenhouse plants at flower shows and always attracts notice because of its tall, feathery plumes of tiny pinkish-brown flowers, often 1·8 m (6 ft) in height. It is a biennial and so must be raised from seed every year. Sow from mid-spring to mid-summer in seed compost, cover very lightly and germinate in a temperature of 15-18°C/59-65°F. Prick off in the same compost as early as possible and then, when the seedlings are 6·2 cm (2½ in) high, pot singly in 7·5 cm (3 in) pots in J.I. No. 1. From these move to 13 cm (5 in) pots and then to 23 cm (9 in) pots, using J.I. No. 2 while being especially careful about drainage. Give plenty of water, damp down around the pots daily in hot weather and grow throughout the summer in an unheated and unshaded greenhouse. In autumn and winter water very carefully and maintain a minimum temperature of 10°C/50°F. Plants sown in mid-spring will flower early the following summer, mid-summer sown plants late the following summer. Plants should be discarded immediately after flowering.

Camellia. Everyone knows and loves the camellia with its large, perfectly formed flowers and glossy, evergreen leaves. It is a shrub which can be planted out of doors in all but the coldest districts and will then grow to considerable size, but in the greenhouse it can be maintained in health for some years in pots no more than 25-30 cm (10 in-1 ft) in diameter. Camellias are excellent subjects for the unheated or slightly heated greenhouse, as the plants are hardy and it is only the flowers, which come in winter or early spring, that benefit from some protection from weather. Grow in J.I. No. 2 or peat potting compost without any lime or chalk and repot every second or third year immediately after flowering. Water freely in spring and summer, moderately in autumn and winter. After flowering the plants should be syringed daily until the end of the summer. They can stand out of doors from early summer to early autumn in a sheltered, partially shaded place and this is better than keeping them in the greenhouse, which is apt to get too hot for them in summer. Return to the greenhouse before the first sharp autumn frosts.

Camellias can be increased by cuttings of firm young growth rooted in a propagating frame within the greenhouse in summer, also by cuttings of mature leaves removed with a growth bud in summer.

There are a great many garden varieties in a colour range from white and pale pink to crimson, some single flowered, some semi-double, some fully double. Most popular are varieties of *Camellia japonica*, which flower in spring. So do the varieties of *C. williamsii* and *C. reticulata*, but those of *C. sasanqua* start in October and continue all winter and so benefit from greenhouse cultivation.

Campanula. The only campanulas which are of much importance for the greenhouse are *Campanula pyramidalis* and *C. isophylla*. It would be hard to imagine two closely related plants more dissimilar in appearance. *C. pyramidalis* makes narrow spires of showy blue or white flowers which may be 1·5 m (5 ft) in height in good soil. *C. isophylla* is a trailing plant with an abundance of thin stems throwing out sprays of starry blue or white flowers. Both flower in summer.

C. pyramidalis is a biennial and so seed must be sown every year. It germinates readily in late spring in seed compost and an unheated frame. Prick off seedlings in the ordinary way and, when they are 6·2 cm (2½ in) high, pot them singly in J.I. No. 1. Subsequently grow them in a frame without protection from early summer to early autumn and with free ventilation during mild weather even in winter. The plants should be potted on by stages in J.I. No. 2, until by early spring they reach their 20-25 cm (8-10 in) flowering pots. Throughout they should be treated as almost hardy plants and are, in consequence, ideal for a cold or cool greenhouse. Give plenty of light at all times and free ventilation whenever the weather permits.

C. isophylla is also practically hardy and requires the same treatment regarding temperature and ventilation. It is easily raised from seed or from cuttings of firm young shoots in spring or early summer. Pot the cuttings or seedlings in J.I. No. 1 as soon as they are growing well and, subsequently, pot on as necessary in No. 2. The plants are ideal for hanging baskets or may be grown in 11·2 cm (4½ in) pots along the edge of the greenhouse staging, which they will festoon with their growth.

Canna (Indian Shot). This perennial plant is grown for its large, broadly lance-shaped green or purple leaves and showy spikes of yellow, orange, pink, red or crimson flowers often speckled with one colour or another. They can be planted out of doors all summer and are popular for giving a sub-tropical appearance to summer bedding schemes. They are also excellent greenhouse pot plants for summer flowering. ·

The fleshy roots rest in winter and can be stored dry in a frost-proof greenhouse over winter. If they are grown in pots it is best to keep them in these to prevent shrivelling. In spring they are started into growth in the greenhouse, temperature 16-18°C/61-65°F, being watered rather sparingly at first but much more freely as leaves appear. Repot in J.I. No. 2 as soon as growth begins and feed in summer once or twice a week with weak liquid manure. Keep in as sunny a place as possible in a slightly moist atmosphere and average temperature of 18°C/65°F. After flowering gradually reduce the water supply until the soil is dry by mid-autumn. Small plants will bloom in 15 cm (6 in) pots, large ones in 21·2 cm (8½ in) pots. Propagation is by division of large roots at potting time or by seeds, which need a temperature of 25-28°C/77-82°F to ensure germination. It is wise to soak the seeds in warm water for 24 hours before sowing after which the seed coat can be punctured with the point of a knife.

Carnation. The greenhouse carnation is a very different plant from the border carnation. For one thing it is much taller, old specimens often reaching 1·6 m (5½ ft) with quite a hard woody stem at the base, for which reason it is sometimes referred to as the tree carnation. Also, instead of flowering for quite a short while in the summer it will continue to bloom for months on end; in fact, by careful management, it is possible to cut blooms throughout the year. It is this characteristic which has given it the popular name of perpetual-flowering carnation. Like the border carnation it has been very highly developed and a great number of named varieties exist, to which new ones are added every year. For this reason I make no attempt to suggest varieties, which should be sought in the most recent catalogues of the trade specialists.

Perpetual-flowering carnations can be raised from seed but, except for the production of new varieties, this is not a very satisfactory method, as seedlings vary greatly in character and some are certain to be very inferior. The usual method of increase is by cuttings, which can be taken at any time from late autumn to early spring, the second half of winter being the most favourable months. Cuttings should be prepared from non-flowering side shoots, the best being those which form about halfway up the flowering stems. These shoots should be pulled off when 7·5 cm (3 in) long. The lower leaves are removed cleanly with a sharp knife and the base of each cutting trimmed just below a joint. The cutting is then ready for insertion in sand in a propagating frame within the greenhouse. The temperature need be no more than 15°C/59°F, but the cuttings should be kept close. When rooted they should be potted singly in 6·2 cm (2½ in) pots and J.I. No. 1 compost and subsequently potted on progressively in No. 2 until by early or mid-summer they reach the 15-20 cm (6-8 in) pots in which they will flower. Alternatively they can, at this stage, be planted in borders of good soil on the floor of the greenhouse. If in pots, they may be stood in a frame outside over summer, protection only being required at night or to ward off heavy rain.

The plants should be stopped at least twice, the first time when they have made about seven pairs of leaves, and again when the side growths resulting from the first stopping have themselves made seven pairs of leaves. Stopping is done by breaking out the topmost joint of each shoot and the effect is to make the plant more bushy. If winter flowers are required, no stopping should be carried out after mid-summer.

Water moderately throughout the spring and summer but very carefully in autumn and winter, though at no time must the soil be allowed to become dry. Ventilate at all times as freely as is compatible with a summer temperature averaging 15°C/59°F and a winter temperature averaging 10-12°C/50-54°F and never falling below 5°C/41°F. Be very careful in winter to avoid excessive use of artificial heat which will cause weak growth and will soon put a stop to flowering. Carnations like a rather dry atmosphere but not a hot one, which will encourage attacks by red spider and thrips, their two worst enemies. Top ventilators should be used freely to maintain a constant circulation of air without draughts.

The flower stems should be disbudded to one bloom each, all the side buds being removed and only the terminal bud retained. Plants that are flowering or about to flower can be fed regularly with a carnation fertilizer or a well-balanced general purpose or liquid fertilizer.

Cassia. *Cassia corymbosa* is a loosely branched evergreen shrub with fine clusters of yellow, pea-type flowers in late summer and autumn. Planted out in a border in the greenhouse it can be trained as a semi-climber beneath the rafters or against the back wall of a lean-to. Alternatively it can be kept to smaller dimensions if its roots are restricted in flower pots 20-30 cm (8 in-1 ft) in diameter. This cassia only requires frost protection in winter and can be stood out of doors for the summer. Grow in J.I. No. 2 compost and water freely from early spring to mid-autumn, sparingly in winter. Increase by cuttings of firm young shoots in spring or early summer in a propagating frame within the greenhouse or by seed sown in spring in a temperature of 18-20°C/65-68°F.

Celosia. Both the plumed celosias, *Celosia argentea*, and the crested types, *C. argentea cristata*, popularly known as cockscomb, make useful pot plants for the moderately heated greenhouse. They should be raised annually from seed sown in spring in a temperature of 18°C/65°F. Pot the seedlings in J.I. No. 1 in 7·5 cm (3 in) pots and later move to 13·7 cm (5½ in) pots in J.I. No. 3 with some extra peat. Water moderately and damp staging daily with tepid water. Keep throughout in a lightly shaded greenhouse with an average temperature of 16°C/61°F or a little more. They will bloom throughout the summer and are extremely decorative. Plants coming into flower can be used for outdoor bedding in the second half of summer but should only be planted out when weather is mild and settled and should then be transferred to the beds with the minimum of root disturbance.

Cestrum. Shrubby plants with long, flexible stems easily trained to wires or pillars. The small, tubular flowers are produced in clusters in summer and autumn. They are nearly hardy and can be grown readily in a cool greenhouse in large pots or tubs in J.I. No. 2 or planted in a bed of good soil on the floor of the greenhouse. Plants can be kept smaller and more bushy by occasionally pinching out the tips of shoots during spring and early summer, or the side growths of larger plants can be cut hard back in early spring. Water freely in spring and summer, sparingly in autumn and winter. Increase by summer cuttings in a propagating frame with bottom heat. Good kinds are *Cestrum aurantiacum*, orange; Newelli, crimson; *C. elegans*, purple; and *C. parqui*, lime yellow scented.

Chamaedorea. *Chamaedorea elegans* is the new name for *Neanthe bella* (dwarf palm, parlour palm). It is neat and graceful, one of the best kinds for an intermediate greenhouse or for growing indoors. It is so slow growing that it can even be planted in a bottle garden. Grow it in J.I. No. 1 or peat potting compost and repot when necessary in early spring. Water freely in spring and summer, rather sparingly in autumn and winter. Shade is not essential but neither is it detrimental. Increase by seed sown in a temperature of 21°C/70°F in spring.

Chlorophytum. *Chlorophytum comosum* makes clumps of narrow, light green leaves usually striped with white in the varieties popular for greenhouse and home decoration. It throws out long, slender, arching flower stems bearing insignificant white flowers and also at the ends little plantlets which often begin to produce fleshy white roots in mid-air. It is a very easy plant to grow and will succeed in any frost-proof greenhouse in sun or shade provided it is watered fairly freely in summer and syringed daily during warm weather. It does not like being baked at any time. It is also an excellent house plant. Grow it in J.I. No. 2, repot in early spring when overcrowded, and increase by division or by pegging the plantlets into small soil-filled pots and severing them from the parent plant when they are well rooted.

Chorizema. These are shrubby Australian trailing plants which can be trained against wires or trellis work on the back wall of a lean-to greenhouse or may be grown over balloon-shaped frames made of wire. They should be grown in a cool greenhouse, in J.I. No. 1 with a little extra peat. Be very careful about watering at all times, keeping the soil moist but never letting it become sodden, particularly in winter. The shoots of young plants should be pinched occasionally to encourage free branching from the base. Increase by either seeds or cuttings, the former sown in peaty sand in spring, temperature 15°C/59°F, the cuttings being prepared from firm side shoots removed with a heel in summer and rooted in sand in a propagating frame. The best kinds are *Chorizema cordatum, C. ilicifolium*, and *C. varium*, all with flowers in shades of red, purple and yellow and all flowering from late spring to early autumn.

Chrysanthemum. See Chapter 20, (p. 504).

Cineraria. There are no showier plants for a winter and spring display in a slightly heated greenhouse than the cinerarias with their fine heads of daisy-like flowers in many shades of blue, pink, red and crimson, often with a zone of white. There are both large-flowered (Grandiflora) and small-flowered (Stellata) varieties, and also varieties of shorter, more compact habit (Nana Multiflora) and double-flowered varieties. All are treated as annuals and are raised every year from seed. At least two sowings should be made, one in mid- to late spring for winter flowers and the other in the second half of summer for spring flowering. Sow thinly in seed compost and germinate at a temperature of 12-15°C/54-59°F. The summer sowings can be germinated in an unheated frame. Prick off the seedlings when they have three leaves into deep seed boxes and grow on with plenty of light and good air circulation. They are almost hardy plants and they do not like being coddled. Pot singly in 7·5 cm (3 in) pots before they become crowded in the boxes and then move them on to 15 cm (6 in) and, in the case of large plants, again into 19 cm (7½ in) pots directly the smaller ones become comfortably filled with roots. The last potting should be made not later than mid-autumn and J.I. No. 1 should be used throughout. The plants will be happiest in a frame until about mid-autumn and should be ventilated freely by day and a little at night, except when the weather is very cold. Even after removal to the greenhouse give as much ventilation as is consistent with a minimum temperature of 7°C/45°F, average 13°C/55°F. Stand the plants on the staging as near the glass as possible and in a light place. Watch closely for attacks by the leaf mining maggot which tunnels the leaves causing white, snaky markings. If observed, search for the tiny maggots in these tunnels and kill them with a pin or spray with HCH. Water fairly freely in summer, moderately in autumn and winter.

Cissus. These are handsome greenhouse climbing plants. *Cissus discolor* has dark green leaves heavily marbled with white and pink and is an excellent plant to train around a pillar in a large greenhouse, or it can be grown on trellis work against the wall of a lean-to. It is easily grown in an intermediate greenhouse at a minimum temperature of 13°C/55°F. Water freely from mid-spring to early autumn, moderately at other times and syringe at least once daily in warm weather. Plants can be grown in large pots in J.I. No. 2 but are really happiest planted out in the greenhouse border. Increase by cuttings of firm young shoots in early summer in a propagating box with bottom heat.

Another species, *C. antarctica*, known as the kangaroo vine, is less handsome but a good deal tougher and is a popular, easily grown house plant. The glossy leaves are heart shaped and shining green and the stems reddish purple. Culture is as for *C. discolor*, except that it can be grown at a minimum temperature of 7°C/45°F.

Clematis. Though most kinds of clematis are hardy plants unsuited to the greenhouse, there are a few species which are tender and make good greenhouse climbers. The best are *Clematis indivisa* and its variety *lobata*, both evergreens with big clusters of showy white flowers in spring. They are vigorous climbers and therefore only suitable for fairly large greenhouses where they can be trained up pillars, under the rafters or against the back wall of a lean-to. They are happy in ordinary soil and require only frost protection in winter. Give free ventilation in summer and plenty of water at this season, with a moderate supply only in winter. Avoid very high temperatures at any period and syringe at least once daily on warm days from late spring to early autumn. Increase is by layers or summer cuttings in a propagating frame.

445

Clerodendrum. From the garden standpoint clerodendrums may conveniently be divided into two groups, the climbing kinds, of which *Clerodendrum thomsoniae* is the most familiar example, and the bushy kinds, of which *C. speciosissimum*, also known as *C. fallax*, is the one most commonly seen. Both will grow in an intermediate or warm greenhouse. *C. thomsoniae* can either be grown in a large pot, in which case it is commonly trained over a dome-shaped wire frame 1·2 m (4 ft) or more across to make a bush-like specimen, or it can be planted out in the greenhouse border and trained on trellis work or around a pillar. In either case use J.I. No. 2 and plant or pot in spring. Water very freely from mid-spring to early autumn, sparingly at other times. Prune plants immediately after flowering, cutting back the flowering shoots to 6·2 cm (2½ in) each. Propagation is by cuttings of firm young shoots in spring in a propagating box with bottom heat.

C. speciosissimum is usually grown from seed sown in late winter or late summer at a temperature of 21°C/70°F. The seedlings are potted on in the ordinary way in J.I. No. 2 until, by mid-summer (or early spring for late summer-sown seedlings) they reach the 14 cm (5½ in) pots with J.I. No. 3 compost in which they will flower. Water freely throughout the summer. Maintain a warm, rather moist atmosphere and, in autumn and winter, keep a minimum temperature of 10°C/50°F, average 15°C/59°F. Under these conditions the plants will produce their vivid scarlet heads of tubular flowers most of the autumn, the late summer-sown ones appearing the following summer. Plants that are about to bloom should be fed every 10 to 14 days with weak liquid manure.

Clianthus (Glory Pea, Parrot's Bill, Lobster Claw). *Clianthus puniceus* is a very beautiful shrub with scarlet or white flowers in late spring/early summer shaped like the claws of a lobster. It will grow 1·8 m (6 ft) or more high and is to be seen trained against sunny walls out of doors in the milder parts of the country. It can also be used effectively in a cold or cool greenhouse in which it may be grown in large pots, tubs, or planted directly in the greenhouse border. It should have J.I. No. 1, or good loamy soil if planted out, and should be watered freely in summer, sparingly in winter. A rather different plant is *C. formosus*, also known as *C. dampieri*, with scarlet, purple-spotted flowers in the second half of spring and a weak, sprawling habit. It is commonly trained over a balloon-shaped wire frame, or may be planted in a large hanging basket and allowed to trail downwards. It is not an easy plant to grow as it needs perfect drainage, very careful watering at all times and is difficult to propagate, many plants being grafted on *Colutea arborescens*. Give it J.I. No. 1 with a little extra peat and lime-free loam. Syringe freely from late spring to early autumn and give plenty of ventilation. A hot, dry atmosphere will encourage red spider, a frequent pest of this plant. Snails are also fond of *C. puniceus* and must be killed with slug bait.

Clivia. These are fleshy-rooted plants, easy to grow and requiring little heat. From mid-autumn to mid-winter they rest and can be kept in their pots almost dry. At this period a temperature of 7°C/45°F is ample. In late winter the plants should be given more water and a little more warmth and can be repotted, if necessary, though overpotting is to be avoided. Use a size which will accommodate the roots comfortably but no more and pot in J.I. No. 1. Thereafter grow on the staging in a sunny place with an average temperature of 12°C/54°F. Water with increasing freedom as leaves lengthen, but in late summer gradually reduce the water supply so that, by mid-autumn, the soil is nearly, but not quite, dry.

From early summer to early autumn the plants may stand in a sunny frame. Ventilation should be free throughout. No syringing is necessary. The plants flower in spring, the flowers themselves being trumpet shaped, in clusters on 60 cm (2 ft) stems. The original species, *Clivia miniata*, has largely been replaced by garden hybrids in various shades of red, yellow and orange. All can be increased by division at potting time and also by seed, though seedlings take several years to reach flowering size.

Cobaea (Cup and Saucer Vine). *Cobaea scandens* is most familiar as a climbing plant for outdoor use during the summer months and is then treated as an annual. It is, however, a true perennial but too tender to survive the winter out of doors. In a frost-proof greenhouse it will make a big plant to cover the back wall of a lean-to or drape the rafters of a span-roofed greenhouse. It will thrive in any ordinary soil and sunny greenhouse that is frost-proof in winter. Artificial heat will be unnecessary most of the year. Ventilation should be free in spring and summer; watering moderate at this period, sparing in winter. The greenish-purple or white flowers are a little like Canterbury Bells and appear in summer. Shoots can be cut back fairly severely in late winter to keep plants within bounds.

Cocos. See **Microcoelum** (p. 483).

Codiaeum (Croton). These are amongst the most popular of all warm greenhouse foliage plants, and justifiably so, for their leaves are of great diversity in shape and colour. The typical croton has long, strap-shaped leaves which may be broader in some kinds, narrower in others, and often waved at the edges. All are heavily variegated, combining greens, yellows, oranges, bronzes and crimsons.

Crotons are not difficult to grow provided one can maintain the necessary temperatures, a minimum of 10°C/50°F, average 15°C/59°F in winter, rising in summer to an average of 21-24°C/70-75°F. From mid-spring to early autumn they need plenty of water, both at the roots and in the air. Syringing and damping down should be discontinued when the weather becomes cold. Little shade is necessary, except in very small houses which tend to become overheated. Use J.I. No. 1 and repot in early spring, but only when pots are full of roots. Good specimens can be grown in 18 cm (7 in) pots. If desired very big specimens can be grown in large pots or tubs but, as a rule, amateurs will prefer to cut plants back each spring as they grow too big to be convenient. Small specimens can be restricted to a single central stem. Cuttings will root in summer if the cut ends are dipped in powdered charcoal to check 'bleeding' and they are inserted in sandy soil in a propagating box with a temperature of about 25°C/77°F and bottom heat. Water freely while rooting. Alternatively they can be air layered in summer.

Coleus. See **Solenostemom** (p. 497).

Columnea. The columneas are trailing plants for intermediate or warm greenhouses. They are seen to best advantage when grown in baskets suspended from the rafters. They will then make cascades of thin stems and soft green or bronzy leaves, with tubular orange-scarlet flowers for half their length in early summer. They should be grown in a mixture of peat and chopped sphagnum moss in equal parts, perhaps with the addition of a little loam and some broken charcoal. Water freely from mid-spring to early autumn and damp down frequently to maintain a fairly moist atmosphere. Water rather sparingly in autumn and winter and maintain a drier atmosphere. Increase by cuttings made from the ends of shoots in mid-spring and rooted in a propagating frame with bottom heat. Repot at the same period. *Columnea gloriosa* is the most popular kind but others worth growing are *C. × banksii* and *C. microphylla*.

Convallaria (Lily of the Valley). Market growers make much money by forcing this plant, but it is not a practice which appeals to amateurs, as the roots are of little use after treatment. For the earliest work, that is to get blooms around Christmas, specially retarded crowns must be obtained and potted eight to ten together in 14 cm (5½ in) pots in the autumn. Keep in a dark place with a temperature of 18-21°C/65-70°F and water rather freely. After about a week gradually give light and reduce the temperature a little. Under these conditions blooms will develop in about a month. For a later supply strong roots can be lifted and potted or boxed in the second half of autumn. These, after a period of five or six weeks in an unheated frame, may be brought into an ordinary greenhouse with an average temperature of 12°C/54°F which a fortnight later may be slowly raised to 18°C/65°F. In all cases it is desirable to reduce the temperature to 12°C/54°F while the plants are actually in bloom to prevent premature fading. After flowering the crowns should be discarded or, if preferred, they can be hardened off and planted in some out-of-the-way corner where some, at least, may establish themselves and make suitable plants for pot culture once again in a few years' time.

Cordyline. These are foliage plants, closely allied to dracaena and frequently erroneously referred to as palms. They have narrow, sword-like leaves and make handsome specimens in pots from 15-45 cm (6 in-1½ ft) in diameter according to the age of the plant. *Cordyline australis* is nearly hardy and is planted out of doors in mild seaside districts where it makes a tall trunk in time with a large rosette of leaves on top. Better for the greenhouse is *C. fruticosa* of which there are numerous garden varieties, with leaves variously striped or marked with pink, purple and cream, with or without green. All can be grown in a cool or intermediate greenhouse in J.I. No. 2. Water very freely in spring and summer, moderately in autumn and winter. Good drainage is important. Give shade on the sunny side of the house during bright days in summer and repot when necessary in early spring. Propagation can be by seeds which will germinate in late winter/early spring at a temperature of about 15-18°C/59-65°F but seedlings will vary in colour and quality. Garden varieties are increased by root cuttings in late winter/early spring started into growth in a temperature of 15-18°C/59-65°F or by stem cuttings made by cutting up the stems into pieces 7·5 cm (3 in) in length in summer, and laying them in moist sand or peat in a propagating frame with bottom heat.

Coronilla. *Coronilla glauca* is an evergreen shrub with small, grey-green leaves and clusters of small, bright yellow, pea flowers most of the year. It is hardy enough to be grown out of doors in some sheltered places but also makes a useful pot plant for the unheated greenhouse. Water freely from mid-spring to early autumn and moderately over winter. Prune in early spring sufficiently to keep plants a good shape and repot, if necessary, at the same time using J.I. No. 1. Give plenty of light and ventilation at all times. Increase by cuttings of firm young shoots in sandy soil in a propagator in the second half of summer.

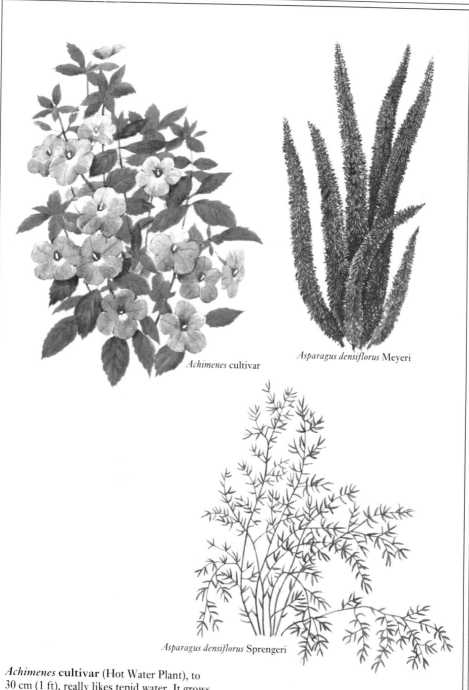

Achimenes cultivar

Asparagus densiflorus Meyeri

Asparagus densiflorus Sprengeri

***Achimenes* cultivar** (Hot Water Plant), to 30 cm (1 ft), really likes tepid water. It grows from small rhizomes set growing in spring and dried off in late summer. Good in pots or baskets in moist peaty compost

***Asparagus densiflorus* Meyeri**, to 60 cm (2 ft) and spread of 90 cm (3 ft), a handsome thickly clothed form making a long-lasting pot plant

***Asparagus densiflorus* Sprengeri**, to 30 cm (1 ft) and spread of 90 cm (3 ft), makes arching growth, fine for a hanging basket or wall-mounted pot. Can be trained as a wall plant to 1.8 m (6 ft) high

Asparagus setaceus

Begonia pendula

Begonia rex

Begonia pendula are pendulous forms of the tuberous begonia with pink, white, red, yellow or orange flowers, ideal for hanging baskets and windowboxes. Keep well watered in summer

Begonia rex, 45 cm (1½ ft), is the most colourful of the begonias grown for their foliage. There are many different patterns and colourings. Easily propagated from leaf cuttings

Asparagus setaceus, to 1.5 m (5 ft) and spread of 1.2 m (4 ft), is often cut to accompany carnations in vases or buttonholes. Fronds quickly brown if it is too hot and dry.

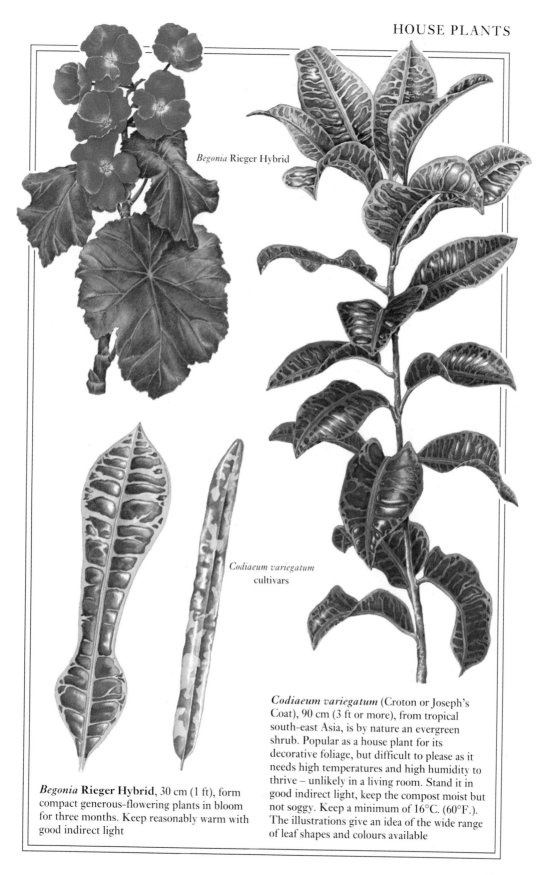

Begonia Rieger Hybrid

Codiaeum variegatum
cultivars

Begonia Rieger Hybrid, 30 cm (1 ft), form
compact generous-flowering plants in bloom
for three months. Keep reasonably warm with
good indirect light

Codiaeum variegatum (Croton or Joseph's
Coat), 90 cm (3 ft or more), from tropical
south-east Asia, is by nature an evergreen
shrub. Popular as a house plant for its
decorative foliage, but difficult to please as it
needs high temperatures and high humidity to
thrive – unlikely in a living room. Stand it in
good indirect light, keep the compost moist but
not soggy. Keep a minimum of 16°C. (60°F.).
The illustrations give an idea of the wide range
of leaf shapes and colours available

451

Columnea x banksii

Columnea microphylla

Cyclamen persicum cultivar

Columnea x banksii (Goldfish Plant – named after its flowers), trails 60 cm (2 ft) from a hanging basket in 13°C. (55°F.) in indirect light. Plant in moist peaty compost and keep air humid.

Columnea microphylla also trails 60 cm (2 ft) but makes less spreading growth

***Cyclamen persicum* cultivar**, 30 cm (1 ft), need moderate conditions. Keep at about 12°C. (54°F.), water only when necessary, give good indirect light. Keep top of tuber above compost. Leaves often patterned silver, flowers can be fringed

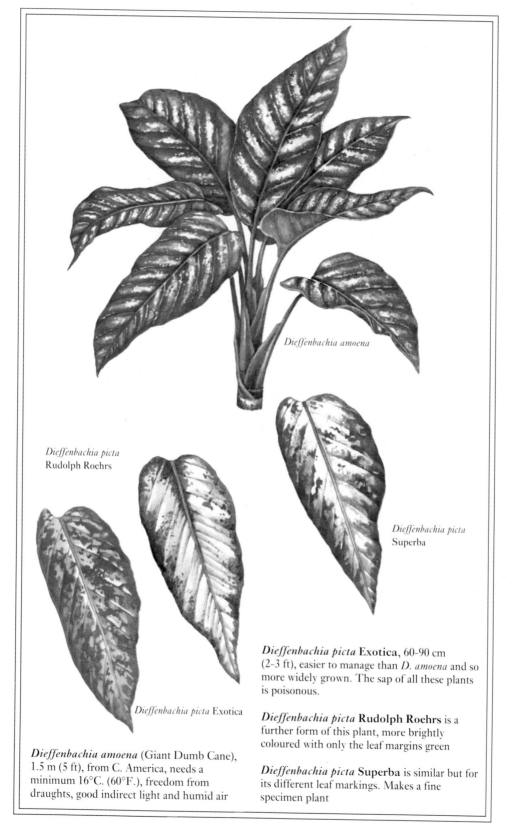

Dieffenbachia amoena

Dieffenbachia picta
Rudolph Roehrs

Dieffenbachia picta
Superba

Dieffenbachia picta Exotica

Dieffenbachia picta **Exotica**, 60-90 cm
(2–3 ft), easier to manage than *D. amoena* and so
more widely grown. The sap of all these plants
is poisonous.

Dieffenbachia picta **Rudolph Roehrs** is a
further form of this plant, more brightly
coloured with only the leaf margins green

Dieffenbachia amoena (Giant Dumb Cane),
1.5 m (5 ft), from C. America, needs a
minimum 16°C. (60°F.), freedom from
draughts, good indirect light and humid air

Dieffenbachia picta **Superba** is similar but for
its different leaf markings. Makes a fine
specimen plant

453

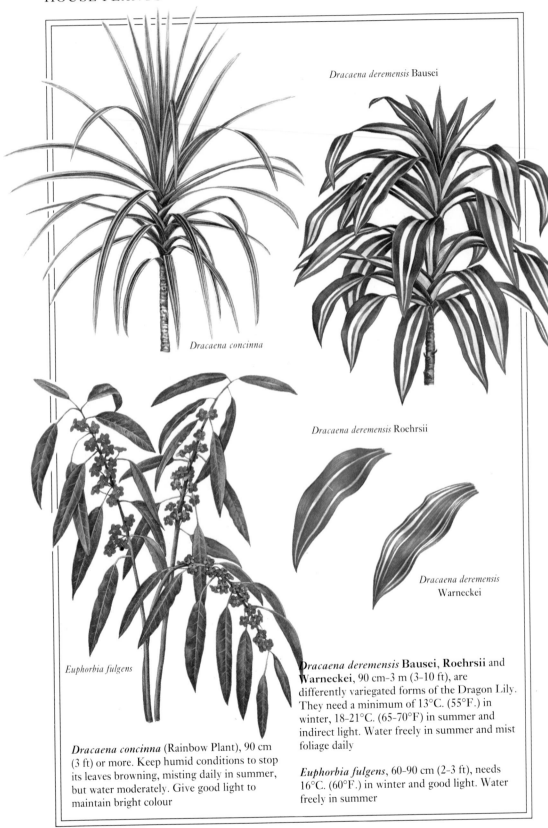

Dracaena deremensis Bausei

Dracaena concinna

Dracaena deremensis Roehrsii

Dracaena deremensis
Warneckei

Euphorbia fulgens

Dracaena deremensis Bausei, Roehrsii and **Warneckei**, 90 cm-3 m (3-10 ft), are differently variegated forms of the Dragon Lily. They need a minimum of 13°C. (55°F.) in winter, 18-21°C. (65-70°F) in summer and indirect light. Water freely in summer and mist foliage daily

Euphorbia fulgens, 60-90 cm (2-3 ft), needs 16°C. (60°F.) in winter and good light. Water freely in summer

Dracaena concinna (Rainbow Plant), 90 cm (3 ft) or more. Keep humid conditions to stop its leaves browning, misting daily in summer, but water moderately. Give good light to maintain bright colour

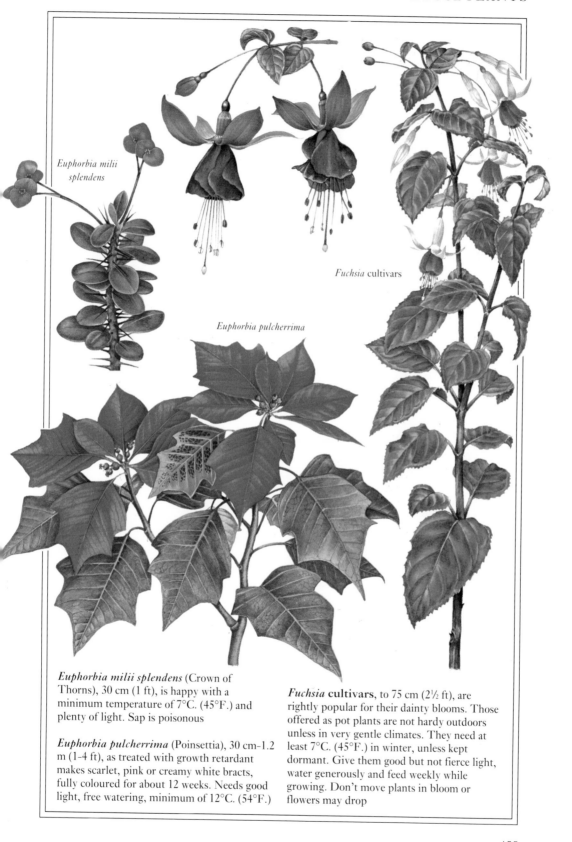

Euphorbia milii splendens

Fuchsia cultivars

Euphorbia pulcherrima

Euphorbia milii splendens (Crown of Thorns), 30 cm (1 ft), is happy with a minimum temperature of 7°C. (45°F.) and plenty of light. Sap is poisonous

Euphorbia pulcherrima (Poinsettia), 30 cm-1.2 m (1-4 ft), as treated with growth retardant makes scarlet, pink or creamy white bracts, fully coloured for about 12 weeks. Needs good light, free watering, minimum of 12°C. (54°F.)

Fuchsia cultivars, to 75 cm (2½ ft), are rightly popular for their dainty blooms. Those offered as pot plants are not hardy outdoors unless in very gentle climates. They need at least 7°C. (45°F.) in winter, unless kept dormant. Give them good but not fierce light, water generously and feed weekly while growing. Don't move plants in bloom or flowers may drop

Hippeastrum cultivars

***Hippeastrum* cultivars** (incorrectly known as Amaryllis), 60 cm (2 ft), grow from bulbs potted in autumn in 16.2 cm (6½ in) pots of moist soil-based compost with top half of bulb exposed. Give good light, a minimum winter temperature of 7-10°C. (45-50°F.). They will flower before the leaves appear. Water discreetly until leaves and roots develop. Continue to water and feed after flowering to build up bulb for next season. Leaves will wither in summer. Replace top 5 cm (2 in) of compost in autumn to provide more food

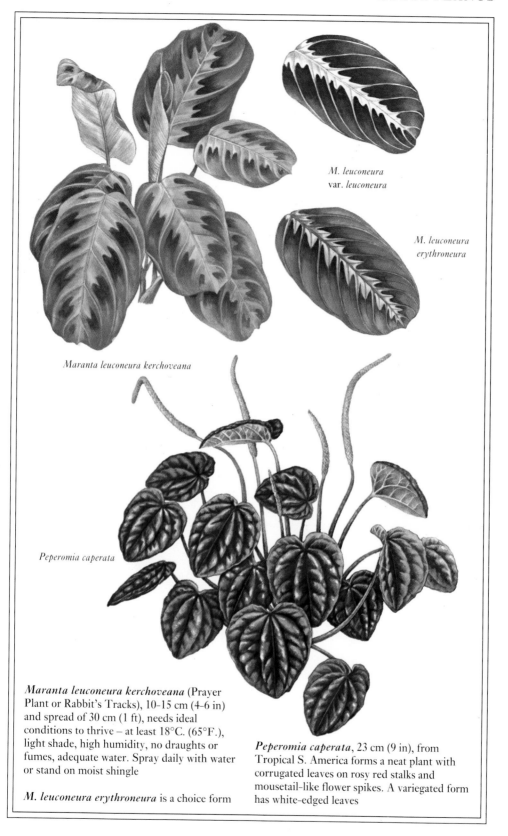

M. leuconeura
var. leuconeura

M. leuconeura
erythroneura

Maranta leuconeura kerchoveana

Peperomia caperata

Maranta leuconeura kerchoveana (Prayer Plant or Rabbit's Tracks), 10-15 cm (4-6 in) and spread of 30 cm (1 ft), needs ideal conditions to thrive – at least 18°C. (65°F.), light shade, high humidity, no draughts or fumes, adequate water. Spray daily with water or stand on moist shingle

M. leuconeura erythroneura is a choice form

Peperomia caperata, 23 cm (9 in), from Tropical S. America forms a neat plant with corrugated leaves on rosy red stalks and mousetail-like flower spikes. A variegated form has white-edged leaves

Peperomia magnoliifolia Variegata

Primula malacoides

Peperomia magnoliifolia Variegata, 23 cm
(9 in), needs good light to colour well, a
minimum winter temperature of 10°C. (50°F.),
preferably 16°C. (60°F.), and moderate
watering. Mist foliage with water daily in
summer. Propagate peperomias from leaf or
stem cuttings in spring or summer

Primula malacoides (Fairy Primrose), 35 cm
(14 in), is grown as an annual. Has similar
needs to *P. kewensis*

Primula kewensis

Punica granatum nana

Rhipsalidopsis gaertneri

Primula kewensis, 30 cm (1 ft), flowers appear early in the year, needs good light, adequate water, average temperature 15°C. (59°F.)

Punica granatum nana, 45 cm (1½ ft), the miniature form of the pomegranate, opens rich orange flowers in late summer sometimes followed by tiny fruits

Rhipsalidopsis gaertneri (Easter Cactus), 15 cm (6 in) high, 30 cm (1 ft) spread, is a tree-dwelling, *not* a desert cactus, so needs a leafy compost, adequate water and a minimum 10°C. (50°F.). Stand outdoors in summer but spray daily with tepid water. Easily increased from stem cuttings

Saintpaulia ionantha cultivar

girl   spoon   variegated

star   crested   bicolour

Saintpaulia ionantha (African violet), 10 cm (4 in), is very popular and not difficult if suited. It needs good indirect light to flower, at least 13°C. (55°F.), preferably 16°C. (60°F.) and hates draughts. It is best watered when necessary – judge by the weight of the pot – by standing in a bowl of water for ½ hr. then draining off. Stand pot on a saucer of damp gravel to keep air humid. Easily propagated by leaf cuttings with stalks in a warm, close propagator or pot covered with a polythene bag

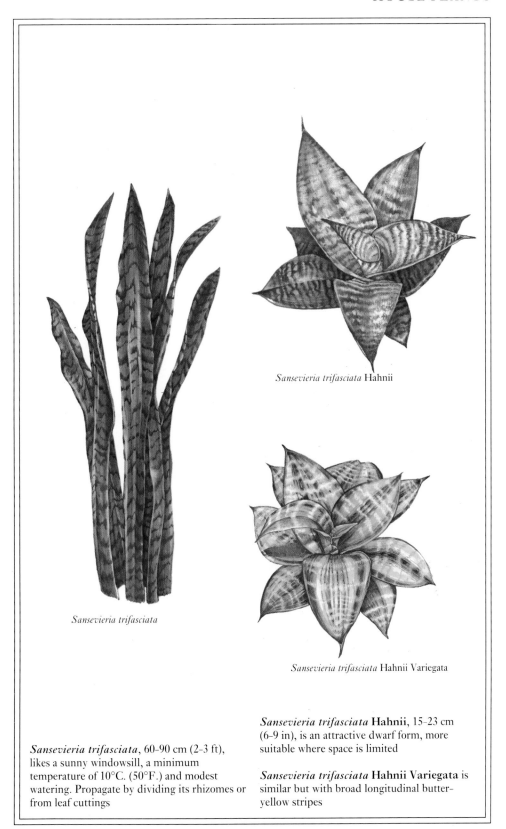

Sansevieria trifasciata Hahnii

Sansevieria trifasciata

Sansevieria trifasciata Hahnii Variegata

Sansevieria trifasciata, 60-90 cm (2-3 ft), likes a sunny windowsill, a minimum temperature of 10°C. (50°F.) and modest watering. Propagate by dividing its rhizomes or from leaf cuttings

Sansevieria trifasciata **Hahnii**, 15-23 cm (6-9 in), is an attractive dwarf form, more suitable where space is limited

Sansevieria trifasciata **Hahnii Variegata** is similar but with broad longitudinal butter-yellow stripes

Sansevieria trifasciata Laurentii

Schlumbergera x buckleyi

Sansevieria trifasciata Laurentii, similar to
the species but with yellow-edged leaves, is the
widely grown Mother-in-Law's Tongue. Only
divisions retain the variegation

Schlumbergera x buckleyi (Christmas or Crab
Cactus), 23 cm (9 in), has similar needs and is
also raised from stem cuttings

Schlumbergera truncata

Sinningia speciosa
cultivar

Smithiantha zebrina

Schlumbergera truncata (Crab Cactus), 30 cm
(1 ft), is similar but larger than *S. x buckleyi*

Sinningia speciosa, syn Gloxinia speciosa,
30 cm (1 ft), needs a minimum of 16°C. (60°F.)
and good indirect light. Stand plant on a tray of
moist gravel or peat and water moderately

Smithiantha zebrina (Temple Bells), 45 cm
(1½ ft), needs at least 15°C. (55°F.) and humid
air to thrive. It is grown from small rhizomes
started in spring

463

Streptocarpus x hybridus cultivar

Streptocarpus x hybridus
Constant Nymph

Stromanthe amabilis

***Streptocarpus x hybridus* Constant Nymph,**
30 cm (1 ft), a hybrid of the Cape Primrose,
blooms from spring to autumn. Stand in good
indirect light in a minimum of 13°C. (55°F.).
Other cultivars have larger flowers in a
variety of colours

Stromanthe amabilis, 30 cm (1 ft), is similar
to the marantas and needs similar conditions

Crassula. Succulent plants often confused with rochea to which they are related. *Crassula falcata* is the most popular kind and makes a branching plant up to 60 cm (2 ft) tall with clusters of showy orange-scarlet flowers in summer. It makes a fine pot plant in J.I. No. 2 with a sixth of its bulk of coarse sand added. It needs plenty of sunshine, a minimum winter temperature of 7°C/45°F and normal watering from spring to early autumn but a very sparing supply in late autumn and winter. It is increased by cuttings from late spring to late summer in sand or very sandy soil.

Crinum. The crinums are all bulbous plants and some are sufficiently hardy to be grown out of doors in sheltered places, but all make excellent pot plants for the cool or even unheated greenhouse. From mid-autumn to late winter the bulbs can be kept almost dry but should not be knocked out of their pots. Repot, if overcrowded, in early spring using J.I. No. 3. Fairly big pots or small wooden tubs will usually be necessary as the bulbs are very large. Water with increasing freedom as leaves lengthen and feed with weak liquid manure while the flower spikes are forming. After flowering in summer gradually reduce the water supply again. Give as sunny a position as possible throughout and as much ventilation as is consistent with a minimum winter temperature of 4°C/40°F and 12°C/54°F in summer. The simplest method of increase is by removing small bulbs at potting time. The best kinds for greenhouse culture are *Crinum longifolium*, pink and white and *C. moorei*, rosy red. Both have white varieties, and the hybrid between them, *C. powellii*, varies from white to pink.

Crossandra. Small evergreen shrubby plants which make excellent pot plants for a warm greenhouse. The most frequently grown species is *Crossandra infundibuliformis* with showy orange-red flowers packed in short spikes in spring. It should be grown in J.I. No. 2 with extra peat or leaf mould or in a peat-based potting compost. It needs plenty of water and a rather humid atmosphere while growing in spring and summer, with shade from direct sunshine in summer, but should be kept much drier in winter and in as light a place as possible. Minimum temperature 18°C/65°F. Increase by cuttings in a warm propagator in spring or summer or by seed in a temperature of 21-23°C/70-74°F.

Croton. See **Codiaeum** (p. 447).

Cryptanthus (Earth Stars). These are low-growing foliage plants with flattish rosettes of usually rather narrow leaves variegated or oddly coloured with bands of white, green, brown or pink. They live largely on air and can be grown on sphagnum moss tied to bark but they can equally well be grown in pots or bottle gardens. Grow in the smallest pots that will contain them in peat potting compost or a mixture of equal parts peat, sand and osmunda fibre. They like intermediate or warm house conditions and the best leaf colours are produced with little or no shading. Water fairly freely in spring and summer, rather sparingly in autumn and winter. Increase by division in the spring.

Cuphea (Cigar Plant). *Cuphea ignea* is a small plant which can be grown in 14 cm (5½ in) pots in a cool greenhouse, average winter temperature 10°C/50°F, summer 15°C/59°F. The little tubular flowers are a vivid scarlet with a dark ring at the mouth and are produced freely throughout the summer. Repot as necessary in early spring in J.I. No. 1 and

465

prune to shape at the same time. Water fairly freely from mid-spring to late summer and feed with liquid manure from late spring to late summer. After flowering gradually reduce the water supply and keep rather dry over winter. *Cuphea ignea* can be increased by cuttings in a propagating box with a little bottom heat in spring or early summer but is often treated as an annual, plants being raised from seed sown in late winter/early spring and discarded in the autumn.

Cyclamen. This is one of the very best plants for the amateur gardener. The greenhouse cyclamen is nearly hardy, can be grown successfully with a minimum amount of heat, and fine specimens can be had in 14 cm (5½ in) pots. Moreover cyclamens flower in winter when colour is most welcome.

Seed may be sown in late summer in an unheated greenhouse and the seedlings grown on to flower 15 months later, or, alternatively, in late winter/early spring in a temperature of 16°C/61°F to flower a little later. It should be sown thinly in seed compost and only just covered. Prick the seedlings off into boxes of the same soil when they have two leaves, spacing them 5 cm (2 in) apart. Germination is often irregular and so forward seedlings may be carefully lifted and pricked off but with as little disturbance as possible of the soil in the seed tray which should not be discarded for several months. Directly their leaves touch in the boxes pot singly in 7·5 in (3 in) pots. Keep in a cool, sunny greenhouse, average temperature 10°C/50°F, minimum 4°C/40°F in winter and pot on in spring and early summer until they reach the 14 cm (5½ in) pots in which they will bloom. For these successive pottings use J.I. No. 1. As the tuber forms take care to keep it on top of the soil. Throughout maintain an equable temperature, average 15°C/59°F in summer, with shade during hot weather, plenty of moisture at the roots and moderate ventilation. Stages can be damped daily in summer, but this should be discontinued in autumn and winter.

For flowering arrange the plants on the staging in a light, sunny greenhouse, average temperature 12°C/54°F. Plants will bloom from about late autumn to early spring. After this remove faded flowers and gradually reduce the water supply. At the end of spring pots may be stood in a shady frame or out of doors and kept almost dry until late summer, when the tubers should be shaken out and repotted. Return to the frame and give a gradually increasing quantity of water as leaves appear. Bring into the greenhouse about the middle of autumn and grow on as before.

The principal point to avoid is too hot and dry an atmosphere, which will encourage attacks by red spider mite. Ventilation should be as free as possible, consistent with the average temperatures given. All the greenhouse varieties are obtained from one species, *Cyclamen persicum*. There are a great many shades of pink, scarlet and purple, also pure white, and in the best strains the butterfly-like flowers are of great size. Some have ruffled petals, there are double-flowered varieties, dwarf varieties and varieties with a narrow 'picotee' edge of a deeper colour to each petal. The leaves can be green or silvered, some strains having been selected specially for the extent and beauty of their silvering.

Cyperus (Umbrella Grass). *Cyperus alternifolius* is known as the umbrella grass because it has a circle of narrow leaves radiating from the top of its 30 cm (1 ft) high flower stem very much like the spokes of an umbrella. It is an attractive foliage plant making clumps of grass-like leaves and it is grown in a cool or intermediate greenhouse. Good plants can be had in 11 cm (4 in) pots in J.I. No. 1. Repot in late winter/early spring and increase by division at the same time, or by seed germinated in a temperature of 15°C/59°F in spring. Shade in summer from strong sunshine. Water freely at this period and syringe frequently. Keep just moist in winter.

Cyrtanthus. *Cyrtanthus* (once known as *Vallota purpurea*) is a bulbous plant with trumpet-shaped scarlet flowers in a cluster on stiff stems in late summer/early autumn. It is easily grown in a cool or intermediate greenhouse. Pot the bulbs after flowering in J.I. No. 2, one bulb in a 11·2 cm (4½ in) pot. Water very sparingly in autumn and winter, freely in spring and summer. Keep throughout in a cool or intermediate greenhouse without shading. Repotting is not essential every year as *cyrtanthus* flower most freely when slightly pot bound. They can be increased easily by removal of small bulbs at potting time. There is a pink-flowering variety.

Cytisus. The shrub which gardeners know as *Genista fragrans* is now listed as *Cytisus canariensis*. It is everybody's plant, easily grown with little or no heat, and also readily forced in a temperature around 15-18°C/59-65°F to get early flowers for Christmas or soon after. Without heat it will bloom in mid-spring. It makes a good bush in a 10-18 cm (4-7 in) pot, according to age, smothered for several weeks on end in bright golden-yellow, lemon-scented, pea-type flowers. Cuttings root quickly in sandy soil in a propagating box in spring or early summer. Pot on through the various sizes of pot first in J.I. No. 1, later No. 2, and pinch occasionally to secure a very bushy habit. The first year keep in a light, slightly heated greenhouse with no more than frost protection. Stand out of doors from early summer to late autumn in a sunny place. The following year some plants can be brought into the greenhouse in late autumn and the temperature gradually raised to 18°C/65°F to produce early flowers, while others can be kept in a practically unheated greenhouse until a couple of months later, when forcing may begin. Yet a third batch can be grown cool, minimum temperature 4°C/40°F, throughout. In all cases water freely while the plants are making their growth and flowering, but more sparingly towards the end of the summer and early autumn before they are started into growth. Plants can also be readily raised from seed sown in the first half of spring at a temperature of 15-18°C/59-65°F.

Daphne. *Daphne odora* is a dwarf, spreading shrub with evergreen leaves and heavily perfumed pink flowers in late winter/early spring. It can be grown out of doors in fairly sheltered places but also makes a good pot plant for the cold or cool greenhouse. It can be grown in 13-18 cm (5-7 in) pots and should be repotted in the first half of spring in J.I. No. 2. Plants may be stood in a frame or sheltered position out of doors from early summer to early autumn. Water freely from early spring to early autumn, rather sparingly from mid-autumn to late winter. No pruning is required but if plants get straggly they can be trimmed after flowering. Propagate by cuttings in summer in a propagating frame within the greenhouse, or layer in autumn.

Deutzia. The deutzia are deciduous shrubs, many of them hardy, but *Deutzia gracilis* is just a little tender and is such a good pot plant that it is usually grown in this way in the cool greenhouse. Pot in autumn in J.I. No. 1. Keep in an unheated frame until mid-winter and then bring into a light, airy greenhouse, average temperature 12°C/54°F. Water moderately at first, more freely as growth lengthens. The sprays of small white flowers will begin to open in early spring if the temperature can be maintained. After flowering cut back fairly severely to points at which new shoots are starting to grow. Keep in the greenhouse or a frame till mid-spring, then stand out of doors in a sunny place. Water freely and feed occasionally with weak liquid manure. In this way plenty of new growth will be made to flower again the following year. Propagation is by cuttings of firm young shoots in summer rooted in a propagating box within the greenhouse.

Dicentra (Bleeding Heart). The familiar bleeding heart of the herbaceous border, *Dicentra spectabilis*, (see p. 126), makes a good pot plant for the cool or unheated greenhouse. Roots can be lifted from the open ground in mid-autumn, potted in J.I. No. 1 or peat potting compost in the smallest pots that will contain them (usually 15 cm (6 in)), placed in a frame for a few weeks to get established and then brought into the greenhouse. Treatment should be quite cool the first year but plants firmly established in pots can be forced in a temperature of 15-18°C/59-65°F to give bloom by late winter/early spring. After flowering harden off and stand out of doors in a sheltered place from early summer to mid-autumn, when the process can be repeated as before.

Dieffenbachia. There are several species all grown for their foliage but the best is *Dieffenbachia picta*, which has several varieties. The leaves are sometimes broad, sometimes narrow, deep green, variously marked with yellow or white. These are tropical plants requiring a minimum temperature of 12°C/54°F in winter, rising to 18°C/65°F or more from mid-spring to early autumn. Water freely from early spring to early autumn, rather sparingly over winter. Shade in summer and syringe daily. Grow in 16·2 cm (6½ in) pots in J.I. No. 2 or peat potting compost. Increase by cuttings of short pieces of stem in spring, rooting these in a propagating frame with a temperature of 21°C/70°F and bottom heat. These plants also do well in fairly warm rooms but do not like draughts.

Diplacus. See **Mimulus** (p. 484).

Dracaena. Foliage plants some of which have rosettes of rather palm-like leaves while others are more laurel-like. They will make shapely plants in pots 15-30 cm (6 in -1 ft) in diameter. Grow in an intermediate or warm greenhouse in J.I. No. 2. Water freely from mid-spring to early autumn and syringe daily in warm weather, also damp between pots to maintain moisture in the air. Keep a much drier atmosphere in winter and water moderately. Repot in early spring. Increase by stem cuttings or pieces of root in sandy peat in spring in a propagating box, temperature 21°C/70°F with bottom heat. Good kinds are *Dracaena deremensis* Warneckei with narrow, dark green leaves striped with silver; *D. marginata*, with narrow leaves edged with red, and *D. fragrans* Massangeana, with broader laurel-green leaves with a wide central band of yellow; and *D. sanderiana* with grey-green leaves edged white.

Echeveria. The best-known species is *Echeveria secunda*, a very popular summer bedding plant. It makes a neat rosette of fleshy, grey-green leaves from which spring, in late summer, elegant little sprays of reddish flowers 23-30 cm (9 in-1 ft) in height. It is half hardy, that is to say it requires the protection of a cool greenhouse or well-made frame from mid-autumn to mid-spring inclusive but for the rest of the year it can be planted out in any sunny place and well-drained soil. Propagation is by division in the spring or by seeds sown in a temperature of 15–18°C/59–65°F in early spring.

Of more interest for the greenhouse owner are the larger species, such as *E. gibbiflora*. This is very much like the bedding type but with rosettes at least twice as big and a series of branches terminated by further rosettes. *E. elegans* has quite small grey rosettes edged with white and the flowers are pink. All are handsome pot plants for the cool greenhouse. They can be propagated like *E. secunda* and should be repotted in mid-spring. Keep all echeverias almost dry in winter but water moderately in summer.

Epacris. These small shrubby plants might easily be mistaken for heathers. Some flower in winter or early spring, some in summer, but the former are the more valuable for the greenhouse owner. Of these the best are *Epacris impressa*, *E. longiflora* and *E. purpurascens* which, with their numerous varieties and hybrids, give a colour range from white to heather red. They grow about 60 cm (2 ft) in height and thrive in an airy greenhouse with an average winter temperature of 12°C/54°F. In summer they can be stood out in a sunny frame. Prune lightly immediately after flowering and then, about three weeks later, repot using J.I. No. 1 without lime and with some extra peat. Some gardeners grow them simply in peat and sand. Pot firmly and water rather sparingly at first, then more freely, but do no more than keep the soil moist from mid-autumn to early spring. After pruning, daily syringing is advisable for a few weeks, but for the rest of the year the atmosphere should be moderately dry. Increase by cuttings of firm shoots in a propagating frame in the first half of summer.

Epipremnum. *Epipremnum aureum* (once known as *Scindapsus aureus*) is a climbing or trailing foliage plant which requires the same treatment as climbing philodendron. The leaves are green flecked with yellow in the common form, almost all yellow in the variety Golden Queen and heavily mottled with white in Marble Queen.

Erica (Heaths, Heather). Many of the best greenhouse heathers flower in winter. They have the neat habit and free-flowering characteristics of the hardy heathers and will grow with a minimum of artificial heat, but are a little difficult to manage because they are very sensitive to watering. The aim should be to keep the soil just moist throughout but never dry or sodden. Plants will thrive in similar conditions and soil to those recommended for epacris. Repot as necessary in spring immediately after flowering. *Erica × hyemalis* can be pruned fairly severely immediately after flowering, but other varieties are best with little or no pruning, though occasional pinching of badly placed shoots will help to keep the plants shapely. During the summer months the plants are best stood out of doors in a sunny, sheltered position, the pots plunged to their rims in peat or sand to reduce the necessity for frequent watering. No syringing or damping is necessary at any time. Propagation is by cuttings of short side growths in the first half of summer, rooted in sand in a propagating box. The best kinds are *E. × hyemalis*, pink and white, *E. gracilis*, heather red or white, and *E. canaliculata*, pink or white with dark anthers.

Erythrina (Coral Tree). *Erythrina crista-galli* is a handsome plant which becomes a shrub or small tree in its native Brazil. In greenhouses if cut back annually in early spring it makes a bushy specimen 1·3 m (4½ ft) high with spikes of scarlet-crimson pea-type flowers in summer. It can be grown out of doors in some very sheltered places but is better in a cool greenhouse watered freely from mid-spring to early summer, but kept dry from mid-autumn to early spring. Repot then in J.I. No. 3 but it needs a big pot or tub and is really happiest planted in a bed of good loamy soil. Propagation is by cuttings in spring, prepared from young shoots with a heel of older wood, rooted in a propagating box with bottom heat.

Eucalyptus (Gum Tree, Blue Gum). Despite the fact that the various species of eucalyptus are all large trees, several can be grown as pot plants in the cool greenhouse provided they are hard pruned in late winter/early spring. One of the best for this purpose is *Eucalyptus globulus*, known in Australia as the blue gum tree with attractive, aromatic, blue-grey leaves. It can be grown in J.I. No. 2 in a light, airy greenhouse with no more than frost protection in winter. In summer the plants can be stood out of doors in a sheltered place. Water freely from mid-spring to early autumn, moderately at other times. Repot as necessary in early spring. Increase by seeds sown in a temperature of 18°C/65°F in spring. Other good kinds for similar culture are *E. citriodora*, *E. coccifera* and *E. gunnii*.

Eucharis (Amazon Lily). The handsome bulbous plant *Eucharis grandiflora* is also known as *Eucharis amazonica*. It has broad, shining leaves and numerous erect stems, terminated in spring (and sometimes again in summer) by large, nodding, pure white and intensely fragrant flowers. The plant is increased by careful removal of small bulbs immediately after flowering. Pot in J.I. No. 2 and water sparingly at first, very freely as growth commences. Keep in a temperature of 22-27°C/72-80°F during spring and summer with shade from direct sunshine, giving abundant water and syringing at least twice daily. Give no shade in the autumn and winter. Keep in a temperature of 13-18°C/56-65°F for a month or so in autumn and water sparingly, but a winter temperature of 18-26°C/65-79°F is desirable.

Euphorbia. This is one of the very large genera of plants and one well provided with weeds but it also includes a few species of outstanding merit. Of these one of the best for the greenhouse owner is *Euphorbia fulgens*, a herbaceous plant with slender, arching stems carrying for half their length in mid-winter small clusters of the brightest orange-scarlet flowers imaginable. It needs intermediate or warm greenhouse treatment. Water freely in spring and summer, moderately in autumn and winter. Grow in J.I. No. 3 throughout. After flowering keep rather dry for a few weeks then, when growth restarts, repot and give more water. Propagation can be effected at about the same time by removing young side growths and rooting in a propagating box in a temperature of 21°C/70°F with bottom heat. *E. splendens*, a stiffly branched, spiny plant with scarlet flowers in summer requires similar temperatures but should be grown in J.I. No. 1 and be kept almost dry from late autumn to late winter. It can be increased by summer cuttings.
For. *E. pulcherrima* see Poinsettia (p. 490).

Exacum. There is no neater pot plant than *Exacum affine*. In a 13·7 cm (5½ in) pot it will make a perfect rounded bush 30 cm (1 ft) high, covered all over with flattish, pale blue flowers each with a centre of bright yellow stamens and with the additional attraction of fragrance. This fine plant is at its best in late summer, but a succession can be had by making several sowings. Seed should be sown in a temperature of 15-18°C/59-65°F from late winter to mid-spring. Pot first in J.I. No. 1, later in No. 2 and keep in a cool, sunny greenhouse throughout, watering fairly freely. The plant is an annual and should be discarded after flowering.

Felicia (Blue Marguerite, Kingfisher Daisy). *Felicia amelloides* is a pretty little plant with small blue daisy flowers produced non-stop all the summer and is sufficiently hardy to be grown out of doors in very warm, sheltered places. It makes an excellent pot plant for a cool greenhouse grown in 10 cm (4 in) pots in J.I. No. 1 compost. Water fairly freely in spring and summer, sparingly in autumn and winter and do not shade. Repot when necessary in early spring. Plant can be raised from seed or by summer cuttings.

Ficus (India-rubber Plant, Fig). These are foliage plants, the best-known kind, *Ficus elastica*, having big leathery leaves, longer than they are broad. There are several varieties, including *F. decora* which is more compact and *F. doescheri* which has white, grey and cream variegation. *F. benjamina*, known as the weeping fig, has much smaller leaves and thinner arching stems, and *F. lyrata* is called the banjo or fiddle-leaved fig from the shape of its large leaves. There is also a useful climbing species known as *F. repens* which will cling to the wall of a greenhouse but this has quite small leaves. All need cool or intermediate house conditions and *F. elastica* is also an excellent house plant surviving even in rooms that are not well lighted. Water freely in spring and summer, syringe frequently in warm weather and shade from strong sunshine. Grow in J.I. No. 2 and repot, when necessary, in early spring. Increase *F. elastica* by removing, in early summer, single eyes or buds with a leaf attached and rooting these in sandy soil in a propagating box, temperature 21°C/70°F with bottom heat. *F. repens* is increased by ordinary cuttings in spring rooted under similar conditions.

Fittonia (Snakeskin Plant, Mosaic Plant). Small foliage plants for intermediate or warm greenhouses or for well-warmed rooms. *Fittonia argyroneura* and *F. verschaffeltii* are the two kinds grown and both have green leaves with all the veins picked out in a different colour, ivory in the first, pink in the second. They should be grown in J.I. No. 2 or peat potting compost, watered fairly freely in spring and summer, moderately in autumn and winter, and shaded from direct sunshine. They like a still, rather moist atmosphere and can be used in bottle gardens. Increase by cuttings from late spring to mid-summer in a propagating frame with bottom heat or divide in spring.

Francoa (Bridal Wreath). The bridal wreath commonly grown is *Francoa ramosa*, a beautiful and easily managed plant with slender 60 cm (2 ft) spikes of white flowers in summer. It is a favourite cottage window plant. The ideal place for it is a greenhouse with frost protection in winter but otherwise it needs no artificial heat but plenty of light and ventilation. During summer the plants can, if desired, be placed in a frame or stood outdoors. Good specimens can be grown in 13-18 cm (5-7 in) pots in J.I. No. 2. They should be watered freely in summer, moderately at other times. Repot annually in early spring and increase by seed sown in warmth in late winter/early spring or by division.

Freesia. There are no more delightful bulbous-rooted plants for the cool greenhouse than freesias. They may be had in bloom from early winter to mid-spring by starting batches in succession and by growing from seed, and are quite easy to grow provided no attempt is made to force them too fast. Obtain bulbs in mid- to late summer and pot, a few at a time, from then until mid-autumn. Place six or seven bulbs in a 13 cm (5 in) pot filled with J.I. No. 3 and just cover with soil. Stand in a cold frame for at least eight weeks, keeping the soil moist, but no more, and ventilating freely except during cold weather. When plenty of roots have been made bring the pots into a well-lighted green-house, average temperature 10°C/50°F which may rise to 15°C/59°F when the flower stems have formed. If a few pots are brought in every week or so from mid-autumn to early winter there will be a continuity of bloom. After flowering grow on under similar conditions for a few weeks and then gradually reduce the water supply until, by early summer, the soil is quite dry. Keep in this condition in a frame or airy greenhouse until late summer, when the cycle recommences. Even earlier flowers can be obtained by sowing seed in the first half of spring. Space the seeds 2·5 cm (1 in) apart in 11·2 cm (4½ in) pots in J.I. No. 1 and do not disturb the seedlings but grow on under similar conditions to those recommended for corms. The species are not now so important as the many named hybrids in a great variety of shades of cream, orange, lilac, blue, pink, rose and salmon. All have the heavy freesia perfume. Increase by seeds or by removing small bulbs at potting time.

Fuchsia. The fuchsia is almost hardy, and no more than frost protection is required, though better plants can be produced under cool or intermediate house conditions. Magnificent specimens can be obtained by growing on from year to year and carefully pinching young growth to build up enormous pyramids or standards, covered throughout the summer with graceful, drooping flowers. There is no difficulty whatsoever about culture. The fuchsia will grow well in J.I. No. 2 or peat potting compost. Light shading will be an advantage on hot summer days, as high temperatures are at all times undesirable. Water freely throughout the season of growth, from about mid-spring to mid-autumn, but keep rather dry in winter, especially if temperatures are low. Feed every 10 to 14 days from late spring to late summer with weak liquid fertilizer. Repotting should be done in early spring. Propagation is easily effected by cuttings of young, non-flowering growth, which will root quickly in a propagating box in spring or summer. There are a great many varieties, some single flowered, some double, in shades and combinations of red, mauve, purple, pink, salmon and white. Some are erect in habit and some semi-weeping.

Gardenia (Cape Jasmine). The fragrant, and usually double, flowers of *Gardenia jasminoides* are chiefly valued for floral decorations and buttonholes, but the plants, which are evergreen shrubs, also make excellent specimens for an intermediate or warm greenhouse. In summer gardenias need shade from strong sunshine and daily syringing and the plants can be fed every 10 to 14 days with weak liquid manure. In autumn and winter keep considerably drier and discontinue syringing. Plants can be had in bloom most of the year if temperatures of 15°C/59°F or more are maintained but should be allowed to rest for a few weeks each winter in a slightly cooler atmosphere and with less water. After this, plants can be repotted in J.I. No. 2 or peat potting compost and moderately pruned to maintain a neat shape. Propagation is by cuttings of firm young wood obtained a few weeks after starting into growth in spring and rooted in sandy soil in a propagating box, temperature 21°C/70°F.

Genista. See **Cytisus** (p. 467).

Geranium. See **Pelargonium** (p. 488).

Gerbera (Barberton Daisy). *Gerbera jamesonii* is a slightly tender South African herbaceous perennial with very attractive daisy flowers with narrow pointed petals in various shades of red, pink, apricot and primrose. Improved garden varieties have sturdier stems, large flowers and often several rows of petals. There are also dwarf strains suitable for pots. All can be grown from seed sown in spring in a temperature of 16-18°C/61-65°F in a rather gritty seed compost. Throughout their life, which is not usually very long, the plants should be grown in a very well drained compost such as J.I. No. 1 with an extra quarter by bulk of coarse sand. Gerberas can be grown in 16·2 cm (6½ in) pots but are often easier to manage in a bed of soil. Grow in a sunny greenhouse with minimum temperature of 7°C/45°F, no shading and plenty of ventilation when the weather is warm. Water fairly freely from mid-spring to early autumn, but sparingly in winter when the soil should be only just moist. The main flowering season is from mid-spring to late summer but it can be longer in really favourable conditions.

Gesneria. See **Smithiantha** (p. 496).

Gloriosa (Climbing Lily, Glory-lily). These are very handsome, climbing, tuberous-rooted plants with reflexed lily-like flowers which, in the two best-known species, *Gloriosa rothschildiana* and *G. superba*, are orange-red and yellow. They do not require very high temperatures and can be stored dry in their pots laid on their sides from mid-autumn to early spring in a temperature of 7-10°C/45-50°F. Then repot in peat potting compost, one tuber in each 18 cm (7 in) pot or three in a 25 cm (10 in) pot, and start in a temperature of about 15°C/59°F. Water sparingly at first, freely later, and place bamboo canes or trellis work for the plants to cling to. Feed frequently with weak liquid manure from late spring to mid-summer. After flowering in summer gradually reduce the water supply until the foliage dies down and the tubers can be stored dry once more. The simplest method of increase is to remove small tubers at potting time.

Gloxinia. Even the tuberous-rooted begonias cannot surpass gloxinias for display during the summer months. The modern garden forms all have large, bell-shaped flowers, mostly in very rich colours, including velvety crimsons and purples, together with many kinds which are heavily spotted or netted with crimson, purple or pink on a white base. The deep green, velvety leaves are also very handsome and the whole habit of the plant, dwarf and compact, is ideal for the small greenhouse. The one drawback is that gloxinias require a little more warmth than the amateur can always manage conveniently. The roots are tuberous and can be stored dry from mid-autumn to late winter. Do not shake them out of their soil but keep them in the pots on their sides in a dry atmosphere and a temperature of 10°C/50°F. In late winter shake the soil from the tubers and arrange them practically

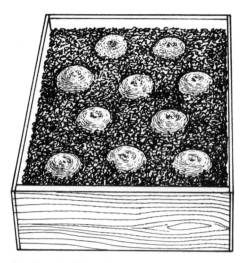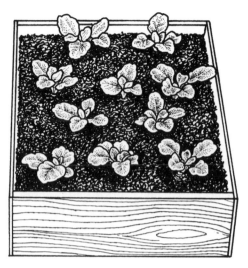

Starting gloxinia tubers into growth. In late winter the tubers are set in boxes of moist leafmould or granulated peat and placed in a temperature of 15-18°C/59-65°F. When they have started into growth plant in 7·5 cm (3 in) pots in J.I. No. 1 or peat potting compost

shoulder to shoulder in seed boxes filled with moist leafmould or granulated peat, but do not cover the tubers. Then place them in a temperature of 15-18°C/59-65°F to start them. Directly they have two or three leaves each, pot them singly in J.I. No. 1 or peat potting compost, first in 7·5 cm (3 in) and later in 13·7 cm (5½ in) pots. Keep them growing in the same temperature and a fairly moist atmosphere. Water freely once established and syringe between the pots (but not over the leaves) daily. From late spring to early autumn give shade on the sunny side of the house. Feed with weak liquid manure every 10 to 14 days as soon as flower buds appear. After flowering gradually reduce the water supply until the soil is quite dry by mid-autumn. The best method of propagation is by seed which should be sown, and the seedlings handled, in the same way as described for tuberous-rooted begonias, but with slightly higher temperatures, about 18°C/65°F.

Grevillea (Silk Oak). The grevilleas are shrubs or trees, a few of which are hardy enough to be grown outdoors in sheltered places. *Grevillea robusta* is, however, invariably treated as a greenhouse foliage plant. It has handsome, deeply divided, ferny leaves and, in an 18·7 cm (7½ in) pot, will make a good specimen 1 m (3½ ft) high. It can be grown in any frost-proof greenhouse without artificial heat for the greater part of the year. Water freely from mid-spring to early autumn, moderately for the rest of the year. Grow in J.I. No. 1 and repot when necessary in early spring. Discard when plants become too large. Increase by seed sown in early spring at a temperature of 18°C/65°F.

Gynura (Velvet Plant). *Gynura sarmentosa* is grown for its violet-purple leaves, the colour being particularly marked on the young growth. It will grow in an intermediate house in J.I. No. 1 and should be watered rather carefully at all times and given a light position. It is also used as a house plant. Increase is by cuttings in spring or summer in a propagating frame.

474

Haemanthus (Blood Flower, Royal Paint Brush). These are bulbous-rooted plants with broad, strap-shaped leaves and globular heads of flowers that look as if they are largely composed of long bristles. All can be grown in a cool or intermediate greenhouse. Water very sparingly from mid-autumn to early spring, then with increasing freedom as growth commences and give full sun throughout. Repot when necessary in mid-spring and increase by removing small bulbs at this period. Summer-flowering kinds are *H. coccineus*, 30 cm (1 ft), scarlet, and *H. katharinae* (now listed as *Scadoxus multiflorus katharinae*), 45 cm (1½ ft), deep red. *H. albiflos*, 30 cm (1 ft), white, flowers in late winter or early spring. *H. magnificus* produces orange-scarlet and yellow flowers on 45 cm (1½ ft) stems in late spring/early summer, requires higher temperatures and is suitable for the intermediate or warm greenhouse.

Hedychium (Ginger-lily). Here again is a family containing some members requiring a fair degree of warmth, though others can be grown in a cool greenhouse. Of these hardier kinds the best is *Hedychium gardnerianum*, with handsome, broadly lance-shaped leaves and large heads of fragrant yellow flowers on 1 m (3½ ft) stems in summer. It should be grown in 20-25 cm (8-10 in) pots in J.I. No. 2. Repot in early spring and water rather freely from mid-spring until after flowering, then reduce the water supply and keep almost dry from late autumn to late winter. It only needs protection from frost and will thrive in a cool or intermediate house. Increase by division at potting time. The best of the more tender kinds is *H. coronarium*, with fragrant white flowers on 1·5 m (5 ft) stems in summer. Culture is exactly as above, but a minimum temperature of 7°C/45°F is essential and intermediate house conditions are preferred.

Heliotropium (Heliotrope). The common heliotrope, or cherry pie, can be grown either as a cool or intermediate greenhouse pot plant or used for summer bedding out of doors over summer. There are various improved garden forms with flowers of extra size or deeper colour. Some of these selected forms must be raised from cuttings which can be prepared from young shoots in spring or summer and rooted in sandy soil in a propagating frame, preferably with a little bottom heat. The common heliotrope, *Heliotropium arborescens*, also known as *H. peruvianum*, can be increased from seed sown in a temperature of 15-18°C/59-65°F in late winter or early spring, and there are also good garden varieties that come reasonably true to colour and habit from seed. Pot on the seedlings or rooted cuttings first in J.I. No. 1, later in No. 2 in the 13·7 cm (5½ in) pots in which they will flower. Alternatively harden them off carefully for planting out in early summer in a sunny position. Water rather freely while in growth.

After flowering reduce the water supply and keep on the dry side from mid-autumn to late winter. Bedded-out plants can be lifted before mid-autumn, pruned fairly hard and potted in the smallest pots that will take their roots, after which they should be returned to the greenhouse and given the same treatment as those grown in pots throughout, but when grown from seed it is really cheaper to discard old plants in the autumn and raise new ones each spring. Very large specimens, or even standards on 60-90 cm (2-3 ft) stems, can be grown by careful training and pinching carried out over several years. The old varieties give the best scent, strongly reminiscent of concentrated vanilla or marzipan.

Hibiscus (Rose Mallow, Rose of China). There are species of hibiscus which are perfectly hardy, and these have been dealt with elsewhere (see pp. 85, 274). Here I am concerned with tropical or sub-tropical species which need greenhouse protection and, in some cases, fairly high temperatures. The grandest of these are undoubtedly the numerous varieties of *H. rosa-sinensis*, a tropical tree in its native habitat, but capable of being grown as a bushy plant in a large pot or tub in an intermediate or warm greenhouse. An alternative is to plant directly in the greenhouse border, so allowing more freedom. The type has very large scarlet flowers produced from late spring to late summer, but there are many varieties, some double flowered, others single, in shades of crimson, scarlet, pink, yellow or buff, and some with white-variegated leaves. All should be grown in J.I. No. 2 and repotted as necessary in early spring. Water very freely from early spring to mid-autumn, moderately for the rest of the year. Syringe frequently in summer and give full sun throughout. Prune at potting time sufficiently to keep plants in bounds. Increase by cuttings of firm young shoots taken in spring or summer and rooted in a propagating frame, temperature 18-21°C/65-70°F with bottom heat.

Hibiscus manihot, with very large yellow and maroon flowers, and a race of hybrids named Southern Belle with large pink or rose and white flowers, are herbaceous perennials best treated as annuals and raised from seed sown in late winter at a temperature of 16-18°C/61-65°F. Seedlings are potted on as necessary in J.I. No. 1 or peat compost and are given intermediate house conditions.

Hippeastrum. These bulbous plants have been much confused with amaryllis, to which they are closely related. They are showy plants for the cool or intermediate greenhouse, flowering from early spring to early summer and resting in winter. The bulbs are big but should not be overpotted; pots 16·2 cm (6½ in) in diameter are adequate for a single bulb. Keep just moist from mid-autumn to late winter in a temperature of 7-10°C/45-50°F. Repot if necessary, directly the bulbs show signs of growing, in J.I. No. 1, but usually bulbs can go for three years with top-dressing only. The bulbs should be only half-buried in the soil. Water with increasing freedom from early spring onwards. Under these conditions the stiff flower stems, terminated by clusters of large, trumpet-shaped flowers in brilliant shades of scarlet and crimson, will soon appear, followed later by the strap-shaped leaves. After blooming, place the pots on a sunny shelf in the greenhouse. As the foliage shows signs of dying down towards the end of the summer, gradually reduce the water supply until, by the autumn, the soil is just moist. Increase by seeds sown in a temperature of 18-21°C/65-70°F in spring, or by removing offsets at potting time. Specially prepared bulbs are available for late summer/early autumn potting to flower in early winter.

Howea. Two of the most useful palms for pot culture are *Howea belmoreana* and *H. forsteriana*. They are both easily grown in a cool or intermediate greenhouse. Give shade from late spring to early autumn and water freely from mid-spring to early autumn, moderately for the rest of the year. Syringe plants at least twice daily in spring and summer. Repot when necessary in early spring, using J.I. No. 1. Increase by seeds sown singly in small pots in early spring and germinated at 21-24°C/70-75°F. In many gardens these popular palms are still known by their old name *Kentia*.

Hoya (Wax Plant). Hoyas are climbing or sprawling plants with very regular clusters of star-shaped flowers which look as if they are made of wax. The climbing species usually grown is *Hoya carnosa*, with very pale pink flowers at their best in the second half of summer. It is quite an easy plant for a cool or intermediate greenhouse. Plants may be grown in large pots in J.I. No. 1, but a better plan is to plant directly in the greenhouse border in good loamy soil with plenty of peat and sand and a little crushed charcoal. The stems twine so they should have suitable support, such as a pillar or trellis. Water freely in spring and summer, moderately in autumn and winter. Thin out overcrowded shoots and shorten weak stems in late winter. Plants in pots or tubs should be repotted every second or third year in early spring. *H. bella* is shorter and more shrubby in growth and has white and purple flowers also in summer. It is a good plant for a hanging basket and prefers the warmer temperatures of the intermediate house. Both kinds can be propagated by cuttings of firm young shoots taken in spring and rooted in a propagating box with bottom heat, or year-old shoots can be layered in autumn, but *H. bella* does better grafted on to young plants of *H. carnosa*.

Humea. See **Calomeria** (p. 441).

Hydrangea. The common hydrangea with its great trusses of blue, pink, red, purple or white flowers is hardy enough to be grown out of doors in sheltered places, but is also a useful shrub for the cold or cool greenhouse. Cuttings of firm young growth root very easily at any time from mid-spring to late summer in a frame or unheated greenhouse. As soon as they are well rooted pot singly in 7·5 cm (3 in) pots in J.I. No. 1. Move on to larger sizes and No. 2 as the small pots fill with roots. Water freely all summer and keep in an unheated and lightly shaded frame, but in mid-autumn move to a greenhouse, minimum temperature 7°C/45°F for the winter. Water moderately till mid-spring, then with increasing freedom. It is almost impossible to overwater hydrangeas in summer provided the soil is porous and drainage good. To produce early flowers the temperature can be raised to an average of 15°C/59°F in mid-spring, or the plants can be grown on without heat to flower in the first half of summer. Bigger specimens can be obtained by growing on plants for two, three or more years. Stand out of doors in a sunny place after flowering, plunging the pots to their rims in peat or ashes, and return to a frost-proof greenhouse early in mid-autumn. Repot in early spring. The only pruning necessary is to cut back flowering stems to side growths or good growth buds immediately the blooms fade.

Blue flowers are only produced in soils that are rather acid, and then only from plants that normally have coloured flowers. White kinds cannot be made to bear blue flowers. Special blueing compounds can be purchased and should be used according to manufacturer's instructions. Alternatively, aluminium sulphate can be mixed with lime-free potting soil at 113 g per 0·03 cu m (4 oz per bushel).

Hymenocallis (Spider Lily). These are bulbous plants with narrow-petalled, sweetly scented white flowers in summer. There are several species but the one that needs least warmth is *Hymenocallis calathina*. This will succeed in intermediate house conditions and even put up with cool house temperatures. Pot bulbs in early spring in 16·2 cm (6½ in) pots in J.I. No. 1 or peat compost. Water moderately at first but freely when leaves appear and feed once a week in summer with liquid fertilizer. Gradually reduce the water supply after flowering and keep the soil quite dry in winter. Increase by division of bulb clusters when repotting in spring.

Hypocyrta. See **Nematanthus** (p. 484).

Hypoestes (Polka Dot Plant). *Hypoestes phyllostachya* is a small tender herbaceous plant with leaves heavily spotted with pink. It is a popular and easily grown house plant and can also be grown in a greenhouse with a minimum temperature of 10°C/50°F. Seed is sown in spring in a temperature of 16-18°C/61-65°F and the seedlings are grown on in small pots in J.I. No. 1 or peat-based potting compost. They should be watered normally and be kept in a light place but with shade from strong sunshine in summer.

Impatiens (Balsam, Busy Lizzie). The balsam is *Impatiens balsamina*, a plant 25-75 cm (10 in-2½ ft) high according to variety with large, double flowers in shades of mauve, pink, salmon, cerise and scarlet as well as white. It is a half-hardy annual which must be raised from seed sown in a warm greenhouse in late winter or early spring. Seedlings are pricked off into boxes and when these are well filled they can either be planted out of doors in late spring or early summer, or be potted singly in J.I. No. 2 in 13 cm (5 in) pots and grown in a sunny greenhouse.

The Busy Lizzie, *I. walleriana* (*I. holstii* or *I. sultanii*) is a bushier plant with flowers produced almost throughout the year. The many garden varieties vary in height from 15-60 cm (6 in-2 ft) and have crimson, scarlet, orange, pink or white flowers. They are perennials but are commonly treated as half-hardy annuals and are much used for summer bedding, especially in shady places where they succeed well. They also make excellent pot plants for cool or intermediate greenhouses; grow in light rooms not too far from a window and grow on for several years. Increase by cuttings if desired.

Ipomoea (Morning Glory). These plants are very closely allied to convolvulus. Here I am concerned with two fine climbing plants for the slightly heated greenhouse, *Ipomoea learii* and *Convolvulus tricolor*, also known as *I. rubro-coerulea*. Both are vigorous twiners which can be trained up a pillar or under the rafters. They flower in summer and the blooms are large and funnel-shaped, Oxford blue in the first named, Cambridge blue in the second. There is an even better form of *C. tricolor* known as Heavenly Blue, in which the colour is paler and purer. *I. learii* is a perennial which can be grown in large pots or tubs, but it is better to plant it directly in the greenhouse border in ordinary well-drained soil. Maintain an average winter temperature of 10°C/50°F, rising to 15-18°C/59-65°F in summer. Water freely in spring and summer, moderately in autumn and winter. No pruning is necessary, though overgrown plants can be cut back in late spring. *C. tricolor* is an annual so it must be renewed from seed each year. Sow the seeds singly in small pots in early spring and germinate in a temperature of about 18°C/65°F. The seedlings should be potted on in J.I. No. 1 as necessary and make useful pot specimens for the greenhouse staging, with the shoots trained around three or four thin bamboo canes stuck into an 18 cm (7 in) pot. *I. learii* can also be grown from seed.

Ixia. See p. 370.

Ixora. These are brilliant evergreen shrubs for the warm greenhouse. They produce their large clusters of vividly coloured flowers in summer. The best is *Ixora coccinea*, with orange-scarlet flowers. Good specimens are to be had in 16·2 cm (6½ in) pots. Grow them in J.I. No. 1. Repot old plants in early spring but young plants, which can be raised from cuttings of firm growth rooted in a propagating box with bottom heat in spring or summer, should be potted on from stage to stage when the smaller pots become filled with roots. Water freely in spring and summer and syringe twice daily in warm weather, but maintain a much drier atmosphere and water moderately in autumn and winter. Plants can be pruned to shape in late winter just before potting.

Jacaranda. *Jacaranda mimosifolia* is a Brazilian tree with handsome blue flowers but as a greenhouse pot plant it is grown mainly for its ferny foliage. It enjoys intermediate house conditions, can be grown in J.I. No. 1 and should be watered freely in spring and summer, rather sparingly in autumn and winter. Plants can be pruned fairly severely in early spring to keep them in shape and within bounds. Propagation is by seed sown in a temperature of 15-18°C/59-65°F in spring or by cuttings of firm young shoots in summer in a propagating frame with bottom heat.

Jacobinia. See **Justicia** (below).

Jasminum (Jasmine). The hardy jasmines will be found in another chapter (see p. 277) but there are also some equally delightful species for the greenhouse. These can conveniently be considered under two headings, cool house and intermediate house kinds. The best species in these two groups are: cool house, *Jasminum polyanthum*, a vigorous climber with fragrant flowers from late winter to mid-spring, and *J. primulinum*, a more shrubby plant with yellow, usually semi-double flowers in winter and spring; intermediate or warm house, *Jasminum sambac* and *J. rex*, both moderate climbers with white fragrant flowers, the first in winter and *J. sambac* most of the year. Grow directly in the greenhouse border in good loamy soil, or in large pots or tubs in J.I. No. 2. Plant or pot in early spring. Water freely in spring and summer, moderately in autumn and winter. No shading should be needed, except from strong sunshine in small houses. Prune sufficiently to keep in bounds, immediately after flowering. Propagate by cuttings of firm young shoots in a propagator in spring or summer or by layering.

Justicia (Shrimp Plant). An easily grown perennial, *Justicia guttata* (once known as *Beloperone guttata*) is 30-45 cm (1-1½ ft) high with arching spikes of white flowers surrounded by shrimp-pink bracts produced throughout the summer. It can be grown in a cool or intermediate greenhouse or in a light room in J.I. No. 1 compost. Water fairly moderately in autumn and winter and increase by cuttings of firm young shoots in summer. It may be necessary to cut off all the flowering stems from one plant to get non-flowering shoots for use as cuttings. There is a dwarf variety and one with lime-green bracts. *J. carnea* is a rather big perennial with crowded heads of hooded pink flowers in late summer/early autumn. *J. rizzini* is a much bushier plant with smaller, more regularly tubular yellow and red flowers all winter. Both require normal watering except that *J. carnea* benefits from being kept a little dry for a few weeks after flowering and then pruned sufficiently to keep it from becoming too tall and straggly. *J. rizzini* will also benefit from a short resting period with reduced water but in late summer/early autumn before it starts to flower. Increase it by cuttings in spring or early summer in a propagator.

Kalanchoë. *Kalanchoë blossfeldiana* is a good greenhouse succulent with showy clusters of small scarlet or yellow flowers in winter or spring. It will thrive in a cool greenhouse in J.I. No. 1 with some additional sand. Water fairly freely in spring and summer, moderately in autumn and winter and do not shade at any time. Increase by seed sown in a temperature of 15°C/59°F in early spring or by cuttings from late spring to mid-summer. There are numerous varieties, some small, compact and bushy, others up to 45 cm (1½ ft) high and also hybrids with rose-pink flowers.

Lachenalia (Cape Cowslip). These deserve to be better known, for they flower in winter or early spring with little artificial heat and are easy to manage. They are bulbous-rooted plants, and the bulbs should be potted five or six together in a 13 cm (5 in) pot in late summer/early winter in J.I. No. 1. Cover with 12 mm (½ in) of soil and place the pots for at least two months in an unheated frame. Then, when plenty of roots have been formed, bring the pots into a sunny greenhouse, minimum temperature 7°C/45°F. Grow on in the same manner as freesias (see p. 472) slowly reducing the water supply after flowering so that, by mid-summer the soil is quite dry. The flowers are yellow or yellow and red, tubular, drooping and arranged in slender spikes remotely like those of the cowslip. Lachenalias may also be grown in hanging baskets very effectively. *Lachenalia aloides* and its varieties are the most popular but there are other good species. Propagation is by seeds sown in a temperature of 15°C/59°F in early spring, or by removal of small bulbs at potting time.

Lampranthus. These showy succulent plants were originally listed as mesembryanthemum and some may still be found under this genus in many nursery catalogues. The annual *Mesembryanthemum criniflorum*, now listed as *Dorotheanthus bellidiformis*, is described on p. 80. Lampranthus are mostly bushy or sprawling in habit with brightly coloured flowers mainly in late spring and early summer. They can be grown very easily from cuttings rooted in summer and grown in a cool or intermediate house in J.I. No. 1 with a little extra sand. Water fairly freely in spring and summer, very sparingly in autumn and winter. Do not shade at any time. Good kinds are *Lampranthus aurantiacus*, orange-red; *L. blandus*, pale rose pink; *L. brownii*, orange-red; *L. coccineus*, scarlet; *L. multiradiatus*, pink; *L. spectabilis*, magenta.

Lantana. There was a time when *Lantana camara* was almost as popular both for summer bedding and for greenhouse display as the verbena, to which it is related and which it resembles in flower. It has slipped out of favour but is, nevertheless, a useful and showy plant, bushy and branching in habit, usually 60-90 cm (2-3 ft) high with bright clusters of flowers throughout the summer. The flowers themselves are in various shades of yellow, orange, lilac, pink, magenta and red, together with white. Lantanas may be raised from seed sown in a temperature of 18°C/65°F in late winter/early spring or from cuttings struck in spring or summer in a propagator. Grow on in a cool greenhouse with plenty of water while they are making their growth but with very little water over winter. No shade is required. Use J.I. No. 1 and prune rather hard in late winter to keep the plants compact. If preferred, lantanas can be planted out of doors in early summer and lifted, repotted and brought back into the greenhouse before mid-autumn.

Lapageria. There are no climbers more beautiful than *Lapageria rosea* and it will grow in any slightly heated glasshouse, minimum winter temperature 4°C/40°F. Plants can be grown in large pots or tubs, but it is better to place them directly in the greenhouse border and train them around pillars or on wires beneath the rafters, from which their waxen, long, bell-shaped red or white flowers will hang throughout the summer. Plant or pot in early spring and water very freely from mid-spring to early autumn but rather sparingly from then on and over winter. Give some shade throughout the summer and syringe daily to maintain a moist atmosphere. In a dry greenhouse plants are likely to be severely attacked by thrips and red spider. Increase by layering in autumn or spring.

Lilium (Lily). A great many lilies can be grown in the greenhouse and, as most of them are hardy, or almost so, they are good subjects for the unheated structure. Few will tolerate much artificial heat, but the various forms of *Lilium longiflorum* can be flowered early in a temperature of 18°C/65°F once they are well established in their pots. All lilies for the greenhouse should be potted in the autumn. In most cases a 15 cm (6 in) pot will accommodate one bulb, or two or three bulbs may be placed in pots 20-25 cm (8-10 in) in diameter. Use J.I. No. 2 and make certain that pot drainage is good. Place the bulbs fairly low in the pots and do not completely fill the pots at first but leave room for topdressing with similar soil as shoots lengthen. After potting, place in an unheated frame for at least two months so that roots may be formed freely before top growth starts. Completely hardy lilies can be left in the frame with advantage until their flower stems are already well formed, and only brought into the greenhouse for the last few weeks. Lilies should have free ventilation throughout and plenty of light, but not strong direct sunshine, from mid-spring to late summer. Water freely while in growth, but after flowering gradually reduce the water supply until, by the time growth dies down, the soil is no more than just moist. Then allow to rest for a month or so before repotting. Those lilies which are hurried along in heat to get early flowers should not be forced two years running.

The best lilies for pot cultivation are *L. longiflorum*, with long, trumpet-shaped, white flowers (this is the popular white lily of the florists' shops); its variety *L. l. harrisii* (or *eximium*) which is both earlier in bloom and finer; *L. speciosum*, with reflexed pink and white flowers in late summer; its numerous varieties, such as Melpomene and *L. s. rubrum*, in which there is more and deeper colouring; *L. auratum*, the immense golden-rayed lily of Japan; *L. formosanum*, which is a little like *L. longiflorum* but with longer and more slender trumpets, and *L. regale*, with widely opened trumpet-shaped flowers, white suffused with gold and purplish brown. This last is one of the easiest of all lilies to grow and, like *L. formosanum*, can be flowered in eighteen months from seed. *L. longiflorum* and its varieties are the best kinds for gentle forcing and by this means can be had in bloom from about late winter to early summer.

Lily of the Valley. See **Convallaria** (p. 448).

Limonium (Statice). In addition to the well-known annual kinds (see p. 88) and the hardy perennial kinds (see p. 136) there are several beautiful species grown mainly as pot plants in the cool greenhouse. The best of these are *Limonium profusum*, which is a perennial with densely branched heads of small purple flowers in late summer, and *L. suworowii*, an annual with pink flowers carried in branched spikes. It is an extremely distinctive plant and well worth growing. *L. profusum* is increased by cuttings prepared in spring from side shoots and rooted in a propagating frame with a little bottom heat. The cuttings are potted on in J.I. No. 1 until they reach 13·7 cm (5½ in) pots in which the plants will bloom. Water freely in spring and summer, but very sparingly for the rest of the year. Old plants can be repotted in early spring. *L. puberulum*, which is similar in appearance but smaller, can be raised readily from seed sown in the second half of winter.

L. suworowii is also raised from seed sown in a temperature of 15°C/59°F in late winter/early spring. The seedlings are potted on first in J.I. No. 1, then until they reach 11·2 cm (4½ in) pots in which they will flower during the summer. After flowering the plants should be discarded. Full sun should be given throughout. Artificial heat is unlikely to be necessary after mid-spring.

Lippia. See **Aloysia** (p. 432).

Luculia. *Luculia gratissima* is a deciduous shrub which deserves to be better known as it has clusters of charming and exceptionally fragrant pink flowers in the autumn. It is rather too big for pot culture, but may be grown in a tub or planted out in the cool greenhouse in any good loam with a little extra peat and sand. Water freely in spring and summer, rather sparingly in autumn and winter. Prune rather hard in late winter to keep plants compact. Increase by seed or by summer cuttings in a propagating frame with bottom heat.

Mandevilla (Chilean Jasmine). *Mandevilla laxa* is a strong-growing, deciduous climber, with fragrant, creamy-white, funnel-shaped flowers in summer. It is nearly hardy and can be grown outdoors in very sheltered places but is quite safe in a greenhouse with minimum temperature of 4°C/40°F. Plant it in a bed of good loamy soil or grow in a large pot or tub in J.I. No. 2. Water normally, provide canes, trellis or wire for its slender stems to twine around and cut back quite severely in late winter. Increase from seed in a temperature of 16-18°C/61-65°F or cuttings in a propagator. *M. boliviensis* is white with a yellow throat, and *M. sanderi*, pink. Grow in J.I. No. 2 in large pots or tubs with very good drainage. Repot, when necessary, in early spring and prune each autumn, but only those shoots which have by then finished flowering, which may be shortened to 2·5 cm (1 in) or so. Water sparingly over winter, moderately during the spring months and freely from mid-spring to mid-autumn. Syringe daily during hot weather to keep down red spider. Increase by short cuttings of young shoots taken in spring or summer and rooted in a propagating frame, temperature 21°C/70°F, with bottom heat.

Manettia. Though one frequently sees *Manettia inflata* at shows, it seldom figures in amateurs' greenhouses, despite the fact that it is pretty and easily grown for the intermediate or warm greenhouse. It is a small, evergreen climber which can be grown in pots 15-25 cm (6-10 in) in diameter and either trained beneath the rafters or wound around a few bamboo canes to form bush-like specimens. The small, tubular, scarlet and yellow flowers are produced freely for the greater part of the year. Grow in J.I. No. 1 and raise readily from cuttings of young shoots which root quickly in a propagator in late spring/early summer. Water fairly freely from mid-spring to early autumn, rather sparingly over winter. Light shade will be needed on hot days.

Maranta (Prayer Plant). Varieties of *Maranta leuconeura* are handsome foliage plants for the intermediate or warm greenhouse where they can be grown quite easily in pots in J.I. No. 1 plus a quarter its bulk of extra peat, or peat potting compost, and they enjoy the still, damp atmosphere of the bottle garden. They need abundant moisture in both soil and atmosphere throughout the spring and summer, but should be watered more moderately from early autumn to early winter, and be kept rather dry for the first two months of the year. Repot, as necessary, in early spring and increase by division at this time. The leaves are large and handsomely variegated with white, grey, purple or pale green on a dark green base. Two popular varieties are *M. l. kerchoveana* and *M. l. massangeana*, the second more spreading in habit and with smaller leaves.

Marguerite. See **Argyranthemum** (p. 433).

Medinilla. The splendid perennial plant *Medinilla magnifica* needs a lot of room and a warm greenhouse so is seldom grown by amateurs, though it is often seen at summer shows in collections of tropical plants. It has large, shining green leaves and hanging trusses of pink flowers on pink stems with pink bracts in late spring and early summer. It should be grown in J.I. No. 2 with extra peat or peat potting compost and be watered freely in spring and summer, sparingly in autumn and winter. Shade from late spring to early autumn and syringe frequently. Plants can be cut back a little before being repotted in mid-summer, after flowering. Propagation is by cuttings in spring.

Mesembryanthemum. See **Lampranthus** (p. 480).

Microcoelum. *Microcoelum weddelliana* (once called *Cocos weddelliana*), is one of the most graceful of palms, with very slender stems and long narrow leaflets. It is easily grown in an intermediate greenhouse, with shade from strong sunshine, from late spring to early autumn. Water freely in spring and summer, rather sparingly the remainder of the year. Syringe at least once daily during summer and also on hot spring days. This palm can be used for short periods as a room plant, but should be returned to the moister and more equable temperature of the greenhouse for recuperation. When indoors sponge the leaves daily with tepid water. Repot, when necessary, in early spring in J.I. No. 1. Increase by seeds sown in early spring at a temperature of 21-26°C/71-79°F.

Mimosa (Sensitive Plant). The plant commonly known in gardens as mimosa is, in fact, an acacia (see p. 429), but there is a genuine mimosa occasionally grown as a pot plant. This is *Mimosa pudica*, a small branching plant with finely cut leaves which have the curious habit of folding up when touched, hence the popular name sensitive plant. It is grown mainly as a curiosity and will thrive in any light, sunny greenhouse with cool or intermediate temperatures. It is usually treated as an annual, seed being sown in early spring in a temperature of 15-18°C/59-65°F, the seedlings being potted singly in 7·5 cm (3 in) pots filled with J.I. No. 1 and moved to larger sizes as necessary. Water and syringe freely in spring and summer and shade from direct sunshine. Plants can be kept for several years if desired, being repotted in early spring, but it is cheaper and more convenient to renew from seed annually.

Mimulus (Musk). The true musk, *Mimulus moschatus*, was once a very popular green-house pot plant on account of its distinctive fragrance, but it fell out of favour in the early part of the century when it lost its scent. It is still worth growing for its yellow flowers, particularly the form of it known as Harrison's Musk, which is rather stronger growing and more showy. It can be raised from seeds sown in early spring at a temperature of 15°C/59°F, or by cuttings of young growth rooted in a propagating frame in spring. Grow on in J.I. No. 1, potting as necessary until the plants reach the 13·7 cm (5½ in) pots in which they will bloom. Water very freely but make certain that the pots are well drained. Grow in a cool, airy, lightly shaded greenhouse, minimum temperature 4°C/40°F. No artificial heat is needed for the greater part of the year.

M. glutinosus, now known as *Diplacus glutinosus*, is an evergreen shrubby plant which needs some support and can be trained around a cane or up a small pillar. It has orange or bronze-red flowers produced during most of the summer and will grow in a cold or cool greenhouse in J.I. No. 2. Prune in late winter sufficiently to keep the plants in shape, repot in early spring if necessary and water freely in spring and summer, moderately in autumn and winter. Increase by seed or by summer cuttings.

Monstera. The vigorous evergreen climbing plant *Monstera deliciosa* has very large green leaves which split into finger-like lobes or form holes. They are favourite house plants as they will put up with a good deal of ill usage and grow in quite poor light. In the green-house the plant enjoys intermediate or warm house conditions and should be watered freely in spring and summer, moderately in autumn and winter. Grow in J.I. No. 2 or peat potting compost, shade from late spring to early autumn and maintain a moist atmosphere during this period. Repot when necessary in early spring. Increase by seed in spring or cuttings of the ends of shoots in summer in a propagating frame with bottom heat in a temperature of at least 21°C/70°F. This plant needs plenty of room.

Myrtus (Myrtle). The evergreen flowering shrub *Myrtus communis* is hardy enough to be grown out of doors in a sheltered position in mild climates, but it also makes an excellent pot specimen for the cool greenhouse, particularly in its variety *M. c. tarentina*, which is more compact in habit. In an open border it will make a compact bush 2·4-3 m (8-10 ft) high, but pot culture restricts it and good specimens, 1 m (3½ ft) high, are to be had in 21·2 cm (8½ in) pots. These will produce their small, but abundant, fragrant white flow-ers in summer. Grow in J.I. No. 2 and repot when necessary in early spring. If desired plants can be pruned to shape at the same time, though pruning is not essential. Water fairly freely in spring and summer, rather sparingly in autumn and winter. If desired the plants can be stood outdoors from early summer to mid-autumn, preferably in a sheltered but not too sunny position. Increase by cuttings of firm young shoots from late spring to late summer, rooted in a propagating frame with a little bottom heat.

Naegelia. See **Smithiantha** (p. 496).

Neanthe. See **Chamaedorea** (p 444).

Nematanthus. *Nematanthus glabra* is the new name for *Hypocyrta glabra* (Clog Plant). It is a small evergreen plant with neat, dark green leaves and orange flowers shaped like tiny clogs and produced mainly in summer. It will grow in a cool or intermediate house and also makes a useful house plant for a fairly light room. Grow it in J.I. No. 1, water freely in spring and summer, moderately in autumn and winter and shade from mid-spring to early autumn. Increase by summer cuttings, preferably with bottom heat.

Neoregelia. These are handsome foliage plants making rosettes of stiff leaves forming an open cup or vase in the centre which becomes bright red. The leaves may also be variegated and in *Neoregelia carolinae tricolor* they are striped with cream and pink. They are favourite house plants as they will succeed in quite poorly lighted rooms. Grow in pots in an intermediate or warm greenhouse in peat potting compost or a mixture of equal parts peat, sand and osmunda fibre. Shade in summer and maintain a moist atmosphere. Always keep the central vase full of water.

Nepenthes (Pitcher Plant). The pitcher plants are so called because some of their leaves have been modified into large, pitcher-like structures which serve as insect traps. They are not only interesting on this account but also distinctly beautiful, as the pitchers are often handsomely marked with crimson, purple and brown. The plants can be grown in either pots or teak baskets, and the best position for them is suspended from the greenhouse rafters. They need a damp, warm atmosphere with abundant moisture during the growing season both in the air and at the roots. Grow them in a compost of about 2 parts by bulk fibrous peat and 1 part sphagnum moss with no soil at all. Place in the pots or baskets in early spring and water rather carefully at first until the roots are established. Subsequently water very freely from mid-spring to early autumn inclusive, but no more than moderately for the rest of the year. Syringing should be continued throughout the year once daily even in winter, and maybe two or three times daily in summer. Temperatures should average 18°C/65°F out of season, 24°C/75°F when growth is active. Shade rather heavily from direct sunshine. Propagation is not very easy but can be effected by means of stem cuttings obtained in spring or early summer and rooted singly in small pots filled with peat and sphagnum moss and placed in a propagating box, temperature 26°C/79°F with bottom heat. Seeds may also be germinated under similar conditions.

Nerine (Guernsey Lily). These bulbous-rooted plants flower in autumn, are very easy to grow and do not require high temperatures but it is sometimes difficult to make them flower regularly. In this respect *N. bowdenii* and its varieties are the hardiest and most reliable. Obtain bulbs from mid- to late summer, and pot them singly in 10 cm (4 in) pots or three or four together in 15 cm (6 in) pots using J.I. No. 1. Place straight away in a sunny, unheated greenhouse. Water very sparingly at first, but with increasing freedom as growth appears. Then, in a month or so, the heads of showy scarlet or pink blooms will develop on stiff 45 cm (1½ ft) stems before the leaves appear in the case of *N. bowdenii*, *N. sarniensis* and their varieties and hybrids. After flowers fade, continue to water fairly freely and grow on in the greenhouse in an average temperature of 7°C/45°F, minimum 4°C/40°F. Give plenty of ventilation and full sunshine throughout. In late spring the foliage will show signs of dying down. Pots may then be stood on a shelf near the glass or in a sunny frame and the water supply cut down but the soil should never be quite dry. Then, in late summer, at the first sign of growth, water more freely again. As plants become pot bound they can then be split up or potted on into larger sizes. Many of the kinds cultivated are hybrids with fancy names and will be found fully described in the catalogues of specialists.

Nerium (Oleander). The oleander, like the myrtle, is an evergreen shrub native to southern Europe and almost hardy. It can be grown in a greenhouse with frost protection only and is a really beautiful shrub which, if planted out in the greenhouse border, will grow in time 1·8-2·4 m (6-8 ft) high and rather more in spread. Smaller plants are to be had in 23 cm (9 in) pots or tubs. The showy flowers of *Nerium oleander*, produced all the summer, are pink, purple or white. Pot or plant in J.I. No. 2 in early spring and only repot when absolutely necessary due to overcrowding. Water freely from early spring to early autumn, rather sparingly for the remainder of the year. In summer plants can be stood out of doors, for a month or so, but must be brought inside before there is a danger of frost. Throughout the warm weather syringe frequently as in too hot and dry an atmosphere red spider may be troublesome. Immediately after blooming prune all young growth rather hard and, subsequently, keep a little dry for a few weeks until growth recommences. In winter it is only necessary to maintain a minimum temperature of 4°C/40°F. Earlier blooms can be obtained by raising the temperature in early spring to about 15°C/59°F, but hard forcing should not be attempted. Propagation is by seed or by cuttings of firm shoots rooted in a propagating frame in late summer.

Nidularium. These plants are closely allied to neoregelia and require similar treatment. The kind commonly seen, *Nidularium innocentii*, has rosettes of stiff leaves that are dark green above and purple below and the centre of the rosette turns crimson around the base. A variety named *N. i. striatum* has leaves striped with pale yellow.

Ophiopogon (Japanese Hyacinth). These are plants grown mainly for their narrow, graceful foliage, which in some varieties, such as *Ophiopogon jaburan* Variegatus and *O. j. aureus* are handsomely variegated with white or yellow. They also produce slender spikes of blue or lilac flowers in summer, but these are of lesser importance. Grow in J.I. No. 1 in the smallest pots that will contain the roots and repot every second or third year in early spring or plant out in the greenhouse border. Water very freely in spring and summer, moderately in autumn and winter. The plants will thrive equally well in full sun or partial shade and all that is required is frost protection in winter. Plants will even grow well under the staging. For most of the year artificial heat is not essential though warmth is not detrimental. Increase by division in early spring.

Oplismenus. See **Panicum** (p. 487).

Ornithogalum (Star of Bethlehem). Both the hardy ornithogalums described on p. 376 may also be grown as pot plants in the cool greenhouse. Pot them in J.I. No. 1 in early autumn. Stand them in a frame for a month or so and then bring them into a light, airy greenhouse. No heat is needed, though if early flowers are required, a temperature of 15°C/59°F can be maintained. There are some other species which are tender and, therefore, only suitable for the greenhouse, notably *Ornithogalum arabicum* and *O. thyrsoides*, the latter being the South African chincherinchee which is grown commercially for cut blooms both with white flowers in summer. Culture is the same as for the hardy kinds, except that protection from frost should be given.

Oxalis (Wood Sorrel). In addition to the hardy species, described on p. 200, there are some slightly tender kinds which make useful pot or basket plants for the frost-proof, but otherwise unheated, greenhouse. Typical of these are *Oxalis deppei*, with rose-red flowers, and *O. purpurata* and its variety *O. p. bowiei* with pink or rose flowers, all flowering in summer. Pot in the autumn in 11·2 cm (4½ in) pots, or place several together in baskets in J.I. No. 1 and grow in a sunny, frost-proof greenhouse. Water sparingly in autumn and winter, but moderately from early spring to about the end of summer, or until foliage dies down. Then keep quite dry for about six weeks until repotting time. Increase them by removal of offsets when potting, starting these in small pots.

Pancratium. These are bulbous-rooted plants related to hymenocallis. All are very showy and make good specimens for large pots in the cool greenhouse. Repot in early spring in J.I. No. 2, but annual repotting is seldom required. Keep in a light, airy greenhouse, average temperature 10°C/50°F, watering rather sparingly at first but freely later. After flowering gradually reduce the water supply and keep almost dry from about late autumn to late winter inclusive. At this period only frost protection is required. Increase by removing small bulbs at potting time. All pancratiums have white flowers. *Pancratium canariense* flowers in early autumn, *P. illyricum* in late spring/early summer, and *P. maritimum* from mid-summer to early autumn. The last two are very sweetly scented.

Pandanus (Screw Pine). The useful foliage plant *Pandanus veitchii* has strap-shaped leaves striped with cream which form a large, palm-like rosette. In decorative value it may be compared with the best of the dracaenas. It can be grown in the intermediate or warm greenhouse or may be used as a house plant, though its saw-edged leaves can be damaging to flesh and clothes. Grow it in J.I. No. 1, repotting when necessary in early spring. Cultural details are the same as for dracaena (see p. 468) except that the best method of propagation is by removal of offsets at potting time.

Panicum. *Panicum variegatum* is the garden name of a useful trailing grass which botanists call oplismenus. With its white-striped, and sometimes pink-tinged, foliage the effect is rather similar to that of *Zebrina pendula* and it makes an equally pretty edging to the greenhouse staging. It will grow in J.I. No. 1 in a cool or intermediate greenhouse or may be used as a house plant. In summer it will thrive in an unheated greenhouse. Water freely in spring and summer, moderately in autumn and winter. Repot in early spring and increase by cuttings rooted in spring or summer in a propagating frame, preferably with a little bottom heat.

Passiflora (Passion Flower). The blue passion flower, *Passiflora caerulea*, can be grown in an unheated greenhouse and is usually more successful there than out of doors. There are also some excellent varieties of it, including Constance Elliot which has white flowers. *P. edulis*, the species which produces the passion fruit, requires more warmth. Most decorative in flower are *P. antioquiensis*, with rose-red flowers, and *P. quadrangularis*, with extraordinary green, white, pink and purple flowers surrounded by long filaments.

P. × *allardii* is a hybrid between the last species and *P. coerulea*. It has blue, pink and white flowers and is nearly hardy. All can be grown in large pots or tubs, but are better planted directly in the greenhouse border in good soil with free drainage. Give them plenty of room and place them where they can climb up a pillar or trellis. The sunnier the position the better. Plant or pot in early spring and water freely from mid-spring to early autumn. Growth can also be syringed daily during hot weather. In autumn and winter keep the soil just moist and the atmosphere dry. A winter temperature of 7°C/45°F will be sufficient. In late winter overgrown plants can be reduced a little and weak shoots removed. Propagation is by seed sown in a temperature of 15-18°C/59-65°F in early spring, or by cuttings of firm young growth rooted in spring or summer in a propagating frame, preferably with bottom heat.

Pelargonium (Geranium). It is a pity that geranium should have been chosen for the popular name of pelargonium for it is also the correct botanical name of a separate genus of plants, some of which are good, hardy herbaceous perennials or rock plants. The familiar scarlet, pink or white-flowered 'geranium' of the summer border is, in fact, a zonal-leaved pelargonium, and in addition there are several other types, including ivy-leaved pelargoniums, which are climbing or trailing plants flowering, like the zonal-leaved kinds, all the summer and well on into the autumn in a mild climate; the show and regal pelargoniums which are mainly greenhouse plants, similar to the zonal-leaved type in habit, but flowering mainly from mid-spring to early summer and with bigger blooms, usually strikingly blotched with maroon or crimson on a red, pink, salmon, mauve or white base; and the scented-leaved pelargoniums, most of which have insignificant flowers but leaves which are not only fragrant but often much divided.

All pelargoniums are easily grown pot plants, thriving in J.I. No. 2 or No. 3, and capable of being raised from cuttings struck in either spring or summer in a temperature of 12-15°C/54-59°F. Cuttings will, as a rule, strike quite readily on the open greenhouse staging or, in late summer, in a frame or out of doors. Too much heat and moisture are not desirable as they may accelerate decay. Pot the spring-struck cuttings singly in 7·5 cm

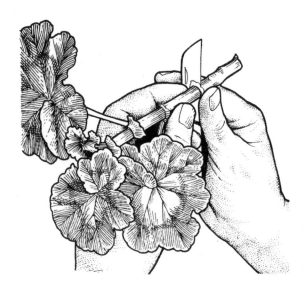

Preparing a pelargonium cutting. The lower leaves are removed cleanly and the cut is made just below a leaf joint

(3 in) pots in J.I. No. 1 directly they are rooted, the autumn-struck cuttings in early spring, and thereafter move them on to larger pots and richer compost as quickly as the smaller ones become filled with roots. Good flowering plants are to be had in 13·7 cm (5½ in) pots though, if desired, old plants can be retained and will eventually make big specimens in pots 20-25 cm (8-10 in) in diameter.

Zonal and ivy-leaved geraniums required for summer bedding should be hardened off in a frame during mid- to late spring and planted out towards early summer in well-drained soil and a sunny position. The ivy-leaved kinds can be trained up sticks about 90 cm (3 ft) in height, allowed to trail over the soil, or they may be grown in baskets or window boxes and allowed to hang down.

The regal and show pelargoniums should be kept in a cool or intermediate greenhouse until they have finished flowering, after which they may be stood in a frame or even out of doors in a sheltered, sunny position. At this period they must be watered rather sparingly for a few weeks, but in late summer the plants should be cut back quite severely and watered with gradually increasing freedom to encourage new growth. They can be repotted directly new shoots appear. A few plants may be pruned and watered in early summer to give a supply of early cuttings which can be rooted in mid-summer and potted singly in 7·5 cm (3 in) pots by early autumn. These cuttings give better results than those taken later.

All pelargoniums require frost protection in winter and should be housed before mid-autumn. Keep in a sunny, airy greenhouse, minimum temperature 7°C/45°F, and water rather sparingly until growth starts again in early spring.

It is also possible to treat zonal-leaved pelargoniums as winter-flowering greenhouse plants, the method being to grow the plants in pots throughout and prevent them from flowering in the summer by pinching off the flower buds as fast as they appear. The plants can stand in a sunny frame from early summer to mid-autumn and then be brought into an intermediate greenhouse minimum temperature 13°C/55°F. From this time onwards blooms can be allowed to develop naturally.

Varieties of all types are very numerous and particulars will be found in the catalogues of specialists. Some varieties of zonal-leaved pelargoniums are grown mainly for the colours of their leaves, which may be green and white or various combinations of green, yellow, red and purple. There are also dwarf varieties no more than 20 cm (8 in) high as well as the normal varieties which can make quite big bushes in time.

Peperomia. These are mostly dwarf plants grown for their handsomely variegated leaves. They can be grown in intermediate or warm greenhouses or in well-lighted well-heated rooms in J.I. No. 1 or peat-based compost but need rather careful watering as they can rot easily if too wet. For the same reason they should be grown in the smallest pots that will accommodate them. They are best increased by summer cuttings in a propagating frame with bottom heat. Good kinds are *Peperomia argyreia*, also known as *P. sandersii*, with silvery green-veined leaves; *P. griseoargentea* with grey and dark green leaves; and *P. caperata* with dark green pleated leaves.

Petunia. The ordinary petunias used for summer bedding (see p. 95) also make excellent pot plants for flowering in the unheated greenhouse in summer. The best kinds for the purpose are the large-flowered hybrids and the double-flowered varieties. All are raised from seed as described on p. 427 and the seedlings are grown on in 11·2 cm (4½ in) pots in J.I. No. 1 in a sunny greenhouse without artificial heat from late spring onwards. Plants should be discarded after flowering.

Philodendron. Evergreen plants grown for their foliage and suitable for intermediate or warm greenhouses. Some are popular as house plants, particularly *Philodendron scandens*, a vigorous climbing species with glossy green heart-shaped leaves and *P. domesticum*, also climbing, has light green arrow-shaped leaves. *P. bipinnatifidum* is not climbing and has large leaves deeply divided into fingers. There are many other kinds. All will grow in J.I. No. 2 or peat potting compost. They should be well watered in spring and summer, moderately in autumn and winter, be shaded from mid-spring to early autumn and syringed frequently during this period to maintain a damp atmosphere. Increase of climbing kinds is by cuttings in summer in a propagating frame with bottom heat and of non-climbers by division at potting time in early spring. It is an advantage to bind sphagnum moss to the supports for climbers and to keep it moist in summer.

Phoenix. A family of large and handsome palms of which the best for the amateur is *Phoenix roebelinii*. This is as useful for decorative purposes like the two howeas described on p. 476 and requires identical treatment. *P. roebelinii* can be used for short periods for indoor decoration but should be returned to the greenhouse to recuperate as it does not thrive for long in the dry atmosphere of a household.

Pilea (Artillery Plant, Aluminium Plant). *Pilea microphylla*, also known as *P. muscosa*, is popularly known as the artillery plant because, when it is about to flower, the buds apparently burst open and throw out a smoke-like puff of pollen. It is worth growing for its ferny foliage as well as this oddity of habit. Another useful species is *P. cadierei* with dark green leaves striped and margined with silver, the whole plant growing to about 23 cm (9 in) high. Both species are easily managed in an intermediate or warm greenhouse, and are also grown as house plants. Water freely while in growth, moderately afterwards. Grow in pots in J.I. No. 1, repotting in early spring. Increase by cuttings prepared from the ends of young shoots, rooted in spring or early summer in a propagating frame with bottom heat.

Plumbago (Cape Leadwort). *Plumbago capensis* is a vigorous climber with big clusters of light blue phlox-like flowers throughout the summer. It is one of the best climbing plants for the cool greenhouse. It can be grown in large pots or tubs, in J.I. No. 3, but is better planted directly in the greenhouse border in rather rich, well-drained soil. Plant it where it can be trained around a pillar, up a wall or beneath the rafters, and be sure to give it plenty of headroom. Plant or pot in early spring. Water freely from mid-spring to early autumn, moderately from mid-autumn to early spring. Foliage can be syringed daily in summer. Prune in early spring, shortening most of the previous year's growths as necessary to fill available space. Increase by cuttings of firm young shoots in a propagating frame in summer.

Poinsettia. The handsome shrubby plant which all gardeners know as poinsettia is a euphorbia, its full name being *Euphorbia pulcherrima*. It is a plant for the intermediate or warm greenhouse and its great merit is that it produces its large scarlet or pink bracts in mid-winter. The flowers, which are at the base of the bracts, are themselves insignificant. Good plants may be grown in 15 cm (6 in) pots in J.I. No. 2. Any repotting necessary should be done in the first half of spring. From then on water with steadily increasing freedom and syringe daily. Give light shade on the sunny side of the house from late spring to early autumn. After flowering prune the year's growth to within a few centimetres of the base and reduce the temperature to an average of 12°C/54°F until it is time for repotting. During this period of comparative rest the soil should be kept just moist.

Poinsettias can also be grown as house plants in fairly warm, well-lighted rooms but not with artificial light in the evenings as this will keep them growing and prevent them flowering.

Propagation is by cuttings, 16·2 cm (6½ in) long, removed in spring and dipped in powdered charcoal to prevent bleeding. Insert these in sandy soil in a propagating frame with bottom heat.

Polianthes (Tuberose). *Polianthes tuberosa* is a tuberous-rooted plant of which one hears a lot, though it is seldom to be seen. The explanation is that, though beautiful and fragrant, it is not a very satisfactory plant in cool climates, even under greenhouse conditions, and tubers usually have to be re-imported every year. The single or double creamy-white flowers are produced in short spikes sometimes on rather overlong stems, though this fault can be avoided by giving the plants plenty of light. Pot the tubers in autumn or spring, one in each 10 cm (4 in) pot in J.I. No. 2. Water very sparingly at first but with increasing freedom as growth lengthens. A temperature of 18°C/65°F will help to start the bulbs into growth, but once this is achieved the plants will do better in a cool greenhouse. Syringe frequently while in growth. After flowering, gradually reduce the water supply and let the tubers ripen well but many gardeners discard them after flowering and make a fresh start with imported tubers. Increase by removing offsets around the old tubers.

Primula. Without the tender primulas the amateur's greenhouse would be a far less interesting place in winter and early spring than it is. Of the four important kinds which are grown, namely *Primula obconica, P. sinensis, P. malacoides* and *P. kewensis*, the first three have given rise to a great number of varieties, and together are the most important group of flowering plants in the cool greenhouse from late autumn to mid-spring. *P. malacoides* and *P. kewensis* are almost hardy and can be grown practically without heat, except during the coldest weather.

These greenhouse primulas are all normally treated as annuals and raised from seed each year. The first sowing should be of *P. kewensis* in late winter/early spring followed by *P. obconica* and *P. sinensis* varieties in mid-spring, all in the greenhouse in a temperature of 15°C/59°F. A further sowing for succession can be made a month or six weeks after the first. *P. malacoides* may be sown from mid-spring to early summer. In all cases sow thinly in seed and cover very lightly. Directly they can be handled, prick off the seedlings 3·7 cm (1½ in) apart into well-drained trays filled with the same compost. Keep them in a light airy greenhouse, shaded on the sunny side and with an average temperature of 15°C/59°F, or in a frame with similar conditions. Pot singly in J.I. No. 1 in small pots directly the seedlings touch in the trays. Pot again into 13 cm (5 in) pots of J.I. No. 2

directly the smaller pots become filled with roots. By mid-autumn frame plants should be removed to the greenhouse with plenty of ventilation, full light and an average temperature of 10-12°C/50-54°F. Make no attempt to force the plants. Water moderately throughout, taking care to avoid wetting the leaves unduly, and above all not allowing water to lodge in the crown of the plants. Pick off any decaying or mildewed leaves. After flowering it is usually best to discard the plants, though *P. kewensis* can be grown on for another year if desired. *P. kewensis* is bright yellow, *P. sinensis* is in various shades of pink, carmine, crimson, salmon orange and blue, together with white, *P. obconica* includes many beautiful shades of pink, rose, mauve, pale blue and white and, though mainly winter and spring flowering, will continue to flower less freely for months. *P. malacoides* has a range from white and palest pink to carmine. *P. obconica* and, to a lesser degree, *P. malacoides*, causes a skin rash in some people.

The show auricula is also a primula and though a perfectly hardy plant must be grown under glass to preserve its flowers and the bloom of its leaves from weather damage. Plants can be raised from seed sown in spring or from divisions in the first half of summer when repotting. Plants may be kept in a cool place out of doors all through the summer and will only need greenhouse protection over winter to mid-spring. Little or no heat should be necessary but it is essential that the plants should be protected from strong sunshine.

Punica (Pomegranate). *Punica granatum* is grown in warm countries for its edible orange-like fruits but it is also a very decorative evergreen shrub up to 4·5 cm (15 ft) high with shiny leaves and scarlet flowers freely produced in late summer/early autumn. There is also a dwarf variety called *P. g. nana*, which grows about 45 cm (1½ ft) high. They make excellent pot or tub plants for a frost-proof greenhouse. Grow in J.I. No. 2 or peat potting compost or in a bed of good loamy soil and water fairly freely from spring to autumn, rather sparingly in winter. No shade is needed at any time. Plants can be raised from seed sown in a temperature of 18°C/65°F in spring or from summer cuttings in a propagator.

Rechsteineria. See **Smithiantha** (p. 496).

Rehmannia. *Rehmannia angulata* is a tender herbaceous plant suitable for the cool greenhouse. It has long spikes of rose-pink, trumpet-shaped flowers in spring and early summer and makes a good specimen in 16·2 cm (6½ in) pots. Grow in J.I. No. 3. Repot in early spring. Water freely from mid-spring to mid-autumn, sparingly for the rest of the year. Give shade from direct sunshine in warm weather. Propagation is usually effected by seeds germinated in late spring in a temperature of 15-18°C/59-65°F, the plants being treated as biennials and discarded after flowering, though, in fact, they are true perennials and can be kept for many years. Division at potting time provides an alternative method of increase.

Rhodochiton (Purple Bell-vine). A slender climber for the cool greenhouse, *Rhodochiton atrosanguineum* has little pink and maroon flowers which hang in lines like tiny skirted dolls in summer. It can be easily raised from seed sown in a temperature of 16-18°C/61-65°F in early spring and is often treated as an annual but is a perennial and can be kept for years. Grow it in large pots of J.I. No. 1 or plant directly in a border within the green-house. Train the stems to wires close to the glass. Water freely in spring and summer, sparingly in autumn and winter.

Rhododendron. The hardy rhododendrons have little place in the greenhouse though small bushes are sometimes potted in autumn and allowed to flower in a cold or slightly heated house in spring. But there are, in addition, a number of slightly tender species and hybrids, which are fine early-flowering evergreen shrubs for a cool greenhouse in which there is plenty of room. They need the same type of peaty acid soil which suits the out-door types, are better grown directly in a border than in pots or tubs and need no more than a winter temperature of 4–7°C/40–45°F. They bloom in late winter and spring and have flower trusses similar to those of the hardy kinds in various shades of pink, salmon, orange and red, together with white. The so-called Javanese rhododendrons require simi-lar soil but a higher temperature, 10°C/50°F being the minimum in winter. Repot when necessary immediately after flowering, which is also the best time for planting. Water freely from early spring to early autumn, moderately for the rest of the year. No pruning is needed, but faded flower heads should be removed. Daily syringing is advisable in hot weather. When grown in pots, the Himalayan and Chinese kinds such as *Rhododendron ciliicalyx*, *R. dalhousiae*, *R. moupinense*, *R. edgeworthii*, *R. taggianum* and hybrids such as × *fragrantissimum*, Lady Alice Fitzwilliam and Countess of Haddington can be stood out of doors in a sheltered place all summer. Increase is as for the hardy kinds (see p. 310).

Rhoeo. See **Tradescantia** (p. 501).

Rhoicissus (Natal Vine). *Rhoicissus rhomboidea* is a climber, very popular as a house plant and also suitable for cultivation in a cool or intermediate greenhouse. The leaves are com-posed of three leaflets, bronze coloured at first but becoming deep shining green as they age. The plant climbs by tendrils and should have trellis or wires for support. Grow it in J.I. No. 2, water fairly freely in spring and summer, and moderately in autumn and win-ter. Pinch out the tips of growths in summer if plants threaten to extend too far. Shade is not essential but neither is it detrimental. Increase by cuttings of firm young growth in summer in a propagator.

Rhynchospermum. See **Trachelospermum** (p. 501).

Richardia. See **Zantedeschia** (p. 503).

Rochea. *Rochea coccinea*, often known as *Crassula coccinea*, is a showy succulent well worth growing. It makes an erect plant, freely branched from the base and 45–60 cm (1½–2 ft) in height. Each stem is closely set with small, fleshy leaves and terminated in summer by a head of vivid scarlet, tubular flowers. It is easily grown in J.I. No. 1 plus one-sixth its bulk of sharp sand in a cool greenhouse. Plants can be repotted in early spring when necessary. Water fairly freely in spring and summer but very sparingly in winter and avoid a damp atmosphere at all times. No shading is required at any time. Cut-tings prepared from the tips of non-flowering shoots in late spring or early summer will root readily in sandy soil on the open greenhouse staging.

Rosa. Though roses are grown in greenhouses in vast numbers by commercial growers to provide cut blooms for market, they are not ideal plants for the amateur. Only the polyantha roses make really showy pot plants, and all need rather careful management or they are apt to become badly infested by red spider and thrips. Just a few climbing varieties thrive well under cool greenhouse conditions, notable amongst these being Marechal Niel, with yellow flowers, and Niphetos, which is pure white. These, however, should not be grown in pots if it is at all possible to plant them directly in the greenhouse border in deep, rich soil. Roses to be grown in pots should be young (maidens are best) and must be potted in autumn, one plant in each 21·2 cm (8½ in) pot, using J.I. No. 3. Make no attempt to force them the first year. They should stand in an unheated frame for at least two months after potting to form roots and, even then, should only be brought into an unheated greenhouse. Prune them in the ordinary way (see p. 330) during mid-winter and water moderately at first, more freely later as growth proceeds. Give full light and plenty of ventilation. When weather is hot syringe at least once daily. After flowering plunge the pots outdoors in a sunny position and continue to water freely. The following year plants well established in pots can be brought into flower early by placing them in a cool greenhouse in the first half of winter and gradually raising the temperature to an average of 15°C/59°F by early spring.

Permanent climbers planted in greenhouses should be pruned when they lose their leaves in the autumn. In most cases it is enough to remove some of the older wood altogether, also weak shoots, and shorten other growths by 60 cm (1 ft) or so. Pests are most likely to be troublesome when the atmosphere in the house becomes too hot and dry in summer. Propagation is as for outdoor roses.

Saintpaulia (African Violet). *Saintpaulia ionantha* is a small but exceptionally beautiful plant with low rosettes of soft, dark green leaves and abundant violet-purple, mauve, pink or white, single or double flowers produced more or less throughout the year. There are no better pot plants for an intermediate or warm glasshouse. Good specimens can be had in pots as small as 7·5 cm (3 in), or several plants can be grown together in a 15 cm (6 in) pot or tray. Pot in the first half of spring in peat potting compost, water moderately in spring and summer, very carefully in autumn and winter, and avoid splashing the leaves. Weak liquid manure can be used occasionally while plants are in flower. Shade plants from direct sunshine, particularly in summer. Propagation can be effected by division at potting time, by seeds sown in late winter in a temperature of 18°C/65°F – the seeds are very small and should be handled in the same way as those of the begonia – or by well-developed leaves which will root readily and soon form new plants if pushed stalk first for about a third of their length into sandy peat in a propagating frame, temperature 21-24°C/70-75°F, and kept moist. Saintpaulias can also be grown from seed in a temperature of 21°C/70°F in spring or summer.

Sansevieria (Bow-string Hemp, Mother-in-law's Tongue). There are several different kinds of sansevieria but by far the most popular is *Sansevieria trifasciata* Laurentii. This has stiff, upstanding strap-shaped leaves, often a little twisted like a corkscrew and always banded and striped with yellow. It is a handsome foliage plant for an intermediate or warm greenhouse or to grow in a room. Grow it in J.I. No. 2 or peat potting compost and feed monthly from mid-spring to late summer with weak liquid fertilizer. Water moderately in spring and summer, very sparingly in autumn and winter. Shade is not essential but neither is it detrimental. Increase by careful division at potting time in early spring.

Saxifraga (Mother of Thousands). *Saxifraga stolonifera* is a perennial plant with roundish leaves which are purplish red on the undersides and veined with silver above. It produces slender pink trailers bearing tiny plantlets complete with roots, hence the popular name mother of thousands. The flowers are white, spidery and produced in summer, but it is grown mainly for its leaves and graceful habit. It is a first-class plant for a hanging basket and, as it is almost hardy, can be grown in a greenhouse without heat. It also succeeds well as a window plant. Water freely in spring and summer, rather sparingly for the rest of the year, and repot when necessary in the first half of spring using J.I. No. 1. Plantlets can be removed and potted separately at almost any time of the year.

Schefflera (Queensland Umbrella Tree). *Schefflera actinophylla* is a popular evergreen house plant which can also be grown in an intermediate or warm greenhouse. Restricted in a pot it makes a shrub rather than a tree. Each shining green leaf is formed of several leaflets which develop as well in dense shade as in lighter places. It should be grown in J.I. No. 2 and be watered moderately from spring to autumn but rather sparingly in winter. Feed in spring and summer with liquid fertilizer. Increase from seed sown as soon as ripe in a temperature of 18-21°C/65-70°F or by air-layering in spring or summer. *S. elegantissima* requires intermediate or warm house conditions and makes a good room plant provided the necessary temperature can be maintained. It can be grown in J.I. No. 2 in 15-25 cm (6-10 in) pots according to the age of the plants. Repot annually in early spring. Water freely in summer, sparingly in winter, and syringe frequently in summer. Propagation is not very easy and probably best left to the expert, though root cuttings can be grown successfully in a propagating frame within the greenhouse, and air layering can be carried out in spring or summer.

Schizanthus (Butterfly Flower). This most graceful flowering plant is an annual and so must be renewed from seed every year. If seeds are sown in small batches from late winter to early summer in a greenhouse with a temperature of 15-18°C/59-64°F, plants will be obtained to flower from mid-summer to mid-autumn. A further sowing made late in summer or early autumn will give plants to flower the following mid-spring/early summer. Sow thinly in seed compost. Prick off the seedlings into a similar mixture as soon as they can be handled and pot singly in 7·5 cm (3 in) pots about three weeks later using J.I. No. 1. Pot on into 13 cm (5 in) and later into 16·2 cm (6½ in) pots as required, using J.I. No. 2 or 3. Some of the best plants may even go into 21·2 cm (8½ in) pots for flowering. Do not pot between late autumn and late winter inclusive. All plants should have their growing tips pinched out when they are 8·7 cm (3½ in) high. As their stems lengthen each plant should be supported with several thin stakes arranged to spread growth out a little like a shuttlecock.

Schizanthus appreciate cool, airy treatment throughout. In winter the temperature may average 10°C/50°F and fall to 4°C/40°F at times without harm. As much air as possible should be given consistent with the maintenance of these temperatures. Water fairly freely in spring and summer but rather sparingly in autumn and winter.

The flowers, produced in large sprays, are usually attractively marked and the colour range includes pink, mauve, purple, carmine, crimson and white with marking of a deeper shade than the ground colour or of yellow or bronze. The large varieties will reach a height of 1 m (3½ ft) but there are dwarf forms up to 45 cm (1½ ft).

Scindapsus. See **Epipremnum** (p. 469).

Selaginella. To most amateurs the selaginellas are either ferns or mosses though, in fact, they have no connection, belonging to a different natural order from either of these. They are grown for their trailing (or in some species erect) moss-like foliage, which in many kinds is bronze, gold or emerald green. Selaginellas can be grown in quite small pots, or several plants together in a 16·2 cm (6½ in) tray. Use J.I. No. 1 with a little extra peat and repot, when necessary, in early spring. Grow in a temperature of 7-10°C/45-50°F in winter, 15-18°C/59-65°F in summer, and give shade from direct sunshine from late spring to early autumn inclusive. Keep the soil fairly moist throughout but make certain that drainage is good. Propagation is effected by division when potting. The trailing kinds are excellent for the front of the staging or for hanging baskets.

Setcreasea. See **Tradescantia** (p. 501).

Smilax. Here is another instance of the botanist and the gardener between them making a grand muddle of naming. There are genuine species of smilax grown in the garden, but they are hot house plants and comparatively rare in cultivation. The cool house plant which every gardener knows as smilax is a usurper of the name, being genuinely an asparagus or, according to some authorities, a myrsiphyllum. I have used the name smilax here as it is the one to which gardeners would turn naturally. This is a trailing, evergreen plant much used in floral decorations and also grown in hanging baskets. It is cultivated solely for its long trails of bright green 'leaves' and is an easily managed plant in any frost-proof greenhouse. It will thrive in sun or partial shade, can be raised easily from seed sown in late winter/early spring in a temperature of 18°C/65°F and should be grown in J.I. No. 1. Water freely in spring and summer, rather sparingly in autumn and winter. During warm weather the plants can be syringed daily and should be fed every 10 to 14 days from late spring to late summer with weak liquid fertilizer. Repotting of young plants should be done when necessary to prevent pots becoming overfilled with roots. Old plants can be repotted in the first half of spring.

Smithiantha (Temple Bells). Tuberous-rooted plants with velvety leaves and 45 cm (1½ ft) sprays of tubular flowers in a variety of colours, including cream, yellow, apricot, pink and red. Plants sold as gesneria and naegelia belong here or require identical treatment. Plant tubers in early spring 12 mm (½ in) deep, one in each 10 cm (4 in) pot in peat potting compost. Start in a temperature of 15°C/59°F, water sparingly at first, freely when roots are well developed and feed every 10 days from the time the flower buds appear. Gradually reduce the water supply after flowering and keep quite dry with the pots on their sides from late autumn to late winter. Grow throughout in a cool or intermediate greenhouse with shade from direct sunshine in summer and a fairly damp atmosphere. The scarlet-flowered plant once sold as *Gesneria cardinalis* is now called *Sinningia cardinalis* and is grown in the same way as smithiantha.

Solanum. There are two totally distinct types of solanum popular as greenhouse plants. The better known is the bushy *Solanum capsicastrum*, often known as the winter cherry because of the bright orange-scarlet fruits about the shape and size of cherries which are produced in mid-winter. It is a very popular plant for Christmas decorations and will make a neat, evergreen bush in 13·7 cm (5½ in) pots. It is usually grown from seed sown in the greenhouse, temperature 18°C/65°F, in late winter/early spring. The seedlings are potted on first in J.I. No. 1, then No. 2 until, by early summer they reach the 13·7 cm (5½ in) pots in which they will flower. Keep well watered during the summer and stand out of doors or in a sunny frame over the same period, as plenty of air will help the flowers to set, and so will daily syringing. From early autumn onwards keep in a light, airy greenhouse, average temperature 10°C/50°F, and water moderately.

If desired, plants can be kept from one year to another, but better results are obtained with young plants. An alternative method of propagation is to take cuttings of young shoots, plenty of which can be obtained in the first half of spring from old cut-back plants placed in a temperature of 15-18°C/59-65°F. These will root freely in sandy soil in a propagating frame with gentle bottom heat.

The other types of greenhouse solanum are vigorous climbing plants, of which the best are *S. crispum* and *S. wendlandii*, both with violet-blue flowers, and *S. jasminoides* Album which bears clusters of white flowers, rather like those of summer jasmine. All are in bloom throughout the summer. They can be grown in large pots, but are better planted out in the greenhouse border in rich, well-drained soil. *S. jasminoides* in particular should have plenty of head room and stems may be trained to wires under the rafters, up a pillar or against a wall. They need frost protection in winter, but can be grown without heat for most of the year, in fact in mild, sheltered places they can be grown out of doors. Water freely from mid-spring to early autumn, sparingly for the rest of the year. Regular pruning is unnecessary, but weak or old stems can be removed and overgrown vines shortened in late winter. Increase by cuttings of young shoots rooted in spring or summer in sandy soil in a propagating frame with gentle bottom heat or by layering in spring.

Solenostemom. All the following were once listed as *coleus*. The most familiar kind, *Solenostemom scutellarioides*, is grown solely for its foliage though two species, *S. thyrsoideus* and *S. frederici* are cultivated for their long, narrow sprays of deep blue flowers which appear in the winter. The many varieties of *S. scutellarioides* all have broad, nettle-shaped leaves which are very handsomely marked in a variety of colours, such as red, bronze, purple, yellow and various shades of green. They make excellent pot plants and good specimens may be had in pots no more than 13 cm (5 in) in diameter. They can be grown in a cool greenhouse but it is easier to overwinter plants in the higher temperature of the intermediate greenhouse. Give full sunlight except on bright, hot summer days. Grow in J.I. No. 2 or peat potting compost and water freely from mid-spring to early autumn, sparingly over winter. Feed with weak liquid manure every 10 to 14 days from late spring to early autumn. Propagation is very easily effected by cuttings of young shoots which can be rooted at almost any time in spring or summer in a propagating frame with gentle bottom heat. Seeds will also germinate easily in early spring at a temperature of 18°C/65°F, but seedlings may vary in the colour of their leaves. Pot on seedlings or rooted cuttings as the smaller pots fill with roots and pinch occasionally to secure a bushy habit. Use J.I. No. 1 for the rooted cuttings, moving on to No. 2. There are varieties whose leaves are curled or deeply divided and also some that are dwarf.

S. thyrsoideus and *S. frederici* require similar conditions. Propagation of the first is as for *S. scutellarioides* but *S. frederici*, an annual or biennial, must be renewed annually from seed sown in early spring at a temperature of 15-18°C/59-65°F.

Sparmannia (African Hemp). *Sparmannia africana* is a useful, if rather large, flowering shrub for the cool or intermediate greenhouse. In habit it looks a little like a large pelargonium with semi-woody growth and clusters of white flowers with yellow stamens which will bloom for most of the year. Left to its own devices it will grow 3 m (10 ft) or more high, but fairly small specimens can be maintained in pots by hard pruning in late winter. Repot in early spring in J.I. No. 2. Water freely from the time growth begins until mid-autumn, but sparingly from then on and over winter. Plants can be stood out of doors in a sunny place all summer, in fact the conditions required are very much the same as for zonal-leaved pelargoniums. Increase is by cuttings of firm young growth in a propagating frame in spring or early summer or by seed in a temperature of 16-18°C/61-65°F in spring.

Spathiphyllum (White Sail). *Spathiphyllum wallisii* is like a miniature arum lily but with more open creamy-white spathes on slender stems in the second half of spring, and often again in mid-autumn. It needs intermediate or warm house conditions and should be grown in J.I. No. 2 or peat compost. Repot each spring, water freely in spring and summer, moderately in autumn and winter, and shade from mid-spring to mid-autumn. Feed with weak liquid fertilizer every 10 to 14 days from mid-spring to late summer and syringe daily during this period. Increase by division at potting time.

Sprekelia (Jacobean Lily). *Sprekelia formosissima* is a slightly tender bulb with spidery, scarlet flowers on short stems in summer. It makes a good pot plant for a sunny frost-proof greenhouse. Pot in spring in 10 cm (4 in) pots and J.I. No. 1, water sparingly at first but freely from the time growth appears until it dies down in autumn when no further water will be needed until the following early spring. Increase by offset bulbs removed when repotting in spring. In sunny, sheltered places this showy and unusual plant can be grown out of doors but may need some winter protection.

Statice. See **Limonium** (p. 481).

Stephanotis (Madagascar Jasmine). *Stephanotis floribunda* is an exceptionally beautiful climber with clusters of intensely fragrant, tubular, waxy-white flowers from mid-spring to mid-autumn or even later according to the amount of warmth available. It is a vigorous twiner and should be planted in J.I. No. 2 for preference, directly in the intermediate or warm greenhouse border in a position where it has plenty of headroom and wires or a trellis up which to climb. Alternatively it can be grown in a large pot. Water very freely from mid-spring to early autumn and syringe at least once daily. In late winter remove weak stems and shorten others as necessary to keep the plants in bounds. Increase by cuttings of firm young growth removed with a heel of older wood in spring and rooted in a propagating frame, temperature 18-21°C/65-70°F with bottom heat.

Strelitzia (Bird of Paradise Flower). *Strelitzia reginae* is one of the most exotic looking of all greenhouse plants. It grows 1·2 m (4 ft) high with a corresponding spread and needs very large pots or small tubs so is not a suitable subject for small greenhouses. The leaves are 60-90 cm (2-3 ft) in length, evergreen and very handsome, while the flowers, which are carried on stout, stiffly erect stems, are shaped rather like the crest of a bird of paradise and are orange and violet. The plant always attracts much comment when in bloom and is at its best in late spring/early summer, though later flowers may be produced intermittently.

Grow in a cool or intermediate greenhouse in J.I. No. 2 and repot, when necessary, in early spring. Water very freely while the plant is making growth from about mid-spring to mid-autumn and maintain a moist atmosphere during this period, but be rather sparing with water for the rest of the year, especially during cold weather. No shade is needed at any time. Increase is by seeds in a temperature of 16-18°C/61-65°F in spring or division at potting time. The divisions should be given a little extra warmth and syringed frequently until the plants are well established.

Streptocarpus (Cape Primrose). These are perennial plants with showy, trumpet-shaped flowers produced freely in loose clusters on erect 30-45 cm (1-1½ ft) stems. Flowers can be obtained for most of the year by varying the sowing time. Sow in a temperature of 18°C/65°F in the second half of winter for late summer and autumn flowering or mid-summer for flowering the following spring and summer. Being very small the seeds should be treated exactly like those of begonia (see p. 435). Plants can also be propagated from mature leaves, which will root readily and form new plants if pushed a little way into sandy peat in a propagating frame with bottom heat in spring or summer, but seed is the better method for the amateur. Grow on in a cool or intermediate greenhouse, first in J.I. No. 1, later No. 2, until the seedlings reach 13·7 cm (5½ in) pots in which they will flower. Water freely throughout this period and give weak liquid manure occasionally when in the final pots. Syringe between the pots frequently in summer to maintain moisture in the atmosphere. Shade from direct sunshine from late spring to early autumn. If plants are to be kept from year to year they should be wintered rather dry in a cool light greenhouse. They are seldom worth keeping beyond their second year. Most of the varieties grown are hybrids and colours include blue, mauve, pink, red, salmon and white. Constant Nymph, lavender-blue, and other small-flowered varieties are particularly floriferous.

Streptosolen. *Streptosolen jamesonii* is a greenhouse climber with brilliant orange flowers in the first half of summer. Good specimens can be grown in large pots or in the border in a cool greenhouse. Grow in J.I. No. 2, giving plenty of water during the growing season and keeping the soil just moist for the rest of the year. A little shade is required from strong direct sunshine. Flowering shoots should be pruned hard immediately the flowers fade to prevent the plant from becoming straggly. Increase by cuttings of young growth rooted in spring or summer in a propagating frame, preferably with a little bottom heat.

Syngonium (Goose-foot Plant). These are climbing or sprawling plants grown for their arrow-shaped leaves which may be either all one shade of green or variegated in two shades of green. They are principally used as house plants but can also be grown in intermediate or warm greenhouses. Treatment is the same as for dieffenbachia, with the exception that plants must have some support to which their long stems can be tied. It is an advantage if this can be covered with sphagnum moss kept moist in spring and summer.

Tecoma. See **Campsis** (p. 252).

Thunbergia (Black-eyed Susan). *Thunbergia alata* is an attractive twining plant with orange, black-eyed flowers throughout the summer. It is usually treated as an annual, plants being discarded in autumn after flowering. Germinate the seeds in a temperature of 18°C/65°F in the first half of spring. Pot on the seedlings in J.I. No. 1 until, by early summer, they reach the 13 cm (5 in) pots or hanging baskets in which they will flower. Put several thin canes around each plant so that stems may twine around them and water freely throughout the growing season. Give all the sunlight possible and ventilate as freely as possible consistent with an average temperature of 12-15°C/54-59°F. If grown as a perennial, give it a minimum winter temperature of 7°C/45°F.

Tibouchina. *Tibouchina semidecandra* is an evergreen shrub with violet-purple flowers from late spring to mid-autumn and long stems which are easily trained to wires so that it is usually grown as a climber. It will succeed in a cool or intermediate greenhouse in J.I. No. 2 either in large pots or planted directly in the greenhouse border. Water it freely in spring and summer, rather sparingly in autumn and winter. No shade is required. Prune in early spring to keep the plant within bounds and repot when necessary at the same time of year. Increase by cuttings of firm young stems in spring or summer. Stems can be thinned or cut back in late winter if necessary to restrict growth.

Tillandsia. These plants have dropped out of favour, but one or two kinds are still worth growing, either for their handsome foliage or for their curiously flattened spikes of flowers with showy coloured bracts. Two of the best are *Tillandsia lindeniana*, with stiff rosettes of deep olive-green leaves and blue flowers surrounded by pink bracts, and *T. cyanea*, with narrower leaves. Both will thrive under the same conditions as aechmea.

Torenia. *Torenia fournieri* is an annual with funnel-shaped flowers in two shades of blue with a yellow throat. It is easily grown from seed and if this is sown in the first half of spring and again in early summer, flowers can be obtained from then to late autumn in a cool greenhouse. Sow in a temperature of 15-18°C/59-65°F, pot three or four seedlings together in 7·5 cm (3 in) pots and later move them to 11·2 cm (4½ in) pots using J.I. No. 1 for both pottings. Place a few twigs or canes and ties to support the rather weak stems. Water moderately, grow in a light greenhouse and discard after flowering.

Trachelium. *Trachelium caeruleum* is a dainty plant with dome-shaped heads of feathery blue flowers on 45 cm (1½ ft) stems throughout the summer. There is also a pure white variety. It is almost always grown as an annual, seed being sown in late winter/early spring in a temperature of 15°C/59°F and the seedlings potted on in J.I. No. 1 until, by early summer, they reach 11·2 cm (4½ in) pots. Stake carefully with a few thin twigs or split bamboo canes. Keep in a sunny greenhouse throughout with free ventilation and an average temperature of 12°C/54°F. Water fairly freely throughout the season. After flowering it is best to discard the old plants.

Trachelospermum. *Trachelospermum jasminoides* is a very beautiful climbing plant. It is evergreen and has clusters of fragrant white flowers, not unlike those of the summer jasmine, at their best in the second half of summer. It requires no more than frost protection, will grow in any cool greenhouse and may be trained on wires under the rafters, up pillars or against a wall. It can be grown in large pots, but is better planted directly in the greenhouse border in fairly rich but light and well-drained soil. Plant or pot in early spring. Water very freely in spring and summer, rather sparingly in autumn and winter, and syringe daily while the weather is warm. Give shade from direct sunshine from late spring to early autumn and avoid high temperatures. Shoots can be thinned out and shortened moderately immediately after flowering. Increase is by cuttings of firm young growth taken in summer and rooted in sandy soil in a propagating frame. There is a good variety with silver variegated leaves.

Trachymene (Blue Lace Flower). *Trachymene caerulea* is a dainty annual with heads of tiny blue flowers on 45 cm (1½ ft) stems in mid-summer. It makes a good pot plant for the unheated or cool greenhouse and can be raised from seed sown in a temperature of 15-18°C/59-65°F in late winter or without artificial heat in mid-spring. Pot seedlings singly in J.I. No. 1 in small pots and move on to 11·2 cm (4½ in) pots for flowering. Water moderately. This plant is sometimes called *Didiscus caeruleus*.

Tradescantia (Wandering Jew). This is one of those plants which has so many synonyms that it is almost impossible to sort things out correctly. *Zebrina pendula* is probably the correct name for the plant which is commonly called *Tradescantia zebrina*. It is one of the most useful small trailing foliage plants with which to drape the front of the staging in greenhouses or to use in hanging baskets. It has oval, glossy leaves of bright green striped with white above and purple beneath. *T. fluminensis* is similar but the leaves are not purple beneath. There are several varieties with names such as Variegata and Aurea describing different kinds of variegation.

Both *T. zebrina* and *T. fluminensis* will grow in the cool or intermediate greenhouse or as house plants. They can be grown in small pots or hanging baskets or may be planted direct in a border of soil. Water freely in spring and summer, moderately in autumn and winter. Shade from strong sunshine in summer and syringe occasionally to keep the air reasonably moist. Pot in spring in J.I. No. 2 and increase by cuttings of young shoots in a propagating frame or by detaching rooted pieces at almost any time of the year.

What was once called *Rhoeo discolor* (Boat Lily), is now *T. spathacea*. It is a compact perennial grown for its foliage, the long, rather narrow leaves being dark green above and purple beneath. There is also a variety with cream variegation. It is an easy plant to grow in an intermediate or warm greenhouse or in a room in J.I. No. 2 or peat potting compost. Water freely in spring and summer, moderately in autumn and winter, and shade from late spring to early autumn. Increase by cuttings or division.

T. pallida (once known as *Setcreasea purpurea*) is a sprawling herbaceous plant with downy purple leaves. It makes a good pot plant for an intermediate or warm greenhouse or a winter heated room. Grow in J.I. No. 1 or peat potting compost and water fairly freely from spring to autumn, rather sparingly in winter. Shade from direct sunshine as this improves the colour of the leaves. Stems can be shortened as necessary to keep them within bounds. Propagation is by cuttings in a warm propagator in spring or summer.

Tritonia (Blazing Star). *Tritonia crocata* is an attractive but rather tender corm grown as a pot plant in cool greenhouses. The flowers are in various shades of cream, orange, salmon, pink and purplish red on slender 30 cm (1 ft) high stems and are at their best in early summer. Pot four or five corms together in spring in J.I. No. 1 in a 10 cm (4 in) pot, and grow in a sunny, frost-proof greenhouse. Water very sparingly at first, but with increasing freedom as growth lengthens. After flowering gradually reduce the water supply so that, by about late summer, the foliage dies down and the corms can be stored dry until repotting time. Propagation is by removal of small corms when potting.

Tropaeolum. Besides the tropaeolums mentioned in Chapters 7 and 8, several kinds make good greenhouse pot plants. These include *Tropaeolum tricolorum*, a twining plant with small scarlet and black flowers in spring, *T. tuberosum*, with yellow and red flowers in late summer, and *T. peltophorum*, with orange-scarlet nasturtium-like flowers, double in some varieties, all summer. The first two have tuberous roots which need to be kept nearly dry for varying periods – those of *T. tricolorum* from the time growth dies down in late spring/early summer until it is time to restart them in autumn, those of *T. tuberosum* for a few weeks in winter. Although *T. peltophorum* has no tubers it needs little water in winter, just enough to keep the soil from drying out.

All kinds will thrive in sunny cool or intermediate greenhouses and should be watered normally while in growth. They need canes or some other support. All except double-flowered varieties of *T. peltophorum* can be grown from seed sown in a temperature of 16-18°C/61-65°F in spring and also from cuttings in a propagator in spring or summer; increase the two tuberous-rooted kinds by division just as they are re-starting into growth.

Vallota (Scarborough Lily). See **Cyrtanthus** (p. 467).

Veltheimia. This is another family of bulbous-rooted plants requiring much the same conditions regarding temperatures as the cyrtanthus. They have spikes of flowers rather like little kniphofias (red-hot pokers), pink and green in *Veltheimia capensis*, the most popular kind, which flowers from mid-winter to mid-spring. Pot in late summer/early autumn in J.I. No. 2. Grow in a cool greenhouse and do not force. Water moderately during the succeeding months and then, after the flowers fade, gradually reduce the water supply until the soil is almost dry by early summer, when the plants may rest until late summer.

Verbascum. Once named celsia, these plants are nearly hardy and are excellent for the unheated greenhouse. The best is *Verbascum arcturus*, with 30-45 cm (1-1½ ft) spikes of clear yellow flowers with purple anthers. *V. creticum* is taller and may reach 1·5 m (5 ft). The plants will bloom in 18 cm (7 in) pots and should be raised annually from seed which can either be sown in late winter/early spring for autumn flowering, or in the second half of summer to flower the following spring and early summer. The seed will germinate readily in a temperature of 15-16°C/59-61°F and seedlings should be potted on in J.I. No. 1 compost. Frost protection only is needed in winter and ventilation should at all times be as free as the weather permits.

Verbena, Lemon. See **Lippia** (p. 281).

Vriesia. These are closely related to aechmea and have similar rosettes of stiff leaves enclosing a central 'vase'. The leaves are mottled and banded in various shades of green and grey and the flowers are borne in distinctive flattened spikes surrounded by bracts which are bright red in *Vriesia splendens*, one of the most popular kinds. Cultivation is the same as for aechmea.

Zantedeschia (Arum Lily, Calla). *Zantedeschia aethiopica* is the familiar white arum lily. There are also other species, some with coloured spathes, notably *Z. rehmannii* with smaller pink or purple spathes, *Z. pentlandii*, which is deep yellow, and *Z. elliottiana*, a slightly paler yellow. All have fleshy roots. *Z. aethiopica* should be repotted in late summer/early autumn in J.I. No. 3 and pots 16·2 cm (6½ in) in diameter. Alternatively two or three roots (each with one strong shoot) can be placed in a 25-30 cm (10 in-1 ft) pot. Stand the pots in a frame until near mid-autumn with free ventilation, though protection is only likely to be needed on cold nights. Water moderately at first, rather more freely as growth lengthens. Directly there is danger of frost bring the plants into a cool greenhouse. Later they can be moved to an intermediate greenhouse if early flowers are required, but over-hasty forcing is undesirable. Plants will flower from early winter to late spring according to the amount of heat employed. After flowering harden off the plants, allowing the temperature to drop gradually and giving increasing ventilation. By early summer the plants can be tapped out of their pots and planted out of doors in any sheltered place or can be put outside in their pots. Continue to water freely during dry weather.

Z. *rehmannii*, Z. *elliottiana* and Z. *pentlandii* require a little more warmth in winter, and intermediate or warm house temperatures suit them. Repotting of the two yellow-flowered kinds is best done in late winter as the flowers are produced in summer. They are kept in a greenhouse throughout.

Propagation in all cases is by seed sown in warmth in spring, or by careful division at potting time.

Zebrina. See **Tradescantia** (p. 501).

Chapter 20

Chrysanthemums Indoors and Out

Few flowers have obtained so great a following as the chrysanthemum. There are chrysanthemum societies the world over holding shows devoted exclusively to these flowers and in addition there are chrysanthemum classes in most of the general autumn flower shows. The literature of the chrysanthemum is extensive and the number of amateur and professional specialists immense.

Types. In formulating any classification of this great family the first division to make is between outdoor (or border) and greenhouse varieties. The distinction is less one of hardiness than of season. All chrysanthemum flowers are damaged by frost. In consequence any variety which blooms towards mid-autumn is unreliable for outdoor cultivation without protection. On the other hand varieties blooming in late summer/early autumn can be flowered out of doors even in cool climates, though they may need some protection to bring them safely through severe winters. The generally accepted classification goes as follows – Early-flowering or Border chrysanthemums include all varieties which normally flower in the open before mid-autumn; Mid-season chrysanthemums include all those that flower during mid-autumn; and Late-flowering or Indoor chrysanthemums include all those that normally flower between late autumn and mid-winter in a greenhouse.

In addition to this seasonal division there are many subdivisions principally based upon the shape and size of the flowers. There are, for example, Single, Anemone-centred (semi-double) and fully double-flowered forms in both outdoor and indoor sections. The doubles may be further grouped into Large-flowered Exhibition types and Small-flowered Decorative types. Then there are forms with the outer petals curving outwards (Reflexed), in contrast to others with all the petals curving inwards (Incurved), and yet others in which the inner petals curl inwards and the outer petals curl outwards (Intermediate). The Exhibition Incurved petals are placed with such accuracy that each bloom makes a perfect globe. The production of the faultless Incurved is perhaps the height of the chrysanthemum grower's art.

Even so the list of chrysanthemum types is not complete. To it must be added the Pompon, with masses of small rounded blooms; the Thread-petalled or Rayonnante type; Spoon-petalled in which the inner section of the petal is rolled and the outer part flattened; Korean, a race of very hardy bushy chrysanthemums with masses of fairly small single or double flowers.

The Cascade chrysanthemum is yet another interesting class. It is its habit that is distinctive, the stems being particularly wiry and freely branched. Left to its own devices it makes a big bush with small single flowers, but with a little skilful training it can be made to hang down in a perfect cascade of growth and flower. The Charm chrysanthemum is similar, but bushy and compact without the tendency to droop.

Propagation. All chrysanthemums can be increased by division of the roots but in practice this method is not used except, occasionally, for the Korean and commoner outdoor types. Increase is by cuttings and results in healthier plants.

Seed, which provides the only other means of increase, germinates readily in a warm greenhouse in spring but seedlings vary greatly in colour and sometimes in type so this is not a satisfactory means of increasing selected varieties except in the case of the Charm varieties. It is, however, the method by which most new varieties are produced.

Cuttings can be taken at any time of the year, from early winter to early spring being the main propagating season with extension to the second half of spring for small plants to be flowered in 11·2 cm (4½ in) pots.

The best cuttings are those prepared from shoots which come through the soil directly from the roots. Shoots from the old woody stems can be used but seldom make such satisfactory plants or produce such good blooms.

Plenty of suitable basal shoots are usually produced by the plant after it has finished flowering. As far as possible work should be started on the greenhouse varieties, particularly those that are to be flowered on second crown buds (see p. 509), the outdoor varieties being left until late winter/early spring.

All the cuttings are taken in exactly the same way. The shoots are severed when about 5-7·5 cm (2-3 in) long. They are cut off below soil level and prepared by being trimmed cleanly just below a joint. The lower leaves are removed, the base of the cutting is moistened and dipped in hormone rooting powder and the cutting is dibbled, about 18 mm (¾ in) deep, into sandy soil. This may be in a pot, box or bed but should, for preference, be in a slightly heated greenhouse. Cuttings can be struck without heat but it is more difficult and there are likely to be more failures than when a temperature of 7-10°C/45-50°F can be maintained irrespective of weather. If the soil itself can be warmed it will speed root formation.

The cuttings need not be kept in a very close, damp atmosphere, but they should be watered fairly freely and shaded from strong sunshine. They usually flag a little at first but pick up after a week or so and begin to root in from two to three weeks after insertion.

Taking a chrysanthemum cutting. The best cuttings are prepared from basal shoots 5-7·5 cm (2-3 in) long. Remove the lower leaves and trim off cleanly just below a joint. Dibble the cuttings about 18 mm (¾ in) deep around the edge of a pot filled with sandy soil

Potting. As soon as the cuttings start to grow they should be lifted carefully and potted singly in small flower pots in either J.I. No. 1 or peat potting compost. Thereafter the plants should be grown on steadily in a temperature of 10–16°C/50–61°F with as much ventilation as the weather allows and all the daylight possible.

They will need to be potted on as the pots become filled with roots. First they will go into 10 cm (4 in) pots and then, in the case of indoor varieties, into the 23 cm (9 in) pots in which they will flower. For each successive potting the soil mixture is made rather coarser than before and more fertilizer is added (see p. 508). Some growers prefer to add a little well-rotted dung to the compost for the final potting and this certainly does help to counteract any mineral deficiencies in the soil, but J.I. No. 2 compost for the intermediate pottings and J.I. No 3 for the final potting will be quite satisfactory.

The final potting for indoor varieties should not be later than mid-summer; usually it is nearly a month earlier than this. Outdoor chrysanthemums can generally be planted out of doors in late spring by which time, as they are rooted late, they may still not have out-grown their first pots.

All potting, and especially the later pottings of indoor varieties, should be very firm unless peat potting compost is used.

Planting Outdoor Chrysanthemums. The ground in which outdoor chrysanthemums are to be planted must be well dug and moderately manured. Well-rotted stable manure is best for this purpose but any form of bulky organic manure may be used at the rate of about 50 kg to 9·6 sq m (1 cwt to 12 sq yd). If this is not available, work in peat at about 2 kg per 0·8 sq m (4 lb per sq yd). Finish this preparatory work at least a month in advance of planting time so that the ground may have time to settle, completing it with a dusting of bonemeal, 113 g per 0·8 sq m (4 oz per sq yd), well raked in.

Potting up rooted cuttings. As soon as the cuttings are growing well place singly in small flower pots in J.I. No. 1 or peat potting compost. By now they will have made good roots

Plant out when the soil is in good working condition, neither too wet nor too dry, and choose a period when the weather seems fairly settled and mild. For two or three weeks beforehand the plants should be in an unheated frame with gradually increasing ventilation to harden them off, and it is unwise to plant them out until they have had at least a week without any protection other than that given by the surrounding walls of the frame.

Plant firmly and space the plants at least 38 cm (15 in) apart. A more usual method for cutting or exhibition plants is to set them this distance apart in double rows with 75 cm (2½ ft) alleyways between.

Summer Treatment. Apart from stopping and disbudding which are described separately (see pp. 508-10), summer treatment consists of staking and tying, necessary for both outdoor and indoor types; watering, usually only necessary with plants in pots, feeding, and keeping a close watch for pests or disease.

Pot plants can usually be stood out of doors by the first week in early summer. A sunny position should be chosen, open but free from cutting draughts. It is an advantage if the pots can stand on a good ash or gravel base or on slates or planks. This will prevent worms entering through the drainage holes, blocking them up.

Water may be needed daily during hot weather. Sufficient must be given at each application to soak right through the soil and run out at the drainage hole in the bottom of the pot. No more water should be given till the soil is drying out.

Support is best given by 1·2 m (4 ft) canes – at least one for each plant and preferably more for big specimens. With pot plants it is a wise precaution to drive stout stakes firmly into the standing ground every 60-90 cm (2-3 ft), with a horizontal wire strained between them 1 m (3½ ft) above ground level. Each cane can then be tied to this wire, which will prevent many breakages during windy weather.

Planting out outdoor chrysanthemums. The plants should first have been hardened off for two or three weeks in an unheated frame to accustom them to outdoor conditions

Feeding. This may be started as soon as the plants are well settled in their summer quarters and continued until the flower buds begin to show colour. Little and often is the rule and feeding should be varied. There are many good proprietary chrysanthemum fertilizers which should be used according to manufacturers' instructions. These may be alternated with natural liquid manure made by steeping well-decayed dung in water and diluting the liquid to the colour of straw. This can then be used freely in the same way as plain water.

A good chemical fertilizer can be made at home with four parts by weight superphosphate of lime, two parts sulphate of ammonia and one part sulphate of potash. Use this mixture at the rate of a teaspoonful per plant or 4·5 l (1 gal) of water every seven to ten days.

Autumn Protection. By mid-autumn most indoor varieties should be removed from their summer standing ground and brought into a greenhouse. Outdoor varieties that have not finished blooming should be protected. A few degrees of frost may be enough to damage the flowers or flower buds though the plants themselves will suffer no harm from much colder weather.

Give the plants as much room as possible in the greenhouse. The more light and air they receive the better. Overcrowding will encourage mildew and grey mould (botrytis) and may spoil the quality of the flowers, though too much heat is equally bad and will weaken the plants. Never forget that they are nearly hardy, that little more than frost protection is required and that the more sturdy the plants are the better the blooms will be.

Treatment after Flowering. When the blooms fade or have been cut, the plants, whether indoors or out, should be cut back to within several centimetres of soil level. This will encourage the production of the basal shoots which provide the best material for propagation. At this stage it is an advantage to lift outdoor varieties and transfer them to a frame or greenhouse. The roots can be packed quite close together providing there is a good dividing mark between one variety and another. This measure of protection will encourage the production of cuttings and insure against losses in the open border, which are likely to occur particularly in wet, cold winters. Since each old plant will provide a number of cuttings it is not necessary to keep all of them unless stock is to be greatly increased.

Stopping. In the linked operations of stopping and disbudding lies much of the art of chrysanthemum culture. To understand either a knowledge of the natural habit of the chrysanthemum is necessary.

Left to its own devices a rooted cutting, after growing a single stem for a while, will produce a small flower bud. This is known as a 'break bud' because it prevents further extension of that particular shoot and causes it to branch or 'break'. Whether this flower bud, or for that matter any subsequent flower bud, develops into a flower depends on a combination of temperature and night length. Normally in cool climates conditions are not right in late spring/early summer when those first buds appear and they simply wither away. The shoots which appear as a result of this breaking will grow on again without further branching until they too are terminated by flower buds which are known as 'first crown buds' and are usually quite capable of developing into good flowers.

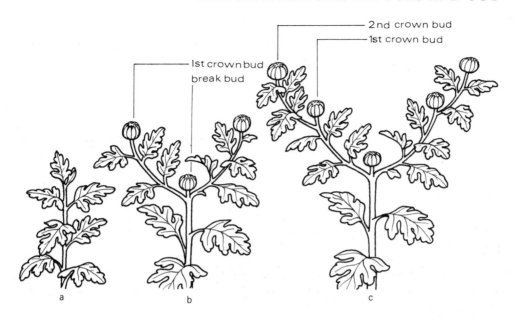

Chrysanthemum stopping and timing diagram. (a) The first single stem made by a rooted cutting. (b) In time a flower bud will appear at the tip of this stem, causing it to branch. This first bud is therefore called a 'break bud'. (c) More flower buds will be formed, the 'first crown buds'. As a result more branches will appear to produce 'second crown buds'. If the plant is allowed to go on branching 'terminal buds', surrounded by more flower buds, will appear

Whether they do so or not the plant, if left alone, will quite likely produce a fresh lot of shoots with more flower buds of similar character. They are known as 'second crown' buds. However, there will come a stage when the plant makes no further upward growth, every shoot, however short, being terminated by a flower bud. The buds of this last group are known as 'terminal buds'.

It will be seen that the gardener usually has a choice of three distinct sets of flower buds. All differ in the time at which they appear and the last differs in kind.

By deciding arbitrarily which of these buds shall flower and which shall not, the gardener can influence to a considerable degree the time at which the flowers are produced. This timing is of importance: it is by this means that the gardener can so manipulate things that a chrysanthemum which would normally be too late or too early for a particular show is, in fact, just right on the day. He can also hasten the outdoor flowering of varieties which might otherwise be damaged by frost.

There is yet another consideration. Experience has proved that, despite the similarity in appearance of the first two stages of this bud series, the quality of bloom produced by each is not always identical. There are some varieties which give a more perfect flower from the first crown bud than from the second crown bud and vice versa. The clever exhibitor will naturally cash in on such knowledge.

Nor is it necessary for the gardener to wait until the plant branches naturally through the production of one or other of these buds. He can hasten nature's process by nipping out the growing tip of the plant at any stage. For example, if he knows that a certain variety will take ten weeks from the production of its break bud to the production of its first crown bud and that this will be a week too late for his purpose, he may pinch the tip out of the young plant a week before the break bud is due to appear. Later buds may be timed in the same way.

Finally there is the peculiarity of the terminal bud to be considered. This seldom produces as good an individual bloom as either of the crown buds but, unlike them, it is surrounded by a lot of other flower buds at practically the same stage of development. If all are left they will together form a spray of small flowers.

Disbudding. So much then, for stopping and timing. Now how does the gardener get the plant to flower on the particular bud or buds he has selected? Simply by removing all other growths which might interfere with this. If it is the crown buds he is after, and these are the best for giving one fine bloom per stem, he will remove all other shoots which appear in the axils of the leaves below them. This kind of disbudding is really little different from that applied to many other kinds of flower though the chrysanthemum grower, perhaps liking to be different, seldom calls it disbudding, but refers to it as 'taking the bud'. However, if it is the terminal buds he wants in order to obtain a nice spray of flowers he may do precisely the opposite, and nip out the central flower bud, leaving the side buds to develop. The virtue of this is that the central bud, if left, would start to open first and its flower might already be fading when the others in the cluster were at their peak.

Stopping and bud-taking suggestions will be found in most catalogues issued by chrysanthemum specialists. They use a peculiar jargon of their own which needs a little understanding. Here are a few of the usual phrases with their meaning:

'Natural break, first crown' means that the plant is to be allowed to grow on and branch once naturally, after which the first bud that appears will be preserved for flowering.

'Stop April 20th, for first crown' is similar to the last except that the tip of the rooted cutting is to be pinched out on April 20th instead of being allowed to grow on until a break bud appears and stops it.

'Natural break, second crown' means that the cutting is to be allowed to branch naturally until the first crown bud appears, when it will be rubbed off and the plant left to branch again and produce second crown buds which will then be preserved for flowering.

'Stop May 1st and June 1st for second crown buds' means that the object is to anticipate the normal branching of the plant twice and so get a second crown, but considerably earlier than by natural means.

It may appear from all this talk about branching that the later the bud is retained the more flowers the plant will carry. Left alone in other respects this is certainly true, but such a result does not always suit the chrysanthemum grower's ideas. Too many flowers means that all will be small. So, if the plant is being grown for exhibition, there is usually a drastic thinning out of shoots after each stopping or natural branching.

If the gardener's object is simply to obtain plenty of good flowers without bothering too much just when they develop these individual stopping and timing instructions can be ignored. Perfectly satisfactory results will be produced by pinching out the tips of all early-flowering varieties when the plants are 21·2 cm (8½ in) high and pinching mid-autumn and late-flowering varieties twice, first when the plants are 21·2 cm (8½ in) high and a second time when the side shoots are 21·2 cm (8½ in) long.

510

Chapter 21

Cacti and Succulents

Although it is customary to talk of cacti and succulents as though they were distinct groups of plants the fact is that the term 'succulents', embracing as it does fleshy plants, includes cacti which merely form a section in the group. Cacti all belong to one family of plants, the *Cactaceae*, whereas succulents belong to many different families, often quite unrelated. The thick, fleshy leaves or stems common to all these plants are constructed to hold moisture and so enable them to withstand long periods of drought. This really gives the key to the cultivation of cacti and succulents. They all come from regions where drought is common and many are desert plants accustomed to a maximum of sunshine and, at any rate for long periods, a minimum of water.

In their native habitats these plants mostly go to rest during the dry season and then grow very actively when rain does fall. Almost all are used to stony or sandy soils and for successful cultivation must have a more open and gritty compost than is common for other classes of greenhouse plants.

Not all cacti and succulents are tender and need greenhouse protection. Some are hardy enough to remain out of doors throughout the year, at any rate in the milder parts of the country and near the coast. Nevertheless, it is as pot plants that cacti and succulents are most familiar.

There is great variety in form and character among these plants and though some seldom produce flowers and are grown principally for their strange shapes, patterned spines or dense covering of filaments, others bloom quite freely and are often of exceptional beauty. It is possible, in a cool greenhouse, to grow a wide selection of these plants and many can be grown successfully inside a sunny window. In summer, they can be stood outside, but in winter they must be brought into the room lest they be damaged by frost.

In general cacti and succulents are very tough plants in the sense that they will put up with a lot of ill treatment, and it is perhaps for this reason that they so often appeal to people who have to garden under unfavourable conditions, such as in the heart of a big city. However, to obtain the best results it is desirable to give the plants what they need, which is plenty of sun and moisture during the growing period, sharp drainage at all times and a rather dry, buoyant atmosphere even in winter. This will involve the use of a little artificial heat at times, as much to keep air on the move and rid it of surplus moisture as to raise the temperature.

Many cacti and succulents are naturally small plants, while others grow so slowly that they can be kept in small pots for a good many years. Such kinds are most useful to the town gardener, who can accommodate a considerable variety of plants in a small area, and for growing on a window-sill.

The things to be avoided for most cacti and succulents are drip, damp and shade which, if permitted for long, will encourage soft growth and eventual decay. However, the epiphytic cacti, of which epiphyllum, schlumbergera and zygocactus are the principal kinds, do appreciate some shade from early summer to early autumn, and, placed outside, can be accommodated during that period in a shelter of slats spaced about 18 mm (¾ in) apart.

It must not be assumed from what has already been said that when the plants are growing, which is usually between mid-spring and late summer, water should be given in dribs and drabs. In desert regions long periods of drought are often interspersed with periods of heavy rainfall, so cacti must usually be watered quite as freely while they are growing as other greenhouse plants. It is only at the end of this period that the watering-can should be put away or used sparingly. Roughly speaking during the active period cacti and succulents will need watering two or three times a week, whereas at other times water may only be required on an average every four to six weeks. If the weather is damp or cold the plants may be left for much longer periods without water. Even if they shrivel slightly during this resting season they will suffer no serious harm and will plump up and start to grow freely again when the spring arrives.

Most cacti and succulents will grow well in J.I. No. 2 plus $\frac{1}{6}$ its bulk of very sharp coarse sand or grit. More drainage crocks should be used in the bottom of each pot than is normal for greenhouse plants. Early spring is the best season for potting and the roots should be made reasonably firm.

Care must be taken not to put cacti out of doors for the summer months until all danger of frost is passed, which usually means not until early summer. For the same reason the plants should be safely housed again at least by mid-autumn. It is usually best to place the plants outside in their flower pots, plunging these to their rims in a bed of ashes or sand, but a few succulents can be planted out in rockeries or sunny borders. Many species of lampranthus (mesembryanthemum) will grow freely in this way and make a splendid display with their brilliant flowers in early summer.

Propagation can in many cases be effected by careful division or removal of offsets at potting time. Some kinds however, and most species of lampranthus are notable examples, have a more shrubby habit with a single woody stem at the base which cannot be divided. With these cuttings often provide a ready means of increase. The cuttings should be prepared from young, non-flowering growths, either side shoots or the tips of stems. The second half of summer is usually the most favourable period for taking these, though propagation can be continued at almost any time of the year. The cuttings should be prepared in the ordinary way and inserted in pure sand or very sandy soil in a propagating frame, preferably within the greenhouse.

In a few instances propagation can be carried out by leaves alone. *Sedum stahlii* is a notable example of this. Its little, globular leaves fall off of their own accord in the autumn and will often root in the sand or gravel on the greenhouse staging without any further attention. Many hundreds of plants can be raised in a short time by this method.

Seed is a universal method of propagation for practically all cacti and succulents though, as the seed is sometimes extremely small, it must be handled with care. Sow it on the surface of seed or peat seed compost and cover either very lightly or not at all. In either case each tray or pot of seed should be protected with a pane of glass. When water is required give it by immersing the pot or tray almost to its rim in water and not by applying water from above, as even through a fine rose the water may wash soil away from the tiny roots.

It is not possible in the scope of this book to give complete lists of desirable cacti and succulents as these run into many hundreds. They will be found in the catalogues of trade specialists and also in books devoted exclusively to this subject. However, here are a few suggestions for the beginner.

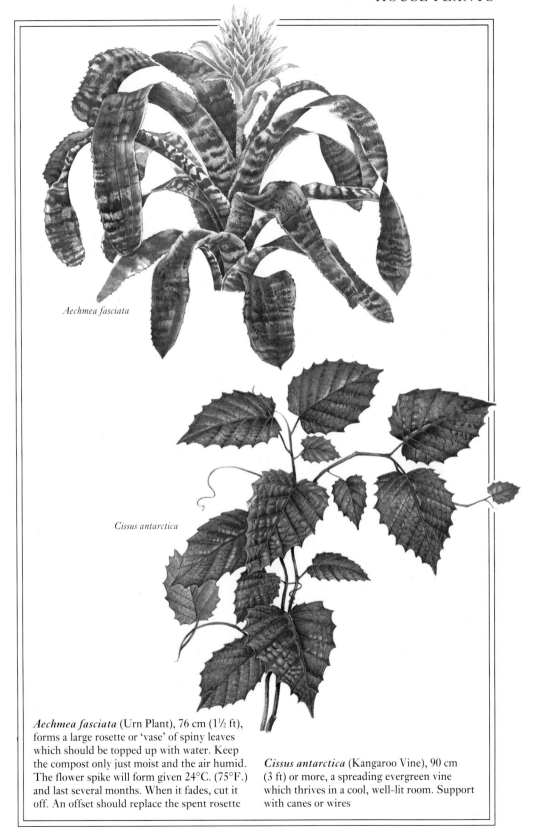

Aechmea fasciata

Cissus antarctica

Aechmea fasciata (Urn Plant), 76 cm (1½ ft), forms a large rosette or 'vase' of spiny leaves which should be topped up with water. Keep the compost only just moist and the air humid. The flower spike will form given 24°C. (75°F.) and last several months. When it fades, cut it off. An offset should replace the spent rosette

Cissus antarctica (Kangaroo Vine), 90 cm (3 ft) or more, a spreading evergreen vine which thrives in a cool, well-lit room. Support with canes or wires

Cryptanthus bromelioides Tricolor

Epipremnum aureum

Cissus discolor

Cryptanthus bromelioides **Tricolor** (Earth Star), 13 cm (6 in), which thrives in good light in a minimum 13°C. (55°F.). 30 cm (1 ft) in diameter

Cissus discolor, 1.5 m (5 ft), comes from the tropics, so needs a minimum 16°C. (60°F.) and high humidity. Stand on moist gravel to keep air moist and provide support

Epipremnum aureum (Devil's Ivy), 1.8 m (6 ft), climbs with support or trails. Care as for monstera

Fatsia japonica Variegata

x Fatshedera lizei

Fatsia japonica

x Fatshedera lizei
Variegata

x Fatshedera lizei (Ivy Tree), to 1.2 m (4 ft) indoors. Pinch tips of its stems to keep bushy

x Fatshedera lizei **Variegata** is more decorative but less vigorous. Give it good light

Fatsia japonica (False Castor Oil Palm), 90 cm-1.5 m (3-5 ft), is a hardy shrub growing as wide across as it is tall indoors, and much larger outdoors. It is valued for its shiny palmate leaves which benefit from misting in summer

Fatsia japonica **Variegata** is similar though less vigorous and marbled creamy white. Keep in good light

515

Hedera canariensis Gloire de Marengo

Glechoma hederacea Variegata

Glechoma hederacea Variegata, 90 cm (3 ft) or more, the variegated form of Ground Ivy, is a hardy trailing plant valued for hanging baskets. Give good light and water well in summer

Hedera canariensis Gloire de Marengo (Canary Island Ivy), 1.8 m (6 ft) or more, grows outdoors but is less hardy than Common Ivy. It has larger leaves and wine-coloured young stems

Hedera helix
Little Diamond

Hedera helix Luzii

Hedera helix Gold Child

Monstera deliciosa

Hedera helix Little Diamond, Lutzii and
Gold Child, 1.8 m (6 ft) or more, are three of
many varieties of Common Ivy to be grown as
pot plants. They are hardy plants so avoid high
temperatures and dry air and roots. Keep them
below 18°C. (65°F.) in good light. Provide
support or let them trail

Monstera deliciosa (Swiss Cheese Plant),
1.8 m (6 ft), grows strongly as a house plant,
given at least 10°C. (50 F.), preferably 18 C.
(65F.), good light and slight shade. By nature
it is a climber. Young or undernourished
plants may have no leaf perforations. Water
freely in summer, cautiously in winter. Mist
daily, feed weekly in summer. Clean leaves
monthly

Philodendron scandens var. oxycardium

Philodendron selloum

Philodendron scandens var. oxycardium (Sweetheart Vine), 1.5 m (5 ft), is a strong climber or trailer, best pinched back to keep it in bounds. It needs support. Water it well in summer, moderately in winter. Spray daily with water, clean foliage monthly

Philodendron selloum (Lacy Tree Philodendron), 1.5 m (5 ft), makes a bold plant with exotic-looking jungly foliage which can spread to 1.8 m (6 ft). It needs a minimum 13-16°C. (55-60°F.), daily misting and generous watering in summer.

Rhoicissus rhomboidea

Rhoicissus rhomboidea Ellen Danica

Solenostemom scutellarioides

Rhoicissus rhomboidea, (Grape Ivy), 1.5 m (5 ft) or more, is grown like *Cissus antarctica*, but more vigorous and notably tolerant of dark corners

Rhoicissus rhomboidea **Ellen Danica** is similar but with deeply cut leaves

Solenostemom scutellarioides, 60 cm (2 ft), needs bright light to maintain good leaf colour and at least 13°C. (55°F.). Water well, feed fortnightly, pinch tips of straggly stems and remove flower spikes. Pot on as necessary in soil- or peat-based compost. Cuttings root easily in heat. Good seed strains available

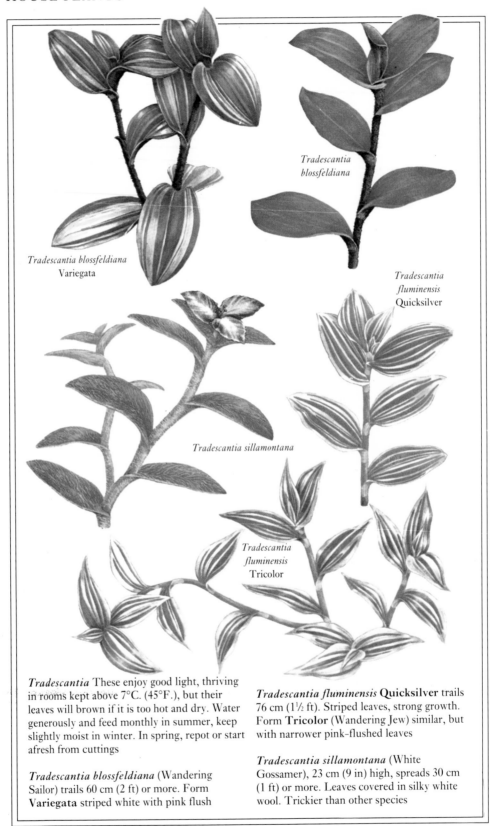

Tradescantia blossfeldiana

Tradescantia blossfeldiana
Variegata

Tradescantia fluminensis
Quicksilver

Tradescantia sillamontana

Tradescantia fluminensis
Tricolor

Tradescantia These enjoy good light, thriving in rooms kept above 7°C. (45°F.), but their leaves will brown if it is too hot and dry. Water generously and feed monthly in summer, keep slightly moist in winter. In spring, repot or start afresh from cuttings

Tradescantia blossfeldiana (Wandering Sailor) trails 60 cm (2 ft) or more. Form **Variegata** striped white with pink flush

Tradescantia fluminensis **Quicksilver** trails 76 cm (1½ ft). Striped leaves, strong growth. Form **Tricolor** (Wandering Jew) similar, but with narrower pink-flushed leaves

Tradescantia sillamontana (White Gossamer), 23 cm (9 in) high, spreads 30 cm (1 ft) or more. Leaves covered in silky white wool. Trickier than other species

Grandpa Dickson

Pascali

Peace

Just Joey

National Trust

Mischief

Mischief, 90 cm (3 ft), has weather-resistant flowers, excellent for bedding

Large-Flowered Roses (Hybrid Teas) form impressive blooms, splendid in the garden, in vases and on the showbench

National Trust, 76 cm (2½ ft), a bright red, is a prolific flowerer

Grandpa Dickson, 90 cm (3 ft), a vigorous grower, is slightly fragrant

Pascali, 90 cm (3 ft), a fine white, is slightly fragrant but susceptible to mildew

Just Joey, 76 cm (2½ ft), is slightly fragrant

Peace, 1.2 m (4 ft), changes from cream to blush-pink as it ages

Pink Favorite

Piccadilly

Wendy
Cussons

Rose Gaujard

Silver Jubilee

Troika

More Large-Flowered Roses:

Piccadilly, 76 cm (2½ ft), is a bright bicolor
with weather-resistant blooms

Pink Favourite, 76 cm (2½ ft), bears specially
handsome slightly fragrant blooms

Rose Gaujard, 90 cm (3 ft), is slightly
fragrant and weather-resistant

Silver Jubilee, 76 cm (2½ ft), a prolific
flowerer, has fragrant disease-free blooms

Troika, 90 cm (3 ft), opens large long-lasting
fragrant blooms. Disease-resistant

Wendy Cussons, 90 cm (3 ft), prolific with
weather-resistant scented blooms

Evelyn Fison

Korresia

Iceberg

Escapade

Elizabeth of Glamis

Eyepaint

Cluster-Flowered (Floribunda) **Roses** for beds crammed with colour:

Elizabeth of Glamis, 76 cm (2½ ft), scented but susceptible to mildew

Escapade, 76 cm (2½ ft), unusual colour, musky scent. Fine among shrub roses

Evelyn Fison, 76 cm (2½ ft), bright red, weather-resistant. Fine for borders

Eyepaint, 1.2 m (4 ft), small brilliant red flowers. Good for hedging

Iceberg, 1.2 m (4 ft), vigorous, free-flowering, susceptible to mildew

Korresia, 76 cm (2½ ft), dwarf with large double scented blooms

Ballerina Frühlingsgold

Chinatown

Frau Dagmar
Hartopp

Fred Loads

Golden Wings

Shrub Roses for informal planting:

Ballerina, 1 m (3½ ft), compact, many tiny flowers in summer and autumn

Chinatown, 1.5 m (5 ft), very vigorous with plenty of double flowers

Frau Dagmar Hartopp, 1.3 m (4½ ft), fragrant single flowers, large red hips, repeat-flowering

Fred Loads, 1.8 m (6 ft), repeat-flowering weather-resistant scented blooms

Frühlingsgold, 2.4 m (8 ft), a large spreading shrub, early flowering

Golden Wings, 1.8 m (6 ft), large single flowers, weather-resistant, repeat-flowering

Galway Bay

Golden Showers

Dublin Bay

Handel

Danse du Feu

Compassion

Climbing Roses for walls and pergolas:

Compassion, 2.4 m (8 ft), strongly scented and ideal for walls, fences, pillars

Danse du Feu, 2.4 m (8 ft), abundant, slightly fragrant, disease-resistant blooms

Dublin Bay, 2.4 m (8 ft), opens plenty of slightly fragrant blooms

Galway Bay, 2.1 m (7 ft), slightly scented. Remove old wood after flowering

Golden Showers, 1.8 m (6 ft), bushy, slightly fragrant but susceptible to black spot.

Handel, 3 m (10 ft), opens its specially fine creamy flowers flushed red at the margins in summer and autumn

Pink Perpetue

Swan Lake

Maigold

Parkdirektor Riggers

Mermaid

More Climbing Roses:

Maigold, 4.5 m (15 ft), vigorous, strongly scented flowers. Also makes a shrub

Mermaid, 6 m (20 ft), very vigorous and thorny, many large single scented blooms

Parkdirektor Riggers, 3.6 m (12 ft), vigorous with weather-resistant blooms

Pink Perpetue, 2.1 m (7 ft), bears many long-lasting weather-resistant, slightly fragrant blooms

Swan Lake, 2.4 m (8 ft), vigorous, weather-resistant, prone to mildew and black spot

Sander's White

Dorothy Perkins

American Pillar

Albertine

Albéric Barbier

Rambler Roses are strong growers, fine for a wall or pergola:

Albéric Barbier, 7.5 m (25 ft), with pale yellow blooms that fade to white

Albertine, 5.4 m (18 ft), is somewhat fragrant but prone to mildew and black spot

American Pillar, 6 m (20 ft), makes strong growth, prone to mildew. Cut out old wood to base

Dorothy Perkins, 4.5 m (15 ft), blooms prolifically but is prone to mildew

Sander's White, 3 m (10 ft), good for an archway or ground cover. Prone to mildew

527

Canary Bird

Rosa moyesii

Rosa rubrifolia

Rosa virginiana

Snow Carpet

Complicata

Swany

Rosy Cushion

Wild Roses have a delicate charm:

Canary Bird (*Rosa xanthina*), 1.5 m (5 ft), is vigorous, blooms early summer

Complicata, 1.8 m (6 ft), is fragrant

Rosa moyesii, 2.7 m (9 ft), opens bright red flowers followed by flask-shaped hips

Rosa rubrifolia, 1.8 m (6 ft), is grown mainly for its glaucous foliage

Rosa virginiana, 1.5 m (5 ft), opens pink blooms, later red hips and autumn tints

Ground Cover Roses are useful too:

Rosy Cushion spreads 90 cm (3 ft)

Snow Carpet flowers until autumn

Swany, semi-prostrate, spreads 1 m (3½ ft)

Aeonium. These are succulents with flat rosettes of fleshy leaves. They need rather more water in winter than most succulents.

Agave. These produce large, upstanding rosettes of stiff, often spine-tipped leaves which may be blue-grey striped or banded with cream or white. *Agave americana* is known as the century plant because it is slow in producing its yellowish-green flowers on very tall stems.

Aloe. These have rosettes of upstanding stiff leaves which are handsomely mottled with grey and white in the popular partridge aloe, *Aloe variegata*.

Aporocactus. This is known as the rat-tailed cactus because of its long, thin, cylindrical stems.

Astrophytum. These are known as star cacti because the more or less globular plants have star-like ribs. They like an alkaline compost containing crushed chalk or limestone.

Bryophyllum. These produce little plantlets on the leaves which fall off and grow into new plants. The most popular kind, *Bryophyllum pinnatum*, is called the air plant, life plant or floppers. These are sometimes known as kalanchoë.

Cephalocereus. Cacti making tall cylinders of growth covered in long grey hairs. The most popular kind, *Cephalocereus senilis*, is known as the old man cactus.

Cereus. These make tall columns of growth bearing large flowers, usually white, which open at night.

Conophytum. This is a genus of stone mimics with small growths like flat buttons. Some kinds have quite showy flowers.

Cotyledon. See p. 184.

Echeveria. See p. 468.

Echinocactus. Large, globular cacti covered in spines. The most popular kind, *Echinocactus grusonii*, is known as the golden barrel cactus or mother-in-law's chair.

Echinocereus. A very varied group of small cacti flowering when quite young and often with very attractive flowers. All are very spiny.

Echinopsis. Small barrel-shaped plants strongly ribbed. Many have showy and some-times scented flowers.

Epiphyllum. These are epiphytic cacti with large and very showy flowers from about mid-spring to early summer. They rest in the first half of winter when they require little or no water. In nature these grow in trees or on rocks and in cultivation they like some shade in spring and summer and a compost containing extra peat or leaf-mould.

Euphorbia. Some kinds are not succulents but this is a very large and varied genus and contains a number of succulent species, some branched like little shrubs, some with snake-like stems, some very swollen. All prefer intermediate to cool house conditions.

Fenestraria. A very curious stone mimic with a little transparent window in the top of each growth to let in light.

Ferocactus. Cacti with short, thick, very spiny growths. They are known as barrel cacti.

Gibbaeum. Another stone mimic known as shark's head because of the shape of the cleft growths.

Gymnocalycium. Small globular plants with quite showy flowers. They like some shade in summer. One kind, *G. mihanovichii*, produces sports with red, yellow, pink or white growth. These are propagated by grafting on to ordinary green-stemmed cacti.

Harrisia. Plants with long, thin sprawling growths and white scented flowers which open at night.

Lampranthus. These are the plants gardeners usually call mesembryanthemum. See p. 480.

Lithops. Pebble-like growths of various colours and markings.

Lobivia. Small globular or cylindrical cacti which flower freely. There are yellow, orange, pink and carmine flowered forms.

Mammillaria. Globular or cylindrical spiny growths with small flowers produced in circles.

Notocactus. Small, more or less globular growths which have red and yellow flowers on top in season.

Opuntia. Big, circular flat growths or pads growing one on top of another to produce a large, branched plant.

Pleiospilos. Stone mimics with pairs of fleshy growths spread outwards, one pair on top of another but at right angles to it.

Rhipsalidopsis. The flattened, arching stems of *Rhipsalidopsis gaertneri* carry very attractive flowers in spring. This plant used to be called *Schlumbergera gaertneri* and is commonly known as the Easter cactus. It is suitable for growing in a hanging basket. Treatment is the same as for epiphyllum.

Schlumbergera. There are several kinds flowering in winter, *S. buckleyi* being known as the Christmas cactus and *S. truncata* as the crab or lobster cactus. These plants were formerly called zygocactus and are similar to rhipsalidopsis bearing flowers in shades of crimson, magenta, lilac and white. Both kinds flower when days are short and nights long and artificial light may interfere with this and prevent flowering. Otherwise cultivation is as for epiphyllum.

Sedum (Stonecrops). See p. 226.

Sempervivum (House Leek). See p. 227.

Senecio. *Senecio articulata* is known as the candle plant because of the shape of its stems.

Stapelia. Plants with thick ribbed growths bearing curious mottled or striped brown, purple and yellow flowers shaped like starfish. The flowers of some kinds have an unpleasant smell.

Trichocereus. Similar to cereus but with spines, not hairs. The flowers are large and white.

Zygocactus. See **Schlumbergera** (p. 530).

Chapter 22
Helpful Tips for House Plants

Almost all house plants are also greenhouse plants and what makes them suitable for cultivation indoors is an ability to grow in relatively poor light and a rather dry atmosphere. Very few plants grown primarily for their flowers will put up with room conditions for more than a few months at a time, so most permanent house plants are grown for their foliage. Some are much tougher and more long suffering than others and a few will even survive well away from windows, but most prefer to be quite close to a window. In Holland and Denmark, where house plants are grown in vast numbers, special large windows with deep tiled ledges inside are often planned specially for displays of house plants.

Another difficulty is that room temperatures often fluctuate greatly. Central heating helps house plants as the temperature is likely to be more constant.

The air in living rooms is usually a good deal drier than in greenhouses, and this can cause leaf scorching and attacks by red spider mites and scale insects. Some improvement can be effected by plunging pots in moist peat or packing damp sphagnum moss around them. Ornamental containers can be obtained for house plants which can be filled with peat or sphagnum moss for this purpose, and some have trays to be filled with sand or ashes or self-watering devices. Climbing plants can be trained around stakes or pillars that have been packed with sphagnum moss held in place with wire netting and kept moist. Leaves can also be sponged frequently with clear water or sprayed lightly with water, not always easy indoors.

Cultivation. The rules for watering, feeding, repotting, pruning and propagation are more or less the same as for these plants when grown in greenhouses and are described in Chapter 19. Because of the lower light intensity in rooms plants cannot make use of so much food and there is some advantage in using rather mild feeds such as seaweed extracts. Just a very little added to the water once a week from late spring to late summer will usually be sufficient, but the rate of growth and the colour of the leaves are the best guide to correct feeding.

Though house plants will grow well in John Innes potting composts there is a tendency to use soilless composts based on peat for them, mainly because these are clean and light. All can be conveniently purchased in plastic bags ready for use. Plastic pots are also favoured because of their lightness and cleanliness. The combination of peat compost and plastic pot helps to retain moisture and means that plants need not be watered quite so frequently as if they were in soil compost and clay pots. All the same, it is wise to look over house plants daily in summer and at least every other day during the rest of the year.

Easily Grown House Plants. Aechmea, *Araucaria excelsa*, aspidistra, *Billbergia nutans*, chlorophytum, *Cissus antarctica*, cryptanthus, fatsia, fatshedera, ficus, *Grevillea robusta*, gynura, hedera, *Impatiens walleriana*, monstera, neoregelia, philodendron, pilea, rhoeo, *Rhoicissus rhomboidea*, sansevieria, *Saxifraga stolonifera*, scindapsus, sparmannia, *Tradescantia fluminensis* and *T. zebrina*, and vriesia.

More Difficult House Plants. Aglaonema, anthurium, aphelandra, *Begonia rex* and *B. masoniana*, beloperone, caladium, calathea, *Chamaedorea elegans*, codiaeum (croton), columnea, cordyline, cyclamen, dieffenbachia, dizygotheca, dracaena, fittonia, *Hibiscus rosa-sinensis*, hoya, *Maranta leuconeura*, *Microcoelum weddellianum*, pandanus, peperomia, *Phoenix roebelinii*, platycerium, saintpaulia, spathiphyllum and syngonium.

Part 4

Vegetables

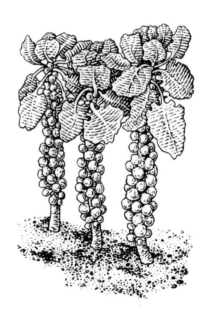

Chapter 23

Planning the Vegetable Garden

In devising a plan for the vegetable garden a great deal must depend on the shape and size of the plot available. However, certain general principles can be laid down. It is, for example, always advisable to make some provision for rotational cropping even though it may not be possible to adhere to this rigidly. The position of 'permanent' crops, such as rhubarb or herbs, must also receive careful attention and, if frames are to be included, these must be given a specially suitable spot.

Rotational Cropping. This is a scheme which is very familiar to the farmer and should be more widely adopted by the gardener. It is based on two principal facts: first that crops make different demands upon the soil, some requiring more of one food, others of another, and second that they suffer from different pests and diseases. If the same crop is grown in the same place every year it is more likely to exhaust the soil or be attacked by some foe or suffer from a soil-borne disease than if it is grown in a different place as often as possible.

Obvious difficulties arise from a haphazard re-arrangement of crops every year and a far better policy is to practise a logical system of rotation. This may be a two-year, three-year or four-year rotation, according to the time that will elapse before any particular crop comes back to the same ground. For garden work the three-year rotation is the one most commonly adopted. There are quite a number of variations of this system but all conform roughly to the same basic plan.

The plot is divided into three approximately equal sections which for the sake of clarity we will designate A, B and C. One of these is devoted mainly to brassicas (cabbages, savoys, Brussels sprouts, broccoli, etc.), another to root crops and the third to peas, beans and miscellaneous small crops. Let us suppose that in the first year brassicas are planted on plot A, root crops on plot B, peas and beans etc. on plot C. The following year all these crops will move on one place, the brassicas going to plot B, the root crops to C, and the peas and beans to A. For the next year they will move on again so that the root crops will be on plot A, the peas and beans on plot B and the brassicas on plot C. In the fourth year they will be back where they started and the rotation begins again

As I have already remarked, there are all kinds of variations of this basic scheme to meet the needs of particular gardens. For example if it is the intention to grow enough potatoes, besides other root crops, to supply the whole family throughout the year, it is highly probable that the root crop section will have to be increased in size out of proportion to the others. In this case the root crop plot may be reserved for potatoes alone and carrots, parsnips and beetroots may go with peas and beans.

Then there is the question of intercropping to be considered and the necessity for allowing reasonable time for cultivation between one crop and another. The chief points to observe are that identical or closely related crops should not follow one another closely, nor those which suffer from the same pests and diseases, and that the scheme followed should be pre-arranged rather than improvised.

Intercropping. This is a device whereby the gardener seeks to increase the cropping capacity of his ground by letting two or more vegetables occupy the same plot of ground at the same time. In theory it is possible to do this without allowing either of them to take up more room than they would if planted alone, but in practice this seldom works out satisfactorily. A good deal of experience is necessary to make intercropping a real success and I think it tends to be more often a snare than a help to the beginner. The trouble is that one or other of the crops almost always grows away too quickly to the detriment of the slow starter which becomes starved and stunted. Nevertheless, provided the ground is in thoroughly good condition and the gardener knows what he is about, it is certainly possible to obtain good results by practising intercropping.

Here are a few suggestions: peas must normally be planted in rows at least as far apart as the height of the pea when fully grown, that is, 90 cm (3 ft) peas should be a minimum 90 cm (3 ft) apart row to row; the same applies to 1·2 m (4 ft) peas and so on. This allows room between the taller varieties for single or even double rows of lettuces, radishes, summer spinach or some other small crop which does not mind a certain amount of shade. Summer turnips and shorthorn carrots may be grown in the same way or between rows of runner beans, which must also be planted with good spacing between them because of the shade they throw.

The trouble arises when the gardener tries to intercrop two vegetables either of which might reasonably be expected to cover the whole area with its foliage. Attempts are sometimes made to plant winter greens between the rows of potatoes. This is only successful if the potatoes are really widely spaced and are almost ready for lifting at the time when the greens are put out. Under other circumstances the greens are almost invariably smothered by the potato haulm.

Catch Cropping. This is another scheme for getting two crops from one plot of ground but instead of the crops being grown at the same time, they follow one another in quick succession. Catch cropping is most useful when ground has been prepared a considerable time in advance for some particular crop.

A good example is celery. The trenches in which it is to be grown are generally dug and manured quite early in the spring, sometimes even in late winter, though the plants are seldom put out before early summer. This means that for two months or more ground is lying idle and there is time to harvest a quick-growing crop such as radishes or early lettuces. Here again, however, considerable forethought is necessary for it is only too easy to find that the first crop is still not ready for gathering when the following crop is already spoiling for want of being put out.

Successional Cropping. The difference between successional cropping and catch cropping is that the following crop is of the same kind as that which preceded it, so lengthening the period of harvesting. It will be sown or planted while the preceding crop is still quite young and so will have to occupy separate ground.

Many vegetables have a comparatively short season when only one sowing or planting is made; peas and lettuces are both good examples of this. Two or three weeks and the crop is over. Unless the gardener practises successional cropping he will be in danger of having a glut at the peak season followed almost immediately by a complete lack of supplies.

The art of successional cropping is to know just how much to sow or plant each time and what time lag to allow between the successive sowings. Knowledge of the average yields may help to solve the first problem while as regards the second, it is a fairly safe general rule to space the sowings of summer crops at two- to three-week intervals from beginning to end of the sowing season.

It should be noted that in many cases succession can also be improved by choosing several varieties which mature at different times, e.g. early, mid-season and late potatoes, broccolis, peas, etc.

Regulating Supply. This is perhaps the most difficult task of all. The only thing to do is to set about the whole planning of the vegetable garden in a methodical way. First to all try to make a rough estimate of the quantity of each vegetable that will be required to supply the household throughout the period when that vegetable is in season. The table on p. 539 is designed to help to this end.

Pay particular heed to two periods, one from about late spring to early summer, and the other during late summer/early autumn. During the first there is liable to be a severe shortage of supplies, or at any rate an almost complete lack of variety. Winter vegetables such as cabbages, savoys and Brussels sprouts are over, spring crops such as broccoli and kale are also over or very scarce and the true summer crops are not yet ready. Very often there is practically nothing but spring cabbage and potatoes left at this season. The difficulty can be overcome by making early sowings of peas and broad beans under cloches and also by carrying over a batch of spinach beet or seakale beet from the preceding year. Summer cabbages raised in warmth and planted out in mid-spring will also help and, if frames are available, shorthorn carrots can be pulled in early summer without artificial heat. Again, a glance at the table on p. 539 will suggest many ways to bridge the gap.

As regards the early autumn period, the trouble is not a shortage but a glut. Almost everything is turning in at once then and only a few of the crops are of a type which can be kept easily. There will be peas, beans of every kind, cabbages, cauliflowers, spinach, carrots, beetroots, lettuces, tomatoes, to say nothing of potatoes, turnips, swedes and possibly an early batch of celery. The way to get over this difficulty is by successional cropping and also by freezing those crops which lend themselves to this method of preservation.

Another difficulty which arises in the regulation of supply is the lack of variety likely to occur in winter. Of course, if the gardener has planned wisely there will be plenty of root crops in store but once mid-winter is past and the main flush of Brussels sprouts and winter cabbage is over, there is often little beyond savoys to provide fresh green vegetables for the table until the spring supplies are ready.

In favoured localities it is possible to grow winter heading cauliflower but there are many places in which these are not successful. Turnips sown in late summer and allowed to stand unthinned in the rows will provide useful supplies of greens from about early spring onwards. There are numerous kinds of kale, notably the Curled Scotch kale and the Thousand Headed kale, which can be picked throughout the winter and early spring. Further variety can be provided by forcing seakale, chicory and salsify in a warm, dark place. If frames are available they may be filled with winter lettuce and endive. Even after the celery is finished the flavour of celery can be maintained in the salad bowl with grated celeriac, a relation of celery.

Manuring the Vegetable Garden. Dung or well-rotted compost should form the basis of all feeding in the vegetable garden, but it does not follow that dung or compost should therefore be applied indiscriminately all over the garden every autumn or winter. For one thing that would be wasteful and for another it might prove positively harmful for there are some vegetables which do best on ground that was manured for a previous crop rather than immediately prior to sowing or planting. Carrots and beetroots both come into this class and it is also true of late summer and early autumn planted brassicas, which are apt to make too much soft growth if planted on newly manured ground.

The rotational cropping scheme will help the gardener to solve such problems in the simplest possible manner as some sections of the garden can be manured right through and others simply treated with appropriate chemicals (see diagram below). Note, however, that even for those vegetables which like freshly manured soil and get it there is generally advantage to be gained by using some chemical fertilizers as well. These as a rule can be applied most conveniently and economically as topdressings just before the crop is sown or planted. Those who like to do things the most scientific way will use separate chemicals, varying them to suit the individual crop and the known deficiencies of the soil. Those who prefer an easier course should use a well-blended fertilizer, with an analysis showing approximately equal quantities of nitrogen, phosphates and potash, for all their crops.

THE UTILITY FRAME

Detailed instructions for the management of each crop in the frame will be found under the headings of the vegetables themselves. The purpose here is to indicate the various uses to which a frame may be put.

SUGGESTED THREE-YEAR ROTATION

A. Cabbages, cauliflowers, Brussels sprouts, kale, savoys, and other brassicas. Preceded by, or intercropped with, lettuces, radishes, and other small salads.
Plot dressed with animal manure or compost and limed (not together). Crops fed while in growth with a high-nitrogen fertilizer.

B. Potatoes. Followed by broccoli, spring cabbage, coleworts, leeks, and late-sown turnip (for tops).
Plot dressed with animal manure or compost, but *not* lime.
Complete artificial fertilizer applied, just prior to planting potatoes.

C. Carrots, parsnips, turnips and beetroots.
Peas and beans with summer spinach and lettuces between.
No animal manure or compost except for pea and bean trenches. Wood ashes forked in. Complete fertilizer (low nitrogen, high phosphoric acid ratio) applied just prior to sowing.

D. Onions.
Plot dressed with animal manure or compost and wood ashes. Nitrate of soda after thinning.

The scheme is applicable to plots of any size or shape, so no dimensions are necessary.
The only essential is that sections **A**, **B**, and **C** should be of approximately the same area though they need not be of the same shape. The second year the order of the crops from top to bottom is **C**, **A**, **B**, **D**; the third year **B**, **C**, **A**, **D**; the fourth year the same as first year. Onions are not included in the rotation because they appear to derive greater benefit from being grown on the same plot for a number of years. If, however, it is preferred to include them, they should go to plot **C**.

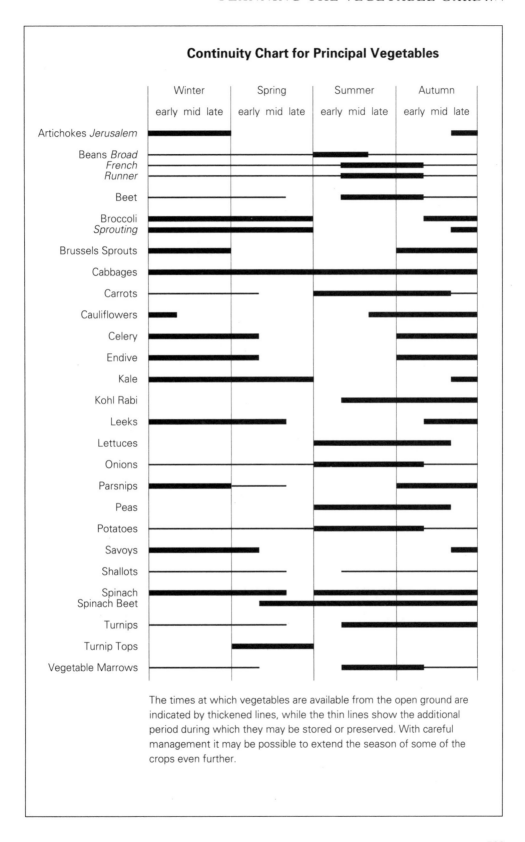

Continuity Chart for Principal Vegetables

The times at which vegetables are available from the open ground are indicated by thickened lines, while the thin lines show the additional period during which they may be stored or preserved. With careful management it may be possible to extend the season of some of the crops even further.

A frame is a great asset to the vegetable garden. It may be either heated or unheated but it will have wider uses if the latter. In any case it should be given a sunny, but reasonably sheltered, position; for example, it may stand at the foot of a wall facing south or on the south side of a greenhouse or potting shed.

There are many different types of frame and almost any of them can be turned to account in the vegetable garden but perhaps the most useful is the standard type of 1·8 × 1·2 m (6 × 4 ft) or 1·2 m × 90 cm (4 × 3 ft) glass panels. This kind of frame may have wooden, brick or concrete walls and should be only a little higher at the back than in front. A 15 cm (6 in) fall from back to front will be sufficient for a 1·8 m (6 ft) panel, and this can be reduced to 10 cm (4 in) for a 1·2 m (4 ft) panel. This will run off water satisfactorily and the advantage of having a rather flat roof to the frame is that all the plants in it can be reasonably close to the glass. If some plants are far from the glass they will tend to get drawn and weak.

There are two distinct purposes for which the frame may be used in the vegetable garden: one to rear seedlings and harden off young plants, and the other to bring crops to maturity at an earlier or later date than would be possible out of doors. Of the two the first is usually of greater importance to the amateur but there is no reason why both objects should not be combined to some extent.

Seed in Frames. Outdoor seed sowing can seldom start before the end of late winter and must often be delayed until early spring. In a frame it is possible to get a good seed bed and satisfactory germination a month earlier even without artificial heat in the case of hardy plants such as Brussels sprouts, cauliflowers, broccolis, leeks, onions, peas and lettuces. Tender vegetables such as tomatoes, cucumbers, vegetable marrows and French and runner beans can also be raised in a frame but as they need protection from frost and a higher temperature to effect germination it will either be necessary to delay sowing until about mid-spring or to provide the frame with some heating (see p. 410).

Seedlings can be raised either in boxes stood on a floor of sand or gravel in the frame or, if preferred, seed can be sown directly into a bed of soil prepared in the frame. With the former method the advantage is that successive batches of seedlings can be passed through the frame more rapidly and easily, but the drawback is that the seeds and seedlings will require more attention, particularly as regards watering. In sunny weather the soil in shallow seed trays dries out rapidly, whereas a good bed of soil rich in humus will retain its moisture for a much longer period.

Taking the crops in chronological order according to sowing date, those which might most advantageously be reared in a frame are onions, leeks, broad beans, lettuces, Brussels sprouts, cauliflowers, early sprouting broccolis, summer cabbages, tomatoes, celery, French beans, runner beans, vegetable marrows and cucumbers.

Frame Crops. Crops to be brought to maturity in a frame can be divided into two groups, summer crops and winter crops. The former will be of greater importance to the amateur as he can combine them readily with the seed raising to which reference has just been made. Winter crops will in general occupy the frame from the first half of autumn until at least early spring, and that really rules out the possibility of any seed raising.

The three best summer crops for the frame are cucumbers, tomatoes and melons in that order of merit. Ordinary varieties of tomato can be grown in frames provided with extra deep sides, preferably removable ones that can be placed in position when the young plants touch the glass, or alternatively dwarf bush varieties of tomato can be used as these do not need much headroom.

Cucumbers are a familiar summer frame crop and usually do very well. Either the ordinary frame cucumber may be grown or the hardier ridge cucumber, which has the merit of being more prolific and easily managed.

Melons are a distinctly tricky crop and I do not recommend them to the beginner. All the same I have seen some very satisfactory and profitable yields obtained by skilful management.

The two most successful winter crops for the frame are lettuces and endive. The description 'winter' is perhaps a slight exaggeration in the case of lettuce for it is unlikely that any crop will be fit for cutting between late autumn and early spring, but mid-autumn and mid-spring supplies can be obtained quite easily and are both very welcome. Endive, being hardier, can actually be cut in winter. Alternative crops are radishes, which can be sown very early in the year for pulling from the end of winter onwards, early carrots and mustard and cress.

CLOCHES

Cloches of many kinds and ingenious patterns can be used with great advantage in the vegetable garden to enable early sowings to be made and to help young plants through the treacherous spring months. Even in summer cloches can be used like miniature greenhouses to hasten the growth of tomatoes, cucumbers, aubergines and other rather tender vegetables, while in autumn they are serviceable as protection against frost and to ripen off tomatoes and onions. Very elaborate cropping schemes are sometimes undertaken so that the cloches are in almost constant use, being passed from one crop to another with the minimum delay. Such schemes require considerable knowledge and careful timing if the whole programme is to be a success. I have referred more fully to these matters on p. 406.

THE UTILITY GREENHOUSE

At the outset it is more important to have a frame than a greenhouse, but if both can be included in the vegetable garden, so much the better. A greenhouse will do many of the things, but not all, that can be done with a frame and it has a few additional functions as well.

It is not possible to harden off satisfactorily plants in a greenhouse and that is where the frame scores. Perhaps this needs a little explanation. Any plant, however naturally hardy, will tend to be made more tender than usual if it is raised under glass. If such a plant is suddenly placed out of doors without any preliminary preparation, it is likely to receive a severe check to growth which may even be sufficient to kill it outright. To overcome this difficulty the gardener uses the process known as hardening off, during which the plant is gradually accustomed to greater degrees of exposure. This begins with increased ventilation during all favourable periods. With the frame there comes a time when the protecting light is dispensed with altogether unless the weather becomes unseasonably cold or rough. Now there is no way of dispensing with the glass in a greenhouse, the most that can be done being to throw the ventilators wide open and open the door and this does not harden the inmates so thoroughly as exposure in an open frame.

With these reservations, however, it may be said that all the seedlings suggested for frame rearing may also be germinated in a greenhouse and many of them several weeks earlier if heating is available. In addition, all the crops suggested for the frame may be brought to maturity in a greenhouse with equal or greater success and, in the case of tomatoes, cucumbers and melons there is a great advantage in the extra head room available.

A wider variety of winter crops can be included with the aid of artificial heat. The skilled grower can even ripen tomatoes and obtain moderate yields of cucumbers at this season. But no amount of artificial heat can make up for lack of daylight, in fact too much heat without balancing light can result in drawn, weakly plants and eventual disaster. Much of the skill of producing winter crops lies in knowing just how much heat can be used to keep plants growing without causing this weakness, and that is knowledge which must be gained by experience rather than from books.

HOTBEDS AND SOIL WARMING

The hotbed is a very ancient method of generating heat. It is based on the observation that a rapidly fermenting heap of dung becomes very warm. Fresh stable manure containing a fair proportion of straw produces the greatest degree of heat over the longest period and is therefore best for hotbed construction, but plain straw or chaff treated with one of the proprietary substances sold for preparing mushroom compost will make quite a good substitute.

The idea is to build a flat-topped heap of well-trodden dung 60–90 cm (2–3 ft) in height and a little larger than a portable garden frame. The frame is then stood on top of this fermenting heap and a 15–20 cm (6–8 in) layer of good soil placed in it. The heat from the rotting manure warms the soil and is trapped by the frame light so converting the frame into a miniature hothouse. Seeds, cuttings or young plants can be placed in the soil.

Sometimes the manure is placed in a pit instead of being built into a heap with the idea that this will conserve the heat better. Care must be taken that the pit does not become waterlogged with the result that the dung is chilled.

It is always wise to wait a few days before putting frames in position so that ammonia fumes may escape.

Because of the difficulty nowadays of obtaining suitable fresh horse manure, hotbeds are not used anything like so much as they once were, their function being taken over by electric soil-warming cables (see p. 410).

Chapter 24
Vegetables and their Cultivation

In this chapter the principal vegetables likely to be grown in the amateur's garden are arranged alphabetically for easy reference and brief cultural directions are given for each, together with some suggestions regarding varieties. It should be noted, however, that new varieties of merit are constantly being introduced and that many large seed firms list own specialities (some from the Far East) which are described in the various trade catalogues. Moreover in some cases strain is more important than variety, so that it is more vital to obtain seed from firms of repute who maintain the highest standard in their stocks than to purchase a name without regard to the source from which it comes.

ARTICHOKE, GLOBE

This is a vegetable for the epicure rather than for the general gardener. Judged on weight of crop per 0·8 sq m (1 sq yd) it is not profitable as the only parts of the plant which are edible are the bases of the scales protecting the inflorescence. The plants are extremely ornamental particularly in foliage and worth growing for this alone.

There are two methods of raising globe artichokes, one from seed and the other by means of offsets or divisions. The former has the merit of being cheap, but the best results are obtained with offsets taken from plants selected for the quality of their produce. These offsets should be detached in mid-spring and planted at once in deeply dug, well-manured ground and a well-drained, sunny position. Space them at least 90 cm (3 ft) apart.

Seed may be sown in a frame or unheated greenhouse in early spring or in shallow drills out of doors a few weeks later. The seedlings are transplanted several centimetres apart in well-broken, reasonably rich soil, directly they can be handled conveniently, and are transferred to their final quarters the following spring, when planting is exactly the same as for offsets.

Subsequent treatment is the same in each case. The ground should be well mulched with decayed manure in late spring and thoroughly watered in summer during dry weather. Weak liquid manure can be substituted for plain water if available. Dead leaves are cut off towards mid-autumn and the crowns covered lightly with bracken or straw as a protection against frost. This should be left in position until the first half of spring.

No crop should be cut the first summer after planting. Subsequently the flower heads are cut as soon as they are of good size and the outer scales feel fleshy. The plants will go on cropping for several years but it is most profitable to replace them after the third year.

It is important to obtain a good strain, that is to say seed or offshoots from plants that are known to have given good results. Vert de Laon is particularly reliable.

ARTICHOKE, JERUSALEM

There could hardly be a greater contrast than between the Jerusalem and the globe artichoke. The latter is a vegetable for the epicure, but the Jerusalem artichoke is for everyone – or at any rate, everyone who likes its rather peculiar flavour and somewhat slushy texture. It is a very profitable crop judged on the basis of weight lifted per 0·8 sq m (1 sq yd), and it can be grown anywhere. It is cultivated for the tubers which are formed in big clumps underground, rather like an immense root of potatoes. Growth above ground is tall, stiffly erect and very similar to that of a sunflower, to which the plant is related.

The Jerusalem artichoke is grown from tubers which can be separated from the parent clump when it is lifted. It is advisable to choose well-shaped tubers of medium to large size for planting. They are put in during the second half of winter, as soon as the ground is in workable condition. Almost any plot will serve but best results are obtained when it is deeply dug and dressed with dung or compost at 50 kg per 9·6-12 sq m (1 cwt per 12-15 sq yd). Plant 38 cm (1 ft 3 in) apart in rows 90 cm (3 ft) apart and cover with 11·2 cm (4½ in) of soil. No earthing up is needed as in the case of potatoes. It is sufficient after planting to keep the plot clear of weeds.

The plants and tubers are perfectly hardy and may be left in the ground all winter if desired, being lifted for use as required, though it is usually convenient to lift at least part of the crop in late autumn and store in a shed or outhouse under a little dry soil. Do not leave the tubers exposed or they will shrivel fairly quickly.

Named varieties in the ordinary sense are seldom offered but there is considerable difference in stocks and it is advisable to exercise care in choosing a good one. There are pink-skinned and white-skinned forms of which I prefer the latter, and the most desirable types have large, roundish, shallow-eyed tubers.

ASPARAGUS

This is another vegetable for the epicure but, unlike the globe artichoke, one which will give a considerable return of food in relation to the ground occupied. The drawbacks with asparagus are that it takes rather a long time to come into being and then continues to occupy the same ground for a number of years, which means that, unless the plot is well manured and cleaned to begin with, it will soon become worked out or covered with weeds. In new gardens it is generally wise to wait a year or so before making the asparagus bed so that the ground can be brought into thoroughly good condition first.

Asparagus can easily be raised from seed sown in a frame or sheltered bed out of doors in mid-spring. Sow thinly in drills 12 mm (½ in) deep and 38 cm (1 ft 3 in) apart. Thin seedlings to 8·7 cm (3½ in) apart. Leave to grow for two years and discard any plants that produce berries as these are females which will not give either the quantity or quality of asparagus that is produced by male plants. At the end of the second year the seedling asparagus plants are transplanted to the beds in which they will crop.

An alternative system is to sow the seed directly in the bed in which the asparagus is to grow and then thin the seedlings to 30 cm (1 ft) apart. The rows themselves should be 38 cm (1¼ ft) apart. With this method the seedlings grow unchecked and attain cropping size more rapidly. Usually, however, the amateur will prefer to start by purchasing two-year-old roots, which can be obtained from most nurserymen. Such roots should be planted in mid-spring 30 cm (1 ft) apart in rows at least 38 (1¼ ft) apart.

Frequently asparagus is grown in long, narrow beds raised a little above the surrounding ground to ensure good drainage round the crowns. A convenient width for such beds is 1·2 m (4 ft), which will allow for three rows lengthwise with 23 cm (9 in) separating the outer rows from the edge of the bed.

Excavate the soil to a depth of at least 60 cm (2 ft), break up the bottom with a fork, replace the top soil and at the same time mix in well-rotted stable or farmyard manure at the rate of 50 kg per 4 sq m (1 cwt per 5 sq yd). Built the bed up at least 15 cm (6 in) above the surrounding level.

Allow the bed to settle for at least a month and then plant the crowns with their roots well spread out and cover with 7·5 cm (3 in) of soil.

Another method is to plant on the flat, spacing the roots 30 cm (1 ft) apart in trenches 15 cm (6 in) deep and 1·2 m (4 ft) apart. Return the soil over the roots and allow the plants to grow for a full year, keeping the soil clear of weeds and topdressing it with well-rotted manure or compost in the second half of winter. Then during the second year draw soil from between the rows towards the plants as they grow, so earthing them up in low mounds rather like potatoes. Thereafter these mounds remain as a permanent feature of the asparagus bed.

Whichever method is adopted, do not take any crop the first year. In subsequent years begin cutting the young shoots in late spring and continue until early summer. The shoots are cut when 7·5-10 cm (3-4 in) high and are severed well below soil level.

After early summer the plants are allowed to grow unchecked and make plenty of top growth which is not removed until it turns yellow in mid-autumn. It is then cut off just above soil level.

The asparagus bed should be fed each spring with a good thick mulch of well-broken and thoroughly rotted manure or garden compost.

There are approximately 17 varieties, one of the most popular and best in size and quality being Connover's Colossal. There are also various pedigree strains offered by asparagus specialists, some of which crop very heavily. Cito is an all-male hybrid.

AUBERGINE (EGG PLANT)
This is grown for its thick sausage-shaped fruits which can be cooked in a variety of ways and are esteemed a delicacy.

Sow from mid-winter to early spring in well-drained trays or boxes filled with an ordinary seed mixture (see p. 427). Germinate in a temperature of about 15-18°C/59-65°F. Pot seedlings singly in 6.2 cm (2½ in) pots as soon as they can be handled and move from these into 16·2 cm (6½ in) pots when the first are nicely filled with roots using J.I. No. 1 for the first potting and J.I. No. 2 for the second. Alternatively plants can be spaced 38 cm (1¼ ft) apart in a bed of good soil on the greenhouse floor.

Grow the plants throughout in a sunny greenhouse (or from late spring in a frame) with an average temperature of 15°C/59°F, which might rise to 26°C/79°F on sunny days but should never fall below 10°C/50°F. Water rather freely. Pinch out the tip of each plant at about 15 cm (6 in) high and subsequently train growths to stakes or wires. When fruits form restrict them to about five or six per plant and thereafter feed liberally with weak liquid manure or a good compound fertilizer.

The fruits are ready for use when they become fully coloured and a little soft, in fact about the condition in which tomatoes would be picked.

Some 27 varieties are usually available, by far the most popular being Long Purple. There are also white, yellow and pale purple varieties.

BEANS, BROAD
Broad beans are hardier than any of the other popular types and, unlike runner and

French beans, are grown solely for their seeds. They are a profitable crop for they give a heavy yield and will thrive with a minimum of attention.

There are few soils in which broad beans will not succeed, though they do best on the richer types of loam. Digging should be as thorough as possible and well-rotted manure or compost worked in at not more than 50 kg per 12 sq m (1 cwt per 15 sq yd) unless the soil is very poor. An alternative is to plant this crop after brassicas, potatoes or some other crop for which the ground has already been well manured and give no further dressing. In any case it is wise to give extra phosphates and potash as, for example, superphosphate of lime, 85 g per 0·8 sq m (3 oz per sq yd), and sulphate of potash, 28 g per 0·8 sq m (1 oz per sq yd), raked in immediately before sowing. Broad beans do best in soils that are neutral or at most only slightly acid, so if there is any doubt on this point, a dressing of lime or chalk should be given at the appropriate rate (see p. 16).

Seed can be sown in three ways: out of doors in the second half of autumn; in deep boxes in a warm greenhouse or frame during the second half of winter; or out of doors in spring. Autumn sowing can be unsatisfactory in cold winters or on wet soils unless the seedlings are protected by cloches until about mid-spring.

Box sowing is very satisfactory provided the seedlings are not subjected to too much heat (a temperature of 15°C/59°F is ample) and are well hardened off before being planted out. This can usually be done with safety during mid-spring. From either an autumn sowing or box sowing a crop of beans can be picked in early summer.

The main crop for use in summer is obtained by sowing in the first half of spring out of doors. Some gardeners make a second sowing in late spring to crop in early autumn and this can be most useful.

For all outdoor sowings the beans should be placed 15 cm (6 in) apart in drills 3 cm (1½ in) deep and 60 cm (2 ft) apart, or alternatively two rows can be spaced at 45 cm (1½ ft) intervals and then a wide alleyway of 75 cm (2½ ft) left between this pair of rows and the next. On heavy soils it is sometimes best to sow the seeds on the surface, not in drills, and cover by drawing the soil over the seeds in a low ridge.

No thinning is required and little aftercare beyond weeding and hoeing until the plants have set their first clusters of beans. Then the growing tip of each should be broken off to prevent further extension and hasten the maturing of the crop.

Seeds raised in boxes are spaced 5 cm (2 in) apart and covered with 18 mm (¾ in) of soil. They are not pricked off but are left to grow undisturbed until they can be planted out of doors. Planting should be with a trowel; the roots must be dropped into good, deep holes and the plants spaced as for beans sown out of doors.

Picking should be started directly the beans inside the pods are of good size. Start from the bottom clusters and work upwards. If a few pods are removed at a time from each plant the rest will be encouraged to develop more quickly.

There are a good many varieties, many of which do not differ greatly. Good standard kinds with green seeds are Imperial Green Windsor and Imperial Green Longpod. Aquadulce Claudia is white seeded, very hardy and recommended for autumn sowing. Green-seeded varieties are to be preferred for deep freezing. Bunyards Exhibition, Express Masterpiece Green Longpod, and The Sutton are all big favourites.

BEANS, FRENCH
French beans start to crop earlier than runner beans, are just a little hardier and take up

less room. There are two principal types, dwarf and climbing, but the former are more popular as they need no staking and are very easy to grow. There are also varieties in which the pods are circular in section, in contrast to the flattened type.

Ground should be prepared in exactly the same way as for broad beans. Outdoor sowing should not be attempted until after mid-spring except in very sheltered places or under cloches. Earlier crops can be obtained by sowing seeds in deep boxes in a greenhouse or frame during early spring and hardening the seedlings off for planting out towards the end of spring. In boxes the seeds should be spaced 5 cm (2 in) apart. Out of doors they should be spaced 8·7 cm (3½ in) deep and 45 cm (1½ ft) apart, the seedlings being thinned to 18 cm (7 in). These distances are also the right ones for planting out greenhouse-raised seedlings.

The secret of producing good French beans is to keep them growing fast throughout. Water them freely if the weather is dry and then mulch with grass clippings, strawy manure or moist peat. Start to pick beans when they are 8·7 cm (3½ in) long and never let any beans get big and coarse on the plants as this checks further production.

Climbing varieties are grown in much the same way but the rows should be 1·2 m (4 ft) apart with bean poles, long canes, trellis work or netting for plants to twine on.

If it turns out that more beans have been grown than are required for use while green, leave some of the plants unpicked altogether and let them ripen their whole crop. The dried seeds can then be shelled out and used as haricots. They will keep in a cool, dry place for years.

Good dwarf varieties of the flat-podded type are The Prince, Canadian Wonder, and Masterpiece. A good climbing variety is Blue Lake White Seeded. Good dwarf stringless varieties (pencil shaped) are Tendergreen and Bush Blue Lake which do not require staking.

Forcing. French beans can be grown under glass in pots or directly in a bed of soil. From a mid-winter sowing in a cool or intermediate greenhouse beans may be had by late spring while late winter/early spring sowings under a frame or cloche will yield early summer pickings. Use a soil mixture similar to that recommended for tomatoes and grow throughout under as even conditions of temperature and moisture as possible. If grown in pots three seeds may be sown in each 20 cm (8 in) pot in J.I. No. 2.

BEANS, HARICOT

The only difference between the haricot bean and the French bean is that the former is grown for the seeds. The pods are all left to ripen, after which the seeds are shelled out and stored in a cool, dry place for winter use. All the details given for the cultivation of French beans apply equally to haricot beans. The crop is not a heavy one, seldom more than 170 g (6 oz) of ripened beans per 0·8 sq m (1 sq yd), and I doubt whether it is a profitable one. It is probably better to leave the cultivation of haricot beans to farmers in warm climates.

There are both dwarf and climbing haricots, just as there are dwarf and climbing French beans. Two of the best varieties I have tried, both dwarfs, are Brown Dutch, with brown seeds, and Comtesse de Chambord with white seeds, but the ordinary dwarf French bean Masterpiece also makes an excellent haricot. Chevrier Vert is also recommended for use green, half ripe or fully ripe.

The wigwam method of supporting runner beans. Four canes are attached at the top to form a wigwam-like structure and the plants climb up each stake

Conventional staking of runner beans. The stakes, lashed to a horizontal pole, should be set in position directly the seedlings appear

Supporting runner beans from a central pole. The beans are sown in a circle about 1.5 m (5 ft) in diameter and a number of pegs inserted around the edge from which strings are looped to the top of the pole

BEANS, RUNNER

There are few crops which will give a greater return for less trouble than the runner bean. It will grow practically anywhere, on heavy or light soils and sunny or partially shaded positions. I have seen quite good crops taken from town gardens with the plants grown in boxes and trained against most unpromising looking fences and walls.

The preparation of the ground is the same as for broad beans. Some people grow runner beans in trenches prepared in much the same manner as for celery and this is not at all a bad plan as it saves labour and materials, but in heavy soils the trenches are apt to serve as drains for surface water with disastrous results for the plants growing in them.

Runner beans are very tender so it is not safe to sow seed out of doors until late spring except in the most favoured localities or where the plants are to be covered by cloches. An alternative is to raise seedlings in boxes in the same way as described for French beans and plant them out in late spring/early summer, after proper hardening. For a late crop a second sowing may be made out doors in early summer.

The spacing for seeds or for plants to be grown on poles out of doors is 20 cm (8 in) apart in double rows 45 cm (1½ ft) apart. At least 1·8 m (6 ft) should be left between each pair of double rows. An alternative method of cultivation is to turn the plants into big, loose bushes by constantly pinching out the points of the runners. This is the method used by most commercial growers and excellent crops can be obtained, though individually the beans seldom achieve the length and straightness of those obtained from staked plants. If the bush method is to be used the plants must be spaced at least 60 cm (2 ft) from plant to plant and 90 cm (3 ft) from row to row. Hammond's Dwarf Scarlet is a naturally low-growing variety which makes a bushy plant without any pinching. It should be grown like a dwarf French bean.

Where beans are to be grown on poles these should be put in position directly the seedlings appear. Poles 2·4 m (8 ft) long are best and should be lashed securely at the top to a horizontal spar running the length of the row. A row of fully grown runner beans presents a tremendous resistance to wind. Yet another possibility is to sow in circles about 1.5 m (5 ft) in diameter, drive one strong upright into the centre of each circle and a number of pegs around the edge, and loop string from the top of the pole to the pegs to form a tent-like support.

It pays to mulch the ground between bean rows with strawy manure or peat early in summer. This not only feeds them but also keeps the soil cool and moist, encourages root growth and helps the setting of the bean flowers. Some growers syringe their beans every evening with clear water while they are in flower as an additional aid to setting, but the main cause of flower dropping is cold at night and it is very much a seasonal trouble about which little can be done.

The beans should be picked young and none allowed to remain to ripen, unless a few plants are set aside especially to supply seed which should be shelled out when the pods become dry and commence to split open.

There are a good many varieties but a well-selected strain of Scarlet Emperor still takes a lot of beating for ordinary kitchen use. For exhibition one of the very long-podded kinds is preferable, such as Enorma, Prizewinner or Streamline. Amongst the dwarf kind is Gulliver.

BEETROOT

There are three principal types of beetroot, the globe, in which the roots are shaped more or less like a cricket ball, the long-rooted, which may be as much as 30 cm (1 ft) in length, gradually tapering to a point, and the tankard or intermediate type, obtained by crossing the other two. This deserves to be better known as it gives a heavy weight of crop without needing very deep soil. The roots are roughly canister shaped, shorter and less tapering than those of the long beetroot.

The beetroot needs a well-tilled and reasonably rich soil but too much dung is liable to cause forking of the roots. The best policy is to choose a plot that was thoroughly manured for a previous crop and then prepare it by digging and topdressing with a well balanced compound fertilizer a week or so prior to sowing, and rake in very thoroughly.

A first sowing out of doors, preferably of a globe-rooted kind, should be made from mid-spring. It should be followed by a main sowing of a tankard or long-rooted beetroot during late spring. In all cases sow in drills 2·5 cm (1 in) deep and 30 cm (1 ft) apart, drop in the seeds in twos or threes, 10 cm (4 in) apart in the case of globe varieties and 15 cm (6 in) with the other types. When the seedlings are 2·5 cm (1 in) high, reduce them to one at each point. If growth is slow give a topdressing of nitrate of soda in early summer, 28 g per 3·6 m (1 oz per 12 ft) of row, and hoe in. No other treatment is necessary beyond an occasional hoeing to keep down weeds. A late sowing of a globe variety may be made in early summer to give young roots in early autumn.

Many people leave beetroot in the ground too long with the result that the roots get coarse and woody and some begin to crack. Globe kinds should be lifted, a few at a time as required, from the period at which they are 5 cm (2 in) in diameter. None should be left to grow beyond the size of cricket balls. If they cannot be used at this stage, lift and store them in a shed or outhouse, covering them with dry soil or sand. Long and tankard-rooted beetroots should be lifted during early autumn and stored in the same way. They will keep till the second half of spring.

There are numerous varieties, particularly of the globe and long-rooted types and many seedsmen list their own specialities. Good standard varieties are Boltardy, Detroit Globe, Cheltenham Green Top and Cylindra.

Forcing. An extra early crop for the first half of summer can be obtained by sowing a globe-rooted variety in a frame or under cloches. Preparation of the soil is exactly as for outdoor culture. Seed can be sown in late winter in drills 20 cm (8 in) apart, seedlings being thinned to 10 cm (4 in). Ventilate freely on fine days from mid-spring onwards. Choose a non-bolting variety, such as Boltardy, for this purpose.

BORECOLE. See KALE (p. 565).

BROCCOLI

This vegetable is closely related to the cauliflower but instead of making a close, white curd it produces a number of separate shoots each terminating in a cluster of greenish, white or purple flower buds. These are cut just before the flowers open and it is these flowering shoots and buds which form the edible part of the plant. Calabrese is a summer broccoli whose central stem usually produces a small head with smaller sprouts following from surrounding stems.

A first sowing of early varieties of the calabrese type can be made in early spring in a frame with a further sowing in mid-spring, and a final small sowing of late sprouting broccoli a few weeks later.

In all cases sprinkle the seed thinly in drills 6 mm (¼ in) deep and 15 cm (6 in) apart. If the seed is sown very thinly the seedlings can be left to grow until they are big enough for removal to their final quarters, but should the seedlings appear crowded they must be pricked off 6·2 cm (2½ in) apart in rows 15-20 cm (6-8 in) apart as soon as they can be handled. The object is to get sturdy, well-rooted plants to put out from late spring to mid-summer.

Meanwhile the final bed should be prepared by deep digging with dung or compost worked in at about 50 kg per 12 sq m (1 cwt per 15 sq yd). In addition after completion of digging give a topdressing of a well balanced compound fertilizer as advised by the manufacturers.

Do not pull the seedlings out of the seed bed but lift them with a fork. Plant firmly, preferably with a trowel rather than a dibber, and space the plants at least 60 cm (2 ft) apart each way. Water in well if the weather is dry and water the seedlings before they are lifted from the seed bed.

Cutting can begin directly the flower shoots are well developed but before any flower buds open. Again, almost daily cutting is necessary.

Good varieties of calabrese for summer cutting are Green Sprouting, Express Corona and Corvet. For spring cutting Purple Sprouting.

BRUSSELS SPROUTS

This is one of the most useful brassicas for the amateur as, unlike so many others of its family, picking can be continued for a considerable time from one batch of plants. For this reason there is seldom any waste as so often occurs with broccoli, cauliflowers, cabbages, or savoys.

Brussels sprouts need a rich, firm soil. It should be dug as long as possible in advance of planting so that the soil may have ample time to settle. Dung or compost can be used with advantage at rates up to 50 kg per 8 sq m (1 cwt per 10 sq yd) and it is almost always desirable to add some extra phosphates and potash immediately prior to planting. These can be in the form of superphosphate of lime, 85 g per 0·8 sq m (3 oz per sq yd), and sulphate of potash, 28 g (1 oz) to the same area, or use a well balanced compound fertilizer.

Seed should be sown in a separate seed bed at least two months before the plants are required for putting out. It is usually desirable to make two separate sowings, one about early spring in a frame or sheltered position out of doors and another in the open during mid-spring. For a very early supply seeds may be sown in an unheated greenhouse or frame in late winter or out of doors in early autumn. In the latter case the seedlings will be transferred to a frame in late autumn and kept there until the following spring.

Sow in drills 12 mm (½ in) deep and 15-20 cm (6-8 in) apart. When the plants have five or six leaves each, transplant them to their final quarters at least 60 cm (2 ft) apart in rows 75 cm (2½ ft) apart. Plant very firmly and water freely if the weather is dry. About two months later topdress down the rows with well-rotted dung and draw soil over this towards the stems. If the plants grow very large and are in an exposed place, it may be necessary to stake them and it is certainly better to do this than to risk their being blown over.

When the bottom sprouts are of useful size cut and use the sprout tops. This will encourage the rest of the sprouts to swell. Then begin to pick them, a few at a time, starting at the bottom and continuing up the stem. Treated in this way one batch of sprouts should continue to yield for two or three months and by growing two batches, one of an early and the other of a late variety, sprouts can be had from late summer to late winter.

The principal difficulty is that many of the sprouts come loose instead of being nice tight buttons. There are three possible causes, a poor strain of seed, loose soil or insufficient potash and too much nitrogen in the soil. If cabbage root fly strikes apply bromophos, phoxim, or pirimiphos-methyl in the seed beds. Club root disease is tackled with thiophanate-methyl or a similar fungicide.

Varieties are numerous as this is an important market garden crop. Peer Gynt is an excellent early variety and Rampart a reliable late one. Citadel and Eveshore Special are equally popular.

CABBAGE

It is possible to cut cabbage throughout the year but it takes a little skill and forethought to do it. The method is to make use of varieties from three separate groups of cabbage; quick-growing varieties that will mature in early summer from a spring sowing, slower growing kinds that will be ready in autumn and winter from a spring sowing, and varieties which can be sown in late summer to heart the following spring.

The first sowing can be made under glass, preferably with a little artificial heat in late winter. Seed should be sown thinly in boxes and the seedlings pricked off 6·2 cm (2½ in) apart into a bed of reasonably rich soil in a frame the following month. Here they are hardened off until in mid-spring they are sturdy enough to go out of doors in rich soil and a fairly sheltered position. If a suitable variety, such as Primo, Golden Acre or Hispi is chosen heads should be ready for cutting from early summer onwards.

A second sowing of a similar variety should be made in early spring in a frame or sheltered place out of doors. Two more sowings, one of an autumn and one of a winter cabbage, should be made in mid-spring, the seeds being sown very thinly in 12 mm (½ in) deep drills and left undisturbed until they can be planted in late spring/early summer. It is sometimes wise to make yet another sowing of a winter kind about late spring treating it in the same way but not planting out the seedlings until mid-summer.

The last sowing, of spring cabbage, is made some time in the second half of summer. The precise date will vary according to district and soil and if you cannot get any local advice on this point it is probably best to make two separate sowings the first season, one early and the other late, and in subsequent years adjust matters according to results. Seedlings from this summer sowing will be treated just like the spring seedlings and planted in their final quarters in the first half of autumn. Some seedlings can be left in the seed bed throughout the winter and used to fill up gaps at the start of the following spring.

In all cases the bed for the final planting should be in an open position and the soil reasonably rich. For summer supplies more dung can be used than for winter and spring cabbage, say 50 kg per 8 sq m (1 cwt per 10 sq yd) for the first and 50 kg per 12 sq m (15 sq yd) for the latter. An alternative is to plant the spring cabbage – that is, those raised from mid- to late summer sowing – after potatoes or some other crop for which dung has already been used, when no further manure need be added but only potash and phosphates in the form of artificial fertilizers. It is, in any case, always wise to give some extra potash and phosphate besides dung as, for example, superphosphate of lime at 85 g (3 oz) and sulphate of potash at 42 g per 0·8 sq m (1½ oz per 1 sq yd) or a balanced compound fertilizer.

Plant spring and early summer maturing cabbages 30 cm (1 ft) apart in rows 45 cm (1½ ft) apart. Autumn and winter maturing kinds make bigger plants and need more room, usually 45 cm (1½ ft) in the rows and 76 cm (2½ ft) between the rows.

Lift the seedlings from the seed bed with a fork, injuring the roots as little as possible, plant firmly with a trowel and water in well. Sprinkle a little bromophos in each hole before planting as a preventative against cabbage root fly maggots and club root disease. It is a good plan to rake a little bromophos into seed beds before sowing if either maggots or club root have been troublesome in previous years. About six weeks after planting, summer, autumn and winter maturing cabbages will benefit from a topdressing of nitrate of soda, 28 g (1 oz) per 1·8 m (6 ft) of row well hoed or watered in. In the case of spring cabbages application of this dressing should be delayed until the first half of spring.

Varieties are extremely numerous and I can only mention a few of the best known. They are grouped according to the classes already described. For summer cutting, Primo, Golden Acre, Hispi, Greyhound and Winnigstadt; for winter cutting Celtic, Rearguard, Holland Winter White, January King and Christmas Drumhead; for spring cutting, Early Offenham, Harbinger, Flower of Spring, Durham Early and Wheeler's Imperial. Red Cabbages, such as Red Drumhead, are grown mainly for pickling purposes. They are summer drumhead types.

CABBAGE, CHINESE
This vegetable is related to the common cabbage but has less fleshy leaves and looks more like a cos lettuce. It can be used raw as a salad or can be cooked like a cabbage. Seed can be sown from late spring to late summer, but mid-summer is probably the best time in most gardens as this plant hearts up when days are short, and runs to flower and seed when days are long. It grows rapidly and can be ready for cutting eight to ten weeks after sowing if given rather rich soil and then thinned to 23 cm (9 in) so that there is no check to growth. Good varieties are Tip Top and Kasumi.

CAPSICUM (SWEET PEPPER, CHILLI)
Capsicums are grown in the same way as tomatoes. Seed is sown in the first half of spring at a temperature of 16-18°C/61-65°F and the seedlings potted singly into 7·5 cm (3 in) pots when they have their first true leaves. They can later be moved into 18·7 cm (7½ in) pots if they are to grow under glass throughout, or they can be planted outdoors in a warm, sheltered, sunny place in early summer. J.I. or peat composts can be used. Capsicums can also be grown in peat-filled growing bags.

They need similar conditions to tomatoes. When the fruits start to swell the plants can be fed with a tomato fertilizer. If plants do not branch naturally, pinch out their growing tips when 30-45 cm (1-1½ ft) high to force them to branch. They will need to be tied to canes or other supports.

Picking can begin as soon as the fruits are large enough and while they are still green, or some can be left to ripen, when they turn red or yellow according to variety. Recommended varieties are Bell Boy, Canape and New Ace, all red-fruited. Goldstar and Yellow Lantern are yellow-fruited.

CARROTS
There are two main types of carrot, stump rooted and tapering, and a number of variations of each differing in size, length of root, colour of the core, etc. The very short, stump-rooted varieties are excellent for forcing in frames or under cloches. Longer stump-rooted varieties are probably the best for general use but the intermediate (tapering) and long (tapering) varieties are favoured by exhibitors because of their good

appearance and the challenge they make to good cultivation if they are to be really well produced.

All carrots do best on rather open, easily worked, reasonably rich soils. Dung, if used at all, should be applied sparingly and several months before sowing, but it is better to provide a site which was manured for a previous crop and to prepare this with artificial fertilizers alone. A suitable dressing is sulphate of ammonia, 28 g per 0·8 sq m (1 oz per sq yd), superphosphate of lime, 85 g (3 oz) to the same area and sulphate of potash, 42 g (1½ oz) to that area, raked in thoroughly just before sowing.

The earliest crops are obtained in frames or greenhouses and sowing can begin in mid-winter if a temperature of 12°C/54°F can be maintained. For these early crops, sow very thinly in drills 6 mm (¼ in) deep and 20 cm (8 in) apart and do not thin out the seedlings. Let them stand until they are big enough to use and then pull out the most forward first, leaving the rest to gain size.

Outdoor sowing can, as a rule, be started in early spring though it is no use sowing if the ground is wet and cold. Better wait for three or four weeks than risk bad germination. Drills should be 12 mm (½ in) deep and 23 cm (9 in) apart for stump-rooted varieties, 30-37 cm (1 ft-1 ft 3 in) apart for intermediate and long-rooted kinds. Successional sowings of stump-rooted varieties can be made every fortnight or so until mid-summer. As a rule it is not wise to sow the main crop for storing until mid-spring and in some districts it pays to wait until early summer for by this means the carrot fly is avoided. This fly lays its eggs in the soil near the seedlings, small white maggots hatch out in a week or so and eat their way into the young carrot roots. The pest is very damaging in some places and at certain seasons, but can usually be controlled by sprinkling bromophos in the seed drills or along the rows after thinning the carrots or when leaves are 5 cm (2 in) high.

Early carrots need not be thinned but maincrop carrots should be singled out to at least 10 cm (4 in) apart in the rows. For exhibition this may be increased to 20 cm (8 in). Do this while the seedlings are still quite small and be careful to press the soil firmly around the roots after thinning. If left loose the carrot fly is encouraged. It often pays to topdress along the rows with sulphate of ammonia or nitrate of soda, 28 g per 1·8 m (1 oz per 6 ft) of row, immediately after thinning.

Early carrots should be pulled as required for use, while the main crop should be dug about early autumn or at latest by mid-season. If left too long the roots get coarse and some will crack. Such roots do not store well.

Maincrop carrots lifted in good condition will keep until the spring if placed in a dry, airy shed and covered with dry sand or fine soil. Alternatively they can be stored in small clamps out of doors. First cut off the tops, then pack the roots in a low ridge with their tops outwards. Finally cover them with about 7·5 cm (3 in) of sand or sifted boiler ashes. The clamp should be made in a sheltered place.

There are a great many varieties of carrot though a good many of these do not differ markedly from one another. Reliable standard kinds are as follows: Stump rooted: Amsterdam Forcing, Chantenay Red Cored, Early Gem, Early Nantes; Tapered: James' Scarlet Intermediate and St Valery.

CAULIFLOWER

Cauliflowers need to be grown steadily without check from start to finish. The soil chosen for them should be rich and well watered and care must be taken that seedlings raised under glass are properly hardened off before they are planted out, otherwise they may be chilled and set back for several weeks.

Cauliflowers can be cut out of doors in early summer from a sowing made in late winter in a warm greenhouse, provided an early variety is chosen. An alternative method is to sow the seed out of doors in early autumn, transfer the seedlings to an unheated frame the following month and allow the seedlings to remain there throughout the winter. In either case the seedlings should be hardened off for planting out as early in spring as the weather allows. Later crops are obtained by sowing seed in a frame or sheltered position out of doors in spring and planting out from mid-spring to mid-summer.

In all cases the position chosen for planting should be open, sunny, but not too exposed. The ground must be dug as deeply as possible, in fact if it can be trenched so much the better, and manure should be used liberally; 50 kg per 4·8 sq m (1 cwt per 6 sq yd) will not be too much for summer and early autumn varieties but not for winter or spring heading varieties. In addition dust with superphosphate of lime, 56 g per 0·8 sq m (2 oz per sq yd) a week or so before planting.

Plant firmly with a trowel, 45 cm (1½ ft) apart for the early varieties and 60 cm (2 ft) apart in rows 75 cm (2½ ft) apart for the late summer, autumn and winter kinds. Topdress with a compound fertilizer when the plants are well established and draw a little soil from between the rows over the fertilizer and around the stems of the plants at the same time. Water freely if the weather is dry. Very weak liquid manure can be used instead of water.

When curds begin to form break some of the inner leaves down over them as a protection from sunlight which will spoil their whiteness. In autumn the broken leaves also serve to protect the curds from frost.

Cauliflowers should be cut directly the curds are of good size and before they begin to open. They tend to turn in all at once and so it is important in small gardens to make successional sowings or plantings every few weeks.

Good crops of early cauliflowers can also be produced under glass. The seedlings are raised in the ordinary way and are planted out in a bed of rich soil on the floor of the greenhouse as soon as they have five or six leaves each. Space them 45 cm (1½ ft) apart each way. Grow them on in an average temperature of 12°C/54°F. Keep well watered and ventilate freely whenever the weather is favourable; the more light and air the plants receive the better. This is quite a good utility crop to precede tomatoes. It will probably be necessary to plant the tomatoes in the greenhouse before the cauliflowers are cut and room should be left for this, but the tomatoes will not be very big by the time the cauliflowers are removed.

Varieties are numerous and are constantly added to. Alpha Polar Ice, Machelse Delta, Snowball Early Super and Snow Crown are recommended for early and mid-summer cutting; Dok, Dominant and Nevada for late summer and early autumn; Barrier Reef, Canberra and Flora Blanca for autumn; and Angers, English Winter, St. George and Walcheren Winter selections for winter and early spring, but these last are only suitable for mild districts. For ordinary conditions the summer and early autumn varieties are easiest and most satisfactory to grow.

CELERIAC

This is a useful alternative to celery and one which can be grown more easily in many gardens. It is cultivated for its thick stem base which, when fully grown, is about the size of a good turnip and has the flavour of celery. This swollen stem can be grated in salads or can be sliced and cooked in stews, soups, etc. It is sometimes stated that celeriac will grow in ground not rich enough for celery. This may be so but it is a comparative distinction only and does not mean that celeriac should be planted in poor, dry places. On the contrary, the ground should be dug thoroughly and well manured, for preference with farmyard or stable manure at about 50 kg per 6·4 sq m (1 cwt per 8 sq yd). The position should be open and not too dry.

Seed is sown in an unheated greenhouse or frame during the first half of spring. The seedlings are pricked off 5 cm (2 in) apart into deeper boxes directly they can be handled and, once well established, are gradually hardened off for planting out in late spring/early summer. Plant 30 cm (1 ft) apart in rows 45 cm (1½ ft) apart and subsequently keep well watered if the weather is dry but do not attempt to earth up in any way. A topdressing of high-nitrogen fertilizer, 28 g per 0·8 sq m (1 oz per sq yd), can be given a few weeks after planting out. No further attention should be necessary until mid-autumn, by which time the swollen stems should be well formed and ready for lifting. In sheltered districts celeriac can be left out of doors all winter and lifted as required, but in exposed places it is better to dig the whole crop in mid-autumn and store in a shed, covering with sand or dry soil.

Marble Ball is a good variety, as is Giant Prague and Tellus.

CELERY

This most useful of autumn and winter salad vegetables is not too easy to grow. It needs very good soil, plenty of moisture while in growth and yet good drainage. To reconcile these needs it is necessary to use plenty of well-rotted dung or, failing this, good compost, together with leafmould and peat to make the soil rather open and spongy.

Celery is reasonably hardy but the seed is so small and germinates so slowly, unless in a warm place, that it is better to raise it under glass in boxes or trays of fine soil than to chance sowing it in the open air. The earliest crops are obtained from early spring sowings made in a greenhouse with a temperature of 12-15°C/54-59°F, while seed for the main crop can be sown in an unheated greenhouse or frame about mid-spring.

Sow in seed or peat seed compost and cover with the merest sprinkling of the same compost. In addition cover each box or tray with a pane of glass and a sheet of brown paper, but this must be removed directly germination takes place.

As soon as they can be handled the seedlings should be pricked off into deeper seed boxes filled with a similar compost. The earlier this can be done the better and the seedlings must be separated out singly at this stage. They are so small and often the roots are so tangled together that it is easy to put them in in small clumps by mistake. Space them 5 cm (2 in) apart. Water them in well and return to the greenhouse or frame for a further fortnight, after which they can be gradually hardened off for planting out some time between late spring and mid-summer. The ground must be prepared for the plants as long as possible in advance and weeds eliminated before planting.

It is customary, though not essential, to grow celery in trenches which may be either 37·5 cm (13 in) wide to take a single row of plants, or 48·2 cm (1 ft 7 in) wide to take a double row. Soil from the trench is dug out to a depth of at least 60 cm (2 ft) and preferably 90 cm (3 ft), the subsoil, if poor, is replaced with good soil from another part of the garden, and then the trench is nearly but not quite refilled with the top soil mixed liberally with well-rotted dung; 50 kg (1 cwt) of dung to 8 m (24 ft) of trench is not too much. Plant with a trowel, 30 cm (1 ft) apart down the middle of the trench for a single row, or at each side if two rows are to be planted.

A few weeks after planting a topdressing of nitrate of soda or sulphate of ammonia can be given down the trenches at the rate of 28 g per 3·6 m (1 oz per 12 ft) and this can be repeated a fortnight later. Water liberally in dry weather and occasionally substitute weak liquid manure for plain water.

Earthing up to blanch the stems should not be started until the plants are fully grown as it checks further progress. As a rule the earliest crop, planted in late spring, is ready for earthing during late summer, while the main crop is earthed during the first half of autumn. First of all remove any offshoots that have formed around the base of each plant. Then tie the stems together and draw the soil from each side of the trench towards the plants and up around them. Some growers tie a brown paper collar round the plants before earthing up to prevent soil falling into their hearts. In the case of self-blanching celery no earthing is necessary but all offshoots should be removed as soon as they appear.

It takes about six weeks to blanch celery properly and subsequently it can be left just as it is to be dug as required. From late autumn onwards it is advisable to place a couple of planks on edge along the summit of each ridge to divert water and prevent it soaking down into the hearts of the plants. After the ridge has been opened at one end and a few sticks removed the soil should be returned and banked up again as a protection against frost.

There are numerous excellent varieties but the main distinction is to be made between white- and pink-skinned types. Of these Solid White, Wright's Giant White, Standard Bearer Pink, Clayworth Prize Pink are good examples. Pink varieties are hardier than white and may be left for later lifting. Celebrity and Ivory Tower are self-blanching.

There are also self-blanching varieties which have naturally pale-coloured stems. If planted 23 cm (9 in) apart in a squarish bed the leaves cast sufficient shade to complete the blanching to a very pale, golden or greenish colour. These varieties are not of the highest quality nor do they make sticks of very great size but they are extremely economical to grow. Because of the close planting it is essential to grow them in very rich soil and to water freely. They are only suitable for summer and early autumn use.

CHICORY

This is grown as a salad for winter use, for which purpose the leaves and stems are forced and blanched. Suitable roots for forcing are obtained by sowing seed out of doors in the second half of spring in drills 12 mm (½ in) deep and 37·5 cm (1¼ ft) apart. Sow the seed very thinly. Previously the ground should have been well dug and given a dressing of dung or compost at the rate of 50 kg per 9·6 sq m (1 cwt per 12 sq yd) followed by a topdressing of superphosphate of lime, 56 g per 0·8 sq m (2 oz per sq yd). The seedlings are thinned to 23 cm (9 in) apart as soon as they have their first true leaves. Subsequently they need little care beyond hoeing and weeding until mid-autumn, by which time they should have formed good roots, 30 cm (1 ft) or more in length and not unlike thin parsnips. These are lifted a few at a time, any remaining leaves are cut off just above the crowns and they are packed 2·5 cm (1 in) or so apart in boxes or fairly large flower pots filled with any old potting soil. They are then brought into a warm greenhouse, shed or

Earthing up celery for blanching. The stems may first be protected by paper or cardboard collars

Blanching chicory by placing the closely packed roots in a dark cupboard

cupboard and kept completely dark. The temperature should be 15°C/59°F or more and the soil must be watered moderately. The blanched shoots are cut off at soil level when 16·2 cm (6½ in) high. They are served in salads in the same way as lettuces or endives or can be cooked and served hot. The forced roots are of no further use and should be thrown away. Alternatively some roots of chicory can be blanched outdoors by earthing them up like celery and these will give a successional crop in late winter or spring.

Brussels, also known as Witloof, is an old variety. Alpha and Crispa are more recent introductions. Sugar Loaf and Red Verona form dense heads of leaves rather like cos lettuce and can be used direct from the ground in autumn.

CHIVES

This member of the onion family is very easily grown and is remarkable for its mild flavour. Many people prefer it on this account to spring onions as an ingredient of salads and it can also be used instead of onions as flavouring in soups and stews.

Chives are exceptionally easy to grow. All that is necessary is to obtain a good clump as early in spring as possible, split it up into small tufts, each with two or three shoots and some roots attached, and plant these firmly 15 cm (6 in) apart in rows about 23 cm (9 in) apart in any ordinary garden soil and reasonably open position. No further attention is required except for occasional hoeing and weeding, until the plants get overcrowded, when they can be lifted, divided and replanted in early spring.

When chives are required for kitchen use, the shoots are simply cut off at soil level. Take a few from each plant and growth will continue unchecked.

There are no varieties.

CORN SALAD (LAMB'S LETTUCE)

Corn salad is a low-growing annual plant which is cultivated for its leaves. These are cut when the plants are several centimetres high, before they begin to flower, and are served in salad with lettuce and the other more familiar ingredients.

Seed should be sown sparingly, either broadcast or in 12 mm (½ in) deep drills, 10 cm (4 in) apart. Thin the seedlings to 10 cm (4 in) apart. Frequent small sowings should be made at fortnightly intervals from about early spring until early autumn. Late sowings for autumn and winter use are best made in a frame or may be covered later with cloches. The ground chosen should be open or slightly shaded and the soil well dug and fairly rich. Water freely in dry weather.

There are no varieties of importance.

CRESS

Cress is usually grown to accompany mustard as a salad, but those who find the flavour of mustard too strong can, if they prefer, have cress alone.

Outdoor crops can be grown from mid-spring to early autumn, while under glass in a temperature of 10-15°C/50-59°F cress can be grown for the remaining months of the year, but many people prefer to grow it in frames, even in summer, in order to keep it clean. No special soil is required so long as it is fine and sandy; in fact it is possible to grow cress in sand alone. Cress should be grown in shallow trays or in pots, the seed being broadcast thinly and evenly all over the surface. No soil covering is needed but glass and brown paper should be laid over the boxes or pots until germination occurs. Then remove this covering and give the cress full light until it is ready for cutting somewhere between the 12th and 18th day from sowing. Cut with scissors just above soil level when seedlings are 6·2 cm (2½ in) high.

Note that cress takes three or four days longer than mustard to grow, a point which must be allowed for when making sowings to cut at the same time. For a constant supply it is advisable to make a small sowing every 7 to 10 days.

CUCUMBER

The frame or house cucumber needs a good deal of warmth to succeed and is a crop only to be grown under glass. In contrast the ridge cucumber is much hardier and good crops can be obtained in the open during the summer months. The fruits are inferior in size and appearance but not in flavour to the glasshouse kind.

Under Glass. Frame cucumbers need a very rich, open-textured soil containing abundant humus. They must have good drainage and yet the compost must be sufficiently spongy to hold ample moisture even when the atmosphere is very warm. The usual practice is to make up a special bed with a mixture of 3 parts by bulk good loam and 1 part well-decayed manure.

Build this into a flat-topped bed 30 cm (1 ft) deep and wide at the top and about 15 cm (6 in) wider at the base. This bed can run the whole length of the house if desired. One cucumber will be planted every 90 cm (3 ft) along its length. In an ordinary greenhouse with side walls 60 cm (2 ft) or more high beds may be on the staging, but if a low-walled forcing house is used or one that is glazed to ground level the bed is best made on the floor.

An alternative method of bed making is to spread a 15 cm (6 in) deep layer of the compost to a width of about 90 cm (3 ft) and any desired length, and make a low mound with 18 l (4 gal) of compost every 90 cm (3 ft) along this shallow bed. One cucumber is planted on the summit of each mound. The advantage gained by this is that of really sharp drainage round the collar of the plant where stem joins root. Decay is liable to occur here if it is kept too wet. The drawback of the mounded bed is that not only the collar but the roots themselves may get dry at times and that will mean a check to growth.

Beds can be made and seed sown at almost any time of the year, according to the period at which the crop is required, but usual practice with amateurs is to make one sowing just after mid-winter for an early crop, another in early spring for the main crop, with possibly a late-spring sowing for a late supply.

The seeds are sown in pairs in small pots filled with J.I. seed or peat seed compost. They are watered moderately and placed in a greenhouse with a temperature of 18-21°C/65-70°F. Stand in a box covered with glass or cover the pots themselves with glass and brown paper. Germination is usually very rapid and may take no more than two days. Directly the seedlings can be seen the covering must be removed and a day or so later the seedlings are reduced to one in each pot, the best being retained.

Plant when the seedlings have two rough leaves each, keeping the top of the ball of soil just level with the surface of the bed, and watering in freely.

The main shoot of each plant is trained directly towards the apex of the house on horizontally strained wires about 30 cm (1 ft) below the glass. As side growths form they are tied along the wires and each is pinched at the second leaf beyond the first fruit formed. The main growth is pinched when it reaches the top of the house or a length of 2·1-2·4 m (7-8 ft). Secondary shoots forming from the first side growths will also carry fruits and must be stopped two leaves beyond these. Later in the season, after the plants have been cropping for some time, some of the older growths that have already carried a lot of cucumbers are cut right out and young shoots are trained in.

Cucumbers produce flowers of two sexes, male and female. They can be distinguished quite easily by the fact that immediately behind the female flower is a tiny embryo cucumber, whereas the male flower is simply carried on a thin stalk. These male flowers should be picked off as soon as they can be distinguished as it is not desirable that the female flowers should be fertilized. If they are the cucumbers will produce seeds and will not be nearly so palatable. There is no need to reduce the number of female flowers unless the plants are weak. No fruits are allowed to form on the main stem, only on side shoots. Some varieties produce nearly all female flowers and this can save time.

Throughout the season the atmosphere should be pleasantly warm and very moist. If it is allowed to become dry the foliage is likely to be scorched and to be attacked by red spider, a minute pest which breeds on the undersides of the leaves, sucks the juice from them and turns them a curiously mottled, greyish-yellow colour. The best preventive for red spider is moisture and this is maintained by damping the floors, walls and stages of the house and syringing the leaves two or three times a day with tepid water.

The cucumber is a surface-rooting plant and after a short time a good many white roots will probably appear on top of the soil. This is the signal for topdressing with a mixture of equal parts well-rotted stable manure and good loam, which should be spread 2·5 cm (1 in) thick all over the bed, mounds included, but not around the stems where they enter the soil. Two or three topdressings can be given during the course of a season, being repeated each time fresh roots appear on the surface.

In winter, spring and autumn cucumbers can usually do with all the light they can get, but in summer some shading should be given. This may take the form of a thin stipple of whitewash or one of the advertised shading compounds applied to the glass from a spraying machine fitted with a fine nozzle.

Cucumbers should be cut regularly when of good size but before they begin to turn yellow. It is a mistake to let them hang too long as this checks cropping; on the other hand immature fruits are bitter.

Sometimes, particularly towards the end of the cropping season, a good many of the fruits will wither back from the end. This is a sign that the plants are weak and may be due to over-cropping, under feeding or a decaying root system, caused by over or under watering and general deterioration of the bed. Sometimes such plants can be encouraged to bear a few more good fruits by being heavily topdressed and thoroughly pruned to get rid of old growth.

Frames. Culture in frames differs in no marked respect from that of cucumbers under glass except in the method of training. Each plant is pinched when it has made about six leaves. Subsequently four new shoots are allowed to form and these are trained towards the four corners of the frame, being pegged to the soil with pieces of wire bent like large hairpins. These runners are in turn pinched when they reach the confines of the frame and most of the fruits are produced on the secondary side growths. As a rule one plant is sufficient for each 1.8×1.2 m (6×4 ft) frame, and should be planted in the centre. It is a great advantage if the frame can stand on a good hotbed or be warmed by electric soil-warming cables. Mid-spring is a suitable time for planting.

There are many varieties of frame cucumber but one of the best for general purposes is Butcher's Disease Resisting. Improved Telegraph has fine-quality fruits but a somewhat shorter season. A variety named Conqueror will thrive in a much drier and cooler atmosphere than any other frame cucumber and in consequence will grow with other plants, such as tomatoes. Modern varieties producing mainly female flowers are Femspot and Pepinex 69.

Outdoor Cultivation. Ridge cucumbers require a rather different system of culture. The seed is sown and germinated in a similar manner but not before the last fortnight in mid-spring, as the seedlings must not be planted out until the first week in summer. The plants are given as sunny and sheltered a position as possible in well-dug soil that has been thoroughly dressed with decayed manure. One may use as much as 50 kg (1 cwt) of manure for 4 sq m (5 sq yd) of bed. Contrary to popular belief, it is not good policy to plant ridge cucumbers on a ridge, as they tend to dry out too quickly, but the bed must be well drained. The plants are pinched as for cucumbers grown in frames, the runners being stopped again when about 90 cm (3 ft) long.

Male flowers are not picked off as with the frame cucumber for it is desirable that the female flowers should be fertilized. In fact, if fruits fail to set properly, it is good policy to fertilize them by hand. This is done by picking off some of the male blooms when fully open and shaking them over the female flowers.

Ridge cucumbers will be killed by the first touch of autumn frost, but are quite capable of giving a heavy crop during late summer/early winter. They should be watered freely during dry weather.

Earlier crops can be obtained by growing ridge cucumbers under cloches. With such protection plants can often be put out safely in late spring in some places. Two shoots per plant instead of four should be retained after the first pinching and these trained in opposite directions along the line of cloches. Towards mid-summer the cloches may be

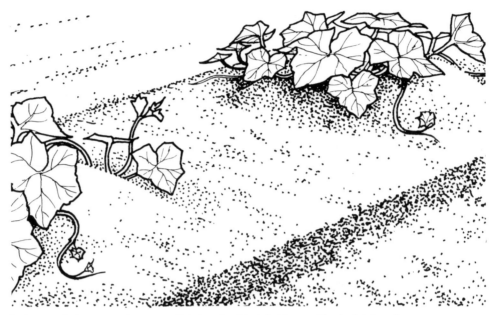

Ridge cucumbers growing on a slightly raised but flat-topped bed of rich soil

removed and the plants allowed to spread more widely. Yet another alternative is to grow ridge cucumbers in frames in which case they are stopped like ordinary frame cucumbers. If the frame is well made and in a sheltered place it is possible to plant about mid-spring.

Good varieties are Burpee Hybrid, Burpless Tasty Green and Bedfordshire Prize. The frame cucumber Conqueror can also be grown as a ridge variety and is particularly good under cloches. Conda is a good gherkin-type.

ENDIVE

This vegetable looks rather like a lettuce and is used in salads in exactly the same way as lettuces. It is rather more bitter in flavour but this is less marked if the endive is grown quickly throughout and is thoroughly blanched. The great merit of this salad vegetable is its hardiness and the fact that it can be grown in winter without artificial heat.

The soil should be reasonably rich and well dug. Well-rotted dung can be used at the rate of up to 50 kg per 8 sq m (1 cwt per 10 sq yd). In addition superphosphate of lime should be raked into the bed immediately before sowing, at the rate of 56 g per 0·8 sq m (2 oz per sq yd). Sow thinly in drills 12 mm (½ in) deep and 30 cm (1 ft) apart. A first sowing can be made in mid-spring, with further sowings at intervals of about three weeks until late summer, but because of its value as an autumn and winter salad it is the later sowings which are most important.

Seedlings should be thinned to 23 cm (9 in) apart and can be transplanted elsewhere if desired. From the last sowing it is a good plan to transplant some of the thinnings to a frame or unheated greenhouse and then to cover the remaining plants in the seed rows with cloches towards mid-autumn.

A week or so after thinning nitrate of soda can be dusted down the rows at the rate of 28 g per 3·6 m (1 oz per 12 ft), and a similar dressing given three weeks later.

No other attention, beyond regular hoeing and weeding, is necessary until the plants are well grown, when they should be blanched either by covering each with an inverted plate or piece of wood or, in the case of frame- or cloche-grown plants, by darkening the glass or throwing sacks over it. The more light that can be excluded the better, for the aim should be to blanch all green colouring out of the leaves. It will take about six weeks to do this and the endives are then ready for use.

Good kinds are Moss Curled and Green Batavian, the former with very curly and deeply cut leaves which have a most attractive appearance, and the latter with almost plain leaves. Green Batavian has the merit, however, of being even hardier than Moss Curled.

FENNEL

There are two kinds of fennel – common fennel, *Foeniculum vulgare*, sometimes grown as a herb for its aniseed flavoured leaves (and a good base on which to roast chicken), and Florence or sweet fennel (finocchio), *F. vulgare dulce*, grown for its swollen bulb-like leaf bases with a similar aniseed flavour which are cooked as a vegetable.

Common fennel is easily grown in any reasonably well drained soil from seed sown in spring where it is to grow, the seedlings being thinned to 30 cm (1 ft) apart. It is a perennial that can be left for several years and is likely to spread by self-sown seed.

Florence fennel is equally easy to grow but not so easy to grow well, as it does not always form its swollen leaf base. This happens when plants bolt (run prematurely to flower and seed), which is controlled to some extent by day length. For this reason early and mid-summer sowing may be preferable to spring sowing, especially for varieties like Sweet Florence and Perfection, but other varieties are less likely to bolt. All should be treated as annuals to be sown every year in well manured, well drained soil and a sunny place. Thin seedlings to 30 cm (1 ft) apart and lift them for use as the swollen stems reach an acceptable size. Water the plants well in dry weather as lack of moisture is another cause of bolting.

GARLIC

The flavour of garlic is strong and most people will find a dozen plants are sufficient for their purpose.

The cultivation of garlic is very similar to that of shallots. At the end of each season of growth the plant forms a cluster of small bulbs, each of the bulbs being known as a clove. This should be split up into separate bulbs and replanted in late autumn or, failing that, in early spring, 15 cm (6 in) apart in rows 30 cm (1 ft) apart. The bulbs should be given a sunny position in well-drained, fairly rich ground and should be barely covered with soil. Thereafter leave them alone, with the exception of weeding and hoeing, until the foliage turns yellow in mid-summer, when the whole plant is lifted and hung up in a cool, airy shed for a week or so to dry off. Some of the cloves can then be kept for kitchen use and others set aside for replanting the following year. All should be stored in a cool, dry, airy, but frost-proof place. There are white and pink varieties.

GOURDS

Botanically these have the same origin as vegetable marrows and from the garden standpoint they are treated in exactly the same manner except that the fruits (gourds) are not cut until they are fully ripe, when the skins turn from green to yellow or orange and become very hard. The gourd can be stored for several months in a cool, dry, airy place.

The fruits are used in the same way as pumpkins but some of the very ornamental varieties have little flesh and are grown more for decoration than utility.

HERBS

Besides those kinds dealt with separately the following could be useful for flavouring.

Balm *(Melissa officinalis)*. A hardy perennial with lemon-scented leaves that can be grown from seed sown in spring where it is to grow. The leaves can be used fresh or dried and stored.

Basil. Generally, two kinds are grown – bush basil *(Ocimum minimum)*, a compact plant, and sweet basil *(O. basilicum)* with taller, looser growth. Both have spicily flavoured leaves and are slightly tender annuals grown from seed sown in early spring in a frame or greenhouse, or outdoors in late spring. Plants should be spaced 15 cm (6 in) apart in well cultivated soil and a sunny position. Specialist seed merchants will sell a wide range of varieties including those from Thailand and Indonesia.

Borage *(Borago officinalis)*. A hardy annual with blue flowers that are much sought after by bees. It can be grown from seed sown outdoors in spring where it is to grow. It likes sunny places and well drained alkaline soil.

Caraway *(Carum carvi)*. A hardy biennial grown from seed sown in mid-spring where it is to grow. Seedlings are thinned to 23 cm (9 in) apart. Its seeds are chiefly valued for flavouring and are harvested as soon as ripe in summer the following year.

Chervil *(Anthriscus cerefolium)*. An annual grown for its aniseed flavoured leaves. Seed should be sown from mid-spring to early summer where it is to grow and seedlings thinned to 15 cm (6 in).

Coriander *(Coriander sativum)*. An annual grown for its small, seed-like fruits which have a spicy flavour, and foliage. Seed is sown from mid- to late spring in a warm sunny place and seedlings thinned to about 15 cm (6 in). The plants are cut and brought inside to be dried when the little fruits become beige-coloured. The kind known as Indian parsley produces more leaf, and is a better choice for many recipes.

Dill *(Anethum graveolens)*. A hardy annual with feathery leaves. Both leaves and seeds can be used for flavouring. It is grown from seed sown outdoors in the second half of spring in a sunny place where plants are to grow and seedlings thinned to 23 cm (9 in).

Hyssop *(Hyssopus officinalis)*. An attractive small shrub with blue flowers grown for its aromatic leaves. It can be raised from seed sown in a frame or outdoors in the second half of spring, seedlings being transplanted 30 cm (1 ft) apart in a warm, sunny place in well drained soil.

Lovage *(Levisticum officinale)*. A rather big, leafy hardy perennial grown for its mid-spring celery-like flavour. It can be grown from seed sown outdoors in mid-spring but old plants can also be divided in spring or autumn. It likes rich, rather moist soil and will grow in sun or semi-shade.

Marjoram. There are several different kinds of marjoram but the one usually cultivated as a culinary herb is sweet or knotted marjoram (*Origanum marjorana*). It is a rather tender perennial usually cultivated as an annual sown under glass in early spring, or outdoors later in the season. It likes good soil and a sunny position and seedlings should be planted out or thinned to about 15 cm (6 in) apart.

Savory. Two kinds are grown, summer savory (*Satureia hortensis*), an annual, and winter savory (*S. montana*), a perennial. Both can be grown from seed sown outdoors in the second half of spring, but winter savory can also be increased from summer cuttings or by division in spring or autumn. Plants need to be 23-30 cm (9 in-1 ft) apart and like well drained soil.

HORSE RADISH

This is one of the easiest of all vegetables to grow badly, thought it is not so simple to grow it well. By this I mean that roots of a sort can be produced merely by planting small roots or even pieces cut from roots in any soil and situation and leaving them alone, but that such samples are likely to be thin, much branched and not of the thick, straight shape which is the most useful for cooking.

The best roots are produced by choosing an open situation, digging the soil deeply and breaking up all large lumps, working in a little well-rotted manure and then, in early spring, making holes with a thick dibber (an old spade handle is ideal) and dropping into each of these one small horse-radish root right way up. The top of each root should be just below soil level. It is not essential that the root should have a crown attached though it is better if it has. No further attention is necessary beyond weeding and hoeing until late autumn, when the whole bed should be lifted, the best roots sorted out for kitchen use and the remainder divided or cut up into suitable lengths for replanting. All should then be laid in sand or ashes in a sheltered place, the planting roots to be put in the following early spring and the others to be used as needed. It is necessary to clear the bed thoroughly of roots as any pieces left may grow and horse radish can become a troublesome weed.

KALE (BORECOLE)

These are members of the brassica family and are thus very closely allied to the cabbage and broccoli. In appearance and habit they are a most varied lot. There are, for example, the Scotch kales with densely curled leaves; in contrast there are varieties with almost plain leaves, such as Cottager's kale and Thousand Headed, others with cut leaves such as Russian kale, an exceptionally hardy kind, and yet others which are grown more for the young shoots than for the leaves, such as the Asparagus kale. Almost all are very profitable and hardy vegetables, particularly serviceable between the New Year and the end of spring, when green crops tend to become scarce and variety is lacking.

Seed should be sown out of doors in mid-spring in any open position and well-broken ground. Sow thinly in drills 12 mm (½ in) deep and 15 cm (6 in) apart. When the seedlings have made four or five leaves each, transplant them to their permanent positions, where they should be spaced 45 cm (1½ ft) apart in rows at least 76 cm (2½ ft) apart for the larger growing kinds, though these distances can be reduced to 30 cm (1 ft) and 60 cm (2 ft) respectively for smaller sorts such as the Dwarf Scotch Curled.

The ground should be prepared exactly as for winter cabbage and planting should be carried out in the same way. It is good policy, though not essential, to topdress along the rows with well-rotted dung about mid-summer and draw soil from between rows over the dung and up around the stems in a low ridge. This helps to steady the plants and encourages them to make further roots into the fresh soil and more vigorous growth.

Alternatively some varieties such as Asparagus kale, Hungry Gap and Russian kale can be sown thinly in early to mid-summer directly where they are to grow, the seedlings being well thinned but not transplanted.

There is a popular idea that no kale should be cut until there has been fairly sharp frost. It is perfectly true that the flavour of the kale is improved after cold weather but it is quite possible to start using the leaves early in the autumn even before there has been any frost at all. The right method is to cut the leaves from the plants, starting from the bottom and working up and allowing a small stump of stalk to remain. The tops should be removed last of all, though even after they have been cut off there may still be some secondary growth from the lower part of the stem. In this way it is possible to gather useful food from a single plantation of kale for several months at a time when there is a scarcity of other green vegetables.

KOHL RABI

This is grown for its swollen turnip-like stems. Its merits are that it has the flavour of a mild turnip but can be grown successfully in soils and during seasons which are too dry for turnips. The kohl rabi, like the turnip, is a member of the brassica family.

Prepare the ground in exactly the same way as for summer cabbages, being fairly generous with dung. The seed can either be sown very thinly where the plants are to grow or, alternatively, can be raised in a seed bed as for cabbages, the seedlings being transplanted to final quarters at an early stage. In either case the plants should be spaced 30 cm (1 ft) apart in rows 45 cm (1½ ft) apart. Keep them growing as quickly as possible during the summer by frequent hoeing and an occasional light topdressing of nitrate of soda, 28 g per 0·8 sq m (1 oz per sq yd). Pull the roots for table use when they are about the size of tennis balls. A common mistake is to let them get too big, when they are strong in flavour and tough.

Kohl rabi cannot be stored for any length of time like turnips and in order to ensure a supply from late summer to about Christmas, small successional sowings should be made every four weeks or so, starting in mid-spring and finishing with the last sowing in mid-summer.

White Vienna has white bulbs and Purple Vienna purple marked bulbs. F_1 Lanro is a good new hybrid.

LEEKS

These can be extremely profitable if well grown but they need a deep and rather rich soil and must have a long season of growth. For exhibition, seed is usually sown in a warm greenhouse in mid- to late winter, the seedlings being pricked off 3·7 cm (1½ in) each way into fairly deep trays as soon as they can be handled and then gradually hardened off for planting out of doors in mid-spring. An alternative is to raise the seedlings in a frame from a late winter sowing. For ordinary kitchen use it is satisfactory to sow seed out of doors in the first half of spring in an open position and well-broken soil, into which superphosphate of lime has been raked at 56 g per 0·8 sq m (2 oz per sq yd), immediately prior to sowing. The resultant seedlings will be lifted and planted in the first half of summer, the earlier the better.

For ordinary purposes plant in rows 45 cm (1½ ft) apart spacing the plants 23 cm (9 in) apart. Make the holes about 25 cm (10 in) deep with a stout dibber – one made out of an old spade handle is excellent. One plant should be dropped well down into each hole so that only the tops of the leaves project above ground level. The soil is not replaced immediately in the hole but instead the plants are well watered in directly from the spout of a watering-can so that some soil is washed down round the roots. Later on the holes will automatically fill up, both from the action of rain and when the bed is hoed. This will blanch the stems for several centimetres and further blanching can be secured by drawing soil from between the rows towards and around the plants.

For exhibition purposes an even greater length of blanched stem is required and this is obtained by planting the leeks in trenches prepared as for single rows of celery (see p. 556) and spaced at least 90 cm (3 ft) apart . The leeks are planted 30 cm (1 ft) apart in these trenches. As the leeks grow, soil is gradually drawn into the trenches and, later, from between the trenches towards the plants to form a steep-sided ridge; in fact in some cases planks placed on edge are used to hold the soil up. In this way the leeks are encouraged to grow a very long stem which is blanched from top to bottom. Pure white stems 90 cm (3 ft) in length may often be seen at shows. Note particularly that the blanching is done gradually throughout the season of growth, not all at once at the end of the season as in the case of celery and endive. Exhibition leeks are usually fed generously during the growing season with weak liquid manure and small topdressings of nitrate of soda or soot well hoed in.

Leeks are in season from about late summer until the following mid-spring. They are quite hardy, so it is unnecessary to lift and store the crop; they can be dug from the open ground at any time during the winter as required for use.

Most firms list their own specialities, but good standard varieties are Musselburgh, Lyon and various selections of Autumn Mammoth. The pot leek is extremely popular and there are special competitions for it. This has a very thick but quite short stem and it is grown in the same manner as leeks for kitchen use, though with special attention to the richness of the soil when extra weighty exhibition specimens are needed.

LETTUCE

It is possible, but not easy, to produce lettuce throughout the year. Outdoor supplies can be obtained from mid-spring to mid-autumn without protection, while in greenhouses, frames and cloches, winter and early spring supplies can be grown. The chief difficulty with the mid-winter lettuce is that there are few varieties which will heart during the short days. Any attempt to force ordinary lettuces by increasing the amount of artificial heat results in disease or in the production of a few big leaves without any hearts. This difficulty can only be overcome by using special winter-hearting kinds such as Dandie or

Planting leeks in holes 25 cm (10 in) deep made with a stout dibber. The holes are partly filled in by watering directly from the spout of a watering-can

Kwiek, though a fair amount of skill is needed to grow even these successfully. There are, in addition, so-called hardy lettuces which can be left out of doors all the winter in sheltered positions, but these are seldom fit to cut before mid-spring.

Apart from this difference between summer- and winter-hearting varieties, there are three principal types, the cabbage, the cos and the loose-leaf lettuce. The first is the familiar, round-hearted lettuce of the greengrocers' shops and by far the most popular type in this country. Some varieties have quite brittle leaves and are known as 'crisphead'; others have leaves of softer texture and are known as 'butterhead'. The cos lettuce has long, boat-shaped leaves of a crisp texture. Loose-leaf varieties do not make any heart but have a mass of leaves.

The secret of success with all lettuces is to grow them swiftly and without check in rather rich, well-watered but open-textured soil. (Lettuces started early in the greenhouse can be grown in small peat pots which are planted outside when the weather improves: the roots grow through the container minimizing disturbance.) Though lettuces can be grown in a certain amount of shade a sunny position is better, especially for early and late supplies. In mid-summer a little shade is sometimes an advantage as it minimises the necessity for watering.

The ground should be dug as deeply as practicable. Well-rotted manure may be used freely up to 50 kg per 6·4 sq m (1 cwt per 8 sq yd). In addition, immediately prior to sowing, rake in at the rate of 113 g per 0·8 sq m (4 oz per sq yd) a mixture of 6 parts by weight superphosphate of lime, 2 parts sulphate of ammonia and 3 parts sulphate of potash, or use a balanced compound fertilizer according to maker's instructions.

Individual sowings should be fairly small but should be repeated at frequent intervals as lettuces will not stand long and must be cut as soon as ready for use. The first sowings are made under glass in a temperature of 12-15°C/54-59°F during the second half of winter. Seed can be sown thinly in boxes or pans and must be very lightly covered. The seedlings are pricked off 5 cm (2 in) apart into deep seed trays as soon as possible and are then hardened off for planting out during a mild, damp spell from early to mid-spring. Take them from the boxes with plenty of soil round the roots and plant firmly but not too deeply with a trowel, spacing the plants 30 cm (1 ft) apart.

Outdoor sowing can be started in early spring as the ground becomes workable and thereafter a small sowing can be made every fortnight or three weeks until late summer. Sow very thinly in drills 12 mm (½ in) deep and 30 cm (1 ft) apart, and thin out the seedlings to 25 cm (10 in) when they have three or four leaves each. The thinnings can be transplanted elsewhere if required and will usually heart up about a week or ten days later than those plants left undisturbed. In early autumn a sowing can be made in a frame or greenhouse or, alternatively, in a very sheltered place out of doors, with the object of transplanting the seedlings to a frame or greenhouse later on.

Once they have been thinned, lettuces require very little attention, though if growth is slow a dusting of nitrate of soda, 28 g per 3 m (1 oz per 10 ft) of row, well hoed in, will help. Trouble is most likely to occur if the weather is very hot and the soil becomes thoroughly dry. In this case watering may be essential but once started must be continued as long as the drought continues. If growth is too slow, the soil poor, or the weather very hot, lettuces are liable to run to seed before they have time to form a heart.

There are a great many varieties. Representative butterhead varieties are All the Year Round, Avondefiance, Continuity and Trocadero Improved; crisphead varieties, Tom Thumb, Avoncrisp, Great Lakes, and Webb's Wonderful; cos varieties, Little Gem, Lobjoit's Green and Winter Density; and a loose-leaf variety, Salad Bowl. For winter and early spring cultivation in greenhouses Arctic King, Dandie, Kwiek and Kloek are recommended.

Forcing. In winter under glass, the chief difficulty is to get enough light to counterbalance the artificial heat and keep the plants growing steadily. The frame or greenhouse should be in the sunniest place available and the glass must be kept spotlessly clean. The bed in which the plants are grown must be near the glass and the temperature should never rise much above 15°C/59°F with 10°C/50°F as the mean. Ventilation must be given freely whenever outside conditions are favourable and there is no fog. In frames ventilation may be even more liberal and temperatures lower, though this will mean slower growth and a later crop.

Sowings for these winter and early spring lettuces should be made from early to mid-autumn in a temperature of about 12°C/54°F. Seedlings should be transplanted when they have three or four leaves and roots must be kept quite close to the surface. Deep planting will encourage disease; so will overcrowding, so adopt the same spacings as for outdoor plants.

For special varieties see above.

MINT

This is one of those odd plants which will grow like a weed in one place and absolutely refuse to take in another. It does best in an open, sunny position and reasonably rich soil which is neither very heavy nor very light. Roots should be obtained in early spring and spread out thinly all over the bed. Then cover them with about 2·5 cm (1 in) of fine soil: old potting soil is admirable for the purpose though ordinary garden soil can be used. After this, leave the bed well alone, simply pulling out by hand any weeds that appear. Neither a hoe nor any other tool can be used on the mint bed with safety.

There may not be a great deal of growth the first year, but as long as the roots do make some shoots and leaves, it is satisfactory. By the second year they should be growing strongly and the bed will soon be a mat of roots covered with dense mint growth, from which shoots can be picked as required.

When the bed becomes so crowded that growth falls off, the roots should be lifted in early spring, divided and replanted in freshly dug, moderately manured ground. Various flavours are available, including ginger and peppermint.

Forcing. To obtain a winter supply of mint lift a few good roots in mid-autumn, break them up into single pieces and strew these thinly in ordinary seed boxes filled with old potting soil. Cover them with 12 mm ($\frac{1}{2}$ in) of the same material, place them in a frame for a month or so and then bring them into a warm greenhouse with a temperature of about 15-21°C/59-70°F. Water moderately and growth should start very quickly. These forced roots are not of much use afterwards and should be thrown away.

There are no important garden varieties of mint but there are several different species cultivated, of which far and away the best is the familiar Spearmint, with smooth, dark green, notched leaves.

MUSHROOMS

This is probably the most difficult crop for the beginner to manage. Sometimes mushrooms crop excellently and at other times, though apparently given identical treatment, they are a failure.

Mushrooms can be grown both indoors and out but the crop in the open is even more risky than that under cover and can only be obtained with any degree of certainty from about late summer to mid-autumn. Under cover it is possible to have mushrooms the whole year round provided a temperature of around 12°C/54°F can be maintained. It is not at all essential to have a greenhouse, as mushrooms can be grown in complete darkness.

At one time it was supposed that mushrooms could only be cultivated in horse manure but nowadays they are usually grown on a compost made by rotting clean straw with a special mushroom compost maker. In using this manufacturers' instructions must be accurately followed.

If horse manure is employed there are two essentials: first, to obtain really fresh manure containing a fair amount of straw and second, to make certain that it comes from healthy, stable-fed animals. There must be no shavings or sawdust in the manure. Take out any pieces of twig or other refuse and then build the manure into a stack 90 cm (3 ft) high, 90 cm (3 ft) wide and of any convenient length. Cover this all over with 2·5 cm (1 in) of soil.

A week later turn the stack completely, bringing the inside parts out and vice versa. At the same time water thoroughly any parts which appear dry. Continue to turn the stack in the same way every fourth or fifth day for three weeks by which time the manure should have decayed to such an extent that the straw can be easily broken and the whole mass appears brown and rotten. If there is any smell of ammonia when the heap is turned, it is not sufficiently rotted.

The prepared compost or decayed manure is either made into beds or placed in boxes of any convenient size and 23-30 cm (9 in-1 ft) in depth. Indoor beds are usually flat, 76 cm (2½ ft) wide, 23 cm (9 in) deep and of any convenient length. Out of doors ridge beds are preferred as they shoot off rain more readily. The ridge is about 90 cm (3 ft) wide at the base, 76 cm (2½ ft) high, a little rounded on top and of any desired length. In all cases the manure should be trodden down firmly layer by layer as the box is filled or the bed made. Plunge a thermometer well down into the manure and take a reading daily. When the temperature falls to between 21°C/70°F and 24°C/75°F the bed is ready for spawning.

It is possible to obtain either manure spawn made from composted manure inoculated with mushroom mycelium or grain spawn in which crushed rye, wheat or barley is used as the base. The spawn should be broken up by hand into small lumps each about as big as a walnut, and these should be buried 2·5 cm (1 in) deep and 23 cm (9 in) apart all over the bed. Grain spawn can be scattered thinly over the bed. Then cover the whole bed with a 15 cm (6 in) layer of clean, dry straw or, if the bed is out of doors, use 30 cm (1 ft) of straw for additional protection. About ten days later, remove a little of the straw and examine the bed. Dig into the manure with a pointed stick. If there are fine, white filaments running this way and that, the spawn is growing and the bed is ready for casing. This should be done with a mixture of equal parts of finely broken chalk and moist peat, or with sterilized soil, spread 2·5 cm (1 in) thick over flat beds or 4 cm (1½ in) over ridge beds and beaten down quite smooth with the back of a spade. This casing is put directly on the manure and the straw covering must be removed while the work is being done but should be replaced directly the whole bed is cased.

For inside beds, if any heating apparatus is available maintain a temperature of about 15°C/59°F until mushrooms appear through the casing and then let the temperature fall to about 10-12°C/50-54°F. Keep the atmosphere damp by syringing paths and walls daily with tepid water. Water the beds also when they become dry but be careful to avoid overwatering.

It usually takes about six weeks from the time a bed is spawned to the time at which the first mushrooms can be gathered and at this stage the straw covering should be removed. With good management the bed will continue to crop for a further month or six weeks. The mushrooms should be gathered regularly directly they are large enough for use and they may either be broken off carefully at bed level or cut with a sharp knife, but cutting is preferable.

Inside beds can be made at any time of the year provided the necessary temperatures can be maintained. The best time for making an outside bed is in the middle of summer.

It is sometimes possible to introduce mushroom spawn to fields and so obtain what is virtually a naturalized crop. This is, however, even more risky than cultivation in outdoor beds. The method is to raise a turf every 90 cm (3 ft) or so with a sharp spade and insert two or three pieces of brick spawn beneath, replacing the turf at once. It will help if a little rotted horse manure can be scattered under the turf with the spawn. The best time for this experiment is in mid-summer and the most favourable place a meadow which has been grazed by horses, advice that will not unfortunately help town gardeners.

If you are only interested in growing relatively small quantities of mushrooms and have a limited amount of time to devote to their requirements, special kits are available.

MUSTARD

Two allied plants are grown in the vegetable garden as 'mustard', *Sinapis alba*, the white mustard, and *Brassica napus*, popularly known as rape, which has a milder flavour. They are grown as salad for cutting while still in the seed-leaf stage of development, at which point they are virtually indistinguishable. They should be grown as quickly as possible so that the leaves may be tender and have a mild flavour. It is possible to have supplies the whole year round by sowing in a warm greenhouse from late autumn to late winter, in an unheated greenhouse or frame from early spring to early autumn and either out of doors or in a frame for the remaining months.

Cultivation is exactly the same as for cress, with which mustard is often combined, but it grows a little more rapidly and should be sown three days later for cutting at the same time.

ONIONS

Onions of ordinary size and quality can be grown in most soils but the big bulbs which one sees at exhibitions require a considerable degree of skill on the part of the gardener.

Bulbs can be produced from small, specially grown bulbs, known as sets, or from seed. The latter can be sown in a special seed bed or in boxes, the seedlings being transferred to their final quarters at a later stage, or it can be sown directly in the ground in which the bulbs are to mature. Good results can be obtained by either method of sowing but, if the second system is to be followed, it is essential to have a finely broken seed bed with a surface texture not liable to become caked after heavy rain. On heavy soils this means working in a good deal of material such as strawy manure, leafmould, peat, wood ashes and sand. Many gardeners place such importance on the texture of the onion bed that they do not allow it to form part of the usual rotational cropping system, but instead keep it in one position for a number of years. This is satisfactory so long as the onions do not suffer from any soil-borne disease or pest, but undoubtedly it is safer to give the onions a fresh plot each year as with other crops.

Rotted manure can be used in the preparation of the onion bed at rates up to 50 kg per 6·4 sq m (1 cwt per 8 sq yd). In addition, rake in superphosphate of lime, 85 g per 0·8 sq m (3 oz per sq yd), and sulphate of potash, 28 g (1 oz) to the same area prior to sowing or planting.

Outdoor sowing can be started as early in spring as the ground is in workable condition. Sow in drills 12 mm (½ in) deep and 30 cm (1 ft) apart. Thin the seedlings when they are about 10 cm (4 in) high to 10 cm (4 in) apart if small bulbs are required, 15 cm (6 in) apart for medium-sized bulbs or 30 cm (1 ft) for very large, exhibition bulbs. The thinnings can be used for salads or may be transplanted elsewhere. Topdress with nitrate of soda, 28 g per 3·6 m (1 oz per 12 ft) of row, a week or so after thinning and give a second, similar dressing in early summer.

Towards the end of summer bend over the leaves just above bulb level and a fortnight or three weeks later loosen the bulbs in the soil with a fork to check growth and encourage ripening. Towards early autumn lift the bulbs completely and spread them out to dry either on the surface of the ground or in a frame or greenhouse. After a further day or so, store in a cool, dry, airy place either on open-slat shelves or strung up in ropes. This roping is done by plaiting the withered onion leaves together with two or three strands of raffia or string.

Onions to be transplanted can either be sown under glass in mid- to late winter or out of doors in late summer. The glasshouse sowing should be made in boxes filled with J.I. seed or peat seed compost and germination effected in a temperature of from 10°C/50°F- 15°C/59°F. The boxes can be shaded at first but the seedlings must have all the light possible once they have germinated. Either sow the seeds singly 2·5 cm (1 in) apart or prick off the seedlings 4 cm (1½ in) apart when they are 5 cm (2 in) high. Transfer to a frame in early spring and harden off for planting out in mid-spring. Plant with a trowel and, contrary to general advice, make rather deep holes so that the roots can be dropped vertically into the soil and the base of the stems covered to a depth of about 12 mm (½ in).

Space 15 cm (6 in) apart in rows for medium bulbs, 30 cm (1 ft) apart for large bulbs. Water in well if the ground is at all dry. Then treat as for outdoor-sown plants but bend down the tops, loosen the bulbs and lift and dry off a week to a fortnight earlier.

Late-summer sowings are made in a sheltered but sunny position and finely broken, well-drained soil. The seedlings are left unthinned throughout the winter, lifted carefully with a small fork during early spring and planted exactly like the greenhouse-raised seedlings. If desired, some of the seedlings can be left undisturbed in the seed bed, the thinnings being used for planting out. Bulbs from these late summer sowings will be ready for use from early summer onwards but should not be stored until the foliage dies down, which will probably be towards the end of summer.

Salad onions are produced by sowing thinly in drills 23 cm (9 in) apart at fortnightly intervals from early spring to early summer, and again in late summer. No thinning is carried out and the onions are pulled as soon as they are big enough for use. A mild-flavoured variety is generally preferred.

Onion sets are planted in mid-spring 15 cm (6 in) apart in rows 30 cm (1 ft) apart and barely covered with soil. Subsequently they are treated in exactly the same way as spring-sown onions though they may be ready for use a little earlier. Sets of special varieties are also available for planting in the autumn, from early autumn until early winter for use at the start of next summer. Cultivation is the same as for spring planted sets.

There are many varieties of onion. For exhibition Ailsa Craig or selections from it are generally preferred. For kitchen use a smaller and more solid-fleshed onion is better, for example Bedfordshire Champion, Rijnsburger and various selections of that variety, Hydura and Hygro. Most of these varieties can also be sown in late summer, but better, because more reliable, are the Japanese varieties Express Yellow, Imai Early Yellow and Senshyu Semi-Globe Yellow. If some onions are required for salad use only, White Lisbon is good because of its mild flavour. Up-to-Date, Rousham Park Hero, Improved Reading and White Spanish appear to be highly resistant to the onion white rot disease so should be used in all gardens in which this disease has proved troublesome. Stuttgarter Reisen is a good variety for sets.

PARSLEY

This is one of the few vegetables that is required in most gardens throughout the year. For this purpose at least two sowings should be made; the first as early in spring as soil and weather conditions will allow and the second in the first half of summer. For each seed should be sown directly in the ground in which the plants are to grow, but an earlier crop can be obtained by sowing in a warm greenhouse in late winter, pricking the seedlings out into boxes and hardening off for planting in a frame, under cloches or in a sheltered place out of doors in mid-spring. The soil need not be particularly rich for parsley but should be well dug and the position should be open and sunny. Quite a common practice is to use parsley as an edging for beds in the kitchen garden. Sow in drills 6 mm (¼ in) deep, or broadcast, covering with 6 mm (¼ in) of fine soil.

Germination is, as a rule, rather slow so there is no need to worry if no seedlings appear for four or five weeks. When the seedlings are 2·5 cm (1 in) or so high, thin them out to 15 cm (6 in) apart and subsequently leave them to grow with occasional weeding or hoeing. Cutting can begin as soon as the plants are nicely grown and if only a few leaves are taken from each plant at a time cropping will continue for many weeks. Some of the seedlings from the last sowing in mid-summer can be transferred at thinning time to a frame or to a very sheltered border in which they can be covered with cloches. The remaining plants can be left where they are, either to take their chance with the winter weather or to be covered later on with cloches or spare frames supported on bricks. As a rule no protection is needed before mid-autumn and even then only light covering is required to keep off the most severe cold.

Varieties are not numerous. Any good strain of Moss Curled will be satisfactory.

PARSNIPS

These have the merit of extreme hardiness, which makes it possible to produce winter crops in districts too cold for turnips or carrots. A drawback is that parsnips grow rather slowly and require a long season if really big roots are to be formed. For this reason the earlier in spring that seed can be sown the better, provided the soil is in good working condition, but the seed bed must be reasonably dry and crumbly. It is better to wait until mid- or even late spring than to sow in a sticky seed bed.

For exhibition purposes ground must be trenched at least 60 cm (2 ft) deep, but for ordinary kitchen purposes deep digging is usually sufficient. Do not use any animal manure but choose a position that was manured thoroughly for a preceding crop such as brassicas or potatoes. Before sowing, dust the surface with superphosphate of lime, 85 g per 0·8 sq m (3 oz per sq yd), sulphate of ammonia, 28 g (1 oz) to the same area, and either sulphate or muriate of potash, 42 g (1½ oz) or use a balanced compound fertilizer according to maker's instructions.

The seeds are comparatively big and the best method of sowing is to drop them in twos or threes 8·7 cm (3½ in) apart in drills 2·5 cm (1 in) deep and 45 cm (1½ ft) apart. Then the seedlings can be singled out to 18 cm (7 in) apart. It is no use trying to transplant the thinnings as they will not produce good roots.

Give a topdressing of nitrate of soda at the rate of 28 g per 3 m (1 oz per 10 ft) of row immediately after thinning. Dust this in a double band 5 cm (2 in) wide along each side of the rows and hoe in at once. Subsequently hoeing will be the only attention required until mid-autumn, when lifting may begin.

Most of the roots can be left in the ground all winter to be dug as needed, but it is convenient to lift a few and store in sand, ashes or dry soil in a shed so that roots are available even when the weather is too unpleasant, or the ground frozen too hard for lifting.

An alternative method of cultivation sometimes practised by exhibitors is, after digging the ground, to bore holes with a crowbar, 30 cm (1 ft) apart in rows at least 45 cm (1½ ft) apart. These holes should be about 60 cm (2 ft) deep and 5 cm (2 in) in diameter at the top. They are almost filled with any old sifted potting soil. Two or three seeds are then sown in each hole and covered with 2·5 cm (1 in) of the same fine soil. Later the seedlings are singled out. The idea is that the root follows the direction of the bored hole and so is exceptionally straight and well formed.

When lifting parsnips for exhibition it is very important to obtain as great a length of root as possible, even including the long, thin 'tail' of the root. This may necessitate opening a trench 90 cm (3 ft) or more deep at one end of the parsnip bed, and working towards the plants with a fork so as to get them out intact and without any injury.

Avonresister, Tender and True, Hollow Crown, White Gem, and Offenham are reliable varieties.

PEAS

Some gardeners grow peas in trenches prepared in much the same way as celery trenches (see p. 556), but a better method is to dig the ground as deeply as possible throughout, working in dung or compost at the rate of about 50 kg per 6·4 sq m (1 cwt per 8 sq yd). The position should always be as open and sunny as possible. Before sowing dust the surface with superphosphate of lime, 85 g per 0·8 sq m (3 oz per sq yd) and sulphate of potash, 42 g (1½ oz) to the same distance. Peas do best in ground that is reasonably well supplied with lime but as lime cannot be given economically at the same time as dung it is advisable to choose a plot that has been previously limed.

There are two methods of sowing, one in the ordinary V-shaped drills drawn with the corner of a hoe, in which case it is usual to draw two such drills about 23 cm (9 in) apart to form a double row and then leave an alleyway at least as wide as the eventual height of the peas. The alternative is to sow in shallow, flat-bottomed trenches scooped out with a spade held almost horizontally. Such trenches should be about 5 cm (2 in) deep and 20 cm (8 in) wide. Two lines of peas are sown in each trench, one on either side, and the trench is then half filled with fine soil, thus leaving a small depression which serves to hold water should the peas require watering in hot weather. The seeds themselves should be sown singly at least 5 cm (2 in) apart.

Peas are split up into Early, Second Early, Maincrop and Late varieties and also into dwarf and tall kinds. The difference between the earliest and later peas is simply in the time they take to reach maturity from a spring sowing date. Roughly speaking, the very earliest varieties will begin to fill their pods about ten weeks from the date of sowing; second early varieties will take twelve to thirteen weeks to reach the same stage of development; maincrop, thirteen to fourteen weeks. This effect depends on a delicate interaction between day length and temperature and so, if very early quick-maturing kinds are sown late when average temperatures are relatively high, they may attempt to crop before they have made adequate growth. In general it is unwise to sow the earliest varieties after mid-spring when later varieties requiring more heat hours to induce maturity would be better.

Whatever kinds are used successional sowing should be practised with the object of spreading the picking season from early summer to at least early autumn and possibly beyond in a favourable year. This will mean a first sowing of an early in late winter, followed by a similar sowing a fortnight later with perhaps a second early sown in early spring and a main crop from late spring to early summer.

Varieties below 60 cm (2 ft) in height need not be staked though I think it best to give some support, even if it is only a string strained between canes down each side of the row. Those over 60 cm (2 ft) in height must be staked and brushy hazel branches are best for this purpose. They should be put in as soon as the seedlings appear, a row of them down each side of the line.

Peas thrive on plenty of moisture, particularly when the pods begin to fill, and it pays then to water freely either with plain water or, better still, with weak liquid manure from the time the pods can be seen unless the weather should be wet. Pick early and regularly as this encourages the plants to go on bearing. Do not allow any of the pods to ripen or turn yellow on the plants. If possible spread a mulch of strawy manure or grass clippings 5 cm (2 in) thick between the rows in late spring.

Pea varieties are classified as round-seeded and wrinkle-seeded, the latter less hardy but sweeter flavoured. It is impossible to name more than a few standard kinds of which these are representative: Those not marked as round-seeded are wrinkle-seeded. FIRST EARLY: Hurst Beagle – 76 cm (2½ ft); Feltham First – 76 cm (2½ ft) round seeded; Little Marvel – 45 cm (1½ ft); Foremost – 1 m (3½ ft); Meteor – 45 cm (1½ ft) round-seeded; Gradus – 1·2 m (4 ft); Pilot Improved – 90 cm (3 ft) round-seeded; Kelvedon Triumph – 60 cm (2 ft) and Kelvedon Wonder – 45 cm (1½ ft). SECOND EARLY: Early Onward – 60 cm (2 ft); Hurst Green Shaft – 75 cm (2½ ft); Hurst Canice – 60 cm (2 ft) and Kelvedon Monarch, also known as Victory Freezer – 75 cm (2½ ft); MAINCROP: Onward – 75 cm (2½ ft); Lord Chancellor 1 m (3½ ft); Alderman – 1·5 m (5 ft).

In addition there are sugar peas such as Sugar Dwarf Sweetgreen` – 45 cm (1½ ft), which are grown for their edible pods to be eaten before peas are well formed in them; snap peas such as Sugar Snap – 1·8 m (6 ft) and Sugar Ray – 90 cm (3 ft) which can be eaten whole even when peas are well developed though they may need stringing; and the asparagus pea – 45 cm (1½ ft), which belongs to a different genus but is grown like a pea, for its little winged pods which are eaten whole.

POTATOES

There are few soils in which potatoes will not grow tolerably well though the ideal is undoubtedly a light, easily worked loam and the nearer one can get to this the better. The position for the potato bed should always be as open as possible. In shade the haulm tends to get excessively long and crops are likely to be light.

Dung can be used freely in the preparation of practically all soils. An average dressing is 50 kg per 9·6 sq m (1 cwt per 12 sq yd), and this can be increased to 4·8 sq m (6 sq yd) on the poorer and lighter types of soil. However, it is seldom wise to rely on dung only. Potatoes need plenty of phosphates and potash, in both of which dung is likely to be deficient. Immediately prior to planting dust the ground at the rate of 113 g per 0·8 sq m (4 oz per sq yd) with a mixture of 5 parts by weight superphosphate of lime, 2 parts sulphate of ammonia and 2 parts sulphate of potash, or use a high phosphate compound fertilizer according to maker's instructions.

Potatoes are grown from tubers which are often known as seed potatoes though in fact they have nothing to do with real seed. Any healthy tubers can be used for the purpose but commercial growers usually try to supply tubers averaging about 56 g (2 oz) in weight, as these give a satisfactory result and are economical. Larger tubers are extravagant unless they are divided, which takes time and is not satisfactory with all varieties, while smaller tubers do not give a sufficiently strong plant. Tubers should be purchased in the first half of winter and stood with their eyes uppermost in shallow trays in a fairly light but frost-proof place to sprout. The temperature should be round about 7°C/45°F. If the place chosen is too hot or too dark sprouts will be long and weakly; if it is too cold the tubers will be chilled or perhaps even frozen and killed. The ideals to aim for are short, sturdy green or purplish sprouts by the time the potatoes are required for planting.

Acer palmatum Dissectum Atropurpureum

Aesculus parviflora

Arctostaphylos uva-ursi

Acer palmatum
Senkaki

**Acer palmatum Dissectum
Atropurpureum**, to 3.6 m (12 ft), one of
several Japanese Maples grown for its dainty
foliage and fiery autumn tints
⊕ ☼ ◐ 🞖 ■ 🞐

Acer palmatum Senkaki (Coral Bark Maple),
6 m (20 ft), is grown for its reddish bark,
showy in winter, and its foliage
⊕ ☼ ◐ 🞖 ■ 🞐

Aesculus parviflora (Dwarf Buckeye), 3 m
(10 ft), a cousin of the Horse Chestnut, is
attractive in flower and provides good autumn
colour ⊕ ❀ Summer ☼ ◐ 🞖 🞐

Arctostaphylos uva-ursi (Red Bearberry),
30 cm (1 ft), forms excellent evergreen ground
cover decorated with white bells and red fruits
△ ❀ Spring ↺ Autumn ☼ ◐ ● 🞖 🞐

Arundinaria viridi-striata, 1.2 m (4 ft), is an elegant Bamboo that prefers a cool shady spot

***Aucuba japonica* Variegata**, 3 m (10 ft), is a female form of this species grown for its gold-splashed evergreen leaves and scarlet fruits. Makes a good pot plant too
△ Spring Autumn

Berberis darwinii (Darwin's Barberry), 2.7 m (9 ft), is clothed in tiny holly-like leaves, with orange flowers and bluish fruits. Makes a good hedge △ Spring Summer

***Berberis* Rubrostilla**, 1.2 m (4 ft), a thorny berberis, is grown primarily for its clusters of large rich red fruits
Spring Summer

Caryopteris x clandonesis Kew Blue

Camellia japonica
Adolphe Audusson

Buddleia globosa

Camellia japonica Adolphe Audusson, to
3 m (10 ft), blooms early so site it away from
early morning sun so its flowers are not
damaged. The shrub itself is hardy. Keep its
roots moist in summer
△ ❀ Spring ☀ ▧ ■

Buddleia globosa (Orange Ball Tree), to 4.5 m
(15 ft), is a vigorous shrub, is distinct from
familiar purple *B. davidii*. Prune after flowering
in summer ⊕ ❀ Summer ☀ ▧ ▮

Caryopteris x clandonensis Kew Blue, 90 cm
(3 ft), is a choice form of this late-flowering
shrub. Prune back to 1 or 2 buds from the old
wood in spring to stimulate flowering shoots
⊕ ❀ Autumn ☀ ▧ ▮

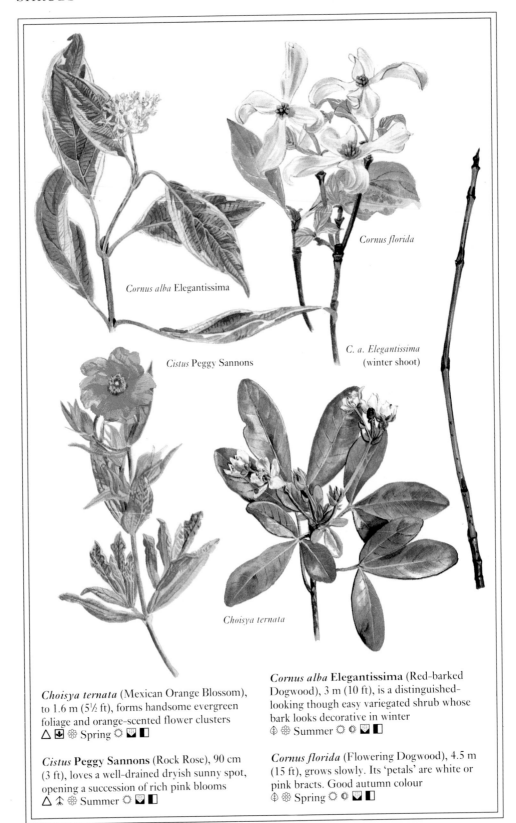

Cornus florida

Cornus alba Elegantissima

C. a. Elegantissima
(winter shoot)

Cistus Peggy Sannons

Choisya ternata

Choisya ternata (Mexican Orange Blossom), to 1.6 m (5½ ft), forms handsome evergreen foliage and orange-scented flower clusters
△ ▣ ✳ Spring ☀ ▨ ▮

Cistus Peggy Sannons (Rock Rose), 90 cm (3 ft), loves a well-drained dryish sunny spot, opening a succession of rich pink blooms
△ ✿ ✳ Summer ☀ ▨ ▮

Cornus alba Elegantissima (Red-barked Dogwood), 3 m (10 ft), is a distinguished-looking though easy variegated shrub whose bark looks decorative in winter
✦ ✳ Summer ☀ ◉ ▨ ▮

Cornus florida (Flowering Dogwood), 4.5 m (15 ft), grows slowly. Its 'petals' are white or pink bracts. Good autumn colour
✦ ✳ Spring ☀ ◉ ▨ ▮

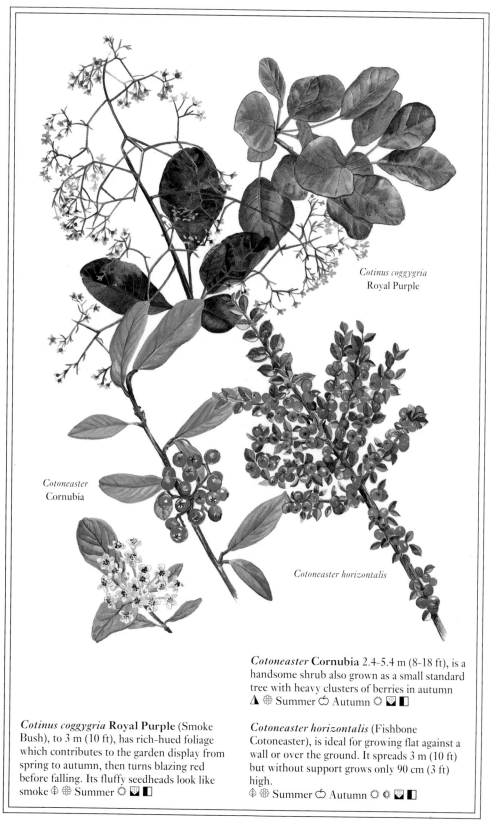

Cotinus coggygria
Royal Purple

Cotoneaster
Cornubia

Cotoneaster horizontalis

Cotoneaster **Cornubia** 2.4–5.4 m (8–18 ft), is a handsome shrub also grown as a small standard tree with heavy clusters of berries in autumn
▲ ❀ Summer ♻ Autumn ☼ ▨ ▮

Cotinus coggygria **Royal Purple** (Smoke Bush), to 3 m (10 ft), has rich-hued foliage which contributes to the garden display from spring to autumn, then turns blazing red before falling. Its fluffy seedheads look like smoke ⊕ ❀ Summer ☼ ▨ ▮

Cotoneaster horizontalis (Fishbone Cotoneaster), is ideal for growing flat against a wall or over the ground. It spreads 3 m (10 ft) but without support grows only 90 cm (3 ft) high.
⊕ ❀ Summer ♻ Autumn ☼ ◐ ▨ ▮

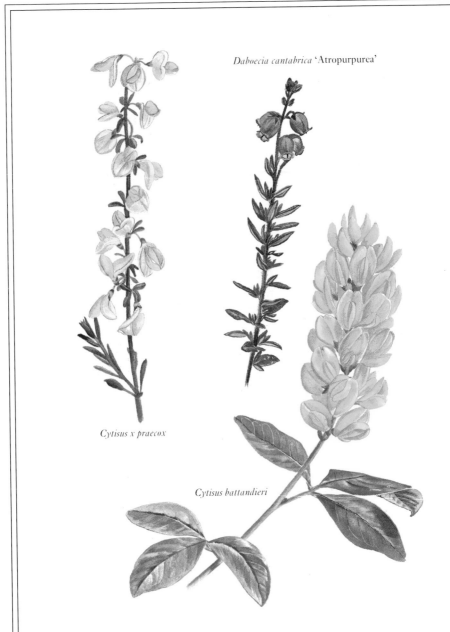

Daboecia cantabrica 'Atropurpurea'

Cytisus x praecox

Cytisus battandieri

Cytisus battandieri (Moroccan Broom), 3 m
(10 ft), a vigorous silver-leaved shrub with
pineapple-scented flowers, is best against a
warm south wall. Cut out spent wood after
flowering ✤ ❀ Summer ☀ 🛡 ∎

Cytisus x praecox (Warminster Broom),
90 cm–1.8 m (3-6 ft), makes a bushy shrub
with pendulous growth smothered in pale
yellow blossom in spring. Cut back, but not
into old wood, after flowering
✤ ❀ Spring ☀ 🛡 ∎

Daboecia cantabrica Atropurpurea
(St Dabeoc's Heath), 60 cm (2 ft), is a form of
heather with unusually large bells that remain
colourful for a long time
△ ❀ Summer ☀ ☀ 🛡 ∎

Elaeagnus pungens Maculata

Daphne retusa

Elaeagnus x ebbingei

Deutzia x hybrida Mont Rose

Daphne retusa, 90 cm (3 ft), grows slowly but produces many clusters of scented flowers and red berries
△ ❀ Summer ↻ Autumn ☼ ◉ ▼ ▮

Deutzia x hybrida Mont Rose, 1.8 m (6 ft), is a most attractive flowering shrub. Prune out old wood after flowering.
⊕ ❀ Summer ☼ ◉ ▼ ▮

Elaeagnus x ebbingei, 3 m (10 ft), with grey-green leaves makes an excellent screen with fragrant flowers
△ ❀ Autumn ↻ Winter ☼ ◉ ▼ ▮

Elaeagnus pungens Maculata, up to 2.7 m (9 ft), is outstanding for its cheerful year-round colouring. Remove any non-variegated shoots
△ ☼ ◉ ▼ ▮

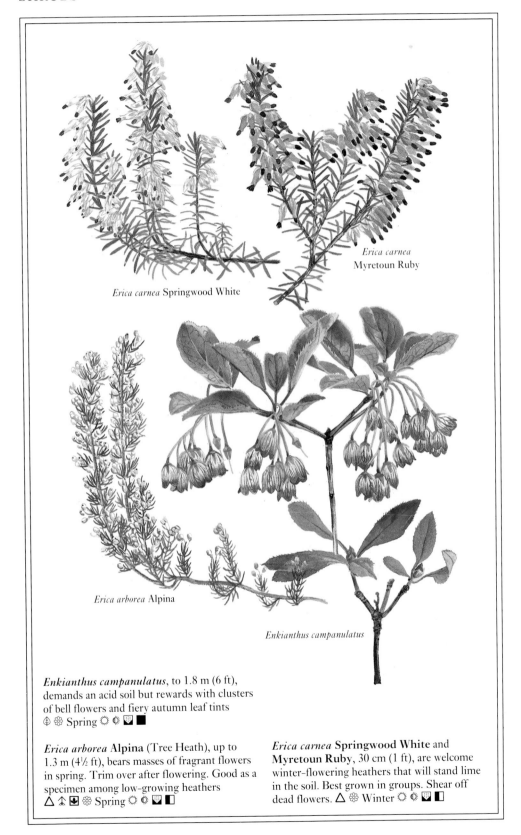

Erica carnea
Myretoun Ruby

Erica carnea Springwood White

Erica arborea Alpina

Enkianthus campanulatus

Enkianthus campanulatus, to 1.8 m (6 ft), demands an acid soil but rewards with clusters of bell flowers and fiery autumn leaf tints ✿ ❀ Spring ☼ ◐ ▨ ■

Erica arborea Alpina (Tree Heath), up to 1.3 m (4½ ft), bears masses of fragrant flowers in spring. Trim over after flowering. Good as a specimen among low-growing heathers △ ⚭ ⬇ ❀ Spring ☼ ◐ ▨ ▐

Erica carnea Springwood White and Myretoun Ruby, 30 cm (1 ft), are welcome winter-flowering heathers that will stand lime in the soil. Best grown in groups. Shear off dead flowers. △ ❀ Winter ☼ ◐ ▨ ▐

Fothergilla major

Fothergilla major
(autumn colour)

Euonymus fortunei Silver Queen

Forsythia Lynwood

Fremontodendron California Glory

Euonymus fortunei Silver Queen, a
handsome slow-growing trailer which can also
climb a wall △ ✿ 🛡 ❑

Forsythia x intermedia Lynwood, 1.8 m
(6 ft), a superior form of the familiar early
spring-flowering shrub. Prune out old wood
after flowering ⊕ ❀ Spring ✿ ✿ 🛡 ❑

Fothergilla major, 2.4 m (8 ft), is grown for its
small white bottlebrush flowers and its
spectacular leaf tints in autumn
⊕ ❀ Spring ✿ ✿ 🛡 ❑

Fremontodendron California Glory will
grow up to 9 m (30 ft) but needs shelter, best
on a warm south wall
△ ❀ Spring ✿ ✿ 🛡 ❑

Fuchsia Mrs Popple

Fuchsia Riccartonii

Gaultheria procumbens

Fuchsia **Mrs Popple**, 75 cm (2½ ft), is hardy but its arching stems carry larger flowers. Cut back to the ground every spring
✦ ❀ Summer ☼ ◑ ▦ ❘

Fuchsia **Riccartonii**, to 1.8 m (6 ft), the hardiest of garden fuchsias, makes a fine specimen bush, or a hedge. Trim back dead growth in spring after frosts
✦ ❀ Summer ☼ ◑ ▦ ❘

Gaultheria procumbens (Creeping Wintergreen), to 60 cm (2 ft), is a vigorous spreading evergreen useful for ground cover. Its white bells are followed by scarlet fruits
△ ⋀ ▼ ❀ Summer ↻ Autumn ◑ ● ▦ ■

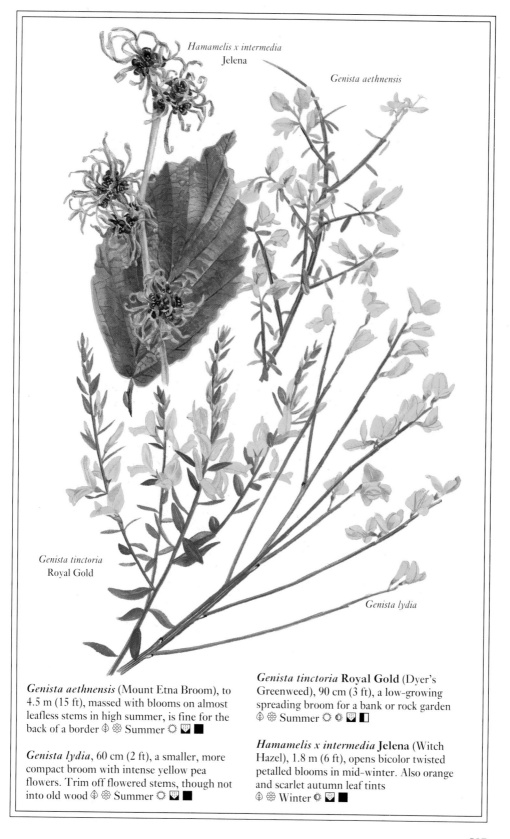

Hamamelis x intermedia
Jelena

Genista aethnensis

Genista tinctoria
Royal Gold

Genista lydia

Genista aethnensis (Mount Etna Broom), to 4.5 m (15 ft), massed with blooms on almost leafless stems in high summer, is fine for the back of a border ✧ ❀ Summer ☀ ▨ ■

Genista lydia, 60 cm (2 ft), a smaller, more compact broom with intense yellow pea flowers. Trim off flowered stems, though not into old wood ✧ ❀ Summer ☀ ▨ ■

Genista tinctoria Royal Gold (Dyer's Greenweed), 90 cm (3 ft), a low-growing spreading broom for a bank or rock garden ✧ ❀ Summer ☀ ✧ ▨ ❑

Hamamelis x intermedia Jelena (Witch Hazel), 1.8 m (6 ft), opens bicolor twisted petalled blooms in mid-winter. Also orange and scarlet autumn leaf tints ✧ ❀ Winter ✧ ▨ ■

Hibiscus syriacus Woodbridge

Hibiscus syriacus
Blue Bird

Hippophae rhamnoides

Hydrangea macrophylla
Madame Emile Mouilliere

Hibiscus syriacus Blue Bird, 2.4 m (8 ft), a fine hardy hibiscus with handsome bloom in late summer. **Woodbridge** is the best red–flowered variety ✦ ⚘ ✿ Summer ☼ 🛡 ◨

Hippophaë rhamnoides (Sea Buckthorn), a 3.6 m (12 ft) seaside shrub that stands high winds and salt spray, so is valuable as a hedge or screen. Plant male and female plants to get berries ✦ ↻ Autumn ☼ 🛡 ◨

Hydrangea macrophylla **Mme. Emile Mouillière**, a choice Mophead hydrangea, forms a rounded 1.8 m (6 ft) shrub. Leave old flower heads to protect buds from frost. Keep roots moist in summer ✦ ✿ Summer ☼ ◑ 🛡 ■

Hydrangea paniculata
Grandiflora

Hydrangea macrophylla
Bluewave

Hypericum x inodorum Summergold

Hydrangea macrophylla Bluewave, 1.3 m
(4½ ft), is one of the best Lacecap Hydrangeas
with fertile flowers surrounded by a ring of
sterile florets. Thin out old growth in mid-
spring if necessary ✤ ❀ Summer ☼ ◕ ▧ ■

Hydrangea paniculata **Grandiflora** makes a
fine shrub up to 3 m (10 ft) with clusters of
florets that turn brown before falling
✤ ❀ Summer ☼ ◕ ▧ ■

Hypericum x inodorum **Summergold** starts
the season acid yellow but turns green. Small
yellow flowers are followed by red to black
berries
✤ ❀ Summer ↻ Autumn ☼ ◕ ▧ ▯

Leycesteria formosa

Lavatera olbia

Kerria japonica Pleniflora

Kerria japonica Pleniflora (the double Jew's Mallow), 1.8 m (6 ft), gives bright colour in spring. Its glossy green stems are decorative in winter ⊕ ❀ Spring ☼ ◐ ▦ ▮

Lavatera olbia (Tree Mallow), 1.6 m (5½ ft), is magnificent in flower but apt to die back in winter. It pays to cut it back to 30 cm (1 ft) from the ground each spring ⊕ ❀ Summer/Autumn ☼ ▦ ▮

Leycesteria formosa (Pheasant Berry), 2.1 m (7 ft), produces strong hollow-stemmed shoots carrying tiny flowers in deep wine-red bracts followed by similar coloured berries. Prune out old wood in spring ⊕ ❀ Summer ♢ Autumn ☼ ◐ ▦ ▮

Mahonia aquifolium

Magnolia stellata

Magnolia x soulangiana

Magnolia liliiflora Nigra

Magnolia stellata, 3.3 m (11 ft), blooms earlier and is daintier. Lovely underplanted with bulbs (e.g. muscari). Protect blooms from frost and wind if possible ✤ ❀ Spring ☼ 🛡❚▮

Magnolia liliiflora Nigra, 3m (10 ft), is similar to *M. soulangiana* but smaller with much darker flowers ✤ ❀ Spring ☼ 🛡❚▮

Mahonia aquifolium (Oregon Grape), to 1.8 m (6 ft), makes a valuable if rather invasive bush with handsome leaves, yellow flowers and blue 'grapes' in summer
△ ❀ Winter ♻ Summer ✤ ● 🛡❚▮

Magnolia x soulangiana, 9 m (30 ft), the most popular magnolia, opens its blooms before the leaves ✤ ❀ Spring ☼ 🛡❚▮

591

Rhododendron Vuyk's Rosyred

Rhododendron Pink Pearl

Rhododendron Blue Tit

Rhododendron Golden Oriole

Rhododendron Blue Tit, 60 cm (2 ft), a dwarf variety, introduced a rather unusual rhododendron colour to a collection △ ✿ Spring ☼ 🛡 ■

Rhododendron Golden Oriole, deciduous azalea, 1.8 m (6 ft), is early into bloom, before its leaves unfurl. Has the distinctive azalea scent ✤ ✿ Spring ☼ 🛡 ■

Rhododendron Pink Pearl, 3 m (10 ft), is one of the most widely planted large-flowered varieties. Like all its family it insists on acid, lime-free soil △ ✿ Spring ☼ 🛡 ■

Rhododendron Vuyk's Rosyred, hybrid azalea, 90 cm (3 ft), opens intensely coloured flowers. Fine for the front of a display ✤ ✿ Spring ☼ ☼ 🛡 ■

Planting should begin in early spring for the earliest varieties and continue throughout mid-spring for the later kinds. The very first planting should be made in as sheltered a position as possible as the growth is tender and likely to be killed by even a few degrees of frost. April plantings are usually quite safe right out in the open.

There are a number of methods of planting, the essential thing being to space the tubers 30-38 cm (1 ft-1ft 3 in) apart in rows 90 cm (3 ft) apart and to cover them with 7·5 cm (3 in) of good soil. Perhaps the quickest method is to dig out a shallow V-shaped trench with a spade, place the tubers in this and then use the soil from the next trench to fill up the preceding one. An alternative is to draw the same soil back into the trench again with a rake or hoe, while some gardeners use a draw hoe to make the trenches.

Earthing up should be started as soon as the shoots appear through the soil. At first only a little soil is drawn from between the rows right over the young potato shoots. A few days later the process is repeated, with a third earthing up ten days or so later so that finally all the soil is drawn up into broad, rounded ridges with the potato shoots growing through their summits. The idea is to give plenty of loose soil into which the potato can grow and form its tubers. On poor soil it is an excellent plan to give a further dusting of the mixed fertilizer already recommended prior to the first earthing up, which should be used at the rate of 85 g per 3·6 m (3 oz per 12 ft) of row.

No further attention should be needed until the earliest varieties are ready to dig, which may be any time in early summer according to season, variety and time of planting. The only way to make sure is to scrape a little soil away from one of the ridges and examine some of the tubers. Start to dig as soon as they are the size of hens' eggs and only lift a few roots at a time, just as many, in fact, as are required for immediate use. These early potatoes soon spoil when out of the ground.

Maincrop and Late potatoes must be left much longer and will need to be sprayed with a copper fungicide, maneb or zineb about the first week in mid-summer as a precautionary measure against potato blight, the commonest and most destructive of all potato diseases. Cover both the upper and undersides of the leaves with the spray and give a second application at the end of the month and a third about three weeks later. Near industrial

Dividing a large seed potato so that each piece contains an equal number of good, sturdy growths to get a larger yield

centres, where the air is polluted by factory smoke, copper fungicides should not be used as under these conditions they can cause severe leaf scorching.

Second Early potatoes are usually ready for digging in late summer as soon as the First Earlies are finished, but if they are to be kept for winter they should be left in the ground until skins are firm and cannot be removed by pressure with the thumb. The same test should be applied to Maincrop and Late potatoes which are usually ready towards early autumn.

Dig with a broad-tined fork and be careful not to bruise or spear any of the tubers. Remove those that are undersized, damaged or diseased in any way. The remainder can be stored for winter use either in a frost-proof shed or in a clamp out of doors.

A clamp is made by spreading clean straw on the ground to a depth of about 30 cm (1 ft), piling the tubers on this, covering them with more straw to the same depth and then with soil at least 23 cm (9 in) thick, beaten down smoothly with the back of a spade. Usually clamps are made in the shape of a ridge 1·5 m (5 ft) through at the base, 1·2 m (4 ft) high and of any desired length, but conical clamps are sometimes more suitable for the small garden. Essentials are a good layer of drainage material underneath and a good thick covering of straw and soil to keep out frost and rain. In the summit of the clamp some provision should be made for ventilation, the usual method being to draw some of the straw through the covering soil. In a well-made clamp potatoes will withstand the coldest weather without injury. Clamps with thin walls are useless. When a clamp is opened to remove potatoes for use the end must be sealed up again with sacks and soil to keep out frost.

When potatoes are stored in sheds they must be kept in the dark. If they are in thin sacks and the shed has windows it will be necessary to cover the sacks in some way, otherwise the outside potatoes will become green and bitter.

Varieties are numerous and tend to change fairly rapidly. This is because many kinds deteriorate with the passage of years. The trouble can be checked to a considerable extent by cultivating seed potatoes exclusively in those areas which are relatively free from virus disease. All the same it is rather important to keep up to date on information regarding

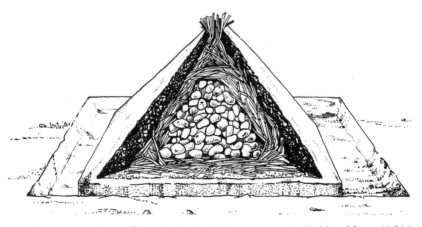

Constructing a potato clamp. The stacked potatoes are covered with a 30 cm (1 ft) layer of straw and a further 23 cm (9 in) of soil beaten down smoothly with the back of a spade. Ventilation is provided by drawing some of the straw through the soil at the top of the clamp

potato varieties and in particular to find out what kinds are known to give good crops in the locality in which they are to be grown.

There are three main groups or subdivisions: First Earlies, Second Earlies and Maincrops. These differ in the time they take to reach maturity. The First Earlies needing something like three months from planting to digging, Second Earlies four months and Maincrop five months. There is usually a considerable difference between the weights of crop lifted from Earlies and Maincrops.

Here are a few of the best kinds at the time of writing. FIRST EARLIES: Arran Pilot, Epicure, Foremost, Home Guard, Maris Bard, Pentland Javelin, Sharpe's Express, Duke of York (syn. Midlothian Early). SECOND EARLIES: Estima, Maris Peer, Wilja. MAINCROP: Cara, Desiree, King Edward, Maris Piper, Majestic, Pentland Dell, Romano.

RADISHES

These are very quick-growing plants and make an excellent catch crop to be taken off a plot of ground prepared well in advance for another crop. For example, radishes can be sown between the celery trenches and on plots prepared for late peas or autumn and winter brassicas. It is hardly possible to have too rich a soil for the purpose for the more quickly radishes can be grown the more tender and crisp they are to eat.

Sowing should be made every fortnight or three weeks out of doors, starting as early in spring as soil conditions allow and continuing until late summer. Earlier supplies can be obtained by sowing in a frame in late winter, while winter radishes can be had either by growing a hardy variety such as Black Spanish or China Rose from a mid- to late summer sowing, or by growing ordinary radishes in a slightly heated frame or greenhouse from early autumn and mid-winter sowings.

Seed can either be sown broadcast or in 12 mm ($\frac{1}{2}$ in) deep drills 11·2 cm ($4\frac{1}{2}$ in) apart. In either case sow very thinly and so avoid the necessity for thinning out. Broadcast seed should be covered with 6 mm ($\frac{1}{4}$ in) of fine soil. Water freely in dry weather.

Radishes should be ready for pulling within six or seven weeks of sowing except in winter and early spring when they will take considerably longer. Use the most forward roots first.

Varieties are not numerous but there are two distinct types, the round or olive-rooted radish, of which French Breakfast is typical, and the long, tap-rooted radish. The former is easily the more popular and better for general cultivation. There are also yellow and white-skinned varieties which can make a pleasant and unusual colour variation in mixed salads, and also the black-skinned varieties known as Black Spanish, Long and Black Spanish which are very hardy and so are suitable for winter cultivation.

RHUBARB

This is one of the small number of perennials grown in the vegetable garden. As rhubarb roots may occupy the same soil for a number of years, initial preparation should be very thorough. Dig the ground deeply, working in dung or compost at 56 kg per 9·6-12 sq m (1 cwt per 12-15 sq yd).

Early spring is the best planting season and good roots can be purchased from nurserymen. They should be spaced 90 cm (3 ft) apart. As they are generally rather big it is most convenient to plant them with a spade. The roots must be planted so that the whole of the woody part of the crown is covered but the shoots on it just appear through the soil. Plant very firmly and water in freely should the ground be at all dry.

Do not pull any sticks the first year and be rather moderate in pulling the second year. If any flowering spikes appear, cut them off at once.

It is also possible to raise rhubarb from seed and some varieties mature surprisingly quickly. Seed should be sown very thinly in a frame in early spring or out of doors a few weeks later in drills 12 mm (½ in) deep and 30 cm (1 ft) apart. Thin the seedlings to 15 cm (6 in) apart and transplant them to their permanent quarters the following spring, after which the same details of cultivation apply as for purchased roots.

Forcing. Early rhubarb is appreciated from mid-winter to early spring. The first supplies are obtained in heated greenhouses or sheds and later ones by covering roots out of doors to exclude the light.

For indoor forcing strong roots (at least two years from planting) should be lifted, as required, from mid-autumn to mid-winter. Allow them to lie out of doors for a day or so exposed to cold, then bring them into a greenhouse or shed, place them in boxes or large pots or even pack them very close together on the floor and surround them with old potting soil. Water moderately and then make the place quite dark. If the roots are in pots they can be covered with other inverted pots; if they are packed on the floor a framework may be built over them and covered with sacks or linoleum, while another excellent method is to plant under the greenhouse staging and hang thick sacks in front to keep out the light.

In a temperature of 18-20°C/65-68°F growth will be rapid and sticks will be ready for pulling within four or five weeks.

For outdoor forcing, roots should be covered with special forcing pots, boxes or barrels where they are growing in their permanent beds. If possible surround and almost cover these pots with dead tree leaves and strawy stable manure, mixed in about equal parts. This will generate some heat and so increase the rate of growth, but it is not absolutely necessary. Again it is essential to exclude all light so the tops of the forcing pots should be covered with lids, while barrels, etc. from which the ends have been knocked, should also

Outdoor rhubarb can be forced by covering the roots in their permanent beds with special forcing pots, boxes or barrels to exclude all light

be suitably covered. As a rule outdoor roots do not require any watering while they are being forced.

There are not many varieties of rhubarb, among the best being Hawke's Champagne, Timperley Early, Sutton and Victoria. Cawood Delight has smaller stems than these but they are exceptionally well coloured and of very good quality.

SAGE

This useful herb is a perennial of shrubby habit. It will eventually make a bush 90 cm (3 ft) high and of equal spread.

Sage can be grown from cuttings of firm, young growth taken in late summer or early autumn and inserted in a frame in rather sandy soil or, alternatively, seed can be sown in a frame in early spring or out of doors a few weeks later. Seedlings should be pricked off 6·2 cm (2½ in) apart in lightish soil and a sunny place as soon as they can be handled, and transplanted the following autumn or spring to their permanent quarters. Cuttings taken in late summer will be rooted and ready for permanent beds the following spring. In all cases the final planting should be in full sun and well-drained, though not necessarily particularly rich, soil. Space the plants at least 45 cm (1½ ft) apart.

Young shoots can be cut or leaves removed from established plants at any time as required for use, provided no plant is heavily stripped at any one time. For drying, sage is cut in early summer, just before the plants come into flower. The young shoots are tied up in small bundles and hung head downwards in a cool, airy place until they are quite dry.

In addition to the common green-leaved sage there are several varieties with coloured foliage, one purple leaved, another purple splashed with pink, cream and green, a third yellow and green. These have the same flavour as common sage and are highly ornamental as well. *Salvia discolor* tastes of blackcurrant, and *S. rutilans* of pineapple.

SALSIFY

This not very common vegetable is grown for its roots, which are rather like thin parsnips in appearance and have, in the opinion of many people, a very good flavour, the plant sometimes being known as the vegetable oyster.

Salsify is grown from seed, which should be sown out of doors in mid-spring in drills 12 mm (½ in) deep and at least 30 cm (1 ft) apart. The position should be open and sunny, the soil deeply dug and prepared as for parsnips. Thin the seedlings to 20 cm (8 in) apart while still quite small and subsequently keep the soil well hoed and free from weeds.

In mid-autumn the whole crop should be lifted, the tops cut off and the roots stored in sand, ashes or fine, dry soil in a shed or outhouse. Varieties include Giant, Mammoth, and Vegetable Oyster.

SCORZONERA

Another of the less well known root vegetables but one which is worth growing for variety. It makes long, tapering roots not unlike those of salsify, but with black skins and it is grown in exactly the same way as salsify. Varieties include Duplex, Habil, Long John, and Maxima.

SEAKALE

This is grown for its young shoots which must be blanched in order to be palatable. If grown in the light they are green and excessively bitter.

Seakale can be raised from seed sown in shallow drills out of doors in mid-spring but it usually takes two years to get plants large enough for forcing in this way. Given very favourable conditions some of the most forward roots may be ready for forcing the first autumn. The more usual method of culture is from root cuttings which are obtained in autumn from the plants that are to be forced. Any side roots from about the thickness of a lead pencil to that of a man's thumb may be used. Cuttings can be from 10-25 cm (4-10 in) long and it is advisable to cut the bottom of each piece on the slant and the top squarely across, so that is possible to distinguish which way up they should be planted.

Tie the cuttings in small bundles and lay them in sand or ashes in any sheltered place out of doors until early spring. Then plant them out in deeply dug, rather rich soil. Dung can be used in the preparation of this bed at the rate of 50 kg per 8·8 sq m (1 cwt per 11 sq yd). Drop the roots, right way up, into dibber holes 30 cm (1 ft) apart in rows 45 cm (1½ ft) apart. The top of each cutting must be about 12 mm (½ in) below the surface. Keep the bed clean and well hoed all summer.

In late autumn lift all the roots, cut off thongy side growths to provide a new lot of cuttings and reserve the strong main roots and crowns for forcing. Alternatively part of the bed may be left intact for forcing out of doors.

Forcing. The earliest crop should be grown in a greenhouse or shed with a temperature of 15-24°C/59-75°F. Pot the crowns, four in each 16·2 cm (6½ in) pot, in any old potting soil, water moderately and place in complete darkness (see notes on forcing rhubarb). It is advisable to force only a few potfuls at a time and to bring a succession of pots into the forcing house every week or ten days from late autumn to late winter.

Later supplies can be had by covering strong outdoor plants with inverted flower pots or by heaping fine sand, ashes, or even sandy soil over them to a depth of 21·2 cm (8½ in). If flower pots are used the hole in the bottom of each must be blocked up in some way to keep out the light.

In all cases the shoots should be cut at soil level when they are 15-23 cm (6-9 in) long.

Roots which have been forced are of little further use.

There are no varieties of any importance but it is desirable to obtain a good strain from a reliable source.

SEAKALE BEET

This is a variety of beetroot which is cultivated for its foliage and not for its roots. The central rib of each leaf is very large and can be separated from the remainder of the leaf and served as a substitute for seakale, while the green part is cooked separately and served as spinach. It is a useful vegetable, capable of giving a big crop for a long period and it has the additional merit of being hardy.

Seed should be sown in the first half of spring and again during late summer. Choose well-cultivated soil that has had a good dressing of manure or a compound fertilizer and sow in drills 2·5 cm (1 in) deep and 45 cm (1½ ft) apart, dropping the seeds in pairs 23 cm (9 in) apart. Single out the seedlings to one at each station. No further attention is required beyond hoeing and weeding.

Leaves can be cut a few at a time as required directly the plants are growing freely. Provided no plant is stripped at any one time, the bed will continue to yield for several months. From the spring sowing it should be possible to gather leaves and mid-ribs from early summer to mid-autumn, while the late summer sowing will give a few leaves in autumn and a lot more in the spring.

Swiss Chard, also listed as Silver Beet, has green leaves and white midribs and Rhubarb Chard has darker leaves and red midribs.

SHALLOTS

Some people prefer shallots to onions because of their milder flavour. They also have the merit of being easier to grow and will often give a good crop in places where onions fail. Small shallots are excellent for pickling, while the larger bulbs can be used for flavouring and some kept for replanting.

It is always better to grow shallots in this way, from carefully selected but not necessarily very large bulbs, than to raise them from seed, as seedlings have a tendency to run to flower, in which case they seldom produce a satisfactory crop. Bulbs should be planted in late winter/early spring. It is necessary only to press them firmly into the soil until they are about half covered. Space them 20 cm (8 in) apart in rows 30 cm (1 ft) apart, giving them an open position and well-dug soil which has been moderately manured. Dung can be used at the rate of about 50 kg per 9·6 sq m (1 cwt per 12 sq yd) and superphosphate of lime, 85 g per 0·8 sq m (3 oz per sq yd); sulphate of potash may be raked in with advantage prior to planting at 50 kg per 0·8 sq m (1 oz per sq yd). A few weeks later go over the bed carefully and firm any bulbs which appear loose. Frost may push them out or sometimes mice or birds will disturb them before they are rooted. Keep the bed well hoed.

Directly the foliage turns yellow, which is usually during mid-summer, lift the plants with a fork and spread them out to dry in an airy shed. A few days later the clusters can be split up into separate bulbs, sorted according to size and some of medium size selected for replanting. Then all can be stored until required in any cool, dry, airy place.

There are both yellow-skinned and red-skinned varieties and also one named Hâtive de Niort that produces particularly shapely bulbs much admired for exhibition, but it is not so prolific as the common varieties.

SPINACH

I have spoken repeatedly of the importance of sowing some vegetables at short intervals for succession and this applies to none more so than spinach, which has a very short season, especially when the weather is hot. If a big batch is sown at one time it is almost certain that most of it will go to seed before it can be used. The ideal for an ordinary family of three or four persons is to sow about a 6 m (20 ft) row of summer spinach every fortnight from early spring to mid-summer and then, a month later, make one sowing in a sheltered position of a winter spinach to be used in autumn and later all spring.

All spinach requires rich, deeply dug ground and summer supplies need, in addition, plenty of moisture. If possible, make the spinach bed in a place where it will be easy to turn the hose on the plants during dry spells. It is not a bad plan to make the spring-summer sowings in a partially shady place as this reduces the need for such frequent watering.

Dung or compost can be used freely in the preparation of the bed; 50 kg per 6·4 sq m (1 cwt per 8 sq yd) will not be too much on dry or sandy soils. While the plants are in growth feed them once or twice with small doses of nitrate of soda, 28 g per 3 m (1 oz per 10 ft) of row. Winter spinach must not be fed too freely or it may grow too soft and be killed by frost. Cut down the application of dung to 12 sq m (15 sq yd); rake in sulphate of potash at 14 g per 0·8 sq m ($^1/_2$ oz per sq yd) prior to sowing and give no nitrate of soda until mid-spring.

All spinach should be sown thinly in drills 2·5 cm (1 in) deep and 23-30 cm (9 in-1 ft) apart. Thin the seedlings to 13 cm (5 in) apart as early as possible. Start to cut as soon as the outer leaves are of a usable size.

Good varieties of the summer type are King of Denmark, Supergreen and Monarch Long Standing. Broad Leaved Prickly is a good variety for winter.

New Zealand spinach is a different plant, sprawling in habit and cropping over a very long period. Seed can be sown out of doors in the second half of spring, and the seed is best soaked for 12 hours before sowing. Treat as for summer spinach but only the one sowing is required.

SPINACH BEET

Practically all that has been said regarding seakale beet applies equally to spinach beet except that the leaves do not have the thick, white midribs which distinguish seakale beet. Consequently spinach beet is purely a spinach substitute, not a seakale substitute as well. It is grown in precisely the same way as seakale beet and has the same capacity for cropping for a very long time.

It is usually listed as Perpetual Spinach.

SWEDES

The garden swede is closely allied to the turnip and is grown in the same way. It has the merit of great hardiness and swedes will often winter out of doors without any protection. It also gives a very heavy crop, though roots of the largest size are not really desirable as they are inferior in texture and flavour to smaller specimens.

Cultivation is the same as for turnips except that rows should be 38 cm (1 ft 3 in) apart and as a rule one sowing, in late spring/early summer, is sufficient. Best of All, Devon Champion and Marian are good varieties.

SWEET CORN

This is grown for the cobs or heads of seed which are gathered for use before they are fully ripe. It is easily grown from seed sown out of doors in late spring. Choose a sunny, rather sheltered position and prepare the soil by digging it deeply and manuring it generously. Well-rotted dung can be used at rates up to 50 kg per 9·6 sq m (1 cwt per 12 sq yd) and additional superphosphate of lime and sulphate of potash given, the former at 85 g (3 oz) and the latter at 28 g (1 oz) per 0·8 sq m (1 sq yd). Drop the seeds into small dibber holes 2·5 cm (1 in) deep, 38 cm (1 ft 3 in) apart in rows 90 cm (3 ft) apart or alternatively sow seeds singly in small pots and germinate in a frame or greenhouse for planting out in late spring. It is better to have several short rows than one long one because the plants are wind pollinated and in a compact block there is more chance of pollination taking place.

Keep well watered in dry weather and feed with weak liquid manure. When the plants come into flower, frequently shake the male tassels which top the stems and so assist in the distribution of the pollen to fertilize the cobs. These are formed low down on the main stems. Sometimes strong plants will produce a number of cobs but as a rule it is wise to restrict them to no more than three.

It is very important to gather the cobs at exactly the right stage of development, which is when the seeds are milky. The test is to open the covering sheath very carefully (it can be slit with a knife if necessary) and push the point of a penknife into one of the seeds. If transparent juice comes out, the cob is too young. If the interior of the seed has the consistency and appearance of a hard-boiled egg, the crop is too old. If a white, milky liquid comes out, it is just right.

It is important to choose a variety which matures fairly quickly, otherwise many of the cobs will be spoiled by frost before they are ready for use. Golden Bantam, First of All, John Innes Hybrid, Earliking and Kelvedon Glory are all reliable varieties.

TARRAGON (*Artemisia dracunculus*)

This is a perennial which can be grown from seed sown outdoors in mid-spring or can be increased by division of old plants in spring, but tarragon does not overwinter well in cold, wet places. It likes sun, warmth, good drainage and a fairly rich soil. Plants should be spaced at least 30 cm (1 ft) apart. Leaves should be cut for drying in late summer before the plants flower. French tarragon has the best flavour but is harder to grow than the Russian kind.

THYME

This most important of garden herbs is a dwarf shrubby perennial which makes an attractive edging for vegetable beds or can be grown in the herb border. The foliage is dark green and variegated.

Thyme can either be raised from seed sown thinly in mid-spring in a frame or sheltered place out of doors, or from cuttings of firm young growth struck in an unheated frame in the second half of summer. Both methods are equally satisfactory but seed is probably the simpler for the amateur. Transfer the seedlings to a bed of fine soil out of doors in late spring/early summer, planting them 6·2 cm (2½ in) apart in rows 23 cm (9 in) apart. From this nursery bed remove them to their final quarters the following autumn or spring, spacing them at least 23 cm (9 in) apart each way. The ground need not be particularly good but it should be well drained and the position as sunny as possible.

For immediate use thyme can be gathered at any period of the year but for drying it should be cut in early summer, just before it comes into flower. Tie the shoots up in small bundles and suspend them in a cool, airy place but not in full sun. When the leaves are quite dry they can be crumbled and stored in stoppered bottles for use during the winter.

TOMATOES

The tomato is a half-hardy plant which can only be grown in the open in cool climate gardens from the start of a good summer to mid-autumn. This is too short a season for anything like a full crop to be obtained and so the tomato is primarily regarded as a glasshouse plant, though in some warm, sheltered places fairly extensive plantations are also made in the open. Under glass it is quite possible to gather ripe tomatoes all year round, but a good deal of skill is required for winter and early spring crops. The reason for this is that artificial heat does not entirely take the place of sunlight and in winter it is lack of light which often brings about disaster. For these reasons I would advise the beginner to concentrate upon producing ripe tomatoes from about mid-summer until early autumn and then, as skill and understanding increase, lengthen the season by earlier and later sowings.

For this main crop under glass seed should be sown towards the end of winter at a temperature of 15-18°C/59-65°F. Seed can be broadcast thinly in ordinary seed trays but a better method is to space the seeds singly 2·5 cm (1 in) apart. I use a piece of glass to carry the seeds and the point of a pen-knife to flick them off on to the soil. Use J.I. seed or peat seed compost and cover the seeds with the same compost to a depth of 0·3 cm (⅛ in). Water through a fine rose and cover each box with a pane of glass and a sheet of brown paper. Within ten days or so seedlings should be spearing through the soil. Remove the brown paper at once and tilt the glass to let in air. A couple of days later remove the glass altogether. Keep the trays on the greenhouse staging in as light a position as possible.

Directly the seed leaves are well formed, prick the seedlings off into other seed trays, spacing them 7·5 cm (3 in) apart each way or, better still, pot them up singly in 6·2 cm (2½ in) pots in J.I. No. 1 or peat potting compost. Keep them on the staging in a temperature averaging 15°C/59°F and not falling below 10°C/50°F at any time. Water fairly freely, always using water warmed to the temperature of the house. As soon as the small pots begin to fill with roots, which will probably be about three weeks after potting, move the plants on into 10 cm (4 in) pots in J.I. No. 2 or peat potting compost.

Meanwhile the soil in which the tomatoes are to fruit should be prepared. This may be in a border on the floor of the greenhouse; in troughs about 30 cm (1 ft) deep and wide and of any convenient length; in flower pots not less than 20 cm (8 in) in diameter or in bottomless pots known as rings. Alternatively tomatoes can be grown in special growing bags, which are bought already filled with a suitable peat compost. Growth is very much under the gardener's control in pots, troughs and growing bags and the earliest crops are usually obtained in this way, but a drawback is that the plants require more frequent attention. This does not apply to ring culture, which is described separately (see p. 604).

For pots and troughs the rich J.I. No. 3 is as satisfactory as any. If desired this can also be used to make up beds on the floor of the house but usually this is impracticable because of the quantity of soil required. The method is then to use existing soil well dug and enriched with rotted stable manure, 50 kg per 8·8 sq m (1 cwt per 11 sq yd). After digging the surface is dusted with bonemeal, hoof and horn meal and sulphate of potash all at 113 g per 0·8 sq m (4 oz per sq yd). Alternatively use a proprietary tomato base

Removing the side shoots of tomato plants. These form in the angle of the leaf stalks and should be nipped out as soon as seen

fertilizer according to maker's instructions. Prepare the bed at least a fortnight in advance of planting time.

The tomatoes should be ready for planting from the 10 cm (4 in) pots or for removal to large pots, boxes or troughs by about the middle of spring. Plant or pot them very firmly and let the top of the old pot ball be a little below the surface of the ground. In beds space the plants at least 38 cm (1 ft 3 in) and preferably 45 cm (1½ ft) apart in rows at least 60 cm (2 ft) and preferably 90 cm (3 ft) apart. If it is a big greenhouse with many rows of plants, it is advisable to have a still wider alleyway between every second or third row.

After planting the tomatoes should be well watered in and subsequently they should receive gradually increasing quantities of water. For the first week or so this will average about 0·5 l (1 pt) per plant per day, but by the time the tomatoes are carrying three or four trusses of fruit this quantity should have been increased to an average of something like 4·5 l (1 gal). But do not try to work entirely by rule of thumb. The ideal is to keep the soil moist right through the pot or box or, in the case of beds, for the full area and depth occupied by the roots, an area which is, of course, steadily increasing. Always water directly from the spout of the watering-can, not through a rose, and never if the surface of the soil is still wet.

As a rule each tomato plant is restricted to a single stem. Side shoots, one of which will form in the angle between each leaf and the main stem, should be rubbed out as soon as seen. The plant itself is generally stopped, that is to say the top is pinched out, when it has formed six trusses of flowers but in that case the uppermost side shoot is retained and allowed to grow on again, so forming a new top. The idea is temporarily to throw the whole strength of the plant into the production of the first six trusses and so hasten the date on which ripe fruits can be gathered.

The plants must be supported in some way. The simplest method is to use a 1·9 m (6½ ft) bamboo cane for each plant. A cheaper and quite satisfactory scheme is to use 4- or 5-ply fillis (a specially made soft string). Loop this round the base of the plant and tie in a non-running knot. Then twist the fillis round the plant two or three times and fasten at its upper end to wires strained horizontally just beneath the rafters of the greenhouse. As the plant continues to grow it will be wound round the fillis in the same direction.

Even if the soil has been well prepared and properly enriched to begin with, more food is likely to be needed directly the fruits begin to swell. Both artificial fertilizers and animal manure should be used for this purpose. Good compound tomato fertilizers can be purchased ready mixed or one can be prepared with 3 parts by weight superphosphate of lime, 2 parts sulphate of ammonia and 2 parts sulphate of potash. Use this mixture at a teaspoonful per plant approximately once every week or ten days from the time the fruits begin to swell until the last trusses are commencing to ripen. In addition give two or three light topdressings of well-rotted manure at intervals of a few weeks, each to be spread all over the bed or surface of pots, boxes, etc. to a depth of about 12 mm (½ in).

If growing bags are used these should be laid flat on any firm level surface and slits made in the upper side of the bag about 38 cm (1 ft 3 in) apart through which the tomatoes are planted. All water and food must be given through these slits. Aim to keep the compost evenly moist throughout. There will be enough food in the compost to keep plants going for about a month, after which weekly feeding with a soluble tomato fertilizer will be necessary and is most simply given in the water. When the flowers are fully developed, syringe the plants daily with clear water to assist in pollination.

The temperature in the greenhouse from late spring to early autumn should average 15°C/59°F, rising to as much as 29°C/84°F on hot, sunny days but never falling below 10°C/50°F. Ventilate freely as soon as the thermometer rises above 15°C/59°F.

In small greenhouses it is sometimes necessary to throw open the door as well as all ventilators on really hot, summer days and some temporary shading may be required in addition as too much heat will cause leaf scorching and make the fruits ripen unevenly. In particular avoid rapid temperature rises on bright mornings following chilly nights.

It is often said that tomatoes require a dry atmosphere. If this means dry by comparison with that needed for cucumbers it is true, but it is quite easy to have too little moisture in the air even for the tomato. This will cause bad setting and particularly the condition known as dry set, in which the tiny fruitlets refuse to swell and remain for weeks like pinheads. The remedy is to splash water about on the paths and walls on sunny days to create humidity within the house or even to syringe the plants themselves.

Begin picking the fruits directly they are half coloured. They can be finished indoors in a sunny window or in a box or drawer and their removal will help the other fruits to ripen quickly. Always pick complete with calyx and stem, breaking the latter off at the knuckle. At the end of the season if there are any green fruits remaining on the plants they can be picked and used for chutney.

Ring Culture. Some plants, notably tomatoes, chrysanthemums and carnations, grow well in bottomless pots standing on a bed of gravel or ashes. Real pots with the bottoms knocked out can be used but most ring culture is carried out in special rings made of bitumenized cardboard or 'whalehide'. Rings 23 cm (9 in) in diameter and depth are suitable for strong-growing plants. They are filled with J.I. No. 3 and stood on a bed of clean washed gravel or well-weathered boiler ashes at least 15 cm (6 in) deep. The plants are raised in the normal way from seed or cuttings and are planted in the rings while still quite small. They are well watered in until water trickles out of the bottom of the rings, but subsequently all water is applied to the bed of gravel or ashes from which some will soak up into the compost in the rings. This water can be applied automatically from a siphon tank or in some other way if desired to save time and labour. Any solid or liquid food required is applied to the soil in the rings from which the plants derive all the chemicals they require, but they get their major water supply from the aggregate into which they will quickly root, forming a much coarser root system in it than in the rings themselves. The gravel or ash bed can be retained for several years but the compost in the rings should be renewed annually.

Outdoor Culture. The cultivation of tomatoes in the open follows the same general principles as under glass but differs in some important details. Seed should not be sown before early spring, and I have often had excellent results from seed sown later that season. If the seed is put in too early the plants get too big before they can be transplanted to their fruiting quarters. The only exception is in the case of plants that are to be protected with special cloches after planting out and for this purpose the seed should be sown right at the start of summer. Otherwise details of germination and early potting of the seedlings is the same as for greenhouse plants.

The tomato plants should be potted in 10 cm (4 in) pots a fortnight or three weeks before planting out. They must be carefully hardened off by being placed in a frame and

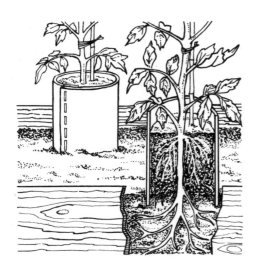

Tomatoes grown by the ring culture method. The plant draws its food from the compost in the ring and water from the aggregate below, in which it forms a coarser root system

given steadily increasing ventilation on all favourable days, but even with the best treatment they will remain susceptible to a few degrees of frost. This means that in the colder sites it is not safe to plant tomatoes out of doors without protection until the start of summer.

Prepare the ground by deep digging and a moderate use of well-rotted dung but not more than 50 kg per 8 sq m (1 cwt per 10 sq yd). If not available, use well-rotted compost at the same rate or plenty of peat or leafmould to supply the necessary humus. In any case use fertilizers as advised for indoor crops.

Plant 38–45 cm (1¼ –1½ ft) apart in rows 76 cm (2½ ft) apart, or alternatively have two rows spaced at 52·5 cm (1¾ ft), and then an alleyway of 90 cm (3 ft). Let the rows run as nearly as possible north and south or, if there is to be one row only, it can run east and west in front of a south-facing wall or fence. The sunnier the position the better but if it can be sheltered from the north and east this is all to the good. Water the plants in but subsequently only give water if the soil appears dry.

Remove side shoots exactly as advised for indoor plants but stop the plants by pinching out the growing point when three, or at the most four, flower trusses have been formed. This is as many as can reasonably be expected to ripen out of doors.

Either stake the plants individually, each with a 1·2 m (4 ft) bamboo cane or similar stick, or alternatively drive strong 1·2 m (4 ft) stakes at 3 m (10 ft) intervals along the rows, strain one wire along the tops of these posts and then string the plants individually from beds to wire.

Start to pick at a rather earlier stage than with greenhouse plants as, even under the most favourable circumstances, it is difficult to ripen a whole crop out of doors.

Topdressings with dung are usually unnecessary out of doors but the plants can be fed with artificials as already described.

Keep a look out for sharp frosts from the beginning of autumn onwards and gather the whole crop, however green the fruits may be, before such a frost occurs. Many of the fruits can be ripened subsequently indoors packed in boxes in a dark place while the very green ones can be used for chutney.

An alternative is to pull the plants up, roots and all, before a sharp frost occurs and hang them in a greenhouse, while yet another method is to untie them, remove the stakes and just lay the plants down lengthwise along the row, where they can be covered quite easily with polythene tunnel cloches. If this is done it is advisable to spread some clean straw on the ground first.

There are also bush varieties of tomato which remain comparatively dwarf but branch freely. The side shoots are not removed from these, nor are the plants staked, but some clean straw can be spread around each plant to keep the ripening fruits out of contact with the soil. It is advisable to plant about 60 cm (2 ft) apart. Bush varieties can be grown under cloches or in frames.

There are a great many varieties of tomato and though some of the old kinds remain good, others lose their vitality after a time and must be replaced, so that it is advisable to keep up to date on these. Here are a few that can be recommended, though note that new varieties are constantly being made available:

FOR GREENHOUSE CULTURE: Ailsa Craig, Alicante, Mirabelle, Moneymaker, Super Roma, Tigerella.

FOR OUTDOOR CULTIVATION: Gardener's Delight, Super Marmande, Yellow Perfection.

BUSH VARIETIES: Red Alert, Tornado, Tumbler.

TURNIPS

Summer turnips are not an easy crop in all gardens because unless they can be grown quickly and without check the roots tend to be tough and strong flavoured. To counteract this the ground should be as rich as possible and well dug, but it is not desirable to use dung immediately before sowing as this tends to cause forking. Either choose a plot that was manured for a preceding crop or give a moderate dressing of well-rotted dung 50 kg per 12 sq m (1 cwt per 15 sq yd) at least three months prior to sowing. In addition dust the ground with superphosphate of lime, 85 g per 0·8 sq m (3 oz per sq yd), sulphate of ammonia, 56 g (2 oz) to the same area, and sulphate of potash, 28 g (1 oz), immediately before sowing.

Make small successional sowings every three or four weeks starting in early spring as the condition of the ground will allow and continuing until mid-summer. This will make it possible to use the roots while they are still fairly small and tender.

The final sowing for winter storing need not be made until towards late summer, provided the ground is in really good order and water can be supplied should the weather become dry. Failing these necessities it is advisable to sow three or four weeks earlier as growth may be delayed.

All seed should be sown in 12 mm (½ in) deep drills 30 cm (1 ft) apart. Thin the seedlings to 10 cm (4 in) apart and for the last sowing to 15 cm (6 in) apart.

The whole remaining crop should be lifted in mid- to late autumn and stored in a shed or outhouse. Cover the roots with a little dry soil, sand or ashes.

Turnip tops make a welcome change in spring from kale and broccoli. They are produced by sowing seed rather more thickly than usual early in autumn, and leaving the seedlings unthinned throughout the winter. Space the rows 23 cm (9 in) apart and cut the tops at ground level as required from early spring onwards.

Reliable varieties for summer use are Snowball, Golden Ball and Milan White. For winter use and providing turnip tops in spring Manchester Market is hardy and reliable.

VEGETABLE MARROW

This is an extremely tender vegetable and one which will be killed by even a few degrees of frost so it is customary to start it under glass. Seeds are sown singly or in pairs in small pots in late spring in J.I. seed or peat seed compost.

They are germinated in an unheated greenhouse or frame, and if frost threatens at night must be well protected with newspaper or polythene. Germination is, as a rule, rapid and within three or four weeks of sowing the pots should be well filled with roots and the plants already 13 cm (5 in) high with several strong leaves each. Unless protection can be given do not plant out of doors before early summer, except in specially mild regions.

The old method of growing marrows was on raised beds composed chiefly of decaying turves with any other vegetable refuse that might be available and a little dung. Excellent crops can be produced in this way but a drawback is that the plants are liable to need a lot of watering in dry weather. For this reason it is really better to plant marrows on the flat in ordinary beds well dug and liberally dressed with dung used at rates up to 50 kg per 5·6 sq m (1 cwt per 7 sq yd).

There are two types of marrow – bush and trailing. The former should be planted 60 cm (2 ft) apart and the latter at least 90 cm (3 ft). Water in well after planting and keep on watering every day or so for the first ten days or fortnight until the plants are growing freely.

Bush marrows will need no further attention beyond fertilizing the female flowers. This is done by picking well-developed male blooms and inverting them over the females, which can be distinguished by the fact that each is attached to an embryo marrow. Do this fairly frequently and, for preference, when the sun is shining and the pollen is dry.

Trailing marrows should be fertilized in the same way; in addition the points of the runners should be pinched out occasionally to encourage the formation of side growths. These are usually more productive of female flowers than the main runners, which often carry nothing but male blooms.

Cut the marrows while they are still quite young and feel a little soft if pressed with the thumbs at the blossom end. In early autumn one or two fruits per plant may be allowed to remain to attain full size and ripen. If they are cut when the skins show a yellow tinge and feel really hard, they will keep for many months in any cool and perfectly dry place, such as on a shelf in a spare room.

To produce very large marrows for exhibition the number of fruits should be considerably restricted and the plants fed freely with weak liquid manure from the time the fruits begin to form.

There are numerous varieties, the most useful being Long White Trailing, Long Green Trailing, White Bush and Green Bush. Table Dainty gives a number of rather small marrows. Varieties specially recommended for use as courgettes are Zucchini, Rondo de Nice, Tondo di Nizza. Custard Marrows and Squashes, some of which are highly ornamental, are grown in the same way.

WATERCRESS

The best watercress is produced in specially made beds flooded with slowly running water, but it is possible to grow it in the garden without any water at all except that which is applied from a can or hose.

To deal with the former first, the beds may be of any convenient size but are not generally more than 1·2 m (4 ft) wide and should certainly not be more than 25 cm (10 in) deep. They are lined with concrete, black polythene or butyl sheeting and provided with valves or sluices to enable the flow of water to be controlled at all seasons. The bottom of each bed is covered with 7·5 cm (3 in) of good loamy soil and a little clean gravel or sand is spread on top of this to keep the soil down. Cuttings from young shoots taken from any good watercress plants during spring, summer or early autumn are dibbled into the bed 15 cm (6 in) apart. Water is then admitted, but only to a depth of 4 cm (1½ in) at first. Later, as the plants grow, a greater depth of water is maintained, but never more than 10 cm (4 in).

Start to cut as soon as the bed is covered with growth. Do not cut the whole of any one plant but leave a few centimetres at the base to throw up fresh shoots. A bed treated in this way will continue to crop for many months.

To grow watercress without running water, dig a trench 30 cm (1 ft) deep and about 60 cm (2 ft) wide and break up the subsoil with a fork. Then put 15 cm (6 in) of rotted manure in the bottom, cover with 7·5 cm (3 in) of soil and either sow watercress seed in this thinly in mid-spring and late summer or plant cuttings as for the water beds. Water the trenches freely whenever the soil appears dry.

There are no varieties of importance.

Part 5

Fruits

Chapter 25

Making a Fruit Garden

Contrary to popular belief, soil is not so important as situation when it comes to growing fruit. Highly successful orchards are to be seen on land varying from stiff clays to quite light sands or gravels, and though it is probably true to say that the ideal soil for an orchard is a medium well-drained loam, this is by no means essential. Any ground that is capable of producing good crops of potatoes, cabbages and similar common vegetables is also suitable for the cultivation of all kinds of fruit.

Situation. The very sheltered position is not, as is frequently supposed, always the most suitable for fruit. The real danger is of frost at blossom time, and frost behaves in peculiar ways. Still, cold air tends to flow downwards like water and in consequence spring frosts are often most severe in valleys and hollows, in fact in just the places which seem so delightfully sheltered and suitable for planting fruit trees. Hillsides, which are exposed to all the winds that blow, are generally relatively free from spring frosts and, provided the altitude is not too great, are often ideal for orchard planting. However, fruit trees are unlikely to crop reliably above certain heights. As a rule it is considered that 213 m (700 ft) is about the maximum for successful fruit growing though in exceptional cases this height may be exceeded.

I do not want to give the impression that fruit should never be planted in low-lying places. Far more depends upon the relative height of the ground to that immediately around it than upon its actual height above sea level. A hollow on a high plateau may be more of a frost trap than a small knoll not much above sea level. Moreover, however frosty the situation, it is still possible that fruit crops will be obtained as frequently as two years out of three on the average, which may be quite enough to satisfy the amateur gardener though it would be fatal to the success of a commercial grower.

Many people have the idea that they cannot include fruit in their garden because of the amount of room it will take up. With modern stocks and forms of training this should be no problem. It is possible to include some fruit even in the smallest gardens by making use of dwarfing stocks and such forms as the single-stem cordon.

Forms of Tree. Any fruit tree left entirely to its own devices would in time form a big branching bush or tree. The gardener sets out to adapt the shape of the tree to his own requirements. So far as the bigger fruits such as apples, pears and plums are concerned there are eight forms of tree in fairly common use. Taking them in the order of the space they occupy, first there is the standard, which has a main trunk 1·8 m (6 ft) high on top of which are a number of branches radiating in all directions, forming a roughly globular head, in fact what we commonly call a tree. Next to this is the half-standard, similar in all respects except that the main trunk is only about 1·2 m (4 ft) in height. Third comes the bush, in which the main stem is still further reduced to about 60 cm (2 ft) though some old specimens may have main trunks as short as 30 cm (1 ft) or less. Again branches radiate in all directions, forming a big, goblet-shaped specimen.

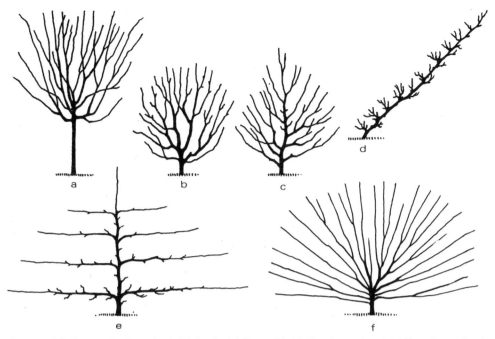

Forms of fruit tree. (a) Standard; (b) Bush; (c) Pyramid; (d) Cordon trained; (e) Espalier trained; (f) Fan trained

The pyramid appears rather similar at first sight but on closer inspection proves to be much more regular in shape. It has a main stem continued vertically right through the centre of the tree and from this, from bottom to top, branches radiate, the bottom branches being longer than those at the top, giving to the whole tree the shape not so much of a pyramid as of a cone. This form was very popular at one time but then fell into disuse, mainly because of the amount of pruning necessary to keep it in trim. Latterly there has been renewed interest in this form particularly when the trees are worked on dwarfing stocks (see p. 612) and so can be kept quite small. A variation on this is the spindle bush. It too has a central stem with radiating branches but the three or four at the bottom are tied downwards to check the flow of sap and encourage fruit bud formation while those at the top are fairly frequently renewed to keep them shorter yet vigorous.

Next in scale are the horizontal-trained or espalier tree and the fan-trained tree. The former has an unbroken central stem like the pyramid with branches or arms at right angles to it but in one plane only and not all round the trunk. The object of the espalier-trained tree, as its name implies, is to occupy a position on an espalier fence, that is to say a series of wires stretched horizontally between uprights embedded firmly in the soil.

The fan-trained tree bears about the same relationship to the horizontally trained tree as the bush does to the pyramid, that is to say it is less formal though it occupies approximately the same amount of space. The name gives a satisfactory description for the branches are roughly arranged like the ribs of a fan, radiating from a short main stem and from one another but in one plane so that the tree can be planted against a fence or wall.

Finally there is the cordon-trained tree which has several variations such as single, double, triple, oblique and horizontal. All are based on the same general idea, namely to have a main stem (or two or three stems in the case of the multiple cordons) to which all side growth is pruned comparatively closely. The great advantage of the cordon is that it occupies very little space and so gives the owner of a small garden the opportunity to grow a considerable variety of fruit.

Distance of Planting. Roughly speaking the standard tree needs a circle 7·5-9 m (25-30 ft) in diameter, that is to say no other tree of similar type can be planted closer to it than that. The half-standard occupies about the same amount of ground, perhaps a little less, much depending upon the type of stock on which it is worked (see below). A bush or pyramid needs from 3-4·5 m (10-15 ft); a spindle bush 2·2 m (7½ ft); dwarf pyramid 90 cm-1·8 m (3-6 ft); horizontal and fan-trained trees 3-4·5 m (10-15 ft); and single-stemmed cordons 60 cm (2 ft) in one direction and 1·8 m (6 ft) in the other, so that if several rows of cordons are to be planted they should be at least 1·8 m (6 ft) apart though the trees in the rows are spaced only 60 cm (2 ft) apart.

The Influence of Stock. Only the tree fruits (apples, pears, plums, cherries, peaches, etc.) are worked on stocks, that is to say grafted or budded to a root system other than their own. Soft fruits, such as currants and gooseberries, and cane fruits such as raspberries and loganberries are grown from cuttings, layers or offshoots and their roots are of their own providing.

The original reason for grafting or budding tree fruits was simply that they could not readily be grown from cuttings or layers and that seedlings varied too much in character to be of any real value. In consequence the only satisfactory method of propagating a good variety was by grafting it either on to a seedling or on to some type of allied tree which could be raised from either cuttings or layers. It was quickly observed that this method of increase has definite advantages because root systems vary greatly and have a marked influence upon the growth and fruiting characteristics of the tree. Standardized stocks have now been produced for several types of fruit, including apples, pears and plums and each of these has a known and predictable influence.

To take Paradise apple stocks as an example, there are now a number of these classified and known under numbers which either bear the prefix M after the East Malling Research Station where much of the original work of collection and identification was carried out, or MM for Malling-Merton, this being applied to stocks raised by the East Malling Research Station in collaboration with the John Innes Horticultural Institution, then situated at Merton. Only a few are of importance to the gardener. M. 9 is notably dwarfing in character. Even a naturally vigorous apple such as Bramley's Seedling, when grafted on it, makes quite a small tree and I have seen ten-year-old bushes of this variety no more than 1·8 m (6 ft) across though on an old-fashioned crab stock they would have been three or four times that diameter at the same age. Moreover M. 9 stock brings apples into bearing exceptionally early. It is no uncommon occurrence for some fruit to be produced the year after grafting, whereas on crab stock it might be eight to ten years before any fruit was produced by the same variety. However on poor soils apples on M. 9 make little or no growth and so it is only suitable for rather good conditions. M. 26 is a little more vigorous than M. 9 but neither of these stocks has a very good root hold on the soil and so trees grafted on them must be securely staked and tied. The most dwarfing rootstock of all is M. 27 which will make little bushes no more than 90 cm (3 ft) in height. It is specially useful for pot- or tub-grown apple trees.

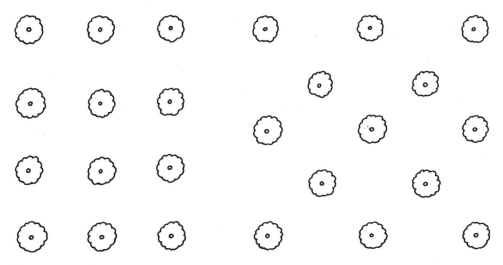

Two systems of planting an orchard, known as the square and the triangular

MM. 106 stock is more vigorous and less precocious than M. 9 but still moderately dwarfing and has been found to produce ideal root systems for a great many apples in private gardens when trees are to be grown as dwarf pyramids, small bushes or are to be espalier trained. M. 2, MM. 111 and MM. 25 carry this vigour a stage further and are sufficiently sturdy to make large bushes or half standards.

It will be seen that by choosing his stock wisely to suit the main peculiarities of the variety and the purpose for which it is required, the fruit grower can solve a lot of his problems and in particular a great deal of unnecessary pruning later on.

PLANNING AN ORCHARD

In very small fruit gardens the question of planning will scarcely arise as fruit trees will probably have to go wherever room can be found for them and, most likely, share the ground with other crops. There is nothing against this except that it should be borne in mind that most fruit, and particularly currants, raspberries, cherries and brambles, make a great many roots near the surface which rules out the possibility of much digging or forking close to them. These roots will generally extend at least as far as the branches. Another point is that some of the sprays used to keep down pests and diseases on fruit trees are damaging to other plants. This is particularly the case with winter washes used to kill insect eggs. The difficulty can be overcome to some extent by covering other crops with polythene sheeting while spraying is in progress.

With bigger orchards the first thing to observe is that whatever system of planting is adopted it should be symmetrical throughout. This is not merely a matter of appearance but also one of utility, for if the trees are evenly spaced and in straight lines cultivation will be easier and the trees themselves will be encouraged to make well balanced growth. Quite a number of different systems of planting have been used, the widely used square and triangular being shown on the next page. Allow at least 1·8 m (6 ft) between rows for easy working.

In small orchards it is probable that only one or two specimens of each variety will be included and the most that can be advised in this case is to keep fruits of a kind together, that is to say all apples in one part of the orchard, pears in another and so on. With bigger plantations this grouping should be extended to varieties since there can be considerable difference in growth and in reaction to spray fluids and fertilizers between varieties.

Fertility. At the same time different varieties of the same kind of fruit should be fairly close together because most fruit trees are to a greater or lesser degree self-sterile. This simply means that they do not set a good crop, or in some cases any crop at all, unless the blossom is fertilized with pollen from another variety of the same kind of fruit. This point must be understood clearly. Apple blossom can only be fertilized with pollen from an apple, pear blossom from a pear, and so on. But the blossom of such a variety of apple as, say, Cox's Orange Pippin needs to be fertilized with pollen from another variety of apple such as Laxton's Superb or Worcester Pearmain. It is important that 'mates' chosen for this purpose shall flower at the same time.

When planting a big orchard it is necessary to intermingle these good mating varieties. There is no need for them to be actually side by side so long as they are within 13·5 m (45 ft) of one another. Quite a usual plan in commercial establishments is to have two or three rows of one variety followed by a single row of the pollinating kind.

Under Planting. Next to be considered is the question of under planting, either with vegetables or with soft fruits. Although there is plenty of room for under crops at the outset, the fruit trees soon fill up all the space and in addition there are the problems inherent in spraying and fertilizing. All the same, interplanting is usually good policy in small gardens for the first five or six years, and for this purpose black currants or gooseberries are frequently used.

Walls and Fences. In private gardens fences and walls can almost always be turned to good account for fruit. There are suitable varieties of fruit for every conceivable aspect from full sun to full shade included in the list at the end of this section. Cleverly used, walls and fences can greatly extend the fresh fruit season, the sunny walls giving a crop earlier than can be obtained in the open and the shady ones extending it after the normal crop has been gathered.

Beware of one point, however. The soil at the foot of a wall or fence is almost always relatively dry and until fruit trees have had time to root out for some distance they may need considerable supplies of water.

SOIL PREPARATION

There is really nothing very special to be said about the preparation of soil for fruit trees. Provided the ground is broken up as deeply as practicable and is in reasonably good condition fruit trees should succeed in it. Contrary to what is often stated it is an excellent plan to add some well-rotted dung prior to planting. A dressing of 50 kg per 12 sq m (1 cwt per 15 sq yd) is ample and should be thoroughly mixed with the soil to a depth of 45 cm (1½ ft) or so. At the same time give coarse bonemeal, 170 g per 0·8 sq m (6 oz per sq yd) and either sulphate or muriate of potash at 28 g (1 oz) to the same area.

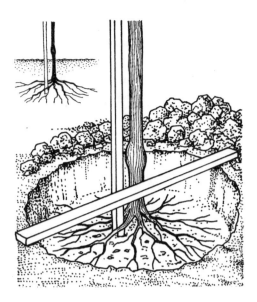

Planting a tree. The roots should be spread out fully and not covered too deeply

Complete the digging as long as possible in advance of the time of planting. An ideal plan is to use the site of the fruit garden for a crop of early potatoes, clearing them as soon after mid-summer as possible and then dig the ground in late summer/early autumn for planting in late autumn.

PLANTING

The chief point to observe about planting is to do it when the soil is in the right condition and not when it is waterlogged or frostbound. In some seasons there are only a few weeks during which this work can be carried out with real success so it is important to make the best possible use of the time when conditions are favourable. Other things being equal, the best period for planting bare-root fruit trees and bushes is usually from mid- to late autumn. By early winter the ground is almost always too wet and cold and this state of things is likely to continue at least until the end of winter, by which date sap is rising and there is little time left to complete planting. Container-grown fruit can be planted at any time when soil is in suitable condition as the plants suffer little or no check to growth.

Dig a few holes and if the soil clings to the spade or if the holes fill with water, planting should not be attempted. The ideal is that the soil should be crumbly; sufficiently moist to bind together when squeezed in the palm of the hand but dry enough for the ball so formed to break up again when tossed on to the surface.

If bare-root trees or bushes arrive from the nursery when soil conditions are unfavourable for planting, they should be heeled in temporarily. This simply means digging a trench large enough to accommodate the roots in which the trees are lined out as close together as possible. The soil is then returned over the roots and made firm. Treated in this way the bushes will take no harm for several weeks.

The vital points to remember in planting are to spread the roots out fully and not to cover them too deeply. A common fault is to make the holes too deep and narrow, though the normal habit of fruit tree roots is to grow out more or less horizontally. Not many roots plunge steeply into the soil and this is, in any case, an undesirable characteristic.

Speaking generally, holes for apples, pears, plums, etc. should be about 90 cm (3 ft) wide and 30 cm (1 ft) deep, but these dimensions may need to be varied a little to suit individual peculiarities of growth. In any case the hole should be wide enough to accommodate the longest root fully extended in a natural manner and deep enough to permit the uppermost roots to be covered with 10 cm (4 in) of soil.

It is wise to drive a stake into position in the centre of each hole before the tree is planted. Even bush trees need staking for a year or so though quite short stakes will suffice. For standards the stakes should be long enough to reach to the top of the main stem where it forks, and go down 60 cm (2 ft) into the soil. It often pays to have a second stake driven in at an angle to the main stake and bound to it as a stay.

Before planting the trees examine the roots carefully and cut off any portions that are badly broken or bruised. These are not likely to be of much use to the tree and if left they may decay and cause trouble.

It is an asset to have assistance when planting. One person can hold the tree and jerk it gently up and down while the other returns the soil a little at a time, the finer and more crumbly portions first. When all the roots are just covered the soil should be trodden down firmly. Then the rest of the soil is returned but left loose.

Tie the newly planted trees securely to their stakes directly planting is finished. Better still use the adjustable plastic straps sold for this purpose.

Container-grown Plants. The above instructions for planting apply to fruit trees and bushes lifted from the open ground. If plants are supplied in containers the method is slightly different and planting can be done at any time of the year when the soil is in workable condition, provided the plants are well established in the containers so that all the soil is bound together by their roots.

The plants must be removed from the containers carefully with a minimum of injury or disturbance to the roots. Polythene film containers can be slit and stripped off and plants in rigid plastic containers can usually be turned upside down and tapped out cleanly. The complete ball of soil and roots is then placed carefully in the prepared hole and surrounded with the displaced soil which should be made firm in the usual way. Only if plants are supplied in containers made of compressed peat through which the roots can grow and which will decompose in the soil can they be planted safely without removing the pots.

Chapter 26

Fruit Propagation

The nurseryman produces fruit trees by five different means: seeds, cuttings, grafts, beds and layers. Seeds are only used to raise new varieties or stocks upon which accepted kinds are grafted or budded. The reason is that there can be no guarantee that a seedling will resemble its parent in any respect except, of course, that an apple will always produce an apple, a pear a pear and so on. But in all the important details of size, colour and flavour it is almost certain that the seedling will differ widely from the fruit from which it was obtained. Moreover the change is seldom one for the better, the chances being in favour of deterioration rather than improvement. This remains true even when careful crosses have been made between parents selected for special points of excellence. Nurserymen who specialize in raising new varieties of fruit have to rear many hundreds of seedlings in order to obtain one or two that are fit to put on the market.

There is, of course, nothing to prevent the amateur from sowing pips and seeds on the off-chance of getting something good as long as he realizes just what the chances are. He should also know that seedlings are, as a rule, slow in giving any fruit. Seedling apples and pears may take ten years to produce a single fruit by which their quality may be judged, and even then further years must elapse before their cropping capabilities can be fully proved. This tardiness can often be overcome by grafting shoots from the seedling on to one of the dwarfing stocks to which I have already referred.

The actual handling of fruit seeds is the same as that for the seeds of other hardy trees and shrubs. The fruits are gathered when they part readily from the tree, and are then stood in a dry and fairly warm place until they become quite ripe. The seeds are then removed from them and stored in a cool, dry spot until early the following spring, when they are sown either out of doors in shallow drills or, a better policy, separately in small pots in a frame. If in pots the seedlings should be planted out in good soil the following autumn and subsequently left to grow with a minimum of thinning or pruning, which would only delay fruit production.

Cuttings. Soft fruits, such as gooseberries and currants, are always raised from cuttings taken in the autumn just before or as soon as the leaves fall. Wood of the current year's growth is used for this purpose, that is to say the young stems which have grown during the preceding summer. They must be firm and well ripened at the base but it does not matter if they are still fairly soft at the tips as these can be discarded. Stems about 30 cm (1 ft) in length are ideal but shorter pieces will serve. Each potential cutting is either severed from the parent plant just below a joint, that is, the point at which a leaf stalk joins the stem, or alternatively, if it is a side growth and not a terminal shoot, it is pulled away from the main branch with a strip of old bark, when it is known as a 'heel cutting' as opposed to a 'plain cutting'. Many gardeners assert that a heel cutting has a better chance of rooting, but a drawback of this method is that it leaves an ugly wound instead of a clean one on the parent plant and so affords greater chance of infection by disease germs.

If a heel cutting is taken the thin strip of bark left at the foot of the cutting must be trimmed neatly back. With the plain cutting no further preparation is necessary providing the cut has been made quite cleanly just beneath a joint. If the cut is ragged or removed from a joint these faults should be rectified.

With gooseberry and red and white currant cuttings it is advisable to nick out all buds on the lower half of each shoot with the point of a knife. The object of this is to prevent any shoots forming below soil level as these are a nuisance, tending to block up the centre of the bush and hindering picking. This precaution is not necessary with black currants because with these as much as possible of the old wood is cut out annually and therefore the sucker growths, which incidentally always produce the best fruit, do not overcrowd the bush.

All these cuttings are inserted in the same way. They are lined out about 15 cm (6 in) apart in straight-backed trenches about 13 cm (5 in) deep in well-broken soil and an open but not too exposed position. These trenches are best chopped out with a sharp spade and the backs should be kept as nearly vertical as possible so that the cuttings stand upright. The soil is returned around the cuttings and made thoroughly firm with the foot. No further treatment is necessary beyond the usual summer watering and hoeing until the following autumn, by which time the cuttings should be sufficiently well rooted to be lifted and planted in fruiting quarters.

A few failures will usually occur and need cause no concern, but if there are many blanks in the cutting bed it is probable that the shoots selected were either too soft or too hard. With a few varieties, particularly of gooseberry, it is difficult to get the right kind of shoot to make a good cutting. The gooseberry Leveller is a notable offender in this respect. The difficulty can be overcome by setting apart a few bushes for propagation early in the year, cutting them back to within several centimetres of the soil level and then, when shoots appear in spring, gradually drawing the soil around them to a height of 20 cm (8 in), much as when earthing potatoes. This will keep the bases of the shoots sufficiently soft to make satisfactory cuttings when they are severed for this purpose the following autumn.

Grafting. This is done just before mid-spring when the sap is beginning to rise freely. The shoots of the fruit tree which is to be propagated are known as scions and the roots to which these scions are to be joined are known as stocks.

Scions can be prepared from any firm, well-ripened young growths, shoots, in fact, identical with those used as cuttings in the case of soft fruits. Very often a sufficient number of these can be obtained in the ordinary course of winter pruning. Fairly strong shoots terminating branches are ideal for the purpose and should be obtained in mid-winter. They should be labelled clearly and heeled in in a shallow trench made in a cool, shady position such as under a north wall. The object of this is to hold them back so that by grafting time they are more backward than the stocks to which they are to be joined.

These stocks should be planted in autumn in well-prepared soil and allowed to grow for at least a year before being grafted. Stocks which are to form young trees should at the time of grafting have one main stem about as thick as a man's thumb and this is cut cleanly through about 38 cm (1¼ ft) above soil level a month before the time of grafting.

There are many different kinds of grafting but as far as the formation of young trees is concerned only one need interest us. This is the whip graft.

To make a successful whip graft one needs a very sharp knife, a supply of soft raffia or soft string and some grafting wax which can be obtained from any dealer in horticultural sundries. Select one of the shoots reserved as a scion and, starting immediately behind a bud, make a long, straight, downward cut coming out on the opposite side of the shoot about 5 cm (2 in) from the point of entry. The effect of this is to shape the bottom of the shoot into a long, thin wedge. Turn the shoot over and, starting about a quarter of the way down the first cut, draw the knife upwards in the opposite direction, so forming a thin slip or tongue as shown in the illustration. Now make two exactly similar cuts in the reverse direction at the top of the beheaded stock. These cuts should be identical in length and width with those made on the scion so that scion and stock can fit together perfectly. Do this and bind them together with raffia or soft string. Then cover the whole wounded area with grafting wax which will need to be warmed to make it work freely.

If the scion is a long one the top can be cut off several centimetres above the top of the stock. Some very strong shoots may be cut into two or three separate scions. There is nothing against this provided all the wood is properly ripened, but avoid using soft, downy-looking wood for this purpose. The tips of even the best shoots have to be thrown away on this account.

Two other methods of grafting are used though not for raising young trees. Both are serviceable for converting older trees to newer or more suitable kinds of fruit. One is known as rind grafting and the other as frame or stub grafting. In both cases a start must be made by gathering scions in winter just as for whip grafting but the method of preparing the trees which are to be grafted is different. For rind grafting each main bough or branch is cut off 30 cm (1 ft) or so above the trunk of the tree, thus leaving a number of short thick stumps. For frame grafting there are two alternatives. Either every side growth along the length of each main branch is removed, leaving the branches bare but unshortened, or no preparation at all is done at this stage.

A rind graft is particularly simple to make. The scion is cut with one long, sloping incision like that made for the whip graft but without the reverse cut. The stock is prepared by slitting the bark vertically from the top downwards for a length equal to that of the cut made on the scion. The flaps of bark on each side of this incision are gently raised from

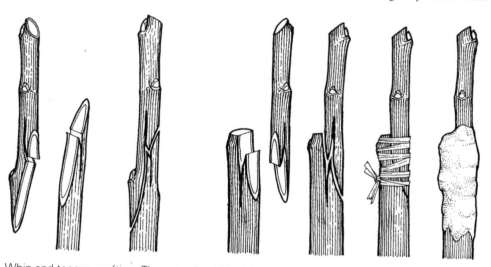

Whip and tongue grafting. The cuts should be identical in length and width so that stock and scion fit perfectly. They are then tied in place and covered with grafting wax

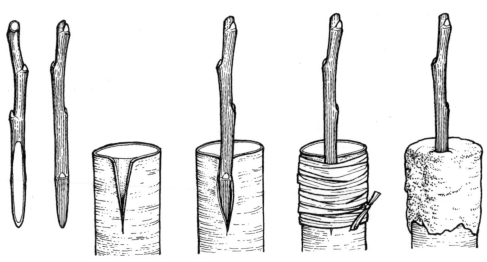

A rind graft is very simple to make. If the stump is large enough two or three scions can be inserted around it.

the hard wood beneath and the tapering wedge of the scion is pressed down beneath them so that its cut surface lies snugly inwards against the moist wood of the stock. Two or three scions can be inserted in this way round the top of each stump if it is a big one. All are then bound in place with a raffia tie and covered with grafting wax.

Frame Working. For frame grafting, if all side growths were removed in autumn, L-shaped incisions are made in the bark every few centimetres along each main branch. Again the flap of bark so formed is raised and the scions, prepared in the same way as for rind grafting, are slipped beneath, bound in and waxed.

If the side growths were not removed in winter a different method is employed. A short, downward incision is made on the upper side of each side growth 12 mm (½ in) above its base. The scion is prepared with a double cut forming a rather blunt wedge. The side growth is then bent downwards to open the cut, the scion is slipped into position and the shoot is immediately released so that it springs back and grips the scion. Finally the shoot is cut off just beyond the point at which the scion was inserted. By this method no tying is necessary and it only remains to wax the wound in the ordinary way.

The advantage of frame grafting is that the whole main framework of the tree, however old, is retained and the conversion is made with the minimum of delay. The tree that has been headed back for rind grafting may take a number of years to regain its former productiveness.

Budding. This is a simple method of making a union between stock and scion. It is the form of grafting nurserymen invariably use first when working young stock for sale, their practice being to bud all their stocks in mid- to late summer following the autumn of planting, and then, the next spring, to graft any which may have failed when budded. Budding is far more satisfactory than grafting for stone fruits as it does not necessitate severe heading back of the stock and consequently does not render it so liable to attack by

Frame working. The scions, prepared in a similar way as for rind grafting, are inserted every few centimetres along each main branch. In this way the main framework of the tree is retained and the conversion made with less delay than is achieved with rind grafting

diseases such as silver leaf. The limitation of budding is that it can only be applied to quite young wood and does not provide a satisfactory method of reworking old trees.

All the work is done in summer, usually from about mid- to the end of summer. The limiting factors as regards time are, at the beginning, the earliest date at which ripe buds can be obtained, and at the end of the period, the latest date at which the bark of the stock will part cleanly from the wood.

The buds referred to are, in fact, dormant growth buds, one of which will be found in the angle between the leaf stalk and stem on practically every young shoot in summer. Suitable wood for budding can be obtained when doing summer pruning for well-developed side growths (laterals) are just what is needed. The tips of these are usually still soft and downy and should be discarded but the lower portion of each should be firm and woody and therefore suitable. The leaves are removed from the selected shoots but the leaf stalks are retained.

The stock should be anything from two to four years old and should for preference be about as thick as a man's thumb. It is prepared by making a T-shaped incision in the bark about 30 cm (1 ft) above soil level. The down cut of the T should be 2·5 cm (1 in) long and the cross cut 12 mm (½ in) wide. The flaps of bark on each side of this down cut are raised with the thin end of a budding knife. Next a bud is cut by inserting the blade of the knife 12 mm (½ in) below one of the leaf stalks on the selected shoot and drawing it in and up beneath the bud and out again on the same side, well above the leaf stalk. This gives a shield-shaped portion of bark and wood with a leaf stalk and bud. Holding this by the leaf stalk turn it over, grip between thumb nail and knife point the slip of wood contained within the bark and whip it out. Now square off the top of the shield-shaped portion of bark 8 mm (⅓ in) above the bud. Still holding the section by the leaf stalk slip it beneath the flaps of bark on the stock, keeping the bud uppermost and outwards. Push it down until the squared top of the bud lies snugly against the top of the T. Finally bind it in position with soft raffia or a special budding tie, being careful to do so well above and below the cut portion.

Six or seven weeks later examine the ties. If, due to its growth, some are cutting into the bark of the stock, remove the old tie and replace with a fresh one.

Nothing further needs to be done until the following late winter when the whole of the top growth of the stock should be cut off just above the point of budding. This concentrates all the sap from the roots on to the inserted bud which by this time should have made a good union and will therefore be ready to grow away strongly. Any shoots coming from the stock below the inserted bud should be removed.

Layering. As a method of propagation layering is not very frequently applied to fruit trees themselves, though a special form known as tip layering is used for bramble fruits, but it is the best method of increasing many fruit stocks, notably paradise and quince stocks. The method for them is very simple. The stocks are planted in the ordinary way in straight rows. Then in late winter they are cut back to within a few centimetres of ground level. The following spring strong basal growth will appear from each beheaded stock. The best shoots are selected and pegged down horizontally to the soil the following winter. The remaining weaker shoots are cut out. Side shoots will soon form freely along the lengths of the pegged stems. Soil is drawn up around these a little at a time, just as when earthing potatoes, until eventually there is a ridge right down the row 60 cm (2 ft) wide and 15 cm (6 in) in height. Most of the shoots will make roots into this soil. The following autumn they can be pulled away from the parent plant with roots attached and be planted up on their own.

Tip layering as applied to blackberries and loganberries is done in the second half of summer. Any strong, young canes can be used. These are bent down so that the tip of each touches the soil and is then weighted in this position with a stone or held down with a peg. In a very short time roots will grow from the tip which will also continue to grow on, producing a further shoot. By the autumn the new plant should be sufficiently well rooted to be severed from its parent just behind the point of layering.

Gooseberries, especially those with a weeping habit, sometimes layer themselves where branches touch the soil. When this happens the rooted layers can be severed from the parent plants and lifted between late autumn and early spring to be replanted elsewhere.

Chapter 27

Pruning Fruit Trees

Before discussing the principles underlying all pruning and outlining the methods employed, it is as well to be quite clear about the reasons for pruning at all. Many people imagine that the object of pruning is to obtain fruit, whereas this is far from being the case. It is almost always the unpruned fruit tree which will bear most rapidly and heavily. In fact one of the big problems which faces the fruit grower is to devise a system of pruning which will achieve the desired ends without unduly delaying or reducing the production of fruit.

What, then, are the objectives? In the main they are four in number, as follows:

1. To form each tree to a specified shape and, in particular, to produce branches where they are most needed to suit the convenience of the gardener.

2. To allow sufficient light to reach leaves and fruits and prevent rubbing of one branch against another.

3. To get rid of dead, diseased and pest-infected wood.

4. To prevent over-cropping and so improve crop quality, and regulate yield from one year to another.

The regulation of yield from year to year requires some explanation. Many fruit growers complain that their trees only carry a crop every second year. So marked in certain instances is this habit of biennial bearing that it was at one time thought to be unavoidable. Further experience has shown this to be wrong. The habit is due to the exhaustion of the tree in the year during which it is carrying a crop. So much strength goes into the actual production of that one crop that the tree is unable at the same time to produce fruit buds to crop again the following year. The next year, having no fruit to ripen, it can make more buds and so the cycle continues. If the strain on the tree in the 'on' year is suitably reduced the tree will make sufficient fruit buds not to have an 'off' year.

Pruning falls into two main stages. First there is the initial pruning, during which the main framework of the tree is formed. Following this comes the permanent pruning of the tree, after the main framework has been formed. Roughly speaking for the first six or seven years of the life of an apple, pear, plum or cherry initial pruning will be carried out, after which there will be a more or less gradual transition to permanent pruning. But common sense must always be used and the actual growth of the trees considered.

Terms. Before considering the actual methods of pruning employed, it is necessary to explain certain technical terms which will constantly crop up. Chief amongst these are 'leader', 'lateral', 'fruit bud', 'growth bud' and 'spur'. 'Dart' is occasionally used for a short growth terminated by a fruit bud.

A leader is any young shoot that is required to extend a main branch or start a new branch.

A lateral is any other young shoot and not necessarily one growing out sideways from a branch. Usually, laterals are of this type but occasionally a terminal shoot may have to be treated as a lateral if it is not required as a leader under the terms explained above.

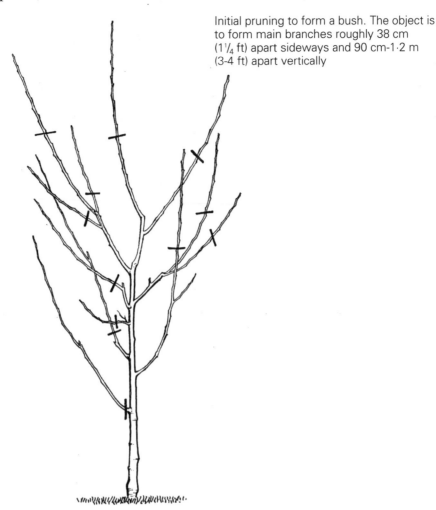

Initial pruning to form a bush. The object is to form main branches roughly 38 cm (1¼ ft) apart sideways and 90 cm-1·2 m (3-4 ft) apart vertically

A fruit bud contains a cluster of flower buds and will only produce fruit if some of these flowers are fertilized with pollen. It is necessary to be able to distinguish a fruit bud from a growth bud (see above) and this is really a matter of experience and observation. Fruit buds are in general larger, fatter and rounder than growth buds and definitely more noticeable in autumn when most pruning is done.

A growth bud is one which will in the normal course of things produce a shoot and not a flower. As a rule a growth bud will be found in the angle formed by every leaf stalk where it joins the stem.

A spur is a group of fruit buds and is a characteristic development on many mature fruit trees. Sometimes spurs become extremely complicated, branching freely and occupying quite a lot of space. As a rule such complex spur systems are undesirable, much simpler systems being more satisfactory.

Initial Pruning. If any young shoot is shortened in autumn or winter it will tend, the following year, to produce new shoots from just below the point of cutting. The gardener makes use of this tendency to obtain branches where he requires them. Let us for a moment consider the early formation into a bush of a maiden apple, that is, one which has just completed its first year of growth after budding or grafting and has only one main stem with perhaps a few small side shoots (feathers, the professional calls them) near the base. A bush is shaped like a goblet standing on a short leg or main trunk. This trunk needs to be about 60-76 cm (2-2½ ft) in length, so, sometime between mid-autumn and early spring, the maiden is beheaded 60-76 cm (2-2½ ft) above soil level and any feathers (small shoots) below this point are removed.

The following spring the tree produces several shoots from just below the point of pruning, and the gardener retains about three of these to make the first main branches as nearly as possible at equal points all round the stem. Other shoots are rubbed out quite early.

From now on the object will be to form main branches roughly 38 cm (1¼ ft) apart sideways and 90 cm-1·2 m (3-4 ft) apart vertically. Note particularly that a greater distance is necessary between branches that overtop one another than between branches which are beside one another. This is because they will gradually be pulled down both by their own weight and that of the fruit they carry.

By the end of the second year the three shoots retained after the first pruning will probably have grown 60-90 cm (2-3 ft) each and be well spaced out at the tips. There is, in consequence, room for more branches, so the three original shoots are cut back to approximately the points at which they are 38 cm (1¼ ft) apart.

The following year still more shoots will come from each of the pruned stems and the gardener will retain sufficient of these, perhaps two per stem, to fill the available space, still bearing in mind that the branches are to be roughly 38 cm (1¼ ft) apart laterally. But by this time it may be possible to add some more branches vertically as well as outwards so adding an inner ring to the tree. This process goes on until the bush covers a circle 2·4-3 m (8-10 ft) in diameter and has, perhaps, 24 branches.

A standard or half-standard is formed in much the same way, except that the main stem of the maiden is allowed to grow on unchecked until it has attained the required height for the trunk of the finished tree, 1·2-1·3 m (4-4½ ft) in the case of half-standards, 1·8 m (6 ft) in the case of full standards. The top is then removed and the head branches allowed to form, as for the bush tree.

The formation of a fan-trained tree follows the same general lines as that of the bush except that instead of selecting shoots situated all round the main trunk they are retained in one plane only. Otherwise the same method of encouraging branches at about 38 cm (1¼ ft) intervals is adopted.

A little more care is called for in forming the horizontally trained tree for in this branches must be placed with considerable accuracy. The usual scheme is to have one pair of horizontal arms every 38 cm (1¼ ft) up the main central stem. The method is as follows: in autumn or winter the maiden tree is pruned back to within 45 cm (1½ ft) of ground level. In the spring three shoots are retained as near the pruning cuts as possible. The two most conveniently placed are bent down to left and right respectively and fixed to canes or wires. The third is trained vertically, usually to a stout cane. The next autumn the vertical growth is cut back to within 45 cm (1½ ft) of the horizontally trained shoots. In the spring three shoots are again retained, two to form a second pair of arms and the third to continue the central stem. The process can go on indefinitely until the desired number of arms has been formed.

Summer pruning a trained fruit tree. Aim to cut back every half-woody shoot to within four or five well-developed leaves of its base. The right condition of growth is generally reached in mid- to late summer for apples and pears, a week or so earlier for plums and cherries

There is some difference of opinion whether the horizontal arms themselves should or should not be pruned. They are not required to branch and therefore it would seem most logical to leave them unpruned but usually they fail to make sufficient new growth when treated in this way. This fault can only be overcome by light cutting back each autumn.

There remains the cordon tree to consider. This has a single (or sometimes double or triple) main stem to which all other growth is kept fairly closely pruned. As branching is not required, no pruning of the leader should be carried out. It is allowed to extend vertically until it reaches the desired height for the completed cordon, when further development is prevented by cutting out all further leader growth when pruning in autumn or winter. If a multiple-stemmed cordon is to be formed the maiden is cut back to within about 30 cm (1 ft) of the ground and two or three stems are trained vertically. Subsequently each stem is treated like a single-stemmed cordon.

In discussing the formation of young trees nothing has been said about the treatment of side shoots. What is to become of these while the main framework is being formed? The answer will depend largely on the variety and form of tree, the kind of stock upon which it is worked and on the character of the soil in which it is grown. If laterals are left unpruned many of them will start to carry fruit along most of their length in their second year. That may seem very nice and a good many amateurs are only too pleased to allow their trees to bear as quickly and heavily as possible. But bearing places a great strain on the tree and may result in a cessation of growth. That must not be allowed while the framework of the tree is being formed. It is therefore almost certain that some of the laterals will have to be removed or shortened to lessen the number of fruit buds. In the case of the trained trees, especially the horizontally trained and cordon-trained types, it will be essential to shorten the laterals to maintain the characteristic shape of the specimen.

This shortening is best done in two operations, one carried out in summer and the other in winter. Summer pruning is done as soon as the laterals become woody near the base. Young growth has a soft, downy appearance which passes slowly with age. With apples and pears the right condition of growth is generally reached from mid- to late summer according to variety and location. Plums and cherries may be a week or so earlier, while gooseberries and currants will probably be ready for summer pruning by mid-summer.

The method is to cut every half-woody shoot to within four or five well-developed leaves of its base. Generally there are a few poorly developed leaves in a rosette near the bottom of the shoot. Take no account of these when reckoning the approximate point of pruning. In the autumn these summer-pruned shoots are either left as they are or, if the tree is a cordon or horizontally trained one, are further cut back to a length of two or three buds.

The following year these side shoots are likely to produce some new growth which can be summer pruned to one leaf. On the older part, below the point of the first summer pruning, they will generally form some fruit buds and when these are observed the shoots can be pruned back to one of them, precisely which one depending upon whether it is wished to keep a strictly formal specimen with very short fruiting spurs or to build up a looser but more prolific tree.

Permanent Pruning. As the tree takes its permanent shape the gardener becomes progressively less concerned with the production of new branches and more with the regulation of fruitfulness. Another point which he must watch is the spacing of the branches, for trees, as they age, tend to spread out and droop. As a result branches which were originally well spaced may with age become too close and some must be removed.

The precise amount of pruning which has to be carried out on the adult tree will vary according to its character. Often bushes, half-standards and standards can go for a number of years with no more than an annual autumn or winter thinning out of stems or branches which rub together and, of course, removal of dead or diseased wood. But as a rule there will be something additional to do. Some branches may be damaged by over-cropping or be showing signs of waning vitality. Either such branches should themselves be cut back quite severely, even if this means going into wood that is several years old, or a neighbouring branch should be cut back. The object is to get strong new shoots from which one or more may be selected to replace the old one and the principle upon which the gardener works is the old one that 'growth follows the knife'.

Elsewhere it may be seen that a tree is making long, thin growths which could not carry the weight of fruit even if they produced it. These should be shortened sufficiently to give them necessary stiffness and in this case each cut should be made, if possible, just beyond a good, plump fruit bud.

Some varieties of fruit, such as apples Worcester Pearmain and Irish Peach and pear Jargonelle, make a great many fruit buds right at the tips of side growths. These should have very little pruning unless they are grown as trained trees, in which case their natural habit will have to be modified by summer pruning. This also applies to naturally vigorous

To encourage old trees to make new growth, many main branches may be headed back quite severely to side branches, a method known as dehorning

varieties such as apples Bramley's Seedling, Newton Wonder and Blenheim Orange which tend to make wood at the expense of fruit if heavily pruned, especially in autumn or winter. But it is really wise to avoid such varieties when choosing trees for training and to select instead varieties of moderate vigour which tend to form fruit spurs easily. Apple Cox's Orange Pippin, Charles Ross, Rival, Beauty of Bath and Laxton's Superb and most choice dessert pears are examples of this type.

Formal specimens such as pyramids and fan, horizontal or cordon-trained trees must always have a considerable amount of pruning, especially of side growths, or they quickly get out of shape. Summer pruning on the lines already indicated will be needed throughout their life whereas it can be largely omitted in the case of bushes and standards after the initial years. It will be followed by winter pruning to keep spurs and fruiting side shoots as compact as possible. Prune to fruit buds wherever these exist but, failing them, to the first, second or third growth bud reckoned from the base of each shoot.

Renovation of Old Trees. Still later in the life of the tree the laterals, which in the early days carried no more than two or three fruit buds each, begin to develop many spurs each crowded with fruit buds. Blossom production in spring may be immense but the high hopes of the gardener when he sees this grand display may not be realized.

The trouble is that the tree is now producing too many fruit buds and not enough new growth. It is in need of renovation. There are several ways in which this may be done.

First of all the spurs themselves can be thinned out or reduced in number. Some can be removed entirely and others left with only two or three fruit buds. Second, many main branches (not just one here and there as already described) may be headed back quite severely (dehorning is the technical term for this) with the object of making them produce new growth and so giving the gardener fresh material upon which to work. Feeding also has a bearing on this problem of excessive production at the expense of new wood, for by increasing the rate of application, particularly of nitrogenous foods, further growth can be encouraged.

Root Pruning. It is not always the branches alone which need pruning. Sometimes the roots also grow too vigorously, with the result that the tree makes too much growth and does not fruit as it should. This is most liable to happen with young trees that are grafted on vigorous stocks or are planted on very rich land.

One remedy is to cut back some of the roots. This is best done in mid- to late autumn. The method is to dig a trench around the tree 90 cm-1·2 m (3-4 ft) away from it and work towards it with a fork, uncovering the roots and severing any thick ones, particularly those which tend to dive down steeply into the subsoil. Finer roots are preserved and, when the pruning is judged to have gone sufficiently far, these are spread out again, covered with soil and made thoroughly firm.

Some gardeners believe that only one half of a fruit tree should be root pruned at a time, the other half being left until the following year. Personally I think that this encourages unbalanced growth and prefer to go right round the tree at one operation. If there is fear that this may prove too drastic, stop some distance from the base of the tree.

Young fruit trees are often most effectively root pruned by lifting and replanting them. This should be done in autumn directly they have lost most of their leaves.

It should be noted that excessive vigour may be caused by incorrect feeding, particularly by giving too much dung or nitrogenous fertilizer. Obviously the best way to counter this is to stop the practice that has caused it. Potash fertilizers only, for a few years, and no pruning at all may bring an over-vigorous tree into bearing.

Specialized Methods of Pruning. In addition to the methods described there are several specialized methods of pruning which have their keen advocates. Notable among these are the Lorette system devised by M. Lorette in France, and the renewal system largely developed in Kent for commercial apple orchards.

The Lorette system is an extremely severe method of pruning most suitable for small, trained trees. Under it the fruiting spurs are produced very close to the main branches and a particularly neat specimen results. It is said to be applicable to all apple and pear varieties but in cooler climates the results have been mixed.

Briefly the Lorette system depends upon forcing into growth and turning into fruit buds certain very tiny buds, known as stipulary buds, which normally remain dormant. These buds are situated at the extreme base of each shoot. In order to force these buds to grow the shoots must be cut back severely – to within 6 mm (¼ in) of the base. The precise condition of growth when this is done is important as it must be fairly ripe but not really hard and woody. Three summer prunings are usually advised. In early summer all side shoots that have attained pencil thickness are cut back to 6 mm (¼ in). Four weeks later the process is repeated on shoots that have attained the required thickness since early summer. In late summer any further shoots that have reached pencil thickness are also cut back in a similar manner. Shoots which are not thick enough to be pruned in mid-summer are tied downwards to check the flow of sap. Leaders of main branches are shortened by about one third in mid-spring. There is no winter pruning at all.

But there are so many qualifications to this general outline of treatment that anyone who really intends to apply the method seriously should study a book on the subject before attempting it.

Renewal pruning is almost diametrically opposed to Lorette pruning in that it is directed towards encouraging the formation of buds throughout the length of young branches. All close summer pruning is eliminated and the work is done entirely in winter.

About two out of every three year-old shoots are then cut back to a length of about 2·5 cm (1 in) and the third is left unpruned. These unpruned shoots should form fruit buds freely the following summer and carry a crop the summer after that. They can be shortened a little and left to bear for a second year after which they are cut right out. Meanwhile the shoots which were severely shortened will have made more strong growths some of which will be retained to provide new fruiting wood.

Great judgement is required when using this method and feeding must be carefully supervised to ensure that the trees make the required amount of strong new growth each year. Moreover, as trees treated in this manner tend to acquire an increasingly weeping habit each year, strong young stems growing upwards from the topmost part of each bent branch must be retained to act as replacement leaders. Each year a few of the very weeping branches are cut back to these replacement leaders.

Once again this is a system for experienced fruit growers rather than for novices, and I would advise any amateurs who are interested to study a book on the subject or see a practical demonstration of the method before trying to put it into effect.

Notching. This is a variation on the foregoing practice applied to individual buds. A dormant bud will be encouraged to start into growth if a triangular notch of bark is removed in mid-spring just above it, whereas a similar notch made just below the bud will check its growth. Such methods are often of service when forming trained trees to obtain shoots and fruit buds just where they are needed and to prevent them occurring where they are not wanted.

Fruit on Young Wood. So far I have written as though all fruit trees and bushes with which we are concerned produce their fruit on spurs and upon the older wood. There are a few kinds which bear either exclusively or mainly upon the young wood, usually that produced the previous year, the raspberry being an obvious example. It throws up fresh canes from the roots every summer and these carry fruit the following summer and then die out. Blackberries and loganberries have exactly the same characteristic and black currants carry it to a lesser degree. Peaches, nectarines and Morello cherries are other common fruits in which year-old wood is more important for fruit production than older wood.

With all these the gardener's endeavour must be to maintain a sufficient production of young growth each year to carry the next year's crop. This is done partly by adequate manuring and soil cultivation and partly by thinning out young growth as it appears, leaving only enough for next year's requirements and so concentrating all the available strength of the plant upon it. Quite a complicated process of disbudding is used in the case of peaches, nectarines and Morello cherries, and I have described this in some detail under the heading 'Pruning' on p. 659.

In all this class of pruning the object is to get rid of as much as possible of the old fruiting wood soon after the crop has been gathered and to retain the best young growth to crop the following year.

Ringing. This is a device for checking excessive vigour and encouraging fruitfulness without going to the labour of root pruning. It works well with apples and pears but is less satisfactory with stone fruits. The work is done early mid-spring. A ring of bark, 6 mm (¼ in) wide, is removed around the main trunk 60-90 cm (2-3 ft) above soil level. In the case of bushes with short trunks it is usually better to cut one ring near the base of each main bough.

The object of ringing is to check the free downward flow of sap from leaves to roots for a limited period, that is, until the ring has healed over again. The effect is to check root growth and so it has much the same result as moderate root pruning.

If the ring is too wide the healing process may take too long and the tree will die of starvation. Some growers prefer to make two half-rings on opposite sides several centimetres apart, while another scheme is to cut a ring which nearly but not quite encircles the trunk. I have not found these precautions necessary providing the width of 6 mm (¼ in) is not exceeded.

It is not essential to protect the ring in any way but there is no harm in coating it with warm grafting wax or binding a piece of adhesive tape around it.

Knife-edge Ringing. This is a special form of ringing used mainly on individual branches with the object of encouraging growth where it has not previously occurred, for example if a young branch fails to develop any fruit buds or laterals over a portion of its length. In late spring the edge of a sharp knife is drawn around the branch at the top of the bare portion in such a way as to cut through the bark and soft tissues without actually removing

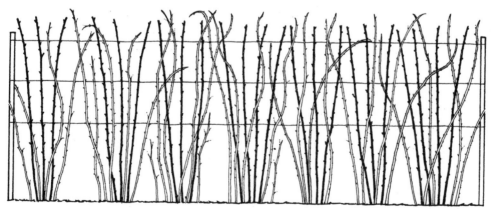

To make room for the young raspberry canes which will bear fruit the darker coloured old canes which have already fruited are cut out at the base in late summer. The young canes can then be thinned to about 23 cm (9 in) apart

anything. The downward flow of certain chemicals or hormones which inhibit the growth of lower buds is thus checked for long enough to allow these buds to start into growth.

Ringing the bark of a fruit tree checks excess vigour and so encourages fruitfulness.
In this example two half-rings are being removed on opposite sides of the trunk. Some fruit growers regard this as safer than cutting one ring completely round the trunk

Chapter 28

A Spraying Programme

Pests and diseases are discussed in detail in a separate chapter (see p. 716) but the spraying of fruit trees is such a special matter and so much of it is carried out purely for prevention, even though no pest or disease is actually seen, that a separate description is necessary here.

Winter Washing. Following the calendar year, work begins in mid-winter with the application of tar-oil wash. This can be given to all fruit trees and bushes but is usually only necessary every second or third year. Its purpose is to clean the trees as thoroughly as possible both from obvious growths such as those of moss, lichen and algae or green scum, and also from the less obvious but more dangerous eggs of pests, chiefly those of greenflies and allied species of aphid and scale insects. Tar oil is damaging to trees once the buds have begun to swell, but the later it can be applied up to this stage the better because insect eggs are more vulnerable as the spring draws near. Generally it is unwise to continue tar-oil spraying after the end of mid-winter on apples and pears, and not much later on cherries and plums.

Anti-Scab Treatment. The next step for apples and pears is to keep scab under control. This is a disease which spots and cracks the skins of these fruits. Though it does not penetrate to the flesh it often checks development and is, in any case, very unsightly. It may also attack the bark of small stems causing them to blister and possibly die.

Scab is controlled with captan, benomyl or thiophanate-methyl, the first application being made when the blossom buds are sufficiently open to show the tiny clusters of green flower buds within. This is known as green bud stage. Further applications are given every ten days to a fortnight. In bad cases where scab has been persistent and attacked twigs further applications are continued in early, mid-, and late summer.

Caterpillars and Grubs. Meanwhile other foes may have been launching an attack. First of all there will be winter moth caterpillars which are small, green or brownish and move by looping themselves. Sometimes they appear almost as soon as the blossom buds open and strip the trees of their first leaves. They can be killed by prompt spraying with derris, permethrin, or malathion which to save time can be mixed with the anti-scab spray.

After the winter moths come the sawflies and codling moths. Apple sawfly is often terribly destructive. It lays its eggs in the fully open blossom and the tiny maggots eat into the fruits, producing the familiar maggoty apple. The codling moth caterpillar attacks apples in just the same way but appears later. There are not often any sawfly maggots left after mid-summer whereas apples may still contain codling moth caterpillars in late summer.

To counter apple sawfly the apple grower mixes HCH, malathion or dimethoate with the anti-scab spray after blossom fall. Codling moth is controlled by spraying with carbaryl, permethrin or malathion when the eggs begin to hatch out, usually in early summer, repeating four weeks later.

In early summer the fruit grower will have to turn his attention to the raspberries. They, too, may become maggoty with the grubs of the raspberry beetle unless the open flowers are dusted with derris and the treatment is repeated, this time on the fruits, towards mid-summer.

Sometimes aphids of various kinds including greenflies and blackflies are very troublesome, infesting the young shoots and leaves, causing them to cockle and curl and covering them with a sticky substance on which sooty mould may soon grow. At the first sign of attack trees should be sprayed with malathion, pirimicarb or pirimiphos-methyl and treatment repeated every seven to ten days until there are no aphids left.

Grease Bands. There is only one other routine measure which should be taken whether foes are seen or not. This is the application of grease bands to all fruit trees about early autumn. The grease band is simply a piece of grease-proof paper about 15 cm (6 in) wide wrapped tightly round the main trunk of the tree about 90 cm (3 ft) above ground level or, in the case of bushes, one band around each main bough at the same height from the ground. The band is then thoroughly smeared with special sticky grease. The purpose of the paper is simply to prevent the grease from injuring the bark. There are some proprietary brands of grease which can safely be applied direct to the bark of mature trees.

The purpose of the grease is to trap any insects which may try to crawl up the trunk from the soil to the branches. Principal among these are the female winter moths, which are wingless. As they pupate in the soil and lay their eggs on the branches the grease band is quite an effective method of catching them. Incidentally codling moth caterpillars often crawl from fallen apples back to the branches of an apple tree to pupate, so if this pest has been troublesome it is worth while getting grease bands in position two months earlier than usual, that is to say in mid-summer instead of early autumn. In any case the grease bands should be kept in position, the grease being renewed from time to time, throughout the winter.

This brief account of routine pest control in a fruit garden does not rule out the possibility of a great deal of extra spraying having to be done. This will depend upon just what foes materialize and full particulars regarding these will be found in the chapter already referred to.

Chapter 29

Cropping Problems

One of the perennial complaints of the amateur is that some of his trees do not bear fruit. I have already referred to some of the possible causes earlier in this section, but as there is so much confusion of thought on the subject of bad fertility it seems wise to assemble all the relative facts in one chapter.

Many trees giving cause for anxiety are simply not sufficiently mature to produce fruits. The actual age at which any tree should begin to fruit will depend upon several things, such as the variety of tree, the type of stock on which it is grafted and, to a lesser degree, the form in which it is trained. Some stocks, such as M. 9 or Malling C induce comparatively early fruitfulness; others, such as crab stock and free pear stock, delay fruitfulness. Naturally slow-fruiting varieties, such as the apples Bramley's Seedling or Blenheim Orange, worked on crab stock, cannot reasonably be expected to produce much fruit until they are fifteen years old. A naturally precocious variety such as Sunset or Greensleeves, worked on M. 9 stock, may quite likely produce a fairly heavy crop at three years. That gives an idea of the kind of difference which may occur from this cause.

Over-pruning may prevent fruiting by destroying most or all the flower buds.

A tree that is growing very vigorously, making perhaps shoots 90 cm (3 ft) long each year, is unlikely to fruit well. Here again, before taking drastic action one must decide whether this vigour is the normal exuberance of youth or due to faulty feeding. A young tree on a sturdy stock should make a good deal of growth and it would be a mistake to check it too soon. However, if the growth really is abnormal and due to too-rich soil, it can be checked by correcting the manurial programme, by root pruning in mid-autumn, by bark ringing in mid-spring (see p. 631) or by growing grass under the trees.

Then there is the question of pollination to be considered. In order that fruit may be formed the blossom must be fertilized with ripe pollen, and in most cases it is far better, if not actually essential, that this pollen should come from another tree of the same kind but a different variety (see p. 614). Sometimes there is even incompatibility between certain varieties. This is most marked in cherries and is fully described under that heading.

Even when there is plenty of pollen of the right kind it may be that the weather prevents bees or other insects from carrying it from flower to flower and tree to tree. Bees are the chief natural agents of pollen distribution in fruit trees. They will not fly far if the weather is bad and in any case in some districts there are not enough bees to give satisfactory pollination even when the weather is good. The remedy is to pollinate by hand; not such a lengthy business as it sounds, if the orchard is not too big. The pollen is collected on a camel-hair brush or rabbit's tail tied to a stick and dusted lightly over the blossoms to be pollinated.

Again there is the possibility that the essential organs of the blossom may be killed by frosts. It is not necessary that the blossom should be killed outright. The most sensitive part of the flower is the stigma or central organ and this may be destroyed by frost even before the blossom opens. Such flowers can be detected by very careful examination as they have a tiny black eye.

Novices are often misled by the fact that fruits form and even, perhaps, grow as big as marbles only to fall off. They think that this could not occur unless the blossom had been pollinated. On the contrary, these fruits are often the result of imperfect pollination, as can be proved by cutting them open. Instead of having plump seeds within they either have empty husks or no seeds at all.

Another cause of failure to fruit may be an early attack by sawfly grubs or other pests which eat into the fruits and cause them to fall prematurely. This can be ascertained by cutting open some of the defective fruits.

Lastly there is the often-overlooked point that big supplies of readily available food, particularly nitrogen, are required during the first few weeks after pollination. If the soil is rather poor or dry this food may not be available. It not infrequently happens that a previously barren tree can be brought into bearing by giving in mid-spring a topdressing of a quick-acting nitrogenous fertilizer such as sulphate of ammonia.

Manuring. A great deal depends upon the correct feeding of fruit trees. Failure to grasp the importance of this accounts for many disappointments. Vigour control is partly a matter of right feeding though it is also influenced by stock (see p. 612) and pruning (see pp. 623–32).

Nitrogen and potash are the two foods which have the most marked effect, the former mainly on growth and the latter on fruitfulness, though to some extent the two are linked. Phosphates play a comparatively small part except with strawberries. Lime does not have anything like so marked an effect as was at one time thought, and lack of lime is seldom if ever the main cause of poor stone formation in plums, cherries, etc. In some districts magnesium deficiency is the cause of poor growth and early defoliation.

Here are a few danger signs. Very vigorous growth with dark green leaves and poorly coloured fruits indicates an excess of nitrogen. Poor growth with small, pale leaves is an indication of too little nitrogen. Potash shortage will cause severe scorching of the leaf edges, a condition which is often erroneously ascribed to disease. Excess of potash is not likely to occur and in any case will probably only cause excessive colouring of fruit with some diminution of growth.

An excessive amount of lime will cause yellowing of the foliage and poor growth. Lack of magnesium will result in an early leaf fall affecting most markedly the young shoots which may only retain a few leaves at base and tip, the middle portions being bare. This deficiency may also be diagnosed by the regular, brown smudging of the leaves between the veins.

Routine feeding must be adjusted to meet the growth of the trees and the known or observed deficiences of the soil, but an average programme from which deviations can be made as seems necessary is as follows:

In winter or early spring a topdressing of well-rotted farmyard or stable manure should be applied at the rate of 50 kg per 12 sq m (1 cwt per 15 sq yd) for apples, pears and gooseberries, 50 kg per 9·6 sq m (1 cwt per 12 sq yd) for plums, cherries and currants and at the same time, or in autumn, sulphate of potash at 28 g per 0·8 sq m (1 oz per sq yd). Every second autumn basic slag or bonemeal should be given at 113 g per 0·8 sq m (4 oz per sq yd). For strawberries apply superphosphate of lime each spring at 56 g per 0·8 sq m (2 oz per sq yd). If no dung is available sulphate of ammonia could be substituted at the same as the last rate for any of these fruits.

If leaf-edge scorching appears, two applications of potash fertilizer could be given per year till the trouble clears up. Should the scorching be of the smudgy, intervenal type associated with magnesium deficiency, sulphate of magnesium could be added to the spring dressings at the rate of 28 g per 0·8 sq m (1 oz per sq yd), or magnesium limestone could be used at 226 g per 0·8 sq m (8 oz per sq yd). This latter is lasting and safe but rather slow in action.

In the case of trees which show a marked tendency to bear one year and miss the next it will often pay to give an extra dressing of sulphate of ammonia, 28 g per 0·8 sq m (1 oz per sq yd) in mid-spring. This is particularly likely to prove beneficial if the trees have not been making much new growth for this is an almost certain indication that the biennial bearing is due to weakness and, in particular, to lack of readily available nitrogen at the critical time when the fruit should be starting to swell. In addition, the fruit buds may be drastically thinned during the spring of each year when heavy cropping is expected – what fruit growers term the 'on' years. The buds can be rubbed out before they open, no more than one being left per spur. This reduces the crop that year and gives the tree a chance to make fruit buds for the next year which would otherwise be a light cropping, or 'off', year.

Chapter 30

Fruits and their Cultivation

In this chapter the principal fruits are arranged alphabetically with concise cultural instructions for each and brief lists of varieties. New varieties of fruit do appear from time to time but they are by no means so numerous as new vegetables, nor do they catch on so readily. The lists given can therefore be taken as including in general the best varieties for planting.

APPLES

The apple is one of the most popular hard fruits grown in cool climates and undoubtedly the most widely planted. Even in places too subject to spring frosts to be suitable for the majority of hardy fruits it is sometimes possible to grow apples successfully by choosing late-flowering kinds. The season of apple blossom is later than that of any other tree fruit, extending through late spring in a normal season, and there are a few varieties such as Crawley Beauty, Edward VII, Royal Jubilee and Court Pendu Plat which often carry on into early summer, by which time there is seldom much danger of damage from frost.

Soils. Apples succeed best on medium loamy soils that are reasonably well drained. They can also be grown on quite light soils but in such places stronger growing stocks should be used and a rather higher rate of manuring practised. Trouble is most likely to occur on very heavy soils, particularly if badly drained. Under such conditions apples may suffer from canker and die back after the first few years.

The two most vital foods are nitrogen and potash. So far in extensive experiments phosphatic fertilizers have not shown much effect, but in view of the importance of maintaining the general fertility of soil it is advisable to give some phosphatic fertilizer even in apple orchards.

When ground is being prepared for planting it should be dug as deeply as appears reasonable, taking into account the character of the subsoil. A moderate quantity – about 50 kg per 12 sq m (1 cwt per 15 sq yd) – of well-rotted dung should be worked in at the same time. It is also advisable to give some extra potash which can be in the form of wood ashes, 168 g per 0·8 sq m (6 oz per sq yd), or any of the potassic fertilizers recommended in Chapter 6. Lime is not essential in any great quantity and provided the pH of the soil (see p. 16) is not below 6 there should be no necessity to add lime.

Types of Tree. Apples can be trained in a number of ways. Where there is ample space and the labour of picking is not a great consideration, full standards may be planted. These are particularly suitable for orchards which are eventually to be grassed down. Half-standards are occasionally favoured but bushes are the most popular type of all. Bushes on a stock of medium vigour, such as M. 7, M. 26 or MM. 106 are suitable for even quite small gardens and may be planted 3·6–4·5 m (12-15 ft) apart. On M. 9 this distance can be decreased to 2·4 m (8 ft) and on M. 27 it is possible to plant 1·5 m (5 ft) apart.

Apples are not as suitable as other fruits for growing against walls, though they will succeed in such a position, particularly if the wall faces west. For this mode of training, and also when grown against wire fences in the open, the horizontal tree rather than the fan-trained is almost invariably used.

For trees on dwarfing rootstocks the dwarf pyramid and spindle bush methods of training can be used. The cultivation of cordon-trained apple trees is also very popular, particularly with the owners of small gardens. The single-stem cordon on M. 9 for rich soils and M. 7 or MM. 106 for poorer soils can be planted as close as 76 cm (2½ ft) in the rows and so offers great scope for variety in a small garden.

What are popularly known as 'family trees' produce several different apple varieties. The only problem is that one variety may prove more vigorous than the rest, and the balance of different varieties is lost.

Stocks and Propagation. I have already had a good deal to say about apple stocks on p. 612. It only remains for me to re-emphasize here the importance of working trees on the right kind of stock for the purpose for which they are intended. The natural vigour and habit of the trees must be taken into account and also the richness of the soil on which they are to be planted. For example, M. 9 would be very suitable for a small bush of Bramley's Seedlings on good soil but would unduly dwarf a weak-growing apple such as Sunset especially if on poor soil. M. 16, M. 25, and Crab C are suitable for big standards that are to be grassed under.

Propagation is either by grafting in the first half of spring or by budding in the second half of summer.

Fertility. There are practically no apples that are fully self-fertile, certainly none in general cultivation. A few are fully self-sterile, that is to say they will set no fruit unless their blossom is fertilized with pollen from another variety of apple. But the great majority of varieties are partially self-fertile: they will set a moderate crop with their own pollen but a much better crop with pollen from another variety. There is no inter-incompatibility amongst apples. This rather formidable term simply means that any variety of apple will pollinate any other, provided of course its pollen is ripe at the correct time.

The blossom season extends over about a month but for any one tree it only lasts about ten days to a fortnight, and it is probable that out of that the effective period for pollination is only five or six days. Varieties which are to act as 'mates' must overlap in their full blossom period during those five or six days.

There are, in addition, a few kinds of apple which produce little or no fertile pollen. Bramley's Seedlings is a notable example. These do not make good pollinators for any variety and are specially indicated in the list on pp. 642-50.

Season. Early apples, such as Gladstone, Beauty of Bath and James Grieve, are ready to eat when picked, or perhaps it would be better to say should not be picked until they are ready to eat. This is not true of the later kinds which must be picked before they are blown off the tree, though they may not be ready for use until many months later. In other words the ripening process for these kinds goes on after the apples have parted from the tree. An extreme example of this kind is Sturmer Pippin, which is usually ready for gathering by mid-autumn but is hard, woody and tasteless at that time though it develops into an excellent dessert apple by the following spring. In the table of varieties (pp. 642-50) and also in most nurserymen's catalogues the season of use of each variety is indicated after the name. It should be understood clearly that this is not necessarily the time at which the fruit should be picked. For varieties in season during late summer/early autumn the dates of picking and using are likely to coincide. Mid-autumn apples are usually picked two or three weeks in advance of their season of use, while later apples are gathered also in mid-autumn.

Age of Tree. For planting, young trees are preferable to old ones. Because of this the expert may be well advised to start with maiden trees, that is, apples at the end of their first season of growth after budding or grafting. Less experienced gardeners will probably prefer a tree which has been formed for a year or so by an expert but four years should be regarded as the maximum age for any tree other than a standard or half-standard. These, because of their greater size, do not begin to take proper shape until about the fifth or sixth year. Because of this greater age there is increased risk in transplanting them and they are more likely to suffer a check to growth

Planting. Apples can be planted at any time between mid-autumn and early spring in a normal season, or, to put it another way, between the times when the leaves begin to fall off fairly freely to the date at which the buds show signs of bursting in the spring. The middle part of this period is seldom favourable owing to poor weather and bad soil condition. Late planting can be very successful if the following spring is damp but may be disastrous if the spring is dry. On the whole the best time for planting is in the second half of autumn.

Trees well established in containers can be transplanted at any time of the year provided the roots are not broken and the soil is undisturbed around them.

There is nothing special to be said about the actual methods of planting beyond emphasizing that the union between stock and scion (see p. 618), which can usually be identified quite distinctly in a young tree as a marked swelling well above the uppermost roots, must not be buried beneath the soil. If it is buried the apple is likely in time to make roots of its own above those of the stock.

Treatment of Young Trees. The first year after planting trees should never be allowed to bear fruit. If they do produce blossom, it should be picked at once. The trees must be pruned fairly severely either immediately after planting or, if planted in the autumn, during the following late winter. In general, leaders (see p. 623) should be cut back by half their length or more and side growths either eliminated or shortened to no more than 2·5 cm (1 in). The object is to reduce the strain on the roots for the first few months of growth and so give the tree a chance to make satisfactory shoots during the first summer. Very often newly planted trees, especially if they have been badly handled and the roots have been allowed to dry out unduly, make very little progress the first year and then it becomes essential to cut right back into two-year-old or even three-year-old wood, which wastes time and useful material.

Every other encouragement should also be given to the trees to make good growth. If the weather in spring is dry, heavy watering will help and may be followed by a mulch of straw or grass clippings to keep the moisture in. If the soil was properly prepared no manure should be necessary this first year. A topdressing of a well balanced compound fertilizer such as Growmore may be given the following late winter/early spring as advised by the maker. In the case of trained trees, particularly cordons and horizontally trained trees, summer pruning should be carried out in the second half of summer and the general rules given on p. 627 must be followed.

Pruning. Once a tree is established, pruning should proceed on absolutely normal lines (see p. 627). For the first five or six years the framework of the tree is built up and then there is a gradual transition to adult pruning with the object of maintaining regular production of fruit.

There are, in apples, certain marked differences of growth between one variety and another which must be taken into account when pruning, especially in the later stages when the trees are coming into full bearing. Broadly speaking varieties can be classified under two headings: (1) varieties which form fruit buds and spurs readily and do not make a great deal of wood; (2) varieties which do not form fruit buds freely and tend to produce a lot of wood. In addition a third group of tip-bearing varieties might be added but I think too much has been made of this characteristic with the result that novices become confused. From the point of view of pruning, tip bearers may be amalgamated with Group 2 above, the principal difference being that they do not usually make a lot of wood and so are likely to need harder leader pruning and more frequent dehorning (see p. 629). The point about the tip bearer is that it tends to produce quite a lot of fruit at the ends of both side growths and, sometimes, leaders as well. In consequence too much lateral pruning may diminish the crop very seriously.

Examples of the two groups are: Group 1. Arthur Turner, Beauty of Bath, Charles Ross, Cox's Orange Pippin, Crawley Beauty, Early Victoria, Edward VII, Ellison's Orange, Exquisite, Golden Noble, Grenadier, James Grieve, King of the Pippins, Lane's Prince Albert, Laxton's Superb, Lord Lambourne, Rev. W. Wilks, Rival and Sunset. Group 2. Allington Pippin, Bismark, Blenheim Orange, Bramley's Seedlings, Encore, Newton Wonder and Warner's King. To these may be added the tip bearers: Irish Peach, Lord Lambourne, Worcester Pearmain.

When pruning for fruit the side growths of all varieties in Group 1 can, if necessary, be pruned a good deal more severely than those of varieties in Group 2. I say 'if necessary' advisedly because it is not essential to prune any apple severely unless it has to be stimulated into fresh growth for some reason or there is a necessity to shorten weak stems or eliminate diseased wood. Obviously it is varieties of Group 1 which will make the best trained trees, especially horizontal-trained specimens, as they will submit more readily to the hard pruning necessary to maintain the characteristic shape of such specimens.

In the case of the more vigorous apples coming under Group 2 it is essential to be as sparing as possible with the secateurs. If side growths are cut back too often and too hard the result will be a thicket of new growth and very little fruit. When such varieties are trained, as much as possible of the pruning should be done in summer as this will tend to check, rather than increase, their natural vigour.

Feeding. Routine feeding for apples resolves itself, as a rule, into the application of dung, or a nitrogenous fertilizer such as sulphate of ammonia in the spring, and potash in the form of wood ashes or any potassic fertilizer in late winter/early spring. The average

FRUIT

Good Varieties of Apple

Abbreviations: C, cooking; D, dessert; CD, cooking or dessert; SS, self-sterile; PSF, partially self-fertile. (Note that self-sterile varieties should not be planted alone nor should they be used as pollinators for other varieties. Even partially self-fertile varieties will give better crops if associated with other varieties of apple flowering at approximately the same time.)

Name	Use	Season	Pick	Type	Colour	Flavour	Pruning	Flowering	Fertility	Cropping
Allington Pippin	D	mid-autumn – mid-winter	mid-autumn	medium, round, conical	lemon, faintly flushed red	good	moderate to upward-pointing buds	rather late	PSF	very good
American Mother	D	mid- to late autumn	mid-autumn	medium, conical	yellow, flushed red	good	moderate	late	PSF	irregular
Annie Elizabeth	D	early winter – early summer	mid-autumn	large, oblong, conical, uneven	yellow, flushed and striped deep red	good, acid	light to outward-pointing buds	rather late	PSF	good when established
Arthur Turner	C	late summer – mid-autumn	late summer – early autumn	very large, even	yellow, flushed brownish red	good, acid	light	mid-season	PSF	very good
Barnack Beauty	CD	early winter – early summer	mid-autumn	medium, conical	golden, flushed and striped red	good, crisp	moderate	mid-season	PSF	irregular
Beauty of Bath	D	late summer	when ripe	medium, flattened	yellow, striped and mottled red	good	light	early	PSF	irregular

642

Name	Use	Season	Pick	Type	Colour	Flavour	Pruning	Flowering	Fertility	Cropping
Belle de Boskoop	D	early winter – mid-spring	mid-autumn	medium, flattened	dull yellow-red russeted	good, sweet	moderate	early	SS	good
Bismarck	C	late autumn – mid-winter	mid-autumn	large, tapering, angular	yellow, flushed deep crimson	good, sub-acid	light	early	PSF	good
Blenheim Orange	DC	late autumn – mid-winter	mid-autumn	fairly large, flattened, round	yellow, flushed and russeted	excellent, crisp and good cooker	light to upward-pointing buds	mid-season	SS	good when established
Bramley's Seedling	C	late autumn – mid-spring	mid-autumn	large, irregular, flat	green	excellent, acid	very light	mid-season	SS	very good
Brownlees Russet	D	mid-winter – mid-spring	mid-autumn	medium, conical, irregular	brownish green russet	good	moderate to outward-pointing buds	early	PSF	irregular
Charles Ross	DC	mid – late-autumn	mid-autumn	large, round, even	yellowish, green, flushed and striped red	moderate	moderate	mid-season	PSF	good
Claygate Pearmain	D	early winter – early spring	mid-autumn	medium, round, flattened	dull green, flushed and russeted	excellent	moderate to upward-pointing buds	mid-season	PSF	good
Cornish Gillyflower	D	mid-autumn – early winter	mid-autumn	large, ribbed, conical	dull green, red flush	excellent	light	mid-season	PSF	fair

Name	Use	Season	Pick	Type	Colour	Flavour	Pruning	Flowering	Fertility	Cropping
Court Pendu Plat	D	mid-winter – mid-spring	mid-autumn	small, round, flattened	yellow, flushed dull red and russeted	good	fairly hard to outward-pointing buds	late	PSF	very good
Cox's Orange Pippin	D	late autumn – early winter	mid-autumn	medium, round, regular	yellow, faintly russeted and striped brownish red	excellent	hard	mid-season	PSF	usually good
Crawley Beauty	C	early winter – mid-spring	mid-autumn	medium, round, regular	greenish yellow, flushed red	good	moderate to upward-pointing buds	very late	PSF	very good
Crimson Bramley	C	late autumn – mid-spring	mid-autumn	large, irregular, flat	deep crimson	excellent, acid	very light	mid-season	SS	very good
Crimson Cox	D	late autumn – late winter	mid-autumn	medium, round, regular	deep crimson	excellent	hard	mid-season	PSF	very good
Cutler Grieve	D	late autumn – mid-winter	mid-autumn	medium, flattened, conical	yellow, covered red flush and stripes	moderate	moderate to outward-pointing buds	mid-season	PSF	good
Delicious	D	late autumn – late winter	mid-autumn	medium, conical	yellow, red stripes	good	moderate to outward-pointing buds	rather late	PSF	good
Devonshire Quarrenden	D	late summer – early autumn	when ripe	small to medium, flat	deep crimson	good	moderate to upward-pointing buds	mid-season	PSF	irregular

Name	Use	Season	Pick	Type	Colour	Flavour	Pruning	Flowering	Fertility	Cropping
Early Victoria (Emneth Early)	C	mid – late summer	as needed	large, conical, irregular	yellowish green	good	moderate	mid-season	PSF	very heavy, needs thinning
Edward VII	C	mid-winter – mid-spring	mid-autumn	large, oblong, regular	green	very good, cooks pink	moderate to outward-pointing buds	late	PSF	very good
Egremont Russet	D	mid-autumn – early winter	early autumn	medium, round, regular	yellow, heavily russeted	good	moderate to upward-pointing buds	early	PSF	very good
Ellison's Orange	D	early – mid-autumn	early autumn	medium, round	golden yellow, striped crimson	good	light	mid-season	PSF	irregular
Encore	C	mid-winter – early summer	mid-autumn	large, oblong	grass green, yellow, flushed brown	good, acid	light	mid-season	PSF	good
Epicure	D	late summer – early autumn	when ripe	medium, conical	yellow, red streaks	very good	moderate	mid-season	PSF	very good
Exquisite	D	early – mid-autumn	early autumn	tall, angular	yellow, red streaks	very good, soft	moderate to upward-pointing buds	mid-season	PSF	fair
Fortune	D	early – mid-autumn	early autumn	conical, irregular	yellow, striped red	good	light	mid-season	PSF	good

645

Name	Use	Season	Pick	Type	Colour	Flavour	Pruning	Flowering	Fertility	Cropping
Gascoyne's Scarlet	D	early autumn – mid-winter	by mid-autumn	large, slightly flattened, oval	brilliant scarlet, heavy bloom	good	light to upward-pointing buds	late	PSF	uncertain
Gladstone	D	mid- – late summer	when ripe	medium	red	good	moderate	rather late	PSF	good
Golden Noble	C	early autumn – mid-winter	by mid-autumn	round, regular	clear yellow	excellent, cooks yellow	light	mid-season	PSF	good
Golden Spire	C	early – mid-autumn	by mid-autumn	tall, conical	clear yellow	good	moderate	early	PSF	good
Gravenstein	CD	mid-autumn – early winter	early autumn	large, irregular	yellow, red flush and streaks	good	moderate to upward-pointing buds	very early	SS	irregular
Grenadier	C	late summer – early autumn	late summer	large, round	yellowish green	good, acid	moderate to upward-pointing buds	mid-season	PSF	very good
Herring's Pippin	CD	mid- – late autumn	mid-autumn	large, conical	bright red	good, soft	light	rather late	PSF	very good
Howgate Wonder	C	mid-autumn – early winter	mid-autumn	large, round, flat	yellow, red stripes	good	light	mid-season	PSF	good

Name	Use	Season	Pick	Type	Colour	Flavour	Pruning	Flowering	Fertility	Cropping
Irish Peach	D	late summer	when ripe	medium, flattened	yellowish, streaked dull red	very good if eaten immediately	light	very early	PSF	irregular
James Grieve	D	early – mid-autumn	early autumn	medium, conical	lemon yellow, striped red	very good, soft	moderate	mid-season	PSF	very good
Keswick Codlin	C	late summer	when ripe	medium, conical	yellow	good	moderate	very early	PSF	sometimes biennial
King's Acre Pippin	D	early winter – early spring	mid-autumn	medium, irregular	greenish, streaked dull red	very good	moderate	mid-season	PSF	good
King of the Pippins	D	mid- – late autumn	mid-autumn	medium, conical	orange, red flush	medium, crisp	moderate to outward-pointing buds	mid-season	PSF	good
Lady Sudeley	D	late summer – mid-autumn	when ripe	large, conical	yellow, scarlet striped	good if eaten immediately	moderate	rather late	PSF	good
Lane's Prince Albert	C	late autumn – early spring	mid-autumn	large, rounded, conical	grass green, red flush	very good, acid	hard to upward-pointing buds	rather late	PSF	very good
Lord Derby	C	mid-autumn – early winter	early autumn	large, conical	green	excellent, cooks red	light to outward-pointing buds	mid-season	PSF	good

647

Name	Use	Season	Pick	Type	Colour	Flavour	Pruning	Flowering	Fertility	Cropping
Lord Lambourne	D	mid– late autumn	early autumn	medium, conical	yellow, deep red flush and stripes	excellent, soft flesh	light	early	PSF	very good
Miller's Seedling	D	late summer – early autumn	late summer	medium, conical	pale yellow, few stripes	good, crisp	light to outside bud	early	PSF	heavy
Monarch	C	early winter – mid-spring	mid-autumn	large, rather square	pale yellow, flushed and striped red	good	moderate	rather late	PSF	very good
Newton Wonder	C	early winter – late spring	mid-autumn	large, broad	yellowish green, red flush and few stripes	very good	very light	mid-season	PSF	irregular
Orleans Reinette	D	mid– late winter	mid-autumn	flat, regular	orange yellow, red stripes	excellent	moderate	rather late	PSF	fair
Peasgood's Nonsuch	C	early – late autumn	early autumn	large, regular	yellow, crimson flush and stripes	good, soft	light to upward-pointing buds	mid-season	PSF	good
Rev. W. Wilks	C	early – late autumn	mid-autumn	large, conical	cream with scarlet dots	good	moderate	early	PSF	very good
Ribston Pippin	D	late autumn – mid-winter	mid-autumn	medium, conical	orange-red with russet	excellent	light to upward-pointing buds	early	SS	good

Name	Use	Season	Pick	Type	Colour	Flavour	Pruning	Flowering	Fertility	Cropping
Rival	CD	mid-autumn – early winter	by mid-autumn	medium, flattened, regular	yellow, carmine flush and stripes	moderate, cooks well	light to upward-pointing buds	mid-season	PSF	good
St Cecilia	D	mid-winter – mid-spring	mid-autumn	medium, oval	yellow, russeted red striped	excellent	moderate to upward-pointing buds	mid-season	PSF	irregular
St Edmund's Pippin	D	early – late autumn	mid-autumn	small, flattish	orange russet	excellent	moderate	early	PSF	good
St Everard	D	early autumn	late summer	round, regular	yellow, red stripes and russet	very good	light	mid-season	PSF	irregular
Saltcote Pippin	D	late autumn – late winter	mid-autumn	medium, conical	brownish red	good	light	mid-season	PSF	good
Stirling Castle	C	late summer – mid-autumn	early autumn	large, round	pea green to pale yellow	good, acid	hard	mid-season	PSF	very good
Sturmer Pippin	D	early spring – early summer	mid-autumn	medium, large	yellowish, brown flush and russet	very good	light	mid-season	PSF	good
S. T. Wright	C	early – mid-autumn	early autumn	large, flat	pale yellow, striped pink	good	moderate	mid-season	PSF	good

Name	Use	Season	Pick	Type	Colour	Flavour	Pruning	Flowering	Fertility	Cropping
Sunset	D	late autumn – early winter	mid-autumn	medium, round	yellow, flushed red	good	moderate	mid-season	PSF	good
Superb (Laxton's)	D	early winter – early spring	mid-autumn	medium, round	yellow, flushed dull red	very good	light	rather late	PSF	sometimes biennial
Tydeman's Early	D	late summer – early autumn	when ripe	medium, conical	reddish, carmine	good	light	mid-season	PSF	good
Wagener	D	mid-winter – late spring	mid-autumn	large, flat	green, brown flush	fair	moderate	mid-season	PSF	good
Warner's King	C	late autumn – mid-winter	early autumn	enormous, flat, conical	bright green to yellow	good, acid	light to upward-pointing buds	early	SS	moderate
Wellington (syn. Dumelow's Seedling)	C	late autumn – early spring	mid-autumn	medium, flattened	pale yellow flushed red	very good, acid	light	rather late	PSF	moderate
Winston	D	mid-winter – mid-spring	mid-autumn	medium, conical	dull red	good	moderate to outward-pointing buds	late	PSF	fair
Worcester Pearmain	D	early – mid-autumn	when ripe	medium, conical	yellow, heavily flushed scarlet	good if left on tree till ripe	light	mid-season	PSF	good

dressing for adult trees of normal vigour would be dung at the rate of 50 kg per 12 sq m (1 cwt per 15 sq yd), or sulphate of ammonia at 28 g per 0·8 sq m (1 oz per sq yd), followed by wood ashes at 85 g (3 oz), or sulphate of potash at the same rate as ammonia. For trees growing in grass these quantities might be doubled since a good deal of the food will be used by the grass. An alternative to individual chemicals is to use a balanced compound fertilizer.

Thinning. If the spring is favourable for fertilization and the trees are in good condition they will very likely set more fruit than they can bring to perfection. Some natural thinning will occur and there is often quite a heavy drop of fruit towards mid-summer for which the gardener must make due allowance. Nevertheless it is often necessary to reduce the fruits still further by hand. This should be done a little at a time during the second half of summer. Dessert varieties can be allowed to carry more fruit than cookers because the individual fruits are not required to be so large. As a rough guide dessert apples should not exceed two per cluster and should be at least 7·5 cm (3 in) apart along the branch, whereas cookers should hang singly and be spaced 18 cm (7 in) apart.

When thinning give preference to the most perfect fruitlets and, other things being equal, remove the central fruit in each cluster, sometimes known as the king fruit, as this is often mis-shapen.

Picking. Apples are ready to pick directly they part readily from the tree. The test is to lift the fruit gently without twisting or tearing it, at the same time pressing down gently on the stalk with the thumb. If it comes away easily, well and good; if not, let it hang a little longer.

It does not follow that all the fruits on any tree will be ready for gathering at the same time. It often pays to go over a tree several times at intervals of a few days. The picking season extends from late summer for early varieties such as Gladstone, to mid-autumn for late kinds, such as Sturmer Pippin. Care should be taken not to bruise or damage the fruit, especially if it is to be kept.

Storing. Early apples should be used as soon as possible after gathering but mid-season and late varieties may be kept for periods varying from a month to eight or nine months, according to variety and condition.

There are several methods of storing apples, the best for the amateur being to wrap each fruit separately in waxed paper and pack fairly tightly in boxes deep enough to contain four or five layers. The boxes should then be placed in a cool, dark place. It is an advantage if the atmosphere is a little moist. A shed with a good roof but an earthen floor is ideal as the floor will hold a little moisture and give just the right degree of humidity to the atmosphere. Failing this an outhouse or spare room may be used. Before the apples are wrapped, however, they should be spread out thinly for a week or so to sweat which they will always do after picking. No attempt should be made to pack them away until all this surplus moisture has evaporated from their skins.

An alternative method of storing apples is to spread them out in a single layer on an open-slatted shelf but this is not so satisfactory as the fruits tend to wither prematurely. However, one advantage is that decaying fruits can be detected at once and removed.

APRICOTS

Apricots do not grow well in the open in cool climates unless planted against sunny walls or in similar sheltered and warm positions. They succeed admirably under glass though, either in unheated houses or with a small amount of artificial heat to start them into growth.

Soils. Their requirements are similar to those of plums, that is to say they grow best in a soil rather richer than desirable for apples. It must be really well drained. They do particularly well on fertile loams overlying chalk or limestone though, despite the popular belief to the contrary, lime is not essential to them.

Types of Tree. Apricots are almost always trained in fan formation. Such trees should be planted at least 4·5 m (15 ft) apart. In the open they may be grown as small bushes or half-standards, but are only likely to succeed in the warmest areas. Planting distances are 3·6-4·5 m (12-15 ft) for bushes, 4·5-6 m (15-20 ft) for half-standards.

Stocks and Propagation. Apricots are increased by budding on to plum stocks such as Brompton, Common Mussel and St Julien. Budding is carried out from mid- to late summer.

Fertility. Unlike many other hard fruits apricots do not appear to suffer from self- or inter-sterility so that trees may be planted singly, but as the blossom is produced very early in the year there are seldom enough bees flying at the time to ensure satisfactory pollination. This should be carried out by hand with a camel-hair brush or rabbit's tail. The work should be done as far as possible on fine, dry days towards noon when the blossom is fully open. Under glass hand pollination is always essential.

Season. Apricots cannot be stored for any length of time. They must be used as soon as they are picked from the trees, unless of course they are bottled or preserved in some similar way. Roughly speaking the season of apricots grown under glass can be extended from about mid-summer until mid-autumn by choosing early, mid-season and late varieties.

Age of Tree. As with apples it is best to start with young trees and the ideal way is to purchase maidens and train them according to their requirements. Less experienced gardeners will no doubt prefer to have a slightly older tree, but should not buy one more than four years old.

Planting. This can be done at any time during the dormant period from approximately mid-autumn until early spring. In greenhouses apricots are best planted in late autumn. The general rules for planting should be observed and the uppermost roots kept fairly close to the surface. Be careful not to injure the roots unnecessarily when planting as this may cause a troublesome production of suckers.

Treatment of Young Trees. After planting, trees should be pruned rather severely, leaders being cut back by as much as two thirds their length and weak shoots removed or shortened to several centimetres. Trees planted under glass should be watered freely in late winter and receive sufficient water subsequently to keep the soil just moist right through. No trees should be allowed to produce fruit the first year after planting. New growth should be restricted to that required to fill the available space.

Pruning. Apricots bear on wood two years old and more in the same way as plums. Pruning should be as light as possible compatible with keeping the trees to the desired form. Quite a lot of the work can be done in summer by shortening side growths to the sixth good leaf reckoned from the base. In the case of trained trees, badly placed shoots which cannot easily be tied back to the training wires can be rubbed or cut out as soon as noticed. In winter it will only be necessary to shorten leaders to points at which branches are required (see p. 623) and, where side growths are overcrowded, to cut some of these still further back.

With old trees it often pays to retain an occasional strong, young shoot at practically full length and tie it in to take the place of an older branch which can be removed the following year. As with plums, hard pruning may encourage silver leaf or gumming.

Feeding. Here again the requirements are very similar to those of plums, nitrogen and potash being the particular requirements but with the emphasis on the former. Good treatment is to give an annual spring mulch of well-rotted dung at the rate of 50 kg per 8 sq m (1 cwt per 10 sq yd) and sulphate of potash at 28 g per 0·8 sq m (1 oz per sq yd).

Thinning. As a rule apricots can carry all the fruit they set but occasionally when the branches are very heavily laden a little thinning out is repaid. It should not be started until the stones are formed, a point which can be determined by cutting through any typical fruit. There is often quite a heavy natural fall just before this period and earlier thinning may leave the gardener with an unsatisfactory crop.

Picking. This should be done as soon as the fruits are well coloured and part readily from the tree. As with other fruits it is advisable to go over any one tree several times rather than strip it at one operation.

Cultivation under Glass. In the main the treatment of apricots under glass is the same as for outdoor trees but a few special points require emphasis. It is vital to give the border a thorough soaking of water each winter. This is the only time at which subsoil reserves can be replenished without injury to the roots. Trees can either be allowed to start naturally into growth, which they will do in a normal season in early spring, or a little artificial heat can be applied in late winter and the ventilators closed at the same time. The temperature at this stage should not exceed an average of 12°C/54°F.

During the summer it is important to maintain sufficient moisture in the atmosphere which can be done by syringing the trees with water morning and evening, and thoroughly damping the paths and walls at the same time. Failure to observe this precaution may result in bad attacks by red spider mites or by frog flies.

Ventilation throughout should be as free as possible, subject to maintaining an average temperature of 12°C/54°F, rising to 18°C/65°F in summer. When the leaves fall in autumn the house should be thrown wide open so that the wood becomes quite dormant in winter.

Varieties. Good apricots are Alfred, late July, inclined to crop biennially unless well thinned; Farmingdale, August; Hemskerke, August and Moorpark, August-September.

BLACKBERRIES AND OTHER BRAMBLE FRUITS

These are very useful for filling odd corners in the garden, and for clothing screens, pillars or even arches, though if the last method of training is contemplated, fairly drastic pruning and frequent tying will be necessary with most varieties. A drawback to blackberries in the small garden is that they take up rather a lot of room and that their extremely spiny and vigorous growth can be a nuisance. There are thornless varieties which may be preferred on this account.

Soils. Blackberries and allied bramble fruits are not fussy regarding soil. They will thrive in light sands and stiff clays but they do respond well to generous feeding. The ground should therefore be dug thoroughly before planting, and well-rotted manure or compost should be incorporated at the rate of 50 kg per 6·4-9·6 sq m (1 cwt per 8-12 sq yd). It will usually also pay to give additional potash either as wood ashes at 168 g per 0·8 sq m (6 oz per sq yd) or as sulphate or muriate of potash at 28 g (1 oz) to the same area.

Types of Plant. Blackberries and the allied bramble fruits are always grown naturally, that is to say they are allowed to make new sucker-like growths from the base every year, though these can be trained in a variety of ways to cover walls or fences, to be grown around pillars or tied to horizontally trained wires. One good method of training is to drive in stout posts 3·3 in (11 ft) apart and strain three horizontal wires between them, 45 cm (1½ ft), 90 cm (3 ft) and 1·5 m (5 ft) above ground level. One plant is grown between each pair of posts and restricted to six main stems which are trained to left and right.

Propagation. The best method of propagation is that known as tip layering. Strong young canes are bent downwards in the first half of summer and their tips are held to the soil either by the weight of a stone or with a forked peg driven into the ground. In a few weeks, roots will be formed and new shoots will start to grow. The parent stem can then be severed and the following spring the young plant may be transferred to a nursery bed to grow on until, by the autumn, it is strong enough to go into its permanent position.

Age to Plant. It is highly desirable to start with young plants. Nurseries usually offer year-old plants from tip layers and these are satisfactory, though they should not be allowed to fruit until their second year from planting.

Planting. Bramble fruits are notably surface rooting. In consequence wide, rather shallow holes should be prepared for them. The best period for planting is from mid- to late autumn, but work can be continued during good weather until mid-spring. Plants should be at least 2·4 m (8 ft) apart; very vigorous kinds such as Himalaya at least 3 m (10 ft) apart. If more than one row is contemplated these should be at least 2·4 m (8 ft) apart.

Treatment of Young Plants. By late winter after planting, or immediately in the case of late-planted canes, all growth should be cut back to within about 23 cm (9 in) of soil level.

As a result, fairly strong young canes should be formed the first summer and these will require no pruning until they have carried fruit the following summer, after which they should be cut out.

Pruning. The last sentence of the preceding paragraph really describes the very simple pruning of bramble fruits; that is to say, once they have started to crop it is necessary to cut out each year all the old fruiting canes to make way for the young shoots from the base. This pruning should be done as soon as possible after the crop has been gathered. During the early summer it is an advantage to tie young growth to one side (or up the centre if the fruiting canes are tied out on each side) to keep them out of the way of the fruiting stems. In this way it will be possible to gather the fruits easily without risk of damaging the rather brittle young shoots. Then, after fruiting, the young canes can be trained in the place of the old ones.

Feeding. A mulch of dung or compost should be applied each spring at about 50 kg per sq m (1 cwt per 10 sq yd) plus sulphate of ammonia and sulphate of potash each at 28 g per 0·8 sq m (1 oz per sq yd).

Picking and Storing. Blackberries can be bottled or frozen.

Varieties. Good varieties of the common blackberry with their seasons of ripening are Bedford Giant, mid-summer; Himalaya Giant, late summer/early autumn; John Innes, early autumn; Merton Thornless, late summer/early autumn; Parsley-leaved, late summer/early autumn and Oregon Thornless, similar to the last but without thorns. Useful hybrid berries are Boysenberry, very vigorous and often not very heavy cropping but with large fruits, red at first but nearly black when fully ripe and also a thornless version of this; Loganberry, with deep red fruits much larger than those of a raspberry; Thornless Loganberry, similar in every respect but without thorns; Tayberry, best planted in a selection named Medana, a hybrid between raspberry and blackberry, which resembles the Loganberry but has even larger fruits, and Wineberry (often known as Japanese Wineberry), perhaps more valuable for ornament than utility.

CHERRIES

There are three distinct types of cherry: sweet, grown for dessert; sour, grown for cooking; and Duke cherries which are intermediate between the other two and may be used both for dessert and cooking. The sour cherries are the easiest to grow for they will succeed in every situation, even trained against walls facing due north.

Soils. All cherries succeed best on medium to light soils, particularly light loams overlying chalk. The sour cherries will also grow on poorer types of soil but no type of cherry likes a heavy, badly drained clay.

Preparation should be thorough and dung can be used fairly freely, at about 50 kg per 0·8 sq m (1 cwt per sq yd). In spite of the fact that cherries do so well on ground overlying chalk this seems to be due less to a liking for lime than for a need of summer moisture which the chalk holds. Cherries will grow quite well in lime-free soils provided they are suitable in other respects.

Types of Tree. Cherries dislike hard pruning and therefore succeed best in the freer forms of training such as standard, half-standard or large bush. They can also be trained against walls and fences, in which case the fan system is best. Occasionally one sees cherries trained as cordons but these are seldom satisfactory. Minimum planting distances are: standards, 9 m (30 ft); half-standards, 7·5 m (25 ft); bushes, 4·5 cm (15 ft); fan trained, 4·5 m (15 ft).

Stocks and Propagation. Cherries, like other tree fruits, are propagated by grafting or budding, usually the latter, on to suitable rootstocks. The Wild cherry and the variety Malling 12/1 are vigorous stocks and Colt is semi-dwarfing and so more suitable for garden trees.

Fertility. The question of fertility assumes particular importance with cherries. Most sweet varieties are fully self-sterile, that is to say they will not set any fruit if pollinated with their own pollen. In addition there is a great deal of inter-sterility, that is to say there are many varieties which will not pollinate one another. Set out below, in table form, are the principal facts as at present known. It will be seen that the varieties are arranged in groups. All varieties in one group are inter-sterile. Varieties from different groups can be planted together as pollinators but even then it is wise to choose kinds that bloom at the same time. However, this is not quite as important as with other fruits because the cherry

---

POLLINATION TABLE FOR SELF-STERILE CHERRIES

Varieties within any one group are not fertile, either individually or collectively. All can be successfully cross-pollinated by varieties from any of the other squares. Letters in brackets mean: (**e**) early flowering, (**m**) mid-season flowering, (**l**) late flowering. The following varieties are known as universal donors since they will pollinate any of the varieties in the 12 groups below and also each other: Noir de Guben (**e**), Merton Glory (**e**), Bigarreau Gaucher (**l**), Florence (**l**) and White Heart (**l**). These varieties are not satisfactory planted singly with no other cherries nearby but Morello or Flemish can be planted in isolation and can also be used as pollinators for any of the other cherries. So can some, but not all, forms of Kentish Red.

1	**2**	**3**
Bedford Prolific (**e**)	Bigarreau de Schrecken (**m**)	Bigarreau Napoleon (**l**)
Black Eagle (**m**)	Black Heart (**e**)	Emperor Francis (**e**)
Black Tartarian A (**e**)	Frogmore Early (**l**)	
Black Tartarian B (**e**)	Waterloo (**m**)	
Early Rivers (**m**)		
Knight's Early Black (**m**)		

4	**5**	**6**
Kent Bigarreau (**l**)	Late Black Bigarreau (**m**)	Elton Heart (**l**)
Ludwig Bigarreau (**m**)	Turkey Heart (**e**)	Governor Wood (**l**)
Merton Premier (**e**)		Merton Heart (**m**)

7	**8**	**9**
Géante d'Hedelfingen (**l**)	Noir de Schmidt (**m**)	Merton Lake (**m**)
Bigarreau de Mezel (**m**)	Peggy Rivers (**e**)	Ursula Rivers (**m**)

10	**11**	**12**
Bigarreau Jaboulay (**e**)	Guigne d'Annonay (**e**)	Noble (**l**)
Black Tartarian D (**e**)		

GOOD VARIETIES OF CHERRY

* There are several different forms of these varieties in cultivation and though outwardly identical they behave differently as regards fertility and pollination.
Some cherries are not only self-sterile but also inter-sterile with certain other varieties. This makes it essential to select cross-pollinating varieties with some care. In the column below headed 'Group' the figures indicate the respective pollination groups of the cherries listed. Those marked 0 may be planted with each other or with any other variety, provided flowering times overlap. With the remainder, varieties bearing the same number should not be planted to pollinate one another but may be planted with any varieties bearing different figures.

Abbreviations: SS, self-sterile; SF, self-fertile; PSF, partially self-fertile.

Name	Use	Season	Colour	Flavour	Flowering	Fertility	Group	Cropping
Archduke	DC	mid-summer	dark red	sweet	late	PSF	0	good
Bedford Prolific	D	mid-summer	dark red	sweet	early	SS	1	very good
Bigarreau de Mezel	D	mid – late summer	black	excellent	late	SS	3 & 7	good
Bigarreau de Schrecken	D	early summer	black	good	mid-season	SS	2	good
Bigarreau Napoleon	D	mid-summer	yellow & red	excellent	late	SS	3	good
Black Eagle	D	mid-summer	black	excellent	mid-season	SS	1	good
Black Heart	D	mid-summer	black	fair	early	SS	2	good
Black Tartarian	D	mid-summer	black	excellent	early	SS	1 & 10*	good
Early Rivers	D	mid-summer	black	excellent	mid-season	SS	2	good
Elton Heart	D	mid-summer	red	excellent	late	SS	6	fair
Emperor Francis	D	mid-summer	deep red	excellent	mid-season	SS	3	good
Flemish	C	mid-summer	red	acid	late	SF	0	very good
Florence	D	late summer	yellow & red	good	late	SS	0	good
Frogmore Early	D	early summer	yellow & red	good	late	SS	2	good
Géante d'Hedelfingen	D	mid-summer	deep red	excellent	late	SS	7	good
Governor Wood	D	mid-summer	yellow & red	good	late	SS	6	good
Kent Bigarreau	D	mid-summer	yellow & red	good	late	SS	4	good
Kentish Red	C	early summer	red	acid	late	SF or PSF*	0	fair
Knight's Early Black	D	early summer	black	good	mid-season	SS	1	good
Late Duke	DC	late summer	deep red	fair	late	PSF	0	good
May Duke	DC	early summer	black	fair	late	PSF	0	very good
Merton Bigarreau	D	mid-summer	black	excellent	late	SS	2	good
Merton Glory	D	mid-summer	pink	good	late	SS	1	good
Merton Late	D	late summer – early autumn	yellow & red	good	mid-season	SS	9	good
Merton Premier	D	mid-summer	dark red	good	early	SS	4	very good
Morello	C	late summer	black or dark red	acid	late	SF	0	fair
Noble (Tradescant's Heart)	D	mid-summer	black	excellent	late	SS	12	good
Peggy Rivers	D	mid-summer	red & yellow	good	early	SS	8	fair
Royal Duke	DC	mid-summer	deep red	good	late	PSF	0	good
Stella	D	mid-summer	black	good	late	SF	0	good
Turkey Heart	D	early autumn	black	fair	early	SS	5	fair
Waterloo	D	early summer	black	excellent	mid-season	SS	2	

blossom season is a short one and many kinds overlap sufficiently for pollination to take place.

Some acid cherries are self-fertile, that is to say will produce fruit when fertilized with their own pollen, and this is true of Morello and Flemish. Other varieties and also Duke cherries are partially self-fertile but produce better crops when fertilized with pollen from another variety of cherry. In addition these varieties are also universal donors, in other words they will fertilize any other variety of cherry in bloom at the same time.

The only other point to observe about cherry fertility is that the flowering season is exceptionally early; therefore the blossom is particularly liable to be cut by frost or to suffer from lack of attention by bees.

Season. Cherries are in season from mid-summer to early autumn and cannot be kept once they are ripe except by bottling or canning. Since sweet cherries are liable to be attacked by birds wall-trained trees should be netted.

Age of Tree. Within reason the younger the tree to be planted the better, but as most amateurs will prefer to start with a specimen that has been formed by an expert it is usually necessary to plant three to five-year-old trees, the greater age for standards or half-standards. Those who feel competent to do their own initial pruning will be well advised to start with one or two-year-old trees whatever the form of training.

Planting. This should be done between mid-autumn and early spring, preference being given to the early part of this period provided the soil is in good order. Cherries generally make many spreading roots and should therefore be planted in wide, rather shallow holes, the uppermost roots being covered with 7·5-10 cm (3-4 in) of good soil.

Treatment of Young Trees. Though established cherries dislike hard pruning it is as a rule necessary to cut them back fairly severely after planting to ensure good growth the first season. Most branches may be shortened by about half the length of growth they made the previous summer. Weak shoots should be pruned to 5-7·5 cm (2-3 in) or cut out altogether.

In the spring following planting it is as well to give a generous mulch of dung. The soil around each tree should be kept clear of weeds and grass even though it is intended eventually to grass the orchard down.

Summer pruning the first year is usually unnecessary except in the case of trained trees in which badly placed shoots may be rubbed out early.

Pruning. The sweet cherry, like the plum, bears on both second-year and older wood and forms spurs freely. The main problems in pruning are to keep an open, shapely tree and avoid silver leaf and bacterial canker. Infection by both is very likely to occur during autumn and winter through wounds made when cutting back, so confine pruning to the summer or early autumn and keep it light.

Side growths can frequently be retained unpruned as they will then form fruit buds throughout their length. If they tend to become overcrowded some can be shortened to five leaves in mid- or late summer.

Leaders can be left unpruned unless they are tending to become weak, in which case they may be shortened by one third in late summer/early autumn as soon as the crop has been gathered. At the same time dead or damaged wood can be removed and overcrowded branches thinned, this being mainly saw work only necessary every few years. All large wounds should be treated at once with a good bituminous wound dressing.

Trained trees will of necessity need rather more pruning. Leaders must be cut back to a point at which they are about 38 cm (1¼ ft) apart. As much as possible of the side growth should be laid in between the main branches but badly placed shoots should be cut out or have their tips pinched out in the first half of summer.

A different system of pruning is necessary in the case of sour cherries, including Morello, because these bear mainly on second-year wood. Pruning is very similar to that of peaches and nectarines. In the early stages while the tree is being formed leaders must be cut back as described to obtain branches where they are needed. But side growths must, as far as possible, be replaced annually. This is done mainly by a process of disbudding carried out gradually from late spring to late summer. Each year-old side growth will, during this period, produce a number of new shoots. Two or three only are retained, one as near as possible to the base of the old growth, one at its tip and perhaps a third somewhere along its length. All the rest are rubbed out as early as possible. The terminal shoot is pinched when it is 7·5-10 cm (3-4 in) long, and so is a middle shoot if retained, their purpose being solely to draw sap through the stem and so help any fruits it may be carrying to swell. The basal shoot is allowed to grow unhampered. As soon as possible after the crop has been gathered all the old side growths are cut out and the new basal shoots are tied back in their places.

Feeding. Nitrogen is the most important food for cherries but must be balanced with a moderate quantity of potash. The usual practice for cultivated orchards is to give a mulch of dung in spring, about 50 kg per 8 sq m (1 cwt per 10 sq yd), together with a potash fertilizer such as sulphate of potash at 42 g per 0·8 sq yd (1½ oz per sq yd). In the case of grass orchards, sulphate of ammonia at 28 g per 0·8 sq m (1 oz per sq yd) may supplement the dung.

Picking. This should be started as soon as the fruits are well coloured and part readily from the spurs. Commercial orchards are usually stripped at one operation but it will pay the amateur to go over his trees several times, so extending the season for a fortnight or more and getting a much higher average quality of fruit.

The wood of cherry trees is rather brittle and in consequence easily broken, so care should be taken not to injure branches and twigs more than is unavoidable.

COBNUTS

Cobnuts, and filberts which are simply a variety of cob with long awns, are not often grown in private gardens, probably because they are not very profitable on a small scale. They have, however, a limited usefulness, especially for forming wind breaks or making hedges which are productive as well as ornamental.

Soils. All will succeed in a great variety of soils. The only places where they cannot be grown successfully are on very thin soils and heavy, waterlogged clays. They are native to the country and therefore well adapted to our climate but fruiting may be irregular in frosty places.

In preparing the ground digging should be thorough and a little well-rotted dung can be used with advantage, about 50 kg per 16 sq m (1 cwt per 20 sq yd).

Types of Tree. Nuts are almost invariably grown as open-centred bushes, with either a very short leg (main trunk) or no leg at all. They have a habit of throwing up strong growths direct from the roots and occasionally it pays to retain one of these to replace an older, worn-out growth, but it is not wise to encourage the production of too many suckers or the bushes will soon become shapeless and overcrowded. Bushes should be spaced at least 3·6 m (12 ft) apart.

Propagation. Unlike most other fruit trees, nuts are grown on their own roots, not budded or grafted on stocks. They are either layered in late winter or spring, or rooted suckers can be detached in the autumn. Layering is done by bending whippy shoots down to soil level, notching them at a joint where they touch the soil and then pegging them down at this point or weighting them with a heavy stone. The layers form roots from the point of notching and if well rooted can be severed in the autumn.

Nuts can also be raised from seeds sown in early spring out of doors but as seedlings vary greatly and are often inferior to their parents, this is not a good method.

Fertility. Despite their hardiness and the fact that they are self-fertile, nuts often fail to crop properly. This is due to the fact that some varieties produce little or no good pollen or few pollen-bearing catkins. Other kinds, such as Cosford and Pearson's Prolific, produce plenty of pollen even when quite young and it is therefore a good policy either to form plantations exclusively of these kinds or to mix them with other kinds, with at least one good pollinator to four others.

Age of Tree. The best method is to start with year-old suckers or layers, which means, of course, that the gardener must form his own tree from the outset. If he prefers to start with a partly formed bush he may purchase three-year-old plants but should not buy any that exceed this age.

Planting. The work is done from mid-autumn until early spring as for most other fruits, and the general instructions given on p. 615 should be followed.

Treatment of Young Trees. Immediately after planting it is wise to prune severely, in fact very much as for black currants (see p. 663). All strong branches are cut back to within about 30 cm (1 ft) of ground level of the main trunk and all weak shoots are removed. No special precautions are necessary the first summer, but the soil around the bushes should be kept clear of weeds and may be mulched with dung or grass clippings in spring.

Pruning. The pruning of established nut bushes is little understood by amateurs and failure to treat the bushes properly often accounts for bad crops. First it must be realized that two distinct types of flower are present: the catkins which are the male flowers and produce pollen only, and the female flowers which are very small and bright red. In spite of the colour of these females it is quite difficult to see them and they are often overlooked although they are most important, as it is from them, and them alone, that nuts will be produced. Both types of flower appear in late winter/early spring, but usually the catkins open a little before the female flowers.

Apart from shaping the bushes, which can be done in late autumn, the important pruning is carried out during the blossom period. Side growths are cut back to the first catkin reckoning from the tip or, if the shoot carries no catkins, to the first female flower. Shoots that are carrying catkins only may be left unpruned until the catkins fade, when they are best shortened to two buds.

During the operation of shaping the bushes in late autumn suckers should be removed unless required to replace old branches as already described.

Feeding. As a rule nuts get on quite well without a great deal of feeding but if dung can be spared a light topdressing can be given each spring. Bushes that are not making sufficient growth can be stimulated with sulphate of ammonia applied in early spring at 56 per 0·8 sq m (2 oz per sq yd), plus sulphate of potash, 28 g (1 oz) to the same area, and superphosphate of lime, 56 g (2 oz), again to the same area, or a well balanced compound fertilizer used at manufacturer's recommendations.

Picking. This should be done in the first half of autumn when the nuts part readily from the bushes and the husks are yellowing.

Storing. Nuts will keep for quite a long time in any cool, dry, mouse-proof place but a better method of storing is to shell and pack them into glass jars, earthenware crocks or tightly fitting polythene containers with plenty of salt sprinkled between and over them.

Varieties. Good cobnuts and filberts are Cosford, Pearson's Prolific, Duke of Edinburgh, Kentish Cob, Red Filbert, and White Filbert. The first two are good pollinators for themselves and for other varieties.

CURRANTS, BLACK

These are among the most satisfactory of small fruits for the amateur gardener. They succeed well in most districts and usually crop heavily from about the third year onwards. The profitable life of a black currant bush is rather short compared with that of some other fruits, seldom extending much beyond the twelfth year, but new stock can be produced easily at home by means of cuttings taken from old plants.

Soils. Black currants succeed best in rather rich soils and can stand more nitrogen than most other fruits. They need plenty of moisture during the growing season but dislike stagnation in winter and therefore require good drainage. The ideal is a deep, well-cultivated, rather light loam and the worst types of soil are those which are very thin and overlie stone or chalk. Cultivation should be thorough prior to planting and well-rotted dung may be worked in at 50 kg per 8·8 sq m (1 cwt per 11 sq yd).

It does not very much matter whether the position is sunny or in partial shade so long as it is open overhead. In fact one method of extending the season is to plant some bushes, preferably of a late variety, in a place with a cool, northerly aspect and so encourage the berries to hang a long time.

Types of Plant. Black currants are usually grown as bushes, without any main stem or leg but with a number of strong shoots coming direct from the roots. Very occasionally black currants are fan trained, usually against walls or fences.

Propagation. This is by cuttings prepared in autumn from well-ripened shoots formed the previous summer. Each cutting should be about 30 cm (1 ft) long, trimmed at the base just below a joint and inserted firmly some 10 cm (4 in) deep in good soil out of doors. The cuttings root readily and can be transferred either to a nursery bed or fruiting quarters the following autumn.

Fertility. All varieties are self-fertile, that is to say any particular plant will set fruit when pollinated with its own pollen. They are, as a matter of fact, usually self-pollinated, either by insects or by the pollen falling from the anthers direct on to the stigmas. Bad fertility is frequently due to cold, damp weather when the flowers are open and to lack of insects to carry the pollen.

Frequently the basal flowers in each truss set berries whereas the tip flowers fail, a fault referred to as 'running off'. This is due to the fact that the flowers at the base of the truss generally have such short pistils that the stigmas are within the anthers so that it is easy for the pollen to fall on to them without the help of insects. In contrast the pistils of the tip flowers are long, the stigmas sticking out beyond the anthers and missing the pollen so that its transference is dependent on insects, which may be scarce if the weather is bad. This can be overcome by hand pollination with a camel-hair brush on fine, dry days when the flowers are fully open.

Season. The only ways in which black currants can be kept is by bottling and deep freezing. The season for fresh fruit extends from mid-summer to early autumn.

Age to Plant. It is advisable to start with quite young plants, certainly no more than two years old.

Planting. This should be done while the bushes are dormant from about mid-autumn until early spring. Late planting is not desirable unless the bushes can be well watered for the first few months. The second half of autumn is usually the most favourable period.

The plants are surface rooting and the uppermost roots should therefore be covered with only 5 cm (2 in) of soil. The bushes generally lift with a mass of fibrous roots which dry out and shrivel rapidly if exposed to the air so the quicker they can be planted the better. Black currants make big bushes and should not be planted closer than 1·5 cm (5 ft) in each direction.

Treatment of Young Bushes. By the late winter following planting or, in the case of spring-planted bushes, immediately after planting, all strong stems should be cut back to within 10-15 cm (4-6 in) of ground level and weak stems removed. No fruit will be produced the first season but the bushes will be encouraged to make strong growth to fruit the following year. No further pruning is necessary until a crop has been gathered.

Black currants benefit from a moderate mulch of strawy manure or decayed garden refuse applied in mid-spring and renewed about early summer.

Pruning. Established black currants should be pruned as soon as possible after the crop has been gathered in late summer or early autumn. The crop is borne on year-old wood so that all old wood that has just carried fruit can be cut right out, together with any weak young growth, the strong young growth being retained at full length to crop the following year. The more strong stems there are coming direct from the roots the better. Suckers are not harmful. One method is to prune the wood with the fruit still hanging, when it may be picked off in the kitchen.

Bushes that are not making a great deal of new wood may either be cut back to within 23 cm (9 in) of soil level, in which case they will bear no fruit the next year but should make strong growth, or alternatively a little of the old wood can be removed and the rest retained with whatever new growth it may be carrying. In either case the bushes should be fed more liberally than usual.

Feeding. Nitrogen is the most important item and can be given in spring in the form of any quick-acting nitrogenous fertilizer such as sulphate of ammonia, which may be used at 56 g per 0·8 sq m (2 oz per sq yd). In addition there should be an annual mulch in spring of well-rotted dung, 50 kg per 8 sq m (1 cwt per 10 sq yd). It is wise to give some extra potash in late winter/early spring as, for example, sulphate of potash, 28 g per 0·8 sq m (1 oz per sq yd). Phosphates may be required on some soils and given in autumn as bonemeal, 140 g (5 oz) to the same area, or in spring as superphosphate of lime, 56 g (2 oz) again to that area.

Picking and Storing. For exhibition the fruits are almost invariably picked on the truss, but for home use it may pay to pick individual berries and go over the bushes several times at intervals of a few days. The fruits at the top of the truss invariably ripen before those lower down and can be removed first. The difference is more marked with some varieties than others. Black currants can be bottled or frozen.

Varieties. Good black currants are Baldwin, late; Ben Lomond, late-flowering, mid-season; Blackdown, mid-season; Boskoop Giant, early; Laxton's Giant, early; Malling Jet, late; Seabrook's Black, mid-season; and Wellington XXX, second early.

CURRANTS, RED AND WHITE

These differ from black currants both in their habit of growth and method of bearing. They crop heavily and succeed in most places but are less useful than black currants and should be planted on a smaller scale.

Soils. Requirements are very similar to those of black currants but they will withstand drought a little better and do not need quite such liberal supplies of nitrogen. In preparing the ground dung can be used at 50 kg per 12 sq m (1 cwt per 15 sq yd), and sulphate of potash should usually be added at 28 g per 0·8 sq m (1 oz per sq yd).

Types of Plant. Unlike the black currant, red and white currants are grown as bushes with a distinct main stem or leg about 13 cm (5 in) high. Occasionally one sees bushes with a good deal of sucker growth coming directly from the roots. This is not definitely harmful but it is not as satisfactory for garden purposes as the more orthodox type of bush. All bushes should be planted at least 1·5 m (5 ft) apart. Red and white currants can also be trained in various ways. Single, double or triple-stemmed cordons are quite popular and very high-class fruits can be produced in this way. Planting distance is 30 cm (1 ft) for single cordons, 45 cm (1½ ft) for twin stems and 60 cm (2 ft) for triple cordons. Rows should be at least 1·2 m (4 ft) apart.

Propagation. This is done by cuttings prepared and rooted in the same way as those of the black currant, except that all buds are nicked out of the lower half of each cutting to prevent the formation of suckers.

Fertility. All varieties are fully self-fertile and in consequence single bushes may be grown with satisfactory results. Red and white currants flower early and are therefore apt to suffer from frost if planted in hollows and similar frost pockets. For the same reason hand pollination is often well repaid as few bees may be flying when the plants are in bloom.

Season. This is a little earlier than for black currants, being mainly in mid-summer, though some fruits may be ready earlier in the season. There is no method of storing other than by bottling or deep freezing.

Age to Plants. As for black currants.

Planting. The same instructions apply as those given for black currants.

Treatment of Young Bushes. It generally pays to cut back rather severely after planting to ensure good growth the first year. However, it is possible to obtain some fruit during the first year by leaving the best branches at half their original length and cutting others back by about two thirds. In other respects treatment is the same as for black currants.

Pruning. Established bushes should be both summer and winter pruned, the main work being done in mid-summer. Unlike black currants, red and white currants fruit on old as well as on second-year wood and form spurs freely like an apple or plum. In mid-summer all strong side growths should be shortened to about six leaves. This will encourage the formation of fruit buds. In winter there will be little further to do beyond shortening the leading shoots by several centimetres each and, where fruit buds are showing prominently on side growths, cutting back to these. An attempt should be made to keep the centre of each bush open, rather like an apple bush on a smaller scale, to allow the free circulation of air.

Cordons are treated very much like apple cordons, that is to say the leading shoot of each plant is left unpruned until it reaches the desired height for the cordon, when any further extension is cut out each autumn; side growths are shortened to six leaves in mid-summer and are further cut back to two or three buds in the second half of autumn.

Feeding. The same general routine may be followed as advised for black currants but with rather less emphasis on nitrogen and more on potash. If dung is available for spring use it will not as a rule be necessary to give a nitrogenous fertilizer as well. Potash should be used fairly freely as red and white currants both show the effects of potash deficiency very quickly. Sulphate of potash is the most suitable form and can be used at 56 g per 0·8 sq m (2 oz per sq yd).

Picking and Storing. As for black currants.

Varieties. The best red currants for garden planting are Jonkheer van Tets, early; Laxton's No. 1, early; Red Lake, mid-season; and Stanza, late flowering.

Good white currants are White Dutch, mid-season, and White Versailles, early.

FIGS

These are not very widely grown in cooler climates except under glass, but in warm, sheltered places good crops can be ripened out of doors most summers.

Soil. The really important points about soil are that it must not be too rich and must be well drained. Dung should be used very sparingly, not more than 50 kg per 16 sq m (1 cwt per 20 sq yd) in the initial preparation of the ground as too much may cause rank growth which will prove unfruitful. If there is any doubt about the drainage it is good policy to remove the soil to a depth of 76 cm (2½ ft) and place a good layer of hard rubble in the bottom. This is almost always a wise precaution when figs are to be grown under glass and often the border is further restricted with bricks or concrete to a width of about 90 cm (3 ft). It is also wise policy to sprinkle a little ground chalk or limestone right through the soil while preparing it.

Type of Tree. Figs are usually grown either as bushes with quite a short central trunk or as fan-trained specimens against walls. Occasionally one sees half-standards in the open but these are seldom satisfactory except in the warmest localities. Allow at least 4·5 m (15 ft) between fan-trained trees; 7·5 m (25 ft) between bushes and half-standards.

Propagation. Figs are raised on their own roots, an easy method being to layer stems in spring or autumn. Alternatively cuttings can be rooted in spring in a propagating frame, preferably with bottom heat.

Fertility. The fig has a curious system of flowering. The flowers, of two separate sexes, are carried inside the young fig and can only be seen if this is cut in half. In the warm Mediterranean countries to which the fig is native these flowers are fertilized by a special kind of wasp which crawls into the fruit through a hole in the end and carries the pollen from male to female flowers. But fertilization is not essential with most cultivated varieties. Perfectly good crops of fully developed figs are produced without any outside agency. When failure occurs and the figs drop off instead of swelling, it is usually due to some fault in management of the bushes and not bad fertilization.

Season. Outdoor figs are in season at the end of summer and in early autumn, but under glass it is usually possible to get two separate crops from the same trees, one quite early in the summer and the other at about the same time as outdoor figs.

Age of Tree. It is best to start with two- or three-year-old trees which should, for preference, be purchased in pots.

Planting. In the case of figs lifted from the open ground between mid-autumn and early spring, the usual instructions for planting (see p. 615) should be followed. With figs purchased in pots or other containers in autumn or winter the only difference is that the roots, which are likely to be bound fairly tightly in a ball, should be carefully loosened and spread out before they are planted. This is not desirable if container-grown figs are planted between mid-spring and early autumn, during which period the ball of soil and roots must be left intact.

Treatment of Young Trees. After planting the trees must be pruned fairly severely. The following spring a moderate mulch of dung should be applied. Trees under glass will need frequent and generous watering from mid-spring to early autumn. Apart from this no special attention is required for the first season and no crop should be allowed to form.

Mode of Bearing. Before describing the pruning of figs it is necessary to understand the way in which the fruits are produced. It is possible for a fig to produce three separate crops in one year and it is usual for it to try to produce at least two crops. Under glass two crops can usually be matured but in the open in a cool climate it is never possible to ripen more than one crop. Pruning must be adjusted accordingly.

The first crop is produced on wood of the previous year's growth, in fact the young fruits are already well formed on the wood in the autumn. They stay there practically without alteration in size until the spring when, if the temperature can be raised to about 15-18°C/59-65°F they begin to swell fairly rapidly and will ripen in about three months. By this method a crop can be obtained quite easily by mid-summer, the trees being started into growth in the first half of spring.

The second crop is carried on the tips of the previous year's growth or from beside the scars left by the removal, while still small, of the first fruits described in the preceding paragraph. The tip fruits will also be present in the autumn but will be no bigger than peas whereas the first-crop figs will be much more forward at that time. This second crop is the only one which can be secured out of doors and all other fruits should be removed.

The third crop is produced on short side growths from the current year's wood. Under glass it may ripen in the autumn but in practice it is seldom obtained, two crops being sufficient for the strength of the tree.

Pruning. This is generally directed towards maintaining a suitable supply of strong, young wood and restricting the tree to those fruits which it is able to ripen. The main pruning is done as soon as the leaves fall in the autumn. Some of the oldest wood is cut right out and any thin or weak shoots removed but the best young branches are trained in at full length. In summer, side growths not required to fill space are rubbed out and in early summer good side shoots can be shortened to five leaves to prevent overcrowding.

With outdoor trees all embryo fruits which form in summer should be rubbed off until the end of summer, after which further fruitlets are left as they are the ones that will over-winter and develop into ripe fruits the following year. Any summer pruning of outdoor trees should be completed by mid-summer.

Trees that are making too much new wood and bearing badly should be root pruned in mid-autumn.

Feeding. Avoid too much dung as this tends to produce rank growth at the expense of fruit. Weak trees can have a light mulch each spring, otherwise artificial fertilizers applied in late winter/early spring will prove sufficient; sulphate of ammonia at 28 g per 0·8 sq m (1 oz per sq yd) in early spring, bonemeal at 113 g (4 oz) to the same area and sulphate of potash at 28 g (1 oz), again to the same area.

Thinning. With all trees, out of doors or under glass, only the best of the swelling fruits should be retained. Smaller fruits should be removed in spring or early summer. This thinning is additional to the removal of all fruits of unwanted crops.

Picking and Storing. Figs are ready for picking when they begin to get soft, a little nectar appears in the eye of the fruit or the skin starts to split. Figs may be bottled or dried.

Varieties. The best all-round variety is Brown Turkey as it crops freely and is hardy. The skin is nearly brown when ripe. White Marseilles has a pale green skin and ripens early but is not as reliable as Brown Turkey. Others sometimes offered are Brunswick, with very large fruits, and Negro Largo, which does well grown in large pots or tubs.

GOOSEBERRIES

Together with black currants these are the most useful bush fruits for the small garden. There are few places in which they will not succeed and they probably have a wider soil range than any other fruit. The flowering season is early so that spring frosts may do much damage in low-lying places.

Soils. The ideal is a medium, well-drained loam and extremes towards sand or clay should as far as possible be avoided. Both heavy and light land can be improved by liberal additions of well-rotted dung to which gooseberries respond well. In all cases it is wise to give some additional potash when preparing the ground as gooseberries are especially sensitive to potash deficiency. The results of the latter will be shown in poor growth and leaf scorching, often followed by premature defoliation.

Gooseberries may be planted under fruit trees or be interplanted with vegetables. They associate well with plums as, like them, they enjoy a generous rate of manuring.

Types of Plant. The bush form is generally adopted and gooseberries are grown with a distinct main stem or leg like red and white currants. It is impossible to form an open, goblet-shaped bush in quite the same manner as with currants but the main stems should be well spaced to allow easy gathering of the crop. Such bushes should be planted at least 1·2 m (4 ft) apart.

Gooseberries are also grown as cordons with one, two or three main stems and very big fruits of exhibition quality are produced in this way. Spacing is as for red and white currant cordons.

Propagation. This is carried out by cuttings taken in exactly the same way as those of the red and white currant. Note particularly that the lower buds on each cutting should be nicked out with the point of a sharp knife to prevent the cutting forming sucker shoots from below ground level. Such suckers are not harmful in the way in which they would be with a fruit cultivated on a stock but they are a great nuisance and make it very difficult to carry out cultural operations.

Fertility. All gooseberries appear to be self- and inter-fertile and so no problems arise on this score but because of the earliness of their flowering it is sometimes necessary to take special precautions to ensure pollination. Individual bushes can be protected during the flowering period with old net curtains or fine mesh nylon netting spread across them and, if few bees are flying, the flowers can be fertilized by hand with a camel-hair brush or rabbit's tail.

Season. By planting early, mid-season and late varieties and starting to pick as soon as the most forward fruits are large enough for cooking, it is possible to have gooseberries from the end of spring until the end of summer. Many varieties which are listed as dessert gooseberries can also be used for cooking in the green state. When the set is heavy it is a distinct advantage to thin fruits towards the end of spring or early in summer by which time the thinnings are usually serviceable. The remaining fruits can be left to grow bigger or to ripen for dessert.

The only methods of storing are by bottling and deep freezing.

Age to Plant. It is wise to start with young stock; year-old rooted cuttings for preference but certainly nothing older than three years.

Planting. This is the same as for red, white and black currants. The uppermost roots should be covered with about 7·5 cm (3 in) of soil. Space bushes at least 1·2 m (4 ft) apart, and single-stem cordons 30 cm (1 ft) in rows with 1·2 m (4 ft) between rows. Double and triple-stem cordons are spaced a minimum of 45 cm (1½ ft) and 68 cm (2¼ ft) apart.

Treatment of Young Plants. Again there is little to add to what has already been said regarding red and white currants, except that it is particularly important to get good growth the first year after planting and therefore more than ever necessary to be rather severe in pruning and liberal with mulches and water.

Pruning. For bush trees after the first year, pruning may resolve itself into thinning out all overcrowded branchlets and shortening all leaders sufficiently to correct any peculiarities in habit. Some gooseberries are satisfactory in this respect but many have a semi-weeping habit while others grow too erect. With the weepers each leading growth should be cut back to the top of the arch and to a bud pointing upwards. With those varieties which are too erect in habit leaders should be shortened by about one third and cut to an outward-pointing bud.

Cordons require more pruning to maintain their distinctive shape. Leading shoots are left untouched until the maximum desired height is obtained, after which they are removed. Side shoots are pruned in mid-summer to six leaves each and are further cut back to two or three buds in the second half of autumn.

Feeding. Potash is of particular importance and has an almost controlling effect on growth. Give a generous mulch of well-rotted dung each spring if possible or, failing this, some other bulky, organic manure such as well-made compost supplemented by a potassic fertilizer such as sulphate of potash, about 42 g per 0·8 sq m (1½ oz per sq yd). If bushes fail to make satisfactory growth or show indications of dying back, the rate of feeding can be increased to as much as 50 kg per 4·8 sq m (1 cwt per 6 sq yd) of dung and 85 g per 0·8 sq m (3 oz per sq yd) sulphate of potash.

Thinning. Do this when the fruits are of usable size. See 'Season', p. 668.

Picking and Storing. For dessert, gooseberries should not be picked until they cease to be hard and acquire their full colour. For cooking they can be picked as soon as of sufficient size. They can be bottled or frozen.

Varieties. Good gooseberries are Careless, white, mid-season; Early Sulphur, yellow, early; Golden Drop, yellow, mid-season; Keepsake, green, mid-season; Lancashire Lad, red, mid-season; Leveller, yellow, mid-season; May Duke, red, early; Whinham's Industry, red, mid-season; and Whitesmith, white, mid-season.

GRAPES

Grapes of high dessert quality cannot as a rule be cultivated very satisfactorily in the open in cool climates. A few of the hardiest varieties will succeed in certain sheltered places but in general outdoor cultivation is a risky business and good crops are only obtained occasionally. Those who require a regular supply of grapes for the table should plant under glass. Some varieties of wine grapes can be grown satisfactorily outdoors in cool climates.

Greenhouse. Vines can be grown satisfactorily in almost any kind of greenhouse, but the ideal vinery should be not less than 3·6 m (12 ft) wide and 6 m (20 ft) long and should have glass extending to within 60 cm (2 ft) of soil level. For early crops a lean-to house against a wall facing south, or a little west of south, is best. For the main crop a span-roofed house running north and south is very suitable.

The vine border may be inside the vinery, outside, or partly in and partly out. The inside border encourages early growth as the soil warms up quickly in the spring. It is, however, entirely dependent upon the gardener for its water supply and therefore taxes his skill and time to a greater extent than the outside border. The latter has the merit of being easy to manage and requiring little attention for the greater part of the year but growth tends to be late and, if rainfall should be excessive, there is no easy means of protecting the roots from it. The border partly inside and partly out has much to recommend it as it combines the advantages of both methods.

Whatever type of house is used it must be provided with suitable training wires. These must be strained horizontally at least 23 cm (9 in) below the glass and should extend the full length of the vinery. There should be one wire every 38 cm (1¼ ft), that is, a wire for each lateral growth of the vines.

Soil. A medium loamy soil is best for grapes. Drainage is of paramount importance, so much so that if there is any doubt about its adequacy a special border should be prepared with drainage trenches in the bottom leading to a properly constructed soakaway (see p. 25), or main drain.

If the ordinary soil of the garden is reasonably good it can be used as the basis of the compost. A fairly liberal addition of very well decayed dung, preferably horse manure, should be made, the precise quantity depending on the known quality of the soil. The average will be one barrow load of dung to every eight barrow loads of soil. In addition mix in about 1·8 kg (4 lb) of well-broken chalk and 0·4 kg (1 lb) of coarse bonemeal. Finish off with a topdressing of sulphate of potash, 42 g per 0·8 sq m (1½ oz per sq yd), forked or raked into the surface.

If the natural soil of the garden is not good or its suitability for vines is in doubt, remove it altogether from the vine border and replace with loam or, better still, chopped turves obtained from a meadow in good condition. The same additions should be made as recommended for garden soil. The border must be at least 1·2 m (4 ft) wide, preferably more, and should extend the full length of the vinery. The depth must not be less than 76 cm (2½ ft). The border should be completed at least two months before planting so that the soil may have ample time to settle.

Types of Training. Two methods are commonly used, one the single-rod system the other the extension or multiple-stem system. In the former a number of vines are planted side by side about 1·2 m (4 ft) apart. Each is restricted to a single main stem which is trained directly from soil level to the apex of the house, following the line of the roof rafters. Under the extension system one vine may fill quite a large house, a notable example being the great vine at Hampton Court in London. The first growth from the roots is trained horizontally beneath the eaves and from it subsidiary rods are trained parallel with the roof rafters to the apex of the house at approximately 1·2 m (4 ft) intervals.

The single-rod system is now most in favour with experienced growers and is certainly the best for the amateur.

Propagation. Vines can be increased by cuttings or single eyes. Cuttings are taken in autumn directly the foliage has fallen. They are prepared from well-ripened growth formed during the previous summer, suitable wood for the purpose being that which has just finished carrying a crop of grapes, in fact the very kind of growth which would in any case be removed at the winter pruning (see p. 690). Each cutting should be about 30 cm (1 ft) in length, severed at the base just below a joint or leaf. The cuttings are potted singly in rather sandy compost in well-drained 11·2 cm (4½ ft) pots. Stand these in the greenhouse or vinery and keep moderately watered. The cuttings should be well rooted by the following autumn when they may be planted in their permanent quarters or, if preferred, can be transferred to larger pots and grown on for another year.

Many growers think that single eyes make sturdier plants than cuttings. This method is certainly economical of material. The best time to obtain these eyes is in mid-winter. The eye in question is in fact a dormant growth bud, and it can either be scooped out with a portion of bark, as when preparing a rose bud (see p. 333) or can be cut with a section of stem about 12 mm (½ in) long. In either case the eyes should be inserted in moist peat and sand in 7·5 cm (3 in) pots in such a manner that they are just level with the surface. Start them growing in a propagating frame with bottom heat, but when well rooted remove to the open greenhouse staging. Pot on into 13·7 cm (5½ in) pots in J.I. No. 2 when necessary and grow on under cool conditions, or in a frame or sheltered place out of doors in summer, for planting the following autumn or spring. Vines can also be increased by layering young stems in spring.

Fertility. Vines are self-fertile, that is to say it is quite possible to grow one variety only in a greenhouse and yet obtain good crops.

Season. By growing early and late varieties and starting the former into growth with artificial heat, it is possible to have ripe grapes from early summer to Christmas or even later, but considerable skill is necessary in producing both very early and very late crops. The beginner will be well advised to be satisfied with an autumn crop for the first few years.

Age of Vine. As with other fruits it is undoubtedly best to start with young plants. Year-old cuttings or rooted eyes transplant without any difficulty and will grow on into fine fruiting vines in time, but it will be several years before a crop is gathered. Most amateurs prefer to start with something more advanced and the nurseryman meets this requirement by offering so-called fruiting vines in pots. These are usually three or four years old and must be planted with considerable care if they are not to receive a severe shock. Such vines should always be purchased in pots.

Planting. Home-grown vines, whether year-old cuttings or well-rooted eyes, can with advantage be planted in the first half of autumn, before growth ceases for the year. Fruiting vines should be purchased in late autumn but not planted until early the following spring. Meanwhile they should simply stand in the vinery in their pots and become acclimatised.

The young vines can be planted with little or no root disturbance but with the older plant, which will probably have its roots bound round in a tight ball, it is essential to disentangle these before planting. This must be done carefully and a pointed stick can be used to tease out the tangled roots which should then be spread out in a wide hole, sufficiently deep to allow the uppermost to be covered with 7·5 cm (3 in) of soil. Work fine soil around and between them and make really firm.

Treatment of Young Vines. Home-grown vines that have been planted in the first half of autumn will require no pruning the first winter. Fruiting vines should be pruned about a month before they are planted. They are cut back to 90 cm (3 ft) from soil level.

The first spring one strong growth is trained under the rafters towards the apex of the house. Any side shoots are pinched when they have made one or two leaves. When the main shoot has grown 1·8 m (6 ft) it is also pinched. Following this further side growths will appear. One of these, as near the end as possible, is trained on towards the apex and the rest of the shoots are allowed to grow unstopped until mid-autumn when they should all be pinched.

By this means the grower will obtain by the end of the first year anything from 2·1-3 m (7-10 ft) of growth, the lower part of which will be beginning to get stout and woody. When all the leaves have fallen he will cut this back to a length of about 1·5 m (5 ft). Any side growths remaining should be cut right back to the main rod.

Meanwhile the vine border should be well watered throughout the summer. No artificial heat should be needed but in hot weather the vine should be syringed daily with tepid water and the path and walls damped down.

Ventilation should be free throughout, subject to avoidance of draughts and rapid falls in temperature.

Treatment of Established Vines. After the first year fruiting vines should be able to carry a small crop which will, of course, increase every succeeding year. Home-grown cuttings will take a further year or so of foundation pruning, on the lines of the first-year treatment, before they are sturdy enough to crop.

Starting into Growth. Vines required for an early crop are started into growth in the second half of winter by closing the ventilators and raising the temperature to about 12°C/54°F. Before this the border, if inside, should have been very thoroughly soaked with water. It is also wise to give a good mulch of well-rotted dung at the time the vines are to be started.

Temperature. Subsequently an average temperature of 12-15°C/54-59°F rising to 21-24°C/70-75°F with sun heat should be maintained, except during the flowering period when an increase of about 3°C/5°F is preferred. As the summer advances and the grapes become well formed, the maximum temperature may rise to 26°C/79°F with sun heat but every effort should be used to prevent higher temperatures than this as they may cause scorching of leaves and berries. For the final week or so, while the grapes are getting their full colour, it is better to have a lower temperature again, with a night average of 15°C/59°F.

Ventilation. Throughout ventilation should be as free as possible and compatible with the maintenance of these temperatures. More ventilation must be given while the flowers are setting even though this means increased artificial heat. There should be another increase in ventilation while the pips are being formed.

Watering. At no time must the vine border be allowed to become dry. If the winter watering has been properly done the soil will be moist throughout to begin with. Subsequently water is likely to be needed every three or four weeks all through the season, depending on the weather. Not less than 22·5 l per 0·8 sq m (5 gal per sq yd) should be given at each application. However, avoid watering by rule of thumb. Watch the soil carefully and give water when it appears to be getting dry.

Humidity. A fairly damp atmosphere must be maintained throughout the season of growth except for a week or ten days when the vines are in flower, and again when the grapes are colouring. For the first few weeks, until the shoots are 11·2 cm (4½ in) long, the vines should be syringed daily with tepid water. Subsequently shallow trays of water

Rosmarinus officinalis

Ribes sanguineum
Pulborough Scarlet

Romneya coulteri

Ribes sanguineum Pulborough Scarlet, to
3 m (10 ft), the richest coloured variety of the
hardy flowering currant, is early into leaf and
flowers with the forsythia
⊕ ❀ Spring ☼ ◐ ▧ ▮

Romneya coulteri (Californian Tree Poppy),
1.8 m (6 ft), a sub-shrub that should be cut
back to ground level in early spring. Its stems
bear pale glaucous leaves and magnificent
poppies. Needs ample moisture
⊕ ⚇ ❀ Summer ☼ ◐ ▧ ▮

Rosmarinus officinalis (Rosemary), to 1.8 m
(6 ft), a native of the warm Mediterranean
clothed in neat aromatic grey-green leaves,
with pale blue flowers in spring. Fine in a
border or as a dwarf hedge. Also used as a
culinary herb ⊕ ❀ Spring ☼ ◐ ▧ ▮

673

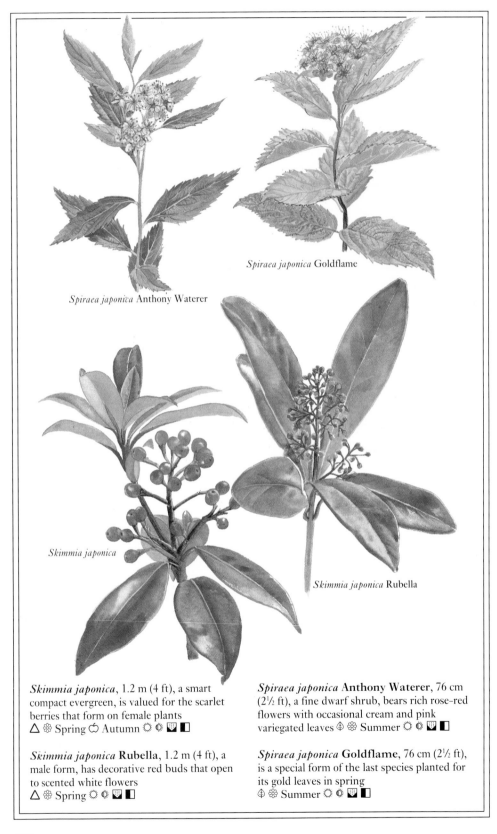

Spiraea japonica Anthony Waterer

Spiraea japonica Goldflame

Skimmia japonica

Skimmia japonica Rubella

Skimmia japonica, 1.2 m (4 ft), a smart compact evergreen, is valued for the scarlet berries that form on female plants
△ ❀ Spring ☙ Autumn ☼ ☀ 🌑 ⬛

Skimmia japonica Rubella, 1.2 m (4 ft), a male form, has decorative red buds that open to scented white flowers
△ ❀ Spring ☼ ☀ 🌑 ⬛

Spiraea japonica Anthony Waterer, 76 cm (2½ ft), a fine dwarf shrub, bears rich rose-red flowers with occasional cream and pink variegated leaves ✦ ❀ Summer ☼ ☀ 🌑 ⬛

Spiraea japonica Goldflame, 76 cm (2½ ft), is a special form of the last species planted for its gold leaves in spring
✦ ❀ Summer ☼ ☀ 🌑 ⬛

Viburnum x bodnantense Dawn

Viburnum davidii

Symphoricarpos orbiculatus

V. davidii (berries)

Symphoricarpos orbiculatus (Indian Currant or Coral Berry), 1.8 m (6 ft), makes bushy growth
✤ ❋ Spring ↻ Autumn ☼ ◐ ● ▦ ▮

Viburnum x bodnantense **Dawn**, to 2.1 m (7 ft), deserves a place in the garden for its fragrant winter flowers. Keep roots moist in summer when flower buds are formed
✤ ⚘ ⬇ ❋ Winter ☼ ◐ ▦ ▮

Viburnum davidii, 90 cm (3 ft), is a low-growing member of this family of shrubs. Its deeply-veined shiny leaves are neat and handsome. Its flowers are followed by unusual bright blue berries
△ ⚘ ❋ Spring ↻ Summer ☼ ◐ ▦ ▮

Viburnum rhytidophyllum

Viburnum tinus

Vinca major Variegata

V. tinus (berries)

Viburnum tinus (Laurustinus), to 2.8 m
(9½ ft), is a widely planted evergreen which
opens its pink-tinged white flowers in mild
spells in winter, followed by dark blue berries.
Good for screening and hedging
△ ❊ Winter ↻ Summer ☼ ◐ ▦ ▮

Viburnum rhytidophyllum, 3 m (10 ft), a more
vigorous relation of *V. tinus*, is remarkable for
its handsome deeply wrinkled leaves △ ❊
Spring ↻ Autumn ☼ ◐ ▦ ▮

Vinca major Variegata is a handsome form of
the vigorous trailing Periwinkle, forming
excellent ground cover. Its variegated leaves
form a pleasing background to its flowers
△ ⚐ ❊ Summer ☼ ● ▦ ▮

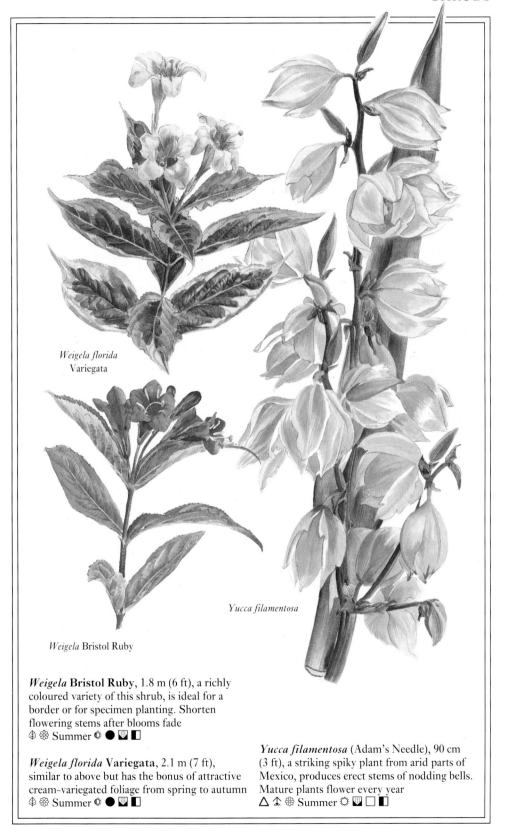

Weigela florida
Variegata

Yucca filamentosa

Weigela Bristol Ruby

Weigela Bristol Ruby, 1.8 m (6 ft), a richly coloured variety of this shrub, is ideal for a border or for specimen planting. Shorten flowering stems after blooms fade
✥ ❀ Summer ☼ ● 🛡️▯

Weigela florida Variegata, 2.1 m (7 ft), similar to above but has the bonus of attractive cream-variegated foliage from spring to autumn
✥ ❀ Summer ☼ ● 🛡️▯

Yucca filamentosa (Adam's Needle), 90 cm (3 ft), a striking spiky plant from arid parts of Mexico, produces erect stems of nodding bells. Mature plants flower every year
△ ⚘ ❀ Summer ☼ 🛡️□▯

677

Wisteria's long pendent clusters of soft lilac flowers add an aristocratic touch to a house,
particularly one of period design. Prune back new growth to encourage flowers

Though it demands a warm sheltered position to survive and flower, *Abutilon megapotamicum* is well worth the trouble for its excellent display of 'lanterns'

Jokingly called the Mile-a-Minute Vine, *Fallopia baldschuanica* is ideal for covering a wall or eyesore quickly, but never plant it where it can become a nuisance

The traditional cottager's 'roses round the pergola' idea is worth imitating and what better than old-fashioned Mme Gregoire Staechelin to provide the blooms?

Climbing roses and clematis are favourites for covering a wall with choice flowers, but the effect can be greatly enhanced by training both together – here New Dawn and Perle d'Azur

Vigorous small-flowered clematis like *Clematis montana* Tetrarose are the ones to plant if you have a large wall or old tree to camouflage. They look magnificent in flower

Clematis are a large and richly varied family. Yellow *C. tangutica* is specially charming.
The others in this group are red Ernest Markham and blue Mrs. N. Thompson

Camellias, like Fascination here, are noble blooms but less trouble than you might expect.
The bushes are bone hardy, though the blooms can get browned by frost

Sambucus racemosa Plumosa Aurea is doubly decorative, having deeply cut foliage that is also a bright gold colour throughout the warmer months of the year

The golden leaves of the Japanese maple, *Acer japonica* Aureum make it an eye-catching feature from spring to autumn, contrasting with the more intricate leaves of *A. palmatum*

Telling contrasts repay the careful planning involved and bring a garden to life. Here the blue spruce *Picea pungens* Koster contrasts with the golden heather, *Erica cinerea* Windlebrook

should be placed near radiators and the floor damped once or twice daily.

In addition to the mulch of dung applied before starting the vine into growth a further mulch should be applied when the berries are set and beginning to swell. It is also advisable to apply a compound vine manure in winter or spring according to manufacturers' instructions.

Stopping and Disbudding. A great deal of the pruning of the vine is done by a process of disbudding and pinching carried out throughout the spring and summer. The ideal is to have one side growth approximately every 38 cm (1¼ ft) on each side of the main rod. Any surplus side growths over and above this number are rubbed out as soon as possible. Each selected side growth is pinched either two leaves beyond the point at which it produces a bunch of flowers or, if it fails to produce flowers, when it has reached a length of 60-90 cm (2-3 ft). Any subsidiary side growths which come from it are stopped at the first leaf. The main rod is stopped when it reaches the apex of the house.

Tying. All young growth must be tied down to the training wires a little at a time. The shoots are very brittle to begin with and if pulled down too quickly will snap off. The method is to loop a piece of soft raffia or fillis around the tip of the growth, attach the other end of the tie to the wire and then shorten the tie daily until the growth lies parallel with the wire.

Fertilization. This can be ensured partly by correct temperature and ventilation and partly by jarring the vines daily while in bloom, or dusting the flowers with a camel-hair brush.

Thinning. About a fortnight after the berries are set, thinning should be carried out. Speaking generally, a vine bunch contains about twice as many berries as it can develop fully. The surplus must be cut out with a special pair of pointed vine scissors. All berries at the tips of the branchlets should be retained and the thinning confined mainly to the

Pruning a vine. Side growths are pinched two leaves beyond the point at which flowers are produced. Secondary growths are pinched at the first leaf

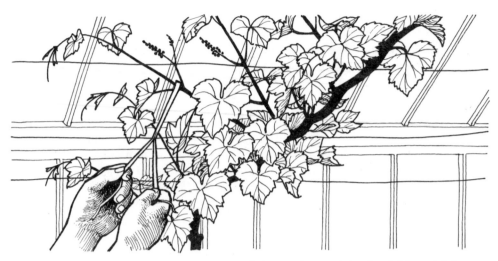

Tying down vine laterals. This must be done a little at a time and the ties tightened daily, as the young shoots are very brittle

interior of the bunch. It should be most drastic towards the point and least severe around the shoulders, which will extend and so give the berries more room to develop.

Great care must be taken not to bruise the very tender fruits. The bunches should not be touched by hand but may be held and turned as necessary with a small forked stick.

Thinning should so far as possible be completed at one operation, but it may be necessary to check the bunches two or three times during the following weeks to make certain that there is no overcrowding.

Pruning. Winter pruning is not done until the leaves have fallen from the vine. It can usually be left with advantage until early winter, later in the case of late vines. Do not, however, delay after mid-winter or sap may be rising in which case the cut surfaces may bleed. When bleeding does occur it must be checked at once. This can be done by treating the cut surface with a styptic.

If the summer stopping and disbudding has been properly done winter pruning is really very simple. All laterals, whether they have carried fruit or not, are shortened to two buds and that is all there is to it. Some growers prefer to cut back to one bud, arguing that as only one new lateral will be required at each spur the following spring, one bud is sufficient. But two seems wiser as an insurance.

Cleaning. Directly pruning has been completed any loose bark on the main rod should be removed by rubbing with the palm of the hand. Then the whole rod should be sprayed with tar-oil winter wash.

Winter Treatment. During the winter from the time the grapes are cut until it is time to start the vine into growth, the freest possible ventilation should be given and no artificial heat should be used. The vine rods themselves are perfectly hardy and should be encouraged to become thoroughly dormant during the winter.

During this dormant period it is an advantage to untie the main rods from the training wires and let them hang down on long strings. If this is done before pruning it will save the use of steps for this operation. The vines should be allowed to continue hanging until the new shoots are 6·2 cm (2½ in) long in the spring, after which the rod should be tied back in the normal position. The purpose of this is to encourage complete dormancy in winter and even out the flow of sap when it starts to rise. With the vines tied in their normal position the sap will tend to flow to the top first with the result that the lower eyes may not start into growth.

Grapes in the Open. Out of doors, grapes are most likely to be successful grown against sunny walls. They can be allowed to spread out almost at will, side shoots being pinched in summer a leaf or so beyond the bunches of fruits and surplus growth being cut out in winter much as for indoor vines but with less restriction. Alternatively vines are planted 90 cm (3 ft) apart and a much more rigorous system of pruning adopted. Each plant is restricted to two stems or rods, one for fruiting and the other for producing new growth. Each winter the fruiting rod is shortened to six dormant growth buds and is tied down horizontally several centimetres above the soil level and the other rod is cut back to two growth buds. Young lateral growths from the first are permitted to bear grapes the following year, each being pinched two leaves beyond the first bunch of flowers. When the crop has been gathered this rod is cut right out. Meanwhile two shoots have been allowed to grow upwards from the second rod and in winter will be shortened respectively to six and two buds to start the process all over again. If desired, the fruiting canes can be covered with cloches. A less restrictive variation of this is to retain two rods for fruiting, one tied down to the left, the other to the right along the row, and a third rod shortened to three or four buds, to provide three replacement growths for the next season. In winter the two rods that have fruited are cut out, two of the replacement rods are shortened to six buds and tied down in their place, and the third is again shortened to three or four buds to provide replacement growth.

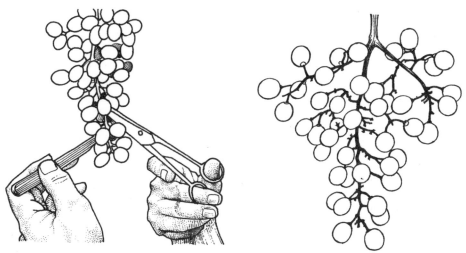

Thinning grapes, using a stick to steady and turn the bunch. All surplus berries are removed giving the others room for development

Varieties. There are many varieties of grape but for greenhouse cultivation probably Black Hamburgh, an easily grown grape of good quality, is the best all-round variety for heated or unheated houses. Muscat of Alexandria is a pale yellow grape which sets the standard for quality but it is more difficult to grow and needs warmth. Gros Colmar is remarkable for the size of the black berries and is very late ripening but is of inferior quality. Foster's Seedling is a good white grape for an unheated or slightly heated greenhouse. Buckland Sweetwater is pale green, hardy and free cropping but not of top quality. Madresfield Court is an early-ripening black grape of good quality and Mrs Pince, Lady Downe's Seedling and Alicante are black grapes which keep well and were once much grown but are not so reliable as some of the others named. For outdoor cultivation early ripening varieties must be used such as Brandt, purple, good autumn foliage; Madeleine Angevine, pale green; Madeleine Sylvaner, pale yellow; Müller Thurgau, greenish white; Seyval Blanc, pale amber, and Siegerrebe.

MELONS

From the cultural standpoint melons more closely resemble vegetables than fruits and it may be argued that if tomatoes and cucumbers are to be included amongst vegetables, melons also should be numbered amongst them, but custom decrees that the melon should be classified with fruits rather than with vegetables. Hence its inclusion here.

Soil. As melons are almost always grown in a greenhouse or frame, the soil can be specially prepared for them in a way that is impossible with more permanent fruits. The compost must be rich and open in texture, in fact very similar to that employed for cucumbers. A satisfactory mixture can be prepared with 3 parts by bulk of turfy medium loam, 1 part well-rotted stable manure and a liberal sprinkling of bonemeal and wood ashes. This should be spread to a depth of about 15 cm (6 in) over a porous base such as a good layer of clinkers or clean straw. The bed should be about 90 cm (3 ft) wide and of any convenient length. Every 90 cm (3 ft) a low, rounded mound should be made with about two bucketfuls of the same compost. One plant will be placed on the summit of each mound. The object of this is to ensure perfect drainage at the collar of the plant, that is, where the stem enters the soil.

Raising Seedlings. Melons are propagated from seed, which is germinated in a warm greenhouse for an early crop or an unheated greenhouse or frame for a late summer crop. A minimum temperature of about 18°C/65°F is necessary for germination, so in the unheated greenhouse it is seldom wise to sow before the end of spring. In a heated house the first sowing can be made in mid-winter, provided the necessary temperature can be maintained throughout.

The seeds are sown singly in small, well-drained flower pots, filled with J.I. seed or peat seed compost. The seed pots should be plunged to their rims in peat in a propagating frame, preferably with bottom heat, and covered with glass or a light, the object being to maintain as damp an atmosphere as possible.

Germination is, as a rule, rapid. As soon as the seedlings appear ventilation should be given and a few days later the pots may be removed to the ordinary staging of the greenhouse.

Growing melons in the greenhouse border. (a) Each plant is placed on a 90 cm (3 ft) mound of rich soil placed on a sheet of polythene to protect it from infection from below. Stems are trained to wires fixed as for vines. (b) Fertilizing a female melon flower with pollen from a male bloom

Planting. By the time the young plants have their fourth true leaf they may be planted on the previously prepared mounds. Be careful not to plant too deeply, in fact the soil in the pot ball should be only just covered. Water in well and decrease ventilation for a few days until growth resumes freely.

Training. The principal shoot of each plant is trained to wires fixed as for vines (see p. 670). It should be led directly towards the apex of the house following the lines of the roof rafters. Side growths are tied out along the training wires and are stopped when they have made about 30 cm (1 ft) of growth each. The main shoot is itself stopped when it has grown about 1·8 m (6 ft).

Fertilizing Flowers. Flowers and fruits will be produced on the side growths only. There are two sorts of flower, male and female, and they can be distinguished easily by the fact that immediately beneath each female flower is an embryo fruit rather like a large pea, whereas the male flower has only a thin stalk.

It is essential that the female flowers which are to produce fruits should be fertilized by pollen from the males. Moreover no fruit must be allowed to get ahead of any other on one particular plant so that as far as possible all the flowers required on one plant must be set on the same day. This is assured by picking off all female flowers until the plant is well developed and four flowers are open approximately together on different side growths. This will usually be about one month after planting out. These four selected female blooms must be fertilized by securing a male flower, not necessarily from the same plant, that has ripe pollen on it, and dusting this over the centre of each female bloom. A good test for the pollen is to stroke the flower across the palm of the hand. If the pollen is ripe, yellow dust-like grains will be seen quite clearly on the skin.

It is advisable to fertilize the same flowers two or three times on successive days. Preferably the work should be done when the sun is shining and towards mid-day. The atmosphere of the house should be allowed to dry a little and the temperature to rise a few degrees. If fertilization is successful the fruits will begin to swell rapidly in a few days. If instead they turn yellow, it will be necessary to look for a fresh set of female flowers and treat them in the same way.

Feeding and General Management. Ventilation throughout should be as free as possible consistent with a minimum temperature of 15°C/59°F, rising to 26-29°C/79-85°F on sunny days.

Throughout the plants should be watered freely but care should be taken to keep the collar of each plant dry. Failure to observe this point may result in canker of the main stem at or just above soil level. Some growers place a zinc collar round the bottom of each plant to protect it from accidental splashes of water. It is also good policy to sprinkle the base of the plant with sulphur from time to time.

After a few weeks, white rootlets will appear on the surface of the compost. At this stage give a topdressing, 12 mm (½ in) thick, of well-rotted stable manure mixed with an equal bulk of good soil. Repeat this dressing as often as roots reappear on the surface. No other feeding is required.

As the fruits gain in size they must be supported. This is done with special melon nets, one to each fruit, the net itself being slung to the wires beneath the rafters.

Cultivation in Frames. The only difference in the treatment of melons in frames from that of melons in greenhouses is in the training. Two plants are enough for an ordinary 1·8 × 1·2 m (6 × 4 ft) frame. They should be set as nearly as possible equidistant on the centre line of the frame, that is to say about 60 cm (2 ft) from each end and 60 cm (2 ft) from each side.

The point is pinched out of each plant when it is about 15 cm (6 in) in height. Subsequently four shoots only are retained per plant and these are trained towards the four corners of the frame. They can be pegged in position with pieces of galvanized wire bent to the shape of hair pins. These primary runners are stopped when they reach the confines of the frame. Fruits can either be produced on them or on secondary side growths from them, whichever is more convenient.

The same instructions apply regarding fertilization of all flowers on one day. Sometimes it is possible to obtain four fruits per plant in frames but as a rule two or three fruits are sufficient. As the fruits ripen they can be raised on slates, tiles or inverted seed trays to expose them more fully to the sun.

Unless the frames are heated it is unwise to plant before early summer.

Melons can also be grown under cloches in much the same way except that it will be best to restrict each plant to two stems, training these in opposite directions under the cloches placed end to end to cover them.

Varieties. Good melons for greenhouse culture are Hero of Lockinge, King George and Superlative. For frames and cloches the hardier Cantaloupe varieties, such as Charentais, Dutch Net and Tiger, should be used.

MULBERRIES

Like the medlar, the mulberry is usually a lone tree in the garden, grown as much for ornament as for utility. Nevertheless it can be extremely profitable, old mulberries in particular bearing very heavy crops.

Soil. This should be rather rich and well supplied with moisture though not waterlogged, in fact very much the kind of soil which would grow culinary plums well. The situation must be open and sunny and plenty of room should be allowed, for though mulberries grow slowly at first, they make big trees in the long run. Preparation should be thorough and a moderate amount of well-rotted dung can be mixed with the soil before planting. Lime is not essential. It is a good plan to add coarse bonemeal at 113 g per 0·8 sq m (4 oz per sq yd) and sulphate of potash at 28 g (1 oz) to the same area before planting.

Types of Tree. Mulberries are almost always grown as standards. Occasionally one may see bushes but these are not so satisfactory because of the spreading habit of the branches.

Propagation. The simplest method of increasing mulberries is by layering. For this purpose fairly young branches should be used and pegged down to the soil in autumn.

Seed is sometimes employed as a means of propagation but it is not very satisfactory. It is germinated out of doors in early spring.

Cuttings will root if prepared partly from well ripened young wood plus a little two-year-old wood. These cuttings should be 30-38 cm (1-1¼ ft) long and must be taken in autumn. They are inserted firmly 11·2 cm (4½ in) deep in rather sandy soil in a sheltered position out of doors.

A fourth method of propagation is by grafting good forms of mulberry on to seedling mulberries. This is done in early spring in the same manner as for apples.

Fertility. Mulberries are self-fertile and usually set fruit freely without any assistance or special precautions once they have reached fruiting age.

Age of Tree. Because mulberries are sometimes slow to come into bearing there is a temptation to start with well-developed trees already five or six years old. This is a mistake as such trees usually suffer a severe check when transplanted and take some years to recover. It is far better to begin with two or three-year-old specimens even though this may mean waiting several years for fruit.

Planting. The dormant period from about mid-autumn to early-spring is the correct time for planting mulberries with the emphasis on the early part of that time. If planting can be completed by mid-autumn so much the better. If more than one tree is to be planted fully 9 m (30 ft) must be left between them.

The roots tend to spread laterally for a considerable distance and must be accommodated in wide, rather shallow holes. The uppermost roots should be covered with 7·5 cm (3 in) of soil and staking should be secure from the outset.

Treatment of Young Trees. This is exactly the same as for young apples but staking is particularly important as mulberries are easily blown over.

Pruning. Young trees are formed and branches obtained where required by the methods detailed in Chapter 27. Bear in mind the ultimate spreading habit of the mulberry and allow ample space between branches that are one above the other. Once the main framework of branches is formed, little further pruning is required. All the work should be done in autumn immediately after leaf fall.

Feeding. Young trees can be fed in the same way as plums but old trees seldom require any attention except possibly an occasional topdressing of dung in spring.

Thinning. Unnecessary.

Picking and Storing. Mulberries are ready to pick when they become a dark crimson in late summer/early autumn. They can only be kept by bottling or deep freezing.

Varieties. It is the black mulberry, *Morus nigra*, that has the most pleasantly flavoured fruits. There are no varieties.

PEACHES AND NECTARINES

These are fruits for sunny regions and they can be grown successfully out of doors only in fairly warm places. They do well under glass if given plenty of light and ventilation and do not overheat in the summer. The nectarine is simply a smooth-skinned form of the peach and is otherwise identical.

Soil. A medium loamy soil gives the best results and good drainage is absolutely essential. In greenhouses it generally pays to make up a special border for the trees, excavating the existing soil to a depth of 60 cm (2 ft) or more, a width of at least 1·2 m (4 ft) and a length of at least 1·8 m (6 ft) per tree, and replacing it with chopped turf mixed with about one twelfth its own bulk of well-rotted dung. In addition give a good sprinkling of coarsely crushed bones, lime or crushed chalk and wood ashes. A good layer of clinkers or land drain pipes should be placed in the bottom of the bed connecting with a main drain or soakaway outside to take away surplus moisture.

Out of doors peaches and nectarines succeed best against walls facing south or south west. In some mild places they can be grown in the open without any protection.

Types of Tree. The fan system of training is almost invariably followed both with glasshouse trees and with those planted against walls out of doors. Such trees should be planted a minimum of 4·5 m (15 ft) apart. Occasionally small bushes are grown in pots, and bushes are also best if peaches or nectarines are to be grown in the open away from walls or fences.

Stocks and Propagation. Peaches and nectarines can be raised easily from stones. Seedlings may differ considerably in quality of fruit though they are often quite good, but for best results named varieties should be obtained and these are increased by budding just after mid-summer in the same manner as for apples or plums. Plum stocks or seedling almonds are most commonly used to provide the necessary roots. Of the former Brompton, St Julien A and Pershore are most satisfactory.

Fertility. All varieties of both peach and nectarine appear to be fully self-fertile though they are dependent on bees for fertilization. In climates where they flower too early to be reliably pollinated by such means, it is advisable to go over the fully open blossom with a rabbit's tail or camel-hair brush. As far as possible this should be done on fine, sunny days when the pollen is dry and parting readily from the anthers.

Season. By planting early, mid-season and late varieties, starting some into growth with artificial heat and leaving others to start naturally in unheated houses, it is possible to pick ripe peaches and nectarines from early summer to mid-autumn. The fruits cannot be stored by any means and the only method of extending the season beyond these dates is by bottling or canning.

Age of Tree. It is best to start with quite young trees, certainly no more than three years old. Maidens or two-year-old specimens transplant even better but, of course, take a little longer to come into bearing. However, peaches and nectarines properly managed are not slow in cropping and will usually give some fruit by their fifth or sixth year.

Planting. This can be done at any time from mid-autumn to early spring, but early planting is desirable, particularly under glass. In other respects planting follows the general lines already detailed on pp. 615–16, the only point to add being that, when planting against walls out of doors, it is desirable to keep the base of the tree at least 23 cm (9 in) away from the wall rather than plant hard up against it.

Treatment of Young Trees. Pruning after planting should be very severe to ensure strong growth the first season. For the same reason two mulches of well-rotted manure may be given, the first in early spring and the second four to six weeks later. Watering should be generous both under glass and for outside trees against walls as here they seldom receive sufficient moisture from natural rainfall.

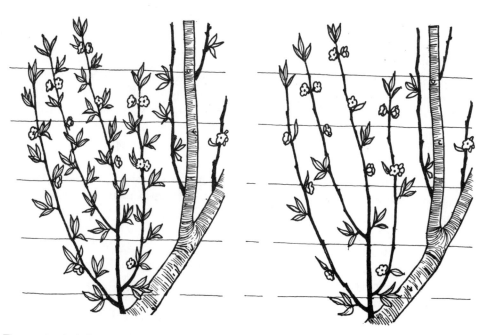

The method of disbudding peach trees is similar to that used for Morello cherries. Two or three new shoots only are retained on each growth, one at the base, one at the tip and perhaps a third along the length

Pruning. In the early stages the framework of the tree is built up as described in Chapter 27. The main branches of fan-trained specimens should be approximately 30 cm (1 ft) apart and side growths may be laid in between these as close to one another as 15 cm (6 in). Avoid having a central stem to a fan tree as this will tend to grow more vigorously than the rest. Fill the centre with secondary branches trained from the main branches laid down on each side.

By about the third year it will be possible to modify this initial pruning and encourage the production of some flowers and fruit. The system employed is the same as that used for Morello and other sour cherries. Peaches and nectarines bear on year-old side growths and a sufficient but not excessive number of these must be obtained annually.

The method is to remove all unwanted shoots, a few at a time, quite early in the season, usually in late spring/early summer. Roughly speaking two new side growths are retained for each fruiting side growth, one as near as possible to its base and the other at its tip. The former will replace it in the autumn whilst the latter is retained solely to draw sap through the fruiting lateral and so assist in the swelling and ripening of the crop.

In the autumn, as soon as the fruit has been gathered, it simply remains to cut out the old laterals entirely and train the young growths in their place. Note particularly that framework pruning to extend the tree further and obtain more branches may be going on concurrently with the pruning for fruit just described.

Watering. The first essential with peaches and nectarines, particularly those under glass, is to give the soil a very thorough soaking of water before they start into growth in late winter. During the spring and summer more water will be required whenever the border shows signs of dryness and enough must be given to soak well down. Under glass the trees should be syringed daily with house-warmed water throughout the growing season, except during the time when they are in bloom and while the peaches are colouring.

Feeding. Just as the trees start into growth a mulch of well-rotted dung, 50 kg per 4·8 sq m (1 cwt per 6 sq yd) should be given. This may be supplemented in the case of old trees that are making insufficient new growth by a nitrogenous fertilizer such as sulphate of ammonia at 28 g per 0·8 sq m (1 oz per sq yd). In addition give sulphate of potash, 56 g per 0·8 sq m (2 oz per sq yd), and in alternate years bonemeal, 113 g (4 oz) to the same area, and hydrated lime 226 (8 oz), again to this area, applied in the autumn.

Thinning. Start to thin fruits as soon as they are of marble size but do not complete thinning until the stones are well formed as there is often a considerable natural fall before this stage. At first reduce fruits to one per cluster but later space out at least 20 cm (8 in) apart.

Temperature. Ventilation should be as free as possible throughout though draughts and sudden drops in temperature should be avoided. Overheating and too dry an atmosphere in the greenhouse will almost certainly result in an attack by red spider mites or frog flies.

Great heat is undesirable at any time. Early peaches and nectarines can be started into growth in late winter by closing the house and raising the temperature to 10°C/50°F. In the summer every effort should be made to keep the temperature below 26°C/79°F. After the crop has been gathered the peach and nectarine house should be thrown wide open, for, as with grape vines, it is essential that peaches and nectarines should become completely dormant during the winter months.

Out of doors fruits may with advantage be exposed to the sun as they ripen by the removal of leaves that shade them or by being propped forward with wooden plant labels or something similar.

Picking. Peaches and nectarines are picked as soon as they are ripe and part readily from the branches. They cannot be kept for more than a few days and bottling or canning provides the only satisfactory means of preserving them.

Varieties. Good peaches are Amsden June, July; Barrington, September; Bellegarde, September; Duke of York, July; Dymond, September; Hale's Early, July-August; Peregrine, August; Rochester, August; Royal George, August and Sea Eagle, September. Of these Peregrine and Rochester are the most reliable for outdoor planting.

Good nectarines are Dryden, August; Early Rivers, July; Elruge, August; Humboldt, August-September; Lord Napier, August; Pine Apple, September and River's Orange, September. Of these Early Rivers is the best for outdoor planting.

PEARS

Pears are not quite so satisfactory in cool climates as either apples or plums but they do well in some districts, particularly those with plenty of sunshine. They are quite suitable for small gardens as they respond to pruning well and can be trained in restricted forms.

Soil. A medium to light, well-drained loam is the best type of soil. In other respects pears need similar conditions to apples. As the flowering season is early it is advisable to choose a sheltered position, otherwise there is danger of the blossom either being killed outright by frost or damaged so badly that fertilization is impeded.

The ground should be prepared in exactly the same way as for apples with a moderate dressing of manure and extra potash, particularly if this is believed to be deficient in the soil. Heavy soils which are liable to become waterlogged in winter must be drained adequately.

The choicest varieties of dessert pear crop most satisfactorily when planted against a wall facing south or south west.

Types of Tree. All the forms commonly employed for apples may also be used for pears but only the less choice varieties should be planted as standards or half-standards. The best dessert pears should be grown as small bushes, pyramids, espalier-trained trees or cordons. Pears make particularly good cordons as most varieties form fruit buds freely and submit to severe pruning readily.

Planting distances are as for apples.

Stocks and Propagation. This is always done by budding or grafting in the same way as for apples. Budding is carried out between mid-summer and early autumn and grafting towards mid-spring.

There are two main groups of stock, the one seedling, which may be obtained from garden pears, perry pears or wildings, and the other quince. The seedling stocks are in general more vigorous than the quince stocks and are therefore more suitable for large trees such as standards and half-standards. However the quince is itself variable and an effort has been made to classify the different types in a manner similar to the Paradise stocks for apples. Two of these types are of importance to the fruit grower and they are known respectively as Quince A and Quince C. The former is the most vigorous, and suitable for bushes; the latter is dwarfing and therefore good for cordons.

Not all varieties of pear make a good union direct with the quince stock in any of these forms. Examples are Jargonelle, Joséphine de Malines, Marguerite Marillat, Marie Louise, Souvenir du Congrès and to a lesser extent Dr Jules Guyot and Williams'. When these varieties are to be grown on quince stocks they are double worked, that is to say first of all another variety that is known to make a good union with quince is grafted to it and then, when it is growing nicely, it is cut back to a convenient height and the incompatible variety is grafted on to it. Pitmaston Duchess and Fertility are often used as intermediate stocks in this way.

Fertility. Most varieties are partially self-fertile, that is to say they will set some fruit with their own pollen but give a better crop if pollinated from another pear tree of different variety. There is little or no incompatibility between one variety and another but a few are unsatisfactory pollinators because they produce little pollen. Provided several varieties of pear are planted fairly near together and they all bloom at approximately the same time, there is unlikely to be much difficulty in securing proper fertilization so long as the weather is favourable at blossom time and the position is a suitable one. The pear, however, like the apple, is dependent on bees to carry pollen and if the weather is cold, damp or windy, or the position very exposed, these insects may not venture far from the hive. Under such conditions it is wise to pollinate by hand with a rabbit's tail or camel-hair brush, bringing the pollen from one tree to another.

Season. By planting early, mid-season and late varieties and storing the two last correctly, ripe pears can be enjoyed from mid-summer until Christmas or later.

Age of Tree. All the remarks made under this heading regarding apples apply equally here.

Planting. This follows exactly the same lines as with apples, with perhaps a little more emphasis on planting only when the soil is in tip-top condition. It is on the whole better to work in the second half of autumn or in late winter/early spring period than in midwinter when weather conditions are seldom favourable.

Treatment of Young Trees. This should be precisely the same as for apples.

Pruning. This should be similar to apples, but as most pears make fruit buds and spurs more readily than apples it is possible to be a little more severe without upsetting the balance of growth. It is for this reason that most pears make such good trained trees. If side growths are shortened to about five leaves in mid- or late summer, most of them will form fruit buds the following year and be further shortened to these the following autumn.

GOOD VARIETIES OF PEAR

Abbreviations: C, cooking; D, dessert; CD, cooking or dessert; SS, self-sterile; PSF, partially self-fertile. Note that Conference is not a suitable pollinator for Beurré d'Amanlis, nor is Seckle for Louise Bonne. Varieties marked sterile should not be planted alone nor used as pollinators for other pears. Even partially self-fertile varieties will give better crops if associated with other varieties of pear flowering at approximately the same time.

Name	Use	Season	Pick	Type	Colour	Flavour	Pruning	Flowering	Fertility	Cropping
Beurré d'Amanlis	D	early autumn	as ripe	medium, pear shaped	yellow, flushed brown	good	moderate to upward-pointing buds	early	SS	good
Beurré Bedford	D	mid-autumn	early autumn	large, tapering	yellow, flushed red	good	moderate	mid-season	PSF	good
Beurré Clairgeau	C	late autumn – early winter	mid-autumn	large, pear shaped	golden brown and red	fair	moderate to outward-pointing buds	early	PSF	very good
Beurré Diel	D	mid-autumn – early winter	early autumn	large, oval	yellow, flushed brown	good	moderate	early	SS	good
Beurré Hardy	D	mid-autumn	early autumn	medium, conical	brown, russet	very good	light	late	PSF	good
Beurré Six	D	late autumn – early winter	mid-autumn	large, pear shaped	light green	good	light	mid-season	PSF	good
Beurré Superfin	D	mid-autumn	early autumn	medium, pear shaped	yellow and russet	very good	fairly hard	mid-season	PSF	good
Bristol Cross	D	mid-autumn	early autumn	large, pear shaped	yellow and russet	good	moderate	mid-season	PSF	good
Catillac	C	early winter – mid-spring	mid-autumn	large, round	green	good cooked	light	mid-season	SS	irregular
Clapp's Favourite	D	late summer – early autumn	as ripe	medium, pear shaped	yellow, striped red	good	moderate to outward-pointing buds	late	PSF	good
Conference	D	mid – late autumn	early autumn	medium, long	green, russet	good	moderate	mid-season	PSF	very good

Name	Use	Season	Pick	Type	Colour	Flavour	Pruning	Flowering	Fertility	Cropping
Dr Jules Guyot	D	early autumn	as ripe	large, oval	yellow, slight flush	good	fairly hard to outward-pointing buds	late	PSF	good
Doyenné du Comice	D	late autumn	mid-autumn	medium, broad pear-shaped	golden russet	very good	fairly hard	late	PSF	unreliable
Doyenné d'Eté	D	mid– late summer	as ripe	small, round	yellow, flushed brown	fair	hard	early	PSF	good
Durondeau	D	mid– late autumn	early autumn	large, pear shaped	brown, flushed red	very good	moderate	mid-season	PSF	good
Emile d'Heyst	D	mid-autumn	early autumn	long, oval	yellow with russet	good	hard, to upward-pointing buds	early	PSF	good
Fertility	CD	mid-autumn	early autumn	medium, conical	russet	poor	fairly hard, to outward-pointing buds	late	PSF	very good
Fondante d'Automne	D	early – mid-autumn	early autumn	medium, round	russet	good	hard to upward-pointing buds	mid-season	PSF	good
Glou Morceau	D	early – mid-winter	mid-autumn	medium, oval	green	very good	fairly hard, to upward-pointing buds	late	PSF	good
Gorham	D	early autumn	as ripe	medium, pear shaped	yellow and russet	good	moderate, to outward-pointing buds	late	PSF	very good
Hessle (Hasel)	D	mid-autumn	early autumn	small, round	brown	fair	light	late	PSF	very good
Jargonelle	D	late summer	as ripe	medium, long	greenish, yellow	good	light	early	SS	very good
Joséphine de Malines	D	early – late winter	mid-autumn	small, conical	greenish, yellow	very good	light	mid-season	PSF	good

Name	Use	Season	Pick	Type	Colour	Flavour	Pruning	Flowering	Fertility	Cropping
Louise Bonne of Jersey	D	mid-autumn	early autumn	medium, conical	yellow, flushed red	very good	moderate, to outward-pointing buds	early	PSF	very good
Marguerite Marillat	D	early – mid-season	early autumn	large, pear shaped	yellow, flushed red	fair	moderate to outward-pointing buds	mid-season	SS	good
Marie Louise	D	mid– late autumn	early autumn	medium, oval	greenish, yellow	good	fairly hard	late	PSF	fair
Merton Pride	D	early autumn	as ripe	medium, pear shaped	green and russet	very good	fairly hard	mid-season	SS	fair
Packhams Triumph	D	mid– late autumn	mid-autumn	large, conical	yellow	good	moderate	late	PSF	good
Pitmaston Duchess	CD	mid– late autumn	mid– late autumn	large, pear shaped	yellow	fair	moderate	late	SS	unreliable
Seckle	D	mid– late autumn	early autumn	small, round	brown	very good	hard to outward-pointing buds	mid-season	PSF	good
Souvenir du Congrès	D	early autumn	as ripe	large, pear shaped	yellow, flushed red	good	fairly hard	mid-season	PSF	good
Thompson's	D	mid– late autumn	mid-autumn	medium, oval	yellow and russet	very good	hard	mid-season	PSF	moderate
Triomphe de Vienne	D	early autumn	as ripe	medium, conical	yellow, flushed red	good	moderate	late	PSF	good
Williams' Bon Chrétien	D	early autumn	as ripe	large, pear shaped	yellow, slight flush	good	moderate	mid-season	PSF	very good
Winter Nelis	D	late autumn – mid-winter	mid-autumn	small, round	green to yellowish	very good	hard	late	PSF	good

However, this severe treatment is not essential and when pears are grown as standards, half-standards or bushes and the main framework of branches has been formed, they can, if desired, be left pretty much alone.

A few varieties have the habit of forming fruit buds at the tips of shoots. With these kinds light pruning is particularly desirable. The most familiar examples are Jargonelle and Joséphine de Malines.

Because of the freedom with which spurs are produced it may be necessary to carry out drastic spur thinning or reduction in the case of old trees. Dehorning (see p. 629) is also beneficial if insufficient new growth is being made.

Feeding. Here again the general instructions given for apples apply also to pears, the two most vital foods being nitrogen and potash. There is, however, if anything a slightly greater necessity for nitrogen with pears than with apples and spring dressings of manure can therefore be a little heavier, say up to 50 kg per 8 sq m (1 cwt per 10 sq yd).

Thinning. This follows the general lines described for apples (p. 651) but should be a little more severe, especially for big dessert pears such as Pitmaston Duchess or Durondeau which may be left as much as 23 cm (9 in) apart.

Picking. Early pears are ready for picking in mid-summer. Like early apples they will not keep and should be used up as gathered. The picking season continues until about mid-autumn and some of the later varieties will store for a period, though few will last as long as the latest apples.

Storing. Pears must be stored in a warmer and drier atmosphere than that necessary for apples. A spare room or airy cupboard is a very good place in which to keep them and they should be spread out in single layers, not packed into boxes like apples. Once ripe they begin to decay from the centre very rapidly, a condition known as sleepiness, and quickly become unfit to eat. Pears in store should therefore be examined frequently and used directly they are in suitable condition before they start to deteriorate.

PLUMS

Plums are easily grown in most parts of the country but on account of their very early flowering season they are apt to crop unreliably in cold or exposed places. Also they do not, as a rule, take kindly to very hard pruning and, as they frequently make a good deal of growth, they are not as suitable for small gardens as are apples or pears. Damsons, being very hard, are sometimes planted as windbreaks.

Soil. The better grades of loam are most suitable. Plums require more nitrogen than apples or pears and more moisture during the growing season. For this reason plum orchards should never be grassed down in the way so common with apple orchards after the first few years. Good drainage is essential. The position should be reasonably open without being too exposed, for the reasons already explained.

The soil can be prepared by thorough digging and the addition of well-rotted dung or compost at the rate of 50 kg per 8·8 sq m (1 cwt per 11 sq yd). At the same time it is desir-

GOOD VARIETIES OF PLUM

Abbreviations: C, cooking; D, dessert; CD, cooking or dessert; SS, self-sterile; SF, self-fertile; PSF, partially self-fertile. Self-fertile varieties should not be planted alone while even partially self-fertile varieties will give better crops if associated with other varieties of plum flowering at approximately the same time.

Name	Use	Season	Type	Colour	Flavour	Flowering	Fertility	Cropping
Belle de Louvain	C	late summer	large, egg-shaped	red	fair	late	SF	good
Black Prince	C	late summer	medium, round	blue-black	good	early	SS	good
Blaisdon Red	C	early autumn	medium, oval	red	poor	mid-season	SF	very good
Bountiful	CD	late summer	large, oval	red	good	mid-season	SF	good
Bryanston Gage	D	early autumn	medium, round	yellowish	very good	mid-season	SS	good
Cambridge Gage	D	early autumn	medium, round	green	very good	late	PSF	good
Coe's Golden Drop	D	early autumn	large, oval	yellow	very good	early	SS	fair
Count Althann's Gage	D	early autumn	large, oval	crimson	good	late	SS	good
Czar	C	late summer	medium, round	black	poor	mid-season	SF	very good
Delicious	D	early autumn	large, oval	red	very good	late	SS	good
Denniston's Superb	D	late summer	medium, round	yellow	very good	early	SF	good
Early Laxton	D	mid-summer	medium, oval	yellow & red	good	mid-season	PSF	fair
Early Transparent Gage	D	late summer	small, round	yellow	very good	late	SF	fair
Giant Prune	C	early autumn	large, oval	purple	fair	late	SF	good

Name	Use	Season	Type	Colour	Flavour	Flowering	Fertility	Cropping
Gisborne's	C	late summer	medium, oval	yellow	poor	late	SF	very good
Golden Transparent Gage	D	mid-autumn	large, round	yellow	very good	early	SF	fair
Green Gage	D	late summer	medium, round	green	very good	late	SS	fair
Jefferson	D	late summer	large, oval	yellow	very good	early	SS	fair
Kirke's	D	early autumn	medium, round	purple	very good	mid-season	SS	fair
Late Transparent Gage	D	early autumn	large, round	yellow	very good	late	SS	fair
Laxton's Gage	D	late summer	medium, round	yellow	very good	mid-season	SF	good
Marjorie's Seedling	CD	mid-autumn	large, oblong	blue-black	good	late	SF	good
Merryweather Damson	C	early autumn	small, round	blue-black	good	mid-season	SF	very good
Monarch	C	early autumn	large, round	purple	fair	early	SF	good
Oullin's Golden Gage	D	late summer	large, round	yellow	very good	late	SF	very good
Pershore	C	late summer	medium, egg-shaped	yellow	fair	mid-season	SF	very good
Pond's Seedling	C	early autumn	large, oval	red	fair	late	SS	good
President	C	mid-autumn	large, oval	purple	good	early	SS	poor
Purple Pershore	C	late summer	medium, oval	red	fair	mid-season	SF	very good
Rivers' Early Prolific	C	mid-summer	small, round	black	good	mid-season	PSF	good
Severn Cross	CD	early autumn	large, oval	yellow	fair	mid-season	SF	very good
Victoria	CD	late summer	large, oval	red	good	mid-season	SF	good
Warwickshire Drooper	C	early autumn	large, oval	yellow	good	early	SF	very good

able to give extra potash either as wood ashes at 196 g per 0·8 sq m (7 oz per sq yd), or sulphate of potash, 42 g (1½ oz) to the same distance.

Types of Tree. Plums succeed particularly well as standards or half-standards as they can be allowed to grow freely with a minimum of pruning once the head of branches has been formed. The drawback is that the trees soon get very large and all cultural operations become difficult, with ladders being required for picking. Both standards and half-standards must be planted a minimum of 6 m (20 ft) apart. Plums can also be grown as bushes planted 4·5-6 m (15-20 ft) apart and choice dessert varieties are often trained against sunny walls, in which case the fan system is usually employed. Such specimens should be at least 3·6 m (12 ft) apart. Even when trained the more freedom plum trees can have the better, for example, a high wall is better than a low one.

Propagation. This is almost invariably carried out by budding in summer though grafting in spring is occasionally employed.

A number of stocks are used. Myrobalan B and Brompton are vigorous and suitable for standard and half-standard trees. Common Plum and St Julien A are moderately dwarfing and suitable for bush or fan-trained trees. Some varieties of plum are incompatible with common Plum but St Julien A is suitable for all varieties. Common Mussell is semi-vigorous, Mariana more vigorous and trees on it are slow to come into bearing. Suckers from the Pershore Plum make good stocks for plums to be grown as small bushes. The most dwarfing stock is Pixy.

There are just a few varieties of plum which are occasionally grown on their own roots and can be increased by suckers. Notable amongst these are Blaisdon Red, Pershore and Warwickshire Drooper. The suckers are removed with roots just after mid-autumn and planted in the ordinary way. It must be stressed, however, that this method of propagation is only possible if the plum is on its own roots. If it has been grafted or budded, the suckers will resemble the stock.

Fertility. Some plums are fully self-fertile, but more are either self-sterile or partially self-sterile and need a mate flowering at approximately the same time.

It should be noted that poor fertility in plums is quite as often due to bad weather at blossom time as to lack of suitable pollen. Hand pollination and the provision of some shelter will often solve the fertility problem.

Season. The earliest plums are ripe in mid-summer and the season continues until mid-autumn. There is no method of keeping plums once they have been picked other than by bottling or canning.

Age of Tree. The remarks already made with regard to most tree fruits such as apples and pears apply equally to plums. Other things being equal, the younger the tree at the time of planting the more likely it is to make a good start. The drawback to planting young trees is that plums are sometimes slow in coming into bearing. If one starts with a maiden it may be six or seven years before any crop is gathered.

Planting. This should be done during good weather from about mid-autumn to early spring. Plums are surface rooting and so must not be planted too deeply. Spread the roots out in wide, rather shallow holes and cover the uppermost with about 10 cm (4 in) of soil. Be sure to plant very firmly and, with large trees, make certain that they are properly staked; in fact two stakes per tree, one vertical and the other inclined towards the direction of the prevailing wind are often desirable.

Treatment of Young Trees. Though established plums do not like hard pruning, it is advisable to be fairly severe after planting. In any case the main shoots must be cut back to the points at which branches are required as explained in Chapter 27.

A good mulch of strawy manure or grass clippings applied in the spring following planting will help to keep the trees growing strongly. This is particularly important with plums in the early stages because if they don't get off to a good start it is sometimes difficult to get them going again. Apart from this no special treatment is called for during the first year.

Pruning. Young trees are shaped by the ordinary methods applied to apples and pears but a changeover should be made to lighter pruning at an earlier stage. This is not difficult because as a rule plums branch quite freely on their own account; in fact by the fourth or fifth year it may be necessary to carry out some thinning of branches to prevent overcrowding, rather than keep on pruning for fresh branch formation.

Once the trees are well formed very little pruning is required except for trained specimens. Watch for dead or diseased wood so that it may be removed promptly. For the rest it is generally sufficient to cut out a crossing branch here and there and keep the centre of the tree reasonably open. It is an advantage to do as much as possible of this pruning directly the plums have been gathered. The reason for this departure from normal pruning practice is that there is less danger of infection by silver leaf, the worst disease of plums, if pruning is done in summer or early autumn than if it is done in winter.

Trained trees can be pruned to a very large extent during the summer months, the system followed being almost identical with that for apples, that is to say side growths which cannot be trained in at full length are shortened to about five leaves when they start to become hard and woody at the base, usually during mid-summer. These summer-pruned side growths can be further cut back when they form fruit buds the following season.

Feeding. This is similar to that carried out for apples but with greater emphasis on nitrogen and less on potash. The plum orchard must never be cultivated deeply because of the number of surface roots formed but a good mulch of dung or compost applied each spring will feed these roots and protect them at the same time. As much as 50 kg per 6·4 sq m (1 cwt per 8 sq yd) can be given to trees that are not making too much new growth. Failing dung or compost use a nitrogenous fertilizer such as sulphate of ammonia at 28 g per 0·8 sq m (1 oz per sq yd). In any case give sulphate of potash at the same rate and every alternate autumn also give bonemeal at 113 g (4 oz) to the same area.

QUINCES

Few quinces are grown in cool climates but perhaps if it were realized what excellent jam and jelly they make and how freely the trees crop they might be seen more often.

Soil. Quinces require precisely the same conditions as pears with perhaps a little more emphasis on moisture during the season of growth. This does not mean, however, that they will thrive in stagnant, waterlogged soils. A good, rich loam with plenty of humus is ideal.

Types of Tree. Quinces could be grown in practically any of the forms used for pears but are almost invariably grown as bushes.

Propagation. The quince can be increased by layering (p. 622), and bushes which are known to be on their own roots can also be propagated by suckers detached with roots in autumn. Occasionally selected quinces are grafted or budded on to common forms, in which case the suckers will be of this common type and cannot be used to increase the improved variety worked on it.

Fertility. Quinces are fully self-fertile and will also pollinate pears or can be pollinated by pears.

Age of Tree. As for pears.

Planting. As for pears.

Treatment of Young Trees. As for pears.

Pruning. After the initial stages of formation, which are the same as for pears, very little pruning is required; just a little thinning out to prevent overcrowding and to preserve the chosen shape of the bush. This can be done in autumn or winter.

Feeding. As a rule very little feeding is required but if the bushes do not make sufficient growth or fail to crop satisfactorily, they can be fed in the same manner as pears.

Varieties. The best variety is Vranja but others sometimes available are Champion, Ludovic, Pear-Shaped and Serbian.

RASPBERRIES

Raspberries flower comparatively late and so it is possible to obtain crops in many places where other fruits fail. It is of the utmost importance to obtain healthy stock at the outset, as raspberries are susceptible to various virus diseases.

Soil. The conditions which suit raspberries best very closely resemble those required for black currants. The soil should be reasonably rich, well supplied with moisture during the spring and summer but not waterlogged in winter. The last point is of vital importance. There is probably no fruit which reacts more quickly to bad drainage and it is one of the commonest causes of failure.

The soil should be particularly well cultivated at the outset as raspberries make masses of fine roots just beneath the surface, so that very little cultivation can be carried out once the plantation has been made. The plot should be dug deeply, dressed with well-rotted dung at the rate of 50 kg per 6·4–8 sq m (1 cwt per 8–10 sq yd), and given additional potash such as sulphate of potash at 56 g per 0·8 sq m (2 oz per sq yd).

The situation may be open or in partial shade but should not be under overhanging trees.

Propagation. The raspberry is increased by means of offshoots or suckers which are freely produced without any special encouragement. These suckers should be removed with roots at any time during the normal planting season. The only important point to note is that suckers must not only be perfectly healthy themselves but must be produced from plants which are also healthy. Failure to observe this point results in the spread of disease and accounts for the weakness of so many raspberry plantations.

Fertility. No problems of self- or inter-fertility occur with raspberries. All varieties will set fruit with their own pollen and as a rule no difficulties occur. Occasionally one meets plantations in which the set is very bad or many of the fruits are malformed. More often than not this is due to a faulty strain, that is to say it is a hereditary characteristic. The only remedy is to scrap the entire stock and replant with good canes. Bad setting may also be due to the raspberry beetle (see p. 758).

Season. The normal raspberry season is mid-summer but there are also kinds which fruit in the autumn and some varieties will bear a double crop, one in summer and another in autumn, but both crops may be reduced so it is more sensible to plant separately for each season.

Age of Plants. Only year-old canes can be used for planting as, after fruiting, the canes die down and only the young growth remains. Indeed the raspberry plantation itself should not be retained too long, a good policy being to remake a quarter of the plantation every year.

Planting. This can be done at any time from mid-autumn to early spring, but the best results are seldom obtained from mid-winter planting. If the work cannot be completed by late autumn it is generally best to leave it until the spring. Late planting often gives very good results provided the plants are well cared for and not allowed to suffer from drought.

Plant the canes singly 60 cm (2 ft) apart in rows 1·8 m (6 ft) apart. Spread the roots out widely and cover the uppermost with only 5 cm (2 in) of soil. Make the soil very firm.

Treatment of Young Plants. After planting the canes must be cut back to within about 23 cm (9 in) of soil level. With autumn-planted stock this can be done late the following winter but if planting is left to the spring pruning should be done immediately. No crop will be produced the first year except in the case of autumn-fruiting varieties but the hard pruning should result in plenty of young growth to fruit the following year. These new canes are generally tied to wires strained between posts, 2·4–3 m (8–10 ft) apart. As a rule two training wires are sufficient, one 60 cm (2 ft) and the other 1·5 m (5 ft) above ground level.

A generous mulch of strawy manure or grass clippings should be spread all over the plantation in mid- to late spring. Weeds should be removed by hand, by very light hoeing or by the use of a safe weedkiller such as glyphosate. At no time must a fork or spade be used near raspberry canes for fear of damaging the surface roots.

No pruning of summer-fruiting varieties will be required the first year, after the initial hard cutting back described above.

Pruning. In subsequent years summer-fruiting raspberries are pruned as soon as possible after the crop has been gathered. All the canes that have just borne fruit are cut out at ground level. Some growers reduce the young canes to six or seven per root at the same time, choosing those that are strongest and nearest to the training wires. My own policy is to allow the plants rather more freedom. The young canes are thinned to about 23 cm (9 in) apart and any which are growing right out in the alleyways between the rows are removed but otherwise each plant is allowed to spread to a considerable extent. After a year or so a row of raspberries presents rather the appearance of a thin hedge, perhaps 60 cm (2 ft) or more wide and with canes evenly spaced throughout. It appears that the fruits benefit from the shade provided by the surrounding canes, though more feeding and mulching is required because of the heavy demands made on the soil.

Some varieties grow very strongly and with these it is desirable to shorten the young canes a little in late winter. They may be cut back to a level height of about 1·8 m (6 ft). With shorter kinds this supplementary pruning is not necessary.

A different system of pruning is needed for autumn-fruiting raspberries. These are left until late winter when all the canes are cut back to within 23 cm (9 in) of soil level.

In the case of Lloyd George and other varieties, which are mainly summer fruiting but may also produce a small autumn crop, the best policy is to prune as for summer raspberries. Then, in late winter, shorten by 30 cm (1 ft) or so any canes which, in autumn, bore fruit at their tips only and remove any canes which, in autumn, fruited throughout their length.

Feeding. The most important item in the routine feeding of raspberries is a good annual mulch of strawy dung applied in the first half of spring at the rate of 50 kg per 5·6 sq m (1 cwt per 7 sq yd). This serves the dual purpose of feeding the roots and protecting them from drought. The dung can be used at the rate of 50 kg per 6·4 sq m (1 cwt per 8 sq yd), but it must be well decayed. If dung is not available, decayed vegetable refuse such as grass clippings can be used in the same way. At the same time sulphate of potash should be applied at 56 g (2 oz) to the same area.

Virus Disease. Raspberries are liable to be attacked by incurable virus diseases which may sap them of strength and greatly reduce cropping. That known as mosaic is particularly common. It produces a yellow mottling or variegation of the leaves and reduced growth. Some varieties are more susceptible than others or suffer more severely. Lloyd George is one of the worst in these respects. Always buy certified virus-free stock.

Picking and Storing. Raspberries can be bottled, canned or frozen.

Varieties. Good raspberries are Autumn Bliss, autumn; Delight, early mid-season; Glen

Pegging down strawberry runners. A small flower pot has been sunk in the ground from which the new plant can easily be transplanted

Clova, early; Glen Moy, early; Glen Prosen, mid to late; Heritage, autumn; Leo, very late; Malling Admiral, late; Malling Jewel, mid-season; Malling Orion, mid-season; Malling Promise, early; September, autumn; and Zeva, autumn.

STRAWBERRIES

Strawberries are not at all difficult to grow. The only trouble is that many plants are required in order to obtain good pickings throughout the season. Most amateurs make the mistake of having too small a strawberry bed with the result that they can only fill a dish with fruit for a few days at the height of the season. A bed of a hundred plants is about the smallest that will be adequate for a family of two adults and two children.

Soil. Most strawberries do well on rich, medium to heavy loams provided they are properly drained in winter. A few varieties, such as Royal Sovereign, do well on sandy loams. If drainage is bad the plants are apt to rot but this difficulty can be overcome by planting along the summits of broad, low ridges. On light soils it is essential to manure heavily, as much to maintain moisture in summer as for the sake of the food which the dung contains. In any case the soil must be dug deeply and it is wise to add dung or compost at the rate of not less than 50 kg per 6·4 sq m (1 cwt per 8 sq yd). Phosphates are of more importance with strawberries than with other fruits and so bonemeal can be used in the initial preparation at 113 g to 0·8 sq m (4 oz per sq yd). Additional potash should be given as for raspberries.

Propagation. Alpine strawberries, which are varieties with very small fruits and a prolonged fruiting season, are usually increased by seed which can be raised in a warm greenhouse in late winter or in a frame in the first half of spring. The seedlings, after hardening off, are planted out in early summer. They fruit a little the first summer and give a full crop the second year.

All the familiar large-fruited strawberries are propagated by runners which are freely produced throughout the summer.

It is good policy to set aside a few plants specially for propagation, removing the flowers and so encouraging the production of runners. If propagation is carried out on the ordinary fruiting bed it is apt to become a tangle of growth by the end of the summer. Anyway it is advisable to restrict plants to no more than six runners each.

Plantlets are formed several centimetres along each runner but only one should be retained and that the nearest to the parent plant. The tip of the runner must be pinched off immediately beyond this.

The plantlets will often root themselves where they touch the soil but a more satisfactory method is to peg them down to the soil with a piece of wire bent like a hairpin. Some growers peg them into small pots filled with potting soil and sunk to their rims in the strawberry bed. This makes it possible to transplant the rooted runners with little or no check.

If all goes well the plantlets will be rooted nicely in about five to six weeks, when the runners can be severed from the parent plants. Wait a further week, then lift the rooted plantlets with good balls of soil and transfer them to the new bed.

It is of great importance to propagate only from thoroughly healthy and vigorous plants which come from a stock of proved cropping capacity. Failure to observe these precautions will result in rapid deterioration of stock.

Fertility. A few varieties of strawberry are partially or fully self-sterile, due to the fact that they produce little or no good pollen of their own, but none of the popular varieties suffers from this fault.

Season. The main strawberry season is early and mid-summer, but there are both early and late varieties as well as so-called perpetual-fruiting or remontant varieties which crop from mid-summer to mid-autumn.

Age of Plants. It is essential to start with young plants, seedlings in the case of alpines and freshly rooted runners with the large-fruited strawberries. The strawberry bed soon wears out and becomes unprofitable and so it is wise to renew it frequently. The usual practice is to replace a third of the bed every year so that no plant is retained for more than three years, though some growers prefer to cut this period to two years.

Planting. This can be done in late summer, early autumn or spring but undoubtedly the best results are obtained from late summer/early autumn planting. If runners are to be ready by this time they must be pegged down early, which is one of the advantages of having a separate bed for propagation.

The vital point about planting is to keep the crown of each plant level with the surface of the soil. If the crown is buried it is almost certain to rot during winter. This means that the uppermost part of the roots is only just covered with soil. Make the plants thoroughly firm, otherwise the soil will settle away from them and leave some of the roots exposed, which is quite as bad as having the crowns covered.

If the planting is to be left until early spring it is a considerable advantage to use potrooted runners. In any case spring-planted strawberries should not be allowed to fruit the first summer. Any flowers which they produce should be cut off at once.

Space large-fruited and remontant strawberries 38 cm (1¼ ft) apart in rows 76 cm (2½ ft) apart. These distances may be reduced a little for alpine kinds.

Care of the Plants. Clean straw or the special mats sold for the purpose should be placed around the plants in late spring, just before they come into flower. The straw serves a double purpose: it keeps the berries clear of the soil and so preserves them from mud splashes and it makes a useful mulch, which encourages root growth. The straw or mats should be removed in late summer as they may harbour pests or disease spores.

Apart from this the principal cultural operation is to remove any runners not required for propagation. This should be done frequently throughout the summer as the runners, if left, make an unnecessary drain on the strength of the plants, reducing their capacity to fruit the following year.

Protection from birds is another essential. Either the strawberry bed can be made in a permanent fruit cage covered with wire netting or small-mesh garden netting can be spread over a suitable framework when the berries begin to colour. Care must be taken to see that there are no holes nor any spaces left at soil level.

Some growers make a practice of burning the straw on the beds instead of removing it. This is done on a dry and rather windy day so that the straw is kept burning briskly and does not smoulder too long around any particular plant. All the strawberry foliage is destroyed but the plants quickly recover and the treatment kills a lot of pests.

Feeding. An annual mulch of dung given in mid-spring in the same way as for raspberries should be the staple item in routine feeding. It may be supplemented by an application made at the same time of superphosphate of lime, 85 g, per 0·8 sq m (3 oz per sq yd), and sulphate of potash, 56 g (2 oz) to the same area.

Strawberries under Glass. Strawberries can be forced quite easily if early rooted runners are transferred in mid-summer to 15 cm (6 in) pots filled with J.I. No. 2 (see p. 423). The pots should be placed in a frame but no protection need be given until mid-autumn. From then onwards protection will be required during very cold weather though ventilation should be given freely during favourable periods.

From mid-winter to early spring the plants can be removed, in suitable batches, to a greenhouse with an average temperature of about 10°C/50°F. Arrange them as near the glass as possible and in a light place. Water sparingly at first but more freely as the plants grow and flowers are produced. These flowers must be fertilized by hand with a camel-hair brush. From this stage onwards the temperature can be raised little by little to a maximum of 21°C/70°F as the fruits swell and colour, but it is advisable to let it drop again to 15°C/59°F for the last few days.

Another method of enjoying early strawberries is to cover some of the plants in the ordinary outdoor bed with cloches placed in position about early winter. Little or no ventilation will be required but if the weather is bright and sunny it may be necessary to shade lightly with whitewash for the last week or so. Polythene tunnel cloches can be used.

Deterioration of Stock. Strawberries often deteriorate rather rapidly largely due to infection by virus diseases. It is unwise to purchase any strawberry plants unless they are known to be healthy or, better, carry a certificate for freedom from virus.

Picking and Storing. Strawberries can be bottled, canned or frozen.

Varieties. Good summer-fruiting varieties are Cambridge Favourite, second early; Cambridge Late Pine, late; Cambridge Vigour, first early; Elista, mid-season; Gorella, early; Grandee, mid-season; Maxim, mid-season; Pantagruella, early; Tamella, mid-season; Totem, mid-season. Good remontant varieties are Aromel, Gento and Rabunda. A good alpine strawberry is Baron Solemacher.

Part 6

Dealing with Foes

Chapter 31

Diagnosis and Treatment

I do not regard it as part of the amateur gardener's job to be able to identify any great number of the multitudinous pests and diseases which may afflict his plants, but I do think that every keen amateur should be able to make a rough diagnosis of those symptoms which will enable him to identify them as characteristic of a certain group of allied troubles, and to recognize at sight a few extremely common foes. The purpose of this chapter is to satisfy these two needs.

GROUP DIAGNOSIS

The value of the general classification is that it will often suggest a line of treatment which can at least be pursued while the advice of an expert is being sought – and I certainly advise that in all cases of doubt advantage should be taken of one of the many services which exist.

When faced with any unusual condition in plants one should first ask oneself the question 'Is this likely to be the work of some animal (including, under this heading, insects), is it a disease caused by an infection of some kind, or could it be put down to weather or faulty cultivation?' As a rule a little investigation will reveal the answer.

Pests. This is a convenient term under which to group all the troubles caused by animals. Quite a lot of this kind of damage is too obvious to need any explanation. A tree that has been badly barked tells its own tale though one may not, at first sight, be quite certain whether the bark has been removed by the gnawing of rabbits or rats, the chewing of cattle or goats, the clawing of cats or the penknife of a mischievous child.

When whole pieces are removed from leaves, stems or fruits one can be fairly certain that a bird or an animal is responsible, though it may be a very small one – for do not forget that throughout I am using 'animals' in its widest sense and including slugs, woodlice, caterpillars, beetles, weevils, etc. Often a close search of the plant or its surroundings will reveal the culprit and if it can be found actually at work all doubt will be set at rest. A good many pests feed at night and hide by day, so when other methods have failed it is always wise to visit the plants after dark and examine them carefully with a torch.

There are many insects which live on plants without ever taking a bite out of them. These are suckers of sap and they usually work with such a fine proboscis or probe that they leave no visible wound. All the greenflies, blackflies and other aphids belong to this group as do the allied capsid bugs which do so much damage to fruit trees and garden plants, also red spider mites, thrips, frog hoppers, leaf hoppers, white fly and scale insects. Fortunately many of these stay put on their chosen host for quite long periods, so are easy enough to identify, though in some cases a small hand lens may be needed to make them plainly visible. Always have a good look at the tender tips of young shoots and the undersides of the younger leaves if you have any cause to suspect that foes of this type are at work. Sucking insects will usually check growth and cause some yellowing, mottling, streaking or silvering, often accompanied by distortion and severe cockling. These will quite likely be the first symptoms to attract the gardener's eye, and it will only be after closer inspection that the insects themselves will be detected.

Diseases. A great many of the diseases which affect plants are caused by fungi. Often the symptoms are easy even for the novice to recognize. Powdery mildew, for example, causes a very obvious powdery white outgrowth on the leaves and stems of plants. Downy mildews are a little less distinctive since the powdering of white mould is usually much fainter and confined to the undersides of the leaves, which turn yellow or develop yellow spots. It is sometimes important to distinguish one group of mildews from the other since the chemicals which control one do not always so effectively control the other. Treat powdery mildew with a benomyl or thiophanate-methyl spray, and downy mildew with mancozeb.

Then there are moulds which produce fluffy white outgrowths similar to those one finds on mouldy jam or bread. Grey mould or botrytis is one of the commonest diseases of this kind, attacking most plants and being most severe in damp, cool conditions. It can work havoc in autumn and winter in inadequately heated, overwatered greenhouses.

Rusts are so called because they produce rusty-looking spots on the leaves or stems attacked and there are a whole host of spot diseases in which brown or blackish spots of varying size develop, usually on leaves or fruits. Spotting can be caused by other agencies than fungi, such as spraying with a caustic fluid, but a tell-tale characteristic of the fungus spot is that it spreads outwards, gradually getting bigger and bigger. If it is examined closely it will be seen that the central part, usually the darkest, is completely dead whereas the marginal area is in process of destruction.

There are also a number of fungi which attack plants at soil level. Damping off is a disease of this type and one which every gardener with a greenhouse or frame will meet before long. The stem rots right through and the plant topples over just as if it had been bitten off at soil level. There are, in fact, soil caterpillars and other creatures which will eat through stems at just this point and at first the beginner may be puzzled to distinguish damage of this character caused by a pest from that due to a disease, but a little experience will teach him that the insect always makes a clean job of it whereas the stem that has been destroyed by fungi is more or less blackened in the process.

There are a few plant diseases which are caused by bacteria and these are not easy for the amateur to diagnose in a general way, though he may learn to distinguish a few specific and common kinds such as the soft rot of cabbages and celery in which the decay starts from the middle and is of a slimy nature. There is also a highly distinctive and rather common bacterial canker of cherries which causes the bark to decay, often in the crotch where main branches join the stem. Other distinctive symptoms are gum oozing from the rotting bark and clean-edged circular holes in the leaves from which this is sometimes called shot-hole disease. But as a rule it would be wise to regard suspected bacterial diseases as requiring the advice of an expert.

The last group of diseases is due to virus infection. There are a great many of these and some of them are difficult for the amateur to diagnose as the symptoms are very much like those caused by bad cultivation, in fact it is quite certain that a great many of the failures which once were ascribed, even by experts, to overwatering, overfeeding and the like were, in fact, caused by unrecognized viruses. Some of the curious leaf deformities caused by virus infections can also be simulated by spray or vapour from hormone weedkillers drifting on to the plants. But it can be said with safety that if a plant is very much deformed or dwarfed, or if its leaves are curiously variegated or streaked, virus infection is likely. Show a sample to an expert as quickly as possible. Viruses are carried from plant to plant mainly by sucking insects such as aphids and thrips so their presence indicates virus infection is likely.

Physiological Disorders. Under this heading are grouped all those ailments which are caused, not by an outside organism be it pest or disease, but by some fault in the actual living conditions of the plant. These troubles are sometimes the most difficult of all to diagnose and it is certainly hard to think of any general rules which will enable the novice to distinguish them from the effects of certain fungi and viruses.

Draughts and drought will both cause leaf scorching and so will exposure to excessive heat (especially under glass) or to some kinds of fumes, notably those from creosote or a badly adjusted paraffin lamp. Creosote and its fumes can cause severe scorching, so it is unwise to use it near plants. Use safe preservatives instead. Scorching can also be due to lack of potash or magnesium in the soil and to an overdose of certain fertilizers, or to the direct effect upon the leaves of some chemicals. In all these cases the damage can be distinguished from the browning caused by fungus disease by the fact that it ends quite cleanly and sharply, and does not tail off to a zone in which the tissue is in the process of destruction as the fungus grows through it. The damaged part of the leaf is, as a rule, quite dry and papery and may even appear transparent when held up to the light. Admittedly dry spotting is a feature of some virus diseases but generally such spots are quite small and accompanied by other symptoms such as distortion or variegation which give them away.

Bad drainage will often produce a progressive yellowing of the foliage until, if the condition is not rectified, the plant dies. This occurs commonly with pot plants grown in badly drained pots and the cause may often be traced to earthworms which have entered the pots through the drainage holes and blocked them with their casts. The remedy, in this case, is to stand the pots on slates, boards or sharp boiler ashes through which worms cannot pass.

A rather special case of drainage trouble is often found in low-lying orchards. Here the trouble occurs in winter when roots die through drowning but it is not noticed at first because the trees are dormant. Growth starts apparently normally in the spring but is, in fact, sustained only by the sap remaining in the branches. Directly this is exhausted the leaves collapse and within a few weeks the trees are quite dead.

Some queer symptoms can be caused by deficiency of certain essential foods in the soil. I have already referred to the scorching which may be caused by lack of potash or magnesium. With potash deficiency it is the leaf margin that is most damaged, whereas with magnesium scorching there is a smudgy discolouration between the veins of the leaves which may look extremely like a fungal disease to an inexperienced eye. A central decay of the roots of beetroots and swedes may be caused by boron deficiency or the growing tips of plants may wither as if scorched. This can be common with sunflowers which are sensitive indicators of boron deficiency. Severe yellowing of many plants may result from a shortage of iron or manganese, a condition known as chlorosis. This is especially likely to occur in chalky or limy soils and must then be rectified by applying iron and/or manganese sequestrols. In all cases where this kind of trouble is suspected it is wise to consult an expert as harm may result from wrong treatment.

As the autumn approaches it is inevitable that the leaves of most outdoor plants suffer an increasing amount of weather damage, which may vary in intensity from a slight spotting to extensive discoloration. In spring late frosts will often play havoc with tender young leaves and shoots, while some plants may be killed outright especially if they have been raised in a warm greenhouse and put out with insufficient hardening off. Chilling at this season may result in a complete cessation of growth and a change in the colour of leaves from normal green to a bluish or purplish shade.

GROUP TREATMENT

While the number of different pests and diseases which may attack garden plants is very great the number of remedial or preventive measures suitable of use in private gardens is comparatively small. In practice the amateur will find that just as he is using the same half dozen or so fertilizers in different combinations for practically all his plants so a very few stock remedies will see him through most of his troubles if applied at the right time and in the right way. Therein lies the value of the group classification outlined, for once the trouble can be placed in its right class it is highly probable that a suitable treatment can be determined without bothering to find out the precise pest or disease responsible.

Biting Insects. Suppose, for example, we decide that the damage is due to an animal which bites holes in the stems or leaves. It may be a caterpillar, a beetle or a weevil but it is highly probable that the quickest way to get rid of it will be to poison it much as one would poison rats or mice. Several suitable poisons are available.

Derris and pyrethrum derivatives are mainly insect poisons which can be used with relative safety, except that derris must not contaminate pools containing fish, to which it is very poisonous. HCH and carbaryl are effective against many biting insects. They are sold under various trade names, invariably combined with other chemicals to increase their range of effectiveness.

The essential in all cases is to apply the appropriate spray or dust to the plants at the first sign of attack and to cover all the leaves as evenly as possible so that the insect, whatever it may be, cannot take a bite anywhere without absorbing a fatal dose of poison at the same time. Some of these chemicals also act by contact with the body of the insect.

Sucking Insects. If diagnosis suggests the sucking rather than the biting type of pest the line of attack may have to be slightly different because the insect lives on the sap direct, without taking pieces out of the surface of the leaf. Either it will be necessary to poison the sap itself with what is known as a systemic insecticide such as dimethoate or the gardener can make use of what are known as contact poisons, that is chemicals which kill merely by coming in direct contact with the body of the insect. HCH, permethrin, malathion, pirimiphos-methyl and derris all operate in this way, so they are very good general insecticides to use when in doubt. Of the systemic insecticides, dimethoate is one of the best to use in the garden.

Fungal Diseases. If a rough diagnosis points to a disease caused by a fungus, the choice of a remedy will be equally restricted. Some compound of copper or sulphur is almost certain to give results and those in most general use are various proprietary fungicides based on copper oxides or copper oxychlorides, colloidal copper and colloidal sulphur sprays. Other useful fungicides which do not contain either copper or sulphur are captan and thiram. The sulphur sprays are particularly effective against mildews of all kinds and for fruit trees, whereas the copper sprays are more suitable for spots and rusts in the vegetable and flower garden. Thiram is an excellent general fungicide with a wide band of effectiveness. Captan is a fungicide which is widely used against rose black spot and apple and pear scab. There are also systematic fungicides like benomyl and triforine which enter the sap and so cannot be washed off by rain.

Though these fungicides – the correct name for any chemicals which kill fungi – can be used to check the further spread of diseases which have already made their appearance they are much more effective as preventives and it is for this reason that many gardeners carry out regular routine spraying year by year whatever does, or does not, turn up. Surface fungicides should always cover the leaves completely, above and below, so that wherever the spore of a fungus starts to grow it will come in contact with a film of chemical poisonous to it.

It is possible to purchase both copper and sulphur dusts for use where a dry powder is more convenient than a wet spray.

Virus Diseases. So far no satisfactory spray has been found to combat virus diseases once plants are infected by them, but as they are spread mainly by sucking insects, principally aphids and thrips, any measures taken to reduce the number of these pests by suitable sprayings or fumigations will also limit the virus. In addition infected plants should be destroyed so that they cease to act as carriers. Healthy plants can sometimes be produced from virus-infected plants by heat treatment or by taking tiny cuttings from the

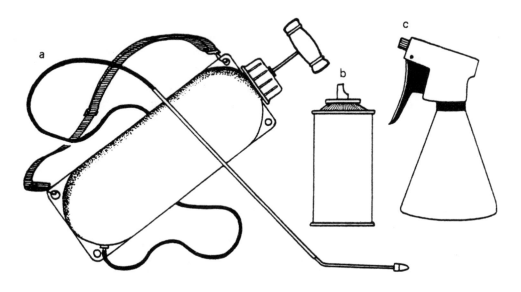

Types of sprayer. (a) Knapsack pressure sprayer; (b) Aerosol sprayer; (c) Hand spray with trigger action

growing tips of shoots, or by a combination of the two, but these are techniques requiring great accuracy and skill and are really only for professional use.

Bacterial Diseases. These mostly defy treatment and leave the gardener with the thankless task of promptly destroying every infected plant as the best possible means of preventing further trouble. Something can also be achieved by keeping down slugs and snails and protecting plants from wounds through which infection may enter.

Physiological Disorders. With these the remedy is almost always the obvious one of removing as quickly as possible the faulty condition which has caused the trouble. However, do not rush from one extreme to another. Because a plant has been in too cold a place it will not help to transfer it to one which is too hot; nor, if the soil has been short of some essential food, is it wise to apply the appropriate fertilizer at rates in excess of those ordinarily recommended. What is needed is to restore matters to normal and keep them there.

Soil Pests and Diseases. So far the treatments suggested have been applicable mainly to those foes which attack the aerial parts of plants. But there are also a number of pests and diseases which are to be found in the soil and in the main attack the roots or lower parts of their victims. Many soil insects can be driven out or killed using treatments which include pirimiphos-methyl or phoxim.

Some pests can be trapped, and such baits as sliced potatoes or carrots are frequently used for the purpose. These are impaled on sharpened sticks and buried just beneath the surface. Then they can be lifted every other day and any insects feeding on them collected and destroyed.

Slugs, snails, woodlice and leatherjackets can be poisoned in various ways. A very little powdered metaldehyde mixed with bran makes a good slug and snail poison. Ready-prepared slug baits are available and also liquid preparations of metaldehyde which can be suitably diluted and applied from a watering-can fitted with a fine rose. Methiocarb is another slug and snail killer which may prove more effective than metaldehyde in wet weather.

To kill fungi in the lawn use a benomyl or carbendazim based treatment. Thiophanate-methyl will tackle club-root, though the best method of ridding land altogether of the club-root organism is to keep it well limed, for this is a fungus which thrives in acid soil. By contrast, the fungus which causes the rough scabs on the skin of potatoes thrives in alkaline soil and so is encouraged by lime.

Where soil is heavily infected with disease-causing organisms or pests some form of sterilization is usually the only method by which they can be cleared completely. Unfortunately this is too costly to be carried out on a large scale and must usually be confined to seed and potting composts (see p. 423) and greenhouse borders. Most amateurs are likely to prefer buying ready-prepared composts at a nursery or garden centre to save the fuss of mixing their own, even though this could be somewhat more expensive.

Either heat or chemicals may be used to sterilize soil, or more accurately, partially sterilize it for that is all that is desirable. Complete sterilization would render it unfit for cultivation for a considerable period.

Heat may be applied dry or wet but extremes either way are to be avoided because

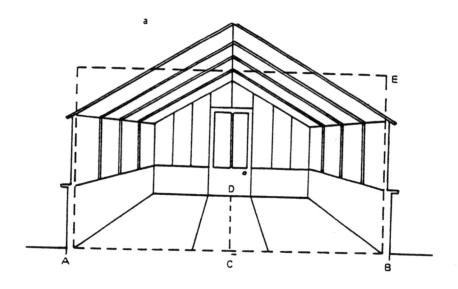

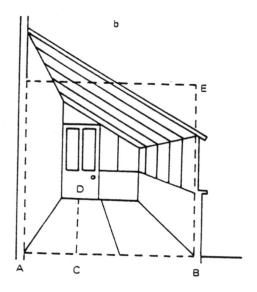

Calculating the volume of a greenhouse for fumigation purposes. (a) A span-roofed house. Multiply the breadth (AB), the length (CD) and the height (BE) to halfway up the roof slope. The result will give the cubic capacity of the house in whatever measurement unit has been chosen. (b) A lean-to house. Here again the breadth (AB) is multiplied by the length (CD) and the height (BE) halfway up the slope of the roof either may have a bad effect upon the texture of the soil. For this reason steam is one of the best sources of heat as it will neither char the soil nor make it sodden. Sometimes special apparatus can be obtained for steaming large or small quantities of soil, but quite satisfactory results can be obtained in a large, closed vessel (the old-fashioned domestic copper was ideal) if the soil is placed in a small sack and suspended over, but not actually in, several centimetres of fast-boiling water. Let the soil be rather dry to begin with and do not try to handle too much at a time – a bucketful will be ample. Get the water boiling fast before the sack is placed in position and then clap a lid over all and cover with further sacks to trap the heat. The ideal is to raise the temperature of the soil as quickly as possible to about 93°C/200°F and keep it at that for 20 minutes or so. Very slow heating or over-long sterilization are equally undesirable.

Paths and Greenhouses. Special formulations of tar oil are marketed for clearing algae, fungi and other undesirable organisms from paths, greenhouses structures and so on. If used strictly according to the maker's instructions, these can also be used to sterilize the soil in greenhouse borders. The soil must then be left unplanted for about two months or preferably more.

GREENHOUSE FUMIGATION

In a closed space vapour or smoke has many advantages over either a liquid or a dust as a pest killer because every nook and cranny is penetrated and there can be no question of some part of the plant being missed.

Some chemicals can be vaporized and small electric vaporizers are available. These and the chemicals supplied by the manufacturers for use in them should be used strictly in accordance with the instructions supplied.

Another method is to combine the insecticide or fungicide with a pyrotechnic achemical to make a little smoke bomb. When ignited the pellet or cone gives off a dense cloud of smoke which carries the insecticide or fungicide with it and deposits it in a fine film all over the plants in the house. Label instructions will state the area each pellet or cone will treat. To find this capacity measure the length, breadth and height of the greenhouse to a point halfway between eaves and ridge and multiply the three figures together. Place the required number of pellets at intervals down the path and ignite them quickly, one after the other, staryting at the far end of the house. Leave the greenhouse at once, making sure it is tightly closed, and do not re-enter until all the smoke has disappeared.

HCH, permethrin and pirimiphos-methyl will kill many insects, other chemicals being necessary to tackle fungi.

Some insecticides are formulated in vaporizing bars which can be suspended in a greenhouse or other closed area and will give off an insect-killing vapour which is effective over a long period.

Yet another method of dealing with pests in greenhouses is by aerosols. The chemical is dissolved in a highly volatile fluid and is applied as a very finely atomized spray. The carrying fluid almost immediately evaporates leaving the insecticide to settle on the plants. Aerosols are mostly prepacked ready for application and so are quick and easy to use. Malathion will control red spider mites and other pests, pirimiphos-methyl is a good general insecticide, and pirimicarb will kill aphids, all being available in aerosol form.

Alternatively, use biological control. *Encarsia formosa* is a parasitic wasp which lays its eggs inside whitefly larvae. The emerging wasps promptly devour their hosts. *Phytoseiulus persimilis* eat red-spider mite and *Cryptolaemus montrouzieri* is an Australian ladybird which preys on mealy bug. The major drawback is that it is likely to eat other ladybirds.

Other natural predators include *Aphidoletes aphidimyza* (which attack aphids), *bacillus thuringiensis* (caterpillars), and nematodes (vine weevil larvae). But note that when using any of the above you cannot also use insecticides.

Chapter 32

Common Pests and Diseases

For simplicity of reference many of the commoner pests and diseases are arranged in alphabetical sequence in this chapter with short descriptions and an account of the best method of dealing with each. Ready made sprays, powders, and liquids are available at garden centres.

American Blight. See **Woolly Aphis** (p. 766).

Ants. These can cause a lot of damage by loosening soil especially in pots, seed boxes, seed beds and around small plants and on lawns they may throw up ant hills. They will sometimes attack and damage blossoms and ripening fruits and also do indirect damage by transporting aphids from one plant to another.

These are several proprietary ant killers which should be used strictly in accordance with manufacturers' instructions. If nests can be found HCH or derris dust can be sprinkled over them or they can be treated with pirimiphos-methyl. Grease bands placed around the trunks or main branches of trees will catch many ants ascending and descending.

Aphids. This is the general name used to cover the numerous plant lice known to the gardener as greenflies, blackflies and so on. They are all small, soft-bodied creatures, some winged but mostly wingless and slow moving. They tend to cluster around the tips of young shoots or on the undersides of leaves, from which they suck the sap. They check growth, often cause severe distortion and frequently carry virus diseases from one plant to another.

A number of insecticides are effective in killing them. Non-systemic kinds include malathion, HCH, derris, and pirimicarb. Spraying with these may need to be repeated at intervals of 10 to 14 days until the attack is over. Systemic insecticides, which enter into the sap, remain effective for a month or more and include dimethoate. Spraying with non-systemics should be started at the first sign of attack, but systemic chemicals can also be used as a preventive when an attack is considered likely but before it has occurred.

On fruit trees the eggs of aphids, which are mostly laid on the ends of the young shoots, can be killed in winter with tar-oil winter wash. This is used while the trees are quite dormant in the first half of winter. Manufacturers' instructions regarding strength should be followed.

A special kind of aphid attacks the roots of some plants, notably auriculas and lettuces. Valuable plants may be lifted and dipped in a solution of derris, for example, some of which may also be poured into the holes from which they have been removed.

For woolly aphis see p. 766.

Bacterial Canker. This is a common bacterial disease of cherries which may also attack plums, peaches and nectarines. The bark is killed, particularly at the crotch where main branches join the trunk, and as a result leaves wither and whole branches die. Gum often oozes freely from the cankered bark. An early symptom may be the appearance of small circular holes in the leaves (hence its alternative name, shot hole).

Infection is most likely to occur through wounds in autumn or winter, so pruning should be completed early, by late summer if possible. Some believe that all wounds should be painted with a good wound dressing or copper fungicide while others argue it's impossible to eliminate all infection and painting seals it in. Withering branches should be cut off and burned at once, and trees sprayed heavily with Bordeaux mixture from late summer to mid-autumn. Cherries budded on such canker-resistant stocks as Seedling Mazzard or F. 12/1 are less likely to contract this disease.

Basal Rot. There are several different fungi which attack the bulbs of narcissi and tulips causing them to rot at the bottom and these are all known by the name basal rot. As the treatment is the same it is not necessary to be able to distinguish between one and another. All bulbs should be very carefully examined before they are planted and any which show signs of decay should be destroyed. Bulbs should always be stored in a cool, dry place as this minimizes risk of infection. The bulbs can be sterilized against eelworm by being immersed in water for 3 hours at 43°C/110°F. As a protection bulbs may be dipped in benomyl prepared as advised for spraying.

Basal Stem Rot. This disease attacks cucumbers and melons. It is often known as canker, and has no connection with basal rot. It is caused by a bacterium and produces a soft decay of the stem, usually just above soil level, as a result of which the plant collapses. Plants grown on low mounds are less likely to suffer and so are those surrounded by a metal collar to protect the main stem from water splashes. The soil in which cucumbers and melons are to be grown should be steam sterilized and the base of plants can be dusted with copper dust.

Bees, Leaf-cutting. Certain species of bee cut pieces out of leaves to form their nests. These pieces are always cleanly removed from the edges of the leaves in the form of semi-circles and so it is usually possible to recognize the culprit from the kind of damage done. Though leaf-cutting bees are seldom sufficiently numerous to constitute a serious danger to the garden they can be most annoying. Unfortunately there is very little that can be done effectively to get rid of them except to catch the bees with a fine-mesh butterfly net and destroy them.

Beetles. In general beetles, in contrast to weevils, tend to be friends rather than foes of the gardener as they are mainly carnivorous. There are, however, one or two notable exceptions such as the raspberry beetle, described on p. 758, the flea beetle, described on p. 736, the asparagus beetle, a small but rather striking insect on black with orange markings, and the pea and bean beetle who is more a worry to seedsmen than to gardeners. The grubs of the asparagus beetle feed on the leaves of asparagus and may leave the stems quite bare. An occasional dusting or spraying with carbaryl, derris, malathion, fenitrothion or pirimiphos-methyl will account for many beetles but not for the pea and bean beetle which drills tiny holes into pea and bean seeds. There is nothing that can be done about it in the garden, but seedsmen have ingenious machines which pick out the holed seeds and discard them.

One other group of beetles that may occasionally prove troublesome are the bark beetles and shot borers, all of which are very small brown or blackish beetles which tunnel into the wood of various trees. Usually only old trees or those that are in poor health are attacked, so good general cultivation is the first line of defence. All wounds should be protected with a good wound dressing such as Arbrex.

Big Bud. This condition is all too common in black currants and is occasionally found in red and white currants and even gooseberries. The dormant buds become swollen and globular instead of being comparatively small and a little pointed. The condition can be detected very easily towards the end of the winter. It is due to the infestation of the buds by great numbers of tiny mites, which later migrate to other buds. Besides destroying many of the buds these mites often carry virus disease, particularly the destructive virus which causes reversion.

The mite is checked by picking off the swollen buds in winter and spraying in spring and early summer with benomyl.

Birds. Many species of birds can be a considerable nuisance in the garden though there are few birds which do not also do some good. Probably one may place completely on the black list jays, wood pigeons and bullfinches and in some districts rooks and crows can be very troublesome. There is no simple or single remedy; netting or similar protective measures are the only ones likely to give complete immunity. Quassia-based sprays may give a little protection by rendering berries too bitter to be palatable but their true value seems very doubtful. The same is true of most bird scarers, for after a while birds become used to even the most terrifying. Proprietary deterrents are also available and grass seed is often pre-treated in this way to prevent birds picking it up.

Bitter Pit. This is a very common physiological disease of apples in which the surface becomes marked with small, darkish depressions. If the skin is peeled it will be found that beneath each 'pit' there is a small area of brown flesh. Closely allied to this is the condition known as 'cork' in which there are small brown bare areas of flesh throughout the fruit and not merely near the surface. Both troubles are connected with calcium and/or boron deficiency. Some varieties of apple are more subject to bitter pit than others.

Spraying with calcium nitrate, 28 g per 4·5 l (1 oz per gal) of water, every three weeks from early to late summer can help and, if the soil is acid, lime or chalk should be given to raise the pH to about 6·5. If boron deficiency is the cause give 3 g of borax to each sq m (1 oz per 11 sq ft) of soil.

Blackfly. The name is given to one of the many kinds of aphid. Blackfly is particularly troublesome on broad beans. With this crop, apart from spraying with one of the insecticides recommended for sucking insects (see p. 720), considerable benefit is to be gained by early sowing and by pinching out the tips of the plants when the first clusters of pods start to form. For other plants and trees remedies are the same as for other aphids (see p. 726).

Blackleg. A disease which attacks the stems of potatoes at and just above soil level, causing them to go black and die, with the result that the foliage withers and the whole plant collapses. As a rule only an odd plant is affected here and there in the potato bed and the disease is seldom very serious. No cure is known, but as the disease is carried in the seed tubers care should be taken to destroy all affected plants and to examine the planting sets closely. Destroy any which are soft or rotten at the end removed from the eyes.

Black Spot. Though a great many diseases cause black spots to appear on leaves or fruits the name 'black spot' is reserved for a specific and extremely serious diseases of roses. The foliage is attacked and the disease progresses rapidly in summer, the blackish spots, at first more or less circular, increasing rapidly in size until eventually the leaf is destroyed and falls prematurely. Badly attacked leaves should be removed and burned. Plants should be treated fortnightly from mid-summer to early autumn with a spray which will include one or more of the following: captan, thiram, propiconazole, benomyl, bupirimate, triforine or thiophanate-methyl, according to maker's instructions. In winter, when all leaves have fallen, the bare branches and the surface soil can be sprayed with copper sulphate, 28 g per 4·5 l (1 oz per gal) of water. In severe cases it will pay to remove the top 2·5 cm (1 in) of surface soil from beneath all affected roses in winter, burn it and replace with fresh soil from another part of the garden where no roses have been grown. In less serious cases it will help to mulch the rose beds with dry grass clippings in mid-spring and maintain this mulch throughout the summer, so checking the rise of disease spores from the soil to the leaves.

Blight (Potato). I have referred to this very widespread disease under the general heading Potatoes on p. 576. The disease is caused by a fungus which first attacks the leaves of potatoes and tomatoes, causing them to develop black spots and patches which rapidly spread until all the leaves and even the stems are killed. On potatoes the disease usually passes quickly to the tubers causing them to develop brown, decayed patches which may extend deep down into the flesh. On tomatoes the fruits are usually attacked and these develop black streaks and blotches which soon cause the whole fruit to go rotten. The disease can be prevented by spraying or dusting potatoes and tomatoes in good time with Bordeaux mixture, copper fungicide, bupirimate or thiram and repeating at intervals until autumn. The first preventive spraying should occur in early summer.

Blossom-end Rot. A physiological disease of tomatoes which sometimes causes heavy loss of crop. The fruits only are attacked and always at the end farthest removed from the stalk. First a dark spot appears. This rapidly gains in size, becomes black and hard and finally the end of the fruit is flattened.

Despite appearances to the contrary the disease is not primarily due to a fungus but is caused by shortage of water. It may be several weeks after the period of dryness before the spots make their appearance. There is no cure for affected fruits but the disease can be prevented by regular and adequate watering. Affected fruits should be removed and burned before secondary infections occur.

Blossom Wilt. This fungal disease of apples, apricots and plums is also known as spur blight, canker, die back and withertip, all of which refer to its appearance. Flowers wilt, and decay spreads back into the spurs and sometimes even to the main stems. All infected growth should be cut out and trees sprayed with tar-oil wash just before the buds begin to swell and open, usually some time in late winter, and twice with benomyl or thiophanate-methyl, first when the flowers are open and again a week later. (See Brown Rot).

Blotchy Ripening. A condition of tomato fruits which prevents them from turning red evenly. Instead the fruits have greenish or yellowish blotches or areas irregularly disposed. This condition is sometimes a symptom of virus disease but more commonly it is due to unbalanced feeding and can be corrected by giving the plants a fertilizer containing plenty of potash as well as nitrogen and phosphates.

Botrytis. This disease is commonly known as grey mould because, as it develops, a fluffy, greyish mould appears all over the affected area. In the early stages the attacked tissue decays, becoming soft and black in the process.

This is an extremely common trouble and one which attacks an unusually wide range of plants. Strawberries are often severely affected, the fruits suffering most and becoming bitter as they rot. Lettuces are frequent victims, the main stem suffering most severely just above soil level, so that the whole plant collapses. In roses it causes serious die back of the year-old wood, most of which may die during the winter. The seed heads of giant sunflowers are often completed rotted. Cucumber, melon and marrow fruits may become infected. Tomato stems and fruits are also attacked and infection is most likely to start at points where leaves or shoots have been cut off. Coleus and pelargonium plants are very susceptible in the greenhouse in winter, especially if the temperature falls below 12°C/54°F.

Botrytis is an almost impossible disease to control once it has secured a firm hold but it needs a damp, cool atmosphere to stimulate it to its worst attacks and is always most troublesome in autumn out of doors, and in winter or early spring under glass. Careful watering and ventilation combined with a little artificial heat will go far to prevent it in greenhouses. Outdoor crops should be harvested so far as possible before the weather becomes cold and wet and should be stored in dry, well-ventilated places. Spraying with captan, thiram, benomyl, bupirimate, triforine or thiophanate-methyl or frequent dusting with flowers of sulphur will help to check botrytis. In the case of winter lettuces, which often suffer severely, great care should be taken not to plant too deeply and to choose varieties suitable for winter cropping. Greenhouse plants can be protected by fumigating with tecnazene.

Brown Rot. A widespread disease of fruits caused by the same fungi as those that produce blossom wilt. Apples, pears, plums, cherries, peaches and nectarines are frequently attacked. First there is a soft brown rot of the flesh which later develops a series of small, whitish pustules often arranged in a series of concentric rings. Eventually the whole fruit withers and may hang for months on the tree in a mummified condition.

Trouble almost invariably starts through some small wound, so that the first line of defence is to eliminate pests and protect the fruits from accidental damage and bruising. In apples brown rot often follows the damage caused by caterpillars of the codling moth or maggots of the apple sawfly. All affected fruits must be removed and burned or buried as soon as noticed. Trees can be sprayed with benomyl or thiophanate-methyl in late summer and again in early autumn. If spurs or stems show disease, treatment as advised for blossom wilt should be carried out.

Bud Blast. The worst disease of rhododendrons, this causes flower buds to turn brown and develop small black, bristle-like sporeheads. All affected buds should be picked off and burned and plants sprayed occasionally in summer with HCH, derris or malathion to keep down leaf hoppers which puncture the buds and so allow the bud-blast fungus to penetrate. Spray also with captan or Bordeaux mixture just before flower buds open, and again every month until late summer.

Bud Dropping. The flower buds of various plants are apt to drop without apparent cause just before they open. This trouble is particularly common with sweet peas, lupins (especially the white varieties), begonias, runner beans and tomatoes. It is usually due to sudden changes in temperature, especially to cold nights, and may be encouraged by draughts and under or overwatering.

Under glass care should be taken to maintain reasonably even temperatures and to water correctly according to the nature of the plant. Out of doors it is more difficult to control the trouble as the gardener is often at the mercy of the weather, but if the soil is dry, a good watering followed by syringing overhead with tepid water may help.

Cane Blight. A damaging disease of raspberries caused by a fungus which attacks the fruiting canes at or near ground level causing the canes to wither and die. Infection usually occurs through wounds and these are often caused by the cane midge so that anything done to kill this pest will also reduce cane blight. Combat this pest with fenitrothion or HCH and the fungus with copper fungicide. In addition all infected canes should be cut right out, not just broken off at the point of infection.

Cane Midge. The tiny pink maggots bore into the tender parts of young raspberry canes near ground level. The direct damage is not usually very serious but the wounds caused by these maggots give entry to the fungus which causes cane blight. The young canes should be sprayed in mid-spring with HCH or fenitrothion and this treatment should be repeated a fortnight later. Dig over surface soil in winter to expose larvae.

Cane Spot. A common, though not usually a very serious, disease of raspberries and loganberries. It is caused by a fungus which attacks the canes causing them to develop numerous small greyish, purple-rimmed spots. The canes are weakened and may, in very severe cases, be killed. Occasionally fruits are also infected and become lopsided. The remedy is to spray in early spring with benomyl or thiram, as directed by the manufacturer and repeat at fortnightly intervals until fruits are set.

Canker. The most troublesome canker is that which attacks apples and, to a much lesser degree, pears, but there is also a distinct form of canker which causes similar trouble on roses. The fungus eats into the wood, often the wood of older branches or main trunk, and causes deep, gaping wounds with gnarled edges. Eventually the flow of sap is so checked that the branch, or even the whole tree, dies.

Small branches, twigs and spurs that are cankered should be removed and burned. Wounds on larger branches may be painted with a proprietary dressing which checks the fungus and helps the wood to heal. Some varieties are much more subject to canker than others and should be avoided in places where the disease has caused much trouble. Canker is encouraged by bad drainage and cold, heavy subsoils and also in apples and pears it follows attacks of scab. Young trees can be sprayed with benomyl when the leaves fall in autumn.

Capsid Bugs. These are insects allied to aphids and are much like them in appearance but mostly more active and less numerous. They often cause an amount of damage quite disproportionate to their numbers. Leaves, stems and fruits are all liable to be attacked and a great variety of plants are affected, fruit trees suffering particularly badly. Leaves and shoots become distorted, flower buds fail to develop or have deformed or missing petals, while fruits show rough, brown uneven scabs and may be greatly stunted.

Spring and summer spraying with fenitrothion, pirimiphos-methyl, HCH, dimethoate or malathion are useful methods of control and in greenhouses HCH smoke generators can be used. With fruit trees additional control can be obtained by spraying with winter petroleum emulsion when the buds are on the point of bursting in late winter/early spring.

Caterpillars. It is not necessary for the amateur to be able to recognise and name the great variety of caterpillars which may invade gardens as all are pests and all may be destroyed by spraying with HCH, derris, pirimiphos-methyl, fenitrothion or permethrin or by dusting with carbaryl. Hand picking is often the quickest and surest method of stopping an attack, especially in the early stages. On fruit trees caterpillar damage can be much reduced by spraying with tar-oil winter wash while the trees are dormant in mid-winter. Grease banding in early autumn will catch the female winter moths but the bands must be fixed tightly round the trunks or main branches at least 60 cm (2 ft) above soil level, and they must be kept sticky all the winter. The threat of cutworm caterpillars can be reduced by spraying with the bacterium *Bacillus thuringiensis*.

Chafers. These are beetles, one of which, the cockchafer, is very common and may often be encountered just after dusk on a summer evening flying rapidly with a droning noise. It lives on the leaves of many trees and can be most troublesome. Even more destructive, however, are the larvae which are found half-coiled in the soil and which attack the roots of a great variety of plants. They are big with brown, horny heads and swollen, white bodies which have a darker hue towards the tail.

Larvae may be killed or driven out by forking HCH into the soil in spring or autumn or by using carbaryl or pirimiphos-methyl. Alternatively, remove by hand-picking in winter.

Chlorosis. One of the commonest of the deficiency diseases, that is, disorders caused by the lack of something in the soil, chlorosis is often due to lack of iron or manganese, resulting in insufficient green colouring matter in the leaves, which consequently become pale yellow in patches or all over. Excess lime will often bring about deficiency of iron by rendering it insoluble and sometimes also of manganese but with the latter an excess of organic matter may also be a contributory factor. Because the deficiency can be caused by the character of the soil applications of ordinary chemicals containing iron or manganese, for example sulphate of iron and sulphate of manganese, are not always satisfactory and special compounds, known as sequestrols, must be used. In these the iron or manganese is chelated, that is, held in such a way that it cannot be rendered insoluble, and therefore of no use to plants by reactions within the soil. Such sequestrols should be applied according to manufacturers' instructions.

Chocolate Spot. One of the numerous spot diseases and extremely common on broad beans. The name aptly describes the condition except that blotch might be a better word than spot. Spraying with benomyl will check the disease but as it is only likely to be serious after severe weather it can be prevented by giving early beans as much shelter as possible. Be generous with phosphatic and potassic fertilizers when preparing the soil as these will tend to harden growth.

Club Root. This is quite the worst disease the gardener has to deal with when growing cabbages and allied crops. Club root is caused by a soil-borne fungus which attacks the roots of all kinds of brassicas and some allied plants. At first there is a notable lack of fibrous roots. Soon the main roots swell, often to an astonishing size, and then they gradually decay with a most obnoxious smell. The small round swellings on the extreme base of the stem caused by the cabbage gall weevil (see p. 753) are often mistaken for club root but are easily distinguished, first by the fact that they are on the base of the stem and not ton the root itself, and secondly because, if they are broken open, they will be found to be hollow, with probably one or two of the white larvae feeding inside.

Club root thrives on acid soils and one of the most effective remedies is to apply so much lime that the soil becomes markedly alkaline (pH 7·5 or thereabouts, see p. 16). This and a thorough rest from cabbage crops for three or four years is the only complete cure. All affected plants should be lifted and burned.

Codling Moth. This is one of the two insects responsible for most maggoty apples, the other being the apple sawfly (see p. 759). The damage is done by the small white caterpillar of the codling moth. It enters the fruit, often by way of the eye, about mid-summer or a little later and feeds in the core and surrounding flesh, leaving the fruit a few weeks later by another tunnel and then forming a cocoon in some sheltered place. Features by which this pest can be distinguished from the sawfly are that the attack starts some weeks later when the fruit is already well formed and that there is no unpleasant smell from the damaged flesh.

This pest can be controlled by spraying or dusting in early summer and again several weeks later with derris, carbaryl, malathion, fenitrothion, permethrin or pirimiphos-methyl. If bands of sacking are tied round the trunks of the apple trees in mid-summer many of the caterpillars will pupate beneath them and can either be collected by hand in the autumn or be killed where they are by soaking the bands with tar-oil wash at the normal winter spraying.

Corticium Disease. This disease of lawns is also known as red thread because of the pinkish filaments of the fungus which causes it. Check it by treatment with benomyl or thiophanate-methyl used according to manufacturers' instructions.

Crown Gall. A very curious bacterial disease which attacks a great variety of plants including fruit trees, ornamental trees and shrubs, roses and occasionally beetroot, causing them to develop large, roughened, tumour-like swellings. Though often extremely unsightly it does not seem greatly to affect the vigour or condition of the plants attacked. No satisfactory remedy has been devised but if individual roots are attacked it is best to remove and burn them.

Cuckoo Spit. This insect has acquired its popular name because it usually appears first of all at cuckoo time and covers itself with a spittle-like mass of sap for protection. In some localities it is known as the spittle bug or the frog hopper, the latter because the adult insect jumps when disturbed. The creature itself is small and yellowish white. It lives by sucking sap but is seldom found in sufficient numbers to do great damage.

HCH, derris, malathion, carbaryl or fenitrothion will kill it but it is wise first of all to hose the plants or syringe heavily with clear water to remove as much as possible of the spittle covering and expose the insect to the insecticide. Hand picking is usually the simplest and most satisfactory method of getting rid of this pest.

Cutworms. This is a general name for all those caterpillars which live in the soil and attack plants at the base so that they topple over with the appearance of having been cut off at or about soil level. There are several different kinds of cutworm, each the caterpillar of a different moth, but treatment for all is the same, namely to hoe frequently so as to expose the cutworms for destroying by hand or by their natural enemies, birds, and to hoe or fork into the soil an insecticide containing carbaryl or HCH. Whenever plants are attacked, search in the surface soil immediately around them as it is highly probable the cutworms will be found.

Damping Off. This is another general term applied to several distinct fungi which attack seedling plants at or just above soil level causing them to rot and topple over. Damping off can spread very rapidly in the damp, stuffy conditions which favour it. Thin sowing and early pricking off or potting are two of the best preventives as are careful watering and adequate ventilation. The disease is unlikely to prove troublesome in sterilized soil (see p. 722). The spread of attacks can be checked by spraying with thiram, benomyl or thiophanate-methyl. Alternatively soil can be watered or sprayed with captan, and seeds can be dusted with captan or thiram seed dressing before they are sown.

Die Back. This is the name given to one of the many manifestations of botrytis or grey mould. Die back affects gooseberries and roses, killing the bark of the main stems and causing whole branches to die. On gooseberries leaves may develop yellowish or whitish edges and fall prematurely and the fruits may turn brown and become soft.

All infected branches should be removed and burned and plants sprayed with Bordeaux mixture in mid- or late spring (for gooseberries as soon as the fruit has set). Gooseberries may also be sprayed in winter, while still dormant but just before the buds burst, with benomyl, or copper fungicide. Roses can be sprayed with thiophanate-methyl at three-week intervals in summer.

Dollar Spot. Another of the common lawn diseases causing small, more or less circular brown or whitish patches on the turf. Treatment is as for corticium disease (see p. 733).

Dry Set. Sometimes the fruits of tomatoes, though apparently set, fail to swell but remain the size of a large pin head. This is known as dry set and is often caused by too hot and dry an atmosphere. Freer ventilation and daily syringing of the plants with water will then soon improve matters but dry set can also be a symptom of mosaic virus (see p. 757).

Earthworms. In the ordinary way earthworms are not pests but are highly beneficial to the soil because they drag decaying leaves into it and pass the soil through their bodies, breaking it up and moving it in the process, and, by making tunnels in it, admitting air. But all these activities, excellent as they are in the right place, can be damaging in the wrong one. Earthworms are a menace in pots and seed boxes, for they block up drainage holes with their casts and disturb roots by their constant tunnelling. On lawns their casts flatten out over the grass and smother it.

On lawns earthworms can be killed with formulated carbaryl, while worms in pots and boxes can be driven out by watering with a deep pink solution of permanganate of potash or with lime water made by pouring 4·5 l (1 gal) of water on 0·2 kg (½ lb) of quicklime, leaving for 24 hours and then decanting the clear liquor. Never use lime water on lime-hating plants.

Earwigs. These are too familiar to need description but the damage they do in the garden is often wrongly ascribed to other causes. Earwigs have a special partiality for petals, which they devour, giving the blooms a very ragged appearance. They also attack leaves, causing them to look rusty and distorted much as capsid bugs do. As the earwigs work by night and hide by day they are often undetected.

Earwigs can be trapped by inverting small, hay-stuffed flower pots on canes, by placing old, hollow broad bean stalks in the branches of the plant attacked or by suspending slightly open match boxes from them. HCH, pirimiphos-methyl, malathion or carbaryl dusts can be scattered where earwigs are seen.

Eelworms. Gardeners sometimes say they have seen eelworms attacking the roots of their plants. In fact this is quite impossible because the harmful species of eelworm are microscopic in size. What has actually been observed are almost invariably larger kinds of nematode worm which are eel shaped and transparent like the harmful eelworms but large enough to be seen with the naked eye – in fact they are often 8 mm (⅓ in) in length.

These big nematode worms feed mainly on decaying matter in the soil. When found on roots they are usually attacking tissue that is already rotting from some other cause, though occasionally they may do some direct damage to living tissue. The really harmful eelworms either attack roots from outside or actually enter the plant and live within it.

A great many plants suffer from eelworms but fortunately most have their particular species so that, for example, the eelworm which damages potatoes will not also attack phloxes, nor will the phlox eelworm infest narcissi, onions or chrysanthemums.

As at some stage in their existence eelworms pass into the soil to attack other plants some soil treatment is necessary in addition to measures applied to the plant itself. Where the quantity of soil is small, sterilization (see p. 722) provides the complete answer but on a large scale out of doors this is impracticable and starvation is the only possible means of destroying the pests. This may mean growing no crop similar to that attacked for three or four years.

As regards the plants themselves burning is often the only course but the stools of chrysanthemums can be cleared of eelworms without injury to the plants by immersing them in water at a steady temperature of 43°C/110°F for 20-30 minutes, followed by immediate immersion in cold water. If the water gets any hotter, the plants or stools may be destroyed while a lower temperature will not kill the eelworms.

Bulbs need a longer period of hot-water treatment varying from 1 hour for irises to 3 hours for narcissi and daffodils. Strawberry runners are heat treated at 46°C/115°F for 5 minutes for leaf and bud eelworms and for 7 minutes for stem eelworms.

One special method of control, applicable to phloxes, is to work up a new stock of plants from root cuttings. This depends upon the fact that the phlox eelworm lives in the stems and the roots are therefore clear. However, the new stock of plants will soon become reinfested if grown in the same soil as the parents.

Fire Blight. A bacterial disease of pears and some other trees and shrubs including apples, quince, amelanchier, cotoneaster, hawthorn, mountain ash, pyracantha and whitebeam. Infection starts from the blossom which withers, but quickly passes back to the stems. Leaves wither and die, bark cracks and gradually the whole plant is destroyed. This is a notifiable disease which in some regions should be reported to the authorities so that appropriate action may be taken to confine the infection.

Flea Beetle. This is a very small, blackish beetle which jumps when disturbed. It attacks all kinds of brassica seedlings including cabbages and turnips, eating small round holes in the leaves so that they look as if they had been perforated. One remedy is to keep the seedlings growing fast by watering them freely and giving them a small dose of nitrate of soda so that they quickly pass out of the seedling stage. A more positive line of attack is to sprinkle the seedlings with HCH, carbaryl or derris dust.

Fly; Carrot, Onion, Cabbage Root. There are a great many flies which are pests of one plant or another, but the term is used here in its common garden application which is to three distinct pests, the cabbage root fly, the onion fly and the carrot fly. Though in fact quite unrelated all three have points of great similarity, at least for the gardener. In each it is the maggot of the fly that does the damage, and in each the maggot is small, white and attacks the roots, or, in the case of the onion, the bulb. In all three the fly responsible lays her eggs in the soil near the base of the plant so that when the maggots hatch out they have food close at hand. Plants that are attacked stop growing, and the leaves of onions and cabbages take on a leaden hue. Sometimes they recover, but small plants are usually killed outright. Maggots of the cabbage root fly also sometimes attack the buttons of Brussels sprouts.

Cabbage root fly can be controlled with HCH, phoxim or pirimiphos-methyl. All brassicas can be protected to some extent from the egg-laying female by fitting felt or plastic discs round the young plants at planting time. Slit the discs to the centre so they fit snugly round the stems and firmly on the soil. Both carrot and onion flies can be controlled with pirimiphos-methyl or HCH, but for carrots the latter is best used as a seed dressing before sowing to reduce the risk of tainting the crop. Late-sown carrots often escape attack as they come through the soil after the fly has finished egg-laying.

For celery fly see Leaf Miners (p. 754).

This is a most attractive combination of plants. In the foreground is *Euphorbia characias* and *Weigela florida* Variegata with viburnum and *Euonymus alatus* just beginning to turn colour

Cotoneasters are widely planted for their cheerful scarlet berries, but *C. x watereri* Rothschildianus is refreshingly different with pleasant yellow fruits

Ornamental trees are fine, but why not enjoy some fruit for your labours? Sunrise is a handsome eater, but needs a pollinator – perhaps the crab Golden Hornet?

Strawberries like Cambridge Favourite are delectable and not difficult if you keep off birds, slugs and mould. Bottom: A clean orderly vegetable garden is surprisingly beautiful

Only one criticism is possible of *Laburnum x watereri* Vossii – it is so good that it has been
overplanted. Contrasts well with purple foliage

Ballet-skirted fuchsias like Swingtime are treasured alike by windowsill gardeners and those with a greenhouse-size collection. They can be enjoyed in baskets and as standards too

The unusual colouring and intricate construction of Passion Flower blooms and the fable linking them with Christ's passion, ensure them many admirers. But this is a strong climber

Everyone who has been to the Mediterranean on holiday is familiar with brilliant magenta bougainvillea. Why not grow a plant in your own greenhouse, provided it is kept frost free?

A lot of heat just isn't necessary for a colourful conservatory display. These calceolarias, cinerarias, primulas and pelargoniums offer a galaxy of colours yet are undemanding

What could look more exotic than a tuberous-rooted begonia in bloom? Yet they are easy enough
to grow from tubers or seeds and their demands for warmth are modest

It is surprisingly simple to pack your greenhouse with brilliant colour in summer. Here are gloxinias, streptocarpus, coleus and fuchsias, none of them specially demanding

747

Lapageria, the national flower of Chile, produces these glorious waxy textured bells in late summer, yet demands little more than to be kept frost free

It's easy to dismiss succulents as plants that conveniently tolerate neglect. This group
demonstrates that they are worth collecting for their great variety of shape and colouring

It is possible to enjoy a dazzling show of colour in a cool greenhouse in late winter/early spring by filling it with hyacinths and narcissi, plus some calceolarias or cinerarias

Autumn can vie for brilliance of colour with summer and spring if you plant the right trees and bushes. These acers provide a brilliant example

This view of a trial fruit garden shows the value of setting everything out in an orderly manner – and protecting it from the depredations of birds with netting

Fly, Narcissus. Another very troublesome group of flies are the narcissus flies, the dirty-coloured larvae of which feed within the bulbs of daffodils and narcissi. With the large narcissus fly only one larva will be found in each attacked bulb, but when the small narcissus fly is involved numerous small larvae may be found. The remedy is the same for both: lift all suspected bulbs, burn those seriously damaged and immerse the remainder for one hour in water kept at a steady temperature of 43°C/110°F. Frequent hoeing and raking of narcissus beds during the spring will fill up cracks in which the flies might lay their eggs and HCH dust can be sprinkled around the necks of the bulbs at fortnightly intervals from mid-spring until mid-summer.

Foot Rot. This disease can easily be confused with basal stem rot since it attacks cucumbers and melons at or near soil level, causing them to collapse. But basal stem rot is caused by a bacterium and produces a soft decay whereas foot rot is caused by a fungus and the affected part turns brown. It also attacks other plants, including annual asters, petunias, cinerarias, salpiglossis and tomatoes. It can also attack the fruits of tomatoes causing them to develop concentric dark rings, a condition known as buckeye. Plants should as far as possible be grown in sterilized soil. The soil around growing plants can be watered with Cheshunt compound, copper fungicide or thiram and the lower trusses of tomatoes can be tied well up or protected with a layer of clean straw from water splashes from the soil.

Frog Flies. See **Leaf Hoppers** (p. 754).

Fusarium Patch. This is a common disease of lawns which causes the grass to die in yellowish-brown patches, sometimes with a pinkish-white outgrowth. A form of this disease known as snow mould can be particularly troublesome after snow has lain over turf for a considerable time. Treatment is as for corticium disease. Avoid excessive use of nitrogenous fertilizer especially in late summer and do not use lime or anything else liable to raise the soil above pH 6·0.

Gall Weevil. The small white grub of this weevil enters the base of the stem of all plants of the cabbage tribe including turnips and swedes, causing small rounded galls to form. These swellings are frequently mistaken for those caused by club root (see p. 733). Gall weevil does little damage and it is usually sufficient to break open any galls noted when planting brassicas and kill the grubs within. A light dusting of HCH along the rows when preparing seed beds and transplanting seedlings will also kill many weevils or grubs.

Greenback. A very common physiological trouble of tomatoes caused by too much exposure of the fruit to strong sunshine. The chief symptom is the refusal of the fruit to ripen properly around the stalk where there is a band of hard green or yellowish flesh. The remedy is to ventilate freely, shade lightly and to leave sufficient foliage to shade the fruits.

Gumming. All stone fruits and particularly plums and cherries are liable to exude large masses of resinous gum from to time to time. Frequently little or no harm results but sometimes the gum is the symptom of a disease, probably of bacterial origin. See Bacterial Canker (p. 726).

Hollow Heart. A condition common in some varieties of potato on certain soils and particularly in wet seasons. The centre of the potato is hollow though not actually decayed. Varieties which naturally produce very large tubers are most likely to suffer and the trouble may be aggravated by an excess of nitrogenous fertilizer with lack of balancing phosphates and potash. Extremes of soil moisture, however, are mainly to blame and improvements in the texture and drainage of the soil will help.

Leaf Curl. One of the commonest diseases of peaches and nectarines, particularly out of doors. Almonds are also affected. The trouble starts in spring when young leaves curl, redden and become thickened. Twigs may also be attacked and die back. The disease is always most troublesome when the weather is cold. Affected leaves and twigs should be removed and burned. If the disease has proved troublesome in former years spray with Bordeaux mixture or copper fungicide after leaf fall in autumn and again just before the buds begin to open in spring.

Leaf Hoppers (Frog Flies). Though very common these troublesome little insects are often overlooked. They are about the size of greenflies, the adults yellowish and winged, the young similar but wingless. They will be found on the undersides of the younger leaves, from which they suck the sap, and they are often mistaken for aphids. Two distinctive features are the white mottling of the attacked leaves, with little or no distortion, and the white, papery, cast-off skins of the growing frog flies which will usually be found attached to the undersides of the leaves even many weeks after an attack has finished. Accurate distinction between frog flies and aphids is not really vital, however, as the treatment is the same for both – spraying with HCH, derris, malathion, fenitrothion, carbaryl, or permethrin, or one of the systemic insecticides such as dimethoate.

Leaf Miners. The grubs of several different kinds of flies attack the leaves of plants by tunnelling within them and eating out the soft, fleshy part without disturbing the skin, which remains as a protection to them. The chrysanthemum leaf miner is a well-known example of this type of pest and it can be extremely troublesome. Badly attacked leaves appear to be covered with snaky white lines which, on closer inspection, prove to be the tunnels left by the grubs in their passage through the leaves. Similar damage is done by the cineraria leaf miner. The celery leaf miner burrows out a blister-like patch rather than a tunnel as do the lilac and holly leaf miners.

If the attacked leaves are run between the fingers the grubs can usually be felt as small lumps. In mild cases the quickest way to check the damage is to go over the leaves in this way one by one and kill the grubs with a pin or the point of a penknife. More extensive damage can be dealt with by spraying or dusting fairly frequently with HCH, carbaryl, malathion, dimethoate, or pirimiphos-methyl.

Leaf Mould. This is one of the commonest diseases of tomatoes grown under glass. It is the foliage that is attacked and the damage is usually at its worst towards the end of the season, encouraged by damp, cold air and lack of ventilation. The first indication that something is wrong is the appearance of khaki-coloured spots on the undersides of the leaves. These spread rapidly and the leaf withers.

If plants are adequately spaced and properly ventilated leaf mould is likely to be at a minimum. Some varieties show considerable resistance. When attacks do occur all badly affected leaves should be removed and burned and the plants sprayed at once with a copper fungicide, or benomyl, etc.

Leaf Scorch. Leaf scorching of various kinds may occur from a great variety of causes including excessive temperatures, lack of water, fumes from gas, paraffin or creosote, an overdose of certain fertilizers and exposure to draughts. The term is also commonly used for a specific disease very common in fruit trees, also occuring in ornamental trees and shrubs and herbaceous plants of many kinds. This kind of leaf scorch is due to lack of potash and the typical symptom is a yellowing of the leaf margin early in summer followed by a brown or ash-grey withering from the outer edge inwards. The remedy is to apply a quick-acting potash fertilizer, such as sulphate of potash, to the soil.

Leaf Spot. An omnibus name given to a number of quite unrelated diseases all of which cause small spots to appear on the leaves. The most important are carnation leaf spot which attacks both carnations and pinks, causing them to develop bleached spots; celery leaf spot which is confined to celery and produces spots which are pale at first but which may eventually cause the whole leaf to wither, and strawberry leaf spot which produces small reddish spots on the leaves of strawberries. Carnations should be sprayed with captan, or thiram. Celery seed should be soaked before sowing in thiram prepared as for spraying. Affected plants should be sprayed with benomyl. In addition celery seedlings, also plants in summer, may be sprayed with Bordeaux mixture, copper fungicide, or benomyl.

Leatherjackets. These may be mistaken for cutworms (see p. 734) as they look rather like caterpillars, live in the soil and attack the roots of plants or bite them off at soil level. Closer examination will show that they are not caterpillars as they have no legs. Leatherjackets are dark grey or almost black, extremely slow in their movements and have soft but very tough skins. They are the larvae of the flies known as daddy-long-legs or crane flies.

Remedies are the same as those recommended for cutworms. When leatherjackets become troublesome on lawns, which they may do by eating the grass roots and causing the grass to die in patches, an effective cure is to broadcast HCH dust over the surface or water with carbaryl or pirimiphos-methyl.

Lily Disease. There are many diseases of lilies but that commonly known as lily disease is a form of botrytis which is particularly liable to attack the white Madonna lily, causing the leaves to wither from the bottom of the plant upwards. If the disease has proved troublesome plants should be sprayed every week or so with benomyl from mid-spring until they are about to come into flower.

Mealy Bug. This is a serious pest in many greenhouses. It attacks vines and a great variety of tender shrubs and ornamental plants, sucking sap from their stems or leaves. It is small, bug-like and covered with a whitish, waxy substance which gives it its popular name. As a rule individual treatment is necessary, each affected plant being sponged with derris, malathion, or dimethoate. A good wetter, such as household detergent, is usually essential if a spray is used to enable it to penetrate the waxy covering but may not be required with systemic insecticides. For biological control use *Cryptolaemus montrouzieri*, an Australian ladybird.

Mice. These universal pests will eat seeds and small bulbs so cleanly that the novice is often left wondering where they have disappeared. Any of the advertised poisons can be used and also the usual household mousetraps baited with fat, nuts or cheese. If peas and beans are dusted before sowing with one of the proprietary seed dressings containing both an insecticide and a fungicide they are likely to be unpalatable to mice.

Midge, Pear. The small yellowish-white maggots of this pest feed within the young fruits of pears causing them to become deformed, turn black and fall. All such fruitlets should be collected and burnt. In addition the trees may be sprayed with HCH or fenitrothion when the blossom is fully open. If poultry are allowed to feed beneath the trees from mid-spring to early summer they will peck up many of the maggots.

Mildew. There are a great many different mildews, most of which attack only one particular family of plants. They may be divided into powdery mildews which produce a white, powdery outgrowth on the part affected, usually the leaves or younger stems though occasionally the fruits, and downy mildews which cause leaves to turn pale green in patches, then yellow and eventually shrivel with only a faint white powdering on the under surface. American gooseberry mildew is peculiar in producing a thick, greyish felt on the gooseberries.

All powdery mildews can be attacked with sulphur. Flowers of sulphur may be dusted over the leaves or propiconazole, benomyl, bupirimate, thiram or triforine may be used as a spray. For gooseberry mildew it is necessary to spray with benomyl or bupirimate when the fruit is set and again three or four weeks later. Alternatively a spray of 336 g (12 oz) of washing soda and 336 g (12 oz) of soft soap in 22.5 l (5 gal) of water may be used. This is very safe but easily washed off so may need to be reapplied every 10 to 14 days from the time the fruit is set until mid-summer or even later.

Downy mildews are usually more difficult to control. Copper fungicide and thiram are amongst the best chemicals to use against them.

Millepedes. These are soil pests which vary a good deal in size and appearance but are thin in proportion to their length with a great number of small legs. They are often confused with centipedes but may be distinguished by the fact that they are relatively inactive and usually comparatively dull in colour, greyish or blackish in contrast to the yellow or orange of centipedes. The centipede is always dashing about and is, in fact, doing the gardener a good turn for he is looking for other insects to eat. Millepedes eat roots though they often follow in the wake of other pests rather than initiate the trouble. They can be trapped in sliced carrots or potatoes buried just beneath the surface of the soil. HCH soil insecticide or carbaryl hoed or forked in will kill these pests.

Moles. These are both friends and foes of the gardener – friends because they live on many soil insects, foes because in tunnelling to find their food they loosen the soil around roots and under seedlings, causing beds to collapse and plants to lose their root hold.

Moreover on lawns they throw up unsightly molehills which, if not immediately removed, will smother and kill the grass.

Fine-mesh wire netting may be buried vertically in the soil around seed beds or plots to prevent moles entering them, or the whole area may be surrounded with naphthalene moth balls dropped into holes 10 cm (4 in) deep and 3·7 cm (1½ in) apart. These should be replaced every three years. Yet another possibility is to use special smoke generators or fuses based on sulphur which are ignited and then inserted in the runs. These runs should be sealed with a turf or piece of wood to trap the fumes. Though sulphur fumes are poisonous, the smokes could be used to scare off moles rather than kill them.

Mosaic. This is a name given to a symptom rather than to a disease, the condition being one of irregular pale green or yellowish mottling of the leaves. It generally indicates virus infection of some kind and a great many plants are capable of showing mosaic symptoms, though it would be mistake to assume on that account that the same virus was at work in all cases. There are, in fact, many different viruses causing mosaic symptoms, some specific to one kind or group of plants, others attacking a variety of quite unrelated plants. Raspberry mosaic is an example of the former kind which attacks raspberries and causes, in addition to the typical mottling, a slow deterioration in the vigour and cropping capacity of the canes. Some varieties are especially susceptible, Lloyd George being one of the worst. An example of the second type is cucumber mosaic which in addition to attacking cucumbers is found in marrows, melons, delphiniums, primulas and many other plants.

There is no cure and no preventive. Affected raspberry canes should always be removed and burned as noted. The disease is not carried in the soil so, provided the infected canes are removed roots and all, others may be planted in their place without danger. Note particularly that yellowing or bronzing of raspberry leaves is common in late summer especially if the weather is hot and is, as a rule, due to failure of surface roots for lack of moisture. True mosaic shows as a distinctive yellow variegation on the normal green background and is most easily detected about mid-summer.

In other plants mild symptoms of mosaic may sometimes be tolerated if the plants are otherwise desirable and difficult to replace but it must be realized that each such plant is a source of infection and that the disease, transferred to other plants, may produce more serious symptoms, so destruction is usually the best policy.

Neck Rot. This is a common disease of onions and one which also attacks shallots and garlic. The name is a good one because the principal symptom is a soft rot starting at the neck of the bulb. The trouble often does not start until after the onions are lifted and placed in store. Bulbs with thick, soft stems are more liable to be attacked than those with thin, dry, well-ripened necks and the principal method of control is to carry out good culture throughout so that the bulbs are properly ripened. Lift in fine, dry weather and do not store while still damp. See that the store is cool, airy and dry.

Rabbits. A vast amount of damage may be done by rabbits especially to young trees and shrubs of all kinds and also in the vegetable garden to young green crops. Trees and shrubs are barked near soil level and die as a result of the interruption to the flow of sap.

There is really only one way of dealing with rabbits on a large scale and that is to enclose the whole garden in wire netting which should have a mesh of not more than 3·7 cm (1½ in) and must be a minimum of 1·2 m (4 ft) in height of which 30 cm (1 ft) should be buried in the soil. Individual trees can be protected with circles of wire netting or bundles of brushwood tied around the trunks. There are also various rabbit deterrents on the market to be painted on the trunks or main stems of trees and shrubs. Foetid animal oil, obtainable from some country chemists, can be used in this way. Failing that, cats are very efficient at killing rabbits.

Raspberry Beetle. The adult beetle, small and greyish, damages the flowers of raspberry canes but its tiny white maggot is the gardener's worst enemy as this enters the raspberry fruits and feeds within them. The remedy is to dust or spray with derris, fenitrothion or malathion just after the blossom period and again when the earliest fruits begin to colour.

Rats. These are seldom as troublesome as mice to the gardener but they will sometimes cause serious damage to roots, bulbs or seeds in store and occasionally may bark young trees and shrubs in a similar manner to rabbits. Remedies are the same as for mice.

Red Spider Mites. There are a number of different kinds of red spider mite, each with its favourite host plants, but there is no need to distinguish between them as all are harmful and all are to be tackled in much the same manner. Red spider mites love a hot, dry atmosphere and are repelled by coolness and moisture so one of the best methods of keeping them under control is to make frequent use of the syringe with nothing more potent than clear water. If this does not prove enough, spray with malathion, derris or dimethoate.

The red spider mite often escapes identification because it is so very small and unlike what its name would suggest. To the naked eye it looks no bigger than a grain of rust, though a pocket lens will reveal it to be a living creature with a roundish body and eight legs. It lives on the undersides of leaves, especially in the angles of the veins. It sucks sap like an aphid and the effect is to check growth and give the leaf a curiously grey or bronze mottled appearance which is immediately detectable by the experienced gardener. Red spider mite can be controlled in the greenhouse by its natural predator *Phytoseiulus persimilis* which is commercially available.

Reversion. This disease of blackcurrants has a most misleading name. It was given because the affected bush gradually changes in character, developing a simpler, less lobed type of foliage, a bunched habit at the top and a progressive loss of fertility. These features were supposed to be typical of a reversion to some primitive type. In fact this is a disease caused by a virus and spread by the big-bud mite (see p. 728). The disease can be identified most readily in the first half of summer. If at that time bushes are producing a great deal of small growth giving them a bunched or nettleheaded appearance, and if it is found that most of the leaves have less than five pairs of subsidiary veins on the main lobe, it is probable that reversion is the cause. Such bushes should be grubbed and burned at once as they are a source of infection. Steps should be taken to eliminate big bud from the plantation.

Rhododendron Bug. One of the commonest pests of rhododendrons. The bug is a small black insect which may not be easy to detect but the damage it causes is distinctive enough, the leaves appearing rusty beneath and mottled above. The remedy is to spray in early summer and again a few weeks later with derris, HCH, dimethoate, or malathion. In very bad cases it may be necessary to remove and burn all terminal growth in early spring though this means sacrificing all bloom for a year.

Root Rot. There are a number of different fungi which attack the roots of plants, causing them to decay. Peas are particularly subject to a form known as black root rot because roots and stem base turn black. Violas, pansies, violets and cyclamen are also attacked by this black root rot. Violet root rot attacks asparagus, beetroot, carrots, chicory, potatoes and seakale. A violet or purplish-coloured mould appears on the surface of roots and quickly kills them.

The most damaging and widespread root rot of all is that caused by the honey fungus or armillaria, which attacks a great variety of plants including most trees and shrubs. The fungus spreads by black, stringy growths from which it gets yet another popular name, boot-lace fungus. Between the bark and wood of badly attacked trees there is a close web of white fungus.

In most cases there is little that can be done except to remove and burn the affected plants. A method of treating honey fungus for which success has been claimed is to remove soil from around the collars and the upper roots of trees and saturate them and the soil with refined creosote. It is also recommended that the soil from which infected plants have been removed should be sterilized with a suitable tar oil formulation and that nothing should be planted there for about two months. Cultivation of the soil appears to destroy the fungus at least for a time, and it may be possible to keep cleaned soil from becoming reinfected by surrounding it with a 'wall' of polythene to a depth of 60–90 cm (2–3 ft).

Rust. A great number of diseases pass under the name 'rust' though some are quite unrelated and most are confined to one family of plants only. The most troublesome are hollyhock rust, antirrhinum rust, rose rust and chrysanthemum rust, each confined to the plant named. They are alike in producing rust-coloured or orange spots or pustules on the undersides of the leaves, which are eventually killed.

All rusts are rather difficult to cure and if only a few plants are attacked it is usually best to destroy them. On a larger scale remove and burn the worst leaves and spray the plants fairly frequently with Bordeaux mixture, copper fungicide, triforine or thiram. Antirrhinums resistant to rust are available.

Sawflies. The larvae of various species of sawfly attack various crops and plants. Some are known as slugworms and are dealt with separately (see Slugworms). Maggots of the apple sawfly attack the fruits of apples, burrowing right into them like the caterpillars of the codling moth. The attack starts earlier, usually in late spring/early summer when the fruits are still very small, and there are often ribbon-like scars on the surface where the maggots have tried to enter. Frass (excreta) is thrown out from the holes and smells unpleasant. The remedy is to spray with HCH, malathion or dimethoate a week after the blossom falls and again a week later to catch the maggots as soon as they hatch out and before they enter the fruits.

759

The leaf-rolling sawfly attacks roses and causes the leaves to roll up tightly so that the little green or grey larvae are completely protected inside them. The leaves may start to roll as soon as punctured by the female flies without even eggs necessarily being laid, so treatment is difficult but fortnightly spraying in late spring/early summer with HCH, fenitrothion or dimethoate will help.

Scab, Apple and Pear. This is one of the most troublesome diseases of apples and pears. It is not a killer, but fruits are much disfigured by the roundish, black, shrunken spots some of which may run together or develop into deep, dry cracks. These spots are only skin deep, but they check the development of the fruit and may make it undersized or lopsided. Moreover the spurs and twigs are also attacked, the bark developing small blisters and eventually dying. These wounds often form a starting place for canker.

Scab must be kept down by routine spraying as it is much too common and widespread to be left for treatment if and when it turns up. Fortnightly spraying from the time the buds burst in spring until about late summer may be necessary to give full control, but in many gardens an early spray when blossom buds are just showing colour followed by a couple more when the blossom falls, and one about mid-summer may prove adequate. The best fungicides to use are benomyl, thiophanate-methyl or thiram. The persistent use of benomyl and/or thiophanate-methyl may result in the build-up of resistant strains of the scab fungus, so it is advisable to alternate these with captan or thiram.

Scab, Potato. One of the commonest diseases of the potato. In attacks the skin, causing it to develop rusty-looking scabs slightly raised above the surface. The flesh remains unaffected but the appearance of the tubers is seriously impaired.

The fungus which causes potato scab is carried in the soil and flourishes in alkaline conditions, such as may exist in naturally chalky soils or those that have been heavily limed. It is seldom a serious problem in fairly acid soils. One preventative, therefore, is to avoid the use of lime on ground that is shortly to receive potatoes. Another is to use liberal quantities of peat or leafmould in the preparation of the ground as these will tend to make it more acid. Gritty soil particles which wound the skin of the potato appear to make it more liable to infection and for this reason also it is wise to surround planting sets with soft, yielding material such as peat, leafmould or grass clippings. Rotational cropping will also help to keep the disease down by starving the fungus.

Scalding. Under glass rapid fluctuations of temperature accompanied by bright sunshine will often cause direct scalding or scorching of young leaves and fruits. Tomatoes and grapes are particularly likely to suffer, the leaves withering from the margin as if they had been burned. The bunches of grapes themselves may also be affected and develop brown, sunken patches on the side exposed to the sun. The remedy in all cases is to give more ventilation while the sun is shining and, if necessary, to give some shade.

Scale Insects. A number of insects attach themselves to the leaves, stems or bark of various plants and trees, looking rather like tiny limpets or mussels, and feeding by sucking sap from their hosts. Fruit trees can be cleared of scale insects by spraying in winter with tar-oil winter wash. This is too strong to use on plants in leaf which must be cleared by dusting, spraying or sponging with dimethoate or malathion. Sponging with soapy water to remove the scales can also be effective.

Sclerotinia Rot. This fungal disease, also known as stem rot, collar rot and storage rot, attacks both growing plants and plants in store. Usually it is the crown of the plant, where stems join roots, that is attacked and this rapidly rots with a fluffy white outgrowth. Sap is cut off and the whole plant collapses. Roots in store may become mummified. Plants affected include artichokes, carrots, parsnips, turnips and swedes, also campanulas, chrysanthemums and dahlias. Soil should be sterilized before use and the soil around growing plants watered with Cheshunt compound. Only sound roots should be stored and then in a dry, airy place.

Shanking. This common disease of old or over-cropped vines may easily be mistaken for scalding. The grapes turn brown and collapse just before they ripen, and on close examination it will be found that the stalk which attaches the berry to the bunch has withered. This is a feature which may be used to identify shanking at once, coupled with the fact that the whole berry collapses, not merely a patch on the sunny or exposed side. Shanking is always an indication that the roots are giving out and this in turn may mean that the vine border has become waterlogged through bad drainage, or that the soil is exhausted. The remedy is then to remake the border the following autumn.

Silver Leaf. This most destructive disease of plums is also found to a lesser extent on other stone fruits, hawthorns, blackthorns, roses and even Portugal laurels. The leaves of an affected branch gradually assume a metallic, silvery sheen which is most obvious about mid-summer. Later the branch dies but this may take a year or so. On the dead wood a plentiful growth of purplish-mauve fungus appears and it is from this that spores are distributed to infect new trees. It is wise policy to cut out all silvered boughs before the autumn, even though they are not yet dead, and to burn this wood at once. Pruning should, as far as possible, be confined to the summer months when danger of infection is least, and all pruning cuts should be painted with Arbrex or some other good wound dressing.

Slugs and Snails. These are universal pests of every garden. Curiously enough slugs seem to be destructive in inverse proportion to their size, it being the small grey and black species which do by far the most damage. Slugs and snails are for the most part night workers, and by day they hide in dark crannies or in the soil so that their depredations are often wrongly blamed upon some other creature. A search after dark with the aid of a torch will usually set doubts at rest. The appearance of ragged holes in the leaves of plants, sometimes with tell-tale slime trails leading to them, will warn the more experienced gardener what he is up against. Both slugs and snails can be killed with a poison bait made with 28 g (1 oz) of metaldehyde finely crushed to 1·3 kg (3 lb) of bran or ready-prepared pellets can be obtained. Metaldehyde can also be obtained in suspension to be mixed with water and applied to soil and plants from a watering-can fitted with a rose.

Another remedy is methiocarb purchased ready for use as small greyish-blue pellets. It is more effective in wet weather than metaldehyde, which kills slugs and snails by dehydration.

Slugworms. These have nothing to do with slugs. They are the larvae of certain species of sawfly and owe their popular name to the fact that they are often blackish, though

sometimes yellow, and somewhat like a small, thin slug in appearance, but a closer examination will show that, unlike a slug, they have legs. Slugworms have the curious habit of
eating the surface of a leaf while leaving a transparent skeleton intact. Roses, cherries and
pears are favourite subjects for attack. They can be killed by spraying with HCH, derris,
malathion, fenitrithion, or dimethoate.

Soft Rot. Every grower of cabbages or celery is likely to meet this troublesome disease
sooner or later. It also attacks carrots, onions, seakale and even bearded irises and arum
lilies. It is caused by a bacterium which produces a soft, slimy decay proceeding from the
centre of the plant outwards.

This disease attacks plants through wounds so one method of controlling it is to avoid
all possible causes of injury, as for example by clearing the ground of slugs and keeping
down caterpillars. With irises cut off and burn infected rhizomes, dust cut surfaces with
copper fungicide or Bordeaux mixture and soil with superphosphate of lime at 56 g per
0·8 sq m (2 oz per sq yd). Cut off affected portions of arum tubers in summer and replant
in sterilized soil.

Sooty Mould. This very descriptive name describes a disease which is often widespread,
especially in greenhouses and on plants that have been heavily attacked by aphids or scale
insects. It appears as a black, dirty-looking film on the surface of the leaf and grows
chiefly on the sticky substance left on the leaf by the insects that have preceded it. It can
be sponged off with warm, soapy water but it is most important to take the appropriate
steps to rid the plants of the pests which have given the mould a chance to grow.

Springtails. The name is given to tiny, whitish insects which are sometimes found in
great numbers on the roots of all kinds of plants, even large trees. When disturbed some
of them jump by means of a rapid movement of the rear part of the body. In the main
springtails, like millepedes, follow in the wake of other troubles, feeding on matter already
dead or decaying, but also like millepedes, they seem to be capable of carrying the damage
still further themselves or perhaps sometimes even initiating it. Good cultivation and
drainage will help to eliminate them, as will correct liming. It is also wise to avoid the use
of half-rotted dung and compost if these pests have proved troublesome. In bad cases use
HCH soil insecticide.

Streak. A troublesome disease of sweet peas and tomatoes which is most likely to occur
under conditions of high cultivation. This is because it is caused by various viruses which
thrive most readily in tissue that has been rendered soft by overfeeding. Avoid the use of
too much food containing nitrogen, give plenty of potash to ensure firm, disease-
resistant growth and spray to keep down aphids and thrips which spread the disease.
Streak is well named for it causes long, sunken brown or blackish streaks on stems and
leaves and, in the case of tomatoes, brown sunken spots on the fruits as well. Badly
affected plants should always be burned.

Tarsonemid Mite. Many gardeners will dismiss the tarsonemid mite as just another red
spider mite. This does not much matter as the same treatment will do for either, but as
the name is sure to be met sooner or later it is as well to know the difference between

these pests. There are several tarsonemid mites and each has its favourite plant, one attacking strawberries, another begonias, a third cyclamen and so on. Like red spider mites they are very small and found mostly on the undersides of leaves. They are whitish or pale brown rather than reddish, and leaves which are attacked become deep purple in colour and very brittle. Flower buds wither and blooms are distorted. Young strawberry plants that are attacked may be immersed before planting for 20 minutes in water at a steady temperature of 43°C/110°F. Strong sprays should be used with care on seedlings or young plants under glass before late spring, or at any time in bright sunshine.

Thrips. Out of doors and under glass thrips are ever ready to give trouble especially when the weather is hot and the atmosphere dry. In fact precisely the conditions which favour red spider mites also encourage thrips and the two may often be found together. Thrips are small, very narrow in proportion to their length, yellow to black and almost always running about actively. A very few seem able to do a quite disproportionate amount of damage. Leaves and stems become distorted and develop silvery or brown streaks. Flower buds turn brown and refuse to open. When thrips are suspected it is always a good plan to shake a plant or flower over a sheet of paper. It is almost certain that a few will be dislodged and be seen scuttling away to safety.

Out of doors the remedy is to spray frequently with HCH, derris or malathion. Under glass these chemicals may be used as smokes. Gladiolus thrips can be controlled by dusting corms with HCH in autumn before they are stored.

Tulip Fire. A highly descriptive name given to a fairly common disease of tulips which withers leaves and buds or open flowers as if they had been burned. It is caused by a fungus and can be controlled by spraying frequently with benomyl or thiram from the time shoots appear through the soil until flower buds are about to open. Bulbs can be soaked in benomyl or thiophanate-methyl for 15 to 30 minutes before planting.

Virus Diseases. These have proved both the most difficult class of disease to investigate and the most troublesome to treat. Viruses are so minute that they cannot be seen with ordinary microscopes, nor can they be trapped in the finest of filters. Their presence can be detected by the peculiar symptoms they produce and the fact that they can be transmitted from one plant to another. This is how many of them are spread, being carried by sucking insects such as aphids and thrips, by eelworms in the soil and also by direct contact of plant stems or roots.

Viruses are seldom outright killers but they gradually weaken the plants which they attack and disfigure them by causing their foliage to become mottled, or to develop dry brown spots, or to become distorted or stunted. Some plants have a considerable degree of tolerance to certain viruses and may show no signs of ill heath even when heavily infected. Such plants can be a potential source of danger in the garden by acting as unsuspected carriers of disease.

So far no satisfactory methods of curing virus-infected plants have been discovered and all such plants must be destroyed as soon as noted to prevent the disease being passed on. Any measures taken to keep down sucking insects will also help to limit the spread of viruses. Care should also be taken in the use of pruning implements, such as knives and secateurs. Virus infection may be carried on the blades so if they are used on any doubtful plants they should be dipped in boiling water or methylated spirit before being used again.

Virus infection is not usually carried in the seed so seedlings, even from infected plants, may be quite healthy. Some plants must be renewed fairly frequently by seed to get rid of virus infections passed on through divisions, cuttings, grafts and buds. Infected fruit stocks will infect clean varieties worked on them, so only use certified virus-free stocks.

It is sometimes possible to raise healthy plants from virus-infected plants, by taking tiny cuttings from the fast-growing shoot tips and rooting them in agar containing nutrients, but this is work only for experts.

Wart Disease. Fortunately this is not a common disease and most readers will probably never see it but it is one of the most serious diseases of the potato, notifiable to the authorities. Attacked tubers develop large, warty outgrowths which may eventually encompass the whole of the potato, reducing it to a shapeless, cancerous-looking mass. This disease must not be confused with scab which causes no more than rusty-looking scabs on the skin and leaves the flesh untouched. There is no remedy for wart disease but fortunately many varieties are immune to it. These are indicated in catalogues by the single word 'immune' after the name and only these should be planted in districts in which wart disease is known to have occurred.

Weevils. A number of weevils can prove troublesome in the garden but four are of outstanding importance as pests. They are the apple blossom weevil, the pea and bean weevil, the clay-coloured weevil and the vine weevil.

The first, as its name suggests, attacks the flowers of apples. The adult weevil is a small dark, beetle-like creature but it is its white grub which does the damage, feeding within the open flower and causing it to turn brown and become capped. HCH, fenitrothion or carbaryl should be applied when the buds are bursting in early spring and the most forward are at the 'mouse-ear' stage, that is the leaves surrounding the flower bud clusters are just emerging from the winter buds like little ears.

The pea and bean weevil also conveniently confines its attentions to the plants indicated by its name, broad beans being a particular favourite. The plants are usually attacked when still quite small and the leaf edges only are eaten so that they quickly acquire a distinctive, scalloped appearance. This time it is the grey, beetle-like adult which does the damage, though it is so active and cunning it may never be seen. Dust the foliage with fenitrothion, HCH, pirimiphos-methyl or derris.

The clay-coloured and vine weevils are so similar from the gardener's standpoint that they can be considered together. Each is destructive in both the adult and larval (grub) stages. The grubs are small, whitish and fond of attacking roots, bulbs and corms, in which they may be found curled up. The adults are beetle-like with the long snouts characteristic of weevils. The clay coloured is ashen grey, the vine weevil black. They eat rugged holes in foliage and the damage is often mistaken for that caused by caterpillars or slugs. A great variety of plants is attacked both out of doors and under glass. If plants are shaken after dark over tarred sacks or paper many feeding weevils will fall off and be trapped. Plants may also be sprayed or dusted with carbaryl. When pot plants are attacked by the larvae of these weevils the only remedy as a rule is to unpot the plants and remove the grubs by hand.

White Fly. White fly is one of the most troublesome pests under glass. There is also a related but distinct form which lives out of doors and has a special fancy for brassicas. In the greenhouse white fly seems to live on anything, though tomatoes are always singled out for early attention. It is not really a fly at all and does not look like one. It is very small, winged and pure white. It flies out when disturbed and, if there is a heavy infestation, the effect is like a cloud of smoke. Scales, representing a stage in the life cycle of the insect, are formed on the leaves and eggs are also laid in great numbers. The white fly and the scales suck sap from the plant and cover it with a sticky grey excrement which often attracts sooty mould, already referred to on p. 762.

Under glass fumigation with HCH is effective if repeated two or three times at intervals of 7 to 10 days or malathion aerosol may be used. HCH, permethrin, pirimiphos-methyl and malathion sprays or dusts may also be used indoors or out. There is also an insect parasite, *Encarsia formosa*, which can be introduced into greenhouses on parasitized leaves when the temperature is at least 21°C/70°F. It attacks and kills the scales, greatly reducing, though not eliminating, infestation.

Wilt. A number of quite unrelated diseases pass under the name of wilt. The most important for the gardener are aster wilt, which is confined to annual asters and has very much the appearance of damping-off disease (see p. 734) except that the main stem may be attacked well above soil level; clematis wilt, which attacks mainly the large-flowered garden varieties of clematis, causing whole stems to wither and die, and spotted wilt, which attacks a number of greenhouse plants.

Aster wilt is best controlled by sterilizing the soil in which the plants are raised and growing them in a different part of the garden each year. Wilt-resistant varieties can be obtained.

Clematis wilt is controlled by cutting out all wilted shoots, painting wounds, however small, with Arbrex or Medo and spraying plants occasionally in spring and early summer with Bordeaux mixture or a copper fungicide. Young large-flowered clematis plants are less likely to die prematurely if encouraged to make strong roots before they carry much top growth, which should be reduced for the first year or two.

Spotted wilt is not caused by a fungus, like the other wilts, but a virus disease fairly common on tomatoes, gloxinias and arum lilies. The first symptom is the appearance of ring-like spots on the leaves. Plants are stunted and the heads of tomato plants become bunched and have a bronzed appearance. Since the disease is uncurable and very catching, infected plants should be burned. Thrips are often active in spreading infection, so appropriate steps should be taken against these pests (see p. 763).

Winter Moths. See **Caterpillars** (p. 732).

Wireworms. These are amongst the most destructive soil pests in the garden. They are to be found everywhere, being the larvae of certain species of small brown beetles, known as click beetles because, if they are rolled over on their backs, they right themselves with a jerk and a distinctive clicking noise. The wireworms themselves are yellow, shiny-skinned, up to 2·5 cm (1 in) long and no thicker than a piece of ordinary string. They are not very active and have only three pairs of legs near the head, points which serve to distinguish them from the very active and many-legged centipedes. Wireworms live on the roots of the plants and on large seeds such as peas and beans. They are particularly fond of potatoes and carrots, and are usually found in great numbers in rough grassland. Often damage is most severe the second year after such land is broken up, the explanation apparently being that the first year they continue to feed on the decaying grass roots and only turn their attention seriously to garden plants when their original source of food is gone.

Good cultivation will reduce the wireworm population by exposing the grubs to birds. Many wireworms can be trapped in sliced potatoes or carrots buried just beneath the surface of the soil and examined every day or so. Potting and seed soil may be sterilized by heat or with one of the advertised chemical sterilizers.

HCH dust may be applied to the soil but if this is to be used for root crops HCH dust should be applied the autumn prior to planting to avoid risk of tainting.

Woodlice. Everyone is familiar with the hard-skinned, grey or blackish woodlouse, with its habit of rolling itself into a ball when disturbed which has given it the name of pillbug in some localities. It feeds mainly on decaying matter but will also attack soft-stemmed plants, and particularly tiny seedlings which may be eaten off so cleanly that they have the appearance of being mown. Many can be trapped in the same way as earwigs (see p. 735) and they can also be poisoned with HCH, pirimiphos-methyl or carbaryl sprinkled where they are seen. In greenhouses fumigation with HCH is effective. Decaying refuse should be removed as it provides a hiding place and breeding ground.

Woolly Aphis. This form of aphid attacks apples and covers itself with a white, wool-like protective material, so that a tree heavily infested appears to be covered with pieces of cotton wool. This makes it difficult to get an ordinary spray into contact with the insects. It is usually best to apply the insecticide direct to the patches with a stiff, old paint brush. Malathion, dimethoate, and HCH may be used or methylated spirits, the last-mentioned having the advantage of being particularly penetrating. Winter spraying with tar oil will also help to clear trees. Buds are often so severely damaged by woolly aphis that they become blind and develop large gall-like swellings. The pest is also known as American blight.

Chapter 33

Useful Remedies

New chemicals to control garden pests and diseases are constantly being tried and hardly a year passes without some introduction that is claimed to be an improvement on older remedies. It is therefore very difficult to keep any list adequately up to date. There is the further difficulty that it may be some years before harmful side effects of new chemicals are observed and in the case of some chemicals pests acquire a resistance to them. The following remedies have all been used sufficiently long to have proved themselves and are safe to use in gardens, provided they are handled with reasonable care and manufacturers' instructions are carefully followed. Some are only available in combination with other chemicals.

Note that chemicals, even those described as non-poisonous, can be harmful under certain circumstances and should always be kept away from food and out of reach of children and animals. It is wise to wear rubber gloves when handling concentrated chemicals, to avoid splashing them on the skin and to prevent spray or dust getting on the face and into the eyes. Hands and face should always be washed after spraying or dusting and equipment should be carefully cleaned out after used.

Benomyl. A systemic fungicide that has proved useful for the control of many plant diseases including botrytis, tomato leaf mould, apple and pear scab, rose black spot, and powdery mildews. If used too frequently it can sometimes induce the appearance of resistant forms of the disease-causing organism so it may be wise to alternate it with other fungicides.

Bordeaux Mixture. This excellent fungicide was developed in the Bordeaux district of France to deal with a troublesome disease of the vineyards. It has proved to be one of the most useful fungus killers with a very wide range of application in the garden, being particularly valuable as a preventive of potato blight on both potatoes and tomatoes. It will also check most mildews and many rust and leaf spot diseases, but it is liable to scorch the foliage of some plants.

Bordeaux mixture in powder form can be purchased ready for mixing with water and manufacturers' instructions regarding strength must be followed.

Bupirimate. A fungicide useful for the control of apple scab, rose black spot, potato blight and mildews. It is mainly available with triforine to give it a wider range of effectiveness and longer control, since the latter is systemic.

Captan. A fungicide available in combination with other chemicals, and particularly recommended for the control of apple and pear scab as it does not scorch leaves or russet or crack fruits. Use to control various diseases including rose black spot, grey mould, peach leaf curl, storage rots and damping off.

Carbaryl. An insecticide used to kill caterpillars, sawflies, weevils, scale insects, earwigs, woodlice, leatherjackets and some other pests. It will also kill bees and therefore should not be applied to open flowers. Crops treated with carbaryl should not be eaten for a week.

Copper Sulphate. By itself this can only be used on hard-wooded plants while they are completely dormant and leafless in winter, as it will scorch foliage severely. It is used on roses in the first half of winter to kill the resting spores of the fungi which cause black spot and orange rose dust diseases. For this purpose it is dissolved in water at the rate of 2·8 g per 4·5 l (1 oz per gal).

Derris. An insecticide prepared from the roots of certain tropical plants which contain rotenone, which is what actually kills insects. Derris-based treatments kill a wide range of pests including aphids, leaf hoppers, thrips, caterpillars, pea and bean weevils, raspberry beetles and red spider mites. It is almost non-toxic to warm-blooded animals, including human beings, but is very poisonous to fish.

Dimethoate. A systemic insecticide, that is, the chemical enters into the sap. Effective against aphids and red spider mites, it is supplied as a liquid to be diluted with water according to label instructions and used as a spray. It is poisonous to bees and fish and should not be used on chrysanthemums. At least a week should elapse before crops sprayed with dimethoate are eaten.

Fenitrothion. An insecticide effective against many garden pests including aphids of all kinds, capsids, codling moth, sawflies, caterpillars, thrips and weevils. For most edible crops an interval of 14 days should elapse between last spraying and harvesting.

HCH. The abbreviation commonly used for a chemical named benzene hexachloride. It is used as an insecticide against a wide range of insects including aphids, caterpillars, cut-worms, weevils and their larvae, scale insects, wireworms and leatherjackets. The active insecticidal portion of HCH is what is known as its gamma isomer which is separated from the other isomers which are apt to impart a musty taint to treated crops, particularly roots and fruits. This extraction is sometimes known as gamma-HCH and, when at least 99 per cent pure, as lindane.

Malathion. An insecticide very effective against all kinds of aphid and apple sucker as well as red spider mites, thrips, white flies, leaf hoppers, scale insects and mealy bugs. It is generally available as an aerosol for use in greenhouses. (In the past malathion could be bought as a dust ready for use, and as a liquid to be diluted with water according to label instructions and applied as a spray. Once mixed it was used without delay as it quickly decomposed. It could be mixed with most fungicides and insecticides but alkaline chemicals usually shortened its period of effectiveness. By itself it is poisonous to bees and fish, and crops sprayed with it should not be eaten for 24 hours. It is liable to damage some plants including antirrhinums, ferns, fuchsias, petunias, sweet peas and zinnias.)

Metaldehyde. Originally this substance was sold exclusively as a solid fuel but later it

768

was discovered to be an excellent slug poison. For this purpose it should be powdered as finely as possible and mixed with any suitable bait. A mixture of 28 g (1 oz) metaldehyde to 1·3 kg (3 lb) of very slightly moistened bran is excellent or ready-prepared pellets can be purchased. Place in small heaps where slugs are likely to feed. It is harmful to fish, birds and animals so take precautions to limit the risk of their being harmed. Crops sprayed with metaldehyde should not be eaten for 10 days.

Methiocarb. A chemical to kill slugs and snails. It is supplied in the form of small grey-blue granules ready for use as a slug and snail bait to be sprinkled lightly wherever these are seen or are damaging plants. Unlike metaldehyde it does not dehydrate the slugs and snails and so is as effective in wet as in dry conditions. It is harmful to fish and crops treated with methiocarb should not be eaten for 7 days.

Permethrin. Another of the synthetic pyrethroid insecticides for controlling white fly, aphids, leaf hoppers, thrips, etc.

Pirimicarb. An insecticide which kills all kinds of aphids very rapidly and effectively. For some edible crops such as lettuce an interval of 14 days is necessary between last spraying and harvesting.

Pirimiphos-methyl. An insecticide effective against a wide range of garden pests including ants, earwigs, aphids of all kinds, beetles, weevils, cabbage root fly, carrot fly, onion fly, caterpillars, sawflies, codling moth, leatherjackets, wireworms and white fly. It is harmful to bees and fish.

Propiconazole. A systemic fungicide for the control of black spot, mildew and rust on roses, rust on antirrhinums, hollyhocks and pelargoniums, and mildew on chrysanthemums, begonias and other plants.

Pyrethrum. This insecticide will kill a wide range of insects including aphids, leaf hoppers and thrips and is only moderately poisonous to warm-blooded animals, including man. It has been largely replaced by synthetic pyrethrins such as permethrin.

Sulphur. Ordinary flowers of sulphur, which can be purchased from any chemist, is an excellent fungicide for use as a dust directly on the foliage of plants. It will do no harm even to tender greenhouse plants, and can be used on grapes, even when ripening, to check the spread of mildew. Special brands of green horticultural sulphur are used in precisely the same way, the only advantage being that they are not so conspicuous on leaves. Wettable sulphur formulations are also prepared for dilution with water and use as sprays.

Tar-oil Winter Wash. This is chiefly used as a winter cleanser for fruit trees. It will kill the eggs of aphids and also overwintering insects, including scale insects, and clear the bark of lichens and green, scummy growths. Tar oil is very damaging to leaves and even to swelling buds so must only be used when the trees are quite dormant in the first half of winter. It is a manufactured article but usually prepared to a standard strength; the correct dilution is 2·8 l (5 pt) concentrated tar oil to 45 l (10 gal) of water.

Special formulations of tar oil emulsion are sold for sterilizing the soil in greenhouse borders. Use them strictly according to the maker's instructions.

Thiophanate-methyl. A systemic fungicide effective in the control of botrytis, mildews, apple and pear scab and some other diseases. This is not a good fungicide to alternate with benomyl as strains of fungi resistant to one are also likely to be resistant to the other.

Thiram. The name given to zinc oxide, a fungicide with a wide band of effectiveness against many diseases including rose black spot, tulip fire, tomato leaf mould and some mildews and rusts, including those of roses and chrysanthemums.

Triforine. A systemic fungicide useful for the control of powdery mildews, rose black spot and some other diseases.

Washing Soda (ready-mix). This mixture is particularly effective against gooseberry mildew provided frequent applications are made during spring and summer. It has the twin merits of being non-poisonous and non-staining but is quickly washed off by rain.

Chapter 34

Weeds and Weedkillers

Weeds may be defined as plants in the wrong place. Thus grass that is highly desirable in a lawn becomes a weed in the vegetable garden or flower border. Blackberries may be cultivated with care in the fruit garden and treated as pernicious weeds in the shrubbery or cultivated woodland.

It follows that no one chemical, or even class of chemicals, can be satisfactory to kill all weeds and yet be harmless to garden plants. Even the term 'weedkiller' can be misleading. Experts do not use it but refer to such chemicals as herbicides, allotting to each its particular characteristics and range of effectiveness.

Herbicides may be classified in various ways. Some are systemic, that is, they enter the sap of the plant and are carried to all parts of it. Some operate by direct contact with the plant, so they must be sprayed, watered or dusted on to its leaves or stems, while others operate through the soil and are referred to as residual, since they may remain present in the soil for a long time. There are also so-called total herbicides that kill almost every kind of plant, and selective herbicides which kill particular types of plant but are harmless, or relatively so, to others. Dalapon and alloxydim-sodium kill grasses and are either harmless or only slightly damaging to other types of plant. Couch grasses are particularly sensitive to alloxydim-sodium.

Some total herbicides can be made to act in a selective way by the manner in which they are applied and even the most selective of herbicides usually have some harmful effects outside the range of plants they are intended to kill. It is therefore important to choose the right method of application, to apply herbicides with great care and to follow to the letter instructions regarding strength and safety precautions.

Herbicides may be used to keep paths, drives and paved areas entirely clear of all growth; to clear ground prior to planting or sowing; to kill weeds in lawns; to kill weeds and grass around trees and shrubs, including fruit trees, or to kill or suppress weeds in flower borders and vegetable gardens. The chemicals used and the methods of application must be chosen to suit these different needs.

Clearing Paths and Drives. For this purpose herbicides that will kill plants of all kinds are required. Sodium chlorate is one of these and it can be applied dry or in solution usually at about 113 g per 4·5 l (4 oz per gal) of water. It is relatively cheap, quick acting and effective but it may be carried for considerable distances in soil water and so reach and injure plants that it is not supposed to touch. It is also highly inflammable, though proprietary formulations can be obtained which contain a fire depressant to reduce the risk of fire or explosion, and only those containing a fire depressant should be used in the garden.

Paraquat and diquat are more or less total herbicides available in granular or liquid form for solution or dilution in water according to label instructions, but only granules are marketed for garden use since both paraquat and diquat are dangerous poisons. Application can be made from a watering-can, from a special applicator fitted with a sprinkle bar which enables the diluted chemical to be applied direct to the weeds without risk of splashing or drifting on to nearby plants or grass which it will kill as readily as the weeds, or from a spraying machine with a hood to prevent drifting. Paraquat and diquat kill by contact with green leaves and are inactivated by contact with the soil. They have no residual effect and so are only useful for clearing paths and drives of weeds, not for preventing more weeds growing in their place.

This, however, is what simazine will do and one application properly made in spring can keep a path or drive clear for the rest of the year. Simazine is dissolved in water according to label instructions and applied in the same way as paraquat but so as to wet the whole surface of the path or drive. In gravel or in the soil in crevices between paving slabs it will form a film, perhaps 2·5 cm (1 in) deep, through which seedlings cannot grow. It is not very effective in killing weeds already established so a mixture of simazine with a contact herbicide is really best for treating paths or drives that are very weedy.

Glyphosate is a systemic herbicide that enters plants through their leaves. It acts rather slowly (most rapidly when plants are actively growing) but it makes a clean sweep of such difficult weeds as ground elder, docks, nettles and oxalis.

Clearing Vacant Ground. Sodium chlorate can be used for this but as long as it remains in the soil it will be unsafe to sow or plant anything there, and it is difficult to estimate just how long it will take for the chemical to be completely washed out. This will depend on rainfall and the type of soil, since the sodium chlorate will be held longer in a close soil such as clay or chalk than in an open one such as sand or gravel.

It is, therefore, safer to use paraquat or diquat which are inactivated as soon as they enter the soil, so that planning or sowing can be started immediately if desired, or glyphosate which seems to have little or no residual effect.

Weeds in Lawns. These are always destroyed with selective herbicides that kill broad-leaved plants but are relatively harmless to grass. The oldest herbicide of this type is lawn sand, a mixture of 3 parts by weight sulphate of ammonia, 1 part sulphate of iron and 20 parts fine silver sand. Lawn sand can be purchased ready mixed. It owes its selectivity to physical rather than to chemical reasons since it is held on the broad, more or less flat leaves of weeds and as it slowly dissolves scorches them by excessive salt concentration whereas it slips off the narrow, more or less upright leaves of grass on to the soil where it acts as a fertilizer. However, this satisfactory effect depends on very even distribution at the correct rate of 113 g per 0·8 sq m (4 oz per sq yd) at a time when there is no heavy rain for 24 hours or so. Too much lawn sand in one place can kill the grass as well as the weeds while rain following too soon after its application can wash it harmlessly away. All the same, application of lawn sand in spring or early summer is still a useful way of killing many weeds including moss and some other weeds that are resistant to other lawn weedkillers.

There are a number of these, including 2,4-D, MCPA, mecoprop, and dicamba. These are all chemically selective and are for dilution with (or solution in) water so that they can be applied through a sprinkle bar, preferably a wide one so that the lawn can be covered quickly. All these herbicides give some check to the grass so it is wise to feed this with a lawn fertilizer a few days before the weedkiller is used. They are also most effective when weeds are young, in spring or early summer, though they can be used at any time when

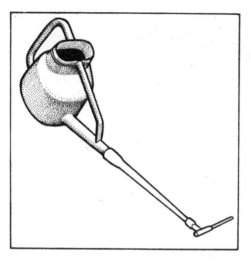

The use of a narrow sprinkle bar enables the gardener to apply herbicide to weeds under the foliage of plants in the border

grass is growing. Most can only be used safely on well-established turf.

It is wise to ring the changes on selective lawn weedkillers since some are more effective than others against particular weeds. Some manufacturers offer mixtures of chemicals to give as wide a band of effectiveness as possible. Some also mix selective herbicides with fertilizers so that the lawn can be fed and weeded at the same time. These are for dry use and may be applied with a mechanical fertilizer distributor. Moss can be killed with lawn sand (it is the sulphate of iron in it which is the effective moss killer) while 2,4-D is also a very effective bindweed (convolvulus) killer.

Killing Weeds Around Plants. The most useful chemicals to kill weeds around growing plants, including trees and shrubs, are paraquat, diquat, glyphosate, dichlobenil and simazine. The first three are total herbicides but can be made selective by application from a watering-can or special applicator fitted with a narrow, 7·5 cm (3 in) sprinkle bar which can be passed under the lowest leaves of the plants and between plants even when growing fairly close together. By this means the herbicide is applied direct to the leaves of the weeds and kills them only.

Simazine is rendered selective by applying it at exactly the right strength and quantity to make a film in the top 2·5 cm (1 in) or so of soil but not to penetrate more deeply where it may do harm to the roots of the garden plants. It is not carried about freely in the soil like sodium chlorate. All the same, it cannot be used safely around all plants and must always be applied with care according to label instructions. It is particularly useful in keeping rose beds free of weeds. Dichlobenil is generally used in granular form and selectivity depends on spreading the correct amount for the particular purpose in hand. Manufacturers' instructions for this and similar herbicides must be followed.

General Precautions. Even minute quantities of some herbicides can damage some plants. Great care should be taken not to allow them to spread where they are not wanted. If a watering-can is used for herbicides it should be set aside for that purpose alone and not used for watering plants, however carefully it is washed out. That is one advantage of having a special applicator for weedkillers as there will be no temptation to use it for any other purpose. Even so, apparatus should be well washed out after each use to prevent residues of one herbicide becoming accidentally mixed with another required for a different purpose.

Lawn mowings from lawns treated with the hormone type of weedkiller (2,4-D, MCPA, etc.) should not be placed on the compost heap for several weeks but should be burned or otherwise disposed of where they can do no harm. It is unwise to use this type of weedkiller on very hot days lest vapour should drift on to surrounding plants and injure some of them. Tomatoes are particularly sensitive.

Index

Page numbers in italics indicate illustrations

Abelia 244
  A. floribunda 244
  A. × *grandiflora* 244
  A. schumanii 244
Abor-vitae, see Thuja
Abutilon 245, 429
  A. megapotamicum 245, *296*,
    429, *679*
  A. striatum thompsonii 429
  A. × *suntense* 245
  A. vitifolium 245
Acacia 429
  A. armata 429
  A. baileyana 429
  A. dealbata 429
  A. drummondii 429
  A. longifolia 429
Acaena 175
  A. buchananii 176
  A. microphylla 176
  A. novae-zelandiae 176
Acalypha 429
  A. godseffiana 429
  A. hispida 429
  A. wilkensiana 429
Acantholimon 176
  A. glumaceum 176, *209*
Acanthus 114
  A. mollis 114, *145*
  A. spinosus 114
Acer 245, 751
  A. capillipes 245
  A. davidii 245
  A. griseum 245, *289*
  A. grosseri 245
  A. hersii 245
  A. japonica Aureum *687*
  A. negundo 245
  A. palmatum 245, *577*, *687*
  A. pennsylvanicum 245
  A. platanoides 245, *289*
  A. pseudoplatanus 245, *289*
  A. saccharum 245
Achillea 114, 176
  A. ageratifolia 176
  A. clavennae 176, *209*
  A. filipendulina 114, *145*
  A. × *lewisii* 176
  A. millefolium 114, *145*
  A. ptarmica 114
  A. taygetea 114
  A. tomentosa 176
Achimenes 430
  A. cultivar 449
acidity 14-16, 32
Acidanthera 340
Acinos alpinus 182
Aconitum 115
  A. fischeri 115
  A. lyoctonum 115
  A. napellus 115, *146*
  A. volubile 115
  A. wilsonii 115
Acorus 388
  A. calamus 388
Acroclinium roseum 85
Actinidia kolomitka *296*
Adams needle, see Yucca
Adonis 69
  A. aestivalis 69
  A. annua 69
  A. autumnalis 69
  A. vernalis 69
Aechmea 430
  A. fasciata 430, *513*
  A. fulgens 430
Aeonium 529
Aesculus 246
  A. × *carnea* 246, *289*
  A. hippocastanus 246
  A. indica 246
  A. parviflora 246, *577*

A. pavia 246
Aethionema 176
  A. armenum 176
  A. Warley Rose *209*
Aethionemas 173
Africa corn lily, see Ixia
African harlequin flower, see
  Sparaxis
African hemp, see Sparmannia
African lily, see Agapanthus
African violet, see Saintpaulia
Agapanthus 61, 115, 430
  A. Headbourne Hybrids *146*
  A. africanus 115, 430
  A. campanulatus 115
  A. umbellatus 115
Agathaea, see Felicia
  A. coelestis 82
Agave 431, *529*
  A. americana 431, *529*
  A. filifera 431
  A. victoria-reginae 431
Ageratum 69, 70
Aglaonema 431
  A. commutatum 431
Agrostemma 70
  A. githago 70
Agrostis 84
  A. nebulosa 84
  A. pulchella 84
Aichryson 431
  A. × *domesticum* 431
Ailanthus 246
  A. altissima 246
  A. glandulosa 246
Aithionema 176
  A. grandiflorum 176
Ajuga 176
  A. reptans 176, *209*
Alamanda cathartica 431
Alchemilla 115
  A. mollis 115, *146*
Alder, see Alnus
Alexandrina laurel, see Danae
Alisma 388
  A. plantago-aquatica 388
alkalinity 16
Alknet, see Anchusa
Allamanda 431
Allium 115, 340
  A. areophilum 340
  A. caeruleum 340
  A. carinatum pulchellum 340
  A. cernum 340
  A. christophii 340, *353*
  A. giganteum *54*, 340
  A. karataviense 340
  A. moly 340, *353*
  A. neapolitanum 340
  A. oreophilum *353*
  A. rosenbachianum 340
  A. siculum 340
  A. spaerocephalum 340
Alnus 246
  A. glutinosa 246
  A. incana 246
Alocasia 431
Aloe 432, *529*
  A. variegata 432, *529*
Alonsoa 70
  A. acutifolia 70
  A. warscewiczii 70
Aloysia 432
  A. triphylla 281, 432
Alstroemeria 115
  A. aurantiaca 116
  A. chilensis 116
  A. haemantha 116
  A. ligtu 116, *354*
  A. psitticina 116
  A. violacea 116
Althaea, see Hollyhock
  A. ficifolia 86
  A. rosea 86
Aluminium plant, see Pilea
Alyssum *52*, 57, 70, 177
  A. maritimum 70
  A. saxatile 177
Amaranthus 70

A. caudatus 70
  A. hypochondriacus 71
  A. tricolor 71
Amaryllis, see Hippeastrum
  A. belladonna 340, *354*
Amazon lily, see Eucharis
Amelanchier 246
  A. canadensis 246
  A. grandiflora 246
  A. laevis 246
  A. lamarckii 246, *290*
  A. stolonifera 246
American blight, see woolly
  aphis
American cowslip, see
  Dodecatheon
American currant, see Ribes
Ampelopsis, see Parthenocissis
Anagallis 71
  A. monelii 71
  A. linifolia 71
Ananas 432
  A. bracteatus striatus 432
  A. comosus 432
Anaphalis 116
  A. cinnamomea *146*
  A. margaritacea 116
  A. nibigena 116
  A. triplinervis 116
  A. yeodensis 116
Anchusa 71, 111, 116
  A. azurea 116
  A. caespitosa 116
  A. capensis 71
  A. myosotidiflora 116, 120
Andromeda 247
  A. polifolia 247
Androsace 173, 177
  A. carnea 177
  A. imbricata 177
  A. lanuginosa 177
  A. primuloides Chumbyi *210*
  A. sarmentosa 177
Anemone 116, 169, 177, 339,
  341
  A. alpina 178
  A. apennina 177, *354*
  A. blanda 177, *341*
  A. coronaria 341, *354*
  A. × *fulgens* 341, *355*
  A. hepatica, see Hepatica
  A. hupehensis 117
  A. × *hybrida* 116, *147*
  A. japonica 116
  A. nemorosa 177, 341, *355*
  A. pulsatilla, see Pulsatilla
    178, 205
  A. sulphurea 178
Anethum graveolens, see Dill
Angels trumpet, see
  Brugmansia
annuals 11, 47-106
  half-hardy 47-106
  hardy 47-106
Antennaria 178
  A. dioica 178, *210*
Anthemis 117, 178
  A. cupaniana 178
  A. marschalliana 178
  A. santi-johannis 117
  A. tinctoria 117
Anthericum 117
  A. lilago 117
  A. ramosum 117
Anthriscus cerefolium, see
  Chervil
Anthurium 432
  A. andreanum 432
  A. scherzerianum 432
Anthyllis 178
  A. montana 178, *210*
  A. vulneraria 178
Antirrhinum 47, 71, 108
  A. asarina 178
  A. glutinosum 178
ants 726
Aphelandra 433
  A. squarrosa louisae 433
Aphidoletes aphidimyza 725

aphids 725, 726
Aponogeton 388
  A. aldenhamensis 388
  A. distachyus 388
Aporocactus 529
Apple Sunrise *739*
Apples 638-51
Apricots 652-54
Aquilegia 111, 117, 179
  A. bertolonii *210*
  A. caerulea 179
  A. glandulosa 179
  A. longissima 117
  A. McKana Hybrids *147*
  A. vulgaris 117
Arabis 179
  A. caucasica 179, *211*
Araucaria 433
  A. heterophylla 433
Arbutus 247
  A. andrachne 247
  A. × *andrachnoides* 247
  A. menziesii 247
  A. unedo 247, *290*
Arctostaphylos uva-ursi *577*
Arctotis 72
  A. grandis 72
Ardisia 433
  A. crispa 433
Arenaria 28, 179
  A. balearica 179, *211*
  A. caespitosa 179
  A. montana 179
  A. purpurascens 179
Argemone 72
  A. grandiflora 72
  A. mexicana 72
Argyranthemum 433
  A. frutescens 433
Aristolochia 433
  A. durior 433
  A. elegans 434
  A. macrophylla 433
Armeria 117, 179
  A. caespitosa 180
  A. juniperifolia 180, *211*
  A. maritima 179
  A. plantaginea 117
Arnebia 72
  A. cornuta 72
  A. echioides 72
  A. pulchra 72
Arrow arum, see Peltandra
Arrow head, see Sagittaria
Artemisia 118, 180, 247
  A. abrotanum 247
  A. absinthum 118
  A. arborescens *147*
  A. caucasica 180
  A. dranunculus, see Tarragon
  A. glacialis 180
  A. lactiflora 118
  A. latiloba 118
  A. ludoviciana 118
  A. schmidtiana *58*, 118
  A. schmidtii 180
  A. stelleriana 118
Artichoke, Jerusalem 543
Artillery plant, see Pilea
Arum, see Zantedeschia
  A. creticum *355*
Aruncus 118
  A. dioicus 118
  A. sylvester 118
Arundinaria, see Bamboo
  A. japonica 249
  A. murielae 249
  A. viridi-striata 249, *578*
Arundo 388
  A. donax 388
Asarina, see Antirrhinum
  A. procumbens 178
Asclepias 434
Ash, see Fraxinus
Asparagus 434, 544
  A. densiflorus Meyeri *449*
  A. plumosus 434
  A. setaceus *450*
  A. sprengeri 434

Asperula 72, 180
  A. azurea 73
  A. gussoni 180
  A. hirta 180
  A. odorata 180
  A. orientalis 73
  A. suberosa 180, *211*
Asphodeline 118
  A. lutea 118
Aspidistra 434
  A. elatior 434
Aster 73, 118
  A. acris 119
  A. alpinus 180
  A. amellus 118
  A. cordifolius 119
  A. ericoides 119
  A. farreri 180
  A. forrestii 180
  A. frikartii 118
  A. hybridus luteus 164
  A. linosyris 119
  A. novae-angliae 118
  A. novi-belgii 118
  A. purdomii 180
  A. sedifolius nanus 180
  A. subcaeruleus 180
  A. tongolensis 119
Astilbe 119, 181, 434
  A. × *arendsii* 119, *148*
  A. astilboides 119
  A. chinensis pumila 181
  A. × *crispa* 181
  A. davidii 119
  A. glaberrima saxatilis 181
  A. japonica 119
  A. thunbergerii 119
Astrantia 119
  A. carniolica 119
  A. major 119, *148*
  A. maxima 119, *148*
Astrophytum 529
Atriplex 247
  A. halimus 244, 247
Aubergine 545
Aubrieta *52*, 181
Aucuba 243, 248
  A. japonica 248, *578*
Auricula, see Primula
Autumn crocus, see Colchicum
Avena sterilis 84
Avens, see Geum
Axclepias curassavica 434
Azalea 12, *52*, 248, 435
  A. amoenum 248
  A. indica 435
  A. kaempferi 248
  A. pontica 248

Babiana 341
Baboon root, see Babiana
Baby blue eyes, see Nemophila
Bacillus thuringiensis 725
bacteria 13-15, 23, 30, 34
bacterial canker 726
Balloon flower, see Platycodon
Balm 564
Balsam, see Impatiens
Bamboo 249
Baptisia 120
  B. australis 120
Barberry, see Berberis
Barberton daisy, see Gerbera
bark 33
Barrenwort, see Epimedium
Bartonia, see Mentzelia
  B. aurea 90
basal rot 727
basal stem rot 727
Basil 564
Batchelors buttons, see Kerria
Bay, see Laurus
Bead plant, see Nertera
Beans 545-48
Bears breeches, see Acanthus
Beauty bush, see Kolkwitzia
Beauty of Nice stocks, see
  Stocks
bedding plants 11, 47, 108, 381

Beech 243, see also Fagus
bees, leaf-cutting 727
beetles 727
Beetroot 549
Begonia 73, 435, 746
  B. haageana 437
  B. lucerna 437
  B. manicata 437
  B. masoniana 437
  B. pendula 450
  B. rex 436, 450
  B. Rieger Hybrid 451
  B. semperflorens 73, 437
  B. socotrana 436
Belladonna lily, see Amaryllis
Bellflower, see Campanula
Bellis 74
Bellium 181
  B. bellidoides 181
  B. minutum 181
Bellwort, see Uvularia
Beloperone guttata 479
benomyl 767
Berberis 249
  B. aggregata 249
  B. buxifolia 249
  B. × carminea 249
  B. darwinii 244, 249, 578
  B. empetrifolia 249
  B. gagnepainii 249
  B. janesiana 249
  B. × ottawensis 249
  B. prattii 249
  B. pruinosa 250
  B. Rubrostilla 578
  B. sargentiana 250
  B. × stenophylla 244, 250
  B. thunbergii 249
  B. verruculosa 250
  B. wilsoniae 249
Bergamot, see Monarda
Bergenia 120
  B. cordifolia 120
  B. purpurascens 120
Betonica, see Stachys
Betula 250
  B. albo-sinensis 250
  B. ermanii 250
  B. lutea 250
  B. nigra 250
  B. papyrifera 250
  B. pendula 250, 290
  B. utilis var. jacquemontii 250
biennials 47, 48, 67-106, 108
big bud 728
Billbergia 437
  B. nutans 437
Birch 50, see also Betula
Bird of paradise flower, see
  Strelitzia
bitter pit 728
black spot 729
Black-eyed Susan, see
  Thunbergia alata
Blackberries 654-5
blackfly 728
blackleg 728
Bladder campion 17
Bladder senna, see Colutea
Blazing star, see Tritonia
Blazing star, see Liatris
Bleeding heart, see Dicentra
Blessed thistle, see Silybum
blight, potato 729
Blood flower, see Haemanthus
Bloodroot 207
blossom wilt 729
blossom-end rot 729
blotchy ripening 730
Blue gum, see Eucalyptus
Blue lace flower, see
  Trachymene
Blue marguerite, see Felicia
Bluebell, see Hyacinthoides
Boat lily, see Tradescantia
Bocconia, see Macleaya
Bog arum, see Calla
Bog bean, see Menyanthes
bog gardens 383

bog plants 393-4
Bog rosemary, see Andromeda
bonemeal 30, 34
Borage 564
Borago officinalis, see Borage
Bordeaux mixture 767
Borecole, see Kale
boron 31-2
Boronia 437
  B. megastigma 437
Boston ivy, see Parthenocissus
  286
botanical names 113, 114
botrytis 730
Bottle brush, see Callistemon
Bougainvillea 437, 744
Bouvardia 438
Bow string hemp, see
  Sansevieria
Box 11, see also Buxus
Brachycome 74
  B. iberidifolia 74
Brachyglottis 250
  B. compacta 250
  B. greyi 250
  B. laxifolia 250
Bramble fruits 654-5
Bramble, see Rubus
Brambles 18
Brandy bottle, see Nuphar
brick 25-8
Bridal wreath, see Francoa
Briza maxima 84
  B. media 84
  B. minor 84
Broccoli 550
Brompton stocks, see Stocks
Bromus briziformis 84
Broom, see Cytisus; Genista;
  Spartium
Browallia 74, 438
  B. speciosa 74, 438
  B. viscosa 74, 438
brown heart 32
brown rot 730
Brugmansia 438
  B. arborea 438
  B. cornigera 438
  B. sanguinea 438
  B. suavolens 438
Brunfelsia 439
  B. pauciflora 439
Brunnera 120
  B. macrophylla 116, 120
Brussel sprouts 551
Bryophyllum 529
  B. pinnatum 529
Buck bean, see Menyanthes
bud blast 731
bud dropping 731
budding 241
Buddleia 250
  B. alternifolia 251
  B. davidii 236, 250
  B. fallowiana 251
  B. globosa 251, 579
  B. × weyeriana 251
Bugbane, see Cimicifuga
Bugle, see Ajuga
Bulbocodium 342
  B. vernum 342, 355
bulbous iris 339
bulbs 11, 47, 50, 108, 338-80
Bulrush, see Scirpus
Buphthalmum 120
  B. salicifolium 120
  B. speciosum 120
Bupirimate 767
Burning bush, see Dictamnus
Busy Lizzie, see Impatiens
Butchers broom, see Ruscus
Butomus 388
  B. umbellatus 388
Buttercup, see Ranunculus
Butterfly flower, see Schizanthus
Butterfly tulip, see Calochortus
Button snakeroot, see Liatris

Buxus 251
  B. sempervirens 251

Cabbage 552
  Chinese 553
Cacalia coccinea 81
Cacti 511-531
  compost 512
  potting compost for 33
  propagation 512
  watering 512
Caladium 439
Calamint, see Calamintha
Calamintha 181
Calandrinia 74, 182
  C. grandiflora 74
  C. umbellata 74, 182
Calathea 439
  C. makoyana 439
Calceolaria 182, 439, 745, 750
  C. burbidgei 440
  C. clibranii 440
  C. darwinii 182
  C. integrifolia 440
  C. polyrrhiza 182
  C. profusa 440
calcium 31-3, 37
Calendula 74
Californian poppy, see
  Eschscholzia
Californian tree poppy, see
  Romneya 161, 313
Calla 388, see also
  Zantedeschia
  C. palustris 388
Callirhoe 182
  C. involucrata 182
Callistemon 440
  C. citrinus 440
  C. salignus 440
  C. speciosus 440
Callistephus, see Aster
  C. chinensis 73
Callitriche 389
  C. verna 389
  C. autumnalis 389
Calluna 251
  C. vulgaris 251
Calochortus 342
  C. splendens 342
  C. venustus 342
Calomeria 441
  C. amaranthoides 441
Caltha 389
  C. palustris 389
  C. polypetala 389
Calvary clover 75
Camassia cusickii 355
Camellia 252, 441
  C. Fascination 685
  C. japonica 252, 441, 579
  C. reticulata 441
  C. sasanqua 252, 441
  C. × williamsii 252, 441
Campanula 120, 182, 441, 442
  C. alpestris 182
  C. caespitosa 120, 182
  C. carpatica 120, 182, 212
  C. cochlearifolia 182, 212
  C. excisa 182
  C. garganica 182
  C. glomerata Alba 121, 149
  C. isophylla 441
  C. lactiflora 120
  C. latifolia 120
  C. latiloba 120
  C. medium 75
  C. muralis 182
  C. persicifolia 120, 149
  C. portenschlagiana 182
  C. poscharskyana 182
  C. pulla 182
  C. × pulloides 182
  C. pusilla 182
  C. pyramidalis 441
  C. raddeana 182
  C. tommasiniana 182
  C. waldsteiniana 182
  C. zoysii 182

Campion, see Lychnis
Campsis 252
  C. grandiflora 252
  C. radicans 252
  C. × tagliabuana 252
Canary creeper, see Tropaeolum
Candytuft, see Iberis
cane blight 731
cane midge 731
cane spot 731
canker 731
Canna 442
Canterbury bell 75
Cape cowslip, see Lachenalia
Cape figwort, see Phygelius
Cape gooseberry, see Physalis
Cape jasmine, see Gardenia
Cape primrose, see
  Streptocarpus
Capsicum 553
capsid bugs 732
captan 767
Caraway 564
carbaryl 768
Cardinal flower, see Lobelia
Cardiocrinum, see Lily
  C. giganteum 356
Carex 389
  C. pendula 389
  C. pseudocyperus 389
Carnation 75, 76, 442, 443
  border 121, 122
Carpenteria 252
  C. californica 252
Carpinus 252
  C. betulus 252
Carrots 553
Carum carvi, see Caraway
Caryopteris 253
  C. × clandonensis 253, 579
  C. incana 253
Cassia 443
  C. corymbosa 443
Cassiope Muirhead 212
Castanea 253
  C. sativa 253
Castor oil plant, see Ricinus
Cat-tail, see Typha
Catalpa 253
  C. bignonioides 253, 290
Catananche 253
  C. caerulea 122, 149
Catchfly, see Silene
caterpillars 725, 732
Catmint, see Nepeta
Caucasian scabious 108
Cauliflower 554
Ceanothus 12, 254
  C. arboreus 254
  C. × delineanus 254
  C. dentatus 254
  C. impressus 254
  C. rigidus 254
  C. thyrsiflorus 254, 296
  C. Topaz 296
  C. × veitchianus 254
Cedar, see Cedrus
Cedrus 254
  C. deodara 254
  C. libani 254
Celastrus 255
  C. orbiculatus 255
Celeriac 555
Celery 32, 556
Celosia 76, 443
  C. argentea 443
Celsia, see Verbascum
  C. arcturus 105
  C. cretica 105
cement 26
Centaurea 122, see also
  Cornflower, Sweet Sultan
  C. dealbata 122, 149
  C. macrocephala 122
  C. montana 122
  C. moschata 103
Centranthus 122
  C. albus 122
  C. coccineus 122

Cephalaria 122
  C. alpina 226
  C. tatarica 122
Cephalocereus 529
  C. senilis 529
Cerastium 123, 183
  C. biebersteinii 183
  C. tomentosum 183
Ceratostigma 123, 255
  C. plumbaginoides 123
  C. willmottianum 123, 255
Cercis 255
  C. siliquastrum 255
Cereus 529
Cestrum 444
  C. aurantiacum 444
  C. elegans 444
  C. parqui 444
Chaenomeles 255
  C. speciosa 235, 255
  C. × superba Knap Hill Scarlet
    297
chafers 732
chalk 14-16, 32, 37, 38
Chamaecyparis 256
  C. lawsoniana 233, 243, 256
  C. macrocarpa 243
  C. nookatensis 256
  C. obtusa 256
  C. pisifera 256
  C. × lawsoniana 243
  C. × leylandii 243
Chamaedorea 444
  C. elegans 444
Chamomile, see Anthemis
Cheiranthis × allionii 76
Cheiranthus 76, 123
  C. cheiri 76
  C. Harpur Crewe 123
  C. mutabilis 123
chelates, see sequestrols
Chelone 123
  C. barbata 123
  C. lyonii 123
  C. obliqua 123
chemicals, 11, 13, 31
  analysis 17
  control of pests and diseases
    767
Chenille plant, see Acalypha
Cherries 655-9
Cherry laurel 243, see also
  Prunus laurocerasus
Cherry pie, see Heliotrope
Cherry plum, see Prunus
  cerasifera
Cherry, see Prunus
Chervil 564
Chestnut, see Aesculus;
  Castanea
Chiastophyllum, see Cotyledon
Chicory 557
Chilean crocus, see Tecophilea
Chilean fire bush, see
  Embothrium
Chilean jasmine, see Mandevilla
Chilli, see Capsicum
Chimonanthus 256
  C. praecox 256, 297
Chincherinchee, see Ornithogalum
Chinese bellflower, see Abutilon
Chiondoxa 342
  C. luciliae 342, 356
  C. sardensis 342
Chives 558
chlorophyll 18, 32
Chlorophytum 444
  C. comosum 444
chlorosis 32, 38, 732
chocolate spot 733
Choisya 257
  C. ternata 257, 580
Chorizema 444
  C. cordatum 444
  C. ilicifolium 444
  C. varium 444
Christmas rose, see Helleborus
Chrysanthemum 62, 77, 123,
  504-510

C. Buckland 62
C. carinatum 77
C. coronarium 77
C. maximum 123
C. parthenium 77
C. rubellum 123
C. segetum 77
C. spectabilis 77
C. uliginosum 123
Chrysogonum 183
C. virginianum 183
Chusan palm, see Trachycarpus
Cigar plant, see Cuphea
Cimicifuga 124
C. japonica 124
C. racemosa 124
C. simplex 124
Cineraria 445, 745, 750
Cinquefoil, see Potentilla
Cissus 445
C. antarctica 445, 513
C. discolor 445, 514
Cistus 12, 257
C. × corbariensis 257
C. crispus 257
C. × cyprius 257
C. incanus 257
C. ladaniferus 257
C. laurifolius 257
C. Peggy Sannons 580
C. × pulverulenta 257
C. × purpureus 257
Cladanthus 77
C. arabicus 77
Clarkia 77, 78
clay 11, 13-15, 22, 24, 29
Clematis 16, 235, 236, 257, 445
C. alpina 297
C. armandii 258, 297
C. Beauty of Worcester 257
C. Belle of Woking 257
C. Comtesse de Bouchaud 257
C. Duchess of Edinburgh 257
C. × durandii 124
C. Ernest Markham 298, 684
C. flammula 257
C. heracleifolia davidiana 124
C. Henryi 257
C. indivisa 445
C. integrifolia 124
C. × jackmanii 298
C. Jackmanii Superba 257
C. macropetala 258
C. montana 257, 298, 683
C. Mrs N Thompson 684
C. Nelly Moser 257
C. Perle d'Azur 682
C. tangutica 258, 298, 684
Clematis, herbaceous 124
Cleome 78
C. spinosa 78
Clerodendrum 258, 446
C. bungei 258
C. falla 446
C. speciosissimum 446
C. thomsoniae 446
C. trichotomum 258
Clianthus 446
C. dampieri 446
C. formosus 446
C. puniceus 446
climbers 235-8, 242
Climbing lily, see Gloriosa
Clivia 446
C. miniata 447
cloches 406-408
Clog plant, see Nematanthus
club root 733
coal ashes 34
Cobaea 78, 447
C. scandens 78, 447
Cobnuts 659-661
Cockscomb, see Celosia
Cocos, see Microcoelum
C. weddelliana 483
Codiaeum 447
C. variegatum cultivars 451
codling moth 733

Codonopsis 183
C. clematidea 183
C. ovata 183
Coix lachryma-jobi 84
Colchicum 343
C. autumnale 343, 356
C. speciosum 343, 356
C. Water Lily 356
Coleus 747, see also Solenostemom
Collinsia 78
C. bicolor 78
Columbine 117, see also Aquilegia
Columnea 447
C. × banksii 448, 452
C. gloriosa 448
C. microphylla 448, 452
Colutea 258
Common immortelle, see Xeranthemum
compost 16, 24, 30, 34
accelerators 34
heap 35
making 34, 35
rate of decay 34
concrete 26-29
Coneflower, see Rudbeckia
Conifers 232
pruning 235
Connemara heath, see Daboecia
Conophytum 529
Convallaria 343, 448, see also Lily of the valley
C. majalis 124, 136, 343
Convulvulus 78, 184, 259
C. annua 78
C. cneorum 184, 259
C. mauritanicus 184
C. tricolor 478, see also Ipomoea
Copper leaf, see Acalypha
Copper sulphate 768
Coral tree, see Erythrina
Cordyline 448
C. australis 448
C. fruticosa 448
Coreopsis 78, 111, 124
C. auriculata superba 124
C. grandiflora 124
C. lanceolata 124
C. tinctoria 78
C. verticillata 124
Coriander 564
C. sativum, see Coriander
Corms 338-380
Corn Cockle, see Agrostemma
Corn salad 558
Cornflower 78, 79
Cornus 259
C. alba 259, 580
C. florida 259, 580
C. kousa 259
C. mas 259
C. nuttalii 259
C. sanguinea 259
C. stolonifera 259
Coronilla 448
C. glauca 448
Cortaderia, see Pampas grass
C. selloana 140
corticium disease 733
Corydalis 184
C. cashmeriana 184
C. cheilanthifolia 184
C. lutea 184
C. thalictrifolia 184
Corylopsis 259
C. pauciflora 259
C. sinensis 260
C. spicata 259
Corylus 260
C. avellana 260
C. maxima 260
Cosmea, see Cosmos
Cosmos 79
C. bipinnatus 79
C. sulphureus 79
Cotinus 260

C. americanus 260
C. coggygria 260, 581
C. obovatus 260
Cotoneaster 260
C. adpressus 261
C. conspicuus 261
C. Cornubia 581
C. dammeri 212, 260
C. dielsianus 260
C. franchetii 260
C. frigidus 260
C. henryanus 260
C. horizontalis 235, 261, 581
C. microphyllus 261
C. salicifolius 260
C. simonsii 244, 260
C. sternianus 260
C. thymifolius 261
C. × watereri Rothschildianus 738
Cotton grass, see Eriophorum
Cotyledon 184
C. oppositifolia 184
C. simplicifolia 184
C. umbilicus 184
cow manure 35, 36
Crab apple, see Malus
Crambe 124
C. cordifolia 124
Cranesbill, see Geranium
Crassula 465
C. coccinea 493
C. falcata 465
Crataegus 261
C. crus-galli 261
C. laevigata 261
C. × lavallei 261
C. monogyna 243, 261
C. oxyacantha 243, 261
C. persimilis 261
crazy paving 28
Cream cups 96, see also Platystemon
Creeping Jenny, see Lysimachia
Crepis 185
C. aurea 185
C. incana 185, 213
Cress 559
Crinodendron 261
C. hookerianum 261
Crinum 343, 465
C. bulbispermum 343
C. capense 344
C. longifolium 465
C. moorei 465
C. × powellii 343, 465
Crocosmia 344
C. × crocosmiiflora 344
C. masonorum 344, 357
C. paniculatus 344, 357
Crocus 50, 339, 344
C. biflorus 345
C. chrysanthus 345, 357
C. imperati 345
C. kotschyanus zonatus 345
C. pulchellus 345
C. sieveri 345
C. speciosus 345, 357
C. susianus 345
C. tomasinianus 345, 358
C. vernus 345, 358
Crossandra 465
C. infundibuliformis 465
Croton, see Codiaeum
crown 110
crown gall 733
Crown imperial, see Fritillaria
Cryptanthus 465
C. bromelioides Tricolor 514
Cryptolaemus montrouzieri 725
Cryptomeria 261
C. japonica 261, 262
cuckoo spit 734
Cucumber 559-561
cultivation 13, 14, 18, 24
autumn and winter 19, 20
spring and summer 19, 22
Cup and saucer vine, see Cobaea

Cuphea 79, 465
C. ignea 79, 465
Cupids dart, see Catananche
× Cupressocyparis 262
Cupressus 262
C. arizonica 262
C. glabra pyramidalis 262
C. macrocarpa 234, 262
C. sempervirens 262
Currants, black 661-665
Cushion pink, see Silene
Cushion saxifrage 173
cuttings 47
autumn 238, 240
summer 238-240
heat for 239
mist propagation 239
rooting medium 239
cutworms 734
Cyananthus 185
C. lobatus 185
C. microphyllus 185
Cyclamen 169, 345, 466
C. coum 346, 358
C. europaeum 346, 358
C. hederaefolium 213, 346, 358
C. libanoticum 346
C. persicum 345, 452, 466
C. pseudibericum 346
C. repandum 346, 358
Cydonia, see Chaenomeles
Cymbalaria 185
C. aequitriloba 185
C. muralis 185
C. pallida 185
Cynoglossum 79
C. amabile 79
Cyperus 389, 466
C. alternifolius 466
C. involucratus 389
Cypress, see Chamaecyparis; Cupressus
Cypripedium 185
C. calceolus 185
C. reginae 185
C. spectabile 185
Cyrtanthus 467
Cytisus 262, 467
C. ardoinii 263
C. battandieri 263, 582
C. × beanii 263
C. canariensis 263, 467
C. dallimorei 263
C. × kewensis 263
C. monspessulanus 263
C. multiflorus 262
C. × praecox 262, 582
C. purpureus 263
C. scoparius 262
C. × spachianus 263

Daboecia 263
D. cantabrica 263, 582
Daffodils 47, see also Narcissus
Dahlia 80, 339, 346, 347, 359
Types 347
Daisy bush, see Olearia
Daisy, see Bellis
Dames Violet, see Hesperis
damping off 734
Danae 263
D. racemosa 263
Daphne 185, 263, 467
D. blagayana 186
D. × burkwoodii 264
D. cneorum 185, 213
D. collina 264
D. mezereum 264
D. odora 264, 467
D. retusa 583
D. rupestris 186

Deciduous cypress, see Taxodium
Delphinium 110, 111, 124, 125, 186
D. ajacis 87, see also Larkspur
D. nuducaule 186
derris 768
Deutzia 264, 467
D. × elegantissima 264
D. gracilis 467
D. × hybrida Mont Rose 583
D. scabra 264
Dianthus 58, 80, 125, 186
D. allwoodii 125, 126
D. alpinus 186, 213
D. barbatus 103
D. chinensis 80
D. deltoides 186
D. freynii 187
D. glacialis 186
D. gratianopolitanus 186
D. heddewigii 80
D. La Bourbrille 214
D. Mrs Sinkins 150
D. pavonius 186
D. plumarius 125
D. superbus 125, 187
Diascia 187
D. barbaria 187
D. cordata 187
D. rigescens 187
Dicentra 126, 468
D. eximia 126
D. formosa 126
D. spectabilis 126, 150, 468
Dictamnus 126
D. albus 126
Didiscus caerulea 501
die back 734
Dieffenbachia 468
D. amoena 453
D. picta 468, 453
Dierama 188
D. pulcherrimum 348, 359
digging 14, 18, 19-22
Digitalis 126, see also Foxglove
D. ambigua 126
D. ferruginea 126
D. grandiflora 126
D. mertoniensis 126
Dill 564
dimethoate 768
Diplacus, see Mimulus
D. glutinosus 484
disease 23, 717-770
bacterial 718, 722
fungal 718, 720
rusts 718
soil 722
symptoms 717
viral 718, 721
disorders 16
deficiency 719
physiological 719, 722
ditches 24
Dodecatheon 187
D. media 187
Dogs tooth violet, see Erythronium
Dogwood, see Cornus
dollar spot 734
Doronicum 126
D. austriacum 126
D. columnae 126
D. Miss Mason 150
D. orientale 126
D. plantagineum 126
Dorotheanthus 80
D. belliiformis 80
Double daisies 47
Double everlasting, see Helichrysum
Douglas fir, see Pseudotsuga
Dove tree, see Davidia
Draba 187
D. bruniifolia 187
D. dedeana 187
D. rigida bryoides imbricata 187

Dames Violet, see Hesperis

Danae 263
D. racemosa 263
Daphne 185, 263, 467
D. blagayana 186
D. × burkwoodii 264
D. cneorum 185, 213
D. collina 264
D. mezereum 264
D. odora 264, 467
D. retusa 583
D. rupestris 186
Datura, see Brugmansia
Davidia 264
D. involucrata 264
Dawn redwood, see Metasequoia
Day lily, see Hemerocallis
Dead nettle, see Lamium
deciduous 232

Dracaena 468
  D. concinna 454
  D. deremensis 454, 468
  D. Massangeana 468
  D. sanderiana 468
Dracocephalum, see
  Physostegia
Dragons head, *see Physostegia*
drainage 14, 23, 24
drains, central 24
dressings 24
Dropwort, *see Filipendula*
dry set 734
dry walls 11, 169-70, 175
Dryas 188
  D. drummondii 188
  D. octopetala 188, 214
  D. × *suendermannii* 188
dung 13, 15, 17, 24, 30
Dutchmans pipe, *see*
  Aristolochia
Dwarf palm, *see Chamaedorea*

Earth star, *see Cryptanthus*
earthworms 30, 735
earwigs 735
East Lothian stocks, *see Stocks*
Eccremocarpus 81
  E. scaber 81, 299
Echeveria 468
  E. elegans 469
  E. gibbiflora 469
  E. secunda 468
Echinacea 127
  E. purpurea 127
Echinocactus 529
  E. grusonii 529
Echinocereus 529
Echinops 127
  E. bannaticus 127
  E. humilis 127
  E. ritro 127, 150
  E. spaerocephalus 127
Echinopsis 529
Echium 81
  E. plantagineum 81
Edelweiss, *see Leontopodium*
Edrianthus 188
  E. graminifolius 188
  E. pumilio 188
  E. serpyllifolius 188, 214
eelworms 113, 735
Egg plant, *see Aubergine*
Elaeagnus 264
  E. argentea 265
  E. commutata 265
  E. × *ebbingei* 265, 583
  E. pungens 264, 583
Elder, *see Sambucus*
elements 14, 17, 33
  major 31
  trace 31
Elm, *see Ulmus*
Elodea 389
  E. canadensis 389
  E. crispa 389
  E. densa 389
Embothrium 265
  E. coccineum 265
Emilia 81
  E. flammea 81
Encarsia formosa 725
Endive 562
Enkianthus 265
  E. campanulatus 265, 584
Epacris 469
  E. impressa 469
  E. longiflora 469
  E. purpurascens 469
Epilobium 188
  E. dodonaei 188
  E. glabellum 188
  E. canum 231
Epimedium 127
  E. alpinum 127
  E. grandiflorum 127
  E. pinnatum 127
  E. × *versicolor* 127
Epiphyllum 529

Epiphytic plants, potting
  compost for 33
Epipremnum 469
  E. aureum 469, 514
Epsom salts, *see* sulphate of
  magnesium
Eragrostis elegans 84
  E. interrupta 84
Eranthis 348
  E. cilicica 348
  E. hyemalis 49, 348, 359
  E. tubergenii 348
Eremurus 127, 348
  E. himalaicus 349
  E. olgae 349
  E. robustus 349
  E. stenophyllus stenophyllus
    349
Erica 265, 469
  E. arborea 266, 584
  E. caniculata 469
  E. carnea 265, 584
  E. ciliaris 266
  E. cinerea 265, 688
  E. × *darleyensis* 265
  E. erigena 265
  E. gracilis 469
  E. herbacea 64
  E. × *hyemalis* 469
  E. mediterranea 265
  E. tetralix 266
Erigeron 127
  E. aurantiacus 127
  E. philadelphicus 127
Erinus 188
  E. alpinus 188, 214
Eriophorum 389
  E. angustifolium 389
  E. latifolium 389
  E. vaginatum 389
Eritrichium 188
  E. nanum 188
Erodium 189
  E. chamaedryoides roseum
    189, 215
  E. chrysanthum 189
  E. corsicum 189
  E. glandulosum 189
  E. guttatum 189
Eryngium 127
  E. alpinum 128
  E. giganteum 128
  E. × *oliverianum* 128
  E. planum 128
  E. × *tripartitum* 128
  E. × *zabelli* 128
Erysimum 81, 189
  E. alpinus 189
  E. hieraciciifolium 76
  E. linifolium 81, 189
  E. perofskianum 81
  E. pumilum 189
  E. suffruticosum 81
Erythrina 469
  E. crista-galli 469
Erythronium 349
  E. californicum 349
  E. dens-canis 349, 359
  E. revolutum 349
  E. tuolumnense 349
Escallonia 266
  E. Iveyi 299
  E. rubra 244, 266
  E. virgata 266
Eschscholzia 65, 81
Eucalyptus 266, 470
  E. citriodora 470
  E. coccifera 266, 470
  E. dalrympleana 267
  E. globulus 470
  E. gunnii 266, 470
  E. niphophila 266
  E. urnigera 267
  E. viminalis 267
Eucharis 470
  E. amazonica 470
  E. grandiflora 470
Eucryphia 267
  E. cordifolia 267

  E. glutinosa 267
  E. × *nymansensis* 267
Eulalia, see Miscanthus
Euonymus 267
  E. alatus 267, 737
  E. europaeus 267
  E. fortunei 267, 585
  E. japonica 267
  E. latifolius 267
Euphorbia 128, 189, 470, 530
  E. biglandulosa 128
  E. characias 128, 151, 737
  E. cyparissias 128, 189
  E. epithymoides 128
  E. fulgens 454, 470
  E. griffithii 128, 151
  E. milii splendens 455
  E. myrsinites 151, 189
  E. pilosa major 128
  E. pulcherrima 455, 490, *see*
    also Poinsettia
  E. robbiae 151
  E. sikkimensis 128
  E. splendens 470
Euryops 189
  E. acraeus 189
Evening primrose, *see Oenothera*
evergreen 232
Evergreen laburnum, *see*
  Piptanthus
evergreens, transplanting 234
Everlasting pea, *see Lathyrus*
Exacum 470
  E. affine 470
Exochorda 268
  E. racemosa 268

F₁ hybrid, definition 48
F_1 hybrid, definition 48
F_2 hybrid, definition 48
Fabiana 268
  F. imbricata 268
Fagus 268
Fallopia 268
  F. baldschuanica 268, 680
False acacia, *see Robinia*
False asphodel, *see Asphodeline*
False daisy 181
False goats beard, *see Astilbe*
False heath, *see Fabiana*
False hellebore, *see Veratrum*
False indigo, *see Baptisia*
× *Fatshedera* 268
  × *F. lizei* 268, 515
Fatsia 269
  F. japonica 269, 515
feathers 36
feeding 15
  balanced 31
Felicia 82, 471
  F. amelloides 82, 471
  F. bergeriana 82
Fenestraria 530
fenitrothion 768
Fennel 563
Ferocactus 530
fertility 14
fertilizer 15-17, 30-33
fertilizers 637
Ficus 471
  F. benjamina 471
  F. decora 471
  F. doescheri 471
  F. elastica 471
  F. lyrata 471
  F. repens 471
Fig, ornamental, *see Ficus*
Figs 667-667
Figwort, *see Scrophularia*
Filbert, *see Corylus*
Filipendula 128
  F. hexapetala 128
  F. purpurea 128
  F. rubra 128
  F. ulmaria Aurea 152
fire blight 736
Fire thorn, *see Pyracantha*
fish guano 36
fish manure 36
fish waste 36
fish, *see* water gardens

Fittonia 471
  F. argyroneura 471
  F. verschaffeltii 471
Flax, *see Linum*
flea beetle 736
Fleabane, *see Erigeron*
Floating heart, *see Nymphoides*
flocculation 16, 32
Flower of the west wind, *see*
  Zephyranthes
Flowering currant, *see Ribes*
flowering plants 47
Flowering rush, *see Butomus*
fly, cabbage root 736
fly, carrot 736
fly, narcissus 753
fly, onion 736
Foam flower, *see Tiarella*
foliage colour 30, 31
foot rot 753
Forget-me-not, *see Myosotis*
forking 14, 18-22
Forsythia 269
  F. × *intermedia* 269, 585
  F. suspensa 269
Fothergilla major 585
Fox-tail lily, *see Eremurus*
Foxglove 82, *see also Digitalis*
frames 47, 406, 408, 411
Francoa 471
  F. ramosa 471
Frankenia 190
  F. laevis 190
  F. thymifolia 190
Fraxinus 269
  F. excelsior 269
  F. ornus 269
Freesia 472
Fremontodendron 269
  F. California Glory 585
  F. californicum 269
  F. mexicanum 269
Fritillaria 349
  F. imperialis 349, 360
  F. meleagris 349, 360
Fritillary, *see Fritillaria*
frog flies, *see* leaf hoppers
Fruit 16, 610-715
  development 32
  bare-rooted 615
  bark-ringing 635
  bird protection 752
  container-grown 615
  cropping problems 635
  cultivation 638
  feeding 636
  fertilizers 637
  frost 635
  manuring 636
  notching 630
  orchards 613
  over-pruning 635
  planting 615, 616
  planting distances 612
  pollination 614, 635
  propagation 617-622
  pruning 623-630
  renovation 628
  ringing 631, 632
  root stocks 610, 612
  scab 633
  situation 610
  soil 610
  soil preparation 614
  spraying 633
  training 610
  tree forms 610, 611
  underplanting 614
  wall-grown 614
  winter wash 633
Fuchsia 47, 190, 270, 472, 747
  F. cultivars 455
  F. magellanica 270
  F. Mrs Popple 586
  F. procumbens 190
  F. Riccartonii 586
  F. Swingtime 742
fusarium patch 737

Gaillardia 82, 111, 128

  G. × *grandiflora* 152
  G. pulchella 82
Galanthus 350
  G. byzantinus 350
  G. elwesii 350, 360
  G. ikariae ikariae 350
  G. nivalis 350, 360
  G. plicatus 350
Galax 190
  G. urceolata 190
Galega 129
  G. officinalis 129
gall weevil 753
Galtonia 350
  G. candicans 350
Gardenia 472
  G. jasminoides 472
Garland flower, *see Daphne*
Garlic 563
Garrya 270
  G. elliptica 270, 299
Gaultheria 270
  G. mucronata 270
  G. procumbens 270, 586
  G. shallon 270
Gay feather, *see Liatris*
Gazania 82
Genista 271, *see also Cytisus*
  G. aethnensis 271, 587
  G. cinerea 271
  G. fragrans 467
  G. hispanica 271
  G. lydia 587
  G. tinctoria 271, 587
  G. virgata 271
Gentian, *see Gentiana*
Gentiana 190
  G. acaulis 190
  G. asclepiadea 152, 191
  G. bavarica 191
  G. farreri 191
  G. freyniana 191
  G. lagodechiana 191
  G. lutea 191
  G. × *macauleyi* 191
  G. septemfida 191
  G. sino-ornata 191, 215
  G. verna 190, 215
Gentianella, see Gentiana acaulis
Geranium 108, 129, 191, *see*
  also Pelargonium
  G. argenteum 191
  G. cinereum Ballerina 191,
    215
  G. dalmaticum 191
  G. endressii 129
  G. grandiflorum 129
  G. lancastriense 191
  G. macrorrhizum 129
  G. pratense 129
  G. psilostemon 129
  G. pylzowianum 191
  G. sanguineum 191
  G. wallichianum Buxtons
    Variety 152
Gerbera 473
  G. jamesonii 473
germination 47, 67
Gesneria, see Smithiantha
Geum 129, 191
  G. borisii 129
  G. chiloense 129
  G. montanum 191
  G. reptans 191
  G. rivale 191
Giant reed, *see Arundo*
Giant scabious, *see Cephalaria*
Giant sequoia, *see*
  Sequoiadendron
Gibbaeum 530
Gilia 83
  G. capitata 83
  G. coronopifolia 83
  G. lutea 88
  G. tricolor 83
Ginger lily, *see Hedychium*
Ginkgo 271
  G. biloba 271
Gladiolus 339, 350-1

G. byzantinus 352
G. callianthus *361*
Glaucium 83
G. flavum 83
G. luteum 83
Glechoma hederacaea Variegata
    516
Gleditsia 271
G. triacanthos 271
Globe flower, *see Trollius*
Globe thistle, *see Echinops*
Globularia 192
G. bellidifolia 192
G. cordifolia 192
Gloriosa 473
G. rothschildiana 473
G. superba 473
Gloriosa daisy, *see Rudbeckia*
Glory lily, *see Gloriosa*
Glory of the snow, *see Chiondox*
Glory pea, *see Clianthus*
Gloxinia 473, 474, 747
G. speciosa *463*
glyphosate 109
Goats beard, *see Aruncus*
Goats rue, *see Galega*
Godetia 65, 83
Gold dust, *see Alyssum*
Golden club, *see Orontium*
Golden feather, *see*
    Chrysanthemum
Golden rod 110, *see also*
    Solidago
Goose foot plant, *see Syngonium*
Gooseberries 667-669
Gorse, *see Ulex*
Gourds 563
grafting 241
Grape hyacinth, *see Muscari*
Grapes 62, 669, 670-2, 689-92
Grasses, ornamental 83, 84
gravel gardens 173
gravel, for paths 26, 28
grease bands 634
green manure 30
greenback 753
greenhouse 10, 406-542
    alumminium 412
    blinds 420
    capillary bench 419, 422
    capillary watering 421
    cold 413
    condensation 418
    cool 413
    circular 412
    damping down 419
    disease control 724
    forcing 412
    fumigation 723, 724
    heating 410, 414-16, 418
    hot house 412
    humidity 419
    insulation 418
    intermediate 413
    lean-to 412
    lime-wash 420
    management 417
    pest control 724
    plants 47, 429
    potting 422-7
    propagation 427-8
    shading 417, 420
    smoke 724
    span-roof 410
    tar oil wash 724
    temperatures 417
    three-quarter span 412
    tunnel 412
    types 410
    ventilation 417, 418, 420
    watering 417, 420-2
    wood 412
Grevillea 474
G. robusta 474
Griselinia 271
G. littoralis 271
ground limestone 37
growmore 31, 33
guano 36, 37

Guernsey lily, *see Nerine*
Gum tree, *see Eucalyptus*
gumming 753
Gunnera 129
G. manicata 129, 394
Gymnocalycium 530
G. mihanovichii 530
Gynura 474
G. sarmentosa 474
Gypsophila 84, 108, 113, 192
G. elegans 84
G. paniculata 130
G. repens 192
G. perennial 130

Haberlea 192
H. ferdinandi-coburgii 192
H. rhodopensis 192, *216*
Haemanthus 475
H. albiflos 475
H. coccineus 475
H. katharinae 475
H. magnificus 475
Halesia 272
H. monticola 272
H. tetraptera 272
Halimium 272
H. commutatum 272
H. lasianthum 272
H. ocymoides 272
Hamamelis 272
H. × intermedia Jelena *587*
H. mollis *64*, 272
H. virginiana 272
hardening-off 410
Hardy orange, *see Poncirus*
Harrisia 530
Hawkweed, *see Hieracium*
Hawthorn, *see Crataegus*
Hazel, *see Corylus*
HCH 768
Heath, *see Erica*
Heather *64*, *see also Calluna;*
    Erica
Hebe 272
H. albicans 273
H. × andersonii 273
H. armstrongii 273
H. brachysiphon 273
H. cupressoides 273
H. elliptica 272
H. × franciscana *63*, 272
H. hulkeana 272
H. ochracea 273
H. pimeloides 273
H. pinguifolia 273
H. salicifolia 273
H. speciosa 272
Hedera 273
H. canariensis 273, 299, *516*
H. colchica 273, *300*
H. helix 273, *300*, *517*
hedges 12, 235, 238, 243, 244
Hedychium 475
H. coronarium 475
H. gardnerianum 475
Helenium 111, 130
H. autumnale 130
Helianthemum 12, *58*, 192
H. oelandicum alpestre *216*
H. Wisley Primrose *216*
Helianthus 130, *see also*
    Sunflower
H. annus 101
H. atrorubens 130
H. decapetalus 130
H. Loddon Gold *153*
Helichrysum 84, 192
H. bellidoides 193
H. bracteatum 84
H. monstrosum 84
Heliophila 85
H. longifolia 85
Heliopsis 130
H. scabra 131, *153*
Heliotrope 47, 85, 108, *see also*
    Heliotropium
Heliotropium 475
H. arborescens 85, 475

H. peruvianum 85, 475
Helipterum 85
H. manglessi 85
H. reseum 85
Helixine, *see Soleirolia*
Helleborus 131
H. atrorubens 131
H. corsicus 131, *153*
H. foetidus 131, *153*
H. niger 131, *153*
H. orientalis 131
Hemerocallis 131
Hemlock spruce, *see Tsuga*
Hepatica 132, 193
H. americana 193, *216*
H. angulosa 132
H. × media 193
H. transsilvanica 193
H. triloba 132
herbaceous 107-168
    borders 107-109
    season of interest 107
    back of border 110
    cut flowers 108
    edging 110
    feeding 109
    hardy 107
    mid-border 110
    pests and diseases 113
    planting 109
    propagation 110-113
    soil preparation 109
    spacing 110
    staking 110
    thinning 110
    watering 109, 110
Herbs 564
Hermodactylus 352
H. tuberosus 352
Herniaria 193
H. glabra 193
Herons bill, *see Erodium*
Hesperis 132
H. matronalis 132
Heuchera 132
H. × brizoides 132
H. sanguinea 132
Heucherella 132
H. tiarelloides 132
Hibiscus 85, 274, 475
H. manihot 476
H. rosa-sinensis 476
H. syriacus 274, *588*
H. trionum 85
Hieracium 193
H. aurantiacum 193
H. villosum 193
Himalayan honeysuckle, *see*
    Leycestria
Himalayan poppy, *see*
    Meconopsis
Hippeastrum 352, 476
H. cultivars *456*
H. pratense 352
Hippophaë 274
H. rhamnoides *590*
hoeing 14, 18, 22
Hoheria 274
H. lyallii 274
hollow heart 754
Holly, *see Ilex* 274, 276
Hollyhock 86, 111, *see also*
    Althaea
Holy thistle, *see Silybum*
Honesty, *see Lunaria*
Honey locust, *see Gleditsia*
Honeysuckle 235, *see also*
    Lonicera
hoof and horn meal 37
hop manure 37
Hop, *see Humulus*
hops, spent 30, 37
Hordeum jubatum 84
hormone rooting powder 241
hormone weedkiller damage 719
Hornbeam 243, *see also*
    Carpinus
Horned poppy, *see Glaucium*
Horse chestnut, *see Aesculus*

horse manure 37
Horse radish 565
Hosta 132
H. fortunei Albopicta *154*
H. lancifolia 132, *154*
H. plantaginea 132
H. sieboldiana 132, *154*
H. undulata medio-variegata
    132
Hot-water plant, *see Achimenes*
Hottonia 390
H. palustris 390
Hounds tongue, *see*
    Cynoglossum
House leek, *see Sempervivum*
House plants 532, 533
Howea 476
H. belmoreana 476
H. forsteriana 476
Hoya 476
H. bella 477
H. carnosa 477
Humea, *see Calomeria*
Humulus 86
H. japonicus 86
H. lupulus aureus *300*
humus 13-17, 24, 33
Hutchinsia 193
H. alpina 193
Hyacinth 47, 339, *750*, *see also*
    Hyacinthus
Hyacinthoides 369
H. hispanicus 369
H. non-scripta 369
Hyacinthus 369
H. amethystinus 369
H. azureus 369
hybrids 47
Hydrangea 275, 477
H. anomala petiolaris 275
H. arborescens 275
H. aspera villosa 275
H. macrophylla 275, *588*, *589*
H. paniculata *61*, *236*, 275,
    589
H. petiolaris *300*
H. sargentiana 275
hydrated lime 32
Hydrocleys 390
H. nympoides 390
hydroponics 13, 14
Hymenocallis 477
H. calathina 477
Hypericum 193
H. calycinum 275
H. coris 193
H. forrestii 275
H. fragile 193
H. × inodorum 275, *589*
H. × moserianum 275
H. nummularium 193
H. olympicum 193
H. patulum 275
H. polyphyllum 193
H. repens 193
H. reptans 193
Hypocyrta, *see Nematanthus*
Hypocyrta glabra 484
Hypoestes 478
H. phyllostacha 478
Hyssop 564
Hyssopus officinalis, *see Hyssop*

Iberis 86, 194
I. amara coronaria 86
I. correifolia 194
I. gibraltarica 194
I. saxatilis 194
I. semperflorens 194
I. sempervirens 194
I. umbellata 86
Iceland poppy, *see Papaver*
    nudicaule
Ilex 276
I. × altaclarensis 276
I. aquifolium 276
I. perado 276
Impatiens 87, 478
I. holstii 478

I. sultanii 478
I. walleriana 478
Incarvillea 132
I. mairei grandiflora 133
India-rubber plant, *see Ficus*
Indian bean, *see Catalpa*
Indian shoot, *see Campanula*
Indigofera 276
I. heterantha gerardiana 276
insects, biting 720
insects, sucking 720
Intermediate stocks, *see Stocks*
Inula 133, 194
I. acaulis 194
I. ensifolia 133
I. hookeri 133
I. magnifica 133
I. oculus-christi 133
I. royleana 133
Ionopsidium 87
I. acaule 87
Ipomoea 87, 478
I. learii 478
I. purpurea 87
I. rubro-caerulea 87, 478
I. tricolor 87
Iris 61, 133, 194, 370, 390
    Dutch 370
    English 370
    Spanish 370
I. chamaeiris 133, 194
I. cristata 195
I. danfordiae *361*, 370
I. douglasiana 134
I. gatesii 133
I. germanica 133
I. gracilipes 134, 195
I. histrioides *361*, 370
I. hoogiana 133
I. innominata 134, 195
I. kaempferi 134, 390
I. lacustris 195
I. laevigata 134, 390
I. latifolia 370
I. ochroleuca 134
I. onocyclus 133
I. pallida 133
I. pseudacorus 390
I. pumila 133, 194, *217*
I. regeliocyclus 133
I. reticulata *361*, 370
I. sibirica 134, 390
I. stylosa 134
I. susiana 133
I. tenax 195
I. tingitana fontanesi 370
I. unguicularis 134
I. variegata 133
I. xiphium 370
Irish heath, *see Daboecia*
Ivy, *see Hedera*
Ixia 370
Ixia lily, *see Ixiolirion*
Ixiolirion 371
I. ledebourii 371
I. montanum 371
I. pallasii 371
Ixora 478
I. coccinea 478

Jacaranda 479
J. mimosifolia 479
Jacobs ladder, *see Polemonium*
Jacobaea 87
Jacobean lily, *see Sprekelia*
Jacobinia, *see Justicia*
Japanese anemone, *see*
    Anemone
Japanese hyacinth, *see*
    Ophiopogon
Japanese moonwort, *see Shortia*
Japanese quince, *see*
    Chaenomeles
Jasmine, *see Jasminum*
Jasminum 277, 479
J. nudiflorum 277, *301*
J. officinale 277, *301*
J. polyanthum 479
J. primulinum 479

779

J. rex 479
J. sambac 479
Jeffersonia 195
J. dubia 195
Jerusalem sage, see Phlomis
Josephs Coat, see Amaranthus
Judas tree, see Cercis
Juglans 277
J. nigra 277
J. regia 277
Juncus 390
J. effusus 390
J. follicularis 390
J. glaucus 390
June Berry, see Amelanchier
Juniper, see Juniperus
Juniperus 277
J. chinensis 277
J. communis 277
J. horizontalis 277
J. × media 277
J. sabina 277
J. scopulorum 277
J. virginiana 277
Justicia 479
J. carnea 479
J. guttata 479
J. rizzini 479

Kaffir lily, see Schizostylis
Kalanchoe 480
K. blossfeldiana 480
Kale 565
Kalmia 278
K. latifolia 278
Kanzan cherry, see Prunus
Kanzan
Kerria 278
K. japonica 278, 590
Kidney vetch, see also Anthyllis
Kingcup, see Caltha
Kingfisher daisy, see Felicia
Kirengeshoma 134
K. palmata 134
Knapweed, see Centaurea
Kniphofia 134
K. caulescens 135
K. galpinii 134
K. Maid of Orleans 155
K. rufa 134
K. Torchlight 155
K. triangularis 135
K. uvaria 134
Knotweed, see Polygonum
Kochia 87
K. scoparia trichophylla 87
Kohl rabi 566
Kolkwitzia 278
K. amabilis 278

Laburnocytisus adamii 278
Laburnum 278
L. alpinum 278
L. anagyroides 278
L. × watereri 278, 291, 741
Lachenalia 480
L. aloides 480
Lads love, see Artemisia
ladybirds 725
Ladys mantle, see Alchemilla
Ladys slipper, see Cypripedium
Lagurus ovatus 84
Lambs ears, see Stachys
Lambs lettuce, see Corn salad
Laminaria, see Seaweed 42
Lamium 135, 195
L. galeobdolen 135
L. maculatum 135, 195, 217
Lampranthus 480, 530
L. aurantiacus 480
L. blandus 480
L. brownii 480
L. coccineus 480
L. multiradiatus 480
L. spectabilis 480
land drains, see drains
Lantana 480
L. camera 480
Lapageria 481, 748

L. rosea 481
Larch, see Larix
Large-leaved saxifrage, see
Bergenia
Larix 279
L. decidua 279
L. × eurolepis 279
L. kaempferi 279
Larkspur 87, 88, see also
Delphinium ajacis
Lathyrus 135, 195, see also
Sweet pea
L. grandiflorus 135
L. vernus 195
Laurus 279
L. nobilis 279
Lavandula 279
L. angustifolia 279
L. dentata 279
L. officinalis 279
L. spica 279
L. stoechas 279
Lavatera 88, 280
L. olbia 280, 590
L. rosea 88
L. trimestris 88
Lavender 11, 244, see also
Lavandula
Lavender cotton, see Santolina
lawns 10, 11, 395-404
layering 121, 240, see also
propagation
Layia 88
L. elegans 88
leaf curl 754
leaf hoppers 754
leaf miners 754
leaf mould 754
leaf scorch 755
leaf spot 755
leafmould 13, 17, 24, 30
leatherjackets 755
Lebanon squill, see Puschkinia
Leeks 566
Lemon-scented verbena, see
Lippia; Aloysia
Lenten rose, see Helleborus
Leontopodium 195
L. alpinum 195
Leopards bane, see Doronicum
Leptinella 195
L. reptans 195
L. squalida 195
Leptosiphon 88
Leptospermum 280
L. scoparium 280
Lettuce 567, 568
Leucanthemum maximum 123
Leucojum 371
L. aestivum 371
L. autumnale 371
L. vernum 371
Levisticum officinale, see Lovage
Lewisia 196
L. columbiana 196
L. cotyledon 196, 217
L. rediviva 196
L. tweedyi 196
Leycestria 280
L. formosa 280, 590
Leyland cypress, see ×
Cupressocyparis
Liatris 135
L. pycnostachya 135
L. spicata 135, 155
Ligularia 135
L. clivorum 135
L. dentata 135
L. stenocephala 136
Ligustrum 280
L. delavayanum 280
L. ionandrum 280
L. japonicum 280
L. lucidum 280
L. ovalifolium 243, 280
L. pratii 280
L. vulgare 280
Lilac, see Syringa
Lilium 371, 481

L. auratum 362, 372, 374, 481
L. brownii 373
L. bulbiferum 374
L. canadense 373
L. candidum 362, 372, 373
L. chalcedonicum 362, 373
L. davidii 373
L. Enchantment 362
L. formasanum 481
L. formosanum 373
L. giganteum 372, 373
L. hansonii 374
L. henryi 374
L. japonicum 373
L. longiflorum 373, 481
L. maculatum 374
L. martagon 362, 374
L. monadelphum 373
L. pardalinum 374
L. pyrenaicum 374
L. regale 372, 373, 481
L. speciosum 374, 481
L. tigrinum 374
L. × testaceum 372, 374
Lily 373-4, see also Lilium
lily disease 755
Lily of the field, see Sternbergia
Lily of the valley 136, see also
Convallaria
lime 11, 15, 16, 24, 32, 33, 37-9,
232
limestone 32, 38
Lime tree, see Tilia
Limnanthes 88
Limnocharis, see Hydrocleys
Limonium 88, 136, 481
L. incana 136
L. latifolium 136
L. profusum 481
L. psyllostachys 89
L. puberulum 482
L. sinuatus 89
L. suworowii 481
Linaria 89, 136, 196
L. alpina 196, 217
L. dalmatica 196
L. maroccana 89
L. purpurea 136
Ling, see Calluna
Linum 89, 196
L. arboreum 196
L. campanulatum 196
L. elegans 196
L. flavum 196
L. grandiflorum 89
L. narbonnense 196
L. perenne 196
L. suffruticosum salsoloides
196
Lippia citriodora 281, see also
Aloysia
liquid manure 39, 40
Liquidambar 281
L. styraciflua 281
Liriodendron 281
L. tulipifera 281, 291
Liriope 136
L. muscari 136
Lithodora diffusa 197, 218
Lithops 530
Lithospermum 197, see also
Lithodora
L. diffusum 197
L. graminifolium 197
L. intermedium 197
L. rosmarinifolium 197
Livingstone daisy, see
Dorotheanthus
loam 15, 17
Lobelia 89, 136
L. cardinalis 137
L. erinus 89
L. fulgens 137
L. hybrida pendula 89
L. syphilitica 137
L. tenuior 89
L. vedrariensis 137
Lobivia 530
Lobster claw, see Clianthus

Lobularia maritima 70
Lonicera 281
L. × brownii 282
L. fragrantissima 282
L. japonica 282, 301, 302
L. nitida 243, 282
L. periclymenum 281, 301,
302
L. sempervirens 282
L. standishii 282
L. × tellmanniana 282, 302
L. tragophylla 282
Loosestrife, see Lysimachia
Lovage 564
Love-in-a-mist, see Nigella
Love-lies-bleeding, see
Amaranthus
Luculia 482
L. gratissima 482
Lunaria 89
L. annua 90
L. biennis 90
Lungwort, see Pulmonaria
Lupin 111, 113, see also Lupinus
Lupinus 90, 137, 282
L. arboreus 137, 282
L. polyphyllus 137
Lychnis 137, 197
L. ceoli-rosa 106, see also
Viscaria
L. chalcedonica 137
L. coronaria 137
L. × haageana 197
L. flos-jovi 197
L. viscaria 137
Lysimachia 137, 197
L. clethroides 137
L. ephemerum 137
L. nummularia 197, 218
L. punctata 137
L. vulgaris 137
Lythrum 138
L. salicaria 138
L. virgatum 138

Macleaya 138
M. cordata 138
M. microcarpa 138
Madagascar jasmine, see
Stephanotis
Magnolia 282
M. campbelli mollicomata 283
M. denudata 283
M. grandiflora 283
M. kobus 283
M. liliiflora Nigra 591
M. sieboldii 283
M. sinensis 283
M. × soulangeana 233, 283,
591
M. stellata 283, 591
M. wilsonii 283
Mahonia 283
M. aquifolium 283, 591
M. japonica 283
M. lomariifolia 283
M. × media 283
Maidenhair tree, see Ginkgo
Maize, see Grasses, ornamental
malathion 768
Malcolmia, see Virginian stock
M. maritima 105
Malope 90
M. trifida 90
Malus 283
M. × atrosanguinea 284
M. baccata 284
M. coronaria 284
M. floribunda 283, 292
M. Golden Hornet 291, 739
M. ioensis 284
M. lemoinei 233
M. × purpurea 284
M. × robusta 284
M. spectabilis 284
Mammillaria 530
Mandevilla 482
M. boliviensis 482
M. laxa 482

M. sanderi 482
Manettia 482
M. inflata 482
Manuka, see Leptospermum
manure 16, 17, 30, 33, 36
Maple, see Acer
Maranta 483
M. leuconeura 483
M. l. erythroneura 457
M. l. kerchoveana 457
M. makoyana 439
Marguerite 108, see also
Argyranthemum
Marigold 103, see also Tagetes;
Calendula
Mariposa lily, see Calochortus
Marjoram 565, see also
Origanum
marl 14
Marsh marigold, see Caltha
Masterwort, see Astrantia
Matricaria 77, see also
Chrysanthemum
Matricaria eximea 77
Matthiola bicornis 100
M. incana 100, see also
Stocks
Mazus 197
M. pumilio 197
M. radicans 197
M. reptans 197, 218
Meadow rue, see Thalictrum
Meadow saffron, see Colchicum
mealy bug 725, 755
Meconopsis 197
M. baileyi 198
M. betonicifolia 198
M. cambrica 198
M. grandis 198
M. integrifolia 198
M. napaulensis 198
M. paniculata 198
M. quintuplinervia 198
M. regia 198
M. × sheldonii 198
Medeinilla magnifica 483
Medicago, see Calvary clover
Medicago echinus 75
Medinilla 483
Melissa officinalis, see Balm
Melons 692-694
Mentha 198, 390
M. aquatica 390
M. requienii 198
Mentzelia 90
M. linleyi 90
Menyanthes 390
M. trifoliata 390
Mertensia 138
M. ciliata 138
M. pulmonarioides 138
M. sibirica 138
M. virginica 138
Mesembryanthemum, see
Dorotheanthus;
Lampranthus
M. criniflorum 80
metaldehyde 768
Metasequoia 284
M. glyptostroboides 284
methiocarb 769
Mexican orange blossom, see
Choisya
Mexican Sunflower, see Tithonia
mice 242, 756
Michaelmas daisies 110, 111,
see also Aster
Microcoelum 483
M. weddelliana 483
midge, pear 756
Mignonette 91
mildew 756
Milfoil, see Achillea
Milkwort, see Polygala
millepedes 756
Mimosa 483, see also Acacia
Mimulus 91, 138, 391, 484
M. cardinalis 138
M. cupreus 91, 138, 218

M. glutinosus 484
M. guttatus 91, 391
M. luteus 138, 391
M. moschatus 57, 91, 484
M. ringens 391
M. tigrinus 91
Mint, see Mentha
Minuartia verna 179
Miscanthus 138
M. sacchariflorus 138
M. sinensis 138
Mixed border 108, 382
Mock lupin, see Thermopsis
Mock orange, see Philadelphus
moles 756
Moltkia, see Lithospermum
molybdenum, effects of 31, 32
Monarda 139
M. didyma 139, 156
M. fistulosa 139
Monkey flower, see Mimulus
Monkshood, see Aconitum
monocarpic 108
Monstera 484
M. deliciosa 484, 517
Montbretia, see Crocosmia
Moon daisy 108
moraine 171
Morina 139
M. longifolia 139
Morisia 198
M. hypogaea 198
M. monantha 198
Morning glory, see Ipomoea
mosaic 757
Mosaic plant, see Fittonia
Moses in the bulrushes, see
Tradescantia
Moss campion, see Silene
Mother of thousands, see
Saxifraga
Mother-in-laws tongue, see
Sansevieria
Mountain ash 11, see also
Sorbus
mountain plants 169
mowing 11, see also lawns
Mulberries 694-696
Mullein, see Verbascum
muriate of potash 40
Muscari 374
M. armenaicum 374
M. aucheri 374
M. botryoides 374
M. comosum 374
M. latifolium 374
mushroom compost 40
Mushrooms 570
Musk, see Mimulus
Mustard 571
Myosotis 91, 199, 391
M. alpestris 199, 219
M. rupicola 199
M. scorpioides 391
Myriophyllum 391
M. spicatum 391
M. verticillatum 391
Myrtle, see Myrtus
Myrtus 285, 484
M. communis 285, 484
M. luma 285

Naegelia, see Smithiantha
Narcissus 51, 339, 374, 750
divisions 375
N. bulbocodium 363, 376
N. cyclamineus 363, 375, 376
N. February Gold 363
N. jonquilla 375
N. Magnet 364
N. poeticus 375
N. Rockall 363
N. Sempre Avante 364
N. Silver Chimes 364
N. tazetta 375
N. triandrus 363, 375
N. Texas 364
Nasturtium 92, see also
Tropaeolum

Natal vine, see Rhoicissus
Neamatanthus 484
Neanthe bella 444
Neck rot 757
Nectarines 696-699
Nectaroscordum siculum 364
Nematanthus glabra 484
nematodes 725
Nemesia 92
N. strumosa 92
Nemophila 92
N. insignis 92
N. menziesii 92
Neoregelia 485
N. carolinae tricolor 485
Nepenthes 485
Nepeta 139
N. × faassenii 139
N. mussinii 139
N. sibirica 139
Nerine 12, 485
N. bowdenii 364, 485
N. sarniensis 485
Nerium 486
N. oleander 486
Nertera 199
N. depressa 199
N. granadensis 199
Nettles 18
neutral 16
New Zealand flax, see Phormium
New Zealand tea tree, see
Leptospermum
Nicotiana 93
N. affinis 93
N. alata 93
N. sanderae 93
Nidularium 486
N. innocentii 486
Nierembergia 199
N. caerulea 199
N. repens 169, 199
Nigella 285
N. damascena 93
N. hispanica 93
Night-scented stocks, see
Stocks
nitrate of lime 41
nitrate of potash 40
nitrate of soda 30, 40
Nitro-chalk 41
nitrogen 17, 31, 33, 34
Norfolk Island pine, see
Araucaria
Notocactus 530
Nuphar 391
N. lutea 391
N. minima 391
N. pumila 391
nursery bed 69
nutrient deficiency 31
nutrient excess 31
Nymphaea 391
N. alba 391
N. candida 391
N. odorata 391
N. Marliacea Chromatella 60
N. laydekeri 392
N. marliacea 392
N. tetragona 391
Nymphoides 392
N. peltata 392
Nyssa sylvatica 292

Oak 285, see also Quercus
Obedient plant, see Physostegia
Ocimum basilicum, see Basil
O. minimum, see Basil
Oenothera 93, 139, 199
O. acaulis 199
O. berlandieri 199
O. biennis 93
O. caespitosa 199
O. lamarkiana 93
O. missouriensis 156, 199
O. pumila 219
O. speciosa childsii 199
O. tetragona 139
Oleander, see Nerium

Olearia 285
O. gunniana 285
O. × haastii 285
O. macrodonta 285
O. phlogopappa 285
O. ¥ stellulata 285
Omphalodes 139, 199
O. cappadocica 139, 200
O. luciliae 199
O. verna 139, 200
Onions 572
Ononis 200
O. rotundifolia 200
Onosma 200
O. alboroseum 200
O. echioides 200
O. stellulatum 200
O. tauricum 200
Ophiopogon 486
O. jaburan 486
Oplismenus, see Panicum
Opuntia 530
Orborus, see Lathyrus
Orchids, potting compost for 33
Oregon grape, see Mahonia
Oriental poppies 113, see also
Papaver
Origanum 200
O. dictamnus 200
O. × hybridum 200
O. marjorana, see Marjoram
O. pulchellum 200
O. rotundifolium 200, 219
O. vulgare 200
Ornamental rhubarb, see Rheum
Ornithogalum 376, 486
O. arabicum 376, 486
O. nutans 365, 376
O. thyrsoides 376, 486
O. umbellatum 376
Orontium 392
O. aquaticum 392
Osmanthus 285
O. × burkwoodii 285
O. delavayi 285
O. heterophylla 285
O. ilicifolius 285
Osteospermum 93
O. Cannington Joyce 94
O. ecklonis 93
Our Lady's Milk Thistle, see
Silybum
overwintering 410
Oxalis 200, 487
O. adenophylla 200, 219
O. deppei 487
O. enneaphylla 200
O. floribunda 201
O. purpurata 487

Pachysandra 285
P. procumbens 285
P. terminalis 285
Paeonia 140, 286
P. delavayi 286
P. lactiflora 140, 157
P. lutea 286
P. mlokosewitschii 140
P. officinalis 140, 156
P. peregrina 140
P. suffruticosa 286
Pampas grass 140
Pancratium 487
P. canariense 487
P. illyricum 487
P. maritimum 487
Pandanus 487
P. veitchii 487
Panicum 487
P. variegatum 487
P. violaceum 84
Pansy 94
Papaver 94, 140, 201
P. alpinum 201, 219
P. orientale 140, 157
Paradisea, see Anthericum
P. liliastrum 117
paraquat 109
parasitic wasp 725

Parlour palm, see Chamaedorea
Parochetus 201
P. communis 201
Parrots bill, see Clianthus
Parrotia 286
P. persica 286, 292
Parsley 573
Parsnips 574
Parthenocissus 286
P. henryana 286, 302
P. inserta 286
P. quinquefolia 286, 303
P. tricuspidata 286, 303
P. vitacea 286
Partridge-breasted aloe, see
Aloe
Pasque flower, see Pulsatilla
Passiflora 286, 487, 743
P. × allardii 488
P. antioquiensis 487
P. caerulea 286, 303, 487
P. edulis 487
P. quadrangularis 487
Passion flower, see Passiflora
Paths 10, 26-29, 724
Paulownia 287
P. fargesii 287
P. lilacina 287
P. tomentosa 287
paving 10, 26, 28
Peaches 696-699
Pear, ornamental, see Pyrus
Pearly everlasting, see Anaphalis
Pears 699-703
Peas 575
peat 13-15, 17, 24, 33, 41, 172,
173
pebbles 26
Pelargonium 47, 56, 488-9, 745
Peltandra 392
P. alba 392
P. undulata 392
Pennisetum longistylum 84
P. villosum 84
Pennywort, see Cotyledon
Penstemon 141, 201
P. barbatus 141
P. fruticosus scouleri 201
P. glaber 141
P. heterophyllus 141
P. isophyllus 141
P. menziesii 201
P. pinifolius 58, 201
P. rupicola 201, 220
Peony, see Paeonia
Peperomia 489
P. argyreia 489
P. caperata 457, 489
P. griseoargentea 489
P. magnolifolia Variegata 458
P. sandersii 489
Perennial statice 113
perennials, hardy 107-168, see
also herbaceous
Perilla 95
P. atropurpurea laciniata 95
P. frutescens nankinensis 95
Periwinkle, see Vinca
permethrin 769
Pernettya, see Gaultheria
P. mucronata 270
Perovskia 287
P. atriplicifolia 287
Persicaria virginiana variegata
165
Peruvian lily, see Alstroemeria
pests 717-770
soil 722
symptoms 717
Petrorhagia 201
P. saxifraga 201
Petunia 56, 57, 95, 489
pH test 16
Phacelia 96
P. campanularia 96
P. tanacetifolia 96
Pheasants Eye, see Adonis
Philadelphus 287
P. Beauclerk 287

P. Belle Etoile 287
P. coronarius 287
P. delavayi 287
P. grandiflorus 287
P. intectus 287
P. × lemoinei 287
P. microphyllus 287
P. pubescens 287
P. × purpureo-maculatus 287
P. Sybille 287
P. Virginal 287
Philodendron 490
P. bipinnatifidum 490
P. domesticum 490
P. scandens 490, 518
P. selloum 518
Phlomis 288
P. chrysophylla 288
P. fruticosa 288
Phlox 96, 111, 141, 202
P. adsurgens 202
P. amoena 202
P. divaricata 202
P. douglasii 202
P. drummondii 96
P. hoodii 220
P. paniculata 141, 157
P. stolonifera 202, 220
P. subulata 202
Phoenix 490
P. roevelinii 490
Phormium 141
P. cookianum 141
P. tenax 141
phosphate 34
phosphate of potash 41
phosphoric acid 30, 33, 34
phosphorous 31, 33
Photinia 288
P. × fraseri 288
P. Red Robin 288
P. serrulata 288
Phygelius 141
P. aequalis 142
P. capensis 141
Phyllostachys, see Bamboo
P. flexuosa 249
P. nigra 249
Physalis 142
P. alkekengi 142
P. franchetii grandiflora 142
Physoplexis comosa 202, 220
Physostegia 142
P. virginiana 142
Phyteuma 202
P. comosum 202
Phytolacca 142
P. americana 142
Phytoseiulus persimilis 725
Picea 288
P. abies 288
P. omorika 288
P. pungens 288, 688
P. sitchensis 288
Pickerel weed, see Pontederia
Pieris 305
P. floribunda 305
P. formosa 53, 305
P. japonica 305
P. taiwanensis 305
pig manure 41
Pilea 490
P. cadieri 490
P. microphylla 490
P. muscosa 490
Pimpernel, see Anagallis
Pine 305
Pineapple, see Ananas
Pink, see Dianthus
Pinus, see Pine
P. ayacahuite 305
P. montezumae 305
P. mugo pimilio 305
P. nigra 305
P. patula 305
P. pumila 305
P. radiata 305
P. strobus 305
P. sylvestris 305

P. wallichiana 305
Piptanthus 305
P. laburnifolius 305
P. nepalensis 305
pirimicarb 769
pirimiphos-methyl 769
Pitcher plants, see Nepenthes
Pittosporum 306
P. tenuifolium 306
P. tobira 306
Plane, see Platanus
planning 10-45
plant food 14, 15, 17, 30
Plantain lily, see Hosta
Platanus 306
P. × acerifolia 306
P. × hispanica 306
P. orientalis 306
Platycodon 142
P. grandiflorum 142
P. mariesii 142
Platystemon 96
P. californicus 96
Pleioblastus auricomus 249
Pleiospilos 530
Plum, ornamental, see Prunus
Plumbago 490, see also
Ceratostigma
P. capensis 490
Plume poppy, see Macleaya
Plums 704-8
Poached egg flower, see
Limnanthes
Pocket handkerchief tree, see
Davidia
Podophyllum 142
P. emodi 143
Poinsettia 490
pointing 28
Pokeberry, see Phytolacca
Pokeweed, see Phytolacca
Polemonium 143
P. caeruleum 143, 158
P. foliosissimum 143
Polianthes 491
P. tuberosa 491
Polka dot plant, see Hypoestes
Polyanthus see Primula
Polygala 202
P. chamaebuxus 202
Polygonatum 143
P. × hybridum 143, 158
P. multiflorum 143
P. odoratum 143
Polygonum 97, 143, 202, see
also Fallopia
P. affine 143, 202
P. amplexicaule 143
P. baldschuanicum 303
P. bistorta 143, 158
P. campanulatum 143
P. capitatum 97
P. superbum 143
P. vaccinifolium 143, 202
Pomegranate, see Punica
Poncirus 306
P. trifoliata 306
Pond weed, see Elodea
Pontederia 392
pools 383-394
poor drainage 17
Poplar, see Populus
Poppy 65
Poppy mallow, see Callirhoe
Poppy, oriental, see Papaver
Poppy, see Papaver
Populus 306
P. balsamifera 307
P. candicans 307
P. × euroamericana Aurea
Serotina 307
P. nigra italica 306
P. tremula 306
P. trichocarpa 307
Portugal laurel 243, see also
Prunus lusitanica
Portulaca 97
P. grandiflora 97
Pot marigold, see Calendula

potash nitrate 42
Potatoes 32, 576, 593-5
Potentilla 143, 203, 307
P. alba 203
P. argyrophylla 143
P. atrosanguinea 143
P. aurea 203
P. fruticosa 307
P. nepalensis 203
P. nitida 203
P. tongei 203
P. William Rollison 158
poultry manure 42
Prayer plant, see Maranta
Prickly poppy, see Argemone
Prickly thrift, see Acatholimon
Primrose 97, see also Primula
Primula 169, 203, 491, 745
P. alpicola 204
P. auricula 204, 492
P. bulleyana 204
P. capitata 203
P. cockburniana 204
P. denticulata 203, 221
P. edgeworthii 204
P. farinosa 204
P. flaccida 204
P. florindae 204
P. frondosa 204
P. glaucescens 204
P. hirsuta 204
P. japonica 204
P. juliae 204, 221
P. kewensis 459, 491
P. latifolia 204
P. malacoides 458, 491
P. marginata 204, 221
P. mooreana 203
P. obconica 491
P. prolifera 204
P. × pruhoniciana 204
P. × pubescens 204
P. pulverulenta 204
P. secundiflora 204
P. sieboldii 204
P. sikkimensis 204
P. sinensis 491
P. veris 96
P. viali 204
Prince's Feather, see
Amaranthus
Privet, see Ligustrum
propagation 238
Prophet flower, see Arnebia
Propiconazole 769
Prunella 205
P. grandiflora 205
P. vulgaris 205
pruning 232
Prunus 307
P. amygdalo-persica 308
P. amygdalus 307
P. avium 308
P. × blireana 307
P. cerasifera 243, 292, 307
P. cerasus 308
P. × cistena 307
P. dulcis 308
P. incisa 308
P. Kanzan 51
P. lannesiana 308
P. laurocerasus 307, 308
P. lusitanicus 307
P. mume 308
P. padus 308
P. persica 307
P. sargentii 308
P. serrula 293, 308
P. serrulata 308, 293, 294
P. subhirtella 294, 308
P. tenella 308
P. triloba flore pleno 308
P. × yeodensis 308
Pseudofumaria lutea 184
Pseudosasa japonica 249
Pseudotsuga 309
P. glauca 309
P. menziesii 309
Pulmonaria 144

P. angustifolia 144
P. argentea 144
P. azurea 144
P. saccharata 144
Pulsatilla 205
P. vulgaris 222
Punica 459
P. granatum 459, 492
Purple bell vine, see
Rhodochiton
Purple cone flower, see
Echinacea
Purple loosestrife, see Lythrum
Purple rock cress, see Aubrieta
Puschkinia 376
P. scilloides 365, 376
Pyracantha 309
P. atalantoides 309
P. coccinea 235, 309
P. rogersiana flava 309
Pyrethrum 108, 144
Pyrus 309
P. salicifolia 294, 309

Queensland umbrella tree, see
Schleffera
Quercus 309, see also Oak
Q. coccinea 310
Q. ilex 310
Q. robur 309
Quick, see Crataegus
Quickthorn, see Crataegus
monogyna
Quinces 708, 709

rabbits 757
Radishes 595
raised beds 170
raking 22, 65
Ramonda 205
R. myconi 205, 222
R. nathaliae 205
R. pyrenaica 205
Ranunculus 144, 205, 339, 376
R. aconitifolius 144
R. acris 144
R. alpestris 205, 222
R. amplexicaulis 206
R. asiaticus 365, 377
R. bulbosus pleniflorus 144
R. ficaria 206
R. gramineus 205
R. lingua grandiflorus 206
R. speciosus plenus 144
Raoulia 206
R. australis 206
Raspberries 709-711
raspberry beetle 758
rats 242, 758
Rechsteineria, see Smithiantha
red spider mite 725, 758
Red valerian, see Centranthus
Red-hot cats tail, see Acalypha
Red-hot poker, see Kniphofia
Redwood, see Sequoia
Reed mace, see Typha
Rehmannia 492
R. angulata 492
Reseda, see Mignonette
reversion 758
Rheum 161, 394
R. palmatum 161
Rhipsalidopsis 530
R. gaertneri 459, 530
Rhodanthe, see Helipterum
Rhodochiton 492
R. atrosanguineum 492
Rhododendron 12, 17, 310, 493
R. arboreum 311
R. augustinii 311
R. Blue Tit 592
R. campylocarpum 311
R. catawbiense 310
R. ciliatum 311
R. cinnabarinum 311
R. dalhousiae 493
R. discolor 311
R. edgeworthii 493
R. falconeri 311

R. × fragrantissimum 493
R. fortunei 311
R. Golden Oriole 592
R. griersonianum 311
R. griffithianum 311
R. hanceanum Nanum 310
R. hippophaeoides 310
R. kiusianum 248
R. loderi 311
R. luteum 248
R. moupinense 311, 493
R. obiculare 311
R. obtusum 248
R. occidentalis 248
R. Pink Pearl 592
R. ponticum 311, 312
R. praecox 310
R. racemosum 311
R. russatum 311
R. simsii 435
R. sinogrande 311
R. taggianum 493
R. thomsonii 311
R. Vuyks Rosyred 592
R. wardii 311
R. williamsianum 311
R. yakushimanum 310
R. yunnanense 311
rhododendron bug 759
Rhodohypoxis 206
R. baueri 206
Rhoeo 501, see also
Tradescantia
R. discolor 501
Rhoicissus 493
R. rhomboidea 493, 519
Rhubarb 595, 596
ornamental, see Rheum
Rhus 312
R. hirta 312
R. typhina 295
Rhynchospermum, see
Trachelospermum
Ribes 312
R. laurifolium 312
R. sanguineum 312, 673
R. speciosum 312
Richardia, see Zantedeschia
Ricinus 97
R. communis 97
ridging 19-21
ripening 32
Robinia 313
R. hispida 313
R. kelseyi 313
R. pseudoacacia 295, 313
Rochea 493
R. coccinea 493
Rock cress, see Arabis
rock gardens 58, 169-231
rock plants 11, 169
planting 173
planting time 173
propagation 174,175
protection 175
watering 175
Rock purslane, see Calandrinia
Rock rose, see Cistus
Rock rose, see Helianthemum
Rodgersia 161
R. aesculifolia 161
R. pinnata 161
R. podophylla 161
Romneya 161, 313
Romneya coulteri 161, 313, 673
roots 13, 18, 23, 30
cuttings 111
development 32
rot 759

R. Dorothy Perkins 527
R. Dublin Bay 525
R. Elizabeth of Glamis 523
R. Escapade 523
R. Evelyn Fison 523
R. Eyepaint 523
R. Frau Dagmar Hartopp 524
R. Fred Loads 524
R. Fruhlingsgold 524
R. Galway Bay 525
R. Gaujard 522
R. Golden Showers 525
R. Golden Wings 524
R. Grandpa Dickson 521
R. Handel 525
R. Iceberg 523
R. Just Joey 521
R. Mischief 521
R. Korresia 523
R. Maigold 526
R. Marechal Niel 494
R. Mermaid 526
R. Mme Gregoire Staechelin
681
R. National Trust 521
R. New Dawn 682
R. Niphetos 494
R. Parkdirektor Riggers 526
R. Pascali 521
R. Peace 521
R. Piccadilly 522
R. Pink Favourite 522
R. Pink Perpetue 526
R. Rosy Cushion 528
R. Sanders White 527
R. Silver Jubilee 522
R. Snow Carpet 528
R. Swan Lake 526
R. Swany 528
R. The Fairy 59
R. Troika 522
R. Wendy Cussons 522
Rosa species
R. × alba 326
R. chinensis minima 206
R. eglanteria 244
R. filipes 326
R. hugonis 326
R. longicuspis 326
R. moyesii 326, 528
R. multiflora 326
R. pomifera 326
R. roulettii 206
R. rubiginosa, see R.
eglanteria
R. rubrifolia 326, 528
R. sericea pteracantha 326
R. setipoda 326
R. spinosissima 326
R. virginiana 528
R. willmottiae 326
Roscoea 206
R. alpina 206
R. cautleoides 206
R. purpurea 206
Rose acacia, see Robinia
Rose mallow, see Hibiscus
Rose of China, see Hibiscus
Rose of heaven, see Viscaria
Rose of Sharon, see Hypericum
Roses 11, 108, 244, 326-337
Rose, see also Rosa
classification 326, 327, 336,
337
disbudding 332
established 332
feeding 332
pruning 330, 331
exhibiting 333
flower shape 326
half-standards 327
mulching 332
pests and diseases 332
planting 327-8
propagation 333-336
spraying 332
standards 327
suckers 332
training 327

Rosemary 11, 244, *see also Rosmarinus*
Rosmarinus 206, 313
  R. × *lavandulaceus* 206
  R. officinalis 206, 313, 673
Rowan, *see Sorbus*
Royal paint brush, *see Haemanthus*
Rubus 313
  R. cockburnianus 314
  R. deliciosus 314
  R. spectabilis 314
  R. trilobus 314
  R. ulmifolius 314
Rudbeckia 98, 161
  R. fulgida 161
  R. laciniata 161
  R. maxima 162
  R. nitida 161
Ruscus 314
  R. aculeatus 314
Rush, *see Juncus*
Russian sage, *see Perovskia*
Russian vine, *see Fallopia*
rust 759

Sage 597, *see also Salvia*
Sagittaria 392
  S. japonica 392
  S. lancifolia 392
  S. latifolia 392
  S. sagittifolia 392
Saintpaulia 494
  S. ionantha 460, 494
Salix 314
  S. alba 63, 233, 314
  S. babylonica pekinensis Tortuosa 314
  S. fargesii 314
  S. hastata 315
  S. herbacea 315
  S. lanata 315
  S. matsudana Tortuosa 295
  S. purpurea 315
  S. × *sepulchralis* Chrysocoma 314
Salpiglossis 98
Salsify 597
saltpetre, *see* nitrate of potash
Salvia 98, 162, 377
  S. argentea 162
  S. farinacea 99
  S. haematodes 162
  S. horminum 98
  S. nemorosa superba 162
  S. patens 162, 377
  S. sclarea turkestanica 162
  S. splendens 98
  S. uliginosa 162
Sambucus 315
  S. canadensis 315
  S. nigra 315
  S. racemosa Plumosa Aurea 686
sand 13, 14, 32
Sandwort 28, *see also Arenaria*
Sanguinaria 207
  S. canadensis 207
Sanguisorba 162
  S. canadensis 162
  S. obtusa 162
Sansevieria 494
  S. trifasciata 461, 462, 494
Santolina 315
  S. chamaecyparissus 315
  S. incana 315
  S. pinnata 315
  S. rosmarinifolia 315
sap 18, 23
Saponaria 99, 162, 207
  S. calabrica 99
  S. ocymoides 207
  S. officinalis 162
Sarracenia 393
  S. flava 393
  S. purpurea 393
Satureia hortensis, see Savory
Satureia montana, see Savory
Savory 565

sawflies 759
Saxifraga 207, 495
  S. × *apiculata* 225
  S. boydii 225
  S. burseriana 223, 225
  S. callosa 208, 225
  S. camposii 208
  S. cochlearis 225
  S. cortusifolia fortunei 225
  S. cotyledon 208
  S. decipiens 208
  S. × *elizabethae* 225
  S. × *geum* 225
  S. granulata 208
  S. grisebachii 223, 225
  S. hypnoides 208
  S. × *irvingii* 225
  S. lilacina 225
  S. longifolia 208, 223, 225
  S. marginata 225
  S. moschata 208
  S. muscoides 208
  S. oppositifolia 223, 225
  S. paniculata 208
  S. stolonifera 495
  S. trifurcata 208
  S. umbrosa 225
  S. urbium 225
Saxifrage, *see also Saxifraga*
  Cushion 207
  Diptera 208
  Encrusted 207
  Engleria 207
  Kabschia 207
  Ligularia 208
  London Pride 208
  Mossy 207
  Oppositifolia 207
  Silver 207
scab, apple 760
scab, pear 760
scab, potato 760
Scabiosa 162, 226
  S. alpina 226
  S. atropurpurea 99
  S. caucasica 162
  S. columbaria 163
  S. graminifolia 226
  S. perennis 226
Scabious 99, 111, 162, *see also Scabiosa*
Scadoxus multiflorus katharine 475
scalding 760
scale insects 760
Scarborough lily, *see Cyrtanthus*
Schizanthus 495
Schizocodon, *see Shortia*
Schizophragma 315
  S. hydrangeoides 315
  S. integrifolium 315
Schizostylis 163, 377
  S. coccinea 163, 377
Schlefflera 495
  S. actinophylla 495
  S. elegantissima 495
Schlumbergera 530
  S. × *buckleyi* 462
  S. buckleyi 530
  S. truncata 463, 530
Sciadopitys 316
Sciadopitys verticillata 316
Scilla 339, 377
  S. bifolia 378
  S. peruviana 378
  S. sibirica 366, 377
  S. tubergeniana 378
Scindapsus, see Epipremnum
  S. aureus 469
Scirpus 393
  S. tabernaemontani Zebrinus 393
sclerotina rot 761
Scorzonera 597
Scotch marigold, *see Calendula*
scree 171
Screw pine, *see Pandanus*
Scrophularia 163
  S. aquatica 163

Scutellaria 226
  S. alpina 226
  S. indica parviflora 226
  S. scordifolia 226
Sea buckthorn, *see Hippophae*
Sea holly, *see Eryngium*
Sea lavender, *see Limonium*
Seakale 597
  beet 598
Seakale, ornamental, *see Crambe* 124
seaweed 42
Sedge grass, *see Carex* 389
Sedum 163, 226
  S. acre 226
  S. album 226
  S. anglicum 226
  S. Autumn Joy 159
  S. caeruleum 227
  S. cauticolum 226
  S. dasyphyllum 226
  S. ewersii 226
  S. hispanicum 226
  S. kamschaticum 226
  S. lydium 226
  S. middendorfianum 226
  S. palmeri 224
  S. pilosum 227
  S. pulchellum 226
  S. reflexum 226
  S. spathulifolium 224, 226
  S. spectabile 159, 163, 226
  S. spurium 226
  S. telephium 159, 163, 228
seed 22, 47, 66-9, 242
Selaginella 496
Self-heal, *see Prunella*
Semiarunidinaria fastuosa 249
Sempervivum 173, 227
  S. arachnoideum 224, 227
  S. × *calcaratum* 227
  S. heuffelii 227
  S. montanum 227
  S. reginae-amaliae 227
  S. soboliferum 227
  S. tectorum 227
Senecio 531, *see also Brachyglottis; Ligularia*
  S. elegans 87
Sensitive plant, *see Mimosa*
sequestrols 43
Sequoia 316
  S. sempervirens 316
Sequoiadendron 316
  S. giganteum 316
Service tree, *see Sorbus*
Setaria italica 84
Setcreasea, *see Tradescantia*
  S. purpurea 501
sewage sludge 43
Shallots 599
shanking 761
Shasta daisy 108, 111, *see also Chrysanthemum maximum*
Shirley poppy 95
Shooting star, *see Dodecatheon*
Shortia 227
  S. galacifolia 227
  S. soldanelloides 227
  S. uniflora 227
Shrimp plant, *see Justicia*
Shrubby cinquefoil, *see Potentilla*
Shrubby germander, *see Teucrium*
shrubs 108, 232-325 240
Sidalcea 163
Silene 99, 228
  S. acaulis 224, 228
  S. alpestris 228
  S. armeria 99
  S. pendula 99
  S. schafta 228
Silk oak, *see Grevillea*
Silver bell tree, *see Halesia*
Silver birch 11, *see also Betula*
silver leaf 761

Silybum 99
Sinarundinaria nitida 249
sink garden 172, 174
Sinningia speciosa 463
Siphonormanthus, *see Osmanthus*
Sisyrinchium 163, 228
  S. angustifolium 228
  S. bermudianum 228
  S. douglasii 228
  S. grandiflorum 228
  S. striatum 163
Skimmia 316
  S. japonica 316, 674
  S. reevesiana 316
Skullcap, *see Scutellaria*
slugs 761
slugworms 761
Smilacina 164
  S. racemosa 63, 164
Smilax 496
Smithiantha 496
  S. zebrina 463
Smoke tree, *see Cotinus*
snails 761
Snakes head iris, *see Hermodactylus*
Snakeskin plant, *see Fittonia*
Snapdragon, *see Antirrhinum*
Snow-in-summer, *see Cerastium*
Snowbell, *see Styrax*
Snowberry, *see Symphoricarpos*
Snowdrop tree, *see Halesia*
Snowdrop, *see Galanthus*
Snowflake, *see Leucojum*
Snowy mespilus, *see Amelanchier*
Soapwort, *see Saponaria*
soft rot 762
soil 11, 13-20, 23-4, 30, 33
Solanum 316, 497
  S. capsicastrum 497
  S. crispum 304, 316, 497
  S. jasminoides 316, 497
  S. wendlandii 497
Soldanella 228
  S. alpina 228
  S. montana 228
Soleirolia 228
  S. soleirolii 228
Solenostemom 497
  S. frederici 497
  S. scutellarioides 497, 519
  S. thyrsoideus 497
Solidago 110, 164
  S. canadensis 164
  S. Goldenmosa 159
Solidaster 164
  × *S. luteus* 164
Solomons seal, *see Polygonatum*
soot 17, 43
sooty mould 762
Sophora 317
  S. microphylla 317
  S. tetratera 317
Sorbaria 317
  S. kirilowii 317
  S. sorbifolia 317
  S. tomentosa 317
Sorbus 317
  S. aria 295, 317
  S. aucuparia 317
  S. discolor 317
  S. domesetica 317
  S. essertauana 317
  S. hupehensis 317
  S. intermedia 318
  S. sargentiana 317
  S. scopulina 317
  S. vilmorinii 317
South Sea myrtle, *see Leptospermum*
Southernwood, *see Artemisia*
spade 20
Spanish broom, *see Spartium*
Sparaxis 378
Sparmannia 498
  S. africana 498
Spartium 318

S. junceum 318
Spathiphyllum 498
  S. wallisii 498
specialized border 108
Specularia, see Venus's looking glass
Speedwell, *see Veronica*
Sphagnum moss, *see Moss*
Spider flower, *see Cleome*
Spider lily, *see Hymenocallis*
Spiderwort, *see Tradescantia*
Spinach 599
  beet 600
Spindle tree, *see Euonymus*
Spiraea 318, *see also Astilbe*
  S. Arguta 318
  S. douglasii 318
  S. japonica 318, 674
  S. prunifolia 318
  S. salicifolia 318
  S. thunbergii 318
  S. × *vanhouttei* 318
sprayers 721
Sprekelia 498
  S. formosissima 498
spring bedding 381
springtails 762
Spruce, *see Picea*
Spurge, *see Euphorbia*
Squill, *see Scilla*
St Bernards lily, *see Anthericum*
St Brunos lily, *see Anthericum*
St Dabocs heath, *see Daboecia*
St Johns wort, *see Hypericum*
Stachys 61, 164, 229
  S. corsica 229
  S. lanata 164
  S. macrantha 164
Stachyurus 319
  S. chinensis 319
  S. praecox 319
Stags horn sumach, *see Rhus*
Stapelia 531
Star of Bethlehem, *see Ornithogalum*
Statice, *see Limonium*
stem cuttings 111
Stephanotis 498
  S. floribunda 498
sterilization 722
Sternbergia 378
  S. lutea 366, 378
Stewartia, *see Stuartia*
Stocks 100, 101
Stokesia 164
  S. laevis 164
Stonecrop, *see Sedum*
Stransvaesia 319
  S. davidiana 319
Strawberries 712-715
Strawberry Cambridge Favourite 740
Strawberry tree, *see Arbutus*
Strawflower, *see Helichrysum*
streak 762
streams 383
Strelitzia 499
  S. reginae 499
Streptocarpus 499, 747
  S. × *hybridus* Constant Nymph 464
Streptosolen 499
  S. jamesonii 499
Stromanthe amabilis 464
Stuartia 319
  S. malacodendron 319
  S. pseudpcamellia 319
Styrax 319
  S. hemsleyana 319
  S. japonica 319
  S. obassia 319
subsoil 15, 20, 21, 24, 25
Succulents 511-531, 749
  compost 512
  propagation 512
  watering 512
Suckers, propagation from 238
sulphate of ammonia 30, 33, 43, 44

sulphate of iron 44
sulphate of magnesium 44
sulphate of potash 44
sulphur 31, 769
summer bedding 381
Summer cypress, see Kochia
Summer hyacinth, see Galtonia
Sun rose, see Helianthemum
Sunflower 32, 101
    perennial, see Helianthus
superphosphate of lime 30, 33,
    44, 45
Swamp cypress, see Taxodium
Swan river daisy, see
    Brachycome
Swedes 32, 600
Sweet bay, see Laurus
Sweet briar, see Rosa eglanteria
Sweet corn 600
Sweet flag, see Acorus
Sweet gum, see Liquidambar
Sweet laurel, see Laurus
Sweet pea 101-103
Sweet pepper, see Capsicum
Sweet rocket, see Hesperis
Sweet scabious, see Scabious
Sweet sultan 103
Sweet William 103
Swiss chard, see Seakale beet
Symphoricarpos 319
    S. albus 319
    S. × doorebossi 319
    S. orbiculatus 319, 675
Syngonium 499
Synthyris 229
    S. reniformis 229
Syringa 319
    S. × chinensis 320
    S. × josiflexa 320
    S. josikaea 320
    S. microphylla 320
    S. × persica 320
    S. reflexa 320
    S. vulgaris 320

Tagetes 57, 103, 104
    T. erecta 103
    T. patula 103
    T. signata pumila 103
Tamarisk, see Tamarix
Tamarix 244, 320
    T. anglica 320
    T. gallica 320
    T. parviflora 320
    T. ramosissima 320
    T. tetrandra 320
tar oil 633, 769
Tarragon 601
tarsonemid mite 762
Tassel flower 81
Taxodium 321
    T. distichum 321
Taxus 321
    T. baccata 321
Tecoma, see Campsis
Tecophilea 378
    T. cyanocrocus 378
Temple bells, see Smithiantha
Ten week stocks, see Stocks
terraces 10, 172
Teucrium 321
    T. chamaedrys 321
    T. fruticans 321
Thalia 393
    T. dealbata 393
Thalictrum 165
    T. aquilegifolium 165
    T. delavayi 160, 165
    T. dipterocarpum 165
    T. flavum glaucum 165
    T. minus adiantifolium 165
Thamnocalamus spathaceus
    249
Thermopsis 165
    T. montana 165
thiophanate-methyl 770
thiram 770
Thistles 18

Thorn, see Crataegus
Thrift, see Armeria
thrips 763
Thuja 321
    T. occidentalis 243, 321
    T. orientalis 321
    T. plicata 233, 243, 321
Thujopsis 322
    T. dolabrata 322
Thunbergia 500
Thyme 28, 58, 173, 601, see also
    Thymus
Thymus 229
    T. carnosus 229
    T. × citriodorus 229
    T. drucei 229
    T. herba-barona 229
    T. nitidus 229
    T. praecox articus 229
    T. pseudolanuginosus 229
    T. richardii 229
    T. serpyllum 229
Tiarella 165
Tibouchina 500
    T. semidecandra 500
Tidy tips, see Layia
Tiger flower, see Tigridia
Tigridia 378
Tilia 322
    T. × euchlora 322
    T. × europaea 322
    T. × platyphyllos 322
tillage 19
Tillandsia 500
    T. cyanea 500
    T. lindeniana 500
Tithonia 104
    T. rotundifolia 104
    T. speciosa 104
Toadflax, see Linaria
Tomatoes 601-605
topsoil 20
top-dressing 14
Torenia 500
    T. fournieri 500
Tovara 165
    T. virginiana variegata 165
Trachelium 500
    T. caeruleum 500
Trachelospermum 501
    T. jasminoides 501
Trachycarpus 322
    T. fortunei 322
Trachymene 501
    T. caerulea 501
Tradescantia 165, 501
    T. × andersoniana 160, 165
    T. blossfeldiana 501
    T. fluminensis 501, 520
    T. pallida 501
    T. sillamontana 520
    T. spathacea 501
    T. virginiana 165
    T. zebrina 501
Tree of heaven, see Ailanthus
trees 10, 11, 108, 232-325
    shapes 223
trench 19-21
Trichocereus 531
Tricholaena rosea 84
Triforine 770
Trillium erectum 229
    T. grandiflorum 160, 229
    T. sessile 229
Tristagma 379
    T. uniflorum 366, 379
Tritonia 502
    T. crocata 502
Trollius 166
    T. europaeus 166
    T. ledbourii 166
    T. pumilus 166
Tropaeolum 104, 166, 502, see
    also Nasturtium
    T. peltophorum 502
    T. peregrinum 104
    T. polyphyllum 166
    T. speciosum 166

T. tricolorum 502
    T. tuberosum 166, 502
troughs 172
Trout lily, see Erythronium
Trumpet creeper, see Campsis
Tsuga 322
    T. canadensis 322
    T. heterlphylla 322
Tuberose, see Polianthes
tubers 338-380
tulip fire 763
Tulip tree, see Liriodendron
Tulip 47, 51, 52, see also Tulipa
Tulipa 339, 379
    T. acuminata 380
    T. batalinii 366
    T. clusiana 366, 380
    T. fosteriana 366, 380
    T. greigii 367, 380
    T. Hollands Glory 367
    T. kaufmanniana 367, 380
    T. Keizerskroon 367
    T. linifolia 380
    T. linifolia batalinii 380
    T. Mrs John Scheepers 368
    T. orphanidea 380
    T. Peach Blossom 368
    T. praestans 368, 380
    T. Queen of Bartigons 368
    T. saxatilis 380
    T. tarda 368, 380
    T. undulatifolia 380
Tunica, see Petrorhagia
Turnips 32, 606
Turtle head, see Chelone
Typha 393
    T. angustifolia 393
    T. minima 393

Ulex 322
    U. europaeus 322
Ulmus 322
    U. glabra 322
    U. stricta 323
Umbrella grass, see Cyperus
Umbrella pine 316
union 241
urea 45
urea formaldehyde 45
Ursinia 104
    U. anethoides 104
    U. anthemoides 104
    U. pulchra 104
    U. versicolor 104
Uvularia 166
    U. grandiflora 166

Vaccaria, see Saponaria
    Venidium
    V. pyramidata 99
Vallisneria 393
    V. spiralis 393
Vallota, see Cyrtanthus
    V. purpurea 467
Vegetable marrow 607
vegetables 534-637
    catch cropping 536
    cloches 541
    continuous supply 537
    cultivation 543
    frames 538, 540
    greenhouse 541
    hotbeds 542
    intercropping 535, 536
    manuring 538
    rotation 535, 538
    seed sowing 540
    soil warming 542
    successional cropping 536
    types 535
Veltheimia 502
    V. capensis 502
Velvet plant, see Gynura
Venidium decurrens 104
    V. calendulaceum 104
    V. fastuosum 104
Venetian sumach, see Cotinus
ventilation 67

Venus's looking glass 104
Veratrum 166
    V. album 166
    V. nigrum 166
    V. viride 166
Verbascum 105, 111, 166, 502
    V. arcturus 502
    V. bombicyferum 105
    V. broussa 105
    V. creticum 502
    V. densiflorum 167
    V. phoeniceum 160, 167
    V. thapsus 105
Verbena 105, 167, 230
    V. bonariensis 167
    V. chamaedrifolia 230
    V. peruviana 230
    V. rigida 167
    V. venosa 167
Veronica 167, 230, see also
    Hebe
    V. cinerea 230
    V. filiformis 230
    V. fruticans 230
    V. gentianoides 167
    V. longifolia subsessilis 167
    V. prostrata 230
    V. rupestris 230
    V. saxatilis 230
    V. spicata 167, 230
    V. virginica 167
Viburnum 323, 737
    V. × bodnantense 323, 675
    V. × burkwoodii 323
    V. × carlcephalum 323
    V. carlesii 323
    V. davidii 323, 675
    V. farreri 323
    V. fragrans 323
    V. grandiflorum 323
    V. opulus 323
    V. plicatum 323
    V. rhytidophyllum 323, 676
    V. tinus 323, 676
    V. utile 323
Vinca 230, 324
    V. major 230, 324, 676
    V. minor 230, 324
Vine, see Vitis
vine weevil larvae 725
Vines 236
Viola 94, 167, 230
    V. bosniaca 231
    V. cornuta 230
    V. cucullata 231
    V. elegantula 231
    V. gracilis 230
    V. labradorica 231
    V. odorata 168
Violet cress, see Ionopsidium
Vipers bugloss, see Echium
Virginia creeper 235, see also
    Parthenocissus
Virginian stock 105
virus 763
Viscaria 61, 106
Vitis 324
    V. Brandt 304
    V. coignetiae 304, 324
    V. vinifera 324
voles 242
Vriesia 503
    V. splendens 503

Wahlenbergia, see Edrianthus
    188, 214
Wallflower, see Cheiranthus 76,
    123
Walnut, see Juglans
Wand flower, see Dierama
Wandering jew, see Tradescantia
wart diseases 764
washing soda 770
water forget-me-not, see
    Myosotis scorpioides
water gardens 383-394
Water hawthorn, see
    Aponogeton

Water lily 60, see also
    Nymphaea
Water millfoil, see Myriophyllum
Water plantain, see Alisma
Water poppy, see Hydrocleys
Water starwort, see Callitriche
Water violet, see Hottonia
water, moving 387
    surplus 25
Watercress 607, 608
waterlogging 14, 23, 24
Wattle, see Acacia
Wax plant, see Hoya
weather 14
weathering 19, 20, 30
weedkiller 18, 771-774
Weeds 17, 18, 22, 30, 109
Weeping fig, see Ficus
weevils 764
Weigela 324
    W. Bristol Ruby 677
    W. floribunda 324
    W. florida 324, 677, 737
Wellingtonia, see
    Sequoiadendron
Western red cedar, see Thuja
White cedar, see Thuja
white fly 765
White sail, see Spathiphyllum
Whitebeam, see Sorbus
Wig tree, see Cotinus
Wild clematis 17
Willow herb, see Epilobium
Willow, see Salix
wilt 765
windbreaks 235
Windflower, see Anemone
Winter aconite, see Eranthis
Winter cherry, see Solanum
Winter hazel, see Corylopsis
winter moths 765
Winter sweet, see Chimonanthus
winter wash 769
wireworms 765
Wisteria 324, 678
    W. floribunda 325
    W. sinensis 304, 324
    W. venusta 325
Witch hazel, see Hamamelis
wood ashes 45
Wood sorrel, see Oxalis
woodland plants 169
woodlice 766
Woodruff, see Asperula
woolly aphis 766
Woundwort, see Stachys

Xeranthemum 106
    X. annuum 106

Yarrow, see Achillea
Yellow archangel, see Lamium
Yew, see Taxus
Yucca 325
    Y. filamentosa 325, 677
    Y. flaccida 325

Zantedeschia 503
    Z. aethiopica 503
    Z. elliottiana 503
    Z. pentlandii 503
    Z. rehmannii 503
Zauschneria 231
    Z. californica 231
    Z. microphylla 231
Zea mays 84
Zea, see Grasses, ornamental
Zebrina, see Tradescantia
    Z. pendula 501
Zenobia 325
    Z. puverulenta 325
Zephyranthes 380
    Z. candida 380
zinc 31, 32
Zinnia 106
    Z. angustifolia 106
    Z. elegans 106
    Z. haageana 106